The INTERNATIONAL CRITICAL COMMENTARY
on the Holy Scriptures of the Old and New Testaments

GENERAL EDITORS:

S. R. DRIVER
Regius Professor of Hebrew, University of Oxford

A. PLUMMER
Master of University College, University of Durham

C. A. BRIGGS
*Edward Robinson Professor of Biblical Theology,
Union Theological Seminary, New York*

THE BOOK OF PSALMS

VOLUME I

A CRITICAL AND EXEGETICAL COMMENTARY

ON

THE BOOK OF PSALMS

BY

CHARLES AUGUSTUS BRIGGS
D.D., D.Litt.

AND

EMILIE GRACE BRIGGS
B.D.

IN TWO VOLUMES

VOLUME I

EDINBURGH
T. & T. CLARK LIMITED, 59 GEORGE STREET

PRINTED IN THE U.K. BY PAGE BROS (NORWICH) LTD

FOR

T. & T. CLARK LTD, EDINBURGH

0 567 05011 4

Latest Impression 1987

To

JOHN CROSBY BROWN

AND

D. WILLIS JAMES

PRESIDENT AND VICE-PRESIDENT OF THE BOARD OF DIRECTORS

OF

THE UNION THEOLOGICAL SEMINARY

THIS WORK IS DEDICATED

IN RECOGNITION OF THEIR EMINENT SERVICES TO THEOLOGICAL

EDUCATION AND TO LIBERTY OF CHRISTIAN SCHOLAR-

SHIP DURING THE THIRTY-THREE YEARS OF

THE AUTHOR'S PROFESSORATE

PREFACE

THIS Commentary is the fruit of forty years of labour. In 1867, when making special studies in Berlin with Dr. Emil Rödiger, I began a critical Commentary on the Psalms, the Ms. of which is still in my possession. In 1872 the translation of Moll's " Commentary on the Psalms " in Lange's *Bibelwerk* was published in the series edited by Philip Schaff. I translated and enlarged the Commentary on Pss. 1–41 51–72 with twenty-five per cent additional matter, and edited the Introduction with additional notes. In 1874 I began teaching as professor of Hebrew and cognate languages in Union Theological Seminary, and lectured on the Psalms every year until 1890 when I became Edward Robinson Professor of Biblical Theology, in which position I continued to lecture on the Criticism and Theology of the Psalter until 1904, when I was transferred to my present chair. In the plan of the International Critical Commentary I undertook the volumes on the Psalms, and have been at work upon them ever since. In addition to my work on the theological terms of the new edition of Robinson's Gesenius' *Hebrew Lexicon*, BDB., I have made a complete lexicon to the Psalter, based on a revised Hebrew text, which I hope ere long to publish. I have spared no pains upon the text of the Psalter, not only in the study of the Versions, but also in the detection and elimination of the glosses in the search for the original texts as they came from their authors. The Theology of the Psalter has been carefully investigated ; only the limits of space prevent me from giving it in this volume.

I have made a careful study of the chief commentaries and have referred to them so far as practicable in the notes, but the most that could be done was to distribute credit to my predecessors in fair proportions. The amount of literature is so vast that no other course was possible. The Commentary will show that Roman Catholic Commentators have rendered valuable service which has been too often neglected by modern Protestants; and that the older British interpreters are the real fathers of much of the material for which modern Germans usually receive the credit. For more than thirty years I have given much attention to Hebrew poetry. For a long time I had to battle for it alone against unreasoning prejudice. I have lived to see a large proportion of American scholars adopt essentially the views which I represent. All of the Psalms have been arranged in this Commentary in measured lines, and the great majority of them in equal strophes. Their literary character has thereby been greatly improved and their historical propriety become more evident. The translations are based on the English official Versions, but whenever important I have not hesitated to forsake them in order to conform to that original which I have determined by the principles of textual criticism. I have not attempted to give a Version for public or private use, but simply one to set forth the original text as I have determined it. A public Version, in my opinion, should be less pedantic and literal than the Revised Version, and not so slavish in its adherence to the Massoretic text. In this respect the older Versions, especially the Version of the Book of Common Prayer, is to be preferred; for while it is less accurate than the later Versions, it preserves many readings of the Greek and Vulgate Versions which later English Versions unwisely rejected, and it is concerned to give the sense of the original in rhythmical devotional language well suited to the character of a book of prayer and praise.

The results which have been reached in Textual Criticism, Higher Criticism, Hebrew Poetry, Historical Criticism, Biblical Theology, and Interpretation of the Psalter have not been stated without long and careful consideration. If I could spend more years in preparation, doubtless I would do much better work. But there is a limit to all things, and I cannot longer withhold my Commentary from the press. Whatever is true and sound in this work will endure, whatever is mistaken and unsound will soon be detected and will perish. I would not have it otherwise.

The Psalms are among the most wonderful products of human

genius. No other writings but the Gospels can compare with
them in grandeur and importance. The Gospels are greater
because they set forth the life and character of our Lord and
Saviour. The Psalter expresses the religious experience of a
devout people through centuries of communion with God.
I cannot explain either Gospels or Psalms except as Books of
God, as products of human religious experience, inspired and
guided by the Divine Spirit.

I could not have completed these volumes without the help
of my daughter, Emilie Grace Briggs, B.D., who has laboured
with me on the Hebrew Lexicon and in the preparation of this
Commentary. It is simple justice to add her name to mine on
the title-page. I have dedicated these volumes to John Crosby
Brown, Esq., and D. Willis James, Esq., who have for more
than the thirty-three years of my professorship served Union
Seminary on its Board of Directors. Their services to Theological Education and especially to the liberty of theological scholarship cannot be too highly estimated.

C. A. BRIGGS.

CONTENTS

C. CANONICITY

D. INTERPRETATION

ABBREVIATIONS.

———◆———

I. Texts and Versions.

𝕬 = The Psalter of Asaph.
Ald. = Aldine text of 𝕲.
Aq. = Version of Aquila.
AV. = Authorized Version.

BD. = Baer & Delitzsch, Heb. text.

Chr. = The Chronicler, author of Ch. Ezr. Ne.
Comp. = Complutensian text.

𝕯 = The Psalter of David.
D. = The Deuteronomist in Dt., in other books Deuteronomic author or Redactor.
𝕯𝕽 = The Psalter of the Director.

𝕰 = The Elohistic Psalter.
EVs. = English Versions.
E. = Ephraemitic sources of Hexateuch.

𝕲 = Greek Septuagint Version.
𝕲B = The Vatican text of Swete.
𝕲A = The Alexandrine text.
𝕲ﬡ = The Sinaitic text.
𝕲R = Psalterium Graeco-Latinum Veronense.
𝕲T = Psalterium Turicense.
𝕲U = Fragmenta papyrocea Londonensia.
𝕲λ = Leipziger Papyrusfragmente.

𝕳 = Hebrew consonantal text.
H. = Code of Holiness of the Hexateuch.
HP. = Texts of Holmes and Parsons.
Hex. = The Hexateuch.

𝕵 = Latin Version of Jerome.
J. = Judaic sources of the Hexateuch.
JPSV. = Jewish Publication Society Version.

𝕶 = The Korahite Psalter.
Kt. = Kᵉthib, the Hebrew text as written.

𝕷 = Old Latin Version.

𝕸 = The Psalter of the Mizmorim.
Mas. = Masora.
MT. = The Massoretic pointed text.

NT. = The New Testament.

OT. = The Old Testament.

P. = The priestly sources of the Hexateuch.
PBV. = Version of the Book of Common Prayer.

Qr. = Qᵉrê, the Hebrew text as read.

R. = The Redactor, or editor.

RV. = The Revised Version.

RV.^m = The margin of the Revised Version.

𝕾 = The Syriac Peshitto Version.

Σ = The Version of Symmachus.

𝕿 = The Targum or Aramaic Version.

𝖁 = The Vulgate Version.

Vrss. = Versions, usually ancient.

WL. = The Wisdom Literature of the OT.

Θ = The Version of Theodotian.

ψ = The Psalter in its present form.

II. Books of the Old and New Testaments.

Am. = Amos.

BS. = Ecclesiasticus of Ben Sira.

1, 2 Ch. = 1, 2 Chronicles.
Col. = Colossians.
1, 2 Cor. = 1, 2 Corinthians.
Ct. = Canticles = The Song of Songs.

Dn. = Daniel.
Dt. = Deuteronomy.

Ec. = Ecclesiastes.
Eph. = Ephesians.
Est. = Esther.
Ex. = Exodus.
Ez. = Ezekiel.
Ezr. = Ezra.

Gal. = Galatians.
Gn. = Genesis.

Hb. = Habakkuk.
Heb. = Hebrews.
Hg. = Haggai.
Ho. = Hosea.

Is. = early parts of Isaiah.
Is.² = exilic parts of Isaiah.
Is.³ = postexilic parts of Isaiah.

Jb. = Job.
Je. = Jeremiah.
Jn. = John.
Jo. = Joel.
Jon. = Jonah.
Jos. = Joshua.
Ju. = Judges.

1, 2 K. = 1, 2 Kings.

La. = Lamentations.
Lk. = Luke.
Lv. = Leviticus.

Mal. = Malachi.
1, 2 Mac. = 1, 2 Maccabees.
Mi. = Micah.
Mk. = Mark.
Mt. = Matthew.

Na. = Nahum.
Ne. = Nehemiah.
Nu. = Numbers.

Ob. = Obadiah.

Phil. = Philippians.
Pr. = Proverbs.
Ps. = Psalms.

Rev. = Revelation.
Rom. = Romans.
Ru. = Ruth.

1, 2 S.	= 1, 2 Samuel.	Zc.	= Zechariah.
		Zp.	= Zephaniah.
1, 2 Thes.	= 1, 2 Thessalonians.		
1, 2 Tim.	= 1, 2 Timothy.	Wisd.	= Wisdom of Solomon.

III. AUTHORS AND WRITINGS.

AE.	= Aben Ezra.	DB.	= Hastings's Dictionary of the Bible.
Ains.	= Ainsworth.		
Aug.	= Augustine.	De.	= Franz Delitzsch.
		De R.	= De Rossi.
Bä.	= F. Baethgen.	De W.	= De Wette.
BDB.	= Hebrew and English Lexicon of the OT., edited by F. Brown, S. R. Driver, C. A. Briggs. The editor specially referred to is designated by BDB. F. Brown, BDB. S. R. Driver.	Dr.	= S. R. Driver, Parallel Psalter.
		Dr.[0]	= Heb. Tenses.
		Dr.[Intr]	= Introduction to Literature of OT.
		Dru.	= Drusius.
		Du.	= B. Duhm.
		Dy.	= J. Dyserinck.
Bar Heb.	= Bar Hebraeus.	EB.	= Encyclopaedia Biblica.
Be.	= G. Beer.	Ehr.	= Ehrlich.
Bi.	= G. Bickell.	Eph. Syr.	= Ephraem Syrus.
Bö.	= F. Böttcher.	Ew.	= H. Ewald.
Bö.[§]	= his *Lehrb. der Heb. Sprache.*	Ew.[§]	= his *Lehrb. der Heb. Sprache.*
Br.	= C. A. Briggs.	Fü.	= J. Fürst.
Br.[MP]	= Messianic Prophecy.		
Br.[MG]	= Messiah of the Gospels.	Genebr.	= Genebradus.
Br.[MA]	= Messiah of the Apostles.	Ges.	= Gesenius, *Thesaurus.*
Br.[SHS]	= Study of Holy Scripture.	Ges.[§]	= his Heb. Gram. ed. Kautzsch.
Br.[Hex]	= Higher Criticism of the Hexateuch.		
		Ges.[L]	= his *Lehrgebäude.*
Bu.	= F. Buhl.	Gi.	= Ginsburg.
Bud.	= K. Budde.	Gr.	= Grätz.
Bux.	= Buxtorf.	Grot.	= Grotius.
Calv.	= John Calvin.	Hengst.	= Hengstenberg.
Cap.	= Cappellus.	Hi.	= F. Hitzig.
Che.	= T. K. Cheyne.	Houb.	= C. F. Houbigant.
ChWB.	= Levy, *Chald. Wörterbuch.*	Hu.	= H. Hupfeld, *Psalmen.*
		Hu.[Ri]	= *Psalmen*[2] ed. Riehm.
Co.	= C. H. Cornill.	Hu.[3]	= *Psalmen*[3] ed. Nowack.

JBL.	= Journal of Biblical Lit-erature.	Ra.	= Rashi.
		Reu. '	= Ed. Reuss.
JE.	= Jewish Encyclopaedia.	Ri.	= E. Riehm.
Jer.	= Jerome.	Ri.*HWB*	= Riehm's *Handwörterbuch*.
Jos.	= Fl. Josephus.	Rö.	= E. Rödiger.
JQR.	= Jewish Quarterly Re-view.	Rob.	= E. Robinson, Biblical Re-searches.
		Ros.	= Rosenmüller.
Kau.	= E. Kautzsch.	RS.	= W. Robertson Smith.
Kenn.	= B. Kennicott.		
Ki.	= Daniel Kimchi (Qam-chi).	Siev.	= E. Sievers.
		Sm.	= R. Smend.
Kirk.	= A. F. Kirkpatrick.	SS.	= Siegfried and Stade, *Heb.*
Kö.	= F. E. König.		*Wörterbuch.*
Kue.	= A. Kuenen.	Sta.	= B. Stade.
Lag.	= P. de Lagarde.	Talm.	= The Talmud.
Lag.*BN*	= his *Bildung der No-mina.*	Tisch.	= C. Tischendorf.
		Tr.	= Tristram, Natural History of
Luz.	= S. D. Luzzato.		the Bible.
Mich.	= J. D. Michaelis.	We.	= J. Wellhausen.
Mish.	= The *Mishna*.	We.*sv*	= his *Skizzen und Vorarbeiten.*
NHWB.	= Levy, *Neuhebr. Wör-terbuch.*	ZAW.	= *Zeitschrift f. alttest. Wis-senschaft.*
		ZMG.	= *Z. d. deutsch. Morgenländ.*
Ols.	= J. Olshausen.		*Gesellschaft.*
		ZPV.	= *Z. d. deutsch. Pal. Vereins.*
Pe.	= J. J. S. Perowne.		

IV. GENERAL, ESPECIALLY GRAMMATICAL.

abr.	= abbreviation.	α.λ.	= ἀπαξ λεγόμενον, word or phr.
abs.	= absolute.		used once.
abstr.	= abstract.	al.	= *et aliter*, and elsw.
acc.	= accusative.	alw.	= always.
acc. cog.	= cognate acc.	antith.	= anthesis, antithetical.
acc. pers.	= acc. of person.	apod.	= apodosis.
acc. rei	= acc. of thing.	Ar.	= Arabic.
acc. to	= according to.	Aram.	= Aramaic.
act.	= active.	art.	= article.
adj.	= adjective.	As.	= Assyrian.
adv.	= adverb.		

Bab.	= Babylonian.	impf.	= imperfect.
B. Aram.	= Biblical Aramaic.	imv.	= imperative.
		indef.	= indefinite.
c.	= *circa*, about ; also *cum*, with.	inf.	= infinitive.
		i.p.	= in pause.
caus.	= causative	i.q	:= *id quod*, the same with.
cf.	= confer, compare.	intrans.	= intransitive.
cod., codd.	= codex, codices.		
cog.	= cognate.	juss.	= jussive.
coll.	= collective.		
comm.	= commentaries.	lit.	= literal, literally.
comp.	= compare.	loc.	= local, locality.
concr.	= concrete.		
conj.	= conjunction.	m.	= masculine.
consec.	= consecutive.	metaph.	= metaphor, metaphorical.
contr.	= contract, contracted.	mng.	= meaning.
cstr.	= construct.	mpl.	= masculine plural.
		ms.	= masculine singular.
d.f.	= dagesh forte.		
def.	= defective.	n.	= noun.
del.	= *dele*, strike out.	n. p.	= proper name.
dittog.	= dittography.	n. pr. loc.	= proper noun of place.
dub.	= dubious, doubtful.	n. unit.	= noun of unity.
		NH.	= New Hebrew.
elsw.	= elsewhere.	Niph.	= Niphal of verb.
emph.	= emphasis, emphatic.		
esp.	= especially.	obj.	= object.
Eth.	= Ethiopic.	opp.	= opposite, as opposed to or contrasted with.
exc.	= except.		
exil.	= exilic.		
		p.	= person.
f.	= feminine.	parall.	= parallel with.
fig.	= figurative.	part.	= particle.
fpl.	= feminine plural.	pass.	= passive.
fr.	= from.	pf.	= perfect.
freq.	= frequentative.	Ph.	= Phoenician.
fs.	= feminine singular.	phr.	= phrase.
		Pi.	= Piel of verb.
gent.	= gentilic.	pl.	= plural.
gl.	= gloss, glossator.	post B.	= post Biblical.
		postex.	= postexilic.
haplog.	= haplography.	pred.	= predicate.
Heb.	= Hebrew.	preëx.	= preëxilic.
Hiph.	= Hiphil of verb.	preg.	= pregnant.
Hithp.	= Hithpael of verb.	prep.	= preposition.

prob.	= probable.	str.	= strophe.
pron.	= pronoun.	subj.	= subject.
ptc.	= participle.	subst.	= substantive.
Pu.	= Pual of verb.	*s.v.*	= *sub voce.*
		syn.	= synonymous.
qu.	= question.	synth.	= synthetic.
q.v.	= *quod vide.*	Syr.	= Syriac.
Rf.	= refrain.	t.	= times (following a number).
rd.	= read.		
refl.	= reflexive.	tr.	= transfer.
rel.	= relative.	trans.	= transitive.
		txt.	= text.
sf.	= suffix.	txt. err.	= textual error.
sg.	= singular.		
si vera	= si vera lectio.	v.	= verse.
sim.	= simile.	*v.*	= *vide*, see.
sq.	= followed by.	vb.	= verb.
st.	= *status*, state, stative.		

V. Other Signs.

† prefixed indicates all passages cited.

‡ prefixed indicates all passages in ψ cited.

‖ parallel, of words or clauses chiefly synonymous.

= equivalent, equals.

+ plus denotes that other passages might be cited.

[ ] indicates that the form enclosed is not in the Hebrew, so far as known.

√ = the root, or stem.

' = sign of abbreviation in Hebrew words.

׳ = *Yahweh.*

( ) Indicates that Massoretic text has not been followed, but either Vrss. or conjectural emendations.

VI. Remarks.

Biblical passages are cited according to the verses of the Hebrew text.

Numerals raised above the line (1) after numerals designating chapters indicate verses (Gn. 6³); (2) after numerals designating lines of strophe indicate measures (2 Str. 6⁴); (3) after proper names refer to sections of grammars or pages of books (Ges.§ 42).

Proper names usually refer to works upon the Psalter given in the History of Interpretation.

In notes numbers in italics (Ps. *1²*) indicate passages in which the word has been fully discussed.

INTRODUCTION.

§ 1. *The Psalter belongs to the third division of the Hebrew Canon, entitled Hymns or Prayers, from its chief contents. The Greek Version named it Psalms from the most frequent sub-title, and in this has been followed by other Versions.*

The Hebrew OT. consists of three divisions, the Law, the Prophets, and the Writings, representing three layers of successive canonical recognition. The Writings were of indefinite extent until their limits were defined by the Synod of Jamnia. Prior to that time there were disputes as to several of the Writings, such as Chronicles, Song of Songs, and Ecclesiastes ; but, so far as we are able to discover, there never was any dispute as to the canonicity of the Psalter as a whole, or as to any one of the Psalms. In the Greek Septuagint (𝔊) these divisions of the Canon were broken up and the books were rearranged on topical principles. The Apocrypha were mingled with the books of the Hebrew Canon, doubtless from a wider and looser view of its character and extent (Br.^HS. 124-130). EV^s. follow the order of the books of the Latin Vulgate (𝔙) of the sixteenth century, which was based on 𝔊, but with several important differences. This order for the three great poetical books is Job, Psalter, Proverbs.

The most ancient order of the Writings, preserved in Literature, is that of the *Baba Bathra* of the Talmud (f. 14^b), which placed Ruth first, because of the theory that it gave the genealogy of David, and therefore should precede the Psalms of David (*v.* Br.^SHS. 252). The modern Hebrew Bibles follow the order of the German codd., which, though of comparatively late date, doubtless preserve the original order in putting the Psalter (ψ) first. The breaking up of the triple division of the Canon in 𝔊, followed by other Vrss. ancient and modern, occasioned various other rearrangements of the books in accordance with different theories about them. The books which were supposed to be historical, Ch., Ezr., Ne., and Est., were arranged with the prophetic histories. Ruth was attached to Judges. These all therefore preceded ψ. The three great poetical books, which in the German codd. are in the natural order, ψ, Pr., Jb., were given in 𝔙 in the order Jb., ψ, Pr., in accordance with a mistaken theory as to their historical order of composition. La. was attached to Je., in accordance with a theory as to date, authorship, or character of the composition. Thus, of the five rolls which in the Hebrew Canon belonged together, only Ec. and Ct. were left to follow Pr. The most serious change, however, was the placing of the three greater poetical books and these two rolls in the middle, between the Historical and the Prophetical Books.

In the Hebrew Canon the Psalter bears the title *Praises*, or *Book of Praises*, because of the conception that it was essentially a collection of songs of praise, or hymn book, to be used in the worship of God ; or else *Prayers*, because it was a collection of prayers, a prayer book. In 𝔊 it is entitled *Psalms*, doubtless because the word " psalm " was in the titles of such a large proportion of the poems. In early Greek writers it received the name *Psalter*, which seems a more appropriate name for a collection of Pss. for use in public worship.

(*A*) The Hebrew title was either תְּהִלִּים or ספר תהלים N.H. or תהלין Aramaic for the proper Hebrew תְּהִלָּה, pl. of הְרְכָּה n.f. *a song of praise*, formed by ת from הלל vb. *praise in sacred song*. The nucleus of the Pss. 90–150 is composed of Hallels, with the title הללויה, originally a collection of songs of praise or hymns (*v.* § 35). Only Ps. 145 has the title תהלה. This title of ψ appears in a writing ascribed to Hippolytus (ed. Lagarde, p. 188) as Σέφρα θελειμ (cf. the gloss σεφρ ἀθελλιμ in Mercati's *Un Palimpsesto Ambrosiano dei Salmi Esapli*, Turin, 1898); in Origen (Euseb. *Hist. Eccl.* VI. 25, ed. Mc-Giffert) Σφαρθελλειμ ; and Jerome (*Psalterum iuxta Hebraeos*, ed. Lagarde, p. 2) *sephar tallim, quod interpretatur volumen hymnorum.* So also Philo always uses the term ὕμνοι or one of its compounds in his citation of Pss. (Hatch, *Essays in Biblical Greek*, p. 174), and in the *De vita contempl.* (II. 475), an early writing attributed to Philo (*v.* Br.SHS. 126), the same usage appears. Josephus (*Antiq.* VII. 12) refers to the psalms as songs and hymns (*v.* § 12).

(*B*) [הלל] vb. Qal only in mng. *be boastful*, which also appears in Pi. and Hiph. *make one's boast* (*v.* 5⁶ 56⁵· ¹¹). Pi. ‡*praise :* (1) obj. God 63⁶ 69³⁵ 119¹⁷⁶; c. לֹ, on account of, 119¹⁶⁴; in summons 148¹· ¹· ¹³; often of public worship in holy place 22²³· ²⁷ 84⁵ 107³² 146¹· ²; ‖ אירך 35¹⁸ 109³⁰; c. ב instr. 149³; (2) obj. שֵׁם, of God 69³¹ 74²¹ 113¹· ¹ 135¹· ¹ 145² 148⁵. Imv. used of temple worship 22²⁴, cf. v.²³· ²⁵, 150²· ²· ³· ³· ⁴ ⁴· ⁵· ⁵, in summons to angels and all creatures 148²· ²· ³· ³· ⁴· ⁷ 150¹· ¹; addressed to all nations 117¹; to Zion

147[12]. Liturgical use: הַלְלוּיָה 135[3]; elsw. as titles of Hallels, at the beginning 106[1] 111[1] 112[1] 113[1] 135[1] 146[1] 147[1] 148[1] 149[1] 150[1]; at the end 104[35] 105[45] 106[48] 113[9] 115[18] 116[19] 117[2] 135[21] 146[10] 147[20] 148[14] 149[9] 150[6]; in other forms 102[19] 115[17] 150[6]. Pu. *be praised:* (1) maidens in song 78[63]; (2) elsw. of God, in ptc. with gerundive force, *to be praised, worthy of praise*, 18[4] (= 2 S. 22[4]) 48[2] 96[4] (= 1 Ch. 16[25]) 145[3]; of His name 113[3]. — ‡ תְּהִלָּה n.f. (1) *praise, adoration*, paid to Yahweh, 22[4] 34[2] 48[11] 51[17] 71[6. 8. 14] 109[1] 111[10] 119[171] 145[21]; as sung 40[4] 106[12], cf. 33[1] 148[14] (?); (2) *act of general public praise* 22[26] 65[2] 66[2. 8] 100[4] 147[1] 149[1], cf, also 22[4] 33[1] 106[12]; (3) *song of praise* in title 145[1]; (4) *qualities, deeds*, etc., of Yahweh *demanding praise* 9[15] 35[28] 78[4] 79[13] 102[22] 106[2. 47].

(*C*) The term תְּפִלּוֹת is used in Ps. 72[20] as a sub-title of the Davidic Psalter (*v.* § 27). ‡ תְּפִלָּה n.f. *prayer*, is used in the titles of Pss. 17, 86, 90, 102, 142, and also Hb. 3[1]. In all these cases it was original before the Pss. were taken up into any of the Psalters. תְּפִלָּה is used elsw. in ψ for prayer 35[18] 66[20] 80[6] 88[14] 102[18] 109[4. 7] 141[5], c. ל 42[9] 69[14], לפני 88[3] 141[2]. Phrs. for hearing prayer: c. שֶׁמַע 4[2] 39[13] 54[4] 65[3] 84[9] 102[2] 143[1]; הקשׁיב 61[2] 66[19]; האזינה 17[1] 55[2] 86[6]; לקח 6[10], פנה אל 102[18]. The vb. ‡ [פלל] is not used in Qal. It prob. had the fundamental mng. *intervene, interpose*, and accordingly the derivatives, *arbitrate, judge*, not used in ψ ; and *intercede, pray*, Pi. 106[3)], Hithp. c. אל 5[3] 32[6], בעד 72[15]. The term הפלה was indeed the most appropriate title for 𝕯, as the great majority of its psalms are prayers. But the term תהלה ultimately prevailed among the Hebrews as among Christians; for prayers when sung in worship naturally are regarded as hymns. Thus, in place of תפלות 72[20] of Hebrew text 𝕲 has ὕμνοι, so 𝔙 *laudes*, showing that at the date of the origin of 𝕲 the conception of the Psalms as hymns had already, among Hellenistic Jews, displaced the older conception. Gr. does not hesitate to regard 𝕲 as giving the original text. 𝔖 omits the passage as an editorial note. But Aq., Σ, Θ, 𝔍, agree with 𝔐, which certainly gives the true reading.

(*D*) In 𝕲, ψ bore the title ψαλμοί, pl. ψαλμός, so Lk. 24[44], or *Book of Psalms* Lk. 20[42] Acts 1[20]; ψαλμός is the translation of מִזְמוֹר used in the titles of fifty-seven Pss. in 𝔐, a n. formed by מ from [זמר] vb. denom. [זָמִיר] n.m. *song* or *poem*, with trimmed, measured words and ornate style, from † זמר vb. *trim, prune*. Qal Lv. 25[34]. Niph. Is. 5[6]. † זָמִיר sg. cstr. Is. 25[5], elsw. pl. 2 S. 23[1] Is. 24[16] Jb. 35[10] Pss. 95[2] 119[54]. † זִמְרָה n.f. *idem*, accompanied with instrumental music Am. 5[23] Pss. 81[3] 98[5]; prob. also, though not mentioned, Ex. 15[2] Is. 12[2] 51[3] Ps. 118[14]. † [זמר] denom. vb. only Pi.: (1) *sing*, c. ל, to God 9[12] 27[6] 30[5] 66[4] 71[23] 75[10] 101[1] 104[33] 105[2] 146[2] Ju. 5[3]. שֵׁם Pss. 18[50] 92[2] 135[3]; c. אל 59[18]; c. acc. sfs. 30[18] 57[10] (?) 108[4] (?) 138[1]; c. acc. God 68[33] 147[1] Is. 12[5]; כֵּס Pss. 7[18] 9[3] 61[9] 66[2. 4] 68[5]; נבורתך 21[14]; משכיל 47[8]; abs. 57[8] 98[4] 108[2]; (2) *play*, musical instruments 33[2] 47[7. 7. 7. 7] 71[22] 98[5] 147[7] 149[3], cf. 144[9]. מִזְמוֹר is a more technical form for שׁיר זמור, and indicates a poem with measured lines and strophes, selected for public worship. It seems probable that all these מזמרים were gathered in an early collection for this purpose (*v.* § 31). The title of this early Psalter subsequently became the title of the whole

Psalter. The term of 𝕲 has been followed by most Vrss. In 𝕲ᴬ the title ψαλτήριον appears; also in Hippolytus, Athanasius, Epiphanius, and other Fathers. On the whole, this seems to be the most appropriate title. Hb. 4⁷ ἐν Δαυίδ seems to be a title of the Psalter, reflecting the popular usage as reflected elsw. in NT. and in ancient and modern usage as a popular personification of the book that bears his name. Here, again, the early Psalter of David gave the name to the entire collection of the Psalter.

A. THE TEXT OF THE PSALTER.

§ **2.** *The original text of the Psalter was written in the Hebrew language, and in letters which were subsequently abandoned for the Aramaic script. This latter text has been preserved in Mss., none of which are older than the tenth century; but they rest upon two important revisions of that century, those of Ben Asher and Ben Naftali, which differ chiefly in Massoretic material.*

The text of the Psalter, as that of all the OT., was written in the ancient Hebrew language. The Pss. were written by many different authors at different periods of time, and also passed through the hands of many different editors. They therefore show traces of several stages in the development of the Hebrew language. The most if not all of the Pss. were written in letters resembling those of the Samaritan language, preserved elsewhere only in inscriptions and on coins. They were subsequently transliterated into the square Aramaic letters through an intermediate form of current Aramaic script (Br.ˢᴴˢ·¹⁷⁰⁻¹⁷³). In all these processes of copying, editing, and transliteration, changes occurred, some of which were intentional, others unintentional, due to mistakes of various kinds. The Hebrew text has been preserved in a large number of Mss. The earliest text of the entire OT. is the St. Petersburg Codex, 1009 A.D. There are a number of codd. of the Psalter, but none of an early date. All these rest upon a revision of the text made by the Rabbi Ben Asher in the early part of the tenth century, who undoubtedly used material no longer accessible, and made such excellent use of it that his text has remained the standard authority for the Massoretic text until the present day; although the variations in pointing of his cotemporary, Ben Naftali, representing another tradition, have been preserved in the Massoretic apparatus which is usually given in Hebrew Bibles.

The earliest text of the OT. preserved is the St. Petersburg Codex of the Prophets, 916 A.D., but this does not contain the Psalter. Ginsburg (*Text of the Heb. Bible*, p. 469 sq.) thinks that a Ms. of the British Museum was written in 820–850 A.D., but, so far as we know, he has found no one to agree with him. Most Hebrew codd., that have been preserved, rest upon a text revised by Rabbi Ben Asher in the early part of the tenth century, and this is the text that has been taken as a standard in all printed editions. The recently discovered codd. of St. Petersburg gives an earlier and simpler system of vowel points and accents, but only slight variations in the unpointed text. The variations in the most important codd. are given by Baer in his text of ψ from two codd. Curtisianus, three codd. Erfurtensis, one cod. each Francofurtensis, Heidenheimianus, Petropolitanus, and Sappiri Parisiensis. The Massora also contains 13 traditional variations between the Palestinian and Babylonian tradition, and 299 variations between Ben Asher and Ben Naftali, none of which are of any serious importance for the interpretation of the ψ.

§ **3.** *The Massora also gives evidences of variations of text, going back to primitive times, in marginal notes and signs, where the text remains unchanged. Citations in the Talmud and other early Jewish writings give little evidence of other variations of text.*

The Massorites devoted themselves to the study of the traditional text of the OT. When the knowledge of ancient Hebrew was confined to scholars, they endeavoured to perpetuate and stereotype the traditional pronunciation, the method of recitation of the OT. in the synagogue, and the connection of words and clauses in the sentence, by the use of vowel points, accents, and other signs. This was necessary because the Hebrew, like other Semitic languages, was in ancient times written only so far as the consonants were concerned.

These Massorites were so called as masters of Massora, or tradition. Their work was based upon the methods of the Syrian schools with reference to Syriac Literature. The differences between the so-called Babylonian and Palestinian systems of vocalisation and accentuation show various stages in their work, which continued for several centuries. The earliest stages have left no record, but they may be inferred from the simpler forms of Syriac and Arabic Literature (Br.[SHS. 180-183]). It is important to notice that all these vowel points and accents are comparatively late in origin, and, although they rest on tradition going back to primitive times, they were still matters of opinion, and by no means have the venerable authority of the consonantal text. The view that they were equally inspired with the consonantal text, held commonly in the sixteenth century, has been universally abandoned. There are several Massoretic notes and signs which are of great importance, for they indicate variations of text in ancient tradition which the Massorites felt obliged to record, although they did not venture to change the traditional text. These are: (1) The variation between the קרי, that which should be read, and the כתיב, that which is written. There are seventy of these in ψ. (2) The inverted נ, parentheses, 107[23. 24. 25. 26. 27. 28. 40] (v. Ochla veochla[179]; Dikduke hateamini[§ 60]; Gemara, Rosch hashana[17b]). (3) The Paseq, which calls attention to a peculiarity of text that sometimes needs correction. There are forty-seven of these in ψ (v. Grimme, Psalmenprobleme, s. 166 sq.; Kennedy, Note Line in Biblical Hebrew, commonly called Paseq or Pesiq). This sign was neglected by the older critics, but has been carefully considered by many moderns, and is often found to be a sign of a corrupt text. (4) The change of the form of letters also probably indicates variations of text, the ר זעירא ר 24[4], כ׳ רבתה 80[16], ק׳ רבתה 84[4], ע׳ תלויה 80[14]. (5) The superfluous letters: נעלם א׳ 99[6] 104[12] 116[6], יתיר ר 51[4], יתיר ר 26[2] 38[21] 89[29] 101[5] 144[13] 145[8], יתיר י 16[10] 21[2] 77[20] 119[147. 161]. These all need attention as suggesting variations in the text. (6) The extraordinary points mark letters as doubtful 27[18]. There are large numbers of citations of ψ in the Talmud and other early Jewish writings, but so far as they have been examined and collated they give no evidence of any important variations besides those indicated in the Mas., which doubtless took the most, if not all of them, into consideration.

§ **4.** *The earliest printed edition of the Hebrew Psalter was published at Bologna in 1477. Independent texts based on Mss. were published at Soncino, in the Complutensian Polyglot, and the second Rabbinical Bible. All subsequent editions were mixed texts, until those of Baer and Ginsburg, which give accurate forms of the Massoretic text of Ben Asher.*

(1) The earliest edition of the Hebrew text of ψ was printed at Bologna, 1477. The whole Bible was first printed at Soncino, Lombardy, in 1488; then at Naples, 1491–1493. Another edition was printed at Brescia in 1494. This was used by Luther in making his version. The same text is used in Bomberg's first Rabbinical Bible, 1516–1517, edited by Felix Pratensis, and in his manual editions 1517 sq.; and also by Stephens, 1539 sq., and Sebastian Munster. (2) The second independent text was issued in the Complutensian Polyglot, 1514–1517, of Cardinal Ximenes. (3) The third independent text was edited by Jacob ben Chayim in the second Rabbinical Bible of Bomberg, 1524–1525. This was carefully revised after the Massora. All the printed texts from that time until recent times are mixtures of these three texts. (4) Baer and Delitzsch undertook a fourth independent text by the use of the entire Massoretic apparatus accessible. The *Liber Psalmorum* was published in 1880. (5) A fifth independent text was published by Ginsburg,

1894. It is essentially "based upon the first edition of Jacob ben Chayim's Massoretic recension." (6) A sixth independent text is in process of publication by R. Kittel (1905), with critical notes, using ancient Vrss. and conjectural emendations. The vol. containing ψ has not yet appeared.

§ 5. *The earliest Version of the Psalter was that of the Greek Septuagint, translated from the Hebrew in the second century B.C. at Alexandria, and preserved in many ancient codices, the earliest of the fourth century A.D., giving evidence as to an original Hebrew text, many centuries prior to any Hebrew authorities. The ancient Latin, Coptic, Gothic, Armenian, and Ethiopic Versions are based upon the Greek Version.*

The OT. was translated for the use of Egyptian and Greek Jews. The earliest writings translated were the five books of the Law in the third century. The Psalter was probably translated in the early second century, for use in public prayer and praise in the Egyptian synagogues. It was made from the best Mss. accessible at the time, and gives evidence as to the original Hebrew text of early second century B.C., three centuries earlier than the text fixed by the school of Jamnia, and twelve centuries earlier than the Mass. text as fixed by Ben Asher and preserved in the earliest Hebrew codd. It is usually called the Septuagint because of the legend that it was prepared by seventy chosen Hebrew scholars (Br.^HS. 188 sq.). The Septuagint Version of the Psalter, referred to in the abbr. ⅊, is one of the best translations of the OT. It shows an excellent knowledge of the original Hebrew, and a good knowledge of Alexandrine Greek. The translator appreciated the poetic character of the Psalter, and also the fact that it was for public use in the worship of the synagogue. He was concerned, therefore, to preserve as far as practicable the metrical form, and to give the sense of the original in intelligible Greek. Where a literal rendering interferes with these objects he departs from the letter and gives the spirit of his original, and so tends toward the method of the later Targums. He shares in the religious and theological prejudices of his times. He has an undue awe of God, and conceives of Him as essentially transcendent. He shrinks from the anthropomorphisms and anthropopathisms of the earlier writers.

The text of 𝕲 has been preserved in several types enabling us to go back, on the genealogical principle of textual criticism, to an original earlier than any of the codices (*v.* Br.[SHS. 231 sq.]). (1) The earliest codex is one preserved in the Vatican Library, usually indicated by B. Pss. 105^{27}–137^6 are missing. This cod. was written in the fourth century A.D. It was the basis of the Sixtine edition of the Septuagint of 1586(7). It was used in the London Polyglot, with critical notes making use of the other known codd.; and so in many manual editions, especially Van Ess, 1823, 1854, and Tischendorf, 1850, 1856. B was published by Mai in 1857, and a facsimile edition by Vercellone and Cozza in 1866 sq., a photographic lithographic edition, 1890. The hands of several later editors may be traced in the text, indicated by B[a. b. c]. (2) About the same time, and under essentially the same influence, the Sinaitic codex was written. It was discovered by Tischendorf in 1844–1859, in the convent of S. Catharine, on Mt. Sinai, and was deposited in the Imperial Library at St. Petersburg. It gives ψ complete. It is known usually as ℵ, but by many Germans as S (*v.* Gregory, *Prolegomena*, pp. 345 sq.). Tischendorf issued a facsimile edition in 1862 (*Bibliorium Codex Sinaiticus Petropolitanus*, Tom I.–IV.). He also used ℵ in his manual editions of 1860, 1869, continued after his death by Nestle, 1875, 1880, 1887. The best text of B has been issued by Swete (3 vols. 1887–1894, 1895–1899), who uses ℵ to supply the missing Pss. The references to B will be given simply as 𝕲[B], those to ℵ will appear as 𝕲[ℵ] (*v.* Intr. Swete's edition). These two codices give what Westcott and Hort term the Neutral Text, based on a text written on separate rolls in the early part of the second century A.D. (*v.* Br.[SHS. 197]). (3) The Alexandrian codex (𝕲[A]), now in the British Museum, was written in the fifth century. Pss. 49^{19}–79^{10} are missing from its text. This codex represents an Alexandrian official text, but later than the revisions of Hesychius and Origen. This text was published by Grabe and his associates in 1707–1720). HP. also cite the *Psalterium purpureum Turicense* (𝕲[T]) as Ms. 262. It has been preserved in the Municipal Library of Zurich. It was published by Tischendorf in his *Monumenta Sacra inedita*, IV. It was evidently written in the seventh century. According to Swete its readings are in frequent agreement with A. The following Pss. are missing: 1–25 30^2–36^{20} 41^6–43^3 58^{14}–59^5 59^{9-10} 59^{13}–60^1 64^{12}–71^4 92^3–93^7 96^{12}–97^8. (4) The text of Origen is represented in the fragments of his Hexapla which have been preserved. A Syriac translation of the text of the Hexapla (Syr. Hex.) was made by Paul of Tella in 616 A.D. A Ms. of this text of the eighth century was discovered by Ceriani in the Ambrosian Library of Milan, and issued in 1874. (5) Lucian the martyr (311 +) made an independent revision of the entire Greek Bible at Antioch. Lagarde issued this text for the Historical books of the OT. in 1883, but died before he was able to publish the rest of the OT. This text rests upon a parent text which is the basis of the old Latin version, is near the Syriac version, and resembles that used in the citations in Josephus (*v.* Br.[SHS. 203-204]). The Codex Vaticanus 330 (HP. 108) was recognised by Field and Lagarde as giving essentially this text. It was the chief authority for the text of the Complutensian Polyglot; but this cod. does not contain ψ. Swete regards 144, 147, 185 HP. as Lucian in their characteristics. (6) The Revision of Hesychius is not so easy to determine. Cornill (*Ezekiel*, 79) and Swete (*Introduction to Old Test. in Greek*, 486) think that the Aldine text gives essentially the text of Hesychius. Four other codices have come into importance in recent times. (7) The *Psalterium Graeco-Latinum Veronense*, 𝕲ᴿ, generally attributed to the sixth century, is preserved in Verona. It was published by Bianchini in his *Vinaiciae canonicarum scripturarum*, I., Rome, 1740; but was not used in HP. It is highly valued by Tisch., Swete, and others. Swete says: "A few portions of the Psalms (1^1–2^7 65^{20}–68^3 68^{26-33} 105^{43}–106^2) have been replaced or supplied by a hand of the tenth century, to which the corrections throughout the Ms. are generally due." (8) The *Fragmenta papyracea Londinensia* (𝕲ᵁ). These are in the British Museum. Only two portions of ψ have been preserved: 10^2–18^6 20^{14}–34^6. It was published by Tisch. in his *Monumenta sacra inedita, Nov. Coll.*, 1855. Tisch. ascribes it to the sixth or seventh century. "Its readings are often unique, or agree with the Hebrew or the Vrss. or patristic citations, against all other known Mss." (Swete, p. xiii). (9) The Leipzig papyrus fragments of the Psalter contain Pss. $30^{5-14, 18-25}$ 31^1 32^{18b}–33^{9a} 33^{13}–34^2 34^{24}–35^3 36^4–55^{14}. They have been published by Heinrici, in *Beiträge zur Geschichte und Erklärung des N.T.*, IV., Leipzig, 1903. According to this scholar, these fragments resemble those of 𝕲ᵁ, and both represent the common text, used by Christians and cited by the early Fathers, as described by Jerome and Origen, before the latter undertook to purify it and establish a correct text (pp. 9, 13, 25).

Many ancient Vrss. were translated from 𝕲. The oldest of these was the ancient Latin. Many Latin Psalters have been preserved, but so far as known, none of them give early texts. We are for the most part dependent on citations in the early Fathers. Jerome made a revision of the Latin Psalter under the auspices of Pope Damasus I. in 383. This is the Roman Psalter still used in St. Peter's at Rome. About 392 Jerome made a second revision on the basis of the Hexapla. This is known as the Gallican Psalter, and is still in use in the Vulgate and the Roman Catholic Breviaries. The Coptic Vrss. were made from 𝕲. The Bohairic Vrs. of the Psalter is of the sixth century (edited by Lagarde, 1875). The Sahidic Vrs. is older, but of uncertain date. The Psalter has been edited by Bridge, 1898. It seems to represent a text of 𝕲 corresponding closely to 𝕲ᵁ (*v.* Brightman, *Journal of Theol. Studies*, II., 275). The old Gothic Vrs. of the sixth and the Slavonic of the ninth century were made from 𝕲 of

Lucian. The Armenian and Ethiopic Vrss. in their present form are based on mixed texts, in which Syriac and Hebraic elements are mingled with the Greek.

The texts of the Psalter in the several codd. of 𝔊 are not always homogeneous with the texts of other parts of OT., especially in the early codd. This was due to the fact that the Psalter was usually on a separate roll, and that the most of these rolls were prepared for ecclesiastical use. Swete remarks quite truly that Pss. of 𝔊ᴬ "are evidently copied from a Psalter written for ecclesiastical use, and it is interesting to notice how constantly A here appears in company with the later liturgical Psalters, R and T, and with the seventh century corrections of ℵ known as ℵ^c. a." He also says: "The first hand of ℵ often agrees with A against B, and the combinations ℵ, A, R, T in the Psalms are not uncommon" (*Intr. to OT. in Greek*, p. 490). To this may be added that in fact it is just these liturgical Psalters which seem to have preserved the most accurate text of 𝔊, whether that was due to the well-known conservatism of liturgical texts, or to a more conservative revision of the ancient faulty texts by Origen and Lucian than has generally been supposed, limited chiefly to the correction of errors. The text of 𝔊 where there is a consensus of readings has a value which has not been estimated by critics as highly as it ought to be, so far as the Psalter is concerned. In a very large number of cases this common text is to be preferred to 𝔥. Where the ancient codd. 𝔊ᴮ· ℵ differ from the other codd. they are almost invariably at fault. It is altogether misleading to take them as the norms of a correct text of the Psalter.

I have carefully examined all the most important variations, and the result is the following. I. Where 𝔊¹ stands alone: (1) there are nine corruptions of Greek words, 17^{14} 27^8 35^{20} 37^{28} 71^{15} 74^8 76^8 84^{11} 105^{36}. (2) There are fourteen omissions of words or clauses of 𝔥 required by measure or else earlier Heb. glosses, 16^2 64^3 $65^{2.6}$ 71^{12} 73^{18} 74^4 75^7 88^{19} 90^{16} 102^{16} 139^{12} 143^3 145^2. (3) There is one insertion injuring the measure, 76^4. (4) There is only a single instance in which the text is correct. That is the omission of a clause of 𝔥, 41^2, which injures the measure. But this may be merely an accidental coincidence in which a careless scribe happened to omit a passage which was a real gloss. II. Where Gᴺ stands alone there are many cases of error, e. g. $110^{3.6.6}$ 115^8 $116^{1.2.5}$ $122^{2.6.9}$ 129^4 130^6 138^8.

The earliest printed editions of the Psalter of 𝕲 rested upon codd. which have not, so far as I know, been determined: Milan, 1481; Venice, 1486, 1489; Basel, 1516. Justinianus issued in 1516 at Genoa his *Octaplum Psalterium*. The text of the Complutensian Polyglot, 1514–1517, was followed by four other polyglots: Antwerp, 1569–1572; Heidelberg, 1586–1587; Hamburg, 1596; Paris, 1645 +. The Aldine text of 1518, the text of the Complutensian Polyglot and of the Octaplum, all agree for the most part with 144, 185, 264, of HP; and although based on late codd., in fact are much nearer the original 𝕲 than the earliest codd. 𝕲^B. N. In a few instances the *Octaplum* differs from the Complutensian text, but in these, so far as the most important readings are concerned, it agrees with 144 HP, which is regarded as Lucian's. A valuable discussion of texts and versions of 𝕲 is given by Swete, *Introduction to the Study of the OT. in Greek*, and by Nestle, *Urtext und Uebersetzungen*, pp. 64–65. A cautious but valuable study of the reading of 𝕲 of Swete's edition is given by F. W. Mozley, *The Psalter of the Church*, 1905. There remains much work to be done in the study of these codd.

§ **6**. *Several other Greek Versions were made in the second, third, and fourth centuries A.D., that of Aquila from the official Hebrew text of the school of Jamnia, that of Theodotion to improve 𝕲 in the direction of that text; and that of Symmachus to give a better Greek style. Other minor Versions, indicated as Quinta and Sexta, were also composed. None of these have been preserved, except in fragments.*

𝕲 was used in a large proportion of the citations in the NT. and Christian writings of the second and third centuries. The Jews of the school of Rabbi Akiba, owing to a literalistic tendency, threw discredit upon 𝕲 among the Jews, and so gradually undermined the confidence even of Christians in its accuracy. Accordingly, many attempts were made to make a better Version. The first of these came from Aquila, a pupil of Akiba, who made a new translation from the official text established by the school of Jamnia. This is exceedingly literal and pedantic, and frequently transliterates rather than translates. This Version, indicated by Aq., is chiefly valuable for its evidence as to the official text which it translates. Theodotion (Θ) undertook a revision of 𝕲 to make it more conformable to the Hebrew text of Jamnia. Its variations from 𝕲 also help to the official Hebrew text of the second century rather than to an earlier text. Symmachus (Σ) had a later and a different purpose; namely, to improve the style and character of 𝕲.

It is therefore of value in helping to a text of 𝔊. It is difficult to determine the purpose of Quinta and Sexta, but so far as appears they do not give evidence of any knowledge of early Hebrew codd. These efforts did not succeed in producing a text suitable for universal adoption; they in fact increased the confusion and corruption among the Greek codd. by mixed texts. This evil was the chief reason for the masterly work of Origen in his Hexapla. Origen's Hexapla was the most important Biblical work in ancient times. It gave in six parallel columns the original Hebrew text, the same transliterated, a purified text of 𝔊, the Versions of Aq., Σ, Θ, and also, as a sort of appendix, Quinta, Sexta.

The Hexapla has been preserved only in parts. The Syriac translation was discovered by Ceriani in the Ambrosian Library of Milan, and published in 1874. Mercati, in the same library, discovered the original Hexapla of Ps. 45 and parts of 17, 27–31, 34, 35, 48, 88, of which he gives an account in *Un Palimpsesto Ambrosiano dei Salmi Esapli*, 1898. He has recently discovered additional material in the Vatican. The publication of all this material is announced for one of the forthcoming parts of *Studi e Testi*, Roma, under the title *Psalmorum Hexaplorum reliquiae e codice rescripto Ambrosiano*, etc. The parts of the several Greek Vrss., so far as they were known to exist at the time, were published by Field, *Origenis Hexaplorum quae supersunt*, 2 vols., Oxford, 1875. Dr. Schechter discovered some fragments of Aq., portions of Pss. 22, 90, 91, in the Genizah at Cairo.

§ 7. *The Syriac Peshitto Version was made from a comparison of the Hebrew text with 𝔊, and shows the influence of an early Aramaic Targum. It has maintained its integrity since the fourth century.*

At an early date, probably in the second or third century, a translation of the Psalter was made for the use of Syrian Christians (𝔖). It was based upon a Hebrew text, but kept 𝔊 constantly in view. It also shows traces of the influence of an oral Aramaic Targum earlier than the existing Targum (*v.* § 13). The author was a good Hebrew scholar, but his purpose was to give a Vrs. for practical use, rather than an exact verbal rendering. He therefore takes liberties with the original from a dogmatic as well as a practical point of view. 𝔖 passed through a number of revisions, but has kept its integrity since the fourth century, as Aphraates in his Homilies uses it essentially in the same form that we now have.

The first edition of the Psalter of $\mathfrak{S}$ was published by Erpenius, Leyden, 1625, from two late codd. Gabriel Sionita in the same year issued a Syriac text based on three other codd., with a Latin translation. This edition was used in the Paris Polyglot, 1629–1645, and the London Polyglot, 1654–1657. In the latter, Herbert Thorndyke in his critical apparatus used two codd. of late date. Dathe in 1768 reissued the text of Erpenius, with variations from the London Polyglot. The text of the London Polyglot was reissued by Lee in 1823, and was translated into English with critical notes by Andrew Oliver, Boston, 1861. The American missionaries, in 1852, published at Urumia, Persia, a Nestorian text of much value. This has been the basis of other texts for use in the East. The Codex Ambrosianus was published by Ceriani, Milan, 1876–1883. F. Bäthgen, in 1878, made a collation of this codex and three later codd. in his *Untersuchungen*. In 1879, in his *Psalterium Tetraglottam*, Nestle reissued the Codex Ambrosianus ; and this edition has been reprinted by W. E. Barnes, in his *Peshitta Psalter according to the West Syrian Text*, 1904. Barnes, however, corrects it occasionally from early West Syrian codd., and gives a rich critical apparatus derived from a collation of a large number of codd. The best estimate of the text of $\mathfrak{S}$ is given by Bä. in the *Jahrbücher für Protestanische Theologie*, 1882. The influence of $\mathfrak{G}$ upon $\mathfrak{S}$ was so great that when these agree it is doubtful whether the testimony of $\mathfrak{S}$ as to the original text of $\mathfrak{H}$ is independent. Especially was $\mathfrak{S}$ influenced by $\mathfrak{G}^L$; but, on the other hand, it belongs to the same family of texts. Agreement with $\mathfrak{H}$ is of greater importance, and disagreement with $\mathfrak{H}$ and $\mathfrak{G}^L$ more important still. It should also be remembered, as Barnes justly says, " We have to deal in the Psalter with a text which was specially transcribed for ecclesiastical use, and accordingly we must not be surprised, if we find it coloured by ecclesiastical phraseology" (p. xxxv). On the one side, it may be said that because of its ecclesiastical use it is more difficult to revise the Psalter than any other book of the Bible ; on the other side, that the Vrss. often preserve early readings. My study of the text of the Psalter shows that while $\mathfrak{S}$ tends to an agreement with $\mathfrak{G}^L$, it nevertheless often agrees with $\mathfrak{H}$ against $\mathfrak{G}$, and sometimes with $\mathfrak{J}$ against $\mathfrak{G}$ and MT. It not infrequently has independent readings, a fair proportion of which are to be preferred as nearer the original text than those of any other Vrss., even of $\mathfrak{H}$; cf. $2^{7.\ 12}$ 16^2 17^{13} 27^8 32^4 46^6 74^3, but especially 4^8 $17^{3.\ 4}$ 59^{10} 69^6 80^{13} 112^4 139^{16}.

§ 8. *Jerome in the early fifth century issued his Latin translation, made from the Hebrew text of his times, but with all the other ancient Versions and Origen's Hexapla in view.*

Jerome, after the completion of the two revisions of the old Latin Psalter already mentioned (§ 5), undertook *c.* 389 a translation of the entire OT. from the original Hebrew, which he completed in 390–405 at Bethlehem. This Vrs. took the place of the old Latin Vrss. in all the books except the Psalter, and is known as the Vulgate (𝕍). This new Vrs. of the Psalter could not overcome the use of the Gallican Psalter in the usage of the Church. Accordingly, 𝕍 of the Psalter is the Gallican Version, and the Version of Jerome is distinguished from it in reference by the abbreviation 𝕁. This Vrs. is exceedingly valuable, especially in the study of the Psalter; for Jerome was not only an able Hebrew scholar, using the best Hebrew texts accessible to him in Palestine, at the time when the Rabbinical School at Tiberius was in its bloom; but he was also familiar with Origen's *Hexapla*, and the full text of all the ancient Vrss. in earlier Mss. than those now existing. 𝕁 in the main gives evidence as to the Hebrew text of the fourth Christian century. Where it differs from 𝕳 and 𝕲 its evidence is especially valuable as giving the opinion of the best Biblical scholar of ancient times as to the original text, based on the use of a wealth of critical material vastly greater than that in the possession of any other critic, earlier or later.

The text of 𝕁 is best given in Lagarde's *Psalterium juxta Hebraeos Hieronymi*, 1874, and also in Nestle's *Psalterium Tetraglottum*, 1879.

§ **9.** *The Aramaic Targum of the Psalter in its present form dates from the ninth century, but it rests upon an oral Targum used in the synagogue from the most ancient times.*

The Targum on the Psalter (𝕋) represents a traditional oral translation, used in the services of the synagogue from the first century A.D. The original Hebrew text was constantly kept in view, for it was the custom to read the original before the Targum was read. Therefore the Targum gives evidence as to the traditional Hebrew text, with all the development that that tradition had from the first till the ninth century, ever restrained, however, by the original text. The Targum, however, was not simply a translation, but at the same time an explanation of the original, enlarging upon it to give the sense by way of paraphrase. It avoids anthropomorphism, and entirely disregards the poetic form and style.

𝕋 of ψ was first published by Bomberg, 1517, with Jb., Pr., and the Rolls. Lagarde's edition *Hagiographa Chaldaice*, 1873, is based on that of Bomberg. It was republished by Nestle, in his *Psalterium Tetraglottum*, 1879. Bacher

(*Das Targum zu den Psalmen*, Grätz, *Monatsschrift*, 1872) states that the 𝔗 of ψ and Jb. came from the same hand.

§ **10.** *The critical use of Hebrew texts and versions leads back in several stages from the official text of Ben Asher of the tenth century, through the text used by Jerome of the fourth century, the official text of the School of Jamnia of the second century, to the unofficial codices of the second century B.C., which gave the Canonical Psalter in its final edition. But it had already passed through centuries of transmission by the hands of copyists and editors. We have to distinguish, therefore, between the original text of the Psalter of the Canon and the original text of the psalms themselves as they came from their authors.*

The existing Hebrew codd. lead us to the official MT. of the tenth century as edited by Ben Asher, with Massoretic notes indicating traditional variations in the text coming down from ancient times. 𝔍 takes us back to a Hebrew text of the fourth century prior to the work of the Massorites, and therefore to a text composed of consonants only. The Hebrew text of Origen's *Hexapla*, and 𝔖, also tend in the same direction, although they are to be used with more reserve, because of modifying influences traceable in these Vrss. The Greek translations of Aq., Θ, are all important helps to determine the official Hebrew text of the Synod of Jamnia of the second Christian century. The text of 𝔊 carries us still farther back, to a Hebrew text of the second century B.C., very soon after the Psalter had received its final editing. In this way, by the use of the genealogical principle of Textual Criticism the original Hebrew text of the Psalter may be determined, at the time when it was finally edited for use in the synagogue and temple, and took its place in the Canon of the Writings. But it is evident that even then we are a long distance from the original text of the Pss. as composed by their authors. The Pss. had passed through the hands of a multitude of copyists, and of many editors, who had made changes of various kinds, partly intentional and partly unintentional. The Pss. were changed and adapted for public worship, just as has ever been the case with hymns, prayers, and other liturgical forms. The personal, local, and historical features were gradually effaced, and additions of various kinds were made to make them more appropriate for congregational use. The text of the Psalter is one thing, the text of the original Pss. is another thing. After we have determined the former as far as possible, we still have to determine the latter by the use of additional internal evidence in the Psalter itself, and of external evidence from other books of OT.

§ **11.** *There are several Psalms which appear in different texts in the Psalter itself, or in the Psalter and other Books of the Old Testament. These give evidence of originals differing in some respects from the varying texts that have been preserved.*

(1) Pss. 14 and 53 are evidently the same Ps. in different texts. The latter betrays more clearly its historical origin, although the original divine name יהוה has been changed to אלהים, as in other Pss. of 𝔈 (*v.* § 32). The former has been generalised and made smoother and more didactic. They both show editorial changes as well as errors of copyists. (2) Ps. 18 is the same song as that given in 2 S. 22. The text of the latter is more archaic, although it has many of the same late glosses as the Ps. The Ps., however, received still later revision, making it more suitable for public use. (These variations are given in the Massora of Baer's text, pp. 130–135.) (3) Ps. 70 is the same essentially as 40¹⁸⁻¹⁷. It was appended to Ps. 40 for liturgical purposes, and adapted to its context. (4) An early Ps. has been used both by 57⁸⁻¹² and 108¹⁻⁶, another by 60⁷⁻¹⁴ and 108⁷⁻¹⁴, these three Pss. being all composite (*v.* § 14). (5) 1 Ch. 16⁸⁻³⁶ gives a Song of thanksgiving, which is composed of Pss. 105¹⁻¹⁵ and 96. The former is part of a tetralogy, 104–107; the latter is a part of the royal Ps. broken up into 93, 96–100. The Song of Ch. is therefore a mosaic of parts of two Pss., to which a doxology was added by a late editor of Ch., who inserted it as a specimen of the temple Pss. of his time.

§ **12.** *The Psalms were composed in the parallelisms, measures, and strophical organisations of lyric poetry. When these have been determined with reference to any particular Psalm it is not difficult to see the changes that have been made in the original text.*

(*A*) Hebrew poetry is dominated by the principle of parallelism of members. The simplest form is seen in the couplet; but it is extended to a considerable number of lines. There are three primary forms of parallelism: (1) the synonymous, (2) the synthetic, and (3) the antithetic; the synonymous having a more ornate variety which may be called (4) emblematic; the synthetic a more vigorous variety which is (5) stairlike in character. An

important variation appears in what is called (6) introverted parallelism. But within these six varieties there are still a great number
of combinations in accordance with the nature of the parallelism,
whether it extends to entire lines or to the more emphatic words
in them.

Bishop Lowth (*De sacra Poesi Heb.* 1753; cf. Preliminary Dissertation to
Isaiah, 1778) was the first to establish the principle of parallelism in Hebrew
poetry, although he based his conclusions on older writers, Rabbi Asarias and
especially Schöttgen (*Horae Heb.* Diss. VI. *De Exergasia Sacra*). Lowth's
views were at once accepted and have maintained themselves. Lowth distinguished three kinds of parallelism, — the synonymous, the antithetical, and
the synthetic. Bishop Jebb (*Sacred Literature*, § IV. 1820) called attention to a fourth kind, which he properly named "introverted." Lowth had
already recognised it (Prelim. Diss. *Isaiah* xiv), but did not name it or
emphasize it. Other scholars have noted the stairlike and the emblematic
(*v.* Br.SHS. 385-414).

Attention may be called to the following specimens: —

(1) *Synonymous.*

15¹   YAHWEH, who shall be a guest in Thy tent?
         Who shall dwell on Thy holy mount?

17¹³⁻¹⁴ᵃ   O RISE, Yahweh, confront him, cast him down;
         O deliver me from the wicked, destroy with Thy sword;
         May they be slain with Thy hand, Yahweh; slain from the world.

7¹³⁻¹⁴   IF not, He whets His sword,
         Doth tread His bow and make it ready,
         And doth prepare for him deadly weapons;
         His arrows He maketh into fiery ones.

6⁷⁻⁸   FOR I am weary with *my* groaning;
         I must complain every night on *my* bed;
         I make dissolve with my tears *my* couch.
         Wasteth away because of grief *mine* eye,
         Waxeth old because of all *mine* adversaries.

19⁸⁻¹⁰   THE Law of Yahweh is perfect, refreshing the soul;
         The Testimony of Yahweh is trustworthy, making wise the simple;
         The Precepts of Yahweh are right, rejoicing the heart;
         The Commandment of Yahweh is pure, enlightening the eyes;
         The Saying of Yahweh is clean, enduring forever;
         The Judgments of Yahweh are true, vindicated altogether.

(2) *Synthetic.*

14²   YAHWEH looked forth from heaven upon the sons of mankind,
         To see whether there was any acting intelligently in seeking after God.

17¹¹⁻¹²   THEY advance, now they march about, they fix their eyes;
         They purpose to camp in the land, they maltreat as a lion;
         They are greedy for prey, they are like a young lion lurking in secret
         places.

23⁵⁻⁶   THOU spreadest before me a table in the presence of mine adversaries
         Hast thou anointed my head with oil; my cup is exhilarating.
         Surely goodness and kindness pursue me all the days of my life,
         And I shall dwell in the house of Yahweh for length of days.

40²⁻⁴   I WAITED steadfastly on Yahweh, and He inclined unto me;
         And brought me up from the pit of desolation, from the clay of the
             mire;
         And set my feet upon a rock; He established my steps;
         And gave a new song in my mouth, a song of praise to my God.
         Many see and they fear, and they trust in Yahweh.

(3) *Antithetical.*

37¹²⁻¹³ THE wicked deviseth against the righteous and gnasheth his teeth at him.
         The Lord laugheth at him; for He seeth that his day cometh.

17¹⁴ᵇ⁻¹⁵ LET their portion be during life; their belly fill Thou with Thy stored up
             penalty.
         May their sons be sated, may they leave their residue to their children.
         But as for me, let me behold Thy face; let me be satisfied with Thy
             favour.

126⁴⁻⁶   O RESTORE, Yahweh, our prosperity, as streams do in the south country.
         They that sow seed in tears, may they reap with jubilation.
         He may go forth weeping, bearing the load of seed;
         Let him come home with jubilation, bearing the load of sheaves.

37⁹⁻¹¹   FOR evil-doers will be cut off; but those that wait on Yahweh will inherit
             the land.
         And yet a little while, and the wicked will be no more, and thou wilt
             attentively consider his place, and he will be no more;
         But the afflicted will inherit the land, and take delight in abundance
             of peace.

38¹⁸⁻¹⁵ THEY also that seek my life lay snares;
         Of my distress they speak, of ruin;
         And utter deceits all the day.
         But I am like a deaf man that heareth not,
         And as a dumb man that openeth not his mouth,
         And in whose mouth are no arguments.

(4) *Emblematic.*

37¹⁻²   FRET not thyself because of evil-doers, and be not envious against them
             that do wrong;
         As grass they will speedily wither, and like the fresh grass fade.

124⁶⁻⁸   BLESSED be Yahweh! who hath not given us over as a prey to their
             teeth.
         Lo, we are like a bird, that has escaped out of the trap of the fowler.
         Lo, the trap was broken, and we escaped from it.
         Our help is in the name of Yahweh, maker of heaven and earth.

129⁵⁻⁸ᵃ LET them be put to shame, and let them be turned backward, all the
             haters of Zion,
         Let them become as grass of the housetops, which, before one can
             draw the scythe, withereth.

Wherewith the reaper does not fill his hand, or he that bindeth sheaves
his bosom.
And they who pass by say not, " The blessing of Yahweh unto you."

(5) *Stairlike.*

24^{8b. c}   YAHWEH, strong and *mighty*,
         Yahweh, *mighty* in battle.

3²⁻³   YAHWEH, how *many* are mine adversaries!
         Many are rising up against me;
         Many are saying of me:
         "There is no salvation for him."

25¹⁻⁷   UNTO Thee, Yahweh, I lift up my soul; O my God, let me not *be
         ashamed.*
         In Thee I trust, therefore let not mine enemies exult, even mine.
         Yea, let none that wait on Thee *be ashamed;* let them *be ashamed* that
         deal treacherously without effect.
         Thy ways make me know, Yahweh, and Thy thoughts *teach* me;
         Lead me in Thy faithfulness, and *teach* me; for Thou art the God of
         my salvation.
         Remember Thy compassion, Yahweh, and Thy kindness, for they are
         of old.
         The sins of my youth *remember* not; according to Thy kindness
         remember me.

In the other two Strs. of this Ps. the stairlike parall. is carried out on the
scheme: $2 + 2 + 3$, Str. II.; $3 + 2 + 2$, Str. III., as Str. I. In every tristich
the middle line does not have the catchword.

12⁴⁻⁵   MAY Yahweh cut off every flattering *lip*,
         And every *tongue* speaking great words;
         Those who say, "To our *tongues* we give might,
         Our *lip* is our own; who is lord over us."

(6) *Introverted.*

30⁹⁻¹¹   UNTO Thee I was crying, and unto my God I was making supplication
         for favour:
             "What profit is there in my blood, when I go down to the Pit?
             Will the dust praise Thee, declare Thy faithfulness?
         Hear and be gracious, become helper to me."

6⁹⁻¹¹   DEPART, ye workers of trouble, from *me;*
             For He hath heard the voice of *my* weeping,
             Yahweh hath heard *my* supplication,
             Yahweh accepteth *my* prayer.
         They will turn back, they will be put to shame in a moment.

34¹⁶⁻²²   THE face of Yahweh is against them that do evil, to cut off their memory
         from the land.
             The eyes of Yahweh are unto the righteous, and His ears unto their
             cry for help;
             They cry and Yahweh heareth, and delivereth them out of all their
             distresses.

> Yahweh is nigh unto the brokenhearted, and the crushed in spirit
> saveth.
> Many are the misfortunes of the righteous, but out of them all Yah-
> weh delivereth him ;
> He keepeth all his bones ; not one of them is broken.
> Misfortune shall slay the wicked, and they that hate the righteous shall
> suffer punishment.

(*B*) The Pss., as Philo, Josephus, Origen, Eusebius, and Jerome tell us, were composed in several kinds of meter. The measures, however, were not of feet, as in classic Latin and Greek, or of syllables as in Syriac poetry ; but of words or word accents, as in Assyrian, Babylonian, Egyptian, and the most ancient poetry of other nations. The simplest measure is : (1) the trimeter, measured by three tonic beats ; (2) the tetrameter, which has four tones, usually with a caesura in the middle ; (3) the pentameter, which has five tones, the caesura usually coming after the third tone, but sometimes for variety of effect after the second ; (4) the hexameter, which has six tones, with the caesura usually in the middle, but sometimes for variety after the second or the fourth tones, and occasionally with two caesuras dividing the line into three parts. In the estimation of tones we have to consider that on the one side monosyllabic words are usually not counted, but are attached to the following word and not accented ; and on the other side that words of four or more syllables have a secondary accent which is counted in the measures. This is true occasionally of words of three syllables.

The statements of Josephus (*Ant.* II. 16 (4); IV. 8 (44); VII. 12 (30)) that Hebrew poetry was composed of trimeters and pentameters and hexameters are so distinct that they cannot justly be questioned. He is sustained by Philo (*de Vita Mosis*, I. 5). Although it may be said that Origen (on Ps. 118, Pitra, *Analecta Sacra*, II. 341), Eusebius (*De praep. Evang.* XI. 5 Migne, XXI. 852), and Jerome (in *librum Job, praef.*) depended upon Josephus, yet they were near enough to the original Hebrew text to have an independent judgment in this matter; and their judgment has been confirmed by modern investigation in the teeth of a stubborn traditional opposition. As Ley shows (*ZATW.* XII. 212), Origen distinguishes between the Hebrew pentameter and hexameter written in one line and the Greek method of dividing them into two. I. Many efforts have been made to measure syllables after classic models : (1) Franc. Gomarus (*Davidis lyra*, 1637), followed by Heinsius, De Dieu, Hottinger, and the younger Buxtorf. (2) Marc. Maibon

(*Davidis Psalmi X. item* VI. 1690).   (3) Francis Hare (*Psalmorum libri in versiculos metrice divisus*, 1736), followed especially by Weisse.   The treatises of Gomarus, Maibon, and Hare were republished in Ugolino, *Thesaurus* (XXXI.).   Lowth severely criticised Hare's measures.   He had no doubt that Hebrew poetry had measured lines, and he distinguished between long and short measures, in the former recognizing the " small rest or interval "; but he thought that it would be impracticable to find more definite measures because the original pronunciation of the Hebrew language could not be known (*v.* Prelim. Diss. to *Isaiah*, xxv.).   (4) William Jones (*Poeseos Asiaticae commentariorum*, 1776) applied the rules of Arabic meter to Hebrew poetry, involving the doing away with the Massoretic system of vowels.   So, essentially, E. J. Greve.   (5) J. J. Bellermann (*Versuch über die Metrik der Hebräer*, 1813), applied the system of morae to Hebrew poetry.   (6) J. L. Saalschütz (*Von der Form der Hebräischen Poesie*, 1853) rejected the Massoretic system and built on the pronunciation of the Polish and German Jews, after the Aramaic method.   II. G. Bickell (*Metrices Biblicae*, 1879; *Carmina Veteris Metrici*, 1882; *Dichtungen der Hebräer*, 1882–1884), followed by G. Gietmann (*de re metrica Hebraeorum*, 1880), finds a Hebrew meter in the number of syllables after the method of Syriac poetry.   There is a constant alternation of rise and fall, so that only iambic and trochaic feet are possible.   The Massoretic system is rejected and the Aramaic virtually put in its place.   The accent is generally, as in Syriac, on the penult.   An elaborate criticism of Bickell's theory is given by Ecker (*Porta Sion*, 1903, pp. 147 sq.).   Doubtless the original Hebrew pronunciation was different from that of the Massoretic system, but Hebrew was not a mere dialect of the Aramaic, still less of so late a form of it as the Syriac.   It has recently been shewn that the earliest Syriac poetry did not measure by number of syllables.   III. The measurement of Hebrew verse by the beat of the accent has been maintained by a great number of scholars with increasing conviction.   This is independent of the doctrine of syllables, whether more like the Arabic, Aramaic, or the Massoretic system.   Moreover, it is independent of the theory on what syllable of the word the accent should fall.   In any case, we have just so many accents in the verse.   The earliest writer to make the accent the determining principle of measurement, so far as I have been able to discover, was C. G. Anton (*conjectura de metro Hebraeorum*, 1770, *Specimen editionis Psalmorum*, 1780).   In this he was followed by Leutwein (*Versuch einer richtigen Theorie von der Biblischen Verskunst*, 1775), Ernst Meier (*Die Form der Hebr. Poesie*, 1853), but especially Julius Ley (*Die metrischen Formen der Hebr. Poesie*, 1866; *Grundzüge des Rhythmus des Vers- und Strophenbaues in der Hebr. Poesie*, 1875; *Leitfaden der Metrik der Hebr. Poesie*, 1887, and other minor writings).   To Ley, more than to any other scholar, is due the credit of leading to a correct conception of the measures of Hebrew poetry. I accepted the principle of measurement of Hebrew poetry by accents soon after I began to teach as Professor of Hebrew and cognate languages in Union Theological Seminary, in 1874 ; and from that time I have given much attention to the subject. My views were published in 1881 (*Homiletic Quarterly*, pp. 398 sq., 555 sq. ; *Biblical Study*, first edition, 1883, pp. 262 sq.). The principles were applied in the study of the *Poem of the Fall of Mankind* (*Reformed Quarterly Review*, 1866), *Poem of the Creation* (*Old Testament Student*, 1884), and of all the poetic Messianic passages (*Messianic Prophecy*, 1886). My views were more fully stated in five articles (*Hebraica*, 1886–1888), and in the tenth edition of *Biblical Study*, enlarged under the title *General Introduction to the Study of Holy Scripture*, 1899. In 1883 I criticised Ley's octameters and decameters as simply double tetrameters and pentameters, and objected to his theory of substitution and compensation, which he has since abandoned. This principle of tonic measures was adopted by Francis Brown (*Measures of Heb. Poetry as an Aid to Literary Analysis*, *JBL*. IX. pp. 91-106) and many other Americans. C. H. Toy (*Commentary on Proverbs*, 1899) uses the tonic principle, but objects to the terms trimeter and tetrameter, and uses ternary, quaternary, etc. W. R. Harper used the method on the basis of my article in *Hebraica*, in the preparation of his *Commentary on Amos and Hosea*, 1905 (*v.* Preface, ix.). Cheyne employs the tonic principle (in his commentaries on the *Psalms*[2, 3], *Book of the Prophet Isaiah*, *SBOT*. 1899). Most Biblical scholars since Jebb have been reactionary in their views of Hebrew poetry. Budde (*Das Hebraische Klagelied*, *ZATW*. 1882) deserves great credit for his investigation of the pentameter in the Old Testament ; but the name, *Kina* verse, that he gave to it, though adopted by many scholars, has little to justify it, for the earliest *Kina* uses the tetrameter measure (2 S. 1[17-27]), and the pentameter measure is used for all kinds of poems, especially for those in praise of the Law, 19[8-15] 119, which are the reverse of *Kina's*. Budde's long hesitation to accept other measures is difficult to understand. He says, however (article *Hebrew Poetry*, DB.), " The vastly preponderating probability appears to belong to the theory of Ley, who counts the 'rises' without taking account of the 'falls.' " Duhm, in his Commentaries on *Isaiah*, 1892, and the *Psalter*, 1899, also uses the tonic principle, but without any explanation of his principles or his relation to others. It is astonishing how exactly his views, as to many passages, correspond with those given previously in my *Messianic Prophecy*, 1886. In the meanwhile the principle of tonic measure was greatly strengthened by the discovery that the same principle determined the structure of the more ancient Egyptian, Babylonian, and Assyrian poetry. F. Brown (*Religious Poetry of Babylonia*, *Presbyterian Review*, 1888), among other examples, shewed that the epic of the descent of Istar to Sheol is pentameter. The Hymn to the Nile was recognised as measured by the tonic accent, by Guieysse (*Records of the Past*, new ed., III. 47-48). Erman also (*Life in Ancient Egypt*, p. 395) stated that Egyptian poetry was measured by the tonic accent. Two recent scholars have endeavoured to fortify the tonic principle by a closer study of the syllable. H. Grimme (*Abriss der Bib. Hebr. Metrik*, *ZDMG*. 1895; *Grundzüge der Hebr. Akzent und Vokallehre*, 1896; *Psalmen Probleme*, 1902) revives the use of morae, but builds essentially on the accents for measurement of lines. His last book has only come into my hands since I completed my Ms. for this Commentary. Our independent work agrees as to the measures of Pss. 1–50, except in 7, 9–10, 11, 17, 19^a 23, 25, 31, 32, 34, 37, 38. Pss. 25, 34, 37, hexameters, he interprets as trimeters, dividing the lines at the caesuras. The other Pss. are full of difficulty, due chiefly to glosses where there is room for difference in reconstruction. E. Sievers in 1901 published his *Metrische Studien*. While building on the tonic principle, he fortifies it by giving it a foundation in the laws of speech, song, and music, and by a careful study of the unaccented syllables. His principles have been adopted for the most part in Bäthgen's *Psalmen*[3], 1904. Sievers, in his double fours and sevens, falls into an error similar to that of Ley. His double fours of Ex. 15, 2 S. 1, Ju. 5 are nothing but tetrameters, and his sevens limited, so far as ψ is concerned, to 4, 9–10, are due to mistaken interpretation of the measures, which in both cases in the original Pss. were trimeters, disturbed, however, by many glosses. Those who have used the principle of tonic measure since Anton, have not failed to recognise that the stress of the accent alternates with a falling of the voice in one, two, or three syllables, in varied relation to the tonic syllable ; but they have not thought it needful to count these syllables as Sievers does. Indeed, Sievers (p. 77) recognises that Anton instinctively came nearest the truth, that his theory needs few modifications, and that he only failed in working it out in detail. But it is just this detail in Sievers' method which is of doubtful value. It is based on the essential accuracy of the Massoretic system, which, as is evident from the transliterations in Origen's Hexapla, was artificial ; and, as many Hebrew scholars since Lowth have recognised, is of doubtful originality. And in fact Sievers' measures, as those of Grimme, really depend upon the tonic accents, which alone are of any great importance even in his system. In the use of the natural laws of speech and music as the basis of the measures of poetry, Sievers was anticipated by the eminent American poet, Sydney Lanier (*Science of English Verse*, 1880), whom I used at an early date. A most thoroughgoing and invariably hostile criticism of metrical theories of Hebrew poetry is given by Ecker (*Porta Sion*, 22–181 ; 1903). A more recent, less complete, more sympathetic, yet uncertain criticism is given by W. H. Cobb (*Criticism of Systems of Hebrew Metre*, 1905).

The following is the result of my study of the measures of the Psalms : —

I. There are eighty-nine trimeter Pss. in the Psalter. This is a favourite measure for lyrics. These Pss. are 2, 3, 6, 7, 8, 9–10, 11, 15, 18, 19$^{2-7}$ 20, 21, 22, 24$^{1-6}$ 24$^{7-10}$ 26, 27$^{7-12}$ 33, 36$^{6-10}$ 38, 44, 47, 49, 51, 54, 55$^{2-3.\ 5-8}$ 56, 57$^{2-5}$ 57$^{6.\ 8-12}$ (= 108$^{2-6}$) 59, 60$^{3-7.\ 12b-14}$ 60^{8-12a} (= 108$^{8-14}$) 63, 66$^{1-9}$ 66$^{13-19}$ 67, 69$^{8-14.\ 20-29}$ 71, 73, 75, 76, 77$^{2-16}$ 77$^{17-20}$ 78, 79, 80, 81^{2-6b} 81^{6c-15} 82, 83, 85, 88, 89$^{4-5.\ 18-46}$ 90, 91, 92, 93 + 96–100, 94, 95$^{1-6}$ 95$^{7-11}$ 102$^{2-12}$ 103, 104, 105–106, 107, 109$^{1-5.\ 16-18.\ 21-27}$ 109$^{6-15}$ 111, 112, 113, 114, 115$^{1-8}$ 115$^{9-16}$ 116, 117, 118, 135, 136, 138, 139$^{1-6.\ 13-16.\ 23-24}$ 139$^{7-12}$ 139$^{17-22}$ 142, 144$^{1-2.\ 7-11}$ 146 147$^{1-6.\ 7-11.\ 12-21}$ 148, 149, 150. We may give as a specimen 24$^{1-6}$: —

ליהוה הארץ ומלואה
תבל וישבי בה
כי־הוא על־ימים יסרה
ועל נהרות יכוננה
מי־יעלה בהר יהוה
מי־יקום במקום קדשו
נקי ובר לבב
לא־נשא לשוא נפשו
ישא ברכה מיהוה
וצדקה מאלהי ישעו
זה דור דרשו
מבקשי פניו יעקב

II. There are twenty tetrameters in the Psalter: 1, 4, 12, 13, 16, 29, 30, 41, 46, 58, 61, 64, 68, 74, 86, 89[2-3. 6-15] 89[47-52] 140, 141, 144[12-15]. Ps. 13 may be given as a specimen. The caesura is always in the middle when it occurs.

עד־אנא יהוה — נצח תשכחני
עד־אנא תסתיר את־פניך ממני
עד־אנא אשית עצות בנפשי
עד־אנא ירום עלי איבי
יהוה אלהי — הביטה ענני
פן־אישן המות — האירה עיני
פן־יאמר איבי — לו יכלתי
פן־יגל כי אמוט צרי

III. There are twenty-five pentameters in the Psalter: 5, 14 (= 53), 17, 19[8-15] 27[1-6] 28, 32, 35, 36[2-5] 39 40[2-12] 42-43, 48, 52, 55[10-16. 21-22. 24] 65, 69[2-7. 15-19. 30-32] 40[14-18] (= 70), 84, 87, 101, 110, 119, 137, 143. Ps. 14 may be given as a specimen. The caesura usually comes after the third beat, but occasionally for variety after the second.

אמר נבל בלבו — אין אלהים
השחיתו התעיבו עלילה — אין־עשה־טוב
יהוה משמים השקיף — על־בני־אדם
לראות היש משכיל — דרש אלהים
הכל סר סג — יחדו נאלחו
אין־עשה־טוב — אין גם אחד
הלא ידעו פעלי־און — אכלו עמי
אכלו לחם — יהוה לא קראו
שם פחדו פחד — כי־אל פזרם
עצמת הביש — כי יהוה מאסם

IV. There are twenty-five hexameters: the alphabetical 25, 34, 37, 145; the pilgrim Pss. 120, 121, 122, 123, 124, 125, 126, 127[1-2] 127[3-5] 128, 129, 130,

131, 132, 133, 134; and 31, 50, 62, 72, 102[13-28, 29]. Pss. 124, 125 illustrate the varied use of the caesura.

לולי יהוה שהיה לנו — יאמר־נא ישראל
לולי יחוה שהיה לנו — בקום עלינו
אזי חיים בלעוני — בחרות אפם בנו
אזי המים שטפוני — נחלה עבר נפשנו

ברוך יהוה — שלא נתננו טרף לשניהם
(הנה) נפשנו כצפר — נמלטה מפח יוקשים
(הנה) הפח נשבר — ואנחנו נמלטנו (ממנה)
עזרנו בשם יהוה — עשה שמים וארץ

הבטחים ביהוה — כהר ציון — לא־ימוט לעוס
ישב ירושלים — הרים סביב לה
ויהוה סביב לעמו — מעתה ועד עולם
כי־לא ינוח שבט הרשע — על־גורל הצדיקים

V. There are long Pss. of varying measures. Ps. 23 has three Strs. of three, four, and five tones, increasing with each Str. Ps. 45 is essentially a tetrameter, but it uses occasional trimeters with striking effect for a more rapid movement of the thought. In this it resembles the Song of Deborah, Ju. 5. Some scholars, as Toy and Duhm, recognise dimeters of two tones, but these are parts of tetrameters or hexameters. The division made by these scholars are at the caesuras. There are no dimeters except in broken lines used at times for a metrical pause (e.g. Pss. 1[1, 4] 8[2, 10]). Many of Grimme's trimeters are really hexameters. Sievers' double threes and double fours are trimeters and tetrameters.

VI. The Hebrew poets seldom accent a monosyllable. It usually loses its tone by being attached to the previous or the subsequent word. Two successive tonic syllables make very bad euphony, especially at the end of l. There were various devices for overcoming this difficulty. At the end of l., the accent of the word before the monosyllable was retracted; e.g. שֹׁפְטֵי אֶרֶץ 2[10], 24[1]. Two tones וְיֹשְׁבֵי בָה 18[20], חָמֵץ בְּי 7[15], וַיֵּלֶד עָשֶׁר‎,יֹהֶבל און 2[12], חֹסֵי בי 2[10], were gained by attaching three short words; e.g. כָּל־חֹסֵי־בָךְ 5[12], כִּי־סָרוּ־בָךְ 5[11], כָּל־יֹשְׁבֵי־הָלֶד 49[2]. The insertion of the conj. ו before a monosyllable makes a sufficient vocalic utterance to justify giving the word a tone. It is sometimes used to make it easier to give a long word two tones; e.g. וְאַל 25[2], וְאַל 41[9], 37[31] וְלֹא, וְיֵל 3[9], 37[1], in all cases given by 𝕲 but omitted by 𝕳.

(C) The Hebrew poets, as poets of other nations, used archaic words and forms for metrical purposes: (a) The archaic case endings softened the transition from word to word and made the language more melodious. (b) The archaic suffixes and modal forms were used partly for the same purpose and partly to give the tone a more melodious position. (*c*) The archaic prepositions were employed in order to get independent words or variation in the tonic syllable (Ley.*Grundzüge,* S. 100 sq.; Br.*SHS. 371*).

(*a*) י 50[10] 79[2] 104[20] 114[8].
 ־ְ 123[1].
 ־ְתָה for ה־ֶ 3[3] 44[27] 63[8] 80[3] 92[16] 94[17] 120[1] 125[8].
(*b*) נּוּ 5[13] 25[12] 41[4] +.
 וּן 5[10] 11[2. 3] 12[9] 35[11] 36[8] +.
 ־ָמוֹ sf. 2[3. 5] 11[7] 21[10. 11. 13] 22[5] +; לָמוֹ for לָהֶם 2[4] 44[4. 11] 49[14] +.
(*c*) בְּמוֹ for בְּ 11[2].
 כְּמוֹ for כְּ 29[6] 58[5. 8. 10] 63[6] 78[13] 90[9] 92[8] +.
 עֲדֵי for עַד 104[23].
 עֲלֵי for עַל 50[5. 16] 92[4] 94[20].
 מִנִּי for מִן 44[11] 45[9] 78[2].
 בְּלִי for בַּל 19[4] 63[2] 72[7].

(*D*) The Hebrew poets ornamented their lines by various devices at the beginning, in the middle, before caesuras, and at the end. At the beginning the order of the alphabet was followed and acrostics were made of various kinds. Certain important words were repeated in several successive lines. At the ends of lines a kind of assonance or rhyme was made, especially by the use of identical suffixes. The same device was also used at times before caesuras.

(*a*) The Alphabetic Pss. are 9–10, 25, 34, 37, 111, 112, 119, 145. Usually the letter of the alphabet begins a l., a couplet, or a Str.; but in 9[2-3] it is repeated at the beginning of each of the four ll. of the Str., and in 119 throughout the twenty-two alphabetical Strs. it is repeated eight times (cf. La. 3). (*b*) Ps. 13[2-3] has עַד־אָנה at the beginning of each of the four lines of the Str.; and v.[4-5] has פֶּן at the beginning of three of the four ll. Ps. 29 repeats קוֹל יהוה eight times and הבו thrice. Ps. 62 repeats אַךְ eight times. Ps. 148 repeats הללוהו six times, and Ps. 150 the same nine times. (*c*) Rhyming with identical suffixes is used as an ornament, rather than as in modern poetry to mark the ends of all ll. of the poem. The following examples may suffice. — מ־ִ 2[3ab. 4ab. 5ab]. — ־ִי 13 throughout, 27[B. 7-8. 9. 11-12] 22[2. b-22] 30[2. 4] 54, 55[A.] 142. — ־ָ 9[2-3] 15[1] 20[2-3] 45[4]. — ־ִךְ 45[11]. — ־ִי 15[2-3]. — ־ָה 24[1-2] 45[13-16] (6 l.). — The Pss. that use this method usually vary in their use of it. — Ps. 6 has ־ִי for the most part 6[2ab. 3ab. 4ab. 5a. 7abc 8ac. 9ab. 10ab], but ך v.[5b. 6ab], ־ָ v.[8b. 11a], — Ps. 31 has ־ִי v.[2-17], but ך v.[20-21. 23]. — Ps. 35 has ־ִי v.[1-4. 11-14], but ־ָ v.[5-6]. — Ps. 119 has a variation, some Strs. ending in ה, others in ־ִי. — (*d*) Ps. 110 has ־ָ after caesura and at end of l. 1, but ך in ll. 2, 3, 4, 5; ־ָם l. 6; י l. 7; ־ִים

ll. 8, 10 ; ‎ה‎ֶ l. 9. At the beginning of six ll. of 45¹³⁻¹⁶ the words end in ‎וֹח‎ֵ.
— Ps. 143 has in ten ll. the first and last words in ‎ֶ‎י, before caesuras ‎ק‎. —
144ᴮ has assonance in every word of the tetrameter hexastich ; all the words
of ll. 1, 3, 5 end in ‎כ‎ִ‎י ; those of 2, 4, 6 in ‎ח‎ֵ. The later scribes and editors
did not care for this ornament of style, and so obscured it and even effaced
it partly by changing the order of words in the sentence, or by glosses of
various kinds.

(*E*) The Pss. were also arranged in regular strophical organization, as was indeed almost necessary for musical rendering in early
lyric forms of song. The reason why this has not been evident is
that the liturgical glosses of later times have obscured or destroyed
them. These strophes are of great variety as coming from so
many different authors and so many different periods of time.
Strophes may be simple or complex, just as in the case of parallelism of lines. The simple strophes are of few lines of one kind of
parallelism. The complex strophes have more lines and two or
more kinds of parallelism. In this case the connection of thought
is usually clear. The strophical divisions may be determined by
a more decided separation in the thought of the poem. Sometimes it is not easy to distinguish between the lesser and greater
separations because of a lack of familiarity of modern scholars with
the delicate shades of parallelism, which constituted the most characteristic feature of Hebrew thought ; and because of the prejudices
due to other rhetorical and logical uses of Western races and modern times. The simple strophes of one kind of parall. only are not
common. They tend to a monotonous style. The usual method
in the strophe is to combine the several kinds. This puts at the
disposal of the poet a very great variety of combinations. These
will appear in the commentary on the particular Pss. As Lowth
well says : " A happy mixture of the several sorts gives an agreeable
variety, and they serve mutually to recommend and set off one
another." (Prelim. Diss. to *Isaiah*, p. xxvi.) I may, however,
sum up the results of my investigation of the strophical structure
of the Pss. as follows : —

The Strs. are arranged on the same principles of parallelism as the ll., in all
its varieties. Poems of single Strs. are uncommon. The most frequent structure
is the pair of Strs. frequently doubled in two pairs, rarely as eight and sixteen
Strs. The triplet of Strs. is also common, less frequent its multiples of six,

nine, and twenty-four Strs. There are also poems of five, and its multiples, ten, fifteen, and twenty Strs. Poems of seven Strs. are uncommon. Poems of eleven and twenty-two Strs. are limited to alphabetical poems. I do not attempt to separate the glosses in the verses given below. Duplicates are not counted. (1) Poems of single Strs. are the Pilgrim Pss., 123, 125, 127$^{1-2}$ 127$^{3-5}$ 128, 131, 133, 134. There are only four others: 15, 36$^{2-5}$ 117, 144$^{12-15}$, which have special reasons. (2) Poems with a pair of Strs. are fifty in number: 1, 7, 8, 11, 13, 19$^{2-7}$ 19$^{8-15}$ 20, 21, 24$^{1-6}$ 24$^{7-10}$ 27$^{1-6}$ 32, 36$^{6-10}$ 39, 40$^{14-18}$ (= 70), 49, 52, 54, 57$^{6.\ 8-12}$ (= 108$^{2-6}$), 58, 59, 62, 65, 66$^{18-20}$ 72, 79, 81^{2-6b} 89$^{47-52}$ 95$^{1-6}$ 95$^{7-11}$ 101, 102$^{13-29}$ 110, 114, 120, 121, 122, 124, 126, 129, 130, 136, 139$^{17-22}$ 142, 143, 144$^{1-2.\ 7-11}$ 147$^{1-6}$ 147$^{7-11}$ 150. Poems with four Strs. are thirty-one in number: 2, 3, 4, 6, 12, 26, 30, 33, 40$^{2-12}$ 41, 44, 48, 51, 56, 60$^{3-7.\ 12b-14}$ 60^{8-12a} (= 108$^{8-14}$) 71, 77$^{17-20}$ 81^{6c-15} 83, 85, 91, 92, 102$^{2-12}$ 107, 113, 115$^{1-8}$ 118$^{2-7.\ 10-12}$ 132, 141, 148. Poems of eight Strs. are: 17, 68, 116; of sixteen Strs. 89$^{4-5.\ 18-46}$. (3) Poems of three Strs. are thirty-six in number: 16, 23, 25, 27$^{7-12}$ 28, 34, 35, 42–43, 45, 46, 50, 55$^{2-3.\ 5-9a}$ 55$^{9b-16.\ 21-24}$ 57$^{2-5}$ 61, 63, 64, 66$^{1-9}$ 67, 69$^{2-7.\ 14-19.\ 30-32}$ 76, 82, 84, 87, 88, 115$^{9-16}$ 118$^{19-26}$ 135, 137, 138, 139$^{7-12}$ 140, 145, 146, 147$^{12-21}$ 149. Poems of six Strs. are: 18, 75, 89$^{2-3.\ 6-15}$ 90, 94, 109$^{1-5.\ 16-18.\ 21-27}$ 139$^{1-6.\ 13-16.\ 23-24}$. Poems of nine Strs.: 74; of twenty-four Strs.: 105–106. (4) There are twelve poems of five Strs.: 5, 14 (= 53), 22, 29, 31, 38, 47, 69$^{8-13.\ 20-29}$ 77$^{2-16}$ 80, 86, 109$^{6-15}$. There is also one of ten Strs.: 73; one of fifteen Strs.: 93 + 96–100; and one of twenty: 78. (5) There are three poems of seven Strs.: 37, 103, 104. (6) Alphabetical poems are two of eleven Strs.: 111, 112; and two of twenty-two: 9–10, 119.

These Strs. vary in number of ll. and in combinations of parall. The Refrains are not counted in the Strs. (1) The only apparent monostichs are in alphabetical Pss.: 25, 34, 111, 112, 145. But these are not really monostichs, but ll. grouped in several kinds of stichs: 25, 34, 145 heptastichs; 111, 112, distichs. (2) Distichs are not common in the Psalter. They are more appropriate to sentences of Wisdom. There are, however, five: 14 (= 53), 62, 66$^{1-9}$ 111, 112. (3) Tristichs are not common: 17, 74, 75, 77$^{17-20}$ 87, 116. (4) The tetrastich is the most frequent lyric form. There are sixty-two of them: 3, 4, 5, 9–10, 12, 13, 23, 26, 27$^{7-12}$ 28, 29, 30, 40$^{14-18}$ (= 70), 47, 48, 55$^{2-3.\ 5-9a}$ 57$^{2-5}$ 57$^{6.\ 8-12}$ (= 108$^{2-6}$), 60$^{3-7.\ 12b-14}$ 60^{8-12a} (= 108$^{8-14}$), 61, 63, 65, 73, 78, 81^{6c-15} 82, 86, 89$^{2-3.\ 6-15}$ 89$^{4-5.\ 18-46}$ 94, 101, 103, 105–106, 109$^{6-15}$ 109$^{1-5.\ 16-18.\ 21-27}$ 113, 115$^{1-8}$ 117, 118$^{19-26}$ 120, 121, 122, 123, 124, 125, 126, 127$^{1-2}$ 127$^{3-5}$ 128, 129, 130, 131, 132, 133, 134, 137, 139$^{1-6.\ 13-16.\ 23-24}$ 139$^{7-12}$ 139$^{17-22}$ 141, 144$^{1-2.\ 7-11}$. (5) There are thirteen pentastichs: 6, 31, 32, 36$^{6-10}$ 40$^{2-12}$ 41, 55$^{9b-16.\ 21-24}$ 64, 67, 81^{2-5b} 90, 110, 143. (6) There are forty-three hexastichs: 1, 19$^{2-7}$ 19$^{8-15}$ 27$^{1-6}$ 36$^{2-5}$ 37, 38, 46, 50, 52, 54, 56, 68, 69$^{2-7.\ 14-19.\ 30-32}$ 69$^{8-13.\ 20-29}$ 76, 77$^{2-16}$ 79, 80, 84, 85, 89$^{47-52}$ 92, 93 + 96–100, 95$^{1-6}$ 95$^{7-11}$ 102$^{2-12}$ 102$^{13-29}$ 114, 115$^{9-16}$ 118$^{2-7.\ 10-12}$ 135, 136, 138, 140, 144$^{12-15}$ 146, 147$^{1-6}$ 147$^{7-11}$ 147$^{12-21}$ 148, 149, 150. (7) There are nine heptastichs: 2, 25, 34, 39, 66$^{18-20}$ 71, 72, 91, 145. (8) There are nine octastichs: 8, 11, 16, 20, 44, 58, 83, 104, 119. (9) There is one nonastich: 42–43. (10) There are

seven decastichs: 7, 15, 22, 33, 35, 51, 142. (11) There are four duodeca-
stichs: 21, 59, 88, 107. (12) There are two fourteen-lined Strs.: 18, 49.
(13) There are several Pss. with varying Strs., 24^{1-6} 24^{7-10}, with responsive
choirs. Ps. 45 has Strs. of increasing length with Rfs. and measures varying
as the Song of Deborah, Ju. 5.

The credit of calling the attention of scholars to the strophical organisation
of Hebrew poetry is usually given to Köster (*Das Buch Hiob und der Prediger
Solomos nach ihrer strophischen Anordnung*, 1813; *Die Psalmen nach ihrer
strophischen Anordnung*, 1837; and especially *Die Strophen oder Parallelismus
der Verse der Heb. Poesie*, S. K. 1831). But in fact many older scholars had
recognised the strophe and antistrophe in Hebrew poetry; so especially
Anton. Even Lowth pointed out that there were stanzas of different numbers
of lines (Prelim. Diss to *Isaiah*). Köster builds on Lowth's system of parallelism and maintains that groups of verses are arranged on the same principles of parallelism as the verses themselves, and thus he gets various kinds of
strophic parallelism corresponding with the various kinds of parallels of lines.
He distinguishes (1) word strophes, (2) thought strophes, (*a*) synonymous,
(*b*) antithetical, (*c*) synthetic, and (*d*) identical. In this he is essentially
correct. De Wette, in the fourth edition of his Commentary, 1836, recognises
that about all the Psalms are divided into strophes; so Ewald, Olshausen,
Delitzsch, and others in their Commentaries. There were, however, great
differences of opinion as to the principles for determining the strophical
organisation, as these scholars, one and all, made the strophical divisions
dependent upon their opinions of the most important breaks in the thought of
the poems. If they had built on Köster they would have been more successful. D. H. Müller (*Die Propheten in ihrer ursprünglichen Form*, 1895, *Strophenbau und Responsion*, 1898) classified the strophes under the terms,
responsion, concatenation, and inclusion. As I said in 1899 ([SHS. 399]): "There
is nothing new in his theory but the terminology and some of the illustrations.
Responsion is simply the antithetical parallelism of strophes, concatenation is
the stairlike parallelism of lines used in strophical relations, and inclusion is
the introverted parallelism of strophes. I have taught all this for thirty years
and given the doctrine of the strophe in the writings above referred to."
Müller was hardly justified in objecting to Zenner (*Chorgesänge im Buche
der Psalmen*, 1896) as appropriating his ideas, for they were common property, the inevitable result of the application, since Köster, of the principles of
parallelism to strophes. Rather Müller himself was to blame for not properly
recognising the work of his predecessors, which would have shown him that
his views were not as original as he supposed.

(*F*) There are also Refrains which some poets use in connection with the various strophes of their poems. These are of several kinds: (*a*) they are often identical in thought and expression;
(*b*) the thought is the same but its expression varies; (*c*) the

thought and expression both vary; (*d*) a number of Pss. were composed and arranged for singing by responsive choirs; and (*e*) some for solo voices and choruses.

(*a*) Ps. 39 has 2 Str. 7⁵ with identical Rf. 1⁵; Ps. 42–43 has 3 Str. 9⁶ with identical Rf. 3⁵. The following also have identical Rfs.: 46, 49, 56, 59, 62, 80, 85, 116, 144ᴬ. (*b*) Ps. 8 has an identical couplet of Rf.; but it is before the first Str. and after the second Str., on the principle of inclusion or introverted parallelism, so 57ᴮ(= 108ᴬ), cf. 58. Ps. 107 has double Rfs. (*c*) Ps. 45 has 3 Str. of increasing length, 2, 6, 18, with a Rf. of one line at the close of each beginning with an identical term, but varying in thought and expression in other respects. Ps. 66ᴬ has two Str. couplets, each introduced by a Rf. varying only in expression. The following Pss. are uniform in structure, with varying Rfs., 50, 84. (*d*) Pss. 20, 21 were sung by responsive choirs. The Rfs. vary in expression. They are trimeter couplets following 2 Str. 8³ in Ps. 20, and 2 Str. 12³ in Ps. 21. Ps. 24⁷⁻¹⁰ was also arranged for responsive choirs with Rfs. in which there is identical expression in part, and in part variation. Pss. 118ᴬ 118ᴮ were also arranged for responsive choirs. (*e*) Ps. 15 has a couplet of inquiry, followed by a decalogue of moral requirement and a monostich of conclusion. Ps. 24¹⁻⁶ has a similar variety of inquiry, response, and statement. The recognition of Refrains and responsive choirs in the Psalter has been quite general. But there has been a great difference of opinion as to particular Pss. Zenner (*Chorgesänge im Buche der Psalmen*, 1896) pushes responsion to extraordinary lengths, and includes in his scheme a large number of Pss. that give no other suggestion of responsive choirs than the principle of responsion, which is, as we have seen, rather a characteristic of one kind of parallelism of Strophes as well as lines of Hebrew poetry. At the same time it is quite possible that the choirs of temple and synagogues made a more extended use of responsive singing than has ordinarily been supposed. This feature of responsion of Strophes certainly made such responsive singing easier; cf. Condamin, *Le Livre d'Isaie*, 1905. The attempt of Baumann (*ZDMG.* 1905, S. 129 sq.) to discredit the Rf. is based on false conceptions of the nature of a Rf., and is made in such a way as to discredit rather the author.

§ 13. *Several Pss. give evidence that they were parts of longer Pss.*

(1) Pss. 9 and 10 were originally one alphabetical Ps., as indeed they are given in 𝕲, 𝔙, and in the uses of the Roman Catholic, Greek, and Syriac Churches, making a difference of numbering of one less Ps. from Pss. 10–113. Ps. 9 in the order of the alphabet reaches the Str. with כ, Ps. 10 begins with ל and continues the alphabetical structure to the end. However, there are several Strs. in which the letter has been lost, partly through mistake, partly from the intentional substitution of other words and sentences by editors.

(2) Pss. 42 and 43 were originally one. This is evident from the Rf., which comes twice in 42 and once in 43, and from the fact that the measures, strophical organisation, and entire character of the Pss. are the same. (3) Pss. 93, 96–100 were originally parts of a great royal advent Ps. of fifteen trimeter hexastichs. It was broken into six Pss., and these were edited with many changes for liturgical purposes. Even in 𝕳 in twelve codd. 93 is part of 92, in nine codd. 95 of 94, in four codd. 96 of 95, in fourteen codd. 97 of 96, in eight codd. 99 of 98. (4) Pss. 105 and 106 were originally one, each having twelve trimeter tetrastichs. (5) 𝕲 also divides 116 and 147 into two Pss. each, followed by 𝕵, so that 117–147 𝕳, EVs., are numbered differently from 𝕲, 𝕵. 148–150 have the same number in all.

§ **14**. *Many Pss. are composite of two or more original Pss. or parts of Pss. combined for liturgical purposes. Usually the original Pss. were of different poetic structure, and they are combined in various ways by editorial seams.*

(1) Ps. 19 is composed of an early trimeter morning hymn in praise of the sun, v.$^{2-7}$, and a late pentameter in praise of the divine Law, v.$^{8-15}$. (2) Ps. 24 is composed of an original choral, v.$^{7-10}$, and a later ethical Ps., v.$^{1-6}$. (3) Ps. 40 is composed of an original Ps., v.$^{2-12}$, of four pentameter pentastichs, to which was appended v.$^{13\ sq.}$ = Ps. 70 with editorial modifications. (4) Ps. 60 is composed of v.$^{8-12a}$, an ancient piece, and v.$^{3-7.\ 12b-14}$, a more modern one. Ps. 108 is composed of v.$^{1-6}$ = 57$^{8-12}$ and v.$^{7-14}$ = 60$^{7-14}$, not that this Ps. actually used parts of 57 and 60, but that it used one of the originals of each of these Pss. (5) Ps. 89 is composed of a paraphrase of the Davidic covenant in four parts, each of four trimeter tetrastichs, v.$^{4-5.\ 18-46}$; a much later tetrameter poem of six tetrastichs in praise of the fidelity of Yahweh in the creation and government of the world, v.$^{2-3.\ 6-15}$. These were combined at a still later date, and given a conclusion of two tetrameter hexastichs expressing an intense longing for divine interposition, v.$^{47-52}$. (6) 𝕲, 𝕾, and even Ki. combine 114 with 115 in their 113; but in fact 115 is composed of four trimeter tetrastichs, v.$^{1-8}$, and three trimeter hexastichs, v.$^{9-16}$. (7) The following Pss. are also composite of two or three earlier Pss.: 27, 36, 55, 57, 66, 69, 77, 81, 95, 102, 109, 118, 127, 139, 144, 147.

§ **15**. *Many early Pss. have been adapted by editors of the several minor and major Psalters for later use by glosses of various kinds. These are usually in different measures from those of the Pss.; and frequently the persons and numbers of nouns and verbs differ from those of the original poems, as if the editors would carefully distinguish their additions from the originals.*

These glosses are of several kinds. The simplest and most natural are liturgical in character, petitions, intercessions, calls to worship, expressions of praise and the like. Pss. expressive of piety and protestations of integrity are modified by the insertions of confessions of sin and pleas for forgiveness. Protestations of innocence are inserted in Pss. which lament the sufferings of the people of God from vindictive and cruel enemies. Personal, local, and earlier national relations are generalised so that earlier Pss. might with propriety be used in the public worship of late times. Early Pss. were adapted to the time of the supremacy of Law by legal glosses, to the times of Hebrew Wisdom by legal glosses, to the Maccabean times by lamentations for defeat, imprecations upon enemies, and other warlike expressions appropriate to a period of persecution and conflict. Early Pss. were enriched by illustrations from earlier literature, or by fuller and expansive statements. Several Pss. were given a Messianic reference in this way. Thus the editors of the various Psalters did exactly what the editors of prayer-books, liturgies, and hymn-books have always done. They had greater interest in editing the Pss. for public worship than in preserving their original literary form and meaning. Accordingly, many of the Pss. have lost their original literary form. They express varied states of mind, differences of experience, inconsistent situations; there are sudden and unexpected changes in tense of verbs, and in person and number of pronouns and suffixes. All this makes the Pss. richer in the expression of religious experience, and in this respect more suited to the varied needs of the congregation, but greatly injures their literary and historical value.

It will be sufficient to call attention to several Pss. in which editorial work of various kinds appears.

(1) The alphabetic Pss. show signs of changes of the text. Ps. 9 has the alphabetical structure preserved with Strs. א, ב, ו, ז, ח. But the Strs. ג, ה, ט, י, כ have been modified. Ps. 10 has the alphabetic structure in ל, ק, ר, ש, ת. But the Strs. מ, נ, ס, ע, צ are confused. Ps. 25 has an additional line with ר for an original ק. Ps. 34 adds two tetrameters. Ps. 37 has the Str. ע confused. Ps. 119 shows evidence of a great number of changes in the uses of terms for divine Law and in their order in the Strs. Ps. 145 lacks the Str. נ. The alphabetic form of La. has been well preserved, but that of Na. 1 has been confused still more than that of Pss. 9–10. (2) Ps. 1³ is a mosaic

from Je. 17[5-8] Ez. 47[12] Jos. 1[8] interposed between two antithetical Strs., making a metrical arrangement of the present Ps. impracticable. (3) Ps. 18 was a graphic ode of the time of David, preserved in another edition 1 S. 22. An editor prefixed a protestation of love, v.[2]. Another inserted an assertion of fidelity to the Deuteronomic Law, v.[21-24]; still another of fidelity to the morals of Hebrew Wisdom, v.[25-28], and there are other expressions indicating a later attitude of Israel to the nations than that represented in the original ode, v.[36. 45b. 46. 50]. (4) Ps. 22 was a graphic plea of suffering Israel. A later editor appended a liturgical gloss, v.[24-25. 27], another v.[28-32], to give the sufferings a world-wide and Messianic significance. (5) Ps. 32, a simple penitential Ps., was enlarged by an ethical gloss, v.[2], a gloss of intensification, v.[7], a gloss of warning, v.[8-9], and a concluding liturgical gloss. (6) Ps. 44, an original Ps. of 𝕳 was edited in 𝕰 with a gloss of adaptation, v.[5. 7]. Maccabean glosses appear in v.[5. 8-9], the exultation of victory, and in v.[10. 12], by another hand, the humiliation of defeat. (7) Ps. 65 is an ancient song of praise in the temple, v.[2. 3a. 5. 6a. 7. 8a 9b]. A gloss makes the worship universal, v.[3b. 6b]; another makes the divine wonders in nature an object of fear, v.[9a]; another thinks of the covering over of transgression, v.[4]. Later editors add fragments of two harvest songs, the one, v.[10-11], of the grain harvest; the other of the richness of flocks, v.[12-14]. (8) Ps. 72[8-12] is a mosaic of citations from Zec. 9[10] Is.[2] Jb. 29[12]. A large proportion of the Pss. have such glosses as these, adapting early Pss. to later uses, in the several successive editings of the Psalter.

§ **16**. *The text of the Psalter shows a large number of errors, just such as one would expect from its transmission through the hands of many different editors and copyists. There are essentially the same kinds of errors and subject to the same rules and principles of classification as those that are found in all Literature.*

The most of the Pss. were composed in the ancient Hebrew script, resembling the Samaritan letters. They were transliterated into the Egyptian Aramaic script, and finally into the later square Aramaic letters. In each of these scripts errors arose from mistakes as to similar letters both in form and in sound; the transposition of letters in a word or of words in a sentence; the wrong attachment of letters to words, or of words to sentences; the transposition of clauses; and conjectures in the case of defective or illegible Mss.

(1) There is a large number of mistakes of letters. A list of these is given in Gr. (*Com. on Pss.*, Vol. I. 128 sq.); cf. Baumgartner (*Étude Critique sur l'état du texte du livre des Proverbes*, 277 sq.). The following specimens of a very large number may suffice: 12[6] יפיח; 𝕲, 𝕾, Σ, עפע. 14[6] כהס = 53[6] מאס. 16[4] נסכיהם; 𝕲 נס־יב. 18[11] ירא = 2 S. 22[11] ירא. 28[7] משירי; 𝕲, 𝕾,

‎בשרי‎. 29² ‎חדרת‎; ‎חצרת‎ 𝕲. 30⁸ ‎הררי‎; ‎הרדי‎ 𝕲. 40¹⁶ ‎ישׁמו‎ = 70⁴ ‎ישׁבו‎. 42⁵ ‎אדרם‎;
‎תשׁב‎. 𝕲, 𝕴, 𝕾, ‎רשׁן‎. 71²¹ ‎הסב‎; 68¹⁶ ‎בשׁן‎; 𝕲, 𝕾, ‎הבלים‎. 40⁵ ‎רהבים‎; ‎אדרם‎. 𝕲
‎זרח‎. 𝕲, 𝕴, 𝕾, ‎זחל‎. 97¹¹ ‎זרע‎; 𝕲, 𝕴, 𝕾, ‎יחל‎. 91¹³ ‎זרעהם‎; 𝕲, 𝕾, ‎זרמתם‎; 90⁶
109¹⁰ ‎וירשׁו‎; 𝕲 ‎יגרשׁו‎. 109¹¹ ‎ינקשׁ‎; 𝕲, 𝕴, ‎יבקשׁ‎. 109¹³ ‎אחר‎; 𝕲 ‎אחד‎.

(2) *Transposition of letters :* 10⁶ ‎לא ברץ‎ for 𝕲, 𝕴, ‎בלא רע‎. 11⁶ ‎פחים‎; Σ ‎פחמי‎.
‎אל‎. 𝕲 ‎לא‎; 25³ ‎ומריד‎, so 144². ‎וידבר‎ = 2 S. 22⁴⁸. 18⁴⁸ ‎בעריו‎ = 2 S. 22¹³. 18¹³
‎קברם‎. 𝕲, 𝕾, 𝕿, ‎קרבם‎; 49¹² ‎פאר‎. 𝕴 ‎אחר‎, 𝕾, 𝕾, ‎אופיר‎; 45¹⁰ ‎נעב‎ 𝕲. ‎מעון‎; 26⁸
‎כתיב‎ 𝕲 ‎בסיהו‎. 104⁶ ‎ויאריך‎ 𝕲; ‎יראוך‎; 72⁵.

(3) *Letters differently connected :* 4³ ‎כברי לב למה‎ for 𝕲 ‎כבורי לכלמה‎. 11¹¹
‎ואלי שׁבי לבם לה‎ for 𝕲 ‎ואל ישׁובו לכסלה‎. 85⁹ ‎גורו הר כמו צפור‎, Vrss. ‎נודו הרכם צפור‎.
‎עליים‎ 𝕲 for ‎על ים‎. 106⁷

(4) *Verses differently connected :* 22³¹ ‎לרור:יבאו‎; but 𝕲, 𝕰, ‎לדור יבוא‎.
‎פני ואליה‎ 43⁵ but v.¹² ‎פניו : אלהי‎. 42⁶ ‎אשׁא אלהי‎ 𝕲 but ‎אשׁא: אלהי‎ 25¹.

(5) *There are many examples of dittography :* 10¹⁰ ‎חלכאים אסרים‎; 10¹⁴
‎הצרני הני‎ 32⁷; 44⁴ ‎כי‎ after ‎ה‎, so v.²⁰. ‎וראתה כי אתה‎.

(6) *The following specimens of haplography may be given :* 38⁹ ‎ארני‎ (א)‎לבי‎;
42² ‎חערג‎ (ה)‎כאיל‎; 28²² ‎אל‎ (ארי)‎; 45⁴ ‎ירך‎ for ‎ורכך‎ required for assonance.

(7) *Displacements :* 5¹³ ‎כצנה‎ displaced from ‎סך עלימו‎, making a confusion
of similes.

(8) *Conflation by error :* 32⁶ ‎מצא רק‎ for ‎מצוק‎ confused with ‎מצור‎; 44³
‎אתה ירך‎, but ‎אתה‎ not in 𝕲, 𝕾; 27¹³ ‎לולא‎, 𝕲 only ‎לו‎.

(9) *Compression by omission :* 3⁹ ‎ליהוה‎ for ‎לך יהוה‎, needed for measure;
4² ‎בצר‎ for ‎בצר לי‎, needed for measure; 7⁸ ‎לרק‎ for ‎אין פרק‎ 𝕲, 𝕾, required
for measure; 14⁸ ‎סר‎ = ‎סג‎ 53⁴ for ‎סר סג‎, both needed for measure; 19⁵ ‎קוה‎ for
‎קולם‎ 𝕲, 𝕴, Σ; 23⁶ ‎ושׁבתי‎ for ‎וישׁבתי‎ 𝕲, Σ, for ‎וישׁבתי‎ 𝕴, 𝕾, 𝕿, required by context; 24¹⁰ ‎יהוה צבאות‎ for ‎יהוה אלהי צבאות‎, required for measure, so 46⁸·¹²;
28⁸ ‎לעמו‎ for ‎למו‎ 𝕲, 𝕾; 39² ‎אשׁמרה‎ for ‎אשׁמה‎ 𝕲, 𝕰; 45³ ‎יפיפית‎ for ‎יפי יפית‎ 𝕲,
Aq., Σ, 𝕾, 𝕴, required for measure.

§ 17. *A very large proportion of the changes in the text of the
Psalms was due to corrections of the scribes and glossators, who for
various reasons endeavoured to improve the text to make it more
intelligible and useful.*

The scribes corrected the text to make it more intelligible.
The older writers were concise, and left many things to be inferred
by the attentive reader. In the unpointed consonant text the
words were not distinctly separated, and forms were written as
briefly as possible, so that various interpretations were possible.
There were also many abbreviations which might easily have been
misunderstood.

(*A*) There is a large number of grammatical glosses. (1) The most frequent change was the addition of suffixes to the noun or verb. In this 𝕲

and 𝕳 differ so frequently that it is improbable that they used different texts. It seems evident that they appended different suffixes to an original text, which was without them. The article in Hebrew, as in Greek, often expresses the possessive, and in poetry the article is frequently omitted. (2) The variations of number in nouns and verbs is due to the failure to distinguish numbers in the originals and the various interpretations of the scribes. It is probable that in the most ancient Hebrew texts, as in Syriac, the number of nouns and verbs was not always distinguished. (3) The same form is sometimes interpreted as a noun, sometimes as a verb, which was quite possible when only the consonants of the form were written. It is precisely the same in unpointed Syriac texts. (4) In 𝕳 and Vrss. forms are interpreted differently, as pf., impf., or ptc., all often for an original inf. abs. (5) Prepositions were often inserted in order to make the relation of nouns and verbs more definite, especially after the older case distinctions had been lost. (6) Particles were inserted to make the connection of clauses more distinct, especially the relative אשׁר and the conjunctions כי and ו. (7) The divine names were inserted very often in order to make it evident that God was the subject or object of the verb. (8) Personal and emphatic pronouns are frequent additions to the text. (9) Other subjects and objects were also inserted in order to make the meaning of the sentences more clear. In all these cases even 𝕳 has been changed from a simpler original. In a very large number of instances the ancient Vrss., especially 𝕲 and 𝕵, are more correct than 𝕳. Modern scholars have greatly erred in a too exalted estimate of the correctness of the unpointed Hebrew text in this regard. The measures make it evident that even 𝕳, by its numerous additions and changes of the original, is as truly an interpretation of an older text as 𝕲 and other ancient Vrss.

(B) The glossators are responsible for many changes in the text. The earliest and simplest glosses are those originally put on the margins of Mss., which subsequently crept into the text. (1) These were often explanations of rare and obsolete words by more familiar ones. In this way doublets arose which are easily detected, especially when they make the line overfull. These sometimes extend to phrases, sentences, and even lines. (2) There are many ejaculations of prayer, or praise, or pious exclamation on the part of devout scribes, which were proper on the margin, but make confusion with measure and sense in the text itself. Many imprecations may be thus explained. (3) There are many minor glosses due to the desire of the scribes to make the expressions stronger or clearer, and so they enlarge upon the original, intensify it, and elaborate it. (4) There are many Qrs. of the divine name in accordance with the uses of *Elohim* and *Adonay* in different periods for an original *Yahweh;* and not infrequently both readings appear as a conflation of the original text. (5) Citations of older Scriptures were made to illustrate and strengthen the force of the original. Sometimes these were originally in the margin and afterward crept into the text. (6) Some of these glosses were absent from 𝕲 and other Vrss., and sometimes 𝕲 and other Vrss. have similar glosses which are not in 𝔐. The measures and strophical organisation give great help in the detection of all such glosses.

(*C*) By far the larger proportion of variations between 𝔐 and the Vrss. consists in differences of interpretation of the same forms in the unpointed text. With these should be associated the variations in the use of the vowel letters and difference of interpretation as to their place in the form. It is altogether probable that vowel letters were much more sparingly used in the codd. of the first century B.C. than in 𝔐. 2⁶ נְסַכְתִּי, but 𝔊 נְסִכְרֵּי; 7⁷ אֵלַי, but 𝔊 אֵלִי; 9¹⁴ רָאֵה, but Aq., 𝔍, רָאֵה; 9¹⁷ נוֹקֵשׁ, but 𝔊, Aq., 𝔖, 𝔗, נִוְּקָשׁ; 9²¹ מוֹרָה, but 𝔊, 𝔖, מֹרֶה; 10⁵ יָחִילוּ, but 𝔍, Aq., יְחוּלוּ, 𝔊, 𝔖, Ψ, יָחֵדּוּ; 12² אֱמוּנִים, but 𝔊 אֵמוּנִים; 14⁷ יְשׁוּעַת, but 53⁶ יְשׁוּעוֹת; 18²⁶ גְּבַר, but 2 S. 22²⁶ גִּבּוֹר; 22⁴ קָדוֹשׁ, but 𝔊, 𝔍, קְרֹשׁ; 22¹⁰ סַבְטִיחִי, but 𝔊, 𝔍, 𝔖, מֵבְטִיחִי, as 71⁵; 27⁶ ירוּם, but 𝔊, 𝔍, יָרִים; 29⁹ אַיָּלוֹת, but אֵלוֹת; 31¹¹ עֵנִי, but 𝔊, 𝔖, חֵנִי; 𝔖 עֵנְוֵי Σ חֵנְוֵי; 32⁴ לְשַׁדִּי, but 𝔊, 𝔍, לְ prep. and שַׁד, 𝔖 שֵׁד; 32⁴ חָיִץ, but 𝔊 קַיִץ; 32⁵ יָלֵי, 𝔊 עֲוֹנִי; 36² פְּשַׁע, 𝔊 פֶּשַׁע. These are a few specimens only of a very great number throughout the Psalter.

B. HIGHER CRITICISM OF THE PSALTER.

§ 18. *Ancient Jewish opinion regarded David as the editor of the Psalter and the author of a great portion of the Psalms, so that David and the Psalter were essentially synonymous terms.*

In a *Beraitha* of the tract *Baba Bathra* of the Talmud, the Psalter is placed second in the roll of Writings; and it is said, "David wrote the Book of Psalms with the aid of the ten ancients, with the aid of Adam the first, Melchizedek, Abraham, Moses, Heman, Jeduthun, Asaph, and the three sons of Korah." The writing of David here is evidently editorship, and the Psalter is represented as containing Psalms from these ten worthies as well as from David. This statement comes from the second century A.D., and is stereotyped in Jewish tradition. But it will not sustain the test of criticism. Moses' name is in the title of Ps. 90; Heman's in 88; those of Asaph and the sons of Korah in groups of Pss.; Jeduthun's in Pss. 39, 62, 77; but in none of these cases can we think of authorship (*v.* §§ 28, 29, 34). The names of Adam and Melchizedek do not appear in the titles, but Melchizedek's name is in 110⁴. Adam's name was possibly thought of in connection with the Ps. of creation, 104. But it is impossible to think of either of them as authors of Pss. Moreover, as will soon appear, no Ps. can be regarded as earlier than David, and few belong to his time.

The apocalypse of Ezra represents that the ancient Psalter was destroyed with the other Writings and restored by Ezra, but that does not affect the question of original authorship. Josephus says that, "David, being freed from wars and dangers and enjoying a profound peace, composed songs and hymns to God of various sorts of meter. Some of those which he made were trimeters and some pentameters." David here stands essentially for the Psalter. This statement is not inconsistent with the Jewish tradition already given that David was aided by others in the composition of Pss., for it is a general and comprehensive statement.

§ **19.** *In the New Testament David is used as the equivalent of the Psalter, and as such personified in the references to particular Psalms. Questions were not raised as to authorship or editorship.*

The Psalter is referred to as *the Psalms*, Lk. 24[44], *the Book of Psalms*, Lk. 20[42], Acts 1[20], and *David*, Heb. 4[7]. The latter passage cites from Ps. 95, which has no title. There are in the NT. many citations, direct or indirect, from the Psalter. Six are cited under the name of David, 2, 16, 32, 69, 109, 110, and these simply use the name as a common designation which amounts to nothing more than " the Psalter " itself. Only one of these Pss. could by any possibility have come from the time of David, and that is altogether improbable.

Ps. 2[1-2] is cited in Acts 4[25-26] as by "the mouth of our father David"; but 2[7] is cited, Acts 13[33] as " in the second Ps.," and in Heb. 1[5] 5[5] as a word of God. Ps. 16[8-11] is cited in Acts 2[25-28] as " David saith "; but 16[10b] in Acts 13[35] as " in another (Ps.)." Ps. 32[1-2] is cited in Rom. 4[7-8] as David's blessing. Ps. 69[23-24] is cited in Rom. 11[9-10] as " David saith "; but 69[5] in Jn. 15[25] as " written in their Law "; 69[10a] in Jn. 2[17] as " it was written "; 69[10b] in Rom. 15[3] as " it is written " ; 69[22] in Jn. 19[28-29] as " that the scripture might be accomplished " ; 69[23] in Acts 1[2)] as " written in the Book of Psalms," though doubtless included under the general statement Acts 1[16] " by the mouth of David." The same is true of 109[8] cited in the same passage. Ps. 110[1] is cited by our Lord as " David himself said in the Holy Spirit," Mk. 12[33]. Cf. Mt. 22[43-44] ; but Lk. 20[42-43] as " David himself saith in the Book of Psalms"; and so Acts 2[34-35] " (David) saith himself "; and in Heb. 1[13] as God's words. Jesus and Peter were arguing with the Pharisees in the *Halacha* method on the basis of received opinion. There were no good reasons why Jesus and his apostles should depart from these opinions, even if they did not share them. There was no reason why Jesus as a teacher should have come to any other opinion on this subject than his contemporaries held. This was not a matter in which his divine knowledge would have influenced his human training. He was doubtless not informed as to matters of criticism which did not confront him in his day. We cannot, therefore, regard this single statement of Jesus as decisive of the authorship of Ps. 110 (*v.* Br. ^{Hex. 28}; Gore, *Lux Mundi*, 360). The other citations (a table of which is given by Kirk. vol. III. 838 sq.) will be considered in connection with the History of the Interpretation of the Psalter ; *v.* § 47.

§ **20.** *There was no consensus of the Fathers, and there was no decision of the Church, as to questions of the Higher Criticism of the Psalter, although the common traditional opinion, in the ancient and medieval Church, was that David was its author.*

Jerome (*Ep.* 140 *ad Cyprianum*) held that Moses wrote besides Ps. 90 also 91–100, on the theory that anonymous Pss. are to be attributed to the author last named. In this he follows Jewish opinion that the Psalter was edited as well as written by David. Augustine (*De Civitate Dei* 17¹⁴) held that the more credible opinion was that David was the author of the Psalter. Theodore of Mopsuestia explains seventeen Pss. as referring to the Maccabean age, but he seems to suppose that they were written by David in the spirit of prophecy.

§ **21.** *Calvin among the Reformers regarded Ezra as the editor of the Psalter, and in this was followed by Du Pin and others; but the prevailing opinion until the eighteenth century was that David wrote the entire Psalter.*

Calvin held that Ezra or some one else edited the Psalter, and made the first Ps. an introduction to the collection. Andrew Rivetus says : " This only is to be held as certain, whether Moses or David or any other composed the Psalms, they themselves were as pens, but the Holy Spirit wrote through them " (prolog. to his *Com. on the Psalms*). Casaubon says, " The truth is they are not all David's Psalms, some having been made before and some long after him, as shall be shown in due place " (preface to *Com. on Psalms*). Du Pin said, " Though the Psalms are commonly called the Psalms of David, or rather the Book of the Psalms of David, yet 'tis certain, as St. Jerome has observed in many places, that they are not all of 'em his, and that there are some written long after his death. 'Tis therefore a collection of songs that was made by Ezra " (*Dissert. Prelim. Bib. des Auteurs eccl.* 1696, pp. 1–5). These represent Protestant and Roman Catholic opinions, freely expressed without censure, against the still prevailing traditional opinion that David was the author of all the Psalms (*v.* Br.[SHS. 262]).

§ **22**. *With the rise of the Higher Criticism, the traditional opinion as to the Davidic authorship of the Psalter was questioned, and soon abandoned by all critics. At first editorship by Ezra and the Davidic authorship of only those Psalms which have David in their titles was proposed; but subsequently internal evidence showed this to be impossible, so that critical opinion gradually came to the result that the final editorship of the Psalter could not have been earlier than the Maccabean period, and that David wrote few, if any, of the Psalms, the most of them being postexilic.*

After the Davidic authorship of the entire Psalter had been generally abandoned, an effort was made to rally about the Davidic authorship of those Pss. which have לדוד in their title, on the theory that the ל is ל of ascription to an author. But this position could not be maintained; for a constantly increasing number of scholars, such as Eichhorn, Ros., Bauer, Jahn, De W., al., recognised many of these Pss. as later than David. Horsley says, " The misapplication of the Psalms to the literal David has done more mischief than the misapplication of any other part of the Scriptures, among those who profess the Christian religion " (*Book of Psalms*, Vol. I., Pref. 14). Ewald recognised 11 Pss. of David, besides a few fragments taken up into later Pss.; Hi. found 14, Schultz 36, De. 44. After De. had abandoned the Davidic authorship of 30 of the 74, and Schultz 38 of them, it was no longer possible to urge Davidic authorship from the titles, and scholars had to depend on internal evidence alone. Many recent critics refuse to recognise a single Psalm as written by David; so Gr., Ku., Reu., Stade, Che., Du.; and the most of them no preëxilic Pss. But other critics, such as Bä., Dr., Kirk., rightly refuse this extreme position, and still think of preëxilic and even Davidic Psalms.

§ **23**. *The Higher Criticism of the Psalter depends chiefly upon the internal evidence of the Psalms themselves. The titles are valuable for traces of the history of their use; but their contents, their interrelation, and their relation to other writings of the OT., give the only reliable evidence as to their origin and transmission.*

The Higher Criticism of the Psalter has made it evident that there is no dependence to be placed upon any of the traditional theories; for it is manifest that they were all conjectural, and rested upon insufficient evidence. We are thrown back first upon the titles. These came from the hands of editors, and with the exception of a few words, were not attached to the original Pss. They therefore give evidence of the different stages in the editing and use of the Pss.; and not of the authorship, date, or character of the originals. For these questions we must depend on a few external evidences of citation and silence, but for the most part on internal evidence alone : the poetic form and spirit, the subject matter in its relation to the development of religion, faith, and morals, the slight traces of historic circumstances and conditions, citations from earlier writings, the use of words and phrases in their relation to the development of the Hebrew language and literature, and other like evidences used in the Higher Criticism of all literature (v. Br.[SHS. 92 sq.]).

The Pss. are divided into two great classes, those with titles and those without. The latter are usually designated as "orphans." The titles certainly came from the hands of editors. There are a few instances in which parts of the titles may have been attached to the original Pss., but these are comparatively unimportant. The titles represent several stages of editing. This process still continued in 𝕲 and 𝕾 after the Hebrew text became stereotyped. These Vrss. do not hesitate to make conjectural additions to the titles, and even, in some cases, to make substitutions. The neglect into which the titles fell, soon after their traditional interpretation was abandoned, was really discreditable to Criticism; for they give the opinion and show the methods of a number of different editors. They are, as it were, the prints of their fingers, which give important evidence as to the condition and use of the Pss., at several different periods. Much work has been given to the subject in more recent times. The views which I shall present are based chiefly on my own private study during the past forty years. I cannot agree with my friend Cheyne in his opinion that the titles are chiefly corruptions of original local and personal references which he restores by purely speculative criticism. Undoubtedly we must resort to speculative criticism when all other means fail us, but there is no such necessity as regards the titles of the Pss. All the evidences used in the Higher Criticism come into play in the investigation of the Pss. There are many citations in the NT. and other later literature, but there are few citations in the OT. books themselves, or in the Apocrypha or Pseudepigrapha. So far as those in the Apocrypha or Pseudepigrapha are concerned, they give no help back of the Maccabean period. The argument from silence has little part in the study of the Psalter, because of the special lyric character and the limited extent of the Pss. Very great importance must be attached to the study of words and phrases. These give evidence of relative position in the development of the Hebrew language and literature. We have to take account of the archaic character of poetic composition; but with due allowance for this feature, great help has been found in this study. I have made a lexicon of the Psalter, giving every word and every use of every word, and comparing these with the uses of other OT. literature. This has cost me an immense labour for some years, but has amply repaid me by the fresh light cast upon the Pss. The study of Biblical Theology in its historical development, to which I have given many years of labour and teaching, has also aided in the Higher Criticism of the Psalter. There are comparatively few historical traces, but these, though often obscure, have sometimes been found illuminating.

§ **24**. *The earliest term to appear in the titles was doubtless "Song," which, in some cases at least, was attached to the originals. It indicated a lyric poem used for singing, especially on joyous occasions; in later times especially in religious worship of praise, and by the Levitical choirs.*

Ps. 18[1] (= 2 S. 22[1]) has in the title, † שִׁירָה n.f., *a song*, especially an *ode*, as that of the crossing of the Red Sea, Ex. 15[1]; the Song of the Fountain, Nu. 21[17]; the Song of Moses, Dt. 31[19, 19, 21, 22, 30] 32[44]; the Song of the Vineyard, Is. 5[1]; love songs accompanied by a lyre, Is. 23[15]. This ancient term, not used after the time of Hezekiah, was in all probability attached to this earliest of the Pss.

‡ שִׁיר *n. m. song*: (1) *of a lyric character*, distinguished from מָשָׁל 1 K. 5[12], antith. to קִינה Am. 8[10], sung on joyous occasions Gn. 31[27] +; of love songs Ps. 45[1] שִׁיר ידידת, cf. Ct. 1[1] title; not suited to sorrow Ps. 137[3]; (2) *of a religious type* used in worship of God: ‖ הפלה 42[9]; usually of praise הלל בשיר 69[81]; הורה משיר 28[7], cf. Ne. 12[46]; שׁ׳ יהוה Ps. 137[4], cf. 2 Ch. 29[27]; שׁ׳ ציון Ps. 137[3]; שׁ׳ חדש 33[3] 40[4] 96[1] 98[1] 144[9] 149[1], cf. Is. 42[10] (indicating a fresh outburst of song); so in titles of Pss.: שִׁיר 46[1]; שׁ׳ המעלות *pilgrim songs* in titles of 120–134; שׁ׳ מזמור 48[1] 66[1] 83[1] 88[1] 108[1]; מזמור שִׁיר 30[1] 65[1] 67[1] 68[1] 75[1] 76[1] 87[1] 92[1]; שׁ׳ משׁכיל 45[1] *v. supr. sub* (1). In all these cases except 30[1] 92[1] 108[1] other terms are added to an original שִׁיר (*v.* Br.[JBL. XVIII. 138]).

Ps. 30[1] has שיר חנכת הבית *song for the dedication of the house* or temple; Ps. 92[1] שיר ליום היבת *song for the Sabbath day*. These indicate liturgical uses, and must have come from editors and not from authors. Ps. 108 is a late composite Ps., and שׁיר in the title may have come from the title of the original, v. 8-14 = 60[8-14], which is an early song of triumph. The character of 83, 88 does not seem to suit the term, for the former is essentially an imprecation upon enemies of the time of Nehemiah, the latter a lament of the early exile. At the same time these terms seem to be original to the Pss. and probably imply a more comprehensive meaning for שׁיר, such as is certainly found in the שׁיר המעלות, Pss. 120–134, a collection of Pss. of great variety, hymns, prayers, and didactic Pss.; a little social song book for pilgrims to the great feasts (v. § 36). 𝔊 also uses ᾠδή for שׁיר in Pss. 91, 93, 95, 96, for reasons difficult to discover, for, while it is appropriate enough in 93, 95, 96, it seems not appropriate to 39, 91.

§ **25.** *Miktam in the titles of seven Psalms indicates that they were taken from an early collection of choice pieces, made in the middle Persian period.*

Pss. 56–60 have *Miktam* in their titles, so also Ps. 16. To these must be added Is. 38⁹⁻²⁰. There were probably other pieces which have been lost because they were not used by the editors of the early Psalters. These all bear on their faces evidences of antiquity. None of them were composed later than the early Persian period.

The most of the Rabbis rightly interpret מכתם, as formed by prefix מ from the noun כֶּתֶם *gold*, and thus think of *golden piece*, in accordance with the ancient custom to name select poems, gems, jewels, choice pieces, and the like. This indeed indicates their character, for they are artistic in form and choice in their contents. Pss. 56, 57, 59, 60, are trimeters; 16, 58, are tetrameters. Is. 38⁹⁻²⁰ is a pentameter. 56, 57, 58, 59, have refrains, catch words, and other ornaments of style. They all have rare words, strange combinations, and a vigorous roughness of style, and express strong emotions. They resemble in this respect the preëxilic prophets, and are among the most ancient of the Pss. Ps. 60ᵃ belongs to the early monarchy; 58, Is. 38⁹⁻²⁰, to the middle monarchy; 56 to the late monarchy; 16, 57ᵃ, 59, to the early Persian period. Five have editorial assignments: 56, 57, 59, 60, to circumstances of David's career; Is. 38⁹⁻²⁾ of Hezekiah's. The מכתב of Is. 38⁹ is probably an error for מכתם. Pss. 16, 56–60, were taken up into 𝔅, the earliest Psalter (v. § 27); Pss. 56–60 were also used in 𝔈 and 𝔅ℜ (v. §§ 36, 37), but 16 was not included in these Psalters. This doubtless explains the separation of 16 from the group. 𝔊 interprets מכתם as στηλογραφία, *inscription on a tablet, tituli inscriptio,* 𝔙; so 𝔗 as if it were מכתב. De. suggests on this basis, *a memorial* or *catchword poem.* Ps. 60 has also ללמד after לדוד. This was evidently ancient, and, standing by itself, is meaningless. It probably has the same meaning as in the title of the Lament of David over Jonathan, 2 S. 1¹⁸, and probably was originally with it and others of the same kind in the Book of Yashar.

§ **26.** *Maskil, in the titles of thirteen Psalms, indicates a collection of meditations made in the late Persian period.*

Pss. 32, 42–45, 52–55, 74, 78, 88, 89, 142, have *Maskil* in their titles. These were separated because of the selections made by the editors of the several minor and major Psalters. None of them, in their original forms, were composed later than the Persian period, and therefore they were probably collected not later than the late Persian period.

מַשְׂכִּיל was formed by the prefix מ from שׂכל in the Hiph. *consider, contemplate*, and is, therefore, probably a *meditation, meditative poem*, so De. "*pious meditation*," cf. Ps. 47[8] אמר משכיל. So essentially 𝔊 συνέσεως or εἰς σύνεσιν; 𝔙 *intellectus*, or *ad intellectum ;* 𝔍 *eruditio*. This suits the character of these Pss. essentially; so Ges., De W., Hi., regard them as poems to enforce piety and wisdom. משכיל is defined by Ew. as a *song with cheerful music* to be accompanied with clear-sounding cymbals, and in this is followed by many moderns ; so Kirk. "a cunning Psalm " ; but this does not suit the internal character of many of these Pss. These Pss. were all comparatively early in their original forms: 45 middle monarchy ; 52, 54, 55, late monarchy ; 42–43, 74, 88, 89[a], 142, exile ; 32, 53, 78, early Persian period ; 44 late Persian. Pss. 32, 52–55, 142, were taken up into 𝔇 ; 42–45 into 𝔎 ; 74, 78, into 𝔄. Of these, 42–45, 52–55, were also in 𝔇𝔎, and these with 74–78 in 𝔈. Moreover, these two pseudonyms are Maskilim ; 88 of Heman, which was also in 𝔇𝔎; and 89[a] of Ethan, which was not in any of the minor Psalters. None of these Pss. are orphans. It is quite probable that there were other Pss. in the original collection, which have been lost.

§ **27**. *David in the titles of seventy-four Psalms indicates, not authorship, but, with few exceptions, the first of the minor Psalters, gathered under the name of David in the late Persian period, from which these Psalms were taken by later editors of the major Psalters.*

1. It is evident from the internal character of these Pss., with a few possible exceptions, that David could not have written them. It is improbable that the word *David* was designed by the early editors to indicate their opinion that these Psalms were Davidic in authorship. The ל is not the ל of authorship, as has generally been supposed. The earliest collection of Pss. for use in the synagogue was made under the name of David, the traditional father of religious poetry and of the temple worship. The later editors left this name in the titles, with the preposition ל attached, to indicate that these Psalms belonged to that collection. This explains all the facts of the case and the position of these Pss. in the Psalter. This view is confirmed by Ps. 72[20], which states that

this Ps. was the conclusion of the prayers of David, and implies that the collection was a prayer-book. This statement is in accordance with the contents of these Psalms, for they are for the most part prayers. Some of the Pss. with David in the titles could not, however, have been in the Davidic Prayer-book. Pss. 86, 103, 108, 122, 124, 131, 133, 145, all belong to the Greek period. David was for various reasons inserted in the titles by later editors. Still later editors continued to attach David's name to other Pss. in 𝔊, 𝔖, and 𝔗. All the other Pss. which bear the name of David were composed, in their original form, with a single exception, not later than the middle Persian period. Ps. 68 seems to belong to the late Persian period, to which, therefore, we may assign the final collection of the Davidic Psalter (𝔇). Thirteen of these Pss. have in their titles references to incidents in the life of David. It seems probable that they were an original collection by themselves, which the editor of 𝔇 used as his nucleus.

The Pss. with לדוד are the following : 3–9, 11–32, 34–41, 51–65, 68–70, 86, 101, 103, 108–110, 122, 124, 131, 133, 138–145. To these we must add 10, whose title does not appear because it was really, as in 𝔊, the conclusion of 9. 𝔊 also gives David in the titles of 33, 43, 67, 71, 91, 93–99, 104, 137, fourteen others ; but 43 is a part of 42 of 𝔎 ; 93, 96–99 are parts of the royal Advent Ps. ; 104 is part of the group 104–107 ; 137 is a Ps. of the captivity not suited to a prayer-book, as 𝔇 ; 71 is dependent on earlier Pss. of 𝔇 ; 33 was given the title as in the midst of Pss. of 𝔇. It is improbable that this would have been omitted in 𝔎 if genuine. 67, 91, 94, 95, have no claim to have been in 𝔇. These insertions of 𝔊 are all conjectures of later editors. But such conjectures appear also in 𝔎. The four pilgrim Pss. 122, 124, 131, 133, could not have been in 𝔇. David came into the title of 145 from its connection with the group 138–144. Ps. 108 is composite of earlier Pss. of 𝔇 ; 86, 103, received David into the titles because of resemblance and use of Pss. of 𝔇. None of these Pss. is earlier than the Greek period. All the other Pss. with David in the titles in 𝔎 were probably in 𝔇 ; and it may be that other Pss. were therein which have been lost, or placed ultimately elsewhere in the OT. Ps. 72, in its original form, was at the conclusion of the Davidic prayer-book, as sufficiently indicated by the subscription v.[20]. It is also probable that Ps. 2 was its introduction, as is most suitable on account of its reference to the Davidic covenant. If now we remove the duplicate 53 (= 14), there are 68 Pss. which we may regard as in 𝔇. These Pss. have been disturbed from their original order by the selections from them made by later editors. Among the Mizmorim appear : 3–6, 8–10, 12–13, 15, 19–24, 29–31, 38–41, 51, 62–65, 68, 101, 109–110, 139–141, 143. For 𝔇𝔎 were selected : 4–6, 8–14, 18–22,

31, 36, 39–41, 51–52, 54–62, 64–65, 68–70, 109, 139–140. In 𝔈 were selected 51–65, 68–70, 72.

(2) Thirteen Pss. of 𝔇 have in their titles references to certain incidents in the life of David. These statements all depend upon the narratives of Samuel, and were subsequent to the Deuteronomic redaction of the prophetic histories: Ps. 3, "when he fled from Absalom his son," cf. 2 S. 15. Ps. 7, "which he sang to Yahweh concerning the words of Cush a Benjamite," cf. 2 S. 16. Ps. 18, "in the day that Yahweh delivered him from the hand of all his enemies and from the hand of Saul," cf. 2 S. 22^{1}. Ps. 34, "when he changed his behaviour before Abimelech who drove him away and he departed," cf. 1 S. $21^{10\,sq.}$. Ps. 51, "when Nathan the prophet came unto him after he had gone in to Bathsheba," cf. 2 S. 12. Ps. 52, "when Doeg the Edomite came and told Saul, and said unto him, David is come to the house of Abimelech," cf. 1 S. $22^{9\,sq.}$. Ps. 54, "when the Ziphites came and said to Saul, Doth not David hide himself with us?" cf. 1 S. $23^{19\,sq.}$ ‖ $26^{1\,sq.}$. Ps. 56, "when the Philistines took him in Gath," cf. 1 S. 27. Ps. 57, "when he fled from Saul, in the cave," cf. 1 S. 22. Ps. 59, "when Saul sent, and they watched the house to kill him," cf. 1 S. 19^{8-17}. Ps. 60, "when he strove with Aram Naharaim and with Aram-zobah, and Joab returned and smote of Edom (error for Aram) in the Valley of Salt twelve thousand," cf. 2 S. 8^{13} 10. Ps. 63, "when he was in the wilderness of Judah," 1 S. $22^{5\,sq.}$. Ps. 142, "when he was in the cave," cf. 1 S. 24. These thirteen Pss. were all in 𝔇, but only 52, 54, 142, are *Maskilim*; 56, 57, 59, 60, *Miktamim*; 3, 51, 63, *Mizmorim*. Therefore the statements can have nothing to do with these collections. Furthermore 𝔈 uses eight: 51, 52, 54, 56, 57, 59, 60, 63, omitting five; 𝔇ℜ also uses eight: 18, 51, 52, 54, 56, 57, 59, 60, omitting five; 3, 7, 34, 142, were used by neither. Therefore these notices could not have come from these editors. 𝔇 is thus the only collection in which all are found, and therefore either the editor of 𝔇 must have been responsible for them, or these statements must have been in his sources. It is improbable that he would assign historical occasions to only thirteen out of his collection of sixty-eight. We must therefore seek them in his sources. But it is evident that they do not belong to the original Pss., for the only one that comes from the time of David is the original of Ps. 18, which gets its title from 2 S. 22^{1}. 2 S. 23^{1} gives another poem which is attributed to David in the same way. These titles of the Pss. came from an editor of the same type as the one who inserted these poems in the book of Samuel. It is probable, therefore, that these thirteen Pss. constituted a little collection of Davidic Psalms. The editor of 𝔇 used them just as he found them, with these titles as the nucleus of his collection. They are not, however, in their original order, if designed to illustrate the life and experience of David. Their order, according to the narratives of Samuel, would be rather: 59, 57, 63, 52, 54, 142, 56, 34, 60^{a}, 51, 3, 7, 18. It is quite possible that 2 S. $23^{1\,sq.}$ was originally at the end, and the lament of David over Jonathan, 2 S. 1^{19-27}, in the middle before 60, making fifteen in all. One of these, Ps. 60^{a}, was probably in the book of Yashar as well

as 2 S. 1[19-27]. These Pss. originated in different periods and in different circumstances, such as accord only in some respects with these titles. Ps. 18 in its original form was probably Davidic, and possibly Pss. 7, 60[a]. Ps. 3 was from the middle monarchy; 52, 54, 56, the late monarchy; 63, 142, from the exile; 34, 57[a], 59, the early Persian; and 51 probably from the time of Nehemiah. It is altogether improbable, therefore, that an editor of the middle Persian period could have thought that his references to experiences of David were historical. He made them to illustrate the Pss., as the editor of 2 S. 22–23 used the Pss. to illustrate the close of David's career (cf. the use of Pss. in 1 Ch. 16). It is noteworthy that not long before the Pseudonyms, Ps. 72, 88, 89, appeared (*v.* § 34).

(3) We may determine the original order of the Pss. in 𝕭 only by the most careful review of all these facts. Ps. 72 was originally the concluding Ps. of 𝕭 (v.[20]). We shall have to suppose, therefore, that 101, 109–110, 138–144, were removed from their original positions before 72. It is altogether probable that 16 was, in 𝕭, still connected with the group 56–60. The groups 51–65, 68–70, 72, selected by 𝕰 from 𝕭, are not in their original places. The Pss. with historical references 3, 7, 18, 34, 51, 52, 54, 56, 57, 59, 60, 63, 142, were, as we have seen, originally in the same group. The key to their order is doubtless in 18, originally the last of the series. It is probable that 𝕯𝕽 followed the original order for the most part, so far as 4–6, 8–14, 19–22, 31, 36, 39–41, are concerned, but the order of 𝕰 in 51–62, 64–65, 68–70. That 109, 139–140, appear so late must be due to a still later editor. The order of 𝕱𝕳 is also substantially original: 3–6, 8–10, 12–13, 15, 19–24, 29–31, 38–41, 51, 62–65, 68, 101, 109–110, 139–141, 143, except as disturbed by later editors. The Pss. with לדוד alone, 17, 25–28, 34–35, 37, 138, 144, which, therefore, did not appear in the intermediate Psalters, and those used by 𝕯𝕽 only, 11, 14, 36, and by 𝕯𝕽 and 𝕰 only, 61, 69–70, are probably out of their original order. Inasmuch as 70 was attached to the end of 40, it is probable that the original order of 𝕭 was 69, 40, 70. The following may therefore be given as a provisional theory of the original order, 2, 4–6, 8–13, 14 (= 53), 16, 17, 59, 63, 52, 57, 54, 142, 56, 34, 60, 51, 3, 7, 18 (30, 55, 58, 61–62, 64–65), 19–24 (15, 101), 25–28 (35, 37, 138–141, 143, 144), 29, 31–32, 36, 38, 39 (68, 109, 110, 69, 40, 70), 41, 72.

The Pss. of 𝕭, in their original, may be dated as follows: (1) The early monarchy, 7, 13, 18, 23, 24[b] 60[a] 110. (2) The middle monarchy, beginning with Jehoshaphat, 3, 20, 21, 27[a] 58, 61. (3) The late monarchy, beginning with Josiah, 19[a] 28, 36[a] 52, 54, 55, 56, 60[b] 62, 72. (4) The exile, 63, 142. (5) The early Persian period, before Nehemiah's reforms, 4, 6, 9–10, 11, 12, 14 (= 53), 16, 17, 22, 25, 31, 32, 34, 35, 37, 38, 39, 40[b] (= 70), 41, 57[a] 59, 64, 69[a] 101, 109[a] 140[a] 143, 144[a]. (6) Middle Persian period of internal and external peace after Nehemiah's reforms, 5, 8, 15, 26, 29, 30, 40[b] 51, 57[b] 65, 69[b] 138, 139[b] 141. (7) Late Persian period of strife and confusion, 68. It is probable, therefore, that 𝕭 was edited toward the close of the Persian period, in Palestine, for use in the synagogues. To these Pss. other Pss.

and glosses were added by later editors, for practical purposes in public worship.

§ 28. *The term " sons of Korah " in the titles of eleven Psalms indicates a collection of religious poems, made in the early Greek period, from which these were taken.*

Two groups of Pss., 42–49, and 84, 85, 87, 88, have in their titles " belonging to the Sons of Korah." The separation of the two groups was due to a selection of the former group by an editor, who united them with 50–83. The other group was appended from the original collection by the final editor of the Psalter. These Pss. have common features which are not sufficient to imply the same author or authors, but yet imply careful selection. These are (1) a desire to engage in the worship of the sacred places ; (2) confidence in Yahweh, the king enthroned in Jerusalem, who watches over the people from thence and saves them ; (3) a highly artistic finish and symmetrical poetic forms. These Pss. were selected from a collection of Pss. gathered under the name of the Sons of Korah, in Palestine, in the early Greek period.

בני קרח is doubtless the same as בני הקרחים, 2 Ch. 20[19], a guild of temple singers distinguished from בני הקהתים, another guild. According to 1 Ch. 6[18 sq. (33 sq.)], Heman, a Kohathite, Asaph, a descendant of Gershom, and Ethan, of the sons of Merari, represented the three sons of Levi. According to 1 Ch. 26[19] the doorkeepers of the temple were Sons of Korah and Merari. Ezr. 2[41] Ne. 7[44] mention only sons of Asaph as singers. According to 1 Ch. 6[7. 18 sq.] Heman was בן קרח, a grandson of Kohath, and so both Kohathite and Korahite. The term "Korahite" seems to have been substituted for " Kohathite," and Heman was the representative of the line, as Asaph was of the line of Gershom. Both were guilds of temple singers in the temple of the Restoration. All of these Pss. except 48 and 87 were taken up into 𝔅𝔎. These have the title למנצח at the beginning, but 88 has two titles, and למנצח is at the beginning of the second. This singularity makes it probable that the first title was a later addition, due to the conjecture that, inasmuch as Heman mentioned in the second title was the chief of the Korahites, his Ps. should have that title also. Ps. 88 was simply a *Maskil* of Heman, as 89 was a *Maskil* of Ethan. Ps. 49 differs so much in character from the other Kora-hite Pss. that it seems probable that it was not originally with that collection, and that the name came into the title by txt. err. or editorial conjecture, because the Ps. was attached to the group 42–48, immediately before 50 of Asaph. It represents an early type of WL. Ps. 43 was originally the third Str. of 42, as is evident from the common Rf. and from internal characteristics which are common. The remaining nine Pss. have been preserved from 𝕳. We are unable to say whether 𝕳 had more of them, or not. The group 42–49 differs from the group 84–85, 87–88, by the use of the divine name *Elohim* in the former and *Yahweh* in the latter. This difference was not in 𝕳, but was due to 𝕰, who changed *Yahweh* into *Elohim*. 𝕳 originally used *Yahweh* throughout. These Pss. represent different periods of history: 45 from the time of Jehu; 46, 87, time of Josiah; 42–43, 84, time of Jehoiachin; 47, middle Persian period after Nehemiah; 44, 48, 85, late Persian period; 42–43, 44, 45 were taken from the collection of משכיל. As none of these Pss. are later than the Persian period, and so many are late in that period, it is probable that the collection was made early in the Greek period. These Pss. are highly artistic in form. Five of them have Refrains: 42–43, 45, 46, 84, 85; three are trimeters, 44, 47, 85; one tetrameter, 46; four pentameters, 42–43, 48, 84, 87, and one varies between tetrameter and trimeter, 45. They are all highly poetic in content, and on the whole the choicest collection in the Psalter from a literary point of view.

§ **29**. *The term "Asaph" in the titles of twelve Psalms indicates a collection of religious poems made in Babylonia in the early Greek period, from which these Psalms were derived.*

The group of Pss. 73–83 and the detached 50 have Asaph in their titles. The separation of 50 from the group was due to a later editor, probably in order to make an appropriate concluding Ps. to the first division of 50. These Pss. have common features: (1) vivid descriptions of nature; (2) emphasis of divine providence in the life of the individual; (3) use of history with a didactic purpose; (4) exalted spiritual conceptions of God; (5) sublimity of style. These features are not sufficient to show a common author or guild of authors, but imply careful selection by an editor with a plan and purpose to set forth those features. The Pss. were originally in a collection by themselves, made in the early Greek period, probably in Babylonia.

אָסָף was a Levite, the son of Berechiah, 1 Ch. 6²⁴ ⁽³⁹⁾, one of the three chiefs of the Levitical choir, 1 Ch. 15¹⁷; a seer, 2 Ch. 29³⁰; associated with David Ne. 12⁴⁶. בני אסף are mentioned 1 Ch. 25¹⁻² as set apart to prophesy with musical instruments. It is evident that this Asaph could not have been the author of the collection, or, indeed, of any of its Pss., for they are all of a much later date. "Asaph" is used as a name of the collection, just as "David" and "Sons of Korah" of the other collections. Only five of the twelve Pss. were used in 𝕯𝕽, but all by 𝕰. The Pss. of 𝕬 are chiefly religious poems, in which the didactic element prevails. These Pss., apart from glosses, were composed probably as follows: 74, 77ᵃ 79, 81ᵇ 82, during the Exile; 75, 76, 78, 80, 83, in the early Persian period; 50 in the late Persian; and 73 in the early Greek period. We may therefore assign the collection to the early Greek period. There are additions, 77ᵇ and 81ᵃ, besides glosses from the later Greek and Maccabean periods. There is nothing in the originals that is opposed to the dates given above. All of the Pss. of 𝔄 were taken up into 𝔈, and were probably used as the basis of that collection. The divine name אלהים seems to have been original to 𝔄, and is not to be ascribed to the editor of 𝔈. This was probably due to the fact that the collection was made in Babylonia, where the use of that divine name prevailed. In this 𝔄 agrees with P of the Hexateuch, which came from the same region. Two of the Pss. of 𝔄, 74, 78, in their original form were taken from the collection of מכלים. These Pss. received many glosses, and in these cases אלהים seems not to have been original.

§ **30**. *The other proper names in the Psalter, Solomon, Ps. 72; Moses, Ps. 90; Heman, Ps. 88; Ethan, Ps. 89; 'Ani, Ps. 102, are pseudonyms.*

The name of Solomon is in the title of Ps. 72, the closing Ps. of the original 𝔇; doubtless placed there as a pseudonym by the author, composing from the point of view of Solomon, for it could not have been written by Solomon himself, even in its original form. Three pseudonyms are together in the midst of the Psalter, doubtless by editorial design: 88 ascribed to Heman, 89 to Ethan, 90 to Moses; all alike with the same purpose, to compose Pss. in the name and from the point of view of these ancient worthies. In no case is the name of an author attached to a Ps. 'Ani, Ps. 102, is probably a pseudonym for the suffering pious of Israel. The Pss. are all, with the exception of these pseudonyms, anonymous.

(*a*) Solomon's name is attached to 72, but it really belongs only to the original v.¹⁻⁷· ¹³⁻¹⁷ᵃ, two hexameter heptastichs constituting a prayer for a king on his accession, probably from the time of Josiah, and therefore appropriately put into the mouth of Solomon, who might be supposed to have just such aspirations for his son. It was originally a Yahwistic Ps. Solomon is also in the title of 127 in 𝔋, but not in 𝔊. This is a pilgrim Ps., and we must ascribe the insertion to the conjecture of a late scribe. (*b*) Heman, the Ezrahite, is in the title of 88, originally in the collection of מכלים. It is a Ps. of national lamentation during the extreme distress of the Exile, and could not have been written either by the sage of Solomon, 1 K. 5¹¹ (4³¹), or the singer of David, 1 Ch. 15¹⁷· ¹⁹ 25⁵. It was put into his mouth by the author as a pseudonym. (*c*) Ethan, the Ezrahite, is in the title of Ps. 89. He was one of the sages of

Solomon, 1 K. 5¹¹ (4³¹). The Ps. in its original form (v.¹⁸⁻⁴⁶) is a paraphrase of the Davidic covenant and a lament as to its failure. It came from one of the companions of Jehoiachin in his exile. It could not have been written by Ethan. It was put into his mouth as a pseudonym. (*d*) Moses, the man of God, is in the title of the prayer Ps. 90, which imitates purposely Dt. 32, 33, songs ascribed to Moses, with the view of putting the Ps. in his mouth. It could not have been written by Moses. It is not an early Ps., but dates probably from the later years of the Exile. (*e*) Ps. 102 has in the title, תפלה לעני כי יעטף ולפני יהוה ישפך שיחו = *Prayer of the afflicted one when he was fainting and before Yahweh pouring out his complaint*. עני is probably a pseudonym. The author writes in the name of afflicted Israel. The Ps. is composite: v.²⁻¹² seems to come from the closing years of the Persian period, but v.¹³⁻²³· ²⁹ is a Maccabean Ps. (*f*) Some codd. 𝔊 of 65, 137, so 𝔙, have Jeremiah in the titles; conjectures of late scribes, based on the similarity of the circumstances of the Ps. with those of Je. and La. (*g*) 𝔊 inserts Haggai and Zechariah in the titles of 146, 147, 148, 149, 𝔊ᴬ also Zechariah in the titles of 138, 139, doubtless for similar reasons. Authorship is not to be thought of in these cases, and not even pseudonyms.

§ 31. *Mizmor, in the titles of fifty-seven Psalms, indicates a collection made for singing in public worship in the early Greek period, from which these Psalms were taken.*

The term *Mizmor*, like the terms *Miktam* and *Maskil*, implies a selection or collection of Pss. of this class. They were made, as the name implies, for public worship in song in the synagogue. As all those whose מזמור is genuine were derived from the earlier Psalters of 𝔇, 𝔎, 𝔄, with the exception of the exilic pseudonym 88 and two orphan Pss., 66–67, of the early Greek period, it is probable that the collection was made about that time.

(*a*) There are 57 Pss. in 𝔚, with מזמור (*v.* § 1); of these there were derived from 𝔇, 35 (36) Pss.: 3–6; 8–9 (+ 10), 12–13, 15, 19–24, 29–31, 38–41, 51, 62–65, 68, 101, 109, 110, 139–141, 143; from 𝔎 5 Pss.: 47–48, 84–85, 87; from 𝔄 9: 50, 73, 75–77, 79–80, 82–83. To these were added 5 orphan Pss.: 66, 67, 92, 98, 100, the pseudonym 88, the gnomic 49, and the composite 108. But the term in 92, 98, 100, was doubtless from later scribes, 98, 100, being parts of the royal advent Ps., which could not have been written, still less broken up, in time to be included in the collection; 92 doubtless received this title in connection with its liturgical assignment. 66 is a composite Ps., but in its earliest form v.¹⁰⁻¹², like 67, was probably composed early in the Greek period, possibly for use in this Psalter by its editor. There is no ground, therefore, on which to go later than this period for this collection of Pss.

(*b*) 𝔊 also attaches ψαλμός to ten other Pss.: 7, 11, 14, 25 of 𝔇; 43, 44, 46 of 𝕂; 81 of 𝔄, and 94, 99, orphans, but omits it from 4, 39 of 𝔇, using ᾠδή instead. Of these it may be rejected from 99 for the same reasons as from 98, 100, of 𝕳. 43 was originally a part of 42, and doubtless was not separated in 𝔐. In 46 למנ is a later substitution for שׁיר. No good reason can be assigned for the omission from 11, 14, 25, 94 of 𝕳 or 44 of 𝕂 or 81 of 𝔄. מזמור was more likely to have been inserted by assimilation to the groups in which they occur.

(*c*) In Ps. 7 the use is peculiar, for מזמור of 𝔊 represents the enigmatical שִׁגָּיוֹן of 𝕳. This term is used elsw. only Hb. 3¹, in pl. שגינות, where it is doubtless an error for נגינות, cf. 𝔊 μετὰ ᾠδῆς. It is derived by Aq., Σ, 𝔍, 𝔗, from שגג and rendered *error, confusion*. Most moderns, as Ew., De., Kirk., al., derive from שוג *go astray, reel*, and think of the wild, passionate dithyrambs, with rapid change of rhythm, cf. Lag.*BN. 201f.* But this Ps. does not really have these characteristics. It is indeed confused by many glosses from different periods, but the original Ps. was less passionate and rambling than many other Pss. The word is doubtless a txt. err., which may have stood for an original נגינות, as in Hb. 3; but in this case it could not have belonged to this Ps., which was not in 𝔇𝕂, and must have come in by mistake from the previous Ps. 6.

(*d*) The original Mizmorim were probably, therefore, 54(5). Of these 𝔇𝕂 used 34. The original order of these Pss. in that collection was doubtless different in many instances from their order in the present Psalter.

§ **32.** *The group of Pss. 42–83, characterised by the use of the divine name Elohim instead of Yahweh, was originally in a major Psalter, edited probably in Babylonia in the middle Greek period, and made up chiefly of selections from the previous minor Psalters.*

This group of 42 Pss. in the midst of the Psalter differs from the preceding group, Pss. 1–41, and from the following, 84–150, by the use of the divine name *Elohim*, which is seldom used in the other Pss., and by an avoidance of *Yahweh*, which is used ordinarily by them. This use was evidently designed, and in the case of the selections from 𝔇 and 𝕂, was not original, but editorial. These Pss. therefore constituted a selection of Pss. made by an editor from the earlier collections. Inasmuch as 𝔄 is given complete so far as known, Pss. 50, 73–83, 𝔄 was probably the basis of the collection. Selections from 𝕭, 42–48, 49 (?), and from 𝔇, 51–65, 68–70, 72, were prefixed to 𝔄, and three orphan Pss., 66, 67, 71, were added. The changed order of these last and of 50 is due to later editors. This collection was probably made in Babylonia, as that of 𝔄 before it, and for similar reasons.

It is convenient to give in this connection the use of the divine names in ψ.

I. יהוה is used c. 6823 t. in OT. יְהֹוָה Qr. = אֲדֹנָי = ὁ κύριος in 𝕲, for an original יַהְוֶה = *Yahweh* (*v.* BD*B.*). It is the proper name of the God of Israel, first revealed to Moses according to 𝔈 as "the One ever with His people" Ex. 3[12-15]. It is not used by P until Ex. 6[3]. But J uses it from the beginning of his narrative, and possibly explains it as meaning "the everlasting God," Gn. 21[33]. It is used cautiously by E (c. 163 t.), but constantly by J (c. 449 t.) and by P after Ex. 6[3] (c. 781 t.). D uses it apart from his phrases c. 211 t. In the prophetic histories it is used sparingly by E, but constantly by J, D, R. The Chr. uses it in his sources, but avoids it in his own composition. It is used throughout the prophetic literature, but in various proportions, and in some writers chiefly in combination with other divine names. The book of Jb. uses it only in the Prologue and Epilogue (27 t.), the seams (4 t.), and in a proverbial expression 12[9]; but in Pr. it is the characteristic divine name. In Dn. it is used only in ch. 9 (7 t.) (source), and in Ec. not at all. It is constantly used in ψ, except in the group 42–83 (E), where it is used 44 t. (chiefly glosses).

יהוה is frequently combined with other divine names. י אֱלֹהֶיךָ is a phr. of D (c. 239 t.) used by Chr. 6 t., Is.[2] 4 t., elsw. seldom; Ps. 81[11] in citation from Ex. 20[2]; י אֱלֹהֵיכֶם is a phr. of D[2] (c. 70 t.) and of H (c. 30 t.), in Jo. 7 t., Chr. 11 t., elsw. seldom, Ps. 76[12] (the law of vows); י אֱלֹהֵינוּ is also a phr. of D[2] (28 t.) used by Chr. 16 t., Je. 18 t., elsw. not uncommon; in ψ 20[8] 94[23] 99[5. 8. 9. 9] 105[7] 106[47] 113[5] 122[9] 123[2]. Uses of יהוה with אלהים and other sfs. are characteristic of Je. (11 t.) and Ch. (26 t.); in ψ י אֱלֹהַי 7[2. 4] 18[29] 35[24] 104[1] (all dub.) 13[4] 30[8. 13] 38[22] 40[6] 109[26], י אלהיו 33[12] 144[15] 146[5]. The combinations אל יהוה 118[27], אל אלהים יהוה 50[1], are conflations of an original יהוה.

† יָהּ is a poetic contraction of יהוה, earliest use Ex. 15[2] (cited Is. 12[2] Ps. 118[14. 14]) Ex. 17[16] Is. 38[11] Ct. 8[6]; יה יהוה Is. 26[4] (?); יה שמו Ps. 68[5] (?); יה אלהים 68[19] (?); elsw. הללו יה 104[35] 105[45] 106[1. 48] 111[1] 112[1] 113[1. 9] 115[18] 116[19] 117[2] 135[1. 8. 21] 146[1. 10] 147[1. 20] 148[1. 14] 149[1. 9] 150[1. 6]; יהלל יה 102[19]; הללו יה 115[17]; הלל יה 150[6]. In other phrs. 77[12] 89[9] 94[7. 12] 115[18] 119[5. 6. 17. 18. 19] 122[4] 130[3] 135[4].

II. ‡ אֵל n.m. *strong one:* (1) angels, בני אלים 29[1] 89[7]; (2) gods, אל זר 44[21] 81[10], אל נכר 81[10] Dt. 32[12] Mal. 2[11]; (3) mighty things in nature, הררי אל Ps. 36[7], ארזי אל 80[11]; (4) used of God as the most primitive term, c. 217 OT. as *the Strong One.* הָאֵל the true God 18[31. 33. 48] 68[20. 21] 77[15] 85[9], cf. Is. 42[5]; אֵלִי *my God* Pss. 18[3] 22[2. 2. 11] 63[2] 68[25] 89[27] 102[25] 118[28] 140[7], cf. Ex. 15[2] Is. 44[17]; אל ישראל Ps. 68[36]; אל יעקב 146[5]; אל השמים 136[26]; אל סלעי 42[10], cf. 43[4]; אל נקמות 29[3]; אל חי 42[9] (prob. also 42[3] 84[3] for אל הי); אל אמת 31[6]; אל הכבוד 94[1. 1]; אל גדול 77[14] 95[3] Dt. 7[21]; אל רחום Ps. 86[15] Ex. 34[6] (J) Dt. 4[31]; אל נשא 94[1. 1]; Ps. 99[8]; (5) אֵל without article, of God: indef. 5[5], elsw. def. 7[12] 10[11. 12] 16[1] 17[6] 19[2] 52[3. 7] 55[20] 57[3] 68[21] 73[11. 17] 74[8] 77[10] 78[7. 8. 18. 19. 34. 41] 82[1] 83[2] 89[8] 90[2] 104[21] 106[14. 21] 107[11] 118[27] 139[17. 23] 149[6] 150[1]; (6) divine name 50[1] (gl.), as Gn. 33[20] (E) Dt. 32[18] 33[26]; אל עליון **Ps. 78[35]**.

III. ‡ אלהים n.m. real pl.: (1) rulers Ex. 21⁶ 22⁷·⁸·⁸·²⁷ Jn. 5⁸ Pss. 82¹·⁶ 138¹; (2) superhuman beings, including God and angels, Gn. 1²⁷ Ps. 8⁶ (cf. Jb. 38⁷); (3) angels, אלהים (ו) בני Jb. 1⁶ 2¹ 38⁷ Gn. 6²·⁴ (J), cf. בני אלים; (4) gods Pss. 86⁸ 136²; אלהי העמים 96⁵ Dt. 6¹⁴ 13⁸ +; כל אלהים Pss. 95³ 96⁴ 97⁷·⁹ 135⁵. (5) *The God of Israel*, pl. intensive, originally with article, *the All Strong*, retaining this mng. when the article was omitted in usage, but subsequently losing its mng. and standing as a common name for the Divine Being, like θεός, *deus*, *God* (*v.* BD*B*.). It is used with article in ψ only in phrs.: איש האלהים title of 90, עיר האלהים 87³, where the article really defines the previous n. It is used in the cstr. in phr. אלהי אברהם 47¹⁰, phr. of J, אלהי ישראל 41¹⁴ 72¹⁸ 106⁴⁸ (benedictions) 59⁶ 68⁹ 69⁷, phr. of E, Je., Chr.; אלהי יעקב a poetic phr. 20² 46⁸·¹² 75¹⁰ 76⁷ 81²·⁵ 84⁹ 94⁷; אלהי יעע with various sfs. 18⁴⁷ א' חסרי 4²; א' צדקי 88²; א' ישועתי 51¹⁶; א' תשועתי 51¹⁶; 24⁵ 25⁵ 27⁹ 65⁶ 79⁹ 85⁵; 59¹¹·¹⁸; א' מעוזי 43² (?); י' אלהי צבאות 89⁹; א' תהלתי 109¹; א' האלהים 136². אלהים is used with sfs. frequently in ψ, because of the emphasis upon personal relations with God in lyric poetry. אֱלֹהַי 3⁸ 5⁸ 18⁷·²²·³⁰ 25² 31¹⁵ 35²³ 40⁹·¹⁸ 42⁷·¹² 43⁵ 59² 69⁴ 71⁴·¹²·²² 83¹⁴ 84⁴·¹¹ 86² 91² 94²² 104⁸³ 118²⁸ 119¹¹⁵ 143¹⁰ 145¹ 146²; אֱלֹהֶיךָ 42⁴·¹¹ 68²⁹; אֱלֹהָיִךְ 146¹⁰ 147¹²; אֱלֹהָיו 37⁸¹ 144¹⁵; אֱלֹהֵינוּ 18³² 20⁶ 40⁴ 44²¹ 48²⁹ 50³ 66⁸ 92¹⁴ 95⁷ 98³ 115³ 116⁵ 135² 147¹·⁷; אֱלֹהֵיהֶם 79¹⁰ 115². For other uses of אלהים with יהוה and אדני, *v.* I. IV. אלהים is used alone for God in 𝕰 c. 180 t., elsw. ψ c. 22 t.; *v.* VII. ‡ אֱלוֹהַּ is a poetic sg. of אלהים, used Dt. 32⁵·¹⁷, and on this basis as an archaism in late poetry Pss. 18³² (for אל 2 S. 22³²) 50²² (gl.) 114⁷ (err.) 139¹⁹ (gl.). It is characteristic of Jb. (41 t.).

IV. ‡ אֲדֹנִי divine name, originating in Judah; syn. of *Baal*, used in North Israel (*v.* BD*B*.); always ὁ κύριος in 𝕲. AV., *Lord*, to be distinguished from LORD for יהוה; also ὁ κύριος in 𝕲. The pointing ָ was to distinguish the divine name from אֲדֹנִי as applied to men. It is intensive pl. *sovereign lord*. In the oldest usage it was: *my sovereign Lord*, so 2⁴ 16² 37¹³ 59¹² 86³·⁴·⁵·¹²·¹⁵ 140⁸; later a proper name *Adonay* 55¹⁰ 57¹⁰ (= יהוה 108⁴) 71⁵·¹⁶ 89⁵⁰·⁵¹ 130²·³·⁶. Its use in ψ elsw. is questionable. It is not certain whether אדני 51¹⁷ was original in either sense or a substitute for יהוה. אדני is certainly a substitute for an original יהוה 40¹⁸ 54⁶ 68²³ 90¹. Seventeen codd. Kenn. rd. יהוה 110⁵. אדני either precedes or follows יהוה in conflation of text for earlier Qr. 68²¹ 69⁷ 73²⁸ 109²¹ 141⁸. It is a real gl., not in 𝕲 38¹¹; and though in 𝕲 a gl. in 22³¹ 35¹⁷·²²·²³ 38¹⁶ 39⁸ 44²⁴ 68¹²·¹⁸·³³ 77³ (𝕲 אירביכ) 77⁸ 86⁸. It is part of a larger gl. in 38²³ 62¹³ 66¹⁸ 68²⁰·²⁷ 73²⁰ 78⁶⁵ 79¹² 86⁹ 90¹⁷. The tendency to use it as Qr. for יהוה in later times, and also its general use for other divine names is illustrated by these editorial changes.

V. צבאות is given 24¹⁰.

VI. † עֶלְיוֹן n. m. *Highest* (1) name of God, Nu. 24¹⁶ Dt. 32⁸ Ps. 18¹⁴ (= 2 S. 22¹⁴), used as an archaism 9³ 21⁸ 50¹⁴ 73¹¹ 77¹¹ 78¹⁷ 83¹⁹ 91¹·⁹ 92² 107¹¹ Is. 14¹⁴ La. 3³⁵·³⁸; with other divine names אל עליון Gn. 14¹⁸·¹⁹·²⁰·²² Pss. 78³⁵ 87⁵ (?), יהוה עליון 7¹⁸ (?) 46⁵ (?) 47³ 97⁹; אלהים עליון 57³ 78⁵⁶; (2) of rulers, either monarchs or angel princes: בני עליון 82⁶.

VII. The group of Elohistic Pss. is composed of selections: —

(*a*) From 𝕶 42–48, 49 (?). These use אלהים 36 t.; some doubtless glosses, a few possibly original in 𝕶, but the great majority editorial substitutions for an original יהוה. יהוה צבאות was retained in the Rf. 46[8. 12], but in 48[9] it is a gl. יהוה in 42[9] 46[9] 47[3. 6] 48[2] is either a gl. or a substitution of later editors for the אלהים of 𝔈. In the Pss. of 𝕶 not in 𝔈, אלהים is used : 84[8. 10] (all glosses or txt. err.), but יהוה v.[3. 12. 12] יהוה צבאות v.[2. 4. 13] צ אלהים י׳ v.[9] is txt. err. for האלהים י׳ אלהי צבאות is used 87[3], but יהוה v.[2. 6]. אלהים is not used in 85 (but יהוה v.[2. 8. 9. 13], ראל v.[9]), or in 88 (?), but יהוה v.[2. 10. 14. 15]. There can be no doubt, therefore, that יהוה was the divine name of 𝕶, and that אלהים was substituted for it by the editor of 𝔈.

(*b*) From 𝕸 were taken 51–65, 68–70, 72. In these, אלהים is used 102 t. יהוה is used : 54[8] 55[17. 23] 56[11] 58[7] 59[4. 9] 64[11] 68[17] 69[14. 17. 32. 34] 70[2. 6]. All these are glosses, or substitutions of a still later editor. It is evident that אלהים of 53 has been substituted for יהוה of 14. In most other cases it was so also ; for in the other Pss. of 𝕸, אלהים is used but 15 t. : 3[3] 5[11] 7[10. 11. 12] 9[18] 10[4. 13] 14[1. 2. 5] 25[22] 36[2. 8] 144[9]; besides 6 t. in 108[2. 6. 8. 12. 12. 14] +, which is a mosaic of two Elohistic Pss. Ps. 86 uses אלהים v.[8. 10. 14], יהוה v.[1. 6. 11. 17], אדני v.[3. 4. 5. 8. 9. 12. 15]. This Ps. is also a mosaic of glosses of different date. The Pss. of 𝕸 in 𝔈 also use אדני 51[17] 54[6] 55[10] 57[10] 59[12] 62[13] 68[12. 18. 20. 23. 27. 33]. אדני ״ 68[21] is gl. י׳ אלהים צבאות 59[6] and אדני צבאות ״ 69[7] are conflations of late scribes. יהוה אלהים 72[18] is conflation in the doxology.

(*c*) All of 𝔄 that have been preserved were taken up into 𝔈: 50, 73–83. The separation of 50 from the group was not made in 𝔈, but by a later editor. These Pss. used the divine name אלהים 40 t. יהוה is used 50[1] 74[18] 75[9] 76[12] 78[4. 21] 79[5] 81[11. 16] 83[17. 19], in all cases either glosses themselves or in larger glosses. Besides אדני is used 73[20] 77[3. 8] 78[65] 79[12]; ארני יהוה 73[28]. אלהים צבאות 80[8. 15], and י׳ אלהים צבאות 80[5. 2)] were originally י׳ צבאות.

(*d*) The orphan Pss. 66, 67, 71, use אלהים 18 t., יהוה only 71[1]; a later substitution for אלהיב used v.[11. 12. 17. 18. 19. 19]. אדני and יהוה in v.[5. 16] belong to different ll. אדני is used 66[18]. These Pss. in 𝔈 doubtless followed 72. It is improbable that an editor who kept the Pss. of 𝕶 and 𝔄 together would not have done the same with the Pss. of 𝕸. These were the only Pss. not in 𝕸, 𝕶, 𝔄. Pss. 66 and 67 were in 𝔐 of the early Greek period; Ps. 71 in its original form, v.[4–9. 14–19], from the Greek period. The Psalter of 𝔈 could not therefore have been earlier, or indeed much later.

§ 33. *Fifty-five* (57) *Psalms have in their titles a reference to the director or choir master, which indicates that they were taken from a major Psalter which bore this title. They were collected in the middle Greek period in Palestine, as a prayer book for the synagogues, selected from the previous minor Psalters.*

The Pss. with למנצח are scattered through the Psalter. The term means, " Belonging to the Director." These Pss. were taken from a Psalter bearing the Director's name. Thirty-five of the fifty-four *Mizmorim* were probably taken as a basis. To these were added sixteen Pss. from 𝔇, four (5) from 𝔎, and one from 𝔄. As no Ps. later than the previous minor Psalters was used, it is probable that the collection was made in the middle Greek period, not long after 𝔐. As the divine name Yahweh was retained, this Psalter was doubtless collected in Palestine. The term *Director* also suggests the period of the Chronicler, who alone elsewhere uses the term. The great majority of these Pss. are prayers. The collection was, therefore, like 𝔇, designed as a prayer-book for use in the synagogues. Hb. 3 also attaches למנצח as part of the title of the song therein contained. This was originally a part of the Psalter of the Director (𝔇𝔎) and was subsequently removed to Hb. The Psalter of 𝔇𝔎 must therefore have been earlier than the final editing of Hb. and the close of the Canon of the Prophets. This also points to the middle Greek period, prior to Simon II. ?219–198 B.C.

למנצח is Pi. ptc. with prep. ל from נצח vb. denom. of נצח, *v.* 9⁶. The vb. is not used in Qal, but only in Pi., with the exception of a single Niph. ptc. וְצַחַ, Je. 8⁵, *enduring* (of apostasy), and in Pi. only in Chr. and titles of Pss., in the mngs. *act as overseer, superintendent, director :* (1) in building or repairing the temple, c. עַל 2 Ch. 2¹ Ezr. 3⁸· ⁹, c. ל 2 Ch. 34¹³, c. ל inf. 2 Ch. 2¹⁷, abs. 2 Ch. 34¹²; (2) in the ministry of the temple, c. עַל 1 Ch. 23⁴; (3) in the organised liturgical service, 1 Ch. 15²¹, six of them overseeing the basses, עַל השמינית, leading them with כנרות, and eight over the sopranos, עַל עלמות, leading them with harps (*v.* § 34). Heman, Asaph, and Ethan were over them all, leading with cymbals. This doubtless represents the temple service of the middle Greek period, and it is altogether probable that למנצח in the titles of the Pss. has the same meaning, especially as these and other musical terms are associated with it in the titles. We may therefore take it as meaning *director*, or *choir master*. The preposition ל has the same meaning here as in other uses in the titles, and indicates that these Pss. were taken from a Psalter collected under the name of the Director or choir master. The modern view that ל indicates assignment to the care of the choir master is improbable, because, as Ols. says, this was a matter of course, and would not be specified in titles. And this would not explain its use in some Pss. rather than in others. 𝔊 interprets למנצח as late form for לָנֶצַח = εἰς τὸ τέλος. This is explained by Eusebius and Theodoret in an eschatological sense : *unto the end* (of the world). 𝔗 renders לְשַׁבָּחָא to *sing in liturgy*, taking it as Aram. inf. with the mng. *use constantly, perpetually*, thinking of perpetual use in the liturgy. The explanation of De., " for the accomplishment, fulfilment, rendering fully," is improbable. It seems most probable that 𝔊 and 𝔗 agree in thinking of these Pss. as selected for perpetual use unto the end, in the liturgy. Another tradition is given in Aq. τῷ νικοποιῷ, Σ ἐπινικίος, Θ εἰς τὸ νῖκος, 𝔍 *victore*. These follow a conceit of the school of Rabbi Akiba (due probably to the Messianic hopes of that period) that they were the triumphal songs of Israel. But this does not suit the character of these Pss., which are prayers rather than hymns. The 𝔗 preserves the older tradition of 𝔊, which is essentially correct so far as the use of the collection is concerned, though it misses the exact sense of the term which is given by the Chronicler.

Fifty-five Pss. have למנצח in the titles. To these we may add 10 and 43, which belong to the previous Pss., 9 and 42. Of these thirty-five were Mizmorim: 4–6, 8–10, 12–13, 19–22, 31, 39–41 of 𝔇; 47, 49 (?) of 𝔎; 51, 62, 64, 65 of 𝔇; 66–67 orphans; 68 of 𝔇 (?) (*v.* § 27); 75–77, 80 of 𝔄; 84–85, 88 (?) (*v.* § 28) of 𝔎; 109, 139–140 of 𝔇. To these were added sixteen Pss. from 𝔇 (four Maskilim, 52–55, five Miktamim, 56–60; one Shir, 18, and six others, 11, 14, 36, 61, 69–70); moreover five (six) Pss. were added from 𝔎; (four (five) Maskilim, 42–45, 88, and the Shir, 46); one also from 𝔄, 81. All of these Pss. were used in previous Psalters, though they were adapted by this editor for use in his time. These Pss. are chiefly prayers, the great majority of them, thirty-three, being of this kind, as compared with eleven hymns and thirteen religious poems. This Psalter was therefore essentially a prayer book, on the basis of the earlier 𝔇 and 𝔐, for use in the synagogues of the Greek period. This is confirmed by the fact that למנצח, in the sense of director or choir master, is characteristic of the service of the temple as described by Chr. 1 Ch. 15, and belongs to his period. It is used elsewhere only in Hb. 3[19], as part of the title of that ode which, doubtless also originally was in 𝔇𝔎, but was separated from it and inserted in Hb. The collection of the Twelve Minor Prophets was closed and fixed in the Canon in the time of Ben Sira (BS. 49[10]) because he mentions the Twelve by that technical name. Daniel 9[2] seems to imply that the Canon of the Prophets was closed. The Psalter of the Director must therefore have been made in the middle Greek period.

§ **34.** *The Director attached to his prayer book instructions to the choir with reference to the tones, the voices, and the musical instruments to be used in the rendering of certain psalms in public worship.*

Twenty-nine of the Pss. of 𝔇𝔎 have musical directions attached. Several tones are mentioned to which special Pss. were to be sung, indicated usually by the initial words of some familiar song. There are several special references to the kind of voice that was most appropriate. There are also several kinds of musical instruments mentioned as suitable for accompanying the singing. These are, in all cases, special directions. Where such do not

appear, it is a reasonable inference that the choirs were left free in
their choice in these respects.   This collection of 𝔇ℜ was doubtless made for the use of some great synagogue in Jerusalem, where
it was possible to fulfil these directions.   There is no reference
to those instruments of music that were especially characteristic
of the feasts and of the more ornate worship in the temple.

Inasmuch as all the musical directions are attached to Pss. of 𝔇ℜ, it is
reasonable to suppose that they were first attached to this Psalter.   They are
of three kinds: (1) designation of tone or melody, (2) of voice, (3) of musical instrument.

(1) The tones are usually referred to by the use of initial words of some
well-known song, in accordance with an ancient usage which continues until
the present time.   The preposition עַל precedes these words, with the mng.
in accordance with, after (the tone of).   In some cases אֶל is used instead
of it, in accordance with a not infrequent misuse of this prep. for עַל (*v.* B*D*B.).

(*a*) אל תשחת is used in the titles of Pss. 57–59, Miktamim of 𝔇, and 75 of
𝔄.   The אל is pointed as negative in MT., and so the two words seem to mean
Destroy not; but the omission of עַל is striking and improbable.   It should be
אֶל for עַל as usual, and the original piece probably began with *Destroy*, referring to enemies of the nation.   RV. does not translate, but transliterates.
These Pss. have a variety of measures.   It is hardly possible that the reference could have been to a melody.   It was doubtless to a tone for cantilation,
as the tones of the early synagogue and early Church, which are capable of
use in pieces of different measure and different strophical length.

(*b*) עַל יונת אלם רחקים is in the title of the Miktam, Ps. 56.   The first line of
the piece referred to was probably, *The silent dove of them that are afar off*,
as in RV.ᵐ.   RV. transliterates, but does not translate.   𝔊 ὑπὲρ τοῦ λαοῦ τοῦ
ἀπὸ τῶν ἁγίων μεμακρυμμένου = *for the people removed far from the sanctuary*,
is doubtless a paraphrase.

(*c*) עַל שושן עדות is in the title of Ps. 60, a trimeter Miktam of 𝔇. עַל שושנים
is in the title of Ps. 45, Maskil of ℜ, and of 69 of 𝔇; אל ששנים עדות is in the
title of 80 of 𝔄.   These all undoubtedly refer to the same piece, a Ps. in
praise of the Law, whose first line was, *my testimony is a beautiful anemone*.
The view that it referred to an instrument of music shaped like a lily has
nothing in its favour, not even the mng. "lily," which cannot be proved in
the usage of this word.   The pl. is the pl. of intensity, " *beautiful* anemone."
It is not translated in the text of RV., but RV.ᵐ has it essentially as I have
given it.   𝔊 ὑπὲρ τῶν ἀλλοιωθησομένων or τοῖς ἀλλοιωθησομένοις = *for those
who shall be changed*, is a misinterpretation.

(*d*) עַל מחלת in the title of 53, a Maskil of 𝔇, and מחלת לענות עַל in the
title of 88, Maskil of Heman, both in 𝔇ℜ, are doubtless the same.   𝔊 ὑπὲρ
Μαελὲθ τοῦ ἀποκριθῆναι takes the first word as a proper name and the second
as inf. cstr. ענה *answer, respond.*   Aq., Θ, 𝔍, " for the dance," is inappropriate

to the sadness of these Pss. MT. מַחֲלַת n. cstr. before inf. is improbable.
𝕲 rd. מֵחֹלָת, Aq. ἐπὶ χορείᾳ, so essentially Θ, Σ, 𝔍, from חלל. It is most probable that we should rd. מַחֲלֶה n.f. *wounding, trouble,* from חלל; and לְעַנּוֹת inf.
cstr. ענה *suffer affliction.* Two words only of the original are preserved, *For
wounding, suffering affliction.* It is transliterated in RV.

(*e*) Ps. 22 has in the title עַל אַיֶּלֶת הַשַּׁחַר *hind of the dawn.* The third word
is missing. We might supply the vb. *leaps,* thinking of the fresh vigour of
the hind in the early morning ; but that does not suit the character of the Ps.
It is more appropriate to think of the hind hunted to death in the early morning. 𝕿 and Midrash regard it as referring to the lamb of the morning sacrifice. But it is improbable that the hind would represent the lamb. The hind
was not used for sacrifice in the OT. This Ps. was in 𝔻, 𝔐, 𝔻𝕽.

(*f*) 𝕲 adds to Ps. 70 the title εἰς τὸ Σῶσαί με Κύριον, *save me, O Lord,*
showing that another tone was added at so late a date. For it is improbable
that it was original and was omitted from the text in 𝖁.

(*g*) עַל הַגִּתִּית is in the title of Ps. 8 of 𝔻, 𝔐, 81 of 𝔄, and 84 of 𝕭, 𝔐.
𝕲 and Σ ὑπὲρ τῶν ληνῶν; so 𝖁, 𝔍, *pro torcularibus, for the wine presses,*
reading גִּתּוֹת, refers therefore to a harvest song at the vintage or treading of
grapes. This suits the triumphant, joyous character of these Pss., and is probably correct. They were to be sung to the tone of some well-known vintage
song. Aq., Θ, have in Ps. ὑπὲρ τῆς γετθίτιδος, but the Syr.-Hex. of Aq. in
81 and 84 ἐπὶ τοῦ ληνοῦ or ἐπὶ τῶν ληνῶν. This is more probable than a Gittite musical instrument. 𝕿 " the harp which David brought from Gath," or
a tone of Gath, the march of the Gittite guard (2 S. 15[18]), explanation of גִּתִּית
MT., both equally improbable.

(*h*) עַל יְדוּתוּן in 62 of 𝔻, 𝔐, עַל יְדוּתוּן in 77 of 𝔄, 𝔐, לִידוּתוּן in 39 of 𝔻, 𝔐,
all doubtless refer to the same thing. ל in 39 is doubtless err. for עַל, and the
variation of י and ו in the penult is a variation of MT., not of the original
of 𝖁. It is probable that Jeduthun, the choir master, is referred to, *v.* 1 Ch.
16[41] 25[3] 2 Ch. 5[12], or his choir, 1 Ch. 25[1, 3] 2 Ch. 29[14] Ne. 11[17]; but it is improbable that this name is in apposition with לַמְנַצֵּחַ as De., in which case עַל
would be err. for ל; rather it refers to a tone of this choir. The reference to
a lily-shaped musical instrument of some Rabbis, though followed by Ges.,
is without justification.

(2) There are two voices referred to, the falsetto and the bass.

(*a*) עַל עֲלָמוֹת is in the title of Ps. 46, tetrameter of 𝕭. 𝕲 interprets it as
ὑπὲρ τῶν κρυφίων = 𝖁 *pro arcanis,* deriving from עלמה n.f. in the sense of
secret, hidden. This was interpreted as in a gentle, quiet style. Σ ὑπὲρ τῶν
αἰωνίων derives as pl. of עוֹלָם, *ever,* in the late sense of *ages.* Aq. ἐπὶ νεανιο-
τήτων and 𝔍 *pro juventutibus* follow MT. and derive from עלמה n.f. abst.,
youth. These last are nearer the correct view, for the explanation is found in
1 Ch. 15[20], where it refers to the maidenlike style. Some think of maidens, as
Ps. 68[26], where they play upon timbrels in the march of Yahweh ; but maidens
took no part in the service of song. Bö. thinks of the tenor voice ; but more
probably it was the falsetto male voice. At the end of Ps. 48[15] עלמות seems

out of place. It probably belongs to 49, from the title of which it has been detached by error, the על being omitted as supposed dittog., or for the opposite reason. It is also probable that על מות לבן in the title of Ps. 9 belongs here. It is usually interpreted on the basis of MT. as a reference to a tone in accordance with (1); this tone being designated by two words of the first line, " Death to the son," or, " Death for the son "; but this is in itself improbable and has no support in Vrss., which all rd. עלמות. 𝕲 ὑπὲρ τῶν κρυφίων τοῦ υἱοῦ, Aq. νεανιότητος τοῦ υἱοῦ, Θ ὑπὲρ ἀκμῆς τοῦ υἱοῦ. These are doubtless correct as to the form. But then we must follow them in interpreting it in the same way as in 46, and refer it to the falsetto voice. לבן is then the fuller designation, showing that it was the maidenlike voice of a son, thinking of a boy or a youth.

(b) על השמינית is in the titles of Pss. 6, 12, both prayers of 𝕱 and 𝕯. 𝕲 interprets it as ὑπὲρ τῆς ὀγδόης, on the octave, so 𝕍 pro octava. This is doubtless correct, as it is in accord with 1 Ch. 15²¹, which refers to the lower octave or the bass voice. The opinion of some that it refers to an instrument of eight strings is a mere conceit, without support in the OT.

(3) There are references to two kinds of musical instruments — stringed instruments and wind instruments.

(a) נגינות is in the titles of Pss. 4, 6, 54, 55, 67, 76, with בְ of accompaniment, and in 61 (sg.) with עַל. Of these, 54, 55, were Maskilim; 4, 6, 67, 76, in 𝕱; 4, 6, 54, 55, in 𝕯; 76 in 𝕬; 4, 6, 54, 55, 61, are prayers; 67, a hymn; 76, a poem. They are of different measures. 𝕲 has ἐν ὕμνοις in 6, 54, 55, 61, 67, 76, and ἐν ψαλμοῖς in 4. The form is pl. f. of נגינה n.f. stringed instrument. נון vb. denom. Pi. to play on stringed instruments, נוגנים players on stringed instruments, Ps. 68²⁶. Hb. 3¹·¹⁹ have in 𝕲 the same word, doubtless in both cases נגינות, correct for 𝕳 שיגינות. These seven Pss. and Hb. 3 were to be accompanied by stringed instruments, such as the lyre and harp.

(b) אל הנחילות is in the title of Ps. 5, a morning prayer of 𝕱 and 𝕯. It is interpreted by 𝕲 and Θ as ὑπὲρ τῆς κληρονομούσης, 𝕍 pro ea quae hereditatem consequitur, Aq., Σ, 𝕴, pro hereditatibus, all deriving the form as pl. n.f. from נחל inherit. The אל is doubtless variation for על as often. No reasonable explanation of this term has yet been given. It is probable that it is a n. formed by נ from הלל, a variation of חליל the reed pipe, as Hu., or abstr., as De., Moll., for flute playing, cf. 1 S. 10⁵ 1 K. 1⁴⁰ Is. 30²⁹. It is probable that instruments of the class of the pipe or simple flute are referred to.

(c) It is noteworthy that these references are not only few, but in general terms, and that no particular musical instrument is referred to. The music especially characteristic of festivals in the temple worship does not appear. The music was probably that of a simple orchestra of two or four pieces of the lighter string and wind instruments, and not the louder music used in the temple courts. And it is also probable that musical instruments were seldom used in the synagogues, or we would have had more assignments of this kind.

(d) There is little reference to musical instruments in the earlier minor Psalters. There is no reference in 𝕯, for 57⁹ = 108³ = 144⁹ were not originally in 𝔇 (v. § 27). In 𝕬 the only reference is in 81³⁻⁴ to a new moon celebration, doubtless in the temple courts, with the use of the נבל and כנור the *harp* and *lyre*, the two chief kinds of stringed instruments usually associated ; the שופר the *horn*, and the תף *timbrel*. In 𝕶 43⁴ the כנור is used in temple worship ; so in the orphan 33² 92⁴ both כנור and נבל. This probably represents the ordinary worship of the Greek period. On great occasions, such as feasts or celebrations of victories, more instruments of music were used ; so in the royal advent Ps. 47⁶ (𝕶) the שופר, and in 98⁵⁻⁶ the כנור, the שופר, and the חצצרה *the straight trumpet*. In the Maccabean Hallels a greater number and variety of instruments appear ; due to the reorganisation of the temple worship with greater pomp than ever before. 147⁷ mentions only the כנור, 149³ the כנור and תף, but 150³⁻⁵ the כנור and נבל, the שופר and תף, and also the instruments not mentioned earlier : עוגב the small organ, מנים stringed instruments, and צלצלים cymbals. The Pss. also mention the use of musical instruments by minstrels apart from public worship ; so the כנור in 49⁵ of 𝕶 (?) and in the orphan 137² ; and both the כנור and נבל in the orphan 71²² 57⁹ (= 108³ = 144⁹ all glosses).

§ 35. *A collection of Hallels, or songs of praise, was made for the temple service in the Greek period. It was subsequently enlarged in the Maccabean period. These Psalms have in their titles the term Hallelujah.*

The term הַלְלוּיָהּ = *Praise ye Yah* is found at the close of Pss. 104, 105, 115, 116, 117, and the beginning of Pss. 111, 112, and at both beginning and end of Pss. 106, 113, 135, 146, 147, 148, 149, 150. 𝕲 gives it also at the beginning of 105, 107, 114, 116, 117, 118, 119, 136. In the case of 105, 107, 114, 116, 117, 136, it seems to have been detached by error from the beginning of these Pss. and attached to the close of the previous Pss. in 𝕳. All of these Pss. are Hallels except 118 and 119, which are only so given in 𝕲, the former being a triumphal Maccabean song, the latter the great alphabetical praise of the Law. Both of these were regarded as Hallels in later usage. These Hallels are in the present Psalter in four groups : 104–107, 111–117, 135–136, 146–150. This separation was due to the final editor of the Psalter. 104–107 constitute a tetralogy, 104 being a Ps. of creation, 105 telling the early history of Israel, 106 of the Exodus, 107 of the Restoration. The second group begins with 111–112, a pair complementary in subject and alphabetic in structure ; 113 begins the special Hallel of the great feasts, according to later liturgical assignment. At the Passover the order was 113–114 before supper, 115–118 after supper. In the third group 136 is the ordinary Great Hallel, with its Rf. repeated twenty-six times in the present Ps., though the earliest text was much simpler. In later times Pss. 119–136 were likewise called the Great Hallel in distinction from the ordinary Hallel 113–118. The last group of Hallels consisted of the doxologies 146–150. All of these Hallels except 147,

149, belong to the Greek period and were doubtless in their original form in the collection of that period, composed for public use by the choirs especially on the great feasts. The collection consisted of sixteen Pss. A Maccabean editor added 147, 149. The final editor of ψ distributed these Hallels in the present four groups. In later liturgical use 118 and 119 were regarded as Hallels and still later 120–134. The technical terms of the Hallels are הללויה, הודו, and ברכו. For הלל and תהלה v. § 1; for יָהּ v. § 32 (I.); for ברכו v. Pss. 5^{13} 184^7. הודו Hiph. imv. 2 pl. ‡ [ידה]. Qal is not in ψ, but only Hiph. † (1) *confess*, a late usage Ps. 32^5, cf. Pr. 28^{13} 1 K. $8^{33. \ 35}$ = 2 Ch. $6^{24. \ 26}$. (2) *praise*: (*a*) the king Ps. 45^{18}, the rich 49^{19}; elsw. (*b*) Yahweh in the ritual: c. acc. יהוה 7^{18} 9^2 109^{30} 111^1, יָהּ 118^{19}, שם י' 44^9 54^8 99^3 138^2 142^8, פלא י' 89^6; sfs. referring to יהוה 18^{50} 28^7 $30^{10. \ 13}$ 35^{18} $42^{6. \ 12}$ $43^{4. \ 5}$ 52^{11} 57^{10} $67^{4. \ 4. \ 6. \ 6}$ 71^{22} 76^{11} 86^{12} 88^{11} 108^4 $118^{21. \ 28}$ 119^7 $138^{1. \ 4}$ 139^{14} 145^{10}; c. לְ, ליהוה 33^2 92^2 105^1 106^1 $107^{1. \ 8. \ 15. \ 21. \ 31}$ $118^{1. \ 29}$ 136^1, cf. v.$^{2. \ 8. \ 26}$, לשם י' 106^{47} 122^4 140^{14}; sfs. referring to Yahweh 6^6(?), cf. Is. 38^{18}, Pss. $75^{2. \ 2}$ 79^{13} 100^4 119^{62}; abs. לזכר קדשו 30^5 97^{12}.

§ 36. *A collection of songs for the use of pilgrims on their way to the three great feasts was made in the middle Greek period. These Psalms have in their titles, " Songs of Pilgrimage."*

Pss. 120–134 have in their titles שִׁיר הַמַּעֲלוֹת. This is rendered in 𝕲 ᾠδὴ τῶν ἀναβαθμῶν, ode of ascents, 𝕵 and 𝕵 *canticum graduum*, gradual psalms, Aq., Σ εἰς τὰς ἀναβάσεις, Θ ᾆσμα τῶν ἀναβάσεων. These variations have given rise to three different theories: (1) The phrase refers to the fifteen steps in the temple leading up from the court of the women to the court of the men of Israel upon which these Pss. were chanted; so Lyra, Luther, Horsley, Gr. The Talmud indeed mentions these Pss. in that connection (*Middoth*, II. 5, *Sukka*, 51 *b*), but simply to compare them with those steps on which the music resounded on the first day of the feast of Tabernacles; it does not explain the Pss. as used thereon (*v.* De., p. 780). Furthermore, the contents of these Pss. were not suited to that purpose. They are not temple Pss. (2) The term has metrical significance indicating the stairlike parallelism, advancing by steps or degrees; so Ges., Köster, De., Moll., De W. This is a modern theory based on the fact that this method of parallelism is frequently used in these Pss. But it is not used in them all, and not in a thoroughgoing manner in any; and certainly not to such an extent as to give titles to the group. There are other Pss. which use this method of parallelism in a more thoroughgoing manner, *v.* § 12. (3) The term refers to the ascents of pilgrimage (*a*) 𝕾 and the ancient Fathers thought of the ascent from the Babylonian exile. Ew., in 1839, called them "the songs of the homeward marches." (*b*) Agellius, Herder, Eichhorn, Ew. in 1866, and most modern scholars, think of the ascents to the feasts of the Law. Street thought that they were simply processionals. Is. 30^{29} Ps. 42^5 shew that it was the custom to make pilgrimages to the temple with song and music, and even sacred dances and shoutings. We would expect, therefore, that a collection of songs suitable for this purpose would be made. These songs have a common social and patriotic character. They are all hexameters composed of one or more hexastichs. They could all have been sung to the same tone. They were all composed in the Greek period, except 129, which is Maccabean. It is probable that this last Ps. was added to the collection, which originally consisted of fourteen Pss. made in the middle Greek period.

§ **37.** *A considerable number of Psalms, especially those of the Greek period, did not find their way into any of the minor or major Psalters, but were used at last by the editor of the present Psalter.*

(*a*) Ps. 1, composed in the middle Greek period, is didactic in character. It was probably used for the first time by the editor of the Psalter as its introduction.

(*b*) Ps. 33 was probably from the Maccabean period. It was given its present position by the final editor of the Psalter.

(*c*) The pseudonyms, Pss. 88, 89, 90, 102 (*v.* § 30), were given their present position by the final editor.

(*d*) Ps. 91 was probably from the early Greek period. It was given its present position because it was conceived as a counterpart to 90.

(*e*) Ps. 92 was probably from the later Greek period. It was originally a song composed for liturgical use. Its contents justify its present position.

(*f*) Pss. 94, 95, were probably from the Greek period. They were given their present position for liturgical reasons.

(*g*) Pss. 93, 96–100, were originally one great advent hymn from the early Greek period. It was broken up into little Pss. for liturgical purposes (*v.* § 13).

(*h*) Pss. 86, 103, 145, from the late Greek period, were given their present position because of resemblances to Pss. of 𝕯, and, for that reason, 𝕯 subsequently crept into the titles.

(*i*) Ps. 137 from the early exile was not taken up into any of the earlier Psalters because of its inappropriateness for worship. It was used by the final editor of the Psalter as an ancient piece which he thought should be preserved. It was inserted after 136 as an appropriate place, on account of the historical references in both Pss.

§ **38.** *The editor of the present Psalter used the two major Psalters as the nucleus of his work. The Babylonian Elohistic Psalter, 42–83, was placed in the middle, and appropriate Pss. 84–89 were added thereto. The first part was based on the Palestinian Director's Psalter, in which were inserted chiefly Psalms from the Davidic Psalter. The third part was arranged about* *the temple Hallels and the Pilgrim Psalter, to which were added the remaining Psalms of the Director's Psalter and other appropriate Psalms, chiefly of late date. This work was accomplished in the Maccabean period, after the reorganisation of the worship.*

There can be little doubt that the editor of the present Psalter used 𝔇𝕽, the prayer-book of the Greek period in Palestine, as the basis of his work. He was compelled to do so if he would produce a collection which would take its place in public use. He also used 𝕰, because that was the Psalter in familiar use in Babylonia and among the Jews of the Dispersion all through the East. It was necessary to combine that collection with the other if he would secure his book a public use in the Orient. He must indeed enlarge both collections by the introduction of Pss. old and new, in order to justify his task. The editor was probably called to his work by public authority and by an understanding between the Jews of the East and the West. It was also in the plan to combine the Pss. used in synagogue worship with those used in the worship of the temple. And so the Hallels and the Pilgrim Psalter were made the nucleus of a much larger collection, suited for this purpose. The editor also added a number of older Pss. of a national character, even though they had not previously been used in public worship. It was just because he thus satisfied all interests in a most comprehensive way, that his book supplanted all others and at once attained universal recognition.

A careful examination of the arrangement of the present Psalter on the basis of what has already been determined as to the several minor and major Psalters and the Pss. not included in them, enables us to trace, to a great extent, the methods of the editor of ψ.

The first part of ψ is 1–41 based on 𝔇𝕽. (*a*) Ps. 1 was made the general introduction to ψ, followed by 2, the original introduction to 𝔇, followed by 3, the first prayer of 𝔇, 𝕸. Then came 4–6 of 𝔇𝕽. The enigmatic 7 of 𝔇 was then inserted. (*b*) Pss. 8–14 of 𝔇𝕽 are followed by 15 of 𝔇, 𝕸, describing the true citizen of Zion (in antithesis with the wicked fool of 14), and 16, a Miktam of 𝔇, and 17, a prayer of 𝔇. (*c*) Ps. 18, the ode of David, introduces the next group of 𝔇𝕽, 19–22. To these were added the following: the shepherd Ps. 23 of 𝔇, 𝕸, the choral 24 of 𝔇, 𝕸, and the group of prayers 25–28 from 𝔇 only, and of hymns 29–30 from 𝔇, 𝕸. (*d*) To 31, the prayer of 𝔇𝕽, was appended 32, the penitential Maskil of 𝔇; and 33, an anon. hymn; 34, an alphabetical hymn of 𝔇; and 35, a prayer of 𝔇. Then follows 36 of 𝔇ℜ; 37, a poem of 𝔇; and 38, a penitential Ps. of 𝔇, 𝕱𝕸, concluding with 39–41 of 𝔇ℜ. Thus the editor of ψ used 20 Pss. from 𝔇ℜ, to which he added in appropriate places, 19 of 𝔇 (including Ps. 2), and 2, anon. Pss. not used in any previous Psalter.

The second part of ψ was 42–89 based on 𝔈. (a) 42–48 𝕶 49 (𝕶?) concluding with 50 of 𝕬, which was transferred to this place for the purpose of giving an appropriate liturgical close to this group before the penitential 51. (b) The group of 𝔇, 51–65, after which 66–67 of 𝕱𝕸, 𝔇ℜ, followed by 68–70 of 𝔇, followed by 71, peculiar to 𝔈, and 72, the original conclusion of 𝔇. (c) The group of 𝕬 73–83. Pss. 42–83 were taken from 𝔈, which was thus inserted bodily in the middle of ψ, without additions, except in glosses. (d) ψ now appended 84–85 from 𝕶 used by 𝕱𝕸, 𝔇ℜ, then 86, a prayer, later ascribed to 𝔇, but really anon. (see §§ 27, 37), 87 from 𝕶, 𝕱𝕸, and the pseudonyms 88, 89, the latter being the conclusion of this second part.

The third part of ψ was 90–150, based on the Hallels and the Pilgrim Psalter. (a) Ps. 90, the pseudonym, was prefixed, 91, 92, 94, 95, anon. were added, then the great advent Ps. 93, 96–100, was broken up for liturgical reasons, 101 of 𝔇 and 𝕱𝕸, and 102, a pseudon. prayer, follow; then 103 an anonym., a late hymn kindred to the first group of Hallels, 104–107, which it precedes. (b) To the second group of Hallels, 111–117, was prefixed 108 of 𝕱𝕸, 109 of 𝔇, 𝕱𝕸, 𝔇ℜ, and 110 of 𝔇, 𝕱𝕸. To these, the Maccabean *Hodu* 118 was added. (c) The group of Pilgrim Psalms, 120–134, was placed in the midst of the third part, preceded by 119, the alphabetical praise of the Law. (d) To the Hallels 135–136 were added 137, the anon. exilic Ps. of vengeance, and 138 of 𝔇, 139, 140 of 𝔇, 𝕱𝕸, 𝔇ℜ, 141 of 𝔇, 𝕱𝕸, 142 Maskil of D, 143 of 𝔇, 𝕱𝕸, 144, 145, anon. alphabetical Pss. (the latter ascribed to 𝔇, *v.* §§ 27, 37). (e) The concluding Hallels, 146–150.

§ **39**. *Liturgical assignments appear in several titles, referring to days of week, kinds of sacrifice, and festivals. These are so few that they must have been prefixed, not by the final editor, but by late scribes.*

(a) Assignment to days of the week in the temple service. ליום השבת = *for the Sabbath Day*, in the title of 92, indicates its assignment for use on the Sabbath. 𝕲 gives several other titles of this kind: in 24, *for the first day of the week;* in 38, *the Sabbath;* 48, *for the second day of the week;* 94, *for the fourth day of the week;* 93, *for the day before the Sabbath.* Doubtless in late liturgical use each day of the week had its appropriate Ps., but only the earliest assignment, that to the Sabbath, appears in 𝔥. In BS. 50[14 sq.] there is an account of these temple services.

(b) Assignments to sacrifices in the temple. לתודה *for the thank-offering* is attached to 100. The Ps. was to be used in connection with that kind of a sacrifice. The word might mean *for praise*, but it would be meaningless in the midst of a multitude of Pss. which, of their very nature, are hymns of praise. לְהַזְכִּיר in the titles of 38, 70, is a Hiph. denom. (Lv. 2^2 + 6^8 Nu. 5^{26}) from אזכרה, the technical term for the offering of the *Mincha*. It doubtless means to make the *Azkarah*. These Pss. were designated for use at that sacrifice. Doubtless other Pss. were used on sacrificial occasions, but references to their use did not make their way into the titles of the Pss.

(*c*) Assignments to festivals. שיר חנכת הבית in the title of 30 indicates its assignment to a festival of the dedication of the temple, probably that of Judas the Maccabee, B.C. 164, when the temple was rededicated after its desecration by Antiochus, 1 Macc. 4^{59} Jn. 10^{22}. 𝔊 gives in the title of Ps. 29 ἐξοδίου σκηνῆς, 𝖁 *in consummatione tabernaculi*, referring to its use on the last day of Tabernacles.

§ **40**. *There are doxologies at the close of the five books into which* 𝕳 *divides the Psalter. But these were designed to be used at the conclusion of every psalm in liturgical service.*

Although these doxologies are counted in the verses of the Pss. in MT., so are the titles, and the former are no more parts of the original than the latter. These doxologies are benedictions, or ascriptions of blessedness to the God of Israel. A series of such benedictions has been preserved as the earliest part of the Jewish Liturgy apart from the Psalter. Such are also of frequent occurrence in the citations from the early Rabbis in the Misnayoth and Beraithoth. Though given usually only at the close of the books, the doxologies were really used at the conclusion of every Ps. or part of Ps. sung in the liturgy.

These are the benedictions in ψ : —

Ps. 41^{14}	ברוך | יהוה אלהי ישראל | מהעולם ועד העולם | אמן ואמן
72^{18-19}	ברוך | יהוה (אלהים) אלהי ישראל | עשה נפלאות לבדו
	וברוך | שם כבורו לעולם | וימלא כבורו (את)־כל־הארץ | אמן ואמן
89^{53}	ברוך | יהוה | לעולם | אמן ואמן
106^{48}	ברוך | יהוה אלהי ישראל | מן־העולם ועד העולם |
	| (ואמר כל־העם) אמן

We also find the last of these in 1 Ch. 16^{36}, where it was used as one of the doxologies of the temple service. It was not cited from this Ps. Rather the reverse is the case : that the doxology was added to ψ from the Chronicler ; for it could not have been used by the editor of ψ in the time of Judas the Maccabee, the early part of the second century B.C., because it divides the group of Hallels 104–107, which were designed as a tetralogy to be used together. These four doxologies began with ברוך Qal ptc. pass., *Blessed,* which was probably uttered by a solo voice, followed by a metrical pause. They close with the double *Amen; verily,* sung by the choir or by the people according to the rubric 106⁴⁸, "Let all the people say *Amen.*" The intervening material is a trimeter couplet, as 41¹⁴ = 106⁴⁸. These differ only in the scribal variation מִן ה׳ for מֵהָ, the former destroying the measure preserved by the latter. 89⁵³ is evidently an abridgment of the same couplet. 72¹⁸⁻¹⁹ gives a double benediction, and therefore a couplet in each v. יהוה is a Qr. for אלהים at the close of Ps. of 𝔈. את is a prosaic insertion at the expense of the measure without affecting the sense. There are virtually, therefore only two doxologies : —

(1) *Blessed be | Yahweh the God of Israel | From everlasting even unto everlasting.*
   Amen and Amen.

(2) *Blessed be | Yahweh the God of Israel, | Doer of wonders alone.*
   Blessed be | His glorious name for ever | And may the whole earth be filled with His glory.
   Amen and Amen.

The first of these is the ancient benediction, and it was probably used in ψ at the close of the first and second divisions. The third division needed no such benediction because it ended with a series of Hallel doxologies. The more elaborate benediction of 72¹⁸⁻¹⁹ and that of 106⁴⁸ were appended subsequently when ψ was divided into five books.

§ 41. *Selah indicates the abbreviation of a psalm in liturgical use, and marks the place where the closing benediction might be sung. The word itself means : Lift up (the voice in praise). This interpretation explains the tradition of 𝔊 that it called for an "interlude," and the Palestinian tradition, which represents it by the last word of the doxology, "forever." The term was first attached to psalms in the Psalter of the Mizmorim. It was used in the Director's Psalter, and in the Collection of the Elohist, and it continued in use at least until the time of the Psalter of Solomon and the earliest portions of the Jewish Liturgy.*

Selah is used in 𝕳 71 t. in thirty-nine Pss. It is also found 3 t. in Hb. 3. As it is used frequently in 𝕯𝕽, it was probably attached to Hb. 3 before the removal of that Ps. from 𝕯𝕽 to its present position. It is used in all the major Psalters, and in 32, 89, in addition. The latest uses of Selah in the Psalter of 𝕳 are in 66ᵇ 67 from the early Greek period ; and in 24ᵃ 89ᶜ, parts of composite Pss. which belong to the later Greek period.

But Selahs continued to be added in 𝔊 after the completion of
that translation.   They also appear twice in the Psalter of Solomon, and twice in the Jewish Benedictions.   This late use makes
it impossible to think that the term was misunderstood either in
the Alexandrian or the Palestinian tradition.   The former translates
the word by διάψαλμα, *interlude*, the latter by *forever*.   Both renderings depend on the same usage, regarded from different points
of view.   The former indicates an interlude at which the benediction should be sung, and the Ps. concluded for that particular
service.   The latter gives the last word of the benediction as an
abbreviation for the benediction itself.   The word סלה calls for
the *lifting up* of the voice in praise.   This interpretation satisfies
all the conditions of the problem, and is in accord with the actual
position occupied by Selah in the Psalms.

סֶלָה is used : (*a*) *at the close of a Str.:* in Pss. 3[3. 5. 9] 4[3. 5] 7[6] 9[17. 21] 24[6. 10]
32[4] 39[6. 12] 46[4. 8. 12] 47[5] 48[9] 50[6] (before Rf.) 15 (𝔊) 52[7] 59[6. 14] (before Rf.) 60[6] 66[15]
67[5] 76[1. 10] 77[4. 10. 16] 80[8] (𝔊) 82[2] 83[9] 84[5] 87[3] 89[5. 38. 46. 49] 140[4. 6. 9] (43 t. in
25 Pss.).   This is evidently the prevailing use.   (*b*) *At the close of a pericope made without regard to measure:* in Pss. 20[4] 21[3] 32[5] 49[14] 52[5] 67[2] 84[9] 85[3]
87[6] 88[8. 11] (om. 𝔊) 143[6] (12 t. in 11 Pss.).   Five of these Pss. have also ס at
close of Str.: 32, 52, 67, 84, 87.   It seems unlikely that both uses came from
the same hand.   The Selahs at end of Strs. are presumably earlier than the
others.   (*c*) *At the close of a gloss:* in Pss. 32[7] 44[9] 49[16] 54[5] 55[8. 20] 57[4a. 7] 61[5]
62[5. 9] 66[4. 7] 68[20] 75[4] 81[8] (16 t. in 12 Pss.).   In more than half of these Pss. ס may
have been earlier than the gl., and may have stood originally at the close of
a Str.   There can be little doubt that this is the case in 54[5] 62[5] 66[7] 75[4];
it may well have been so in 32[7] 61[5].   The Selah in 68[20] may also originally
have followed the last l. of Str. if v.[21] be an independent gl.; but if these vs.
form one gl. ס is probably the insertion of a later editor.   The use of the term
in 55[8] 57[4a] is difficult to explain, as the gl. is short and the ס immediately
precedes the last l. of Str.   Was the gl. intended to take the place of the
closing l.? or are these examples of displacement?   𝔊 gives Selah in 57[3] in
some codd., showing a fluctuating usage for this Ps.   It is possible that these
Selahs also stood originally at close of Str.   In any case there are upward of
six Selahs to be added to the list given above under (*a*).   There remain
seven Selahs that seem inseparable from the glosses which they follow :
44[9] 49[16] 55[20] 57[7] 62[9] 66[4] 81[8].   As these Selahs cannot be earlier than their
gls., the use must be a late one.   49[16] may be a gl. of 𝔈, or it may come from
a later hand.   81[8] is a gl. of 81[b], 57[7] of 57[b].   These Pss. were probably joined
to their present mates in 𝔈, and these Selahs may all be due to 𝔈.   So 55[20] and
62[9] also preserve late gls. and late uses of ס.   44[9] 66[4] are gls. later than 𝔈,

and their Selahs may be later still. The use of ׳ס in $68^{8.33}$ is probably due to error, v.^{33} to txt. err. (*v.* Ps.), and v.^{8} to err. of transposition, as ׳ס stands here in the midst of a citation from Dt. 5^{4-5}. It may have stood originally at end of citation, or else of Str., or it may be due to dittog. So many uses of the term in this Ps. have been preserved in the different Versions, that it is difficult to form any opinion as to its genuineness in 𝔥. סֶלָה was used in all three of the major Psalters. (1) There are 28 (26) of the Selah Pss. in 𝔐: 3–4, 7 (𝔊), 9, 20–21, 24, 39, 47–50, 62, 66–68, 75–77, 80 (𝔊), 82–85, 87–88, 140, 143. The term is used in these Pss.: (*a*) *at close of Str.:* 3–4, 9, 24, 39, 47–48, 50, 66–67, 76–77, 80, 82–84, 87, 140 (19 Pss.); and prob. also in 62^{5} 66^{7} 68^{20} 75^{4} before the insertion of gl. (*b*) *Regardless of measure:* 20^{4} 21^{3} 49^{14} 67^{2} 84^{9} 85^{3} 87^{6} $88^{8.11}$ 143^{6} (9 Pss.). As this usage could hardly have come from the same hand, it must be regarded as later than 𝔐. (*c*) *At close of gloss:* in 49^{16} 62^{9} 66^{4}. These gls. are all from time of 𝔈 or later, so that these Selahs could not have been in 𝔐. The characteristic use of ׳ס in the Mizmorim is therefore at the close of Str., and the editor of 𝔐, when he would shorten a Ps., did so by leaving off one or more Strs. (2) There are 29 of the Selah Pss. in 𝔇ℜ. All of these are found in 𝔐 save: 44, 46, 52, 54, 55, 57, 59, 60, 61, 81 (10 Pss.). In this collection ׳ס stands: (*a*) *at close of Str.:* in 4, 9, 39, 46–47, 52, 59–60, 62, 66–68, 75–77, 80 (𝔊), 84, 140 (18 Pss.). Four of these Pss. were not in 𝔐: 46, 52, 59, 60. 𝔇ℜ seems therefore to have continued the use of ׳ס begun in 𝔐. To these may be added Pss. 54^{5} 61^{5}, as ׳ס prob. antedates gl., and stood originally at end of Str. The use in 55^{8} 57^{4a} is doubtful, as has been seen, and may be rather that of (*c*) or (*b*) *regardless of measure:* 20, 21, 49, 52, 67, 84, 85, 88 (8 Pss.). All of these are in 𝔐 save 52; but as it seems unreasonable to ascribe a regard for measure and a disregard of it to the same editor, it is necessary to consider this usage as later than 𝔐, and hence as due to 𝔇ℜ. It is true that two of the examples given in Pss. of 𝔐 are lacking in 𝔇ℜ, 87^{6} 143^{6}; but 87 has another Selah at close of Str., so that the use of the term in v.^{6} must in any case be due to a later hand. As to 143^{6}, there is no special propriety in the use of ׳ס here, and if genuine, it may well be late. A similar use is to be found in 32, one of two Selah Pss. outside the major Psalters. (*c*) *At the close of gl.:* 44^{9} 49^{16} 55^{20} 57^{7} 62^{9} 66^{4} 81^{8}. All of these Selahs are in Pss. of 𝔇ℜ; but, as has been shown, they can hardly be separated from their gls. and must therefore belong to the time of 𝔈 or later. The Selahs added by 𝔇ℜ seem to have been placed with less regard for the strophical organisation of the Ps. than was shown by 𝔐, the musical or liturgical interest being paramount. It is worthy of note that 𝔇ℜ has added musical notes to the titles of many of the Selah Pss., including all those wanting in 𝔐, excepting 52, 61, and 44 (whose ׳ס is too late for 𝔇ℜ). (3) Twenty-four of the Selah Pss. appear in 𝔈: 44, 46–50, 52, 54–55, 57, 59–62, 66–68, 75–77, 80–83. All of these Pss. are also in 𝔇ℜ save 48, 50, 82, 83, which are Pss. of 𝔐 and use ׳ס only at close of Str. There seems to be no independent use of ׳ס in 𝔈 apart from gls. All the examples of ׳ס *at end of gl.* are in Pss. of 𝔈: 44^{9} 49^{16} 55^{20} 57^{7} 62^{9} 66^{4} 81^{8}.

These could hardly have been earlier than 𝕰, and may all have been later.
The Selahs in 49[16] 55[20] 57[7] 62[9] 81[8] are possibly due to 𝕰. Those in 44[9] 66[4]
seem to be from a later hand. It is possible that 𝕰 is responsible for some
of the gls. inserted between Selah and the last l. of the Str. in Pss. of 𝕯𝕽. If
𝕰 added any Selahs to his Psalter, he did so only at the close of gls. Thus of
the three distinct uses of ‫ס‬, one is characteristic of each of the major Psalters.
There remain for consideration 2 Pss. excluded from the major Psalters: 32,
89. Both are Maskilim; 32 was in 𝕯, and 89 was a pseudonym. In 32[4]
‫ס‬ stands at close of Str.; so also in v.[7], the gl. being a later insertion. In
v.[5] Selah appears in the midst of a Str., though at an appropriate place in
liturgical use. This Selah is doubtless later than the others. The usage of
the Ps. corresponds with that of 𝕵𝕳, 𝕯𝕽. It is classed among the Mizmorim
in 𝕲[A]. 89 is a composite Ps. 89[b] is from the time of the Exile, 89[c] from
the late Greek period. This Ps. and 24[a] are the only Selah Pss. later
than the major Psalters. All of the Selahs in 89 stand at the close of Strs.
The ‫ס‬ in 89[c] and that at the close of 24[a] imply a continuation of the use of
the term through the Greek period. Additional late uses are furnished by
the Versions. 𝕲 always translates ‫סלה‬ by διάψαλμα, *interlude* (9[17] διαψάλ-
ματος). It omits the term from 3[9] 24[10] 46[12] at close of Ps., and would doubtless have done so in 9[21], if it had not combined 9–10 in one. 𝕲 also omits
‫ס‬ from 88[11], but some cod. H and P give it in 88[13]. 𝕲 gives ‫ס‬ in 57[3] instead
of 54[4], and in 61[5a] instead of 61[5b]. It also inserts the term in 2[2] 34[11] 50[15]
68[4. 14] 80[8] 94[15]. Of these, Pss. 2, 34, 94 certainly represent a late Alexandrian usage. Other uses are to be found in codd. of H and P, and in Psalterium Vetus. The *Psalter of Solomon* uses διάψαλμα in 17[31] 18[10]. Many
codd. begin a new Ps. at the latter passage. The use in 17[31] corresponds
with those in the Psalter. It is evident that this editor must have understood the mng. and use of Selah; so also the later scribes of 𝕲. There are
additional uses of the term in the Jewish Liturgy. The Selahs in the third
and eighteenth benedictions of *Shemoneh Esreh* or *Eighteen Benedictions*
stand in the earliest portions of the Liturgy, and are, in all likelihood, genuine
and ancient.

‫סלה‬ is imv. ‫סלל‬ *to lift up* (the voice in praise), cf. Ps. 68[5] and it indicates
that a benediction might be sung after the pericope thus designated. The
explanations of Ew. "loud," a strengthening of the voice or instruments,
De. *forte*, as opposed to *piano*, Bö. "a playing with full power," do not suit
all the passages where it is used, and imply a use of instrumental music
which is not justified by the titles of the Pss., or by their contents. The
explanation of Ges., after Rosenmüller, deriving it from ‫סָלָה‬ = *rest, be quiet*,
and thinking of a *pause*, is conjectural, and does not explain the problem.
Fürst, followed by Ley, derives from ‫סלה‬ = *separate*, and thinks it indicates
section. None of these theories explain the Jewish traditions. Σ, Θ, usually
follow 𝕲 in the rendering διάψαλμα. 𝖁 does not translate, but omits. 𝕾 usually abbreviates. 𝕲 διάψαλμα indicates an interlude, but does not imply its
purpose. Aq. ἀεί followed by Quinta, Sexta, 𝕾 occasionally, and always by

א *semper, iugiter*, also 𝕿 and Jewish tradition cannot be explained by any of the older theories. A hint is, however, given by Jerome in his letter to Marcella (Ep. 28), where he compares the use of the word with that of *Amen* or *Shalom* to mark the end of a passage and confirm its contents. So Jacob of Edessa, as cited by *Bar Heb.* in his Com. on Ps. 10[1] in a passage quoted but not understood by Bä. (Lagarde's *Praetermissorum*, p. 109). The ἀεἱ = עולם was an abbreviation of the second line of the couplet of the Benediction מעולם ועד עולם, used for the benediction itself, which was to be sung at this place. This interpretation for Selah agrees with and harmonises the ancient traditions, the Alexandrian and the Palestinian ; it is in accordance with the most natural explanation of the Hebrew word, and it accounts for every instance of its use as standing at the close of a pericope or liturgical selection.

§ **42**. *The Psalter in the middle of the second century, shortly before its translation into Greek, was divided into five books, after the division of the Pentateuch, and was numbered as 150 psalms, with variation of numbering to suit the variations needed for the three years' course of Sabbath readings.*

The division of the Psalter into five books was doubtless made to accord with the five-fold division of the Law, and was in some way connected with the five great feasts of Judaism. Subsequently the Five Rolls were arranged in the same way and assigned for reading at these feasts. The second division of the Psalter was divided into two at 72, and a doxology was inserted. The third division of the Psalter was also divided at 106 and a doxology added.

The Pss. of 𝕳 are 150 in number. But, as we have seen, the numbering in 𝕳 differs from that in 𝕲. This has caused endless confusion in citations, as Jewish and Protestant Vrss. and usage follow 𝕳; Roman Catholics, Greeks, and Orientals 𝕲. But neither 𝕳 nor 𝕲 number according to the originals. The arrangement of the numbering of both was for liturgical purposes. The differences appear: (1) at Ps. 10 (𝕳), which in 𝕲 goes with 9, but in 𝕳 is separated. This makes 𝕲 number one less than 𝕳 until we come to (2) 114 (𝕳), which is combined with 115 to make 113 of 𝕲. But this difference is at once adjusted in (3) 116 of 𝕳, which combines 114, 115 of 𝕲. The difference of one now continues till (4) 147 of 𝕳, which combines 146, 147 of 𝕲. The concluding Pss., 148–150, have the same number. We then have in four cases variations which make it possible to number the Pss. from 148 to 152. These variations were probably indicated in Mss. which lie at the basis of 𝕳 and 𝕲. They remind us of the 153 lections of the Thorah, the oldest division of sections, made for a three years' course of Sabbath readings. It is probable that the numbering of the Pss. and the variations recognised was for the same purpose. Each reading of the Thorah had its accompanying Ps. It should be noted that 𝕲 adds Ps. 151, which evidently is a late composition, probably to give an additional variation for Sabbath readings. It was originally written in Hebrew, and describes the anointing of David and his combat with Goliath. It was probably of Maccabean origin.

§ **43.** *The Psalter represents many centuries of growth in the historical origin both of its Psalms, extending from the time of David to the Maccabean period, and of the various minor and major Psalters through which they passed, from the early Persian to the late Greek period, before the present Psalter was finally edited and arranged, in the middle of the second century* B.C.

We may assign seven Pss. in their original form to the early Hebrew monarchy, before Jehoshaphat : 7, 13, 18, 23, 24^b 60^a 110 ; seven to the middle monarchy : 3, 20, 21, 27^a 45, 58, 61 ; and thirteen to the late monarchy : 2, 19^a 28, 36^a 46, 52, 54, 55, 56, 60^b 62, 72, 87 ; thus twenty-seven to the period of the Hebrew monarchy. During the Exile thirteen were composed : 42–43, 63, 74, 77^a 79, 81^b 82, 84, 88, 89^b 90, 137, 142. In the early Persian period there was a great outburst of psalmody. As many as thirty-three Pss. were composed : 4, 6, 9–10, 11, 12, 14 (= 53), 16, 17, 22, 25, 31, 32, 34, 35, 37, 38, 39, 41, 57^a 59, 64, 69^a 70 (= 40^b) 75, 76, 78, 80, 83, 101, 109^a 140, 143, 144^a. This was due to several influences. The conquest of Babylon by Cyrus, which aroused the enthusiasm of the exilic Isaiah, called forth lyric songs. The rebuilding of the altar and temple, with the restoration of the worship in Jerusalem, as it was accompanied by prophetic voices, so also by those of lyric poets. The struggles of the pious with the unfaithful in the community, and with the neighbouring little nations, whose jealousy and hatred constantly interfered with the growth and prosperity of the people in Jerusalem, also naturally expressed itself in song. Toward the close of this period the collection of *Miktamim*, or golden poems, was made after the example of the older collection of the book of Yashar. To the middle Persian period, the times of Nehemiah, we may assign sixteen Pss. : 5, 8, 15, 26, 29, 30, 40^a 47, 51, 57^b 65, 66^a 69^b 138, 139^a 141 ; to the late Persian period, in which internal and external trouble was renewed, eleven Pss. : 27^b 36^b 44, 48, 49, 50, 68, 81^a 85, 89^a 102^a. In this last period the collection of *Maskilim*, or religious medita-

THE EVOLUTION OF

Dates.	Pss. apart.	Miktam.	Maskil.	David.
Early Monarchy.		60^a.		7, 13, 18, 23, 24^b 60^a 110.
Middle Monarchy.		58.	45.	3, 20, 21, 27^a 58, 61.
Late Monarchy.		56.	52, 54, 55.	2, 19^a 28, 36^a 52, 54, 55, 56, 60^b 62, 72.
Exile.	90, 137.		42–43, 74, 88, 89^b 142.	63, 142.
Early Persian.		16, 57^a 59.	32, 53 (= 14), 78.	4, 6, 9–10, 11, 12, 14 (=53), 16, 17, 22, 25, 31, 32, 34, 35, 37, 38, 39, 40^b (=70), 41, 57^a 59, 64, 69^a 101, 109^a 140, 143, 144^a.
Middle Persian.				5, 8, 15, 26, 29, 30, 40^a 51, 57^b 65, 69^b 138, 139^a 141.
Late Persian.	89^a 102^a.		44.	27^b 36^b, 68.
Early Greek.	86, 91, 95, 93 + 96–100, 108, 145.			
Later Greek.	1, 19^b 24^a 77^b 89^c 92, 94, 103, 119, 139^b 144^b.			
Maccabean.	33, 102^b, 109^b 118, 139^c.			

The final collection of the Present
The division into five

THE PSALTER.

Asaph.	Korah.	Mizmor.	Director.	Elohist.	Hallel.	Pilgrim.
	45.	Selections from 𝔇, 𝔈, 𝔄+ ☞	Selections from 𝔇, 𝔈, 𝔄, and 𝔐+ ☞	Selections from 𝔇, 𝔈, and 𝔐, with all of 𝔄+ ☞		
	46, 87.					
74, 77^a 79, 81^b 82.	42–43, 84.					
75, 76, 78, 80, 83.						
	47.	66^a.				
50, 49(?).	44, 48, 85.			81^a.		
73.		67.	66^b.			
				71.	104–107, 111–117, 135–136, 146, 148, 150.	120–128, 130–134.
					147, 149.	129.

Psalter out of all the above material.
books and 150 Psalms.

tions, was made ; also 𝔇 was edited as a prayer-book for use in the synagogues, and soon after 𝕂, more ornate in character. The conquest of Alexander introduced the Greek period, which in its early part was advantageous to the Jews. At the beginning of this period the great royal advent Ps. was composed, 93, 96–100, and soon after eight other Pss. : 66ᵇ 67, 73, 86, 91, 95, 108, 145. The Psalter of 𝔄 was prepared in Babylonia ; and later in Palestine the Psalter of the *Mizmorim*, the first of the major Psalters, as a hymn-book for use in the synagogues. Toward the close of this period 𝔇𝕂 was made, using all the earlier Psalters, as a prayer-book for the synagogues, and directions were given for musical rendering. The later Greek period was troublous in Palestine, owing to the constant strife between the kings of Egypt and Syria, and to internal dissensions resulting therefrom. But in the East the Jews were less troubled. There in the early part of this period 𝔈 was prepared for synagogue use. To this period we may ascribe eleven Pss. : 1, 19ᵇ 24ᵃ 71, 77ᵇ 89ᶜ 92, 94, 103, 139ᵇ 144ᵇ, and the elaborate praise of the Law, 119. In addition fourteen Pilgrim Pss., 120–128, 130–134, were composed, and the Pilgrim Psalter collected in this period. Also sixteen of the Hallels, 104–107, 111–117, 135–136, 146, 148, 150, were composed and edited in a collection. The Maccabean period began with the persecution of Antiochus and the rise of the Maccabees at the head of the patriotic party. They gradually triumphed, and organised the Maccabean dynasty and kingdom. To this period we may ascribe Pss. 33, 102ᵇ 109ᵇ 118, 139ᶜ; also 129 of the Pilgrim Psalter, and 147, 149 of the Hallels. After the rededication of the temple the present Psalter was prepared, combining Pss. appropriate for use in the synagogue and in the temple, and using all the previous Psalters, especially 𝔇, 𝔇𝕂, 𝔈, the Hallels, and the Pilgrim Pss. The collection was divided into three books. Toward the close of the second century the final editor divided it into five books and 150 Pss., in accordance with the same divisions of the Law, allowing for variations in usage.

C. CANONICITY OF THE PSALTER.

§ **44.** *The Psalter was the first of the Writings to win canonical recognition, and it has maintained this recognition in the unanimous consent of Jew and Christian until the present day. The testimony of representative Jews and Christians in all ages is that the Psalter is a holy Book, divinely authoritative, the norm and guide of worship and religious experience.*

The Pss. were collected for the purpose of public worship in the synagogues and in the temple, some being appropriate for the latter, but the most of them evidently more suitable for the former. There were several minor Psalters, and then later several major Psalters, long before the present Psalter was edited. These collections were all made for use in public worship, and it is altogether probable that each one, as it was adopted, gained recognition as canonical. This gave the Pss. their first place in the Canon of the Writings, though they did not receive their final form until a long time after others of the Writings had been composed and had also been received into the Canon. The division of the Psalter into five Books is doubtless based on the same division of the Pentateuch, and it is probable that the numbering of the Pss. had a similar motive to the arrangement of the Pentateuch for a three years' course of Sabbath readings. These liturgical motives are strong indirect evidences of canonical recognition.

The Psalter was used in the synagogues in the time of Jesus and his apostles alongside of the Law and the Prophets, and is quoted by him and his apostles as prophetic and authoritative (Lk. 20[42] 24[44] Acts 1[20]), and used by them in worship (Mt. 26[30] Acts 16[25] James 5[13] 1 Cor. 14[26] Eph. 5[19] Col. 3[16]). The Jews have always used the Pss. in the worship of the synagogue and still continue its use (Schiller Szinessy, in *Prayer Book Interleaved*, p. 255). The Christian Church in all its branches has used the Pss. as the basis of its ritual and the common expression of divine worship. It is a tradition of the Church of Antioch that Ignatius introduced antiphonal singing of the Pss. (Socrates, *Hist. Eccl.* 6[8]). At all events it is certain that the use of the Pss. in the synagogues passed over into the Christian churches in all parts of the world (Tert. *Apol.* c. 39 ; Jerome, *Ep. Marcella*, xlvi.), and has continued in unbroken succession to the present time. In the celebration of the Eucharist, the most sacred institution of the Christian religion, the use of appropriate Pss. has continued as an essential part of the liturgy from the most primitive times, doubtless based on their use at the Jewish feasts, especially the Passover. Chrysostom thus describes the use of the Pss. in his day : " If we keep vigil in the church, David comes first, last, and midst. If early in the morning, we seek for the melody of hymns, first, last, and midst is David again. If we are occupied with the funeral solemnities of the departed, if virgins sit at home and spin, David is first, last, and midst. . . . In monasteries, amongst those holy choirs of angelic armies, David is first, midst, and last. In the convents of virgins, where are bands of them that imitate Mary ; in the deserts, where are men crucified to this world and having their conversations with God, first, midst, and last is he " (Neale and Littledale, *Com. on the Psalms*, p. 1). In the Ambrosian rite, still used in Milan, the Psalter is recited at the hours of prayer, once a fortnight ; in the Roman or Gregorian rite once a week : Pss. 1–109 at Matins, 110–150 at Vespers ; and fixed Pss. are assigned for use at Lauds, Prime, Tierce, Sext, Nones, and Complines. So also the Benedictine rite prescribes a weekly recitation of the Pss., and this usage has been followed by monastic, mendicant, and other religious orders in the Roman Church. In the Greek Church the Psalter is recited once a week, except in Lent, when it is recited twice. Similar uses are in the Coptic, Syrian, Armenian, Abyssinian, and other Churches. Proper Pss., or parts of Pss., are also assigned for the Mass in all rites ; some fixed, others varying with the kind of Mass or the feasts and fasts of the ecclesiastical year. The Church of England, when it condensed the hours of prayer into two, matins and vespers, arranged the Pss. for recitation once a month, besides assigning proper Pss. for use daily, or for the varying sacred days of the ecclesiastical year at Holy Communion. The Lutheran and Reformed Churches also make the Psalter an essential part of their Liturgies. In the Reformed Churches in the sixteenth and seventeenth centuries, and, in some of them even in the eighteenth and nineteenth centuries, the Psalter was the only hymn-book apart from a few paraphrases of Holy Scripture. The multiplication of Christian hymns in the eighteenth and nineteenth centuries brought about a gradual disuse of the Psalter in Great Britain and America in several religious denominations, but toward the close of the century a reaction began in the form of responsive readings of the Psalter, for which purpose many arrangements have been prepared.

§ **45**. *The canonicity of the Psalter is attested by its contents. Its religious, doctrinal, and ethical materials give evidence to its holy character as coming from God and leading to God.*

The Psalter contains, in the usual numbering, 150 Psalms, of great variety of form and content ; but all within the limits of a hymn-book and prayer-book, composed for religious worship, public in the synagogue and temple, and private in the household and in the closet. It is therefore by its very nature essentially religious, and indeed in the lyric form. (*A*) Its religion is at

once simple and comprehensive, equally appropriate to all classes
and conditions of mankind in all nations and in all ages. It expresses the child-like yearnings of the simple-minded, and the
loftiest aspirations of the mature man of God. It plays upon all
the chords of the human soul, and evokes from each and all that
which is most appropriate to union and communion of the individual or the community with God.

Many of the Pss. in their original form were composed as an expression
of private devotion. These features remained even after they were adapted
by editorial revision for use in the synagogues. Many others were composed
for use in public worship in the synagogues, to express the worship of the
congregation. In the synagogue the ceremonies of religion were reduced
to a minimum, and therefore such ceremonies do not appear in these two
classes of Pss., notwithstanding the fact that the most of them were composed
long after the fully developed ritual of the Priest's code had become fixed in
usage in the temple service. Only a few of the Pss. were composed for or
even adapted to worship in the temple, and these, especially the Hallels, were
songs of praise suited to the ritual of the thank-offerings, votive offerings, or
whole burnt offerings. These offerings are mentioned in appropriate places
in the Psalter. The sin-offerings and the trespass-offerings do not appear,
even in the Penitential Pss., doubtless because these offerings were not accompanied with sacred song. Furthermore, local and temporal references were
gradually eliminated by editorial revision from the older Pss., making them
more and more appropriate for worship. Therefore the Psalter became a
hymn-book and prayer-book, having so little of the ceremonial side of religion that it was lifted above all that was local, temporal, and occasional, and
made appropriate for the worship of all places, all times, and all occasions
and persons.

(*B*) The doctrines of the Psalter do not appear in a dogmatic
form, demanding acceptance by the intellect and will; but in a
concrete form, expressing the faith already entertained or established. From this point of view, while on the one side the doctrines are not so complete in detail and not so clearly defined in
their relations as in the Prophets, yet on the other side they rise
to the loftiest heights in their conception of God, sink to the lowest
depths in searching the soul of man, expand to the greatest breadths
in their comprehension of the union of God and man and the
world in the divine ideals of redemption. For these reasons the
Psalter is the nearest to the NT. of all the writings of the OT.

Few of the Pss. are didactic, and these are ethical rather than dogmatic. The Pss. are chiefly lyrics, expressing religious emotions, experiences, aspirations. They are contemplative or intuitive, using the religious imagination and fancy rather than the logical faculty and the reasoning powers. They are also with few exceptions quite limited in extent, and doctrines appear in them in bold, graphic, realistic statement, in detached form, and out of connection with any system of belief. The Psalter represents in its various Pss. many different periods of Hebrew Literature. The temporal characteristics have to a great extent been obscured by editorial revisions; but at the same time these are in fact, though not on the surface, really embedded in the Pss., so that it is quite possible to distinguish the several stages in the development of doctrine in correspondence with those that appear in the Prophets.

The doctrine of God is especially rich in the attributes. The kindness, goodness, and love of God stand out more distinctly in the Psalter than in any other part of the OT. The vindicatory, saving righteousness of Yahweh and His discriminating justice are no less prominent. The doctrine of creation appears in simple, beautiful, poetic conceptions, which might have modified the rigid dogma of the theologians, based on the early chapters of Genesis, if the theologians had been sufficiently comprehensive in their study of the Bible to take account of it. It is the divine providence in history as well as the experience of the individual upon which religious poets delight to dwell.

The doctrine of man is especially prominent in the Psalter from the very fact that the Pss. give expression to human experience, whether of the individual, or of the nation. This is well expressed by Calvin. "This Book not unreasonably am I wont to style an anatomy of all parts of the soul, for no one will discover in himself a single feeling whereof the image is not reflected in this mirror. Nay all griefs, sorrows, doubts, fears, hopes, cares, and anxieties, in short all those tumultuous agitations wherewith the minds of men are wont to be tossed, the Holy Ghost hath here represented to the life. The rest of Scripture contains the commands which God gave to His servants to be delivered unto us. But here the prophets themselves holding converse with God, inasmuch as they lay bare all their inmost feelings, invite or impel every one of us to self-examination, that of all the infirmities to which we are liable and all the sins of which we are so full none may remain hidden."

The doctrine of redemption is richly unfolded, especially on its experimental side, in the personal deliverance of the individual from sin and evil. The Penitential Pss. have always been and still are found to be the most suitable expression of Christian penitence and the joy of divine forgiveness. The elegies express the depths of woe that surge up about the reflective soul in all ages as he contemplates the brevity of life, the limitations of man, and the certainty and speedy approach of death. The Pss. of expostulation express, though often in a daring way, venturing close upon the brink of irreverence and despair, the writhings of the soul under the sense of injustice and wrongs that the faithful servants of God have so often to suffer in this life.

The Pilgrim Pss. are the most suitable expression of social religion that have ever been composed. The Guest Pss. sound a note of religious joy in the communion with God that has been attained by no other poets so thoroughly well.

In the Psalter the Messianic ideal is in some respects richer than in the Prophets. The royal Messiah, the son of David, appears in most vivid, dramatic situations in Pss. 2 and 110, which find their only realisation in the resurrection, enthronement, and reign of Jesus Christ. The suffering servant of Pss. 22, 40, 69, transcends that of Is. 53 in his vivid, lifelike picture of the suffering Saviour. The royal Pss. have ever been used in the Church as the most suitable expression of her longing for the second advent of her Lord. The future life of man in a state of redemption after death is more clearly depicted in Pss. 16, 49, 73, than anywhere else in the OT. It is not surprising therefore that Jesus and his apostles used the Psalter so much as reflecting and depicting the Messianic redemption.

(*C*) The ethics of the Psalter are relatively not so high as in the Wisdom Literature, which is essentially ethical. And yet from the point of view of ethical experience they are rich enough to give very important complementary material to the Law, the Prophets, and even Hebrew Wisdom. The ethics of the Law are summed up in the terse and comprehensive experience depicted in Pss. 1, 19, while Ps. 119 presents the Law as a mirror in which the pious man sees himself and others in such a wondrous variety of ethical experience that he is overwhelmed with a sense of a divine presence and influence. The ethics of the Prophets are summed up in that chaste and beautiful guest of Yahweh of Ps. 15.

All along the line of religion, doctrines, and morals the contents of the Pss. have always been found to be just what they are to-day; such unique, exalted, comprehensive, and satisfactory expressions in lyric form of what mankind needs for union and communion with God, that men in all ages and countries have been convinced that the Psalter is a divinely inspired Book, a rule of faith and life.

§ **46.** *The only objections to the canonicity of the Psalter seriously entertained are based on a number of imprecations upon enemies and protestations of righteousness on the part of suffering servants of God. These objections are invalid because they fail to apprehend that these imprecations and protestations belong necessarily to earlier stages of religion and to certain historic situations where they have their essential propriety.*

These objections to the canonicity of the Psalter are quite modern. They have arisen in the Protestant world in connection with the stress laid upon the doctrine of justification by faith only, which makes any form of self-righteousness impossible ; and by the growth of individualism, with its liberty of conscience and opinion, which is necessarily opposed to any kind of persecution or violence, even toward the enemies of religion.

The protestations of righteousness are in the Pss. which appeal to God for help from sufferings of body or of mind in connection with the experience of injustice and wrong. These protestations do not imply sinless perfection, or absolute conformity to the divine ideal of conduct, for they not infrequently are connected with the confession of sin ; they are rather protestations of fidelity to God and His religion, which is essentially righteousness (cf. Gn. 15⁶ Hb. 2⁴). Such fidelity demands divine interposition on its behalf, vindication from enemies and deliverance from sufferings and trouble. Though these protestations sometimes rise from plaintive expostulation with God to complaint of injustice and wrong, which seem in their intensity of passion to the modern mind to come close to irreverence, they do not really go so far, for it is in these very Pss. that are found the most sublime conceptions of the righteousness and justice of God, and it is to their God that they appeal in sublime confidence as they plead in intense and agonising petitions which will not be refused.

It is not without significance that the strongest protestations of this kind are found in Pss. 22, 40, 69, which are usually regarded as Messianic, and which Jesus himself used to express his own feelings in his most trying hours, and which his apostles regarded as most aptly suited to the situation of the Passion of their Lord. It is quite true that Jesus Christ was exceptional in his righteousness; but that does not in any way impair their propriety of use for others, for Jesus and his apostles used these Pss. as familiar to them from the liturgical use of the synagogue and the home, and thereby gave their sanction to the legitimacy of this experience for suffering Christians. Notwithstanding the fact that these protestations of righteousness seem to be inconsistent with the experience of sin and ill-desert that are felt by many of the best of men, yet there is no real inconsistency between general fidelity to God and occasional faults and failures. The Christian Church, in the greater part of its history and in the greater part of its membership at the present time, finds no inconsistency between the experience of merit and the experience of sin. Such a sense of inconsistency is a peculiarity of the Protestant world. And even among Protestants it is the common experience, notwithstanding the recognition of personal sinfulness and that justification is by faith only, that suffering and trouble are not in accord with demerit, and that there is injustice and wrong in the sufferings that the God-fearing often have to endure, and which the wicked often escape. Jesus Christ in the endurance of suffering and wrong taught his disciples how to undergo the sad experience, but that does not remove from him or from his disciples the injustice that there is in the sufferings of the righteous and the inconsistency that there is in the greater welfare of the wicked and their triumph over the righteous. The pious are justified, as Jesus was, in pleading with God against it, and it is not self-righteousness to do so.

It is an exaggeration of the doctrine of justification by faith only, which excludes from Christian experience the consciousness of personal righteousness and merit. Luther misled in his interpretation of Gn. 15⁶ and Hb. 2⁴. The former represents that God accounted Abraham as really righteous because of his trust in Him. The latter states that the pious live by fidelity, faithfulness, אמונה, and not by faith only. When Nehemiah prayed to God to remember his faithfulness and acts of kindness in His behalf and spare him in the greatness of His kindness, Ne. 13¹⁴· ²², he was not self-righteous, but acting in accordance with the common experience of the OT. His prayer of penitence (Ne. 9) is among the finest in the Bible. Jesus distinctly taught the meritoriousness of deeds of love. The only passage that can be adduced to the contrary in his teaching, Lk. 17¹⁰, is wrongly interpreted in this regard (v. Br. *Ethical Teaching of Jesus*, pp. 218 sq.). St. Paul, the apostle of justification by faith, did not hesitate to say, as his hour of martyrdom drew near, "I have fought the good fight, I have finished the course, I have kept the faith ; henceforth there is laid up for me the crown of righteousness which the Lord, the righteous judge, will give me at that day: and not only to me, but also to all them that have loved his appearing," 2 Tim. 4⁷⁻⁸, cf. Acts 26²⁶ ˢᵠ· 23¹.

The imprecations are not so frequent in the Pss. as in the Law and the Prophets. Although they have a lyric intensity of passion, they are not more bitter than those of other parts of the OT. If imprecations are inconsistent with canonicity, the whole OT. is excluded, and not the Psalter especially. The imprecations of the OT. are connected with the sense of the solidarity of the interests of the individual servant of God with those of the nation of Israel, and with the religion of God itself ; so that all personal and national considerations are merged in those of the kingdom of God, whose aggressive, unscrupulous, and deadly foes must be remorselessly crushed in order that the holy religion may continue to exist and accomplish its sacred mission to the world. Whenever and wherever this sense of solidarity of interests has existed, or still exists, these imprecations express the religious feelings of God's people toward the enemies of God.

It is the modern discrimination between the religion of the individual and that of the nation, and between both of these and the ideal religion of mankind that makes these imprecations impossible to the experience of many moderns. These discriminations certainly belong to a later stage in the development of religion than the indiscriminating sense of solidarity. But individualism, however important, whether we think of the person or the denomination or the nation, ought not to impair the higher interests of the organism of the kingdom of God, as the embodiment of the divine religion of mankind. It is indeed excessive individualism with its lack of appreciation of organic religion, that sees no place for imprecations against the enemies of the kingdom of God. Jesus Christ taught the exceeding value of the soul of the individual and gave an example of self-sacrificing love in dying for his enemies with the prayer for their forgiveness upon his lips ; but these enemies knew not the wrong they did to him, to the world, and to themselves. Jesus Christ distinguishes between sins of ignorance and sins of self-will, sins repented of and sins glossed over by self-righteousness and hypocrisy. He pronounced woes upon the Pharisees because they were hypocrites, tempters to sin, and obstructors to the kingdom of God. He denounced them as blind guides and serpents, and dooms them to Gehenna (Br., *Ethical Teaching of Jesus*, pp. 175 sq., 184 sq.). He announced the doom of the traitor Judas. He proclaimed the judgment of the cities that rejected him and his apostles, culminating in the destruction of Jerusalem and the world. The Apocalypse does not misinterpret the spirit of Christ, when it tells of the wrath of the Lamb and describes him in his second Advent as treading the wine-press of the wrath of Almighty God ; and when it pictures the martyrs underneath the altar crying aloud : " How long, O Master, the holy and true, dost thou not judge and avenge our blood on them that dwell on the earth?" (Rev. 6[10]). The righteousness of God is on the one side vindicatory and saving, on the other retributive and destructive. The unfolding of vindicatory righteousness into the highest conception of self-sacrificing love is accompanied with the development of retribution into the most intense hatred and awful wrath. No one knows what love is, who cannot truly hate. It is a weak and sickly individualism which shuts its eyes against the wrath of God, and of the Lamb, and of the Church, the Bride of the Lamb, against evil and incorrigible sin. There is a place, therefore, for imprecation in the highest forms of Christianity, only it is more discriminating than in the OT. religion and much more refined. In substance, the imprecations of the Psalter are normal and valid ; in their external form and modes of expression they belong to an age of religion which has been displaced by Christianity.

The imprecations of the Psalter belong to four historic situations: (1) The persecutions of Jeremiah and his associates by those who were pushing the national religion to destruction, Ps. 52[4 sq.], cf. Je. 11[18 sq.] 15[15 sq.] 17[18] 18[19 sq.] 20[11 sq.]. (2) The brutal cruelty of Edom and Moab toward the Jews at the time of the destruction of Jerusalem by the Babylonians, Ps. 137, cf. Ob.[10 sq.]. (3) The treachery of Sanballat and Tobiah, Ne. 2–6, which threatened the very existence of the congregation of the Restoration. The imprecations of Ne. 4[4–5] 6[14] 13[29] are in accord with those of Pss. 9[20–21] 10[15] 69[23–29] 83[10–18]. (4) The persecution of Antiochus, which aimed at the extermination of the worshippers of Yahweh. To this period the majority of the imprecations belong, many of them glosses in older Pss. At that time, if ever, imprecations were appropriate, cf. Pss. 79[10. 12] 109[6–15. 19–20. 28–29]. Thus all the imprecations of the Pss. are upon just such treacherous hypocrites, traitors, and bloodthirsty enemies of the kingdom of God, as Jesus himself pronounces imprecations upon, who aim at nothing else than the wilful destruction of the true religion. It is the form and general character of these imprecations which are most obnoxious to the modern mind, especially the physical sufferings that are invoked, the dishonouring of wives and daughters, and the slaughter of babes, even of the unborn. This is from the point of view of the solidarity of interest in the family, tribe, and nation ; and especially from the ancient principle of the duty of revenge which was inherited by sons and kinsmen ; so that the only way to avoid future peril of revenge was the extermination of all who would be likely in the future to undertake it.

D. THE INTERPRETATION OF THE PSALTER.

§ **47.** *Jesus and his apostles interpreted the Psalter usually in accordance with the methods of their time, literally or allegorically, as they had need. But they chiefly used it either for practical exhortation, for dogmatic or ethical instruction, or for prophetic anticipations of the life and work of Jesus and his Church.*

(1) Jesus used the Psalter more than any other part of the OT. He used it to describe his own state of mind: Ps. 6[4] in Jn. 12[27], Ps. 22[2] in Mt. 27[46] = Mk. 15[34], Ps. 31[6] in Lk. 23[46], Ps. 35[19] (= 69[5]) in Jn. 15[25], Ps. 42[6] in Mt. 26[38] = Mk. 14[34]; his actions, Ps. 6[9] in Mt. 7[23] = Lk. 13[27]; and the actions of others in his time, Ps. 8[3] in Mt. 21[16], Ps. 41[10] in Jn. 13[18]. He also used it for authoritative teaching, Ps. 37[11] in Mt. 5[5], Ps. 48[3] in Mt. 5[35], and for historical reference, Ps. 78[24] in Jn. 6[31]. He used Ps. 82[6] in argument with the Pharisees after the Halacha method in Jn. 10[34], arguing from less to greater. He used Ps. 110[1] in Mt. 22[44] = Mk. 12[36] = Lk. 20[42. 43], in argument with the Pharisees, to show that the Messianic son of David must be at the same time his Lord; cf. 1 Cor. 15[25] Eph. 1[20] Col. 3[1] Heb. 1[8] 8[1] 12[2] 1 Pet. 3[22]. He also

applied Ps. 118$^{22-23}$ to himself as the headstone of the spiritual temple, Mt. 21^{42} = Mk. 12$^{10, 11}$ = Lk. 20^{17} (cf. Acts 4^{11} 1 Pet. 2$^{4-7}$).

(2) The Gospels use the Pss. freely, applying them to Jesus and his work: (*a*) to his entrance into the world. Ps. 91$^{11-12}$ is cited by the devil Mt. 4^6 = Lk. 4$^{10, 11}$; (*b*) to his experience in life Ps. 69^{10} in Jn. 2^{17}, his teaching Ps. 78^2 in Mt. 13^{35}, his entrance into Jerusalem Ps. 118$^{25-26}$ in Mt. 21^9 23^{39} Mk. 11^9 Lk. 13^{35} 19^{38} Jn. 12^{13}; (*c*) to his passion Pss. 22$^{8-9, 19}$ Jn. 19^{24}, cf. Mt. 27$^{35, 39, 43}$ = Mk. 15$^{24, 29}$ = Lk. 23$^{34-35}$, Ps. 34^{21} in Jn. 19^{36}, Ps. 69^{22} in Mt. 27$^{34, 48}$ = Mk. 15^{36} = Lk. 23^{36} = Jn. 19$^{28-29}$, Ps. 109^{25} in Mt. 27^{39}. The canticles Lk. 1 are also chiefly mosaics of the Pss. (3) *In the book of Acts:* (*a*) Ps. 89^{20} is cited by Paul in Acts 13^{22} in historical reference, so Ps. 132^5 by Stephen Acts 7^{46}; (*b*) Ps. 2$^{1, 2}$ in Acts 4$^{25-26}$ is applied to the persecution of Christ in his disciples, Ps. 69^{26} 109^8 in Acts 1^{20} as fulfilled in Judas; Ps. 2^7 is applied in Acts 13^{33} to the resurrection of Jesus; so Ps. 16$^{8-11}$ in Acts 2$^{25-32}$ 13^{35}, and Ps. 110^1 in Acts 2$^{34-35}$, Ps. 132^{11} in Acts 2^{30} to his reign; (*c*) in liturgical use Ps. 146^6 in Acts 4^{24}, cf. 14^{15}. (4) *In the epistles of Peter:* (*a*) as practical exhortation Ps. 34$^{13-17}$ in 1 Pet. 3$^{10-12}$, Ps. 55^{23} in 1 Pet. 5^7; as realised in Christian experience, Ps. 34^9 in 1 Pet. 2^3; (*b*) as authoritative doctrine Ps. 90^4 in 2 Pet. 3^8.

(5) St. Paul uses the Psalter freely: (*a*) as practical exhortation Ps. 4^5 in Eph. 4^{26}, Ps. 112^9 in 2 Cor. 9^9, Ps. 116^{10} in 2 Cor. 4^{13}; (*b*) as authoritative teaching Ps. 24^1 in 1 Cor. 10$^{26 (28)}$, Ps. 32$^{1-2}$ in Rom. 4$^{7-8}$, Ps. 51^6 in Rom. 3^4, Ps. 94^{11} in 1 Cor. 3^{20}. Pss. 5^{10} 10^7 14$^{1-3}$ (= 53$^{2-4}$) 36^2 140^4 are cited as descriptive of the utter wickedness of mankind, in Rom. 3$^{10-18}$; (*c*) Ps. 44^{23} is cited Rom. 8^{36} as realised in Christian experience; (*d*) Ps. 69^{10} is cited Rom. 15^8 and applied to the humiliation of Christ. Ps. 8^7 is cited in 1 Cor. 15^{27} Eph. 1^{22} and applied to the resurrection and reign of Christ; so Ps. 68^{19} in Eph. 4^8. Ps. 69$^{23-24}$ is cited Rom. 11$^{9-10}$ and applied to the fall of Israel. Pss. 18^{50} 117^1 are cited Rom. 15$^{9-11}$ and applied to the conversion of the Gentiles. Ps. 19^5 in Rom. 10^{18} is applied to the preaching of the Gospel. (6) The epistle to the Hebrews makes great use of the Pss.: (*a*) as practical exhortation Ps. 95$^{7-11}$ in Heb. 3$^{7 \text{ sq.}}$, Ps. 118^6 in Heb. 13^6; (*b*) as authoritative teaching Ps. 104^4 in Heb. 1^7; Ps. 135^{14} in Heb. 10^{30}; (*c*) Ps. 2^7 is applied to the resurrection and reign of Christ Heb. 1^5 5^5; so Ps. 8$^{5-7}$ in Heb. 2$^{6-8}$, Ps. 97^7 in Heb. 1^6, Ps. 45$^{7-8}$ 102$^{26-28}$ in Heb. 1$^{8-13}$, Ps. 110^4 in Heb. 5^6 6^{20} 7$^{17, 21}$. Ps. 18^8 22^{23} are applied to his redemptive work in Heb. 2$^{12-13}$; so Ps. 40$^{7-9}$ in Heb. 10$^{5-7}$. In Heb. 4$^{1-11}$ Ps. 95$^{7-11}$ is interpreted at length in an allegorical way. (7) *In the Apocalypse:* the Psalter is often used in hymns and incidental allusions. Besides these it is cited as predictive of the reign of Christ, Ps. 2$^{8-9}$ in Rev. 2$^{26-27}$ 12^5 19^{15}.

§ **48.** *In the ancient Catholic Church the Apostolic Fathers and Apologists used the Psalter for practical purposes. The School of Alexandria emphasized the allegorical method of interpretation, the School of Antioch the typical method.*

The Christian writers of the second Christian century followed the example of the apostles in using the Psalter for practical purposes. Nothing at all resembling a Commentary, so far as we know, was composed by any of them. The citations of the Pss. in the Apostolic Fathers, Apologists, and early Fathers, Tertullian, Irenaeus, Cyprian, and others, are similar to those in the New Testament, using the same methods of interpretation, with a more decided tendency to the allegorical method and less restraint from its exaggeration. The School of Alexandria was established by Pantaenus, c. 200, and made famous by the great teachers and theologians, Clement and Origen. Pantaenus is said to have composed the first Commentary (Eusebius, *Ecc. Hist.* 5^{10}). Clement distinguished between the body and soul of Scripture, and called attention to its fourfold use. Origen made a Commentary on the Psalms, using the allegorical method of Philo, which he worked out in a Christian form and became its father in the Church. He distinguished a threefold sense, body, soul, and spirit, and used thirteen of Philo's rules (*v.* Br.[SHS. 448-449]). The School of Antioch was established by Lucian and Dorotheus at the close of the third century. Its fundamental principles of interpretation were: (1) Every passage has its literal meaning and only one meaning; (2) alongside of the literal sense is the typical sense which arises out of the relation of the Old Covenant to the New (Kihn, *Theodor von Mopsuestia, s.* 29). The most of the Commentators on the Pss. in the Greek Church were from writers of this school. Jerome occupied an intermediate and not altogether consistent position. He strives for historical and grammatical exposition, yet it is easy to see that at the bottom he is more inclined to the allegorical method. Thus there grew up in the ancient Church three exegetical tendencies, the literal and traditional, the allegorical and mystical, the historical and ethical, and these became gradually interwoven in the writings of the Fathers, and in all sorts of abnormal forms of exegesis in others (*v.* Br.[SHS. 453]).

Corderius (*Expositio Patrum Graecorum in Psalmos,* 3 Tom. 1643) uses the following Greek Commentators: Athanasius, Ammonius, *Anonymous,* Apollinarius, Asterius, *Basilius,* Gennadius, Geo. Alexandrinus, *Gregorius Nazianzenus,* Gregorius Nyssenus, *Didymus,* Dionysius Areopag., *Eusebius Caesariensis,* Hesychius, *Theodoretus, Theodorus Antiochenus,* Theodorus

Heracleota, Isidorus, Cyrillus Alexandrinus, Maximus, Pachymera, *Chrysosto-mus*, Psellus, *Origines*. I have italicised those most frequently cited. Jerome (*ep. ad August.* cxii.) mentions the following Greek interpreters of the Psalter up to his time : Origen, Eusebius of Caesarea, Theodore of Heraklea (the Anonymous of Corderius), Astelios of Skythopolis, Apollinaris of Laodicea, Didymos of Alexandria. All of these interpretations of the Psalter, so far as preserved, are given by Migne in his Greek Patrology. For additional information we may refer to Pitra, *Analecta Sacra*, Bäthgen, *ZATW.*, 1886, Lietzmann, *Der Psalmencommentar Theodore von Mopsuestia*, 1902. The work of the great Syrian scholar, Gregory Bar Hebraeus († 1286, given by Lagarde, *Prae-termissorum*, 1879), must be added here as the noblest representation of the late Syrian School. The work of Jerome on the Pss. is given in his Epistles, XX., XXVIII., XXX., XXXIV., LXV., CVI., CXL. (Migne, XXII.), and his commentary (edited by Morin, *Anecdota Maredsolana*, III., 1895).

§ **49.** *In the Latin Church the allegorical method of interpreting the Psalter prevailed, chiefly through the influence of Ambrose and Augustine, although Junilius and Cassiodorus exerted a modifying influence in the use of the principles of the Antiochan School.*

Ambrose may be regarded as the father of the interpretation of the Psalter in the Western Church; but Augustine, his pupil, was the one who dominated all subsequent times. He distinguishes four kinds of exegesis, — the historical, aetiological, analogical, and allegorical, — and laid down the principle that whatever cannot be referred to good conduct or truth of faith must be regarded as figurative. Junilius, and still more Cassiodorus, exerted a wholesome influence by the introduction into the West of the principles of the Schools of Antioch and Nisibis. He urged the comparison of Scripture with Scriptures, and points out that frequent and intense meditation is the way to a true understanding of them (*v.* Br.[SHS. 449-453]).

Jerome (*ep. ad August.* cxii.) mentions the following Latin interpreters of the Pss. : (1) Hilary of Poitiers, based on Origen and Eusebius ; (2) Eusebius of Vercelli, who translated the Commentary of Eusebius of Caesarea ; (3) Ambrose. Ambrose († 397) is the only one who was independent and original. Ambrose was a practical prelate, possessed of the true Roman spirit, and he gave the allegorical method a Western practical turn. His *Enarrationes* have had great influence on the Church. Augustine († 430) built his *Enarrationes* on those of Ambrose, and became the basal authority for all subsequent writers. The most wholesome commentary of the times is that of Cassiodorus († 563). Other early Western writers on the Psalter were Hippolytus († 235), Arnobius

(† c. 406), Asterius († 410), Gregory of Tours († 594), Gregory the Great († 604), Prudentius (eighth century).   All of these are given by Migne in his Latin Patrology.

§ **50.** *In the Middle Ages the Commentaries were chiefly compilations of the earlier writers, called Epitomes, Glosses, Postilles, Chains, which appeared in great numbers, all under the domination of the allegorical principles of Augustine, often in exaggerated forms.*

The compilers of the Oriental Church were Euthymius Zigabenus († 1118, *v.* Pitra, *Analecta*, IV.); Nicephorus, thirteenth century (given by Migne). A host of writers on the Pss. appear in the West: *Beda* († 735); *Alcuin* († 804); *Walafrid Strabo* († 849); *Haymo* († 853); *Rhabamus Maurus* († 856); *Paschasius Radbertus* († 866); *Hincmar* († 882); *Remigius* (ninth century); *Bruno Herb.* († 1045); *Komualdus* († 1027); *Anselm* († 1109); *Bruno Carth.* († 1101); *Richard St. Victor* († 1173); *Innocentius III.* († 1216); Hugo S. Caro, *Postillae* († 1263) (commentaries 1496 attributed wrongly to Alexander Hales, † 1245); Antonius Patavinus († 1231, *Sermones in Pss.*, 1757); Thomas Aquinas († 1274, *In Psalmos Expositio*, 1876); Albertus Magnus († 1280, *Comm. on Pss.*, Col. 1536); Ayguanus († 1396, *Com. on Ps.*, 1524 +); Nicolaus de Lyra († 1340, *Postillae*, Rom. 1471; *Biblia cum glossa ordinaria*, 6 v., Basel, 1506); Herenthal († 1400, *Catena*, Col. 1483); Turrecremata († 1468, *Expositio*, 1474). Those italicised are found in Migne's Patrology.

§ **51.** *In the Middle Ages Jewish Commentators distinguished themselves as compared with the Christian by a fuller use of the literal and historical methods of interpretation, although no less dependent on Rabbinical tradition than Christian scholars were on Christian tradition.*

The earliest important interpreter of the Pss. whose writings have been preserved was Saadia († 942), author of the Arabic translation of the OT. His Commentary was published in Cracow in 1660.   Raschi's Commentary (R. Solomon Isaaki, † 1105) was published in the Rabbinical Bibles, also a Latin translation by Breithaupt, 1710.   Aben Ezra's Commentary († 1167) was published in the Rabbinical Bibles.   His Commentary on the first ten Pss. was published in Latin and Hebrew by P. Fagius, 1542.   David Kimchi's Commentary († 1235) was published, Naples, 1487; Venice, 1518; Isny, 1541; Amsterdam, 1765; Latin translation by Janvier, 1566.   The first book of Psalms was published according to the text of the Cambridge Ms. Bible with the larger Commentary of R. David Kimchi, critically edited from nineteen

Mss. and early editions by Schiller Szinessy, Cambridge, 1883. The most important of later commentaries was by Obadiah Sforno, teacher of Reuchlin, Venice, 1586; Amsterdam, 1724.

§ 52. *The Reformation involved a great revival of Biblical study, and especially of the Psalter, the chief book of the OT. The allegorical method was pushed in the background by the Humanists in the interests of the grammatical sense, and so by Roman Catholics as well, and Protestants who were influenced by them. The chief difference was that the Protestants resorted to the Hebrew text as the original supreme authority, the Roman Catholics based themselves on the Vulgate Version, and interpreted it in submission to the authority of the Church and the Fathers. The successors of the Reformers fell back into pedantic and dogmatic methods.*

The Humanists revived the study of the ancient languages and the ancient literatures, and thus the grammatical and literary study of the original texts was employed over against the allegorical method. Lyra and the Jewish Commentators were used more than the Christian Commentators of the Middle Ages. The Protestant Reformers were great exegetes. Luther began his academic lectures with an exposition of the Psalter in 1513. These lectures were published by Seidemann in 1876, under the title, *Dr. Martin Luther's erste und älteste Vorlesungen über die Psalmen aus den Jahren 1513–1516 nach der eigenhändigen lateinischen Handschrift Luthers auf der Königlichen öffentlichen Bibliothek zu Dresden.* Reuchlin published his *Auslegung der sieben Psalmi poenitentiales,* 1512; Bugenhagen, his *in lib. Psalmorum,* 1524; Bucer (Aretius), *Psalmorum libri 5,* 1526. Calvin's *Commentary on the Psalms,* 1564, was by far the best up to his own time. Other commentators of the time of the Reformation were Pellican, 1532; Münster, 1534–1535; Musculus, 1550; Castalio, 1551 +; Marloratus, 1562. The Moravian Rüdinger also issued a valuable Commentary in 1580–1581. The Protestants of the next generation fell back from the vital principle of the Reformers and became dependent on Protestant rules of faith, and were dogmatic and pedantic in their Commentaries. In the following lists, I give, so far as I know, the first edition; when there were subsequent editions, it is indicated by +. The works of Selnecker, 1581; Moller, 1573; Menzel, 1594; Gesner, 1609; Piscator, 1646 +; Quistorp, 1648; Amyraldus, 1662; Bakius, 1664+; Geier, 1668 +; Carlov, 1672+, though with valuable and useful material are reactionary and of no permanent value. The Roman Catholics vied with the Protestants in the sixteenth century in their work on the Psalter: Clarius, 1542 +; Vatablus, 1545; Palisse, 1548; Cajetan, 1530; Campensis, 1533 +; Flaminius, 1558; Gennebradus, 1577 +; Jansenius, 1586. In the early seventeenth century R. C. exegetes employed better methods, and were more able and fruitful than Protestants, as is evident in Agellius, 1606 + ; Faber Stapulensis, 1609 ; Lorinus, 1612 + ; Bellarmin, 1611 + ; Mariana, 1619 + ; Torinus, 1632 + ; Muis, 1636 + ; Corderius, 1643 + ; Drexelius, 1643 ; Hulsius, 1650 ; Heser. 1654 +.

§ 53. *In the middle of the seventeenth century the English Puritans emphasized grammatical and practical exegesis; Grotius, Hammond and the Arminians, the historical method; Cocceius and the Federalists, the allegorical. The dogmatic method still prevailed to some extent.*

Ainsworth is the prince of Puritan Commentators. His Commentary on the Pss., issued in 1626, is a monument of learning. He was too much influenced by Rabbinical subtilties, but he employed the grammatical method with great practical skill. Thomas Smith, Thomas Pierson, and especially William Gouge issued practical commentaries introducing a long and valuable series in Great Britain. Hugo Grotius in Holland and Henry Hammond in England revived the Humanistic spirit and laid stress on the literal and historical sense. The Commentaries on the Pss. of Grotius, 1645, and of Hammond, 1653, especially the latter, introduce a new epoch in the interpretation of the Psalter. Cocceius, the founder of the Federal School of Holland, 1660, revived the allegorical method, but with sobriety and practical sense. The *Criticorum Sacrorum*, 1660, sums up the chief material of previous authors, using Munster, Vatablus, Castalio, Clarius, Drusius, and Grotius. This was followed by Poole's *Synopsis Criticorum*, 1669, which uses Muis, Geier, Ainsworth, Hammond, Rivetus, Cocceius, Genebradus, Calovius. The *Biblia Magna*, 1643, and the *Biblia Maxima*, Paris, 1660, both by John de la Haye, are a magnificent summing up of R. C. exegesis, embracing a thorough study of texts and Vrss., and the expositions of Nic. de Lyra, Gagnae, Estii, Menochii, and Tirini. Vol. VI. of the latter contains the Psalter. There was then a lull in work on the Pss. which continued for a century. We may mention, however, the R. C., Le Blanc, 1682 + ; Ferrandus, 1683 ; Bossuet, 1691; Berthier, 1788 + ; Calmet, 1791 + ; Camponi, 1692 + ; the Protestants, Bythner, 1664 ; J. H. Michaelis, 1720 ; Clericus, 1731 ; Venema, 1762.

§ 54. *The study of the Psalter was enriched through the work of Kennicott upon the text and of Hare and Lowth upon Hebrew poetry, connected in all these with original work upon the Psalter which influenced all subsequent scholars.*

I have already called attention to the work of Hare, Lowth, and Kennicott on the text and Hebrew Poetry. These scholars carried on the grammatical and historical exegesis of Grotius and Hammond. Lowth in his notes attached to Merrick's Version, 1768, supported also by an Anonymous. made contributions which were often original and of great value. Kennicott, in his notes on the Psalms, 1772, also greatly advanced the study of the Psalter. All this material was used by Street, 1790, with independent and excellent judgment, resulting in the best Commentary on the Psalms of the eighteenth century. Bishop Horsley, 1815 (posthumous), inherited their spirit. These scholars are the real fathers of a large number of emendations of the text and of new interpretations for which later scholars, especially Germans, have received the credit. Many practical commentaries of great value appeared in this period, such as Henry, 1710; Horne, 1771; Gill, 1774–1776. The Commentaries of Dathe, 1787, and especially Rosenmüller, 1798–1804, represented this period in Germany.

§ **55.** *The study of the Psalter has been improved in the last century by a more comprehensive and thoroughgoing study of all the material by Textual Criticism, Higher Criticism, Historical Criticism, and Biblical Theology, with a just estimate of Exegesis in its different phases.*

De Wette, 1811 +, began this most fruitful period, and was followed by Ewald, 1836 +, both with remarkable critical sagacity and profound historical sense. Hitzig, 1836 +, and Olshausen, 1853 +, opened wide the field of Textual Criticism; Hupfeld, 1855 +, and Böttcher, 1864, grammatical and lexicographical exegesis. Delitzsch, 1859 +, shows a deep spiritual sense and a thorough understanding of the genius of the ancient Hebrew people. Hengstenberg, 1842 +, is the father of the reactionaries. On these princes of modern German exegesis a great number of scholars build. Among these we may mention on the continent of Europe: Tholuck, 1843 +; Köster, 1837; Vaihinger, 1845; Reuss, 1879 +; Grätz, 1882–1883; Hirsch, 1882; Moll, 1884 +; Schultz, 1888 +; Bachmann, 1891; Bäthgen, 1892 +; Wellhausen, 1895; Duhm, 1899; Valeton, 1903. Among R. C. scholars, we may mention Alioli, 1832 +; Aigner, 1850; Schegg, 1857[2]; Crelier, 1858; Rohling, 1871; Thalhofer, 1889[5]. Migne, *Cursus Completus,* 1841, and Cornely, Knabenbauer, and Hammelauer in *Cursus Completus,* 1885, give a thesaurus of interpretation of many scholars, ancient and modern. Many British and American interpreters of the Pss. have been reactionary in the spirit of Hengstenberg, such as Phillips, 1846; Neale, 1860; Wordsworth, 1867; Alexander, 1868+; Murphy, 1875; Cowles, 1872. The Puritan spirit was inherited in Spurgeon, 1870, and Barnes, 1871. Perowne, 1864 +, deserves the credit for the introduction into the English-speaking world of the modern spirit, which indeed is only a rebuilding on the work of the older English scholars of the eighteenth century. The following Commentators deserve mention: *The Psalms Chronologically arranged by Four Friends,* 1867; Kay, 1871; Cook, 1873; Jennings and Low, 1875; Burgess, 1879; Aglen, 1884; Cheyne, 1888+;

Maclaren, 1893–1894 + ; Montefiore, 1901 ; Kirkpatrick, 1903 ; W. T. Davidson, 1903 + ; Ehrlich, 1904. Cheyne and Kirkpatrick are preëminent, the former for his brave investigation of the most difficult problems and his generous recognition of the work of other scholars, the latter for his sound judgment and excellent exegetical method. These scholars easily outrank all their predecessors. Their occasional faults and failures are cordially overlooked in view of their magnificent contributions to Biblical Science.

§ **56.** *English Versions of the Psalms began with Wycliffe in 1382. The Version of Coverdale of 1535, revised for the great Bible of 1539, has been used since as the Version of the Book of Common Prayer. The Version of 1611 was made from the Hebrew, with a limited study of other versions. It supplanted all other English Versions except that of PBV. The Version of 1885 was a revision of that of 1611, in closer conformity to the Massoretic text. The R. C. Version is that of Douay.*

John Wycliffe made the first English translation of the Bible from the Vulgate Version, 1382. It was revised by John Purvey in 1388 (*v.* Forshall and Madden's text, 4 v., 1850; Skeats, reprint of Purvey's revision in 1879). Coverdale published a translation of the whole Bible in 1535. His translation of the Psalter was taken up into Matthew's Bible in 1537, and into the Great Bible in 1539–1541. Coverdale, in his dedicatory Epistle to the King and in Prologue, states that he had followed largely five sundry interpreters; to judge from internal evidence, the Vulgate, Luther, the Zurich Version, Pagninus, and Tyndale, the latter not giving the Psalter. The Zurich Version was completed in 1529 by Zwingli, Pellican, Leo Juda, and others. Pagninus' version was a translation of the Psalter into Latin (1527). The Psalter of the PBV. is from the last revision of the Great Bible of 1540 (*v.* Westcott, *The Paragraph Psalter*; Earle, *The Psalter of 1539 a Landmark in English Literature*, 1892; Driver, *The Parallel Psalter*, Int. 1904[2]; Fry, *Description of the Great Psalter*, 1865). The Genevan Version of 1560 was translated into English and used by the Puritans from that time onward. The Bishop's Bible of 1568 was used in the scriptural readings in the Church of England, but not in the recitations of the Psalter. In 1611 the Authorized Version was made by a select company of scholars under the authority of the crown. It displaced all other Vrss. for Protestants in the public and private reading of the Scripture: but did not succeed in displacing the Vrs. of the Great Bible in the recitation of the Psalter. The Roman Catholics continued to adhere to the Douay Version, which was a literal translation of the Vulgate, whereas the AV. was translated from the Hebrew. The AV. has maintained its hold on the English Protestant world until the present time. The RV. of 1885, prepared by a joint British and American Committee, under the authority of the convocation of Canterbury, has thus far been unable to replace it. The RV. is a more accurate rendering of the Hebrew text of Ben Asher ; but it is literalistic and pedantic. It was prepared in a period of transition of Hebrew scholarship and does not satisfy the present conditions of OT. scholarship or the needs of the Church or people. Furthermore, it does not sufficiently consider the Ancient Vrss., and is not based on a revision of the Hebrew text. The margin of the RV. gives the most important part of the work of the Revisers and is of great value. Several independent versions have been made in recent times: John De Witt, 1884 ; T. K. Cheyne, 1888 ; Furness, 1898 ; S. R. Driver, *The Parallel Psalter*, 1904[2] (an important and valuable revision of PBV.). The Jewish Publication Society of America, 1903, gave a new and excellent translation from the Massoretic text. There is no sound reason why Roman Catholics, Protestants, and Jews should not unite and agree in a Version far better than any that has yet been made.

Many metrical versions of the Psalter have been made for use in Christian worship in the service of song, the chief of which are those of Sternhold and Hopkins, and Tate and Brady, used in England; Rouse, used in Scotland; and Watts, used by the Nonconformists of England and their children in America. From a literary point of view the most valuable paraphrase is still that of Merrick, 1765. The fault of all these versions is that they are based either upon English Versions or the Massoretic text. None of them were made with any knowledge whatever of the measures of Hebrew poetry. It is now quite possible to reproduce the poetry of the Psalms in essentially the same measures in English poetry. Scholars who have the poetic gift should undertake this task, which when accomplished will greatly enlarge the use of the Psalter for English-speaking peoples, and enrich their devotion, public and private, with a finer literary flavour.

A COMMENTARY ON THE BOOK OF PSALMS.

A COMMENTARY ON THE BOOK OF PSALMS.

PSALM I., 2 STR. 6⁴.

Ps. 1 is a didactic Ps. of the Greek period, introductory to the Psalter. In two antith. Strs. it contrasts the happiness of the righteous man (v.$^{1-2}$) with the ultimate ruin of the wicked (v.$^{4-6}$). The righteous man avoids the company of wicked men, and diligently studies the Law. An intermediate gloss compares the righteous to a fruitful tree in a well-watered garden (v.^{3}).

HAPPY the man!
Who doth not walk in the counsel of wicked men,
And in the way of sinners doth not stand,
And in the session of scorners doth not sit down;
But rather in the Law of Yahweh is his delight,
And in His Law he studies day and night.
NOT so the wicked!
But rather they are as the chaff which the wind driveth away;
Therefore wicked men will not rise up in the Judgment,
And sinners (will not enter) into the congregation of righteous men;
For Yahweh knoweth the way of righteous men,
But the way of wicked men will perish (everlastingly).

Ps. 1 is orphan (Intr. § 37) and therefore was not in any of the Psalters prior to the last. It was doubtless later than any of them. It was not counted originally, for 2 codd. DeR. do not number it; and 5 codd. Kenn., 3 DeR., some codd. 𝕲, Justin (Ap. 1^{40}), and many fathers (especially Western), and rabbis, combine it with Ps. 2; according to the ancient saying that the first Ps. begins and closes with beatitude (Talm. *Berakoth* f. 9^{b}). In Western texts and Vrss. of Acts 13^{33}, Ps. 2 is cited as Ps. 1; so Meyer, Tisch., Blass; but the great Uncials have δευτέρῳ, so Westcott and Hort, and Wendt. It was selected as an introduction to ψ by the final editor. The date of Ps. 1 may be determined by the following considerations: (1) It is characteristic of late writings that they make much use of earlier ones. V.^{3} is based on Je. 17$^{5-8}$ and Ez. 47^{12}, and is therefore postexilic. If v.^{3} be original, it gives

3

evidence of date of Ps.; if a gloss, only as to date of the gloss. The argument of Bä. that the prose writer uses the poet and not the poet the prose, is without force if v.[3] is a prosaic gloss. V.[2b] is based on Jos. 1[8] (D), and is post-deuteronomic; for the Ps. substitutes for the external, "depart out of thy mouth," the first clause of Jos. 1[8], the internal "delight in," indicating a later and more matured conception. The language of the Ps. is that of the Greek period: פלגי מים v.[3a], מושב לצים v.[1d], עצת רשעים v.[1b]. The syntax is also late: יורע v.[6], והיה v.[3a]. (2) The רשעים and צדיקים are classes in the Jewish community. The earlier antitheses between wicked rulers and an oppressed people, characteristic of preëxilic writings; and of righteous Israel and her wicked foes, characteristic of the long period of foreign domination, do not appear; the antithesis is between two classes among the Jews, the righteous, the strict students of the Law, who keep apart from the company of the wicked; and the wicked, who scorn the ethical teachings of Wisdom and transgress the Law. All this implies a fully developed school of Wisdom, as well as an intense scribal devotion to the Law. There is not that exclusive devotion to the Law of Pss. 19[8-15] 119, or to Wisdom of Pr. 1–9; but the author blends the teachings and practice of these two types. He lived in peaceful times before the antagonisms of religious parties, and thus probably in the late Greek period. A similar situation is in BS 6[37] 14[20-21], which seem to be based on this Ps. (3) The reference to the Judgment, v.[5a], implies a judicial interference of Yahweh; not as between Israel and her oppressors, as in the prophetic books, but as between the righteous and wicked in Israel itself. As the result of that Judgment the righteous will rise up, an organized congregation, v.[5b], from which the wicked will be excluded. The wicked will not rise. If the rising here is to be interpreted as a resurrection, then the exclusion of the wicked implies an earlier date than Dn., which includes wicked Israelites in the resurrection, Dn. 12[2], and is more in accord with Is. 26[14-19], where the wicked oppressors do not rise with God's people. The apocalypse, Is. 24–27, seems to belong to the time of Alexander the Great. The resemblance in doctrine between Ps. 1 and Is. 26 would favour the putting of our Ps. between that apocalypse and Dn.; that is, in the Greek period before the persecutions of Antiochus. This Ps. was probably the basis of the doctrine of the Two Ways which plays such an important part in Jewish and early Christian Literature (Mt. 7[13-14]. V. Br. Ethical Teaching of Jesus, pp. 82 sq.).

The Ps. has two antith. Strs. of six tetrameter lines each. This has not been observed by Du. or Siev., both of whom regard v.[3] as original to the Ps. The former says: "Keine Strophen, wie mir scheint, sondern nur unregelmässig gebildete Stichen, die sich auch in Stil und Ausdruck der Prosa nähern." The latter says: "Ps. 1 enthält so viel metrisch Anstössiges oder Auffälliges, dass man nicht über den Zweifel herauskommt wie viel davon späterer Verderbnis oder persönlichem Form-ungeschick des Verfassers entstammt." The real difficulty is with both that they did not discern the gloss, and so could not understand the measure, which is really one of the simplest and finest in the Psalter.

Str. I. 1. The poet, in view of the description of the righteous man he is about to give, exclaims: *Happy the man !* He uses a dimeter, or half line, to allow a metrical pause after the exclamation. He is not thinking of mankind, men, women, and children ; but of men only. He has not in mind all men, or all Jews, or all pious men ; but specifically that kind of a man he is about to describe, one devoting his whole time, night and day, to the study of the Law ; that is, the ideal scribe such as Ezra. Jerome tells us the pious Jews thought of King Josiah as the ideal. The righteous man is described first negatively in three syn. tetrameters which yet gradually became more intense, reaching a climax in the last line : *who doth not walk*] cf. Mi. 6[16] Je. 7[24] ; *doth not stand*] cease from walking and so remain standing ; *doth not sit down*] continual participation in. — *in the counsel*] while walking, listening to and receiving counsel or advice, *in the way*] the moral conduct, the course of life, *in the session*] not settling down in the session, or assembly of the scorners, and so being in entire accord with them. — *Wicked men*] a class in antithesis to righteous men, who studied and practised the Law ; *sinners*] antith. to upright, a more general term referring to all who fail from or do not conform to the ethical and religious goal or way of life ; *scorners*] antith. to wise men ; those who mock at and scorn the discipline of wisdom. The righteous man abstains from all such conduct and avoids the company of all such men. — **2.** The righteous man is described positively in two syn. lines antith. to the previous three. — *In the Law of Yahweh*] embracing the entire legislation compacted in the Pentateuch, and so called the Law as the first layer of the Canon, in the Greek period when this Ps. was composed (*v.* Br.[SHS 120]), repeated for emphasis. — *his delight*] the good pleasure the righteous man took in the Law, ‖ *studies day and night*] reading it over and over again in the low, murmuring tone of one reading to oneself, to impress it upon the mind and commit it to memory, a method characteristic of oriental students, rather than meditating or musing upon what had been previously read. This study is habitual not only during the day but also during the night. The second line is cited from Jos. 1[8] (D).

3. The editor of ψ inserts four lines of illustration before the antistrophe.

A ND he is like a tree transplanted beside channels of water,
 Which yieldeth his fruit in his season,
 Whose leaf withers not;
 So all that he doeth, he carries through successfully.

The happiness of the righteous man is illustrated by the simile
of a tree, which is removed from its native soil and transplanted
to the most favoured soil, in a fertile garden irrigated by many
channels of water, such as Wady Urtas, where were the gardens
of Solomon ; Engedi, famed for its fertility (Rob.[I. 477, cf. 556]) ; the
gardens of Damascus, Egypt, and Babylon, irrigated by canals
drawn from the great rivers ; and it is probable that the story of
the streams of Eden, Gn. 2, was in the mind of the poet ; for he
adapts and combines from Je. 17[8] the beautiful and fully stated
simile of the man trusting in Yahweh ; from Ez. 47[12b] the description of the living trees on the banks of the river of life in the
future paradise, which bear fruit monthly and whose leaves are
ever green and medicinal (cf. Rev. 22[2]) ; with the irrigated gardens of his own time, for a condensed simile, suggesting a comprehensive ideal to one familiar with the sacred writings. He
then interprets the simile of the last line by an adaptation of
Jos. 1[8b]. The righteous man has in him such life and vigour from
his study of God's word that he makes everything that he does to
succeed and be prosperous. This verse is thus a mosaic of three
earlier passages. The lines are irregular and prosaic (5. 4. 3. 4).
The two middle lines are synonymous but synthetic to the first
line, and the last line is a synthetic explanation of the simile.

Str. II. is an antistrophe to Str. I. V.[4] is composed (*a*) of a
dimeter line, v.[4a], with metrical pause antithetical to v.[1a], contrasting the wicked with the righteous man ; and of a tetrameter
simile, v.[4b], likening *the wicked* to *chaff* on the threshing floor.
This, in Palestine, is usually on flat, open places on hilltops, so
that when the ears of grain are thrown up, the heavy grain falls
to the ground, while the *wind drives away* the light chaff. This
simile is antith. to that in v.[3], so far as a fruit-bearing tree may be
to chaff of grain ; but the original antith. was probably of " driveth
away " to deliberate walking in counsel, v.[1b]. — 5. *Rise up in the
Judgment*] is antith. to standing in the way, v.[1c] ; *enter into the congregation*] antith. to the sitting down in the session, v.[7d]. Wicked

men will not rise up, that is, in the resurrection which takes place in the Judgment, at the end of the age of the world. Only the righteous share in that resurrection. So Is. 26$^{14-19}$, the people of God rise, their wicked oppressors do not. So Jesus speaks of the resurrection of the just, Lk. 14^{14}, without mentioning that of the unjust; and St. Paul sets forth the resurrection of Christians 1 Cor. 15, those who are not, apparently, being in the background of his thoughts and so unmentioned (*v.* Br.$^{MA 113 sq.}$). The resurrection of the wicked appears in OT. only Dn. 12^2, and in NT. explicitly only Jn. 5$^{28-29}$ Rev. 20$^{11-15}$ (*v.* Br.$^{MG 273}$). This interpretation, given by 𝕲, 𝖄, 𝕿, Bä., is more suitable, in view of the late date of the Ps., than the usual modern interpretation, " stand in the judgment," that is, God's providential judgment in the course of human history. The congregation of the righteous men may be conceived as the congregation of the zealous Jews from which the wicked would be kept apart by divine judgment; but better, of the congregation after the judgment of the resurrection, in which there can be no wicked, for they have not been permitted to rise. — **6.** The Str. concludes with two antith. tetrameters summing up the contrast already drawn. There are two ways. *The way of the righteous* is a way which *Yahweh knoweth;* not merely theoretically and ideally, but practically and really by personal acquaintance with and attentive supervision of it, so that it is Yahweh's way, leading unto true and lasting happiness. *The way of wicked men* is a way which goeth on to everlasting ruin, cf. 69^{29}. The Ps. begins with happiness and concludes with ruin, cf. Ps. 112. All is comprehended between these two ends and in these two ways.

1. † [אַשְׁרֵי] cstr. pl. abstr. אֶשֶׁר or אָשֵׁר √אשר Ew.§ 179, Lag.$^{BN 143}$, BDB., 33 t. always exclam., of man (never of God), *O the happiness, happy is* or *be,* c. אִישׁ elsw. 112^1; אדם 32^2 84$^{6. 13}$ Pr. 3^{13} 8^{34} 28^{14}; גבר Pss. 34^9 40^5 94^{12} 127^5; הגוי 33^{12}; העם 89^{16} 144$^{15. 15}$; ptc. 2^{12} 32^1 41^2 84^5 106^3 119^2 128^1 Is. 30^{18} Dn. 12^{12}; other words Dt. 33^{29} 1 K. 10$^{8. 8}$ (= 2 C. 9$^{7. 7}$) Jb. 5^{17} Pss. 65^5 119^1 128^2 137$^{8. 9}$ 146^5 Pr. 8^{32} 14^{21} 16^{2}) 20^7 29^{18} Ec. 10^{17} Is. 32^{20} 56^2. — [אֲשֶׁר] rel. pron., usually omitted in ψ, dub. here; often gloss of prosaic copyists. — הלך, ישׁב, עמד] Pfs. abstr. emphatic presents of characteristic and established state or condition, Ew.§ 135, Ges.§ 106. 2, usually expressed in Eng. by auxiliary *do.* — [עצת רשעים] Jb. 10^8 21^{16} 22^{18}. ‡ עֵצָה *counsel,* either as (1) *advice, guidance,* when used of God, Pss. 33^{11} 73^{24} 106^{13} 107^{11}, cf. 119^{24} of His Law; or (2) *purpose,* *design, plan,* of men, 1^1 13^3(?) 14^6(?) 20^5 33^{10} 106^{48}. — ‡ רָשָׁע adj. *wicked;* in ψ either (1) guilty of hostility to God or His people, syn. *enemies;* sg. 17^{18} 71^4 $109^{2. 6. 7}$ $140^{5. 9}$; coll. $9^{6. 17}$ $10^{2. 3. 4. 13. 15}$ 55^4 58^{11} 94^{13} 139^{19}; pl. 3^8 7^{10} 9^{18} $11^{2. 6}$ 12^9 17^9 28^3 31^{18} 58^4 68^3 $75^{5. 11}$ $82^{2. 4}$ 91^8 92^8 $94^{3. 3}$ 97^{10} 104^{35} $119^{53. 61. 95. 110. 112}$ 129^4 141^{10} 145^{20} 147^6; or (2) guilty of sin against God or man, ethically wicked: sg. 11^5 32^{10} 36^2 $37^{10. 12. 21. 32. 35}$ 112^{10}, coll. 34^{22} 39^2, pl. $1^{1. 4. 5. 6}$ 26^5 36^{12} $37^{14. 16. 17. 20. 28. 34. 38. 40}$ 50^{16} $73^{3. 12}$ 106^{18} 112^{10} 146^9; רִשְׁעֵי (ה)אָרֶץ 75^9 101^8 119^{119}. This word is little used in preëx. Lit. and not at all in sense (2). It is chiefly used in Ez., W. L., and ψ, antith. צַדִּיק. — [בְּדֶרֶךְ חַטָּאִים] phr. α.λ. ‡ דֶּרֶךְ in ψ, (1) *way, road, path,* 2^{12} 77^{20} 80^{13} 89^{42} $107^{4. 7. 40}$ 110^7, (2) fig. of course of life or action, undertaking 10^5 18^{33} 35^6 $37^{5. 7. 23}$ 91^{11} 102^{24} 119^{37} 128^1 139^3 146^9, (3) esp. of moral action and character 5^9 39^2 49^{14} 50^{23} $119^{5. 26. 59. 168}$, (4) of duty (commanded by God) $25^{8. 12}$ 32^8 119^1 143^8, (5) specif. in good sense 1^6 37^{14} $101^{2. 6}$ 119^{30} 139^{24}, or (6) in bad sense $1^{1. 6}$ 36^5 107^{17} 119^{29} 139^{24}; (7) way of God, His moral administration, 18^{31} 77^{14} 85^{14} 103^7 138^5 145^{17}, or His commands 18^{22} $25^{4. 9}$ 27^{11} 37^{34} 51^{15} 67^3 81^{14} 86^{11} 95^{10} $119^{3. 14. 27. 32. 33}$. — ‡ חַטָּאִים pl. adj. [חַטָּא]. Sg. only f. חַטָּאָה Am. 9^8; alw. in ψ in ethical sense, more comprehensive than רְשָׁעִים, and antith. יְשָׁרִים, those who fail or err from the norm of right $1^{1. 5}$ 25^8 26^9 51^{15} 104^{35}; used both in earliest and latest Lit. — [בְּמוֹשַׁב לֵצִים] phr. α.λ. ‡ מוֹשָׁב might be *seat, place of sitting down,* as 𝔊, 𝔙, cf. עִיר מוֹשָׁב city as dwelling-place $107^{4. 7. 36}$, or Zion as place of enthronement of God 132^{13}; but better *sitting, session, assembly,* as 107^{32}, Ain., Kirk. — † לֵץ *scorner* Pr. 1^{22} 3^{34} $9^{7. 8}$ 13^1 14^6 15^{12} $19^{25. 29}$ 20^1 $21^{11. 24}$ 22^{10} 24^9 Is. 29^{20}, a term characteristic of fully developed *Wisdom,* not used prob. till Greek period. 𝔊 λοιμῶν is interpret. and does not imply a different text. 𝔙 *pestilentiae,* takes the word as abstr. = *homines pestiferi.* Aug. "whose word spreadeth as a canker." — 2. [כִּי אִם] = v.⁴ *but rather, on the contrary,* stronger than כִּי, *but,* BDB. *Makkeph* alw. used after אִם except Gn. 15^4 Nu. 35^{33} Ne. 2^2 (*v.* Intr. § 12). — [בְּתוֹרַת י־] cstr. sg. ‡ תּוֹרָה n.f. √ירה/ (1) the Law in its completion, as 19^8 $78^{5. 10}$ 89^{31} 94^{12} 105^{45} 119^1 + 21 t. (*v.* txt.); תּוֹרָה elsw. ψ, (2) of instruction of poet 78^1, (3) of divine teaching, in the mind 37^{31} 40^9. Lag. Du. rd. בְּיִרְאַת, cf. 19^{10}, on ground that the poet would not repeat himself in syn. lines. But the use of identical words in syn. lines is not uncommon to emphasize the variation in other words. — ‡ [חֵפֶץ] c. בְּ. (1) *delight* as 16^3, so usually, but (2) 𝔊 θέλημα, 𝔙 *voluntas, will, purpose,* as Is. 44^{28} 46^{10} 48^{14}; elsw. (3) *desire, longing,* Ps. 107^{30}. — Jos. 1^8 has לֹא יָמוּשׁ סֵפֶר הַתּוֹרָה הַזֶּה מִפִּיךָ וְהָגִיתָ בּוֹ יוֹמָם וָלַיְלָה. The change from בִּי to בְתוֹרָתוֹ was necess. because of omission of סֵפֶר in previous line, otherwise it would have furnished a good tetrameter. — [וְיֶהְגֶּה] Qal impf. frequentative ‡ הגה: (1) *growl, groan, moan,* not in ψ. (2) *utter* c. acc. rei. 38^{13}, subj. לָשׁוֹן 35^{28} 71^{24}; פֶּה 37^{30} *speak* abs. 115^7. (3) *utter* indistinct sound as in soliloquy, meditations, c. בְּ, ‖ שִׂיחַ 63^7 77^{13}; so prob. 77^7 as 𝔊 for הֶ נְגִינָתִי 143^5; so possibly Jos. 1^8 and here. (4) But better of the low, murmuring sound of reading aloud to oneself, or the repetition of study, Ains.; (5) *imagine, devise,* c. acc. 2^1, as Pr. 15^{28} 24^2. — ‡ [יוֹמָם]

= יוֹם + ‏ם‏ַ adv. *in the daytime, by day*, sq. ‏לילה‏, also 32⁴ 42⁴ 55¹¹, possibly 13⁸ 𝔊, also 88² (for יום rd. ‏יומם‏); ‖ ‏לילה‏ 22⁸ 42⁹ 78¹⁴ 91⁵ 121⁶. — 3. ‏והיה‏] cannot be ‏ו‏ consec., for there is no previous impf. upon which it can depend. The only previous impf. is frequentative. It cannot be consec. to the str. as a whole, for it introduces a simile, not a consequence. In fact, it is a simple citation from Je. 17⁸, where it is ‏ו‏ *consec.* in its context. But taken from its context it can only be ‏ו‏ conj. of late style, introducing a new and independent clause. — ‏כעץ שתול על פלגי מים‏] is the same as Je. 17⁸ except for the insertion of ‏פלגי‏. Je. cannot have cited from Ps., for the clause in Je. is part of a beautiful simile, and necessary both in syntax and idea; whereas it is loosely attached to Ps., the first clause of a mosaic of three earlier passages, without measure and disturbing the symmetry of Ps. — ‏שָׁתוּל‏ Ptc. pass. = Je. 17⁸. √† ‏שׁתל‏ *transplant* (not *plant*) 92¹⁴ Ez. 17⁸·¹⁰·²²·²³ 19¹⁰·¹³ Ho. 9¹³(?). † [‏שָׁתִיל‏] *transplanted shoot* Ps. 128³. — † ‏פַּלְגֵי מָיִם‏ artificial watercourses used to irrigate gardens, parks, and arable land; so here Is. 32² Pr. 5¹⁶ 21¹, cf. Ps. 46⁵; fig. of tears from eyes Ps. 119¹³⁶ La. 3⁴⁸, cf. Jb. 29⁶ of outrun of oil from vat; ‏פלגים‏ elsw. of overflow of river Is. 30²⁵, sg. of downfall of rain Ps. 65¹⁰. — ‏פריו יתן בעתו‏] is generalization of Ez. 47¹²ᵃ. — † ‏בעתו‏ *in his season*, *i.e.* of ripe fruit Ho. 2¹¹ Jb. 5²⁶, when food is needed Ps. 104²⁷ 145¹⁵, of rain Dt. 11¹⁴ 28¹² Je. 5²⁴ Ez. 34²⁶, appearance of constellation Jb. 38³², appropriate time Pr. 15²³ Ec. 3¹¹. — ‏ועלהו לא יבול‏] direct citation from Ez. 47¹²ᵇ. — ‏עָלֵהוּ‏ archaic poetic sf. ‡ ‏עָלֶה‏ *leaf, foliage*, only here ψ, usually of fading Is. 1³⁰ 34⁴ 64⁵ Je. 8¹³ Ez. 47¹². — ‏יבול‏ Qal impf. † ‏נָבֵל‏ (1) *sink, drop down*, 18⁴⁶ = 2 S. 22⁴⁶, of exhaustion of Israel's foes Ex. 18¹⁸ (E) Jb. 14¹⁸. (2) *fall* like leaf or flower, *wither, fade* Is. 1³⁰ 24⁴ 28¹·⁴ 34⁴ 40⁷·⁸ 64⁵ Je. 8¹³ Ps. 37², so here and Ez. 47¹². — ‏וכל‏] not subj. as AV. after 𝔊, which prob. rd. Qal of Vb.; but obj. after Hiph., so Dr. accord. to Jos. 1⁸ on which the clause is based. See v.²ᵇ. — ‏יַצְלִיחַ‏] Hiph. impf. ‡ ‏צלח‏ Qal *have success* 45⁵, Hiph. *carry a thing through to success* or *victory*, of man 37⁷ as here; of God 118²⁵. — 4. ‏לֹא־כֵן‏] *not so*, strong antithesis to v.¹ᵃ. It is repeated in 𝔊. So We., Oort, Bä., Che., but by dittog.: exact antith. to v.¹ᵃ requires dimeter. — ‏הרשעים‏] *article*, here only in Ps. because of antithesis to ‏האיש‏ v.¹ᵃ. — † ‏כַּמֹּץ‏] *as chaff*, always as driven by wind, and c. ‏כ‏ of sim.; of wicked 35⁵ Ho. 13³ Jb. 21¹⁸ as here; of hostile nations Is. 17¹³ 29⁵, of Judah's power Is. 41¹⁵, of passing time Zp. 2². — ‏אשר‏] relative unnecessary prosaic gloss, destroys measure. — ‏הֲדְּפֶנּוּ‏] Qal impf. 3 f. with *strong* sf., Ges.§ 58(4). √† ‏נדף‏ Qal *drive about*, here chaff, but smoke 68³, man Jb. 32¹³, Niph. *be driven*, of smoke by wind Ps. 68³, cf. Pr. 21⁶; various things Lv. 26³⁶ Is. 19⁷ 41² Jb. 13²⁵. 𝔊, 𝔙, PBV add ἀπὸ προσώπου τῆς γῆς, so Bi., Du., in order to get rid of abruptness of first line. But 𝔊 is an explanatory gloss. — 5. ‡ ‏עַל־כֵּן‏] *"upon ground of such conditions, therefore*, introducing, more generally than ‏לָכֵן‏, the statement of a *fact*, rather than a *declaration"* BDB; also 18⁵⁰ 25⁸ 42⁷ 45³·⁸·¹⁸ 46³ 110⁷ 119¹⁰⁴·¹²⁷·¹²⁸·¹²⁹. — ‏יָקֻמוּ‏] def. written Qal impf. 3 pl. *rise up*, of resurrection, 𝔊 ἀναστήσονται, 𝔙 *resurgunt*, 𝕿, 88¹¹ Is. 26¹⁴·¹⁹; most moderns, because of supposed early date of Ps., *stand, abide*, c. ‏ב‏ as 24³; no other mng. of Qal suits context. —

בְּמִשְׁפָּט‎] *in the judgment*, the time when God will pronounce His final judgment at His advent, as Ec. 11⁹ 12¹⁴ = דִּין‎ Dn. 7¹⁰· ²²· ²⁶. It is usually interpreted by moderns of any historic judgment. ‡מִשְׁפָּט‎ (1) *act of judgment*,
deciding a case, by God, in historic time 9⁸ 35²³ 76¹⁰, of Davidic kings 122⁵;
(2) *the process, procedure, litigation*, before the judge 112⁵ 143²; (3) *the
sentence* or *decision* 7⁷ (if צִוָּה‎ is used, otherwise as (1), so possibly original),
17²; (4) *the execution of the judgment* 9⁵· ¹⁷ 119⁸⁴ 146⁷ 149⁹, acts in execution
of 10⁵ 48¹² 97⁸ 103⁶ 105⁵· ⁷. (5) attribute of the שֹׁפֵט‎, *justice;* of God 33⁵
37²⁸ 99⁴· ⁴ 111⁷, also 36⁷ 72¹ (יָהּ‎ pl.), צדק ומ׳‎ bases of divine throne 89¹⁵ = 97²;
of man 37⁶· ³⁰ 72² 94¹⁵ 101¹ 106⁸; (6) *ordinance* promulgated by שֹׁפֵט‎, judgment as law 19¹⁰ 25⁹ 81⁵ 119⁷ ⁺ ²¹ ᵗ· 147²⁰. (7) *decision* of the שֹׁפֵט‎ in a case
of law (v. Br.Hex. ²⁵²sq·); pl. of series of decisions; in Covt. code and D,
collection of pentades in conditional or temporal clauses, c. כי‎ or אם‎ in D, in
combination חקום ומ׳‎ Dt. 4¹+, in Code of H and after in combin. חקות‎
ומ׳‎ Lv. 18⁴+, cf. Ps. 18²³ (= 2 S. 22²³) 89⁸¹ 147¹⁹; (8) that which belongs
to one by justice or law, his *right, due*, 140¹³; (9) *the time of judgment*,
only here ψ as above. For other uses than those of ψ see BDB. —
עֵדָה‎] cstr. sg. ‡עֵדָה‎ *congregation*, or *company*, properly assembled by appointment, √יעד‎. (1) of nations 7⁸, of angels 82¹, of evil-doers 22¹⁷, cf.
106¹⁷· ¹⁸, of bulls, fig. nobles 68³¹, עֲרִיצִים‎ ע‎ 86¹⁴; (2) specif. of the congrega-
tion of Israel. 𝕲 συναγωγή 74² as usual in P, also 62⁹ (𝕲), 111¹ (|| סוד‎), so
here. 𝕲 has here ἐν βουλῇ as v.¹ᵇ, בעצת‎, by editorial assimilation is error.
This line is trimeter; we should probably supply vb. יבואו‎. It is improb. that
poet shortened his line to make both lines dependent on יקמו‎. That looks
more like the work of a prosaic copyist. — צַדִּיקִים‎] pl. ‡צַדִּיק‎, (1) *just,
righteous* in government, of God, in general 119¹⁸⁷ 129⁴, in discrimination
7¹⁰· ¹² 11⁷, in redemption 116⁵, in all His ways 145¹⁷; (2) *righteous*, as vindicated and justified by God, (*a*) his people over against enemies sg. coll. 11³· ⁵
14⁵ 31¹⁹ 55²³ 58¹¹· ¹² 64¹¹ 75¹¹ 92¹³ 94²¹ 97¹¹ 141⁵, pl. 33¹ 52⁸ 68⁴ 69²⁹ 97¹²
118¹⁵· ²⁰ 125³· ³ 140¹⁴ 142⁸ 146⁸, passing over into, and not always distinguish-
able from, (*b*) because of zeal for righteousness of Law, sg. coll. 37¹²· ¹⁶· ²¹· ²⁵· ³⁰· ³²
34²⁰· ²², pl. 34¹⁶ 37¹⁷· ²⁹· ³⁹ and here 1⁵· ⁶; (3) *just, righteous* in conduct and
character, more ethical than above, as in W. L. sg. coll. 5¹³ 7¹⁰ 72⁷ 112⁴· ⁶,
pl. 32¹¹. — 6. יוֹדֵעַ‎] Qal ptc. In classic usage ptc. would imply continuous
knowledge as disting. fr. impf. frequentative, oft-repeated action, but || impf.
תּאבַד‎ suggests in such a late Ps. the late Heb. usage of ptc. for verbal action
without distinction of kind or sphere of time. ידע‎, vb. ‡Qal in ψ has but two
classes of mng., (1) *know, learn to know* things, of man *know, understand*
73¹⁶ 74⁹ 81⁶, *know so as to estimate and tell* 71¹⁵, *know by experience* 9²¹ 14⁴
(= 53⁵) 39⁵· ⁷ 73²² 78³· ⁶ 82⁵ 89¹⁶ 90¹¹ 92⁷ 139¹⁴; *be conscious, aware of* 35¹¹· ¹⁵,
recognize, admit, acknowledge 51⁵, *anticipate, expect* 35⁸, *know that* c. כִּי‎ 4⁴ 20⁷
41¹² 46¹¹ 56¹⁰ 59¹⁴ 83¹⁹ 100³ 109²⁷ 119⁷⁵· ¹⁵² 135⁵ 140¹³; the sun knows his
setting 104¹⁹; (2) *know* a person, *be acquainted with* him and his affairs,
(*a*) subj. man, *know* God in intelligent worship and obedience 36¹¹ 79⁶ 87⁴,
His name 9¹¹ 91¹⁴, His ways 67³ 95¹⁰, His testimonies 119⁷⁹· ¹²⁵, His judg-

ments 147^{20}; be acquainted with men 18^{44} 101^{4}; (*b*) subj. God, *know* a person, *be acquainted with* him, personally interested in his actions and affairs, taking notice of him and regarding him, *c. acc.*, so here as 37^{18} 44^{22} 69^{20} 94^{11} 103^{14} 138^{6} 139$^{2. 4. 23, 23}$ 142^{4} 144^{3}, fowls 50^{11}, c. בצרות נפשׁי 31^{8}, c. ל 69^{6}, abs. 40^{10} 73^{11} 139^{1}. — [תׇאבֵר Qal impf. i.p. for תׇאבַר, c. דֶּרֶךְ only here, elsw. אבר vb. ‡ Qal, (1) *perish, vanish away, die* 49^{11} 119^{92}, emphasis on mortality 146^{4}, the wicked by divine judgment 37^{20} 68^{3} 73^{27} 92^{10} so here; stronger meaning *be exterminated*, of Israel 80^{17}, other nations 2^{12} 83^{18}, cf. 9^{4}; of inanimate things, a vessel 31^{13}, heavens and earth 102^{27}; (2) fig. the memory 9^{7}, name 41^{6}, hope 9^{19}, desire 112^{10}, place of flight 142^{5}; (3) *be lost, strayed*, of sheep, fig. 119^{176}. A trimeter line at the end is possible, but not probable. The inf. abs. אׇבֹד has probably been lost by copyist error because of identity of letters with תאבר. This is so appropriate metrically and intensively that it is altogether probable.

PSALM II., 4 STR. 7^{3}.

Ps. 2. was the Messianic introduction to 𝔅. It describes the nations plotting against Yahweh and His Messiah (v.$^{1-3}$); and in antistr. Yahweh Himself laughing at them and telling them of His installation of His king (v.$^{4-7a}$). The Messiah then cites the word of Yahweh constituting him Son of God and giving him the nations as his inheritance (v.$^{7b-9}$); and in antistr. warns them to serve Yahweh (v.$^{10-12c}$). A liturgical addition pronounces all happy who seek refuge in Him (v.^{12d}).

WHY do nations consent together,
And peoples devise plans in vain ?
Kings of earth take their stand,
And princes do consult together,
Against Yahweh and against His anointed:
" Let us tear apart their bands,
And let us cast away from us their cords."
ONE throned in heaven laughs (at them),
My sovereign Lord mocks at them :
Then in His anger He speaks unto them,
And in His burning anger terrifies them :
(Declaring) the decree (of Yahweh),
" Now I, I have set My king,
Upon Zion, My sacred mount."
YAHWEH said unto me :
" My son art thou,
I, to-day, have begotten thee;
I will give nations for thine inheritance,
And for thy possession the ends of the earth.

> Thou shalt rule them with an iron sceptre,
> As a potter's vessel thou shalt dash them in pieces,"
"NOW therefore act prudently, O kings,
> Be admonished, governors of earth,
> Serve Yahweh with fear,
> And rejoice in Him with trembling.
> Kiss sincerely, lest He be angry,
> And ye perish from the right way,
> For quickly His anger will be kindled."

Pss. 2 and 72 are without 𝔅 in titles in 𝔥. But 𝔊 has ψαλμὸς τῷ Δαυίδ in title of Ps. 2 in 𝔊ᴿ Ald. Compl., and in title of Ps. 72 in 42 codd. HP. none earlier than eleventh century. These rest probably on editorial conjecture. Ps. 72²⁾ after doxology, and therefore after attachment of doxologies to ψ, ends with a statement which implies that Ps. 72 concluded 𝔅 (v. Intr. § 27). Ps. 2 was therefore introductory to 𝔅 and Ps. 72 its conclusion, and being used for the same purpose by the editor of ψ, he omits the reference to 𝔅. The Ps. describes an ideal situation, in the universal dominion of the monarch and the vain plotting of the nations. Such a situation never emerged in the history of Israel before the exile, in David and his successors; or subsequent to the exile, in the Greek kings of Palestine or the Maccabean princes. The situation is rather that of the Assyrian and Babylonian world-powers, against which there was continual vain rebellion, according to the Hebrew prophets, and the cuneiform monuments of these kings. The same world-wide dominion was held by Persia and Alexander, but there was not the same situation of plotting and rebellion. It is probable that the poet idealizes the dynasty of David into just such a world-power as Assyria or Babylonia, and that he wrote during the supremacy of one of them. The seat of the dominion is Mt. Zion, and therefore we cannot think with Hi. of a Greek king, such as Alexander Jannaeus, or with Du. of Aristobulus I. The king cites a divine word as his title to his dominion. This is based on the covenant made by Yahweh with David, 2 S. 7¹¹⁻¹⁶ = 1 Ch. 17¹⁰⁻¹⁴, adopting the seed of David as son of God. This is paraphrased Pss. 89²⁾ ˢᑫ· 132¹¹⁻¹² (Br.ᴹᴾ ¹²⁶ ˢᑫ· ²⁵⁸ ˢᑫ·). The king, Messiah and Son of God, of this Ps. must be of the dynasty of David. Therefore we cannot think of Maccabean princes who were not of the line of David. The Ps. refers to a birthday, a time of the installation of the king on Zion. We must therefore think of the day of the institution of the covenant, which is ideally combined with the installation of the dynasty in Jerusalem. It is probable that the Ps. represents David as himself speaking for himself and his seed in Strs. III. and IV.; just as in Str. II. Yahweh speaks, in Str. I. the nations. It is true that, in fact, David was not installed in Jerusalem and on Zion, but at Hebron first by Judah 2 S. 2¹⁻⁴, and then some years after by all the tribes 5¹⁻³; after seven years' reign in Hebron he captured Jerusalem and removed his capitol thither 5⁴⁻⁹ without any further installation; and the covenant established by Yahweh confirmed him in his dominion there. But the poet combines all these several things in one picture and regards them all as the installation of the dynasty on Zion. Under these circumstances, it is not so important to determine when the Ps. was written, for in any case the Messianic dynasty is in view. It must, however, be later than the covenant which thinks only of an everlasting dominion and not of a world-wide dominion ; and so must be in the period of the supremacy of the world-powers, when first universal dominion could be conceived in connection with the universal rule of God. Therefore we cannot think of the time of David (older scholars even Pe.), or of Solomon (Ew., Bleek, Kirk.), or of Uzziah (Meier), or the time of the prophecy of Immanuel (De.). The earliest time conceivable would be the reign of Hezekiah (Maurer, Gr.); but many arguments point rather to the reign of Josiah, or the time of Jeremiah. These are also against the views that it was composed in the pre-Maccabean times (Che.) or the Maccabean (Bä.). The language does not favour a late date, unless רגשׁוּ v.¹, תִּרְעֵם v.⁹ and בר v.¹² be Aramaisms. But they are all good Heb. words appropriate to the age of Je., to which also the phrase ננתקה את מוסרותימו v.³ points. There is no departure from strict classic style of syntax. The style, rhythm, and poetic conception are of the best types. There is no dependence on other Lit.; the Ps. is throughout original in conception. Ps. 59⁹ has essentially the same two lines as 2⁴ quoting our Ps.; Ps. 59 is a מכתם, probably the oldest group in ψ (v. Intr. § 25). This would prove the preëx. date of the Ps., were it not that Ps. 59⁹ is probably a gloss. Ps. 110 has the same essential theme. There is a possible connection between the חק of v.⁷ᵃ and the נאם יהוה 110¹, נשׁבע יהוה 110⁴, although the situation of the king is dissimilar. There is possibly a verbal correspondence between ילדתּיך v.⁷ᶜ and ילדתך 110³ᵇ. It is difficult to show dependence; but probably 110 is earlier; at least it reflects a more warlike condition of the Davidic monarchy. Ps. 89²⁸ has the same idea of extensive dominion and sonship in בכור firstborn and עליון למלכי ארץ. However, with Ps. 132 it laments the failure to realize the covenant and is probably later than Ps. 2, which is so confident of its realization. The Ps. is composed of four strs. of 7 trimeters each. There are two parts each of two antith. strs. The two parts are in introverted parall. or inclusion. Str. IV. is synon. with Str. I.; these include Str. III. synon. with Str. II. The parall. of the lines of strs. with the corresponding lines of synon., or antith. strs. has nothing to surpass it. A number of lines are in assonance in מו — v.³ᵃ ᵇ, ⁴ᵃ. ᵇ, ⁵ᵃ ᵇ. The Ps. is Messianic because it presents a world-wide dominion of the Son of David, such as was not a historical reality in the time of the poet or in any previous or subsequent time in history, but remains an ideal at the goal of history. Jesus of Nazareth is represented in the NT. as the Son of David and heir of this ideal. God at his baptism recognized him, "*Thou art my beloved Son*" (that is, Messianic Son) Mk. 1¹¹, and at his transfiguration (Mk. 9²⁻⁸). In his reign from heaven over the world he is gradually fulfilling it. When he ascended into heaven and sat down on the right hand of God, he was installed as Son of God in his world-wide dominion as Messiah. So St. Paul Acts 13³⁸, Rom. 1⁴, applies this Ps. to him. Also Heb. 1⁵ combines our Ps. with 2 S. 7¹⁴, and refers them to the enthroned

Christ, cf. Heb. 5⁵. Acts 4²⁵ applies the fruitless rebellion of the nations to the gathering together of Herod and Pilate, the Gentiles and the people of Israel against the crown rights of Jesus. The universal dominion of the Messiah is stated in connection with the enthronement Phil. 2¹⁰⁻¹¹. It is only gradually realized, for he must reign until he hath put all his enemies under his feet, 1 Cor. 15²⁰⁻²⁸. At the Second Advent he is to rule with a rod of iron, Rev. 2²⁷ 12⁵ 19¹⁵. The Ps. is a proper Ps. for Easter.

Str. I. The Ps. conceives of Yahweh as sovereign of all nations; and of the king anointed by Him, as ruling over the kings of the earth. His kingdom is world-wide, cf. 89²⁸. The nations, like those subjected by the world-power Babylon, are impatient of this dominion, and accordingly they secretly plot together to throw it off. This is graphically described in 4 syn. lines. — **1.** *Why do nations consent together ?*] meet in council and come to a common agreement in their desire of rebellion; so most probably from mng. of Heb. stem and context; "rage" AV., RV., JPSV, "rage furiously " PBV, "tumultuously assemble " RVᵐ, Kirk., and so variously, most moderns, are not sustained by usage or context. — *peoples devise plans*] to make their rebellion successful all *in vain*] for no plan that they can think of, is possible of realization. **2.** *Kings of earth take their stand*] at the head of their nations, to embolden them and arouse their courage; finally, *princes do consult together*] in order for common action in real rebellion. They regard themselves as in bondage, bound by bands and tied by cords, as captives and slaves; and with one voice they resolve : **3.** *Let us tear apart their bands ‖ And let us cast away from us their cords*] This is the outcome of their plotting, the climax of their efforts, words and nothing more. They never get so far as actual rebellion. The reason appears in the antistrophe.

Str. II. describes, in 4 syn. lines, **4–5,** *One throned in heaven*] in sublime contrast with the plotting nations. He *laughs at them*] those nations consenting together. — *My sovereign Lord*] giving the word its original mng. which is more suited to the context than the proper name *Adonay*, of Vrss. — *mocks at them*] those peoples devising plans in vain. — *In His anger He speaks unto them*] those kings taking their stand; and finally *in His burning anger terrifies them*] those princes consulting together. Nothing more is necessary. The nations are ready to revolt, but Yahweh is ready for war; and He terrifies the plotters so that they can do nothing. Yahweh's words sound forth in antithesis to the words of the plotters. **6.** *I, I have set My king*] he is already installed, Yahweh's response to v.³ᵃ — *upon Zion, My sacred mount,*] the sacred capitol, to which the vassal nations and kings are bound, His response to their resolution, v.³ᵇ. **7a.** *Declaring the decree of Yahweh*] so 𝕲; these are, however, the words of the poet depending on v.⁵, and probably originally immediately following it, the decree being the words of Yahweh v.⁶, the inviolable law binding all vassals to His dominion: in antith. to v.²ᶜ. The transposition of this line led 𝕲 to interpret it as words of the king beginning, however, v.⁶, and 𝕳 to make the words of the king begin with v.⁷, both at the expense of the parall. and strs. The Ps. in this decree is thinking of the covenant which Yahweh made with David through Nathan the prophet, constituting David and his seed an everlasting dynasty. That dynasty was set or installed in David, and continued in his seed forever. This covenanted dominion cannot be thrown off. Though it be limited in the time of the poet to a small territory and to a small people, it is, in his ideal, world-wide, universal, over all the nations and kings of the earth. The ideal will certainly be realized, for it is a divine decree; and though nations and kings may plot to overthrow the dominion, as they did that of the world-powers of Assyria and Babylonia, they will not succeed; for the world-power of the king is so identified with Yahweh's dominion that that very thought will terrify the rebellious into submission. Zion the *sacred mount*, consecrated by the theophanic presence of Yahweh in His temple, is the seat of the dominion, the residence, of the anointed king, the capitol of the world, to which all nations and kings are bound, whether by cords of love or bands of iron, cf. Is. 2²⁻⁴; Mi. 4¹⁻⁴ where the mountain of the house of Yahweh is the resort of all nations for instruction and government, in order to universal peace.

Str. III. 7b. *Yahweh said unto me*] David himself speaks as the father and representative of his dynasty, quoting Yahweh's words to him by Nathan the prophet. These words are in three progressive couplets, each in syn. parall. within itself. — *My son art thou ‖ I, to-day, have begotten thee*] David and his seed were adopted as Yahweh's Son on the day of the institution of the

Davidic covenant, when first David reigned by right of divine sonship. The poet ideally combines the installation of David, 2 S. 2⁴, with the covenant recognition of sonship, 2 S. 7¹¹⁻¹⁶; although the former took place some years earlier. This was an unfolding of the earlier covenant with Israel which constituted Israel as a people, the firstborn son of God, Ex. 4²²⁻²³ (J.), a kingdom of priests, Ex. 19³⁻⁶ (E.). Now the Davidic line, by divine institution, becomes the son and king in a nation, which remains both son and kingdom in larger relations. — **8.** *The nations* ‖ *the ends of the earth*] A universal, world-wide dominion over them was not contemplated in the covenant with David. The *inheritance* ‖ *possession* of the kingdom of Israel was the holy land, Gen. 12¹⁻³, 49¹⁰ ˢq· (*v.* Br. ᴹᴾ ⁴⁸¹ ˢq·) ; that of David's seed, the holy land and holy people. The rule of David extended over Ammon, Moab, Edom, Syria, Philistia ; but never reached the extent of the old empires of Egypt, Babylonia, or the Hittites. Subsequently the kingdom of David was divided, each section was reduced, and finally destroyed, the Northern kingdom by Assyria, the Southern by Babylon. These arose successively as the great world-powers ; making it evident that if the Davidic kingdom was to be in fact an everlasting kingdom, it must be a world-power, and have ultimate and universal dominion. This logical result of the Davidic covenant, in the light of the history of Babylonia, becomes to the poets of Pss. 2, 89 an essential part of the original covenant, and is put here ideally in the mouth of David himself. — **9.** The rule of the Messiah is to be with *an iron sceptre*, because he has to do with rebellious nations, and these will only obey an iron rule ; even though all their array of kings and nations are as *a potter's vessel* when brought in conflict with the power of the one king who rules as the son of God.

Str. IV. If we take the last line of the Psalm as original, it is necessary to think of the poet as speaking the warning ; but then we are struck by the absence of the Messiah. If, however, we regard that line as a liturgical addition, it is better to think of David himself as warning the kings. There are three couplets of warning, with a concluding line giving the reason for it. The first and second are syn. couplets, progressive one to the other ; the third is a synth. couplet progressive to the second. Line by line this antistr. corresponds with its str. **10–11**. *Act prudently, O kings*]. You have to deal with Yahweh's words, v.⁷ᵃ ‖ *be admonished, governors of earth*]. You have to do with Yahweh's son, v.⁷ᵇ ‖ *Serve Yahweh with fear*], as vassals, not in the usual religious sense of worship and obedience to the Law; to serve Yahweh's son is to serve Him, v.⁷ᶜ. — *rejoice in Him with trembling*]. Yahweh has given the nations for the king's inheritance, v.⁸ᵃ, that is a reason for rejoicing; but that joy should be accompanied with trembling lest He be displeased. — **12**. *Kiss sincerely*] the kiss of the hands in worship, cf. Jb. 31²⁷. Worship in purity and fidelity, "with a pure heart" JPSV. because He has given the ends of the earth for the possession of His king, v.⁸ᵇ. ⅁ paraphrases or had a different text in rendering "lay hold of instruction." EVˢ. "kiss the son," the Messiah, cannot be justified by usage or context, and is based on a misinterpretation due to Syriac and Aramaic influence. If the rulers do not render sincere homage, they may fear *lest He be angry* ‖ *lest ye perish*]. He rules with an iron sceptre, v.⁹ᵃ; you cannot resist it successfully, you will perish if you try, therefore submit in joy and fear. The reason for this warning is now given, *For quickly His anger will be kindled*]. This is the climax corresponding with the climax of the previous str., v.⁹ᵇ. A liturgical editor adds a general statement which does not suit the ideal situation of the Ps., but which is appropriate to the congregation when they use it in worship. — *Happy are all seeking refuge in Him.*

1. ‡לָ֫מָּה] *2¹* 42¹⁰ 43² 44²⁴· ²⁵ 49⁶ 68¹⁷ 74¹¹ 79¹⁰ 80¹⁸ 115²; but ‡לָמָה 10¹ 22² 42¹⁰ 43² 74¹ 88¹⁵; no satisfactory explanation of difference has yet been given (Ges.§ 102 (2) *l*, Ges.ᴸ 49. 2 ʀ; 102 ʀ, Kö. I. p. 144; II. pp. 461b, 517 (2), B*D*B.). (*a*) expostulation, *for what reason, why, wherefore:* c. pf. of God 22² 42¹⁰ 43² 74¹ 80¹⁸; of nations *2¹*; impf. of God 10¹ 44²⁴· ²⁵ 74¹¹ 88¹⁵; of man 42¹⁰ = 43²; mountains 68¹⁷. (*b*) Deprecating, *why should*, c. impf. of man 49⁶ 79¹⁰ = 115². — †רָגְשׁוּ] *a.λ.* Qal pf. 3 pl. √רגש usually explained as cog. with רעשׁ and so *a noisy, tumultuous assembling*, after 𝔙 *turbabuntur;* but in late Heb. this mng. is confined to Hithp., and it is doubtful whether the mng. *tumultuatus est* of 𝔖 is early. At all events this mng. is not suited to the context in any of the forms from the stem in the Heb. or Aram. of OT. The ordinary mng. of the simple form of the stem in Aram. and Syr. is *observe, experience*, so Hiph. of late Heb. It is better to build on this. The noun [רָגֶשׁ ‖ סוד] 55¹⁵ must mean either *company, companionship*, or *concord;* so

𝕲 ἐν ὁμονοίᾳ *in concord*, AV. *in company*; but 𝕵 *cum terrore*, RV. *with the throng* are both unsuited to the intimate fellowship of friendship in syn. line. The noun [רִגְשָׁה ‖ רֶגֶשׁ] סוד 64⁸ = 𝕵 *a tumultu*, 𝕲 ἀπὸ πλήθους, AV. *insurrection*, RV. *tumult*; but none of these is so appropriate as *companionship, concord*, or possibly *conspiracy*, for some such mng. seems to be required by the synonymous סוד. It is noteworthy that in our Ps. רגשׁ vb. is synonymous with נוסרו from יסר denom. סוד (see below), and the syn. parall. urges a similar mng. such as *be in concord, consent together*, for *consensus* is an easy derivative from *sensus*, the normal mng. of stem in Aram. This mng. best suits the context. Such a poet as the author of our Ps. would hardly begin with an anticlimax. It should also be said that these three uses, the only ones in Bibl. Heb., are all in 𝕳. It may also be said that the Aphel of רגשׁ Aram. Dn. 6⁷·¹²·¹⁶ cannot with propriety have the strong mng. of *tumultuous assembling*. The Persian officials would hardly come to their king עַל ר׳ v.⁷·¹⁶ in such a fashion, nor would they be likely in this way to assemble to watch Daniel at prayer, v.¹². The context and the situation would suit better their coming together *in concord* or *in common consent, with one accord*, to watch Daniel and to influence the king. 𝕲 ἐφρύαξαν *behave arrogantly* seems to be a paraphrase, rather than a translation. Since writing the above I have noticed that Ehr. takes essentially the same view with me. — [גוים] pl. 53 t. in ψ, always of foreign nations; sg. coll. of foreign nations 43¹ 105¹³·¹³ 147²⁰; of Israel 33¹² 83⁵ 106⁵. — [לאמים] pl. of לְאֹם prop. *common, vulgar people* (BDB.); poet. sg. *people*, both of Israel and Edom Gn. 25²³ (J), elsw. of Israel Is. 51⁴; usually pl. of foreign peoples 2¹ 7⁸ 9⁹ 44³·¹⁵ 47⁴ 57¹⁰ 65⁸ 67⁵·⁵ 105⁴⁴ 108⁴ 148¹¹ 149⁷. — [יֶהְגּוּ] Qal impf. 3 pl. הגה (see 1²) frequentative of repeated action, in the discussion and elaboration of devices over against the emphatic present רגשׁ. The tetrastich begins and closes with pf., including the two impfs. The change of tense is awkward in a question. It is probable that the question closes with v.¹, and that v.² is a statement of fact. — רִיק and [רֵיק] are mixed in MT., both adj. [רִיק] vb. Hiph. (1) *pour out* or *down*, of rain, *empty* vessels, not in ψ. (2) c. acc. *draw* sword, either from scabbard (emptying it) or as using to pour out blood, common in Ez., not in ψ, which uses, however, ‖ *draw out* lance Pss. 35⁸ 18⁴³ (text err.). רִיק adj. is not used in 𝕳 of ψ either in mng. *empty* of vessels, or *vain, idle, worthless* of persons or things. רִיק adj. is usually † adverbial לריק *in vain*, of labour without benefit or advantage Lv. 26¹⁶·²⁰ (H.) Is. 49⁴ 65²³ Jb. 39¹⁶, abbreviated ריק Ps. 73¹³ Is. 30⁷ Je. 51⁵⁸ = Hb. 2¹³. It is prob. that רִיק in Ps. 2¹ belongs here = *in vain*, and that רֵיק 4⁸ should be pointed רִיק *vain, unprofitable thing* ‖ כזב as Pr. 12¹¹ = 28¹⁹. If Ps. 2¹ is to have that mng., it also should be pointed רִיק. — 2. [יִתְיַצְּבוּ] Hithp. impf. of graphic description √[יצב], Niph., Hiph., Hoph. are derived from [נצב]. Both Niph. (√נצב) and Hithp. (√יצב) have the same mng., *station oneself, take one's stand*. ‡ Hithp. abs. here (2²) and 1 S. 17¹⁶ *taking a stand to fight*, elsw. in ψ *taking a stand for* one against the workers of iniquity 94¹⁶; *holding one's ground* 5⁶; in a way of life 36⁵. ‡ Niph. *take one's stand*: c. ב of place, God to plead 82¹; queen at right hand of monarch in ceremony of marriage 45[10] ; *stand firm*, of man 39[6] (text dub.); of Yahweh's word 119[89]. ‡ Hiph. (1) *set, station* 41[18] ; (2) *fix, establish*, boundary 74[17], cf. Dt. 32[8] ; (3) *cause to stand erect*, of waters 78[18]. There is no sufficient reason to substitute here יחיעצו as Lag., We., Oort. — † מַלְכֵי אֶרֶץ] *kings of earth :* 2[2] 76[18] 89[28] 148[11] Ez. 27[33] La. 4[12] ; with כל prefixed Pss. 102[16] 138[4] 1 K. 10[23] = 2 Ch. 9[22. 23] ; earlier kings of the land Jos. 12[1. 7] ; similar † שֹׁפְטֵי ארץ] Ps. 2[10] Is. 40[23], with כל prefixed Ps. 148[11] Pr. 8[16] ; also † כָּל מַמְלְכוֹת הָאָרֶץ *all the kingdoms of earth* Dt. 28[25] 2 K. 19[15. 19] (= Is. 37[16. 20]) Ezr. 1[2] (= 2 C. 36[23]) Is. 23[17] Je. 15[4] 24[9] 25[26] 29[18] 34[1. 17], without כל Ps. 68[33]. Chr. uses rather † (כל) מַמְלְכוֹת הָאֲרָצוֹת 1 Ch. 29[30] 2 Ch. 12[8] 17[10] 20[29]. The phrases centre in the time of Jeremiah. † רוֹזְנִים] *princes*, Qal ptc. [√רזן], only pl. ‖ מלכים here (2[2]) Ju. 5[3] Hb. 1[10] Pr. 8[15] 31[4] ; ‖ שפטים Is. 40[23]. — † נִיסְרוּ] Niph. pf. emphatic present יסר denom. סור Ges.§78 (v. רגש above), *treat about, discuss, consult*, 𝔍 *tractabunt*, 𝔖 συσκέπτονται, so Bä., Bu., Du., so הִוָּסְרוּ 31[14]. 𝔊 (of 2[2]) συνήχθησαν seems to have rd. נֵיעֲדוּ, so Lag., Oort, *BDB*.; Ges., SS., *al.* derive from יסר *fix, establish*, Niph. *sit in conclave*. ‡ יַחַד] as adv. *together :* (1) community, in action, consult. 2[2] 31[14] ; place, *in same place* 88[18] 133[1] ; in time, *at the same time* 141[10]. (2) *all together, altogether* 33[15] 40[15] 41[8] 62[10] 74[6. 8] 98[8]. (3) together in the sense of *alike*, the one as well as the other 49[3. 11]. See *BDB.* — עַל] *against*, repeated before מְשִׁיחוֹ, separates him emphatically from יהוה. There are two beats of accent on וְעַל־מְשִׁיחוֹ. — מָשִׁיחַ] n. m. sf. *His anointed*, sf. referring to Yahweh. √משׁח *anoint*, spec. *consecrate* to an office. † מָשִׁיחַ is used of high priest of Israel Lv. 4[3. 5. 16] 6[15] (P) Ps. 84[10] ; of Cyrus as commissioned by Yahweh Is. 45[1] ; of the prince Dn. 9[25. 26] ; of patriarchs Ps. 105[15] = 1 Ch. 16[22] ; elsw. of kings of Israel anointed by divine command 1 S. 12[3. 5] 16[6] 20[7] 24[7. 7. 11] 26[9. 11. 16. 23], 2S. 1[14. 16] 19[22] 23[1] La. 4[20] Hb. 3[13] Pss. 20[7] 28[8], and esp. of Davidic dynasty with Messianic ideals Pss. 2[2] 18[51] (= 2 S. 22[51]) 89[39. 52] 132[10] (= 2 Ch. 6[42])[17], 1 S. 2[10. 35]. — 3. וְנַתְּקָה] Piel impf. cohort. 1 pl., expressing resolution, *we will*, or exhortation, *let us tear apart.* ‡ נתק Piel *tear apart, snap :* c. acc. מוֹסְרוֹת Je. 2[20] 5[5] 30[8] Na. 1[13] Ps. 2[3] 107[14]. — מוֹסְרוֹתֵימוֹ] 3 pl. sf., fuller form for יְהֶם, used to soften, make more euphonious the ending ; espec. for the assonance which continues for six successive lines. † מוֹסֵר] = מַאסָר *bond* (√אסר *tie, bind*); subj. *bonds made strong* (those imposed by Assyria) Is. 28[22] ; elsw. obj. made to symbolize those of Babylon Je. 27[2] ; פתח מ׳ *loose bonds* Ps. 116[6] Is. 52[2] Jb. 39[5] ; cf. 12[18] ; elsw. נתק מ׳ 2[3] 107[14] Je. 2[20] 5[5] 30[8] Na. 1[13]. — וְנַשְׁלִיכָה] Waw coörd. with Hiph. cohort. 1 pl. — מִמֶּנּוּ] reduplication of מן with strong sf. 1 pl. 2[3] 103[12] ; same as 3 mpl. (but Orientals point 1 pl. מִמֶּנּוּ Baer[Jb. p. 57], Kö.[I. 290]). — ‡ עֲבֹת *twisted cord, rope :* 2[3] 118[27] 129[4]. — 4. יוֹשֵׁב] Qal ptc. nominal force : the ordinary mngs., *sit, sit down, dwell*, do not suit here, only the ‡ pregn. *one sitting enthroned :* (1) usually of God 9[8] 29[10] 55[20] 102[18] 132[14] ; also מכון שברו *place of His sitting enthroned* (heaven) 33[14] ; המגביהי לשבת *He who exalts to sit enthroned* 113[5] ; ההר חמד לשבתו *the mount on which He desired to sit enthroned* 68[17] ; בשמים 2[4] 123[1] ; c. ל *loci* 80[2] (ה) כרובים 9[12] ציון ; acc. *loci* על כסא 47[9] ; c. על *loci* 29[10] לַטֲבוּל 9[6] לכסא

99¹; ישראל תחלות 22⁴. (2) of Davidic king, before God 61⁸; at His right hand 110¹; successive kings לכסא 132¹²; c. acc. כסאות 122⁶. — [וְיִשְׁחָק] impf. Qal i. p. graphic description. √‡ שׂחק *laugh at*, of God, c. ל 37¹⁸ 59⁹; of man, c. על 52⁸. As 59⁹ depends on *24*, it is prob. that למו followed ישׂחק in original text. This is sustained by 𝕲 and rhyme of previous and subsequent lines. Piel *sport, play* 104²⁶. — אֲדֹנִי (pointing ־ֲ to disting. from ־ִ, used of men): originally *my sovereign lord* 16² 86³·⁴·⁵; so here ‖ one enthroned (though 59⁹ cites as יהוה); subsequently *Adonay*, as proper name (*v*. Intr. § 32). — [וְיִלְעַג] Qal impf. 3 p. cited as 2 p. 59⁹ √‡ לעג *mock, deride;* also 80⁷ and prob. 35¹⁶ (𝕲). Hiph. 22⁸ same mng., prob. also Qal originally. —
5. ‡[אָז] adv. *v*. B*D*B. (1) *temporal* (*a*) past, *then*, sq. pf. 89²⁰; (*b*) future, sq. impf. 56¹⁰(?); (*c*) emph. of particular features of description *2⁵* 40⁸(?) 96¹²; (*d*) pointing back with emph. to inf. with בּ 126²·²; (2) *logical sequence*, sq. impf. 19¹⁴ 51²¹·²¹ 69⁵(?) 119⁶·⁹². — [אֲלֵימוֹ] full sf. for rhyme, prob. therefore original close of line: usual prep. with רבר. — [בְּאַפּוֹ] prep. בּ and sf. ‡ אַף: (1) *nostril* as organ of breathing 18⁹·¹⁶, smelling 115⁶; אֶרֶךְ אפים prolonged breathing, *long suffering* of God 86¹⁵ 103⁸ 145⁸, based on Ex. 34⁶ (J); elsw. (2) *anger*, (*a*) of man Pss. 37⁸ 55⁴ 124³ 138⁷; usually (*b*) of God *2¹²* 10⁴ 74¹ 76⁸ 78²¹·⁸¹·⁸⁸·⁵⁰ 85⁶ 90¹¹ 106⁴⁰ 110⁶, באף *2⁵* 6² 7⁷ 21¹⁰ 27⁹ 30⁶ 56⁸ 77¹⁰ 90⁷ 95¹¹, אף חרון 69²⁵ 78⁴⁹ 85⁴; denom. vb. †אנף is term of D. Qal *be angry*, of Yahweh, c. בּ 85⁶ 1 K. 8⁴⁶ (= 2 C. 6³⁶) Is. 12¹ Ezr. 9¹⁴, abs. Ps. *2¹²* 60³ 79⁵ Hithp. *id*. of Yahweh c. בּ Dt. 1⁸⁷ 4²¹ 9⁸·²⁰ 1 K. 11⁹ 2 K. 17¹⁸. — [בַּחֲרוֹנוֹ] prep. בּ sf. חרון nm. √‡ חָרָה with אף subj. 106⁴⁰ 124³ *anger burn agst.*, but without and so impers., c. ל 18⁸; term of EJD. chiefly with preëxilic writers, not of HP., Je., Ez., Is.² † Hithp. *heat oneself* in vexation Ps. 37¹·⁷·⁸ Pr. 24¹⁹, ‡ חרון alw. of God's burning anger, usually in phr. אף חרון 69²⁵ 78⁴⁹ 85⁴ as Ex. 32¹² Nu. 25⁴ 32¹⁴ Jos. 7²⁶ (all J) +, phr. chiefly preëxilic prophets; אף is omitted only Ex. 15⁷ (song) Ne. 13¹⁸ Ez. 7¹² (del. Co.)¹⁴ Ps. 58¹⁰ (dub. text) 88¹⁷ (pl. *bursts of burning anger*). It is quite prob. that in *2⁵* originally the text was חרון אפו which is certainly more rhythmical. — [וִיבַהֲלֵמוֹ] Piel impf. full sf. for rhyme. ‡ [√בהל] not in Qal but Niph. *be disturbed, dismayed, terrified* 6³·⁴·¹¹ 30⁸ 48⁶ 83¹⁸ 90⁷ 104²⁹ Gn. 45³ (E) Ex. 15¹⁵ (song). Piel subj. Yahweh, *dismay, terrify* Pss. *2⁵* 83¹⁶, elsw. late 2 C. 32¹⁸ Dn. 11⁴⁴ Jb. 22¹⁰. — **6.** [וַאֲנִי] ו introd. 𝕲, 𝔜, 𝔍, pron. emphatic, solemn proclamation. — † [נָסַכְתִּי] pf. Qal aorist of single historic act. Vb. variously explained: (1) *pour out*, of libation and of molten metal, and so *anoint* king; so 𝕮 Σ ἔχρισα (cf. Acts 4²⁷ ἔχρισας) Ges., Ew., JPSV. (2) *weave a web*, after Is. 25⁷, so ἐδιασάμην Aq. Quinta 𝔍. (3) 𝕲 κατεστάθην, 𝔜 *ordinatus sum*, 𝔖 *set, install*, cf. As. *nasâku*, whence *nasîku prince*, cf. Heb. † [נָסִיךְ] Jos. 13²¹ Ez. 32³⁰ Mi. 5⁴ Ps. 83¹²; so AV., RV., most moderns, who differ only as to whether (3) is derived from (1) as De., Pe., Bu., SS., or whether it was an independent original stem, BDB. There are but two examples: here (*2⁶*) Qal pf. and Pr. 8²³ Niph. pf. נִסַּכְתִּי; but 𝕲 rds. Niph. here also ἐγὼ δὲ κατεστάθην βασιλεὺς ὑπ' αὐτοῦ = ואני נסכתי מלכי *now I, I was installed His king*. This is preferred by Du. There has been an assimilation by 𝕲 of Ps. *2⁶* to

Pr. 8²⁸, which required קרשו for קרשׁ of 𝔅 v⁶ᵇ and subordination of אֶסְפְּרָה in ptc. clause. However, 𝔈 rds. *sanctum eius*. 𝔅 suits context and division of strophes. Introduction of the king, as speaking in v.⁶ instead of Yahweh, destroys parall. with Str. I. and makes v.⁷ᵇ tautological. — [מַלְכִּי] *my king*, so as Yahweh's representative = משיחו v.²; 𝔊 מלכו = 𝔏, both interp. of original מֶלֶךְ.—הַמֶּלֶךְ. nm. (1) for kings other than the line of David 33¹⁶ 45¹⁴ 105²⁰· ³⁰ (rd. sg.) 135¹¹· ¹¹ = 136¹⁹· ²⁰ ; pl. see v.² ‡ (2) for king of David's line (either real or ideal of Mess. promise) ⨀⁶ 18⁵¹ 20¹⁰ 21². ⁸ 45². ⁶· ¹². ¹⁵· ¹⁶ 61⁷ 63¹² 72¹· ¹ 89¹⁹ 144¹⁰ (rd. sg. מ֯.). ‡ (3) of God as *the king* 5⁸ 10¹⁶ 24⁷· ⁸· ⁹· ¹⁰· ¹⁰ 29¹⁰ 44⁵ 47²· ⁷· ⁸ 48³ 68²⁵ 74¹² 84⁴ 95³ 98⁵ 99⁴ 145¹ 149². There is no usage in ψ justifying the opinion of some recent scholars that מלך was used for the nation as the kingdom of God. — [עַל צִיּוֹן] *upon Zion*, poetic name for the city of God, where He resides as king and from whence in theophanic presence He rules. ‡ צִיּוֹן usually in ψ alone 9¹²· ¹⁵ 48¹³ 51²⁰ 65² 69³⁶ 76³ 84⁸ 87²· ⁵ 97⁸ 99² 102¹⁴· ¹⁷· ²² 126¹ 129⁵ 132¹³ 137¹· ³ 146¹⁰ 147¹² ; מציון 147⁷ (= 53⁷) 20⁸ 50² 110² 128⁵ 134⁸ 135²¹ 149² ; הר ציון 48³· ¹² 74² 78⁰⁸ 125¹ Is. 24²³ + ; ז הָרֲרֵי יֹ 133³. — [הַר קָדְשִׁי] *my holy mount;* cstr. best translated in Eng. by adj., not *mount of my holiness.* 𝔊 ἅγιον αὐτοῦ is a diff. interp. from 𝔅 of an original הקרשׁ. † הר קרשׁ as seat of Yahweh's presence 3⁵ 15¹ 43⁸ 48² 99⁹, elsw. Is. 11⁹ 27¹³ 56⁷ 57¹³ 65¹¹· ²⁵ 66²ᴵ, Zp. 3¹¹ Jo. 2¹ Ob.¹⁶ Zc. 8³ Ez. 20⁴⁰ Je. 31²³ Dn. 9¹⁶· ²⁰; in Ez. 28³⁴ the reference is to the Oriental Olympus in N.W. Asia ; ציון הר קרשׁ only Ps. ⨀⁶ Jo. 4¹⁷, הר צבי קרשׁ Dn. 11⁴⁵. The sacred mount elsw. הר ציון (see above), הר יהוה 24³, הר האלהים 68¹⁶, and (ה)הר defined by context 68¹⁷ 78⁵⁴ ; cf. יֹ הָרֲרֵי ק 87¹ 110³ (?) also 30⁸ (?) 76⁵ (?). — 7. [אֶסְפְּרָה] Pi. impf. I sg. cohort. ספר; attached by 𝔊 as ptc. clause to previous v.; so Aq., 𝔈, Du., and by 𝔖 as a final clause impf. 3 sg. As usual in such cases they are varied interpretations of an original text which in this case would be ספר inf. abs., *v.* Ges.§ ¹¹³. Str. II. is one line too short, which is improb. in such an artistic poem. Either it has been omitted by copyist, or is to be found in v.⁷, which is too long. v.⁷ᵃ seems more appropriate before v.⁶, where it gives fine antith. to v.²ᶜ ; so Bi., Che. ; prob. it was transposed by scribal error. This occasioned all the difficulties. — [אֶל חֹק] ‡ חֹק n. m. *something prescribed, a statute*, or *due,* (1) *prescribed limit, boundary*, of heavens 148⁶, (2) *enactment, decree, ordinance*, law of festival 81⁵ ; so here, decree of Yahweh respecting Mess. king; covenant with Jacob 105¹⁰ ; law in general 94²⁰ 99⁷, pl. הֻקִּים *statutes,* of the Law 50¹⁶ 105⁴⁵ 119⁵⁺ ²¹ ᵗ· ⁽ᵉᵐ· ᵗˣᵗ·⁾ 147¹⁹. חֻקָּה pl. of חֹק n.f. *statutes* of type of Holiness code (see Br.ᴴᵉˣ· ²⁵¹) 18²³ 89³² 119¹⁶ (?). It is prob. that, with Houb., Bi., Gr., We., Du., Oort, original reading here was חק יהוה *decree of Yahweh,* which is favoured by Vrss. ; τὸ πρόσταγμα κυρίου. κύριος εἶπεν 𝔊, *praeceptum eius. dominus dixit* 𝔈, *dei praeceptum. dominus dixit* 𝔍. חק without article is too indefinite. אֶל is prob. interp. of 𝔅, as it was not in text of 𝔊 and is a late use of אֶל for עַל. The emendation אֶת, Houb., Bi., We., is improbable. 𝔍, Aq., Θ, 𝔖, 4 codd. De R. have אֵל = *God,* which may be, by an error of transposition, for an original חק אל. This, however, gives bad measure. 𝔊 is in all respects the best reading. — [בְּנִי אַתָּה] is a defective line; add הָיִיתָ after 2 S. 7¹⁴ (והוא יהוה לי לבן); the vb. omitted by prosaic copyist because unnecessary to the sense, the copula often being implied in pers. pronouns. אַתָּה with *pattach* in pause, for אָתָּה, an early copyist's mistake to which attention is called by Mas. — אֲנִי] emph. as above, v.⁶ᵃ. — ‡ הַיּוֹם] *to-day, this day:* 2⁷ 95⁷ 119⁹¹. — יְלִדְתִּיךָ] Qal perf. of completed action in time of speaker for יְלַדְתִּיךָ, which is explained by Ew.§ ¹⁹⁹ᵇ from attraction of antecedent ·; by Ges.§ ⁴⁴ᵈ as possibly derived from יָלַד; by Hu. as due to removal of accent (cf. יְלִדְתַּנִי Je. 15¹⁰; יְלִדְתִּיהוּ Nu. 11¹²); prob. copyist's mistake. ‡ ילד vb. Qal used (1) c. 208 t. for mother bearing child, so Ps. 48⁷, fig. 7¹⁵; (2) of father begetting child, in J 11 t. (= 1 C. 1¹⁰ ⁺ ⁵ ᵗ·) Dt. 32¹⁸ (song) Nu. 11¹² (E both dub.); elsw. only Pr. 17²¹ 23²². ²⁴ Dn. 11⁶; P. and Ch. use Hiph. הוֹלִיד in this sense, so Ru. 4¹⁸ ⁺ ⁸ ᵗ· Ju. 11¹ 2 K. 20¹⁸ = Is. 39⁷ Je. 16⁸ 29⁶ Ez. 18¹⁰. ¹⁴ 47²² Ec. 5¹³ 6³ Is. 45¹⁰. The usage of our Ps. is either early or very late, not in accord with that of exilic literature. Niph. *be born:* Pss. 22³² 78⁶. Pual *be born:* 87⁴. ⁵. ⁶ 90². — **8.** שְׁאַל מִמֶּנִּי] is prob. a gloss. It makes line too long, however we may divide vers.; and str. is complete without it as additional line. It was natural that a gloss of petition should come on the margin of such a divine promise yet unrealized; cf. for similar gloss 110²ᵃ.—וְאֶתְּנָה] ו introducing apodosis of שְׁאַל, but prob. it came into text with gloss; vb. Qal impf. cohort. of נתן, corresponding with cohortative of two previous strophes v.³. ⁷ᵃ.—נַחֲלָתֶךָ] *inheritance,* cf. 111⁶; a term esp. characteristic of D. and Je., but also used by P. and later writers. ‡ אֲחֻזָּה] *possession,* α.λ. ψ, but term of P., Ez., Chr.—†אַפְסֵי־אָרֶץ] *ends, extreme limits of earth.* There should be a secondary accent here. The phr. elsw. 22²⁸ 59¹⁴ 67⁸ 72⁸ (= Zc. 9¹⁰) 98³ᵇ (= Is. 52¹⁰ᵇ) Is. 45²² Je. 16¹⁹ Dt. 33¹⁷ 1 S. 2¹⁰ Mi. 5³ Pr. 30⁴. — **9.** תְּרֹעֵם] Qal impf. 2 m. sf. 3 pl. of רעע *break in pieces,* so Σ, ℭ, Aram. of רצע, not used elsw. in ψ; Qal only Jb. 34²⁴ and other very late passages of Greek period (see BDB.) Je. 11¹⁶ 15¹² Pr. 25¹⁹. Hithpo. only Is. 24¹⁹ (?) Pr. 18²⁴. But 𝔊 Rev. 2²⁷ ποιμανεῖν, תִּרְעֵם 𝔖,𝔘,𝔍 *rule as shepherd king over them,* is more suited to the context of the sceptre, even if it be of iron; so 78⁷¹. ⁷², cf. 28⁹ 49¹⁵ 80² 2 S. 5² 7⁷ Je. 3¹⁵ Mi. 5³ Ez. 37²⁴ Na. 3¹⁸ +. — שֵׁבֶט בַּרְזֶל] phr. α.λ. ‡ שֵׁבֶט n. *rod:* (1) *sceptre* of monarch 2⁹ 45⁷. ⁷ 125³, of rod of Yahweh 23⁴ 89³³; (2) *tribe* 74² 78⁵⁵. ⁶⁷. ⁶⁸ 105⁸⁷ 122⁴. ⁴.—תְּנַפְּצֵם] Piel impf. sf. √† נפץ. Qal *shatter,* vessels Ju. 7¹⁹, fig. Je. 22²⁸ Dn. 12⁷ (possibly Piel). Piel *dash in pieces,* c. acc. infants, Ps. 137⁹ agst. rock; nations with Babylon as a war club Je. 51²⁰ ⁺ ⁸ ᵗ·, people like jars Je. 13¹⁴ 48¹², so here like pottery cf. 1 K. 5²³. Pual pass. Is. 27⁹ altar stones pulverized. — † כְּלִי יוֹצֵר] *potter's vessel,* made by the potter out of clay, and so easily broken 2 S. 17²⁸ Je. 19¹¹. — **10.** וְעַתָּה] as 27⁶ 39⁸ 119⁶⁷, cf. וְעַל 74⁶ ‡ עַתָּה 12⁶ 17¹¹ 20⁷. ‡ מַעַתָּה 113² 115¹⁸ 121⁸ 125² 131⁸.—הַשְׂכִּילוּ] Hiph. imv. 2 pl. √‡ שכל (1) *consider, regard, give attention to,* c. acc. 64¹⁰ 106⁷, c. אל pers. 41² (?), c. ב *rei* 101², abs. 94⁸; (2) *have insight* 119⁹⁹; (3) *act with circumspection, prudence, insight* 2¹⁰ 36⁴, ptc. משכיל 14² = 53³ Am. 5¹³ Pr. 10⁵ ⁺ ⁵ ᵗ· Pr. Jb. 22²; (4) *later, give insight, teach* Ps. 32⁸; cf. משכיל n. in titles (*v.* Intr.§ ²⁶).—הִוָּסְרוּ] imv. Niph. ‡ יסר Qal *discipline,* subj. God 94¹⁰ Ho. 10¹⁰. † Niph. *let oneself be admonished, cor-*

rected Ps. 2¹⁰ as Pr. 29¹⁹, chastened by discipline of God Je. 6⁸ 31¹⁸ Lv. 26²⁸.
Piel (1) *discipline, correct* the moral nature, with more or less severity acc.
to circumstances, subj. God 94¹² 118¹⁸˙ ¹⁸, subj. man's reins 16⁷; (2) more
severely, *chasten, chastise*, subj. God 6² (= 38²) 39¹² Je. 10²⁴ 30¹¹ 31¹⁸ 46²⁸
Lv. 26¹⁸˙ ²⁸; common in WL. — שְׂפָתֵי אָרֶץ] retracted accent on acct. of following monosyl.; so הֹאבדו v. ¹²ᵃ, חֹוסי v.¹²ᶜ: for phr. *v.* v.². — **11.** [עִבְדוּ אֶת־יהוה
Qal imv. √‡ עבד (1) the primitive mng. *serve* with service, work, is not in ψ;
but (2) as vassals of Davidic king 18⁴⁴ 72¹¹, of Yahweh 2¹¹ 102²⁸; (3) with
worship, as His people 22³¹ 100²; so idols 97⁷ 106⁸⁶. — [בְּיִרְאָה ‡ n.f.
(1) *fear, terror* 2¹¹ 55⁶; usually *fear* of God, *reverence, piety* 5⁸ 34¹²
90¹¹ 111¹⁰ 119³⁸; so for מורא, the Law as object of reverence 19¹⁰, cf. 76¹².
— [וְגִילוּ] Qal imv. ‡ גיל vb. Qal *rejoice:* abs. 13⁵ 51¹⁰; ‖ שׂמח 14⁷ 16⁹ 32¹¹ 48¹²
53⁷ 96¹¹ 97¹˙ ⁸; c. בְּ 149²; בישועתך 9¹⁵ 13⁶ 21²; ביהוה 35⁹; בשם י' 89¹⁷;
גיל וישׂמח ב 31⁸ 118²⁴ Ct. 1⁴ Is. 25⁹ Jo. 2²³; all these with pers. subj., but subj.
לב Ps. 13⁶, נפשׁ 35⁹, כבוד (‖ נפשׁ) 16⁹, ארץ 96¹¹ 97¹; such overwhelming usage
makes it improb. that 2¹¹ and Hos. 10⁵ should have the exceptional mng.
tremble (cf. Ar. stems with the mng. *go round* or *about, be excited to levity*, etc.),
although supported by Ges., Ew., Hi., Che. for Ps. 2¹¹ and by Ges. and most
moderns for Ho. 10⁵; but 𝔊, Hu., De., Pe., AV., RV., *rejoice* for Ps. 2¹¹, and
AV., RV. for Ho. 10⁵ (the latter possibly error for חיל Ew., Gr.). ‡ גִיל n.
rejoicing: 43⁴ 45¹⁶ 65¹³. 𝔊 rds. ἀγαλλιᾶσθε αὐτῷ, which implies גילו בו.
This completes the line and makes it entirely synonymous with the preceding.
בי גילו was omitted by txt. err. because of confusion of בו with לו in גילו. —
† [רְעָדָה] n.f., c. ב; cf. 55⁶; ‖ פַּחַד Jb. 4¹⁴; elsw. Ps. 48⁷, cf. Is. 33¹⁴ also Ex. 15¹⁵.
— **12.** [נַשְּׁקוּ] Pi. imv. of ‡ נשׁק Qal *kiss* (1) of affection, usually c. לְ pers.
Gn. 27²⁶˙ ²⁷ 29¹¹ 50¹ Ex. 4²⁷ (J) Gn. 48¹⁰ Ex. 18⁷ (E) 2 S. 14³³ 15⁵ 19⁴⁰ 20⁹
1 K. 19²⁰ Pr. 7¹⁸ Ru. 1⁹˙ ¹⁴; c. acc. pers. Gn. 33⁴ (JE dub. form) 1 S. 10¹ 20⁴¹
Ct. 1² 8¹; *lips* Pr. 24²⁶; of divine attributes, abs. Ps. 85¹¹; (2) of idolatrous
worship: c. לְ 1 K. 19¹⁸ Jb. 31²⁷ (hand to the mouth); c. acc. calves Ho. 13²:
עַל פִי Gn. 41⁴⁰ (dub.). Pi. *kiss:* (1) of affection; c. לְ pers. Gn. 29¹⁸ (J)
31²⁸ 32¹ 45¹⁵ (E); (2) here only of worship; Aq. καταφιλήσατε, Σ προσκυ-
νήσατε, 𝔍 *adorate.* Hiph. *kiss:* c. אל of wings of cherubim gently touching
Ez. 3¹³. But Hu. regards vb. in our Ps. as from other stem נשׁק with supposed mng. *lay hold of, handle*, which is elsewhere in Heb. only as Qal ptc.
pl. cstr. נֹשְׁקֵי קשׁת *equipped with bow* 1 C. 12² 2 C. 17¹⁷ (possibly also Ps. 78⁹,
BDB.); so here *submit yourselves sincerely*, "*füget euch aufrichtig*"; and
thus he explains 𝔊 δράξασθε, 𝔙 *apprehendite*; so Ew., Hi., Reuss. — [בַּר] dub.
mng. *son* (𝔖, AE., Maimonides, Ges., De W., Pe., Bä., and most moderns),
elsw. only Pr. 31²˙ ²˙ ² (a passage very late, full of Aramaisms); absence of
article and use of בֵּן v.⁷ insuperable objections, and no reference to the king
in this str., the following as well as preceding context referring to Yahweh.
Rd. † בֹּר n. *cleanness:* of hands Ps. 18²¹˙ ²⁵ (= 2 S. 22²¹˙ ²⁵) Jb. 9³⁰ 22³⁰; so Aq.,
Σ, 𝔍 here *worship in purity*, possibly reading נבר ‖ ברעדה ‖ ביראה; 𝔊 δράξασθε
παιδείας, 𝔗 קבילו אולפנא rest upon a different text. Bä. thinks the 𝔗 paraphrases in reference to Law, for it translates in the same way שׁמע תורה Is. 30⁹.

Possibly בר of the Law in Ps. 19⁹ suggested this reference. παιδεία of ⅏ might rest upon מוסר or be a paraphrase as ⅏. Lag. rds. מוּסָר as v.³, מו וֹ, מוסר having fallen out after קו of נשקו, so Now. Marti suggests בר as abbr. ברעדה and then נשׁקו as variant of גילו; so Prince; but these radical changes are unnecessary. Dy., Oort, Hu.: נשׁקו בו has little in its favour. — פֶּן] *lest:* final clause with subj. יֶאֱנַף. ⅏ inserts Κύριος. ‡ פֶּן *conj.* always neg. with impf. subj. 2¹² 7⁸ 13⁴·⁵ 28¹ 38¹⁷ 50²² 59¹² 91¹². — וְתֹאבְדוּ] coord. impf. ‖ subjunctive dependent on פֶּן. — דֶּרֶךְ] acc. of reference Ri., Bä., Du., acc. of limitation Hi., De., local acc. *on the way.* ⅏ ἐξ ὁδοῦ δικαίας = דֶּרֶךְ צְדָקָה. This might be interpretation, but it makes the line a trimeter, and gives a complete and excellent parall. חוֹסֵי בוֹ cstr. before prep. Ges.§¹³⁰·⁽¹⁾. † חסה vb. Qal *seek refuge in :* c. ב, always in ψ in God 2¹² 5¹² 7² 11¹ 16¹ 18³·³¹ (= 2 S. 22³·³¹) 25²⁰ 31²·²⁰ 34⁹·²³ 37⁴⁰ 57² 64¹¹ 71¹ 118⁸·⁹ 141⁸ 144²; ב to be supplied in thought at least 17⁷; בְּצֵל כְּנָפֶיךָ 36⁸ 57²; בְּסֵתֶר כְּנָפֶיךָ 61⁵; תַּחַת כְּנָפָיו 91⁴ (= Ru. 2¹²); apart from ψ seldom used : בְּצֵל Ju. 9¹⁵ Is. 30²; in Zion Is. 14³²; in gods Dt. 32³⁷ (poem); in God Is. 57¹⁸ Nu. 1⁷ Pr. 30⁵ 14³² (without ב); בְּשֵׁם ' Zp. 3¹². † מַחְסֶה *n. m.* also common in ψ of God as *refuge* of His people 14⁶ 46² 61⁴ 62⁸·⁹ 71⁷ 73²⁸ 91²·⁹ 94²² 142⁶ Pr. 14²⁶ Je. 17¹⁷ Jo. 4¹⁶; so rocks for conies Ps. 104¹⁸; falsehood as refuge Is. 28¹⁵·¹⁷; from rain and storm Is. 4⁶ 25⁴ Jb. 24⁸.

PSALM III., 4 STR. 4³.

Ps. 3 is a morning prayer ; the first in the order of the Davidic prayer book. The poet exclaims at the number of his adversaries and their denying salvation to him from God (v.²⁻³) ; asserts that Yahweh was his shield and had answered him (v.⁴⁻⁵). He had slept without fear sustained by Yahweh (v.⁶⁻⁷), Who had smitten all his enemies, and was his salvation (v.⁸⁻⁹).

YAHWEH, how many are mine adversaries !
    Many are rising up against me ;
    Many are saying of me,
    There is no salvation for him.
BUT Thou art a shield about me,
    My glory and the lifter-up of my head.
    Unto Yahweh I called with my voice,
    And He answered me from His holy mountain.
I LAID me down and slept ;
    I awaked, for He kept sustaining me.
    I am not afraid of myriads of people,
    Which round about were arrayed against me.
FOR Thou hast smitten all my enemies,
    The teeth of the wicked Thou hast broken off,
    To Thee Yahweh belongeth my salvation ;
    And upon Thy people rests Thy blessing.

The Ps. was in 𝕯 (לדוד *v.* Intr. § 27) and 𝕸 (מזמור *v.* Intr. § 31). The title mentions an event in the life of David which in many respects suits the experience of the poet. His derision as one forsaken by God 2 S. 16⁷⁻⁸, the danger by night 2 S. 17¹ ˢᵠ·, the myriads of people 2 S. 15¹⁸, 17¹¹, and his high and honourable position. The Ps. certainly expresses the experience of a monarch, or some chief of the people, whose blessing was wrapt up in his salvation v.⁹ and whose enemies were a myriad, in arms against him v.⁷. He is a Davidic chief far from the holy hill of Zion. Yahweh has answered him v.⁵ and smitten his enemies v.⁸. The language and style of the Ps. are simple and of the best type. There is no reference to other scripture unless possibly to Gen. 15¹ (E) in the imagery of the shield; but though the word is the same, the construction is different. The expression " sacred hill " is used in preëx. writings. The use of שׁית v.⁷ in the sense of *set in battle array*, is elsewhere Is. 22⁷. The Ps. is one of the earliest, and cannot well be later than the period of the monarchy, when it was exposed to the attack of the minor surrounding nations. It would suit well the situation of Jehoshaphat 2 Ch. 20. But, as this is only given in Chr. and not in the parallel of K., it is probable that many other historical experiences, such as that in our Ps., are not recorded in the condensed narratives of the historians. The Ps. gives individual experience, but this became characteristic for the nation, and so the Ps. was adapted to common use, although the language was left in its individual form.

Str. I. 2–3. The poet vividly describes *adversaries* in four synth. trimeters as *many*, as *rising up against him*, as *saying of him*, and what they say, *There is no salvation for him*] he does not possess it, and there is no prospect of his ever having it.

Str. II. 4–5. The antistr., in four synth. trimeters, contrasts his real experience with the actions and words of the adversaries : Yahweh *a shield about me*] antith. v.²ᵃ ; *my glory and the lifter up of my head*], that is, the one in whom I glory, and the one who has exalted my head in victory over adversaries, antith. v.²ᵇ ; — *Unto Yahweh I called*] in oft-repeated pleading, aloud *with my voice*] antith. v.³ᵃ ; *He answered me*] as an historical fact, the climax, antith. v.³ᵇ. — *From His holy mountain*] from Zion (*v.* 2⁶) ; salvation has come in response to my prayer and I am in possession of it.

Str. III. 6–7 has two synth. couplets. The poet had not been in such peril and anxiety as his adversaries supposed. He had not been wakeful during the night : far otherwise, he says, *I laid me down*], calm and undisturbed ; *and slept*] ; and when I had sufficient refreshment, *I awaked, for*], all night long Yahweh *kept sustaining me*]. Under such an experience of the support of Yahweh, *I am not afraid,* even *of myriads of people.* The poet is a king, these myriads are enemies who have come up against him in war; they are foreign people in very great numbers. They are *round about*], so numerous are they, they surround the king and his army. — *they were arrayed*] his adversaries put these myriads in battle array against him.

8a. *O rise up, Yahweh, Save me, my God*] appeal to Yahweh to rise up to activity : a gloss, giving the plea of the people of Israel in troublous times, when surrounded by myriads of enemies, and when they were in a less calm and confident frame of mind than the author of the Ps.

Str. IV. 8b–9. The antistr. gives the well-grounded reason for the calm confidence expressed in the previous str. Yahweh had already given victory and wrought salvation. *Thou hast smitten all mine enemies*] they have been defeated in battle ; that is a reason why he has had a calm and refreshing sleep v.⁶ᵃ ; — *The teeth of the wicked Thou hast broken off*], so severely have they been smitten, that they are no longer able to bite. This is the reason for the assurance that God kept sustaining him all night long, v.⁶ᵇ. — *To Thee belongeth my salvation*] Yahweh was his protector, and it was His affair to save him. Therefore he was not afraid of the myriads of enemies, v.⁷ᵃ. — *Upon Thy people rests Thy blessing*] ; What matters it then if the enemies are arrayed in arms against them, v.⁷ᵇ? Yahweh's blessing not only saves them from evil, but bestows upon them every good that is needful.

2–3. מָה] adv. ‡ *how* exclam. as 8². ¹⁰ 21² 31²⁰ 36⁸ 66³ 84² 92⁶ 104²⁴ 119⁹⁷. ¹⁰⁸ 133¹. ¹ 139¹⁷. ¹⁷, in indirect questions 39⁵, *why* 42⁶. ¹². ¹² 43⁵. ⁵ 52³. — רבו] Qal pf. 3 pl. √‡ רבב *be many* in numbers, of enemies 3² 25¹⁹ 38²⁰ 69⁶, works of Yahweh 104²⁴, *be much* in quantity 4⁸. — צָרָי] n. pl. sf. i.p. ‡ צַר n. m. sg. coll., *adversaries* 44¹¹ 74¹⁰ 78⁴². ⁶¹ 107², pl. 3² 13⁵ 27². ¹² 44⁶. ⁸ 60¹⁴ (=108¹⁴) 81¹⁵ 89²⁴. ⁴³ 105²⁴ 106¹¹ 112⁸ 119¹³⁹. ¹⁵⁷ 136²⁴, agst. God 78⁶⁶ 97³. — אֹמְרִים, קָמִים] ptcs. of continual action Dr.§ ¹³⁵. — ‡ אמר לִי] usually *say to* 11¹ 16² (= 140⁷) 35⁸ 40¹⁶ (?) 42¹⁰ 50¹² 52² 54² 66³ 75⁵ 122¹ ; but also *of, about, concerning* 3³ 41⁶ 71¹⁰ 91². — נַפְשִׁי] ‡ paraphrase for personal pronoun *me* JPSV. so 3³ 7³ 11¹ 17¹³ 26⁹ 31⁸ 34⁸ 35⁸. ⁷. ¹² 41⁵ 54⁶ 57². ⁵ 62². ⁶ 66¹⁶ 69¹⁹ 71¹³ 86² 88¹⁵ 94¹⁷ 103¹. ². ²² 104¹. ³⁵ 109²⁰ 116⁷ 119²⁵. ¹²⁹. ¹⁶⁷ 120². ⁶ 130⁵. ⁶ 141⁸ 142⁵. ⁸ 143¹¹. ¹² 146¹ ; נפשך *thee* 121⁷, נפשו *he* 25¹³ 105¹⁸ 109³¹, נפשנו *we* 33²⁰ 124⁷ (*v.* BDB., Br. JBL. 1897, 17 sq.). — אֵין] n. cstr. אֵין ‡ (1) *nothing, naught,* seldom, כָּאֵן *as nothing*

39⁶ 73², (2) cstr. or with sfs. frequent in sense of *denial* of thing, ‡ sq. לְ of possession 3³ 34¹⁰ 55²⁰ 119¹⁶⁵ 146⁸ *v.* B*DB.* — [וִישׁוּעָתָה] n. f., fuller form ישׁועה ancient case ending (Kö.ᴵᴵ ¹· §124 (3) Ges.§ 90 (2), Dr.§ 182ᵒᵇ·) not used with grammatical mng. but euphonic to retract accent before לֹו. ‡ יְשׁוּעָה n. f. [√ישׁע] (1) *salvation* from God 3³· ⁹ 14⁷ (= 53⁷) 22² 35³ 62² 67⁸ 69⁸⁰ 70⁵ (= תּשׁועה 40¹⁷) 78²² 80³ 91¹⁶ 96² 98²· ³ 106⁴ 119¹²³· ¹⁵⁵· ¹⁶⁶· ¹⁷⁴ 140⁸, with vbs. of rejoicing c. בְּ 9¹⁵ 13⁶ 35⁹, ישׁ׳ אלהי 88² (dub.). צור ישׁ׳ Dt. 32¹⁵ Ps. 89²⁷, cf. 62³· ⁷, pl. *saving acts* 42⁶· ¹² 43⁵ 116¹⁸. (2) *victory* wrought by God for His people Ex. 15² Is. 12² Hb. 3⁸ Pss. 20⁶ 21²· ⁶ 68²⁰ 118¹⁴· ¹⁵· ²¹ 149⁴, pl. 18⁵¹ 28⁸ 44⁵ 74¹². The cognate יֵשַׁע see 18⁸, תּשׁועה 33¹⁷ BD*B.* — [בּאלהים· is gloss; makes line too long and is improbable in 𝔐. 𝔊 ἐν τῷ θεῷ αὐτοῦ = לו בּאלהים shows that some codd. inserted the divine name before, others after לו. — **4.** [וְאַתָּה] *emphatic* is sufficiently definite in reference to Yahweh without need of יהוה which is gloss, making line too long. — ‡ מגן] *shield* carried by warrior for defence 76⁴; of רי as warrior 35²; fig. of king 89¹⁹, rulers 47¹⁰, elsw. of Yahweh's defence of His people 3⁴ 7¹¹ 18³· ³¹· ³⁶ 28⁷ 33²⁰ 59¹² 84¹⁰· ¹² 115⁹· ¹⁰· ¹¹ 119¹¹⁴ 144². — [בַּעֲדִי] *about me* ‡ בעד always with sfs., here of shield; 139¹¹ of light; 72¹⁵ 138⁸ *on behalf of:* other mngs. though more fundamental not in ψ BD*B.* — [כְּבוֹדִי] *my glory*, the one in whom I glory, cf. כבודם 106²⁰. — [מֵרִים Hiph. ptc. ‡ רום with ראשׁ elsw. 27⁶ 110⁷ (*v.* 9¹⁴). — **5.** [קוֹלִי] acc. of closer definition, *with my voice* (most) as 142²· ² cf. 77²· ². Hi., Bö., Hu. regard it as giving vb. double subj., active member coming first. The emph. position of קולי is without good reason. The lines rhyme in ־ִ and it is prob. קולִי originally came last in line. — אֶקְרָא Qal impf. freq. oft repeated calling with the result expressed by וֹ consec. impf. וַיַּעֲנֵנִי· *aorist* single act. — ‡ קרא] (1) usually in ψ, *cry, call out for help* to God 147⁹ (ravens), in prayer, abs. 4² 20¹⁰ 22⁸ 27⁷ 34⁷ 56¹⁰ 69⁴ 81⁸ 102⁸ 116² (?) 119¹⁴⁵ 120¹ 138³; c. acc. sf. 17⁶ 31¹⁸ 50¹⁵ 86⁵· ⁷ 88¹⁰ 91¹⁵ 119¹⁴⁶ 130¹ 141¹ 145¹⁸· ¹⁸; יהוה 14⁴(= אלהים 53⁵) 18⁴· ⁷, יה 118⁵; c. לְ pers. 57³ 141¹, אֶל 3⁵ 4⁴ 28¹ 30⁹ 55¹⁷ 61⁸ 66¹⁷ 86³ 99⁶, in worship כ׳ בשׁם 79⁶ 80¹⁹ 105¹ 116⁴· ¹⁸· ¹⁷, cf. קֹרְאֵי שֵׁם 99⁶. (2) *call unto* c. אל one to another 42⁸. (3) *call, summon* c. acc. 50¹, c. אל 50⁴, c. על 105¹⁶. (4) *call, name* 49¹² 89²⁷ 147⁴. — ‡ ענה] (1) usually God's *answer* to prayer, abs. 38¹⁶ c. acc. pers. 13⁴ 20²· ⁷ 22²² 60⁷(= 108⁷) 69¹⁴· ¹⁷ 81⁸ 99⁸ 118²¹ 119²⁶ 143¹, מַהֵר עֲנֵנִי 69¹⁸ 102⁸ 143⁷, after קרא 3⁵ 4² 17⁶ 20¹⁰ 22⁸ 86⁷ 91¹⁵ 99⁶ 102⁸ 118⁵ 119¹⁴⁵ 120¹ 138⁸, other vbs. 18⁴² 27⁷ 34⁵ 55³· ²⁰ 86¹. (2) *respond*, c. acc. pers. 18³⁶ (?) 119⁴², acc. rei. 65⁶. — **6.** [אֲנִי] emph. antith. ואתה v. ⁴ᵃ. — [שָׁכַבְתִּי] pf. aorist sq. וֹ consec. impf. result : וָאִישָׁנָה cohort. for jussive 1st p. ‡ שָׁכַב vb. *lie down* to sleep 3⁶ 4⁹, in ease 68¹⁴, prostrate in peril 57⁵, in death 41⁹, in the grave 88⁶. — [יִישַׁן] vb. *go to sleep, be asleep, sleep* 3⁶ 4⁹ of רי 44²⁴ 121⁴, in death 13⁴ cf. ‡ יָשֵׁן adj. רי 78⁶⁵. — [הֱקִיצוֹתִי] Hiph. pf. aorist ‡ √קיץ only Hiph. *awake* from sleep 3⁶ 73²⁰ 139¹⁸, of death 17¹⁵, רי subj. 35²³ 44²⁴ 59⁶. — [יִסְמְכֵנִי] Qal impf. freq. oft repeated, sustain during the night Dr.³⁰ᵃ ⁿᵒᵗ ³³⁵. ‡ סָמַךְ Qal (1) trans. *lean* or *lay hand upon* 88⁸. (2) God *upholds, sustains* His people 3⁶ 37¹⁷· ²⁴ 51¹⁴ 54⁶ 119¹¹⁶ 145¹⁴, pass. ptc. 111⁸ (Yahweh's Law) 112⁸ the mind. Niph. *support oneself* 71⁶. — **7.** [לֹא אִירָא] Qal impf. present

‡ c. מִן *afraid of 3*[7] 27[1] 65[9] 91[5] 112[7] 119[120].—[רְבָבוֹת] cstr. pl. † רְבָבָה n. f. *myriad* c. *3*[7] 91[7], Gn. 24[60] Nu. 10[36] (J) Lv. 26[8] Dt. 32[30] 33[2] (?) Ju. 20[10] Is. 18[7. 8] 21[12] 29[5] Ct. 5[10] Ez. 16[7. 17] Mi. 6[7], cf. denom. Pual Ps. 144[13].— ‡ עַם] *people* in ψ (1) sg. coll. *the people of God* 3[9] 14[47] (= 53[5. 7]) 18[28] 28[9] 29[11. 11] 33[12] 35[18] 44[13] 50[4. 7] 59[12] 60[5] 62[9] 68[3. 36] 72[2. 3. 4] 73[10] 77[16. 21] 78[1. 20. 52. 62. 71] 79[18] 80[5] 81[9. 12. 14] 83[4] 85[3. 7. 9] 89[16. 20] 94[5. 14] 95[7. 10] 100[3] 105[24. 25. 43] 106[4. 40. 48] 107[32] 111[6. 9] 113[8] 116[14. 18] 125[2] 135[12. 14] 136[16] 144[15.15] 148[14. 14] 149[4], the future generation 22[32] 102[19], so people of king 110[3]; in no case hostile to king or God, and therefore it cannot be interpreted in v.[7] of that portion of Israel hostile to David. (2) sg. coll. of foreign nations 18[44. 44] 47[10] 74[18] 94[8] 105[13] so בְּזוּי עָם 22[7] and *3*[7] of hostile foreign people, also 144[2] (עמי for עַמִּים) 18[48] as 𝕊, Aq., 𝕴, 𝕿. (3) sg. of single people 45[11], prob. also 45[13] 114[1] [עם לציים 74[14] dub.). (4) pl. עַמִּים always foreign nations 7[9] 18[48] 33[10] 45[6. 18] 47[4. 10] 56[8] 67[5] 68[31. 31] 89[51] 96[5. 7. 10. 13] 98[9] 105[20] 106[34], often conceived as taking part ultimately in worship of ״ 66[8] 87[6] 99[1] 102[23], subj. הגוים 9[12] הורו 57[10] 67[4. 4. 6. 6] 108[4], הוריע 77[15] 105[1], כל הגוים 47[2] 49[2] 96[8] 97[6] 99[2].—[אֲשֶׁר] is unnecessary and dub. —[סָבִיב] adv. *round-about*, emph. [שָׁתוּ עָלַי] phr. α.λ. Qal *real* pf. indef. subj. *they have arrayed against me*, cf. Is. 22[7], best given in English as passive. The context indicates an *army* composed of myriads *set* or *put* in battle array. —**8.** [קוּמָה] Qal imv. cohort., urgent entreaty.—[הוֹשִׁיעֵנִי] Hiph. imv. sf. 1 sg. — √‡ [ישׁע] Niph. *be saved*, placed in freedom (1) from evils by God 80[4. 8. 20] 119[117] c. מִן 18[4], (2) in battle and so be *victorious* 33[16]. Hiph. (1) *deliver*, *save* in peril 36[7] 72[13] c. ל pers. 72[4] 116[6] from evils 18[42], of heroic man, frequent in early Lit.; usually of God, who saves His people from external evils 28[9] 69[36] 106[8] 118[25], or the pious among them *3*[8] 6[5] 7[2. 11] 12[2] 17[7] 18[28] 34[19] 37[40] 54[3] 55[17] 57[4] 69[2] 71[2. 3] 76[10] 86[2. 16] 106[47] 109[26] 119[94. 146] 138[7] 145[19], the king 20[7. 10]. God is saviour 106[21] and is with His people to save them 31[3]; Israel prays, *O save with Thy right hand*, 60[7] = 108[7] cf. Is. 59[1]. That from which one is saved c. מִן 22[22] 34[7] 44[8] 59[3] 106[10] 107[13. 19] 109[31]; there is no other salvation, the sword saves not 44[7]; (2) *save* from moral troubles or sin; not in ψ or OT. except Ez. 36[29] 37[23]; (3) *give victory*, of man 31[17] 44[4], God 98[1]. —[כִּי הִכִּיתָ] the reason with Hiph. pf. 2 m. action just completed. — √[נכה] Hiph. *smite* (1) with a single blow *3*[8], if לְחִי original, as La. 3[30] but it is not found elsw. in ψ, it is not in 𝕲 which rds. ματαίως = לְחִנָּם. Both are glosses, 𝕳 to make the enemies into later religious enemies; therefore the smiting is the defeat of enemies as in battle as 78[66] 135[10] 136[17].—[כָּל־אֹיְבַי] Qal ptc. pl. sf. 1 p. ‡ [איב] Qal pf. only אָיַבְתִּי Ex. 23[22] (E) elsw. ptc. *enemy* (1) sg. of nation 9[7] 74[3. 10. 18] 89[23] 106[10] coll. 7[6] 31[9] 42[10] 43[2] 55[4] 61[4] 64[2] 143[9], individual only 55[13] (but cf. 55[4]) אֹיְבִי is always coll. 13[3. 5] 18[18] 41[12] (possibly all should be pointed ־ִ) אוֹיֵב וּמִתְנַקֵּם 8[3] = 44[17]; (2) pl. preceded by כל *3*[8] 6[11] 18[1] 21[9] איבי יהוה 37[20] איבי המלך 45[6], elsw. simply general 9[4] 17[9] 18[4. 38. 41. 49] 25[2. 19] 27[2. 6] 30[2] 31[16] 35[19] 38[20] 41[3. 6] 54[9] 56[10] 59[2] 66[3] 68[2. 22. 24] 69[5. 19] 71[10] 72[9] 78[53] 80[7] 81[15] 83[3] 89[11. 43. 52] 92[10. 10] 102[9] 106[42] 110[1. 2] 119[98] 127[5] 132[18] 138[7] 139[22] 143[9. 12].—[שִׁנֵּי שְׁבַּרְתָּ] phr. α.λ. cf. 58[7] La. 3[16] also comparison of their teeth with weapons Ps. 57[5] cf. Pr. 30[14], other phr. (עַל) חרק שנים *gnashed teeth* upon 35[16] 37[12] 112[10] La. 2[16] cf. Jb. 16[9]

טרף לשניהם 124[6]. — 9. [ליהוה] rd. לְךָ יהוה to get the missing word of measure [עַל־יְמֵךְ] — 𝕲 has ועל עמך which gives us the missing accent for measure. In both lines היה is understood in the sense of present and abiding experience. — ‡[בְּרָכָה] n. f. (1) *blessing* of God 3[9] 21[4] 24[6] 129[8] 133[8], of the people in recognition of good men 109[17]; (2) *source of blessing*, seed of righteous 37[26], king 21[7]; (3) *blessing, prosperity* 84[7].

PSALM IV., 4 STR. 4[4].

Ps. 4 is an evening prayer. The poet is confident that the God of his right has answered his prayer (v.[2-3]). He tells his adversaries that Yahweh hath shewn extraordinary kindness to him, and warns them to tremble and not sin (v.[4-5]). He then urges his followers to offer the right sacrifices, trust in Yahweh, and pray for prosperity and the priestly benediction (v.[6-7]); then affirms his own gladness and peace and goes to sleep in safety (v.[8-9]).

WHEN I call, answer me, O God of my right;
    In my distress Thou hast made room; shew me favour (by hearing) my prayer.
    Ye sons of men, how long shall my honour be a reproach,
    Will ye love a vain thing, seek after a lie?
BUT know that Yahweh hath shewn extraordinary kindness,
    Yahweh heareth when I call unto Him.
    Tremble and sin not (ye sons of men).
    Say (it) in your heart, (lying) upon your bed, and be still.
(YE sons of mankind) sacrifice right sacrifices,
    And trust unto Yahweh, ye many.
    Keep saying: "O that He would shew us prosperity,
    Lift the light of Thy countenance upon us."
YAHWEH, Thou hast put gladness in my heart
    More than that of the season when their corn and new wine were abundant.
    In peace at once will I lay me down and I will sleep,
    For Thou makest me dwell apart, in safety.

Ps. 4 was originally in 𝔻 as a mate to Ps. 3, an evening prayer following naturally a morning prayer. It was then taken up into 𝕱𝕽 and 𝔻𝕽 and assigned for rendering with the music of stringed instruments בנגינות. (See Intr. § 39.) The date of the Ps. depends upon a variety of considerations: (1) The high priestly benediction Nu. 6[24-26] is familiar to the author, for two of its clauses melt together in נסה אור פניך v.[7b]; and בשלום v.[9a] is suggested by it. This blessing belongs to the sources of P, and was familiar, especially in priestly circles, long before the Exile. (2) The blessing of Moses Dt. 33 is familiar to the author in the phrs. זבחי צדק v.[6] = Dt. 33[19]; דגנם ותירושם v.[8b];

לברד לבטח תושיבני v.⁹ᵇ = Dt. 33²⁸. These favour an early date. (3) The language is of best classic type. בני איש v.³ *men of high degree* in antith. with בני אדם *men of low degree*, elsw. in Pss. 49³ 62¹⁰; הפלה חסד v.⁴ elsw. Ps. 17⁷ = הפליא Ps. 31²². If הפלה were from √פלה a dependence upon Ex. 8¹⁸ 9⁴ 11⁷ (J) would appear; but this derivation is improbable. אמר בלבב v.⁵ is a phr. of D, here only in ψ. There are two resemblances to previous Ps., cf. v.⁷ᵃ with 3³, and v.⁹ᵃ with 3⁶ᵃ; but these are not sufficient to establish common author or date. The language favours a date not earlier than Je. (4) The historical situation is entirely different from that of Ps. 3, where a monarch was in peril from hostile peoples. Here a ruler, probably not a king, is sustained by the people, but oppressed by men of station and influence. By lying, and empty, baseless misrepresentation, they have changed his position of honour to one of reproach. This does not suit the experience of David during the rebellion of Absalom; for the adversaries were not men of rank. These were with David, but the common people were against him, having been seduced by Absalom 2 S. 15¹⁻⁶; and David was not in fact in peace and safety 2 S. 17²⁴⁻18. The experience of the Ps. is that of a reformer. The language of the Ps. favours a priest such as Amariah 2 C. 19¹¹, Jehoiada 2 K. 11, Hilkiah 2 K. 22; but all of these excepting the last are too early and none of them were probably sustained by the people over against the princes. The situation is well given in Ezr. 4, where Zerubbabel and Jeshua were opposed at the court of Persia by lies and slanders, which had no basis in fact; and their honour was clouded by such attacks and their work really stayed. This would suit all the conditions of the Ps.

Str. I. 2. The poet prays that when he *calls*, Yahweh will *answer* him. It is just because Yahweh is the *God of my right*] the God who vindicates his cause against his adversaries and establishes his right, that he can so address Him and pray with confidence to Him. This is fortified in the syn. line by past experience; the God of his right has vindicated his right, *when in distress*, and has *made room for* him. Distress is here a being constrained into narrow limits; pressed from rightful freedom, and shut in on every side. The antith. is the removal of such restraint and pressure, giving room and freedom. The request for answer is strengthened into *shew me favour (by hearing) my prayer*. "The word suggests the free bestowal of favour rather than the exercise of forgiving clemency" (Kirk); or pity for sufferers. — **3.** The call upon God is followed by antith. remonstrance with his adversaries, who refuse his right and have brought him into distress. They are *sons of men*] men of rank, of high degree, and so have had the power to reduce his *honour* ‖ right, to *reproach*, ‖ distress.

They have done this because they are themselves false and dishonourable men. — *Will ye love a vain thing ?*] empty and without reality, more specific — *seek after a lie*]. The reproach that they have brought upon him is thus branded as false, without foundation, and a lie. The charge is concrete and specific; "falsehood" (RV., Dr., JPSV) is too general; "leasing" (PBV, AV.) is obsolete for lie.

Str. II. 4. In the antistr., the poet gives his adversaries to *know*, in the first syn. couplet, that *Yahweh hath shewn extraordinary kindness*] as 17^7 31^{22} renewing the experience of v.². 𝔥, though sustained by Vrss. ancient and modern and most critics with the mng.: hath separated, set apart, or distinguished, for Himself, the pious, godly man, is not so well suited to context and is not sustained by good usage. — *Yahweh heareth when I call unto Him*] constant experience resuming v.²ᵃ. 5. In the second syn. couplet, he warns them that had brought his honour to reproach, to *tremble* and not *sin*] by taking the steps necessary to realise their thoughts, make them effective in conduct. Over against their loving a vain thing and seeking out a lie against him, the poet warns them ; *say* (what you have to say) *in your heart*, to yourselves, in secret, while lying *upon your bed*, and *be still*] give no expression to your wicked thoughts.

Str. III. The poet now turns to his discouraged people. 6. They are *sons of mankind*] men of low degree over against the sons of men, men of high degree v.³; the measure as well as the antith. requires this insertion. He exhorts them to *sacrifice right sacrifices*] while he is calling on the God of his right, v.²ᵃ. These were the normal sacrifices, in accordance with law and custom (Du., Bä.), rather than " of righteousness " offered in a right spirit (Pe., De., Hu., Kirk) or symb. of righteous acts (Aug, Chrysostom) or which justify, cf. v.², Genebr. 7. He reminds his followers that they are *many* in numbers, and they should *trust unto Yahweh*, Who has made room for him in the past and Who shews favour to him in his prayer v.²ᵇ. He urges them to *keep saying*] expressing the wish, the strong desire, "*O that He would shew us prosperity* "], so JPSV, antith. to the reproach that has come upon their chiefs, cf. v.³ᵃ. This is better suited to the context than the question "Who will shew us?" of EVˢ. They should beg the bestowal of the divine benediction, *Lift the light of Thy countenance upon us*, in place of the vain thing and the lie, that the adversaries have sought out against him. The poet is thinking of the blessing of the high priest, Nu. 6[24-26] (P), which wishes that the light of Yahweh's face may shine upon His people with favour, bestowing peace and prosperity. This blessing the Psalmist seeks directly from Yahweh Himself, so 67[2], cf. 44[4] 89[16].

Str. IV. The antistr. asserts the poet's gladness, peace, and safety, over against the prayers of his people in the previous str., in introverted parallel clauses. *Yahweh, Thou hast put gladness in my heart*] the response to the prayer v.[7b]. This joy is greater than that of those who in harvest season rejoice that *their corn and new wine were abundant*]. This is in response to the petition v.[7a]. He resolves to *lay* him *down* and go to *sleep at once, in peace*, in the experience of that same trusting unto Yahweh which he has commended to his followers v.[6b]. He enjoys the calm peace which is imparted in the priestly benediction for which they had asked. *Thou makest me dwell apart in safety*] response to the offering of right sacrifices by his people v.[6a]. In calm, peaceful trust he goes to sleep upon his bed with this evening prayer upon his lips.

2. בְּקָרְאִי] Qal inf. cstr. sf. 1 p., temporal clause ; imv. Qal sf. 1 p. in apodosis v. 3[5].— אֱלֹהֵי צִדְקִי] phr. α.λ. *God of my right*, who rights me, vindicates my right, cf. אלהי ישעי 18[47]; א׳ חַסְדִּי 59[11. 18]. ‡ צֶרֶק n.m.: (1) *what is right, just*, 'צ מַעְגְּלֵי *right paths* 23[3], 'צ וְזִבְחֵי 4[6] 51[21] Dt. 33[19]; (2) righteousness in government (*a*) of rulers 58[2] 94[15], (*b*) of laws 119[7. 62. 75. 106. 138. 144. 160. 164. 172], (*c*) of king 45[6] 72[2] Is. 11[4. 5], (*d*) of God's attitude as sovereign : personified agent 85[11. 12. 14], foundation of His throne 89[15] = 97[2], in His government 9[9] 65[6] 96[13] = 98[9], administration of justice 7[18] 48[11]. 50[6] = 97[6], vindication of His people 9[5] 35[24. 28], אלהי צדקי 4[2], it is everlasting 119[142]. (3) righteousness, justice in a cause 35[27] Is. 59[4], שפט כ׳ 7[9], גמל כ׳ 18[21], השיב כ׳ v.[25], הוציא צ׳ 37[6]; (4) rightness in speech 52[5]; (5) ethically right 17[15] 45[8] Je. 22[13] Ho. 10[12] W.L. עשה צ 119[121], פעל 'צ 15[2]; (6) righteousness as vindicated in deliverance 40[10] 119[123]; (7) שַׁעֲרֵי צֶרֶק *gates of* the God *Zedek* 118[19]; cf. Is. 1[26] Je. 31[23] 50[7].— בַּצָּר] emphatic position ; בְּ temporal c. צָר for usual ‡ צַר n. in ψ *straits, distress* 32[7] 60[13] 108[13] 119[143], alw. elsw. either לְ 18[7] 66[14] 106[44] 107[6. 13. 19. 28] = בְּצַר לְ 59[17] 102[3], or כי צר לי 31[10] 69[18] : therefore here also בצר-לי, the transposition of לי a copyist's error. Moreover, this construction improves the measure, for the superfluous tone disappears.— הִרְחַבְתָּ] Hiph. pf. 2 sg. *hast made room*, only

here in this fig. sense, but cf. 18³⁷. The pf. prob. refers to past experience,
Dr.§⁹. It is tempting with Bö.§ ⁹³⁹⁽ᵍ⁾ ⁹⁴⁷⁽ᵍ⁾ to think of a *precative* pf. here;
but, as Dr.§ ²⁰, there is lack of evidence of such a usage in Heb., *v.* Ges. § ¹⁰⁶⁽³⁵⁾;
although Ew.§ ²²³ᵇ sustains it. — חָנֵּנִי] Qal imv. sf. 1 p. ‡√חנן (1) *shew favour,
be gracious;* so usually of God as bestowing redemption from enemies, evils
and sins c. acc. 4² 6³ 9¹⁴ 25¹⁶ 26¹¹ 27⁷ 30¹¹ 31¹⁰ 41⁶· ¹¹ 51³ 56² 57²· ² 59⁶ 86⁸· ¹⁶,
all 𝔅; elsw. 67² 102¹⁴ 119⁵⁸· ¹³² ₁23²· ⁸· ⁸; not used in 𝔎 or 𝔄 exc. abs. 77¹⁰;
(2) of God in bestowal of favours in more general sense : הוֹרָתְךָ חָנֵּנִי preg.
with two acc. *be gracious to me* (in giving) *Thy Law* 119²⁹; (3) of man in
dealing with poor, alw. ptc., abs. חוֹנֵן 37²¹· ²⁶ 112⁵, c. ל 109¹². Poel *direct
favour toward* 102¹⁵ as Pr. 14²¹. Hithp. אֶתְחַנָּן אֶל *seek* or *implore favour* of
God 30⁹ 142². — וְשָׁמַע] makes line too long; is a gloss, being implied in
pregnant clause; cf. 119²⁹. — חפלה] v. Intr. § 1. — 3. ‡ בְּנֵי אִישׁ] pl. cstr.,
vocative, n. of relation c. coll. sg. אִישׁ. This phr. in ψ elsw. only antith.
בְּנֵי אָדָם 49⁸ 62¹⁰, where men of high degree are contrasted with men of low
degree : so here, esp. if we insert בני אדם in v.⁶. In fact אִישׁ in ψ usually
means man as a self-respecting individual with a certain amount of dignity
62⁴, having talent 105¹⁷, sometimes pious 25¹² 34¹³ 109¹⁶ 112¹· ⁵, sometimes an
enemy or wicked 31²¹ 37⁷ 38¹⁵ 92⁷. ‡ בְּנֵי אָדָם in ψ alw. *mankind* 11⁴ 12²· ⁹
14² (= 53³) 21¹¹ 31²⁰ 33¹³ 36⁸ 45³ 66⁵ 89⁴⁸ 90⁸ 107⁸· ¹⁵· ²¹· ³¹ 115¹⁶ 145¹². In
57⁵ 58² it must have the special sense of בני איש if subj., but this is improb.
It is obj., and so has same mng. as all other passages. — ‡ עַד־מֶה] *how long*
as 74⁹ (?) 79⁵ 89⁴⁷. — כְּבוֹדִי] antith. with כְּלִמָּה, only here ψ. כבוד in the mng.
honour, reputation, character of man is elsewhere only 2 Ch. 26¹⁸ Pr. 20⁸ 21¹
25²⁷ Ec. 10¹; but cf. 7⁶. — לְ] before כלמה is preg., implying היה become. —
‡ כְּלִמָּה] n. f. in its original sense of *insult*, not in ψ, but as *reproach;* elsw.
35²⁶ ₄44¹⁶ 69⁸· ²⁰ 71¹³ 109²⁹; cf. 89⁵¹. 𝔊 ἕως πότε βαρυκάρδιοι ἵνα τι =
כִּכְבְרֵי לֵב לָמָה, though sustained by Houb., Genebr., We., is better explained as
due to a mistake quite common, esp. in Egyptian Aramaic script, of ב for
כ; J *incliti mei* after Aq. οἱ ἐνδόξοι μου = כְּבָרַי = נִכְבָּרַי 149⁸ *my honourable men.*
But MT followed by Σ, 𝕿, 𝔖 suits rhythm and context. — הֶאֱרָבוּן] Qal impf.
2 pl. אהב, fuller archaic form to get full-toned penult before monosyl.; obj.
רִיק (*v. 2¹*): cf. 11⁵ 52⁵· ⁶ 109¹⁷ for loving other forms of evil. — תְּבַקְשׁוּ כָזָב]
phr. *a.λ.* Vb. Piel impf. 2 pl. cf. ב׳ רע Ps. 17¹¹. ‡ כוב *lie, falsehood* 4⁹, 5⁷ 40⁵
58⁴ 62⁵· ¹⁰. — 4. הפלה י׳ חָסִיד לוֹ] phr. *a.λ.* vb. Hiph. pf. aorist. The line is
too long in 𝔐, either י׳ or לוֹ must be a gloss. But it is the latter, bec. we
should rd. † הפלא חֶסֶד as 17⁷ 31²², *shew extraordinary kindness.* The misinterpretation as חסיד occasioned the addition of לוֹ; 37 codd. Ken. 28 De Rossi
rd. הפלא. Most recent critics, Dy., Che., Gr., We., Oort, Du. rd. חֶסֶד, but
differ as to חסרו לי or חסרו לו or הסר לי. The use of חסר is so important
in ψ that it seems best to give the complete usage here. †(חסר) vb. denom.
only Hithp. *shew oneself kind :* Ps. 18²⁶ = 2 S. 22²⁶. ‡ חֶסֶד n.m. (1) of man
kindness (*a*) toward men in doing favours and benefits 141⁵, (*b*) especially as
extended to the lowly, needy, and miserable 109¹²· ¹⁶; (2) of God *kindness,
lovingkindness,* in condescension to the needs of His creatures. He is חַסְדִּי

144²; אֱלֹהֵי חַסְדִּי 59¹⁸; אֱלֹהֵי חסדו 59¹¹ (so 𝔊, 𝔙, Ew., Hup., De., Pe., Che., Bä.);
His is the kindness 62¹³; it is with Him 130⁷; specifically (a) *in redemption
from enemies and troubles*: 21⁸ 31¹⁷· ²² (= 4ᵇ)32¹⁰ 33²² 36⁸ 42⁹ 44²⁷ 48¹⁰ 59¹⁷
66²⁰ 85⁸ 90¹⁴ 94¹⁸ 107⁸· ¹⁵· ²¹· ³¹ 143⁸· ¹²; men should trust in it 13⁶ 52¹⁰; rejoice
in it 31⁸; hope in it 33¹⁸ 147¹¹. (b) *in preservation of life from death*: 6⁵
86¹³. (c) *in quickening spiritual life*: 109²⁶ 119⁴¹· ⁷⁶· ⁸⁸· ¹²⁴· ¹⁴⁹· ¹⁵⁹. (d) *in
redemption from sin*: 25⁷ 51³. (e) *in keeping the covenants with David and
his dynasty*: 18⁵¹ 89²⁹· ³⁴. (f) grouped with other divine attributes: הס־ ואמת
Pss. 25¹⁰ 40¹¹· ¹² 57⁴ 61⁸ 85¹¹ 89¹⁵ 115¹ 138² Gn. 24²⁷ (J); רב חסד ואמת Ex. 34⁶
(J) Ps. 86¹⁵; אמת Pss. 26³ 117² Mi. 7²⁰; אמונה Pss. 88¹² 89³· ²⁵ 92⁸; רחמים 77⁹
98³ 103⁴; חסד ומשפט 101¹ Je. 9²³; צדקה Ps. 36¹¹; טוב וחסד 23⁶. (g) The
kindness of God is (a) *abundant*: רב חסד *abundant, plenteous in kindness*
Nu. 14¹⁸ (J) Ne. 9¹⁷ (Qr.)Jo. 2¹³ Jon. 4² Ps. 86⁵ 103⁸ (cf. Ex. 34⁶ (J) Ps. 86¹⁵);
רב חסדֶּךָ Ne. 13²²Pss. 5⁸ 69¹⁴ 106⁷ (𝔊, 𝔙, Aq., 𝕋 to be preferred to MT.
חֲסָרֶיךָ); רֹב חֲסָדֶיךָ La. 3³² Ps. 106⁴⁵ (Kt., 𝔊 in both preferable). (b) *great in
extent*: גדול חסד 145⁸; great as the heavens 57¹¹ 103¹¹; cf. 36⁶ 108⁵; the
earth is full of it 33⁵ 119⁶⁴. (c) *everlasting*: לעולם חסדו Je. 33¹¹ 1 Ch. 16³⁴· ⁴¹
2 Ch. 5¹³ 7⁸· ⁶ 20²¹ Ezr. 3¹¹ Pss. 100⁵ 106¹ 107¹ 118¹· ²· ³· ⁴· ²⁹ 136¹⁻²⁶(²⁶ᵗ·); cf. 52⁸
103¹⁷ 138⁸. (d) *good*: 63⁴ 69¹⁷ 109²¹. (h) pl. *mercies, deeds of kindness*:
the historic displays, mostly late: Pss. 25⁶ 89² Is. 63⁷; promised in Davidic
covenant Ps. 89⁵⁰; in general La. 3²² Ps. 17⁷; cf. 31²² 4ᵇ (sg.) 107⁴³.
‡ חָסִיד adj. (1) *kind*: of man 18²⁶ = 2 S. 22²⁶; of nation Ps. 43¹; of God, only
145¹⁷ Je. 3¹². (2) as n. *pious, godly*: because kindness, as prominent in the
godly, comes to imply other attributes and be a designation of the godly
character, piety; sg. 4⁴ 12² (?) 32⁶ 86²; *Thy pious one* 16¹⁰ (Kt. pl.) pl. *the
pious, godly*, those of the people who were faithful, devoted to God's service,
only in ψ and chiefly if not entirely in late Pss. 149¹· ⁵; *His pious ones* 30⁵ 31²⁴
37²⁸ 85⁹ 97¹⁰ 116¹⁵ 148¹⁴ 149⁹; *Thy pious ones* 52¹¹ 79² 89²⁰ 132⁹ 145¹⁰; *My
pious ones* 50⁵; *her* (Zion's) *pious ones* 132¹⁶. In the Maccabean age συναγωγὴ
Ἀσιδαίων denoted, technically, the party of the pious who opposed the Helleni-
sation of Judaea. See 1 Macc. 2¹² 7¹⁸ 2 Macc. 14⁶; so perhaps Pss. 116¹⁵
149¹· ⁵· ⁹. — 5. רָגְזוּ] imv. Qal 2 pl. refers to בְּנֵי אִישׁ v.³ ‡ רגז Qal *be agitated,
quiver, tremble*, of foundations of mountains 18⁸, depths of sea 77¹⁷, of the earth
77¹⁹, peoples 99¹, so here most suitably. 𝔊, Σ ὀργίζεσθε = Eph. 4²⁶, 𝔍, *be angry*,
AV. is sustained by Is. 28²¹ of God's anger and Pr. 29⁹ of man's. But in these
cases it is rather the quivering and trembling of passion, which is justifiable;
and is regarded by many as Hiph. v. BDB. — וְאַל־תֶּחֱטָאוּ] two tones, neg.
Qal impf. pl. 2 m. jussive ו conj. *and* not advers. *but*, as required by interp. of
𝔊, 𝔍. 𝔍 *nolite* (*peccare*) might imply תאבו and so give us the missing word of
this tetrameter. But 𝔊 has ἃ λέγετε. This may be an interp. to get an obj. for
אמרו or it may rest upon an original אשר = ‡ אֲשׁוּר *step, going*, for mode of life
as 17⁵ 37³¹ 40³ 44¹⁹ 73² cf. 17¹¹. Probably בן אדם is the missing word which
must be supplied in thought and might have been omitted by prosaic copyist as
unnecessary. ‡ חטא vb. Qal in ψ alw. *miss the goal* or *path of right and duty,
sin* (agst. God): abs. 4⁵ 78³², in confession 106⁶; c. לְ 78¹⁷ 119¹¹ in con-

fession 41[6] 51[6]; c. ב of instr. 39[2] cf. Jb. 2[10]. Piel in ψ only †*purify from uncleanness* 51[9]; elsw. in this sense Lv. 14[49. 52] Nu. 19[19] (P). Hiph. *bring to condemnation* or *punishment* Dt. 24[4] Is. 29[21], possibly Ps. 59[13] (insertion in text). — אמרו בלבבכם [†]. phr. a.λ. ψ, but Dt. 7[17] 8[17] 9[4] 18[21] Is. 14[13] 47[8] 49[21] Je. 5[24] 13[22] Zp. 1[12] 2[15] cf. Ho. 7[2] (?), cf. † אמר בלב Ps. 10[6. 11. 13] 14[1] (= 53[2]) 35[25] 74[8], elsw. Gn. 17[17] (P) 27[41] (JE) 1 K. 12[26] Est. 6[6] Ec. 2[1. 15] 3[17. 18] Is. 47[19] Ob.[3] Zc. 12[5] cf. Gn. 8[21] (J) 1 S. 27[1]. † דבר בלבב ל Ps. 15[2] כלב Ec. 2[15]. The use of לֵב is so important in ψ that the entire usage is given below:

‡ לֵבָב n.m. *the inner, middle or central part:* usually *of men* (1) *the inner man* in contrast with the outer, שאר ולבב 73[26]; hands 73[13] (La. 3[41] ?); speech 28[3] 78[18]. (2) *the inner man* indef. *the soul*, comprehending mind, affections and will; or in connection with certain vbs. having more specif. reference to some one of them 62[9] 73[26] 86[11] 139[23]; בכל לבב 86[12] 111[1] 1 S. 7[8] 12[20. 24] 1 K. 14[8] 2 K. 10[31] 2 Ch. 15[15] 22[9] 31[21] Je. 29[13] Jo. 2[12]; abbr. from phr. בכל-ל ובכל-נפש characteristic of D. בל־ Ps. 84[6] (?); עם ל 77[7] (rd. c. הנה as 𝔊); כל־ 20[5] 1 S. 13[14] 14[7]. (3) specif. ref. to *mind* (characteristic of לבב); (a) *knowledge:* ל חכמה 90[12] (cf. Jb. 9[4]). (b) *thinking, reflection:* 73[7] (77[7] supra 2). (4) specif. ref. to moral character (charact. of לבב): יָשָׁר ל 119[7](?) Dt. 9[5] 1 Ch. 29[17], cf. 2 Ch. 29[34] 1 K. 3[6] 2 K. 10[15]; תָּם־ל Ps. 78[72] 101[2] Gn. 20[5. 6] (E) 1 K. 9[4]; בר ל Ps. 24[4], cf. בָּרֵי ל 73[1]; as seat of erring 95[10]; as froward 101[4]; as seat of pride 101[5]; הקשה ל 95[8]. (5) = *the man himself* (mng. charact. of נפש); so here (4[5]) and in all uses of phrases with לבב given above, including 15[2]; also יְחִי לְבַבְכֶם *let your heart* (you yourselves) *live* (late) 22[27] 69[33], cf. 119[175]. (6) specif. as *seat of the appetites* (for which usually נֶפֶשׁ) 104[15]; סְעַד ל *stay the heart* (with food) 104[15] (Ju. 19[8] (?)). (7) specif. as *seat of the emotions and passions* (for which usually נפש); of trouble 13[3] 25[17] 73[21] 109[16]. (8) *seat of courage* (for which usually רוּחַ) 31[25], elsw. only Dn. 11[25]. — עַל־מִשְׁכַּבְכֶם preg. *lying upon your bed.* ‡ מִשְׁכָּב n.m. 4[5] 36[5] 41[4] 149[5]. — וְדֹמּוּ [ו conj., Qal imv. 2 p.; ‡ דמם vb. (1) *be silent, still* 4[5] 30[13] 35[15] (prob.); (2) *be still = perish* 31[18]; c. ל *resigned to* 37[7] 62[6] (?). Poal *be quieted, composed* 131[2]. — 6. וְזִבְחוּ [זָבְחֵי Qal imv. 2 pl. The subj. cannot be בני איש, but their antithesis. That is elsewhere בני אדם, v.[3]. It was omitted by prosaic copyist in text, making measure at fault. ‡ זבח vb. *slaughter sacrifice*, espec. for communion meals; c. acc. of the kind of sacrifice 4[6] 27[6] 50[14. 23] 107[22] 116[17], c. ב, 54[8]; all made to God, but of sons and daughters offered to idols 106[37] (Qal) [88] (Piel, as usual of such sacrifices). ‡ זֶבַח n.m. *sacrifice*, esp. of the class, peace offerings (a) for communion meals ‖ מנחה, עוֹלה, 40[7] 51[18]; (b) covenant 50[5], cf. v.[8]; (c) הודה זבחי thank offerings 107[22] 116[17]; (d) זבחי תרועה [ו phrs. זבחי אלהים 51[19]; זִבְחֵי צֶדֶק *right, normal sacrifices* here as Dt. 33[19] Ps. 51[21]; (f) heathen sacrifices 106[28]. — † וּבִטְחוּ אֶל יהוה] Qal imv. 2 p. phr. 2 K. 18[22] (= Is. 36[7]) Pss. 4[6] 31[7] 56[4] 86[2] Pr. 3[5] to God; to persons Ju. 20[36]; things Je. 7[4]; disting. from בטח בְ, v. Ps. 9[11]; בטח על *rely upon, v. 31[15].* This line is also defective. Gr. attaches רַבִּים in sense of *nobles;* but these were the בני איש, v.[3a], and that mng. of רבים is rare and very late. We might, however, take it in the usual sense of *the*

many, the common multitude ‖ בְּנֵי אָדָם. The displacement was due to the influence of 3² upon copyist. — 7. אֹמְרִים] ptc. pl. verbal force as 3⁸. — מִי יַרְאֵנוּ] Makkeph should be stricken out; for there are two tones, not one, if רבים goes with previous line. The מִי might be question: *Who can* or *will shew us?* expressing discontent and despair; but better as wish, Ges.§ 151 (1).

‡ טוֹב n.m. (1) *welfare, happiness*, obj. ראה 4⁷ 34¹³ Ec. 2²⁴ 3¹³ Jb. 7⁷ (cf. Je. 29³²), בקש Ps. 122⁹, cf. 34¹¹ 84¹² 85¹³, טוֹב וחסד 23⁶, בטוֹב in prosperity 25¹⁸, מטוֹב *afar from happiness* 39⁸; (2) *good things*, sg. coll. 21⁴, obj. שׂבע 104²⁸, cf. 103⁵, מלא 107⁹; (3) *good, benefit*, 119⁶⁵. ¹²²; (4) moral good in autith. to רע 34¹⁵ 37²⁷ 52⁵ Dt. 30¹⁵ Is. 5²⁰ Am. 5¹⁴. ¹⁵, עשׂה טוֹב Ps. 14¹. ³ (= 53². ⁴) 37⁸. ²⁷ Ec. 3¹² (?) 7², רדף טוֹב *pursue good* Ps. 38²¹. — וְסָה] a.λ. Qal imv. cohort.; incorrect for נָסָה. √נסס denom. נס *banner, standard*, and so *wave* the same, Σ ἐπίσημον ποίησον. 𝕲 ἐσημειώθη, 𝔜 *signatum est* = נִסָּה Niph. pf., so Genebr., cf. 60⁶. לְהִתְנֹסֵס Hithp. *that it may be displayed*, of the banner, 𝕲 ἔδωκας σημείωσιν. This suits לֵ־, but not the *light of the divine countenance*. Moderns after ἔπαρον Aq., Θ, *leva*, 𝔍, 𝔗, AE., De W., Ges.§ 76 (2)a, Ew.§ 227b, Kö.I. 42 (10)c regard it as error for נְשָׂא 10¹², so cod. 245 Kenn., נשה cod. 30, usually שׂא 25¹⁸, שׂאו 24⁷. ⁹ 81³ 96⁸ 134². It refers to the blessing of the high priest, Nu. 6²⁴⁻²⁶ (source of P) in the syn. clause יָאֵר פָּנָיו אֵלֶיךָ Nu. 6²⁶, the two melting together in the phr. נְשָׂא אוֹר פָּנֶיךָ, cf. 67²; the prep. על is a late inexactness for אֶל, cf. also 44⁴ 89¹⁶. ‡ אוֹר n.m. (1) *light* as diffused, created 104²; (2) *light* of luminaries, stars 148³, cf. 136⁷; (3) *daylight* 49²⁰, cf. 139¹¹; (4) *light* of fire 78¹⁴; (5) of life 56¹⁴; (6) of prosperity 97¹¹ 112⁴; (7) of instruction 37⁶ 119¹⁰⁵; (8) of face 38¹¹, of God's enlightening face 4⁷ 44⁴ 89¹⁶, cf. 27¹ 36¹⁰ 43⁸. — פָּנִים as used ‡ of God in anthropomorphic and theophanic sense (*a*) *His face* in favour פ׳ אור 4⁷ 44⁴ 89¹⁶, מאור פ׳ 90⁸, האיר פ׳ 31¹⁷ 67² 80⁴. ⁸. ²⁰ 119¹³⁵, indifference (מן) הסתיר פ׳ 10¹¹ 13² 22²⁵ 27⁹ 30⁸ 44²⁵ 51¹¹ 69¹⁸ 88¹⁵ 102⁸ 104²⁹ 143⁷, in hostility c. ב 34¹⁷ 80¹⁷; (*b*) *His presence* בקש פ׳ 24⁶ 27⁸. ⁸ 105⁴, חלה פ׳ 119⁵⁸, קרם פ 89¹⁶ 95², אראה פ׳ 42⁸, חזה פ׳ 11⁷ 17¹⁵, סתר פ׳ 31²¹, in anger 21¹⁰ La. 4¹⁶, על פ׳ in judgment Ps. 9²⁰. — יהוה] at close of line makes it too long. It should go with next line to make that a tetrameter; so 𝔖, Che., Du. —

8. וְנָחֲתָה] fully written Qal pf. 2 m. √נחת. — שִׂמְחָה] n.f. *joy, gladness* 4⁸ 16¹¹ 21⁷ 30¹² 43⁴ 45¹⁶ 51¹⁰ 68⁴ 97¹¹ 100² 106⁵ 137⁸. ⁶. — בְּלִבִּי] short form; cf. long form לבבכם v.⁵. The difference was due to the carelessness of a copyist. The long form is unusual in ψ, therefore more prob. original here. The לֵב as ‡ seat of emotions and passions; of joy in some form of שׂמח 4⁸ 16⁹ 19⁹ 33²¹ 105⁸ (= 1 Ch. 16¹⁰) Ex. 4¹⁴ (J) Pr. 15¹⁸. ³⁰ 17²² 27⁹. ¹¹ Ec. 2¹⁰. ¹⁰ 5¹⁹ Ct. 3¹¹ Is. 24⁷ Zc. 10⁷ (cf. לבב Dt. 28⁴⁷ Is. 30²⁹ Je. 15¹⁶ Ez. 36⁵), שׂישׂ Ps. 119¹¹¹, גיל 13⁶, עלו 28⁷; of desire 21⁸ 37⁴; of trouble 38⁹. ¹¹ 55⁵; other emotions 22¹⁵ 27⁸ 39⁴ 40¹³ 61⁸ 107¹² 109²² 143⁴; of courage 27¹⁴ 76⁶ 119³². — מֵעֵת] pregn. = טוב משׂמחת העת אשר; 𝕲, 𝔖 add ἔλαιον = ויצהרם. This makes line too long, and is gloss to make statement of harvest more complete, as Ho. 2²⁴ —— סְ־ sf. indef., acc. to Ew., Ol., Bä., as proverbial comparison of the Psalmist's personal joy in God with the harvest joy of others, cf. Is. 9². Moll., Pe., think of the prosperous harvest of the enemy as contrasted with the joy in God of the Psalmist. It is better to think of the former prosperity in harvest, and that which they have been urged to pray for = שוב v.⁷ᵃ. — 9. בְּשָׁלוֹם] emph. suggested by ישם לך שלום Nu. 6²⁵, the other parts of formula used v.⁷ᵇ (v. 28³). ‡יַחְדָּו] adv. *together:* (1) of community of action 34⁴ 55¹⁵ 71¹⁰ 83⁶(?) 102²⁸; of parts of building 122³; (2) *at once, at one and the same time,* joining both vbs. in action of same persons, only here 4⁹ in this sense, elsewhere (3) emph. *all together* 14³ (= 53⁴) 19¹⁰ 35²⁶ 37³⁸ 48⁵. — אֶשְׁכְּבָה] Qal impf. 1 p. s. cohort. resolution *I will lie down* or *lay me down.* וְאִישָׁן, because of adv. coördinating two vbs. must be ו coörd. and the form should be אִישָׁנָה, as 3⁶. Coördination may be expressed by repeating the subj. in English. — אַתָּה] emph. pr. 2 m. referring to יהוה v.⁸ᵃ ⁽⁷ᵇ⁾, therefore יהוה, unnecessary in this line and making it too long, is a gloss. — לְבָדָד] adv. *apart, in solitariness,* Nu. 23⁹ Mi. 7¹⁴ (both with שכן), here emphasized by לָבֶטַח *in security* n.m. with לְ prep., with ישב not elsw. ψ, but Lv. 25¹⁸·¹⁹ 26⁵ Ju. 18⁷ 1 K. 5⁵ Je. 32³⁷ 49³¹ Zp. 2¹⁵, c. שכב Pr. 3²⁹ Is. 47⁸ Ez. 28²⁶ 34²⁵·²⁸ 38⁸·¹¹·¹⁴ 39⁶·²⁶ Zc. 14¹¹ Dt. 33¹² Ps. 16⁹ Je. 23⁶ 33¹⁶; לְ omitted with ישב Dt. 12¹⁰ 1 S. 12¹¹ with שכן Dt. 33²⁸ Pr. 1³³. This passage is prob. based on Dt. 33²⁸, espec. as there it is in a land דגן ותירוש as v.⁸. — תֹּשִׁיבֵנִי] Hiph. impf. 2 m. sf. 1 s. *make to dwell* as in Je. 32³⁷.

PSALM V., 5 STR. 4⁵.

Ps. 5 is a prayer composed for public worship. The choir, at morning sacrifice, prays Yahweh to hearken to the cry for help (v.²⁻⁴); for evil and wickedness of speech and action have no place in His presence and are abhorrent to Him (v.⁵⁻⁷). Standing in the court and worshipping towards the temple, they pray for guidance (v.⁸⁻⁹); because the adversaries have abundant wickedness in mind, speech, and act, they plead that God would thrust them forth from His people (v.¹⁰⁻¹¹); and they intercede for blessing upon all who seek refuge in Him (v.¹²⁻¹³).

O GIVE ear to my words, Yahweh; consider my murmuring;
   O hearken to the voice of my crying for help, my King, and my God;
   For unto Thee I pray in the morning, Thou hearest my voice;
   In the morning I set in order (my prayer) for Thee and I keep watch (for Thee).
FOR Thou art not a God taking delight in wickedness, evil cannot be Thy guest;
   Boasters cannot take their stand before Thine eyes;
   Thou dost hate all workers of trouble, speakers of a lie;
   Men of blood and deceit Thou abhorrest, Yahweh.
BUT as for me through the abundance of Thy kindness I enter Thy house;
   I worship with the reverence that is due Thee, towards Thy holy temple.
   Yahweh lead me in Thy righteousness because of those lying in wait for me;
   Even before me Thy way: (before Thee are my ways).

FOR there is no right in their mouth, in their heart is ruin;
    An open grave is their throat, with their tongue they flatter.
    Declare them guilty, O (my) God, let them fall from their plans:
    In the abundance of their wickedness thrust them out, for they rebelled against
        Thee.
BUT let all that seek refuge in Thee, rejoice, forever shout for joy;
    And let them exult in Thee, all that love Thy name;
    For Thou on Thy part blessest the righteous, Yahweh,
    And Thou coverest them over with a great shield, with favour crownest them.

Ps. 5 was in 𝔇 as the 2d morning prayer, then in 𝔐 and also in 𝔇𝔎 as its 1st morning prayer (*v.* Intr. § 27. 31. 33). There seems to be a designed antithesis between the assignment of Ps. 4, an evening prayer בנגינות *with stringed instruments*, and Ps. 5 a morning prayer אל הנחילות *for flute playing* (*v.* Intr. § 39), probably because the former was regarded as more suited to evening prayer, the preparation for sleep; and the latter to morning prayer, the preparation for work. The antith. between the righteous and the wicked differs much from that of Ps. 1 and implies a much earlier date. The Ps. lacks the personal experience of Pss. 3–4, and is throughout that of the congregation of righteous worshippers. The wicked are wicked men in Israel itself. They are chiefly wicked in tongue: expressions are heaped up for this, *boasters*, v.⁶, *speakers of a lie*, *men of deceit*, v.⁷, *no right in their mouth*, *an open grave their throat*, *with their tongue they flatter*, v.¹⁰. Such do not appear in Preëx. or Exil. Literature; but in the peaceful times of Persian and Greek dominion. They are also men, who in their *mind* plot ruin, v.¹⁰, and have *plans* against the righteous, v.¹¹, and they are also *workers of trouble*, v.⁶, *men of blood*, v.⁷; *they rebel* against Yahweh, v.¹¹. The righteous on the other hand are those who observe morning prayer and sacrifice in the courts of the temple, v.⁴·⁸, from which evil is excluded from being a guest, v.⁵; they seek refuge in Yahweh and love His name, v.¹². The author may have been one of the Levitical singers of the 2d temple. If so, his Ps. must have been composed earlier than those Levitical Pss. which appear in 𝔎 and 𝔄. It must have been written in times of external peace and internal strife; after the second temple had been long built; and sacrifices were habitual in its courts — thus in the middle Persian period.

Str. I. 2. The choir, standing in the court of the temple, v.⁸, prays: *O give ear to my words, Yahweh*], those of this Ps., which has as its complement, *consider my murmuring*], the faint utterance which accompanies the words, and also has its petition. This makes better parall. than EV⁴ "meditation." — **3.** The syn. clause is *O hearken to the voice of my crying for help*]. The righteous need help as the next Str. shows; and their words are a cry, aloud with the voice to Yahweh for it. The complement of l. 2 is syn.

with Yahweh, who is here in the plea, *my King and my God*], in
personal special relations to the righteous petitioners, and in the
double relation as King of the kingdom of Israel, and God of His
people. — **4.** The reason for hearing is given in the syn. couplet,
which is also syn. to the previous couplet. *For unto Thee I pray
in the morning*], at the appointed hour of sacrifice, when Yahweh
was accustomed to hear the *voice* of His worshippers in the liturgical morning prayer at the morning sacrifice. — *I set in order*]
arrange, supplying " my prayer " EV[s.] JPSV, " my case," Dr.,
" cause," Kirk, possibly of the parts of prayer with an allusion to
the parts of the sacrifice. — *and I keep watch*], for God's manifestation of His acceptance of the prayer as it ascends to Him, with
the flame of the sacrifice of the altar.

Str. II. 5–7. The reason for the prayer for help is given in
four syn. lines. Those who occasion the cry for help are described as having *wickedness* and its complement *evil*, syn. with
which are *boasters* of the evil which they plan and do, *workers of
trouble*, with its complement, *speakers of a lie;* and *men of blood
and deceit.* Wickedness and evil of speech are chiefly emphasized
in these boasters, characteristics of wickedness in postex. Israel;
but wickedness of violent action is also involved in men of blood
and workers of trouble. God's attitude towards these men is graphically stated in the syn. clauses : *Thou art not a God taking delight
in*], but the very reverse, as is brought out in the complementary
statement, *evil cannot be Thy guest*], be welcome in the house, in
the courts of Yahweh, among His worshippers ; ‖ *stand before
Thine eyes*], in the choir of worshippers, standing before the
temple building; followed by the positive statement, *Thou dost
hate;* and the climax, *abhor.* This attitude of God towards those
against whom the choir of Israel cries for help, gives strong reason
for the assurance that He will give that help.

Str. III. 8. The choir returns to the direct petition of the first
Str. ; stating in a syn. couplet, parall. to the second couplet of the
first Str., the fact : *I enter Thy house* ‖ *I worship towards Thy holy
temple*], indicating with sufficient clearness that the choir is in
the precincts of the temple, and prostrating themselves in the
court, looking towards the temple, the throne room of Yahweh's
abode. These clauses are qualified with the recognition of the

abundance of kindness of Yahweh which permitted this entrance, and a devout statement of the *reverence* with which the worship was accompanied. — **9.** The second couplet is parallel with the first couplet of Str. I., only the petition, " give ear, consider, hearken," advances to, *lead me*, with its syn., *even before me*, and the sphere of it, *Thy righteousness* ‖ *Thy way*. Guidance in life is needed *because of those lying in wait*, the insidious foes described above in the previous Str. and again in the following. The last clause omitted by MT., but suggested by Vrss., is the climax, *before Thee are my ways*] complementary of, *Even before me Thy way*,] even them, make them Thy way.]

Str. IV. 10–11 is syn. with the second Str. and is a stronger representation of the attitude of God towards the wicked. There are two couplets, making four syn. lines. The emphasis upon wickedness of speech is still stronger ; *There is no right in their mouth*], with its complement *in their heart*], that is in their mind, — *ruin*], the *plan* in their mind is to engulf the righteous in ruins ; cf. 52^4 and so ‖ *an open grave is their throat*, with its complement, *with their tongue they flatter*. There is yet in the last line wickedness of action, *in the abundance of their wickedness*, with its complement, *for they rebelled against Thee*. The attitude of God towards them passes over, from their exclusion from the temple worship, God's hatred and abhorrence of them, in Str. II., to the stronger and more aggressive ; *declare them guilty*, with its complement, *let them fall from their plans*], fail in them, and the climax, *thrust them out*.

Str. V. 12–13 is a final intercession which is parall. with Str. I. and III. ; but needs no subsequent Str. parall. with II. and IV. ; for the wicked have been left behind, thrust out from the community, as well as excluded from the temple. The choir accordingly rises, from petition for help, to intercession for the righteous. This is in two couplets, which again are syn. throughout. They are described as those *that seek refuge in Thee*], in the temple worship ‖ ; *love Thy name*], the holy name of Yahweh, as connected with His holy temple. They are finally designated as the *righteous*. These, in the syn. clauses ; *rejoice*, with its complement, *forever shout for joy;* ‖ *exult in Thee;* three terms for the liturgy of temple worship. The climax is reached in the more comprehensive *blessest*, and its specific double simile of tender care and loving attention ; *coverest them over with a great shield*], so guarding from all evil and adversaries ; and its complement, *with favour crownest them*], as favoured guests rejoicing at a feast in their honour, cf. 23⁵, 103⁴.

2. אֲמָרַי] pl. sf. 1. p. emph. ‡ אֹמֶר n.m. (1) *utterance, word* 19⁴, of men esp. in prayer 5² 141⁶. אִמְרֵי פִי Dt. 32¹ Ps. 19¹⁵ 54⁴ 78¹ 138⁴, fig. day to day 19³; of God, אמרי אל 107¹¹. (2) promise of God 77⁹, command 68¹². — הַאֲזִינָה] Hiph. imv. cohort. — ‡√ [אֵן] denom. אֹזֶן n.f. *ear*, only Hiph. (1) *give ear to*, of God's listening to prayer, c. acc. rei 5² 17¹ 55² 86⁶ 140⁷ 141¹, c. אֶל rei 39¹⁸ 143¹, c. לְ rei 54⁴; אֶל pers. 77², Dt. 1⁴⁵, abs. Pss. 80² 84⁹. (2) *perceive by ear, hear*, abs. 135¹⁷, listen to; of men, abs. 49², c. עַל rei 78¹. — בִּינָה] Qal imv. cohort. בִּין *observe, mark, give heed to*, c. acc. as Dt. 32⁷ Pss. 50²² 94⁷·⁸, but only here in connection with prayer. — ‡ הֲגִיגִי] 5² 39⁴ *my musing, my murmuring*, faint utterance, rather than *meditation* of EVˢ. 𝕲 κραυγῆς μου, 𝖁 *clamorem meum*. The former is too weak, the latter too strong. — 3. הַקְשִׁיבָה] Hiph. imv. cohort. ‡ קֹשׁב] Hiph. *hearken*, לְקוֹל only here ; but c. לְ pers. 55³, c. בְקוֹל 66¹⁹ 86⁶, c. אֶל 142⁷, c. acc. 17¹ 61², abs. with אָזְנֶךָ 10¹⁷, dub. (אֵן gloss), cf. 130². — שׁוּעִי] Piel inf. cstr. BDB., Ols.§ ¹⁸²ᵈ, so Du. for שַׁוְּעִי. — ‡√ [שׁוּע] only Piel *cry for help*, abs. 5³ 18⁴² 72¹² 119¹⁴⁷ Jb. 19⁷ 24¹² 29¹² 30²⁸ 35⁹ 36¹³ Is. 58⁹ La. 3⁸, Jon. 2⁸ Hb. 1², so prob. 88², c. אֶל pers. Pss. 18⁷ 22²⁵ 28²(= 31²³) 30⁸ 88¹⁴ Jb. 30²⁰ 38⁴¹. Bä. regards it as n., for usual שׁוּעִי 18⁷, cf. Kö.II. 1, p. 50. — ‡ [מַלְכִּי וֵאלֹהָי = 84⁴, מלכי אלהים 44⁵ (ואלהי 𝕲). ‡ God as King of Israel, Dt. 33⁵ Pss. 10¹⁶ 29¹⁰ 48³ 68²⁵ 74¹² 145¹ 149², מלך הכבוד 24⁷·⁸·⁹·¹⁰·¹⁰, universal king 47³·⁷·⁸ 95³ 98⁶ 99⁴ Je. 10⁷·¹⁰. — כִּי־אֵלֶיךָ] emph. beginning a new line. — אֶתְפַּלֵּל] Hiph. impf. 1 sg. present. ‡ התפלל c. אֶל *pray unto*, elsw. 32⁶, c. בְּעַד *intercede for* 72¹⁵. — 4. יהוה is attached by 𝕲 Du. to previous clause, and properly, if original, but it is a gloss making line too long. — בֹּקֶר תִּשְׁמַע קוֹלִי] belongs with previous clause to complete pentameter. בֹּקֶר acc. time in the morning, the hour of prayer, so 59¹⁷ 88¹⁴ 92³, the three hours of prayer 55¹⁸. It belongs with אתפלל and not with תשמע. — אֶעֱרָךְ] shortened form due to Makkeph, which, however, is an erroneous combination. Separate words are needed for measure. ‡ עָרַךְ (1) *arrange*, used Gn. 22⁹ (E) for arranging wood of sacrifice, Ex. 40⁴·²³, (P) of shew bread, so here in fig. sense as most, or as Jb. 32¹⁴ 33⁵ 37¹⁹ *arrange, set forth*, words in order; elsw. arrange lamp Ps. 132¹⁷, table 23⁵ 78¹⁰, *set forth in order* thoughts 40⁶, a case 50²¹. (2) c. לְ *resemble* 89⁷ (‖ דמה). — לְךָ] should be repeated with אֲצַפֶּה for the completion of the line. This is necess. to get two tones after caesura, and gives better euphony. Moreover, this prep. is required by the vb. — אֲצַפֶּה] Piel impf. 1 p. ‡ צפה Qal *watch*, c. לְ 37³², c. בְּ 66⁷. Piel c. אֶל La. 4¹⁷, c. בְּ Mi. 7⁷, so c. לְ Ps. 5⁴. — 5. This v. is too long, a Makkeph should combine לֹא־אֵל, and if original כִּי also. אַתָּה if original, is out of place separated from לֹא. It is doubtless a prosaic gloss. —

אֵל] n.m. archaic name of God as the *Strong* one (for use in ψ *v.* Intr. § 36).—
‡ חָפֵץ] vb. adj. cstr. acc. of God only here, but of man 34¹⁸ 35²⁷, pl. cstr. before
names 35²⁷ 40¹⁵ = 70³ with sf. 111². The vb. itself ‡ used of God, c. with בְּ pers.
18²⁰ 22⁹ 41¹², rei. 147¹⁰, c. acc. rei. 37²³ 40⁷ 51⁸·¹⁸·²¹ 115⁸ 135⁶, all in mng.
delight in, have pleasure in. For syn. רצו v. v.¹³.— ‡ רֶשַׁע] n.m. *wickedness* (1) in
violence and crime 141⁴ Pr. 12³ ; (2) of enemies Ps. 125³ (but ⅏ SS. רָשָׁע) ;
(3) in ethical sense 5⁵ 10¹⁵ 45⁸ 84¹¹ (?), cf. Pr. 8⁷ Jb. 34⁸·¹⁰ 35⁸ Ec. 7²⁰ 8⁸.
(For רָשָׁע v. Ps. 1¹.) — יִגְרְךָ] Qal impf. 3 sg. sf. 2 sg. defective for יגורך potential mood, Ges.§107 (8b), Dr.§37. ‡ גור Qal (1) *sojourn* in land, c. בּ loci
105¹²·²³, of Israel in Egypt and patriarchs in Canaan, cf. Gn. 26³(J) ; (2) fig.
be a guest of Yahweh, c. בּ loci, in His temple Pss. 15¹ 61⁵, c. acc. pers. fig. 5⁵,
cf. 120⁵. ‡ גֵר n.m. only in sense of *sojourner*, c בּ loci 119¹⁹, c. עִם pers. 39¹³ :
abs. ‖ widow and orphan 94⁶ 146⁹.— רָע] either adj. *evil man* ⅏, ᴣ, Hu., De.,
Ki., al. as 10¹⁵ ‖ הולְלִים v.⁶ ; or n.m. *evil* ‖ רָשָׁע, EVˢ., Dr. most, in accord with complementary part of a pentameter.— ‡ רַע] adj. : (1) *bad, disagreeable, malignant*
144¹⁰ (sword) ; *fierce* 78⁴⁹ (messenger of God). (2) *unpleasant* 112⁷ Je.
49²³. (3) *evil, wicked* ethically, of pers. רע אדם Ps. 140², רָע *evil man* 10¹⁵ Jb.
21³⁰ Pr. 11²¹ 12¹⁸, *thing* עשה הרע בעיני Ps. 51⁶ phr. of D. Dt. 4²⁵ +, c. 60 t.; of
deeds Pss. 55¹⁶ 64⁶ 141⁴. ‡ רַע n.m. : (1) *evil distress, adversity* 23⁴ ; † יְמֵי רע
49⁶ 94¹⁸, cf. Am. 6³ ; ברע *in adversity* Ps. 10⁶, cf. 121⁷ 140¹². (2) *evil, injury,
wrong* 7⁵ 41⁶ 54⁷ 73⁸ 109²⁰ ; לרע *for harm* 56⁶ Je. 7⁶ 25⁷ Is. 59⁷. (3) *evil*, in
ethical sense, Pss. 7¹⁰ 34¹⁴·¹⁷ 36⁵ 52⁵ 97¹⁰ 101⁴ 119¹⁰¹, prob. also 5⁵ (others
adj. *evil man*) ; סור מֵרָע 34¹⁵ 37²⁷ Is. 59¹⁵ Pr. 3⁷ 13¹⁹ 14¹⁶ 16⁶·¹⁷ Jb. 1¹·⁸ 2³ 28²⁸,
cf. רעה Ps. 21¹².— 6. יִתְיַצְּבוּ] Hithp. impf. 3 pl. potential v. 2².—הולְלִים] ptc. pl.
‡ הלל] vb. Qal *be boastful* 75⁵, elsw. only ptc. *boasters* 5⁶ 73⁸ 75⁵ ; Piel same
mng., c. עַל 10⁸ (?) and in good sense, c. בּ 44⁹ 56⁶·¹¹ ; Hithp. *make one's boast*
c. בּ in bad sense 49⁷ 52³ 97¹, in good sense 34⁸ 105⁸, abs. 63¹² 64¹¹ 106⁵. v. Intr.
§ 35 for the use of vb. in the sense of *praise.*— ‡ לְנֶגֶד עֵינֶיךָ] *before Thine eyes*,
locally, in temple worship ; elsw. ideally of God 18²⁵, of man 26³ 36² 101⁸.—
שָׂנֵאתָ] Qal pf. 2 sg. emph. present √ שׂנא *hate*, cf. 11⁵ where alone, elsw. in ψ God
hates evil. But the idea is common in Prophets. The vb. is frequently used
of righteous men hating evil 26⁵ 31⁷ + 10 t. ψ.— † כָּל־פֹּעֲלֵי אָוֶן] *all workers of
trouble*, Qal ptc. pl. cstr. nominal force phr. 6⁹ 14⁴(= 53⁵ without כל) 92⁸ 94⁴
101⁸ (without כל) 28³ 36¹³ 59⁸ 64⁸ 94¹⁶ 125⁵ 141⁴·⁹, elsw. Ho. 6⁸ Is. 31² Jb. 31⁸
34⁸·²² Pr. 10²⁹ 21¹⁵. Text is wrongly divided here, giving only first part of
pentameter. The second or complementary part is v.⁷ᵃ. דִּבְרֵי כָזָב. The separation, or else prosaic view of a copyist, occasioned the insertion of the vb.
תֹּאבֵד, which is inappropriate between שׂנא and חעב.— 7. ‡ דֹּבְרֵי כָזָב] = 58⁴ Qal
ptc. pl. √/[דבר] *speak* Qal only inf. and ptc. cf. antith. ד׳ אמת 15², elsw. 28⁸
31¹⁹ 51⁶ 63¹² 101⁷ 109²⁰ ; v. 4³ for † כָזָב.— אִישׁ דָּמִים] n. of relation coll., cf. 2 S.
16⁷·⁸, for usual † אַנְשֵׁי דָמִים *those guilty of bloodshed* Pss. 26⁹ 55²⁴ 59⁸ 139¹⁹ Pr.
29¹⁰, cf. Pss. 9¹⁸ 51¹⁶. There should be no Makkeph after אִישׁ, and possibly
we should rd. אַנְשֵׁי as usual.— ‡ וּמִרְמָה] is also dependent on אִישׁ, cf. Pss. 43¹
55²⁴. Other uses of מִרְמָה *deceit* 10⁷ 17¹ 24⁴ 34¹⁴ 35²⁰ 36⁴ 38¹⁸ 50¹⁹ 52⁶ 55¹²
109².— יְתָעֵב] Piel impf. 3 sg. יהוה subj. is an unnatural change of tense

though in 𝔏, 𝕾. But 𝕴 *abominaberis* has preserved the original תְּחָעֵב, the weak ת having been omitted in other texts by txt. err. on acct. of the following ת, which would then very easily be interp. as 3 pers. ‡ [√תעב] not in Qal, but Piel : *abhor* (1) in ritual sense, of God, Israel 106⁴⁰ ; (2) in ethical sense, of God 5⁷, man 119¹⁶³ ; (3) in physical sense 107¹⁸. Hiph. in ethical sense 14¹ = 53² *make abominable, cause* their evil deeds *to be abhorred.* — **8.** [וַאֲנִי] emph. antith. 2 pers. v.⁵. — † [רֹב חֶסֶד] *abundance of kindness* as 69¹⁴ 106⁷ (𝕾, 𝔙, Aq. 𝔗 to be preferred to 𝔏 (הסריך Ne. 13²², רב חסרו 106⁴⁵ (?) La. 3³², cf. † רב חסד 86⁵. ¹⁵ 103⁸ based on Ec. 34⁶ Nu. 14¹⁸ (J.) and later Ne. 9¹⁷ Jo. 2¹⁸ Jon. 4². — [בְּיָתְךָ] acc. loci after אבוא Qal impf. 1 p. sg. present, *I enter Thy house* for ordinary worship, so 66¹⁸, cf. entrance of processions 42⁵ 55¹⁵ 122¹, in other phr. see 23⁶. בוא c. acc. loci seldom in ψ, elsw. 71⁸ 105²⁸, more common with ב or אל (264). — [אֶשְׁתַּחֲוֶה] Hithp. impf. 1 p. ‡ √(שחה) only Hithp. (1) *do homage to* a king c. ל 45¹² 72¹¹ ; (2) (*a*) *bow down in worship* of God c. לפני 22²⁸. ³⁰ 86⁹, c. אל, looking towards 5⁸ 138², c. ל 99⁵. ⁹ 132⁷; (*b*) in the more general sense of *worship*, abs. 95⁶, c. ל 29² 66⁴ 96⁹ 97⁷; (*c*) idolatrous worship, c. ל 81¹⁰ 106¹⁹. — [הֵיכַל קָדְשֶׁךָ] refers to the hall of the temple into which priests only were admitted to worship with the holy incense, as the place unto which worship was directed. 5⁸ = 138² Jon. 2⁵. ⁸ without prep.; as place defiled by enemy Ps. 79¹. קדש היכלך as source of blessing 65⁵. היכל קדשׁ is used 11⁴ Mi. 1² Hb. 2²⁰ in more general sense for the heavenly temple in which God resides. Other uses of ‡ היכל without קדש are (1) palace of king Ps. 45¹⁶, fig. of ivory boxes 45⁹, of well-shaped daughters 144¹²; (2) of the hall of the temple 27⁴ 48¹⁰, of the heavenly temple 18⁷ 29⁹ 68⁸⁰. — [יִרְאָתֶךָ] obj. sf. Ges.§¹³⁵ (*a*) *reverence due Thee,* cf. 34¹² 90¹¹ 111¹⁰ 119⁸⁸, v. *a*¹¹. — **9.** [נְחֵנִי] Qal imv. sf. 1 p. sq. ‡ נחה Qal *lead* sq. acc. usually, God subj. Ex. 15¹⁸ Ps. 77²¹, fig. 5⁹ 27¹¹, c. ב 139²⁴, man subj. c. אל 60¹¹ = 108¹¹, Hiph. *lead, guide* 78¹¹. ⁵³. ⁷² 107⁸⁰, esp. in path of blessing 23³ 31⁴ 61⁸ 67⁵, 73²⁴, cf. 43³ 139¹⁰ 143¹⁰. ‡ צְדָקָה n.f. *righteousness:* (1) in government of king 72¹. ³, of God, as attribute 33⁵ 36⁷ 71¹⁹ 99⁴ Je. 9²³ ; (2) *righteousness,* as ethically right Ps. 106⁸. ³¹, cf. Gn. 15⁶ (JE); (3) as vindicated, *justification, salvation* (*a*) of God || ברכה 24⁶, חסד 36¹¹ 103¹⁷. בצ He guides, delivers, exalts His people 5⁹ 31² 71² 89¹⁷ 119⁴⁰ 143¹. ¹¹, cf. 69²⁸ (denied to wicked). His saving righteousness 22⁸² 40¹¹ 51¹⁶ 71¹⁵. ¹⁶. ²⁴ 98² 145⁷, ירע צ 88¹³, עמרת לער 111³ 112⁸. ⁹, cf. 119¹⁴²; (4) pl. the *righteous acts* (*a*) of God in vindication of right 103⁶ ; (*b*) of man's moral conduct 11⁷ (*si vera*) Is. 64⁵ Je. 51¹⁰. — [לְמַעַן] prep. *because of,* referring to enemies, שוררים 5⁹ 27¹¹, צוררים 8⁸, איבים 60¹⁹. — [שׁוֹרְרָי] Polel ptc. pl. sf. 1 p. sg. מ prefix elided BDB. Ges.§⁵². ‡ √שׁור, always in same form 5⁹ = 27¹¹ 54⁷ 56⁸ 59¹¹; 𝕾 ἐχθρῶν 𝕴 *insidiatores,* Dr. *watchful foes* = more strictly *liers in wait for me.* — [הוֹשַׁר] Kt. הַיְשַׁר Qr. Ges.§⁷⁰ ⁽²⁾ Hiph. imv. ‡ √יָשַׁר Qal *be smooth, straight, right,* Piel *esteem right* 119¹²⁸, † Hiph. *make smooth, even* only here, elsw. *look straight,* only Pr. 4²⁵. Vrss. differ 𝕾, Bar. Heb. ἐνώπιόν σου τὴν ὁδόν μου, some codd. 𝕾 ἐνώπιόν μου, few ὁδόν σου, Aq. Σ, 𝕴, 𝖘, 𝔗 agree with 𝔏. It is prob. as the line is defective, that the difference represents two parts of an original complete line הישר לפני דרכך לפניך דרכי. This gives us rhyme in

-*kd* and -*t*. — **10.** [פירהו] txt. err. for פימו 17¹⁰ as 𝔊, 𝔍; sg. improb. in the midst of pls. — [נכוֹנָה] Niph. ptc. fem. √ כון *v.* 7¹⁰ *what is right*, as Jb. 42⁷· ⁸ 𝔊 ἀλήθεια 𝔍 *rectum.* — [קרבם] *their inward part* (𝔊 καρδία interprets, 𝔍 *interiora* is literal), as the seat of thought, and so local acc. antith. פה 49¹² (?) 62⁵ 64⁷ (?) 94¹⁹ 103¹; seat of לב 39⁴ 55⁵ 109²², of רוח 51¹², בקרב לב 36². — [הַוָּה] pl. ‡ הַוּה n.f. in ψ always pl. of intensity, *ruin* into which one has fallen and been engulfed, either as meditated 5¹⁰ 52⁴, spoken 38¹⁸, or accomplished 55¹² 57², all 𝔇; elsw. of pestilence 91⁸ and of wicked throne 94²⁰. Ps. 52⁹ הַוָּתו 𝔚 error for הונו 𝔊, 𝔗 and most moderns. — † [חֶבֶר פָּרוּחַ] There should be no Makkeph, phr. elsw. Je. 5¹⁶ (of quiver). ‡ קֶבֶר n. *tomb* 88⁶· ¹², cf. 49¹² (Vrss. not 𝔚). — [יַחֲלִיקוּן] Hiph. impf. 3 pl. fuller form. ‡ √ חלק Qal *be smooth, slippery*, of deceptive words 55²². Hiph. *flatter* with tongue 5¹⁰ Pr. 28²³, abs. *deal smoothly*, c. אל Ps. 36⁸. — **11.** [הַאֲשִׁימֵם] *a.λ.* Hiph. imv. sf. 3 pl. √ אָשֵׁם Qal (1) *commit an offence, do a wrong ;* (2) *be* or *become guilty*, not in ψ ; but (3) *be held guilty, bear punishment* 34²²· ²³. Hiph. *declare guilty* 5¹¹. 𝔊 κρῖνον αὐτούς, Aq. Σ κατάκρινον αὐτούς, 𝔍 *condemna eos.* — [אלהים] is surprising in a petition of 𝔇, though sustained by 𝔊, 𝔍 al. It is probable that the original was אֱלֹהַי. — [יפלוּ מ] Qal impf. juss. pl. 3 m. either (1) *fall from*, as 𝔊, 𝔍, DeW., Ew., Hi., Bä., as BS. 14² ψ Solomon 4¹⁶ ; or (2) *fall, perish, because of* by, as Pe., Che., Dr., Kirk, Du., which suits parall., so 27². — [ממעצותיהם] should have two accents in measure, pl. sf. 3 pl. with prep. מן. — † [מועצה] n.f. only pl. *counsels, plans* 5¹¹ 81¹³ Mi. 6¹⁶ Ho. 11⁶ Je. 7²⁴ Pr. 1⁸¹ 22²⁰. — [ברב פשעיהם] is attached by 𝔊 to previous clause, but that destroys the measure. 𝔊, 𝔍 κατά, *juxta* = כ not so good as ב 𝔚. — ‡ [פֶּשַׁע] n.m. *transgression* against God 107¹⁷, personified as evil spirit 36², recognised by sinner 32⁵ 51⁵, God visits it 89³³, forgives 32¹, removes 103¹², covers it over 65⁴, blots it out 51³, remembers it not 25⁷, delivers from it 39⁹; (2) *guilt of transgression* 5¹¹ 19¹⁴ 59⁴. — [הַדִּיחֵמוֹ] Hiph. imv. with full sounding sf. 3 pl. for מ above. ‡ √ נדח *thrust out, banish*, here the wicked, but 62⁶ the good man from his position. Hiph. *be thrust out* 147². — [כִּי־מָרוּ בָךְ] should have two accents for measure. נָרוּ because of following monosyl. 𝔊 adds κύριε = 𝔍 *domine*, but this is gloss making line too long. ‡ מָרָה vb. Qal *be disobedient, rebellious*, c. ב Ho. 14¹ and here, elsw. c. acc. pers., also words of God Ps. 105²⁸ abs. 78⁸. Hiph. *shew disobedience*, alw. towards God, abs. 106⁷· ⁴³, c. acc. 78¹⁷· ⁴⁰· ⁵⁶ 106³³ 107¹¹, prob. also 139²⁰ (acc. 𝔍, Σ, Aq., not 𝔚). — **12.** ו] adversative to previous Str. — [וְיִשְׂמְחוּ] Qal impf. 3 pl. juss. שׂמח vb. Qal *be glad, rejoice :* ‡ in relation to God and sacred things: (a) abs. 5¹² 9⁸ 14⁷ (= 53⁷) 16⁹ 34⁸ 35²⁷ 48¹² 67⁵ 68⁴ 69³³ 90¹⁴ 96¹¹ 97¹· ⁸ 105³ 107⁴² 119⁷⁴; (b) c. ב *rei vel pers.* 31⁸ 32¹¹ 33²¹ 40¹⁷ (= 70⁵) 63¹² 64¹¹ 66⁶ 85⁷ 97¹² 104³⁴ 118²⁴ 149²; in other relations *v.* BDB. — [חוֹסֵי בָךְ] Qal ptc. pl. cstr. with retracted accent, *v.* ²¹². — [וִירַנְּנוּ] Piel impf. juss. ‡ רנן vb. Qal *be jubilant, shout for joy :* only 35²⁷, for which 40¹⁷ = 70⁵ substitute שׂושׂ. But Qal is 8 t. in Is. ²· ³. Piel same mng. more intensive (1) abs. 5¹² 63⁸ 67⁵ 71²³ 90¹⁴ 96¹² 98⁴· ⁸ 132⁹· ¹⁶· ¹⁶ 149⁵; (2) c. ב of theme 20⁶ 33¹ 89¹³ 92⁸, c. acc. 51¹⁶ 59¹⁷ 145⁷, c. ל 95¹, c. אל 84³(?). Hiph. (1) same mng.: abs. 32¹¹, c. ל 81²; (2) *cause to jubilate*

6⁹. For nouns *v. 17¹.* — [וְתִסָּךְ עָלֵימוֹ] is out of place, destroying the measure of this line and making the construction difficult. It is needed in v.¹³ᵇ to complete the line and give an appropriate vb. to הָסֵךְ. — צִנָּה Hiph. impf. 2 p. juss. form appropriate to its present context; but it should correspond with תְעַטְרֵנוּ v.¹³ if transferred, and be pointed as *indicative.* ‡ סָכַךְ vb. Qal *screen, cover,* c. לְ 140⁸(?) usually c. עַל in other Lit. Hiph. same c. עַל, here, לְ 91⁴. — [וְיַעְלְצוּ] Qal impf. juss. as syn. verbs. † עָלֵץ vb. *exult* c. בְּ 5¹² 9³ 1 S. 2¹, abs. Ps. 25² 68⁴ Pr. 11¹⁰ 28¹² 1 C. 16³² (= עלז Ps. 96¹²), cf. עלז 28⁷, עלס Jb. 20¹⁸, diff. forms of same word, softened in later usage. — [אֹהֲבֵי שְׁמֶךָ] ptc. pl. cstr. nominal force אהב. Phr. elsw. 69³⁷ 119¹³², cf. 9¹¹ 61⁶ 83¹⁷. 𝕲 has πάντες, which represents an original כל, needed for measure. ‡ Love to God is post Deuteronomic 31²⁴ 97¹⁰ 116¹ 145²⁰, to house 26⁸, to salvation 40¹⁷ 70⁶, to law 119⁴⁷ ⁺ ¹⁰ᵗ, Jerusalem 122⁶. — 13. [כִּי אַתָּה] causal with emph. pro. There should be no Makkeph: the two tones are needed for measure. 𝕲, 𝕵 attach יהוה to second clause, 𝔐 to first; that suits the measure. — [תְּבָרֵךְ צַדִּיק] Piel impf. 2 ms., general statement. This phr. is α.λ., but cf. 115¹⁸ — ‡ בָּרַךְ (1) *bless* Yahweh 16⁷ 26¹² 34² 63⁵ 103¹·². ²⁰· ²¹· ²². ²² 104¹· ³⁵ 115¹⁸ 134¹·² 135¹⁹· ²⁰ 145²· ¹⁰, שֵׁם ב׳ 96² 100⁴ 145¹· ²¹, Elohim 66⁸ 68²⁷; (2) Piel used of God abs. 109²⁸, c. acc. the king 45³, the people 29¹¹ 67²·⁷·⁸ 107⁸⁸ 115¹²· ¹²· ¹³ 128⁵ 134³ 147¹³, His inheritance 28⁹, house of Aaron 115¹², vegetation 65¹¹, provisions 132¹⁵· ¹⁵, as well as those given above; (3) used of men, *bless* 118²⁶ 129⁸; (4) congratulation 10³(?) 49¹⁹ 62⁵, homage 72¹⁵. For *Qal v. 1¹.* — [כַּצִּנָּה] belongs to חסך עלימו *v.* v.¹². ‡ צִנָּה is the large shield; מָגֵן 3⁴, the smaller one, elsw. 35² 91⁴. — ‡ [רָצוֹן] ‖. צִנָּה (1) of the *good will,* *favour* of God, elsw. 30⁶· ⁸ 51²⁾ 69¹⁴ 89¹⁸ 106⁴ Is. 49⁸; (2) *acceptance* of persons offering sacrifice, לרצון Ps. 19¹⁵ as Je. 6²⁰ Lv. 22²¹ Is. 56⁷; (3) of God's *will* Pss. 40⁹ 103²¹ 143¹⁰, of man's *desire* 145¹⁶· ¹⁹ as 2 C. 15¹⁵. — [תַּעְטְרֶנּוּ] Qal impf. 2 m. sf. 3 pl. † [עָטַר] vb. *surround,* elsw. only 1 S. 23²⁶. This is necessary according to arrangement of 𝔐, but if not connected with צִנָּה it is better to take it as ‡ [עָטַר] vb. *crown* Pss. 8⁶ 65¹² 103⁴, denom. of ‡ עֲטָרָה *crown* 21⁴, and point as Piel תְּעַטְרֶנּוּ. So 𝕲, 𝕵.

PSALM VI., 4 STR. 5³.

Ps. 6 is a penitential prayer. The congregation prays Yahweh not to chasten in anger; but to heal the long-continued languishing and dismay (v.²⁻⁴ᵃ); pleads that the peril of death may cease, for there can be no ritual commemoration of Yahweh in Sheol (v.⁴ᵇ⁻⁶). The sufferings are indeed extreme: weariness, nights of complaining, bursts of tears, and eye wasting because of the adversaries (v.⁷⁻⁸). But Yahweh has heard the prayer, and the enemies must depart in shame (v.⁹⁻¹¹).

YAHWEH, do not in Thine anger rebuke *me*.
Do not in Thy rage chasten *me* :
Be gracious to me, for *I* am languishing;
Heal me, for dismayed are *my* bones;
Yea exceedingly dismayed is *my* soul.

BUT Thou, O Yahweh, how long (shall it continue)?
O return, deliver *my* life;
Save me for the sake of *Thy* kindness;
For in death there is no commemoration of *Thee;*
In Sheol who can give *Thee* (ritual) praise?

(FOR) I am weary with *my* groaning;
I must complain every night on *my* bed;
I make dissolve with my tears *my* couch.
Wasteth away because of grief *mine* eye;
Waxeth old because of all *mine* adversaries.

DEPART, ye workers of trouble from *me* ;
For He hath heard the voice of *my* weeping,
Yahweh hath heard *my* supplication,
Yahweh accepteth *my* prayer;
They will turn back, they will be put to shame in a moment.

Ps. 6 was in 𝕯, its first penitential prayer. It was taken up into 𝕸 and 𝕯𝕽 (*v.* Intr. §§ 27, 31, 33), and appointed to be sung with the bass voice על־השמינית to the accompaniment of stringed instruments בנגינה (*v.* Intr. § 39), both peculiarly appropriate to the musical expression of penitence. The Ps. was composed for the congregation, and there is no trace in it of the experience of an individual. It is doubtless the earliest of the seven penitential Pss. 6, 32, 38, 51, 102, 130, 143, and prior to the penitential prayers Ezr. 9; Ne. 9; Dn. 9. The church appropriately assigns these Pss. to Ash Wednesday. Ps. 6 is related to several other passages of OT. (1) v.² differs from Ps. 38² only in that the latter omits אל in second clause, and substitutes the late קצף for the earlier and simpler אף. Je. 10²⁴ has a similar thought, and possibly was in the mind of the author. (2) v.⁶ᵇ is similar to Is. 38¹⁸ (מכתם = מכרב, *v.* Intr. § 25), where we have בשאול מי יודה־לך = כי לא שאול תודך v.⁶ᵇ; but the measure shows that we must read יודך. Is. 38 is pentameter, Ps. 6, trimeter, therefore changes were necessary. In ‖ line of Ps. 6 זכר is used, and in the other half of line of Is. 38¹⁸ הלל. The latter is the simpler and probably the earlier usage. זכר in the sense of *commemoration* is only elsw. Pss. 30⁵ 97¹² 102¹³ 111⁴. The thought is more natural and more appropriate to the context of Is. 38 than to Ps. 6; it was essential there, but not so essential here. The Ps. is therefore later. (3) v.⁷ᵃ is identical with Je., which latter is certainly original. (4) v.⁸ᵃ is the same as Ps. 31¹⁰ᵇ, except that מן takes the place of ב. We may safely conclude that Ps. 6 was later than Je. and Is. 38, but earlier than Pss. 31 and 38. The adversaries, who caused so much grief to the congregation, were not wicked rulers of Israel or hostile nations, but workers of trouble in Israel itself. They are not represented as a class over against the צדיקים and חסידים (cf. Ps. 1³); but in a simpler and more primitive way. They were probably the enemies of the congregation of the Restoration, who were restoring the ritual worship in Jerusalem, in the midst of great hostility on the part of their neighbours and also of the lower grade of people, who did not cordially unite in their reform. The Ps. is one of the choicest specimens of the use of assonance. The lines require but few transpositions to have them all end in יִ‑, except in the Str. II. v.⁵ᵇ· ⁶ᵃ⁻ᵇ, which purposely end in ךְ for the expression of formal antithesis, and in the last lines of Strs. III. and IV. v.⁸ᵇ· ¹¹ᵃ, where intentionally pl. יִ‑ takes the place of sing. יִ‑ for the other four lines of these strs. Besides, there is assonance in הַ‑ in v.⁷ᵇ· ᶜ· ⁸ᵃ· ᵇ. Several trimeters were injured by later scribes by the insertion of יהוה for greater clearness of meaning, v.³ᵃ· ᵇ (not in 𝔊) ⁵ᵃ· ⁹ᵇ, and by amplification, by insertion of כל v.⁸ᵃ and מאד v.¹¹ᵃ. Only one line is too short in 𝔐, occasioned by the omission of כי after לך.

Str. I. 2. The congregation prays Yahweh in two syn. couplets ; negatively, *do not rebuke ‖ do not chasten, in thine anger ‖ in thy rage ;* thus recognising that Yahweh had sufficient reason to be angry with them and to be in rage against them ; and that their sufferings were due to His rebuke and chastisement. — **3.** They have now suffered sufficiently, and so, in a second syn. couplet, also syn. to the first, they pray positively *be gracious to me*, more specifically, *heal me*, the reason for which is their great need : *I am languishing ‖ I am dismayed*. This latter is in the last line limited to the *bones*, which does not imply physical injury ; but, as in other Pss. of penitence and lamentation, the sympathy of nerves and bones with the emotions and passions ; and so the aching of the bodily frame in accord with the internal emotional agony, which now is expressed in climax. — **4a.** *yea exceedingly dismayed is my soul.*

Str. II. 4b. The prayer becomes more intense. The first line expostulates with Yahweh for the long continuance of the chastisement, with its suffering and peril. — *How long ?*] shall it yet continue ? This is followed by two syn. couplets, the second synth. to the first, giving the reason for it. — **5.** In the first couplet is the plea, — *O return*] with favour, condensing the thought of the previous line. The long continuance of suffering seems to imply divine absence or inattention. — *Deliver ‖ save*] make the return effective by redemptive interposition. It is the *life* of the congregation that is in peril by the continuance of this chastisement, and the kindness of Yahweh which is strained by it. — **6.** The motive proposed for this deliverance is, that if the life of the community is destroyed, the *commemoration* of Yahweh ‖ His *praise*, in the worship of the ritual, will be destroyed; and though the congregation may continue their existence in the realm of *Death* and the cavern of *Sheol*, the abode of the dead, they will be no longer a congregation worshipping Yahweh in the ritual of the temple, as prescribed by Yahweh in His Law, and so well pleasing to Him. The *Sheol* of the Hebrews corresponds with *Hades* of the Greeks, the subterranean region whither all mankind go at death and live in a shadowy state of existence.

Str. III. 7. The congregation now intensifies the plea in five syn. lines, describing their sad condition, which again subdivides into an introductory line and two syn. couplets. The *groaning* has continued so long, and has become so intense, that they are *weary*, worn out with it. — *Every night* on the *bed*, ‖ the *couch*, they *must complain*, and with such an intensity of grief, that *tears* burst from the eyes in a flood, wet the *couch*, and cause it to *dissolve*, as in a stream of rushing water. The figure seems extravagant to Western taste, but not to the Oriental. But it is still more extravagant in MT. and Vrss. in the previous line: "make my bed swim." This, by a change of vocalisation merely, gives the more suitable mng. "must complain," as we have given it above. — **8.** *The eye wasteth away* by this continual weeping, *because of grief;* and it *waxeth old*, becomes like the weakened, enfeebled eye of an old man, with little power of vision, — *because of all mine adversaries*] whose actions cause such *grief* and such bursts of tears.

Str. IV. 9–11. — The congregation have not been overwhelmed by their grief and the divine chastisement; their prayer receives its answer while they are making it. They express their confidence in a Str. of introverted parall. wherein the first and last lines are syn., and find their reason in the intervening syn. triplet. The reason is that *Yahweh hath heard* (repeated in emphasis) ‖ *accepteth*]. That which he heard was *the voice of my weeping* ‖ *my supplication* ‖ *my prayer*. Therefore the congregation warns the *workers of trouble* = adversaries, v.[8b]: *Depart from me;* and expresses the assurance that *they will turn back, they will be put to shame*, and that *in a moment*, instantly without delay. This shaming of the enemies in the climax is in striking antith. to the anxiety they have caused the congregation, v.[3b. 4a]. A later editor, wishing to emphasise this still more, inserts v.[11a].

They shall be shamed, and they shall be dismayed exceedingly, all mine enemies.

2. אַל] with Hiph. juss. חוּכִיחֵנִי is usually attached to vb., here separated for assonance in נִי so l.2. — ‡יכח] vb. Hiph. (1) *decide, judge* 94[1]; (2) *convince, convict* 50[21]; (3) *reprove, chide* 50[8] 105[14]; (4) *correct, rebuke* 6[2] = 38[2] 141[5] Jb. 5[17] 13[10. 10] Pr. 3[12]. — [וְאַל־בַּחֲמָתְךָ] has two beats. ‡חֵמָה n.f. (1) *venom*, of serpents 58[5(5?)], as Dt. 32[24. 33], of arrows 140[4]; (2) *burning anger, rage*, of man 37[8] 76[11. 11], of God 6[2] 38[2] 59[14] 78[38] 79[6] 88[8] 89[47] 90[7] 106[23]. — יהוה] is a gloss in both lines. In 3[b] it is not in 𝔊. — **3.** †אָמְלָל] a.λ. adj. = †אֻמְלַל Ne. 3[34]; but better ptc. מְאֻמְלָל with מ omitted as frequently in intensives when with shewa. — רְפָאֵנִי] Qal imv. ‡רפא vb. *heal* from peril of death as 30[8] 41[5] 103[3] 107[2)], more general mng. 147[3]. — ‡עֶצֶם] n.f. *bone* for bodily suffering as 22[15. 18] 31[11] 32[8] 34[21] 35[10] 38[4] 42[11] 51[10] 102[4. 6] 109[18], for skeleton of the dead 53[6] 141[7]. — **4.** מְאֹד] adv. *exceedingly* 35 t. in ψ. — וְאַתְּ] Kt. וְאַתָּה Qr 𝔊 σὐ dub. — עַד־אָרַי] 𝔊 ἕως πότε, abs. *how long* (shall it be). ‡מָתַי adv. *when* 41[6] 42[8] 94[8] 101[2] 119[82. 84]. — עַד־מָתַי *until when, how long?* sq. pf. 80[5], impf. 74[10] 82[2] 94[3], abs. 6[4] 90[13] 94[8]. It is difficult to see with this interp. why 𝔊 connects with previous line. By connecting with subsequent context we get 2 str. of 5 l. each, which is evidently correct. We might read וַיָּאת עַד־מֹתִי Qal impf. ı consec. ‡אָתָה vb. *come* Ps. 68[32] Dt. 33[21], c. עַד Mi. 4[8] and מֹתִי n. ı sf. *my death* (v. v.[6]) and render, *And so it is come unto my death*, I am at the point of death, which admirably suits the context (Br.[SHS 374]). — **5.** שׁוּבָה] Qal. imv. cohort. שׁוּב as 7[8] 80[15] 90[3] all of God. — יהוה] is a gloss as v.[3ab]. — חַלְּצָה] Piel imv. cohort. ‡√חלץ Qal *draw off*, not in ψ but †Niph. *be delivered* 60[7] = 108[7] Pr. 11[8. 9] Piel *rescue, deliver* sq. וְרֶשׁ *life* 6[5] 116[8], c. acc. p. 18[20] (= 2 S. 22[20]) 34[8] 50[15] 81[8] 91[15] 119[153] 140[2] (Ps. 7[5] dub.). — נֶפֶשׁ] ‡ in the sense of *life*, elsw. הִצִּיל נ׳ 22[21] 33[19] 56[14], מִלֵּט נ׳ 89[49] 116[4], פָּדָה נ׳ 34[23] 55[19] 71[23], cf. 49[9], שָׁמַר נ׳ 25[2)] 97[10], בִּקֵּשׁ נ׳ 35[4] 38[13] 40[15] 54[5] 63[10] 70[3] 86[14]; other uses 7[6] 31[11] 56[7] 59[4] 69[2] 71[10] 72[13. 14] 74[19] 78[50] 119[109] 124[4. 5]. For נפש with other mngs. v. 3[3] 10[3] 16[10] 17[9] 22[30] BDB. Br.[JBL 1897, 17 sq.]. — לְמַעַן הַסְדֶּךָ] = 44[27] v. 4[4]. — **6.** בַּמָּוֶת] ב local, in the place or state of death. ‡מוּת n.m. (1) *death* as opp. life 13[4] 33[19] 49[18] 56[14] 68[21] 73[4] 78[5)] 116[8. 15]; (2) *death by violence* 7[14] 18[56] 22[16] 55[5] 116[3], as penalty 118[18]; †(3) *state or place of death* 6[6] 49[15] Is. 28[15. 18] 38[18] Ho. 13[14] Hb. 2[5] Ct. 8[6] Pr. 5[5] 7[27] ‖. אברון Jb. 28[22], שַׁעֲרֵי מָ׳ *gates of death* Pss. 9[14] 107[18] Jb. 38[17]. — †שְׁאוֹל n.f. *the underworld* Dt. 32[22] Is 14[9] Pr. 15[24]; under mts. and sea Jb. 26[6] Jon. 2[3], contrasted with height of heaven Am. 9[2] Jb. 11[8] Ps. 139[8] Is. 7[11]. Thither men descend at death Gn. 37[35] (E) 42[38] 44[29. 31] (J) ı S. 2[6] ı K. 2[6. 9] Jb. 7[9] 21[13] Is. 14[11. 15] Ps. 88[4], Korah and his associates by divine judgment Nu. 16[30. 33] (J) cf. Ps. 55[16]. It has a mouth Ps. 141[7] and is a city with gates Is. 38[10] and has bars Jb. 17[16(?)].

It is syn. with מוח Pr. 5⁵ 7²⁷ Ct. 8⁶ Ps. 89⁴⁹. It is personified Is. 28¹⁵·¹⁸, as insatiable monster 5¹⁴ Hb. 2⁵ Pr. 1¹² 27²⁰ 30¹⁶, and has snares Ps. 18⁶ (= 2 S 22⁶), cf. 116⁸. It is dark and gloomy and from it there is no return Jb. 17¹³ (cf. v.¹⁶ 7⁹); earthly distinctions cease there Jb. 3¹⁷⁻¹⁹ 21²³⁻²⁶. Ec. 9⁵·⁶·¹⁰ represent the dead as without work or knowledge or wisdom: but these gloomy passages of Jb. and Ec. are not to be taken too seriously, for they do not correspond with the ordinary representation of other passages. In postex. Lit. the condition of the righteous and the wicked is often distinguished. The wicked, whether nations or individuals, descend to Sheol Pss. 9¹⁸ 31¹⁸ (cf. Nu. 16³⁰·³³); death acts as their shepherd, and they waste away without power or honour Ps. 49¹⁵·¹⁵. Sheol consumes them as drought-water Jb. 24¹⁹. The righteous dread to go thither because there is no ritual worship there Ps. 6⁶, cf. 88⁶ Is. 38¹⁸; deliverance from Sheol is a blessing Pss. 30⁴ 86¹³ Pr. 23¹⁴. In Ez. it is a place of reproach, the abode of uncircumcised 31¹⁵·¹⁶·¹⁷ 32²¹·²⁷. The righteous will not be abandoned to Sheol Ps. 16¹⁰, cf. 17¹⁵, but will be ransomed from it 49¹⁶, cf. 73²³·²⁵ Is. 57¹·² Jb. 14¹³ 17¹³. In latest Lit. there is a distinction in Sheol. It has depths to which the wicked fools descend Pr. 9¹⁸. It is contrasted with אברון Pr. 15¹¹. בור, שחת when ‖ שאול are in the bad sense of a pit or place of the lost v. 7¹⁶ which prepares the way for local distinction in later Judaism as reflected in Lk. 16¹⁹⁻³¹. שאול is also used fig. of degradation in sin Is. 57⁹ and of place of exile for Israel Ho. 13¹⁴·¹⁴. — זְכָרְךָ] sf. obj. ‡ זֵכֶר n.m. (1) *remembrance*, *memory* of person or people 112⁶ blotted out by their destruction 9⁷ 34¹⁷ 109¹⁵; (2) *commemoration* of Yahweh in the ritual 6⁶ 30⁵ 97¹² 102¹³ 111⁴ 145⁷; (3) *memorial* by which one is remembered 135³. — מִי] *who can*, implying neg. answer (v. 4⁷). — [יֵֽרֶה לָךְ Hiph. impf. 3 m. ידה (v. Intr. § 39). — לָךְ makes the line too long. It is an error of late style for earlier יֶֽרֶךָ of Is. 38¹⁸. — 7. יָגַֽעְתִּי] Qal pf. 1 p., of *state* or *condition* Dr. §11 ‡ יָגֵעַ c. ב 6⁷ 69⁴ Is. 43²² 57¹⁰ Je. 45³. — [אַנְחָתִי n.f. sf. 1 p. ‡ אֲנָחָה n.f. *sighing*, *groaning*, in distress, physical or mental 6⁷ 31¹¹ 38¹⁰ 102⁶. The line lacks a word. Du. rightly prefixes כי, giving reason of foregoing. It was omitted because of previous לָךְ. — אַשְׂחֶה] Hiph. impf. 1 p. frequentative, √שָׂחָה vb. *swim*, elsw. Is. 25¹¹ Ez. 47⁵, so here 𝕲 λουσω, 𝕵 *natare faciam*. This suits subsequent context, but not the previous, or mention of time, and is indeed an extravagant metaphor. It is more natural to take it as parallel with the next line. Therefore we should point it אָשִׂיחָה, Qal impf. cohort. שׂיח as 55¹⁸ 77⁴ Jb. 23². — [בְּכָל־לָֽיְלָה] *in every night*, phr. α.λ. dub., a later intensification by inserting כל. Rd. ‡ בלילה as 42⁹ 77⁷ 88² 90¹¹ 119⁵⁵ 121⁶ 136⁹. — [מִטָּתִי] n.f. sf. *my couch* ‡ מִטָּה n.f. α.λ. ψ ‖ ‡ עֶרֶשׂ 6⁷ 41⁴ 132⁸. — [אַמְסֶה Hiph. impf. freq., tr. to beginning of l. in order to assonance, of יְרֵשׂי in .ׁ., † מסה vb. *melt* for usual מסס Hiph. *cause to melt*, dissolve elsw. of ice 147¹⁸, *cause to vanish* 39¹², fig. לֵב, *intimidate* Jos. 14⁸. מסס Hiph. only Dt. 1²⁸. It is possible that we should rd. here cohort. אֶמְסֶה ‖ אֶשִׂיחָה in order to assonance with יִתְּקָה, יְשֵׁשָׁה. — 8. [עָשְׁשָׁה] vb. Qal pf. 3 f. denom. עָשׁ n.m. *moth*, as waster, consumer 39¹²; vb. elsw. 31¹⁰·¹¹. — ‡ [כַּעַס n.m. *vexation*, as (1) *grief* 6⁸ 10¹⁴ 31¹⁰ Ec. 1¹⁸ 2²³ 7³ 11¹⁰; (2) as *anger of*

Yahweh Ps. 85⁵, cf. Dt. 32¹⁹· ²⁷ 1 K. 15³⁰ 21²² 2 K. 23²⁶. — ‡ [עָתְקָה] vb. Qal pf. sf. *advance in years,* grow old, as Jb. 21⁷. — [צֹרְרָי] Qal ptc. pl. sf. 1 p. † צרר vb. *be an adversary* Nu. 10⁹ 25¹⁷· ¹⁸ 33⁵⁵ (all P) Is. 11¹³ Ps. 129¹· ² Est. 3¹⁰ 8¹ 9¹¹· ²⁴; ptc. sg., usually single person, but Ps. 7⁶ prob. coll.; pl. of God's adversaries 8⁵ 74⁴· ²³, man's Ex. 23²² (E) Am. 5¹² Pss. 7⁷ 23⁵ 31¹² 42¹¹; c. כל 10⁵ 69²⁾ 143¹²; so prob. here except that assonance in ־ִי is then abandoned. —

9. [סורו שׁ] Qal imv. ‡ ס ור vb. Qal (1) *turn aside* Ps. 119¹/², † מֵרָע 34¹⁵ 37²⁷ Jb. 28²⁸ Pr. 3⁷ 13¹⁹ 16⁶· ⁷, *revolt* Ps. 14³ Je. 5²³ Dt. 11¹⁶ 17¹⁷; (2) *depart,* c. מִן pers. Ps. 6⁹ 119¹¹⁵ 139¹⁹; (3) *be removed,* c. מִן pers. 101⁴. Hiph. (1) *remove,* take away, c. מִן 18²⁸ 39¹¹ 81⁷ 119⁹ Ex. 8⁴· ²⁷ (J) 23²⁵ (E) Is. 3¹; (2) *put aside,* reject, Ps. 66²⁰, cf. Is. 31². — [אֱלֵי אָוֶן] v. 5⁶. כל is gloss, as 28³ 36¹³ 59⁸ 64³ 125⁵ 141⁴· ⁹ unnecessary amplification. — [אֹמְנִי] should be tr. to the end of the line for assonance. — [ירוה] is a gloss, destroying the measure. — [שָׁמַע קוֹל בִּכְיִי] phr. α.λ. but שִׁמְעַ קוֹל 18⁷ 55¹⁸ 64² 119¹⁴⁹ v. 4⁴. ‡ בְּכִי n.m. *weeping* 30⁶ 102¹⁰. —

10. [שָׁמַע רַחֲנוּנִי] cf. שׁ· קוֹל רַחֲנוּנַי 28²· ⁶ 31²³ 116¹. ‡ הַחִנָּה n.f. sf. 1 p. alw. this form Pss. 55² 119¹⁷. — **11.** [יִבֹּשׁ וְיִבָּהֵלוּ] Qal impf. בוֹשׁ coördinate by simple ו with Niph. impf. בהל as 83¹⁸. For other uses of בהל v. v.⁸ 2⁵. ‡ בושׁ vb. Qal (1) *feel shame* 22⁶ 25³· ⁸ 31¹⁸ 37¹⁹ 86¹⁷ 97⁷ 109²⁸ 119⁶· ⁴⁶· ⁷⁸· ⁸⁰ 127⁵, אל אבישׁה 31² (= 71¹)¹⁸ 25², cf. 25²⁾; (2) *bc ashamed, put to shame* 6¹¹ 71¹³, sq. הכלם 35⁴ 69⁷ Je. 14³ 2·²² Is. 41¹¹ 45¹⁶· ¹⁷ Ez. 16⁵² 36³² Ezr. 9⁶, חפר Pss. 35²⁶ 40¹⁵ 70⁸ 71²⁴ Je. 15⁹ Mi. 3⁷ Jb. 6²⁰, ס מ Ps. 129⁵, נבהל 6¹¹ 83¹⁸. Hiph. put to shame 14⁶ 119⁸¹· ¹¹⁶, enemies by defeat 44⁸ 53⁶. — [יָשֻׁבוּ יֵבֹשׁוּ] impfs. without ו coördinate more emphatic. ¹ is given, however, 𝕲. בושׁ preceded by שׁוּב α.λ. It evidently has the mng. here of turn back in defeat, as 9⁴· ¹⁸ 56¹⁰. — [רָגַע] i.p. ‡ רֶגַע n.m. *moment* of time 30⁶, elsw. adv. acc. in a moment 6¹¹, כרגע 73¹⁹ as Nu. 16²¹ = 17¹⁰. 𝕲 inserts σφόδρα מְאֹד as above. Du. thinks v.¹⁰ᵃ a gloss as variation of v.⁹ᵇ. It suits the measure and assonance better than v.¹¹ᵃ. The Str. is just one line too long, and one of the lines must be thrown out. V.¹¹ᵃ is a pentameter and least suitable to the context.

PSALM VII., 2 STR. 10⁸.

Ps. 7 is a prayer for deliverance from a personal enemy: (1) a petition for salvation from his pursuer, with an imprecation of death upon himself, if he had done the wrong charged against him (v.²⁻⁶); (2) expressing confidence that Yahweh was preparing weapons against his pursuer, and that his mischief and treachery would receive just retribution (v.¹³⁻¹⁷). Subsequent editors inserted a plea for the judgment of the nations in an ultimate world judgment (v.⁷⁻⁸), a judgment between the righteous and wicked in Israel (v.⁹ᵇ⁻¹²), and a liturgical couplet of praise (v.¹⁸).

MY God, in Thee do I seek refuge;
  Save me from him that pursues, and deliver me;
  Lest, like a lion, he tear me,
  While there be (none) to tear away and none to deliver.
  My God, if I have done this,
  If there be iniquity in my palms,
  If I requited him that was at peace with me with evil;
  Let him pursue me, and let him overtake me,
  And let him tread to the earth my life,
  And my honour let him lay in the dust.
IF not, He whets His sword,
  Doth tread His bow and make it ready,
  And doth prepare for him deadly weapons;
  His arrows He maketh into fiery ones.
  Lo! he travaileth with iniquity,
  And conceiveth mischief and bringeth (it) forth.
  A pit he hath dug and dug out,
  And he will fall into the hole he is making.
  His mischief will return on his own head,
  And upon his own pate his violence come down.

Ps. 7 was in 𝔇, but only in its original form. In that form the historical reference in the title "which he sang to Yahweh because of the words of Cush, the Benjamite" has some propriety; although there is no mention of such a person in the history of the times of David. This fact gives some force to the correctness of a tradition only preserved here; for we know of nothing in the Literature upon which it could be based. There is nothing in the original form of the Ps. that prevents the composition by David under some such circumstances, when he was pursued by Saul and his Benjamite warriors. The traditional circumstance may, however, have been an editorial conjecture. This prayer appropriately follows Ps. 6 in 𝔇. It was not included in 𝔈 or 𝔇ℜ. Accordingly, no musical assignment was made. 𝔊, 𝔍 have מזמור, implying its use in 𝔐 (v. Intr. § 31) instead of שגיון of 𝔥 which was probably a txt. err. The word has not yet been explained (v. Intr. § 34). There is a striking inconsistency between the plea for interposition against an individual enemy in v.2-6. 13-17 and the judgment of nations v.7-9a, and between the righteous and wicked in Israel v.10-12 (v. Bi., Che.). This can only be explained by the insertion of these latter as glosses, to give the Ps. a more general reference for congregational use under later circumstances. Moreover v.2-6. 13-17 are trimeters: v.7-12 in the main at least pentameters. Che. is mistaken in regarding v.7-12 as homogeneous. There is a difference between Yahweh's judgment of the nations v.7-8 and Elohim's judgment of the wicked in Israel v.10-12. The original Ps. is very early, possibly as early as David; the Yahwistic gloss belongs to the Persian period, the Elohistic gloss to the Greek period. Other minor glosses harmonized in a measure the differences, and a liturgical addition made the Ps. more appropriate for use

Str. I. is composed of a trimeter tetrastich followed by two trimeter tristichs. — **2–3**. The tetrastich has a synth. couplet stating, *My God, in Thee do I seek refuge*] followed by the petition, *save me from him that pursues me and deliver me*]. The poet was pursued by a personal enemy, an individual; and has sought refuge in Yahweh for deliverance, possibly at the sanctuary itself. A synth. couplet gives the reason for the plea, *lest, like a lion, he tear me*]. The pursuer will tear him, as a lion his prey, unless his God saves him. *There is none* (other) *to tear* him *away*, from this lion, *and none* (else) *to deliver* him. The pursuer seems to have some pretext for this pursuit: he charges the poet with violation of covenant and personal injury. This the poet repudiates before his God, in a syn. tristich of conditional clauses, followed by a syn. tristich of imprecation upon himself if the condition which he denies be true. — **4–5**a. *If I have done this*] the specific thing charged against him by his pursuer; *if there be iniquity in my palms*] a phr. usually referring to the acceptance of bribes: it can hardly be physical injury by the hands, for there could be no dispute about that. — *if I requited him that was at peace with me with evil*] that is, one in a covenant of peace, a friend who had a right to look for good treatment, involving therefore treacherous breach of friendship and covenant, justly exciting the penalty of pursuit and death. He recognises the rightfulness of the pursuit if his statement be false. — **6**. *Let him pursue me*] as he is doing, v[2b], and furthermore, *let him overtake me*], do not save me from him, v[2b], and *let him tread to the earth my life*], trample me under foot and kill me as v[3a], *and my honour*], phr. for living soul, life, *let him lay in the dust*], throw down prostrate in the dust of death, cf. v[3b]. A later editor, adapting the Str. for congregational use, makes the pursuer pl.: "all that pursue me" v[2b], inserts "enemy" v[6a], and makes a premature renouncement of treachery.

Nay, I used to rescue them that were my adversaries to no purpose (v[5b]).

7–12 constitute a series of glosses separating the two Strs. of the original Ps. They take a wider outlook than the rescue of an individual from his personal enemy; they contemplate the judgment of the nations, and of the wicked adversaries of the righteous in Israel. There were probably three separate stages in these glosses v.[7-8], v.[9a], and v.[9b-12].   **7-8** were probably three pentameters in the original text. They are syn. lines of beauty and power written by a real poet.

> O arise, Yahweh, in Thine anger; lift Thyself up in outbursts of rage;
> O rouse Thyself, Yahweh my God, to the judgment Thou hast commanded,
> While the congregation of peoples assemble around Thee, on high O sit enthroned.

Yahweh is urged in a pressing appeal: *O arise, Yahweh,‖ lift Thyself up ‖ O rouse Thyself, Yahweh my God ‖ on high O sit enthroned.*] These were probably the original readings. (For variations see textual notes.)   It is an invocation of the congregation of Israel to their national God to intervene on their behalf; to sit on His throne of judgment and convoke all parties to His judgment seat.   It is assumed that the decision will be in favour of His people, *in anger ‖ outbursts of rage*] manifested in striking ways.   It is also affirmed that such a *judgment* has been already *commanded.*   The people of God were sure that it would eventually take place, they are in such straits that they urge that it shall be at once. — *While the congregation of peoples assemble around Thee*].   It is a judgment of nations, gathered from all parts about the divine throne for that purpose.   This reflects an entirely different situation from that of the original Ps., and a state of mind represented in Pss. 96–100, cf. Jo. 3.

9a, a trimeter line, *Yahweh judgeth the peoples*], is entirely apart from previous or subsequent context, stating a fact in the midst of earnest entreaties for judgment.   It is a marginal gloss.

9b–12 is a series of pentameters of a different type from the original Ps. and also from v.[7-8].

> JUDGE me, Yahweh, according to my righteousness, according to the integrity
>   that is upon me.
>   O let the evil of the wicked come to an end, and establish the righteous.
>   A trier of hearts and reins is the righteous God.
>   My shield is upon God, a Saviour of the upright in mind.
>   God is a righteous judge, an 'El taking vengeance every day.

The antith. is now, not between the individual and his pursuer, nor between Yahweh and the nations, but between the righteous and the wicked in Israel itself; and so is of a much later date. The judgment is not an ultimate one, but a daily testing and taking vengeance; and the divine name is *Elohim* and not **Yahweh.**

This gloss is not earlier than the Greek period (cf. Ps. 1). The author represents the righteous in Israel. The key word of the five lines is righteousness, *according to my righteousness* v.⁹ᵇ, *the righteous* v.¹⁰ᵃ, *the righteous God* v.¹⁰ᵇ, *the upright in mind* v.¹¹ᵇ, *righteous judge* v.¹²; cf. the syn. terms for judgment: *judge me* v.⁹ᵇ, *establish* v.¹⁰ᵃ, in the sense of vindicate, cf. 99⁴; *trier* v.¹⁰ᵇ, *Saviour* v.¹¹, *judge* v.¹². In the other parts of the lines *according to the integrity that is upon me* v.⁹ᵇ has as its antith., *O let the evil of the wicked come to an end* v.¹⁰ᵃ; *trier of hearts and reins* has as its antith. *taking vengeance every day.* — *My shield over me is God*], protecting me from all enemies as 3⁴. 𐤄 " upon God " makes God the shield bearer of His people, a conception which all EV.ˢ shrink from, in their varied modes of paraphrase. It is possible that the text of 𐤄 v.¹²ᵃ is correct: *strong and patient;* if so, the pentameter line is complete without " El taking vengeance every day," and that must be regarded as a minor gloss. But it is better suited to the context than the additional words of 𐤄, and gives a better climax. Rather 𐤄 is a gloss.

Str. II. 13 sq. is an antistr. The condition of the imprecation in the previous Str. is taken for granted as false, in the abrupt *if not*] without vb. in the original, (" if it is not so, and it is not "; explained by gloss, *if he*, the pursuer, *turn not*). Yahweh becomes the pursuer of the poet's pursuer. This is expressed in four syn. trimeters in antith. with v.²⁻³, so ancient Vrss. EV.ˢ and most comm., but many moderns Che., Bä., Du., Ehr. make the enemies of Str. I. the actor here also. — **13-14.** *He whets His sword*] in behalf of the one who has sought refuge in Him v.²ᵃ; *He doth tread His bow and make it ready*], to save from the pursuer v.²ᵇ; *He doth prepare for him deadly weapons*], to kill the lion ready to tear his prey v.³ᵃ; *His arrows He maketh into fiery ones*], in response to the apparent abandonment of v.³ᵇ. This tetrastich is followed by two trimeter tristichs v.¹⁵⁻¹⁶ᵃ v.¹⁶ᵇ⁻¹⁷, bringing out the true character of the pursuer and his ultimate ruin. — **15-16a.** *Lo! he travaileth with iniquity*], over against the false charge against the poet v.⁴ᵃ; and *conceiveth mischief and bringeth it forth*], in antith. with v.⁴ᵇ. A gloss gives an object " falsehood " to the third vb., but that makes the line too long and mars the effect of the single word, mischief, syn. with iniquity. The pursuer is compared to a woman in childbirth : mischief is the babe which is born. — *A pit he hath dug and dug out*], passing over from the metaphor of childbirth to the metaphor of making a pit to ensnare animals, common in ψ. This is antith. to v.[5a]; instead of the poet being the treacherous violator of covenant and friendship, the man, who pursues him with false charges, has tried to take him like an animal in the covered pit. — **16b-17**. The final tristich is in antith. with the imprecation v.[6] ; the imprecation falls on the pursuer and not on the pursued. *He will fall into the hole he is making*] antith. with v.[6a] ; *his mischief will return on his own head*] antith. with v.[6b] ; and *upon his own pate* will *his violence come down*] over against v.[6c]. And so, seeking refuge in God, the poet sees God pursuing his pursuer, and bringing upon him the retribution which he demanded for the wrong which he himself had done.

18. A later editor added a liturgical gloss as a suitable close of the Ps. in its final form after it had been generalised and adapted for public worship.

> I will praise Yahweh according to His righteousness
> And I will make melody to the name of Elyon.

This liturgical couplet is a trimeter like the original Ps. It is syn. — *I will praise*] in public praise ‖ *I will make melody*. *Yahweh* is the object of the first line, *Elyon*, the Most High, of the second line. The second *Yahweh* has been inserted as gloss. *The name*] of the second line is syn. with *according to His righteousness* of the first.

2. † יהוה אֱלֹהַי] 7[2. 4] 13[4] 18[29] 30[3 ? 13] 35[24] 40[6] 104[1] 109[26] Nu. 22[18] (JE) Dt. 4[5] 18[16] 26[14] Jos. 14[8. 9] 2 S. 24[24] 1 K. 3[7] 5[18. 19] (= 2 Ch. 2[3]) 8[28] (= 2 Ch. 6[19]) 17[20. 21] Je. 31[18] Hb. 1[12], thus phr. of D; elsw. Postex. 1 Ch. 21[17] 22[7] Ezr. 7[28] 9[5] Is. 25[1] Dn. 9[4. 2)] Jon. 2[7] Zc. 11[4] 13[9] 14[5]. The line is too long both here and in v.[4], therefore יהוה is a gloss; so also Pss. 18[29] 35[24] 104[1]. — מְפַל] כֹּל is intensification, only מ is original. — לְרֹדְפִי] Qal ptc. pl. sf. 1 s.; pl. later interpretation for an original sg. ‡ √רָדַף vb. Qal: (1) *pursue* enemy in war 18[38] 31[16] 35[3. 6] 71[11] 83[16]; so here, for v.[3. 6] favour reference to pursuit of warrior. (2) *persecute* 69[27] 109[16] 119[84. 86. 157. 161] 142[7] 143[3]. (3) *follow after*, in good sense 34[15] 38[21], in bad sense 119[150]. (4) *follow after* in order to benefit 23[6]. Pi. *pursue ardently*, possibly v.[6], but prob. = 143[3]. יְרַדֵּף is a Massoretic conceit prob. giving choice of יִרְדֹף Qal or יְרַדֵּף Pi., Ges.§ 63[n], Kö.[I.] § 16[0]. — וְהַצִּילֵנִי] וֹ coörd. Hiph. imv. sf. 1 p. [√נצל] not used in Qal, but Hiph.:

(1) *snatch away* words from mouth 119⁴³; (2) *deliver* from enemies and troubles, c. acc. 7² 22⁹ 25²⁰ 31³ 40¹⁴ 70² 71² 72¹² 106⁴³ 109²¹, c. מִן 18¹⁸·⁴⁹ 22²¹ 34⁶·¹⁸·²⁰ 35¹⁰ 54⁹ 59²·³ 69¹⁵ 91³ 107⁶ 120²¹42⁷ 143⁹ 144⁷, מִיד 31¹⁶ 82⁴ 97¹⁰ 144¹¹, מכף 18¹ (= 2 S. 22¹), abs. אֵין מַצִּיל 7⁸ 50²² 71¹¹ Is. 5²⁹ 42²² Ho. 5¹⁴ Mi. 5⁷; (3) *deliver* from, c. מִן death 33¹⁹ 56¹⁴, Sheol 86¹³; (4) *deliver* from sin and guilt 39⁹ 51¹⁶ 79⁹ 119¹⁷⁰, Niph. pass. *be delivered*, abs. 33¹⁶, c. מן 69¹⁵.—
3. [פֶּן־יִטְרֹף] negative final clause, *lest.* ‡ טרף *tear, rend*, of wild beasts Gn. 37³³ 44²⁸ (J) Ex. 22¹² (E), elsw. only in metaphor in Pss. 7³ 17¹² 22¹⁴ of men compared to lions, and Ps. 50²² of God.—‡ [אַרְיֵה] *lion* 7³ 10⁹ 17¹² 22¹⁴·²², cf. אֲרִי 22¹⁷(?).—[נַפְשִׁי] *me* (*v. 3³*).—[פֹּרֵק] Qal ptc. ‡ פרק: (1) *tear away from, deliver,* c. מן 136²⁴ La. 5⁸, so here if after 𝔊, μὴ ὄντος λυτρουμένου, we read פָּרֵק; so 𝔖, Gr., We., Du., al.; but 𝔥 interpreted as (2) *tear in pieces,* in same sense as Pi. 1 K. 19¹¹.—**4.** [אִם־עָשִׂיתִי] is Qal pf. 1 s. protasis conditional clause continued in v.⁴ᵇ·⁵ᵃ with apod. v.⁶ in juss. of imprecation.—[זאת] is neuter, *this thing,* with עָשָׂה, phr. α.λ. ψ, but Gn. 3¹⁴ (J) 20⁶·⁶ 45¹⁹ (E).—[אִם־יֶשׁ] conditional, implying neg. answer. ‡ יֵשׁ originally n. but in usage subst. vb. *is, are, was,* etc., "not as a mere copula, but implying existence with emphasis" BDB.; elsw. (1) affirmative, יֶשׁ יֵשׁ 58¹², † יֵשׁ יֵשׁ 135¹⁷ (pleonastic). (2) interrogative הֲיֵשׁ 14² = 53³ without הֲ 73¹¹.—‡ [עָוֶל] n.m. *injustice* antith. צדקה 7⁴ 53² 82².—**5.** [גָּמַלְתִּי] Qal pf. 1 p. s. ‡ √גמל (1) c. עַל *deal bountifully* with 13⁶ 116⁷ 119¹⁷ 142⁸, so prob. 57² as 𝔊. (2) c. acc. pers. et rei *requite* 7⁵ 18²¹; elsw. c. לֹ pers. 137⁸ Dt. 32⁶, עַל Ps. 103¹⁰ Jo. 4⁴ 2 Ch. 20¹¹. (3) *wean* a child, only ptc. Ps. 131²·² Is. 11⁸, נמלרע elsw. Pr. 31¹², cf. השיב הרע Ps. 54⁷.—[שׁוֹלְמִי] Qal ptc. שׁלם denom. שלום peace, the *one in covenant of peace with me;* but prob. error for שְׁלוֹמִי obj. sf. as שׁלומי אִישׁ 41¹⁰ 55²¹, שלומים 69²³.—[וָאֲחַלְּצָה] Pi. impf. cohort. 1 s., c. ו consec. √חלץ (v. 6⁵). ו consec. after three syn. lines with אם and before three syn. lines of apodosis, suspicious, esp. as sense of vb. *rescue* is antith. to the protasis and must be of the nature of a parenthesis. But such a parenthesis would not be expressed by ו consec., and has more of the nature of a gloss than the thought of the poet, who seems to balance the three lines of apodosis over against the three of protasis. Such a parenthesis would use ו coörd. and perfect for single act, or imperfect for frequentative; but then why cohort. form? Ges., De., Bä. think of a derivative mng. *spoil, despoiled* not known to Heb. elsw. exc. in n. חליצה *plunder* 2 S. 2²¹ Ju. 14¹⁹; but found in Aram. 𝔖, 𝔗, Houb., Dy., Gr., Che., Du., rd. וָאֶלְחָצָה, √לחץ *oppress* Pss. 56² 106⁴². But this is not in accord with other lines of protasis, where the one supposed to be injured is a friend and ally, and not an adversary, still less an adversary who has not succeeded in accomplishing anything. The line is not consistent with the context. It is really an antith. gloss which anticipates the apodosis. The glossator means to say, he has done the very reverse of injury to his friend: he has delivered habitually his adversaries, while they have vainly and without result striven against him.—‡ [רֵיקָם] adv. *in vain,* without accomplishing anything, *v.* Ps. 25³ 2 S. 1²² Is. 55¹¹.—**6.** [אוֹיֵב] is a gloss, *v.* 3⁸.—[נַפְשִׁי] *me,* as v.³—[וְיִשֵּׂג] ו coörd. with Hiph. juss. 3 s. ‡ [נשׂג] vb., not found in Qal. Hiph. *overtake,* c. acc. after רדף in

Ex. 15⁹, often J Pss. 7⁶ 18³⁸, fig. of battle 40¹⁸ 69²⁵. — [וַיִּרְפֹּם ו] coörd. Qal juss. ‡ רמס, elsw. 91¹³ *tread under foot.* — [לָאָרֶץ] *down to the earth* 74⁷ 89⁴⁰, the life 143³ ‖ עָפֶר] 44²⁶. — [חַיָּי] n. pl. sf. 1 m. *my life.* ‡ חַיִּים only, n.m. pl. abst. life: (1) *physical* 7⁶ 17¹⁴ 21⁵ 26⁹ 31¹¹ 34¹³ 63⁴ 64² 66⁹ 88⁴ 103⁴, כל ימי ח׳ 23⁶ 27⁴ 128⁵, בה׳ *during life* 49¹⁹ 63⁵ 104³³ 146²; (2) as welfare, happiness 30⁶ 133³, אֶל הַיָּי 42⁹ (so also by emendation 42⁸ 84³), מעֶוֹ ח׳ 27¹, מקור ח׳ 36¹⁰ Pr. 10¹¹ 13¹⁴ 14²⁷ 16²², ארח ח׳ Ps. 16¹¹ Pr. 5⁶ 15²⁴. — [כְּבוֹדִי] *my honour,* ‡ of seat of honour. ‖ ונפ׳; as 16⁹ 108² ‖ לב, cf. 30¹⁸ c. זמר, 57⁹ c. עוּרָה. — [לֶעָפָר] *down to the dust,* of death, as 22³⁰ 30¹⁰, cf. Is. 26¹⁹; or possibly of humiliation, as 44²⁶ 113⁷ 119²⁵, as Is. 47¹ Mi. 7¹⁷. — 7. [קוּמָה] Qal imv. cohort. *v. 3⁸,* so עוּרָה v.⁷ᶜ, שׁוּבָה v.⁸ᵇ — [הִנָּשֵׂא] Niph. imv. cohort. נשא ‡ Niph. of God, *lift oneself,* elsw. 94²; of gates personified 24⁷. — [בְּגַבְרוֹת] pl. cstr. obj. *against adversaries.* ‡ עֶבְרָה *overflow,* usually of anger and only such in ψ, and of divine anger, *rage, fury* 78⁴⁹ 85⁴ 90⁹·¹¹; pl. *outbursts of rage* here, cf. Jb. 21³⁰, contr. חַבְרוֹת אַפֵּך Jb. 40¹¹. — [עוּרָה] Qal imv. cohort. ‡ עור] vb. Qal *rouse oneself* to action: of God 7⁷ 44²⁴ 59⁵; of man 57⁹, as Ju. 5¹²; harp and lyre Ps. 57⁷·⁹ = 108³; rage Ps. 78³⁸. Polel. *rouse, incite* to activity, subj. Yahweh 80⁸. Hiph. as Qal 35²³, prob. also 73²⁰. — [אֵלַי] usually interpreted as prep. אל ℑ sf. 1 *ad me, for me,* but ⅌ κύριε ὁ θεός μου = יהוה אֱלַי as in v.²ᵃ·³ᵃ, י׳ אלהי gives us needed word for pentameter and prob. occasioned the אלהי י׳ v.²ᵃ·³ᵃ, where יהוה was not needed. — 8. [הָסִיבֶּךָ] Polel impf., might be juss., relating to יהוה, ‖ imvs.; but is prob. circumstantial clause, *while they assemble, v. 17¹¹.* — [עָלֶיהָ] *over, above it,* sf., refers to the congregation, prob. gloss of interp. — ‡ [מָרוֹם] n.m. *height;* poetic (1) *on high,* elevated place 75⁶, cf. Jb. 39¹⁸; (2) elsw. ψ *height* of heaven 10⁵ 18¹⁷ (= 144⁷) 68¹⁹ 71¹⁹ 73⁸ 93⁴ 102²⁰ 148¹, so here; (3) without prep., *The One on High,* pred. of יהוה 56⁸ 92⁹. — [שׁוּבָה] Qal imv. cohort., of *God,* implies His absence from His heavenly throne of judgment. So ⅌, Vrss. and most, but this seems not to suit context. Rd. with Ra., Dy., Oort, Gr., al. שֵׁבָה, vb. *sit enthroned,* which suits context better, as 9⁵, and was prob. in original. — 9. [י׳ יָדִין עַמִּים] is a gloss from 96¹⁾. The original Ps. thought of a controversy between friends. This is generalized into a conflict of Israel with the nations. ‡ דִין vb. Qal: (1) *act as judge, minister judgment,* עמו 50⁴ 135¹⁴ = Dt. 32³⁶, עמים Pss. 7⁹ 96¹⁰, לאמים 9⁹, so the king 72²; (2) *execute judgment,* vindicate in battle, of God 54³, the king 110⁶. This vb. is syn. with the more comprehensive ‡ שׁפט: (1) *act as lawgiver, governor,* and *judge,* in the most comprehensive sense, of early date before Jehoshaphat established שׁפטים, — only of men in ψ, כבטי ארץ 2¹⁰ 148¹¹; (2) *decide controversies,* discriminating betw. persons, of God 7¹² 9⁵ 82¹. There is no reference to judgment by men in ψ. (3) *execute judgment;* (a) discriminating, of man only 58² 82²; (b) vindicating, of God, c. acc. pers. 10¹⁸ 26¹ 43¹ 58¹². כַצֶּרֶק 9⁷ 35²⁴, of man, c. acc. 72⁴ 82³; (c) condemning, punishing, of man 109³¹ 141⁶(?), of God 51⁶; (d) esp. of God's theophanic advent to judge 50⁶ 75⁸ 94². Vb. c. acc. חבל 9⁹ 96¹⁸ 98⁹, ארץ 82⁸ 96¹⁸ 98⁹, עמים 67⁵, מישרים 75³. Niph. *be judged* 9²⁰ 37³³ 109⁷. For משפט *v. 1⁶.* A series of pentameters begins here, all of which are glosses. —

‏[מִצִּדְקִי‎] cf. 18²¹·²⁵ 17¹⁽?⁾ 35²⁷ 37⁶ and *v. 4²*. — ‏[כָּחְמִי עָלֵי‎] phr. a.λ. ‡ ‏חם‎ n.m. *integrity* 7⁹ 25²¹ 41¹³. † c. ‏הלך‎ Ps. 26¹·¹¹ Pr. 10⁹ 19¹ 20⁷ 28⁶. † ‏חם לבב‎ Pss. 78⁷² 101² Gn. 20⁵·⁶ (E) 1 K. 9⁴. — 10. ‏[יַעֲמָר־נָא‎] Qal impf. juss. with particle. ‡ ‏נא‎ particle of entreaty or exhortation: (1) attached to imv. 80¹⁵ 118²⁵·²⁵ 119¹⁰⁸, ironically 50²², cf. Is. 47¹² Jb. 40¹⁰; (2) to impf. *now I pray Thee* Pss. 7¹⁰ 118²·³·⁴ 119⁷⁶ 122⁸ 124¹ = 129¹; (3) with particles 115² 116¹⁴·¹⁸. — † ‏וְגָּמַר‎ vb. Qal: (1) *come to an end, be no more* 7¹⁰ 12² 77⁹; (2) *bring to an end, complete* 57³ (?) 138⁸. It is a late word. In New Heb., Aram., and Syriac, *complete.* — ‏[בֹּחַן לִבּוֹת וּכְלָיוֹת‎] phr. a.λ. For ‏רַע v. 5⁵‎, *1.*— ‏רְשָׁעִים‎ is based on Je. 11²⁰, where, however, the order of nouns is reversed, and ‏לב‎ is used for ‏לבות‎, which has been here assimilated in form to ‏כְּלָיוֹת. לבות‎ is used elsw. only Is. 44¹⁸ Ps. 125⁴ and Pr. 4 t., and is late. ‡ ‏כְּלָיוֹת‎ n.f. only pl.: (1) physical organ, *kidneys* 139¹³; (2) the *reins*, as seat of affections and emotions 16⁷ 73²¹ Je. 12², and so obj. of divine scrutiny, alw. ‖ ‏לב‎ Pss. 7¹⁰ 26² Je. 11²⁰ 17¹⁰ 20¹². — ‏בֹחַן‎ ptc. with nominal force ‡ √‏[בחן]‎ *examine, scrutinise, test:* (1) God subj. 11⁵ 26² 66¹⁰ 81⁸ 139²³ Je. 9⁶, eyelids of God Ps. 11⁴, c. acc. ‏לב‎ 17² Je. 12³ and ‏כליוח‎ 7¹⁰ Je. 11²⁷, cf. 20¹² +; (2) subj. man, *test, tempt*, God Ps. 95⁹ Mal. 3¹⁰·¹⁵. — ‏[אֱלֹהִים צַדִּיק‎] late style, as v.¹¹, cf. Je. 11²⁰ ‏שׁפֵט צֶדֶק. 𝔊‎ did not use ‏אלהים‎ in such phrases. — 11. ‏[עַל אֱלֹהִים‎] cf. 62⁸ that is resting upon God as shield-bearer. 𝔊 attaches ‏צַדִּיק‎ to this v., and renders δικαία ἡ βοήθειά μου, reading ‏מָעֻזִּי‎ for ‏מָעוּנִי‎. But as Che. exclaims, "Yahweh, his servant's shield-bearer!" ‏על‎ is as Bä., Dy., Gr. for ‏עלי‎ expl. as ‏עֲלֵי‎ instead of ‏עָלַי‎ *over me, covering me*, cf. 3⁴. — ‏[יָשְׁרֵי‎] pl. cstr. ‡ ‏יָשָׁר‎ adj.: (1) *straight*, of a way 107⁷ Je. 31⁹; (2) *just, upright*, (*a*) of God Pss. 25⁸ 92¹⁶, His laws 19⁹ 119¹³⁷, ‏דבר‎ 33⁴; (*b*) of man 37³⁷, ‏יִשְׁרֵי דֶרֶךְ‎ 37¹⁴ 𝔊 (‏לֵב‎), ‏יִשְׁרֵי בַל‎ 7¹¹ 11² 32¹¹ 36¹¹ 64¹¹ 94¹⁵ 97¹¹, cf. 125⁴; (3) as noun sg. coll., of men 11⁷ (dub.), cf. Jos. 10¹³, elsw. pl. of the upright among the people over against the wicked, common in WL. and late Pss. 33¹ 49¹⁵ 107⁴² 111¹ 112²·⁴ 140¹¹; (4) abstr. *uprightness* 111⁸, prob. error ‏יֹשֶׁר‎ for ‏יָשָׁר‎ 𝔊, 𝔖, 𝔗, 𝔍, Hi., Bä. — 12. ‏[שֹׁפֵט‎] Qal ptc. nominal force, see v.⁹; 𝔊 adds καὶ ἰσχυρὸς καὶ μακρόθυμος, PBV. *strong and patient*, which makes a good pentameter. But this leaves ‏וְאֵל זֹעֵם בְּכָל־יוֹם‎, for which 𝔊 μὴ ὀργὴν ἐπάγων καθ᾽ ἑκάστην ἡμέραν, which would need still further enlargement to make another pentameter. ‏אל‎, if negative would require juss. and could not be with ptc. ‏אֵל זֹעֵם‎ a.λ., but *v. 5⁶* for ‏אֵל‎. ‏זֹעֵם‎ Qal ptc. nominal force, ‡ ‏זָעַם‎, vb. *be indignant*, only here ψ, but Zc. 1¹² Is. 66¹⁴ Mal. 1⁴ +. ‡ ‏זַעַם‎ n.m., *indignation*, of God 38⁴ 69²⁵ 78⁴⁹ 102¹¹. ‡ ‏בְכָל־יוֹם‎ *every day*, as 88¹⁰ 145². — 13. ‏[אִב־לֹא יָשׁוּב‎] is suited to the gloss. ‏יָשׁוּב‎ was inserted as a seam. It is not suited to context of v.²⁻⁶ in the original Ps., and it makes the line tetrameter instead of trimeter. ‏אִב־לֹא‎ is protasis antith. to ‏אב‎, cf. v.⁴⁻⁵, followed by apodosis. — ‏[חַרְבּוֹ יִלְטוֹשׁ‎] Qal impf. c. ‏חרבו‎ emph. in position. This phr. is a.λ. † ‏לָטַשׁ‎ vb. Qal: (1) *hammer* Gn.4²²; (2) *whet* sword here, cf. 1 S. 13²⁰, of eyes Jb. 16⁹. Pu. ptc. 52⁴, sharpened razor, as sim. of tongue. — ‏[הִשְׁתִּי דָרַךְ‎] n. emph. ‏דָּרַךְ‎ ק *tread the bow*, the ancient method of bending it with the foot instead of with the arm, 7¹³ 11² 37¹⁴, cf. Je. 51³ La. 2⁴, 3¹² Zc. 9¹³, cf. also ‏דרך חֵץ‎ 58⁸ (?) 64⁴. — ‏ו [וַיְכוֹנֲנֶהָ‎] consec. Polel ‏כון‎

impf. 3 m. sg. sf. 3 f., continuation of previous action. The pf. with ו consec.
impf. instead of impf. of first clause was to emphasize over against the
repeated action of whetting a sword, the immediateness of the single act of
treading the bow and getting ready to shoot; both are graphic. — **14.** [וְלוֹ
emph. לְ sf. 3 sg. refers to enemy. — [כְּלֵי־מָוֶת] *a.λ.*, but cf. כִּי חָמָס Gn. 49⁵,
כִּי מִשַׁחתוּ Ez. 9¹. — [דֹּלְקִים] Qal ptc. pl. nominal force. ‡ [רָדַק] *burn, hotly pursue*, either mng. suitable here, cf. Ob.¹⁸, of Israel ravaging Edom, Ps. 10², of
enemies as La. 4¹⁹. — [יִפְעָל] Qal impf. freq. as in v.¹³ of whetting of sword. —
15. [הֵיָּה] *lo, behold*, of graphic description v. BDB. — [יַחֲבָּל־אָוֶן] Retracted
accent on acct. of monosyl. that follows, so יָהַר v.¹⁵ᵇ v. 2¹²; both accents are
needed for measure. Vb. Pi. impf. 3 m., graphic description, ‡ חבל, elsw.
Ct. 8⁵·⁵, denom. חֶבֶל *birth pangs*, and so *writhe* in travail. — [וְהָרָה] ו consec.
Qal perf. 3 m. carries on יַחֲבָל ‡ הָרָה *conceive* only here ψ, but in fig. sense
also Is. 59⁴ Jb. 15³⁵. ‡ עָמָל n.m.: (1) *trouble*, of sorrow 10¹⁴ 25¹⁸ 73⁵· ¹⁶ 90¹⁰;
(2) *trouble, mischief*, as done to others 7¹⁷ 94²⁰ 140¹⁰ ‖. אוֶן 7¹⁵ 10⁷ 55¹¹;
(3) *toil, labour*, very late WL. Pss. 105⁴⁴ 107¹². — ‡ שֶׁקֶר n.m. in pause:
(1) *falsehood*, in testimony, doing one hurt. עֵד שֶׁ׳ 27¹² Ex. 20¹⁶ Dt. 19¹⁸.
דבר שֶׁ׳ Pss. 52⁵ 63¹² Mi. 6¹² Je. 9⁴ 40¹⁶. † שְׂפַת שֶׁ׳ Pss. 31¹⁹ 120² Pr. 10¹⁸
17⁷. † שֶׁ׳ מְפֵל Ps. 119⁶⁹ Jb. 13⁴; (2) *deceit, fraud,* איבי שֶׁ׳ Pss. 35¹⁹ 38²⁰, cf. 69⁵
119⁷⁸· ⁸³; (3) *deception*, what deceives, disappoints, and betrays 33¹⁷
119²⁹· ¹⁰⁴· ¹¹⁸· ¹²⁸· ¹⁶³ 144⁸· ¹¹; (4) *lie*, of speech in general, late usage 101⁷
109², as WL. Here שֶׁקֶר in unusual sense makes the line too long, and is
interpretative gloss. — **16.** ‡ [בוֹר] emph. The early mngs. *cistern, well,
dungeon* are not in ψ, but (1) *pit*, as dug out 7¹⁶ 40⁸ + ; (2) *the Pit*, in local
sense ‖ שְׁאוֹל, not, however, another name for Sheol, but a distinct place in
Sheol, subsequent to Ez., Ez. 32²³ La. 3⁵³· ⁵⁵ Is. 14¹⁵· ¹⁹ Pss. 30⁴ 88⁵· ⁷, יוֹרְדֵי בִיר
28¹ 143⁷ Is. 38¹⁸ Ez. 26²⁰ 32²⁵· ²⁹· ³⁰, so also Ez. 26²⁰ 31¹⁴· ¹⁶ 32¹⁸· ²⁴ Pr. 1¹²
28¹⁷. — [וַיַּחְפְּרֵהוּ] ו consec. Qal impf. carrying on the action, still further continued as result in וַיִּפֹּל — [יִמְדֹּל] Qal impf. i.p. rel. clause, rel. omitted, as
frequent in Poetry. — ‡ [שַׁחַת] n.: (1) *sink, hole, pit*, elsw. 9¹⁶ (?) 35⁷ 94¹³
+ 4 t.; (2) *Pit*, of Sheol, syn. בוֹר, subsequent to Ezr. 16¹⁰ 30¹⁰ 49¹⁰ 55²⁴ 103⁴
+ 10 t. — **17.** [יָשׁוּב בְּרֹאשׁוֹ] phr., elsw. 1 K. 2³³ Ob.¹⁵; Qal impf. of future
expectation. שׁוּב in the sense of ‡ requital, c. בְּ, elsw. c. עַל 35¹⁸ (?), עַר 94¹⁵,
לְ 54⁷ (Kt.). — ‡ [קָדְקֹד] n. *pate*, top of head, as 68²². — ‡ [חָמָס] n.m. *violence,
wrong,* ‖ עָמֵר 7¹⁷, רִיב 55¹³, גאוה 73⁶ interp. of הִיךְ 72¹⁴, other uses 11⁵ 25¹⁹ 27¹²
35¹¹ 58³ 74²⁰. † חָמָס אִישׁ *violent man* 18⁴⁹ (= אִישׁ חסטיס 2 S. 22⁴⁹) 140¹²
Pr. 3³¹ 16²⁹. אִישׁ חסטיס Ps. 140²· ⁵ *men of violent deeds.* — **18.** [אוֹדֶה] Hiph.
impf. ‖ וַאֲזַמְּרָה Pi. impf., both cohort. united by ו coörd. זמר denom. זָמִיר
song (*v.* Intr. § 31). — [יהוה] is gl., makes line too long, and is not needed
with עֶלְיוֹן (*v.* Intr. § 32).

PSALM VIII., 2 STR. 8^3 + RF. 2^3.

Ps. 8 is an evening hymn in two synth. trimeter octastichs, contrasting the glory of man as creature with the glory of the Creator. The Strs. are enclosed by identical trimeter couplets, praising the name of Yahweh as widespread in all the earth (v.$^{2a. 10}$). **An initial prayer that Yahweh would set His splendour above the heavens, is followed by a contemplation of His strength, in the speech of sucklings, overcoming His enemies; and of the insignificance of man when compared with moon and stars** (v.$^{2b-5}$). **Man made lower than the gods is yet sovereign of all creatures** (v.$^{6-9}$).

> *YAHWEH, our Sovereign Lord,*
> > *How magnificent is Thy name in all the earth.*
>
> O SET Thy splendour above the heavens!
> Out of the mouth of little children and sucklings
> Thou dost establish strength, because of Thine adversaries,
> To still the enemy and the avenger.
> When I see the work of Thy fingers.
> Moon and stars which Thou hast prepared;
> What is man that Thou shouldst be mindful of him?
> Or the son of mankind that Thou shouldst visit him?
>
> WHEN Thou didst make him a little lower than the *Elohim,*
> With glory and honour crowning him,
> Making him to have dominion over the works of Thine hands;
> All things Thou didst put under his feet;
> Cattle small and large, all of them,
> And also beasts of the field,
> Birds, and fish of the sea,
> Those that pass through the paths of the sea.
>
> *YAHWEH, our Sovereign Lord,*
> > *How magnificent is Thy name in all the earth.*

Ps. 8 was originally in 𝕭, and then taken up into 𝕸 and 𝕯𝕽 (*v.* Intr. §§ 27, 31, 33). In the latter it received the assignment על הגתית, probably to be sung to a well-known vintage song (*v.* Intr. § *39*). The linguistic evidence favours the Persian period י' אדנינו v.$^{2. 10}$, elsw. only Ne. 10^{30}; the glory of God על השמים v.^{2}, cf. 57$^{6. 12}$ (= 108^6) 83^{19} +, all late; אויב ומתנקם v.^{3} elsw. 44^{17}, צנה v.^{8} α.λ., for צנא. The relation of v.$^{6-9}$ to Gn. 1$^{26-28}$ is evident. בצלם אלהים Gn. 1^{27} and מאלהים v.^{6} must be interpreted in the same way as referring to gods, that is God and angels, in accordance with usage; cf. Pss. 86^8 97^7 136^2; cf. v.^{7} with Gn. 1^{28}. We can hardly suppose that Gn. 1 derived its conception from Ps. 8, for it is there part of the larger conception, and is therefore original and Ps. 8 derivative. The mode of creation is, however, different. Moon and stars are not created by command, but by the fingers of God, v⁴. This is more like the mode of creation in Gn. 2⁷˙ ¹⁹ ; and there seems to be a reference to the superiority of man in speech of Gn. 2¹⁶˙ ²⁾, in the emphasis upon the speech of sucklings v³. This free use of both of the poems of creation, originally in separate documents of the Hexateuch, but first compacted in the age of Ezra, is best explained by the supposition that, when the Ps. was composed, the Pentateuch had already been compacted in essentially its present form. The Ps. must therefore be subsequent to Ezra. The Ps. is an evening hymn ; with no personal or historic references, but entirely general, adapted to the whole congregation of Israel ; and therefore we may conclude that it was composed for the congregation, and for purposes of public worship. It is admirably suited for this purpose, being symmetrical in structure, of two equal Strs., having an introductory and concluding Rf. The Ps. was probably composed in time of peace and prosperity, for the tone is peaceful and joyous.

Rf. **2a, b** is a trimeter couplet, the first line however without the last beat, in order to get a metrical pause before the utterance of the supreme thought. This is the Rf. which also closes the Ps. v¹⁰ and so encloses it. *Our Sovereign Lord*] pl. emph. Heb., not sufficiently expressed by " Lord " EVˢ. — *How magnificent*] the majesty of God in its wide extent, amplitude, *in all the earth*] throughout its entire extent, cf. 76⁵ 93⁴. " Excellent," EVˢ., suggests ethical rather than physical extent ; " glorious," Dr., " majestic," Kirk. are too general. — *Thy name*] summing up God's manifestation of Himself as the object of commemoration and praise.

St. I. is a trimeter octastich, composed of an introductory line of petition, a synth. tristich, and a tetrastich of two syn. couplets, the second synthetic to the first. — **2c.** *O set*] so most easily the Heb. cohort. imv. But a later scribe, wishing to connect with previous lines, and overlooking their independence as the Rf., inserted the relative, without venturing to change the form, and so has given difficulty to interpreters from the most ancient times. — *Thy splendour*] rich and brilliant display of majesty ; " glory," EVˢ., " majesty," Dr., JPSV. are too general. — *above the heavens*] PBV., AV., as in all other passages ; " upon the heavens " RV., Dr., JPSV., Kirk., al., though grammatically correct, is not justified by usage. The heavens are antith. to earth of the Rf. The poet would say : "Thy name is widespread in all the earth, magnify it still more, set it above the heavens in the splendour of its manifestations." — **3.** *Out of the mouth of little children*] those just able to speak, and in this respect, notwithstanding their weakness especially as *sucklings*, superior to all other creatures, — a conception based on the naming of the animals by Adam Gn. 2^{19-20}. — *Thou dost establish*] emph. present. "Ordain" PBV., AV. in modern usage is too strong and specific. — *Strength*] over against the enemies of God, sufficient to silence them if not destroy them. The poet may have been thinking of the creative strength of God's speech, of Gn. I, and so of the strength that God had established in human speech even of little children as superior to physical prowess. It is probable that he was thinking of the divine strength as recognised and praised by children, in accord with the rendering of 𝔊. — *because of thine adversaries*] RV., in accord with Heb., and not "enemies," PBV., AV., which so translate two different Heb. words. — *to still*] to silence their hostile speech by the praise of children. — **4.** *When I see the work of Thy fingers.*] The poet looks up to the heavens by night, above which he would have the splendour of Yahweh set, and sees there the work of His fingers. — *the moon and stars*] sufficiently indicate, in the absence of the sun, that it is night, and that the author is thinking of the heavens. A prosaic copyist inserted *heavens* in the first line, and so destroyed its measure. Moon and stars were created, and put in their places in the heavens by the fingers of God. Gn. 2^{7-19} seems to underlie this conception of the mode of creation ; only there man and animals were formed by the hand of God, as a sculptor carves out images or as a potter moulds them into clay. Here fingers are used with reference to moon and stars, and the verb *prepared* suggests the builder of 24^2 65^7 119^{90} Pr. 3^{19} 8^{27}, the most frequent conception of the mode of creation, especially in later poets ; only the builder in this particular reference to moon and stars is an artist executing the finest kind of work by the artistic skill of his fingers. The "ordained" of EV⁵. is not suited in modern usage (as it was in old English) to the conception of the use of the fingers of God. — **5.** *What is man.* ‖ *The son of mankind*] not any particular man, but the human kind, man as a race. When compared with moon and stars created by

God and manifesting His splendour, what does mankind amount to, that God should take any account of him? — *that thou shouldst be mindful of him.* ‖ *that thou shouldst visit him*]. These in Heb. are final clauses, with subjunctive mood, and not to be rendered with EV⁸. by the indicative mood as statements of fact.

Str. II. is also a trimeter octastich, composed of an introductory line as protasis, and an apod. consisting of a syn. distich, and a synth. pentastich, all in one sentence. — **6.** *When Thou didst make him*]. The Heb. Waw consec. does not admit of the rendering as an independent clause, "Thou madest" PBV., or causal, "for Thou hast made" AV., RV., or adv., "and yet" JPSV.; but requires either "and thou hast" Dr., going back to the historic act of creation of moon and stars of v⁴, and carrying it on into this new act of creation of man; or else protasis of temporal clause as given above. — *a little lower than the Elohim*] referring to the creation of man in the image of *Elohim* Gn. 1²⁷, and the consultation of God with other *Elohim*, "Let us make" Gn. 1²⁶. As the context is strictly monotheistic, and the whole passage is so late in origin that polytheism is not to be thought of in the mind of the poet, we must think of the *Elohim* as comprehending God and angels, the latter being in their historic origin, the ancient polytheistic gods, degraded to ministering servants of the one God Yahweh. Therefore, they are not merely "angels" Heb. 2⁷, PBV., AV., or "God" RV., JPSV. and most moderns, or "divinity," as abstract Heng., Hu., Pe.; but God and angels, divine beings, gods. — *With glory and honour crowning him*]. When man was created in the image of the *Elohim*, Gn. 1²⁶⁻²⁷, he was crowned with their glory and honour, at his inauguration as sovereign of the creatures. The splendour of Yahweh set above the heavens is reflected in His image, man, whom He has crowned as His representative to rule over the earth. — *Making him to have dominion*] as crowned king of the animal and vegetable kingdom man has rule over them. — *Thou didst put under his feet*] a paraphrase of Gn. 1²⁶⁻²⁸; two different but syn. verbs are used with essentially the same meaning. — *Over the works of Thine hands* ‖ *all things*] on earth antith. moon and stars, the work of Yahweh's fingers in heaven. These works are described by specimens, using syn. words to those of Gn. 1²⁶⁻²⁸. — *those that pass through*] doubtless refers to the sea monsters of Gn. 1²¹.

2. יהוה אֲדֹנֵינוּ] line shortened for metrical pause as 1¹. ‡ אָדוֹן n.m. *lord* (1) master 12⁵ 105²¹, intensive pl. 123²; (2) husband 45¹², intensive pl.; (3) king 110¹, pl. 136⁸; (4) God אדון 114⁷, † ארון כל הארץ 97⁵ Jos. 3¹¹·¹⁸ (J) Zc. 4¹⁴ 6⁵ Mi. 4¹³; intensive pl. *sovereign lord* אדני האדנים Ps. 136⁸ = Dt. 10¹⁷, אדנינו 135⁵ 147⁵ Ne. 8¹⁾, יהוה אדנינו Ps. 8²·¹⁰ Ne. 10³⁰. For אֲדֹנִי *v.* Intr. § 32. — ‡ אַדִּיר] adj. *wide spread, magnificent, majestic,* of waters of sea 93⁴ Ex. 15¹⁰, of kings Ps. 136¹⁸, of Yahweh 76⁵ 93⁴, His name 8²·¹⁰; of nobles 16⁸ (舉) (as Ju. 5¹³·²⁵ Je. 14⁸ 25⁸⁴ Is. 10⁸⁴), but better 𝕲 vb. אדר. — ‡ בְּכָל־הָאָרֶץ] as v.¹⁰ 19⁶ 45⁷ 105⁷. — אֲשֶׁר־תְּ־נָה] rel. c. Qal imv. cohort. √נתן, rel. defined by הוֹרָה. Bö. interprets as permissive "*mayst thou set.*" Ki., Genebr., al. as infin. cstr. for usual תֵּת, as רְבָה for רֶבֶת Gn. 46³, "*the setting of whose splendour.*" 𝔍 *qui posuisti,* 𝔖, 𝕿, Σ, Hu., De., Pe., Gr., al., RV. This would imply וַ־רְבָה, Ammon, Köster, Oort, al., unless as Bä. these Vrss. interpreted thus an inf. cstr. 𝕲 ὅτι ἐπήρθη suggested to Ew., Ri., al. רָנָה = תנן, *extend, stretch out;* but these vbs. do not exist in Heb., and this mng. does not correspond with 𝕲. Schultens rd. תנה n. = *praise;* Michaelis, הנה Qal pf. = *sonat,* Dy. רָנָה = Pu. pf. *be praised;* cf. Ju. 5¹¹, so Kö.ᴵᴵ·⁽¹⁾ § ⁵⁹⁵ = *quod narratur.* Buhl suggests the familiar נכה, but this would be so difficult textually that it would be just as easy to think of נשׂא, which corresponds exactly with 𝕲. It is best to suppose with Che. that אשר is gloss of a prosaic copyist who wished to connect with previous line, not knowing that it was a Rf., and therefore should be as independent here as in v.¹⁾. Then the cohort. imv. is most appropriate at beginning of the Str. This also corresponds with the usage of עַל־הַשָּׁמַיִם, which is alw. *over, above* the heavens 57⁶·¹² = 108⁶ 113⁴, cf. 83¹⁹. — ‡ הוֹד] n.m. *vigour, splendour, majesty,* (1) of king הוד והדר 21⁶ 45⁴ 111³; (2) of God 8² 148¹³, הוד והדר 96⁶ 104¹; cf. 145⁵ — **3.** יִסַּדְתָּ] Pi. pf. 2 ms. God subject, possibly aorist referring to creation of man; but prob. pf. of general truth. ‡ יָסַד vb. Qal *found,* of creation c. acc. *earth* 24²; cf. 78⁶⁹ 89¹² 102²⁶ 104⁵, cf. v.⁸ sq. לְ, God's commands 119¹⁵²; Pi. *establish* 8³. — ‡ עֹז] n.m. *strength,* (1) material and physical 30⁸ 62⁸ 68⁸⁴ 71⁷ 89¹¹ 110² 150¹, עֹז 61⁴ Ju. 9⁵¹ Pr. 18¹⁰; (2) personal, social, political, bestowed by Yahweh 1 S. 2¹⁰ Pss. 29¹¹ 68³⁶ 84⁶ 86¹⁶ 138³, Yahweh the strength of His people 81², for defence 28⁷·⁸ 46² 59¹⁾·¹⁸ 84⁶ 89¹⁸, ‖ ישועה 118¹⁴ = Ex. 15² = Is. 12², cf. 140⁸; (3) strength of Yahweh as attribute 62¹² 68⁸⁵ 93¹ 99⁴, as theme of praise 29¹ 96⁷ (𝕲 τιμήν) 68³⁵ (𝕲 δόξαν), so 8³ (𝕲 αἶνον, 𝔙, 𝔍, 𝔖, Σ, Bar. Heb., Mt. 21¹⁶) 59¹⁷, in connection with sacred places 63⁸ (‖ כבוד), cf. 96⁶, exerted against enemies Ex. 15¹³ Pss. 21²·¹⁴ 66⁸ 68²⁹ 74¹³ 77¹⁵ 78²⁶ 90¹¹ 105⁴, manifested in connection with the Ark 78⁶¹ 132⁸ Aq., Σ κράτος 8³. 𝕿 עושנא. — אויב ומתנקם] elsw. 44¹⁷. אויב *v.* 3⁸. מתרוגם Hithp. ptc. nominal force, ‡ נקם vb. Qal *take vengeance,* subj. God c. על 99⁸. Hithp. ptc. 8³ 44¹⁷, *avenge oneself,* of men. — **4.** כִּי־אֶרְאֶה] Temporal clause apod. v.⁵. — שָׁמֶיךָ] is a gloss; it makes line too long, and is unnecessary for mng. — אֲשֶׁר־הֲכִינוֹתָה אֶצְבְּעֹתֶיךָ] phr. α.λ.

work of God in creation Pss. 103²² 104¹³· ²⁴· ³¹ 139¹⁴, of God's hands 8⁷ 19²
102²³ 138⁸.— [אֲשֶׁר] unnecessary gl., it makes line too long.— [פִּינְנָה] *fully*
written Polel pf. 2 m. i.p. כּוּן.— 5. [זֶה] in antithesis to כֹּה v.²ᵃ; cf. 144³ (אָדָם).—
‡ אֱנוֹשׁ (1) coll. for *mankind* 8⁵ 90³ 144⁸, antith. אלהים 73⁵, cf. 103¹⁵ 104¹⁵· ¹⁵,
antith. Yahweh and Israel, *mere man* 9²⁰· ²¹ 10¹⁸ 56² 66¹²; (2) of individual
man 55¹⁴, pl. 26⁹ 55²⁴ 59³ 76⁶ 119²⁴ 139¹⁹.— ‖ [בֶּן־אָדָם] ‡ אָדָם n.m. (1) *mankind*, coll. 17⁴ 22⁷ 36⁷ 49¹³· ²¹ 56¹² 58¹² 60¹³ 68¹⁹ 73⁶ 76¹¹ 78⁶⁰ 82⁷ 94¹⁰· ¹¹ 104¹⁴· ²³
105¹⁴ 108¹³ 115⁴ 118⁶· ⁸ 119¹³⁴ 124² 135⁸· ¹⁵ 140² 144⁴, כל האדם 116¹¹, כל אדם
39⁶· ¹² 64¹⁰, also בֶּן אָדָם 8⁵ (= אָדָם 144³) 80¹⁸ 146³, usually בְּנֵי אָדָם 11⁴ 12²· ⁹
14² (= 53³) 21¹¹ 31²⁰ 33¹³ 36¹⁸ 45⁸ 57⁵ 58²(?) 66⁵ 89⁴⁸ 90³ 107⁸· ¹⁵· ²¹· ³¹ 115¹⁶
145¹², antith. בני איש, elsw. 49³ 62¹⁰ to אלהים; (2) individual man, only 32²
84⁶· ¹³.— [כִּי] *that*, introducing final clauses with Qal impf. 2 s. c. sf. 3 m.
תִּפְקְדֶנּוּ ,תִּזְכְּרֶנּוּ in rhyme.   ‡ זָכַר vb. *remember, recall to mind* I. (1) *man* subj.
(*a*) past experience 42⁵ 137¹, cf. 77⁷, neg. 137⁶; (*b*) doings of Yahweh 77¹²
(Qr. Kt. Hiph. better) 105⁵ 143⁶, neg. 78⁴² 106⁷, obj. clause with כִּי 78³⁵,
style of D; (2) *remember* persons 109¹⁶; (3) *remember* Yahweh, keep
Him in mind 42⁷ 63⁷ 77⁴, abs. 22²⁸, name of Yahweh 119⁵⁵, His laws,
103¹⁸ 119⁵². II. *God* subj. (1) remember persons with kindness, neg.
88⁶, c. acc. 9¹³ 74² 106⁴ 115¹², mankind 8⁵, c. לְ pers. 25⁷ 136²³; (2) *remember* the devotion of His servants, c. acc. 20⁴ 132¹; (3) His covenant 105⁸ 106⁴⁵ 111⁵ 119⁴⁹, His mercy 25⁶ 98³, His word 105⁴², extenuating
circumstances 78³⁹ 89⁴⁸ 103¹⁴; (4) sins 25⁷ 79⁸, reproach 74¹⁸· ²² 89⁵¹, the day
of Jerusalem 137⁷. Niph. *be remembered*, c. אֶל 109¹⁴; neg. = no longer
exist 83⁵. Hiph. (1) *cause to be remembered, keep in remembrance*, c. acc.
rei 45¹⁸; (2) *mention*, c. בְּ 20⁸, c. acc. 87⁴, works of Jahweh 77¹² (?), His
righteousness 71¹⁶; (3) *make an Azkara*, titles of, 38¹ 70¹.— [פָּקַד] vb. Qal
(1) *visit* graciously 8⁵ 65¹⁰ 80¹⁵ 106⁴; (2) *to search* 17⁸, *punish* 59⁶ 89³⁸.
Hiph. (1) *entrust*, c. בְּיַד 31⁶; (2) *appoint* over, c. עֲלִי 109⁶.— 6. [וַהְחַסְּרֵהוּ] וּ consec. Pi. impf. 2 s. with sf. 3 s., introduces a new Str., and is a change of tense
and cannot carry on previous impfs., protasis of temporal clause with apod.
v⁷ᵇ תְּשַׁוֵּהוּ, the intervening clauses being circumstantial.— [מֵאֱלֹהִים] 𝕭, 𝕾, 𝕿, Heb.
2⁷ AV. *angels;* Aq., Σ, Θ, 𝔍 *God;* so most moderns. Hu., Pe. *divinity*, abst.,
but there is no usage to justify it. אלהים n.m. pl., ‡ as real pl.: (1) *rulers*
Ex. 21⁶ 22⁷· ⁸· ⁸· ²⁷ Ju. 5⁸ Pss. 82¹· ⁶ 138¹; (2) *superhuman, divine beings*, including God and angels. This is the most natural interp. of Gn. 1²⁶· ²⁷ with
1 pl. vb., so here, cf. Jb. 38⁷, where the בְּנֵי אֱלֹהִים take part in the creation;
(3) *angels* Ps. 97⁷ = (ה)אלהים בני Jb. 1⁶ 2¹ 38⁷ Gn. 6²· ⁴ (J); (4) *gods* Pss. 86⁸
136², אלהי העמים 96⁵ Dt. 6¹⁴ 13⁸, כל א' Pss. 95³ 96⁴ 97⁷· ⁹ 135⁵. For use of אלהים
for *God* (*v*. Intr. § 32).— [כָּבוֹד וְהָדָר] phr. a.λ., cf. הוד יהדר 21⁶ of king.—
‡ [כָּבוֹד] n.m. (1) *abundance, riches*, 49¹⁷· ¹⁸ Gn. 31¹ (J) Is. 10⁸ +. (2) *honour,
splendour, glory:* of extern. conditional circumstances, (*a*) of man, at his creation as crowned by God with וְהָדָר Ps. 8⁶; the king is given כ' (‖ הוד והדר)
21⁶; (*b*) of things: the restored holy land 84¹²; (*c*) of God's glory in historic and ideal manifestations to the pious mind: Yahweh's name is a name
of glory 72¹⁹; in the temple His glory is seen 26⁸ 63⁸; it is עַל שָׁמַיִם 113⁴;

על כל הארץ 57⁶·¹² = 108⁶; in a thunderstorm He is אל הכבוד 29⁸; His glory is לעולם 104⁸¹; great 138⁶; the heavens declare כ׳ אל 19²; with refer. to the divine reign 145⁵·¹²: He is מֶלֶךְ הַכָּבוֹד 24⁷·⁸·⁹·¹⁰. He will appear in glory 102¹⁷; His glory will dwell in the land 85¹⁰; the earth will be filled with it 72¹⁹; it will be declared among the nations and all will see it 97⁶; and peoples and kings revere it 102¹⁶. (3) *honour:* of position, רום בכ׳ 112⁹; לקח כ׳ 73²⁴. (4) *honour, reputation,* of character: of man, antith. כְּלִמָּה 4⁸ (also 2 Ch. 26¹⁸ Ec. 10¹ Pr. 20⁸ 21²¹ 25²⁷). (5) *my honour:* poet. of seat of honour in the inner man, the noblest part of man, ‖ נפש 7⁶; ‖ לב 16⁹ 108²; called upon to זמר 30¹³ (rd. כבודי for כבוד); עוּרָה 57⁹. (6) *honour, reverence, glory:* as due or ascribed to one: (a) *of man:* ‖ ישע 62⁸; (b) *of God:* כ׳ שמך 79⁹; 96⁸; 29² יהב כ׳ שמו ל׳ 96⁷; 29¹ יהב כ׳ ועז ל׳ 66²; שים כ׳ תהלתו 115¹; נתן כ׳ ל׳ 29⁹; אמר כבוד 145¹¹; אמר כ׳ מלכותך 96⁸; ספר כבודו בגוים 66²; זמר כ׳ שמו יעלזו בכ׳ *exult with* (ascription of) *glory* 149⁵. (7) *glory:* as object of honour and reverence: *my glory* (the one I glorify) 3⁴; כבורם *their glory* 106²⁰; for כבודה *v.* 45¹⁴. ‡ הָדָר n.m. (1) *ornament,* כְּהַדְרֵי קֹדֶשׁ, priestly robes as sacred ornaments 110⁸ (but rd. הררי *mountains,* after 𝔊, Σ). (2) *splendour:* majesty conferred on man 8⁶, king 21⁶, cf. 45⁴·⁵; but esp. of Yahweh Himself 29⁴ 90¹⁶ 96⁶ 104¹ 111⁸ 145⁵, His kingdom 145¹². (3) *honour, glory:* for saints of Yahweh 149⁹. — [תְּעַטְּרֵהוּ] Pi. impf. 2 m. sf. 3 s. circumstantial. — **7.** [תַּמְשִׁילֵהוּ] Hiph. impf. 2 m. sf. 3 s., prob. originally at end of line for rhyme, and most proper for circumstantial clause. ‡ מָשַׁל vb. Qal, *rule, have dominion,* over: c. ב of man 19¹⁴ 105²¹ 106⁴¹, cf. ptc. מֹשֵׁל עַמִּים 105²⁰; of God 22²⁹ 59¹⁴ 89¹⁰ 103¹⁹; abs. 66⁷. † Hiph. *cause to rule,* c. acc. pers., ב rei 8⁷ Jb. 25² Dn. 11⁸⁹. — כֹּל־] emph. in position; abs. without article elsw. 74⁸ 145¹⁵ comprehending all that context suggests. — [שַׁתָּה] fully written Qal pf. 2 m. שִׁית. — **8.** † צֹנֶה] n.m. *flock,* cf. צֹנְאֶם Nu. 32²⁴ (JE), variation of צאן *small cattle.* — † אֲלָפִים] *large cattle, oxen,* as Dt. 7¹³ 28⁴·¹⁸·⁵¹ Is. 30²⁴ Pr. 14⁴. — כֻּלָּם] summing up, "made more independent and emphatic by being placed . . . *after* the word which it qualifies," BDB. — כל ‡ with suffixes 8⁸ 34²⁰ 62⁴ 67⁴·⁶ 82⁶ 102²⁷ 104²⁴·²⁷ 139⁴·¹⁶ 147⁴; כלו "referring to the mass of things or persons meant," BDB. 29⁹ 53⁴ (= הכל 14⁸). — [וְגַם] *and also* 8⁸ 71¹⁸ 78²¹ 84⁸ 148¹². — [בַּהֲמוֹת שָׂדָי] Jo. 2²², בהמות שרה Jo. 1²⁰, cf. 1 S. 17⁴⁴. ‡ בְּהֵמָה n.f. (1) *beast,* antith. man 36⁷ 104¹⁴ 135⁸, as inferior to man 49¹⁸·²¹ 73²²; (2) antith. wild beasts 148¹⁰, associated with field 8⁸, mountains 50¹⁰, cf. 107³⁸; (3) seldom *wild beast* 147⁹. — **9.** [צִפּוֹר שָׁמַיִם] phr. α.λ. takes place of עוף השמים Gn. 1²⁶ to which it is assimilated. שָׁמַיִם is unnecessary here, and makes line too long. — [עֹבֵר] Qal ptc. עָבַר vb. *pass over, through:* large body of water, Is. 33²¹ of ship; here of water animals. It is a poetic substitute for רְמֶשׂ, Gn. 1²¹·²⁸; cf. Lv. 11⁴⁶ (H) Ps. 69³⁵. — [אָרְחוֹת יַמִּים] phr. α.λ. ‡ אֹרַח n.m. *path:* (1) literal, of sea-animals 8⁹, of sun 19⁶; (2) fig., *path of life,* fortune 139⁸ 142⁴, א׳ מישׁור 27¹¹; (3) fig., *mode* of life 119⁹, ways of Yahweh 25¹⁰, as norm for man 25⁴ 44¹⁹ 119¹⁵, ארח חיים 16¹¹ Pr. 2¹⁹ 5⁶ 15²⁴, *path of wickedness* Pss. 17⁴ 119¹⁰¹·¹⁰⁴·¹²⁸; cf. syn. דֶּרֶךְ *v¹.*

PSALMS IX. AND X., 22 ALPHABETICAL STR. 4³.

Pss. 9 and 10 were originally one. The congregation thanks
Yahweh in temple worship for His wondrous works of deliverance
from the nations, and that He has become a high refuge to His
oppressed people ($9^{2-5, 10-11}$). They pray that He, who has in the
past lifted them from the gates of death, may be gracious and ter-
rorise the nations now afflicting them ($9^{14-15, 20-21}$). He seems to
stand afar off, while the nations are contending, and ignoring Him;
and with craft are crushing His host with impunity (10^{1-11}). They
plead that Yahweh, their everlasting king, will arise, destroy the
nations from the land, and do justice for the oppressed (10^{12-18}).
Later editors substitute for the original, detailed statements of a
more external and dogmatic kind: that Yahweh had given over
the nations to everlasting destruction (9^{6-7}), that He was the everlasting king, ruling in justice (9^{8-9}), that the nations were caught
in their own pits and snares (9^{16-17}), and that they were doomed to
Sheol (9^{18}); but that Yahweh's people would not be forgotten (9^{19});
and the congregation are invoked to praise their king enthroned in
Zion (9^{12-13}).

I WILL give thanks with all my mind unto Thee,
 I will tell all Thy wondrous works,
 I will be glad and I will exult in Thee,
 I will make melody, 'Elyon unto Thy name.
BECAUSE mine enemies turned backward,
 They stumble and they perish at Thy presence;
 For Thou hast done judgment and right in my favour,
 Thou didst sit on Thy throne judging righteously.
  · · · · · · · · · · · · · · · *
AND so Thou art become a high refuge for the oppressed,
 A high refuge for times of dearth;
 And they that know Thee trust in Thee;
 For Thou dost not forsake them that seek Thee.
  · · · · · · · · · · · · · · ·
BE gracious to me, see my affliction;
 Thou that liftest me up from the gates of death;
 In order that I may tell Thy praise.
 In the gates of the daughter of Zion may rejoice.
  · · · · · · · · · · · · ·

---

* These marks indicate that parts of the Ps. have been omitted. *V.* Comments
and notes.

YAHWEH, let not (mere) men prevail;
    Let the nations be judged before Thy face.
    O appoint Terror for them
    That the nations may know that they are (mere) men.

· · · · · · · · · ·

WHY standest Thou in the distance,
    Hidest in times of dearth?
    In their pride they hotly pursue the afflicted;
    Let them be caught in that they have planned.

THE wicked doth contemn Yahweh:
    "According to the height of His anger, He will not require,
    There is no God," are his devices.
    His ways are defiled at all times.

ON high are Thine acts of judgment, at a distance from him;
    As for his adversaries, he puffeth at them;
    He saith in his mind, "I shall not be moved,"
    (He doth swear) "In all generations (I shall be) without evil."

HIS mouth is full of deceits,
    Under his tongue is mischief;
    He sitteth down in the places of ambush of settlements,
    In secret places he slayeth the innocent.

HIS eyes spy on Thy host,
    He lieth in ambush in his secret place as a lion,
    In his covert to seize the afflicted,
    That he may seize hold of the afflicted, dragging him away.

(HE doth hunt) the oppressed with his net, and he sinks down,
    And Thy host falls because of his great numbers;
    He doth say in his mind, "'El hath forgotten,
    He hath hidden His face, He doth not see."

O ARISE, lift up Thy hand,
    Forget not, 'El, the afflicted.
    Wherefore doth the wicked contemn,
    Say in his mind, "Thou dost not require it"?

THOU hast seen the trouble and grief,
    Thou beholdest to requite with Thy hand;
    Upon Thee Thy host leaveth it,
    Of the orphan Thou art the helper.

BREAK the arm of the wicked,
    Let his wickedness be sought out, let it not be found;
    O King, forever and ever,
    Destroy the nations out of the land.

THE desire of the afflicted Thou hast heard,
    Thou settest Thy mind (upon them), Thou harkenest;
    To judge the orphan and oppressed,
    To terrify (mere) man from the land.

Pss. 9–10 were originally one as in 𝕲, 𝔙, 𝔍. They were separated for liturgical purposes as in 𝕳, and therefore Ps. 10 was left without title, and in modern Protestant and Jewish Vrss. the Pss. are numbered one higher than in the Oriental, Greek, and Roman Churches from Ps. 10 to Ps. 147 (*v.* Intr. § 42). The סלה at the close of Ps. 9 is an additional evidence of the original unity of the two Pss., for it indicates a place where a selection might close (*v.* Intr. § 41). The Ps. was in 𝔇, then in 𝔐, and subsequently in 𝔇ℛ (*v.* Intr. §§ 27, 31, 33), in which last it was appointed to be sung by male sopranos, or falsettos (עלמות לבן [לִ.] *v.* Intr. § 34). As Che. says, the Ps. is "partly trimeters, partly tetrameters, indicating either the imperfect skill of the psalmist in the management of his metre, or the interference of a second writer with the original poem. The second hypothesis is the more probable. Originally the poem was, no doubt, a perfect alphabetical psalm, at least so far as relates to the consistency of the metre and the number of stanzas." The nine strophes with א, כ, י, ח, ל, ק, ר, שׁ, ה are essentially in their original form. Six others may be recovered from the present text. (1) Str. י in the present text is 9¹⁸⁻¹⁹; but this is really composed of a trimeter couplet, v.¹⁸, and a tetrameter couplet, v.¹⁹, and is a late addition. The Str. is really v.²⁰⁻²¹, disguised by the prefixing of קומה prematurely before 10¹², in order to make a suitable close for the Ps. (2) Str. ג is disguised in 𝔐 in the last clause of 10³, but in 𝔊 it rightly begins v.⁴. (3) Str. מ is disguised in the midst of 10⁵, its מרום is at beginning of l. 2 of v.⁵. (4) Str. פ is also disguised as second word of 10⁷. ארה is vb., belonging to previous line. (5) Str. ע is disguised at beginning of l. 3 of 10⁸. (6) Str. צ lacks the first word, the first line being defective. It may be restored by conjecture as צר. Three Strs. have been displaced by others which have been substituted for them. It is possible to conjecture originals as underlying them; but only by entire reconstruction, and even then the form and substance of the thought is different from the original. (1) The Str. ג is a tetrameter with cæsura, evident in the midst of three of the lines, less evident but probable in the other. (2) Str. ט is also a tetrameter with cæsuras. (3) Str. ז is a trimeter; a call to praise, not suited to the context of the original Ps., but adapted to later liturgical use, and using late liturgical terms. The remaining Strs. are more difficult to find. Many efforts have been made to find them by reconstruction and conjecture. I have made several such efforts myself, accepting them provisionally, only to finally abandon them as unsatisfactory. (1) The Strs. with ד and ה have disappeared. In place of them is a trimeter tetrastich, beginning with יהוה in third person. But it uses terms of the royal Pss. 98⁹, 96¹⁰·¹³, and these are statements, in liturgical language, of the general truth of the divine dominion, cognate with the idea of the Ps., but in more objective and less personal relations. (2) Str. כ is missing. Possibly a relic of it is present in 10³, in the clause beginning כי הלל, but only one trimeter line and two words of a second line are there; and it is out of place between ל and ג. It is therefore more probable that the verse is a prosaic gloss. (3) Str. ס has disappeared entirely. We can only make it by a readjustment of the lines about where it should come, and at the expense of other Strs. The order of the Strs. is the usual one of the Heb. alphabet, except that ע, צ come together as in La. 2, 3, 4, probably an older order. ג and כ are transposed.

This is probably an editorial change and not original. The historical situation of the Ps. is indicated by internal evidence. The Temple worship was carried on 9^{2-15}. The people suffer from crafty and cruel enemies, who ignore and contemn Yahweh. These are nations, 9^{20-21}, 10^{16}, described by coll. רשׁע $10^{2.4.13.15}$, אנושׁ $9^{20.21}$, 10^{18}, who invade the land and imperil its existence. They are not the great conquering nations, but lesser ones, such as those which troubled Jerusalem before the walls were built by Nehemiah ; Moabites, Ammonites, Arabs, and Philistines, Ne. 2^{10}, 4^7, 6^1. The glosses indicate a later time of calm historical retrospect and confidence in Yahweh, the King enthroned in Zion; and therefore probably in the Greek period.

Str. א. 2–3. Each line begins with א and closes with *kah*. The four lines are syn., using cohortatives, expressing resolutions or determinations. — *I will give thanks* ‖ *tell* ‖ *exult* ‖ *make melody*], terms indicating in their usage public songs of praise. Each vb. has syn. obj. — *unto Thee*], so 𝔊, adding also the divine name, *Yahweh*, which 𝔥 substitutes for it, and so destroys rhyme. ‖ *Thy wondrous works*], as context shows, of deliverance from enemies, cf. Ex. 3^{20} (J) Ju. 6^{13} Pss. 26^7 78^{11} +. ‖ *unto Thy name*], cf. Pss. 61^9 66^4 68^5. The qualifying ideas are *with all my mind*], better than " heart," EVs., which in modern usage rather suggests affections, ‖ *all*] intensifying wondrous works, ‖ *I will be glad*] intensifying " exult." — '*Elyon*], divine name, " Most High," EVs., intensifying Thy name.

Str. ב has two syn. couplets. — 4. The *enemies* are in subsequent context, not private but public enemies, nations. — *Because*] giving a reason for the praise of the previous Str. — *turned backward*], in retreat. The context indicates a historical reference and not present experience or general truth. It is true *stumble* and *perish* are impfs., but they give graphic description of past events. They intensify the retreat as disastrous. — *At Thy presence*], the presence and power of Yahweh brought about the retreat ; the whole credit of it is due to Him. — 5. *For*], causal particle with pf., either syn. with v.⁴ as second ground of praise, emphasizing Yahweh's dealing with His people over against His dealing with their enemies, or else reason of previous couplet, possibly not distinguished in author's mind. The syn. words *judgment and right* intensify the idea. The sf. is objective, and can only be expressed by paraphrase : *in my favour*], that is, of the congregation speaking in its solidarity as an individual. — *Thou hast done judgment ‖ judging righteously*], executed it on the enemies. — *Thou didst sit on Thy throne*], in heaven, as Pss. 11^4 45^7 47^9 89^{15} 93^2 97^2, from which God executes judgment on earth in favour of His people and against their enemies.

Str. ‏ב‎ is a syn. tetrameter tetrastich, substituted for an original trimeter, giving a more comprehensive and general statement, and so differing from the personal experience expressed throughout the original Ps.

> Thou hast rebuked the nations. Thou hast destroyed the wicked;
> Their name Thou hast blotted out forever and ever.
> As for the enemy, they have come to an end. The ruins are forever.
> And cities Thou didst uproot, — their memory is perished.

6. *Thou hast rebuked the nations*]. This was probably in the original Str., but is now followed by a cæsura and a complementary phrase : *Thou hast destroyed the wicked*], of two beats, instead of one complementary word, as in the original Ps. Both phrs. are further expositions of v.⁴. The term wicked is coll. for nations, as 9^{17} $10^{2.\ 3.\ 4.\ 13.\ 15}$ 55^4 139^{19} Is. 11^4 Hb. 3^{13} pl. Pss. $9.^{18}$ 3^8 7^{10} $17^9 +$. — *Their name Thou hast blotted out*], so utterly have they been destroyed that their names are no longer known, save to the antiquarian. The author was thinking probably of the nations exterminated by Israel at the Exodus, as it is a phr. of D., Dt. 9^{14} 29^{19} 2 K. 14^{27}. — **7.** *As for the enemy*], coll. for nations. The position of noun and the article are emph., cf. pl. v.⁴. — *they have come to an end*], so that they exist no longer as nations. The cæsura requires an independent clause. — *Their ruins are forever*], possibly their land, as Je. 7^{34} 44^{22}, but more probably cities, as v.⁷ᵇ and Je. 49^{13}, cities of Bosra; Ez. 26^{20}, of Tyre ; Is. 61^4, of Judah. There is no sufficient authority in usage for referring these to enemies. — *And their cities*], the possessive here and above is not expressed but implied in the context. — *Thou didst uproot*], only here of cities, but of nations Dt. 29^{27} Je. $12^{14} +$, fig. of tree or plant. We might think of the use of cities for inhabitants. — *Their memory is perished*], syn. v.⁶ᵇ, cf. Dt. 12^3 Is. 26^{14} Ps. 41^6.

8–9. This Str. is a syn. trimeter tetrastich, generalising v.⁵, as the previous Str. did v.⁴. It takes the place of Str. ‏ה‎ of the original Ps. The initial ‏ה‎ might be gained by reading ‏הנה‎ " Lo," with Du.

for the המה at close of previous line ; but this would make the line too long, unless we reject *Yahweh* as a gloss. But in any case we do not overcome the use of 3 sg. for 2 sg. of previous Strs. and the generalisation and late liturgical phrasing.

> Yahweh sitteth enthroned forever,
> He hath set up His throne for judgment:
> He judgeth the world in righteousness,
> He governeth the peoples with equity.

8. *He hath set up His throne*], phr. here of divine throne, cf. 103[19], but 2 S. 7[13] of David's. — *He judgeth the world in righteousness*] = 98[9] ; ‖ *He governeth the peoples with equity*] cf. 96[10] ; both implying a late comprehensive view of Yahweh, as sovereign of all nations, and of the entire habitable world.

Str. ו is a syn. trimeter tetrastich. — **10.** It has been changed to 3d pers. and assimilated to previous Str., and *Yahweh* has been inserted as gloss ; and so most Vrss. and commentators, " Yahweh also will be," some ignoring the juss. form, others recognising it, as Dr. " So may Yahweh be." But Du. after 𝔊 reads rightly ו consec. ; but then better, if connected with original Strs. v.[2-5. 14-15], 2d pers. : *And so Thou art become*] referring to historical experience, as in previous Strs. — *A high refuge*], a high place of refuge, cf. Pss. 18[3] 46[8. 12] 48[4] 59[10. 17] 62[3. 7] 94[22] 144[2]. — *for the oppressed*], coll. referring to the congregation, as so oppressed by the enemies as to be literally crushed, elsw. † 10[18] 74[21] Pr. 26[28], in this form, but cog. forms also 10[10] 34[19] 51[19] Is. 57[15]. — *for times of dearth*], phr., elsw. 10[1], cf. Je. 14[1] (*v.* *B*DB), the exact mng. uncertain. — **11.** *They that know Thee*, so originally, syn. *them that seek Thee*.] " Thy name " has been substituted for sf. at such an early date as to appear in all Vrss., but it makes the line too long in its measure, and is in accord with later tendency to interpose something between God Himself and His people, as obj. of knowledge, cf. 91[14] Is. 52[6] Je. 48[17]. Knowing Yahweh Himself is an earlier idea, cf. Ex. 5[2] (J) Ho. 2[22] 5[4] 8[2] Ps. 79[6].

Str. ו is composed of two trimeter couplets, and is a call to the congregation, to the praise resolved upon in Str. א. It is the same kind of a generalised explication of previous Str. as we have seen in v.[6-8], and probably came from the same later hand.

Make melody to Him who is enthroned in Zion,
Declare among the peoples His doings;
For He that requireth blood doth remember;
He doth not forget the cry of the afflicted.

12. *To Him who is enthroned in Zion*], in the Holy of Holies of temple, the throne room of the king of Israel, cf. Am. 1^2 Mi. 4^2 Pss. 76^3 102^{22} 135^{21} 147^{12}, added to the conception of throned in heaven of v.$^{8-9}$. — *Declare among the peoples His doings*], universal proclamation of the interposition of Yahweh in behalf of His people. — **13.** *For He that requireth blood*], as Ez. 33^6, from the enemies of His people as their avenger, based on the primitive conception of relationship of blood, and the obligation to avenge blood.

Str. ה is composed of two couplets, the former synth., the latter syn. — **14.** *Be gracious to me*], intensified by *see my affliction*], the past experience of previous Strs. being the basis for second part of Ps., which now, as Calv., becomes petition for deliverance in present needs. — *Thou that liftest me up*], past experience renewed to enforce the plea. — *from the gates of death*], cf. 107^{18} Is. 38^{10} Jb. 38^{17}, all referring to the abode of the dead, conceived as a city with gates. The nation had been in peril of death, and so of going down into Sheol the place of the dead; but Yahweh hath lifted the nation up from that awful descent. — **15.** *In order that*], final clause, expressing object of lifting up to life. — *In the gates of the daughter of Zion*], the gates of Zion or Jerusalem, over against gates of Sheol. The daughter of Zion is a personification of the people of Zion, cf. Is. 1^8 10^{32} Mi. 1^{13} Je. 4^3 Zc. 2^{14}; cf. daughter of Tyre Ps. 45^{13}, daughter of Babylon 137^8 Is. 47^1, daughter of Jerusalem Is. 37^{22} Mi. 4^8 La. $2^{13.15}$. The conception here is as Ps. 6^6 Is. 38^{18-20} that the public praise of Yahweh in His temple, or royal residence in Jerusalem, is something unique, and of such special acceptance with Him, that it can be had nowhere else, not in Sheol any more than outside the Holy Land, or apart from the divine residence in Jerusalem.

Str. ט is composed of two tetrameter couplets, and is the same kind of substitution, and doubtless by the same editor, as Str. ג.

The nations are sunk down in the pit that they made;
In the net which they hid is their foot caught.

> Yahweh hath made Himself known, He hath executed judgment;
> In the work of His hands the wicked are trapped.

16. *The nations are sunk down in the pit*]. This is probably
from the original Ps., where the pit referred to is the pit of Sheol
as usual subsequent to Ez., Pss. 16^{10} 30^{10} 49^{10} 55^{24} 103^4, and so antith.
to the lifting up of the congregation of Israel from Sheol v.^{14}.
But the editor, by the addition of *that they made*], refers it to a
pit dug by the nations into which they hoped Israel would fall,
cf. 7^{16}; syn. with *in the net which they hid*], cf. 10^9 31^5 35$^{7.\,8}$ 140^6.
— *is their foot caught*], the nations snare themselves instead of
Israel and receive retribution in kind. — **17.** *Yahweh hath made
Himself known*], reflex., cf. 48^4, expl. *hath executed judgment*],
cf. v.^{5}, so RV., Pe., Dr., Bä., Kirk., cf. JPSV. as emphatic independent classes; better than AV., which explains the second
clause as dependent and so relative : " by the judgment which
He executeth," cf. PBV. after $\mathfrak{G}$. — *In the work of His hands*],
Yahweh's put forth in judgment, syn. with previous line of the
couplet ; and not those of the nation, hiding nets and digging pits,
of previous couplet, as EV^s., though sustained by Dr., Che., and
JPSV. — *are trapped*], by Yahweh's hands, who lays traps for
them.

18–19. This Str. begins with ', but it is not the original Str. ',
which we find rather in v.$^{20-21}$. It was inserted by an editor. It is
composed of a trimeter syn. couplet and a tetrameter syn. couplet.

> The wicked shall turn back to Sheol,
> All the nations that forget God.
> For the poor shall not always be forgotten,
> Nor the hope of the afflicted perish forever.

18. *The wicked*], pl. for sg., coll. above, v.^{17}, but not, however, individuals, but syn. with *all the nations.— turn back to Sheol*], antith.
v.^{14}. The wicked nations turn back in defeat and slaughter. So
disastrous will be their fate that they will suffer national death
and so descend as nations to the abode of the dead. There is no
reference in this passage to the future destiny of individuals, cf.
Is. 26$^{14-19}$ Ez. 37$^{7-14}$ Ho. 13^{14} (*v.* Br.$^{MP.\,176,\,276,\,307}$). — *That forget
God*], here of nations, cf. Ps. 50^{22} of wicked Israelites ; (*v.* 10$^{4.\,11}$),
an ignoring of the presence of God and His interest in His

people. —**19**. *For the poor* ‖ *the afflicted shall not be forgotten*],
by God, antith. to their enemies forgetting Him. — *Perish forever*], the *hope* of God's people will not perish, but will be realised
in renewed life in the Holy Land when the nations perish in death
and Sheol.

20–21. Str. ᵕ is disguised by prefixing *O arise* to 9²⁰ in order
to make a suitable close for the Ps. before the *Selah;* but it
destroys the measure. It is a trimeter tetrastich, having three
lines syn., the fourth synth. — *mere men*, syn. *nations*], cf. v.²¹
10¹⁸ 56² 66¹² all referring to enemies conceived, over against
Yahweh and His people, as mere men. The congregation plead
that the nations *may know* this at last, through the exposure of
their weakness. — *prevail*], be stronger than Israel, cf. 52⁹ 89¹⁴, to
prevent which *let* them *be judged*, cf. v.⁵. — *before Thy face*], the
divine face looking in wrath upon them. — *O appoint Terror*]
Their defeat will be that of a panic-stricken army. Terror is
personified as an angel of vengeance appointed by God to drive
them on to their doom. 𝕲, 𝖄, 𝕾, RC.Vrss. render "appoint a
lawgiver," with a slightly different text; so Luther "*einen Meister*,"
which is usually interpreted in a bad sense, as tyrant, Genebr.;
Antichrist, Aug., Cassiodorus; but by some in a good sense, as
Christ, Theodoret, Euthymius; as Yahweh Himself, Bä.

Str. ל is composed of two trimeter distichs, the first syn., the
second synth. It expostulates with Yahweh for delay in interposition, already suggested in previous Str.—**X. 1**. *Why standest
Thou*], as looking on with indifference, ready, but slow to act. —
in the distance], phr. only here, stronger than the usual afar
off. — *Hidest*]. The divine presence, not being manifest when
so greatly needed, seems to imply a deliberate hiding from His
people. — *in times of dearth*], resuming 9¹⁰. — **2**. *In pride*], emph.
in position, to lay stress on this as a chief characteristic of the
enemies. — *hotly pursue*], cf. La. 4¹⁹, RV., *B*DB., so essentially
Kirk., al.; "persecute," PBV., AV., is too general; "set on fire,"
Dr., Bä., after Vrss., is too strong. Most think of the heat of
anxiety, but some of the heat of affliction. — *Let them be caught*],
the wicked nations, in accordance with the expostulation of
previous context, so EVˢ., JPSV., Bä., al. But 𝕲, 𝖄 render as
indicative, "they (the afflicted) are caught, taken," so Pe., Dr.;

"a further description of the wrongs of the poor," Kirk. — *that they planned*]. They planned to catch the afflicted ; but Yahweh is entreated to catch them in their own crafty schemes.

X. 3. This syn. trimeter distich resembles the sentences of Heb. Wisdom, as Du. suggests, and is a late gloss. Its original meaning was obscured by an early copyist who by dittog. of suffix inserted the conjunction *waw*, and so divided the sentence after the fourth tone, making it into a prose sentence, difficult of explanation.

> For the wicked doth boast about (his) covetousness,
> The robber doth congratulate himself.

3. *For the wicked*, syn. *the robber*] so Pe. ; " covetous," EVˢ. is too weak. If a gloss, then it is no longer the nations, but the individual Jew, of the period of Heb. Wisdom. — *Doth boast about his covetousness*], in a bad sense, as 112¹⁰, Pr. 21²⁵⁻²⁶, cf. Ps. 32⁵, " desire " of EVˢ. is too general. — *congratulate himself*] as 49¹⁹, on his success in gaining what he coveted, cf. 36²⁻³.

Str.] was recognised by 𝔊, which begins with ץאנ, but obscured by 𝕳, which attaches this vb. to previous line with Yahweh, prob. in order to avoid a blasphemous expression, and get the thought, "whom Yahweh abhorreth," PBV., AV. It is composed of a trimeter tetrastich, two syn. lines enclosing a syn. couplet. — **4.** *The wicked*] sg. coll., refers to *nations* of original Ps. as v.². — *doth contemn Yahweh*] as shown in their thoughts, words, and deeds, v.⁴⁻¹¹, cf. v.¹³, where the same expression is resumed in expostulation. — *According to the height of His anger*]. It is difficult to think of the wicked man's anger in such a connection, and therefore most moderns think of loftiness of nostrils (*Hochnäsigkeit*, Bä.), or " face " *B*DB., or " looks " Dr. ; as of eyes, 101⁵, mind, Pr. 16⁵, disposition, Ec. 7⁸ ; but Du. rightly explains of divine anger ; and so as included in the thoughts of the wicked as well as the phr. : *He will not require*]. Yahweh may be very angry, as His people claim ; but however great or exalted He may be in anger, He will not interpose on their behalf, He will not require satisfaction from their enemies. — *There is no God*] not a denial of the divine existence, but of His presence and interposition. The PBV. " careth not for God," and AV. " will not seek after God," supply the object of vb. and

take the wicked as subj. after most ancients. — *his devices*] his
evil thoughts, that he is devising, his calculations, what he is
saying to himself, in self-flattery, syn. with his contemning. —
5a. *are defiled*] so 𝕲, 𝔖, 𝖁 " His thoughts and counsels are unclean," Aug. " He always acts badly," Genebr. This is well suited
to context though resting on a different interp. of the form from 𝕳,
which may be read *parturiunt* as 𝔍, Aq., or " strong," " sure," Pe.,
" stable " Dr., " firm " RV., " prosperous " JPSV. after 𝕿, " His
plans succeed ; he is never harassed by the vicissitudes of fortune," Kirk.

Str. 𝕯 is disguised by 𝕳, which puts the first line as second, in
v.[5]; and also in all texts by letting it follow Str. 𝕴. This order
cannot be original, but is due to editorial transposition, and possibly the insertion of the gloss v.[3]. It is composed of two trimeter
couplets, the one synth., the other syn. — **5b.** *On high*] in heaven,
cf. 92[9], where Yahweh is standing v.[1], not yet interposing v.[12]. —
at a distance from him], cf. v.[1]. — *Thine acts of judgment*], they
are still with Yahweh, not yet executed on earth against the
wicked. — *As for his adversaries*] emph. in position. — *He puffeth
at them*], possibly snorting, as gesture of contempt. — **6.** *He saith
in his mind*], so v.[11], cf. v.[4], syn. *he doth swear*], interp. as perf.
vb. and not as noun, " cursing," as beginning of v.[7], so disguising
Str. 𝕯 and destroying its measure. — *I shall not be moved*], phr.
frequently used of the righteous 15[5] 16[8] 21[8] 62[3-7] 112[6]; presumptuous words of the pious when in prosperity 30[7]; here
presumptuous words of the wicked enemies of God and His
people. This is intensified in syn. clause, *in all generations without evil*], so 𝕲, 𝔍. 𝕳 has another reading with relative, which
is disregarded in PBV., RV., Pe., Kirk., but given in AV. as
causal " for," by Dr. " I who." Both these are interpretations
and were not original.

Str. 𝕯, disguised in ancient texts, is composed of a tetrameter
syn. couplet, and a syn. trimeter couplet, the former stating what
seems to be a general truth in a proverbial form ; the latter speci-
fying action of the enemies against innocent Israel. The former
is therefore a substitution of the editor for the original couplet,
which doubtless began with the same word, and set forth the craft
and deceit of the enemy, but hardly in this form and in this gen-

eral way. — **7.** *His mouth is full of deceits ∥ mischief*], so in the
original, expressing the craft of the enemy. — *and oppression*
∥ *trouble*] were added by later editor to indicate the actual injury that they had done to the people of God. — *Under his*
tongue], secreted as Aug., and ready to spring forth ; and not as
Che., Dr., Kirk. after Jb. 20[12], as a delicious morsel, which suits
the context of that passage, but not of this. — **8.** *In places of am-*
bush], as Jos. 8[9] Ju. 9[35] 2 Ch. 13[13], enemies lying in wait to surprise, syn. *in secret places*], where they remain in secret until the
time for attack. — *of settlements*], that is near settlements, whether
of tents, Gn. 25[16] (P), or houses, Lv. 25[31], referring to the un-
walled villages exposed to sudden attacks of treacherous foes. —
slayeth], his object is murder as well as robbery. — *the innocent*],
those who have done them no wrong, who were not at war with
them.

Str. ע is disguised by the ancient texts, because its first line is
in the middle of the verse. It follows פ as in La. 2, 3, 4, an
older order of the alphabet. It is composed of a trimeter tetrastich of stair-like parall. — **9.** *His eyes spy*], cf. 56[7], carrying on
the thought of previous verse. — *Thy host*], as v.[10. 14], the people
of Yahweh regarded as a host or army, however small, when compared with the enemy. — *He lieth in ambush*], vb. for noun of
v.[8a], *in his secret place*], sing. for pl. of v.[8b], article for possessive,
thus taking up both previous words of that verse, in order to stairlike advance in thought. This is made still more definite by unnecessary insertions of later editor. — *as a lion*], frequent simile
for enemies, see 7[3] 17[12] 22[14], and accordingly, *in his covert*], cf.
76[3] Jb. 38[40]. — *to seize*], by the paws of the lion. — *dragging him*
away], as a lion does his prey to his den. 𝕳 attaches *in his net*
to this vb. and is followed by most versions and interpreters, thus
adding the simile of the hunter to that of the lion, and so losing
the force of the stair-like parall., graphically describing the lion's
mode of dealing with his prey. 𝕲, 𝖁 attach it to subsequent v.,
where it is needed for measure.

Str. צ lacks initial word with צ in ancient texts. If with 𝕲,
"in his net" goes with this Str., we may supply the cognate vb. צוד
"hunt." The Str. then is composed of two syn. trimeter couplets
resembling v.[5. 6]. In the first, the simile of the hunter takes the place

of the lion of the previous Str. — **10.** *The oppressed*] as 9[10] 10[13],
the Kt. here which is better sustained by usage and context than
vb. of Qr., which is variously rendered " he falleth down " PBV.,
"croucheth," AV., RV., (of lion) without justification from usage
of vb. ; better " is crushed," JPSV., Pe., Kirk. But Qal is not used
elsewhere, and so is improbable here. — *and he sinks down*], cf.
35[14] 38[7] 107[39], that is overpowered, *because of his great numbers*],
in accordance with usage referring to great numbers of the enemy,
rather than their strength and prowess, " his captains," PBV., " his
strong ones," AV., RV., Dr., *i.e.* ruffians, Kirk. ; or with reference
to the claws of lion, as Ew., De., Che., Bä., *B*DB., as if this carried
on the simile of previous Str. — **11.** The enemies now say, to themselves as in v.[6a–13b], *'El hath forgotten*], cf. v.[18. 19]. — *He hath hidden
His face*], cf. the expostulation of v.[1], where the congregation
make a similar statement and complaint ; and therefore *He doth
not see*], cf. 9[14]. And so the enemy afflict His people with impunity.

Str. ק is preserved in its original form. It is an expostulation
renewing v.[1], and taking up the most important terms in the intervening Strs. It is composed of two trimeter syn. couplets. —
12. *lift up Thy hand*], in order to interpose and smite the enemy
with it. — *Forget not 'El*], plea over against the word of the
enemies, v.[11]. On account of this exact antith., as well as the
requirement of measure, 'El belongs in this line and not in
previous one, though so given in all ancient texts, cf. 9[13]. —
13. *Wherefore doth the wicked contemn ?*] taking up the statement of the fact v.[4a], and also the words of the wicked to themselves, *Thou wilt not require*], already given in third person v.[4b].

Str. ר is composed of two syn. trimeter couplets. — **14.** *Thou
hast seen,* ‖ *Thou beholdest*], an appeal to the divine knowledge
over against the words of the wicked, v.[11] — *the trouble and grief*]
that caused Yahweh's host by the crafty enemies described above.
— *To requite with Thy hand*], antith. with v.[13]. — *Upon Thee*],
emph. in position, implying reliance on their God only. — *Thy
host*] as v.[9–10], — *leaveth it*], that is in trust that God will attend
to it, strengthened by past experience. — *Of the orphan*], emph. ;
the nation is conceived as fatherless, without a ruler of their own,
dependent upon the caprice of governors appointed by the world

power Persia, cf. La. 5^3. — *Thou art the helper*], cf. 37^{40} 46^6 109^{26}.

Str. שׁ is composed of a trimeter tetrastich with introverted parall. — **15.** *Break the arm of the wicked*], cf. 37^{17} Jb. 38^{15}. make them powerless, smiting them with the hand, cf. v.$^{12-14}$. — *Let his wickedness be sought*], as most ancient Vrss., cf. v.$^{4.\ 13}$, taking vbs. as Niphal, that is in vain, *let it not be found*], it will no longer exist; so complete has been the requital, that further requisition finds nothing more to be requited. But EV^s. follow 𝔐, 𝔍 and regard the vb. as Qal with juss. force and render "seek out till Thou find none," AV., RV., or more exactly as Dr., "mayest Thou require." "When God 'makes inquisition' and holds His assize, He will find no crime to punish," Kirk. — **16.** *O King*], vocative, in order to give force to the plea, and not "Yahweh is king," EV^s., for Yahweh is a gloss. The conception of Yahweh as king is frequent, Pss. 29^{10} 44^5 47^7 48^3 68^{25} +. — *for-ever and ever*], antith. to the disappearance of the wicked nations when called to account. — *Destroy the nations*], Pi. imv. syn. "break," v.^{5} as Du., cf. 5^7 9^6 21^{11}, not Qal perf., "the nations are perished," as 𝔐, AV., RV., and most Comm.; or impf., "will perish," as 𝔊, 𝔍, Gr. — *out of the land*], as v.^{18}, the holy land of Israel.

Str. ת is composed of a syn. trimeter couplet and an antith. trimeter couplet. It expresses confidence that the plea has been accepted by Yahweh. — **17.** *Thou hast heard*], more fully: *settest Thy mind*], as 78^8, and so preparatory to *Thou harkenest*]. The sf. "their" with mind (𝔐) is a mistake of an early copyist, due to the *desire of the afflicted* in previous line. It has given trouble to all interpreters by a phr. not known elsw. and difficult to explain. — **18.** *To judge*], execute justice in favour of as 9^5, *the orphan* as v.^{15}, and *oppressed* as 9^{10}; *to terrify*, cf. 9^{21}; *mere man*, cf. 9^{20-21}; *from the land* as v.^{16}, summing all these up in the final Str. An early copyist inserted in the margin a cognate thought in a familiar phrase "he shall not do it again," namely the mere man, that is, what he had done as described in the Ps., because he will no more be in the land. This was subsequently incorporated in the text, destroying the measures of the last couplet, and so confusing the meaning of the clause as to give trouble to all subsequent readers.

2. [אוֹרֶה בְּכָל־לְבִי] = 138[1]. יהוה is substitute for an original לְךָ = σοι 🜚
which should be for rhyme at end of line. אוֹדֶה Hiph. impf. cohort. 1 p.
v. 6[6] ‖. אֲסַפְּרָה Pi. impf. cohort. 1 p., *v.* 2[7]. [בכל לב †] 1 K. 8[23] = 2 Ch. 6[14] Pss. 9[2]
119[2. 10. 34. 58. 69. 145] 138[1], Pr. 3[5] Je. 3[10] 24[7]. — [נִפְלָאוֹת] Niph. ptc. pl. f. √פלא
vb. denom. ‡ פֶּלֶא *wonder* of God's acts of judgment and redemption 77[12]
88[18] 89[6], עשׂה פ׳ 77[15] 78[12] 88[11] Ex. 15[11] Is. 25[1], of Law 119[129]. ‡ [פָּלָא] vb.
Niph. (1) *be difficult* to understand 131[1] Dt. 17[8]; (2) *extraordinary, wonderful*, Pss. 118[23] 119[18. 27] 139[14]. Pt. pl. נִפְלָאוֹת *wonderful acts* of Yahweh in
redemption and judgment 9[2] 26[7] 71[17] 75[2] 78[32] 96[3] 105[2] 106[7] 107[8. 15. 21. 24. 31]
111[4] 145[5] Ex. 3[21] (J) Je. 21[2]; עשׂה נ׳ Pss. 40[6] 72[18] 78[4] 86[10] 98[1] 105[5] 106[22] 136[4]
Ex. 34[10] Jos. 3[5] (J); הראה נ׳ Ps. 78[11] Mi. 7[15]. Hiph. *make wonderful* in phr.
הפ׳ הסרו לי Ps. 31[22], cf. 4[4] 17[7]. — **4.** [בְּשׁוּב אָחִיר] = 56[10]. Qal inf. cstr. not
protasis temporal clause as AV., RV. but *causal*. Pe., Dr. *turn back in defeat*,
so v.[18] 6[11] 70[4], Hiph. 44[11]. — [וְיִכָּשְׁלוּ] Niph. impf. 3 pl. apodosis. ‡ כָּשַׁל Qal.
(1) *stumble* sq. נֵפֶל 27[2], in anxiety and distress 107[12], Is. 59[10]; (2) *totter* of
knees Ps. 109[24]. כּוֹשֵׁל *tottering one* 105[37] Jb. 4[4]; fig. *fail* of strength, Ps. 31[11]
Ne. 4[4]. Niph. *stumble* sq. אבר Ps. 9[4], cf. Ho. 5[5] Je. 6[15]. Hiph. *cause to
stumble* in punishment Ps. 64[9]. — ו [וְיֹאבְדוּ] coörd. Qal impf. 3 pl. *v.* 1[6]. —
[מִפָּנֶיךָ] *at Thy presence*. ‡ מִפְּנֵי (1) *from the face of, because of* peril 61[4], ברח
3[1] 57[1] (titles) 139[7], נוּס 60[6(?)] 68[8], הסתיר 17[9]; (2) *from the presence of*,
enemies banished 78[55] 89[24]; (3) *before, at the presence of* God 9[4] 68[2(3. 9 +)] 96[9],
Je. 4[26] Na. 1[5] Is. 63[19], of fire Ps. 68[3]; (4) *by reason of, because of* 38[4. 4. 6] 44[17]
55[4] 102[11]. — **5.** [מִשְׁפָּטִי] obj. sf. *execute judgment in favour of me*, cf. 146[7]
Mi. 7[9]. For מִשְׁפָּט *v.* 1[5]. ‖ ‡ [דִּין] n.m. *judgment, cause* 9[5] 76[9] 140[13]. For vbs.
דין and שָׁפַט *v.* 7[9]; צֶרֶק 4[2]; יָשַׁב 2[4]. — **6.** [שֵׁם מחה †] phr. elsw. Dt. 9[14] 29[19]
2 K. 14[27], from remembrance. ‡ מָחָה vb. Qal *blot out*, elsw. † sins, by God,
51[8. 11] Is. 43[25] 44[22]. Niph. (1) *be wiped out* from a book 69[29], the name
109[18], sins 109[14], Ne. 3[37]. — † [לְעוֹלָם וָעֶד] 9[6] 10[16] 21[5] 45[7. 18] 48[15] 52[10] 104[5]
119[44] 145[1. 2. 21] Ex. 15[18] Mi. 4[5] Dn. 12[3], to emphasize long-continued duration,
cf. עַד לְעוֹלָם 111[8] 148[6]; other uses of ‡ עַד in ψ from √עָדָה *advance, pass on* and
so *advancing, passing* time, (1) of future time לְעַד *forever*, during lifetime
9[19] 21[7] 22[27] 61[9]; (2) of continuous existence עֲדֵי עַד 83[18] 92[8] Is. 26[4] 65[18];
(3) of divine attributes לָעַד Pss. 19[10] 37[29] 89[30] 111[8. 10] 112[3. 9], also 🜚 of 84[8],
עֲדֵי עַד = 132[12. 14]. עִילָךְ is more frequently used: n.m. √[עוֹלָם]. It may be the
same as עָלַם, *conceal*, as many suppose, and so *hidden, mysterious time;* or
possibly עָלַם, *be mature, ripe* sexually and so *fulness, ripeness of time;* or an
independent stem of unknown meaning. The n. means *long duration*: (1) of
past time, *ancient* gates 24[7. 9], the long dead 143[3] La. 3[6], former acts of God
מֵעוֹלָם Ps. 25[6] 119[52], long silence Is. 42[14] 57[11], God's past existence Ps. 93[2],
years of ancient time 77[6]. (2) (*a*) indef. *futurity*, always at ease 73[12], of
King עֵי יֵשֵׁב 61[8], of *duration* of pious לְעוֹלָם 128[15] 30[7] 37[18. 27. 28] 41[13] 55[23] 73[26]
112[6] (long life), sq. *ever* 89[2] (as long as I live), הורה לע׳ 30[13] 44[9] 52[11] 79[13],
other emotions and activities *during life* 5[12] 31[2] 71[1] 75[10] 86[12] 119[93. 98. 111. 112];
(*b*) *continuous existence* of things 78[69] 104[5] 148[6], nations 81[16], families 49[12]
106[31], Jerusalem 48[9] 125[1] Je. 17[25], reproach Ps. 78[66], memory 112[6]; (*c*) of

divine blessing and praise 72¹⁹ 135¹³, of Yahweh Himself 89⁵⁸, His attributes הסר 89⁸ 138⁸, לעולם חסרו 100⁵ 106¹ 107¹ 118¹· ². ³· ⁴· ²⁹ 136¹⁺²⁵ᵗ·, כבור 104³¹, אמת 117² 146⁶, צדק 119¹⁴², עזה 33¹¹, His reign 10¹⁶ 66⁷ 92⁹ 146¹⁰ Ex. 15¹⁸ (E) Je. 10¹⁰ Mi. 4⁷, ישב לע Ps. 9⁸ 29¹⁰ 102¹³ La. 5¹⁹, His covenant Ps. 105⁸· ¹⁰ 111⁵· ⁹ 2 S. 23⁵, laws Ps. 119⁸⁹· ¹⁴⁴· ¹⁵²· ¹⁶⁾, promise to David 18⁵¹ 89⁵· ²⁹, other blessings 133⁸, אֶרֶךְ יָ׳ 139²⁴, God's relations with His people לע׳ 85⁶ 103⁹ 145²¹, עד עולם 28⁹, Davidic dynasty 45³· ⁷· ¹⁸ 72¹⁷ 89³⁷· ³⁸ 110⁴. (3) indefinite *unending* future 49⁹ phr. עד(ה)עולם(ו) (ו)עד(ה)עולם כ 41¹⁴ 90² 103¹⁷ 106⁴⁸, *see above*, מעתה ועד עולם *from now on and forever* 115¹⁸ 121⁸ (as long as one lives), hope in God 131⁸, God's acts and words 113² 125² Mi. 4⁷ Is. 59²¹, לער ולעולם Ps. 111⁸ 148⁶. Pl. † עולמים abstr. *everlastingness, eternity* 61⁵ 77⁸ 145¹³ 1 K. 8¹³ = 2 Ch. 6² Is. 26⁴ 45¹⁷ 51⁹ Ec. 1¹⁰ Dn. 9²⁴. For completeness here we may consider ‡ נצח n.m. √נצח with the conception of preëminence, so that the noun is time as enduring, *perpetuity*, משאות ב׳ *perpetual desolations* 74⁸, עד נ׳ *unto perpetuity* 49²⁰ Jb. 34³⁶, cf. נצח Ps. 13² 16¹¹ elsw. לָנֶצַח *forever* 9⁷· ¹⁹ 10¹¹ 44²⁴ 49¹⁾ 52⁷ 68¹⁷ 74¹· ¹⁰· ¹⁹ 77⁹ 79⁵ 89⁴⁷ 103⁹. None of these terms have in themselves the conception of never-ending and always-enduring existence. That mng. can only come from context of the passages. — 7. [האויב] emph. in position sg. coll. *v.* v.⁴. — ‡ [חרבות] pl. f. *ruins* 102⁷ of cities Je. 25⁹ as Bosra 49¹⁸, Tyre Ez. 26²⁰. There is no evidence for the reference to nations in usage. Ps. 109¹⁰ ruined dwellings. — [רכו] goes with האו׳ר, coll. interpreted as pl. It is not homogeneous with חרבות which requires vb. or copula understood. Du., Marti, suggest רכו absorbed in similar רכו־. This is tempting but unnecessary. — [זָכְרָה] unnecessary gl., supposed by Du. to be relict of Str. ה and to stand for זְ׳ה, but improb. Besides, it is difficult to explain. It cannot be copula, and the emphatic definition of sf. is not justified by any example in ψ; *v. 16³*. — 8. [ויהוה] ו adver. יהוה emphatic in antith. with האויב. — 9. [והוא] unnecessary and improbable. — [יָדִין לאֻמִּים בְּמֵישָׁרִים] = 98⁹. = [יִשְׁפֹּט תֵּבֵל בְּצֶדֶק] = 96¹⁰ (רִבִיד:). ‡ תֵּבֵל n.f. *world* 9⁹ 18¹⁶ 19⁵ 24¹ 33⁸ 50¹² 77¹⁹ 89¹² 90² 93¹ 96¹⁰· ¹³ 97⁴ 98⁷· ⁹. — ‡ [מֵישָׁר] n.m. pl. abst., in ψ alw. ethical; of government 9⁹ 58² 75³ 96¹⁰ 98⁹ 99⁴, adv. 17². — 10. [ויהי] ו coörd. juss. Dr., but this is against context, an abrupt change. Usually juss. form is interpreted as of late style and without force. Du. points ויהי after 𝕲 καὶ ἐγένετο. But then if v.⁶⁻⁹ are glosses of late editor, it is best to return to 2d pers. of v.²⁻⁵ and rd. וּתְהִי. — יהוה] is an unnecessary gloss. — ‡ [מִשְׂגָּב] n.m. *inaccessible place*, of refuge in physical sense Is. 25¹² 33¹⁶, of God 9¹⁰· ¹⁰ 18³ (= 2 S. 22³) 46⁸· ¹² 48⁴ 59¹⁰· ¹⁷· ¹⁸ 62⁸· ⁷ 94²² 144². — † [דַּךְ] adj. *crushed, oppressed*, 9¹⁰ 10¹⁸ 74²¹ Pr. 26²⁸; cf. דכא Ps. 34¹⁹, נרכה 51¹⁹, דכה 10¹⁰. — [לְעִתּוֹת בַּצָּרָה] = 10¹, cf. דְּבָרַי בְּצָרוֹת Je. 14¹, but עתות is a.λ., עתּתי 31⁶ for usual עִתֹּ; and בַּצָּרָה *dearth, destitution*, BDB. might be interpreted as prep. ב and צָרָה. Gr. would rd. לעזרת בצרה as 46². — 11. [ויבטחו] ו coörd. Qal impf. 3 p., *v. 4⁶*. — [יוֹדְעֵי שְׁמֶךָ] Qal ptc. nominal force. ידע *v. 1⁶*. Earlier usage, know Yahweh Ex. 5² (J) Ho. 2²² 5⁴ 8² ψ 79⁶; so shorten here to יוֹדְעֶיךָ to get proper measure. ידע שם elsw. 91¹⁴ Is. 52⁶ Je. 48¹⁷. — [דֹרְשֶׁיךָ] Qal ptc. pl. sf. 2 s. ‡ דָּרַשׁ vb. (1) *resort* to God to consult or inquire of Him 24⁶ 78³⁴, older mng. Gn. 25²² (J) Ex. 18¹⁵ (E); (2) *seek* in prayer and worship Pss. 9^{11} 14^2 (= 53^3) 22^{27} $34^{5.11}$ 69^{33} 77^8 105^4 $119^{2.10}$ Am. $5^{4.6}$ Ho. 10^{12} Dt. 4^{29}; (3) *ask for, demand, require,* subj. God Pss. 9^{13} $10^{4.13.15}$; (4) *seek* with application, *study,* late, 38^{13}, cf. Pr. 11^{27} in bad sense; Pss. 111^2 $119^{45.94.155}$ in good sense ; (5) *seek for, care for,* 142^5. — **12.** [יִמְרוּ Pi. imv. 3 pl. c. ל for acc. v.^{3}.— [הִגִּידוּ בעמים עלילותיו cf. 105^1 = Is. 12^4 = I Ch. 16^8 (הודיעו).— [יֹשֵׁב צִיּוֹן phr. α.λ.; cf. $2^{4.6}$. — **13.** [דֹּרֵשׁ דָּמִים Qal ptc. דָּרֵשׁ nominal force, *v.* v.^{11}; *avenger of blood,* cf. Gn. 9^5 (P) Ez. 33^6, cf. Ps. $10^{4.13}$ for similar mng. with דמים omitted. — [אוֹיְבָ is prosaic gl. — ‡שָׁכַח vb. *forget.* (1) God subj. : abs. 10^{11}, c. acc. His people, their cry or needs 9^{13} 10^{12} 13^2 42^{10} 44^{25} $74^{19.23}$ 77^{10}; (2) man subj.: (*a*) forget God 44^{18} 50^{22} 106^{21}, divine name 44^{21}, deeds $78^{7.11}$ 106^{13}, benefits 103^2, laws 119^{16+8t}, abs. 59^{12}; (*b*) forget persons 45^{11}, things 102^5 $137^{5.5}$. Niph. *be forgotten* 9^{19} 31^{13}.— ‡[צְעָקָה n.f. *cry* of distress, as Ex. 3^7 (J) 22^{23} (E).— [עֲנִיִּים Kt., עֲנָוִים Qr., so 10^{12}; the reverse 9^{19}, עֲנָוִים 10^{17}, עָנִי sg. coll. $10^{2.9.9}$, עָנִי abst. 9^{14}. These variations illustrate confusion in MT. 𝕲 has $9^{18.19}$ $10^{12.17}$, for the pls. of both forms, πένητες; elsw. it uses for both pls. without discrimination : πένητες 22^{27} (עָנָוִים) 74^{19}; (עֲנִיִּים); πτωχοί 69^{33} (עֲנָוִים) 12^6 $72^{2.4}$ (עֲנִיִּים); πραεῖς $25^{9.9}$ 34^3 37^{11} 76^{10} 147^6 149^4 (only for עֲנָוִים); for sg. uniformly πτωχός. It is doubtful whether the difference in form of pls. is any more than variation of same pl. from the sg. עָנִי. עָנָו, the supposed sg. of עֲנָוִים, does not exist. Nu. 12^3 Kt. is improb.; *v.* BD*B.* However, many think them different (cf. Rahlfs, עָנִי *und* עָנָו *in d. Psalmen,* 1892, Dr.$^{DB. art. Poor}$). ‡עָנִי is usually coll. for Israel as afflicted by enemies, or the pious in Israel afflicted by the wicked, the latter later than the former; not alw. easy to determine. The sg. coll. is usually earlier than pl. The usage of ψ is (*a*) coll. sg. as above $10^{2.9.9}$ 14^6 22^{25} 34^7 35^{10} 68^{11} 102^1 (unless n. pr.) Hb. 3^{14}, [עני ואביון Pss. 35^{10} 37^{14} 40^{18} (= 70^6) 74^{21} 86^1 $109^{16.22}$, || אביון 140^{13}, [עני וכואב 69^{39}, עני ורש 82^8, [עני ונוע 88^{16}, [עני יחיד ועני 25^{16}, || דל Is. 26^6 Zp. 3^{12}, cf. [עני ונכה Is. 66^2, [עניה of Zion Is. 51^{21} 54^{11}; pl. in this sense Pss. $9^{18.19}$ $10^{12.17}$ 12^6 22^{27} $25^{9.9}$ 34^3 37^{11} 69^{33} 74^{19} 76^{10} 147^6 149^4, cf. Is. 14^{32} 41^{17} 49^{13} Zc. $11^{7.11}$; (*b*) of the people as subjects, *poor* and *needy* Ps. $72^{2.4.12}$; (*c*) *humble,* over against proud 18^{28} (= 2 S. 22^{28}) gl. as Pr. 3^{34} 16^{19} Zc. 9^9. — **14.** [חָנְנֵנִי Qal imv. sf. error for usual חָנֵּנִי 4^{2+17t}, Kö.$^{II. 1. 560}$ BD*B.*, but *v.* Ges.^{§205}, Ew.^{§251c}. [רְאֵה 𝕲, 𝕿, 𝕾, in accord with 2d pers. of original Ps. But Aq., 𝕵, Bä., Now., Du., would rd. pf. חָנְנֵנִי and רְאֵה in accord with immediate context. — ‡[עֳנִי n.m. *affliction* 44^{25} 88^{10} $107^{10.41}$ $119^{50.92}$, obj. ראה 9^{14} 25^{18} 31^8 119^{153} Gn. 31^{42} (E) Ex. 3^7 4^{31} (J). — [מִשֹּׂנְאַי prep. מן causal. Qal ptc. pl. sf. I s. i.p. It is an explanatory gl. — [מְשַׁעֲרֵי מָוֶת = 107^{18} Jb. 38^{17} || צַלְמָוֶת, שׁ׳ שאול Is. 38^{10}. For מָוֶת as abode of the dead *v.* 6^6. — **15.** [לְמַעַן אֲסַפְּרָה final clause Pi. cohort. impf. I p. c. acc. as v.^{2}, obj. — [כָּל־תְּהִלָּלֶיךָ *v.* Intr.^{§1}. [שַׁעֲרֵי בַת־צִיּוֹן phr. α.λ., cf. עיר ציון 87^2. — בַּת צִיּוֹן not elsw. in ψ, but Is. 1^8 10^{32} Je. 4^{31} Mi. 1^{13} +.— [אָגִילָה בִּישׁוּעָתֶךָ is vb. Qal cohort. impf. I p., also dependent on למען, *v.* 2^{11}. The line is complete without noun, which is a gl. — **16.** ‡[טָבְעוּ c. ב as $69^{3.15}$. The change to 3 p. and tetrameter indicates a gl. שַׁחַת is the Pit of Sheol, or a *pit* dug out, v. 7^{16}; v.^{14} suggests the former, and that was probably the original mng. But when the Str. was

changed to tetrameter the relative clause with עָשׂוּ made the latter mng. necessary. The remaining three lines of the Str. were in no part original. — † זוּ]
pron. poetic: (1) demonstrative 12⁸ Hb. 1¹¹, so here 𝔊, Aq., Σ, PBV.; but
𝔖, 𝔍, and most moderns, as (2) rel. as Pss. 10² 17⁹ 31⁵ 32⁸ 62¹² 68²⁹ 142⁴ 143⁸
(all 𝕯) Ex. 15¹³·¹⁶ Is. 42²⁴ 43²¹. — 17. ‡ נִירַע] vb. Niph. pf. refl. as 48⁴ 76²
and not pass. as elsw. of things 74⁵ 77²⁰ 79¹⁰ 88¹³. — פֹּעַל כַּפָּיו] phr. α.λ. sf.
ref. to Yahweh and not to רָשָׁע, sg. coll. ‖ גוים as 10². ³. ⁴. ¹³ (v. 1¹). — נוֹקֵשׁ]
pointing favours Qal ptc. ‡ נקשׁ vb. knock down, c. Yahweh subj. elsw. Pi.
38¹³ 109¹¹; so Hu.,³ De. But rd. with 𝔊, Aq., 𝔖, 𝕿, Ols., Ew., Bä., We.,
Buhl, נִיקַשׁ Niph. ‡ יָקַשׁ vb. be trapped; elsw. Qal lay snares 124⁷ 141⁹. —
18. יָשׁוּבוּ] future; not return to the place from which they came, but as v.⁴
56¹⁰ turn back in defeat; cf. 6¹¹ 70⁴. לִשְׁאוֹלָה ,ל of late style with local acc.,
v. 6⁶. — שְׁכֵחֵי] adj. pl. cstr. elsw. Is. 65¹¹, cf. Ps. 50²². — ‡ אֶבְיוֹן] adj. needy,
poor, in Hex. J, E, D, mostly poetic; as adj. 109¹⁶, elsw. n. 49⁸; subject to
oppression and abuse 37¹⁴; to be cared for by the righteous 82⁴ 112⁹, by God
35¹⁰ 107⁴¹ 113⁷ 132¹⁵ 140¹³, by king 72⁴·¹²·¹³·¹³; needing help from God 9¹⁹
12⁶ 40¹⁸ (= 70⁶) 74²¹ 86¹ 109²² (all ‖ עָנִי) 69⁸⁴ 109³¹. — 20. קוּמָה] imv. cohort.
is a gl. adapted to 10², destroying measure and the proper beginning of
Str. ר. — אֱנוֹשׁ] sg. coll. of enemy as mere man antith. Yahweh; so v.²¹ 10¹⁸ 56²
66¹² (v. 8⁵). — עַל־כְּנֶיךָ] "more def. and distinct than לְפָנֶיךָ," BDB; cf. 18⁴³
Je. 6⁷. — 21. יהוה] is a gl. — מוֹרֶה] ctr. מוֹרָאָה txt. err. for ‡ מוֹרָא n. terror 76¹²,
so 𝔍, Aq., Θ, 𝕿, BDB., Dr., Du. But 𝔊, 𝔖, νομοθέτην = מוֹרֶה teacher, so Bä.
after Luther, "Meister." But there is no usage to justify the use of teacher in
such a severe sense. — יֵדְעוּ] final clause. — הֵמָּה] prosaic gl., making l. too long. —
X. 1. רָמָה] as 22² 42¹⁰ 43² 74¹ 88¹⁵ with impf. expostulation; cf. לָמָה 2¹. —
יהוה] is a gl. — בְּרָחוֹק] adj. c. בְ, α.λ. possibly txt. err. for מֵרָחוֹק 𝔊, 𝔍, as elsw.
38¹² 139². — 2. בְּגַאֲוַת רָשָׁע] is gl. defining subj. vb., but making l. too
long; rd. בגאותו. — בִּמְזִמּוֹת] is an explanatory gl. ‡ מְזִמָּה n.f. devices, alw. in
bad sense, elsw. 21¹², wickedness, in act 37⁷ 139²⁰. — חָשָׁבוּ] i.p. ‡ חשׁב vb. Qal
(1) devise, plan, c. acc. alw. evil in ψ, elsw. 21¹² 35⁴·²⁰ 36⁵ 41⁸ 52⁴ 140³·⁵;
(2) c. ל pers. 40¹⁸ (good?); (3) impute iniquity 32². Niph. be accounted
44²³ 88⁵, imputed 106³¹. Pi. (1) consider, be mindful of 77⁶ 119⁵⁹ 144⁸;
(2) devise, c. ל inf. 73¹⁶ Pr. 24⁸. — 3. כִּי הִלֵּל] might begin Str. כ, but it has a
different tone and is gnomic in character (v. 5⁶). — תַּאֲוַת נַפְשׁוֹ] makes a prose
sentence, improb. because of parall. vbs. and gnomic style. Rd. תאותו, then
נַפְשׁוֹ is its syn., obj. of בֶּרֶךְ of l. 2; and ו before בֹּצֵעַ is error of interpretation. — בֶּרֶךְ] syn. הִלֵּל, c. נַפְשׁוֹ as 49¹⁹, congratulate self (v. 5¹³). 𝕳 by attaching
נאץ to this v. as rel. clause mutilated Str. ו and made an awkward sentence. —
It is possible then that ברך was originally interpreted in bad sense as curse,
euphemism for קלל, as Gr., to avoid the cursing and contemning of Yahweh
even by the wicked (v. Br.SHS. p. 178). But all these difficulties are due to
err. of 𝕳 in arrangement of lines. — וְאֵץ] Pi. pf. ‡ וְאֵץ vb. Qal contemn 107¹¹
Je. 33²⁴ Dt. 32¹⁹, Pi. elsw. v.¹³ 74¹⁰·¹⁸ Nu. 14¹¹·²³ 16³⁰ (J) Je. 23¹⁷ +. It begins
Str. ו as 𝔊. — 4. זוֹבַהּ אכי] phr. α.λ. ‡ גֹּבַהּ n.m. only here ψ interp. BDB. of
haughtiness of the wicked; cf. גֹּבַהּ עֵינִים 101⁵, vb. גֹּבַהּ לֵב 131¹. But 𝔊 κατὰ τὸ

πλῆθος τῆς ὀργῆς αὐτοῦ; 𝕵 *secundum altitudinem furoris sui;* so Du., who, however, thinks 𝕲 rd. רב, but this is improbable; it rather interprets the difficult phr. Du. is correct in thinking of the greatness of divine anger, and these as words of wicked just as in next clause. — [אֵין אֱלֹהִים] 14¹ = 53², not a denial of the existence of God, but of His presence and interest in the matter. — [כָּל־מְזִמּוֹתָיו] the noun as v.²ᵇ; but כי is a gl., making l. too long. 𝕲 ἐνώπιον αὐτοῦ, as 9²⁰ is prob. interpretation. — 5. [יָחִילוּ] a.λ. Qal impf. ‡ [חָיַר]=be *strong;* cf. חַיִר *strength;* so RV., Ols., De., Pe., Che., Bä., Du., Dr. But 𝕵 *partureunt;* so Aq., Quinta impf. חוּר. 𝕲 βεβηλοῖνται, so 𝔖 *be profaned* = יָחֵנּוּ. Niph. impf. ‡ חָרֵר. 𝕿 מצלחין is followed by Gr., Lag., We. in reading יצליח, but that was probably interpretation. The text of 𝕲 best suits context. The ways of Yahweh are defiled here, as holy places Ez. 7²⁴ 25⁸, name of God Is. 48¹¹ Ez. 20⁹·¹⁴·²², even God Himself Ez. 22¹⁶·²⁶. — רכו] Kt. err. for דְּרָכָיו, Qr., 𝕲, as 25⁴·⁹ 27¹¹ 37³⁴ 51¹⁵ +, term of D for divine laws (*v. 1¹*). — † [בְּכָל־עֵר] elsw. 34² 62⁹ 106⁸ 119²⁰. — [עָרוֹם] n.m. *height* (*v. 7⁵*) begins Str. מ. 𝕳 wrongly attaches this n. to the previous context. — כל] is gl., spoiling measure. — 6. [אָמַר בְּרַבּוּ] phr. v.¹¹·¹³ 14¹ (= 53²) 35²⁵ 74⁸. — [בַּר־אֱמוֹט] Niph. impf. ‡ מוט vb. Qal *totter, slip* of foot 38¹⁷ 94¹⁸, mts. 46³, kingdom 46⁷, land 60⁴. Niph. *made to totter, be shaken, overthrown,* usually with neg., earth 104⁵, its foundations 82⁵, רֵבַל 93¹ 96¹⁰, the holy city 46⁶, Mt. Zion 125¹, usually of men, espec. the righteous, with neg. כל, elsw. 15⁵ 16⁸ 21⁸ 30⁷ 62⁸·⁷ 112⁶, without neg. 13⁵ 140¹¹, fig. of steadfast obedience 17⁵. Hiph. *dislodge, let fall* 55⁴ 140¹¹. — [לְדֹר וָדֹר] at close of l. 33¹¹ 49¹² 77⁹ 85⁶ 102¹³ 135¹³ 146¹⁰, at beginning *10⁶* 79¹⁸ 89² 106³¹ 119⁹⁰, in the middle 89⁵. Therefore Du. is not justified in saying "gehört das לדר ודר *nach stehendem Sprachgebrauch zum Vorhergehenden*." — [אֲשֶׁר לֹא־בְרָע] is awkward. 𝕲 ἄνευ κακοῦ, 𝕵 *sine malo* = בלא רע without rel. is more prob. — 7. [אָלָה] is vb. *swear,* syn. אָבַר, and not noun *cursing,* as 𝕳 59¹³, with subsequent clause, which makes an awkward sentence, gives a line too long, and obscures the Str. פ which began with פיהו. — [פִּיהוּ מָלֵא] phr. α.λ. — [מִרְמוֹת זָהוּ] phr. α.λ., but cf. תֹּךְ וְמִרְמָה 55¹². — [עָמָל וָאָוֶן] phr., elsw. 90¹⁰ Jb. 4⁸ 5⁶ Is. 10¹; cf. Ps. 55¹¹. For עמל *v. 7¹⁵.* און *v. 5⁶.* This couplet is tetrameter and gnomic, and if original there must be a gl. But it takes the place of Str. פ, and *deceit* is suited to the context. The original was doubtless without והון and ואון, which were amplifications. — 8. ‡ [הֲצֵרִיכ] n. pl. *settlements* of tents Gn. 25¹⁶ (P), or houses Lv. 25³¹ (H), so Bä., Du., Dr. 𝕲 μετὰ πλουσίων, 𝕵 *cum divitibus* = בַּעֲשִׁירִים (cf. Is. 53¹³), is improb. 𝕿 רצהוס suits the context, but would be prosaic. — ‡ [בְּסָרְדִיכ] n. pl. *secret places* for hiding, elsw. 17¹² 64⁵, sg. v.⁹ dub. — [עֵינָיו] begins Str. ע, which follows פ, as La. 2, 3, 4 acc. to ancient order of Heb. alphabet. MT. neglects it by appending this l. to v.⁸. — [לְחֵילָה] = לְחֵילָה. 𝕵 *robustos tuos,* Aq. τὴν εὐποριαν σου, as 48¹⁴, הֵלְכָה v.¹⁴; cf. כאיב חֵל Qr. v.¹⁰; this last as Gr. dittog. for אים of הלך leaving אבר. But 𝕲 εἰς τὸν πένητα, so 𝔖, 𝕿 חֵלְכָה adj. *hapless, B*DB.; הֵלְכָה Ew.§ ¹⁸⁹ (³); חֵלֶכָה Kö.ᴵᴵ· ⁽¹⁾¹¹⁸. But these are the only possible passages, and the derivation from √ הָרָה after Arabic is dub. — ‡ [נָקִי] adj. *innocent,* elsw. 15⁵ 24⁴ 94²¹ 106³⁸ Dt. 19¹⁰ 27²⁵. — 9. [נסכה] Kt. ב

c. ‡ סֻכָּה n. f. *thicket, booth,* as 18[12] 31[21] and Kt. 27[5], but Qr. סֹך, sf. c. ‡ סֹך 76[8] Je. 25[38], Qr. Ps. 27[5].— יֶאֱרֹב] repeated l. 2 at expense of measure.— לַחֲטוֹף] inf. fully written, also יחטף impf. † חטף vb. *catch, seize,* elsw. Ju. 21[21].— בְּמֶשְׁכוֹ] inf. cstr. c. בּ temporal. ‡ מָשַׁךְ vb. (1) *drag away;* cf. 28[3], both of lion; (2) *draw out, prolong* 36[11] 85[8] 109[12].— בְּרִשְׁתּוֹ] is usually attached to נשכו, but the use of a net is not suited to a lion. ⅏ attaches it to next Str. The initial צ of Str. is missing. We might supply ‡ צוּד Qal pf. צוד vb. *hunt* as 140[12] La. 3[52].— ורנכה Kt. adj. כֶּה], so Aq., Σ, 𝔍, 𝔖, Hu.[3], Bä., *confractus;* cf. דָּךְ 9[10] 10[18]; but Qr. יִדְכֶּה. Qal impf. [נכר] = רכא vb. *crush,* elsw. Pi. 44[20] 51[1]; so ⅏ ταπεινώσει, 𝔙 *humiliabit,* Gr.; Niph. *be crushed* 38[9] 51[19]. Ew., Ols., De. al. interpret וְדָכָה as ו consec. Qal pf. = *and he is crushed.* Such a vb. does not suit the use of a net, and does not yield the needed צ. It is prob. that the original reading was צד־דְּרָךְ ברשתו וְעָח. The צד fell off owing to haplog. of ר. The ו is txt. err. for צ originally in the Egyptian Aramaic script. The ה added to דך was interpretation of form. ברשתו was transposed, and thus easily went into previous v.— בַּעֲצוּמָיו] בּ of instrument and pl. ‡ עָצוּם adj. acc. to usage (1) *strong numbers,* here as 35[18] Am. 5[12], cf. vb. Ps. 38[20] 40[5. 13] 69[5] 139[17]; elsw. (2) *mighty* 135[10].—11. ‡ הִקְתִּיר חֶלְכָאִים] phr. elsw. 13[2] 22[25] 27[9] 30[8] 51[11] 69[18] 88[15] 102[3] 143[7]; cf. 44[25] 104[29].— הֶרֶץ] is gl., destroys the measure.—12. קוּמָה] Qal cohort. imv. urgent entreaty, *v.* 7[7].— יהוה אל] makes l. too long; the former is a gl., the latter goes into the next line. It is an early error, for ⅏, 𝔍 have it.— נְשָׂא] Qal archaic strong imv. for usual שָׂא from נָשָׂא, *v.* 4[7]. *Lift up the hand,* to smite, as 106[26], usually in prayer 28[2] 63[5] 134[2].— עֲנוּים Kt. עַנְוים, Qr., *v.* 9[13], so v.[17], עָנוּים for an original עָנִי.— 13. ‡ עַל־מֶה] *wherefore,* as 89[48].— אלהים] is a gl.—14. רָאִתָה] Qal pf. 2 m., fully written ־, defective אי.— כִּי אַתָּה although in ⅏, is yet dittog. of ראתה.— צָבָל וָכָעַס] phr. a.λ., cf. עָמָל ואון v.[7] 90[10].— לָתֵת בְּיָדֶךָ] Qal inf. cst. of נתן, ל נ:תן purpose, to require with the hand, the hand lifted up, as v.[12]. נתן in the sense of requital 28[4. 4] 120[3]. The usual rendering, as syn. of *taking into the hand,* has no justification in usage.— עָלֶיךָ] emph.— ‡ יָתוֹם] n. (m.) *orphan:* (1) of individuals 68[6] 82[3] 94[6] 109[9. 12] 146[9]; (2) of nation 10[14. 18] La. 5[3].—15. רָע] is a gl., though in ⅏. It makes l. too long, is dittog. of רָשָׁע *v.* 5[5].— דָּרוֹשׁ] interpreted by 𝔅, 𝔍 as Qal impf.; by AV., Dr., JPSV. as juss., and following vb. as in final clause; by ⅏, 𝔙, Aq., Σ, 𝔖, Θ, Gr., Du. as Niph. impf., so also תִּמָּצֵא.— 16. יֶלֶךְ] but ⅏ βασιλεύσει, 𝔙 *regnabit;* so Gr. יִמְלֹך.— יהוה] is a gl. defining יֶלֶךְ.— אָבְדוּ] Qal. pf., *v.* 1[6]. ⅏ ἀπολεῖσθε, 𝔙 *peribitis;* so Gr. יאברו, better as Du., Pi. imv.— מֵאַרְצוֹ] The sf. is an interpretation of the original אֶרֶץ *v.* v.[18].— 17. הוה] is gl., makes the l. too long.— תָּכִין לִבָּם] Hiph. impf. 2 m. כון *set the mind, give attention to,* as 78[8] Jb. 11[13] 2 Ch. 12[14]. The sf. is a misinterpretation. Hi., Du. would rd. 2d pers. תָּכִיר] is used with תַּקְשִׁיב, elsw. only Pr. 2[2], and is here an unnecessary gl., *v.* 5[3] 17[6].—18. בַּל־יֹסִיף עוֹד] is a marginal gl. which has crept into the text. It disturbs the sentence, and makes the line too full.— לַעֲרֹץ] ‖ יָגִיר Qal inf. cstr. expressing purpose of Yahweh. ‡ יָרַץ vb. Qal (1) usually intrans, *tremble, be in terror* Dt. 1[29. 7]21 20[3] 31[6] Jos. 1[9] Jb. 31[34], but this does not suit context; (2) trans., *cause to tremble, terrify* Is. 2[19. 21] suits this passage and gives intensity to v.[16b]. Niph. ptc. of *'El*, as *terrible, exciting terror*, Ps. 89[8]. — [אנוש] as 9[20. 21]. — [מן הארץ] 𝕲 על הארץ. This is interpretation, and not suited to v.[16b].

PSALM XI., 2 STR. 8³.

Ps. 11 is a guest Ps. The Psalmist has taken refuge in Yahweh (v.[1b]), and expostulates with those who urge him to flee from his enemies to the mountains (v.[1c-3]). Yahweh is in His heavenly temple (v.[4]), testing the righteous (v.[5a]), hating the wicked (v.[5b]), and about to destroy them (v.[6]). A liturgical couplet states the general truth that Yahweh loveth the righteous, and they will behold His face (v.[7]).

> IN (Thee), Yahweh, have I taken refuge.
>> How say ye to me:
>> "Flee to (the) mountain as a bird;
>> "For lo they tread the bow,
>> "They have prepared their arrow on the string,
>> "To shoot in darkness at the rightminded.
>> "When the foundations are being thrown down,
>> "The righteous — what has he done?"
>
> YAHWEH is in His holy temple;
>> Yahweh is in heaven, His throne;
>> His eyes behold (the world),
>> His eyelids try the sons of mankind.
>> Yahweh trieth the righteous,
>> But the wicked His soul doth hate;
>> He will rain upon the wicked coals of fire,
>> Brimstone and a burning wind will be the portion of their cup.

The Ps. was in 𝔇 and then subsequently in 𝔇ℜ (*v.* Intr. §§ 27. 33). It is a Ps. of refuge, giving the experience of an individual, and stating it objectively. It was generalised by glosses and a concluding couplet, and so adapted to public worship. The following are the evidences of date: (1) There is no reference to earlier literature, except possibly to the story of the destruction of Sodom: Gen. 19[24] (J), in the original v.[6]. (2) The words: השחות v.[3], elsw. Is. 20[4] 2 S. 10[4] in a different sense; זלעפות v.[6], elsw. La. 5[10] Ps. 119[53]; and syntax, יַמְטֵר v.[6] showing neglect of juss. characteristic of Is.[2] give evidence of a date not earlier than the Exile. (3) The צדיק v.[3; 5. 7] is one who seeks refuge in Yahweh and is rightminded; there is no trace of legal or gnomic conceptions. The enemies are not foreign but domestic, and are men of disorder. (4) (*a*) The reference to the heavenly temple and neglect of the earthly, points to a time when the earthly temple had little religious influence. (*b*) The wide outlook of the divine inspection of the world implies the world-point of view rather than the provincial. (*c*) The conception of the disciplinary testing of the righteous and the sure destruction of the violent enemies is post-deuteronomic. On the whole the Ps. seems to be subsequent to J, D, and Is.², and to precede the legal attitude of Ezra and his times. It is best explained as from the circumstances of the feeble community in Jerusalem shortly after the Restoration.

Str. I. 1. The Psalmist states emphatically, *I have taken refuge*], probably in the original less objectively. — *in Thee, Yahweh*], as 31² 71¹, condensed by a late editor to " in Yahweh," cf. Vrss. Therefore he is not dismayed by his perils or the anxieties of his advisers, but on the contrary expostulates with them. — *How say ye to me ?*]. The remainder of the Str. is taken up with their advice, in which the poet describes the perilous situation. — *Flee (thou)*], so all ancient Vrss. and Qr., over against Kt. " flee ye," which originated from " your mountain," an error of MT., for *mountain as* of Vrss. — *as a bird*]. This is thought to be a proverbial popular phrase by Ew., Hu., al. Birds flee to forests when in peril, and as these in Palestine were on mountains, naturally to the mountains. The mountains of Judah were especially places of refuge on account of numerous caves, steep cliffs, and inaccessible rocks ; therefore from the earliest to the latest times they have been refuges of the persecuted ; so for David 1 S. 24, 26 ; for Mattathias 1 Mac. 2²⁸. — **2.** The reason for this advice is *they tread the bow ‖ they have prepared their arrow on the string*]. The enemies are archers, they are all ready to shoot, he is in deadly peril. — *to shoot in darkness*]. They are not in battle array, they are not face to face with him ; but they are hidden, concealed in the darkness, so that he cannot tell when they will shoot or from what direction ; they are secret, treacherous, though deadly enemies. They are probably not real archers, but they are compared to bowmen in ambush. — *at the rightminded*]. They are not only the enemies of the Psalmist, but of all the rightminded, and for the reason that they are rightminded. Their purpose is to destroy the righteous. The poet is in peril just because he is righteous. — **3.** *When the foundations are being thrown down*] : the foundations are the established institutions, the social and civil order of the com-

munity. 𝕲, 𝕾, 𝖁 interpret as vb. with rel.: "For what Thou hast
established they throw down," which thinks of the institutions as
divine. These enemies are not only enemies of the righteous,
but they are pulling down all the institutions and good order of
society. These institutions protect the rightminded righteous:
when they are destroyed the righteous are exposed to violence
of all kinds. — *The righteous*], emph. in position, for his righteousness is the real issue. That describes the Psalmist in the
statement of his timid advisers. — *what has he done*], so PBV.,
Kirk. rightly. Experience shows that he has not accomplished
anything under such circumstances; therefore in such a time,
and in such peril, the best advice is "flee," take refuge in the
mountains — in striking antith. to the Psalmist's action in taking
refuge in Yahweh. The translations: "What *can* the righteous
do?" AV., RV., though sustained by Dr.[§19]; "*shall* do," JPSV.,
are difficult to reconcile with the Heb. perfect tense. The
eight lines of this Str. are synth. each to the previous in regular order.

Str. II. The advisers have stated strongly what the enemies
are doing. The Psalmist now in antith. states more strongly what
Yahweh is doing, as a justification of his seeking refuge in Him.
It is therefore an antistr. to the previous one. This Str. is composed of four couplets, three syn. v.[4a. b, 4c. d, 6], one antith. v.[5]. —
4. *Yahweh is in His holy temple*], sometimes Yahweh is conceived as resident in His holy temple in Jerusalem, in the throne
room of that temple, as 5^8 79^1 138^2; but here from the syn.
Yahweh is in heaven, the temple is the heavenly one, as Mi. 1^2
Hb. 2^{20} Ps. 18^7. — *His throne*], either in apposition with heaven
as a closer definition of heaven itself as the throne, cf. Is. 66^1, or
local accusative on His throne; in either case, seated on His
throne in His heavenly palace. Enthroned there He is not indif-
ferent to what transpires on earth and among men. — *His eyes
behold*], the object has fallen out of 𝕳, but is given in some Vrss.
as *the world*, which is most appropriate to the context. It is
especially favoured by the syn. *His eyelids try the sons of mankind*]. The eyelids are strained in the severe scrutiny, which
marks closely and accurately all that men do in the world. This
tetrastich is in antith. to v.[1], the statement of the Psalmist that he

has taken refuge in Yahweh, and the advice to seek refuge in the mountains. He has in fact sought refuge in heaven, a place infinitely higher and more secure than the mountains; and in Yahweh, the heavenly King, who is investigating just this situation in which he is involved. — 5. *Yahweh trieth the righteous*]. If, as his advisers admit, he is righteous v.[3b] and rightminded v.[2c], Yahweh is scrutinising him, trying him and his case thoroughly. — *but the wicked His soul doth hate*]. This exact antith. to the previous line is weakened by a later editor, at the expense also of the measure, in his effort to describe the wicked more particularly by *him that loveth violence*. They are the archers of v.[2]. Their treacherous preparations to shoot the righteous are all observed by Yahweh, and He hates them from His very soul. The soul is the seat of the passion of anger and hatred, for God as well as for man. If, therefore, Yahweh is trying the righteous man, and hating his deadly enemies, the reason given by the advisers for fleeing to the mountains is not a sound one; it is rather a reason why he should do what he has done : take refuge in Yahweh. — 6. This couplet is synth. to the previous one and in antith. to v.[3]. — *He will rain upon the wicked*]. The figure of rain is suggested by the fact that Yahweh is on His heavenly throne and is looking down from heaven upon the earthly situation ; and also by the fact that divine interpositions are ordinarily conceived as coming from heaven. — *Coals of fire*], so after Σ. For an image of lightning flashes and thunderbolts in similar terms, *v.* Ps. 18[13-15]. ᕯ *snares and fire* gives a heterogeneous combination, and it is difficult to understand what snares have to do with this storm of judgment. The syn. *brimstone* reminds of the destruction of Sodom Gn. 19[24] (J), and *a burning wind* of the *Samum* or *Sirocco* of the East. — *will be the portion of their cup*], not that they were to drink in their cup such a mixture of brimstone and burning, but the cup is fig., as Ps. 16[5], of what one enjoys at a feast. Yahweh rains from heaven upon these wicked men, and they drink their portion. Instead of a draught of joy, it is a draught of burning judgment. In antith. to these wicked men casting down the foundations of society v.[3a], is Yahweh raining fire from heaven upon them ; and so in response to the final question of the previous Str. *"What has he done"* v.[3b] is the answer —

there is no call for him to do anything. Yahweh has done it for him. The wicked have their portion already in hand.

7. The Ps. has reached its splendid climax. There was nothing more to be said. But a later editor, thinking he might give it a better devotional ending, appends an appropriate couplet. —

> For the righteous Yahweh loveth;
> The upright will behold His face.

This is a synth. couplet enhancing the privileges of the righteous of the Ps. *The righteous ‖ the upright*] are the "rightminded" (v.²ᶜ). A still later editor, probably on account of the unusual emph. position of "the righteous," regards it as predicate of Yahweh, or adjective, and so either "Yahweh is righteous" or "the righteous Yahweh," and accordingly supplies an object to the vb.: "*righteous acts*," which may be interpreted either of righteous acts of the righteous man, as Is. 64⁵, or of the righteous acts which Yahweh Himself loves to do. — *behold His face*], so RV., Dr., that is, see the face of Yahweh, as His guest in the temple, Kirk., cf. 5⁵⁻⁶, or after death, cf. 16¹¹ 17¹⁵. That is the highest privilege of the one whom Yahweh loves. But it may be rendered "His face beholdeth the upright," so essentially AV., JPSV., which is a rather tame repetition of v.⁴ᶜ, and is improbable, even in a liturgical addition to the Ps.

---

1. בְּיהוה] emph. — חָסִיתִי] Qal pf. action completed in present, *v. 2¹².* This l. is defective. It is probable that the original was בך יהוה חסיתי as 31² 71¹. — ‡ אֵיךְ] adv. (1) interrog. *how?* in expostulation 137⁴ as Gn. 39⁹ 44⁸·³⁴ Jos. 9⁷ (J), † (ו)אֵיךְ תאמר how canst thou (or you) Ps. 11¹ as Ju. 19¹¹ Je. 2²³; (2) exclam. *how!* in satisfaction Ps. 73¹⁹ Is. 14⁴·¹² Je. 48⁸⁹. — לְנַפְשִׁי] *to me, v. 3³.* — נודו] Kt. Qal imv. m. pl. originated from sf. הָרְכֶם which is not sustained by context nor by Vrss. which rd. הר כמו צפור. Accordingly נוּדִי Qr. fs. is correct. ‡ נוד vb. Qal *move to and fro, flutter* as bird 11¹, elsw. in sympathy 69²¹ Jb. 2¹¹ 42¹¹, Hiph. *cause to wander aimlessly* as fugitives 36¹² 59¹² *v. txt.* — הֲרְכֶם] is fuller archaic form of prep. כְּ sim. *v. 29⁶.* — **2.** הרשעים] a class as v.⁵·⁶ antith. צדיק, *v. 1¹,* here an unnecessary gl. — יִדְרְכוּן קֶשֶׁת] Qal impf. 3 pl. full form in ן descriptive, *v. 7¹³.* — כּוֹנְנוּ] Polel pf. 3 pl. proper perfect. — צֶל־יֶתֶר] i.p. without pausal vowel as indicated by Mas. — לִירוֹת] Qal inf. cstr. c. לְ purpose. ‡ יָרָה vb. Qal (1) *shoot arrows* c. acc. p. 64⁵, c. לְ p. 11². Hiph (1) same c. acc. p. 64⁵·⁸ prob. also 45⁵ (*v. txt.*). (2) *direct, teach* ברדך 25⁸ 32⁸, of God c. acc. p. 119¹⁰²; also acc. rei 27¹¹ 86¹¹ 119³³, ברדך 25¹². — † בְּמוֹ] poetic, archaic for בְּ elsw. Is. 25¹⁰ (Qr.) 43² 44¹⁶·¹⁹ Jb. 9⁸⁰ (Kt.) 16⁴·⁵ 19¹⁶ 37⁸. Before אפל

more euphonic than כ. — † [וְיַשְׁרֵי לָכ] *v. 7¹¹* 32¹¹ 36¹¹ 64¹¹ 94¹⁶ 97¹¹. — **3.** [יְ]
conj. *when.* — [הָשָׁתוֹת] n. pl. emph. † שֵׁת n. : (1) *sitting place, buttocks* 2 S 10⁴
Is. 20⁴. This does not suit our passage. 𝔍 has *leges.* Σ. θεσμοί, so usually
foundations, Dr. *buttresses* (Is. 19¹⁰) 𝔐 is interpreted as same; but 𝔊, 𝔗
שַׁתֶּיהָ, so Bu.). 𝔊, 𝔖 interpret ὅτι ἃ κατηρτίσω here, ה article for relative and
verb, שׁתוֹת = *what Thou hast established,* שִׁית *v. 8⁷.* This is tempting but
improb. — [יֵהָרֵסוּן] Niph. impf. 3 pl. full form, cf. v.² 𝔊 interprets as Qal.
‡ הָרַס Qal: (1) *throw down* 28⁵; (2) *break away* teeth 58⁷. Niph. *be thrown
down,* so here of walls of city Je. 50¹⁵, cities Ez. 36³⁵. — [מַה־פָּעָל] cf. Jb. 11⁸.
Two tones are needed; there should be no Makkeph. — [עֵינָיו יֶהֱזוּ] phr. α.λ.;
n. emph.; vb. Qal impf. 3 pl. of habitual action. The obj. is needed for measure. 𝔊 has εἰς τὸν πένητα = לְהֶלְכָה as 10⁸· ¹⁰· ¹⁴ probably assimilated to that
passage; Θ Syr. Hexapla לַחֶֽרֶל to *world* is better suited to context *v. 17¹⁴.* —
4. ‡ [חָזָה] vb. Qal *see, behold :* (1) (*a*) c. acc. rei 58⁹· ¹¹, God's face *11⁷* 17¹⁵;
(*b*) God subj. His eyes *11⁴* 17²; (*c*) c. בְ *look on,* בִיֽם in temple 27⁴. (2) *see,
perceive* c. acc. Yahweh in His temple 63², in His providential working 46⁹
Is. 26¹¹· ¹¹ Jb. 23⁹. — ‡ [עַפְעַיָּיו] n.m. pl. *eyelids* 11⁴ 132⁴. — **5.** [צריק יבחן ."]. 𝔐,
𝔍 make this a complete sentence attaching וְרָשָׁע to next line. 𝔊 followed by
Du. attaches it to previous clause, making two tetrameters. But the testing
is more appropriate to the righteous, and we get a better antith. by contrasting
God's dealings with the righteous and the wicked in the two lines. ורשע is
the proper antith. to צדיק. Then ואהב חמס must be a gl. of specification. —
[וְשֹׂנֵא נַפְשׁוֹ] Qal pf. 3 f. נפש subj.; but 𝔊 μισεῖ τὴν ἑαυτοῦ ψυχήν (cf.
Pr. 8³⁶) must have rd. שֹׂנֵא. In 𝔊 נפשו is *himself;* in 𝔐 וְרָשׁ is the seat
of anger. 𝔊 makes the antith. in the person of the wicked, 𝔐 with the
previous line. נֶפֶשׁ n.f. as ‡ reflexive 49¹⁹ 69¹¹, for paraphrase of pers. pronouns
v. 3³, as seat of emotions and passions *v. 10³.* — **6.** [יַמְטֵר] Qal impf., in form
juss.; but it has lost its juss. force, as often in later poetry after Is.².
‡ מָטַר vb. denom. *rain,* Qal, Am. 4⁷. Hiph. in ψ only fig.; manna 78²⁴, flesh
78²⁷, cf. bread Ex. 16⁴ (J) and coals of fire Ps. *11⁶.* — [פַּחִים] is scribal error for
פַחֲמֵי after Σ, Ew., Bä., 𝔅DB., Du. † פֶּחָם *coal* Pr. 26²¹. אֵשׁ פחם Is. 54¹⁶, cf. 44¹².
‡ פַּח n.m. *bird trap,* in ψ only fig. of calamities and plots 119¹¹⁰ 124⁷ 140⁶ 142⁴
Je. 18²², פּ יקוֹשׁ Pss. 91³, cf. 124⁷ 141⁹ Ho. 9⁸; as source or agent of calamity
Ps. 69²³ Ho. 5¹ Is. 8¹⁴ Jos. 23¹³; so here if correct, but altogether improbable.
— ‡ [אֵשׁ] n.f. *fire,* of conflagration, antith. מים 66¹², as consuming 68³ 74⁷
118¹²; subj. בערה 83¹⁵, שרף באשׁ 46¹⁰ 80¹⁷, תנור אשׁ 21¹⁰; (2) of lightning,
(*a*) natural 29⁷ 104⁴ 105⁸² 148⁸; (*b*) theophanic, וחלי אשׁ 18¹³· ¹⁴, cf. 140¹¹, so
here if אשׁ פחמי. It precedes Yahweh 50³ 97³. (3) The historic theophanies
of the Exodus 78¹⁴ 105⁸⁹, consuming Korah אשׁ תבער 106¹⁸. (4) Fire of anger
אכלה 18⁹ 21¹⁰ 78⁶³, בערה כאשׁ 79⁵ = 89⁴⁷, cf. 78²¹, of strong emotion תבער אשׁ 39⁴. —
‡ [גָּפְרִית] n.f. *brimstone,* fig. of judgment, with הַמְטִיר also Gn. 19²⁴ (J) Ez. 38²².
— † [וְזִלְעָפוֹת] n.f. pl. *raging heat,* fig. zeal sg. Ps. 119⁵³, pl. of the wind Samum
11⁶, no need however of רוּחַ, which makes 1. too long; of fever of famine La. 5¹⁰.
— ‡ [מְנָת] n.f. *portion,* cstr. מְנָית. √מנה (*v.* Ges.§⁹⁵ⁿ Lag.ᴮᴺ ⁸¹· ¹⁵⁰) in good sense,
of Yahweh 16⁵, in bad sense *11⁶* 63¹¹, cf. 68²⁴. It was contr. for euphony and

should be connected with כוסם by a Makkeph for a single tone. † כּוֹס n.f. *cup* in good sense as given by Yahweh 23⁵ 116¹³, Yahweh Himself 16⁵; in bad sense given the wicked to drink *11⁶* 75⁹ Je. 49¹² La. 4²¹ Is. 51¹⁷ Ez. 23³³. — **7.** כִּי צַדִּיק יהוה אָהֵב] cf. v.⁵ᵃ. The position of צדיק is unusual. Accordingly it was regarded by 𝕳, 𝕲, 𝕵 as an attribute of Yahweh, and a cognate obj. was supplied in צְדָקוֹת *righteous acts*, of divine acts 103⁶ + 6 t., but if correct here of human acts as Is. 64⁵ Je. 51¹⁰ + 4 t. But it is doubtless a gl. making the l. too long. — יָשָׁר יֶחֱזוּ פָנֵימוֹ]. יָשָׁר *v.* 7¹¹ here only coll., and therefore doubtful. 𝕲 interprets as יֹשֶׁר. The vb. may be pl. if connected with צדיק, coll. as subj.; if not it may be an interpretation and not original with יְשָׁר, as subject.   פָנֵימוֹ archaic suffix for פָנָיו, usually pl., but here sg. as Jb. 20²³ 27²³, *v.* Ges. § 103 (2) n. 3. This form of suffix gives a more melodious ending to the Ps. These two lines expressing a general truth are a later gl. for congregation, not suited to the original Ps.

PSALM XII., 4 STR. 4⁴.

Ps. 12 is a prayer, in which the congregation implores Yahweh to save them, for the faithful vanish away and liars prevail (v.²⁻³) ; and to cut off the liars (v.⁴⁻⁵). Yahweh Himself says that He will arise, and set the afflicted in safety (v.⁶· ⁷ᵇ). The congregation finally expresses confidence that Yahweh will preserve them from the wicked round about (v.⁸⁻⁹).

O SAVE, Yahweh, for (kindness) is no more;
 For (faithfulness) is vanished from among the sons of mankind;
 Empty lies they speak, each with his neighbour,
 With flattering lip, with double mind they speak.
M AY Yahweh cut off every flattering lip,
 And (every) tongue speaking great words :
 Those who say, " To our tongues we give might,
 Our lip is our own ; who is lord over us ? "
" B ECAUSE of the spoiling of the afflicted, because of the sighing of the poor,
 Now will I arise," saith Yahweh.
 " I will set (him) in safety, I will (shine forth for) him,
 (When thrust down) to the earth he shall be purified seven times."
T HOU, Yahweh, wilt preserve (his life),
 Wilt keep (him) from this generation forever.
 (Though) round about the wicked walk,
 (When Thou risest up), (Thou dost lightly esteem) the sons of mankind.

The Ps. was in 𝕯, then in 𝕸 and 𝕯𝕽 (*v.* Intr. §§ 27, 31, 33). In the latter it received the assignment עַל־הַשְּׁמִינִית, indicating that it was to be sung an octave lower, that is, by the bass voice (*v.* Intr. § 34). The Ps. is unusually symmetrical in structure, 4 × 4 × 4. This is disturbed by the gnomic gl. in v.⁷. The date of the Ps. cannot be too late because of juss. v.⁴, cohort v.²; but demonst. זו without article v.⁸ is not classic. גמר v.²ᵇ as 7¹⁰ 77⁹ and פסו v.² = אפסי 77⁹; the use of חסיד אמונים v.², עניים, אביונים v.⁶, for the righteous members of the congregation over against wicked members, all indicate a time of religious declension, in which the pious were in great suffering and peril, especially from slander and violence. It was a time of external peace and internal corruption. The great stress laid upon sins of speech, v.³, cf. 41⁷ 144⁸ Pr. 6²⁴ 1 Ch. 12³³; v.⁴ cf. 131¹; indicates the influence of Persian ethics. V.⁶ gives a citation from Is. 33¹⁰, and not the reverse. All this favours the Persian period, at the time when the people were corrupted by mingling too freely with the neighbouring nations, subsequent to the building of the second temple and prior to the reforms of Ezra and Nehemiah.

Str. I. is composed of two tetrameter syn. couplets. The couplets themselves are antith. — **2.** *O save*], cohort. imv., earnest entreaty to *Yahweh.* — *for*], giving the reason. — *kindness ‖ faithfulness*] as suggested by chief ancient Vrss. and best suited to context. 𝕳 and other Vrss. followed by EV⁸. have " godly " and " faithful." — *is no more*], have come to an end as 7¹⁰ 77⁹. — *is vanished*], has disappeared, ceased, as 77⁹. According to the interpretation adopted, kindness, trustworthiness seem no longer to exist in the community, cf. Ho. 4¹ Je. 7²⁸. In the other case the persons themselves who should have these characteristics are no more, cf. Mi. 7² Is. 57¹. — **3.** *Empty lies they speak*], frequentative, of their custom or habit, cf. 41⁷ 144⁸, ¹¹. — *each with his neighbour*]. Unfaithfulness has so spread throughout the congregation that it has become a personal matter of man with man. — *With flattering lip*], as v.⁴, cf. Pr. 6²⁴. — *with double mind*], with two different minds, cf. 1 Ch. 12³³ Ja. 1⁸.

Str. II. has two syn. couplets. — **4.** *May Yahweh cut off*]. The juss. takes place of imv. of previous Str. — *every flattering lip ‖ every tongue speaking great words*]. These do not refer to the character of the words as related to the speaker, and so " proud things " PBV., boastful; but as related to the hearer, greater than the reality, and so flattering, deceiving, and misleading. — **5.** *Those who say*], referring to persons who use lip and tongue. — *To our tongue we give might*], as 𝕲, 𝕵, Hi., De., Dr., Kirk., that it may speak these great words. We are mighty, with no one mightier than we are. — *who is lord over us?*] implying negative answer,

no one. We are our own lord, *our lips are our own*], in our own
possession and power, and therefore we may make them as mighty
as we please. " Proud hypocrites are meant, putting confidence
in their speech to deceive men, and not submitting themselves to
God," Aug. The translation "with our tongue will we prevail,"
EV^a., JPSV., after 𝕋, though followed by Bä., Du., al., is grammatically not so easy and not so well suited to context.

Str. III. is a synth. tetrastich disordered by a gnomic gloss. —
6. *Because of the spoiling*]. The crafty enemies were also violent.
They had attacked the people unprepared and had taken spoils
from them. — *sighing*], indicating a sad condition as the result of
this grievous wrong. — *the afflicted ‖ poor*], as 35^{10} 37^{14} 40^{18} ($= 70^6$)
74^{21} 86^1 $109^{16. \ 22}$; the prey of the liars and flatterers among their
neighbours.   These are the words of Yahweh Himself, who is resolved to interpose on their behalf — the reason for which is mentioned first for emphasis. — *Now will I arise, saith Yahweh*], an
exact quotation from Is. 33^{10}. Yahweh rises up, when He would
interpose on behalf of His people or the righteous among them,
cf. 10^{12}. — *I will set in safety*], phr. only here, an exact response
to the entreaty v.^{2a}. — *I will shine forth for him*], in theophanic
manifestation as Dt. 33^2 Pss. 50^2 80^2 94^1, in accordance with Vrss.
The three vbs. without conj. give emph. utterance to the purpose
of Yahweh. But 𝕳 gives a vb. that occasions great difficulty,
which is interpreted as a relative clause ; " from him that puffeth
at him " AV. ; " at whom they puff " RV., as 10^5 ; " at whom they
scoff " JPSV., or, " that he panteth for " RV.^{m}, Dr., or temporal
" when they pant for him " Kirk. ; none of which are satisfactory.
— **7.** *The words of Yahweh are pure words, silver refined*]. This
clause constitutes a gl., interrupting the words of Yahweh and
destroying the structure of the Str., which has its fourth line at
the close of v.^{7}. It is a glossator's expression of admiration of
the words of Yahweh uttered in the Str. It is, moreover, a gnomic
sentence, cf. Pr. 30^5 Pss. 18^{31} 19^{10}. His words are as pure as refined silver. — *When thrust down to the earth*], referring to the
afflicted among the people, continuing the words of Yahweh,
cf. 74^7 143^3 La. 2^2 Jb. 16^{15}. The usual interpretation, referring
this clause to the silver, is difficult in every respect. The translations : " As silver tried in a furnace of earth " AV ; or " on

earth" RV.; "refined in an earthen furnace" JPSV., are not sustained by etymology or syntax. The Vrss. and interpreters differ greatly, without in any case finding the sentence appropriate to the context. — *he shall be purified*], that is the afflicted, by sufferings; cf. Mal. 3³. — *seven times*], the holy number of complete purification.

Str. IV. is composed of a syn. and a synth. couplet. The pious now express their confidence in Yahweh, who has spoken with so great promptness and decision. — **8.** *Wilt preserve ‖ wilt keep*]. The obj. is dub. in text. The suffixes in 𝔐 are 3 pers. This is better suited to context than 1 pers. of 𝔊, 𝔍. Probably both are interpretations, the Heb. vbs. being without suffixes in the original text. This is confirmed by the absence of one word in the first line, shortening the measure without reason. We should supply the usual object in such cases, probably *his life*. — *from this generation*], the class of men described above as liars and deceivers, cf. Dt. 32⁵ Ps. 78⁸·⁸ Pr. 30¹¹·¹²·¹³·¹⁴. — **9.** *Though*], the conjunction is needed for measure and meaning. — *round about the wicked walk*], familiar association with the righteous as in v.³, close neighbourly conversation, and also publicity and boldness of their wicked life. — *When Thou risest up*], going back upon the promise of Yahweh v.⁶, after 𝔊, which interprets it of Yahweh, though regarding the form as noun. It is usually regarded as infin. with prep. in a temporal clause, referring to the wicked, according to the interpretation of the subsequent context as "the vilest men" 𝔍, AV. But 𝔐 makes it abstr. "vileness" RV., Kirk., "worthlessness" *B*DB. Such a word is, however, unknown elsw. in Heb. It is best therefore to follow 𝔊, and to regard it as vb. and refer it to Yahweh: *Thou dost lightly esteem*], so Gr., cf. La. 1⁸. This gives an appropriate climax to the Ps.

---

2. הוֹשִׁיעָה] Hiph. cohort. imv. √ישׁע *v. 3⁸*. 𝔊 σῶσόν με, so Che. is prob. interpretation. — כִּי־נָמַר] causal conj. Qal pf. √גמר *v. 7¹⁰* real pf., subj. — חָסִיד] 𝔐, 𝔊 ‖. אֱמוּנִים 𝔐, 𝔍, 𝔗, pl. ptc. pass. Qal, √אמן, cf. 31²⁴, *v. 19⁸;* but 𝔊 pl. αἱ ἀλήθειαι = 𝔙 *veritates* = *truths*, cf. 𝔖, Σ, RV.ᵐ. †אֹמֶן n.m. *faithfulness* sg. Dt. 32²⁰, pl. abstr. Pr. 13¹⁷ 14⁵ 20⁶ Is. 26². 𝔊 and 𝔐 differ also Ps. 31²⁴. Probably 𝔊 is correct in interp. of form, but they were both abstract. In this case we should rd. דְּסֵר as We. For similar mistake *v. 4ᵇ*. We should remember that in original Mss. only חסד was written, and it might be interpreted either as חָסִיר or חֶסֶר. —

דְּאֵי] is prob. error for †אָדַם צָרַם *fail, come to an end* as 77⁹ Gn. 47¹⁵ ¹⁶ Is. 16⁴ 29²⁰.
𝕲 ὠλιγώθησαν. The pl. of vb. may be as often elsw. an interpretation.—
3. ‡שָׁוְא] emph.: (1) *emptiness, nothingness, vanity, a vain expectation* 60¹³
(=108¹³) 89⁴⁸ 119³⁷ 127². שׁ׳ הַבְלֵי *vanities, mere nothings, idols* 31⁷ = Jon. 2⁹;
לשׁוא *in vain*, Ps. 139²⁰, so שׁוא 127¹· ¹ Mal. 3¹⁴; (2) *emptiness of speech here*
as Pss. 24⁴ 41⁷ 144⁸· ¹¹; (3) of conduct, שׁ׳ מְתֵי *worthless men* 26⁴ Jb. 11¹¹.—
אִישׁ אֶת־רֵעֵהוּ] *one with another*, cf. שׁ אח־א 49⁸, אישׁ ואישׁ 87⁵.—שְׂפַת חֲלָקוֹת] emph.
= שְׂפָתֵי ח׳ v.⁴, prob. both should be sg. syn. לשׁון.—†[חֶלְקָה] n.f.: (1) *slippery
place* 73¹⁸; (2) *smoothness, flattery* 12³· ⁴ Pr. 6²⁴ Is. 30¹⁰; (3) *smoothness*
Gn. 27¹⁶.—[בְּלֵב וָלֵב] *with two minds*, cf. δίψυχος Ja. 1⁸.—4. [יַכְרֵת] Hiph.
juss. ‡כָּרַת Qal *cut* or *conclude a covenant* 50⁶ 83⁶ 89⁴ 105⁹. Niph. *be cut off*, of
wicked 37⁹·²²·²⁸·³⁴·³⁸ Ho. 8⁴ Is. 29²⁰ Na. 2¹. Hiph. *cut off, destroy* Pss. 12⁴ 101⁸
109¹³, מארץ 34¹⁷ = 109¹⁵.—[לָשׁוֹן] as used for evil purposes v. 5¹⁰. It should
have כל for good measure as in syn. l.—[גְּדֹלוֹת] adj. f. pl. *great, grand words*,
𝕲 μεγαλορήμονα, 𝕵 *magniloquam*, cf. קשׁות *rough words*, Gn. 42⁷·³⁰, גבהה *proud
words* 1 S. 2⁸, טובות *friendly words* Je. 12⁶.—5. [לִלְשֹׁנֵנוּ נַגְבִּיר] α.λ. n. is emph.
vb. is Hiph. impf. 1 pl., and construction difficult. 𝕲 τὴν γλῶσσαν ἡμῶν
μεγαλυνοῦμεν = 𝕵 *linguam nostram roboremus*, suits context and is followed by
Hi., De., Dr. "*our tongue will we make mighty*," and most. 𝕿, "*through our
tongue are we strong*," so Bä., Du. But Ew., Ols. after Dn. 9²⁷ would supply
בְּרִית, but this makes l. too long. ‡גָּבַר vb. Qal: (1) *be strong, mighty*, c.
מִן 65⁴; (2) *prevail*, of divine חסד, c. עַל 103¹¹ 117². Hiph. here only, c. לְ.—
[אָתָּנוּ] prep. אֵת, c. sf. 1 pl. *with us, on our side or in our own possession.*—
6. [מִן־מַשֹּׁד] causal. †שֹׁד n. *spoiling* as Je. 6⁷ 20⁸.—[אֲנָקָה] n.f. *groaning*
79¹¹ 102²¹ Mal. 2¹³.—[בְּיֵשַׁע] in *safety*. ‡יֵשַׁע n.m. elsw.: (1) *salvation*,
18⁸·³⁶ 27¹ 50²³ 51¹⁴ 62⁸ 69¹⁴ 85⁸·¹⁰ 95¹ 132¹⁶, אֱלֹהֵי יִשְׁעִי 18⁴⁷ (cf. 2 S. 22⁴⁷)
24⁵ 25⁵ 27⁹ 65⁶ 79⁹ 85⁵ Mi. 7⁷ Hb. 3¹⁸ Is. 17¹⁰ 1 Ch. 16⁸⁵; (2) *victory* Ps. 20⁷.—
[יָפִיחַ לוֹ] is usually taken as rel. clause, either *against whom one puffs*, cf. 10⁵,
RV., Ges., Hi., or *that he panteth for* Ew., De., Bö., Ols., Dr., RV.ᵐ. Du.
would rd. אפיה. But 𝕲 παρρησιάσομαι as 94¹ presupposes אפע, 𝕾, Σ, הופע.
Both may be explained as interpretations of an inf. abs. *shine forth*, in theophanic or ideal manifestation as Dt. 33² Pss. 50² 80² 94¹. 𝕵 *auxilium eorum* =
עזר(ה) לו is probably a paraphrase.—7. [אֲמָרוֹת] pl. cstr. ‡אִמְרָה n.f. *utterance,
speech*, of man in prayer 17⁶, elsw. of God's word 12⁷·⁷ 18³¹ 105¹⁹ 119¹¹⁺²¹ ᵗ· 138²
147¹⁵.—‡[טְהֹרוֹת] f. pl. טָהוֹר adj. ethically *clean, pure*, of the heart 51¹², words
of Yahweh 12⁷, Law 19¹⁰.—[צָרוּף] Qal ptc. pass. ‡צָרַף vb.: (1) *smelt, refine*, of
silver 12⁷ 66¹⁰, words of Yahweh 18³¹ 119¹⁴⁰ Pr. 30⁵; (2) *test*, the mind, Yahweh
subj. Pss. 17⁸ 26² 66¹⁰ Je. 9⁶ Is. 48¹⁰ Ze. 13⁹; (3) *test, prove* Ps. 105¹⁹.—[בַּעֲלִיל] α.λ.
dub. 𝕿 כבורא interprets as בְּ loc. and עֲלִיל n. *furnace;* but then לארץ must be
pregnant, Dr., Bä., *flowing down to the earth*. Gr. thinks the last לְ dittog. and
rds. עֲלִי as Pr. 27²². Houb. rds. וְחָרוּץ for לארץ; Dy., Gr. כְּחָרֻץ, Oort, Ehr. חרוץ.
Vrss. had a different text. 𝕲, 𝕾 δοκίμιον τῇ γῇ; 𝖁 *probatum terrae;* 𝕵 *se-
paratum a terra;* Aq. χωροῦν τῇ γῇ. All seem to depend on ברל vb. *be
divided, separate*, not used in Heb. in Qal, but only in N.H. and Aramaic. In
Egyptian Aramaic script ר and ‌ע were so similar that interchange was easy.

We might retain בעלל, but instead of interpreting it as בעליל interpret as בעולל, Polal inf. cstr. †עלל with בְ, as Jb. 16¹⁶, *thrust down;* cf. חלל לארץ Pss. 74⁷ 89⁴⁰, דכא לארץ 143³, הגיע לארץ Is. 25¹² La. 2². It would then refer to the afflicted of v.⁶ and introduce the last line of the tetrastich. The intervening six words would then be a gnomic gl. — מְזֻקָּק] Pu. ptc. †זקק vb. Qal, *refine, purify* Jb. 28¹ 36²⁷; Pi. same, Mal. 3³; Pu. *be refined,* only ptc. of metals, elsw. 1 Ch. 28¹⁸ 29⁴, of settled wines Is. 25⁶. — שִׁבְעָתָיִם] i.p. dual form of ‡שֶׁבַע adj. *seven* 119¹⁶⁴, dual *sevenfold,* elsw. 79¹², pl. *seventy* 90¹⁰. — **8.** [אֵיכָה emph. — תִּשְׁמְרֵם] Qal impf. 2 m. sf. 3 pl. || תִּצְּרֶנּוּ sf. 3 sg.; but ⅊ in both cases has ἡμᾶς. 𝔍, Aq., Θ agree with 𝔥, and refer sf. of the first vb. to the divine words. Probably all are interpretations of originals without any sfs. at all. The first line lacks a tone. The missing word was prob. וַפְשׁוֹ, as 25²⁰ 97¹⁰, either *his life* or as poetic paraphrase of pron., v. 3³. — זוּ] without article as adj., Ges.§ 126 *g,* v. 9¹⁶. ⅊ inserts καί in order to give דור a temporal force. — **9.** [סָהִיב emph., v. 3⁷, begins the line too abruptly, stating a fact which is singular in view of כ before רָב; moreover a tone is missing from the line. Probably an original כִי has fallen out by copyist's error. — יְתְהַלָּכוּן] Hithp. impf. 3 pl. full form in conditional clause with כִי *though.* — בְּרֻם] inf. cstr. defectively written with בְ temporal. — †זֻלֹּת] a.λ. *worthlessness.* √[זלל] *be worthless* Je. 15⁹, 𝔍 *vilissimi filiorum hominum.* ⅊, vb. ἐπολυώρησας, Sexta, ἐξουθένησας. Bä., building on χαρμ. of Origen's Hexapla, thinks of כֶרֶם *vineyard,* as Is. 5⁷ 27² Je. 2²¹ 12¹⁰, a vineyard lightly esteemed by the wicked. Gr. rightly rds. זַלּוֹתָ, pf. 2 sg. †[זלל] Qal, trans. *Thou dost lightly esteem,* as La. 1⁸ (Hiph.) for intrans. La. 1¹¹ Je. 15⁹ and trans. *lavish, squander* Dt. 21²⁰ Pr. 23²⁰·²¹ 28⁷.

PSALM XIII., 2 STR. 4⁴.

Ps. 13 is a prayer expostulating with Yahweh for long-continued neglect (v.²⁻³); and petitioning for deliverance from deadly peril from an enemy (v.⁴⁻⁵). A liturgical addition rejoices in salvation already enjoyed (v.⁶).

> HOW long, Yahweh, wilt Thou continually forget *me?*
> How long wilt Thou hide Thy face from *me?*
> How long (must) I put (grief) in *my* soul?
> How long shall mine enemy be exalted over *me?*
> YAHWEH, my God, O look, answer *me;*
> Lest I sleep in death, O lighten *mine* eye,
> Lest mine enemy say, "*I* have prevailed over him,"
> Lest he rejoice that I am moved — even *mine* adversary.

Ps. 13 was in 𝔇 then in 𝔐 and 𝔇ℜ (*v.* Intr. §§ 27, 31, 33). In its present form, it has three Strs. of 5, 4, 3 lines in 𝔥; in ⅊ the last Str. has an additional line. It is tempting therefore to think of gradually decreasing strophes as De. "Das Lied wirft gleichsam immer kürzere Wellen, bis es, zuletzt nur noch freudig bewegt, still wird wie die spiegel-glatte See." But closer examination shows that the man responsible for the present form of the Ps. had not such a fine poetic sense for form. The original Ps. was composed of two tetrameter tetrastichs, rhyming in *i*, the first Str. also in its four lines begins with עד־אנה; the second in three lines with פן. In the Ps. as it now is, the tetrameter measure is changed to trimeter in v.⁶ᵃᵇ, the extra line in v.³ᵇ is without עד אנה; the assonance of פן is neglected in v.⁴; פן is omitted altogether in v.⁵ᵇ; and rhyme is disregarded in an unnecessary change of order of words in both Strs., and also in change of sg. sf. to pl. in v.⁴·⁵. It is quite easy to restore the Ps. to its original form in these respects. It is true עד אנה might be prefixed to v.³ᵇ (Br.SHS. 380), and it is possible with Du. to make over the trimeter in v.⁶ to tetrameter; but even then there is a lack of harmony between v.⁶ and v.²⁻⁵, which is best explained by regarding v.⁶ as a liturgical gl. In that case the rejection of v.³ᵇ as expl. gl. is necessary. The Ps. in its present form is doubtless a congregational Ps. of prayer closing with praise. But if v.⁶ be a gl., the two Strs. are most naturally explained as the prayer of an individual; and in that case the evidences favour an early date. The Ps. was not composed for public worship; but was adapted for the purpose, when it was taken up into 𝕭. There is no evidence of late date apart from gls. There is no intrinsic evidence against as early a date as the time of David. The Ps. is brief, terse, simple, and yet symmetrical and ornate in style and form. The author of 2 S. 1¹⁹⁻²⁷ might have written it. The use of פן there v.²⁰ is similar to its use in this Ps. v.⁴⁻⁵. Hi., De., Kirk., refer it to Saul's persecution of David, and it admirably suits that historic situation.

Str. I. is a syn. tetrastich. — **2.** *How long ?*] emph. repetition in four lines ; earnest expostulation with Yahweh because of long-continued neglect of His servant. *Wilt Thou forget me ?* ‖ *hide Thy face from me ?*], so as not to see, as 10¹¹, where we have same parall. terms in mouth of the enemy. — *Continually*] as 16¹¹ Pr. 21²⁸, and not "forever," RV. after Vrss. which is not suited to the sentence. There is no sufficient reason to break the sentence in two as AV. or paraphrase by "utterly" as JPSV. — **3.** *Must I put in my soul*]. The change from second person, referring to Yahweh, to the first person of psalmist, before third person of enemy is striking in these lines of expostulation. We may be sure this action was not a simple fact feared for in the future, but involuntary action ; and so the mood of vb. cannot be indicative as EVˢ., but must be juss. — *grief*], so by an easy emendation of many scholars in accordance with context, and also with the usual meaning of *nephesh*. But the conception, of a person putting grief in his own soul, was so unusual, that an early scribe by the omission of a letter read " counsels," " advices," so EV⁴. This is thus explained by Pe. : " plan after plan suggests itself, is resolved upon, and then abandoned in despondency as utterly unavailing." But *nephesh* is seldom used of mental states, and this thought is not easy to adjust to the context. It had to be explained by the gl. : *sorrow daily in my mind.* — *Mine enemy*], personal in the original Ps., but congregational in the present text. — *be exalted over me*], in success, supremacy, and triumph : elsw. of God or His people ; here only of enemy over a pious man : all the more therefore emphasising the abnormal situation, the reverse of what it should be.

Str. II. is a tetrameter tetrastich, three syn. lines, synth. to the first line, and is all petition to Yahweh. — **4.** *My God*], to emphasise personal relation of psalmist to Him. — *O look*] earnest entreaty followed by imv. *answer me*, without conj. expressive of urgency, antith. to v.²ᵃ. — *Lest*], in three lines antith. " how long," Str. I. — *O lighten mine eye*], cf. 19⁹, to which it has been assimilated by copyist in use of pl. *eyes* destroying rhyme. The antith. with " hide Thy face " v.²ᵇ indicates that it is here the turning of Yahweh's face upon the psalmist that lightens his eye as 4⁷ 31¹⁷ 67² 80⁴·⁸·²⁰ 118²⁷ 119¹³⁵, all on basis of the High-priest's blessing Nu. 6²⁵. The use of the phr. 1 S. 14²⁷·²⁹ Pr. 29¹³ Ezr. 9⁸, as well as context, favours the enlightenment of the eyes in the sense of the revival of physical strength and moral energy. But it is due here to the light of Yahweh's countenance, so that probably lighten is here pregnant, comprehending both conceptions. — *I sleep in death*]. Death is often conceived as sleep 76⁶ 90⁵ Je. 51³⁹·⁵⁷ Jb. 14¹², not implying that the dead continue in a state of sleep in Sheol, but that the state of dying is a falling asleep to awake in another world. The psalmist is in peril of death, unless the favour of God shine forth from the divine face upon him, with its quickening power. — **5.** *Mine enemy say*], boastfully, antith. " grief," which the poet was obliged to put in his own soul v.³ᵃ. — *I have prevailed over him*], have the ability and power to overcome him, slay him, as parall. implies. — *that I am moved*], shaken, overthrown, removed from my place : the theme of the rejoicing of the adversary, who looks upon his plans as already accomplished. The poet is in grave peril of this result, but it has not yet transpired; and his urgent plea to Yahweh is that he may be delivered in good time. Elsw. in ψ this vb. is used of man with a neg. in the assurance that one "will not be moved" 10[6] 15[5] 16[8] 21[8] 30[7] 62[3.7] 112[6].

6. An editor, desiring to make the Ps. more appropriate for public use, adds a trimeter couplet of faith and joy:

> But I in Thy kindness trust;
> My heart rejoices in Thy salvation.

A still later editor, with the same purpose, adds a resolution of public praise:

> I will sing to Yahweh, because He hath dealt bountifully with me.

𝔊, 𝔙 give a fourth and still later liturgical line from 7[18], preserved in PBV.:

> Yea I will praise the name of the Lord Most Highest.

2. ‡ עַד־אָנָה] 4 t. repeated for assonance at beginning of each l. of original Str.; elsw. 62[4] Ex. 16[28] Nu. 14[11] (J) Jos. 18[3] (E).—נֶצַח] 16[11] Pr. 21[28] *ever, continually*, and not contr. of לנצח *forever*, v. 9[7], the usual term, wh. is not suited to עַד־אנה.—**3.** אָשִׁית] c. בְּנַפְשִׁי, a.λ. and difficult. MT. is an erroneous interp. connected with use of עֵצוֹת, wh. is not suited to context, or the ordinary use of נפש, often the seat of emotions and passions, seldom of mental states; v. BD*B*. Although this text is so ancient and universal as to be in most Vrss., yet it is better after 𝔖 with Dy., Gr., Che., Bu., Du., to rd. עַצְּבֹת *hurts, griefs* (v. 16[4] 147[3]), or sg. עֶצֶב as more suited to נפש and context. Then rd. vb. as juss.—יָגוֹן] n.(m.) *grief, sorrow*, elsw. 31[11] 107[39] 116[3] Gn. 42[38] 44[31] (J) Je. 4 t., is an early word; but also late, Est. 9[22]. It is not, however, suited to לבב, which usually is seat of mental and moral states, seldom of emotions and passions, and then in careless style.—בִּלְבָבִי] long form; cf. short form לְבִי v.[6b]; hardly from same writer, v. BD*B*.—יוֹמָם] v. 1[2], where followed by לילה, added here 𝔊[A], so Bä., Du., Gr., Che., al. We., Lag., Hu.[Now], Kirk., al., rd. יום. We must choose between the two, acc. to Dr. The whole clause is a gl. of emph. repetition, making Str. just this l. too long. —**4.** הַבִּיטָה] Hiph. cohort. imv., sq. imv. emph. coördination.—י אֱלֹהָי] seldom in ψ, v. 7[2]. Rhyme requires that the divine names should begin the l. and יְהוָֹי close it.—פֶּן] neg. final clause, v. 2[12], thrice repeated, the last time omitted by prosaic editor; properly sq. subjunctive cohort. form, but combination with פן requires shortened form for measure.—רָמָה] is acc. of state. —**5.** יְכָלְתִּיו] Qal pf. 1 sg. with sf. 3 sg. a.λ. ‡ יָכֹל vb. (1) *be able* to do a thing, sq. inf. 18[39] 36[13] 40[13] 78[19. 20], abs. 21[12]; *able* to endure 101[5], as Is. 1[13];

able to reach, c. לְ Ps. 139⁶; (2) abs. *have power over, prevail* Gn. 30⁸ (E) 32²⁹ (J) Ho. 12⁵, sq. לְ Gn. 32²⁶ (J) Ps. 129²; so here, as 𝕲 πρὸς αὐτόν, 𝕾, and measure require. Rhyme requires the order לוֹ וכלתי, first neglected by copyist and then by later copyist reduced to sf. — צָרָי] pl. improb., rd. sg. as אֹיְבִי, and transpose to close of l. for rhyme. — וְיָגִילוּ] is improb. without פֶּן. Rd. לֹ פֶּן־יָגֵל; pl. due to double error, the omission of פֶּן and pl. צָרָי. — כִּי אֱמֹט] temporal, AV., Kirk.; causal, Dr.; or better obj., subject-matter of exulting; *v. 10⁶.* — **6.** וַאֲנִי] emph. of personal determination; here for congregation, in liturgical gl. which is trimeter couplet. — בְּחַסְדְּךָ בְטַחְתִּי], pf. state, phr. 52¹⁰, elsw. usually *in God* Himself. If this were original to Ps., we might with Du. insert יהוה, and so get tetrameter. — יָגֵל] juss. with modal sense, if parall. with אָשִׁירָה Qal cohort., so Dr.; but if parall. with previous line has lost modal sense as usual in late style. Subj. לֵב Pr. 24¹⁷ Zc. 10⁷, more properly נפש Ps. 35⁹ Is. 61¹⁰, כבוד Ps. 16⁹. — בִּישׁוּעָתֶךָ] might be given either one accent or two, acc. to good usage and design of poet as to measure; *v. 3³.* — כִּי־גָמַל עָלָי] *deal bountifully with,* as 116⁷ 119¹⁷ 142⁸, *v. 7⁵.* כִּי gives ground or reason of exultation. This l. is a tetrameter and is a still later gl. 𝕲 adds a tetrameter l., καὶ ψαλῶ τῷ ὀνόματι κυρίου τοῦ ὑψίστου = ואזמרה שם יהוה עליון, a liturgical addition from 7¹⁸. יהוה עליון elsw. 47³. If this Str. is to be taken as original, this line is needed to make up tetrastich. But it is difficult to explain its omission from 𝔐. It implies public worship of congregation. But if it be gl., the previous three lines are also gl., because they imply the same situation and a later date than the previous parts of Ps.

PSALM XIV. = LIII., 5 STR. 2⁵.

Ps. 14 describes dramatically the impudent nations, acting abominably, saying to themselves, " There is no God to interfere " (v.¹) ; Yahweh from heaven inspecting them (v.²), and declaring that there is not a single well-doer among them (v.³) ; the devourers of His people, ignoring Him in careless indifference (v.⁴) ; Yahweh suddenly scattering them, and putting their plan to shame (v.⁵⁻⁶). At a later date the congregation prays that salvation may come forth from Zion (v.⁷ᵃ) ; and still later, summons to the worship of Yahweh, because of the restoration of prosperity (v.⁷ᵇ).

THE impudent said to themselves, " There is no God (here)."
 They corrupted their deeds, they acted abominably, there was no well-doer.
YAHWEH looked forth from heaven upon the sons of mankind,
 To see whether there was any acting intelligently in seeking after God.
THE whole have turned aside, have drawn back, together are become tainted.
 There is no well-doer, there is not even one.

HAVE the workers of trouble no knowledge — devourers of my people ?
    They eat bread: Yahweh they do not invoke.
THERE feared they a fear; for God scattered them;
    Their plan was put to shame: for Yahweh rejected them.

Pss. 14 and 53 both have לדוד and למנצח, and so were in 𝔇 and 𝔇𝕽 (*v.* Intr. §§ 27, 33). Possibly the למנצח of 14 was a later assimilation. To 53 is prefixed משכיל, possibly owing to the use of משכיל in v.⁸, but probably original, indicating that the Ps. was also in the little collection of Maskelim (*v.* Intr. § 26). 𝔇𝕽 added a direction for the melody על מחלת (*v.* Intr. § 34). Ps. 53 was also in 𝔈 (*v.* Intr. § 32), where אלהים was substituted for an original יהוה throughout. Thus the Ps. had several editings before it received its present positions in two different texts. There are several minor differences: (*a*) עול 53² = עלילה 14¹; (*b*) the insertion of ו before התעיבו 53²; (*c*) כלו 53⁴ = הכל 14⁸; (*d*) סג 53⁴ for סר 14³; (*e*) כל before פעלי 14⁴; (*f*) ישעית 53⁷ for ישועת 14⁷. These are such variations as might readily occur in different texts without changing the sense. In most cases Ps. 14 seems to be nearer the original. Ps. 53⁶ is different from 14⁵ after the first clause שם פחדו פחד. This difference is due not to design, but to different interpretations of a difficult text, for the same consonant letters lie at the basis of both texts (*v.* v.⁵ notes). In this v. Ps. 53 is nearer the original, as it points to an actual event of experience, where Ps. 14 generalises. 𝔊^{B. א. R}, 𝔈, Syr. Hexapla, PBV, have a number of additional lines, cited in Rom. 3¹⁰⁻¹⁸ from Pss. 5⁹ 10⁷ 36¹ 140⁴ Is. 59⁷· ⁸. They came into 𝔊 at an early date by a marginal reference to Rom. 3¹⁰⁻¹⁸, and in cod. Kenn. 649 of 𝔥 were translated back into Heb.

> Their throat is an open sepulchre;
> With their tongues they have used deceit;
> The poison of asps is under their lips;
> Whose mouth is full of cursing and bitterness.
> Their feet are swift to shed blood;
> Destruction and misery are in their ways,
> And the way of peace have they not known.
> There is no fear of God before their eyes.

It is impossible that these lines should be original, because of the textual evidence. They are absent from 𝔥, other Vrss., 𝔊^A and later codd. 𝔊, and are rejected by Origen and Jerome. Moreover, they do not accord with the thought of the Ps.; they entirely destroy the strophical organisation, and are of several different measures. The Ps. reflects the same situation essentially as Pss. 9–10; cf. 14¹ with 10⁴· ⁶· ¹¹· ¹³. The נבל here is the same as the רשע there. It was a time when the congregation of the Restoration was in great peril from the surrounding nations contemning and treating with contumely their religion and their God: before the reforms of Nehemiah. The language is in general similar to D, Je., Zp., Ez., and Is. One word has no example in this list, נאלח v.³, elsw. Jb. 15¹⁶; but this is an Arabism, and may well have been of this time rather than later, when Aram. influences prevailed. The divine inspection from heaven v.[2] implies the doctrine that Yahweh is not merely the God of Israel, but the God of the nations, the only real God; and therefore the triumph of monotheism over polytheism, such as is evident in Is.[2, 3]. The original reference of the Ps. to the nations, which is evident in 53 because of the more general interpretation of the situation, became in 14, in the worship of the congregation, adapted to the impudent contemners and ignorers of God in Israel itself. The Ps. is composed of five pentameter couplets, but there are three lines of different measure at the end. These represent two different liturgical additions: the one a petition for salvation from Zion the capital of Yahweh, as in 110[2]; the other a call to worship because the salvation had been accomplished. Both imply the temple worship of the Restoration.

Str. I. A synth. couplet describes the nations in their attitude to the people of Yahweh. — **1.** *The impudent*]. They ignore God, treating His people with contempt, and acting in a shameful manner towards the religion of Yahweh and Yahweh Himself. The *Nabhal* is not a "fool" EV[s]. in any of the meanings of this word, but a more aggressive personality, one who, in an earlier religious stage, represents the scorner of WL. (*v.* Ps. 1[1]). He is not the antith. of the wise, but of the one acting intelligently v.[2]. The word is here sg. coll., and so is followed by pl. vbs. In Ps. 14 there is a generalisation of the earlier historical situation, referring to impudent nations hostile to Israel and the God of Israel, which, while not altogether destroying, yet so obscures it as to make it easy for the congregation in later worship to think of the impudent in Israel itself, who act contemptuously towards the pious portion of the congregation and their religion ; and later still to think of the unbeliever and infidel. — *Said to themselves*], in their mind, as 10[6]. — *There is no God (here)*], not a denial of the existence of God, — these nations were polytheists and not infidels, — but a denial of the presence of God, to interfere with their actions, to interpose on behalf of His people, as 10[4]; interpreted by "He will not require" 10[14] and by "God hath. forgotten, He hath hidden His face, He doth not see" 10[11]. Accordingly these nations, in a most impudent manner, went to the utmost length with apparent impunity. — *They corrupted their deeds, they acted abominably*]. Some, even Kirk., think that the psalmist has in mind the corruption that preceded the deluge

Gn. 6^{12} (P) ; indeed, he uses the first of these vbs., but in a different phr. The phrasing here is in accord with Zp. 3^7, all the more if we transpose the noun to be the obj. of the first vb., although the reference in Zp. is to corrupt Israel, and here to the nations. The reference to the universal sinfulness of mankind before the deluge is possible only by a generalisation of the text of the original even beyond the changes of Ps. 14. The abominable deeds towards Israel are more fully described in Ps. 10^{7-10}. — *There was no well-doer*], among these hostile nations ; there was no exception, they were all alike ; they had attained a climax, the utmost possible limit in their impudent and abominable actions.

Str. II. A synth. couplet, describes Yahweh's attitude, antith. to that of the nations, of the first couplet. — **2.** *Yahweh looked forth from heaven*]. He was in heaven, cf. 10^5, at a distance from the nations. They could not see Him ; they might ignore Him, and contemn Him, and to themselves deny His presence ; but in fact He was there. He was intensely interested in what was going on ; so much so that He was looking forth *upon the sons of mankind*], these impudent nations, which yet belong to the race of mankind and not to the order of divine beings, — *to see whether*], making a careful, thorough, scrutinising inspection, — *there was any acting intelligently*], in order, if possible, to single out one from among these impudent ones that was their real antith. in *seeking after God*], in prayer and worship, cf. 9^{11}.

Str. III. A synth. couplet, still further describing the character of the impudent nations. The result of the divine inspection corresponds entirely with the psalmist's description (v.^{1}). — **3.** *The whole*, $14^3 = all$ *of them*, 53^4], variations of style merely, intensified in *together*, of joint action. They all alike share in the same characteristic doings. — *have turned aside* 14^3 ‖ *have drawn back*] 53^4 : syn. vbs., both needed for measure, the two different prosaic editors preferring, one the one term, the other the other term ; both further explication of v.^{1b}. Instead of seeking after God and doing good, they have drawn back and away from God and good. — *are become tainted*], corrupt, spoiled, altogether bad. This is not, as has been commonly supposed, an assertion of universal human corruption ; but, as the context shows, of the total depravity of the impudent oppressors of the people of Yahweh, described in v.¹·⁴. — *There is no well-doer*], showing in the climax the exact agreement of Yahweh with the psalmist as to the character of these nations, intensified, however, by the additional clause : *there is not even one.*

Strs. IV. and **V.** are synth. couplets, giving the psalmist's description of the final result of the antithetical situation described in the previous couplets. — **4.** He first expostulates with these nations : *have (they) no knowledge ?*]. Is it possible that they do not know that Yahweh is inspecting them, and declaring their character and doom ? How can they go on ignoring God as they have done ? It seems incredible that they should act so. — *The workers of trouble*] take the place of "sons of mankind" v.² and "the impudent" v.¹, as a more suitable term to sum up all that has been said about them. — *Devourers of my people*]. The bitter enmity and severe attacks made upon the people by their enemies to destroy them are compared to eating, devouring, as Hb. 3¹⁴ Ps. 27². This suggests the corresponding thought resuming that of v.¹, that they so ignore God, are so impudent and contemptuous in their attitude towards Him, that *they eat bread*], partake of their ordinary food without regard to Him, without at all considering Him. — *Yahweh they do not invoke*], renewing the thought of v.² They have no thought of seeking after God, or of recognising Him at all, even in the enjoyment of His benefits. — **5.** *There*], pointing to a place and a historic event known to the original psalmist, but not indicated. — *feared they a fear*]. This is mentioned abruptly and dramatically, as if they were taken by surprise. It is still further emphasised by the gloss 53⁶, "*where no fear was*" ; that is, either, when there was no apparent reason for fear, suddenly it came upon them without warning, or they were seized with a panic without external cause, due to the sudden realisation in their minds of the real situation described above. — *For God scattered (them)*], so 53⁶, in accordance with the panic of the previous context. The vb. admirably suits that scattering in all directions which takes place whenever a sudden panic comes upon a body of men, cf. 89¹¹. But 14⁵, by error of copyist, has : "for God is in the generation of the righteous," which gives, indeed, a general reason why the nations should fear Yahweh, and stay their evil deeds against His people, but no reason for this sudden fear that has come upon them. Ps. 53⁶ gives as the obj. of " scatter " : " the bones of Thy besiegers." This conceives of the nations as besieging the people of Yahweh when the panic suddenly came upon them. This admirably suits the context and is tempting as a historical basis of the Ps., but in fact it is due to a misreading of the original, and destroys the measure. — **6**. *Their plan was put to shame*]. This underlies and best explains both texts. Their plan was, as the previous context shows, to devour, utterly destroy, the people of God ; and their deeds were most impudent, abominable, and corrupt. Their plan was frustrated and put to shame, because they were scattered in a disgraceful panic. Ps. 14 misreads so as to give either a statement of fact : "Ye put to shame the counsel of the afflicted," or a hypothetical clause : " Ye may put to shame " ; but in either case it is difficult to adjust to the context. It is true that this clause might be regarded as a reiteration of the impudent conduct of the nations, but there is no apparent reason for it here, and we still lack, according to that interpretation, any explanation of the sudden panic with which the verse began. Ps. 53⁶ takes the vb. as abs. and 2 sg. with God as subject, " Thou hast put to shame," which suits the vb. " scattered," but leaves the obj. to be supplied ; while the 2 pers. sg. is strikingly out of place in the midst of 3 pers. sg. in previous and subsequent lines, all pers. alike referring to God. — *For Yahweh rejected them*], so 53⁶, in accord with its context ; 14⁶, " is his refuge," is due to the mistake of a single letter of the original word, though it is quite well suited to the previous context. The original Ps. came to an end with this couplet.

7. A later editor, probably of 𝔻, adds, as a liturgical prayer, a tetrameter line.

> Oh, that the salvation of Israel might come forth from Zion!

Zion is here conceived as the capital seat of Yahweh's dominion, from whence therefore salvation comes. This implies a well-ordered worship in the temple and a strongly defended city, as in Pss. 46, 47. Here is an entirely different situation from that of v.², where salvation comes from Yahweh in heaven; cf. 110² for a similar gloss.

A still later liturgical addition, a tetrameter couplet, was made, probably in ψ, calling upon the congregation in public worship : —

In that Yahweh hath restored the prosperity of His people,
Let Jacob rejoice, let Israel be glad.

The juss. form probably has juss. sense, although at this late date it might be regarded as having lost its distinctive mng., and so be translated as indicative future, "shall rejoice," "shall be glad," EVˢ. ; the former is more suited to a liturgical gloss, the latter is tolerable only in the view that it was original to the Ps., and then the early date would be against this interpretation of the jussive. — *In that*]. The infinitive cstr. with prep. may be interpreted as temporal clause, "when" 𝔍 and most Vrss. and interpreters, but better as giving ground or reason for the exhortation, cf. 9⁴. — *Yahweh hath restored the prosperity of His people*]. This is to be preferred, especially at this late date, to the more specific and earlier rendering of the phr., "bring back the captivity," EVˢ., which does not suit a late liturgical addition.

---

1. †נָבָל] adj.; not ἄφρων 𝔊, *stultus* 𝔍, *fool* EVˢ., but *impudent, contumelious, shameless,* as *impudens* with the double sense of *immodest* and *impudent :* (*a*) towards God 14¹ = 53² 74¹⁸·²² Dt. 32²¹ all of heathen, Dt. 32⁶ of Israel ; (*b*) towards men, antith. to נָדִיב *nobleminded,* and so *shameless, baseminded* Is. 32⁵·⁶ 2 S. 3³³ 13¹³ Je. 17¹¹ Ez. 13³ (?); coll. of the contumelious חֶרְפַּת נָבָל Ps. 39⁹, cf. Pr. 17⁷·²¹ 30²² Jb. 2¹⁰ 30⁸. This mng. is confirmed by נְבָלָה n. f. *wanton, immodest, impudent deed,* not in ψ, but Gn. 34⁷ (J) Ju. 19²⁸ 2 S. 13¹² +, and the denom. vb. †נבל not in ψ, but Qal *be impudent* Pr. 30³², Pi. *treat with impudence* or *contumely :* God Dt. 32¹⁵, father by son Mi. 7⁶, the divine throne Je. 14²¹, Nineveh by Yahweh Na. 3⁶. — הִשְׁחִיתוּ] Hiph. pf. 3 pl. action completed in present. ‡שחת vb. Hiph. (1) *destroy* 78⁸⁸·⁴⁵ 106²³ and prob. 57, 58, 59, 75 (titles); (2) *corrupt* in moral sense Gn. 6¹² (P) Zp. 3⁷, *act corruptly* Ps. 14¹ = 53² Dt. 4¹⁶ 31²⁹ Is. 1⁴ Je. 6²⁸. — הִתְעִיבוּ] Hiph. pf. pl. 3 m. without conj., emph. coördination, *v. 5⁷.* — וַעֲלִילָה] *v.* 9¹². Ps. 53² has עָוֶל, *v.* 7⁴, but this is prob. an error of copyist. The conj. ו between the vbs. in 53² is prosaic and not original. The resemblance of the passage to Zp. 3⁷ favours the view that the noun is really obj. of both vbs. — אֵין עֹשֵׂה־טוֹב] = v.³ᵇ antith. to אֵין אֱלֹהִים. The phr. = 53²·⁴, cf. 37³ Ecc. 7²⁰. The ptc. has nominal force, *well-doer.* טוֹב, *good* is seldom in an ethical sense 34¹⁵ 37²⁷ 52⁵, *v.* 4⁴. 𝔊 adds οὐκ ἔστιν ἕως ἑνός, assimilated to v.³ and not original. — **2.** יהוה]

emph. antith. נבל]; the situation is dramatic as Ps. 2. — [מִשָּׁמַיִם] also emph., the heavenly residence in antith. with earthly men. — [הִשְׁקִיף] Hiph. pf. emph. present. ‡ שָׁקַף vb., Niph. *look forth* from heaven 85¹², ‡ Hiph. same, elsw. 102²⁰ La. 3⁵⁰ Dt. 26¹⁵; cf. הִבִּיט same, 33¹³ 80¹⁵ 102²⁰. — [מַשְׂכִּיל] Hiph. ptc. nominal force, as שׂוּב עֵשׂה, *acting with understanding* or *having insight*, antith. to נבל; cf. 2¹⁰. — 3. [הַכֹּל] *the whole* = כֻּלּוֹ 53⁴ *the whole of it.* ⅏ in both πάντες. The former as 49¹⁸ 103¹⁹ 119⁹¹ 145⁹, the latter as 29⁹. — [סָר] Qal pf. 3 m. סוּר *v. 6⁹,* of *revolt* as Dt. 11¹⁶ 17¹⁷ Je. 5²³. For this 53⁴ has סָג Qal pf. 3 m. ‡ סוּג Qal *backslide, prove recreant,* to Yahweh, abs. *53⁴* Pr. 14¹⁴, c. מִן Ps. 80¹⁹. Niph. (1) reflexive *turn oneself back, prove faithless,* c. מאחרי Zp. 1⁶, אחור Is. 50⁵ Je. 38²² Pss. 44¹⁹ 78⁵⁷ (prep. omitted); (2) passive, *be turned back, repulsed* by foes, with אחור 35⁴ 40¹⁵ (= 70³) 129⁵ Is. 42¹⁷ Je. 46⁵. This l. lacks a tone. We might think that in the original both vbs. סר and סג stood, as two vbs. v.¹ᵇ; and that one copyist took one vb., the other the other. — [יַחְדָּו] *v. 4⁹, together,* of joint action. — [נֶאֱלָחוּ] Niph. pf. 3 pl. † [אלח] an Arabism, *be tainted, corrupt,* elsw. ptc. נֶאֱלָח Jb. 15¹⁶. — [אֵין גַּם אֶחָד], *there is not even a single one.* גַּם in the sense of ‡ *even* 38¹¹ 78²⁰ 132¹², וְגַם *v. 8⁸.* — 4. [הֲלֹא] interrog. with neg. expostulation. — [יָדְעוּ] emph. present, *v. 1⁶.* — [כָּל־פֹּעֲלֵי אָוֶן] so ⅏ of 53⁵, but 𝔐 omits כל there. It is an easy and frequent insertion, *v.* 5⁶ 6⁹, and it makes the l. too long. — [אֹכְלֵי עַמִּי] Qal ptc. pl. cstr. nominal force. ‡ אכל (1) *eat:* man subj. 128²; (*a*) manna 78²⁴·²⁵, birds 78²⁹, אכל לֶחֶם *take a meal 14⁴* (= 53⁵) 41¹⁰ 102⁵ 127² Gn. 3¹⁹ 31⁵⁴ 37²⁵ 43²⁵·³² 2 K. 4⁸; (*b*) sacrificial meals Pss. 22²⁷·³⁰ 106²⁸, even of God, in question 50¹³; (*c*) in mourning, fig. ashes 102¹⁰, cf. 80⁶ (Hiph.); (2) animals subj.: insects 78⁴⁵ 105³⁵·³⁵, dogs 59¹⁶, ox 106²⁰; (3) enemies, *devour,* עַם *14⁴* = 53⁵, Jacob 79⁷, the flesh of the people 27²; (4) subj. things, *devour,* fire 18⁹ 21¹⁰ 50³ 78⁶³, zeal 69¹⁰. Hiph. *give to eat,* God subj. מַחֲלֵב הִטָּה 81¹⁷, fig. לֶחֶם דִּמְעָה 80⁶. Usage makes it plain what is meant here, — a taking of the ordinary meal. — 5. [שָׁם] adv. dem. *there:* (1) simple designation of place after ישב 69³⁶ 107³⁶ 137¹, defining אשר 104¹⁷; שְׁ relative 122⁴; (2) pointing to a place at the end of the clause 48⁷ 87⁴·⁶; (3) emph. at beginning of sentence, pointing to a place where something important had happened or will happen, especially in description, *14⁵* (= 53⁶) 36¹³ where defeat had taken place, 66⁶ rejoicing, 68²⁸ procession, 104²⁵·²⁶ movement of animals or ships in the sea; other conceptions 132¹⁷ 133⁸ 137³ 139⁸·¹⁰. שָׁמָּה, same with ה local, place 122⁵, emph. 76⁴; *v.* B*D*B. — [פָּחֲדוּ פָחַד] vb. Qal pf. 3 pl. aorist ‡ פָּחַד. Vb. *dread,* abs. 78⁵³ Dt. 28⁶⁶ Je. 36²⁴, פחד פחד cog. acc. Pss. *14⁵* = 53⁶ Dt. 28⁶⁷ Jb. 3²⁵; c. מִן Pss. 27¹ 119¹⁶¹. ‡ פַּחַד n. elsw. ψ (1) *dread,* before Yahweh 105³⁸ 119¹²⁰, the enemy 64², peril at night 91⁵; (2) obj. of dread 31¹² 36² 53⁶. 53⁶ adds לֹא הָיָה פָחַד, an explanatory addition to emphasise either that the calamity came when there was no apparent reason for dread, or else that there was no real reason for it. — The great difference between 14 and 53 now appears. [כִּי אלהים] *14⁵ᵇ* 53⁶ᵇ is parallel with כִּי יהוה *14⁶ᵇ* = אלהים כִּי 53⁶ᵈ, both causal clauses with God subj. It is, however, improbable that אלהים was in the original Ps. of 𝕰. — [פֻּר עֲצָמוֹת חֹנָךְ הֱבִישׁתָה] *14⁵ᵇ·⁶ᵃ* for which בָּרוֹר צַדִּיק עֲצַת עָנִי תָבִישׁוּ

53[6b. c]. These variations are evidently due to a copyist's error, and not to intentional change. The texts were written originally thus in 𝔐:

14. ברר צדק עצת עני תבש
53. פזר   עצמת חנך הבשת

There is nothing to correspond with צדק in 53, therefore it was an explanatory addition to דור, which without it is unintelligible. ברר might be interpreted as Aram. בְּרַר *scatter* = פזר, and it might have been an unconscious substitution or interpretation of the form of the original ‡ פָּזַר vb. Niph., bones are scattered at the mouth of Sheol 141[7]. Pi. subj. Yahweh, *scatter, disperse*, enemy 89[11], hoar frost 147[16]; subj. man, his ways, so to run hither and thither to other gods Je. 3[13], scatter money Ps. 112[9] Pr. 11[24]. פזר in the sense of *scattering* enemies is most suited to context, and in all probability original here. עֲצָתָם, *their counsel, plan* (v. 1[1]), best explains both readings. In the one text it was explained as against the עָנִי, *the afflicted* (v. 9[13]); in the other, it was rd. as עֲצָמוֹת *bones* (v. 6[3]), due possibly to 141[7]. This then had to be explained, and so the gl. originated either חנף, 𝔊 ἀνθρωπαρέσκων, 𝔙 qui homines placet, or חֹנֶךְ *thy besieger*, Qal ptc. sf. 2 s. ‡ חָנָה vb. Qal *encamp*, of army, c. על 27[3]; סביב ל metaphor for protection 34[8]; here c. acc. *besiege*. But sf. 2 pers. and acc., both suspicious, and improbable in original. 14 has רְבִישׁוּ Hiph. impf. 2 pl. בוש (v. 6[11]). 53 has הֵבִישׇׁתָה Hiph. pf. 2 m. fully written form. But neither of these is suited to context, which requires 3 sg. The Hiph. in the sense of *be put to shame* is common, as 119[31. 116] Je. 2[26] 6[15] 46[24] 48[1. 1. 20] 50[2. 2]; then עצה might be subj. and the form have been תביש. The 2 pl. is a later interpretation. The 2 sg. pf. is also an interpretation. — מַחְסְרוּ] 14[7] for wh. מָאַס 53. Here again the resemblance is so great in form that the difference must be due to interpretation and not intention. The sfs. are in both cases later interpretations; the difference between מחס and מאס is slight in ancient scripts and in some dialects in pronunciation. ‡ מַחֲסֶה n.m. *refuge*, esp. of God, elsw. 46[2] 61[4] 62[8. 9] 71[7] 73[28] 91[2. 9] 94[22] 142[6], rocks for conies 104[18]. This is suited to the context of 14 in part, but not to the original Ps. — ‡ [מָאַס] Qal *reject, refuse*, c. acc., subj. God 53[6] 89[39], subj. men 36[5] 118[22]; c. ב subj. God 78[59. 67] subj. men 106[24]; Niph. *be rejected 15[4]*. This vb. in perf. 3 m., suits context and the original Ps. — 7. מִי־יִתֵּן] expressive of *wish* = 53[7] 55[7] (v. 4[7]) and introduces a liturgical addition, as 110[2]. — וִישׁוּעַת] sg. cstr. = 53 יְשׁעוֹת pl. cstr., the former *salvation*, the latter *saving acts*, the former more probable, v. 3[3]. — יַעֲקֹב || יִשְׂרָאֵל] poetic terms for the nation and later for the religious community, v. BDB. — בְּשׁוּב] inf. cstr. temporal, Hu., Bä., Du., Dr., Kirk.; but this is not so well suited to context as causal, giving reason of rejoicing; cf. 9[4]. The phr. † שׁוּב שְׁבוּת is technical, 14[7] (= 53[7]) 85[2] 126[1. 4] Dt. 30[3] Je. 29[14] 30[8. 18] 31[23] 33[26] 48[47] 49[39] Ho. 6[11] Am. 9[14] Zp. 2[7] 3[20] Ez. 16[53] 29[14] Jo. 4[1] Jb. 42[10]. In most of these passages we might render, *restore captivity*, bring back captives; but some of them must have the more general mng. *restore prosperity*. If the former here, the liturgical addition must have been very early, after the restoration of Zion to the centre of the Jewish religion; if the latter, it may have been at a much later date. Possibly there are two stages of liturgical addition in this verse.—[יִשְׂמַח] $v. 5^{12}$, ‖ יָגֵל, $v. 2^{11}$, both juss., the latter in form. They should be interpreted as real juss. If, however, the previous clauses be temporal, it would seem necessary to interpret them as future indicatives, and to regard the juss. form as having lost its significance.

PSALM XV., STRS. 2^3 10^3 1^3.

Ps. 15 is a didactic poem, inquiring what sort of a man is qualified to be a guest of Yahweh (v.¹); describing him in accordance with a decalogue of duties (v.²⁻⁵ᵇ); and declaring such a man secure (v.⁵ᶜ).

> *YAHWEH, who shall be a guest in Thy tent?*
> *Who shall dwell on Thy holy mount?*
> HE that walketh perfect in his righteousness;
> He that speaketh truth in his mind;
> Who hath not played the spy upon his neighbour,
> Hath not done harm to his friend,
> Hath not taken up a reproach against the one near to him
> Despised in his eyes is the reprobate;
> But them that fear Yahweh he honoureth.
> He doth swear to (his friend) and changeth not.
> His silver he hath not given in usury,
> Nor taken a bribe against the innocent.
> *WHOSO doeth these things shall not be moved.*

Ps. 15 was in 𝔇 and 𝔐 (v. Intr. §§ 27, 31). It was not taken up into the earlier major Psalters, because it was neither hymn nor prayer, but simply didactic in character, and so less suited for public worship. It resembles Ps. 24³⁻⁶, which has a similar couplet of inquiry and a similar response; now a tristich, but probably originally a couplet, with a concluding couplet; and therefore more artistic than Ps. 15. The measure of Ps. 24 is also trimeter, the response is simpler and earlier. The language and phrasing are so different that there seems to be no interdependence. The situation is entirely different with Is. 33¹⁴⁻¹⁶, where there is a couplet of inquiry, a pentastich of response and a concluding tristich. These are tetrameters. But the language and phrasing are so similar to Ps. 15 that there is interdependence; and probably the briefer ethical conception of Is.³ is earlier than the more complete one of the Ps. The question has the same conception of guest גור; although in Is.³ Yahweh is a consuming fire, in the Ps. He has a hospitable tent. The different situations at the time of composition explain this variation. Three of the ethical requirements are the same: (1) הלך צדקות $v. 2^a$ = הלך תמים Is. 33¹⁵ᵃ. This is all the more the case if we read in $v. 2^a$ הלך תמים בצדקו.

נער כפיו מתמך בשחר‎ v.⁵ᵇ=‎ שחד לא לקח‎ (3).   Is. 33¹⁵ᵇ. ‎דבר מישרים‎=v.²ᵇ ‎דבר אמת‎ (2)
Is. 33¹⁵ᵈ. The conclusion v.⁵ᶜ may be regarded as a summary statement of
Is. 33¹⁶. The *Gemara* (*Makkoth* f. 24*a*) states: "David compresses the
613 commands of the Law in eleven, Isaiah in six, Micah (6⁸) in three;
Amos (5⁴) and Hb. (2⁴) each in one." The comparison is good though the
conception of the author is unhistoric. V.²ᵇ shows such a highly developed
sense of mental truthfulness, that it implies the influence of Persian ethics, and
therefore the Persian period. The form of the decalogue implies familiarity
with its use in the earlier Heb. codes, and a legal habit of mind. This decalogue does not include duties to God as the primitive Decalogue; but is
rather like those decalogues of E, D, H, which comprehend duties to man.
V.⁵ᵇ ‎שחד על־נקי לא־לקח‎ implies ‎ארור לקח שחד להכות נפש דם נקי‎ Dt. 27²⁵, one
command of a primitive decalogue among the sources of D; cf. also Ex. 23⁸.
V.⁵ᵃ ‎כספו לא־נתן בנשך‎ implies ‎את־כספך לא תתן לו בנשך‎ Lv. 25³⁷ out of one of
the groups of laws of H; cf. Ex. 22²⁴ (*v.* Br.Hex. 224. 229. 239). The codes of D
and H were familiar to our psalmist, but he betrays no knowledge of P. The
Ps. seems to give an appropriate answer to the demand of Samaritans to
participate with the Jews in the rebuilding of the temple, Ezr. 4² sq.

Str. I. is a couplet of inquiry, as 24³·⁸·¹⁰ Is. 33¹⁴.—**1.** *Who*]
not, what person? but as often, what sort of a person? what shall
be his character?—*shall be a guest in Thy tent*], *v.* Ps. 5⁵. The
tent is a poetic term for the temple 27⁵⁻⁶ 61⁵, based upon the
ancient sacred tent of Yahweh, prior to the building of the temple
78⁶⁰·⁶⁷. The temple was really the house or palace of Yahweh;
sometimes conceived as the place of sacrifice and worship, sometimes as the place of His royal presence, to which He admits His
servants, either as guests or to shelter them from their enemies.
—*dwell on Thy holy Mount*], parall. with previous line, but not
entirely synonymous. The privilege of access to the sacred tent
as guests is one thing; the privilege of a residence on the holy
mountain as citizens is another. The holy mount is here as elsewhere Jerusalem or Zion (*v.* 2⁶).

Str. II. is a decalogue composed of two pentades of ethical
requirements. The first, **2–3**, comprehends a couplet and a triplet. The couplet is more general, requiring: (1) Moral walk or
conduct. In this the guest of Yahweh should be *perfect in his
righteousness*], complete, faultless, so probably the original, to
rhyme with the other lines of the pentade. These two kindred
words seemed to a later prosaic editor to require each its own
verb, and so he inserted "worketh" before "righteousness," and

destroyed the measure. (2) Moral speech. — *He that speaketh truth*], not merely of external speech to others as 1 K. 22[16] Je. 9[4] Zc. 8[16], where truth and falsehood are conceived in the preëxilic sense as connected with injury to others; but, internal speech, to himself, *in his mind*], the later and much higher conception of truthfulness, due to Persian influence; the Persians, from an earlier date than their contact with Israel, being distinguished above all other ancient nations for the stress they put upon moral truthfulness. The more general attitude of this first pair of ethical requirements passes over into the more specific negative conduct in the triplet, which is progressive in order of thought. The relationship becomes constantly closer in the order : *his neighbour, his friend, the one near to him*, so also in the actions. — *play the spy upon*]. This is the ordinary meaning of the Heb. phr.; but a copyist in the omission of a single letter of the original "neighbour," substituted a Hebrew word meaning "tongue," and so made an obscure and unexampled phr. and construction, which has been rendered in various ways. Those most familiar to English readers, are : " He that hath used no deceit in his tongue " PBV., " He that backbiteth not with his tongue " AV., " He that slandereth not with his tongue " RV.; none of which is well sustained. — *Hath not done harm to*]. The evil disposition, as expressed in spying, has passed over into an active doing of injuries, and reaches its climax in : *hath not taken up a reproach against the one near to him*.

The second pentade, **4–5***b*, is also composed of a couplet and triplet, the couplet general, the triplet specific. The couplet is antith. — *The reprobate*], the one rejected by Yahweh (*v. 14[6]* (revised txt.) = 53[6]), antith. *them that fear Yahweh*], His worshippers, cf. 22[24] 25[12] 34[10] 112[1] 115[11. 13] 118[4] 128[1. 4] 135[20]. The former are *despised in his eyes*], his eyes look upon them with contempt; the latter *he honoureth*. The triplet is progressive, as the previous one, in the rejection of degrees of wickedness. — *He doth swear to his friend*], so 𝕲 "neighbour" PBV.; which is easier and more suited to the context than the stronger and tempting, " to his own hurt " 𝕵, AV., RV., JPSV., and most moderns. This rests upon a different interpretation of the same original consonant letters, which in the unpointed text may be interpreted by two different words — *and changeth not*], that is, adheres to his oath and does not violate it. This probably refers in accordance with the subsequent context to a promise made to a friend of some benefit or help. The violation of the oath of promise now passes over to the more positive usury, and more guilty bribery, in violation of the ancient codes; the former of Ex. 22²⁴ (E) Lv. 25³⁷ (H) Dt. 23²⁰, cf. Ez. 18⁸·¹³·¹⁷ Pr. 28⁸; the latter of Ex. 23⁸ (E) Dt. 27²⁵ (Decalogue) Dt. 10¹⁷ 16¹⁹ 1 S. 8³, cf. Is. 1²³ 5²³ 33¹⁵ Ez. 22¹² Ps. 26¹⁰ Pr. 17²³.

Str. III. is a monostich, summing up the decalogue in final response to Str. I. — **5**c. *Whoso doeth these things shall not be moved*]. This phr. is often employed to indicate the firm, secure condition of the people of God, in Zion, *v. 10⁶*. A later editor thought that he strengthened it by adding " forever."

1. יהוה] unnecessary gl. — [בְּהַר קָדְשֶׁךָ] the sacred mountain Zion; see 2⁶. This couplet rhymes in *ka*. and is syn. throughout. — **2.** [הוֹלֵךְ] ptc. fully written, rel. indefinite, so הלך, דבר. of moral, religious walk, course of life; *v. 1¹.* — ‡[תָּמִים] adj. ; the physical mngs., *whole, entire, sound,* are not in ψ, but only the ethical mng., *sound, innocent, having integrity :* (*a*) of God's way 18³¹, as Dt. 32⁴, law Ps. 19⁸; (*b*) of man 18²⁴, his way 101²·⁶ 119¹, cf. 18³³, without דֶּרֶךְ בתמים 84¹², תמים acc., of way *15²* Pr. 28¹⁸. Other constructions Pss. 18²⁶ 119⁸⁰, adj. for noun late; pl. 37¹⁸ Pr. 2²¹ 28¹⁰; *v.* לֹב 7⁹, חמם 9⁷. — צֶדֶק [פֹּעַל] antith. און פעל, *v. 5⁶.* This makes a tetrameter with cæsura, and also a double requirement at the beginning; whereas in every other line there is a single trimeter requirement. פֹּעֵל is therefore a gl. to separate צֶדֶק and חמים, which originally belonged together. We should rd. צִדְקוֹ for *rhyme.* For צֶדֶק, *v. 4² :* cf. Is. 33¹⁵ צְדָקוֹת הֹלֵךְ. — ‡[אֱמֶת] n.f. (1) *faithfulness, reliableness,* (*a*) of man 45⁵ 51⁸ 119⁴³; (*b*) of God : באמת as the sphere in which man may walk 26⁸ 86¹¹, cf. 25⁵; (2) attribute of God 30¹⁰ 31⁶ 54⁷ 71²², associated with חֶסֶד 25¹⁰ 40¹¹·¹² 69¹⁴ 86¹⁵ 115¹ 138² Gn. 24²⁷ (J) Is. 16⁵, as messenger of God Pss. 57⁴ 61⁸ 85¹¹ 89¹⁵, cf. 43⁸; His faithfulness endureth forever 117², cf. 146⁶; it reacheth unto the skies 57¹¹ 108⁵, is shield and buckler 91⁴; used with ישר 111⁸, צדק 85¹², משפט 111⁷; (3) seldom *truth,* and then not in an abstr. sense, but rather *faithfully, truly,* דבר אמת *15²* 1 K. 22¹⁶ Je. 9⁴ Zc. 8¹⁶; so the divine laws are *true, reliable,* Pss. 19¹⁰ 119¹⁴²·¹⁵¹·¹⁶⁰ Mal. 2⁶; (4) adv. *in truth, truly,* Ps. 132¹¹ Je. 10¹⁰, באמת Ps. 145¹⁸, cf. אָמֵן 12², אֱמוּנָה *334.* — [בִּלְבָבוֹ] the long form for the usual בְּלִבּוֹ; c. דבר only here, elsw. c. אמר, *v. 4⁵*; cf. דבר בלב Ec. 2¹⁵, עם לב Ec. 1¹⁶, אל לב Gn. 24⁴⁵ (J), עַל לב 1 S. 1¹³ (?); cf. Is. 33¹⁵. — **3.** [לֹא־רָגַל] the ptcs. of previous v. pass over into Qal pf. of general truth, in negative rel. clause, אשר omitted as usual in poetry. † רָגַל *a.λ.* Qal pf. denom. רֶגֶל *foot, v. 8⁷,* dub. mng. ⑥ ἐδόλωσεν also for הֶחֱלִיק 36⁸ is prob. interpretation; so 𝔍 *non est facilis in lingua.* It is better to render *play the*

spy upon. This is urged by the mng. of Pi. in Gn. 42⁹ ⁺ ⁶ ᵗ· (E) Nu. 21³²
Dt. 1²⁴ Jos. 2¹ 6²². ²⁵ 7². ² 14⁷ (JE) Ju. 18². ¹⁴. ¹⁷ 1 S. 26⁴ 2 S. 10³ 15¹⁰ 1 Ch. 19³,
go about as spy or *explorer*. 2 S. 19²⁸ is usually rendered *slander*, but it might
just as well have the mng. *play the spy*, and usage urges it. The only other
use of vb. is Tiph. Ho. 11³ *teach to walk* (dub.). The difficulty with רגל is
due to על לשנו‎, which is not homogeneous to the vb. The context suggests
עַל שְׁכֵנוּ *upon his neighbour*, Che. The ל of לשנו originated from dittog. after
the omission of ב‎. We should probably also rd. עלי for better measure. It is
possible that some of the Vrss. interpreted רגל as Aram. דגל *lie, deceive*. —
‡ [רָעָה] n. f. (1) *evil, distress*, 34²² 90¹⁵ 91¹⁰ 107²⁶. ³⁹, יום רעה 27⁵ 41² Je. 17¹⁷. ¹⁸
51², רָעוֹת *evils* Pss. 34²⁰ 40¹³ 71²⁰ 88⁴ 141⁵ Dt. 32²³, עֵת ר׳ Ps. 37¹⁹ Je. 2²⁷. ²⁸ 11¹²
15¹¹ Am. 5¹³; (2) *evil, injury, wrong*, Pss. 21¹² 28³ 35²⁶ 50¹⁹ 52³ 109⁵,
c. עשה ל 15³, חשב 35⁴ 41⁸ 140³ Gn. 50²⁰ (E) Je. 36³ 48², בקש Pss. 71¹³. ²⁴
1 S. 24¹⁰ 25²⁶, דרש Ps. 38¹³, חפץ 40¹⁵ = 70³, שלם 35¹² 38²¹ Gn. 44⁴ (J) Je. 18²⁰
51²⁴; (3) *evil* in ethical sense Pss. 94²³ 107³⁴. — ‡ [חֶרְפָּה] n. f. emph. (1) *reproach*
(a) against man, *taunt, scorn*, of enemy 69²⁰. ²¹ 71¹³ 89⁵¹ 119²², נשא חרפה
Je. 31¹⁹ Ez. 36¹⁵ Mi. 6¹⁶ all against, so Ps. *15³* (no reason to suppose a special
sense of slander here), נשא ח׳ c. על *bear reproach for* 69⁸ Je. 15¹⁵ Zp. 3¹⁸,
העביר ח׳ 119³⁹; (b) against God 69¹⁰ 74²² 79¹²; (2) object of reproach 22⁷
39⁹, היה ח׳ ל *become an object of reproach to* 31¹² 79⁴ 89⁴² 109²⁵, cf. 44¹⁴ 69¹¹
78⁶⁶. — [נָשָׂא] in the sense of ‡ *take up, utter;* elsw. זמרה 81³, לשוא 139²⁰, cf.
24⁴, names 16⁴, covenant 50¹⁶. — [קְרֹבוֹ] *the one near to him*, of relationship, as
38¹², cf. Ex. 32²⁷ *neighbour*. — **4.** [וְנִבְזֶה] and וְנִמְאָס Niphs. may be either pfs. or
ptcs. The impf. יַבֵּר does not help. It is itself doubtful. The connection
of בְּעֵינָיו with נִבְזֶה and the antith. with יַבֵּר make it most probable that this is
the chief vb., and that there is another antith. between the obj. of נִמְאָס and
יְרֵאֵי. — ‡ [בָּזָה] vb. *despise, regard with contempt*, subj. God 22²⁵ 51¹⁹ 69³⁴ 73²⁰
102¹⁸; ptc. pass. 22⁷ Je. 49¹⁵; Niph. *be despised* Pss. *15⁴* 119¹⁴¹ Is. 53³. ⁸
Je. 22²⁸. — [וְאֶת־יְרֵאֵי י׳] emph.; but אֶת dub. in measure. *v. 3⁷.* — [יַבֵּר].
The change of tense was due to change of order of words in sentence and is
of doubtful originality. — [נִשְׁבַּע] Niph. pf. 3 m. ‡ שָׁבַע Niph. (1) of man, *swear
a solemn oath*, abs. 119¹⁰⁶, למרמה 24⁴, להרע *15⁴*; c. ב by God 63¹², by man in
imprecation 102⁹, ליהוה 132²; (2) of God, abs. 110⁴, לדוד 89⁴. ⁵⁰ 132¹¹, בקרש
89³⁶, כ אף 95¹¹. — [לְהָרֵע] may be *to his hurt*, article for sf. and רֵעַ *hurt, v. 5⁶*;
so ₵, Ew., Hu.; inf. Hiph. רעע, *v. 22¹⁷*, Aq., Θ. ℑ *ut se affligat;* so De.,
Bä., as Lv. 5⁴. ₲ τῷ πλησίον αὐτοῦ, ℣ *proximo suo*, so ₴, Gr., Dathe; = לְרֵעַ
as v.³ᵇ. This is easier and more suited to the context, though not so noble
a conception as is MT. At the same time it would be difficult to prove
the existence of such an ethical conception at so early a date as this Ps. —
[יָמֵר] Hiph. impf. 3 m. defectively written ‡ מור, vb. not used in Qal; but
Hiph. *change* of earth in earthquake 46³ (?), c. acc. חֵלֶק Mi. 2⁴, here abs.;
(2) *exchange*, Ps. 106²⁰ Ho. 4⁷.

PSALM XVI., 3 STR. 8⁴.

Ps. 16 is a psalm of faith. The psalmist has sought refuge in Yahweh his sovereign Lord, and supreme welfare (v.¹⁻²); whose good pleasure is in His saints (v.³). The apostates have many sorrows, and he keeps apart from them and their impious worship (v.⁴). Yahweh is his portion and his inheritance in pleasant places (v.⁵⁻⁶); he enjoys His counsel (v.⁷) and continual helpful presence (v.⁸); he is glad and secure (v.⁹), confident that Yahweh will not abandon him in Sheol (v.¹⁰), but will grant him life and joy forever in His presence (v.¹¹).

KEEP me, 'El; for I have sought refuge in Thee.
   I said to Yahweh: "Thou art my sovereign Lord,"
   For my welfare is not (without) Thee.
   To the saints who are in the land,
   (Yahweh) makes wonderful all His good pleasure in them.
   They shall multiply their sorrows who hurry backwards.
   I will not offer their drink offerings, because of bloodshed;
   I will not take up their names upon my lips.
YAHWEH is my share, (my) portion, and my cup;
   (Yahweh is) the maintainer of my lot (for me).
   The lines are fallen for me in pleasant places;
   Yea, mine inheritance is (mighty over) me.
   I will bless Yahweh, who hath given me counsel:
   Yea, in the dark night my reins admonish me.
   I have set Yahweh continually before me:
   Since He is on my right hand, I shall not be moved.
THEREFORE my heart is glad (in Yahweh);
   (Also) my glory rejoiceth (in Yahweh);
   Also my flesh dwelleth securely:
   For Thou wilt not leave me to Sheol;
   Thou wilt not suffer Thy pious one to see the Pit;
   Thou wilt make known to me the path to Life.
   Fulness of gladness is in Thy presence;
   Loveliness is on Thy right hand forever.

Ps. 16 was in 𝔍 belonging to the group of מכתמים (*v.* Intr. §§ 25, 27). It was not in 𝔇�. That is the reason probably why it was separated from the other Miktamim, 56–60, which have been preserved, all of which were in 𝔇�. This favours an early date for the Ps. (1) There is a use of Je. 23⁶ 33¹⁶ Dt. 33¹², שכן לבטח in v.⁹ᵇ; (2) a dependence upon Ez. in the conception (*a*) of *saints, consecrated ones*, for faithful Israelites in accordance with the code of H v.³, and (*b*) of the pit in Sheol v.¹⁰; (3) a much greater dependence upon

Is.[2. 3] (a) in the phrase, *His good pleasure in them* v.[3b], cf. Is. 44[28] 46[10] 48[14];
(b) apostasy expressed by hurrying backwards v.[4a], cf. Is. 50[5]; (c) *the drink offerings* v.[4b] if of blood, correspond with the abominations described in Is. 57[5 sq.] 65[11] 66[3]; and it may be that v.[4c] finds its best illustration in Is. 65[15], as Bä. suggests. The worship there repudiated is that of Palestine and Syria, not that of Babylonia or Egypt. If the situation is the same, we must think of the late days of the Exile or the early days of the Restoration. But it is more probable that these drink offerings were repudiated because those who made them were guilty of bloodshed, of murder of innocent persons. This favours a time when there was no strong government to repress such disorders. (4) The reference to a share or portion in the land (v.[5]) also favours one who has recently returned to the Holy Land. The expression "Saints who are in the land" implies an antith. to those who were not in the land, those still in exile, such as would be quite natural for one recently come to the land from among the exiles. (5) The tone of the Ps. is one of calm trust in Yahweh and the enjoyment of prosperity attributed to Yahweh. The author calmly separates himself from the apostates; but there is no evidence of active hostility, still less of peril or warfare. This does not favour the times of hardship and poverty described by Hg. and Zc., or the times of conflict of Ne. and Ezr. The Ps. was composed either between these times or subsequent thereto. (6) There is a single Aramaism, v.[6b] שפרה עלי, which is found elsewhere only Dn. This might have been used at any time in the Persian period; but most likely not at its beginning. However, it is a copyist's error. 𝕲 has the correct text in a common word גברה. (7) The calm view of death and the expectation of the presence of God and blessedness after death imply an advance beyond Is. 57[1-2]; but prior to the emergence of the doctrine of the resurrection of the righteous Is. 26[19], that is, in the Persian period. The same point of view is in Pss. 17[15] 49[16] 73[23-26] Jb. 19[25-27]. (8) The author was one of the חסרים v.[10b], the pious who distinguished themselves carefully from those who were not faithful to Yahweh, and kept apart from them. (9) There is no trace of the observance of P, or of the practice of temple worship, in this profession of piety, probably, therefore, the date was prior to these. On the whole the composition of the Ps. is best assigned to the time subsequent to Zerubbabel and prior to Nehemiah. The Ps. is tetrameter and of three strophes. It is doubtful whether these are of eight lines or seven. If the text of Str. III. v.[9-11] is the test, it is not difficult to find glosses in v.[3a. 5a] with Du. If these are regarded as original, it is not difficult to reconstruct v.[9] into three lines and regard v.[9ab] as condensed by a prosaic scribe into one line, leaving a trace of it in having one word too many. V.[8-11b] is cited Acts 2[25-32] from 𝕲, and applied by St. Peter to the resurrection of Christ; so v.[10b] by St. Paul, Acts 13[35]. The hopes of the Ps., which apply only to the enjoyment of the presence of God after death, in view of the subsequent emergence of the doctrine of the resurrection, are realised in the eternal life of the resurrection, and so first in Christ, the first fruits of that resurrection.

Str. I. is a tetrameter octastich ; three synth. lines giving the psalmist's attitude toward God, two Yahweh's attitude toward the saints of the land, and three the attitude of both toward the apostates. **1–2.** *Keep me*], a plea for protection based on : *I have sought refuge in Thee*], cf. 2^{12} 5^{12} 7^2 11^1 +. — *I said to Yahweh*], so Vrss., RV., JPSV., Dr., Kirk. ; and not "(O my soul) thou hast said," MT., PBV., AV., which is not well sustained by text or context. — *Thou art my sovereign Lord*], "my Master" JPSV., "my Lord " AV. ; pl. intensive, as 2^4 8^1, and not the divine name "Adonay," "the Lord " RV.[m] — *My welfare*], prosperity, is to be preferred to " my goods," possessions, ᅟ, ᅟ, PBV., elsw. only Ec. 5^{10} ; or to "goodness" AV. "Good " RV. is too general. — *is not (without) Thee*], as ᅟ, is most prob. "Nothing unto Thee" PBV., "(extendeth) not to Thee " AV., cannot be sustained. RV. "beyond Thee " is dub. (Dr.) ; though urged by Ew., RS., Kirk. : "Not merely is God the source of all his weal, but everything which he recognizes as a true good, God actually contains within Himself." The simpler idea that the psalmist is entirely dependent on Yahweh, the source of all good, for his welfare, and cannot prosper without divine favour, is much more probable. — **3.** *To the saints who are in the land*], as distinguished from those abroad, those of the dispersion. — (*Yahweh*) *makes wonderful all His good pleasure in them*], so ᅟ, ᅟ ; preferable to ᅟ, which is so difficult to interpret that there is no agreement among later Vrss. or commentators. Yahweh takes good pleasure in these saints, and He magnifies His good pleasure in them in a wonderful manner. — **4.** *They shall multiply their sorrows, who hurry backwards*], cf. 44^{19} Is. 50^5 ; apostates who turn away from Yahweh and go backwards in apostasy from Him. This is better sustained by ᅟ and Vrss. than "hasten after another (God)" AV., "run after " PBV., "make suit unto " JPSV., which are not sustained by Hebrew usage ; or than "exchange (the Lord) for another (god)" RV., Kirk., so essentially Dr., which requires unnecessary emendation of text. The psalmist, having represented that the saints enjoyed the wonderful good pleasure of Yahweh, now turns to the apostate Israelites who have gone backwards from Yahweh to the worship of other gods, and represents that they, in reverse of enjoying Yahweh's good pleasure, incur a multitude of sorrows. — *I will not offer their drink offerings because of bloodshed*] ; that is, participate with them in their drink offerings to Yahweh, which were abominable because they were associated with bloodshed, the murder of innocent persons. Bä. thinks of the offering of children Is. 57[5 sq.] 65[11] ; Du. of the blood-guiltiness of such offerings as they make, cf. Is. 66[3]. — *I will not take up their names upon my lips*], cf. 50[16], in order to speak to them or about them, — not the names of the gods so worshipped, according to the law, Ex. 23[13] (E), or their names as the names these apostates take on their lips, Ri., but the names of the apostates themselves, Bä., as Is. 65[15]. The poet repudiates them utterly, he will have nothing to do with them, will not even mention them in conversation. The psalmist was undoubtedly influenced by Is.[2]. If the Ps. belongs to the Persian period, we may think of the apostates to idolatry described in antith. with the pious, the saints, v.[3].

Str. II. is composed of four syn. couplets. — **5.** *Yahweh is my share*], in assonance with (*my*) *portion* and *my cup*, rather than " share of my portion " 𝔥, though sustained by Vrss. and most authorities. — *Yahweh is the maintainer of my lot (for me)*]. This was probably the original text, according to the context. The change to the 2d person is improbable. It was doubtless due to supposed editorial improvement of style. The poet here en-larges upon v.[2b]. Yahweh, the source of welfare, also embodies in Himself the share which He gives to His people, the portion assigned them, the cup of pleasure which they enjoy ; and all this He maintains for them against all enemies and perils. " The language used here reminds us of the Levites who had no portion or inheritance, but Jehovah was their portion, Nu. 18[20] Dt. 10[9] 18[1]," Kirk. " Let others choose for themselves portions, earthly and temporal, to enjoy ; the portion of saints is the Lord eternal. Let others drink of deadly pleasures, the portion of my cup is the Lord," Aug. — **6.** *The lines*], the measuring lines of the portion, or share in the land, cf. Ps. 78[55] Mi. 2[5] Am. 7[17]. — *are fallen for me in pleasant places*], the lot in the holy land is a delightful one. — *Yea, mine inheritance is (mighty over) me*], the inheritance in Yahweh, Yahweh Himself as the inheritance, ‖ share, v.[5a], as 𝔊, and so similar to 103[11] 117[2], where the mercy of

God is mighty over His people. The "goodly heritage" of EV⁸. is a paraphrase based on 𝕳 which cannot be sustained.— **7.** *I will bless Yahweh who hath given me counsel*]. The psalmist passes over from his portion in the land to his more intimate relations with Yahweh, whom he has sought as his sovereign Lord, v.¹²ᵃ ; He has counselled him in his life and conduct. — *My reins admonish me*]. The reins are the seat of the emotions and affections, cf. Jb. 19²⁷ Pr. 23¹⁶ Ps. 73²¹ Je. 12² ‖ *mind*, Je. 11²⁰ 17¹⁰ 20¹² Pss. 7¹⁰ 26². His own experience corresponds with Yahweh's counsel. This admonition is *in the dark night*], as 92³ 134¹, intensive pl., rather than "night seasons," AV., RV.— **8.** *I have set Yahweh continually before me*], before the mind, keeping Him continually in mind. — *since He is on my right hand*], present, near at hand, as close as possible to help. This is the reason why, *I shall not be moved*], the usual expression of confidence in God, Pss. 10⁶ 15⁵ 16⁸ 21⁸ 30⁷ 62³·⁷ 112⁶, cf. Pr. 10³⁰ 12³.

Str. III. is composed of a syn. couplet between two syn. triplets. — **9.** *Therefore*], because of confidence in Yahweh's presence as sovereign Lord and portion. — *my heart is glad ‖ my glory rejoiceth*]. In both lines, *in Yahweh*, was probably in the original, completing the measures. A prosaic copyist condensed the two lines into a simple line, too long for the measure of the Ps. — *also my flesh*], the body in antith. with "heart" and "glory," so making up the entire man, body and soul. — *dwelleth securely*], liveth without anxiety, without fear of enemies, cf. Dt. 33¹² Je. 23⁶ 33¹⁶.— **10.** *For thou wilt not leave me to Sheol*]. *Nephesh* is here, as often, the person of the man himself. The poet is not thinking of the soul as distinguished from the flesh, but of himself as composed of both soul and body. It is true the flesh does not go to Sheol at death, but only the soul. The psalmist is here thinking of his entire self and not specifically of that part of himself which goes to the abode of the dead. He expects to die and to go to Sheol, but he prays that God will not abandon him there ; will not leave him in the power of Sheol; but will go with him and remain with him there. — *Thou wilt not suffer Thy pious one to see the Pit*]. The Heb. שחת is not abstract "corruption," which, though given in 𝕲 and 𝕴, and followed by EV⁸., has no authority in the usage of OT.

The Pit is not the tomb, but is syn. with Sheol, usually understood as another name of Sheol itself as a pit or cavern under
the earth ; but usage favours the opinion that it is a Pit in Sheol,
as a deeper place than Sheol, syn. Abaddon, the dungeon of Sheol.
The psalmist will see Sheol, but he will not be abandoned there ;
he will not see the Pit, the dungeon of Sheol, the place of the
wicked.   The pious could hardly go there.   In antithesis with
this, the psalmist has hope and confident expectation of the
presence and favour of God after death. — 11. *Thou wilt make
known to me the path to Life*].   This might imply resurrection
if the Ps. were late enough, a path leading up out of Sheol to
eternal Life.   But the context does not suggest this; the path
rather leads to the presence of God in the abode of the dead.
The path to life is antith. to the Pit in Sheol. — *Fulness of gladness
is in Thy presence*].   The presence of Yahweh, to which the
path to life leads, gives gladness to the full, and complete satisfaction, leaving nothing more to be desired.   It is possible that
the glossator had this in mind as the supreme good or welfare, v.[2b]. — *Loveliness* ‖ *gladness, on Thy right hand*], as the
place of honour, ‖ in Thy presence, antith. to Yahweh's being on
his right hand in life, v.[8b]. — *forever*].   Such a hope he could not
express for this life ; he is thinking of everlasting life in the
presence of Yahweh and on His right hand, after he has departed
this life and gone to Sheol.

1 . [שָׁמְרֵנִי] Qal imv. sf. 1 sg. שמר, see *12[8]*. The metheg of 𝕳 interprets
quametz as *ā*, but this is erroneous, and should be corrected to *ŏ* as Ges.§ 9 v.
Kö.[I. s. 101]. — אֵל poetic for God (*v.* Intr. § 32). — 2. [אָמַרְתְּ] Qal pf. 3 f. implying נפש as subj., so 𝕿, Rabb., RV.[m].   But it should be אָמַרְתָּ, defectively
written 1 pers., as 22 codd. De R., 𝕲, 𝕴, 𝕾, Houb., Ols., Ges.[§ 44i] Kö.[I. s. 151]
Ew., al., cf. Ps. 140[13] Jb. 42[2] 1 K. 8[48] Ez. 16[59]. 𝕵, *dicens* also favours this
form. — [אֲדֹנָי] refers to God as distinguished from אֲדֹנִי referring to men.   But
it is not necessarily *Adonay*.   The context suggests the original mng. *my
sovereign lord*, as predicate of אַתָּה *v. 2[b]*. — ‡ [טוֹבָה] n.f.: (1) *welfare, prosperity, happiness 16[2]*, as Dt. 23[7] Je. 33[9], obj. ראה Ps. 106[5] Jb. 9[25] Ec. 5[17] 6[6];
(2) *bounty, good*, as bestowed by God, Pss. 65[12] 68[11] 86[17]. רעה החת טובה 35[12]
38[21] 109[5] Gn. 44[4] (J) 1 S. 25[21] Je. 18[20] Pr. 17[13]. *v.* טוב *4[7]*. This clause is not
in 𝕲[B], but in 𝕲[א, A, R], where טובה is interpreted as *my goods*, 𝕴 *bonorum*, a
mng. very late, Ec. 5[10]. 𝕵 translates *bene mihi*, Σ ἀγαθὸν μοι, 𝕿 טובתי. —
[עָלֶיךָ] is difficult and is variously interpreted: (1) 𝕲 [·] A, R ὅτι οὐ χρείαν ἔχεις,

thou hast no need or *advantage*, in a causal sentence. The ὅτι may be an interpretation or imply כִּי in the original. The עַל is interpreted in the sense of *for the sake of*, as ‡ 45⁵ 79⁹ 105¹⁴. (2) 𝔍 *sine te*, Σ ἄνευ σοῦ, paraphrased by 𝔖 "from Thee," is a translation of בלעדי, which Houb., Hi., Du. think was in the original text. (3) *Over, beyond,* Ew. " *Thou art my highest good*," Dr. " *My welfare is not beyond (?) Thee.*" BDB. gives in this mng. of *excess* ‡ 138², *above* all Thy name (dub.), in the sense of *above, beyond* Gn. 48²² Ex. 16⁵ Nu. 3⁴⁶ Dt. 25³ Jos. 3¹⁵ Ec. 1¹⁶ Dn. 1²⁰, in local relations, Lv. 15²⁵ of time. But none of these have precisely the sense proposed for this passage. (4) The more usual mng. of עַל, *incumbent on*, of duty, or care ‡ 7¹¹ 10¹⁴ 37⁵ 40⁸ 56¹³ 62⁸, c. השליך 22¹¹ 55²³ 71⁶ is adopted by Ra. But it is then necessary to make the clause interrog. or get a mng. the reverse of the context. Pe. avoids this by changing בל to כל. (5) The mng. ‡ *in addition to* 61⁷ 69²⁸ 71¹⁴ 115¹⁴ is adopted by Ri., Moll., but it is improbable. The line is too short in 𝔐. It is better to rd. as the original a real tetrameter כי שובתי בל בלעדיך. This explains 𝔍. The err. of 𝔐 is chiefly the omission of בל of בלעדי by haplog. and then the err. of עָלֶיךָ for עָדֶיךָ. — **3.** [לִקְרוֹשִׁים] is also difficult and is variously interpreted: (1) לְ in the sense of *as for, as regards* 17⁴, 𝔊, 𝔍, De W., Ew., Dr.; (2) *belonging to*, Calv., Hengst., Hu., Pe., Moll; (3) depending on אמר as a second indirect obj. in antith. ליהוה Ki., De., RV.ᵐ. This is most suitable to context if the present text be correct. קָרוֹשׁ pl. ‡ קְרוֹשִׁים adj. *sacred, holy :* (1) used of God, as exalted on theophanic throne 22⁴ Is. 6³, exalted in victory Ps. 99³·⁵·⁹ Is. 5¹⁶ 1 S. 2², His name Ps. 111⁹, קדוש ישראל, a divine name originating in the Trisagion, Is. 6³, used in Is. 1⁴⁺¹⁰ t. Is.2·3 41¹⁴⁺¹²ᵗ·, elsw. Je. 50²⁹ 51⁵ 2 K. 19²² Is. 37²³ Pss. 71²² 78⁴¹ 89¹⁹; (2) of sacred place of temple in Jerusalem 46⁵ 65⁵; (3) of persons, Aaron, 106¹⁶, קרשים *sacred ones*, either † *angels* 89⁶·⁸ Jb. 5¹ 15¹⁵ Zc. 14⁵ Dn. 8¹³·¹³, or Israelites Dt. 33³ Pss. *16³* 34¹⁰ Dn. 8²⁴. — [בְּאָרֶץ] 𝔊 ἐν τῇ γῇ αὐτοῦ = בארצו : sf. is doubtless an interp., as 10¹⁶. — ‡ [הֵמָּה] *they ;* this fuller, more euphonic form is alw. in ψ, except 38¹¹ נַס־הֵם and 95¹⁰ᶜ וְהֵם, to which הֵם 95¹⁰ᵇ has been assimilated by copyist: (1) emph. *they*, (*a*) antith. to other persons אני 120⁷, אנחנו 20⁹, אתה 102²⁷ 109²⁸, with ו adv., *but they* 55²² 63¹⁰ 106⁴³, at close of sentence emph. previous sf. *even theirs* 9⁷ without justification in usage, and doubtless txt. err.; (2) resuming subj. with emphasis at the beginning of a new sentence 22¹⁸ 23⁴ 27² 37⁹ 43³ 48⁶ 56⁷ 59¹⁶ 62¹⁰ 107²⁴, stronger נס־הם 38¹¹; (3) as copula, properly at end of clause, *they are* or *were* 9²¹ (?) 25⁶ 78³⁹ 94¹¹ 95¹⁰ 119¹¹¹, after אשר only *16³*; (4) in circumstantial clause והמה 88⁶, והם 95¹⁰. — [וְאַדִּירֵי] is also difficult. 𝔍 *et magnificis* ‖ לקרשים, but the word is too distinct to dispense with the prep., and it is cstr., not abs., unless we suppose that 𝔍 had אַדִּיר sg. coll. אדיר (*v.* 8²) is not used elsw. in ψ in this sense, though not infrequent in early poetry. Ges.⁴ §176*d* allows an occasional cstr. in the sense of abs., but this is not allowed by more recent grammars. We might, however, regard the cstr. as before a rel. clause, De W., RV., Dr., and ו as introducing an apod. 𝔊 renders as vb. ἐθαυμάστωσεν πάντα τὰ θελήματα αὐτοῦ = יאדיר. More than 90 codd. HP., so

Theodoret, give κύριος after the vb. This might be regarded as a gl. of interpretation, but it may also be an interpretation of the final י as an abr., for יהוה. This would, moreover, give us a needed tetrameter and a suitable couplet : —

לקרשים אשר בארץ המה
יאדיר יהוה כל־חפצו בם

† [אדר] vb. is used in Niph. ptc. Ex. 15¹¹ of the majesty of God, cf. v.⁶ and Is. 42²¹ in the Hiph. *make glorious*, which is appropriate to this passage. This is the view essentially of Koehler, Schnurer, Bä., Hu.³.— **4.** [עֲצְבוֹתָם] is regarded by 𝕿, Θ, Quinta, 𝕵, Mich., Ols., Ew., Du. as fpl. for usual ‡ עֲצַבִּים n.(m.) *images, idols, v.* 106³⁶. ³⁸ 115⁴ 135¹⁵; but עַצֶּבֶת elsw. pl. †[עַצֶּבֶת] n.f. *hurt, injury* 147³ Jb. 9²⁸, sg. Pr. 10¹⁰ 15¹³, so doubtless here after 𝕲, 𝔖, Aq., RV., and most, *v.* 13³. The lack of agreement between n.f. and vb. m. still remains difficult. The sf. מ‍ַ cannot refer to previous context, but to the rel. clause which follows. The vb. is interpreted by 𝔖, 𝕿 as Hiph., and so the neglect of agreement is avoided, and this is to be preferred, though 𝕲, Aq., Σ, Θ, 𝕵 take it as Qal.— [אַחַר] is variously interpreted: (1) by 𝕵, Θ *post tergum* as אָחוֹר adv. *backwards, v. 9⁴*. This is most prob. (2) 𝕲 μετὰ ταῦτα *ἐτάχυναν,* 𝔙 *postea acceleraverunt* אַחַר, either having sf. or Vrss. supplying it, cf. 49¹⁸ 50¹⁷ 63⁹. (3) 𝕳, Aq. as adj. Aq. refers to one's neighbour. But most think of another god in accordance with subsequent context. — ‡ אַחַר adj. *another*, properly *one coming behind, successors* 49¹¹, *aliens* 109⁸, עם אחר 105¹³, אֶל אַחֵר Ex. 34¹⁴ (J), אַחֵר Is. 42⁸, so Ps. *164* (𝕳). It is used of time דור אחר 109¹³ Jo. 1³.— [מהרו] Qal pf. 3 m. i.p.; ‡ מהר denom. מֹּהַר *purchase price* of wife Gn. 34¹² (J) Ex. 22¹⁶ (E) 1 S. 18²⁵, so vb. *acquire by purchase* Ex. 22¹⁵ (E.) But there is no evidence of such a generalisation of the mng. as is necessary if that is to be used here with De., Dr. (2) 𝕲, 𝕵, 𝔖, Θ, Σ, 𝕿 take it as Pi. pf. ‡ [מהר] vb. Pi. (*a*) *hasten* Gn. 18⁶ Na. 2⁶ Is. 49¹⁷. It is not used in ψ unless here in this sense; but (*b*) as auxiliary having adv. force, sq. perf. 106¹³, elsw. imv. מַהֵר עֲנֵנִי 69¹⁸ 102³ 143⁷, so also prob. 79⁸ sq. impf. (3) Aq. οἱ ἄλλον ἐκάκωσεν implies הֵמֵרוּ Hiph. pf. מרר *act bitterly towards*, a vb. used nowhere in ψ unless here. (4) It is possible to think of such a transposition as the foregoing and then rd. הֵמִירוּ Hiph. pf. מור, as 106²⁰. The conception would be similar if אחר referred to another god, but the construction would be different, and so condensed as to be necessarily obscure. This is the view of Gr., once held by Bä., but subsequently abandoned. (5) Dy., followed by Du., rds. אחרים הרו; but where is הורה used for worship of other gods ? *v. 6⁶*. We must choose between (2) and (4).— [בַּל אַסִיךְ וָפְּכֵיהֶם] Hiph. impf. 1 p. of *resolution* in classic style should have cohortative. ‡ נֶסֶךְ vb. Qal cog. acc. *pour out libation* Ex. 30⁹ (P), יֵין Ho. 9⁴, Hiph. same cog. acc. Gn. 35¹⁴ (E) 2 K. 16¹³ Nu. 28⁷ (P), so prob. here, to other gods Je. 7¹⁸, + 7 t. Je. The noun ‡ נֶסֶךְ only here ψ. 𝕲 συναγάγω τὰς συναγωγὰς αὐτῶν, 𝔙 *congregabo conventicula=* אֲסֵף נסכים Qal impf. 1 p. אסף *gather together, collect*, cf. 39², and Niph. ptc. in shortened form, as נספה Is. 13¹⁵, cf. Gn. 49²⁹ 1 S. 13¹¹, inter-

preted of *assemblages* in accordance with אֲסִיפָה NH. ס and פ were easily confused in Egyptian Aram. script. — נָסִכָּם]. It is interpreted by RV., Dr. as
מן of material, *consisting of blood.* Bä. compares Is. 57⁶ 65¹¹, and thinks of
drink offerings connected with the sacrifice of children. De. thinks of the
guilty hands of the offerer. Moll. and Du. refer to Is. 66³ " he that killeth an
ox is as he that slayeth a man." Kirk., "their libations are as detestable as
though they were composed of blood." The usage of מִדָּם favours bloodshed
and not drink offerings of blood, which are unknown to OT. The מן is never
used of material in connection with blood; it is therefore, in the common
sense, of *on account of, because of bloodshed,* as Hb. 2⁸·¹⁷. For this mng. of
prep. v. 5¹¹ 12⁶ 107¹⁷. — [וּבַל אֶשָּׂא אֶת־שְׁמוֹתָם עַל־שְׂפָתָי] phr. *a.λ.* יָשָׂא, in the sense
of *utter, v. 15³,* paraphrased by 𝕲 μνησθῶ, 𝖄 *memor,* so 𝕾, 𝕿. The sf. may
refer to gods, in accordance with Ex. 23¹³ (E), if we interpret אחר of foreign
gods; but if not, it must refer to the apostates, in accordance with Is. 65¹⁵. —
5. מְנָת] *v. 11⁶.* It is prob. that in this case it was originally מְנָתִי *my portion,*
the three words each with sf. in emph. coördination. ‡ חֵלֶק n.m. : (1) *portion,*
acquired possession, of Yahweh as the possession of His people 16⁵ 73²⁶ 119⁶⁷
142⁶; (2) *chosen portion,* in bad sense, 50¹⁸; (3) *portion, award* from God,
punishment 17¹⁴, as Is. 17¹⁴ Jb. 20²⁹ 27¹³. — [תּוֹמִיךְ] is variously explained. It
is pointed as Hiph. impf. 2 sg. after אַתָּה, which is then emph., but without
apparent reason. יָמֵךְ is not, however, used in OT., and the Arabic stem does
not sufficiently explain its use here. 𝕲 σὺ εἶ ὁ ἀποκαθιστῶν τὴν κληρονομίαν
μου ἐμοί, 𝖄 *restitues hereditatem meam mihi,* is based on גּוֹרָלִי לִי הֵמֶךְ, which
gives the missing tone of the tetrameter line and a form which is known and
suits the context. 𝕵 has *possessor sortis meae.* — ‡ תמך vb. Qal: (1) *hold*
fast, c. acc. Am. 1⁵·⁸ as here, c. בְ Ps. 17⁵ Is. 33¹⁵; (2) *sustain,* subj. God,
c. כ pers. Pss. 41¹³ 63⁹ Is. 41¹⁰ 42¹. The conjectural emendations of Ols.
תוֹסִיף, of Hi., Bi. תָּמִיד are not so suited to the context as the above. — [גּוֹרָלִי
sf. 1 p. — ‡ גּוֹרָל] n.m. *lot:* (1) as cast over garments to distribute them 22¹⁹;
(2) as portion assigned by Yahweh 16⁵, espec. the land of the righteous
125³. לִי of the original has fallen out by haplog. The change to אַתָּה is striking and out of harmony with context. It prob. was a substitution for an
original יהוה. — **6.** [נְעִימִים] defective pl. ‡ נָעֵים adj.: (1) *delightful* 133¹ 135³
147¹, as *delightful things* or *places 16⁶·¹¹,* cf. 141⁴ 2 S. 1²³; (2) *lovely,*
beautiful Ps. 81³ 2 S. 23¹ Ct. 1¹⁶. — [אַף] *also, yea,* "introducing emph. a new
thought " B*DB.* — [נַחֲלָת] acc. to 𝕵, 𝕿, Ges.§ 80*g,* Ki., De., a stronger fem. form
for usual נַחֲלָה *(v. 2⁸).* But 𝕲, 𝕾, Hu.³, Ew., We., Kö.ᴵᴵ·⁽¹⁾⁴²⁵, Dr. defectively
written נַחֲלָתִי. — [שָׁפְרָה] Qal pf. 3 f. שפר *a.λ.* in Heb.; in Aram. Dn. 4²⁴ 6²,
be agreeable, acceptable, beautiful; cf. † שֶׁפֶר n. *beauty* Gn. 49²¹. But 𝕲 κρα-
τίστη μοι = יְנָעֲרָה; cf. 103¹¹ 117². 𝕲 gives a well-known word, a usual construction and an appropriate meaning. — **7.** [אֲבָרֵךְ] Pi. impf. 1 p. resolution
would be cohort. form in classic style. *Bless Yahweh,* common in ψ, 26¹²
34² 63⁵ 103¹·²·²⁰·²¹·²²·²² 104¹·³⁵ 115¹⁸ 134¹·² 135¹⁹·²⁰ 145²·¹⁰, אלהים for an
original יהוה 66⁸ 68²⁷; *v. 5¹³* for other uses of ברך. — [יְעָצָנִי] Qal. pf. 3 m. i.p.
sf. 1 pers. ‡ יָעַץ. Vb. Qal *advise, counsel,* c. acc. pers. 16⁷ sq. inf. 62⁵, abs. with

עין, secondary subj. 32⁸. Niph. *consult together,* יהדו 71¹⁰ 83⁶. Hithp. sq. על,
conspire against 83⁴. — [לֵילוֹת] pl. emph. *night seasons,* better *dark nights,* as
pl. abst. intensive; cf. 92³ 134¹. — [יְסְרוּנִי] Pi. pf. 3 pl. sf. i.p. יסר, *v. 2¹⁰,*
discipline, correct, as 94¹² 118¹⁸, subj. God. — 8. [שִׁוִּיתִי] Pi. pf. 1 s. ‡ שׁוה vb.
Pi. *lay, set 16⁸* 119³⁰, *lay upon* 21⁶ 89²³, *set* or *make like* 18³⁴. — [לְנֶגְדִּי] *in front
of, before,* intellectually and morally as 54⁵ 86¹⁴, *v. 5⁶ 10⁵.* — ‡ [תָּמִיד] in ψ only
adv. *continually* 25¹⁵ 40¹² 69²⁴ 71³·⁶·¹⁴ 73²³ 74²³ 104⁴ 109¹⁵·¹⁹ 119⁴⁴·¹⁰⁹·¹¹⁷;
נגדי ת׳ (ל) *16⁸* 38¹⁸ 50⁸ 51⁵, in prayer 34² 72¹⁵; ויאמרו תמיד 35²⁷ = 40¹⁷ = 70⁵, a
favourite term of Is.² 49¹⁶ + 5 t., seldom elsw. apart from ritual, Je. 6⁷ Ho. 12⁷
Dt. 11¹² + 16 t OT., common, however, in P, Ez., Ch. for the *perpetual burnt
offering.* — 9. [לָכֵן] *therefore* "according to such conditions, that being so,"
B*DB.* 200 t. in OT., *16⁹* 73⁶·¹⁰ 78²¹ 119¹¹⁹, *v. 1⁵.* — [שָׂמַח לִבִּי עַל כֵּן] same phr.
105³, c. בי 33²¹. The line has three tones unless we use Makkeph, which
makes rather a long word for one accent, and then add וַיָּגֶל כְּבוֹדִי to complete
the tetrameter. But then the Str. would be one line less than the others.
Du. reduces them by finding a gl. of one line in each Str. We may easily
complete this l. after 33²¹ by adding בי for ביהוה, which fell out by haplog.
of לבי. — [וַיָּגֶל] ו consec. Qal impf. גיל, *v. 2¹¹.* 𝔍 has *et* here as well as for אף
of next line, and also renders by *future,* ignoring the ו consec. It is the only
use of such a ו in the Ps., and is, indeed, against its style. Rd., therefore,
אף יגיל; then the juss. must be abandoned for the indicative. — [כְבוֹדִי] is here
used for the inner man, as 7⁶ ‖ נפש, 108² ‖ לב, 30¹³ subj. זמר, 57⁹ subj. עורה.
We should add also ביהוה. The two lines have been condensed into one by a
prosaic copyist. ‡ [בָּשָׂר], n.m. *flesh* (1) of body, (*a*) of animals 50¹³, (*b*) of
man 27² 38⁴·⁸ 79² 102⁶ 109²⁴; (2) *for the body itself,* antith. נפש 63² Is. 10¹⁸,
Jb. 14²², antith. לב Pss. *16⁹* 84³ Pr. 14³⁰, subj. *trembling* Ps. 119¹²⁰; (3) as
frail over against God 56⁵ 78⁸⁹; (4) כָּל בָּשָׂר *all flesh, all mankind* 65³ 136²⁵
145²¹ Je. 12¹² 25³¹ Ez. 21⁴·⁹·¹⁰ Dt. 5²³. — [וַיִּשְׁכֹּן לָבֶטַח] *v. 4⁹,* † phr. Dt. 33¹² Je. 23⁶
33¹⁶; cf. Dt. 33²⁸ Pr. 1³³. — 10. [נַפְשִׁי] *my soul.* נפש is usually interpreted as
‡ the *inner* being of man as distinguished from the body, 31¹⁰. נַפְשִׁי וּבִטְנִי, sometimes conceived as resting together with the בשר upon a common substratum,
עָלַי 131²; cf. 42⁵·⁷, and especially in ψ as in need of deliverance from שאול
16¹⁰ 30⁴ 49¹⁶ 86¹³ 89⁴⁹; but some of these might be interpreted of another
mng. of נפש, the paraphrase for the personal pronoun, *me, v. 3³.* — [שאול] *v. 6⁶.*
— [לֹא תִתֵּן] Qal impf. 2 m. indic. c. neg. נתן in the sense of *permit,* c. acc.
+ infin. Gn. 20⁶ (E) as here, or acc. + ל nomen. Ps. 132⁴ Pr. 6⁴. — [חֲסִידְךָ]
Kt. pl. is scribal interp. of הֲסִירָךְ, Qr. and Vrss. sg., referring to an individual
pious man, *v. 4⁴.* — [שָׁחַת] the *Pit* in Sheol as distinguished from Sheol itself,
v. 7¹⁶, and not another name for Sheol, or the abstract διαφθοράν 𝔊, *corrup-
tionem,* 𝔍, *corruption* or *destruction,* which are interpretations of the name of
the place. — 11. [ארח חיים] *the path to life.* It might imply resurrection, if the
Ps. were late enough, but at its probable date it implied a path leading to the
presence of God, ‖ את־פניך; a joyous state, antith. שחת, both yet conceived as
parts of the more comprehensive שאול. — [שֹׂבַע] n.m. *fulness* 16¹¹ Dt. 23²⁵
Ru. 2¹⁸, לשׂבע Ex. 16⁸ Lv. 25¹⁹ 26⁵ Pr. 13²⁵ Ps. 78²⁵. — [שְׂמָחוֹת] pl. שִׂמְחָה, *v. 4⁸,*

either *joys*, or abst. pl. *gladness.* — אֶת־פָּנֶיךָ] 21⁷ 140¹⁴, 𝔊 μετὰ τοῦ προσώπου σου, in association with, communion with the divine face or presence, and not *ante vultum tuum* 𝔍, a weakened explanation.

PSALM XVII., 8 str. 3⁵.

Ps. 17 is a prayer for divine interposition in behalf of the righteous (v.¹⁻²). The psalmist has been tested by God in mind and conduct, and approved (v.³⁻⁴ᵃ); he has kept the divine ways and avoided wicked deeds (v.⁴ᵇ⁻⁵), therefore he invokes God with confidence (v.⁶ᵃ). He prays again that his Saviour may show kindness and keep him as the pupil of the eye (v.⁶ᵇ⁻⁸ᵃ); that he may be sheltered from his greedy and arrogant enemies (v.⁸ᵇ⁻¹⁰), who surround him to prey upon him (v.¹¹⁻¹²). Again he prays for the divine interposition and deliverance by the slaying of the wicked (v.¹³⁻¹⁴ᵃ); that penalty may be visited on them to the third generation, but that he himself may enjoy the divine presence (v.¹⁴ᵇ⁻¹⁵).

O HEAR, Yahweh (a righteous man) ; attend to my yell ;
  O give ear to my prayer, which is without lips of deceit ;
  Let my judgment come forth from Thy presence, that mine eyes may behold it.
IN equity Thou hast proved my mind ; Thou hast visited me by night ;
  Thou hast tested me, and Thou findest no evil purpose in me ; my mouth transgresseth not.
  As to deeds of man, (I intend) according to the word of Thy lips.
I ON my part have kept from the ways of the violent ;
  My steps hold fast to Thy tracks, my footsteps slip not ;
  I invoke Thee : for Thou answerest me, 'El.
INCLINE Thine ear to me, hear my speech ;
  Show Thy kind deeds, O Saviour from those who rise up in hostility ;
  I am seeking refuge on Thy right hand ; keep me as the pupil, the daughter of the eye.
HIDE me in the shadow of Thy wings from the wicked,
  Those mine enemies that assail me, with greed encompass me.
  They shut up their gross heart, with their mouth they speak arrogantly.
(THEY advance), now they march about, they fix their eyes ;
  (They purpose) to camp in the land, (they maltreat) as a lion ;
  They are greedy for prey, they are like a young lion lurking in secret places.
O RISE, Yahweh, confront him, cast him down ;
  O deliver me from the wicked, destroy with Thy sword ;
  May they be slain with Thy hand, Yahweh ; slain from the world.
LET their portion be during life ; their belly fill Thou with Thy stored-up penalty
  May their sons be sated, may they leave their residue to their children :
  But as for me, let me behold Thy face ; let me be satisfied with Thy form.

Ps. 17 was in 𝔇, but not in any of the subsequent collections until ψ. It
is rightly termed a תפלה, *prayer* (*v.* Intr. § 1). This probably is original,
because the greater portion of Pss. of 𝔇 were prayers, and there could have
been no reason why the editor of 𝔇, or any subsequent editor, should have
singled out this Ps. as a prayer, rather than a multitude of others. The Ps.
resembles Ps. 16 in words and phrases : שְׁמָרֵנִי v.⁸ = 16¹; communion with God
at night v.³ = 16⁷; the use of אֶל in prayer v.⁶ = 16¹; the vb. תמך v.⁵ = 16⁵;
the reference to the hand of God as protecting and defending v.⁷·¹⁴ = 16⁸;
the contrasted portions of the poet and the wicked v.¹⁴⁻¹⁵ = 16²⁻⁶; the longing
for the divine presence v.¹⁵ = 16¹¹. All this favours a similar situation, if not
the same author. The use of חלר v.¹⁴ is the same as that of 49², cf. Is. 38¹¹,
although the phr. of the latter and the conception are different. There is a
reference in the use of פנים and תמונה of God, v.¹⁵ to Nu. 12⁸ (E). The
visitation of penalty on the third generation v.¹⁴ is based on the Ten Words
Ex. 20⁵ = Dt. 5⁹. The conception of righteousness v.⁴⁻⁵ is that of D, and prior
to P. And yet the conception of truthfulness v.¹ and the testing the mind
v.³, show the higher ethical conception of the Persian period. The phr.
הפלה חסר v.⁷ = 4⁴, בצל כנפיך v.⁸ = 36⁸ 57² 63⁸, cf. 61⁵ 91⁴ (all post-exilic
Pss.) Ru. 2¹², implies the existence of the temple and probably the cherubic
throne. The pupil of the eye v.⁸ = Dt. 32¹⁰. The Ps. must belong to the
Persian period subsequent to the Restoration and prior to the reform of Ezra,
a time of greater peril than that of Ps. 16, and therefore later than Zerubbabel. The Ps. was originally the prayer of an individual. It has been
generalised and made into a congregational prayer.

Part I. has three pentameter tristichs, the first of these a petition in two syn. lines followed by a synth. line. — **1–2**. *O hear* ‖
attend ‖ *give ear*], the usual terms for importurate prayer, v. 4⁴ 5²·³.
— (*a righteous man*)], so 𝔍 in accordance with v.³⁻⁶, more probable than " my righteousness," 𝔊, 𝔘, or simply " righteousness."
𝔥, Dr., or inexactly " the right " EVˢ., " righteous cause " JPSV.
— *my yell*], shrill, piercing cry for help, ‖ *my prayer*, as 61² 88³. —
without lips of deceit]. The lips which utter the prayer are sincere, entirely truthful. — *My judgment*], either my just cause, or
judgment in my favour. — *come forth from Thy presence*], from the
judgment throne of Yahweh in heaven, cf. 9⁵. — *that mine eyes
may behold it*]. He desires a visible manifestation from God that
He has vindicated him. — *In equity*] properly goes with the next
line as qualifying the divine proving. To make it an object of
behold, with 𝔥 and Vrss. destroys the measure of both lines. —
3–4a. The second tristich is composed of three lines essentially
syn. : yet there is synth. in part, in the second line, and in greater

degree in the third. — *Thou hast proved ‖ hast tested*], v. 7^{10} 12^{7}.
This has been by a personal visitation. Yahweh has not remained
afar off on His throne in heaven ; but has come down in spiritual
presence to the bed of the psalmist. — *visited by night*], during the
quiet hours, when he was alone by himself, and so most open to
inspection ; and especially so, as the inspection had to do not only
with acts done during the day, the usual time of activity, but still
more searchingly with the mind, which often is most active while
the body is at rest. — *Thou findest no evil purpose in me*], as 10^{4}
26^{10} 119^{150}. There was no evil in the mind after the most searching examination. — *My mouth transgresseth not*]. This statement,
intermediate between the purpose of the mind and *the deeds of
man*, external actions, supplements the previous clause and is still
connected with the test by night. It probably refers to private,
secret utterances, rather than words spoken publicly to other persons. And so, while deeds of men are mentioned, that is ordinary
human actions, yet these are deeds not as done, but as intended,
purposed ; for so we should translate, inserting in the text the vb.
(*I intend*). This insertion removes the difficulty of the verse
and explains the antith. between " deeds of man " and *according
to word of Thy lips*. The intent of the psalmist was that his
deeds should be according to the word which came forth from
the lips of God. Having set forth the righteousness of his mind,
as attested by divine inspection, he now turns to a justification of
his conduct. — **4b–6a.** The third tristich is composed of an antithetical couplet followed by a synth. line returning to v.^{1a}, the
ground of assurance in prayer having been given. — *I on my part*],
emph. personal asseveration, on the negative side, *have kept from
the ways of the violent*], the deeds of those who commit robbery or
murder, or both. On the positive side, *My steps hold fast to Thy
tracks*], those prescribed by God in the Deuteronomic laws. — *My
footsteps slip not*]. The context suggests the complement of the
previous clause ; the steps hold fast on the positive side and do
not slip from the divine tracks on the other. Elsewhere the phrase
is used for the firm standing, the security of the righteous under
the divine protection, *v.* 10^{6}. If we follow that meaning here, we
have an expression of confidence in accordance with v.^{6a}.

Part II. has three pentameter tristichs, setting forth the rela-

tion of the poet to his enemies, antith. to the previous part,
setting forth his relation to his God.   The first tristich is petition
∥ v.¹⁻², an introductory line and a syn. couplet synth. thereto. —
6b–8a. *Show Thy kind deeds*], cf. 4⁴, literally " make them mar-
vellous," or " wonderful," in accordance with v.²ᵇ ; let them be
visible in acts of vindication of the righteous. — *O Saviour*], title
of Yahweh as one whose character and habit it is to save His
people from their enemies ; especially characteristic of Is.² — *I
am seeking refuge*].   By an unfortunate transposition of the
original text it has been attached as an object to the ptc., forcing
the rendering with verbal force as ptc. absolute " savest," and then
as a general truth applying to all persons seeking refuge, without
specification of the place of refuge.   This also destroys the
measure of the two lines and makes their interpretation difficult.
Attaching it to, *on Thy right hand*], we get the place of refuge,
recover the measures, and find an easy and natural explanation
in accordance with good usage.   The right hand of God is often
the instrument of judgment and blessing, but also the place of
safety, as 16⁸⋅ ¹¹.   The resemblance of Pss. 16 to 17 in so many
other respects favours the same meaning of right hand of God
here.   This also is a proper basis for the closer and affectionate
care indicated in the phr. : *Keep me as the pupil of the eye*], as
Dt. 32¹⁰ Pr. 7² ∥ *the daughter of the eye*, a Hebraism as La. 2¹⁸, expressing a filial relation, implying affectionate care.   The second
tristich has also an introductory line with a synonymous couplet
synthetic to it. — **8b–10.** *Hide me in the shadow of Thy wings*],
a favourite conception of poets of the Restoration 36⁸ 57² 63⁸,
cf. 61⁵ 91⁴ Ru. 2¹².   It is usually referred to the care of the
mother bird for her young ; not, however, the hen, Mt. 23³⁷, which
is not used in OT., but rather the eagle, cf. Dt. 32¹¹, though the
working out of the simile is different.   It probably, however,
refers to the cherubic wings of the most Holy Place of the temple
in accord with the frequent conception that the temple itself is
a sure refuge for the people of God, involving the idea that the
protecting cherubic wings extended their influence to the holy
temple and the holy city and its inhabitants. — *from the wicked*].
These are, as the context shows, not wicked Israelites, but wicked
nations, who oppress and maltreat the Israelites, cf. 9⁴⋅ ⁶⋅ ¹³. —

Mine enemies that assail me]. They assault, act violently. — *with greed*], cf. 107⁹. They are not only violent, but greedy for their prey. — *encompass me*], surround so as to make escape impossible, *v.* v.¹¹. — *They shut up their gross heart*]. They are not only greedy, but pitiless. They are so greedy that they have become fat and gross; their midriff, the seat of feelings, has become exceedingly insensible. "They have closed it against every influence for good and all sympathy" Kirk. It is necessary in accordance with English usage to substitute heart for midriff. — *with their mouth*], antith. with the mouth of the poet, v.³ᵇ. — *they speak arrogantly*], v. 10² for the same kind of enemies and a similar situation. — **11–12.** The third tristich describes the action of these enemies in three progressive pentameters — (*They advance*)], as 𝕵, resuming the thought of v.⁹. This is much better suited to the context than "our steps" MT., EVˢ., which is not well sustained, and is difficult to construct and understand in this context. The enemies advance to the attack. —*now*], graphic description. — *they march about*], the people of God, probably the holy city, as 55¹¹. — *they fix their eyes*], watching intently, so that no movement of Israel may escape them, showing their greed v.⁹ᵇ. — (*They purpose*) *to camp in the land*]. This is a most difficult clause in the original, and is variously explained in Vrss. and commentaries. The difficulty may be removed by finding the verb, missing in this line, to complete the measure. The infinitive that follows then becomes intelligible, having the ordinary meaning, "pitch," which is used without its usual object "tent," syn. with English "encamp." We then have the enemy purposing to encamp in the land, and so besiege the people, cf. Jb. 19¹², and a very natural and appropriate progress in the activity of the enemy. The various renderings: "turning their eyes down to the ground" PBV., "bowing down to the earth" AV., "to cast us down to the earth" RV., "to spread out in the land" JPSV., all depending on MT., show how impracticable it is to get a good sense on that basis. — *they maltreat as a lion*]. This refers to the acts of violence of a besieging army ravaging for prey, seizing it with violence and abusing it without pity. — *They are greedy for prey*], reiterating v.⁹ᵇ. — *like a young lion lurking in secret places*]. They lie in ambush and lurk for their prey, to fall on it unawares.   This situation resembles very much that of Ps. 10⁸⁻¹⁰.

Part III. has two pentameter tristichs, a petition that Yahweh may by theophanic interposition destroy the wicked enemies and let the people see His presence. — **13–14a.** The first tristich is syn. — *O rise, Yahweh*], as frequent in such prayers 3⁸ 7⁷ 9²⁰ 10¹². — *confront him*], in hostility, cf. 18⁶· ¹⁹. — *cast him down*], overthrow and prostrate in death, as 18⁴⁰. — *O deliver me from the wicked*], the enemies, cf. v.⁹ᵃ. — *destroy with Thy sword*]. Yahweh interposes as a warrior, and so uses His sword, as 7¹³ (cf. 35¹⁻³ for God's use of other warlike weapons). It is necessary, however, to supply a missing verb to complete the measure of line. This was probably "destroy." The omission lies back of 頄 and Vrss., several of which take "sword" as in relative clause, "who is Thy sword" PBV., AV. The idea, though a good one after the analogy of Is. 10⁵, is yet inappropriate to the context, and calls attention needlessly from the main thought and its ready advance to a climax. RV., JPSV. rightfully render " by Thy sword." — *May they be slain by Thy hand*]. This rendering is in accord with the context, the use of the sword by Yahweh, and with a strict interpretation of the unpointed Hebrew text, and is favoured by ancient Vrss. The MT. is pointed so as to give the rendering "men," both here and in the next clause, "from men of Thy hand — from the men" PBV., "from men which are Thy hand" AV., "from men by Thy hand" RV., JPSV., none of which are satisfying. — *from the world*], away from the world, so as no longer to live in the world, *v.* 49², cf. Is. 38¹¹. "O Lord, destroy them from off the earth, which they inhabit" Aug. The usual rendering "from the evil world" PBV., "men of the world" AV., RV., implies an antith. between the world as evil and the righteous Israelite, which while in accord with the NT., Jn. 15¹⁹, is not in accord with the OT. religion and has no justification whatever in OT. usage. This supposed antith. has occasioned a general misinterpretation of the subsequent context, as if it contrasted the earthly joys of the wicked with the heavenly joys of the righteous; which also is a later Biblical conception, but not justified at such a date as that of our Ps. The idea can only be gained by awkward adjustments and renderings. This closing tristich is indeed a continuation of the petition for divine interposition, and contrasts the visitation upon the wicked in a synth. couplet with the vindication of the righteous in the closing line, and so is harmonious with the petition with which the Ps. opens. — **14b–15.** *Let their portion be during life*] ; that is, the portion allotted to them as penalty, as Is. 17^{14} Jb. 20^{29} 27^{13}, and not a good portion enjoyed by them in this life, but no longer to be theirs. — *their belly fill Thou with Thy stored-up penalty*], as Jb. 21^{19} ; and not treasures of wealth, in accordance with other interpretations. This penalty they are to partake of to the full extent of their capacity. Their belly is to be filled with it, and yet it will not be exhausted. It passes over to their sons. — *may their sons be sated*], may they also be so filled that they cannot partake of any more ; and still further in the climax — *may they leave their residue to their children*]. There still remains to the sons a residue of this penalty that they cannot appropriate. This they transmit as an inheritance of woe to their children ; and so the ancient law is fulfilled, in a visiting of the iniquity of the fathers upon the children unto the third and fourth generation, Ex. 20^5 = Dt. 5^9. In antith. with this dreadful punishment of the enemies, the poet prays for himself — *let me behold Thy face*], unfolding the thought of v.^{2}. A later editor, doubtless influenced by v.^{1}, inserts " in righteousness " as a qualification ; thereby destroying the measure, making the first half of this line of four tones instead of three. — *let me be satisfied with Thy form*], the form of God ; that is, as seen in the theophanic vindication, based on the conception of the privilege of Moses, Nu. 12^8. The form of God gratifies and satisfies the psalmist, while the wicked are sated with the divine penalty. This conception of beholding the face and form of God, gave difficulty to later editors ; and so 𝕲, 𝕵, paraphrase " when Thy glory appears," thus interpreting it correctly as theophanic in character. In 𝕳 a scribe inserted " when I awake " so EV^s., which he probably meant to be interpreted, as awakening from the sleep of death, when the vision of the face and form of God was conceived as possible to the highly privileged righteous. But the vb. without suffix leaves other interpretations open, such as awakening from the sleep of anxiety and sorrow, or awakening in the morning from a night of anxiety

and petition.   The insertions of 𝕲 and 𝕳 make the last half of
the line into three tones instead of the needed two, and thus
destroy the measure of the closing part of the Ps. as well as the
return to the conception of the petition with which it began.

1. צֶדֶק] as obj. of hearing.   צִדְקִי 𝕲, 𝖁 is novel and dub., rd. with 𝕵 *justum*
צַדִּיק, *v. 1⁵ 4².* —   רִנָּתִי] sf. 1 pers.   ‡ רִנָּה n.f.: (1) *jubilation*, antith בְּכִי 30⁵,
רמעה 126⁵ᐟ⁶, הודה || 107²², שִׁשׂוּן 105⁴⁸, שׂחוק 126², קוֹל רִנָּה קיל 42⁵ 47² 118¹⁵;
(2) *yell* for help 106⁴⁴ 119¹⁶⁹ 142⁷, || הִפְדָּה 17¹ 61² 88³. — בְּלֹא] α.λ. ψ unless
possibly 10³ acc. 𝕲, 𝕵; but Je. 22¹³ Is. 55¹+ in the sense *without* (Ps. 44¹³
בלא is different, לא belonging to משפט). — **2.** דִּלְפָנֶיךָ] emph. compound prep.
with sf. 2 m. *from before.*   ‡ מלפני: (1) *at the presence* of God 97⁵ᐟ ⁵ 114⁷ᐟ⁷;
(2) *away from* 51¹³, cf. use with נכרח Je. 16¹⁷ 31³⁶ 33¹⁸ Is. 48¹⁹; (2) *pro-
ceeding from* Ps. *17²*. — מִשְׁפָּטִי] also emph., *my just cause* or *judgment in my
favour, v. 1⁶.* — יֵצֵא] juss. *continuing petition*, as Dr., Bä.   The sentence
coming forth from the decision of the judge, cf. Hb. 1⁴ᐟ⁴ for Qal and Ps. 37⁶
Je. 51¹⁰, Hiph. — עֵינֶיךָ] emph. 𝕲 עֵינֵי prob. both interpretations of noun
without sf. — תֶּחֱזֶינָה] final clause. subjunctive not juss. — וְיִשָׁרִים] makes the
l. too long and is needed in next l.   If with חזה, it must be adv. *rightly*, a
mng. elsw. Ct. 1⁴.   In ψ it is used in the ethical sense of equity in government, *v. 9⁹.* — **3.** תִּמְצָא] statement of fact, result of divine inspection as Dr.,
rather than conditional clause without usual particles as Bä., Du. — זַמֹּתִי]
Qal pf. 1 m. Kö.*Syntax, p.124* Ges. §*67ee*.   ‡ זמם vb. *devise*, in bad sense as 31¹⁴
37¹², cf. Je. 4²⁸.   Bä. regards it as inf. cstr. Ew.§ ²³⁸.   But 𝕲, 𝖁, Aq., Σ, 𝕵
and most comm. rd. זַמֹּתִי or זְמֹתִי, better זמה בי for measure as 𝕾, Grimme.   𝕲
properly attaches it to מצא as obj.   ‡ זִמָּה n.f. *evil device, purpose* elsw. 26¹⁰
119¹⁵⁰, cf. מְזִמָּה *104*. — בַּל־יַעֲבָר־פִּי] the two Makkephs enable one to distribute
the two accents better for euphony.   פִי is prob. subj. and not obj.   This is
not a final clause, as Dr., but statement of fact, as Bä., Kirk.   עבר is then in
the sense of *transgress*, abs. only here, but c. acc. 148³ Nu. 14⁴¹ Jos. 7¹¹ᐟ ¹⁵
Dt. 17²+. — **4.** לִפְעֻלּוֹת אָדָם] the prep. ל has the force of *as for, as regards*
Dr.   This is to be preferred to the temporal force *at*, Bä., cf. 32⁶.   ‡ פְּעֻלָּה]
n.f.: (1) *work*, pl. *deeds* of men *174*, of Yahweh 28⁵; (2) *wages* in punishment 109²⁰.   It is a favourite word of Is.², of actions of wicked 65⁷, of wages
40¹⁰ 49⁴ 61⁸ 62¹¹, infrequent elsw.   Dy., Du. rd. אֶדֹּם *I keep silent.* The l. is
defective; a word is missing; rd. אָרָם אֶדֹּם, the latter omitted by haplog.   אָרָם
is contr. of אֲדַמֶּה Pi. impf. 1 pers.   ‡ דָּמָה Qal *be like, resemble* sq. ־ 89⁷ 102⁷
144⁴; Pi. *liken, imagine, think* c. acc. 48¹⁰, obj. clause 50²¹, here *intend* as
Nu. 33⁵⁶ (J) Ju. 20⁵ Is. 10⁷.   This gives an appropriate sense.   𝕲 by its different division of verses increases the difficulty. — אָרְחוֹ־] *v. 8⁹.*   𝕾 prefixes
כְּמֹ.   This may be explanatory; and yet it gives us the missing tone, removes
a difficult phrase, and enables us to explain after Jos. 6¹⁸, cf. Dt. 4⁹ *take heed,
beware of.* — † פָּרִיץ] n.m. *violent one*, robber or murderer elsw. Is. 35⁹ Je. 7¹¹
Ez. 7²² 18¹⁰ Dn. 11¹⁴. — **5.** תָּמֹךְ] Qal inf. abs. תָּמַךְ *v. 16⁵.*   𝕲, 𝖁, Σ, Θ, 𝕵, 𝕿

have imv. — הַעֲגָלוֹתֶיךָ] f. pl. sf. 2 m., cf. Pr. 5²¹ from sg. — ‡ מַעֲגָּל] n. *track* in fig. sense of snares of wicked 140⁶, course of life 23⁸, prescribed by Yahweh 17⁵, those traversed by Him 65¹². — **6.** הַט־אָזְנֶךָ] vb. imv. Hiph. נטה c. acc. אֹזֶן; phr. elsw. of man 45¹¹ 49⁵ 78¹, of God 17⁶ 31⁸ 71² 86¹ 88⁸ 102³ 116². — **7.** הַפְלֵה חֲסָדֶיךָ] *v. 4ᵇ.* — מוֹשִׁיעַ] should be connected with מְמָקוֹמְמִים (with two tones). — הֹקִים] rd. חוֹסָה and attach to בִּימִינֶךָ. It has been transposed by txt. err. These two words then belong to the next line in v.⁸ to make both lines of normal measure. — **8.** אִישׁוֹן] n.m. diminutive of אִישׁ *pupil* of eye, elsw. Dt. 32¹⁰ Pr. 7²; *midst* of night Pr. 7⁹, cf. 20²⁰(?). — בַּת־עַיִן] syn. term elsw. La. 2¹⁸. — בְּצֵל] emph. ‡ צֵל n.m.: (1) *shadow*, *shade*, protection from sun, fig. 80¹¹, of Yahweh 91¹ 121⁵, צ כְּנָפֶיךָ 17⁸ 36⁸ 57² 63⁸, cf. 91⁴ Ru. 2¹², where כָּנָף alone is used; (2) *shadow* as symbol of the transitoriness of life 144⁴, cf. 102¹² 109²³. — **9.** מִפְּנֵי רְשָׁעִים] depends on previous context to complete its line. — זוּ] rel. as 9¹⁶. — שַׁדּוּנִי] Qal pf. 3 m. pl. sf. 1 sg. ‡ שדד: *act violently towards 17⁹; lay waste* 91⁶ 137⁸. — בְּנֶפֶשׁ] *with greed* Bä., Dr. נכש in this sense ‡ as seat of appetite: (a) hunger 78¹⁸ 107⁹, with some form of שׂבע 63⁶ 107⁹ Is. 56¹¹ Je. 50¹⁹ Ez. 7¹⁹, with other terms Pss. 106¹⁵ 107¹⁸; (b) thirst for God 42².³ 63² 143⁵; (c) more general *greed 17⁹*, cf. 107⁵, v. 103. — יַקִּיפוּ] Hiph. impf. 3 pl. ‡ נקף Hiph.: (1) *go round about* a city 48¹⁸; (2) *surround, encompass* c. על pers. 17⁹ 88¹⁸, c. acc. pers. 22¹⁷. — **10.** חֶלְבָּמוֹ] emph. ‡ חֵלֶב *fat* (1) of human body, of *midriff*, v. RS. *Religion of Semites* 360; so here, unreceptive mind; sf. archaic for ◌ָם for better rhythm, also 119⁷⁰ and prob. 73⁷; (2) of beasts as rich food 63⁶; (3) *choicest, best* of wheat 81¹⁷ 147¹⁴, cf. Dt. 32¹⁴ Is. 34⁶. — פֵּימוֹ] פֶּה c. archaic sf. emph. v. v.³ — ‡ גַּאוּת] n.f.: (1) *swelling* of sea 89¹⁰; (2) *majesty* of God 93¹; (3) *pride, haughtiness, arrogance 17¹⁰*, possibly 74²⁰, v. גֵּאֶה 10². — **11.** אֲשֻׁרֵנוּ] n. sf. 1 pl. so 𝕿. † אַשֻּׁר] n.f. *step, going* elsw. Jb. 31⁷. It is improb. that it is different from אָשׁוּר v.⁵; the pointing here might be either txt. err. or a conceit of the punctuators, but is prob. a relict of tradition that it was Pi. of vb. Vrss. have vb., 𝕲 ἐκβάλλοντές με, 𝖅 *projicientes me* = גֵּרְשׁוּנִי, 𝕴 *incedentes*, Σ. μακαρίζοντές με, so 𝕾. אֲשֻׁרֵנִי in both mngs. prob. original in sense of 𝕴, as Cap. — סְבָבוּנִי] Kt., 𝕲, 𝕴, 𝕾 סְבָבוּנוּ Qr. The sfs. with both vbs. in all texts and Vrss. are interpretations and were not original. ‡ סָבַב vb. Qal *turn about*, of Jordan לְאָחוֹר *back* 114⁸·⁵; c. impf. almost auxil. as שׁוּב 71²¹(?); (2) *march* or *walk about* a city 48¹⁸ so here; (3) *surround, encompass*, fig. c. acc. 18⁶ 22¹⁸·¹⁷ 49⁶ 88¹⁸ 118¹⁰·¹¹·¹²; c. double acc. 109⁸. Polel: (1) *encompass* c. acc., subj. divine הסר 32¹⁰, cf. v.⁷(dub.); (2) *assemble round* c. acc. pers. 7⁸; (3) *march* or *go about* a place 55¹¹ 59⁷·¹⁵, an altar 26⁶. — יְעֵינֵיהֶם] emph. construe with יָשִׁיתוּ graphic impf., cf. 48¹⁴ 62¹¹ (c. לֵב). — לִנְטוֹת בָּאָרֶץ] belongs to the next v. to make measures correct. The inf. cstr. נטה with ל is emph. dependent on some vb. given or understood. נטה c. בָּאָרֶץ v.⁶, cf. Jb. 15²⁹ c. לָאָרֶץ. It is prob. that in both נטה is contr. of נטה אהל *pitched the tent* Gn. 12⁸ 26²⁵ 35²¹ (J) 33¹⁹ (E). *To pitch the tent, camp in the land*, suits the context and is especially appropriate after previous vbs. as I have interpreted them. — **12.** דְּרְ־] n. sf. 3 sg. † דִּמְיוֹן] a.λ. *likeness*, so 𝕴, 𝕿, Aq., 𝕾, but 𝕲 ὑπέλαβον με, 𝔙 *susceperunt me* = רְמוּנִי Cap. רמה Pi. *think, purpose* as v.[4]. A word is missing in the line. If now we separate ינו from (ו)דְמ, we get the missing word: then דְּמוּ is the principal vb. upon which לנטוה depends, coming at close of clause, as frequent in this Ps. *To pitch (their tents) in the land they intended* or *thought, v.* v.[4]. Then ינו is Qal pf. 3 pl., prob. for הוּנוּ Hiph. ‡ יָנָה vb. Qal *oppress* 123[4] Qr., *suppress* 74[8] (?). Hiph. *oppress, maltreat*, as Is. 49[26] Je. 22[3] Ez. 18[7]. — [יִכְסִיף] txt. err. for יכספו by transposition of ו. † כסף vb. Qal *long for* c. ל 17[12] Jb. 14[15], Niph. same Ps. 84[3] Gn. 31[30], abs. Zp. 2[1] (?). — ‡ כְּפִיר n.m. *young lion* 17[12] 104[21], ‖ שחל 91[13], of bloodthirsty enemies 34[11] 35[17] 58[7]. — **13**. [הַרְדִּמָה] Pi. imv. cohort. ‡ קדם vb. Pi. denom.: (1) *meet, confront* c. acc. 18[6. 19] 17[13]; come to meet as friend 21[4] 59[11] (?) 79[8], ‖ 88[14], face of Yahweh 95[2], cf. 89[15]; *go before, in front of* 68[26]; *be beforehand* 119[147]; *anticipate, forestall* 119[148]. — [הַכְרִיעֵהוּ] Hiph. imv. cohort. with sf. 3 m. ‡ כָּרַע vb. Qal *bow down* in worship 22[30] 72[9] 95[6], of enemies in death 20[9]. † Hiph. *cause to bow down* in death 17[13] 78[31], c. תַּחַת 18[40] (= 2 S. 22[40]) Ju. 11[35] (in grief). — [פַּלְּטָה] Pi. imv. cohort. ‡ [פלט] vb. Pi. *deliver* esp. of Yahweh, c. acc. pers. 22[5. 9] 31[2] 37[40] 71[2] 82[4] 91[14], c. מִן *from* 17[13] 18[44. 49] 43[1] 71[4], ptc. c. sfs. 18[3] 40[18] 70[6] 144[2]; elsw. in this sense Mi. 6[14]. — [וּנַפְשִׁי] *me, v. 3[3]*. — [רָשָׁע] coll. as 9[6], *v. 1[1]*. — [חַרְבְּךָ] acc. instrument with sf. 7[13]. 𝔖 *has and from the sword;* but 𝔊, 𝔍 take it as relative clause, *who is Thy sword*. The line is defective; insert חֶרֶב Qal imv. as Je. 50[21. 27] omitted by haplog. — **14**. מְמְתִים *bis* emph., so 𝔍 has *a viris manus tuae* interp. as prep. מִן. ‡ [מַת] *male, man*. מְתֵי מִסְפָּר *men of number* Gn. 34[30] (J) Dt. 4[27] Je. 44[28] Ps. 105[12], *men*, simply 17[14. 14], מתי שוא 26[4], Jb. 11[11], מ' און 22[15] מ' סורי 19[19]. The testimony of 𝔍 is vitiated by the rendering *qui mortui sunt* in the second instance; Σ ἀπὸ νεκρῶν, so 𝔖, Aq. ἀπὸ τεθνηκότων, point to מְמֵתִים *from the dead.* 𝔊 ἀπὸ ἐχθρῶν, 𝔙 *inimicis* for the first, and for the second ὀλίγων 𝔊ᴺᴬᴿ, 𝔙 *paucis*. But 𝔊ᴮ has in the second case ἀπολύων, so Aug. It is better to read in both instances Hoph. ptc. of vb. מומתים, as 2 K. 11[2] defectively written as ממתים *may they be slain with Thy hand.* ‡ מות vb. Qal: (1) *die* of natural causes, man 41[6] 49[11] 82[7] 118[17], מֵת *dead man* 31[13], מֵתִים 88[6. 11] 115[17], מתי עולם 143[3] = La. 3[6], זְבְחֵי מֵתִים Ps. 106[28]. (For מות 9[1] 48[15] *v.* Intr.§34.) Polel *kill, put to death*, c. acc. 34[22] 109[16] Ju. 9[54] 1 S. 17[51] Je. 20[17]. Hiph. *kill, put to death* Ps. 37[32] 59[1] Ez. 13[19], fish Ps. 105[29]. Hoph. *be put to death* would then be here and 2 K. 11[2] +. — † [חֶלֶד] n.m. *duration:* (1) of life 39[6] 89[48] Jb. 11[17], cf. Ps. 39[5]; (2) of world Ps. 17[14] 49[2], cf. 11[4] Is. 38[11]. מֵחֶלֶד *out of the world*, removed from it by death. — [צְפִינֶךָ] α.λ. Kt. n.(m.) *treasure*, but Qr. צפונך Qal ptc. pass. *treasured*, in either case stored-up penalty as Jb. 21[19] *v. 108*. — [וְהִנִּיחוּ] ו conseq. pf. Hiph. 3 pl. ‡ נוח Qal *rest, settle down*, sq. על 125[3], cf. Gn. 8[4] 2 S. 21[10] Is. 7[2]. Hiph.: (1) *let remain, leave, bequeath* 17[14], cf. Ec. 2[18]; (2) *abandon* c. ל pers. Ps. 119[121]; (3) *permit* c. acc. pers. 105[14]. — **15**. [וַאֲנִי] emph. — [בְּצֶדֶק] emph. *v.* v.[1]. It is a gl. of qualification, making line too long. — [בְּהָקִיץ] Hiph. inf. cstr. בְּ temporal. קיץ *v. 3[6]*, here sleep of death as Is. 26[19] Dn. 12[2]. It is a gl. of interpretation. 𝔊 has a different gl. ἐν τῷ ὀφθῆναι — † [תְּמוּנָה] n.f.: (1) *likeness, representation* of idols Ex. 20[4] = Dt. 5[8], cf. 4[16. 23. 25];

(2) *form*, *semblance* of Yahweh here, so Aq., Σ as Nu. 12⁸, cf. Dt. 4¹².¹⁵, of apparition at night Jb. 4¹⁶. 𝕲 interprets τὴν δόξαν σου, 𝖁 *gloria tua*, Θ δεξιάν σου = יְמִינֶ֑ךָ, 𝖘 אֱמוּנָתֶֽךָ, all these due to a shrinking from the thought of a *form* of God. Aq., Σ, 𝕵, 𝕿 all regard תְּמוּנָה as obj. of שׂבע and the parall. demands it.

PSALM XVIII., 2 PTS. OF 3 STRS. 14³.

Ps. 18, originally an ode of victory of David over his enemies, was subsequently adapted to public worship. I. David praises Yahweh as his Saviour from a deadly peril described under the metaphor of drowning. He heard his cry for help (v.³⁻⁷) ; His anger caused earth and heaven to quake ; He descended upon a cherubic chariot in a storm cloud (v.⁸⁻¹³). Thunder, lightning, and earthquake were His weapons, and He delivered David from his peril and became his stay (v.¹⁴⁻²⁰). II. David praises God as his lamp and shield, who girded him with strength for war (v.²⁹⁻³⁵), giving him a broad position on which to pursue his enemies and exterminate them (v.³⁷⁻⁴³) ; delivered him from the strivings of his own people, made him head of nations, and doeth kindness to the anointed seed of David forever (v.⁴⁴⁻⁴⁵ᵃ·⁴⁷⁻⁴⁹·⁵¹). The ode was generalised for public worship by several changes in the body of the song ; but especially (1) by prefixing an assertion of love to Yahweh (v.²) ; (2) by inserting two glosses, the first teaching that God rewards according to righteousness (v.²¹⁻²⁴) ; the second, that God acts towards men just as they act towards others, especially in saving the humble and humiliating the lofty (v.²⁵⁻²⁸) ; (3) a reference to nations cringing, in the spirit of later times (v.⁴⁵ᵇ⁻⁴⁶) ; and (4) a resolution of liturgical praise (v.⁵⁰).

PART I.

MY crag and my fortress and my deliverer,
  My God, my Rock in whom I seek refuge,
  My shield and horn of my salvation, my high tower,
  (My Saviour, from violence Thou savest me).
  Worthy to be praised I proclaim Yahweh,
  Since from mine enemies I am saved.
  The (breakers) of death encompassed me,
  And torrents of Belial fell upon me ;
  Cords of Sheol came round me,
  Snares of Death came to meet me ;

In my distress I called upon Yahweh,
And unto my God cried for help;
And He heard from His palace my voice,
And my cry for help (came) before Him in His ears.
THEN the earth swayed and quaked,
And the foundations of (the heavens) trembled,
And tossed to and fro because He burned with anger;
Smoke went up in His nostril,
And fire from His mouth devoured;
Coals were kindled from Him.
Then He bowed the heavens and came down,
Thick darkness under His feet;
And He rode upon the cherub and flew,
And swooped down upon wings of wind;
And put darkness round about Him,
A covering (of) darkness of waters,
Thick clouds of the skies without brightness;
Before Him passed His thick clouds.
THEN Yahweh thundered (from) heaven,
And Elyon gave forth His voice;
And sent forth His arrows and scattered them,
And (flashed) flashes and made them rumble;
And the channels of the (sea) appeared,
(And) the foundations of the world were laid bare.
He sends from on high, He takes me,
He draws me out of many waters;
He delivers me from my strong enemy,
And from those hating me; for they were too strong for me:
Who came to meet me in the day of my calamity.
And so Yahweh became a stay to me,
And led me forth into a wide place,
And rescued me, because He took pleasure in me.

Part II.

FOR Thou art my lamp, Yahweh,
My God who lightens my darkness:
For in Thee I run up to a troop,
And in my God I leap a wall.
The 'El whose way is perfect,
A shield is He to the one seeking refuge in Him.
For who is a God (like) Yahweh?
And who is a Rock (like) our God?
The 'El who girdeth me with strength,
And made my way perfect;
Who setteth my feet like hinds,
And upon high places made me hold my ground;
Who teacheth my hands for war,
And maketh mine arms bronze.

THOU broadenest my steps under me,
    And my limbs do not slip;
    I pursue mine enemies and I overtake them;
    And I return not until I have finished them.
    (And) I smote them down so that they could not rise,
    (And) they fell under my feet.
    And Thou girdest me with strength for war,
    Thou causeth them that rise up against me to bow down under me;
    And mine enemies Thou madest give the back to me,
    And them that hate me I exterminated.
    And they cry for help, but there is no saviour,
    Unto Yahweh, but He doth not answer them;
    And I beat them small as dust of the earth,
    And as clay of the streets pulverised them.
THOU deliverest me from the strivings of (my) people;
    Thou settest me to be head of nations;
    A people I knew not serve me,
    At the hearing of the ear shew themselves obedient to me.
    Liveth and blessed is my Rock,
    And the God of my salvation is exalted.
    The 'El who giveth to me deeds of vengeance,
    And who bringeth down peoples under me,
    And who bringeth me forth from mine enemies,
    And lifteth me up above them that rise up against me,
    From the man of violence rescueth me;
    Who magnifieth acts of salvation to His king,
    And doeth kindness to His anointed,
    To David and to his seed forever.

The Ps. is described in the title as הַשִּׁירָה *the song*, just as other odes of victory over enemies bear this title, Ex. 15[1] (ode of victory over the Egyptians); Dt. 31[30] (Moses' ode of the triumph of Yahweh); cf. Ju. 5[1] (Deborah's ode, where vb. שִׁיר is used). The original form of the title is given in 2 S. 22[1], " And David spake unto Yahweh the words of this song in the day that Yahweh delivered him from the hand of all his enemies and from the hand of Saul." This has been adopted by an editor of the Ps., only changing the second כַּף to the familiar יד for richness of expression, and removing the name of David into the principal clause, making the rest a relative clause and prefixing אשר לדוד יהוה לעבד. This raises the question whether לדוד here has the same meaning as in the other titles of Pss., all the more that the term *servant of Yahweh* precedes it. The titles both represent David as the speaker in the ode, and probably also designate him as the author. It is doubtful, therefore, whether the ode was in 𝔇. It was in 𝔇𝔯, and was probably taken from 2 S. 22. The text of 2 S. has many variations from that of the Ps. It lacks its Aramaisms: רחם v.[1], גְּבַר v.[26], הרג v.[46], דבר v.[48]. It also uses many ו consec. impfs. as historical aorist, which in the Ps. are simply impf., with more general reference to present or future, v.[7c. 12. 30a-b]. In other respects the text of 2 S. is more archaic. The ode, in both forms

of the text, gives many evidences of late date. (1) There are late words
עם עני v.²⁸, ענוה v.³⁶ᵇ (but 2 S. ענה), בני נכר v.⁴⁵ᵇ·⁴⁶ᵃ; but these are all in glosses.
(2) The ode is cited (a) Ps. 116¹⁻⁴ in the text of Ps., חבלי מות v.⁵, and
ומריר || ארחמך v.²; (b) Ps. 144¹⁻⁷ in the text of 2 S., הרודד 144² = ומריר 2 S. 22⁴⁸,
not וירבר Ps. 18⁴⁸; מפלטי לי 144² = 2 S. 22² = מפלטי Ps. 18³; (c) Hb. 3¹⁹ cites v.³⁴,
only changing vbs. שוה, העמיד into more common ones, שים, הדריך; (d) Pr. 30⁵
cites v.³¹, giving an earlier form of text, לכל החוסים בו for לחוסים בו, and
אמרת אלוה for אמרת י׳; (e) Is. 55⁵ cites v.⁴⁴ in two lines in fuller and more
comprehensive style, using also גוי for עם. The Ps. is, therefore, preëxilic.
(3) The ode cites (a) Mi. 7¹⁷ in v.⁴⁶; the texts of Ps. and 2 S. vary as to the
vb., both best explained by the vb. of Micah רגז as the original, but this is a
gloss. (b) 2 S. 7¹²⁻¹⁶ in v.⁵¹. (c) It is not easy to determine whether v.³¹ or
Dt. 32⁴ is the original. The evidence of citation favours a preëx. date for
the ode. (4) There are many late doctrinal conceptions in the ode :
(a) The affectionate love of Yahweh, v.², is post-Deuteronomic ; but it is not
in text of 2 S., and was a later addition to the ode. (b) The doctrine of the
absoluteness of Yahweh as the only God is stated, v.³², in terms of Is.² ; but
this statement is incongruous to the context, which favours the assertion of the
incomparableness of God, as in other early poetry. This couplet has probably
been adapted to later conceptions. (c) The legal righteousness and its
exact retribution of v.²¹⁻²⁴ with the terms שמר דרכים v.²²ᵃ, סור מ׳ v.²³ᵇ, characteristic of D.², בר ידי v.²¹ᵇ, רשע מ׳ v.²²ᵇ, חקות v.²³ᵇ still later. But this passage
is evidently a gl. from its smoothness, calmness, and didactic character, as
compared with the rapid, passionate movement in the ode. This gloss comes
from the period of the reign of Levitical law, and states the doctrine questioned in the Book of Job. (d) The gnomic couplets, v.²⁵⁻²⁸, are still later,
implying the supremacy of Hebrew wisdom, and are ethical as compared with
the legal character of the previous context. They begin with a line similar to
v.²¹ᵃ. (e) The cringing of foreign nations, v.⁴⁵ᵇ⁻⁴⁶, suits the conceptions of
postex. Judaism, and is favoured by Is.²·³. This is a gl. also. (f) The
liturgical formula, v.⁵⁰, is similar to corresponding liturgical additions to other
Pss. This is a gl. (5) On the other hand, (a) the conception of the cherubic
chariot in the storm cloud, v.¹¹, is more primitive than the cherubic chariot
of Ez. 1. (b) The theophany to decide battles is a primitive conception in
the ancient odes, Ex. 15, Ju. 5; cf. Jos. 10¹²⁻¹⁴; as with Moses, Joshua,
Deborah, so also with David. (c) The high places as battle fields is also
an expression of the old songs, 2 S. 1¹⁹·²⁵ Dt. 32¹³ 33²⁹. If the ode in its
present form, in text either of 2 S. or of Ps., is regarded as a unit, one composition without interpolation, there can be no escape from the opinion that
it was composed at the earliest in the late Persian period, more probably in
the early Greek period. But if we remove the glosses, which have adapted
an ode of victory of David to later religious uses, the ode stands out in
simple grandeur as fitting appropriately to the historical experience of David,
whether he wrote it or another wrote it for him by historic imagination,
entering into the experience of the heroic king. After removing the glosses

there is nothing that bars the way to his authorship. The Ps., with the glosses removed, is divided into two parts, each part of three fourteen-lined trimeters; the first part sets forth his deliverance by theophany from peril of death, the second part his strengthening for war by his God and his victory over all his enemies. The two chief glosses, the legal gloss, v.²¹⁻²⁴, and the ethical gloss, v.²⁵⁻²⁸, are inserted between the two parts. Remove them, and the unity and harmony of the ode appear. The other minor glosses are easy to distinguish. Their removal improves the poetic conception and movement of the poem. There are very few departures from the trimeter measure, and these are clearly due to textual errors.

An editor, wishing to adapt the ancient ode to congregational use, in view of the entire thought which follows, prefixes the exclamation *I love Thee, Yahweh, my strength*]. This line is not in the text of 2 S., taking the place of its v.³ᶜ, which was intentionally omitted from Ps. The words for love and strength are Aramaisms, and the conception of loving Yahweh is post-Deuteronomic.

Pt. I., Str. I. The Str. is composed of six trimeters, followed by eight. **3.** Four syn. lines heap up terms to emphasise David's God as his Saviour from an enemy in war. — *my crag* and *my fortress, my high tower*], a place of refuge inaccessible to an enemy, too strong for him. — *My God* and *my Rock* are divine names, Rock being an ancient term for God, also v.³².⁴⁷ Dt. 32⁴.³¹.³⁷. — *My shield*]. God is a warrior with a shield covering David's body. — *horn of salvation*]. God is like a great bull guarding him with his horns; cf. Gn. 49²⁴. The syn. *my deliverer, in whom I seek refuge*, attain their climax in *my Saviour, Thou savest me*. One word, *from violence*, or possibly in the earliest txt. of the Ps., *from the man of violence*, cf. v.⁴⁹, is the only indication of the peril in this part of the Str. A personal enemy who sought to use violence upon him and put him to death, is the reason of his seeking refuge in God. This situation aptly suits that of David when pursued in the wilderness of Judah by the violent Saul. **4.** A synth. distich, synthetic to the tetrastich which precedes, in the first line proclaims Yahweh as the one *worthy to be praised*], a summing up of all the titles given to Him, v.³; and in the second line gives the reason for it. — *Since from mine enemies I am saved*]. The man of violence was accompanied by a number of enemies. — **5-7.** Two tetrastichs, the first, v.⁵⁻⁶, describes the

peril of death, the second, v.⁷, the cry for help and its answer.
The peril of death is graphically described in four syn. lines.
David conceives of himself as in a rushing stream, like the rapids
of the Jordan or the Kishon, which is hurrying him on to death
(cf. Pss. 32⁶ 42⁸ 69²). These are the agents of Death. *Death*
has its synonym *Belial* because of the destruction and ruin involved in it, and *Sheol*, the ordinary name for the place of the
dead. David is, as it were, in the stream, rushing on to death.
He says, *breakers*, agitated waves, breaking on me, *encompassed
me* on every side, *torrents fell upon me*, attacking me as lines
of an army to destroy me. And under the surface of the stream,
cords came round me, the waters seemed like cords binding my
limbs fast so that I could not move them ; *snares came to meet me*,
to ensnare me like an animal, draw me down so that I could not
escape. — **7**. In this deadly peril he cries for help to Yahweh in
a syn. couplet, and the answer is stated in another syn. couplet. —
from His palace], in heaven, where Yahweh was enthroned ; sometimes conceived as a heavenly temple, where He is worshipped
by heavenly beings ; but here as a palace because royal help is
given, rather than response to worship.

Str. II. The salvation of David from his peril of death was
through a theophany. — **8-9**. This is first described in two trimeter tristichs, the first of syn. lines picturing the heaven and
earth in agitation. *Then the earth swayed and quaked ‖ and the
foundations of the heavens trembled*]. The heavens share in
the agitation as in subsequent context and in usage in connection
with theophanies ; see Is. 13⁹⁻¹⁰. ¹³ Jo. 4¹⁵⁻¹⁶. So 2 S., but the Ps.
"mountains" limits agitation to earth. — *Tossed to and fro*],
both earth and heaven, *because He burned with anger*, in behalf
of the one who sought refuge in Him against his enemies. The
second tristich is composed of two syn. and one synth. line, the
former describing the anger ; He breathed hard and rapidly and
His breath like *smoke went up in His nostril*, and so hot was it
that it appeared like a flame of *fire from His mouth*, and (like
a flame), *devoured* whatever came in its way. The last line in
synthesis represents that *coals were kindled*] ; whatever the fiery
breath of His anger reached became coals, were kindled, and
burned like coals *from Him*, that is, from the breath that issued

from Him. — **10–13**. The theophany itself is described in two tetrastichs; in the first as a coming down of God from heaven to earth. — **10**. *He bowed the heavens and came down*]. God, enthroned above the physical heavens, the blue expanse, bends them when He would descend in theophany. He comes down on them. So Ex. 24^{10}, the elders of Israel "saw the God of Israel; and there was under His feet, as it were, a work of bright sapphire, and as it were the very heaven for brightness." The very heaven, its sapphire-blue expanse, was the base on which the feet of the theophanic God stood. Here, however, *under His feet* was *thick darkness*, because the theophany was in a storm of wrath; there it was in the bright sunshine of favour to establish a covenant with His people. So Solomon, in the snatch of an ancient poem preserved from the book of Yashar (according to 𝕲), says, "Yahweh dwelt in thick darkness," 1 K. 8^{12} = 2 Ch. 6^1; cf. Ps. 97^2 and the cloud of the theophany at Horeb, Ex. 20^{18} (E), Dt. 4^{11} 5^{22}. — **11**. *And rode upon the cherub*]. The cherub, coll. sg. for usual pl. cherubim, is conceived as the living chariot upon which God rides when He descends from heaven to earth. So Ez. 1$^{4-28}$ 9^3 10 11^{22}, describe four cherubim inseparably attached to the living chariot of Yahweh; and 1 Ch. 28^{18} connects the cherubic chariot with the cherubim of the Holy of Holies of the temple. They were the guards of Eden, Gn. 3^{24} (J), and of the tabernacle and temple, in which two of them with outstretched wings sustained the base of the divine throne. They always have wings. The conception of the Ps. is a primitive one, but harmonious with the other representations. — *And flew*]. The cherubim constitute a winged chariot. — *And swooped down upon wings of wind*]. The wings of wind may be conceived as wings which the wind has, in which case wind and cherub seem to be synonymous, and we may think of Ps. 104$^{3-4}$. But the thick cloud of Ps. 104^3 appears in 18^{13} as "thick clouds of the skies," and the cherubim are the chariot here in a different sense from the thick clouds there. The conception here is that heaven, thick darkness, cherub, wings of wind, are all under the feet of God, all constitute the platform on which He descends to earth. The cherubim are the living beings of the theophany as in other passages mentioned, and there is no sufficient reason to identify them with the thick storm cloud.

The second tetrastich, **12–13**, in three syn. lines describes what
was *round about* God in His descent, as the previous lines what
was *under His feet*. The texts of Ps. and 2 S. differ greatly here,
and it is difficult to find the original text and interpret it. — God
put darkness round about Him], enveloped Himself in darkness
when He descended ‖ *a covering of darkness of waters*], a dark
mass of waters was the covering; He was bringing with Him a
great storm cloud heavily heaped up with waters, ‖ *thick clouds
of the skies without brightness*]. The Str. concludes with a line
stating what preceded Him — *before Him passed His thick clouds*.
Theophanies in storm for salvation in battle are reported for
Israel under Moses at the crossing of the Red Sea, Ex. 14[19-25]
15[1-18]; Joshua at Bethhoron, Jos. 10[11]; Barak and Deborah at the
Kishon, Ju. 5[20-21]; and so also for David against the Philistines, for
2 S. 5[20], "Yahweh hath broken forth upon mine enemies before
me, like the breaking forth of waters," implies the breaking forth
of a storm; 5[24], "when thou hearest the sound of marching in
the tops of the mulberry trees," the onward march of Yahweh
in a storm manifested first in the tops of the trees.

  Str. III. 14–16. The theophany is still further described as a
storm in a syn. tetrastich and a syn. couplet synth. thereto. The
approach of Yahweh in the storm has been described in the previous Str.: now the storm bursts forth. — *Yahweh thundered from
heaven* (so 2 S. better than " in heaven " of Ps.) ‖ *and Elyon gave
forth His voice*], the sound of thunder as Ps. 29[3]. — *And sent forth
His arrows*]. The thunderbolts are compared with arrows shot forth
from a bow ‖ *flashed flashes*], so 144[6], citing this passage, preferable to Ps., whose text was corrupted into " many " flashes. The
resulting clause, *and scattered them*, is usually referred to the
enemy; but the enemy has not been mentioned since v.[4] and
does not appear again till v.[18], so the reference is here premature.
It is rather the arrows which are scattered, so many are the
thunderbolts in this great storm. — *made them rumble*], the long
reverberating rumbling of the thunder which accompanies the
flashes of lightning, all representing a terrible thunder-storm. The
result of this terrific storm is described in the closing syn. couplet.
— *And the channels of the (sea)*] 2 S. better than the weaker
" waters " of Ps. — *appeared;* ‖ *(and) the foundations of the world*

were laid bare]. This is a return to the thought of the earth-quake as preceding the storm, and now renewed during the storm. A later editor added a gloss corresponding with v.⁹ᶜ, only stronger : *because of Thy rebuke, Yahweh, because of the breathing of the breath of Thy nostrils.* — **17–19.** The second section of the Str. is composed of a couplet and two triplets. The couplet con-tinues the description of the theophany and gives the result of it. *He sends from on high, He takes me ‖ He draws me out of many waters*], that is, the waters described in v.⁵. — The first triplet of syn. lines then explains the imagery. *He delivers me from my strong enemy, ‖ from those hating me ; for they were too strong for me ‖ who came to meet me in the day of my calamity*], the same as the enemies and man of violence of v.³⁻⁴. — The last triplet is also syn. — *And so Yahweh became a stay to me*], a firm prop and support referring back in correspondence of thought to v.³ᶜ. — *and led me forth into a wide place*], giving breadth and freedom of action without peril, and so antith. to his seeking refuge on a crag and in a fortress and high tower v.³ᵃ·ᶜ. — *and rescued me, because He took pleasure in me*], the climax resuming the thought of v.³ᵇ. Thus this part of the Ps. reaches a good conclusion, returning on itself, as is frequent in Hebrew poetry.

21–24. An entirely new conception now appears which is ex-pressed in four syn. couplets. These set forth the doctrine of the reward of righteousness, and especially of legal righteousness, a doctrine which did not originate till after the Deuteronomic Law and which did not attain its height till after the giving of the priestly Law. It is doubtless a gloss from the Persian period. It has nothing in keeping with the previous thought of the Ps. The original Ps. is hot with passion ; this section is calm and placid.

> Yahweh rewards me according to my righteousness,
> According to the cleanness of my hands returns to me ;
> Because I have kept the ways of Yahweh,
> And have not acted wickedly (in departing) from my God.
> For all His judgments are before me,
> And His statutes I did not depart from them ;
> And I was perfect towards Him,
> And kept myself from mine iniquity.

21. *Yahweh rewards me ‖ returns to me*], exact retribution, *according to my righteousness ‖ according to the cleanness of my* *hands*], not using the hands for unclean purposes. This seems to imply not Levitical purity or purity from bribery, which never are expressed in this way ; but, in accordance with Jb. 9³⁰ 22³⁰, innocence from unrighteousness and so ∥ "righteousness." — **22.** *The ways of Yahweh*], *ways* for ways commanded Dt. 8⁶ 10¹² 11²² 19⁹ 26¹⁷ 28⁹ 30¹⁶ Jos. 22⁵. — **23.** *For all His judgments*], legal decisions in law codes ∥ *and His statutes*], f. pl. usage of code of H. — *depart from*], Deuteronomic expression Dt. 9¹² + 7 t. — **24.** *And I was perfect towards Him and kept myself from mine iniquity*]. This is given as a single pentameter line. It may be arranged as two trimeters by separating the preposition from its noun ; but it was probably not so intended by the glossator. These verses can hardly be earlier than the later Deuteronomic writers.

25–28. This section constitutes another and still later gloss, gnomic in character, from the period of Hebrew Wisdom, and so probably as late as the Greek period. They begin with a couplet which is essentially the same as v.²¹. The retribution in the following couplets is ethical rather than legal.

> And Yahweh returned me according to my righteousness,
> According to the cleanness of my hands before His eyes.
> With the pious Thou shewest Thyself kind ;
> With the perfect Thou shewest Thyself perfect ;
> With the clean Thou shewest Thyself clean ;
> But with the crooked thou shewest Thyself crooked:
> For Thou savest humble folk ;
> But (Thine) eyes are (against) the lofty.

26. *With the pious Thou shewest Thyself kind ∥ with the perfect Thou shewest Thyself perfect*]. The pious are those who are devoted to God and His law of kindness ; and who are also complete, entire in their devotion to Him, and are so without blame. To such God is kind and perfect in His dealings. — **27.** *With the clean Thou shewest Thyself clean* in antith. with *but with the crooked* (cf. Pr. 22⁵) *Thou shewest Thyself crooked.* — **28.** *For Thou savest humble folk*]. The antith. compels the meaning "humble," elsw. only Pr. 3³⁴ 16¹⁹, possibly also Zc. 9⁹ ; the earlier sense, "poor, needy, afflicted," is not appropriate here. — *But (Thine) eyes are (against) the lofty*]. The texts of this line are difficult to explain : " lofty eyes Thou humblest" of Ps. is too easy and does not explain 2 S. : *Thine eyes are upon the lofty that Thou mayest bring them down.* The translation given above best explains both variations.

Pt. II., Str. I. begins with a personal reference to Yahweh reminding one of v.[3]. The Str. describes what God had done for David in war, in two parts of three and four couplets. — **29-31.** has three syn. couplets advancing one upon another. — *For Thou art my lamp, Yahweh*], changed in Ps. to " lightest lamp " in order to better parallel. with : *My God who lightens my darkness.* Yahweh was the lamp, as in v.[3c], horn of salvation ; the lamp to light up a dark path, fig. of a difficult task, so of prosperous way through it, cf. Ps. 132[17], probably based on this passage. — *For in Thee* (through Thy help) *I run up to a troop*], a hostile marauding band of the enemy, to attack them. — *and in my God I leap a wall*], to get at them behind the wall. These expressions seem to refer to some difficult campaign in which personal courage, strength, and valour were required. — *The 'El whose way*], providential way of acting, cf. Dt. 32[4]. — *is perfect*], in help and defence, as appears from ‖ *a shield is He to the one* (made more comprehensive by a later editor by insertion of " all") *seeking refuge in Him*] ; cf. v.[3b] for both expressions. — **32-35.** The second part of the Str. is composed of four syn. couplets, setting forth in relative clauses what sort of a God Yahweh is and what He has done for David. The first couplet asks, *For who is a God like Yahweh?* ‖ *and who is a Rock like our God?*], implying a negative answer : there is none like Him, the incomparable One. ('El and Rock are as in v.[3b].) So Ex. 15[11], cf. 1 S. 2[2] Dt. 33[26. 29]. A later editor, adapting the Ps. for congregational use, substitutes for the comparison the terminology of Is.[2] 43[11] 44[6. 8] 45[21], asserting that God is the only God ; that is, monotheism, a doctrine without anything to suggest it in the context, which rather holds up Yahweh as the incomparable One in what He has done for David. — *The 'El who girdeth me with strength*]. Strength is compared to a girdle wrapt about him by his God. — *Who setteth my feet like hinds*], swift to run, as v.[30] ‖ *And upon high places*], battlefields, as Dt. 32[13] 33[29] 2 S. 1[19. 25]. — *made me hold my ground*], stand firm in battle, cf. Am. 2[15] 2 K. 10[4]. —

Who teacheth mine hands for war]. As a warrior of Yahweh he has been trained by Yahweh Himself. — *And maketh mine arms bronze*]. The arms by divine discipline become so strong that they are like bronze weapons ; so essentially ancient Vrss. The "bow" is an ancient interpretation which spoiled the measure and misled as to the sense, and in 𝔐 led to a change in the form of the vb., which is followed by AV. "so that a bow of steel is broken by mine arms" and RV. "mine arms do bend a bow of brass," neither of which suits the context.

36. These two lines are doubtless a gloss. They are not in accord with the previous or following context, which describe what God enabled David to do and not what God was to David.

And Thou gavest me the shield of Thy salvation,
And Thy right hand supported me, and with docility to Thee Thou broughtest me up.

The shield is suited to the previous bronze weapon and the hands and arms, but then it should be a shield of victory and not *shield of salvation*. But the glossator was evidently influenced by the horn of salvation v.^{3c} and the shield v.^{31c}. The last two lines vary in texts and Vrss. 2 S. omits : And Thy right hand supported me ; and the first word of the next clause is pointed so as to read "Thy response," or "Thy docility," which suits better the vb. than MT. of Ps. "Thy condescension" or "Thy humility." So also we may read the vb. "either made me great" or *brought me up*. But in either case the conceptions are later than those of the Ps. as a whole. Two different stages of glosses are represented by the two texts.

Str. II. describes the triumph of David over his enemies. It is composed of a couplet followed by a tetrastich in the first section, and of a tetrastich and two couplets in the second. — **37.** The first section begins with a synth. couplet : *Thou broadenest my steps under me*], taking up the thought of v.^{34}. The step is the place on which the feet step or stand ; it is broadened so as to give ample room for standing, cf. v.^{20b}, plenty of room for exercise and development. — *And my limbs do not slip*]. They stand firm on the broad stepping place. This may refer to the enlargement of the power of David after his final defeat of the Philistines. — **38.** David now describes his victorious pursuit of his enemies.

He is no longer on the defence. — *I pursue mine enemies and I overtake them*]; cf. v.³⁰ of his running and leaping against them; || *and I return not* (from the pursuit) *until* (I have overtaken them and) *I have finished them* (destroyed them completely). — **39.** *And I smote them down so that they could not rise* || *and they fell under my feet*]. This, in the original poem, described a historic experience of David, probably in his wars against Edom and Moab; but an editor, wishing to make future triumphs possible to the thought of the congregation, omits the waws consecutive, so that the verbs may be either futures or presents. The second section opens with a tetrastich: **40–41.** *And Thou girdest me with strength for war*], resuming the thought of v.³³ᵃ, then synth. as result of this warlike strength, *Thou causest them that rise up against me to bow down under me*]; they rise up only to bow down under my blows; || *And mine enemies Thou madest give the back to me*], turn the back of their necks in flight; || *and them that hate me I exterminated.* — **42.** The pitiful condition of the helpless enemy is now stated in a couplet: *And they cry for help, but there is no saviour* || *unto Yahweh, but He doth not answer them.* — **43.** The Str. concludes with a couplet bringing to a climax the final victory: *And I beat them small as dust of the earth*]. An editor substitutes for *earth*, "before the wind," thinking of pursuit. — *And as clay of the streets pulverized them*]. This is probably an indirect reference to captured cities. The entire Str., describing victories over enemies, may be regarded as a poetic representation of the wars of David described in 2 S. 8, 10.

Str. III. sums up and generalizes all that has gone before; but it is mingled with two glosses, which make it more appropriate for congregational worship in later times. — **44–47.** The first section is a hexastich as usual. — **44–45 a.** It begins with a single line: *Thou deliverest me from the strivings of* (*my*) *people*], which, if the text of 2 S. is correct, is the only reference in the ode to civil commotions. This is generalized in the text of Ps. to "people," but the strivings are more suited in usage to civil commotion than to external war, cf. Ps. 55¹⁰. The three lines that follow are syn., referring to foreign nations. — *Thou settest me to be head of nations*]; the conquered nations submit to him

as their head or chief. — *A people I knew not serve me*], unknown
distant foreign peoples, such as the Syrians of Hamath, 2 S. 8⁹ ;
‖ *At the hearing of the ear shew themselves obedient to me*]. This
is followed by a gloss, in the hostile spirit to foreign nations of
later times. — **45b–46**. *Foreigners come cringing unto me* ‖ *foreigners fade away and come trembling out of their fastnesses*].
These lines are in both texts, but there has been a transposition
of v.⁴⁵ᵃ⁻ᵇ in the text of 2 S. There is nothing in this part of the
Str. apart from the gloss that transcends the experience of David ;
although naturally in later times it was given a more general
reference, in accordance with the royal Pss., to a world-wide
dominion of the Davidic dynasty. — **47**. A concluding couplet
ascribes life and blessedness to God. — *Liveth and blessed is my
Rock*]. "Yahweh" has been inserted after "liveth," but elsewhere
"Yahweh liveth" is the formula of the oath, and here it seems
to balance two clauses with two beats each, making a tetrameter.
It is not expressive of a wish, as one says, "May the king live ;"
but is a statement of fact, as to the "Rock," the divine name
of the Song. — *And the God of my salvation is exalted*] ; cf. v.³ᶜ
and this exclamation of the fact to the couplet of challenge, v.³². —
48–51. The second section is constructed somewhat as v.³²⁻³⁵ in
relative clauses. — **48–49**. *The 'El who giveth to me deeds of
vengeance*], such as those described in v.³⁸⁻⁴³. — *And who bringeth
down peoples under me*] ; cf. v.⁴⁰⁻⁴¹. An editor of the Ps. substituted a later Aramaic word "subdueth" for this ptc. — *From
the man of violence rescueth me*]. This is the climax, going back upon
v.³ᵈ, which is left out of text of Ps., but is preserved in text of
2 S., probably referring to Saul, as indicated in title. It was quite
natural that the first reference in the ode to the peril, and the last,
should refer to him ; and as "a man of violence" rather than as
classed with the other enemies. — This is followed by a gloss, **50**,
which is left in the text as a hexameter, a liturgical addition
suitable for congregational worship at this point. — *Therefore will
I praise Thee, Yahweh, among the nations, and to Thy name will
I make melody*]. All the terms are common liturgical terms. —
51. The final triplet of the Str. is individual in its reference to
David as the anointed king over against the man of violence. —
Who magnifieth acts of salvation to His king, ‖ *And doeth kindness*

to His anointed]. There is a reference here to the covenant of David, 2 S. 7¹⁵ˢq·. "My kindness shall not depart from him, as I took it from Saul," cf. also Ps. 89²⁹· ³⁴; and so the climax is appropriate in the mouth of David, *To David and to his seed forever.*

1. [אֶרְחָמְךָ] *I love thee*, Qal impf. 1 p. sf. 2 m. of ‡רהב, a.λ. in Qal; Pi. *have compassion*, frequent ‡ Pss. 102¹⁴ 103¹³· ¹³ 116⁵ and elsw. However, in As., Ar., Aram., Syr., used in Qal with mng. *love*. Possibly an early and rare use in Heb., but prob. a later one, an Aramaism. The idea itself is not earlier than Hosea, and is only common with אהב subsequent to D. This l. is cited Ps. 116¹; but אהבתי is there substituted, or else gives evidence of an original אהבתי in poem. This vb. is not found in 2 S. and is doubtless a gl. — [חִזְקִי] *my strength*: † חֵזֶק a.λ. (2 S. 22² 𝕲ᴸ has ἰσχύς μου, but this is gl. from Ps.); cf. חֶזְקַת Is. 8¹¹, חִזְקְתוֹ 2 Ch. 12¹ 26¹⁵ Dn. 11². † חֹזֶק is used Ex. 13³· ¹⁴· ¹⁶ Am. 6¹³ Hg. 2²²; חָזָק adj. is used of the hand and arm of ˙˙ in delivering Israel from Egypt, especially in D. Cf. Ps. 136¹² and Is. 40¹⁰ (וּזְרֹ־ *as in the character of a strong one*). — **3.** [סַלְעִי] *my crag;* ‡ סֶלַע n.m. fig. of ˙˙ 18³ (= 2 S. 22²); also 31⁴ = 71³ (both וּמְצוּדָתִי אַתָּה (ס; 42¹⁰ (אֶל סַלְעִי); fig. of security 40⁸; in physical sense 78¹⁶ 104¹⁸ 137⁹ 141⁶. — † [צוּרָה] n.f. *fastness, stronghold*, used in ψ of God 18³ (= 2 S. 22²) 31³· ⁴ = 71³ (all ‖ סֶלַע), 91² (‖ מַחְסִי), 66¹¹ 144² (both dub.); elsw. common in narrative of 1 S. 22⁴· ⁵ 24²³ 2 S. 5⁷· ⁹· ¹⁷ (= 1 Ch. 11⁵· ¹⁶) 23¹⁴; also in Ez. 12¹³ 13²¹ 17²⁰ Jb. 39²⁸. It is therefore an early word, extremely suitable in the mouth of David. — [מְפַלְּטִי] *my deliverer*, Pi. ptc. sf. 1 (*v.* 17¹³); elsw. in this ptc. form v.⁴⁹ (for which 2 S. more correctly מוֹצִיאִי); 40¹⁸ = 70⁶, 144², as above, agreeing with 2 S. in adding לִי, which is doubtless original. But Bä., Du., rd. מְחַלְּטִי, as Ps. 55⁹, more in accord. with context. The Ps. is without doubt a trimeter; therefore the initial יהוה must be a gl., though in both texts. — [אֵלִי] *my God;* אֱלֹהַי of 2 S. is prob. later; cf. צוּרִי אֵל סַלְעִי 42¹⁰. — [צוּרִי] *my rock*, here as in Dt. 32³⁷ sq. חֹסֶה בּוֹ. In that poem it is a divine name, given in 𝕲 there as elsw., v.¹⁸· ³⁰· ³¹· ³¹· ³⁷, by θεός; so 𝕲 of 2 S. 23³ Ps. 18³²· ⁴⁷. This usage and the personal reference favours its interpretation as a divine name here, although 𝕲 renders βοηθός; 𝕲 of 2 S. has ὁ θεός μου φύλαξ ἔσται μοι, showing that 𝕲 rd. אֱלֹהַי. ‡ צור n.m. *rock;* used elsw. (1) in late Pss. for God as refuge of His people 19¹⁵ 28¹ 31⁸ (= 71³) 62³· ⁷· ⁸ 73²⁶ 78³⁵ 89²⁷ 92¹⁶ 94²² 95¹ 144¹; (2) in physical sense 27⁵ 61⁸ 78¹⁵· ²⁰ 81¹⁷ 105⁴¹ 114⁸; (3) of *edge of sword* 89⁴⁴. — [קֶרֶן יִשְׁעִי] phr. a.λ. *horn of my salvation.* ‡ קֶרֶן n. horn (1) of animal 22²² 92¹¹, so fig. of God here; (2) of altar 118²⁷; (3) fig. of exaltation. הרים ק׳ *lift up the horn* is used fig. of men of power and honour, compared with the wild bulls; so of wicked 75⁵· ⁶· ¹¹; of God's people, with God as subj. 89¹⁸ 148¹⁴; intrans. רום ק׳ 89²⁵ 112⁹ 1 S. 2¹; so of the king הֵצְמִיחַ ק׳ לְדָוִד 132¹⁷; cf. ירם ק׳ משיחו 1 S. 2¹⁰ (Song of Hannah). — [מִשְׂגַּבִּי] *my high tower:* always fig. of God except Is. 25¹² 33¹⁶ (of forts). 2 S. adds וּמְנוּסִי, but this makes line too long;

prob. a gl. 2 S. 22³ᵈ משעי מחמס תשעני is not in Ps. We need it to make up six lines of Str. It was doubtless original, Ols., Ley, Gr., Bi., Che., Bä., Ecker. Its place was taken by the first line of Ps. — **4.** מְהֻלָּל] Pual ptc. gerundive, *worthy to be praised*, always of ˙; elsw. 48² 96⁴ (= I Ch. 16²⁵) 145³, of name of ˙ 113³. For הלל vb. *v.* Intr. § 35. — וּמֵן אֹיְבַי] is to be preferred to 2 S. וּמֵאיבי on account of rhythm. — **5.** כִּי] of 2 S. is unnecessary; not in Ps. — אֲפָפוּנִי] Qal pf. 3 pl. sf. 1 S. (of past experience) † אפף *surround, encompass:* waters Jon. 2⁶; fig. evils, misfortune רעות Ps. 40¹³, משברי מות 2 S. 22⁵ = חבלי מ' Ps. 18⁵ = 116³ (where it is cited). חבלי of Ps. has come in from next couplet v.⁶. It is improbable that the original was so unnecessarily tautological. — † מֹשְׁבְּרֵי] n. pl. cstr. *breakers, waves* breaking on the shore, gives a beautiful metaphor, which is found elsw., lit. מִשְׁבְּרֵי יָם 93⁴; fig. of תהום 42⁸ = Jon. 2⁴; of מְצוּלָה Ps. 88⁸. 2 S. 22⁵ is prob. the original of all these fig. uses, as תהום and מצולה refer to מות and שאול. — וְנַחֲלֵי בְלִיַעַל] *torrents of Belial*. — ‡ נחל] n.m. (1) *torrent* of rushing water, ‖ breakers, so sim. of foes 124⁴; fig. of ruin here, of pleasures 36⁹; elsw. in ψ lit. 74¹⁵ 78²⁰ 83¹⁰ 110⁷, cf. Ju. 5²¹; (2) *torrent bed, wady*, Ps. 104¹⁰. ‡ בְּלִיַּעַל *worthlessness:* (1) דְּבַר ב' *base, wicked thing*, 101³; † (2) *ruin, destruction*, Na. 2¹; יָעַץ ב' Na. 1¹¹; and so here *destruction* ‖ מות and שאול; דבר ב' Ps. 41⁹ (destructive thing) deadly injury. 2 S. omits ו without reason. — יְבַעֲתוּנִי] Pi. impf. varies from pf. of previous and following lines to express the oft-repeated action. † בעת vb. Qal not used. Niph. *be terrified* 1 Ch. 21³⁰ Est. 7⁶ Dn. 8¹⁷; not in ψ. Pi. (1) *fall upon, overwhelm, assail*, 1 S. 16¹⁴˙ ¹⁵ prose, elsw. poetry, Ps. 18⁵ (= 2 S. 22⁵) Jb. 3⁵ + 6 t. Jb. Is. 21⁴; (2) *terrify* Jb. 7¹⁴ (‖ חתת). — **6.** ‡ מוֹקֵשׁ] n.m. *snare* 18⁶ (= 2 S. 22⁶) 69²³ 106³⁶, of plots of wicked 64⁶ 140⁶ 141⁹ (v. 9¹⁷). — **7.** בַּצַּר־לִי] *in the distress which I had* (v. 4²). — אֶשַׁוֵּעַ] Pi. impf. 1 p. (v. 5³). This is original; אֶקְרָא of 2 S. 22⁷ᵇ is error of repetition from previous line. — יִשְׁמַע] impf. (of vivid description); 2 S. has better יִשְׁמַע, ו consec. of result. — Ps. has two words לְפָנָיו תָּבוֹא, which are not in 2 S., inserted betw. the two words וְשֵׁוְעָתִי and בְּאָזְנָיו. 2 S. is one word too short. תבוא may be explained as a gl. implied by באזניו; but לפניו is not a natural gl. and is therefore probably original. — † שֵׁוְעָה] n.f. *cry for help;* not found abs., but cstr. 1 S. 5¹² Je. 8¹⁹, שַׁוְעָתִי Ps. 18⁷ (= 2 S. 22⁷) 39¹³ 40² 102² La. 3⁵⁶, שׁוְעָתָם Pss. 34¹⁶ 145¹⁹ Ex. 2²³ (J). — **8.** וַתִּגְעַשׁ] Qal impf. 3 f. c. ו consec. of result. † געשׁ Qal α.λ., Dr. = *sway;* but 2 S. Qr. Hithp. וַיִּתְגָּעֵשׁ which is found also of waters *tossing* Je. 5²² 46⁷, and of mountains (2 S. heavens) *swaying* here, v.⁸ᶜ = 2 S. 22⁸ᶜ; so Hithpolel of waters Je. 46⁸, and of drunken men *reeling* Je. 25¹⁶. Pu. Jb. 34²⁰, a people *convulsed*. There is no sufficient reason to doubt the Qal, which is the more difficult form. — וַיִּרְעַשׁ] Qal impf. c. ו consec. *quaked*. ‡ רעשׁ vb. Qal *quake:* of earth 18⁸ 68⁹ 77¹⁹, mountains 46⁴ 72¹⁶ (dub.). Hiph. *cause to quake*, earth 60⁴. — וּמוֹסְדֵי הָרִים] 2 S. omits ו. In that case it is difficult to explain ו consec. with יִתְגָּעֲשׁוּ. ו may be taken as circumstantial, or we may think that it has consec. power notwithstanding the change of order. It certainly would be more natural to read וַיִּרְגְּזוּ, and possibly that was the original. There was a tendency in later times, when ו consec. had lost its force and usage, to change order of vbs. in the older poems. מוסדות השמים of 2 S. is α.λ. and as the more difficult reading is to be preferred; that of Ps. is favoured by the use of חָרָה לוֹ] v.¹⁶ (= 2 S. 22¹⁶), and ארץ over against הרים Dt. 32²². — retracted accent (v. 2¹²). ‡ חרה vb. Qal *burn in anger :* of man אף subj. 124³, God 106⁴⁰; אף omitted, impersonal *18⁸*. Hithp. *heat oneself in vexation* 37¹. ⁷. ⁸ Pr. 24¹⁹. — **9.** עָשָׁן בְּאַפּוֹ] *smoke in his nostril,* because of hard breathing in anger. So אֵשׁ מִפִּיו *fire from his mouth ;* the breath of his mouth in hot anger was a breath of fire. — הָאֻכָּל at end, instead of with ו consec. at beginning. — גֶחָלִים] n.m. pl. ‡ נַחֶלֶת n.f. *coal ;* in ψ only pl. ב בָּעֲרוּ ג׳ *18⁹* = 2 S. 22⁹; so בָּעֲרוּ וַחֲלֵי אֵשׁ 2 S. 22¹³ = וְחֲלֵי אֵשׁ עָבְרוּ בָּרָד עָבָיו Ps. 18¹³ (corrupt txt.), cf. v.¹⁴ (gl.). נַחֲלֵי אֵשׁ also used of cherubim Ez. 1¹³; so rd. Ps. 140¹¹; cf. 120⁴ (of coals of broom plant). — **10.** וַיֵּט שָׁמַיִם] Qal impf. c. ו consec. carrying on result; so also 2 S., but Ps. 144⁵ Hiph., and this is the more probable pointing. Cf. Ex. 24¹⁰. — וַיֵּרַד] Qal impf. c. ו consec., *and descended,* as context shows, in theophany. In this sense only here *18¹⁰* = 144⁵ in ψ, but common in early writers Ex. 19¹¹. ¹⁸ (E)²⁾ 3⁸ 11⁶. ⁷ 18²¹ (J) Nu. 11¹⁷ (JE); sq. בְּעָנָן Ex. 34⁵ Nu. 11²⁵, cf. 12⁵ (all JE); pillar of cloud Ex. 33⁹ (JE); historical references in later writers Ne. 9¹³; prophetic anticipations of future theophanies Mi. 1³ Is. 31⁴ 63¹⁹ 64² Jb. 22¹³. — †עֲרָפֶל] n.m. *heavy cloud ;* 1 K. 8¹² = 2 Ch. 6¹ (poet.), God dwells in it, so Ps. 97². It is used of the cloud in which יהוה descended in theophany at Sinai Ex. 20²¹ (E) Dt. 4¹¹ 5¹⁹, so to David Ps. 18¹⁰ (= 2 S. 22¹⁰); of advent in judgment Je. 13¹⁶ Zp. 1¹⁵ Jo. 2²; in more general sense of clouds Jb. 22¹³, as swaddling bands of sea Jb. 38⁹; of a stormy day Ez. 34¹²; fig. misery Is. 60². — **11.** וַיִּרְכַּב] *and rode,* ו consec. carrying on the thought. ‡ רכב vb. Qal, *ride in chariot ;* so of monarch into battle 45⁵; elsw. in ψ of יהוה in theophany; in the heavens 68³⁴; on a highway in the עֲרָבָה 68⁵; so here the כרוב is conceived as His chariot 18¹¹ = 2 S. 22¹¹; cf. use of רכוב in Ps. 104⁸ and of רֶכֶב collective of the army of God in theophany, רכב רבתים 68¹⁸. Hiph. *cause to ride* 66¹². ‡ כְּרוּב n.m. only here in this relation as chariot of יהוה in the clouds; but Ez. describes four cherubim as inseparably attached to four wheels of chariot and supporting a throne platform, Ez. 1⁴⁻²⁸ 9³ 10 11²²; so 1 Ch. 28¹⁸ connects this cherubic chariot with the cherubim of the Holy of Holies of the temple. They are always conceived as having wings, even when stationary on the slab of gold constituting the throne of יהוה in the tabernacle of P; and also in the temple cherubim. They are also conceived as guards of the tabernacle and temple, and so woven into the texture of the curtains and carved on the golden planks; also in the poem of J, as the guards of Eden Gn. 3²⁴ They are always theophanic. Elsw. in ψ 80² 99¹; cf. 2 K. 19¹⁵ = Is. 37¹⁶ 1 S. 4⁴ 2 S. 6² = 1 Ch. 13⁶ (refer. to the cherubim of the throne) יֹשֵׁב הַכְּרוּבִים. — וַיָּעֹף] *and flew,* subj. God, flew by means of the wings of the cherubic chariot, which He rode. ‡ עוּף vb. Qal, *fly ;* in ψ of God only here *18¹¹* = 2 S. 22¹¹; elsw. fig. of arrow 91⁵, of a man as a dove 55⁷, of men as birds, at end of life 90¹⁰. — וַיֵּרֶא] = in 2 S. וַיֵּרָא, which latter is an error of transcription, ר for ד, as old as 𝔊. ראה, as rare word and suited to context, is to be preferred as original. †ראה vb.

Qal, *dart through the air;* here only in ψ; elsw. Dt. 28⁴⁹ (of eagle), fig. Je. 48⁴⁰ 49²². Dr. *swoop down* is the most prob. rendering. —

12. Ps. = ישת חשך סתרו סביבותיו סכתו חשכת מים

2 S. = וישת חשך — סביבתיו סכות חשרת מים

ו consec. of 2 S. is evidently correct, for the movement of thought goes right on. סביבותיו in both texts suits the clause. Then סתרו of Ps. must be either an addition or out of place. It was prob. a gl. to get a synonym of סכתו. סכה in this sense of *booth,* of God in storm, only here and Jb. 36²⁹, where it is prob. borrowed from Ps. cf. 10⁹. In Ps. 27⁵ (Kt.) 31²¹ Yahweh is booth and shelter to the psalmist. The idea of a booth on a chariot of cherubs is not congruous. We might derive סכה from the other stem סכך = *overshadow, screen* (v. 5¹²). It is true that from this stem no form סכה is known, but only מסך כסה and מסכה, both in sense of *covering;* but there is no reason why סכה *covering, screen,* should not be derived from this סכך, as well as סכה *booth* from the other סכך. Besides, this explanation would bring into comparison La. 3⁴⁴, where of Yahweh it is said, ס׳ בענן לך *Thou hast covered Thyself with a cloud;* so of anger La. 3⁴³. — ‡ [סתר] n.m. frequent in ψ as *hiding-place.* ס׳ רעם *hiding-place of thunder* 81⁸; elsw. in sense of shelter in ׳ 27⁵ 31²¹ 61⁵ 91¹, cf. 32⁷ 119¹¹⁴, secret place of womb 139¹⁵, secrecy 101⁵. It is an easy gl. here; so ἀποκρυφῆς has gone into 𝔊 of 2 S. — חשרת of 2 S. a word unknown elsw., and from stem unknown in Heb.; mng. conjectural, *collection, mass.* As. *asâru, collect, gather;* prob. txt. err. for חשכת, Hi., Gr., כ mistaken for ר, all the more that 𝔊 has σκότος. † חשכה *darkness:* opposed to light 139¹²; of theophany only here (18¹²), cf. Gn. 15¹² (JE); fig. lack of understanding 82⁵, distress Is. 8²² 50¹⁰. חשך is more common. סכת is an original out of which both סכתו of Ps. and סכות 2 S. might be derived; rd. it, therefore, as cstr. sing. and connect it with next word, סכת חשכת מים. Then the covering of darkness of waters is syn. with *He put darkness about Him, i.e.* He came enveloped in dark storm clouds, as in subsequent content. עבי שחקים goes therefore with next v. and takes as its complement מהנגה. — [עבי] pl. cstr. of ‡ עב n.m. *thick, dense cloud:* (1) rain cloud 77¹⁸ 147⁸ Ju. 5⁴ Is. 5⁶; (2) *cloud mass;* so chariot of ׳ Is. 19¹ Ps. 104³; connected with theophany 18¹². ¹³. — ‡ [שחקים] *skies,* the region of thin clouds; this phr. α.λ.; elsw. in ψ pl. שחקים (of the divine faithfulness reaching) 36⁶ = 57¹¹ = 108⁵, עוו כ׳ו (God's) 68³⁵, ש׳ ממעל 78²³ Pr. 8²⁸, קול נ־נו ׳ Ps. 77¹⁸; sg. *sky* 89⁷·³⁸. † שחק vb. Qal, *grind to powder* or *dust:* of the fine incense of sanctuary Ex. 30³⁶ (P), of waters wearing away stones and reducing them to dust Jb. 14¹⁹, of crushing enemies כעפר Ps. 18⁴³ = 2 S. 22⁴³. — **13.** נגה] emph. נ, *without brightness,* referring to th· dense clouds of the sky. If taken as beginning next line, inconsistent with context and only to be justified in connection with a new conception of lightning, but that would be premature here. ‡ נגה n.f. *brightness:* α.λ. in ψ, but cf. 2 S. 23⁴; after rain Is. 60³ 62¹. † נגה vb. Qal, *shine,* of light Is. 9¹ Jb. 18⁵ 22²⁸. Hiph. *cause to shine,* of moon Is. 13¹⁰; *enlighten* Ps. 18²⁹ = 2 S. 22²⁹.

נגרו עביו עברו | ברד וגחלי אש = .Ps

נגרו   בערו   נחלי אש = .S 2

Ps. gives two lines, 2 S. one line. ברד וגחלי אש is given again in v.[14e], but
not in 2 S. It is an easy assimilation, עברו .Ps = 2 S. נ;רו, a transposition of
כ by txt. err. עביו is not appropriate to בערו, but is needed with עברו and
vould be easily suggested by עבי of previous line. ב;ר is more appropriate to
נחלי אש, if alone without ברד, and goes back upon v.[9c], *coals of fire were kindled
from Him*. This reference back to v.[9c], the closing line of first six lines of
Str., is similar to the reference in previous Str. of v.[7ab] back to v.[4ab]. But the
reference to hailstones and coals of fire here seems premature in connection
with the descent of Yahweh in the storm cloud, and before the storm bursts
in subsequent Str. It is best, therefore, to think that the Ps. has preserved
the original of the first line. The transposition of עבר into ב;ר has occasioned the insertion of נחלי אש from v.[9c], and the omission of עביו is by error
of not observing similar letters. — **14.** [ויַּרְעֵם] Hiph. impf. c. ו consec. continuing the movement of thought. ‡ רעם vb. Qal, *thunder:* of the sea 96[11] 98[7].
Hiph. *let it thunder*, trans. *thunder* of י 18[14] (= 2 S. 22[14]) 29[3] 1 S. 2[10]; cf.
בקול 1 S. 7[10] Jb. 37[4. 5] 40[9]. — [בַּשָּׁמַיִם] not so suited to יתן קולו as 2 S. מן. —
[ב;ר וַיַחֲלִי אש] not in 2 S., is a gl. — **15.** [ויתֵּיצֵם] Hiph. impf. c. ו consec. ‡ פוץ
Qal 68[2], where enemies are *scattered* by God. Hiph. *scatter*, only here (18[15])
and 144[6] (quoted from this Ps.). Usually sf. is referred to enemies, but these
have not yet appeared in Ps. It is better with Gr., Du., to think of the scattering
wide the arrows (of thunderbolts); Ps. 144[6] reverses the order of ברק and חץ in
the verse. The ו of Ps. is not in 2 S. and not original. 2 S. has בָּרָק וַיהֻ.ם (Kt.,
ויהם Qr.) for וּבְרָקִים רָב וַיְרֻמֵּם of Ps. 2 S. is one word too short. But Ps. 144[6]
= בריק בָּרָק וּתְפִיצֵם שְׁלַח חִצֶּיךָ וּתְהֻמֵּם. We may explain text of Ps. 18 as an
attempt to improve בריק ברק, and the text of 2 S. as resulting from the omission of one of these. When Ps. 144[6] was written the text must have been
בריק ברק, so Che., Bu. ‡ בָּרָק n.m. *flash of lightning* 18[15] (= 144[6]) 77[19] 97[4]
135[7]. — [רב] before ו consec. impf. is prob. vb. as in parallel line, 𝔊 ἐπλήθυνεν,
𝔍 *multiplicavit*, from רבב vb. *be many*, trans. sense, but not found elsw. It is
usually taken, after Ki., Qal pf. of † רבב vb. *shoot*, cf. Gn. 49[23]; also cf. Je. 50[29]
Jb. 16[13]. It is taken by Hu., De., al., as רב adv. *much, exceedingly*, as Ps. 123[3],
but it is doubtless a relict of בריק, as Bä., Che., al. — [וַיְרֻמֵם] Qal impf. c. ו consec. ‡ המם trans. *make a noise*, drive with rumbling noise, as a wagon in
threshing Is. 28[28]; so here, *cause thunder to rumble* (18[15] = 2 S. 22[15] =
Ps. 144[6]), necessarily so if we refer sf. to thunderbolts, and the conception is
much more poetic than the usual rendering *discomfort*, justified by usage,
Ex. 14[24] (J) 23[27] Jos. 10[10] (E) Ju. 4[15] 1 S. 7[10]. — **16.** [ויֵּרָאוּ] Niph. impf. c. ו
consec.; ראה ‡ Niph. *appear:* of God 84[8] 102[17], of things 18[16] 90[16], of men
י 42[3] Ex. 23[15] (E) 34[20. 23. 24] (J) +; possibly all originally Qal. — [אֲפִיקֵי מַיִם]
2 S. יָם, or מַיִם Ecker, is better on account of || אֲ;בֵ;י. ‡ [אֲפִי;ה] n.m. *channel;*
elsw. אפיהי מים Ps. 42[2] Jo. 1[20] Ct. 5[12]; without defining word Ps. 126[4], as
Ex. 31[12] 32[6] +. — [ויֵּגָלוּ] Niph. impf. ו consec.; this better than יִגְלוּ: of 2 S.

‡ גלה vb. Niph. *be uncovered*, a.λ. in ψ. Pi. *uncover* eyes 119[18]; *make known* righteousness of God 98[2]. — [מִגְּעָרָתְךָ] = 2 S. בְּגַעֲרַת, in accordance with which אַפֶּךָ = אַפּוֹ 2 S. The text of Ps. changes to 2 pers. without sufficient reason. The line lacks one word. This we may get by reading וּמֵן גְּעָרַת יהוה.

† גְּעָרָה n.f. *rebuke;* alw. of God in ψ, *18[16]* (= 2 S. 22[16]) 76[7] 80[17] 104[7], also Is. 50[2] 51[20] 66[15] Jb. 26[11], of man Pr. 13[1. 8] 17[10] Ec. 7[5] Is. 30[17. 17]. — [רוּחַ] in sense of ‡ *breath* of mouth or nostrils (= 2 S. 22[16]), elsw. Pss. 33[6] 135[17]; cf. Ex. 15[8] Jb. 4[9]. — **17.** [יַקְחֵנִי] Qal impf. emph. coördination. — [יַמְשֵׁנִי] Hiph. impf. of graphic description. † מָשָׁה Qal, *draw out:* of water Ex. 2[10]; Hiph. only Ps. *18[17]* = 2 S. 22[17]. — ‡ [מַיִם רַבִּים] (= 2 S. 22[17]) elsw. Pss. 29[3] 32[6] 77[20] 93[4] 107[23] 144[7]. — **18.** [יַצִּילֵנִי] Hiph. impf. of graphic description. — [אֹיְבִי עָז] a.λ. cf. 59[4], where alone elsw. in ψ עָז adv. is used. — **19.** ‡ [אֵיד] n.m. *distress;* in ψ only in this phr. which is found also Dt. 32[35] Je. 18[17] 46[21] Jb. 21[30] Pr. 27[10]. — [וַיְהִי] ו consec. in place of previous impfs., emph. change of tense to express result. — † [מִשְׁעָן] n.m. prop. *support* (= 2 S. 22[19]), elsw. Is. 3[1]. — **20.** [וַיּוֹצִיאֵנִי] ו consec., carrying on previous line. 2 S. has וַיֹּצֵא אֹתִי, which gives proper measure and is doubtless original. — † [לַמֶּרְחָב] cf. במרחב 31[9]; also 118[5] Ho. 4[16] Hb. 1[6]. — [וְיְחַלְּצֵנִי] Pi. impf. חלץ (*v. 6[5]*), a return to impf. of vivid description. — [כִּי חָפֵץ בִּי] reason of previous deliverance. ‡ חפץ vb. Qal: (1) of men (*a*) *take pleasure in, delight in;* c. בְּ 109[17] 112[1] 119[35], c. acc. 68[31] 73[25] Is. 58[2] Ec. 8[3]; (*b*) *delight, be pleased to* do a thing, Ps. 40[9] Dt. 25[7. 8]; (2) of God, *delight in, have pleasure in;* c. בְּ pers. *18[20]* (= 2 S. 22[20]) 22[9] 41[12], horse 147[10]; c. acc. 37[23] 40[7] 51[8. 18. 21] 115[8] 135[6] Pr. 21[1]. — **21.** [כְּצִדְקִי] = 2 S. כְּצִדְקָתִי; so also same variation v.[25]; צדק is the older form (*v. 4[2]*). — [כְּבֹר יָדַי] *cleanness of my hands* = v.[25] (contracted in 2 S. to כְּבֹרִי); elsw. כַּף בֹּר Jb. 9[30] 22[30] (later usage); cf. בַּר from בר(י)/לבב adj. 24[4] 73[1] (*v. 2[12]*). — [יָשִׁיב] Hiph. impf. in sense of ‡ *return, recompense;* c. לְ, here (= 2 S. 22[21]) v.[25] 28[4] 54[7] (Qr.) 79[12] 116[12]; c. עַל 94[2. 23]. — **22.** [כִּי שָׁמַרְתִּי] causal clause, Qal pf. of action completed in present, *keep, observe:* laws of ' (post-Deuteron.), elsw. in this sense דרך 37[34], הוֹרָה 119[34. 44. 55. 136], בְּרִית 78[10] 103[18] 132[12], עֵדוּת 78[56] 99[7] 119[88. 146. 167], דבר 119[17. 57. 101], אִמְרָה 119[57. 158], מִצְוֹת 89[32] 119[60], מִשְׁפָּטִים 106[3] 119[106], חֻקִּים 105[45] 119[5. 8], פִּקּוּדִים 119[4. 63. 134. 168], in general 19[12]; all late Pss. — [דְּרָכִים] pl. of Yahweh's commands; Dt. 8[6] 10[12] 11[22] 19[9] 26[17] 28[9] 30[16] Jos. 22[5] (D. *v. 1[1]*). — [רָשַׁעְתִּי מ'] pregnant, *acted wickedly* (in departing) *from;* vb. denom. ‡ רשׁע a.λ. in this phr.; elsw. a late word, in Qal 1 K. 8[47] Dn. 9[15] 2 Ch. 6[37] Ec. 7[17] Jb. 9[29] 10[7. 15]; Hiph. *condemn as guilty* Pss. 37[33] 94[21], as Qal 106[6]. For רֶשַׁע *v. 5[5]*. — **23.** [מִשְׁפָּטִים] *judgments* (*v. 1[5]*), a type of law in form of judicial cases (introduced by אִם or כִּי, with protasis and apodosis (*v. Br.*[Hex.] *pp. 252-255*). ‖ דרכים (above); earlier usage in code of E = Ex. 21-23. Kt. of 2 S. מִשְׁפָּטָו is possible. — [חֻקֹּת] *statutes*, in fpl. characteristic of the code of 𝔓 (*v. Br.*[Hex.] *pp. 251-252*). — [אָסִיר מֶנִּי] Hiph. impf. frequentative; but 2 S. = מֶנָּה אָסוּר *depart from it*, is simpler, except for lack of agreement in number, which might be explained by an original חֻקֹּתוֹ. Departing from laws of God is an expression of D. in Qal which is prob. original, Dt. 9[12] + 7 t., מִמִּשְׁפָּטֶיךָ Ps. 119[102]; not elsw. in ψ in this sense. — **24.** [וָאֱהִי] = 2 S. וָאֶהְיֶה; shortened

form is earlier and more suited to ו consec. — עָמוֹ] = 2 S. לִי, the latter better, more likely עם assimilated to subsequent context. — וָאֶשְׁתַּמְּרָה] Hithp. cohort. impf. c. ו consec. שׁמר with two accents. This form of 2 S. is older and better than the וָאֶשְׁתַּמֵּר of Ps. Two accents are needed, unless we separate מ and rd. מן עוני; but the rhythm is not so good. — ‡ עָוֹן] n.m. (1) *iniquity* 18²⁴ (= 2 S. 22²⁴) 107¹⁷, as recognised ע׳ הגיד 38¹⁹, ע׳ כסה לא 32⁵; (*a*) *of punishment:* 89³³ פקר על ע׳, 39¹² יפר על לנגדך, 90⁸ שַׁנֵי ע׳, 103¹⁰ גמל כע׳, ע׳ שמר 130³; (*b*) *of forgiveness* or *removal:* 25¹¹ 103³ Ex. 34⁹ Nu. 14¹⁹ (J) Je. 31³⁴ 33⁸ 36³, ע׳ נשא Pss. 32⁵ 85³ Ex. 34⁷ Nu. 14¹⁸ (J) Is. 33²⁴ Ho. 14³ Mi. 7¹⁸; (*c*) *of covering over:* ע׳ כפר Ps. 78⁸⁸ Pr. 16⁶ Is. 22¹⁴ 27⁹ Dn. 9²⁴, cf. 1 S. 3¹⁴ Je. 18²³; (*d*) *of cleansing from:* מע׳ כבס Ps. 51⁴, ע׳ מחה v.¹¹; (*e*) *of imputing, reckoning to one:* ל ע׳ חשב 32² 2 S. 19²⁰, (ל) ע׳ זכר Ps. 79⁸ Is. 64⁸ Je. 14¹⁰ Ho. 8¹⁸ 9⁹, ע׳ יָכֵר Ps. 109¹⁴; (*f*) *of ransoming from:* מע׳ פרה 130⁸. (2) *Guilt of iniquity* (not always easy to distinguish from (1)), ע׳ מצא Ps. 36³ Gn. 44¹⁶ (E), ע׳ בלי Ps. 59⁵; as *great, increased,* 38⁵ 40¹³ 49⁶ 65⁴; † as a condition בע׳: c. חולל Ps. 51⁷; c. גוע Jos. 22²⁰ P; c. מות Je. 31³⁰ Ez. 3¹⁸·¹⁹ 18¹⁷·¹⁸ 33⁸·⁹. (3) *Consequence of,* or *punishment for iniquity:* בע׳, הנה ע׳ על ע׳ Ps. 69²⁸, c. various vbs. 31¹¹ 106¹³ Gn. 19¹⁵ (J) Lv. 26³⁹ (H) Je. 51⁶ Ez. 4¹⁷ + 3 t. — **25.** [וַיָּשֶׁב יהוה לִי כְצִדְקִי] vb. = Hiph. impf. c. ו consec. of שׁוב. This phr. repeats essentially v.²¹; it begins another and still later gl. of a gnomic type, coming from the Greek period of WL. — בְּבֹר יָדַי] reduction to בֹּרִי in 2 S. is a unique expression and doubtless txt. err. — **26.** [הִתְחַסָּד] Hithp. impf. 2 m. חסד vb. denom. (v.4⁴). — [גְּבַר תָּמִים] = 2 S. תמים גבור. Neither גבר nor גבור is needed; in all other lines there is a single word. נְבַר is an Aramaism for גֶּבֶר and not original. גבור is an interpretation of a גבר which has come in by mistake from the line below. — **27.** [וְעִם־נָבָר] Niph. ptc. of ‡ ברר vb. *purify,* and so Niph. *be purified, pure;* α.λ. in ptc.; in pf. Is. 52¹¹ of ceremonial purification of those bearing sacred vessels. Hithp. here and Dn. 12¹⁰. These three lines are in exact parallelism, with same preposition עם, syn. nouns, and syn. vbs. reflexive of the nouns, חסד, תמם, ברר. — תתברר, תתמם, תתחסד. — [עִם־עֵקֵשׁ תִּתְפַּתָּל] † עֵקֵשׁ adj. *twisted, perverted:* (1) as adj. Dt. 32⁵ Ps. 101⁴; (2) as noun masc., of persons Ps. 18²⁷ = 2 S. 22²⁷ Pr. 22⁵, of things Pr. 8⁸, cstr. Pr. 17²⁰ 19¹ 28⁶, pl. 2¹⁵ 11²⁰. Hithp. of vb. עקשׁ is not used, so the glossator substituted the kindred תִּתְפַּתָּל Hithp. of † [פתל] *twist,* α.λ. in Hithp. and only usage of this vb. in ψ. 2 S. has corrupted it תִּתַּפָּל = *shew oneself perverse,* or *crooked;* elsw. found only in Niph. Gn. 30⁸ (E) of struggling in a circle, Jb. 5¹³ of acting falsely; so also Pr. 8⁸ (‖ עִקֵּשׁ). — **28.** [כִּי אַתָּה] = 2 S. יָאֵת. The two readings may best be explained on the basis of an original ואת. The ו is intensive and so expressed by כי in the Ps., and the את is אַתָּ, as usual in most ancient Hebrew. — [עַם־עָנִי] phr. α.λ. For עני *v.* 9¹³. — [רָמוֹת] = 2 S. רמים, Qal ptc. pl. רום (*v.* 9¹⁴) for *the lofty, powerful* (*v.* also Jb. 21²², where Di., Bu., refer to angels); of enemies exalting themselves against, c. על Ps. 13³ 27⁸; c. מן Nu. 24⁷ (poet.). עינים על of 2 S. here is justified by Ps. 32⁸. It is impossible to explain txt. of Ps. from txt. of 2 S.; but if we start with the latter, עֵינֶיךָ עַל רָמִים *thine eyes are upon the lofty,* we may regard the txt. of Ps. as a paraphrase, תשׁפיל being exegetical

of עֲלֵי and 2 pers. sf. of עֵינֶיךָ, and then עֵינִים רָמוֹת explanation of רָמִים in terms
of WL. The line is complete without הַשְׁפִּיל; we may suppose that it came
into the text of 2 S. from text of Ps. The original would then be:

ואת עם־עני תושיע
ועיניך על רמים

Ps. = 29. — כי אתה תאיר נרי יהוה אלהי יגיה חשכי
2 S. = כי אתה   נירי יהוה ויחוה יגיה חשכי

The vb. תאיר in Ps. is unnecessary; it is doubtless a paraphrase. אֱלֹהַי is the
usage of the Ps., and is more probable than double יהוה. ‡ נֵר *lamp*; in ψ
only fig.; of prosperity here and 132[17] (עָרַכְתִּי נֵר לִמְשִׁיחִי), latter prob. based
on this passage; of the Law as guide 119[105]. הֵאִיר Hiph. impf. 2 m. אר vb.
shine (v. 13[4]). Hiph. *light a lamp* only here, but *light wood* Is. 27[11] altar
fire, Mal. 1[10]. — 30. נֵּר] instrumental, emph. — אָרֻץ גְּדוּד] *I run up to a band.*
Bä., after Lag., Ki., rds. ארץ גדור, *I break down a walled* (town); so Lucian
of 2 S. πεφραγμένος; Du. favours רצץ, but doubts גדור. But there is no
usage to justify רצץ גדור. There is more to justify רוץ vb. Qal, *run;* in
1 S. 17[22] David runs c. acc. הַמַּעֲרָכָה up to the army; although this is not in
hostility, yet there is no reason why acc. should not be used in case of hostility, as well as in case of friendly running; so fig. Pss. 19[6] 119[32]; *run and
prepare* (in hostility) 59[5]. — ‡ גְּדוּד n.m. *troop*, or *band* of marauders; this is
suited to early hostile relations; cf. Gn. 49[19] (poem), also vb. Ps. 94[21]. —
אֲדַלֶּג שׁוּר] vb. = Pi. impf. of ‡ דלג Qal, *leap*, not in ψ, 1 S. 5[5] (𝕲) Zp. 1[9]. Pi.
leap a.λ. in ψ (18[30] = 2 S. 22[30]); as a stag Is. 35[6]; c. עַל loci Ct. 2[8]. It is
nowhere else connected with שׁוּר, or cstr. with acc. ‡ שׁוּר n. *wall*, rare
word in Heb., but same in Ar. and Aram. = 2 S. 22[30]; elsw. Gn. 49[22]. —
31. אֵל רָמִים דַּרְכּוֹ] cf. Dt. 32[4] [אִמְרַת יהוה צְרוּפָה. — הַצּוּר תָּמִים פָּעֳלוֹ] although in
2 S. also, yet an early gl. from Pr. 30[5]. — מָגֵן הוּא לְכֹל הַחֹסִים בּוֹ] It might be
that this l. was taken from the same place. Certainly it has been influenced
by Pr. 30[5], although כֹל is a later expansion, marring the rhythm. But this
section of Ps. is composed of couplets, and v.[31a] needs its complement, and
that is found in v.[31c]; v.[31b] is a late gnomic utterance, out of harmony with
the Ps., but v.[31c] is suited to it. God as a shield מָגֵן is an early idea (v 3[4]).
For ב הֹסֶה v. v.[30]; but the original was prob. sg., as context is 1 sg.; rd.
לֹחֹסִי בוֹ. — 32. [כִּי מִי אֱלוֹהַּ מִבַּלְעֲדֵי]. 2 S. has אל, an earlier form of the divine
name, and doubtless correct. — 2 S. repeats [וּמִי צוּר זוּלָתִי]. ‡ בִּלְעֲדַי
(composite בַּל neg. and עֲדֵי *unto*) used in the sense *besides, except,* elsw.
Jos. 22[19] (P) Is. 43[11] 44[6, 8] 45[21]. ‡ זוּלָתִי is more common, 2 S. 7[22] Ho. 13[4]
Is. 45[5, 21] 64[3]. The term is monotheistic like Is.[2], and not like מִי כָמוֹכָה בָּאֵלִם
Ex. 15[11]. It seems prob. that the original was מ, and that an editor under
influence of Is.[2] adapted it by inserting מִבַּלְעֲדֵי, which appears in both ll. in
2 S., while the second l. of Ps. in better style uses זוּלָתִי. The ll. are too long
with these words inserted. — ‡ אֱלוֹהַּ] *God;* used Dt. 32[15, 17], and on this basis
as archaism in late poetry Pss. 50[22] 114[7] 139[19] Jb. 3[4] + 40 t. Jb. Pr. 30[5] Is. 44[8]

Hb. 3⁸ Ne. 9¹⁷ (v. Intr. § 32). — **33**. [הַמְאַזְּרֵנִי] Pi. ptc. of אזר, rel. with art. 2 S. מְעוּזִי; אזר is sustained by וַתְּאַזְּרֵנִי v.⁴⁰ᵃ of Ps. and וַתַּזְרֵנִי contr. from תאזר of 2 S. אזר vb. Qal, *gird, gird on*, not in ψ; but Pi. *18³³. ⁴⁰* (c. acc. חַיִל); 30¹² (שִׂמְחָה); elsw. Is. 45⁵ 50¹¹. Hithp. Ps. 93¹ c. acc. עֹז; cf. Is. 8⁹·⁹. — [וַיִּתֵּן דַּרְכִּי] = 2 S. וַיַּתֵּר דַּרְכִּי, but text of latter uncertain and it makes no good sense. נתן in sense of *make* elsw. v.⁴¹ 39⁶ 69¹² 135¹², etc. דרך here is the way for the feet. ו consec. expresses result here and below, *and so*. — **34**. [אַיָּלוֹת] pl. of אַיָּלָה† n.f. *hind, doe, 18³⁴* (= 2 S. 22³⁴) 29⁹ (?) Hb. 3¹⁹ Jb. 39¹ Gn. 49²¹ (?) Ct. 2⁷ 3⁵; cf. אַיָּל Ps. 22¹ Pr. 5¹⁹ Je. 14⁵. — [עַל בָּמֹתַי יַעֲמִידֵנִי] emph. noun first. בָּמוֹת for *battle-fields*, pl. of בָּמָה‡ n.f. *high place* 2 S. 1¹⁹·²⁵ (poem) Ps. 78⁵⁸, of Israel Ps. *18³⁴* = 2 S. 22³⁴ Dt. 32¹³ Is. 58¹⁴, cf. Dt. 33²⁹ Hb. 3¹⁹; of God Am. 4¹³, cf. Mi. 1³ Jb. 9⁸ Is. 14¹⁴. — [יַעֲמִידֵנִי] Hiph. only here in this connection with mng. *cause to hold one's ground* in battle. Qal is used in sense of *making a stand, holding one's ground*, Am. 2¹⁵ 2 K. 10⁴ Mal. 3², לכני Ju. 2¹⁴ et al., c. עַל for one's life Est. 8¹¹ 9¹⁵. — **35**. מְלַמֵּד יָדַי [לַמִּלְחָמָה] adopted in 144¹ and enlarged: הַמְלַמֵּד יָדַי לַקְרָב אֶצְבְּעוֹתַי לַמִּלְחָמָה. [וְנִחֲתָה קֶשֶׁת נְחוּשָׁה זְרוֹעֹתָי]. The l. is too long. קֶשֶׁת is a gl. explaining נְחוּשָׁה, *copper, bronze*, as material of bow, elsw. Jb. 20²⁴, from which קֶשֶׁת may have come into the text. וְנִחֲתָה = 2 S. וְנִחַת, usually explained after AE. as Pi., the latter 3 m. sg., c. ו consec. for 3 f. sg. of Ps. — [נַחַת‡] vb. Qal, *go down, descend*: to attack Je. 21¹³, into Sheol Jb. 21¹³, fig. in chastisement (hand of י) Ps. 38³; c. בְּ *descend into, make an impression* (of reproof) Pr. 17¹⁰. Niph. sq. בְּ *penetrate* Ps. 38³ (arrows of י). Pi. *press down*, furrows of land Ps. 65¹¹, so *B*DB (but with doubt), *press down, stretch* bronze weapon (bow) *18³⁵* = 2 S. 22³⁵, but bow was not stretched with hands, but with feet, *v.* 7¹³. Ki. regards the forms as Niph. of חתת *be broken*, cf. Je. 51⁵⁶. 𝕲 ἔθου, 𝕵 *posuisti;* so essentially 𝕾, 𝕵, 𝕿, all suggest וְהָרַבָּה, which is most prob. — **36**. [וְעַנְוַתְךָ תַרְבֵּנִי] = 2 S. וַעֲנֹתְךָ תַּרְבֵּנִי; וַתִּתֶּן לִי consec. as v.³³ᵇ. — וַיִמִינֶךָ ו circumstantial. — [וִימִינְךָ‡] ; 𝕲, Θ, ἡ παιδεία σου; 𝕵 *et disciplina tua;* so 𝕾, Aq., ἡ πραΰτης σου; 𝕵 *mansuetudo tua;* Ols., We., rd. עֶזְרָתְךָ. The shorter text of 2 S. is alone sustained by both Vrss. and the unpointed וענותך תרבני; but this makes too short a line. — [עֲנָוָה†] n.f. (1) *humility, meekness*, 45⁵; so 22²⁵ (Aq., 𝕵); elsw. Pr. 15³³ 18¹² 22⁴ Zp. 2³; (2) *condescension*, usually given here is without authority, and to be rejected; the idea itself is a late one. וַעֲנֹתְךָ Qal inf. cstr. c. sf. 2 sg. of ענה *answer* (v. 3⁵) in the sense of response, in docility to the divine guidance, is sustained by Ho. 2¹⁷, and this is near to 𝕲 of 2 S. ὑπακοή. 𝕲 of Ps. παιδεία suggests עֲנּוֹת *afflicting, disciplining;* cf. Ps. 132¹. The sf. would then be objective. תַרְבֵּנִי Hiph. impf. 2 m., c. sf. 1 sg. of רבה in the sense of *educate*, found in Pi. (of the bringing up of children) La. 2²² Ez. 19², but in its application to the training of men it is late; so that in this case also we get a late conception. The 𝕲 of Ps. gives us a conflation: ἡ παιδεία σου ἀνώρθωσέν με εἰς τέλος, καὶ ἡ παιδεία σου αὐτή με διδάξει. — **37**. [תַּרְחִיב] *enlarge;* Hiph. impf. 2 m. (of graphic description, *v.* 4²). — [צַעַד‡] n.m. *step;* so 2 S. 22³⁷ for place of stepping, not elsw. in ψ. ‡ צָעַד vb. Qal, *step* Ps. 68⁸ = Ju. 5⁴ of י stepping in theophany. † [כָּצְדֵי]

n.[m.] *step* Dn. 11⁴³ (*at his steps*); fig. of course of life Ps. 37²³ Pr. 20²⁴. —
וּמְעָדוּ קַרְסֻלַי phr. a.λ. †[מעד] vb. Qal, *totter, shake :* of ankles Ps. *18*³⁷ =
2 S. 22³⁷ Jb. 12⁵; subj. אֲשֻׁרִים Ps. 37³¹; cf. 26¹. Hiph. *cause to totter, shake,*
Ps. 69²⁴ Ez. 29⁷ (?). Pu. not in ψ, but Pr. 25¹⁰. הָרְסֹי pl. c. sf. 1 sg. of [קרסל]
n.f. *ankles* (*B*DB.) a.λ. — **38.** [עַר כָּלִיתָם] Pi. inf. cstr. c. sf. 3 pl. ‡ כלה vb. *be
complete, at an end, finished.* Qal in ψ only: (1) *waste away, be exhausted,
fail,* 31¹¹ 71⁹ 73²⁶ 102⁴ 143⁷; *pine, languish,* 69⁴, cf. 119⁸²·¹²³; with longing
84³ 119⁸¹; (2) *come to an end, vanish, perish* (by judgment of יֿ) 71¹³;
hyperb., by severe discipline 37²⁰·²⁰ 39¹¹ 90⁷. Pi. (1) *put an end to, cause
to cease,* 78³¹; (2) *cause to fail, use up, spend,* years 90⁹; (3) *destroy, exterminate,* subj. man 119⁸⁷; † עַד כְּלוֹת = 2 S. 22³⁸, also 1 S. 15¹⁸, 1 K. 22¹¹ =
2 Ch. 18¹⁰; subj. God, abs. Ps. 59¹⁴·¹⁴ 74¹¹ (?). Pual, *be finished, ended,* 72²⁰. —

39. Ps. = אֶמְחָצֵם וְלֹא יֻכְלוּ קוּם
2 S. = וָאֲכַלֵּם וָאֶמְחָצֵם וְלֹא יְקוּמוּן

𝕲 of 2 S. has καὶ θλάσω αὐτοὺς καὶ οὐκ ἀναστήσονται. וָאֲכַלֵּם is a repetition
of כלות by error of enlargement and addition to the text; but ו consec. is
possibly expressive of result, and original. וְלֹא יֻכְלוּ is also an interpretation
of the modal force of יְקוּמוּן. אֶמְחָצֵם Hiph. impf. 1 sg. c. sf. 3 pl. of ‡ מחץ vb.
Qal, *smite through* foes; elsw. in Ps. 110⁵, their heads 68²² 110⁶ Hb. 3¹³ Ju. 5²⁶,
loins Dt. 33¹¹; cf. Ps. 68²⁴ (?). — [וַיִּפְלוּ] in 2 S. more correctly וַיִּפְלוּ; the Ps.
would make it future, for Israel; 2 S. makes it past, of David's experience.
40. וַתְּאַזְּרֵנִי חַיִל לַמִּלְחָמָה (= 2 S. וַתַּזְרֵנִי) is so near v.³³ᵃ as to be suspicious;
however, it is in both texts, and it might be a resumption of thought at beginning of new Str. — [תַּכְרִיעַ] Hiph. impf. 2 m., ו consec. omitted here and in
2 S. also. ‡ Hiph. of כרע *cause to bow down* in death; in ψ elsw. *17*¹³ 78³¹. —
[וְאֹיְבַי] 2 S. הַכְרֵנִי older form. — **41.** [וְאֹיְבַי], ו is either emph. or circumstantial.
— [נָתַן עֹרֶף] phr. elsw. Ex. 23²⁷ (E) 2 Ch. 29⁶; of hand on neck of fleeing
foe Gn. 49⁸, הָפַךְ ע׳ Jos. 7⁸, פָּנָה ע׳ 7¹² (JE); עֹרֶף n.m. not elsw. in ψ. —
[וּמְשַׂנְאַי אַצְמִיתֵם] = 2 S. מְשַׂנְאַי וְאַצְמִיתֵם. The transposition of ו is all the more
significant that 2 S. attaches מִשַּׂנְאַי to עֹרֶף; but that makes the previous line
too long. If 2 S. be correct, it is best to take ו as ו consec. emph. change of
tense, so making two tones for measure. If Ps. be correct, ו is probably circumstantial, but a tone is missing. †[צמת] vb. *put an end to, exterminate :*
Qal only La. 3⁵³. Niph. only Jb. 6¹⁷ 23¹⁷. Pi. only Ps. 119¹³⁹. Pilel only
Ps. 88¹⁷ (?). Hiph. only in ψ; of man's extermination of enemies *18*⁴¹ (=
2 S. 22⁴¹), of wicked 101⁵·⁸ 69⁵ (txt. err.), of God's exterminating 54⁷ 73²⁷
94²³·²³ 143¹². 𝕲 has here, both in Ps. and 2 S., ἐξωλέθρευσας; 𝔙, 𝔍, *disper-
didisti,* 𝔖 refer. to God, but Aq., 𝔖, Σ, and 𝔗 1 p. as 𝕳. — **42.** [יְשַׁוְּעוּ]
they cry for help, Pi. impf. 3 m. pl. (*v.* 5³), for which 2 S. has יִשְׁעוּ impf. of
שׁעה *look about* (for help), but this sense elsw. only in Hithp. Is. 41¹⁰. Du.
suggests יִשְׁעוּ as a play upon מוֹשִׁיעַ; this is tempting (*v.* 3⁸). — [עַל] of Ps. err.
of late style for אֶל of 2 S. — **43.** [וְאֶשְׁחָקֵם] ו coörd.; but original was ו consec.
as above. — [כְּעָפָר עַל־פְּנֵי־רוּחַ] of Ps. is a later metaphor for the simpler כַּעֲפַר אָרֶץ

of 2 S.—כְּטִיט חוּצוֹת] *mud of the streets*, always sim. of ignominious defeat or treatment; elsw. Mi. 7¹⁰ Zc. 9³ 10⁶; cf. Ps. 69¹⁵ of a bog, fig. of distress; ט׳ הַיָּוֵן Ps. 40³; כִּיט n.m. not elsw. in ψ.—[אֲרִיקֵם = 2 S. אֲרִקֵּם אֶרְקָעֵם. The second word in 2 S. is gl. of first. 𝔊 λεανῶ, 𝔙 *delebo*; so 𝔖, 𝔗, of Ps. give אֶרְקָּם, for which אריקם ,ארקכ is a txt. err. ריק (v. 35³) does not suit טיט, but ארקם does = Hiph. impf. 1 sg. c. sf. 3 pl. of ‡דקק. Qal not in ψ. Hiph. *make dust of, pulverise:* לעפר 2 K. 23⁶ (of Ashera) ‖ 2 Ch. 34⁴·⁷; so of the במה 2 K. 23¹⁵; fig. Mi. 4¹³ (עמים רבים); so here also.—44. [תְּפַלְּטֵנִי = 2 S. מְרִיבֵי עָם ‡; ו consec. original, makes new start as v.²⁸·³³·³⁶·⁴⁰.—[וַתְּפַלְּטֵנִי 2 S. עַמִּי is original; the Ps. generalises. מִן prep., רִיבֵי pl. cstr. ‡ ריב n.m. (1) *strife:* ר׳ בעיר 55¹⁰; (2) *a cause* ר׳ לשׁנות 31²¹; 35²⁸ 43¹ 74²² 119¹⁵⁴; רִיבֵי עַמִּי 2 S. 22⁴⁴ seems to imply civil contention, and so was generalised in Ps. to refer to foreign peoples.—[תְּשִׂימֵנִי = 2 S. הִשְׁמַרְתַּנִי; the latter presupposes David already chief of nations; the former, his being set there by Yahweh for the first time. The text of Ps. is simpler and more probable. שׁים is also more suited to לְרֹאשׁ.—[ראשׁ] in sense of *chief* not elsw. in ψ, but in early writers Dt. 33⁶ 1 S. 15¹⁷ Ju. 11⁸ Ho. 2²; cf. Jb. 29²⁵.—45. ‡ [נֵכָר n.[m.] *that which is foreign:* † בְּנֵי (ה)נֵכָר 18⁴⁵·⁴⁶ = 2 S. 22⁴⁵·⁴⁶ Ps. 144⁷·¹¹ Ez. 44⁷ Is. 56⁶ 60¹⁰ 61⁵ 62⁸, בֶּן (ה)נכר Gn. 17¹²·²⁷ Ex. 12⁴³ (P) Lv. 22²⁵ (H) Ez. 44⁹·⁹ Ne. 9² Is. 56³, none earlier than Ez.; elsw. in ψ, אַדְמַת נ׳ 137⁴, אֵל גֵּכָר 81¹⁰ Dt. 32¹² Mal. 2¹¹. ‡ נָכְרִי *a foreigner* 69⁹. This phr. implies either an insertion not earlier than the Persian Period, or else that the whole ψ is so late.—[יְכַחֲשׁוּ־לִי = 2 S. יִתְכַּחֲשׁוּ־לִי. ‡ כחשׁ vb. †Qal, *grow lean* (of flesh) only 109²⁴; usually Pi. in early writers *deceive*, but in ψ only *cringe* sq. לְ pers. 18⁴⁵ 66³ 81¹⁶. Cf. †Niph. *cringe* sq. לְ pers. only Dt. 33²⁹. †Hithp. only 2 S. 22⁴⁵. —46. [יִבֹּלוּ] Qal impf. 3 pl. of נבל (v. 1³) *sink, drop down exhausted;* elsw. in this sense Ex. 18¹⁸ (E) Jb. 14¹⁸.—[וַיַּחְרְגוּ = 2 S. וְיַחְגְּרוּ, ו coörd. †חרג vb. Qal, *quake;* Aramaism, a.λ. חגר of 2 S. *gird, gird on*, is a common vb., but gives no sense; rd. either יֶרְגְּזוּ as Mi. 7¹⁷, which greatly resembles this passage (v. 4⁵), or יחרדו *tremble*, which is often used pregnantly with מִן, *come trembling* Ho. 11¹⁰·¹¹ and with other prep. 1 S. 13⁷ 16⁴ 21² Gn. 42²⁸ (E).— [מִמִּסְגְּרוֹתֵיהֶם = 2 S. מִמְּסִנְּרוֹתָם has two accents as long word with prep. מִן. ‡ מִסְגֶּרֶת n.f. *fastness;* in this sense elsw. Mi. 7¹⁷, but in sense of *border, rim*, in Historical Books. Cf. ‡ מַסְגֵּר *dungeon* Is. 24²² fig. of exile 42⁷ Ps. 142⁸.— 47. [חַי יהוה] *Yahweh liveth*, elsw. formula of oath (Ju. 8¹⁹ +). ‡ חַי adj. *alive, living:* (1) (a) of God, as *the living One*, fountain of life; so here = 2 S. 22⁴⁷; cf. אֵל חַי Pss. 42³ 84³ (rd. חיו both cases, and so חייב), also Jos. 3¹⁰ (J) Ho. 2¹; cf. אלהים חי 2 K. 19⁴·¹⁶ = Is. 37⁴·¹⁷, א׳ חיים Dt. 5²³ 1 S. 17²⁶·³⁶ Je. 10¹⁰ 23³⁶. (b) Of man, usually pl. חיים *alive, living*, Ps. 55¹⁶ 124⁸; ארץ (ה)חיים *land of the living* Pss. 27¹³ 52⁷ 142⁶, also Is. 38¹¹ 53⁸ Je. 11¹⁹ Ez. 26²⁰ 32²³⁺⁵ᵗ. Jb. 28¹³; ארצות הח׳ Ps. 116⁹; ספר ח׳ 69²⁹; אור הח׳ 56¹⁴ Jb. 33³⁰. (c) Animals and man, phr. for either or both, כל חי Pss. 143² 145¹⁶ Gn. 3²⁰ 8²¹ (J) Jb. 12¹⁰ 28²¹ 30²³; cf. Gn. 6¹⁹ (P). (d) Vegetation, as thorns, *green* Ps. 58¹⁰ (dub.). (2) *Lively, active:* איבו חי ם Ps. 38²⁰ (dub.); elsw. in this sense only 2S. 23²⁰ (but Qr. preferable. — יהוה comes with following phr. in Ps. 144¹, which has

162 · PSALMS

בָּרוּךְ · us ‏י; this, being in a pentameter line, one word must be omitted. If יהוה be omitted, we have the citation בָּרוּךְ צוּרִי. יהוה has prob. been inserted after ברוך in 144¹ and before it in 18⁴⁷. בָּרוּךְ Qal ptc. pass. of ברך (*v. 5¹³*): ‡ בָּרוּךְ י׳ *blessed be* or *is Yahweh* 28⁶ 31²² 41¹⁴ 72¹⁸ 89⁵³ 106⁴⁸ 119¹² 124⁶ 135²¹ 144¹ (but *v.* above); אלהים ב׳ 66²⁾ 68³³; ב׳ אדני 68²⁾; cf. ב׳ אל עליון Gn. 14²⁾; ב׳ צורי Ps. 18⁴⁷ = 2 S. 22⁴⁷ (also Ps. 144¹, *v.* above); ב׳ שֵׁם כְּבוֹדוֹ Ps. 72¹⁹. — [וְיָרוּם = 2 S. וְיָרֻם *be exalted*, of God; elsw. 21¹⁴ 46¹¹·¹¹ 57⁶·¹² = 108⁶ 113⁴ 138⁶ (*v. 9¹⁴*). — [אֱלֹהֵי צוּר יִשְׁעִי = 2 S. אֱלֹהֵי צוּר יִשְׁעִי. צוּר is more primitive and the term of original Ps. It may, however, have come into text from line above, as it is tautological. Cf. אלי צורי v.³, קרן ישעי v.³. — 48. [נְקָמוֹת *deeds of vengeance*, pl. of ‡ נקמה n.f. *vengeance*: c. ‏נקם Ps. 18⁴⁸ = 2 S. 22⁴⁸ 4⁸ Ez. 25¹⁴·¹⁷ (of God); Nu. 31³ (P) of Israel נתן נ׳ ר׳; elsw. נ׳ רם Ps. 79¹⁰; אל נ׳ 94¹·¹; of Israel and its chiefs נ׳ עשׂה 149⁷. — [וַיַּדְבֵּר = 2 S. וַיֹּרִיד. Text of Ps. gives an Aramaic word, Hiph. of דבר *subdue*, elsw. only 47⁴. But text of 2 S., Hiph. of ירד, gives a good ancient word in sense of *bring down, lay prostrate*, Am. 3¹ Is. 10¹³ 63⁶ Ps. 56⁸. הורד is favoured by 144², which is based on this Ps. and reads הָרוֹדֵד עַמִּי תַחְתָּי (Aq., 𝔍, 𝔖, 𝔗, all have pl.). — [תַחְתָּי = 2 S. רַחֲנִי as above, v.⁴⁰. — 49. [מְפַלְטִי = 2 S. וּמוֹצִיאִי. This is intentional variation מְפַרְטִי v.³ᵃ, תפלטני v.⁴⁴ᵃ. 2 S. gives better parallel with תְּרוֹמְמֵנִי. — [מִן קָמַי] contracted from וּמִן אִיְבַי needed for third beat as in v.⁴⁹ᵇ. — [מֵאִיְבַי] for 2 S. מְקָמָי; only אַף of Ps. is explanatory of ו of 2 S. — [מֵאִישׁ חָמָס = 2 S. מֵאִישׁ חֲמָסִים. This makes third l. of verse and is suspicious. The sg. is usual 140¹² Pr. 3⁸¹ 16²⁹; but pl. 140²·⁵ *man of violent deeds*. The pl. is favoured by נְחֻמוֹת v.⁴⁸ᵃ, יְשׁוּעוֹת v.⁵¹ᵃ (*v. 3³*); but the sg. by the individual reference of the original Ps. — 51. [מַגְדִּל וְשׁוּעוֹת phr. α.λ. מַגְדִּל Hiph. ptc. גדל vb. Qal, *become great* 92⁶ +, *be magnified* 35²⁷ +. Hiph. (1) *make great* 41¹⁰ (?) Ob.¹²; (2) *magnify*, here as Gn. 19¹⁹ (J) Is. 42²¹ Ps. 138². 2 S. מגדיל Kt., but מגדול Qr. n.m. *tower*, α.λ. for מִגְדָּל 48¹³ 61⁴.

PSALM XIX.

Ps. 19 is composed of two originally separate poems: (*A*) a morning hymn, praising the glory of 'El in the heavens (v.²⁻⁵ᵇ), and glorious movements of the sun (v.⁵ᶜ⁻⁷); (*B*) a didactic poem, describing the excellence of the Law (v.⁸⁻¹¹), with a petition for absolution, restraint from sin, and acceptance in worship (v.¹²⁻¹⁵).

A. v.²⁻⁷, 2 STR. 6³.

THE heavens are telling the glory of 'El,
His handiwork the firmament is declaring;
Day poureth forth speech unto day,
Night maketh known knowledge unto night;
In all the earth their voice is gone out,
And in the bounds of the world are their words.

FOR the sun there is set up *his* tent.
As a bridegroom he is going forth from *his* canopy.
He rejoiceth as a hero to run *his* course.
From the bound of the heavens is *his* going forth,
And unto their bounds is *his* circuit,
And there is nothing hidden from *His* sun.

B. V.[8-15], 2 STR. 6[5].

THE Law of Yahweh is perfect, refreshing the soul;
The Testimony of Yahweh is trustworthy, making wise the simple;
The Precepts of Yahweh are right, rejoicing the heart;
The Commandment of Yahweh is pure, enlightening the eyes;
The (Saying) of Yahweh is clean, enduring forever;
The Judgments of Yahweh are true, vindicated altogether.
MOREOVER Thy servant is warned by them; in keeping them there is much
reward.
Errors who can discern? Clear me from hidden ones.
Moreover from presumptuous ones restrain Thy servant; let them not rule
over me.
Then shall I be perfect, and cleared from much transgression.
Let the words of my mouth be for acceptance, and the musing of my mind,
Before Thee continually, Yahweh, my Rock and my Redeemer.

Ps. 19 was in 𝔇, then in 𝔐 and 𝔇ℜ (*v.* Intr. §§ 27, 31, 33); but this only
applies to the first half of the Ps. v.[2-7], for the second half was originally a
separate poem. The first half has the trimeter measure, the second half the
pentameter. The first half is a morning hymn of praise of the glory of 'El as
witnessed by heaven, and especially of the sun. The second half is not a
hymn, but a didactic poem in praise of the Law. These were combined in
order that, in public worship, a synthesis of the two might be made, and that
it might be seen that the glory of Yahweh in the Law transcends His glory in
the heavens. The latter is used as a foil to emphasize the former by its
antithesis. The date of the first half is not difficult to determine. Its conception of the creation v.[2], as the work of God's hands, resembles that of
Ps. 8, yet without betraying the influence of the conceptions of creation
either of Gn. 1 or of Gn. 2. It has a single Aramaism מדה v.[5]; but that is
found in 2 S. 23[2], and cannot therefore be regarded as very late. חמה v.[7] is
also, as a poetic term for sun, not earlier than Is. 30[26], used elsw. Is. 24[23],
Jb. 30[28], Ct. 6[10]. This is, however, a poetic term which might have been
used first in this Ps., and may be due to the circumstances out of which it
was composed. The author was a true poet; an enthusiastic admirer of the sun,
which is here personified, as are days and nights, the heavens and the firmament. It may have been written as a protest of a monotheist against the
worship of Shemesh as a deity, described in Ez. 8[16], and common among the
Jews in the Babylonian period. At the same time it must be admitted that
the sun in the second Str. is not declaring the glory of 'El, as are the heavens

and firmament, days and nights of the first Str., but is himself the object of admiration; and therefore it is quite possible that in the original the Ps. was a hymn to the God Shemesh, and was subsequently adapted to the worship of Yahweh. In either case we must put the composition in the Babylonian period, when such sun worship was characteristic and prevalent among the Hebrews and the nations which influenced them. Since writing the above I have read Gunkel's *Ausgewählte Psalmen*, s. 24, and find that he has independently come to a similar conclusion. The second half of the Ps. v.[8-15] is of an entirely different character. It is a pentameter in praise of the divine Law, using six different terms for it. In this respect it resembles Ps. 119, which is also a pentameter, but uses eight terms. The limitation in Ps. 19 is due to the number of lines in the Str. D. H. Müller (*Strophenbau und Responsion*, s. 60), followed by Che., supplies the other two terms for Law by prefixing them to the two tetrameter lines that follow, thus making them pentameters. This is tempting from that point of view. But it would be difficult to explain their omission from all texts and Vrss.; and, furthermore, as will appear in textual notes, this couplet is a gloss, making the Str. just so much too long as compared with the subsequent Str. In other respects these Pss. are so alike that they must be attributed to the same period, when the legislation of P was the great central and substantial fact in the Hebrew religion. The term and conceptions of the priestly legislation are evident: שגנות, sins of ignorance or inadvertence ‖ נס־תרות, over against זדים רב פשע v.[13. 14]. The use of the sacrificial term לרצון v.[15] is to be noted. The term ערות v.[8] is characteristic of P, and is emphasised by having the second place after תורה. רקורים v.[9] is used elsw. only Pss. 119[4 + 20 (21) t.] 103[18] 111[7], and is very late. This part of the Ps. cannot be put any earlier than the Greek period. V.[11] is gnomic in character, using terms and conceptions characteristic of WL. If original, it implies the Greek period also. But it is a tetrameter couplet. It makes the Str. just these two lines too long; it is therefore a gloss. This part of the Ps. was probably earlier than Ps. 119.

PSALM XIX. *A.*

Str. I. is composed of three syn. couplets, the first and second syn. to each other v.[2-3], the third synth. v.[5] to them. A prosaic gloss has been inserted between them v.[4]. — **2-3**. *The heavens, the firmament, day and night*, are all personified; as the heavens 50[6] 97[6], the morning stars Jb. 38[7], the hills and trees Is. 55[12], and nature in general Ps. 148[2 sq.] Jb. 12[7 sq.]. — *are telling ‖ is declaring*]. The participles indicate that this action goes on continually without interruption. These pass over into imperfects, *poureth forth ‖ maketh known*], because it is necessary to express the oft-repeated action of one day pouring forth unto

another day, and one night making known to another night; and
these latter taking up the strain and passing it on to their successors in an endless chain of praise, which Ros. compares to a ring
of dancers repeating the song in a series, and Horne, "like two
parts of a choir chanting forth alternately the praises of God."
These are illustrative conceptions from usages of other nations;
but there is no evidence that the Hebrews had these usages, or
that the poet thought of them. The theme is *the glory of 'El*,
especially as manifested in *His handiwork. The firmament*, the
expanse of heaven, is conceived as having been spread out by the
hands of God at the creation, as elsewhere the earth Is. 42^5 44^{24}
Ps. 136^6, and so as ever after exhibiting and praising the master
workman's power and honour. This is a different conception of
their creation from that of Gn. 1, where they are created by word
of command. It rather resembles Ps. 8^4. It is tempting under
the circumstances, with Ges., to think of the speech in the more
specific sense of hymn; but this has no authority in Hebrew
usage, and is too specific for the subsequent as well as the previous syn. terms. The *speech* and the *knowledge*, though undefined by suffix, must, from the context, mean speech about 'El,
and knowledge of 'El. — **4.** *There is no speech and there are no
words, their voice is not heard*], so most naturally translated, is
rather a tame explanation of the previous lines. "This seems to be
a kind of correction or explanation of the bold figure which had
ascribed language to the heavens," Pe. It is difficult to see, then,
why Pe. did not draw the reasonable inference with Ols., followed
by Du., that it is a prosaic gloss. This internal reason is fortified
by the external one that these two lines make this Str. just two
lines too long in proportion to its antistr. The numerous attempts
to get an appropriate meaning out of the verse have all failed to
give satisfaction; as indeed they are all awkward and entirely out of
place in a Ps. of such wonderful simplicity, terseness, and graphic
power. There is no agreement of EV^s. in their translations. —
—**5ab.** *In all the earth*], emph., in antith. to the heavens v.^{2a}.
The heavens are telling to the earth, and their message extends
throughout the earth ‖ *in the bounds of the world*], that is in the
extreme limits of the inhabited world. — *their voice*], in accordance with the parallel, *their words*], but this requires, with most

modern scholars, after the ancient versions, the correction of the Hebrew text, which by the change of a single letter reads "their line," instead of "their voice." The Hebrew word translated "their line" admits only of the meaning measuring line, which, while it is suited to the thought of extension to the earth's limits, and might spring into the mind of a copyist whose attention was confined, in copying, to this single line, is yet out of harmony with the thought which is emphasised in each of the other five lines of the Str. The proposal to render the Hebrew word "string" of a musical instrument, and so the string, for the sound of it, though urged by Ew. and others, and possibly in accordance with usage in other languages, is not justified by Hebrew usage.

Str. II. is progressive throughout, and is an antistr. to the previous one. As the previous Str. sets forth the glory of 'El, this Str. describes the glory of the sun. — 5c. *For the sun is set*]. The sun is personified, as were heavens and firmament, day and night, of the previous Str., yet not as praising the creator, but as the theme of the praise of the poet. The *'El* of the previous Str. does not appear at all in this Str., unless we suppose Him to be the unexpressed subject of the verb "set," and so render "He hath set." The vb. may, however, be more properly regarded in the present context as having a general subject expressed in English by the passive, "is set." The sun is emphasised at the beginning and also at the close of this Str. v.[7b], as the great theme of its praise. It is therefore really put in parall. with the *'El* of the previous Str., while the poet puts himself in parall. with the personified heavens, firmament, day and night. It seems most natural, therefore, to identify the sun with *'El*. Was the Ps., then, originally a hymn in praise of the god *Shemesh*, who was worshipped in Jerusalem just before the exile, Ez. 8[16]? or is *Shemesh* used for the God of Israel, as in Ps. 84[12]? The praise of God by the sun, so conspicuous in 148[3], is here conspicuous by its absence. On the whole, it seems probable that the Ps. was originally composed in honour of the god *Shemesh*, and that it was subsequently adapted by a few changes to the worship of the God of Israel, by interpreting *'El* in accordance with Hebrew usage, and by interpreting the vb. as having *'El* as subject, and so giving the sun a subordinate position. It is probable that the

preposition ל was prefixed by the editor, and was not original.
The original probably read, "Shemesh has set up his tent."
𝕳 makes a still further modification of the original in order to
connect with the previous Str. by adding "in them," which was
not in the original of 𝕲, and makes the line too long for the
normal measure. The reference to the heavens, which was doubtless designed by this addition, can only be made proper by following 𝕳, and attaching this line to the previous one, and so
destroying the strophical organisation of the Ps. All other explanations give grammatical difficulties. De W. thinks of the
End of the world as the dwelling of the sun. Thus Helios turns
into Thetis ; and Ossian gives the sun a shady cave in which to
pass the night. But all this is in the realm of mythology, and in
so far as these ideas are based on primitive worship of the sun,
rather favours the thought that the Ps. was originally a hymn to
Shemesh = *Helios.* We may think of the *tent* of the sun as in
Hb. 3¹¹, where sun and moon have their dwelling ; or of the
tent of the god *Shemesh*, in accordance with the constant conception of the heavenly temple or abode of God. — **6.** "And he,"
emph. reference to the sun, is unnecessary and difficult to justify
from the context, and it destroys the measure. It is doubtless a
gloss due to the effort to distinguish between '*El* and the sun. —
As a bridegroom], not implying a marriage of the sun, but setting
forth the freshness, the vigour, and the joy with which the rising
sun appears in the East. — *He is going forth from his canopy*].
During the night he has been in his tent, or abode, and behind
and beneath his canopy ; at daybreak he comes forth from the
night's retirement with fresh, youthful, full-grown vigour. — *He
rejoiceth as a hero to run his course*]. The path of the sun in
the heavens is conceived as a racecourse. The ancient warrior or
hero was a runner as well as a fighter, and he enjoyed running as
well as fighting. — **7.** *From the bound of the heavens*], the extreme
East, *is his going forth*], rising. - *unto their bounds*], the extreme
limits of the West, *is his circuit*], the fully rounded course. — *And
there is nothing hidden*], all things throughout the earth come
under his inspection during his circuit ; nothing on the earth's
surface escapes from his rays. — *from His sun*], that is God's
sun ; so the Hebrew word is elsewhere always translated, and in

this sense it gives the most appropriate climax in antith. to the beginning of the Str. The usual rendering, "from his heat," while etymologically possible, has no usage whatever to justify it, and unduly limits the thought to heat, when the term "hid" would more naturally suggest light of the sun, which is thought of also under the more general word "His sun." At the same time it seems likely that the editor, who adapted the Ps. to the worship of the God of Israel, was responsible for the addition of the suffix, and that the original simply used *Hamah* as a parallel word to *Shemesh*, both alike referring to the same god. This, then, gives us the most appropriate climax, that all things earthly are under the eye of God, in accordance with a conception common to the OT., that God, enthroned in heaven, sees, knows, and inspects all things earthly. It is also common to the hymns to the god *Shemesh*, that he is the great inspector and judge of all the earth.

PSALM XIX. *B.*

Str. I. 7–10 has six syn. lines in praise of the Law. There are six different terms for Law, one for each line of the Str., each technically expressing some one special type of Law in ancient usage; but it is doubtful how far those distinctions were felt in the time when this Ps. was composed. *The Law of Yahweh* is the Law conceived as teaching, doctrine, and is especially characteristic of special laws of priestly origin. *The Testimony* is a term characteristic of the priestly legislation, and is the Law conceived as giving testimony for Yahweh, and so is appropriate as a mate of "Law." *Precepts* are types of Law known only to late psalmists. They are divine prescriptions of Law. This term is, indeed, a late syn. for *Commandment*, which is characteristic of the prophetic commands of the Deuteronomic code. — *The Saying*], for so we must correct the text, for "The fear of Yahweh," which is unknown elsw. as a term for Law, and was a mistake for the similar Hebrew word, which is a poetic synonym of "Word" in the usage of Ps. 119, a characteristic term of the most ancient type of prophetic Law, and one which least of all could be omitted from the series. It is, moreover, most appropriate as a mate for *Judgments*, which is also an ancient pre-Deuteronomic type of Law, characteristic of the Code of the Covenant, Ex. 21–22, and also of the recently discovered code of the ancient king Hamurabbi. The only terms of Ps. 119 absent are the " Word," the syn. of " Saying," and the " Statute," an earlier type of the " Judgment " ; the terms most likely to be omitted by a late Hebrew poet, if he must make an omission, due to the limitations of his Str. Each one of the terms for Law has its adjective. These do not seem specially appropriate to the particular terms. There seems to be no good reason why they should not be used interchangeably here, as in Ps. 119 on a much larger scale, extending through twenty-two strophes. These adjectives are : *perfect*, complete, entire, without defect, *v.* 18[31] ; *trustworthy*, firm, reliable, to be depended upon ; *right*, equitable, just ; *pure*, spotless ; *clean*, without impurity or contamination ; *true*, in their exact conformity to justice. Each of the legal terms has also its beneficent activity: " *refreshing the soul*," or " restoring " it, RV., imparting refreshment to the inner man, his true soul-food, as Dt. 8[a] Mt. 4[4]. The translation " converting the soul," PBV., AV., while true enough in itself, and in accordance with other uses of the term, is too specific here and not in accord with the context. — *making wise the simple*], imparting the divine wisdom contained in the Law to those who are so open-minded that they are capable of receiving it. — *rejoicing the heart*], taking hold of the affections and imparting gladness as well as instruction. — *enlightening the eyes*], the eyes of the mind, so that they may see and understand, cf. 119[105, 130] Eph. 1[18]. — *enduring forever*], not transient, but permanent ; not changeable, but standing firm and immovable. — *vindicated altogether*], cf. 51[6] ; so in accordance with all the previous lines, and not " righteous " as a quality ; for statements as to quality are reserved in all the other lines for the first half of the verse. The Str. has come to an appropriate conclusion. If it were to be continued, the two missing words for Law would be used with appropriate adjectives and verbal clauses.

11. These two words are indeed supplied by D. H. Müller, and Che. at the beginning of the two lines of the following couplet, but even then these lines would be entirely different in character from the previous ones.

> They are to be desired more than gold, yea than much fine gold;
> They are sweeter than honey, and the droppings of honeycombs.

A similar thought to v.^{11a} is indeed in 119$^{72, 127}$; but the couplet resembles more closely Pr. 3$^{14-15}$ 8$^{10-11}$ Jb. 28$^{15-19}$, and its thought may be regarded as characteristic of Hebrew Wisdom rather than of Hebrew Law. The use of it here was doubtless on the basis of the uses of Hebrew Wisdom and from a glossator whose enthusiasm for the Law justified him in ascribing to it the characteristics also of Wisdom.

Str. II. has six progressive pentameters. — **12.** *Moreover*], emphasizing following words. — *Thy servant*], emphatic in position, whether we think of the individual Israelite as a worshipper of God, or of the nation as in a special sense the servant of Yahweh, in accord with the conception of Is.^{2}. — *is warned*]. The positive benefits of the Law, in the previous Str., now pass over into negative benefits, in relation to transgression, in warning against it. — *in keeping them*], observing the Law by obedience. — *there is much reward*], in consequence of a beneficent kindness. — **13.** *Errors*], transgressions of Law, due to ignorance or inadvertence; characteristic of the distinctions of the priestly legislation. These committed unconsciously trouble the psalmist; for, *who can discern*], either their number or their enormity, and the extent of their departure from the norm of duty. — *Clear me*], is the prayer; acquit, absolve, or possibly, as often, leave me unpunished. — *from hidden ones*], those errors which are so hidden from the psalmist that he cannot discern them, and which yet he knows are not hidden from God, and therefore may imperil his relations to God. He knows of no other way of deliverance from them except the divine gracious acquittal. — **14.** *Moreover*], increased emphasis, calling attention to another class of transgressions. — *from presumptuous ones*], proud ones; known, clearly discerned, boldly and wilfully committed, corresponding with "highhanded" of the code of P, Num. 15^{30}. — *restrain Thy servant*], hold him back, for he knows his peril of committing them and the serious consequences. — *let them not rule over me*]. Such transgressions overpower the man and reduce him to servitude. The phrase so greatly resembles that of Gn. 4^7 that it is probable the author had in mind the story of Cain, where sin like a wild beast couches at the door greedy to take possession of him and rule him, which it actually did, with terrible consequences. So here the presumptuous sins are personified; they strive to dominate the man, cf. 36[2] Jn. 8[34]. — *Then shall I be perfect*], that is, if cleared from sins of ignorance, and restrained from sins of knowledge and intention, he will be free from all sin, and so be complete, entire, faultless. — *and cleared from much transgression*]. This does not naturally refer to some great extreme transgression as parallel with the presumptuous ones, but rather to the transgressions hidden and to the errors to which he is so sensitive that he fears they may be many, and in their sum amount to much; for *clear* in the passive seems to refer to the same kind of sins as *clear* in the active, and to those from which he would be absolved, rather than to those from which he would be restrained. — **15.** *Let the words of my mouth be for acceptance*], namely, those of the prayer which accompany the sacrifice made in the temple, making the sacrifices real earnest sacrifices, and so acceptable to God; as in Ho. 14[2] the calves (or fruit, *v.* Br.[MP. 177]) of the lips are thus offered, and Ps. 141[2] prayer as sacrifice. — *and the musing of my mind*], the mind acting in harmony with the mouth, as the mouth with the hand that presents the sacrifice. — *Before Thee*], all the activities of devotion, of mind, mouth, hand, tend to the divine presence where alone acceptance can be found. — *continually*], so 𝔊, as the measure requires, but omitted by 𝔐 and most Vrss. by error. The psalmist is not thinking of one single sacrifice, but of oft-repeated, continual approaches to God in sacrifice. All this is fortified and reaches its climax in the plea which gives assurance of success; *my Rock and my Redeemer*], cf. 18[3] 69[19]. The Rock is the negative refuge; the Redeemer is the one who grants the positive redemption from the sins so dreaded in the previous context.

XIX. A.

2. מְסַפְּרִים] Pi. ptc. pl. of ספר; with verbal force, *are telling* constantly; ‖ מַגִּיד — ‡ רָקִיעַ] n.m. *firmament*, expanse of physical heaven, elsw. in ψ, 150[1], ‖ הַשָּׁמַיִם — מַעֲשֵׂה יָדָיו]. Bä. interprets as applying to God's government of the world, ‖ כָּבוֹד; but usage (8[7] 102[23] 138[8]) favours creation. The measure is most easy as tetrameter, although first line is pointed as trimeter. ו is prob. a gl. Possibly אלהים stood in original; it makes better measure. — **3.** יַבִּיעַ] Hiph. impf., habitual action for ptc. of continuous action of previous clause. ‡ נבע vb. Hiph. *pour forth* as from a spring, *bubble:* of speech, in bad sense

59⁸ 94³; in good sense 78² 119¹⁷¹ 145⁷ and here, ‖ יְחַוֶּה Pi. impf. † [חָוָה] vb. Pi. poetic, *tell, declare, make known :* only here in ψ (unless we correct 52¹¹ with Hi., Che., *et al.*); but Jb. 15¹⁷ 32⁶· ¹⁰· ¹⁷ 36². — [אֹמֶר] Ges. renders ἔπος *hymn,* but really it is *saying, speech, utterance,* as v.⁴ ‖ דְּבָרִים. — ‡ [דַּעַת] n.f. *knowledge :* here = their knowledge of the glory; elsw. in ψ only of knowledge as possessed by God 139⁶; as taught by God to man 94¹⁰ 119⁶⁶. These two lines are most easily tetrameters, but might be taken as trimeters by use of Makkephs. — **4.** [אֵין דְּבָרִים ‖ אֵין אֹמֶר] are most easily explained as a denial of the use of speech and words in this praise of the heavens; then בלי נשמע would assert the same thing more strongly. ‡ בלי neg. adv. with vb. only here in ψ; but with n. = *without* 59⁶ 63² (*v.* עַד בְּלִי 72⁷). Their voice is not heard, *is inaudible, i.e.* except for the intelligent, pious mind. But why this qualification? It seems in direct antith. to v.³ ᵃⁿᵈ ⁵ and is tame. 𝔊 takes it as a relative clause : οὐκ εἰσὶν λαλιαὶ οὐδὲ λόγοι ὧν οὐχὶ ἀκούονται αἱ φωναὶ αὐτῶν. 𝔍 also : *non est sermo et non sunt verba, quibus non audiatur vox eorum.* This seems a roundabout, unpoetic way of asserting that their speech was intelligible, although it is followed by De., Moll., Now. Ew. attaches to next v. : "without talk, without words, without their voice being heard, their sound becomes loud throughout the whole earth." The measure of the last line can be only trimeter. This Str. is just the two lines longer than the second Str., and, therefore, in all probability they are a gl.; so Ols., Bi., Bä., Du. — **5.** [בְּקָצֵה הֵבֵל ‖ בְּכָל הָאָרֶץ] emph., the first a spreading abroad, the second a reaching unto the utmost limits. בְּכֹל הָאָרֶץ also in 8²· ¹⁰ 45⁷ 105⁷. — [קַוָּם] sf. of 3 pl. ‡ קַו n.m. *line, string :* (1) *measuring line,* extending over wide territory, as Je. 31³⁹ Ez. 47³ and elsw. Aq. κανών, so Ra., Bä., and most here. Hi. = "line or chain of musical instrument, so Ew. 𝔍 *sonus,* 𝔊 φθόγγος, Σ ἦχος, but there is no usage to justify this mng. Cap., Ols., Ge., Bö., Dy., Bi., Gr., Che., Du., SS., *B*DB rd. קֹלָם, but 𝔊 renders this by φωνή and 𝔍 by *vox,* and not by words they actually use here. — ‡ [קָצֶה] n.[m.] *end, bound, extremity :* מְקָצֵה הָאָרֶץ 61³ 135⁷ Is. 5²⁶ 43⁶ Dt. 28⁴⁹; עַד קְ הָאָרֶץ Ps. 46¹⁰ Je. 25³¹ Is. 48²⁰ 49⁶; בִּקְ תֵבֵל Ps. *19⁵*; מְקְצֵה הַשָּׁמַיִם 19⁷. ‡ [קָצָה] n.f. *end, bound,* in ψ pl. קְצֹותָם (of שָׁמַיִם) *19⁷,* prob., therefore, only pl. of קָצֶה. — [אֲמָרֵיהֶם ‖ מִלָּה ‡ מַם] n.f. *word, speech, utterance :* elsw. 139⁴ 2 S. 23² Pr. 23⁹ Jb. 34 t. This line is trimeter as it stands. — [לְשֶׁמֶשׁ] emph., 𝔊 ἐν τῷ ἡλίῳ. ‡ [שֶׁמֶשׁ] n. *sun :* 58⁹ 72¹⁷ 74¹⁶ 121⁶ 136⁸; זֶרַח שׁ׳ *rise* of sun 50¹ 104²² 113³; fig. of long duration עִם שׁ׳ 72⁶, נֶכַח שׁ׳ 89³⁷; personified *19⁵* 104¹⁹ 148³; fig. of God 84¹². — [בָּהֶם] *in them, i.e.* שָׁמַיִם Hu., Pe., Bä., Kirk., not indefinite, as De W., Ges., Hi., De. But בהם not in 𝔊, and is prob. a gl αὐτοῦ with σκήνωμα of 𝔊 is possibly an interpretation, as ὁδὸν αὐτοῦ for ארח v.⁶ᵇ; but as most of the lines of the Str. end in , the original was prob. אוֹ לוֹ. — **6.** [וְהוּא] emph., referring to שֶׁמֶשׁ personified, masc. usually. There is no need of it, and it should be stricken out, if verse is trimeter. — [יֵצֵא] *as a bridegroom,* a.λ. ψ. — [הֻפָּתוֹ] *his canopy,* a.λ. ψ; elsw. Jo. 2¹⁶ (of bride), Is. 4⁵ (of God's protection). — [וְיָשִׂישׂ] Qal impf. of ‡ שִׂישׂ, vb. Qal, *rejoice :* usu. with בְּ 35⁹ 40¹⁷ 68⁴ 70⁶ 119¹⁴; c. עַל 119¹⁶². — [כְּגִבּוֹר] *as a hero,* ‡ גִּבּוֹר (1) adj., *strong,* *mighty :* ‫ג׳ בארץ‬ 112[2]; ‫אל נבור‬ (of the Messiah) Is. 9[5]; attribute of God fighting for His people Ps. 24[8.8]; cf. Dt. 10[17] Is. 10[21]+. (2) n.m. *strong, valiant man* Pss. *19*[6] 33[16] 45[4] 52[3] 78[65] 89[20] 120[4] 127[4]; ‫גבּרי כֹח‬ 103[20]. — ‫[רוּץ ארח‬ *run along a path :* acc. of measure; cf. ‫בוא א׳‬ *go a path* Is. 41[3]; 𝕾 ‫ארחו‬, prob. correct. — 7. ‫[מוֹצָא‬ sf. 3 sg. ‡ ‫מוֹצָא‬ n.m. (1) *act of going forth :* of sunrise *19*[7], so of the place, the East 75[7]; ‫מוצאי בקר‬ 65[9]; (2) *that which goes forth, utterance* of lips 89[35] Je. 17[16]; (3) *place of going forth, source of water* Ps. 107[33. 35] 2 K. 2[21] Is. 58[11]. — ‫[תּתקוּפתו‬ *his circuit* (√ ‫קוּף‬), a.λ. ψ. BS. 43[7] (of moon); Ex. 34[22] (J) 2 Ch. 24[23] (of year); 1 S. 1[20] (of days of year). This should for assonance come at end of line. — ‫[עַל קְצוֹתם‬ 𝕾 ἕως ἄκρου τοῦ οὐρανοῦ, cf. 48[11] ‫על קצוי ארץ‬, ‫על קצה ארץ‬ late style for ‫אל‬. The measure is difficult with MT., but easy if, after 𝕾, we transpose and rd. ‫ואל קצוחם תקופתו‬. The τοῦ οὐρανοῦ of 𝕾 is interpretation. — ‫[מחמתו‬ rel. clause as 𝕾, 𝔍. — usually *from his heat* (*v.* ‫חמה‬ 6[2]), but † ‫חמה‬ *sun* Jb. 30[28] Is. 24[23] 30[26. 26] Ct. 6[10]; so also here *His sun* = 'El's sun, but originally ‫חמה‬ ‖ ‫שמש‬.

XIX. *B.*

8–10. ‫[תּורה‬ the Law as *instruction*, most common and comprehensive term from earliest time (*v. 1*[2]). — ‡ ‫[עֵדוּח‬ n.f., the Law as *testimony*, characteristic term of P, so 78[5] 81[6] 119[14 + 21 t. (em. txt.)] 122[4], and titles 60[1] 80[1]. — ‡ ‫[פּקּודים‬ n. pl., the Law as *precepts*, only pl. cstr. and sfs. elsw. 103[18] 111[7] 119[4 + 21 t. (em. txt.)]. — ‡ ‫[מצוה‬ n.f., the Law as *commandment*, characteristic of D.; elsw. in ψ always pl., 78[7] 89[32] 112[1] 119[6 + 21 t.]. — ‫[יראה‬ the Law as *object of reverence*, only here in this sense, but frequently for *piety, reverence*, 34[12] 111[10] + (*v. 2*[11]). Though 𝕳 is sustained by Vrss., it is improb. A term for Law is needed. Rd. ‫אמרת‬, as Gr., D. H. Müller, Kau., Che. — ‫[מִשְׁפּטים‬ *judgments*, decisions of rulers in the cases brought before them. A collection of such judgments is the *Covenant Code*, Ex. 21–22. They are also scattered through the Deuteronomic Code (*v. 1*[5]). We notice the absence of the most ancient terms ‫דברים‬ *words*, and ‫חקים‬ *statutes*, given in the Psalm of the Law, **119.** For uses of these technical terms *v.* Br.[Hex. 242 sq.], and BD*B*. — ‫[תּמימה‬ adj. f. (*v. 15*[2]), *whole, sound, having moral integrity, perfect;* of God's way 18[31]. — ‫[וּאמנה‬ Niph. ptc. f. ‡ ‫אמן‬ vb. *confirm, support :* Qal ptc. pass. ‫אמוּנים‬ intrans. *faithful* (as firm, stable), † as subst. m. *faithful ones* 12[2] (> 𝕾, 𝔖, al. *faithfulness*), cf. 2 S. 20[19]; *faithful ones Yahweh keepeth* Ps. 31[24] (but ‫א‬ is here taken by 𝕾, Ri., De., Che. as n. abstr., *v.* ‫אמן‬). Other mngs. not in ψ. Niph. (1) *be verified, confirmed :* precepts of God 111[7], His testimonies *19*[8] 93[5], covenant 89[29]. (2) *be reliable, faithful, trusty :* persons 89[38] 101[6]; ‫רוּח‬, c. ‫את‬ 78[8] (cf. Pr. 11[13]); c. ‫ב‬ rei Ps. 78[37]. Other mngs. not in ψ. Hiph. *trust, believe :* abs. 116[10]; c. ‫ל‬ rei 106[24]; c. ‫ב‬ pers. *trust in, believe in* (the usual construction with God) 78[22]; c. ‫ב‬ rei 78[32] 106[12] 119[66]; c. infin. 27[13], cf. Jb. 15[22]. — ‫[ישׁרים‬ adj. pl. m., *right* (*v. 7*[11]). — ‫[ברה‬ adj. f., *pure* (*v. 2*[12]). — ‫[טהורה‬ adj. f., *clean* (*v. 12*[7]). — ‫[אמת‬ 𝕾 ἀληθινά, 𝔍 *vera*, adj. is required, but ‫אמת‬ has frequently force of an adj., and is frequently rendered by adj. in

𝕲; cf. Dt. 13¹⁵ 17⁴ 22²⁰ Je. 42⁵ (v. 15²). The ptc. clauses, v.⁸⁻¹⁰, constitute complementary parts of pentameters, with two tones.— [שִׁיבַת וְלֹ֯] Hiph. ptc. cstr. of שׁוּב, may be taken with nominal force *refresher of,* or with verbal force *refreshing.* Hiph. in sense of ‡ *restore, recover,* elsw. in ψ, c. acc. 80⁴· ⁸· ²⁰; c. מִן 35¹⁷. וְנֶפֶשׁ is here the animal life in the sensuous nature (v. 10³). — [מַחְכִּימַת] Hiph. ptc. cstr. of ‡ חכם = *making wise;* form only here; why not מַחְתְּפַת, Pi., as 105²² 119⁹⁸ Jb. 35¹¹? Qal not in ψ. Pu. *made wise* 58⁶, cf. Pr. 30²⁴. — † פֶּתִי] adj. *simple:* as subst., open to the instruction of wisdom or folly Pr. 9⁴· ¹⁶, believing every word 14¹⁵, needing חָכְמָה Ps. 119¹³⁰, 19⁵ Pr. 21¹¹, lacking עׇרְמָה 1⁴ 8⁵· 19²⁵, in good sense שֹׁמֵר י׳ פְּתָאִים Ps. 116⁶, but usual tendency is to bad sense Pr. 1²² 14¹⁸ + 6 t. Pr., Ez. 45²⁰.— [מְשַׂמְּחֵי לֵב] Pi. ptc. cstr. of שׂמח *giving joy to* (v. 5¹²).— [מְאִירַת עֵינָיִם] Hiph. ptc. cstr. of אור *light up, cause to shine;* also *give light to, lighten* (v. 13⁴). — [עֹמֶרֶת לָעַד] Qal ptc. of עמד *stand firm, endure.*— [צָדְקוּ] Qal pf. 3 pl. Change from ptc. is striking and improbable. 𝕲 has δεδικαιωμένα, 𝕵 *justificata,* which implies ptc. צֻדָּקִים. Hare rds. צֶדֶק.— **11.** This verse has two tetrameters. These appear in an awkward change of construction.— [הַנֶּחֱמָדִים] Niph. ptc. pl. of ‡ חמד with article, nominal force = *the things to be desired,* or relative force = *they are the things to be desired;* only here with the article, † Niph. ptc. elsw. = *desirable* Gn. 2⁹ 3⁶ (J) Pr. 21²⁰; vb. elsw. in ψ only Qal, *desire* 68¹⁷ (of God), *desired, taken pleasure in* 39¹².— † [זָז] n.m., *refined, pure gold:* of crown of king 21⁴, of Law 19¹¹ 119¹²⁷, elsw. La. 4² Jb. 28¹⁷ Is. 13¹² Ct. 5¹¹· ¹⁵ Pr. 8¹⁹. — [רָב] *much* in quantity, also v.¹⁴ 25¹¹ 119¹⁶². — [וּמְתוּקִים] pl. of ‡ מָתֹוק, adj., *sweet:* of honey, as Ju. 14¹⁴, here ‖ מְתוּקִים; article required as much for the one as for the other. Du. suggests that it be prefixed.— † [נֹפֶת] n.m., *flowing honey,* from the comb: elsw. Pr. 5³ 24¹³ 27⁷ Ct. 4¹¹.— [צוּפִים] pl. of צוּף, n.m., *honeycomb:* elsw. Pr. 16²⁴. This verse is a gl. from the period of WL. It makes the previous Str. too long, if attached to it, and mars the uniformity of its use of legal terms. It is not suited to the second Str.— **12.** [גַּם] *moreover:* ‡ as emphasising the following word 19¹² 71²² 83⁹ 133¹; as emph. *and* 37²⁵ 107⁵ 137¹; also 8⁸ 14³. — [עַבְדְּךָ] *Thy servant,* prob. Israel as nation; cf. Je. 30¹⁰ and Is.². — ‡ [עֶבֶד] n.m. (1) *slave* 105¹⁷ 123²; (2) *worshipper,* עֲבָדָיו 34²³ 69⁸⁷ 135⁹· ¹⁴ (= Dt. 32³⁶); ‖ עַמּוֹ 105²⁵; עֲבָדֶיךָ 79²· ¹⁰ 89⁵¹ 90¹³· ¹⁶ 102¹⁵· ²⁹ 119⁹¹; עַבְדְּךָ 119¹⁷ ⁺ ¹² ᵗ· 143¹²; ‖ בֶּן אֲמָתֶךָ 86¹⁶· cf. 2. 4 116¹⁶· ¹⁶; Abraham 105⁶· ⁴² Gn. 26²⁴ (J); Moses Ps. 105²⁶; David 18¹ 36¹ 78⁷⁰ 89⁴· ²¹· ⁴⁰ 132¹⁰ 144¹⁰. (3) in special sense, *Levitical singers,* עַבְדֵי יהוה 113¹ 134¹ 135¹. (4) *Israel as a people* 136²², as Is. 41⁸· ⁹ 44²¹ 49³. (5) *addressing God in prayer,* sometimes (4), sometimes (2), and sometimes simply honorary address 19¹²· ¹⁴ 27⁹ 31¹⁷ 35²⁷ 69¹⁸ 109²⁸ 143². — [יֻזְהָר] Niph. ptc. of ‡ זהר, † Niph. *be instructed, warned:* elsw. Ez. 3²¹ 33⁴· ⁵· ⁶ Ec. 4¹³ 12¹². — ‡ [עֵקֶב] n.[m.] *consequence.* (1) adv. acc., *in consequence of* 40¹⁶ = 70⁴; (2) *reward, gain* 19¹² Pr. 22⁴; (3) *end* Ps. 119³³· ¹¹². — **13.** [שְׁגִיאוֹת] ἀ.λ., doubtless error for שְׁגָגוֹת, *sins of error, inadvertence,* † שְׁגָגָה, n.f., *error,* characteristic of P. Lv. 4² + 16 t. (P); elsw. Ec. 5⁵ 10⁶. ‡ שׁגג, vb. Qal *err,* from Law Ps. 119⁶⁷. ‡ שׁוּה, vb. Qal *err,* from Law 119²¹· ¹¹⁸. Hiph. *let err,* from Law 119¹⁰. — [מְרִיבִים] exclamation,

implying negative answer (*v.* 4⁷).—[מִנִּסְתָּרוֹת] Niph. ptc. pl. with מִן from סתר
here of secret, hidden sins, but *hide oneself* 55¹³ 89⁴⁷; *be hid* v.⁷ 38¹⁰ —[וַתֵּנִי]
Pi. imv. sf. of ‡ נקה. Pi. (1) *hold innocent*, or *acquit* here and Jb. 9²⁸ 10¹⁴,
both c. מִן; Dr. renders *absolve*, 𝔊 καθάρισον, 𝔍 *munda;* elsw. (2) *leave unpunished*, by God Ex. 34⁷ = Na. 14¹⁸ (J) = Na. 1³; c. acc. Ex. 20⁷ = Dt. 5¹¹
Je. 30¹¹ = 46²⁸. Niph. *be clean*, *free from guilt*, *innocent*, וְנִקֵּיתִי v.¹⁴, only
here ψ; cf. Nu. 5³¹ (P) Je. 2³⁵; 𝔊 καθαρισθήσομαι, 𝔍 *mundabor.*—**14.** [גַּם]
begins second couplet, dealing with grosser sins, used as ‡ introducing the
climax here and in 25³ 41¹⁰ 84⁴·⁷ 85¹³ 118¹¹ 119²³·²⁴ 139¹·¹² (*v.* v.¹²).—
[זֵדִים] pl. of ‡ זֵד, adj., *proud*, *presumptuous*, here of men, Ew., Ols., Hup., Che.,
RV., BDB., Bä., Du., but De., Dr., AV. of sins; elsw. in ψ of men 86¹⁴
119²¹⁺⁵ᵗ·—[חֲשֹׁךְ] Qal imv. of ‡ חשׂךְ, vb. Qal, *restrain*, *hold back*, ממת 78⁵⁰.—
[אַל־יִמְשְׁלוּ־בִי] Qal juss. of משׁל (*v.* 8⁷), involving personification of זֵדִים just as
in Gn. 4⁷, where חטאת is personified as wild beast with same vb. and same
construction. אז, implying a condition (*v.* 2⁵).—[אֵיתָם] Qal impf. 1 sg., fully
written, אֶיְתָם; המס intrans. Ges.§ 67 (3) (*v.* 9⁷).—[וְנִקֵּיתִי] Niph. pf. of נקה, *free
from*, *innocent of*, Dr. *absolved* (*v.* v.¹³).—[מִפֶּשַׁע רָב] *much transgression
(iniquity)*, so רב in 19¹¹·¹² 25¹¹ 119¹⁶²· פֶּשַׁע (*v.* 5¹¹).—**15.** [לְרָצוֹן] the sacrificial term for acceptance by Yahweh of sacrifices Lv. 1⁸ +; cf. Ho. 14³
Ps. 141².—‡ [אִמְרֵי פִי] *words of my mouth:* elsw. 54⁴ 78¹ 138⁴ Dt. 32¹ +.—
[הֶגְיוֹן] cstr. of † הִגָּיוֹן, n.m., *meditation*, or *musing*, of prayer, so here; cf. La. 3⁶²
(in bad sense of plotting); elsw. Pss. 9¹⁷ 92⁴ (dub., *v.* Intr. § 34); cf. הָגוּת
49⁴.—[לֵב] n.m., *inner part*, *midst:* † I. seldom of things, בְּלֶב יָמִים 46³.
בְּלֵב אֹיְבֵי, *in the midst of the enemies* of Ps. 45⁶. II. Of men: ‡ (1) (*a*) *the
inner man* in contrast with the outer 55²² 64⁷ 84³ 102⁵, as within the breast,
בלב 37¹⁵ 119¹¹ 2 S. 18¹⁴, cf. Ps. 40¹¹; (*b*) *the inner man*, indef. *soul*, comprehending mind, affections, and will, 33¹⁵, with occas. emphasis of one or the
other by means of certain vbs., † בכל לב 9² 119²·¹⁰·³⁴·⁵⁸·⁶⁹·¹⁴⁵ 138¹ 1 K. 8²³
= 2 Ch. 6¹⁴ Pr. 3⁵ Je. 3¹⁰ 24⁷; *secrets of the heart* Ps. 44²². ‡ (2) specif.
reference to *mind:* (*a*) *knowledge*, c. ראה 66¹⁸ Ec. 1¹⁶; (*b*) *thinking*, *reflexion*,
Pss. 33¹¹ 49⁴ 83⁶ 140³, so here, cf. 45²; שׁת לב 62¹¹ Pr. 22¹⁷ 24³², c. לְ Ps. 48¹⁴
Ex. 7²³ JE, 1 S. 4²⁰ Pr. 27²³ Je. 31²¹, and c. אֶל Jb. 7¹⁷; (*c*) *memory* Pss. 31¹³
37³¹; (*d*) spec. refer. to *inclinations*, *resolutions*, *determinations of the will:*
† הכין לב *set the mind on* 10¹⁷ 78⁸ 2 Ch. 12¹⁴ Jb. 11¹³; נכון לב Ps. 57⁸·⁸ (= 108²)
78³⁷ 112⁷; other phrs. 44¹⁹ 105²⁵ 112⁸ 119³⁶·¹¹² 141⁴. For other uses of לב
v. 4⁸ 10⁶ 12³.—[לְפָנֶיךָ] goes with last line. 𝔊 has διὰ παντός = תָּמִיד or לְעוֹלָם,
which is required by measure, so Du., Bä., Che.—[גֹאֲלִי] *my redeemer*, cf. Jb. 19²⁵.
‡ גאל vb. Qal, *redeem*, *act as kinsman:* in ψ only *redeem* with God as subj.,
implying pers. relationship : (*a*) *individuals* from death Ps. 103⁴ La. 3⁵⁸
Ho. 13¹⁴, מכל רע Gn. 48¹⁶ (E poem), נפשׁ Pss. 69¹⁹ 72¹⁴, ואלני ריבי ריבה 119¹⁵⁴,
גֹאֲלִי 19¹⁵ Jb. 19²⁵; (*b*) *Israel*, from Egyptian bondage Ex. 6⁶ (P?) 15¹³ (song)
Pss. 74² 77¹⁶ 78³⁵, מיד אויב 106¹⁰; † (*c*) *from exile* (chiefly Is.²·³ the vb., not
in Is.¹), Is. 43¹ + 5 t. Is., Mi. 4¹⁰, מיד Ps. 107² Je. 31¹¹, גֹאֵל גּו יִ Is. 41¹⁴ + 12 t.
Is., and the people גְּאוּלִים Ps. 107² Is. 35⁹ 51¹⁰ 62¹² 63⁴(?).

PSALM XX., 2 PARTS 8^3 + RF. 2^3.

Ps. 20 is a Litany before a battle, in two parts: (1) **During the offering of sacrifice, the leaders of the choir make a petition for the king that he may be victorious in the day of trouble** (v.$^{2-5}$), **and a chorus sums it up with a vow of exultation and praise** (v.^{6}); (2) **the leaders make a declaration of the certitude of victory, accomplished by Yahweh's hand rather than by the army** (v.$^{7-9}$), **which is enthusiastically reaffirmed by the chorus** (v.^{10}).

IN the day of trouble may He answer *thee*,
   May the God of Jacob set *thee* on high;
   May He send from the sanctuary help to *thee*,
   And from Zion sustain *thee*;
   May He be mindful of all *thy* grain offerings,
   And accept as fat (all) *thy* whole burnt offering(s);
   May He give thee according to *thy* mind,
   And fulfil all *thy* plan.
      We will be jubilant in thy victory,
      And in the name of our God will we (rejoice).
NOW (the hand of Yahweh is made known);
   Yahweh hath given His anointed victory.
   He answereth him from His sacred heavens,
   By the mighty deeds of victory of His right hand.
   These by chariots and by horses;
   But by Yahweh our God are we strong.
   They, on their part, bow down and they fall;
   We, on our part, stand and are established.
      Yahweh hath given victory to the king;
      He answereth us in the day we invoke Him.

Ps. 20 was in 𝔇, then in 𝔐 and 𝔇ℜ (*v.* Intr. §§ 27, 31, 33). It is a prayer for a king going forth to battle; implying the existence of the Hebrew monarchy v.^{7}. It is a prayer at a sacrifice in the temple, with whole burnt offerings and accompanying grain offerings, and the use of ritual language v.^{4}. The use of לבב v.^{5} indicates, in preëx. literature, the period prior to Je. The use of chariots and horses by the enemy v.^{8} might refer to the Syrians, Assyrians, or Egyptians, and therefore gives no evidence of date. Theodore of Mopsuestia, and many since his time, have thought of Hezekiah; but the history of Hezekiah gives us no such situation as that described in the Ps. The victory of Jehoshaphat in the neighbourhood of Jerusalem, cf. 2 Ch. 20, gives us a most appropriate historical situation; and the promise of victory, given by the prophet, gives an appropriate explanation of the change from petition to certitude in the two parts of the Ps.

Pt. 1. is composed of five couplets, sung by the choir. Leading voices make the petition for the king, in eight trimeter lines, arranged in four synonymous couplets, all rhyming in *Ka*, which in English must be expressed sometimes by the personal pronoun *thee*, sometimes by the possessive *thy*. The reference to the king is not evident in this petition, but comes out clearly in the chorus v.[10]. Although we cannot suppose that the Levitical choruses were organised at so early a date, in accordance with the usage projected by the chronicler back even into the time of David, we may yet suppose that, with the institution of temple worship, some kind of an official choir was also instituted among the priests in Jerusalem, as in the ancient temples of other religions. — **2.** *In the day of trouble*], implying a serious situation. The nation was in straits and in peril, and victory doubtful so far as their own ability to repel the invaders was concerned ; their only hope was in divine assistance. — *The God of Jacob*]. The reference to the God of the ancestor of the nation, often used in such pleas, enforces the petition, especially as the name of their national and ancestral God was the pledge and security for their national existence and perpetuity. The honour of their God was necessarily involved in the honour of His people, according to the conception of the ancient Biblical writers. — *set thee on high*], in the exaltation of victory. — **3.** *From the sanctuary* ‖ *from Zion*], the source of divine assistance, according to the conception that it was God's place of residence among His people, the place of His theophanic presence, and therefore not only the place of prayer and sacrifice, but also the place from which His people may expect help in answer to prayer. — **4.** *all thy grain offerings*], specific offerings of some kind of grain, which usually, especially in public sacrifices, accompanied all kinds of sacrifices of animals ; the kind of grain offering differing, whether the simple grain, or roasted in the ear, or ground into meal for wafers or cakes or loaves, all depending upon the kind of sacrifice as discriminated in a later priestly legislation, not probably applicable at this early date. — *all thy whole burnt offerings*], special kinds of sacrifice of animals which differed from all other sacrifices of animals in that the entire victim, or rather all the parts that were in their nature clean, or that could be cleansed by washing, were entirely

consumed on the altar and went up in the flame to God. Tl is
ancient form of sacrifice of animals, with its associated sacrifice of
grain, was appropriate for the expression of worship, in the form
of prayer. The nation were assembled, led by priests and choirs
of singers, to participate in the sacrifice and prayer for the victory of their king and army. — *May He be mindful*]. There is
little reason to doubt that this is a sacrificial term as truly as the
‖ *accept as fat*], for it was characteristic of the grain offerings
that they were offered *Azkarah*, to bring the offerer to the remembrance of Yahweh. For that service in the later ritual various
Psalms were assigned (38^1 70^1, *v.* Intr. § 39). There is no good
reason why we should not think that this conception of the
grain offering was ancient. Such a conception does not by any
means involve the numerous distinctions of the later priestly legislation. So also the phrase, "accept as fat," is a sacrificial term,
which indicates the essential thing in the sacrifice of animals,
already recognised in the primitive story of Cain and Abel, Gn. 4^4,
that fat ones should be selected in order to find acceptance with
God, implying that sacrifices, without such selection, would be
regarded as niggardly and unacceptable. To accept or recognise
the whole burnt offerings of animals as fat is, therefore, saying, in
ritual terms, that they are entirely acceptable to God. — **5.** *According to thy mind* ‖ *all thy plan*], the plan devised already in the
mind of the king for conducting the campaign or making the
battle. — **6.** The chorus now sings as it were a refrain, summing
up the contents of the petition in a vow of jubilation and praise.
That the chorus speaks is evident from the introduction of the
first person plural, now for the first time, into the Psalm; as well
as by the change of tone. — *in thy victory*]. The Hebrew word
often means salvation from enemies, and so victory, which alone
is appropriate to the context. The word may, however, be rendered "salvation," in general, as Vrss., which was preferred for a
liturgical use of the Ps. — *will rejoice*]. So some ancient codd. of
𝕲 and many modern scholars, which is more natural than the
unusual word of 𝔥, which is due to a copyist's mistake of a single
letter. The word of 𝔥 is used elsewhere Ct. $6^{4.10}$; but here it
can only be interpreted in a different sense, whether as "set up
our banners," AV., RV., or "wave" them, Kirk. and most. A late

editor appended a line, " may Yahweh fulfil all thy askings," which is only a repetition of v.^{5b}, in the use of an unusual word of late formation and out of harmony with the thought of the couplet. It might, however, be more appropriate for later congregational use to resume the tone of prayer, as indeed the editor aims to do at the close of the Ps. v.^{10}.

Pt. II. 7. The leading voices again sing, not a soloist, as a late editor supposed, who wrote the first singular in place of the first plural of the chorus in an introductory statement which is prosaic. This destroys the symmetry of the couplets of the Ps. It is doubtless a textual error for the original line, which we have ventured to restore by conjecture. — *Now*], as the result of the petition. The time has come in which certitude takes the place of anxiety. — *The hand of Yahweh is made known*]. We may think of certitude born of internal evidence of answer to prayer, or due to the promises of a prophet intervening between the parts of the Ps. in accordance with 2 Ch. 20$^{14-17}$, or to some external token of the acceptance of the sacrifice just offered. This last is most probable, if the restoration of the line given above is correct. The hand of Yahweh is displayed in behalf of His people ; cf. for the use of the hand Is. 66^{14}, of the arm Is. 52^{10}, and of both Ps. 98^{1}. This also makes the tetrastich one of introverted parallelism. — *Yahweh hath given victory*], not that the victory has actually taken place, but that it has already been given to the king in answer to the prayers of his people, and will surely take place. — *His anointed*], as anointed, installed on his throne by Yahweh, in accordance with 2^{2}. — *from His sacred heavens*], the heavens as the sacred place in which God resides, and from which He gives victory to His people, especially in theophanic manifestations, when He would throw His enemies into a panic, such as those described in 2 Ch. 20, at the crossing of the Red Sea Ex. 14–15, at the battle of Bethhoron Jos. 10$^{12-14}$, at the battle of the Kishon Ju. 5, at the battle of Rephaim 2 S. 5$^{22-25}$; cf. also Ps. 18, Hb. 3, Jb. 38^{23}. This turning toward heaven is not inconsistent with the previous turning toward the sanctuary as the source of help, for the conception of theophanic residence in sacred places on earth did not, from the earliest times of the Hebrew religion, lead them away from the thought that the real residence of Yahweh was in heaven. — *mighty deeds*], by acts of God Himself putting forth His might. — *of victory*], gained by those acts of might and overwhelming strength. — *His right hand*], theophanic and anthropomorphic expressions, frequent, especially in poetic literature, in connection with the divine deliverance of His people and judgment upon their enemies, from Ex. 15⁶·¹² onward. — **8**. *These by chariots and by horses*]. These were the chief reliance of the ancient enemies of Israel in their wars from the earliest times. Israel, living chiefly in hilly and mountainous districts, had little use for them. The law of the king (Dt. 17¹⁶) forbids them, although Solomon and other luxurious monarchs made use of them. The sentiment of the prophets was ever against their use. — *But by Yahweh our God*]. Yahweh is the chief, if not the sole, author of victory to His anointed king and people, cf. 33¹⁶⁻¹⁹. — *are we strong*], suited to the context, so 𝔊 and many critics. 𝔥, followed by "we will remember" PBV., AV.; "we will make mention" RV., does not suit the context. — **9**. *They on their part*], the enemy, in strong antith. to *we on our part*], the worshipping people of God. — *bow down and they fall*], a graphic description of the enemy as the mighty hand of God lays hold upon them, bending them down to the ground and prostrating them on the ground; frequent expressions for humiliation of enemies in defeat, *v.* 7¹⁶ 17¹³ 18⁴⁰. — *stand and are established*], stand firm, upright and immovable. Each verb is in direct antith. to its mate in the previous line, to set forth the exaltation of the victorious king and people. — **10**. The chorus now bursts forth in a couplet of enthusiasm, the climax of the Ps. *Yahweh hath given victory*], a renewal of the statement of the leading voices v.⁷ᵃ. — *to the king*], taking the place of "His anointed," in accordance with the context. A later editor, whether because of dittog. of a copyist, changing a perfect into a cohortative imperative, or by intentional alteration to make the close of the Ps. more appropriate for public worship, as in v.⁶ᶜ, changes the certitude as to the victory, which pervades and dominates the entire second half of the Ps. up to this verse, into a petition for victory, in accordance with the first half of the Ps. — The texts vary in the second line. But 𝔥 is doubtless correct in the impf. *He answereth us*, which resumes v.⁷ᵇ, and asserts the assuring fact that Yahweh habitually answers His people in their need. — *in the day we invoke Him*], in the very day, at the very time, they call upon Him in their distress. The whole Ps. is thus included between the day of trouble v.[2] and this day of prayer.

2. [יַעֲנֵךְ] juss. of עָנָה (*v. 3⁵*). — [יהוה] is a gl. making line too long. — [בְּיוֹם צָרָה] *in the day of trouble*, ‡ צָרָה n.f. *strait, distress*: sg. 22¹² 78⁴⁹ 116³ 138⁷ 142³, pl. 25¹⁷ 71²⁰, מכל צרה 54⁹, מכל צרות 25²² 34⁷, ¹⁸ מצרה 143¹¹, יום צ׳ 20² 50¹⁵ 77³ 86⁷ Gn. 35³ (E), עת צ׳ Ps. 37³⁹ Is. 33², נצרה Ps. 81⁸, cf. 31⁸ 46² 91¹⁵ 120¹, also 9¹⁰ 10¹ (?). — [יְשַׂגֶּבְךָ] Pi. juss. of ‡ שׂגב *be high, inaccessible*, in ψ only, Niph.: (1) *be exalted in glory* 148¹³, cf. Is. 12⁴; (2) *be inaccessible of divine knowledge* 139⁶, Pi. *make inaccessible* to an enemy, *unassailable*, c. acc. 20² 69³⁰ 91¹⁴, c. מן 59² 107⁴¹. — [שֵׁם] *name* of God (*v. 5¹²*), is a gl., as Hare, making line too long, so v.⁸ from a late point of view. — † [אלהי יעקב] 2 S. 23¹ Ps. 20² 46⁸, ¹² (59¹⁴ ⑮) 75¹⁰ 76⁷ 81². ⁵ 84⁹ 94⁷ Is. 2³ = Mi. 4², cf. אלוה יעקב Ps. 114⁷, אל יעקב 146⁶, אביר יעקב 132². ⁵ Gn. 49²⁴ Is. 49²⁶ 60¹⁶. — **3.** [עֶזְרְךָ] obj. sf. = *help to thee*. ‡ עֵזֶר n.m.: (1) *help, succour*, from ר 20³ 121¹, ² 124⁸, cf. 89²⁰ (?); (2) concrete, *one who helps*, espec. ר Dt. 33⁷, with מגן Pss. 33²⁰ 115⁹, ¹⁰, ¹¹, מפלט 70⁶, בעזר 146⁶ Dt. 33²⁶. — [צִיּ] should be written for measure צִיּוֹן, cf. 24⁸ 63⁸ 68²⁵. — [סִיעָדֶךָ] juss. strong sf. *v. 18³⁶*. — **4.** [יִזְכֹּר] Qal impf. juss. continued, זכר (*v. 8⁵*). This has doubtless a sacrificial mng., corresponding with the term אזכרה, which belongs espec. to the מנחה in P, and is expressed in the הזכיר in titles of Pss. 38, 70. — [כָּל מִנְחֹתֶיךָ] the grain offering accompanying the עולה, both expressing worship and prayer. The offering here is a special one for the king, and not a sacrifice which he might make during his reign. The use of pl. for grain offering and sg. for whole burnt offering is improbable, the one accompanied the other; rd. either both sg. or both pl. כל is also needed for measure in 2d line. — ‡ [מִנְחָה] n.f.: (1) *gift, present* 45¹³ Gn. 32¹⁴ (E) Is. 39¹ + ; (2) *tribute* Ps. 72¹⁰ Ju. 3¹⁵ Ho. 10⁶ + ; (3) *offering* made to God, of any kind, Ps. 96⁸; (4) *grain offering* (as ‖ עלה and accompanying it) 20⁴ in common use OT., so also 40⁷ 141²; the special grain offering of P not in ψ unless in 141². ‡ [עֹלָה] n.f. *whole burnt offering* 20⁴ 40⁷ 50⁸ 66¹⁸, רצה עלה 51¹⁸, ²¹, העלה 66¹⁵. — [יְדַשְּׁנֶה] cohort. (unusual form in Heb. in 3 pers.) Ges. §48d De.; but Hare, Hi., Bä. sf. יֶהּ or יָהּ. In this case sf. is a later addition of glossator after the order of the words was changed. ‡ [דשׁן] vb. Qal *be fat, grow fat*, not in ψ. Pi. *make fat*, בשׁמן anoint 23⁶; of offering rich in fat parts and so acceptable 20⁴. Gr., Che. rd. יִרְצֶה *accept as well pleasing*; AE., Ki. make it denom. דֶּשֶׁן *reduce to ashes*. It may, however, be conflation of two readings, יִדַשְּׁרֶ Pi. imv. and יְדַשֵּׁן juss., the latter alone suited to context. — **5.** [יְרַבְּרֶ] long form for usual רָב, doubtless original to this Ps. = *according to thy mind*. — [עֲצָֽרְךָ] *counsel, design, purpose* (*v. 1¹*), here *for war*, as Is. 36⁵. These eight lines are in syn. parall. ה is in each one and also juss. of vb. This gives assonance, and it is probable that the lines all began or else closed with words ending in ר, most probably the latter. 1 pl. now takes the place of 3 sg.; there is prob. a different

speaker, a chorus. — **6.** בִּישׁוּעָתֶךָ] *in thy victory, i.e.* the victory given thee (by
יָ). — ישׁועה (*v. 3³*). — נִרְגֹל] Qal impf. **1** pl. of † [רגל] vb. denom. from דֶּגֶל
standard (not in ψ) only here in Qal = *set up standard*, in Niph. Ct. 6⁴· ¹⁰.
Gr., Che., Ehr. rd. נָגִיל, after 𝔊^(B. a. b. א A) ἀγαλλιασόμεθα, which best suits
parall. 𝔊^B μεγαλυνθησόμεθα, 𝔙 *magnificabimur,* so 𝔖. נגדל *shall he be mag-*
nified Ecker., Houb., Lowth. Ew., Bi., Du., We. נִוְדָּר ב (Pi.). Bä. objects
that there is no Heb. usage to justify the construction of Pi. with ב, but Du.
refers to the use of the syn. הגל 44⁹, cf. v.²ᵇ (*v.* 18⁵¹). — † [מִשְׁאֲלוֹתֶיךָ] *askings,*
form, elsw. 37⁴, late. The whole clause is a mere repetition of v.⁵ᵇ. — **7.** עַתָּה]
= *now,* temporal (*v.* 2¹⁰). This part of Ps. was sung later than the first part,
after the sacrifice. — יָדַעְתִּי] *I know,* present emph. (*v.* 1⁶). אֲנִי should be
added to complete the measure. **1** pers. sg. for **1** pers. pl. is striking here.
Does it indicate a soloist, or should we read ידענו? This is certainly prosaic
and not at all suited in the parall. of poetry. The original was prob.
יד יהוה ידעה, cf. Is. 12⁵ מִירעַת, 66¹⁴. נורעה יד י·. יהוה was, as often in ancient
codd., abbreviated to י·; this by haplog. fell out before ידעה. יד still later
fell out for a similar reason. ידעה Pu. ptc. f. without ת, as often in Pi. and
Pu., was wrongly interpreted as pf. Qal **1** sg. כי was inserted as often. —
הושׁיע] Hiph. pf. sure anticipation, assured future (*v.* 3⁸). — [מְשִׁיחוֹ] *His*
anointed one = king (*v.* 2²). — יַעֲנֵהוּ] impf. freq. (*v.* v.²). — [מִשְּׁמֵי קָדְשׁוֹ] phr.
a.λ. ‖ מְקֹדֶשׁ v.³; more suited to the giving of victory on battlefield, as the
sanctuary was more suited to the offering of sacrifices. — [בִּגְבוּרוֹת] = *acts of*
might, pl. of ‡ גְּבוּרָה n.f. in ψ only : (1) *strength, might,* of horse 147¹⁰, body
of man 90¹⁰; (2) *might,* of God 21¹⁴ 54³ 65⁷ 66⁷ 71¹⁸ 80³ 89¹⁴ 106⁸ 145¹¹, pl.
mighty deeds 20⁷ 71¹⁶ 106² 145⁴· ¹² 150² Is. 63¹⁵. — **8.** וָאֵלֶּה, [אֵלֶּה] in antith.
אֲנַחְנוּ. But there is too much emphasis for the measure. The second אלה
and אנחנו are glosses of intensification. — [נַזְכִּיר] Hiph. impf. **1** pl. *mention,*
c. acc. 71¹⁶ 77¹² 87⁴, here only with ב. 𝔊 has μεγαλυνθησόμεθα, as in v.⁶ᵇ =
נגדל, so 𝔖, Aug., Cassiodorus, Psalt. Rom., Lowth. Now., Bä., Du., Oort,
Che. rd. נוביר *we are strong.* All other Vrss. agree with 𝔐, even 𝔊^(א c. a),
and most Greek fathers. — **9.** כָּרְעוּ וְנָפָלוּ] ו coörd. with pf., referring to the
defeat of enemy, cf. 18⁴⁰. — וַנִּתְעוֹדָד] Hithpol. impf. with · consec. † [עוד]
only intensive : Pi. *surround* 119⁶¹, Pol. *restore, relieve,* c. acc. pers. 146⁹
(antith. עוה), 147⁶ (antith. הִשְׁפִּיל), both ἀναλαμβάνω 𝔊. Hithpol. *be restored*
20⁹, and so *are established, stand upright,* AV., RV., PBV., Dr.; ἀνωρθώθημεν
𝔊, ὑπομένομεν Σ, *erecti sumus* 𝔍. — **10.** הוֹשִׁיעָה] cohort. imv. *O save, give*
victory, but the pf. without ה is more prob., as v.⁷. ה of cohort. is dittog. —
[הַמֶּלֶךְ] = כִשִׁיחוֹ v.⁷ᵇ, cf. 2², obj. of vb., as 𝔊, 𝔙, and most moderns. MT. and
other Vrss. refer כ to God as king and attach it to יַעֲנֵנוּ. However, Jerome
(Com.) says that in the Heb. text of his time it was *Domine salvum fac*
regem. — יַעֲנֵנוּ] impf. freq., as v.⁷ᵇ. 𝔊 has יַעֲנֵנוּ imv., so Hare), Bi., Che., Bä.,
al., which is an assimilation to previous imv. and less prob. The uncertainty
of the interpretation of this text in 𝔐 and the Vrss. is due probably to ar
editorial change, making an original statement of the assurance of victory
into a petition more appropriate for later congregational use.

PSALM XXI., 2 PARTS $12^3 +$ RF. 2^3.

Ps. 21 is a Te Deum for the victory won by the king through divine help; composed of two parts, each of twelve trimeters, and a couplet of refrain; the former during sacrifice rehearsing the reasons for thanksgiving (v.[2-7]), with a chorus asserting the king's trust in Yahweh (v.[8]); the latter after sacrifice, expressing certitude of future victories of the king (v.[9-13]) with a fresh chorus of praise (v.[14]).

YAHWEH, in Thy strength the king is glad,
And in Thy victory he greatly rejoiceth;
Thou hast given him his heart's desire,
And the request of his lips Thou hast not withheld;
For Thou camest to meet him with blessings of good things;
Thou settest on his head a crown of fine gold.
Life he asked Thee, Thou gavest it him,
Length of days forever and ever.
His glory is great in Thy victory;
Honour and majesty Thou layest on him;
For Thou givest him everlasting blessings;
Thou makest him joyful in Thy presence with gladness.
Yea, the king is trusting in Yahweh,
And through the kindness of 'Elyon he cannot be moved.
Thine hand will find all thine enemies,
Thy right hand find all those hating thee;
Thou wilt put them in a furnace of fire,
In the time (of the setting) of thy face (against them).
Yahweh will swallow them up in His anger,
And the fire (of His rage) will devour them;
Their offspring thou wilt destroy from the earth,
And their seed from among the sons of men.
Though they have extended evil unto thee,
Thought an evil device, they shall not prevail;
For thou wilt make them turn their shoulder in flight,
With thy bowstrings thou wilt aim against their faces.
Be Thou exalted, Yahweh, in Thy strength;
We will sing and we will praise Thy might.

Ps. 21 was in 𝔇, then in 𝔐 and 𝔇ℜ (*v.* Intr. §§ 27, 31, 33). It is a royal Ps. like the 20th and its complement: the former a litany before a battle, the latter a *Te Deum* after a victory. It was therefore probably composed for the same occasion. That which was the theme of the petition was afterward the theme of the thanksgiving. As Ps. 20 it has two parts: one of thanksgiving made during sacrifice, one of certitude after the sacrifice; each with its chorus. Some have thought of a Coronation Ps. because of the

reference to the crowning v⁴. But it is not necessary to think of that coronation as connected with the thanksgiving; we may suppose that it was at an
earlier date, as was the request that follows it. It was only natural that the
poet should go back to the coronation, a previous experience of blessing on
the part of the king, as a prelude to the additional blessing of victory now
enjoyed.

Part I. has six couplets, all syn. except v. 5, which is synth. —
2. *In Thy strength*], God's, exerted against the enemy in defeating
them, and for the *king*, in giving him the *victory*, in which he
greatly rejoiceth. The second line has been intensified by the insertion, by a later editor, of the exclamation "how" which was
not in 𝕲, 𝕵, 𝕾. — **3.** *His heart's desire* ‖ *the request of his lips*],
that specified in 20⁵, for victory over enemies. — **4.** *For Thou
camest to meet him*]. This causal clause, with imperfects between
perfects, changes the tense as well as construction, in order to go
back to the inauguration of the king which it vividly describes.
The poet conceives that Yahweh Himself came to that festival
with appropriate gifts. — *blessings of good things*], the general welfare of the monarch in property and government. — *Thou settest
on his head*]. Yahweh Himself was the chief actor, though the
ceremonial was performed by His agents, probably the priests.
The king was Yahweh's king, His son, in accordance with the
covenant of David, making David's seed an everlasting dynasty for
His people. — *a crown of fine gold*], the choicest gold for the
royal crown. — **5.** *Life he asked*], not because of previous illness
or peril, but *length of days*], a petition for a long reign, undisturbed
by perils of succession, as expressed in the usual address to kings,
not only in Hebrew, cf. 72¹⁵ 1 S. 10²⁴ 2 S. 16¹⁶ 1 K. 1²⁵ 2 K. 11¹²
Ne. 2³, but also among Egyptians, Babylonians, and other ancient
nations. — *forever and ever*], not in the absolute sense of a never-
ending life, and so realised alone in the Messiah, according to later
conceptions; but in the ordinary concrete sense of a very long
time. — **6.** *His glory* ‖ *honour and majesty*], heaping up terms to
represent the exaltation and renown of the king due to *Thy victory*],
recognising that it was Yahweh's gift to the king and that all this
majesty was put upon him by his God. — **7.** *For Thou givest him*].
returning to the causal clause of v.⁴, in order to make a more general reference to the king's entire career; now in the climax de-

parting from the specific reference to the victory. — *everlasting blessings*], sums up the blessings of good things of v.⁴, and the life, forever and ever of v.⁵. — *in Thy presence*]. The king as the son of God is conceived as not only enjoying the presence of Yahweh at his coronation and in the hour of victory ; but also as living in the presence and favour of Yahweh, and so as ever *joyful* and *with gladness*. — **8**. The chorus, in a couplet of refrain, asserts that *the king is trusting in Yahweh*], the reason for all his experience of divine favour and blessing. It is *through the kindness*] as thus exhibited that he has the confidence that he *cannot be moved;* he will be in the future, as in the past, firm and immovable, and not be shaken by any wars or troubles that may arise in his realm. — *'Elyon*], the name of God as the most High, the Exalted, is most appropriate in the mouth of the chorus, in the exaltation of His victory.

Part II. is an antistr. to the first part. It seems to have been sung after the sacrifice had been made. It thus resembles the second part of Ps. 20. On that account it probably expresses certitude with reference to the future, and the imperfects should be conceived as futures ; although they might grammatically be rendered as jussives, expressing wish, as many interpreters would have them. Where the grammar does not decide, we have to depend upon the context and the circumstances of the Ps. This Str. has the same number of lines as the previous one, although 刈 has abridged one of them ; there are also six couplets, all syn. but v.¹⁰, which is synth. — **9**. *Thine hand* ‖ *Thy right hand . . . find*], in pursuit in battle, overtaking, laying hold of *thine enemies* ‖ *those hating thee.* — **10**. *Thou wilt put them in a furnace of fire*], not as some, fig. of fiery indignation as expressed by the ‖ *in the time of the setting of thy face*]. This is the angry countenance, in accordance with the conception of God's wrath as a consuming fire, Is. 31⁶, and the fiery furnace of the day of judgment, Mal. 3¹⁹ ; but inasmuch as these passages refer to God's anger, and this Ps. to the kings, the furnace is probably literal, in accordance with the cruel methods of war of the early Davidic monarchy, as shown in David's treatment of the Ammonites, 2 S. 12³¹. " He put them under saws, and under harrows of iron, and under axes of iron, and made them pass through the brick kiln." What David did to the Ammonites his successors in the monarchy might be conceived as doing to other enemies. This interpretation, which is confirmed by v.[11], was softened by a later editor into a simile, whether by mistaking ‫ ב‬ *in* for ‫ כ‬ *as*, or intentionally, we may not be able to determine. V.[10] in the present text and Vrss. is two pentameters. We cannot regard it as a gloss because the entire conception of the verse is primitive, and not such as a glossator would insert. The loss of this verse would reduce the Str. by four lines, and so destroy the exact proportion of the two parts of the Ps. The difficulty originated by the condensations of a prosaic copyist, if not by mistakes of copying. The verb has fallen out of the clause : *In the time (of the setting) of thy face (against them)*; and the noun has fallen out of the clause : *and the fire (of His rage) will devour them*. The poet emphasizes the angry face of the king by putting in parall. with it the divine activity : *Yahweh will swallow them up in His anger.* — **11.** *Their offspring ‖ their seed*]. The cruelty of ancient warfare, based on the principle of blood vengeance, which required children to avenge the blood of their parents, and descendants of a tribe to avenge the blood of their tribe, involved the apparent necessity of putting to death all male children in war in order to make such vengeance impossible. The poet simply shares these ancient conceptions, as expressed in the wars of extermination of the Canaanites at the conquest, Jos. 6[21] 10[28-39] 11[14], and even in Pss. 9[6] 137[9]. — **12.** *Though they have extended unto thee ‖ thought*], completed action in the future, in a hypothetical clause. — *evil ‖ evil device*], the plan, the purpose, the attitude of enemies in the future may be evil. Even if they have planned a campaign of injury, *they shall not prevail*], they cannot succeed any more in the future than they have in the past. They will be defeated with humiliation. — **13.** *For thou wilt make them turn their shoulder in flight*]. The reason for their flight is given in the parallel clause which otherwise would be inconsistent with it. — *With thy bowstrings*]. The bow was one of the chief weapons of Israel in the royal period, especially of the king, *v.* 2 S. 1[18. 22], Ps. 45[5-6]. — *thou wilt aim against their faces*]. This deadly peril to the faces of the enemy, as the king and his army advanced against them, is, in the climax, in antith. to their backs as seen in retreat. — **14.** The chorus appropriately concludes the festival by praising the *strength* ‖ *might* of Yahweh, which has given the king the victory.   They are impelled therefore not only to honour and magnify their king, but also to recognise that honour is due to Yahweh, and therefore they sing a glad choral: *Be thou exalted, Yahweh.*

2. מַה־יָּגֵל Kt., מַה־יָּגֵל Qr. But מה is not translated by 𝕲, 𝕾, 𝕵; prob. as Hare, gl. to strengthen the text: original reading = יַגֵּל־מְאֹד. — **3.** [הַאֲוַת cstr. of תַּאֲוָה n.f. *v. 10^{17}*, in ψ usually of physical appetite; but *thing desired* in bad sense 78², here in good sense. — [־בִּי] 𝕲 has τῆς ψυχῆς αὐτοῦ = נַפְשׁוֹ more suitable to usage (*v. 4^8 10^3*). [נָחֵתָּ] fully written for נָחַתָּ so v.⁵. לוֹ is poss. a gl.; no more needed here than in v.³ᵇ, but cf. v⁵ᵃ; if original must have Makkeph [אֲרֶשֶׁת־†]. — †[עָרַךְ־לִי] n.f. cstr. *request a.λ.* √ארש not in Heb., but cf. As. *êrêšu.* — ‡[יַעֲרֹךְ] vb. Qal *withhold;* usually sq. מִן 84^{12}, sq. ־לְ. — **4.** [כִּי תְקַדְּמֶנּוּ] Pi. impf. referring to past between pfs. v.^{3.5}, *come to meet, c.* ב 95² Dt. 23⁵; double acc. here.   Hare thinks the בְּ has fallen off by haplog. — [בְּרְכוֹת טוֹב] blessings consisting of welfare, prosperity Ps. 4⁷ 23⁶ 34^{11} 39³ 85^{13}, or better, *good things* 103⁵ 104^{28} 107⁹ v. 3⁹ 4⁷. — [עֲטֶרֶת־] *crown a.λ.* ψ for עֲטָרָה. — **5.** [חַיִּים] emph. *life, long life.* — [מִמְּךָ] a gl., explanation not needed, impares measure; for an original שָׁאַל, 𝕲 ᾐτήσατό σε. — †[אֹרֶךְ יָמִים] Dt. 30^{20} Jb. 12^{12} Pr. 3². ¹⁶ La. 5²⁾ Pss. 21⁵ 23⁶ 91^{16} 93⁵. — [עוֹלָם וָעֶד] 9⁶ 10^{16} 21⁵ 45^{7.18} 48^{15} 52^{1)} 104⁵ 119^{44} 145^{1.2.21} Ex. 15^{18} Mi. 4⁵ Dn. 12³. — **6.** [תְּשַׁוֶּה] impf. descriptive of past victory, cf. *16⁸.* — **7.** [כִּי־תְשִׁיתֵהוּ] cf. v.⁴ᵇ here c. double acc. in sense of *give to;* c. לְ pers. 9²¹. — [בְּרָכוֹת לָעַד] *blessings forever* ‖ ברכות טוב, therefore blessings given to the king and not "most blessed forever" AV., RV., taking ברכות as abst. pl. intensive.   The usual sense of שִׁית (8⁷) with double acc₁ is, however, to *make* a thing *over into* another 18^{12} 21^{13} 84⁷ 88⁹ 110¹; and c. acc. + כ 21^{10} 83^{12.14}. — [תְּחַדֵּהוּ] Pi. impf. 3 f., c. sf. 3 sg. of †חרה vb. Qal *rejoice* Ex. 18⁹ (E) Jb. 3⁶ (dub.). Pi. *make joyful a.λ.* here. — **9.** [תִּמְצָא] Qal impf. 3 f. of מצא *come* or *light upon* (often unexpectedly); so here c. ־לְ; *befall,* c. acc. 116³ 119^{143}, cf. 89²¹.   Return to 2d pers., referred to Yahweh by some, to king by others, the latter better.   The repetition of מצא in this sense is rather tautological.   Du. would change to תָּבוֹא. 𝕲 has כל before שׂנְאֶיךָ, this prob. the correct text. — **10.** [תְּשִׁיתֵמוֹ] Qal impf. 2 m., c. sf. archaic 3 pl. as v.^{13}. — [כְּתַנּוּר אֵשׁ] *a.λ. as an oven of fire,* כ improb. rd. בְּ. ־וָיּוּר *furnace, a.λ. ψ;* but not uncommon elsw. — [לְעֵת פָּנֶיךָ] *at the time of thy presence, i.e.* in anger, from context, cf. La. 4^{16}.   The line is defective. Insert ־רְ as Lv. 20^{3.6} 26^{17} Ez. 14⁸, ניּרן מנים of angry looks. יהוה is attached to previous words to complete the line against 𝔐 by Bä, but Vrss. and most scholars attach it to subsequent words. — [יהוה בְּאַפּוֹ יְבַלְּעֵם וְהֹאכְלֵם אֵשׁ] as it stands is of a different measure, also 3d pers. appears for 2d pers. of preceding and following context.   It interrupts either as gl., so Bä., Be., or as another voice, as above v.⁸.   Two lines are needed here to make the second half of Ps. equal with the first half.   We have only five words in the text where we need six. The second l. might easily be restored by inserting עברתו as Ez. 21⁹⁶ 22³¹ 38¹⁹.

יהוה באפו יבלעם

ותאכלם אש עברתו

‡[בלע] vb. Qal *swallow up, engulf;* subj. ארץ 106¹⁷ as Ex. 15¹² Nu. 16³⁰, etc.; of devastation of enemy Ps. 124³ Ho. 8⁷ Je. 51³⁴; of calamity Ps. 69¹⁶. Pi. *swallow up, engulf 21*¹⁰ 55¹⁰ subj. ', 35²⁶ subj. enemies. Hithp. *be swallowed up,* their wisdom Ps. 107²⁷.— **11.** [רְיֵמוֹ] archaic sf. 3 pl. of פְּרִי n.m. *fruit.*— **12.** [נֽשׁוּ רָעָה] antith. to נטה הס־: *stretch out, extend hand,* so *extend unto* in the hand, cf. הסר Gn. 39²¹ (J), שלום Is. 66¹².— ‡ רָעָה n.f.: (1) *evil, misery, distress* 34²² 91¹⁰ 107²⁶·⁸⁹; יום רעה 27⁵ 41² Je. 17¹⁷·¹⁸ 51²; רָעוֹת *evils* Pss. 34²⁰ 40¹³ 71²⁾ 88⁴ 141⁵ (cf. Dt. 32²⁸); עֵת רִ־' Ps. 37¹⁹ Je. 2²⁷ + 3 t. Am. 5¹² Mi. 2³ Ec. 9¹²; ראה רעה Ps. 90¹⁵, cf. Je. 44¹⁷. (2) *Evil, injury, wrong* Pss. 21¹² 28⁸ 35²⁶ 52³ 109⁵, c. עשׂה ר' לְ 15⁸ +. Obj. vbs. † השׁב 35⁴ 41⁸ 140³ Gn. 50²⁰ (E) Je. 36³ 48² Mi. 2³; בקשׁ Ps. 71¹⁸·²⁴, cf. 1 S. 24¹⁰ 25²⁶ 1 K. 20⁷; דרשׁ Ps. 38¹³; חפץ 40¹⁵ = 70³; † שׁלב 35¹² 38²¹ Gn. 44⁴ (J) Je. 18²⁰ 51²⁴. (3) *Evil* in ethical sense: שׁלח בר' 50¹⁹ of speech, 94²³ 107³⁴.— [כָּל־יוּכָלוּ] relative clause, *which they cannot* or *could not,* e.g. יכל; לעשׂות (*v.* 13⁵).— **13.** [פִּי הִשִׁיחָמוּ שָׁכֶם] vb. with double acc. *v.* Ges.§117 ਜੱ, Dr.§189 obs.. The *shoulder* here for *back,* cf. [מְיתָר].— 1 S. 10⁹. הפנה שכם Ps. 18⁴¹; נתן ערף Ps. 18⁴¹; פנה עֹרֶף Jos. 7¹² Je. 48³⁹ (Hiph.); n. *bowstring,* a.λ. in this sense; elsw. *tent cords,* but not in ψ, cf. יֶתֶר 11².

PSALM XXII., 5 STR. 10⁸.

Ps. 22 is the lamentation of a great sufferer in peril of deadly enemies. In five strophes, the situation is vividly described: (1) He is forsaken by God in his extremity (v.²⁻³), notwithstanding the fathers had ever been delivered by Him (v.⁴⁻⁶). (2) He is despised by the nations, as a mere worm, and mocked for his trust in God (v.⁷⁻⁹), who has cared for him hitherto since his birth (v.¹⁰⁻¹¹). (3) He is abandoned to bulls and lions (v.¹²⁻¹⁴), and is wasting away body and soul in agony (v.¹⁵). (4) He is about to die by the cruelty of dogs (v.¹⁶⁻¹⁷), who are greedily gazing on him, anxious for their prey (v.¹⁸⁻¹⁹). (5) His life is abandoned to all these enemies, and in despair he prays for deliverance (v.²⁰⁻²²), with the vow to praise Yahweh in the congregation of the temple (v.²³·²⁶). A later editor makes the deliverance more distinct by stating it as a fact (v.²⁴⁻²⁵·²⁷). A still later editor gives the deliverance a world-wide significance, with a meaning to subsequent generations (v.²⁸⁻³⁹).

I.

MY 'El, why dost Thou forsake me?
 Far from my salvation is my roaring.
 I cry in the daytime, but Thou answerest **not**;
 And in the night, there is no respite for me.
 But, O Thou (Yahweh), Holy One,
 Enthroned upon the praises of Israel;
 In *Thee* our fathers *trusted*,
 (In *Thee*) they *trusted*, and Thou didst deliver **them,**
 Unto *Thee* they cried and they escaped,
 In *Thee* they *trusted* and were not ashamed.
BUT I am a worm, and no man,
 A reproach of mankind, and despised of peoples.
 All seeing me deride me;
 They let out (words), they shake their head,
 (Saying) "Roll on Yahweh, let Him deliver him;
 Let Him rescue him, seeing that He delights in him."
 But, O Thou who drewest me forth from the belly,
 (My trust) upon the breast of my mother;
 Upon Thee was I cast from the womb.
 From the belly of my mother Thou art my 'El.

II.

BE not far from me, for there is distress;
 Be near, for there is no helper.
 Many bulls encompass me,
 Mighty ones of Bashan encircle me.
 They open wide upon me their **mouth,**
 As a lion rending and roaring.
 As water I am poured out;
 Yea, all my bones are parted;
 My heart is become like wax.
 It is melted in the midst of mine inwards.
MY strength is dried up like a potsherd,
 And my tongue is made to cleave to my **jaws;**
 And in the dust of death (they) lay me.
 (Many) dogs encompass me,
 An assembly of maltreaters enclose me;
 They dig into my hands and my feet.
 I count all my bones;
 While they look, they stare upon me.
 They divide my garments among them,
 And on my clothing they cast lots.

III.

OH Thou, put not afar off *my* (hind);
 Yahweh, O haste to *my* help;
 O deliver from the sword *my* life,
 From the power of the dog *mine* only one.

From the mouth of the lion save *me*,
From the horns of the yore ox, *mine* afflicted one.
Then will I declare Thy name to my brethren;
In the midst of the congregation will I praise Thee.
From Thee will be my praise in the great congregation;
My vows will I pay in Thy presence.

Ps. 22 was in 𝔇; then in 𝔐 and 𝔇ℜ (*v.* Intr. §§ 27, 31, 33). The latter designated the melody to which it was to be sung אילת השחר (*v.* Intr. § 34): *a hind in the dawn* (*leaps*). This is referred by some Rabbins to the dawn itself as a hind leaping in fresh vigour; by others to the hind hunted in the early morning (*v.* De., *Psalmen*[4] s. 225). The former would be a joyous melody not suited to the Ps.; the latter is most suitable, especially if there be a connection between the hind in the title and the אילת v.[20]. The Ps. is composed of five trimeter decastichs, each of two sections, hexastich and tetrastich v.[2-6, 7-11, 12-15, 16-19, 20-23, 26]. These are arranged in three parts, each characterised by the use of רחק v.[2, 12, 20]. The first two parts consist of Str. and Antistr., the third of a single Str. It is possible that the third also had an antistr. whose place has been taken up by the later additions to the Ps. The Ps. is a simple, graphic, and powerful description of a sufferer, trusting in God, though apparently forsaken by Him and left in the hands of cruel enemies, who have already brought him to the point of death. He yet continues his plaintive cry for deliverance, and concludes with a vow of thanksgiving in the congregation assembled in temple worship. The description is too varied for any individual experience. It heaps up similes and situations which are not always consistent, and which cannot be attached to any real historical event, either of a heroic sufferer, or of the pious part of the community, or of the nation itself. It is indeed an ideal situation such as that described in Lam. with reference to Jerusalem, and that of Is.[2] with reference to Mother Zion and the servant of Yahweh. In these writings many different situations are described in which individuals might be conceived as suffering, and are combined with national experiences, and the whole made into a mosaic of affliction to represent the woes of a pious community, abandoned by God to their cruel foes. The ideal of the Ps. is so nearly related to the suffering servant of Is.[2] that there must be dependence of the one upon the other: קרוש v.[4], cf. Is. 40[25]; תולעת v.[7], cf. Is. 41[14]; בזוי עם v.[7], cf. Is. 49[7] 53[3]; ולא איש v.[7], cf. Is. 52[14]; חרפת אדם v.[7], cf. Is. 51[7]. But the poet is also independent; for his use of animals, lions, bulls, dogs, for enemies, and probably also of the hind for himself is characteristic, and while not without example in Pss., is yet beyond anything else in the OT. The authors cannot be the same. The poets use, however, the same trimeter measure, and in the main the same ideals; and the historical situation which occasioned the poems is similar. If the suffering servant of Is.[2] is exilic, that of the Ps. is post-exilic, for, (1) the reference to the fathers v.[5] is in the style of post-ex. writers, (2) the existence of the temple is implied in the assembly for worship, v.[23, 26]; the payment of vows, v.²⁶; and probably also the cherubic throne idealised in the תהלות of Israel, v.⁴, which in itself seems to imply the temple hymns. But we cannot go too far from the exile because, (1) Ps. 71⁵⁻⁶ cites from v.¹⁰⁻¹¹. (2) The use of אח v.²³ for the brethren of the קהל, cf. 133¹, Pr, 6¹⁹, implies a time when the people were compacted by persecution into a brotherhood. (3) The kingdom or nation no longer exists. The persecutors are foreign nations, עדת מרעים v.¹⁷, an organised body, over against the קהל of the people of God. They are compared to bulls v.¹³·²², lions v.¹⁴·²², and yet also to dogs v.¹⁷·²¹; thus implying a number of enemies, and enemies of different characteristics. This is the situation of the infant community of the restoration, when they were exposed to the cruel and treacherous attacks of the minor nations as described in many Pss. of the period (v. Pss. 9–10 and Ne.). There is, in the fifth Str., the same kind of a distinction between the poet and the sufferer that we find also in Is. 53. This is due to the fact that the poet is not speaking altogether for himself, but for the pious community as the servant of God. And so he speaks of *my hind* ‖ *mine only one* ‖ *mine afflicted one*, as of *my help*, *my life*, and *me*, v.²⁰⁻²². The sufferer is thus the ideal community, and the sufferings are idealised in a mosaic of varied experiences. The Ps. received additions in order to give it a wider outlook: (1) the fact that the sufferer was heard and answered, and that the entire seed of Jacob united in the praise of Yahweh in sacrificial meals, is stated in v.²⁴⁻²⁵·²⁷. In this section v.²⁷ in its use of ענוים, at the sacrificial meals at the temple, particularly in public praise, and the use of the phrase יחי לבבכם for יהי נפשכם, Is. 55³, implies a later period of composition. The vbs. in v.²⁷ have been changed from original imvs., as v.²⁴, into 3 pl. in accordance with the subsequent pentameter. This was made easier by the separation of v.²⁷ from v.²⁴·²⁵ by v.²⁶. (2) The world-wide significance of this deliverance is brought out in a pentameter heptastich. This addition was probably earlier than the other, and is similar to the combination of the trimeter and pentameter poems in Is.² (v. Br.^{MP 339}). This heptastich also has features of resemblance to the last parts of Is.³, especially in the conversion of the nations and their participation in the worship of Yahweh in sacrificial meals in Jerusalem, v.²⁸⁻³⁰, cf. Is. 66¹⁹⁻²³. The conception of Yahweh as the universal king, v.²⁹, is in accordance with that of the royal group of Pss. 93, 95–100. For דור יבאו, עם נולד, דור נולד, v.³¹⁻³²; cf. דור אחרון, עם נברא, 102¹⁹. All this indicates a period in which the minor persecuting nations have passed out of view, and the greater and more distant nations, who are not persecutors, but friendly, have come into the range of thought as hopeful converts to the God of Israel. This addition gave the earlier Ps. a wider outlook and made the deliverance of the sufferer of world-wide importance. The Ps. has been regarded by the Church from the most ancient times as the great Passion Ps., and it is the proper Ps. for Good Friday. This was due: (1) to the use of v.² by Jesus Himself when dying on the cross, Mt. 27⁴⁶ Mk. 15³⁴; and the remarkable resemblance in the situation of Jesus at that time to the situation described in the Ps.; (2) the casting lots for His garments, v.¹⁹, Mk. 15²⁴ Jn. 19²³⁻²⁴; (3) the parching thirst, v.¹⁶, Jn. 19²⁸⁻⁹;

(4) the agony of the stretched bones on the cross, v.[15] and the digging into the hands and feet by the nailing to the cross, v.[17]; (5) the cruel gazing on His sufferings, v.[18], Mt. 27[36-44]; (6) the mocking of His enemies in the words of the Ps., v.[9], cf. Mt. 27[43] Lk. 23[35]. It seems to the Christian that the psalmist indeed gives a more vivid description of the sufferings of Christ on the cross than the authors of the Gospels. Has the psalmist's description of the suffering servant of Yahweh an accidental coincidence with the sufferings of Christ, or is the coincidence due to prophetic anticipation ? We cannot think of direct prophecy. The reference to a historical situation is unmistakable. But inasmuch as the poet, like the author of the conception of the suffering servant of Is.[2], idealises the sufferings of Israel, and gives his sufferer a mediatorial relation to the nations, and does this in order to hold up to the pious a comforting conception of a divine purpose in their sufferings, we may suppose that this ideal was designed to prepare the minds of the people of God for the ultimate realisation of that purpose of redemption in a sufferer who first summed up in his historical experiences this ideal of suffering. In this sense the Ps. is Messianic (v. Br.[MP 322 sq.]).

Pt. I., Str. I. is composed of a trimeter tetrastich antith. to a trimeter hexastich. In the tetrastich, the experience of the sufferer is described, as the reverse of the experience of the fathers. — **2–3.** *My 'El*], the ancient poetic name of God, intensified by repetition by a later editor, but at the expense of the measure. — *why dost Thou forsake me*], expostulation with God for a situation which to the sufferer seems inexplicable, cf. Is. 49[14]. EV[s]. continue the question through the next line, so Dr., Kirk.; but it makes a difficult construction in Hebrew. The ancient Vrss. regard the second line as the beginning of the description of suffering, and this is easier and more natural. It begins a syn. tristich as the basis of the expostulation. — *Far from my salvation*]. There is an awful gap and appalling distance between the agony and the salvation from it. It is this long distance in time, this prolonged postponement of salvation, which the psalmist cannot understand. — *is my roaring*], the loud continued outcry of intense suffering, lengthened by a prosaic copyist at the expense of the measure, and weakened into " words of my roaring." ǁ *I cry in the daytime,* which passes over into, *and in the night,* all day and all night long. A later editor inserted " O my God," to emphasize the appeal to God, but at the expense of the measure. — *Thou answerest not*]. God is silent in this long interval. —

— there is no respite for me]. His agony continues without interruption, his cry for help has no pause. **— 4–6.** The expostulation is
strengthened by a reference to the past experience of the fathers
which was so different; an appeal to Yahweh in a syn. couplet,
and a statement of the experience of the fathers in a syn. tetrastich.— *O Thou (Yahweh), Holy One*], an exclamation, not a statement of fact, "Thou art holy," which is tame and unpoetical, and
not in accord with the state of mind of the sufferer. The divine
name "Yahweh" is necessary to the measure; it was omitted by
an unpoetic copyist. The term "Holy One" is characteristic of
Isaiah, and represents God in His majestic aloofness, a conception peculiarly appropriate here; rather than in accordance with
later ideas, God as the ethically complete and perfect Being. —
Enthroned upon the praises of Israel], a poetical spiritualisa-
tion of the more physical idea that He was enthroned upon the
cherubim in the Holy of Holies of the temple, cf. Ps. 80^2.
Thither the praises of Israel were directed in temple worship;
thither they were conceived as entering, with the clouds of incense
from the altar of incense, which stood in front of this most sacred
place. This incense, whose very idea is to give efficacy to prayer
and praise, sweetens them and makes them acceptable to Yahweh,
goes up and envelopes the cherubic throne so that the throne
of Yahweh is conceived as sustained by them. 𝕲, 𝔙, 𝕴 give a
simpler text, "O Thou enthroned in the sanctuary, the praise of
Israel," which is tempting, and followed by Genebr. and R. C.
scholars generally; but not by modern Protestants, who follow Calv.
in the interpretation given above. Aug., Euthymius, al., interpret
the holy as of holy persons. Horsley follows 𝕲 except that he
thinks of the abstract "holiness" instead of holy place. PBV.
"And Thou continuest holy; O Thou worship of Israel," is an
intermediate rendering, which though advocated by the older
English scholars such as Ham., Jebb, "is based on an untenable
construction of the words," Kirk.— *In Thee*], emphatic in position, repeated in the second line, though omitted in 𝕳 by a
copyist's mistake at the expense of the measure; so also in the
fourth line, with the syn. *unto Thee*], required by its verb in
the third line. — *our fathers*], the common subject of the verbs
of the four lines, and so emphasized over against their suffering

descendants. — *trusted*], repeated for emphasis in the second and fourth lines, with the intervening *cried*, of the third line, so plaintively expressed, in view of the present situation. The fathers were not forsaken, as is their son. *Thou didst deliver them* ‖ *they escaped* ‖ *they were not ashamed*. This is the climax ; the shame of his present position was in its being so much the reverse of theirs.

Str. II. is composed of a hexastich, describing his miserable situation, and a tetrastich of expostulation, based on his own previous experience. — **7.** *But I am a worm, and no man*], taking up the sense of shame, expressed in the last vb. of the previous str. He has lost his manhood and is become a miserable worm. — *a reproach of mankind*], an object of reproach to mankind in general. — *despised of peoples*], the nations by whom he was surrounded. Such is also the description of the servant of Yahweh in Is.[2] : "thou worm Jacob" 41^{14}, "whom man despiseth," "despised of person," "abhorred of the nation " 49^{7}, "the reproach of men " 51^{7}, "so disfigured more than man was his appearance and his form than the sons of men " 52^{14}, "despised, and forsaken of men ; a man of sorrows, and acquainted with grief" 53^{3} (*v.* Br.[MP 349-357]). — **8.** *All seeing me*]. These same nations, looking upon the affliction of the people of God, have no compassion, but deride in word and gesture ; *they let out* (*words*), so essentially ⑹, words that they would not venture to speak to a self-respecting people able to vindicate themselves ; they do not restrain themselves, but give full vent to their maliciousness. This seems more appropriate to the use of the Hebrew term, and more in accordance with their words given in v.[9], than the usual rendering, "shoot out the lip " EV[.]., explaining the original as an insulting gesture, although apparently sustained by similar expressions 35^{21} Jb. 16^{10}. This interpretation was due to the insertion of the word "with the lip " in the text, with the same motive, at the expense cf the measure. But this is difficult to reconcile with the other uses of the Hebrew word, or with any known gesture of that time. — *they shake their head*]. This is the gesture of derision accompanying their words. The same gesture appears in those who mocked the crucified Jesus. "And they that passed by railed on him, wagging their heads, and saying " Mt. 27^{39}. — **9.** *Roll on*

Yahweh], so 肬 imv. ; " commit thyself " RV. ; " cast thyself "
JPSV. ; which is better than ancient Vrss., which render as pf.,
so " He trusted " PBV., AV. The enemies say this in derision.
The burden, to be rolled off on Yahweh, for Him to bear for His
people, was the agony and reproach. — *Seeing that He delights in
him*]. The people were well known to be trusting in Yahweh,
their God, and as therefore presumably acceptable to Him, and
delighted in by Him, cf. Wisd. $2^{16 sq.}$. The derision of suffering
Israel is here, as ever, accompanied with the derision of Yahweh
their God by the hostile nations. — **10.** *But, O Thou*], emphatic
repetition of personal address to Yahweh in antithesis to *But I*
$v.^{7}$; better than the usual interpretation stating a fact, " Thou art
He." This syn. tetrastich emphasises the previous experience,
that Yahweh had not only taken an active part at the birth and
during the infancy of the nation, but had continued to be their
God without ceasing until the present, cf. Is. 46^{3-4}. — **11.** *My 'El*],
at the close of this Str. and at the beginning of the Ps., incloses
the entire first part within this most comprehensive relation.

Pt. II., Str. III. begins with a description of the external
situation in three couplets, and concludes with the effect upon
the person himself in two couplets. — **12.** *Be not far from me*],
renewing $v.^{2b}$, and renewed in $v.^{20a}$ ‖ *Be near*], the negative
transformed into a positive, more probable than the present
text, which makes " near," an adj. predicate of distress, at the
expense of the measure and parallelism. — *for there is distress
‖ for there is no* (other) *helper*], the reason for the plaintive
appeal to God. — **13.** *Many bulls*], intensified in *mighty ones of
Bashan*]. Bashan was famed for its rich pastures, fat cattle, and
powerful and fierce bulls. The enemies are compared to them,
cf. Am. 4^{1}. They *encompass ‖ encircle*], enclose and shut in on
every side with their horns, cf. $v.^{22}$, so that there is no escape, no
one within that enclosure to help. — **14.** Leaving the bulls and
reverting to the enemies : *they open wide upon me their mouth*],
in order to devour, swallow up. This statement is appropriate
not to bulls, but to beasts of prey, and so *as a lion rending and
roaring*], opening the mouth to roar as well as to devour. Cruel
enemies are frequently compared to lions, see $v.^{22}$ 7^{3} 10^{9} 17^{12}. —
15. *As water I am poured out*], so Jos. 7^{5}, " the hearts of the

people melted and became as water." — *all my bones are parted*],
each one distinct in pain, all aching and seeming as if they had
broken apart ; both graphic descriptions of feverish anxiety.
The reference to the heart is renewed and enlarged as the principal thing.   It melts as if it were *wax* within him, cf. 68³.

Str. IV. The antistr. is composed of two tristichs and two
couplets. — **16**. The agony of the previous tetrastich is continued,
the result of the feverish anxiety is still further described. — *My
strength is dried up*], is sapped ; the blood is dried up and the
body is become brittle and breakable, *like a potsherd*, a piece of
pottery. — *My tongue is made to cleave to my jaws*].   By intense
thirst, the tongue adheres to the roof of the mouth so that he
cannot use it, cf. Jn. 19²⁸. — *In the dust of death*], a phrase
especially appropriate not only to the previous context, the dry,
brittle potsherd, but also because it involves the idea of the formation of the original man out of dust, as a potter makes his
pottery, Gn. 2⁷, and also the conception of death as a return of
the body to the dust, Gn. 3¹⁹.   This is probably the reason why
the 2 pers. sg. is given in 𝕳, " Thou layest me," referring to God
as the primary agent, instead of the simpler and more natural 3 pl.
referring to the enemies, cf. v.¹³. — *they lay me*].   The enemies
have been active against the sufferer, while his God, through it
all, has remained afar off. — **17**. (*Many*) *dogs*], so 𝕲, 𝕵, PBV.
∥ " many bulls " v.¹³ more suited to parallel.   " For dogs," 𝕳,
AV., RV.   The enemies are now compared to the more ignoble
animals.   Dogs in the OT. are the fierce prowlers of the night
and scavengers of the streets, *v.* 2 K. 9³⁵⁻³⁶ Pss. 59⁷·¹⁵ 68²⁴ Je. 15³.
They come in a pack, and so are called *an assembly of maltreaters*], cf. 86¹⁴, greedy to seize, maul, and in every way maltreat
their victim. — *They dig into*], the dogs with their teeth. — *my
hands and my feet*].   The extremities are first gnawed by the dogs.
This is the translation best sustained by the Vrss. and the context.
EVˢ. " pierce " is not justified by the Hebrew word, and was due
to a desire for a specific reference to the crucifixion.   𝕳 " as a
lion," used a word for lion not found elsewhere in ψ for the usual
word given above v.¹⁴, and not suited to the previous mention of
dogs, or of hands and feet.   The sufferer here v.¹⁶ᶜ is lying in the
dust in extreme peril of death, and his enemies have already

begun to devour him. — **18.** *I count all my bones*], renewing v.[15b].
Each one stands out with its own special ache. — *While they look
|| they stare*], a circumstantial clause. While the enemies are
looking with intense eagerness, staring greedily upon him, he is
aching all over from head to foot, in all his framework of bones.
The usual rendering, as an independent and emphatic clause,
makes two lines in this verse, in no proper relation of parallelism,
and justifies in a measure the proposal of some moderns to trans-
fer v.[18a] to the beginning of the Str. — **19.** *They divide || cast lots*],
returning from the dogs to the enemies they represent, as above
v.[16c]. They have stripped him of *garments || clothing*, and they
divide these as their spoil in the usual way by lots.

Str. V. is composed of a hexastich of petition and a tetrastich
of vows. — **20–22.** The Str. begins with a plea similar to that of
v.[12]. — *O Thou, put not far off*], as 𝕲, required by the object and
to be preferred to 𝕳 " be not far from." Yahweh has been transposed with *my hind*, because of a misconception of the meaning
of the Hebrew word, which is usually interpreted after 𝕲 as " my
help " or " succour," by EV[s]. and most after 𝕵 as " my strength."
But really it is the same word as that in the title translated by
𝕲 as " help," but pointed by 𝕳 as " hind." Indeed the suffix, in
accordance with Hebrew usage, which regards the soul as well as
the body as resting on a common substratum, the person himself,
(*v.* 42[5.7] 131[2]) objectifies the soul as the seat of his suffering. It
is first compared to a hind, hunted until its strength fails and it
pants, ready to perish, cf. 42[2]; just as in the parallel v.[21a] *my life*,
v.[21b] *mine only one* (cf. 35[17]), as his unique priceless possession,
and again in v.[22b] after 𝕲, *mine afflicted one*. Here also later
copyists, not understanding the original usage, interpret it in MT.
as vb. pf. 2 m. " Thou hast answered me," making a very abrupt
conclusion to the petition, by a single word of divine response,
and making it difficult to explain the phrase *from the horns of the
yore ox*, which occasions great difference of opinion among interpreters. In fact the six lines all rhyme in *i*. Each couplet has
its verb. — *O haste to my help*], a phrase frequent in Pss. of
lamentation || *deliver* || *save*. The four kinds of enemies of the
previous Str. appear also in this climax of petition : the *sword* of
the enemies themselves, *the dog, the lion, the yore ox*. The latter

is an intensification of the bulls of Bashan, and refers to that large, fierce bull of ancient times which has now become extinct. — **23, 26.** The petition is sustained by a vow in four lines : *I will declare Thy name*], make it known as a saving name, *praise* ‖ *pay vows*], make votive offerings. The declaration is to be to *my brethren*], those associated in the community of God's people. See Heb. 2¹², where these words are put in the mouth of Christ. — *the great congregation*] assembled for worship in the temple. — *in Thy presence*], before the sacred place where Yahweh dwelt, in the most Holy Place of the temple. The phrase, *From Thee*] is probably to be interpreted as the source of the deliverance, and therefore of the praise for it. This last couplet, which is parall i to the previous couplet, has been separated by the insertion of a gloss v.²⁴⁻²⁵ which changes the reference to God to the 3d pers , and so makes awkward changes to and from 2d to 3d pers., and also destroys the organisation of the Str. The original Ps. comes to an appropriate close here with a vow of public recognition and thankoffering in the temple for the deliverance, the prayer for which has been the theme of the Ps.

24–25. This piece is composed of two syn. trimeter triplets. It is a call upon the congregation to praise Yahweh because of His deliverance of the afflicted people. It is a generalisation of the situation by a later editor.

> Ye that fear Yahweh praise Him,
> All the seed of Jacob glorify Him,
> All the seed of Israel stand in awe of Him ;
> For He hath not abhorred to answer the afflicted,
> And He hath not hid His face,
> But when he cried unto Him He heard.

24. *Ye that fear Yahweh*], those that have the religion of Yahweh and are in the habit of doing reverence to Him. — *All the seed of Jacob* ‖ *seed of Israel*], phrases for the people Is. 45¹⁹·²⁵ Je. 31³⁶·³⁷ 33²⁶. — *praise* ‖ *glorify* ‖ *stand in awe*], usual phrases of public worship. — **25.** *For He hath not abhorred*]. This strong and unusual term, in this connection, received a milder variant in the margin, " He hath not despised," which subsequently came into the text by conflation and so destroyed the measure. The uncommon expression is weakened in the following line to the usual one, *hath not hid His face*, and the ordinary one, *heard*. — *to answer the afflicted*]. This seems to be the best interpretation of the unpointed text, taking the first word as infin. construct of the vb. " answer " after 𝔊. But 𝔐 points it as abstract noun from the stem meaning affliction, which gives us the tautological " affliction of the afflicted," AV., RV., 𝔍 *modestiam*, so Aq. takes it as another abstract noun, PBV. " low estate," which gives a better sense, but is not suited to the context.

27. This tristich resembles in form the previous two, v.$^{24-25}$, of which it was originally a continuation ; but it changes from 2d to 3d pl., and in this respect agrees with subsequent context.

> The afflicted will eat and be satisfied;
> Those who seek Him will praise Yahweh,
> Saying, " Let your heart live forever."

The afflicted], pl. for the sg. v.^{25a}. — *will eat and be satisfied*], partake of the thankofferings in the temple, as Calv., Ges., De W., Hi. ; and not to be understood in a merely spiritual sense, as Ew., De., or in the still more general sense of refreshment by divine blessing Hu., cf. 23^5. — *Those who seek Him*] are worshippers in general ; they praise Yahweh. — *Let your heart live forever*]. Owing to the change of person this can only be words of those who seek Yahweh, addressed to the afflicted ; and therefore congratulatory, and wishing perpetual health and prosperity to them, as an antidote to their previous affliction. The heart stands here for the man himself, in late usage, confounding לב with נפש.

28–32. This is a pentameter heptastich, a later addition to the Ps., composed of a triplet and two couplets.

All the ends of the earth will remember, and they will turn unto Yahweh,
And all the families of the nations will worship before Him;
For unto Yahweh belongs the kingdom, and He rules over the nations.
Have all the fat ones of earth eaten and worshipped,
Then will bow down all about to descend to the dust, and he who doth not keep himself alive.
A seed will serve Him. It will be told to a generation to come;
And they will declare His righteousness to a people to be born, that He hath done (it).

28. *All the ends of the earth*], as 2^8 67^8 72^8 Is. 45^{22} 52^{10}, to comprehend the entire earth. — *all the families of the nations*], cf.

Ps. 96[7] : all the families or clans into which the nations may be subdivided, with a probable reference to the patriarchal blessings, Gn. 12[3] 28[14]. — *will remember*], call to mind their obligations to Yahweh, whom they have forgotten in going after other gods, and so, *will turn*, in repentance for previous neglect, in entire change of attitude, *unto Yahweh*, so that Yahweh will be recognised as the universal God. — *and worship before Him*], unite in the pre-scribed worship in His temple. 𝕳 " before Thee " is certainly an error of a copyist. 𝕲 has the correct text. — **29**. *For unto Yah-weh belongs the kingdom*]. The reason for the conversion of the nations is that they all are in His kingdom, subject to His dominion. He rules over the nations as the universal king. — **30.** Two classes of worshippers are brought into sharp antithesis : *all the fat ones of earth*], the rich, prosperous, powerful nations, and *all about to descend to the dust*], those decaying, dying, who are going down to the Pit 28[1] 30[4. 10] 88[5] 143[7], to Sheol 55[16], an expression used frequently of dying nations, Is. 14[15] Ez. 26[20] 32[18-30]. — *He who doth not keep himself alive*], the nation unable to protect its life against more powerful neighbours seeking to destroy it. The Vrss. and interpreters have many suggestions here, but none of them are so simple as 𝕳, which gives an explanatory complement to the previous clause. This does not refer to the nations in Sheol after death, in contrast with those still alive on earth, for this would leave us with only the rich nations worshipping Yahweh on earth. The context demands poor, feeble nations, and that is admirably expressed in the terms above where they are represented as dying. The ptc. represents rather the process than the result. The rich and prosperous come first, in a clause which is conditional in form. Have they *eaten and worshipped*], taken part in the sacrificial meals of the temple, and worshipped in connection with these sacrifices ; *then will bow down*], in the prostration of worship, the other class also, the poor and perishing nations, and so the worship of Yahweh will be universal. The universality of worship having been stated as to its comprehending all nations and classes, it is now represented in temporal forms. — **31.** *A seed will serve Him*], a seed descending from the nations mentioned above, their next generation. — *It will be told to a generation to come*], either the

seed previously mentioned, or more probably a generation to
come after them, a second generation. The measure and parallelism requires the exclusion of "*of the Lord*" as a gloss, and the
attachment of "come" to this line with ⅏, rather than to the
next with ℌ. — **32**. *And they will declare His righteousness*], His
vindication of His suffering servant, His salvation of His people,
in accordance with the usual meaning of righteousness in ψ and
Is.[2][3]. — *to a people to be born*], a people in the distant future,
beyond the second generation, after this universal conversion of
the nations; a people not yet born, but ultimately to be born,
probably conceived as summing up all the nations in itself, in
accordance with concept, cf. Ps. 87, where one after another is
born in Zion and all inscribed as citizens. — *That He hath done
(it)*], the salvation He has wrought; in the full sense of this
universal conversion, and worship of Yahweh in Jerusalem. This
ideal is a Messianic ideal, as connected with a sufferer whose
suffering is mediatorial, and whose salvation mediates universal
salvation.

2–3. אֵלִי אֵלִי לָמָה עֲזַבְתָּנִי. [אֵלִי אֵלִי לְמַה חוּשָׁה־לִי]. ⅏ has ὁ θεὸς ὁ θεός μου πρόσχες μοι =
v. v.[20]. Che. and Du. think that ℌ has been shortened and rd. הַקְשִׁיבָה לִי; but
⅏ gives the clue to the insertion, if one is thought necessary. Toy thinks ⅏
rd. second אלי as a prep., *My God unto me* (*attend*), so Hare אֵלַי. חַט אֵלַי. This
would make two trimeter lines instead of one in first half of v. — מִישׁוּעָתִי] Hi.,
Dy., Gr., Ehr. rd. מְשַׁוְּעָתִי. — דִּבְרֵי שַׁאֲגָתִי] ⅏ has οἱ λόγοι τῶν παραπτωμάτων
μου = דִּבְרֵי שְׁוָאַי *affairs of my errors*, so 𝔙, cf. 19[18]. — [אֱלֹהַי] is a gloss. It
certainly does not go with v.[3]. V.[2a] is given in NT. in:

Mt. 27[46] { ἐλωὶ ἐλωὶ λεμὰ σαβαχθανεί;
            { = Θεέ μου Θεέ μου, ἵνα τί με ἐγκατέλιπες; (as ⅏).

Mk. 15[34] { ἐλωὶ ἐλωὶ λαμὰ σαβαχθανεί;
            { = ὁ Θεός μου [ὁ Θεός μου], εἰς τί ἐγκατέλιπές με;

𝔗 אֵלִי אֵלִי מְטוּל מַה שְׁבַקְתַּנִי. Cod. D for Mt. and Mk. rds.: ἥλεὶ λαμᾶ ζαφθανεί,
which, according to Resch, implies a Heb. original עֲזַבְתָּנִי; for Aram. שבק.
If Ps. is a trimeter, it is not difficult to explain the glosses, which destroy the
measure. It was natural that אֵלִי should be repeated for greater emphasis.
The רחוק is sustained by its use in v.[12, 20]; therefore we must regard דִּבְרֵי as
an unnecessary addition. אלהי is the usual insertion of the divine name.
Therefore read:

אֵלִי לָמָה עֲזַבְתָּנִי
רָחוֹק מִישׁוּעָתִי שַׁאֲגָתִי
אֶקְרָא יוֹמָם וְלֹא־תַעֲנֶה

πρὸς σὲ of 𝕲 after κεκράξομαι is a prosaic addition. שׁ דִּבְרֵי is taken by AV. as ‖ ישׁעותי and so the force of למה is retained. It is better to regard the l. as statement of fact upon which the anxious plea is based: so 𝕲, 𝕵, Θ, Aq., 𝕿, Σ, Quinta and Sexta, also Horsley, Bä., al. — † שְׁאָגָה n.f. *roaring* in agony, of person Ps. *22²* 32³, pl. Jb. 3²⁴; elsw. of lion Is. 5²⁹ Ez. 19⁷ Zc. 11³ Jb. 4¹⁰ (*v.* vb. in v.¹⁴). — † דּוּמִיָּה] n.f. *silence:* elsw. 39⁸ 62² 65² (all dub.); 𝕵 *silentium*, 𝕲 εἰς ἄνοιαν = *folly.* Hatch (*Essays in Biblical Greek*, p. 174) rds. ἀνείαν (from ἀνίημι, rare word, not in Lex. of Liddell and Scott); not silence from groanings or complaint, but from trouble; no remission of, no respite from, pain. — **4.** וְאַתָּה קָדוֹשׁ] shortened l. in 𝕳. But 𝕲 σὺ δὲ ἐν ἁγίῳ κατοικεῖς ὁ ἔπαινος τοῦ Ἰσραήλ; 𝕰 *in sancto habitas, laus Israel:* 𝕵 *et tu sancte: habitator, laus Israel*, rd. קְרֹשׁ and רְהִלַּת sg., " habitans in loco, nempe tabernaculo, quae Israelis laus est," Hare; Σ ἐν ἁγίοις κατοικεῖς; Du. follows this and adds after Israel בך, omitted because of בְּךָ in next l. Gr. inserts הכרובים after ישׁב and נורא before תהלות. But this is unnecessary. קָדוֹשׁ is a favourite term for God in Is.[1, 2, 3] (*v. 16³*), cf. Pss. 71²² 78⁴¹ 89¹⁹. Insert יהוה as Bi. to make up l. as in v.²⁰. — תְּהִלּוֹת] *praises* regarded as a cloud upon which Yahweh is enthroned (*v. 2⁴* and Intr. § 1). — **5.** בָּטְחוּ]. בְּךָ should be prefixed to v.⁵ᵇ before as in 5ᵃ and 6ᵇ to make up measure; in all these cases it is emph. בכ׳ (*v. 4⁶* 9¹¹). — וַיְהִינְקֵמוֹ] ו consec. expressing result; full sf. for ־כ. For פלט *v. 17¹³*. — **6.** נִמְלָטוּ] ו coörd., Niph. pf. 3 pl. of מלט. Niph. *slip away, escape* 124⁷·⁷, as often in early Lit. Ju. 3²⁹ 1 S. 19¹⁰ Am. 9¹; so here, no sufficient reason for later pass., *be delivered* (WL. and Dn. 12¹). Pi. *deliver* Ps. 41², c. מן 107²⁰. מלט נפשׁ *save life* 89⁴⁹ 116⁴ 1 S. 19¹¹ Je. 48⁶ Am. 2¹⁴·¹⁶; נפשׁ omitted Ps. 33¹⁷, as Am. 2¹⁵. — **7.** אָנֹכִי] emph. antith. אַתָּה v.⁴; full form as 46¹¹ 50⁷ 81¹¹ 91¹⁵ 104⁸⁴ 141¹⁰ (*v.* Br.ᴴᵉˣ·⁷⁰). — תּוֹלַעַת] *worm*, cf. Is. 41¹⁴ תּוֹלַעַת יעקב. — וְלֹא־אִישׁ] to make it more emph.: *no man* as he should be (antith. with animals), cf. 147¹⁰. — חֶרְפַּת אָדָם] object of reproach by mankind, cf. 39⁹ נָבָל ה׳, also חרפה ר׳ 31¹² 79⁴ 89⁴² 109²⁵ Je. 6¹⁰(+ 5 t. Je.), *v.* also 15⁸. — בָּזוּי־עָם] ptc. pass. of בזה *one despised*, cf. Is. 49⁷ בְּזֹה נפשׁ, 53³ נִבְזֶה וחֲדַל אִישׁים, Je. 49¹⁵ בָּזוּי בָאדָם. — **8.** יַלְעִגוּ לִי] Hiph. impf., לעג *mock, deride*, cf. 2⁴ 59⁹ 80⁷ for Qal., not elsw. in ψ but Hiph. late. Ne. 2¹⁹ 3³³ +; Qal is early, Hiph. late. There is no good reason for pointing Hiph. here; יַלְעִינוּ is just as good here as in Ps. 80⁷. Hiph. pointing assimilated to next vb. יַפְטִירוּ Hiph. Impf. of פטר Hiph. *separate with the lip, open wide with an insulting expression*, only here (22⁸), elsw. Qal. *set free* from duty 2 Ch. 23⁸, *let out* waters Pr. 17¹⁴ (*e.g. in strife*). 𝕲 ἐλάλησαν ἐν χείλεσιν, 𝕰 *locuti sunt labiis:* " blasphemy " Genebr., cf. *rip out* (an oath), 𝕵 *dimittunt labium.* בְשָׂפָה is a gl.; without it the mng. is simply *let out.* — יָנִיעוּ רֹאשׁ] phr. 109²⁵ 2 K. 19²¹ = Is. 37²², sq. עַל Jb. 16⁴, of mocking, cf. Mt. 27³⁹; form of vb. Hiph. impf. 3 pl. of נוע. Hiph. in above phr. and in 59¹² (dub.) *cause to stagger along*, elsw. Qal *stagger*, as a drunkard 107²⁷, as a vagabond 109¹⁰·¹⁹, cf. 59¹⁶ Am. 4⁸. — **9.** גֹּל] imv. of גלל vb. *roll*, so De., Bä., Dr., but 𝕲, 𝕵, 𝕾, Mt. 27⁴³, Ew., Bi., Du., AV., RV.ᵐ גַּל pf. 3 m. Kö.ˢʸⁿᵗᵃˣ ²¹⁷ᶜ inf. abs., גלל in ψ only 119²² (sq. ־עַל) 37⁵ (c. ר׳ עַל), and here, אֶל incorrect for עַל. Vb. לאמר is implied as often in poetry. —

10. [כִּי־אַתָּה] begins a new Str., ci. v.⁴ᵃ antith. v.⁷ᵃ, 𝕵 *autem*, 𝕲 ὅτι, so Aq., 𝖅. — [גֹחִי] = גוּחִי 71⁶ (derived from this passage, but prob. error for גֹחִי). גָּחִי ptc. of גחה *draw forth*, so 𝕲, 𝕮: ‖ גיח Jb. 38⁸ *burst forth* of babe from womb; *propugnator meus* 𝕵, similarly Aq. is after Aram. mng. of גיח also transitive. But Kö.^{I.505} regards it as ptc. — מַבְטִיחִי [גיחי] Hiph. ptc. of בטח (cf. v.⁵), but 𝕲 has ἡ ἐλπίς μου, 𝕵 *fiducia mea* = מבטחי, so 𝖅, 𝖘, PBV., cf. 71⁵ מִבְטַחִי מִנְּעוּרָי and that is doubtless correct. ‡ מִבְטָח n.[m.] in ψ only, obj. of *confidence* elsw. 40⁵ 65⁶ 71⁵. — **11.** [עָלֶיךָ] emph. as v.⁵. — אֵלַי אֱלָהָה Du. would rd. אבי for אלי, but that would be an anachronism in biblical theology. The l. is too long, unless we connect with Makkeph, אלי־אהה. — **12.** [אַל־תִּרְחַק כִּי־צָרָה קְרוֹבָה]; juss. of רחק, cf. v.²ᵇ. ‡ רחק vb. Qal *be* or *become distant*, Yahweh subj. 22¹². ²⁰ 35²² 38²² 71¹², blessing 109¹⁷, elsw. 103¹² 119¹⁵⁰. Hiph.: (1) intr. *remove* 88⁹. ¹⁹ 103¹²; (2) trans. 55⁸. L. 1 is too long and l. 2 too short. Du. inserts יהוה to get three lines, but l. 3 still has but four syllables for three tones. Better divide at צרה and rd. קָרְבָה imv. of קרב; then we have antith. parall. — **13.** [יְתָרוּנִי] *enclose me:* Pi. pf. ‡ [כהר] vb. *surround*, Pi. elsw. Ju. 20⁴³, of surrounding enemy. Hiph. Hb. 1⁴ (as Pi.) Ps. 142⁸ (?). — [אַבִּירֵי בָשָׁן] *bulls of Bashan.* ‡ אַבִּיר adj. *mighty, valiant:* (1) אַבִּירֵי לֵב Ps. 76⁶ Is. 46¹²; (2) of angels Ps. 78²⁵, cf. 103²⁰; (3) of bulls, elsw. for princes 68³¹, and so in sacrifice 50¹³. ‡ בָשָׁן n. pr. country E. of Jordan, esp. between sea of Galilee and Mts. of Hauran, and from Jabbok north to Hermon, elsw. in ψ, 68¹⁶. ¹⁶. ²³ 135¹¹ 136²⁰. — **15.** [פָּצוּ נִשְׁפַּכְתִּי] cf. Jos. 7⁵, also La. 2¹⁹ Ps. 58⁸. The l. is too short. Prefix ואנכי as v.⁷ᵃ or let אנכי follow. — ו [וְהִתְפָּרְדוּ] coörd Hithp. pf. ‡ פרד *divide.* † Hithp. *be divided, separated, parted* from each other, elsw. Jb. 41⁹ of scales of crocodile, Jb. 4¹¹ Ps. 92¹⁰ *be scattered, dispersed.* — [כַּדּוֹנַג] *like wax,* alw. sim. of melting, cf. 68³ 97⁵ Mi. 1⁴. — [נָמֵס] Niph. pf. of ‡ מסס] vb. *melt,* not used in Qal except Is. 10¹⁸, but Niph. *melt away* 68³ 97⁵ 112¹⁰, fig. *faint, grow fearful* 22¹⁵, as frequently in D. Hiph. *cause to melt, intimidate* Dt. 1²⁸, elsw. Hiph. formed from מסה כסה (v. 6⁷). — ‡ [מֵעֶה] n.m. only pl. *inwards, intestines,* usual mng. not in ψ, but, (1) womb 71⁶; (2) ‖ לב *inner man,* elsw. 40⁹. — **16.** כֹּחִי] sf. 1 pers. ‡ כֹּחַ, n.m. *strength, power:* (1) *human strength:* (a) physical vigour in general 31¹¹ 38¹¹ 71⁹ 102²⁴, so here 𝕲, 𝕵; but Ols., Ew., Bä., Kau., Oort, Ehr., JPSV. rd. חִכִּי *palate,* on account of ‖ לְשׁוֹן; *power* opp. to that of God 33¹⁶; (2) *strength of angels* 103²⁰; (3) *power of God* in creation 65⁷; כֹּחַ מַעֲשָׂיו 111⁶; God is רַב כֹּחַ 147⁵, cf. רַב כֹּחַ Is. 63¹ Jb. 23⁶, בְּכֹחַ י׳ קוֹל Ps. 29⁴ (of thunder). — [מַלְקוּחָי] a.λ. pl. sf. √לקח: *jaws* as taking, seizing food. — [עֲפַר מָוֶת] *dust of death,* phr. a.λ., but cf. יוֹרְדֵי עָפָר v.³⁰, שֹׁכְנֵי עָ׳ Is. 26¹⁹, יְשֵׁנֵי אַדְמַת עָ׳ Dn. 12². — [הִשְׁפְּתֵנִי] Qal לֵעָ׳ אִשְׁכָּב Jb. 7²¹, c. עַל Jb. 20¹¹ 21²⁶. — impf. 2 m., c. sf. 1 sing. of † שפת vb. Qal *set, fix, put, lay:* here impf. for present, referring back to God as primary agent, *thou art laying me;* this seems strange in the midst of the description: rather rd. 3 pl. as above; vb. elsw. Is. 26¹² 2 K. 4³⁸ Ez. 24³. ³. — **17.** ‡ [כְּלָבִים] *dogs,* as ignoble animals, elsw. in ψ, v.²¹ 59⁷. ¹⁵ 68²⁴; here ‖ פָּרִיץ as noble ones v.¹⁸ᵃ. 𝕲 has κύνες πολλοί = כְּלָבִים רַבִּים, so Jer. in Com., Hare, Horsley; this prob. correct, but then כי should be stricken out. — [צָרַת כְּרֵיעֶיךָ] fig. passes over into reality, cf. עָ׳ עָרִיצִים 86¹⁴, עָ׳ חֵנַף Jb. 15³⁴,

‡ רעע vb. Hiph. ptc. pl. מְרֵעִים (*v. 1⁵*). עֵדָה (fig. nobles). Ps. 68³¹ עֲ אבירים
Qal *be injurious, evil,* c. לְ 106³². Hiph.: (1) *do an injury, hurt.* here abs.,
c. לְ 105¹⁶ (= c. בְּ 1 Ch. 16²²), c. acc. pers. Ps. 44³, c. בְּ 74³. להרע *do something
to one's own hurt* 15⁴ (cf. Lv. 5⁴ P), but improb. rd. לְרֵעַ as ⅁; (2) *do evil
wickedly* abs. 37⁸, pl. ptc. 27² 37¹·⁹ 92¹² 94¹⁶ 119¹¹⁵, קְהַל מר׳ 26⁵, סוּר מר׳ 64⁸.
— [כְּאֲרִי] *as a lion,* Rabbins, Hi., Köster, Hu., Ehr., al.; but ארי is not elsw. ψ
only אריה as v.¹⁴. Moreover the fig. of lion and bulls has been left for that of
ignoble dogs. ⅁ ὤρυξαν, 𝔙 *foderunt* = כארו = כרו or כורו BDB, Bu. *dig,* so
Compl., Cap., Ham., De., Bä., Oort, al. Others as Pocock, Phillips, Pe., Moll.,
Kö.ˢʸⁿᵗᵃˣ, ᵖ· ⁶⁸¹, interpret as ptc. pl., either cstr. כָּאֲרִי or defective. 𝔍 *vinxerunt,*
Aq.² ἐπέδησαν, Σ ὡς ζητοῦντες δῆσαι = כארו = *they bound;* so 𝔖 and among moderns Ew. Aq.¹ ᾔσχυναν, Aram. כאר = בָּעַר *they soiled,* or *marred,* so Du., who rds.
כָּאֲרוּ. 𝔗 has a conflation of noun and vb. showing an uncertainty in early
Jewish opinion. Ols., Bruston, We. regard the l. as a gl., but without ground,
for it is needed to complete the Str. — **18.** [אֲסַפֵּר] Pi. impf. 1 sg. The l. is
‖ v.¹⁵ᵇ. The interposition of 1 sg. between lines of 3 pers. leads some to transpose l. to the beginning of Str. v.¹⁶ᵃ; but it is more forceful as it is. — [הֵמָּה]
emph. summing up, or better, to indicate circumstantial clause. — [יַבִּיטוּ] impf.
of description — **19.** יִרְאוּ ‖ [יַפִּילוּ גִירָל] *cast lot,* cf. 16⁵ *lot* for portion assigned
by ר, also 125³ וגורל הצדיקים. — **20.** [וְאַתָּה] emph. introducing a new section,
cf. v.¹·⁷ᵃ. — [אֱיָלוּתִי] α.λ. ⅁ τὴν βοήθειάν μου, obj. of μὴ μακρύνῃς. 𝔍 *fortitudo
mea* connecting with לעזרתי as 𝔥. The word is abstr. in form, but improb.
in itself and difficult to explain, whether from אול or איל. This v. is used in
essentially the same terms:

38²²·²³ אלהי אל תרחק ממני חושה לעזרתי אדני;
40¹⁴ = 70² יהוה לעזרתי חושה;
71¹² אלהים אל תרחק ממני אלהי לעזרתי חושה.

In 38²³ אדני stands for an original יהוה; therefore the last clause has always
יהוה except in 71¹² 𝔈, which has changed an original יהוה in the first clause to
אלהים. The יהוה in the original of the first clause here would sufficiently
account for the אלהי in the second. Accordingly Gr. thinks the original here
was אלי אתה compressed into אילותי. It is noteworthy that ⅁ interprets אילת
of title as ὑπὲρ τῆς ἀντιλήψεως, the same word that it uses for עזרתי here.
This shows that in the original text the two words were regarded as syn., and
that the ו of v.²⁰ is fully written ו of interpretation. If the original was אילי,
we might in both cases rd. אֱיָלֵת and think of the נפש as the אַיָּלָה in accordance
with 42². In this case it goes with l. 1 ‖ יְחַיְּדִי of v.²¹ᵇ, and we would have a
rhyme in ־ִ for each l. of this Str. if עזרתי also is transposed to the end of l.
יהוה would then go with לעזרתי חושה as in the other similar passages. We
must then follow ⅁ and make the vb. Pi. or Hiph. with *hind* the obj. —
‡ [עֶזְרָה] n.f.: (1) *help, succour* from ר, elsw. 38²³ 40¹⁴ 70² 71¹², מצר 60¹³ = 108¹³;
(2) *embodied help, one who helps,* of ר 27⁹ 35² 40¹⁸ 44²⁷ 46² 63⁸ 94¹⁷. —
[לְעֶזְרָתִי חוּשָׁה] phr. elsw. 40¹⁴ = 70² 71¹² with words transposed 38²³. ‡ חוּשׁ vb.
Qal *haste, make haste* 119⁶⁰; imv. as above, elsw. sq. לי 70⁶ 141¹. Hiph. trans.

hasten 55⁹.— **21.** יְחִידָתִי] *my only one.* ‡ יָחִיד adj. ‖ נֶפֶשׁ:, also 35¹⁷ as the one unique and priceless possession, elsw. in ψ *solitary, alone* 25¹⁶ 68⁷ 141¹⁰ (ⅅ). — **22.** הוֹשִׁיעֵנִי] Hiph. imv. (*v. 3⁸*) should go to the end of l. for rhyme. — רֵמִים = רְאֵם *the yore ox,* the gigautic bull of ancient times, cf. 29⁶ 92¹¹ Nu. 23²² 24⁸ (E) Dt. 33¹⁷, ⅅ μονοκέρως, *unicorn,* so ℨ. — עֲנִיתָנִי] pf. statement of fact: *thou hast heard me,* so Aq., ℭ, cf. v.¹⁶ᶜ impf.; ⅅ τὴν ταπείνωσίν μου, ℌ, ℬ, cf. Σ τὴν κάκωσίν μου, cf. עֱנוּת 18³⁶ (?) a late word. Thrupp, Oort, We., Bä. עֲנִיָּתִי *my poor soul.* This is doubtless correct and was prob. in text of ⅅ.—
23. אֲסַפְּרָה] Pi. impf. cohort. expressing resolution (*v.* v.¹⁸ᵃ), obj. שֵׁם of Yahweh (*v.* 5¹²), so 102²², כָּבוֹד 19² 96⁸, נִפְלָאוֹת 9² 26⁷ +. — ‡ אָח] n.m.: (1) *real brother* 49⁸ 50²⁾ 69⁹; (2) *friend* 35¹⁴ 122⁸ 2 S. 1²⁶ 1 K. 9¹³ 20³².³³; (3) *member of the congregation* Pss. 22²³ 133¹˙ of the unity of the brotherhood Pr. 6¹⁹. This is public worship in the ‡ קָהָל n.m. *assembly, convocation, congregation :* (1) of evil doers 26⁵, cf. 22¹⁷; (2) assemblage for worship, so here, 107³², קהל רב v.²⁶ 35¹⁸ 40¹⁰˙¹¹; (3) of the pious 149¹; (4) of angels 89⁶.— **24.** יִרְאֵי י׳] = *the god-fearing* (*v. 3⁷*). A change here to 3 pers. from 2 pers.; not original. — כָּל זֶרַע יַעֲקֹב] phr. ɑ.λ., cf. זרע יעקב Is. 45¹⁹ Je. 33²⁶. ‖ כָּל זֶרַע יִשְׂרָאֵל, elsw. 2 K. 17²⁰ Is. 45²⁵ Je. 31³⁷, without כל Ne. 9² Je. 31³⁶ 1 Ch. 16¹³; Post-deuteron. usage shewing influence of Je. and Is.². — וְגוּרוּ מִמֶּנּוּ] ı coörd. Qal imv. ‡ גור vb. Qal *stand in awe of,* c. מִן, elsw. 33⁸, usually *be afraid of,* sq. מפני Nu. 22³ Dt. 1¹⁷ 1 S. 18¹⁵, מִן Jb. 19²⁹; but Dt. 32²⁷ c. acc., therefore rd. here וְרוּחוּ in assonance with כברוהו and הללוהו. A later copyist followed the more common prosaic usage with מִן. The measure requires the change.— **25.** כִּי לֹא־בָזָה]. בזה (15⁴) usually *despise, regard with contempt :* so 51¹⁹ 69³⁴ 73²⁰ 102¹⁸, cf. v.⁷. This is either a defective l. in which עכרו should be inserted, or, as Du., an explanatory gl. to next vb. — ‡ שִׁקֵּץ] vb. denom. *abhor,* elsw. Lv. 11¹¹˙¹³˙⁴³ 20²⁵ Dt. 7²⁶˙²⁶.— עֱנוּת] ɑ.λ. usually explained as n.f. *affliction;* ⅅ δεήσει, ℌ, ℭ imply another word such as שׁוּעִי ‖ צַעֲקָה. But צִעְקַת is not easily changed into עֱנוּת in any transliteration. We might take it as עֱנוּת, inf. cstr. of עָנָה *answer,* abhor to answer, paraphrased into the petition answered. ℨ *modestiam,* prob. rd. עֱנוּת from עֲנָוָה *humility, meekness,* so Aq. עֲנִי (*v. 9¹³*). — הִסְתִּיר פָּנִים] subj. י׳, c. מִן 51¹¹, abs. 10¹¹, *withdraw from* 13² 22²⁵ 27⁹ 69¹⁸ 88¹⁵˙102³ 143⁷, abs. 30⁸.— מִמֶּנּוּ] so ℨ, ⅅ has ἀπ᾿ ἐμοῦ, ℬ *a me,* prob. both gl. of interp. — בְּשַׁוְּעוֹ] Pi. inf. cstr. sf. 3 m., c. בְּ temporal (*v. 5³*). ⅅ, ℬ בשועי, better suited to their interpretation of עֱנוּת. Sfs. in all cases interp.—
26. מֵאִתְּךָ] *from thy presence,* of God, cf. 109²⁰ 118²⁸. ‡ מֵאֵת *from proximity with = de chez,* cf. מֵעִם: נשׂא מאת 24⁵, *bear away from,* as a gift; שׁאל מאת 27⁴ Ju. 1¹⁴ 1 K. 2¹⁶ *ask from ;* הסיר מאת Ps. 66²⁰ *remove from ;* היה מאת 118²³ *come from ;* source in Yahweh 22²⁶ 109²⁰. This return to the 2 pers. is diffi-cult in the midst of the 3 pers. It seems to go with v.²³; if so, the intervening matter is a gl. — בְּקָהָל רָב] phr. elsw. 35¹⁸ 40¹⁰˙¹¹ (*v.* v.²³) *numerous congregation.*— אֲשַׁלֵּם] Pi. impf. † שׁלם vb. *be completed, finished.* Pi. in ψ only (1) *pay* or *perform :* c. acc., vows נדרים שׁ׳ 22²⁶ 61⁹; c. לְ of God 50¹⁴ 66¹⁸ 116¹⁴˙¹⁸, obj. omitted 76¹²; תּוֹדוֹת לְ שׁ׳ (to God) 56¹⁸. (2) *requite, recompense, reward :* subj. man, c. לְ pers. 41¹¹ 137⁸; c. acc. pers. et rei שׁ׳ רעה

שׁ׳ לאישׁ ‎,‎ c. ‎; ‎ שׁ׳ עשׂה גאוה ‎31²⁴‎; c. acc. pers. of God, ‎ תחת טובה ‎35¹²‎, cf. ‎38²¹‎; c. acc. pers. of God, ‎ כמעשׂהו ‎62¹³‎. (3) *Repay debt* ‎37²¹‎. Pu. *be paid* or *performed:* vow ‎65²‎.—
‡ ‎[נדר‎ n.m. *votive offering* ‎22²⁶ 50¹⁴ 56¹³ 61⁶·⁹ 65² 66¹³ 116¹⁴·¹⁸‎ (class of peace
offerings). The ‖ requires 2 pers. here: rd. ‎מאתך‎ ‖ ‎נגדך‎. The editor has
assimilated to v.²⁴ by insertion of ‎יראיו‎.— 27. ‎[יהי‎] Qal impf. juss. ‡ ‎חיה‎ vb.
Qal. *live:* (1) *continue in life*, antith. die ‎49¹⁰ 89⁴⁹ 118¹⁷‎; (2) *live in divine
favour* ‎119¹⁷·⁷⁷·¹¹⁶·¹⁴⁴‎; (3) *live prosperously*, of king ‎72¹⁵‎, others ‎22²⁷ 69³³‎.
Pi. (1) *preserve alive* ‎33¹⁹ 41³ 138⁷‎, ‎ח׳ נפשׁ ‎22³⁰‎; (2) *quicken, restore to life*
‎30⁴ 71²⁰‎; (3) *revive*, by divine favour ‎80¹⁹ 85⁷ 119²⁵·³⁷·⁴⁰·⁵⁰·⁸⁸·⁹³·¹⁰⁷·¹⁴⁹·¹⁵⁴·
¹⁵⁶·¹⁵⁹·¹⁷⁵ 143¹¹‎.— ‎[לבבכם‎] full form, ‎לבב‎ (*v. 4⁵*) in the sense of *selves*, syn. ‎נפשׁ‎,
a late and dub. usage, sf. refer. to the worshippers, participants in the feast,
who are the objects of congratulation and good wishes by all without. 𝕲 *αἱ
καρδίαι αὐτῶν*, 𝖁 *corda eorum*, is doubtless a correction of the awkward
change of persons, making the l. syn. with the previous l. But it neglects
the juss., and also would require ‎לבכם‎, not so easy to explain as ‎לבבכם‎. The
long form may be due to the sf. This awkwardness is removed by Gr., who
changes all the previous vbs. into imvs., and so makes this triplet harmonious
with the other two.— 28. Here begins a series of pentameters, certainly a
later addition to the Ps.— ‎[וישׁבו‎] Qal impf. ‎ו‎ coörd. may be juss. or predictive.— (*v. 2⁸*).— ‎[וישׁתחוו‎] Hithp. impf. 3 pl. of ‎שׁהה‎ (*v. 5⁸*)
‎ו‎ coörd., possibly preceded by ‎ואכלו‎, as v.³⁰, c. ‎לפני‎, also ‎86⁹‎ Dt. ‎26¹⁰‎ 1 S. 1¹⁹
Is. ‎66²³‎, here ‎לפניך‎ 𝕳, but 𝕲 ‎לפניו‎, 𝖁 *in conspectu eius*, so Du.— 29. ‎[הפלוכה‎]
= *royalty*, not elsw. in ‎ψ‎, but Ob.²¹ 1 S. 10¹⁶·²⁵ Is. 34¹² +.— 30. ‎[אכלו וישׁתחוו‎]
eating and so worshipping in the festal sacrifice, as v.²⁷; either a predictive
pf., which is difficult here, or pf. of protasis of condition, prob. latter. ‎לפניו‎
should be attached to vb. in first half of l., as in v.²⁹. There is no good
reason to change ‎אכלו‎ to ‎אך לו‎, as Oort, Bruston, Bä., Du., Kau., Kirk., al.
With this goes the substitution of ‎רשׁי‎ for ‎דשׁני‎ in Du., but ‎דשׁני‎ is quite appropriate; pl. cstr. of † ‎דשׁן‎ adj. = *fat ones, rich, prosperous, flourishing*, cf. ‎92¹⁵‎
for fat trees, Is. ‎30²³‎ for fat grain.— ‎[כל-יורדי עפר‎] phr. α.λ. ‖ *the dying*, cf.
‎יורדי בור ‎28¹ 30⁴ 88⁵ 143⁷‎, ‎שׁכני עפר‎ Is. ‎26¹⁹‎, ‎עפר מות‎ Pr. ‎22¹⁶‎. This is explained
by ‎נפשׁו לא חיה‎ *who doth not preserve alive his life*, vb. with this mng., *revive*
‎80¹⁹ 85⁷‎ +, cf. ‎33¹⁹ 41³ 138⁷‎. This does not satisfy many scholars. 𝕲 has
*καὶ ἡ ψυχή μου αὐτῷ {ῆ}‎ = ‎חיה לו נפשׁי‎, 𝕵 *anima eius ipsi vivet*, so Quinta,
Sexta; 𝕲, 𝕾, 𝖁 ‎נפשׁו‎; Σ, Θ, 𝕵, 𝕮 ‎נפשׁו‎; 𝕲, Aq., 𝖁, Σ, Θ, 𝕵, 𝕾 ‎לי‎. All the
Vrss. take the vb. as Qal pf. 3 f. ‎חיי‎, so Bä. "*aber meine Seele lebt ihm.*" Du.
retains the neg. and translates "*dessen Seele kein Leben hat.*" There is
antith. in this couplet—two classes, the rich and prosperous, and the poor
and perishing.— 31. ‎[זרע‎] indefin., so 𝕵, Σ, 𝕾, 𝕮, but 𝕲, Θ, 𝖁 ‎רעי‎, the latter
is explanatory.— ‎[לאדני‎] is striking here; ‎יהוה‎ and ‎אל‎ are used in the original
Ps., so ‎יהוה‎ v.²⁸·²⁹ in this addition. The word is prob. a gl.— ‎[לדור‎] is difficult as undefined. 𝕲 adds from next line ‎יבוא‎ and rds. it ‎ἡ ἐρχομένη‎, ‎יבוא‎,
so 𝖁 *generatio ventura*, cf. ‎דר אחרון ‎102¹⁹‎, so Hare, Bä., Du., Ehr., al. ‖ ‎לעם נולד‎.
For ‎דור‎ *v. 12⁸*.— 32. ‎[כי עשׂה‎] statement of the fact that he hath done it,
𝕲. 𝕾 add ‎יהוה‎, so Bä. It is not, however, in other Vrss., is explan. and not

needed for sense or measure. עָשָׂה in this emph. sense, of God's accomplish-
ing something, is common in ψ, elsw. 37^5 39^{10} 52^{11} 109^{27} 111^8 115^3 119^{126} 135^6
147^{20}.

PSALM XXIII., 3 STRS. 4^3, 4^4, 4^5.

**Ps. 23 is a guest psalm. It expresses calm confidence in
Yahweh: (1) as shepherd, providing His sheep with plentiful
pasture and water (v.$^{1-3a}$); (2) as guide, conducting His com-
panion safely in right paths through a gloomy ravine (v.$^{3b-4}$);
(3) as host, anointing His guest for the banquet and granting
him perpetual hospitality (v.$^{5-6}$).**

YAHWEH is my shepherd, I have no want.
  In grassy pastures He maketh me lie down ;
  Unto refreshing waters He leadeth me ;
  He restoreth (forever) my soul.
HE guideth me in right tracks for His name's sake.
  Yea, when I walk in a gloomy ravine,
  I fear no evil, for Thou art with me ;
  Thy rod and Thy staff, they comfort me.
THOU spreadest before me a table in the presence of mine adversaries.
  Hast Thou anointed my head with oil; my cup is exhilarating.
  Surely goodness and kindness pursue me all the days of my life ;
  And I shall dwell in the house of Yahweh for length of days.

Ps. 23 was in 𝕯 and 𝕱𝕽 (*v.* Intr. §§ 27, 31). No other statement appears
in the title. Its structure is artistic. The three Strs. are tetrastichs, with
parallel themes: shepherd v.$^{1-3a}$, guide v.$^{3b-4}$, host v.$^{5-6}$. It is a mistake to
suppose that the theme of the shepherd extends into the 2d Str. While it is
true that the shepherd may conduct his flocks through the gloomy wadys
safely, yet there is nothing in any terms used to suggest a flock. The flock
is conducted into safety in Str. I. Why take the flock back to a gloomy
wady in Str. II.? The new and parallel figure of the guide takes the people
to the same safety as that to which the shepherd had taken his sheep already
in Str. I. We then have three syn. Strs., each with its own simple and
beautiful imagery to set forth the central idea of the Ps. The Strs. have
the unusual feature that the measure changes from a trimeter in the first
Str. to a tetrameter in the second, and a pentameter in the third. This is an
advance towards a climax of joyous faith in Yahweh. The language and
syntax of the Ps. and all its ideals are early. There is not the slightest trace
of anything that is post-deuteronomic. The historical circumstances of the
poet must have been peaceful and prosperous. We cannot go down so late
as the prosperous times of the Greek period, or the late Persian period.
We cannot think of the Exile, or early Restoration, for the literature of those

times is full of trial and sorrow. Absence from the temple is indicated by 𐤔𐤄,
but that is due to a textual error. The temple was the habitual resort of the
poet. He was a guest there. We cannot, therefore, think of the Exile, or
of the time of David, the traditional author of the Ps. That he was a shepherd before he became king affords no evidence, for the conception of Yahweh
as shepherd is as early as the story of Jacob, Gn. 48¹⁵ 49²¹, is used in Mi. 7¹⁴
Zc. 11⁴ of the early prophets, Is. 40¹¹ 63¹¹, and especially in 𐤀 74¹ 78⁵² 79¹³ 80¹,
and in the royal Pss. 95⁷ 100³, and also in the NT. Lk. 15³⁻⁷ Jn. 10¹⁻¹⁶. In
fact, the three figures, shepherd, guide, host, are all simple, natural, and characteristic of the life in Jerusalem and its vicinity at any period in Biblical
history. A short walk from Jerusalem at any time would lead to gloomy
wadys and the pastures of shepherds. We cannot think of the period of
conflict with the Assyrians and Babylonians. We must, therefore, go back
to an earlier and simpler period, the days of the early monarchy, not earlier
than Solomon, or later than Jehoshaphat.

Str. I. is a trimeter tetrastich expressing the confidence and
joy of the sheep in the shepherd. — **1.** *Yahweh is my shepherd*],
as frequently in OT., a conception which doubtless originated
in the pastoral life of the early Israelites, especially that of the
ancestor Jacob, which was also the employment of David when
a youth, and which was ever one of the chief occupations of the
inhabitants of Bethlehem ; cf. 1 S. 16¹¹ Lk. 2⁸. Yahweh was conceived as taking the same patient, unwearying care of His people
as the shepherd of his flock. — *I have no want*], because the
shepherd has provided for all wants. The imperf. is not future,
but a present of habitual experience. — **2.** *In grassy pastures*],
those where the tender grass, the young herbage, was abundant.
— *makes me lie down*], in the midst of plenty, so that it may
be enjoyed with ease and comfort. — *Unto refreshing waters*],
not " beside," " along side of," AV., RV., thinking of a stream,
which is not easy to find in the grazing lands of Palestine except
in the rainy season ; but " unto," thinking of the wells, or foun-
tains, from which flocks are usually watered, Gn. 29¹⁰⁻¹¹ Ex. 2¹⁶⁻²¹
(*v.* Tristram, *Natural History of the Bible*, 142). These waters
are not merely drinking water, but choice water ; not only satisfying thirst, but giving refreshment, implying the same kind of
rich provision for the sheep as the grassy pastures. — *He leadeth
me*]. The shepherd, in the East, leads his flock, and they follow
him. He does not drive them as in the West, *v.* Jn. 10⁴⁵ (Thom-

son, *The Land and the Book*, 202 sq.).— **3** a. *He restoreth (for ever) my soul*]. By the rich provision for eating and drinking, He revives, strengthens, restores to full activity and enjoyment; passing over from the figure of the sheep to the man himself. The soul is here, as usually in Hebrew, the seat of the appetites and desires. The original text has but two tones, when three are needed for measure. It has also an unusual verbal form for the usual one in this phrase. This was probably due to a copyist's error in condensing two similar words, the infin. absolute, expressing temporal intensity, "for ever," after its verb, and the usual Hiph. imperf. form.

Str. II. is a progressive tetrameter tetrastich with a cæsura in each line. The guide takes the place of the shepherd in a parallel conception.— **3** b. *He guideth me*], on a journey, in which it is easy to stray from the right path. A guide was needed. Yahweh is the guide.— *in right tracks*], those that lead directly and safely to the place of destination, as distinguished from wrong tracks that would lead astray. The moral and religious reference is involved in the whole figure, and is not to be gained by departing from it in the rendering "righteousness" of EV⁵., after the ancient Vrss.— *For His name's sake*]. The divine name, or honour is involved in guiding rightly.— **4**. *Yea, when I walk in a gloomy ravine*]. The hill country of Judah is broken up by narrow and precipitous ravines, or wadys, difficult to descend and ascend, dark, gloomy, and abounding in caves, the abode of wild beasts and robbers (*v.* 1 S. 24). To pass through these wadys was still more difficult than to find the right path over the hills. The desire to depart from the figure of speech too soon is probably responsible for the pointing of צַלְמָוֶת, so as to get "death shade," "shadow of death," as if it implied the peril of death; which interpretation, through the EV⁵. and Bunyan's use of it in his *Pilgrim's Progress*, has become well nigh universal in English Literature until recent times.— *I fear no evil*], harm, or injury of any kind, either from falling or going astray, or from wild beasts, or robbers.— *for Thou art with me*]. The companionship of his trusty guide removes all fear.— *Thy rod and Thy staff*]. The rod for giving blows in defence, the staff for support in walking. The reference to the shepherd's crook,

though justified by an occasional use of the word translated "rod,"
has no usage to justify it in connection with the word translated
"staff." It involves the continuation of the figure of the shepherd throughout this Str., which is improbable. — *they comfort
me*]. The presence of the guide with rod and staff in hand
ready for use in his defence, assures him of safety, of true guidance, and of eventually reaching his destination. Any tendencies
to fear are at once checked, and any agitation or anxiety is
soothed and calmed.

Str. III. is a progressive pentameter tetrastich, in which the
host takes the place of the shepherd and the guide of the previous
Strs. — **5.** *Thou spreadest before me a table*]. The host welcomes
his guest to a feast all prepared for him on the table. — *in the
presence of mine adversaries*]. The psalmist is not without
adversaries, but they are not dangerous. He has guest-right
with Yahweh. He is safe and secure, because, in accordance with
Oriental customs, the host is obliged to protect his guest from
all enemies, at all costs. — *Hast Thou anointed my head with oil*].
A temporal clause with an apodosis subsequent thereto. It was
the custom in the Orient to honour guests by anointing the head
with oil, or scented grease, before entering the banqueting room ;
cf. Am. 6[6], *v.* also Lk. 7[46]. It was also the custom to sprinkle the
guests with perfumes (Lane, *Modern Egyptians*, p. 203). The
entertainment here conceived is royal. — *My cup is exhilarating*],
the cup given to me by my host, the wine cup of welcome.
It is conceived here not so much as a cup full to overflowing,
as EV[s]. and most moderns, but as one whose wine saturates,
drenches, or soaks the one who drinks it, so excellent its quality
and so ample its quantity, intoxicating, as the ancient Vrss. ; so
Aug., explaining *inebrians*, "And Thy cup yielding forgetfulness
of former vain delights." "*Inebrians,* irrigans, laetificans, con-
solatione plenus, exuberans, redundans excellentissimo liquore,"
Genebr. ; cf. Ps. 104[15] "wine that maketh glad the heart of man."
The Fathers generally find here a mystic reference to the cup
of the Eucharist. — **6.** *Surely goodness and kindness*], of the host
to his guest. — *pursue me*]. These attributes are personified, as
attendants waiting upon the guest, just as other attributes,
43[3] 85[11-12. 14] ; cf. Is. 35[10]. — *all the days of my life* ‖ *for length of*

days]. This one is not a guest who is to be entertained once, and then depart; or one who is permitted occasionally to return; but a guest who is to have a permanent and perpetual place at the table of Yahweh. Kindness is to follow him about, to wait on him continually throughout his life; and so in the parallel. — *I shall dwell in the house of Yahweh*]. He takes up his continual residence as guest in Yahweh's house. This which is given in 𝕲, 𝕵 is more suited to the context than 𝔥, which by another pointing of the same consonant gives another vb. and construction, "and I will return." This is difficult to explain grammatically, and also is not in accordance with the context which emphasises presence in the house and not absence from it. The house of Yahweh is, indeed, the temple, and the feasts are the sacrificial feasts continually provided in the temple. The conception that Yahweh is the host to those partaking of the sacrificial meals in His temple is not uncommon, *v.* 5^5 15^1 27^4 61^5 84^5.

1. רֹעִי] Qal ptc. c. sf. 1 sg. רעה (*v.* 2^9); taken by 𝕲, 𝕵, with verbal force, ποιμαίνει με, *pascit me*, as parall. requires. It is prob. that for rhyme in ◌ִ it originally stood last in l. like the other vbs. of the Str. For Yahweh as shepherd cf. Gn. 48^{15} 49^{24} Mi. 7^{14} Ez. 34^{11-19} Is. 49^{9-10} Ps. 80^2. — 2. נְאֹות] pl. cstr. of ‡ נָוֶה n.f. *pasture, meadow*, נָוֹת Zp. 2^6, נְאֹות 12 t.; elsw. in Pss. 65^{13} 74^{20} 83^{13}, cf. Je. 9^9 23^{10} 25^{37}. — ‡ דֶּשֶׁא] n.m. *tender grass, young herbage*, as 37^2 Dt. 32^2. — יַרְבִּיצֵנִי] Hiph. impf. 3 m. c. sf. 1 sg. of † רבץ vb. Qal *lie down*, of lion 104^{22} Gn. 49^9, Hiph. *cause to lie down*, of flock Ps. 23^2 Je. 33^{12} Ez. 34^{15}. — עַל] for אֶל of late style, *unto*, as 𝕲 ἐπὶ, not *by, alongside of*, or even *down to* from above. — מְנֻחֹות] pl. abstr., *rest, refreshment*, cf. Is. 28^{12}. ‡ מְנוּחָה n.f., elsw. *resting place* 95^{11} $132^{8. 14}$ Is. 11^{10}. — יְנַהֲלֵנִי] Pi. impf. ‡ נהל vb. Pi. *lead* or *guide*, of flock here, prob. after Is. 49^{10}, cf. Is. 40^{11}; subj. Yahweh Ps. 31^4 Is. 51^{18}. — 3. נַפְשִׁי] not *soul* as distinguished from body, but paraphrase for pers. pron. *me* (*v.* 3^3), or *soul* as seat of emotion and passion, *v.* BD*B*. — יְשׁוֹבֵב]: Polel impf. of שׁוּב (*v.* 18^{21}) phr. α.λ., but cf. הֵשִׁיב נפשׁ Pr. 25^{13} Ru. 4^{15} La. $1^{11. 16. 19}$ Ps. 19^8. This is a defective l., rd. prob. ישׁב שׁב (inf. abs. after the vb., intensifying its temporal idea, *forever*, cf. Ju. 5^{23}), and put נפשׁי at end. We have thus far four trimeter lines with rhyme. — מַעְגְּלֵי] cstr. pl. of מַעְגָּל, *track* (of waggon or cart), of snares of wicked 140^6, course of life Pr. 4^{26} 5^{21}, here כִּי צדק in physical sense, *right* as ‖ leading to the proper place. — לְמַעַן שְׁמוֹ] supplementary; phr. also in 25^{11} 31^4 79^9 106^8 109^{21} 143^{11} Is. 48^9 Ez. 20^{44}. — 4. גַּם כִּי] *even when*, or *if*, or *yea though* (Dr.), 𝕵 *sed et*, cf. Is. 1^{15} Ho. 8^{10} 9^{16}; *v.* for other uses of גם 88^{14^3} $19^{12. 14}$. — ‡ גַּיְא] n.m. *valley, wady*, elsw. ψ only 60^2, חֶלָה גְ, as 2 S. 8^{13}. — צַלְמָוֶת] compound, צֵל *shadow* and מָוֶת *death*, as pointed; but this is a rabbinical conceit. It should be pointed ‡ צַלְמֻת.

n.m. *dense darkness*, elsw. 44²⁰ 107¹⁰·¹⁴ Ew.§²⁷⁰ᶜ Kö.II·¹· p. 204(1). 415. — [מִשְׁעַנְתֶּךָ
n. sf. i.p. ‡ מִשְׁעֶנֶת n.f. (√שׁען) *that on which one rests, walking-stick, staff*,
not elsw. ψ, but Ex. 21¹⁹ Nu. 21¹⁸ Is 36⁶ Ez. 29⁶ Zc. 8⁴. — [רְבֵּה] resuming
subj. with emph., so 27² 37⁹ 107²⁴ (*v. 16³*). — [יְנַחֲמֻנִי] Pi. impf. 3 pl. c. sf. 1 sg.
‡ [נחם] vb. Niph.: (1) *be sorry, have compassion*, c. על 90¹³ = אל Ju. 21⁶;
(2) *rue, regret* one's doings Pss. 106⁴⁵ 110⁴ Je. 20¹⁶ Ex. 13¹⁷ (E); (3) *comfort oneself* Ps. 77³ Gn. 38¹² (J); Pi. *comfort, console*, abs., Ps. 69²¹, c. acc.
pers. 23⁴ 71²¹ 119⁷⁶·⁸² ‖ עזר 86¹⁷. Hithp.: (1) *be sorry, have compassion*,
c. על 135¹⁴ = Dt. 32³⁶; (2) *comfort oneself* Ps. 119⁵² Gn. 37⁸⁵ (J). These
four lines are tetrameters. — **5.** ‡ [שֻׁלְחָן] n.m. *table*, mat or piece of leather
spread on ground, elsw. 69²³ 78¹⁹ 128³. — [דִּשַּׁנְתָּ] Pi. pf. 2 m., prot. conditional
clause, *hast thou made fat, greased*, cf. Lk. 7⁴⁶. דשׁן (*v. 204*), here of anointing with oil for banquet. — † [רְוָיָה] n.f. *saturation*, elsw. 66¹² (?). ‡ רוה Qal
drink to satiety 36⁹, Pi. *drench* 65¹¹. 𝔊 καὶ τὸ ποτήριόν σου μεθύσκον, 𝔙 *inebrians*, so 𝔖. These two lines are pentameters. — **6.** [אַךְ טוֹב]. In 𝔅, 𝔖, 𝔍
begins v.⁶, but in 𝔊 ὡς κράτιστον, 𝔙 *quam praeclarus est*, are at the end of
v.⁵. They are needed for measure in v.⁶. The phr. טוב וחסד is α.λ. For טוב
(*v. 4ᵗ*), הֶסֶד (*v. 4ᵗ*). They are personified and so subj. of vb. יִרְדְּפוּנִי. — [וְשַׁבְתִּי]
Qal pf. 1 sg. c. consec., שׁוב pregnant *return to dwell*, Maurer, Baur, Köster,
De.; but 𝔊 τὸ κατοικεῖν με, so Σ, 𝔙, as 27⁴ 84⁵. שִׁבְתִּי בבית יהוה coörd. inf.
cstr. c. sf. 1 sg. of ישׁב (*v. 24*) *my dwelling*, so Ros., Geier, De W., Hu.,
Heng., Dr., Kirk. 𝔍 *habitabo*, so 𝔖, 𝔗, ויֵּשַׁבְתִּי, Hare, De Muis, Hi., Oort,
Che., Bä., Ew.§²³⁴⁽³⁾, Ges. §⁶⁹ᵐ⁽¹⁾. — [בַּית יהוה], בַּית *house* ‡ for dwelling of God,
temple 36⁹ 52¹⁰ 65⁵ 92¹⁴ 93⁵ 118²⁶ 122⁹; חָנֻכַּת הבּ׳ dedication of 30¹ (title),
חצרות ב׳ 116¹⁹ 135², מעון ב׳ 26⁸, קנאת ב׳ 69¹⁰; of entrance for worship, acc. after
בא 5⁸ 66¹³; of processions, acc. after הלך 122¹, c. ב 55¹⁵, דרה עד ב׳ 42⁵,
עמדים בב׳ 134¹ 135²; of permanent residence for worship, acc. after ישׁב, 23⁶ 27⁴
84⁵, cf. 84¹¹, אֹרֶךְ יָמִים (*v. 215*). This verse is a pentameter.

PSALM XXIV.

**Ps. 24 combines two Pss., originally independent, in the one
theme, entrance into the holy temple and city. The first is a
didactic choral. A choir within the court of the temple praises
Yahweh as creator and owner of all things (v.¹⁻²). A choir at the
gate inquires what sort of a man may enter the holy place (v.³).
The choir within responds, giving both the characteristics of the
man and the benefits he will receive (v.⁴⁻⁵). The choir without
asserts the claims of Jacob to such a character, and to an entrance
(v.⁶). The second Ps. is a triumphal choral. Yahweh has come
to the holy city after a victory. The choir without the city demands that the gate be raised that the glorious king may enter**

into Jerusalem (v.⁷). The choir within inquires who he is, and
is answered that it is the victorious Yahweh (v.⁸). Entrance is
again demanded (v.⁹), the same inquiry is renewed, and the effec-
tual reply is made that it is Yahweh, God of hosts (v.¹⁰).

$$A. \text{ v.}^{1-6}, \quad 2 \text{ STR. } 4^3 + 2^3.$$

TO Yahweh belongs the earth and its fulness,
 The world and those that dwell therein;
 For He founded it upon the seas,
 And upon streams establisheth it.
  Who may ascend the hill of Yahweh?
  Who may stand in His holy place?
ONE clean, and pure of mind,
 Who hath not lifted up his soul to a lie;
 He shall bear away a blessing from Yahweh,
 And righteousness from the God of his salvation.
  This is a generation which resorts to Him;
  Those who seek His face are Jacob.

$$B. \text{ v.}^{7-10}, \quad 2 \text{ STR. } 3^3 + 1^3 + 2^3.$$

LIFT up, O gates, (your) heads;
 And exalt yourselves, ye ancient doors:
 And the King of glory will enter.
  Who, then, is the King of glory?
 Yahweh, strong and mighty,
 Yahweh, mighty in battle.
LIFT up, O gates, (your) heads;
 And (exalt yourselves) ye ancient doors:
 And the King of glory will enter.
  Who, then, is the King of glory?
 Yahweh, (God of) hosts,
 He is the King of glory.

Ps. 24 was in 𝔇 and 𝔐 (*v.* Intr. §§ 27, 31). 𝔊 adds to the title an
assignment to the first day of the week, which corresponds with the statement
of the Talm. as to its liturgical use (*v.* Intr. § 39). In Christian usage it is
a proper Ps. for Ascension day. The Ps. is composed of two Pss. of entirely
different character, composed at widely different periods. The older of these
is evidently the second, v.⁷⁻¹⁰, which probably alone bore the title. The first,
v.¹⁻⁶, was probably inserted subsequent to the prefixing of the title to the
second. The combination was made in order to make a Ps. appropriate to
some special occasion in the late Greek or the Maccabean period, otherwise
the Ps. would have been taken up into 𝔈 and 𝔇𝔅 (*v.* Intr. §§ 32, 33). The
second Ps. alone would hardly be suitable for worship either in the temple or
synagogue. The second Ps. in its use of צבאות (אלהי) יהוה, v.¹⁰, and its em-

phasis upon His warlike characteristics, v.[8], implies the warlike Yahweh of David's time. The entrance into the city is that of Yahweh at the head of a victorious army, which suits the removal of the ark to Jerusalem; cf. 2 S. 6. There is no mention in the history of any subsequent going forth of the ark to war, and it is improbable. From that time on, Jerusalem was the holy city, the capital of Yahweh the king, from whence He granted victory; cf. Ps. 20[3]. But He is not conceived as going forth from the city to make war. Moreover, the entrance is into the city, and not into the temple, as we would expect in later times after the temple was built. The פתחי עולם, v.[7, 9] the ancient gates, are the gates of the city, which, though a recent conquest of David, had been a royal city for centuries earlier than his time, and whose gates might justly be named ancient, reaching back into an antiquity beyond the memory of man. There is nothing in the Ps. which requires a later date. It is difficult to see how a Ps. could better fit a historical situation. V.[1-6] are entirely different. It is the temple, not the city, which is to be entered. It is not Yahweh who enters, but men into His presence. He is enthroned in the city, and is not at its gates. The mountain is the mountain of Yahweh, His sacred place, v.[3]. His face they seek, v.[6], from Him they are to receive a blessing, v.[5] But not only is the city His; the earth and all the inhabitants of the world are His, v.[1]. That implies the later postex. conception that Yahweh is king of the whole world, and that His temple is the central place of worship for the world. The conception of creation is that of the erection of a building, an idea which we find Pss. 89[12], 104[5], Jb. 38[4 sq.] Is. 48[13], although here it is conceived as upon subterranean seas. The characteristics of the one privileged to enter the sacred place are not external conformity to Law, but internal, in the mind and soul, v.[4], implying a lofty ethical conception, not earlier than the late Persian period, and sufficiently late to be influenced by Heb. Wisdom rather than Law. The emphasis upon Jacob as the name of the nation is based upon the Is.[2]; but the implication that he has such ethical characteristics as are required by Yahweh, is a conception which could only have originated in peaceful times, when Pss. of lamentation and penitence were no longer written, and when the pious might attend to their internal, ethical development. On the whole, this Ps. seems to belong to the Greek period subsequent to 𝕯𝕽, the early time of Heb. Wisdom.

PSALM XXIV. *A.*

Str. I. 1–2 was sung by a choir within the outer court of the temple, praising Yahweh as creator and owner of all things. It is a trimeter tetrastich of two syn. couplets, the latter giving the reason for the former. — 1. *To Yahweh belongs*]. He is the possessor and owner, cf. 89[12]. — *the earth and its fulness*], all that fills it, its contents, its creatures. — *the world*], with the special signification that it is habitable. and accordingly associated with

it are *those that dwell therein*], its inhabitants. Thus is asserted
the universal ownership of Yahweh, in accordance with the postexilic conception that Yahweh is the universal God and the only
God for the whole earth. His ownership is based upon the fact
that He had created them. The creation is conceived as the erec-
tion of a great building, as in 89^{12} 104^5 Jb. $38^{4\,sq.}$ Pr. $8^{25\,sq.}$. — **2**. *For
He*], emphatic, He and no other. — *founded it* ∥ *establisheth it*].
The single act of creation passes over, as usual in OT., into the
habitual act of God's sustaining providence; both later and more
comprehensive ideas than those given in the poems, Gn. 1–2,
although the primitive conception of subterranean seas and
streams is still retained, cf. Gn. 7^{11} Ex. 20^4 Ps. 136^6. For various other conceptions of the relations of sea and dry land, cf.
Gn. 1^9 Pr. 8^{29} Jb. $26^{7\,sq.}$. — **3** is a trimeter couplet sung by a choir
outside the gate, inquiring the conditions of entrance. — *Who
may*], not what person, but what sort of a person, as 15^1. —
ascend], go up the hill, which is called *the hill of Yahweh*, because His temple or residence was upon it, as Is. 2^3 = Mi. 4^2
Is. 30^{29}. — *may stand*], among the accepted worshippers, admitted
to the sacred precincts. — *in His holy place*], as consecrated to
His worship.

Str. II. 4–5 is the response of the choir within, in two syn.
couplets, the first giving the characteristics of the one who might
be admitted to Yahweh's presence. These are two in number.
— **4**. *One clean*]. An innocent man, as 10^8 15^5. This one is still
further defined as *pure of mind*. He is characterized by internal
innocence, cleanness, and purity. This has been weakened in
the ancient texts by the insertion of " hands " after " clean," which
makes it refer to action, giving two characteristics and making the
line into a tetrameter. — *Who hath not lifted up his soul*], in
desire, cf. 25^1 86^4 143^8. — *to a lie*], falsehood, in accordance with
12^3 41^7 $144^{8.\,11}$. This is an internal desire, harmonious with the
previous purity of mind. This explanation is favoured not only
by the parallel. of the previous line, but also by the subsequent
line, 狂, and Vrss. — *and hath not sworn to deceit*]. This was
doubtless an explanatory gloss ; but it changes the tetrastich into
a pentastich, and so destroys the symmetry of the Ps. — **5**. The
second couplet sets forth the benefits to be derived from Yahweh

in His house. — *He shall bear away*], take with him, when he
departs from the temple. — *a blessing*], suited to the pure in mind,
‖ *righteousness*, suited to the sincere desire. This latter is not in
the sense of alms, as ⑮, a meaning not known to OT.; or in the
sense of that which is ethically right, which could hardly be
bestowed upon him; but in the meaning urged by the phr. *God
of his salvation*, saving righteousness, righteousness of vindication,
as usual, Pss. 5⁹ 22³² 36¹¹ + and Is.² 45⁸ 46¹³ 51⁶ +. — **6.** The choir
without claims the right of entrance in a couplet responding to the
demand as to character, by stating the privilege belonging by
inheritance to the seed of Jacob. They are not strangers who
seek access to Yahweh, but His own people. — *This is a generation*], a class of men whose characteristic it is, that they *resort to
Him* ‖ *seek His face*]. The ptcs. express continual resort to the
sacred place for worship. ℍ has "Thy face," which gives an
abrupt change of person and makes it difficult to explain the
context. "O Jacob," PBV., is an adaptation to ℍ of some texts
of 𝕵 which have "face of Jacob." But the context makes it evident that these are not strangers seeking Jacob, but Israel resorting to his God. "Thy face, O God of Jacob," RV., adapts ℍ to
⑮, which gives "the face of the God of Jacob," but the insertion
of "God" looks like an interpretation and it leaves the subj. out
of the parall. The subj., syn. with generation, is exceedingly for-
cible in the climax if it is defined as Jacob, with all the historic
rights to the covenanted promises contained in the name. Inasmuch as the suffix "they" is not in ⑮, 𝕾, 𝕵, it is an interpreter's
addition. It is easy to correct the text after the parall. and read
"His face," and to regard the couplet as inclusive, "generation"
beginning and "Jacob" closing it.

PSALM XXIV. *B.*

Str. I. is a trimeter tristich, the first two lines syn., the third
synth. A triumphal army, with Yahweh at its head, is at the
gates of Jerusalem demanding entrance. The choir summons the
gates to open to admit the king. — **7.** *O gates*], personified and
addressed as persons, ‖ *Ye ancient doors*], as reaching back in
history into hoary antiquity. Jerusalem was a very ancient city

before David captured it, whose origin is so remote that it is earlier than all historical accounts of it. — *lift up your heads ‖ exalt yourselves*]. The reflexive is more in accord with the parallelism than the passive " Be ye lift up," EV⁸. It is well explained by Ewald : " A new king is about to enter the ancient and venerable city, and indeed the highest and mightiest conceivable, Yahweh Himself, enthroned upon the ark of the Covenant. Such a king has never entered this city, and the gray gates, although venerable with age, are too small and mean for Him." — *And the King of glory*], a phr. only here ; but Yahweh is frequently conceived as king, Ex. 15^{18} Pss. 5^3 10^{16} 29^{10} 44^5 47$^{3.7.8}$ 48^3 68^{25} 74^{12} 84^4 95^3 98^6 99^4 145^1 149^2; and glory is one of the most common attributes of Yahweh, 29^3 72^{19} 145^{12}. Here the glory is that of warlike achievements, such as that ascribed to the king of David's dynasty, 21^6. — **8**. The choir within the gates responds to the summons in a monostich of inquiry. It is not necessary to think of the gates as speaking. It is the challenge of the sentinels, who must demand the password officially, even if they know what the answer will be. It is the poet's art to thus get a reason for the glorification of Yahweh the king. The choir without respond in a couplet setting forth who the king is. — *Yahweh*], the God of Israel, is this king, and not David, God's son, the divine representative in kingship. — *strong and mighty*]. These attributes are those of a warrior, as defined in the stairlike parall. *mighty in battle*. The king is a valiant hero, victorious in battle, a great conqueror. He has returned from a glorious war ; cf. " Yahweh is a man of war " Ex. 15$^{2.3}$; cf. also Num. 10^{35} 1 S. 4$^{21\,sq.}$ for the warlike character of the Ark, as bearing the divine presence.

Str. II. 9–10. The choir of the army repeats the trimeter triplet, renewing the demand for entrance in identical terms.

10. The sentinels make an identical challenge. The choir respond in terms that cannot be questioned, by giving the divine name, characteristic of the Davidic dynasty. The longer and more ancient title, *Yahweh (God) of Hosts*, is required by the measure. It was shortened by an early editor at the expense of the measure, in accordance with the usage of his time, into " Yahweh Sabaoth," and so in all Vrss. after ⅊ " Lord of Hosts." The original title of Yahweh, given as the countersign or military password for

entrance to the royal city, is used here in accordance with the
original meaning of this divine name as given in 1 S. 17⁴⁵, " God
of the battle array of Israel." It was especially appropriate if we
suppose that the entire army of Israel was then at the gates of
Jerusalem with king David at their head, conducting the Ark
of Yahweh to the sacred place consecrated for it. — *He*], emphatic,
and no other, *is the King of glory*, cf. v.[7, 9]

XXIV. *A.*

1. ליהוה] ל of possession, emph. — ‡ [הָאָרֶץ וּמְלֹאָהּ phr. Dt. 33¹⁶ Is. 34¹
Mi. 1² Je. 8¹⁶ 47² Ez. 19⁷ 30¹²; cf. הבל וּמ׳ Pss. 50¹² 89¹², היﬦ וﬦ׳ 96¹¹ 98⁷. —
[יֹשְׁבֵי בָהּ] retracted accent because of final monosyl. ⑥ inserts πάντες =
כל; but it is absent in this same phr. 98⁷ 107³⁴, and is interp. הבל (*v. 9⁹*).
יֹשֵׁב (*v. 2⁴*). V.¹⁻² rhymes in final ‑ָהּ. — **3.** [וּמִי. ו is a prosaic addition impairing the measure. — [הר יהוה] the temple mount, elsw. Is. 2³ (= Mi. 4²) 30²⁹;
of Horeb, Nu. 10³³ (JE), הר י׳ צבאות Zc. 8³, cf. Ps. 15¹. — **4.** [וְהִי כַּרַיﬦ *a.λ.*,
but נקי used for innocent person, *v. 10⁸*. כפיﬦ is a gl. of interpretation, making the l. tetrameter. — [בַּר־לֵבָב] cf. ברי לבב 73¹, לבב v. 4⁵. — [אֲשֶׁר rel. is a
gl. balanced with כפיﬦ, making this l. also tetrameter. A tetrameter couplet
in the midst of trimeters is altogether improbable. — [וְלֹא נָשָׂא לַשָּׁוא נַפְשׁוֹ Kt.,
⑥, ℐ. But Qr. יַפְשִׁי, as if it were a citation from Ex. 20⁷ = Dt. 5¹¹. נפש for
שֵׁﬦ, cf. Ps. 139²⁰. שוא *v. 12³*. Syn. is [וְלֹא נִשְׁבַּע לְמִרְמָה. For שבע *v. 15⁴.*
מרמה *v. 5⁷*. This favours falsehood in the previous l. rather than the dishonouring of the name of God. It is prob. that this l. is an explanatory gl.,
so Bi., Bä. It makes the only tristich in the Ps. ⑥ adds the gl. τῷ πλησίον
αὐτοῦ, 𝔙 *proximo suo.* — **5.** [צְדָקָה. ⑥ has ἐλεημοσύνην, but this is a late mng.
of צדקה not used in OT. Here צדקה || ברכה is || ישׁע, as in Is.² (espec.) and
subsequent writers, *v. 5⁹*. — [אֱלֹהֵי יִשְׁעוֹ cf. 18⁴⁷ 25⁵ 27⁹ 65⁶ 79⁹ 85⁵, and for
other uses of ישׁע *v. 12⁶*. ⑥ σωτῆρος is concrete for abstr. — **6.** [דֹּרְשׁוֹ Kt.,
Qr., both ptc. as rel. clauses, || מבקשׁי, ⑥, ℐ, both pl., as in 9¹¹. דרשׁ vb. *seek*,
consult, by resorting to a sacred place, so acc. of י׳ 78³⁴ Gn. 25²² (J) Ex. 18¹⁵
(E) +. — [מְבַקְשֵׁי פָנֶיךָ יַעֲקֹב. Jacob is not vocative, the suffix cannot refer to
him. It is not the face of Jacob that is sought, but God's face. It is possible
to make יעקב an independent clause, *it is Jacob*, but that is harsh. ⑥ has
τοῦ Θεοῦ Ἰακώβ, so 𝔖, 𝔙, and most moderns, which makes the l. too long
unless with Hare and Grimme אֱלֹהֵי. It gives good sense in accordance
with parall. ℑ in text of Lag. has *faciem tuam Jacob*, as 𝔚, but in text of
Nestle, *faciem Jacob*, פני יעקב, cf. PBV. But it is not foreign peoples seeking
the face of Jacob, as in the conception of second Isaiah and Zechariah, but
faithful Israelites seeking the presence of their God in the temple in Zion.
A simple and natural interpretation would be to regard this l. as in introverted
parall. with previous l. :

> This is a generation which resorts to Him ;
> Those who seek His face are Jacob.

ךְ in פניך is txt. err., not in 𝔊, 𝔖, rd. פניו ‖ דרשיו. י has been omitted in the
one place, ו in the other, and ךְ has been inserted in 𝔐, 𝔍 as interpretation.
— 7. [שְׂאוּ שְׁעָרִים רָאשֵׁיכֶם] so Aq., 𝔍, 𝔖, 𝔗. 𝔊, Σ make ראשיכם = οἱ ἄρχοντες
ὑμῶν here and in v.⁹ the subj., and שערים obj., so 𝔙 *principes;* the chiefs are
to lift the gates instead of their spreading themselves open; but the sf. with
ראשיכם is not easy; in this case it ought to be with *gates.* Prob. both sfs. were
interp. and the original had none. — [יָבִא]. The ו might be subordinate with
subjunctive, *that he may enter :* better introducing apod. of imv., *and he will
enter, v.* Dr.§152. — 8. [זֶה־זֶה] enclitic, *who then,* so v.¹⁾ 25¹². — [עִזּוּז] adj. only
here of ר, and Is. 43¹⁷ of army; vb. for ר Ps. 68²⁹, cf. זרוע עֹזֶך 89¹¹, and עַז as
attributive 62¹² 63⁸ 68³⁵ 93¹ 96⁶, עֹז מֶלֶךְ 99⁴. — [וְגִבּוֹר] adj. for *might* of God
fighting for His people, elsw. Dt. 10¹⁷ Ne. 9³² Is. 10²¹ Je. 32¹⁸; of valiant
man, *v. 19⁶.* — [גִבּוֹר מִלְחָמָה] stairlike parall., for this l. completes what the
previous l. began, defining mighty as mighty in battle. — 9 = v.⁷ save that
הֲרִימוּ gives place to שְׂאוּ; but this is doubtless txt. err., for there is no obj.
𝔊 had Niph., so Hare, al. 𝔍 changes to *erigite* from *elevamini.* But a
change is improb. in this word only. — 10. [מִי הוּא זֶה]. The inquiry is repeated,
differing only from v.⁸ᵃ by insertion of הוּא, but this makes the l. too long.
הוּא is copula and interpretative. 𝔊 is same as v.⁸ᵃ, so also 𝔍. — [יהוה צְבָאוֹת]
so 𝔊 and 𝔍, makes a dimeter. This is possible, but it is more likely that it
was a copyist's shortening of the older phr. יהוה אלהי צבאות, which gives a
good trimeter, into the phr. used in his own time. — ‡ [צָבָא] n.m.: (1) *army,*
organised for war 44¹⁰ 60¹² 68¹³ 108¹²; (2) *of angels* 103²¹ 148²; (3) fig. *of
heavenly bodies* 33⁶; (4) *war* 68¹² (?), others fig. (1); (5) צבאות as name of
God of David and dynasty, based on 1 S. 17⁴⁵, ר מערכות ישראל א' צ' א', originally
ר' אלהי הצבאות, Am. 6¹⁴ Ho. 12⁶, usually ר' אלהי צבאות Ps. 89⁹, reduced to
ר' צבאות 24¹⁰ 46⁸· ¹² 48⁹ 84²· ⁴ ¹³, preceded by ארני 69⁷ Is. 3¹⁵ Je. 2¹⁹ +.
אלהים צבאות Ps. 80⁸· ¹⁵, preceded by יהוה 59⁶ 80⁶· ²⁰ 84⁹; in all cases אלהים for
an original יהוה and where preceded by יהוה conflation. — [הוא מלך הכבוד]
emph. conclusion. 𝔊 has αὐτός ἐστιν οὗτος = הוא זה.

PSALM XXV., 3 STR. 7⁶.

**Ps. 25 is a prayer of the congregation in three parts. (1) Peti-
tion, that they that trust in Yahweh may not be shamed, but
rather those dealing treacherously (v.¹⁻³) ; that Yahweh will teach
His ways (v.⁴⁻⁵), and remember His compassion rather than sins
of youth (v.⁶⁻⁷). (2) Confidence, that Yahweh will teach the
afflicted His way (v.⁸⁻⁹) ; that His paths are kindness and faithfulness (v.¹⁰) ; and that He will instruct and give His intimacy
to those fearing Him (v.¹²⁻¹⁴). (3) Petition, that Yahweh will
bring out of distresses (v.¹⁵⁻¹⁷) ; that He will see his enemies (v.¹⁹) ;**

and that He will deliver those that wait on Him (v.$^{20-21}$). Petitions for pardon were inserted by an editor in place of lines which
he threw out (v.$^{11.\ 18}$).   A liturgical addition makes a general plea
for the ransom of Israel (v.^{22}).

UNTO Thee, Yahweh, I lift up my soul; (O my God,) let me not be *ashamed*.
   In Thee I trust, (therefore) let not mine enemies exult; even mine;
   Yea, let none that wait on Thee *be ashamed;* let them *be ashamed* that deal
      treacherously without effect.
   Thy ways make me know, Yahweh, (and) Thy paths *teach* me;
   Lead me in Thy faithfulness and *teach* me; for Thou art the God of my salvation.
   Remember Thy compassion, Yahweh, and Thy kindness, for they are of old.
   The sins of my youth *remember not;* according to Thy kindness, *remember* me.
GOOD and upright is Yahweh: therefore will He instruct in the *way :*
   He will lead the afflicted in (His) judgment, and He will teach the afflicted
      His *way.*
   All the paths of Yahweh are kindness and faithfulness to them that keep His
      covenant.
*.   .   .   .   .
   Who then is (he) that *feareth* Yahweh ?   He will instruct him in the way He
      chooseth;
   He himself will dwell in prosperity; and his seed will inherit the land.
   The intimacy of Yahweh have they that *fear* (His name), and His covenant,
      to make them know it.
MINE eyes are continually unto Yahweh, that He may *bring forth* my feet.
   Turn unto me and be gracious unto me; for desolate and afflicted am I.
   As for the troubles of my mind, O make room from my distresses; O *bring me
      forth.*
*.   .   .   .   .
   O see mine enemies; for they are many, and they hate me with a hatred of
      violence.
   O keep me and *deliver* me; let me not be ashamed, for I seek refuge in Thee.
   Let integrity and uprightness (*deliver* me) ; for, Yahweh, I wait on Thee.

Ps. 25 was in 𝔻 (*v.* Intr. § 27). 𝔊 has ψαλμός; but it is not in 𝔥, and
it is improbable that it would have been omitted if original. The Ps. is an
acrostic hexameter; all the letters of the alphabet appear except ו and ק.
The ו might be found if with 𝔊 we read ואתך for 𝔥 אורך v.^{5c}; but then only
three of the six words would be given, and that at the expense of the strophical organisation of the Ps. These words are more like a gloss of intensification. The analogy of Ps. 34 favours the opinion that the omission of ו was
intentional. With twenty-two letters it was impracticable to get symmetrical
Strs. without such an omission. The ק Str. might be restored by substituting
קראה for ראה, v.^{18}, regarding the repetition of the latter word as due to dit-

---

* This indicates the omission of an original line. The words italicised indicate
the stairlike parallelism characteristic of this Ps.

tography. But it is probable that this line was a later substitution for the original line, as was v.[11], in order to introduce into the Ps. two petitions for forgiveness of sins. For these two lines are awkward in their relation to their context, interrupting the movement of the thought; and they lack the catch-word of the stairlike parallelism (v. Intr. § 12 A) characteristic of the Ps. in every other line: בוש v.[1, 3], לכר v.[4, 5], זכר v.[6, 7], דרך v.[8, 9], ירא v.[12-14], הוציא v.[15, 17], and it is probable נצל v.[20, 21], the נצר v.[21] being due to a copyist's error or a stylistic change. It is noteworthy that the catchword is in both lines of the distichs, but only in first and third lines of the tristichs, v[1-3, 12-14, 15-17].

V.[22], as Ps. 34[23], is a liturgical addition. It is improbable that any writer would omit a letter of the alphabet from his acrostic, and then add a supplementary line to rectify the omission. Moreover, the use of אלחים for יהוה of the Ps. is evidence of a later hand, as well as the use of ישראל by way of generalisation of the petition and confidence of the Ps. The Ps. has three Strs., the first and the third petitions, separated by the second, expressing trust in Yahweh. It shows no dependence on earlier writings. It is entirely original as a composition. The language is not early and not very late. The phrase חטאות נעורי v.[7], cf. Ez. 23[21] Jb. 13[26], looks back on the youth of the nation. The terms הוריע (דרך) v.[4, 14], למר ארחות v.[4], הדריך v.[5, 9], יורה v.[8, 12], all show the influence of D. There is no evidence of the influence of P save in ערתיו v.[10], which is a gloss. נצרי ברית v.[10] is elsewhere only Dt. 33[9], and may be regarded as a poetic synonym of שמר ברית. The use of לבב v.[17], as 15[2] 24[4] 90[12] 104[15], is that of the Prophets of the Restoration Zc. 1-8 Hg., Jo. There are phrases and words peculiar to the Ps.: טוב וישר י׳ v.[8], the ethical use of טוב for God elsw. ψ 119[89, 68]; ברית for alliance or friendship with God v.[14], שנאת חםם v.[19], תם וישר v.[21] personified attributes. Other noteworthy words and phrases are: תלין בטוב v.[13], cf. Jb. 21[13] 36[11] Ec. 7[14]; סור י׳ v.[14], cf. Jb. 29[4] Pr. 3[32]; פנה אלי וחנני v.[16] 86[16] 119[132]; יחיד alone, solitary v.[16] 68[7]; הרחיב v.[17] dubious meaning, cf. Ps. 4[2]; † מצוקה v.[17] 107[6, 13, 19, 28] Jb. 15[24] Zp. 1[15]. These tend to the terminology of Job. The language and style favour the Persian period prior to Nehemiah.

Str. I. is a hexameter heptastich of petition, composed of a tristich and two distichs, each with its catchword, in stairlike parallelism. — **1-3.** *Unto Thee ‖ in Thee*], both emphatic in position, to indicate that *Yahweh, ‖ my God*, was the only person to whom it could be said, *I lift up my soul*, in longing desire, ‖ *I trust*, of confidence and reliance, ‖ *wait on Thee*, cf. v.[21], hoping, expecting help. — *let me not be ashamed*], by being overcome by enemies: the catch-word of the tristich, repeated both negatively and positively in v.[3]. — *let not mine enemies exult*], in triumph. These two vbs., originally in synonymous clauses in two different lines, were by a prosaic editor brought together in one line in 𝔊 and so in EV⁸., at the expense of the parall., the measure, and the acrostic of the second line. — *them that deal treacherously*], they are crafty, intriguing, treacherous enemies. — *without effect*], without accomplishing anything, as 7⁵, "disappointed of their expectations," Ham. ; "without cause " of EVˢ. is not justified by usage.   All this is not the prayer of an individual, but of a community in peril from crafty enemies. — **4-5.** *Thy ways* ‖ *Thy paths*], terms of the legislation of D., in which the people were to walk in their course of life. — *make me know* ‖ *teach me*], the latter the keyword, reappearing therefore in v.⁵ ‖ *lead me ;* all bringing out the divine discipline of Israel on its positive side of instruction and guidance in the Law.   This is enforced by an appeal to historic experience, *in Thy faithfulness*], that is, to the promises of the covenants with the fathers. — *God of my salvation*], whose character it is to save, and from whom salvation comes.   A later editor adds, either to the text or originally on the margin, so that it subsequently came into the text, *on Thee do I wait all the day*].   This is parallel in thought to the previous clause, and a repetition of that of v.³, without any proper motive in the Ps. itself, and at the expense of the measure and strophical organisation. — **6-7.** *Remember*], the keyword of the distich, repeated therefore in both negative and positive form in v.⁷ ; cf. v.³. — *Thy compassion*], the sympathetic attitude of Yahweh towards His people as their Sovereign and Father ; ‖ *kindness*, as in v.⁷, which is the only measure of the remembrance.   This is more probable than the pl. " loving kindnesses " EVˢ., more properly " loving deeds " JPSV., which, though sustained by 𝔊 and Vrss., is a late and uncommon usage, and is probably an assimilation to the previous plural, which, however, is an abstract plural and not, as this would be, a plural of number. The difference is one of interpretation and not of an originally different text. — *They are of old*].   These gracious attributes of Yahweh have characterised Him from the most ancient times in the historical experience of His people.   This suggests in antithesis, *The sins of my youth remember not*], the sins that the people had committed in former generations, in the beginning of the national existence, as in Ez. 23²¹ in connection with the abode in Egypt. — *and my transgressions*] is a gloss of amplification, making the line over full.   " Remember not sins " is a prophetic term,

Je. 31³⁴ Ez. 18²² 33¹⁶ Is. 43²⁵ Ps. 79⁸ +, to indicate that Yahweh, in His sovereign grace, puts them out of mind, treats them as if they had never existed. It is parallel to "not impute" Ps. 32², "not reward according to" 103¹⁰. It is also syn. with "passing over, overlooking, ignoring" them, Acts 17³⁰ Rom. 3²⁵. — *O Thou for Thy goodness sake*]. This is a gloss, introducing an additional plea, and adding a prosaic short sentence to a line and a Str. which are already complete.

Str. II. expresses trust and confidence in Yahweh, intervening between Strs. of petition. It is composed of a distich, v.⁸⁻⁹, and a tristich, v.¹²⁻¹⁴, with catchwords and stairlike parallelism, and two intervening lines, v.¹⁰⁻¹¹. — **8–9.** *Good and upright is Yahweh*]. The ethical character of Yahweh is here emphasised, at the beginning, in order to indicate that His disciplinary guidance is ethical. Usually God is good, as benignant ; here, as 119³⁹·⁶⁸, seldom elsewhere in OT., ethically good. — *Therefore*], on the basis of this character of Yahweh. — *will He instruct ‖ lead ‖ teach*], stating as a fact what was prayed for in v.⁴⁻⁵. — *the way*], the keyword of this distich, therefore, repeated in v.⁹, which also takes up the term of v.⁴⁻⁵, *the afflicted ;* pious Israel, as afflicted by enemies, v.² ; *v.* 9¹². Therefore *sinners* v.⁸ is improbable in the parallelism. It is a later gloss, making the line over full, and preparatory to the petition for pardon v.¹¹ — **10.** *All the paths of Yahweh*], not the paths in which Yahweh goes, but the paths which Yahweh teaches His people, as v.⁴ — *are kindness and faithfulness*], as in v.⁵·⁷. He leads in faithfulness, and kindness is the norm of His remembrance of His people. — *to them that keep His covenant*], the covenant between Yahweh and His people, whose substance is the Deuteronomic instruction in those ways and paths already spoken of. The keeping of this covenant is a walking in its ways under the guidance of Yahweh. — *and His testimonies*], a gloss of amplification from the point of view of the later priestly legislation, making the line over full. We should now expect, in accordance with the method of this psalmist, a synonymous line with the catchword of this line repeated, and that *covenant* would be this word. In fact the expression of trust and confidence which characterises this Str. is suddenly abandoned, and petition abruptly appears. — **11.** *For Thy name's sake*], an urgent plea, as the basis of the petition, thrown before for emphasis, that the good name, the honour of Yahweh may not suffer in His people. — *pardon mine iniquity*], lift it up as a burden, and bear it away from me and from Thee; syn. "forgive," as v.[18]. — *for it is great*], not in intensity, but in amount, cf. 19[14]. All this is well suited to a worshipping congregation; but it is not in accord with the context, or the course of thought of the Ps. It doubtless was a liturgical substitution for the original line, which was parall. with v.[10] — **12**. *Who then is he?*] This inquiry is in order to prepare the mind for the emphatic answer, *that feareth Yahweh*], the keyword of this tristich, reappearing therefore in v.[14] — *He will instruct him in the way*, as v.[8], ‖ *make them know it*, as v.[4]. — *He chooseth*], relative clause with Yahweh subj., as 33[12] 65[5]. It is usually interpreted as "he should choose," with man as subject. The context favours the former interpretation. — **13**. *He himself*] antith, to *his seed*, or posterity; the former *will dwell in prosperity*, in accordance with the blessedness and prosperity promised to those who fear Yahweh and walk in His ways, cf. Dt. 28; the latter *will inherit the land*, the promised land of Canaan, as Pss. 37[9-34] 44[4], in accordance with Gn. 15[7] Num. 13[30] 21[24. 35] Jos. 18[3] (JE) Dt. 1[8. 21. 39] +. — **14**. *The intimacy of Yahweh*], the intimate, secret fellowship granted to those admitted to the inner circle of friendship or alliance, cf. Pr. 3[32], Jb. 29[4]; ‖ *covenant*, which, while referring to the Deuteronomic covenant, as above v.[10], has yet in this connection the more fundamental meaning of an alliance, as Ps. 55[21]. — *they that fear (His name)*], as 61[6] 86[11] 102[16], for so the text originally read, as the measure requires, instead of "fear Him" of 𝕳, followed by EV[s]., which leaves the measure defective by just one word, which appears, however, in 𝕲, although "His name" is there expanded into a clause, practically identical in other respects with the previous one.

Str. III. is composed of a tristich, v.[15-17], and a distich, v.[20-21], with the usual catchwords and intervening lines, v.[18-19], of a different character; cf. v.[10-11]. — **15**. *Mine eyes*] in antithesis with *my feet*. The former look *continually unto Yahweh;* the latter, Yahweh on His part, in response to the pleading look, brings forth from a place of peril. — *that He may bring forth*], in accordance with the petition which is characteristic of the entire Str., as distinguished from the calm statement of fact which is characteristic of the previous Str. The EV⁸. and interpreters generally regard the clause as causal in accordance with previous context, " for He shall pluck," a loose but poetic rendering of vb. meaning " bring forth," which is the keyword of the tristich. — *from the net*] in 𝕳 and Verss. is due to an interpretative gloss after 9¹⁶ ; but it is at the expense of the measure and has nothing to suggest it in the context, and really is too specific, leading away from the more general thought of the tristich. — *from my distresses*], the parallel of v.¹⁷, where the vb. is repeated, also syn. with the adj. *desolate*, abandoned to enemies, left alone (*v.* 22²¹ 68⁷), and *afflicted*, suffering from words and deeds of the enemies, as v.². ⁹ ; so also with *troubles of my mind*, mental distress, anxiety caused by the treachery of the enemies. — **16.** *Turn unto me and be gracious unto me*]. The turning unto the people on the part of Yahweh is an appropriate response to their eyes continually directed unto Him. — **17.** *O make room*], in accordance with the usage of 4² ; give breathing-place, breadth of position, in contrast to the straits, the cramped and narrow position, in which they were now situated, a mng. entirely appropriate between the verbs " bring lorth." The rendering of 𝕲, 𝕵, EV⁸., al., " the troubles of my heart are enlarged," has no usage in Heb. to justify it ; and the interpretation of the vb. as perfect, while justified by 𝕳, is against the context, and due to an ancient misreading of the text, attaching the letter Waw to the preceding instead of the following word. — **18.** *O see mine affliction and my travail*]. This line is rendered suspicious at the start by its substitution of a vb. with ר, and indeed the same as that of v. 19, for the expected one with ק, which should appear here in the order of the alphabet. An easy emendation would give us this ; but there remain the same objections that we have found against v.¹¹, namely, the unexpected plea, *and forgive all my sins*, and the absence of the catchword of the distich. It is probable, therefore, that we have a liturgical substitution for the original line syn. with v.¹⁹. — **19.** *O see mine enemies*], the same as those mentioned v.², only there they were treacherous, and so dangerous ; here *they are many*, numerous, and so outnumbering the people of Yahweh that they need reinforcement. — *and they hate me*]. This is probably the catchword of the distich, and was to be found in the original mate to this line; intensified by *with a hatred of violence*, a hatred that prompts to deeds of violence. — **20–21.** *O keep me and deliver me*], the latter probably the keyword of the distich, reappearing in v.[21] in the original text; but an early copyist by the mistake of a single letter read it " preserve me," which really implies a previous deliverance, and is not so well suited to *wait on Thee* ‖ *seek refuge in Thee*, which imply that the deliverance has not yet been granted. — *Let me not be ashamed*] goes back to the beginning of the Ps. v.[1-3], and implies the continuance of the same situation. — *Let integrity and uprightness*], personified as messengers of God sent forth to deliver His people, cf. 23[6] 43[3]. — *Yahweh*] concludes as well as begins the Ps., according to 𝔊; but 𝕳 omits it, and so loses one tone from the measure. — **22.** This is a liturgical addition by a late editor, as 34[23]. — *O God*] is characteristic of 𝔈 and an Elohistic period of composition. *Yahweh* was this psalmist's God. — *ransom out of all his troubles*], cf. 78[42] 130[8]. — *Israel*], the name of the people of God, cf. 14[7]. This final petition was suited for the congregation in worship at all times; it generalises the Ps., which was based upon a particular historical experience.

1–2. [אֵלֶיךָ] emph., so also נַפְשִׁי as the seat of desire; נשא נפש *lift up the soul, in desire*, אל יהוה 86[4] 143[8]; אל rei 24[4] Dt. 24[15] Ho. 4[8] Pr. 19[18]. The l. is defective, lacking two words to make up the hexameter characteristic of this alphabetical Ps. One of these is אֱלֹהַי, after 𝔊; the other is the superfluous אַל־אֵבוֹשָׁה of next l., which a prosaic editor has attached to the juss. that follows, bringing the two together. Then l. 2 begins with its letter, בְּךָ, also emph., and has its right measure. בוש is the keyword of the first tristich, thrice repeated (*v.* 6[11]), this poet showing a liking to the stairlike parallelism (*v.* Intr. § 12 A). — [בָטַחְתִּי] emph. present (*v.* 4[6]). — [אַל יַעַלְצוּ] Qal 3 pl. neg. juss. אל should be וְאַל as 𝔊 in order to be a separate word with tone. 𝔊 also has καταγελασάτωσάν μου, 𝖁 *irrideant me*, יִלְעֲזוּ, so Che. לִי is not constructed with the vb., which elsw. is always with בְּ, but with the noun, to intensify personal reference. — **3.** [כָּל־קוֶֹיךָ] vb. Qal ptc. pl. sf. 2 m. ‡ קוה, † Qal ptc., *those waiting for* Yahweh 25[3] 37[9] 69[7] Is. 40[31] 49[23] La. 3[25]. Pi. (1) *wait, look eagerly for*, c. acc. rei Ps. 39[8] La. 2[16], sq. inf. Ps. 69[21] Is. 5[2. 4]; c. acc. Yahweh Ps. 25[5. 21] 40[2] 130[5]; שֵׁם 52[11] (?); abs. 130[5]; c. אֶל Yahweh 27[14. 14] 37[34] Is. 51[5]. (2) *Lie in wait for*, c. acc. Ps. 56[7], c. לְ pers. 119[95]. כֹל should be attached by Makkeph to וּ and not to following ptc. for better euphony. — [לֹא יֵבשׁוּ] Qal. impf. 3 pl. indic., with neg. לֹא is not suited to cou-

text. 𝔊 had juss. with אֶל, which is much more probable. The אל should be
attached by Makkeph to the vb. to make one tone.— [הַבּוֹגְדִים] Qal ptc. pl.,
article with force of rel. ‡ בגד, vb. Qal, *act* or *deal treacherously*, ptc. pl.,
25³ 119¹⁵⁸ Is. 21² 24¹⁶ 33¹ Je. 3⁸˙ ¹¹ 9¹ +; בגדי און Ps. 59⁶, abs. 78⁵⁷, c. acc.
pers., 73¹⁶, elsw. c. ב pers. — [רֵיקָם], not *without cause*, for which no usage can
be shown; but *without accomplishing anything*, as 7⁵; cf. 2 S. 1²² Is. 55¹¹. —
4. [דְּרָכֶיךָ] emph. Str. ר, pl. sf. 2 m. דֶּרֶךְ *ways* for *laws*, so v.⁹ (*v. 1¹*), term
of D. — [אֹרְחוֹתֶיךָ] pl. sf. 2 m., ארח (*v. 8⁹*), *paths* for *laws*. This word has to
bear two beats in the measure, therefore it should be preceded by ו, as 𝔊. —
[לַמְּדֵנִי] Pi. imv. sf. 1 p. למד (*v. 18³⁵*), *teach*, the keyword of the distich, v.⁴⁻⁵. —
5. This v. is overfull. The three words of the last clause are suspicious. Are
they a gl. or part of the missing Str. ו? If with 𝔊 we read וְאֵיהֶךָ we might
begin with ו. However tempting it may be to find Str. ו here, yet the arguments against it are irresistible. The last clause is a gl. — **6.** [זְכֹר] (*v. 8⁵*),
the keyword of the distich, v.⁶⁻⁷. [רַחֲמֶיךָ] pl. sf. 2 m. ‡ רחם, n.m. only abst.
intensive pl.: *compassion*, (1) usually of God 77¹⁰ 79³ 119⁷⁷˙ ¹⁵⁶, || הסד 25⁶
40¹² 103⁴ Ho. 2²¹ Je. 16⁵; phr. נרב רחמיך Pss. 51³ 69¹⁷; c. על 145⁹; (2) of man
106⁴⁶. — [הֲסָדֶיךָ] *Thy deeds of kindness* (*v. 4⁴*), pl., mostly late 17⁷ 89²˙ ⁵⁰ 107⁴³ La.
3²² Is. 63⁷, improb. in view of its use with an attribute here and the use of the sg.
in parall. l.; rd. הַסְדְּךָ. It has been assimilated to רחמיך.—[כִּי] though sustained
by 𝔊 ὅτι, is prob. a gl. of interpretation. — **7.** [חַטֹּאות נְעוּרַי] pl. emph., phr.
α.λ., but cf. Jb. 13²⁶ Ez. 23²¹. ‡ נעור, n.m., only pl. abst., *youth*, elsw. 103⁵
127⁴, שנ׳ 71⁶˙ ¹⁷ 129¹˙ ², *from youth up*, cf. בני 144¹². — [פְּשָׁעַי] pl. sf. 1 sg. (*v. 19¹⁴*).
𝔊 has ἀγνοίας, which is better suited to context; but both are probably
glosses, as are also the words that follow לִי, for the l. is just so much overfull.
אתה is not in 𝔊, 𝔍. It is an emph. reference to Yahweh in connection with
the imv., due to the insertion of לבען טובך, which is only an emph. reiteration
of כחסרך. ‡ טוב n.m. (1) *good things*, coll. as given by Yahweh 27¹³ 65⁵;
(2) abst. *prosperity* of Jerusalem 128⁵, *goodness* of taste 119⁶⁶; (3) *goodness*
of God, in salvation of His people 25⁷ 145⁷, cf. Is. 63⁷; stored up for His
saints Ps. 31²⁰. — **8.** [ט ב וְיָשָׁר יהוה] phr., α.λ. ‡ טוב, adj. (1) *good, pleasant*
45² 133¹; (2) *excellent* of its kind, oil 133²; (3) *appropriate, becoming* 73²⁸
92² 147¹; (4) c. מן, comp. *better than* 37¹⁶ 63⁴ 84¹¹ 118⁸˙ ⁹ 119⁷²; (5) *well,
prosperous* 112⁵; (6) *good*, understanding 111¹⁰, as 2 Ch. 11¹⁰ Pr. 3⁴ +;
(7) *benign*, of God 86⁵; phr. כי טוב 34⁹ 106¹ 107¹ 118¹˙ ²⁹ 135³ 136¹ Je. 33¹¹ +;
cf. Ps. 100⁵; c. לְ 73¹ 145⁹; attribute of divine Spirit 143¹⁰ = Ne. 9²¹, of divine
name Pss. 52¹¹ 54⁸, of divine kindness 69¹⁷ 109²¹; (8) *good, right*, ethically,
(*a*) of man 125⁴, the way 36⁵; (*b*) of God 25⁸ 119⁸⁹˙ ⁶⁸. יָשָׁר (*v. 7¹¹*), יְלֹ־בֵּי
(*v. 1⁵*).— [חַטָּאִ־ם] (*v. 1¹*) is prob. gl., as the l. is overfull and the thought
of sinners is not suited to the context, for v.⁸ begins the second heptastich
of the poem and is closely related not to v.⁷ but to v.⁹, and ־רֶךְ is the key-
word of the tristich || אֹרַח, v. v.⁴. — **9.** [יַדְרֵךְ] Hiph. juss. form, but improb. that
it has juss. mng., *v.* v.⁶. [עֲנָוִים] *v. 9¹³*. [בַּמִּשְׁפָּט] in the Law of the type of
judgment; usually in pl. (*v. 1⁵*). — **10.** [הֶסֶד וֶאֱמֶת] phr., Gn. 24²⁷ (J) Pss. 40¹¹˙ ¹²
57⁴ 61⁸ 85¹¹ 86¹⁵ 89¹⁵ 115¹ 138²˙ (*v. 4⁴ 15²*).— [נֹצְרֵי בְרִיתוֹ] phr., elsw. Dt. 33⁹,

usually שׁמר ברית Pss. 78¹⁰ 103¹⁸ 132¹². ‡ בְּרִית, n.f. (1) *treaty, alliance, league*, of nations against Israel 83⁶ Ho. 12² Ez. 17¹³⁻¹⁹; (2) *alliance of friendship* Ps. 55²¹ 1 S. 18³ 20⁸ 23¹⁸, so with God ‖ סוד Ps. 25¹⁴; (3) *covenant, (a)* with patriarchs 105⁸· ¹⁰ Gn. 15¹⁸ (J) 17²· ²¹ (P), (*b*) with Israel at Horeb Pss. 25¹⁰ 44¹⁸ 50⁵· ¹⁶ 74²⁰ (?) 78¹⁰· ³⁷ 103¹⁸ 106⁴⁵ 111⁵· ⁹, (*c*) with David 89⁴· ²⁹· ³⁵· ⁴⁰ 132¹²; cf. 2 S. 7 = 1 Ch. 17 Je. 33²¹. — [וְעֵדֹתָיו] makes l. overfull and is a late gl.: a late term characteristic of P, and found only in writers subsequent to P (*v. 19⁸*). — 11. [רְמְעַן־שִׁמְךָ] emph., as 23³ 31⁴ 79⁹ 106⁸ 109²¹ 143¹¹. — [וְסָלַחְתָּ] ι consec. pf. carrying on juss. implicit in previous clause. ‡ סלח, vb., *pardon* (syn. of נשׂא *forgive*), Qal, c. ל of sin 25¹¹ 103⁸ Ex. 34⁹ Nu. 14¹⁹ (J) Je. 31³⁴ 33⁸ 36⁸. — [עֲוֺנִי] *v. 18²⁴*. This l. was probably a later substitution for an earlier l. that has been thrown out. It lacks the catchword. — 12. [מִי זֶה] *who, then* (*v. 24⁸*) should be connected by Makkeph. — [הָאִישׁ] (*v. 4³*) is unnecessary. The l. is more euphonic without it. — [יוֹרֶנּוּ] Hiph. impf. 3 m. strong sf. 3 s. ‑נּוּ for ‑הוּ. There is word play here with previous יִרָא. — [יִבְחָר] Qal impf. i.p. rel. clause, without rel. ‡ בחר, vb., Qal *choose:* (1) c. ב, divine choice, Aaron 105²⁶, not Ephraim 78⁶⁷, espec. David 78⁷⁰, Zion 132¹³; (2) rel. clause, subj. God 25¹² 33¹² 65⁵; (3) c. acc. and ל, *choose something* or *some one for*, divine choice 47⁵ 135⁴; (4) c. acc. divine choice 78⁶⁸, human choice 84¹¹ 119⁸⁰· ⁷³; (5) ptc. בָּחוּר, *chosen*, of ruler 89²⁰; cf. בחורי ישׂראל 78³¹ = 1 S. 26². — 13. [בְּטוֹב] *in prosperity* Jb. 21¹⁸ 36¹¹ Ec. 7¹⁴ (*v. 4⁷*). — [תָּלִין] vb., Qal future. ‡ לִין, vb., Qal, *lodge, dwell* 30⁶ 59¹⁶⁽?⁾; c. ב 25¹³ 55⁸; abs. *continue, endure* 49¹³. Hithp., *dwell, abide*, c. ב of man 91¹, of eagle Jb. 39²⁸. — [יִירַשׁ] Qal impf. ‡ ירשׁ, vb., Qal, (1) *take possession of as an inheritance*, usually Israel subj., c. acc. the land of Canaan 25¹³ 37⁹· ¹¹· ²²· ²⁹· ³⁴ 44⁴, cf. 105⁴⁴; enemies, subj. 83¹⁸; (2) *dwell and inherit* 69³⁶. Hiph., *dispossess* 44³. — 14. ‡ סוֹד n. (1) *council*, of a divan, in bad sense 64³, good sense Jb. 15⁸ 19¹⁹; *assembly*, of angels Ps. 89⁸; (2) *counsel*, intimate friendship, of men 55¹⁵ 111⁷, with God 25¹⁴ Pr. 3³² Jb. 29⁴, in bad sense of crafty plotting Ps. 83⁴. 𝔊 יסור is misinterpretation. 𝔊 has a parall. clause, καὶ τὸ ὄνομα κυρίου τῶν φοβουμένων αὐτόν, which might be regarded as a variant; but a word is missing from l., and it is probable that the clue to it is given in ὄνομα = שׁם; then we should rd. לְירָאֵי שְׁמוֹ, the ו in יראיו being dittog. from ובריתו; cf. 61⁶ 86¹¹ 102¹⁶. — 15. [עֵינַי] c. אֶל־, as 123² antith. to רַגְלָי. — [כִּי] not causal *for*, as usual, but final *that*, as 8⁵, as the subsequent context requires. — [מֵרֶשֶׁת] is doubtless a gl., making l. too long. It is not suggested by the context. — 16. [פְּנֵה] Qal imv. ‡ פנה, vb., Qal, *turn*, (1) of days of life 90⁹; לפנות הבקר *at the turn of the morning* 46⁶ Ex. 14²⁷ Ju. 19²⁶; (2) *turn* and look, c. אֶל, man, subj. Ps. 40⁵; Yahweh, subj. 69¹⁷; פְּנֵה אֵלַי וְחָנֵּנִי, the two imvs. with ι coörd. 25¹⁶ 86¹⁶ 119¹³²; אל תפלה 102¹⁸ 1 K. 8²⁸ = 2 Ch. 6¹⁹. Pi., *turn away, put away* 80¹⁰ (?). — יחיד adj., *solitary*, as 68⁷ 141¹⁰ (𝔊) (*v. 22²¹*); עָנִי (*v. 9¹³*). — 17. [צָרוֹת] emph. v.²² (*v. 20²*), not elsw. connected with לבב as the seat of anxiety and trouble (*v. 4⁵*). This clause is not the obj. of vb. הִרְחִיבוּ. Hiph. pf. 3 m. indef. subj., and so passive, *they have enlarged, increased*, for the vb. is not elsw. in this sense, but only in the sense of *increase extent, make more room*, and so in the

sense of deliverance from troubles (v. 4²). The ו should go with the next
word, and then the form is Hiph. imv. ‖ הוציא, and so *make room*, as Lowth,
Horsley. The previous clause is then acc. abs., *as for, as regards the troubles.*
— [מִמְּצוּקוֹתַי], מן prep. *out of* with † צוּקָה, n.f. *straitness, straits 25¹⁷* 107⁶·¹³·¹⁹·²⁸
Jb. 15²⁴ Zp. 1¹⁵. — **18.** [רְאֵה] at the beginning of l. where we would expect ק
is suspicious, especially as it is repeated v.¹⁹. It was either an intentional
change of editor or txt. err. Various suggestions have been made as to the
initial word of Str. ק, so קרב Du., קשב Che., קצר Houb., Kenn., Horsley; but
the easiest and most suitable is קראה, cohort. imv. ‡ קרא, vb., Qal *meet:*
(1) in hostility 35³, (2) in helpfulness 59⁵; so prob. here. — [וְיִשָּׂא] ו coörd. Qal
imv. נשׂא *forgive*, syn., סלח *pardon* v.¹¹. The l. lacks the catchword so characteristic of the Ps., and it is probably a later substitution for a l. that has been
thrown out. — [חַטֹּאת] n.f. in ψ alw. *sin* against God v.⁷ 32⁵ 38⁴·¹⁹ 51⁵ 59⁴,
of the mouth 59¹³; acc. after נשׂא 32⁵, כחה Ps. 109¹⁴ Is. 44²² Je. 18²³, כסה
Ps. 85³, with prep. נשׂא לח 25¹⁸, כפר על ח׳ Ps. 79⁹, מהר מח׳ 51⁴. נשׂא is not used
in this sense in D, P, Je., Is.², La., Ch., and is therefore either before D or else
later than P. — **19.** [שֹׂנְאַי חָמָס] phr. α.λ., but ‡ שֹׂנְאָה n.f., *hatred 25¹⁹* 109⁸·⁵
139²². — **20.** [הֲסִיּ] Qal pf. 1 p.s. emph. present, retracted accent because of
following monosyllable (v. 2¹²). — **21.** [הֹם וָיֹשֶׁר] phr. α.λ., personified qualities.
הֹם (v. 7⁹). ‡ יֹשֶׁר n.m., *straightness, rightness, right*, elsw. ישׁר לבב 119⁷ Dt. 9⁵
1 Ch. 29¹⁷. — [יִצְּרוּנִי] Qal impf. 3 pl. sf. juss., נצר. But this prob. an err. for
the catchword צַלֵּנִי, txt. err. ר for ל in Egyptian Aram. script. — [הֹוִיתִיךָ] Pi. pf.
1 s. sf. 2 m. emph. present (v. v.³). 𝔊 has יהוה omitted by H, but necessary
to the measure. — **22.** [פְּדֵה] Qal imv. ‡ פָּדָה vb., Qal *ransom* from violence
and death, man subj. 49⁸ 1 S. 14⁴⁵; God subj., from enemies and troubles
Pss. 25²² 26¹¹ 31⁶ 34²³ 44²⁷ 55¹⁹ 69¹⁹ 71²³ 78⁴² 119¹³⁴, from Sheol 49¹⁶, from
iniquities 130⁸. This is a liturgical appendix. The Ps. has come to an end
with Str. ר. Str. ו was omitted by design, and therefore there was no reason
to complete the alphabetical number of lines. Ps. 34 has the same situation.
אלהים is not the divine name of the Ps., but of a later editor.

PSALM XXVI., 4 STR. 4³.

Ps. 26 is a profession of integrity by a Levite, engaged in worshipping Yahweh in the temple choir. (1) He professes integrity
in walk, and unwavering trust in Yahweh, as attested by Yahweh
Himself (v.¹⁻²). (2) Ever conscious of the divine kindness and
faithfulness, he abstains from all association with the wicked (v.³⁻⁴).
(3) He hates the company of the wicked and purifies himself for
sacrifice (v.⁵⁻⁶). (4) He loves the temple (v.⁸), and stands in
its choir blessing Yahweh (v.¹²). A later editor by additions
and changes introduces the elements of prayer (v.¹ᵃ·⁹⁻¹¹) and worship (v.⁷).

I HAVE walked in mine integrity;
In Yahweh I have trusted without wavering.
Yahweh hath tested me and proved me;
Tried out are my reins and my mind.
YEA, Thy kindness is before mine eyes;
And I walk in Thy faithfulness.
I do not sit down with worthless men;
And with dissemblers I will not come.
I HATE the assembly of evildoers,
And with the wicked I will not sit down.
I will wash my hands in innocency,
And I will march around Thine altar, Yahweh.
I LOVE the habitation of Thine house,
And the place of the tabernacle of Thy glory.
My foot doth stand in the level place,
And in the choirs I bless Yahweh.

The title has only לדוד, as the entire group 25–28. This Ps. was not taken up into 𝔐, 𝔇ℜ, or 𝔈. It was, in its original form, not appropriate for worship in the synagogue, for it was a profession of right conduct from an ethical point of view, as required by Pss. 15, 24^{3-6}, rather than from the legal of Ps. 1, which in other respects it resembles in v.$^{4-5}$ by repudiation of any association with the wicked. רשעים v.^{5} are not wicked nations, but wicked Israelites מתי־שוא, נעלמים v.^{4}; קהל מרעים v.^{5}, whom the author is only anxious to avoid. The חטאים, אנשי דמים v.^{9}, with their זמה and שחד v.^{10}, are of an entirely different type, who are in deadly hostility. These terms represent a different situation and come from a later editor. The author of the Ps. is in no other peril than that of ethical contamination. Therefore he purifies himself by Levitical purifications for participation in the service of the altar v.^{6}, and worship in the temple choir v^{12}. מישור v.^{12} is probably the level place of the court before the temple where the choir took its stand. The במקהלים, elsw. only 68^{27}, might mean assemblies but more probably choirs. This ethical and religious situation in times of peace and prosperity is best suited to the middle Persian period, before Hebrew Wisdom had become the mould for Hebrew ethics. This profession of integrity is not so inappropriate as many moderns think. It is not self-righteousness. It is not so much self-conscious, as conscious of the divine presence and the requirements that invoke it. It is the ethical answer to the requirements of Pss. 15, 24^{3-6}, Is. 33^{14-16}. It reminds us also of Dt. 26^{1-11} on the one side and of Jb. 31 on the other. The language of the Ps. has no other special features than those mentioned above. The Ps. is a trimeter. The first line has prefixed a petition which makes the line too long, or, if regarded as an abbreviated line, makes the Str. too long. It is an editorial change in order to begin with a petition. It is also probable that original perfects v.^{2} as implied by the Kt. צרופה, have been changed by pointing as imv. for the same reason. V.^{7}, for similar reasons, introduces praise, and v.$^{9-11}$ urges petition again, all of which make the Ps. more suited to public worship in the synagogue, and so later in the church; but spoil the simplicity and symmetry of the original, which was two pairs of trimeter tetrastichs.

Str. I. 1 a. *Judge me, Yahweh*]. This in the present context must be interpreted in the sense of vindication. But it is difficult to see in what respect vindication was needed. The context shows that the psalmist was assured of his integrity, and all that he really needed was divine recognition and acceptance in worship. This petition is not in harmony with the context; but it is an appropriate one in liturgical worship, where various emotions of the congregation mingle together, and logical consistency is the last thing that is thought of. It is an editorial gloss. The first half of the Ps. is composed of two trimeter tetrastichs, as Str. and Antistr., each composed of two syn. couplets. — **1 b.** *I have walked*], the course of life, conduct. This has been *in mine integrity*], in entire accord with ethical requirements], complete and perfect; not in the absolute sense, but in the plain, popular sense that, so far as he knew, he was unconscious of any wickedness in his conduct. This he asserts as a fact, professes it in the presence of his God. He makes not a profession of faith, but a profession of morals, as Job 31. The ancient Hebrew was not a philosopher and had no thought of speculative ethics. The editor is obliged to introduce this by " for " and make it a reason for the plea for vindication ; but the connection is remote. — *In Yahweh I have trusted*], inner disposition, as parallel with outward conduct; the God-ward attitude of soul, corresponding with the man-ward attitude of body, faith and works united in one. — *without wavering*], steady, unshaken, uninterrupted was his communion with Yahweh, in faith, as the counterpart of the integrity, completeness of conduct. The faith and the works were both alike complete, entire, unimpeachable. — **2.** *Yahweh hath tested me*], with its complement, *proved me*, and its parallel, *tried out*, as by the refining of metals, *v.* 17^3. A most searching examination has been made by Yahweh Himself, and that has been complete, for it has extended to *my reins and my mind*], v. 7^{10} Je 11^{20} 17^{10} 20^{12}, the seat of emotions and passions as well as the seat of the intellectual and moral nature. The profession of faith and morals therefore rests upon the divine examination and approval. This assertion of fact did not suit the requirements of a later worship, and therefore

probably the Ps. was left out of the collection made by 𝔇𝕽 and
𝕰. But by changing the pfs. of the vb. to the imvs. "test me
‖ prove me ‖ try out," especially when introduced by "judge me,"
the Ps. was made more suited to the worship of the synagogue and
so also for the Christian congregation.

Str. II. 3. *Yea*], if our interpretation of the foregoing is correct;
but doubtless the editor interpreted it as " for " in accordance
with v.¹ᵇ which it resumes; so all Vrss. — *Thy kindness*], as usual
parallel with *Thy faithfulness;* the former in accordance with the
trust of v.¹ᶜ, although it is *before mine eyes;* the latter in accordance
with the walk, which is indeed expressed in this clause. This
latter is not a qualification of the psalmist, or of the way in which
he walks, and so to be rendered " Thy truth " as EVˢ. because this
Hebrew word seldom has the meaning of " truth," and never when
it is connected with the divine kindness. The "faithfulness" is
syn. with the " kindness," both of which divine attributes as
present with him, before the eyes of his mind, enable him to walk
in his integrity. — **4.** *I do not sit down with*]. In this and the
syn. line, so also in v.⁵, the poet repudiates any association whatever
with the wicked. This reminds us of Ps. 1¹, where walking, standing,
and sitting down with the wicked are repudiated. Here only two
of these actions are mentioned. The action of sitting down with,
is greatly emphasised here because it is repeated in v.⁵ᵇ, as indeed
it is the climax of the actions in Ps. 1¹. Such a sitting down with
them would imply prolonged association and greater intimacy
and responsibility for companionship, than walking with them or
standing with them. — *I will not come with*], that is, be seen
approaching in company with. The vb. has been intentionally
changed from that of v.¹ᵇ· ³ᵇ and implies a movement the reverse
of going; therefore it is improbable that it should have the specific
meaning " go in " of EVˢ. implying entrance to a house or assembly,
which is awkward without designation of place. — *worthless men*],
men whose speech and conduct is empty, false; their speech and
professions empty of reality; with nothing in them that is reliable;
and so parallel with *dissemblers*, those who conceal their thoughts
so that they may appear differently from what they are.

Str. III. The second part of the Ps. is composed of two trimeter tetrastichs, Str. and Antistr., contrasting what the psalmist

loves and hates, the first couplet of each syn., the second couplet of each synth. — **5.** *I hate*], in antithesis with " I love " v.⁸. The object of the former is the *assembly*, or congregation *of evildoers* ‖ *wicked*, more general and positive terms for those of v.⁴ ; the object of the latter is the assembly of the worshippers of Yahweh in the temple choir, although that is not brought out distinctly until the closing line of the Str. — **6.** *I will wash my hands*], doubtless referring to the ceremonial purifications prescribed by the Law for those who were to serve in the temple worship ; the use of pure, running water from the sacred lavers of the temple courts. This washing was not made symbolical by the use of the ethical term, *in innocency*, which recurs to the integrity of v.¹ᵇ ; but in order to show that the external ceremonial purification was only expressive of an internal purity of mind, as indeed the Law and the Prophets require. — *And I will march around Thine altar*], in festal procession, with music and song, while the sacrifice was being made by the priests. There is no good reason to doubt this ceremonial among the Hebrews, although the direct evidence for it is slight. But there are many indirect references, cf. 42⁵ 118²⁷ 1 S. 16¹¹ 30¹⁶ ; and the usual meaning of the Hebrew word favours this interpretation, as well as the reference to choirs v.¹². There is still less justification, from anything we know of Hebrew customs at sacrifice, to interpret it of the psalmist's taking his place in the ring of worshippers around the altar.

7. This v. is a couplet of gloss.

> To cause the sound of thanksgiving to be heard
> And to tell of all Thy wondrous deeds.

This couplet is attached to v.⁶ as an explanation of the march about the altar, to show that it was accompanied with song and music. The contents of the song were thanksgiving and praise ; thanksgiving, sounding forth from human voices and musical instruments so as to be heard far and near. The *wondrous deeds* of Yahweh, especially in the redemption of His people, are what these Pss. of praise commonly tell. This addition is quite appropriate and in accordance with v.¹² ; but it is hung on to v.⁶ by an infinitive, so that it must go with v.⁵⁻⁶. It makes the Str. just these lines too long, as compared with other Strs. ; and it is also overfull in state-

ment as compared with the simplicity of thought and expression
of the previous context. The motive of the addition was evidently
to introduce the missing element of praise to Yahweh, and so
make the Ps. more appropriate for public worship.

Str. IV. 8. *I love the habitation of Thine house*], that is, the
divine abode itself in the temple, the *Debir* or *Holy of Holies*,
behind the curtain of which Yahweh was conceived as in residence ; and so syn. with *place of the tabernacle of Thy glory*]. The
glory of the divine presence was centred there.

A late editor inserts a hexastich gloss —

> Gather not my soul with sinners,
> Or with men of blood my life ;
> In whose hands is an evil device,
> And whose right hand is full of bribery.
> Since I in mine integrity walk,
> Redeem me and be gracious to me, (Yahweh).

This hexastich is composed of a tetrastich of two syn. couplets,
the latter synth. to the first, followed by an antith. synth. couplet.
This is also a gloss introduced for the purpose of making the Ps.
more appropriate for public prayer. — **9.** *Gather not*], as the
context shows in order to take away the soul in death ‖ *life*,
cf. 104²⁹, antith. v.¹¹ᵇ *Redeem me*, and its complement, *be gracious
to me.* *Yahweh* is needed here for the measure, unless we are to
regard v.¹¹ as a pentameter appended still later than v.⁹⁻¹⁰, without
regard to the measure of the previous or subsequent context. —
With sinners ‖ men of blood], violent men who shrink not from
bloodshed, implying a different set of men from the false and dis-
sembling of v.⁴ — **10.** *In whose hand*] emphasised in the parallel
right hand, as stretched out to give *an evil device*, or plan. In the
hand it is something tangible, defined by *full of bribery*, a gift of
money, or jewels, or something valuable, to purchase immunity
from crime. These are probably criminals who bribe, and not
judges or rulers accepting bribes. — **11.** *Since I in mine integrity
walk*], a repetition of v.¹ᵇ in order to get an antith. with the bloodthirsty men, as a basis for the final plea for redemption. The
construction is, however, changed from the perfect to the imperfect of the habit of life, and the whole is put in a circumstantial
clause.

12. *My foot doth stand in the level place*]. This couplet is closely associated with v.[8] as its complement, although separated by the intervening gloss. The psalmist is standing on his feet in the levelled place of the court, where the sacrifices were made at the divine altar. — *And in the choirs*], the group of singers, who unite in the chorus of the benediction. This is more probable than assembly of worshippers in general, especially as *I will bless Yahweh* is not merely an attitude of the soul in worship, but doubtless refers to the benedictions as sung. These benedictions were sung in full chorus at the close of every Ps. or liturgical selection (*v.* Intr. § 40). We may either think of them or of the entire liturgy as sung by the choir.

1. אֵלֵךְ emph.; אֲנִי [אֲנִי בְּתֻמִּי הָלַכְתִּי] emph.; בְּרֻמִּי also emph. (*v.* 7[9]). V.[11] has אֵלֵךְ, otherwise the clause is the same. The l. is too long. Du. thinks this v. has been assimilated to v.[11], and therefore rds. שָׁפְטֵנִי יהוה חם־אני. But the parall. l. requires אני בתמי הלכתו, and therefore שָׁפְטֵנִי י׳ כי is the gl.— [ביהוה] emph., antith. אני.— [לֹא אֶמְעָד] not future of independent clause, but circumstantial, *without slipping, shaking, wavering.*— **2.** [נסה] ‡ Pi. imv. [וַחֲנֵנִי] Pi. vb. only Pi. *test, prove*: (*a*) God subj. 26[2] Dt. 33[8] Ex. 15[25] +; † (*b*) Israel *tests, tries,* God Pss. 78[18. 41. 56] 95[9] 106[14] Ex. 17[2. 7] Nu. 14[22] (J) Dt. 6[16], so Ahaz Is. 7[12]. ‖ [צָרְפָה] Qr. Qal imv. cohort. of צרף (*v.* 12[7] 17[3]), Kt. צְרוּפָה Qal ptc., prob. implies an original txt. in which previous vbs. were pfs. — [כִּלְיוֹתַי וְלִבִּי] *v.* 7[10] Je. 11[20] 17[10] 20[12].— **3.** [וְהִתְהַלַּכְתִּי בַּאֲמִתֶּךָ] cf. 25[5] 86[11], ו coörd.; Hithp. pf. 1 p. of הלך, as v.[1]. 𝔊 εὐηρέστησα is prob. paraphrase.— **4.** [מְתֵי־שָׁוְא] cf. Jb. 11[11], *men of emptiness of speech, falsehood; worthless men.*— [וַעֲלָמִים] Niph. ptc. pl. α.λ., *those who conceal themselves* or *their thoughts, dissemblers.*— אָבוֹא] Qal future, not *go,* for which there is no certain usage, but *come.* The rendering of EV[s]. *go in,* though possible, is without example apart from designation of place, and to have force should be emphasised by some such particle as נָם *v.* 14[3].— **5.** [קְהַל מְרֵעִים] phr. α.λ., *assembly of evildoers,* cf. עֲרַת ש׳ 22[17], סוֹד מ׳ 64[3]. For קהל *v.* 22[23], מרעים Hiph. ptc. of רעע *v.* 22[17].— **6.** [אֶרְחַץ בְּנִקָּיוֹן כַּפַּי] = 73[13], of purification before sacrifice. ‡ רחץ Qal *wash,* elsw. ψ 58[11] (feet with blood in vengeance). ‡ נִקָּיוֹן n.[m.] *innocency,* in ψ only in this phr., cf. Gn. 20[5] (RJE).— [וַאֲסֹבְבָה אֶת־מִזְבַּחֲךָ] *march about* in solemn procession, cf. 1 S. 16[11]. ‡ מִזְבֵּחַ n.m. *altar,* as place of sacrifice, elsw. 43[4] 51[21] 84[4] 118[27].— **7.** [לְשְׁמִעַ] Hiph. inf. cstr., defectively written for להשׁמיע = to *cause to be heard,* the song of thanksgiving; here gerundive, but then the Str. must be six lines. Du. proposes to transpose v.[7] with v.[8], and then inf. becomes dependent on אהבתי. This seems necessary because of the antith. of אהב and שֹׂנֵא. But it looks like an expansive gl. We would, however, expect קוֹל, as 66[8]. בקוֹל is elsw. connected with Qal, and it may be that was the original txt. as interpreted by 𝔊. 𝔍 interprets as Hiph., and בקוֹל

as *clara voce.* — ‡ [תּוֹדָה] n.f.: (1) *thanksgiving in song,* קוֹל תּ׳ 26⁷ 42⁵ Jon. 2¹⁰, ‖ שִׁיר Ps. 69³¹, זִמְרוֹת 95², תְּהִלָּה 100⁴, כִּנּוֹר 147⁷; (2) *thankoffering* תוֹדָה (וזבחי] סִפֵּר כָּל־נַפְלְאוֹתֶיךָ — ¹³.56, זבח תּ׳ 50¹⁴·²³, שֵׁם תּ׳ 56¹³. — [100¹ (title), לתורה 116¹⁷, 107²² contents of תוֹדָה sung by procession, as 9² 73²·⁸ 75². — 8. [יהוה] gl., makes l. too long, due to the insertion or transposition of the previous distich. — ‡ [מָעוֹן] n.[m.] *dwelling,* of יהוה in heaven, מ׳ קֹרֶשׁ 68⁶ Dt. 26¹⁵ Je. 25³⁰ Zc. 2¹⁷; in the temple, מ׳ בֵיתֶ Ps. 26⁸; usually 71³ 90¹ 91⁹ are interpreted fig. of יהוה as the abode of His people, but all dub. ⑮ εὐπρέπειαν = נֹעַם, error of transposition of original מַעֹן. [מִשְׁכַּן כְּבֹדֶךָ] *Thy glorious tabernacle,* poetic for temple. ‡ מִשְׁכָּן n.m. *dwelling-place, tabernacle,* of P, not used in ψ; of Shilo 78⁶⁰; elsw. (*a*) of temple in a more general sense as dwelling-place of יהוה; in sg. מ׳ כְּבוֹדֶךָ 26⁸, מ׳ שְׁמֶךָ 74⁷, cf. 46⁵; (*b*) pl. מִשְׁכְּנוֹת, used of tabernacles of Israel 78²⁸ 87²; of the tomb 49¹² (cf. sg. Is. 22¹⁶); of divine residence in Zion 132⁵·⁷; holy mountain 43³; courts of temple 84². — 9. [אַנְשֵׁי דָמִים] elsw. 55²⁴ 59⁸ 139¹⁹ Pr. 29¹⁰, cf. אִישׁ דמים 5⁷. — 10. [אֲשֶׁר] rel., referring back to *men of blood,* defined by בִּידֵיהֶם. V.⁹⁻¹⁰ are a late gl. — 11. A repetition of v.¹ᵃ. — ¹ [ואני] circumstantial *since,* or *in that, seeing that.* — [אֵלֵךְ] Qal freq., antith. to actions of *men of blood.* — [רָֽצְנִי וְחָנֵּנִי] both Qal imv. ¹ coörd. The l. is defective in the midst of trimeters. Supply יהוה unless it be a gl., and possibly even then. This l. may have been added subsequently to v.⁹⁻¹⁰, and so have been really pentameter. — 12. [רְוֹלִי] emph. subj. vb. — [יָֽעֵידָה] Qal pf. 3 f., c. ב loci as usual, *take one's stand,* cf. בבית 134¹ 135². — ‡ [יָשׁוּר] n.m.: † (1) *a level place* 26¹² 27¹¹ 143¹⁰, prob. also 68⁷ (for כֹּשָׁרוֹת); † (2) abstr., *uprightness* 45⁷ 67⁶ Is. 11⁴ Mal. 2⁶; (3) the prose mng., *level country,* not in ψ. — † [מַֽהֲלֵיב] n.[m.] pl. 26¹² = 68²⁷, either *choirs* or *assemblies for worship.* — [אֲבָרֵךְ] Pi. impf. 1 sg. ברך (*v.* 5¹³). This distich seems to be the complement of v.⁸.

PSALM XXVII.

Ps. 27 is composite. (1) A guest Ps. expresses confidence in Yahweh in time of war (v.¹⁻³), and in the security afforded by the temple to worshippers (v.⁴⁻⁶). (2) An anxious petition urges Yahweh to answer prayer (v.⁷⁻⁸), not to forsake His servant (v.⁹), but to give instruction and deliverance (v.¹¹⁻¹²). (3) Glosses adapt the Ps. for congregational worship (v.¹⁰·¹²ᵇ·¹³⁻¹⁴).

A. v.¹⁻⁶, 2 STR. 6⁵.

YAHWEH, my light and my salvation, of whom shall I be afraid ?
   Yahweh, the refuge of my life, of whom shall I be in dread ?
   When evildoers drew near against me to eat up my flesh,
   Those who were mine adversaries and enemies to me, stumbled and they fell,
   Though a camp encamp against me, my heart will not be afraid ;
   Though battle rise up against me, I shall be trusting.

ONE thing I ask from Yahweh, that will I seek after;
  To gaze on the loveliness of Yahweh (in the morning) in His temple.
  For He will conceal me in His covert in the day of distress;
  Hide me in the hiding-place of His tent, (in straits) lift me up.
  Now therefore He will lift up mine head above mine enemies round about me;
  And I will sacrifice in His tent sacrifices of shouting to Yahweh.

B. v.[7-9. 11-12], 3 STR. 4[3].

HEAR, Yahweh, *my* voice.
  I call, therefore be gracious to me and answer *me.*
  To Thee said *my* heart:
  "Thy face, Yahweh, (do) *I* seek."
HIDE not Thy face from *me ;*
  Turn not in anger (against *me*).
  My help, abandon *me* not;
  Forsake me not, *my* salvation.
IN Thy Way instruct *me,*
  In an even path lead *me ;*
  Give me not over to the greed of *mine* adversary,
  He that breatheth out violence to *me.*

Ps. 27 was in 𝕯. There is nothing else in the title of 𝕳, but 𝕲
has in addition πρὸ τοῦ χρισθῆναι 𝔙 *priusquam liniretur.* Jerome in
his Commentary has *antequam ungueretur ;* but says that it was not in
𝕳 and omits it from 𝔍. Since Kenn. the Ps. has been generally regarded
as composite, the second Ps. beginning v.[7]. So Horsley, Che., Kirk.,
Dy., Ew., Ols., Reu., De., al. As De. says: "Aber auch übrigens sind die
zwei Hälften einander sehr unähnlich. Sie bilden ein Hysteronproteron,
idem die *fides triumphans* der 1 in der 2 in *fides supplex* umschlägt und mit
Beginn der δέησις v.[7] der Stil schwerfällig, die strophische Anlage unklar
und sogar die Begrenzung der Verszeilen unsicher wird." The first Ps. v.[1-6]
has two pentameter hexastichs. It was composed in time of war, when the
army of the enemy was to be feared v.[3]. The enemies were national אכל בשׂר
v.[2] as 14[4]. The refuge was the היכל v.[4], סכה v.[5a], סתר אהל v.[5b]. The worship
was carried on by sacrifice זבח with הרועה v.[6]. לבקר v.[4], if a verb, is an
Aramaism and implies postex. date; but it is doubtless a noun, *in the morning,* referring to morning sacrifice as 5[4], and the אור of v.[1] may be compared
with 4[7]. The Ps. is then preëxilic. The calm confidence in connection with
extreme peril from enemies, apparently besieging the city, reminds us of the
situation of Jerusalem in the time of Hezekiah and Isaiah, *v.* 2 K. 18–19.
The second Ps., v.[7-9. 11. 12], has three trimeter tetrastichs of prayer for deliverance. Nothing indicates any particular occasion. It was probably added to
the first Ps. in the Persian period at the time of the editing of 𝕯 in order
to make this ancient Ps. appropriate for synagogue worship. The difficulties
to which De. alludes are due to glosses of a still later date, adapting the Ps.
by generalisation for later situations. (*a*) The forsaking of a person by his

parents, v.[10], suits a time of persecution such as the Maccabean period, when families were divided. (*b*) v.[13-14], at the conclusion, seem to be an effort to harmonise the two parts by combining the elements of trust and petition. They bring the composite Ps. to a more appropriate conclusion. This was probably the work of the final editor.

Str. I. is composed of three syn. pentameter couplets, progressive one to another in their order. — **1.** *Yahweh*], not probably, " is " EV[s].; but vocative. — *my light*], light to me, that is light coming forth from the face of Yahweh, turned toward the people in favour, in accordance with the priestly blessing, Nu. 6[24-26], cf. 4[7] 44[4] 89[16]; here conceived as in its source, the face of Yahweh being itself a light-giving body or luminary, as in 84[12] Yahweh is a sun. The light is a saving light, and so the source of it is, *my salvation ∥ refuge of my life*], or for my life. The people seeking refuge in Yahweh found their life secure, safe from the enemy. — *of whom*], is therefore a triumphant challenge, implying a negative answer, of none. — *shall I be afraid ∥ be in dread*]. However great the external reasons for fear, because of the numbers and strength of the enemies; under divine protection His people are sure that they are absolutely safe. We are reminded of the sublime challenge, Is. 37[21-35]. — **2.** *When evil doers*], here as elsw. referring to cruel, ruthless enemies, who maltreat their foes; ∥ *mine adversaries ∥ enemies to me*], not private enemies, individuals; but public enemies engaged in war. — *drew near against me*], in hostility and probably to besiege. — *to eat up my flesh*], as in 14[4], as beasts of prey to devour, consume utterly. What the enemies expected did not come to pass, but the reverse. The latter is reserved therefore for stronger antith. in the complementary section of the second line of the couplet. — *stumbled*], over obstacles they did not anticipate, *and they fell*, that is to the ground in defeat and death. — **3.** *Though a camp encamp against me*], surround the people of God in siege, as the army of Assyrians, 2 K. 18[17 seq.] It is better to preserve the identity of words in English than to use the syn. " host " EV[s]. — *Though battle rise up against me*]. The specific meaning is more probable here than the general meaning war. The battle was something to be feared as the consequence of the siege already begun. In these circumstances, justifying fear, *my heart will not be afraid*], resuming v.[1];

but the reverse, *I shall be trusting*], the ptc. expressing the uninterrupted, unbroken continuance of the trust in Yahweh.

Str. II. is composed of two synth. couplets, and an intermediate
syn. couplet. — **4.** *One thing*], emph. at the beginning. He is
confident of deliverance from the enemy ; he need not ask for
that ; but there is one, and one only thing, he desires : *I ask*],
emph. of present experience and not of past experience, or experience just completed. — *that*], resuming the one thing with
the syn. vbs.: *ask* ‖ *seek after*. — *To gaze on*], defining the one
thing, the privilege of beholding steadfastly, contemplating with
a joyous gaze, *the loveliness of Yahweh*], His glory as manifested
to the devout mind in public worship. — *in His temple*], the place
where Yahweh resides and where He manifests Himself to His
worshippers. This worship, especially in early times, was chiefly
in the morning, the chief time of sacrifice, as 5^4 59^{17} 88^{14}. This Hebrew word has been interpreted, by a difference of vowel points,
as a vb. which properly means "inquire" AV., RV. ; but this is
so unsuited to the context and so difficult to explain satisfactorily
that Vrss. are compelled to resort to speculative mngs. : " visit "
PBV., " consider " RV^m., " contemplate " *B*DB. ; some such meaning being required to suit the parall. A later editor, not satisfied
with this designation of the one thing, proposes another, though
similar thing, from 23^6 : *dwell in the house of Yahweh all the days
of my life*, at the expense of the strophical organization. — **5.** *For
He will conceal me* ‖ *hide me*], renewed expression of confidence.
— *in His covert* ‖ *the hiding-place of His tent*], both referring to
the temple as a place of refuge ; not that the enemy might capture the city, but be compelled to respect the sacred right of
refuge in the temple ; for no such respect for the temple appears
among the historic enemies of Israel. The conception is rather
that the temple is such a covert and hiding-place that it protects
the entire city in which it is situated, so that God's people, when
they resort to the temple for worship, will be kept in safety from
all enemies. Accordingly, this is definitely asserted, *in the day
of distress*]. The siege has caused distress, notwithstanding the
courage and confidence of the people. — *in straits*], as the parall.
suggests ; but an early editor has interpreted the Hebrew word by
a different pointing, as " upon a rock " ; and this has gone into

Vrss. ancient and modern, introducing a thought which, however appropriate in itself, is difficult to reconcile with the context. The people have their refuge in the temple. The rock was the refuge of those who were pursued by enemies away from the city and temple, in the country, where by climbing a lofty rock they would be inaccessible. — *lift me up*], in victory, the same antith. to the previous vbs., as is found in the couplet v.². — **6.** *Now therefore*], logical sequence and not temporal. — *He will lift up mine head above mine enemies*], in victory, repeating the previous vb. in stair-like parall. in accordance with 𝕲, 𝕴, PBV., Pss. 3⁴ 110⁷, interpreting it as Hiphil of vb., which is much more probable than 𝕳, though sustained by other ancient and modern Vrss. "shall mine head be lifted up," interpreting it as Qal. — *round about me*]. The enemies are besieging the city, in accordance with v³; so most Vrss. to be preferred to 𝕲, interpreting it as vb. "go about in procession" as 26⁶, attaching it to the next line, at the expense of the measure of both lines. — *And I will sacrifice*] in the morning hour of worship, as v.⁴ᵇ. — *in His tent*], poetic for temple as v.⁵, including the court of the brazen altar, the place of sacrifice. — *Sacrifices of shouting*], sacrifices of peace-offerings in the form of thank-offerings for the victory granted by Yahweh, whose chief characteristic was feasting on the flesh of the victims together with bread and wine in joyful festivity, and therefore accompanied with the sacred shout to Yahweh. A later editor, at the expense of the measure, inserts two vbs.: "I will sing, yea I will sing psalms," more appropriate to the fully developed temple service of later times.

PS. XXVII. *B.*

Str. I. is a syn. tetrastich. — **7.** The first two lines are composed of usual phrases, *v.* 3⁵ 4². ⁴. — *I call*] is attached by MT., 𝕲, 𝕴, and all Vrss., to the first line, usually as a relative or temporal clause; but they differ as regards the connection of *my voice*. 𝕲, 𝕴, PBV. make it the object of *hear*, but AV., RV., and most moderns attach it to *call*. The former is required by the measure, and then it is better to attach *call* to the second line as the antecedent of the two vbs., and so the first trimeter couplet is simple and harmonious. — **8.** *To thee*], emph., referring to Yahweh. —

said my heart], a late expression instead of the usual "in my heart." We would expect at once what was said. — *Thy face, Yahweh, do I seek*], that is, resort to the temple, the place of the divine presence. This simple trimeter couplet was disturbed by an early marginal exclamation "seek ye My face." This marginal exhortation eventually, as in so many other cases, came into the text at the expense of the rhythm.

Str. II. is a syn. tetrastich. — **9.** *Hide not Thy face*], in indifference, not looking at me, ignoring my need of Thee ; ‖ *abandon me not* ‖ *forsake me not*] ; so the intermediate, *turn not*, as 𝕲, 𝔍, interpreting the verb as Qal. But 𝕳 followed by EVˢ. and most moderns interpret it as Hiphil, "cast away" PBV. ; "put away" AV., RV. None of these has any sure warrant in Hebrew usage, and all are against the parall. — *in anger against me*], so probably in the original. But as often "Thy servant" has been substituted for "me" by an editor. This is more natural than to take "servant" as obj. of verb, in accordance with the interpretation rejected above, or "from Thy servant" of 𝕲, 𝔍, which requires the insertion of a preposition in the original text. — *my help* ‖ *my salvation*] : the assertion of past experience is the basis of the plea.

10. *When my father and my mother have forsaken me*], as PBV., AV. is more probable than "for" RV., though sustained by 𝕲, 𝔍. It is then the protasis with perfect of vb. This most naturally is to be referred to a time of religious persecution, such as the times of Antiochus and the early Maccabees, when families were divided, and subsequently when parties in Israel became bitterly antagonistic even in families, an idea hardly suited to the Ps in this context. The apodosis is : *then will Yahweh take me up*]. This is a late meaning of the Hebrew word. The verse may be regarded as a pentameter, but more probably is a mere prose sentence. In either case it does not correspond with the rhythm of the simple trimeter in which it is embedded, or the construction of its Strs. This verse is therefore a gloss, not earlier than the Maccabean period.

Str. III. is composed of two syn. couplets in antith. — **11.** *In Thy way instruct me*]. In 25$^{8, 12}$, this phr. refers to the Deuteronomic legislation ; but that does not suit the present context, which suggests rather a way of safety from enemies. This is favoured by the ‖ *In an even path lead me*], a path leading to a level place, a place upon which one can stand securely. This was certainly the interpretation of the glossator, who at the expense of the measure, added from, 5[9] : *because of those lying in wait for me.* — **12.** *Give me not over*], taking up the abandonment of v.[9] and putting it in another syn. form. — *to the greed*]. The soul of the adversaries, as the seat of greedy desire, is all greed. Parallel with this is, *he that breatheth out*], the greed is expressed by excited, eager, hot breath. The greed of soul is expressed in *violence* of word and deed. The same glossator, probably, as the one who inserted v.[10], also inserted between the two lines of the couplet the words : *For false witnesses have risen up against me*, which suits quite well the situation in the strife of parties in the Maccabean times.

13-14. An editor, probably earlier than the glossator mentioned above, possibly the one who combined the prayer with the original Ps., made that combination more appropriate by summing up the essential ideas of both parts in these verses.

> I believe that I shall look on the good things of Yahweh in the land of the living.
> Wait on Yahweh. Be strong and let thy heart take courage.

𝕳 "unless" followed by EV[s]. is marked in MT. as doubtful by extraordinary points, and it is not justified by most ancient Vrss.

13. *I believe*,] emphatic present with infin. const. of obj. — *that I shall look on the good things of Yahweh*], those given by Yahweh ; which takes the place of the loveliness of Yahweh of v.[4] as a practical interpretation of it. — *in the land of the living*] : cf. 142[6], as distinguished from the realm of the dead, emphasising continuance of life on the earth. This also generalises the more specific and devout thought of v.[4]. — **14.** *Wait on Yahweh*], in faith, confidence, and hope ; paraphrased in PBV. "the Lord's leisure " ; repeated at the close of the verse for emphasis, probably added by a much later hand. As the previous line expressed the confidence of the first Ps. by the perfect of the vb., this line expresses the prayer of the second Ps. by imperatives : *Be strong*, intensified in, *let thine heart take courage*], cf. 31[25], which is a more probable interpretation of the vb., as 𝕲, 𝕵, RV., Dr., Kirk., al., than PBV. "He shall comfort thine heart," interpreting the vb. as apodosis of imv. and giving it a causative force.

XXVII. *A.*

1. [אוֹרִי וְיִשְׁעִי] phr. *a.λ.* sfs. obj. אוֹר *v. 4*[7]; יֵשַׁע *v. 12*[6]. — [מָעוֹז חַיַּי] phr. *a.λ.*; ‡ מָעוֹז n.m. *place* or *means of refuge, safety :* (1) place, not in *ψ* ; but (2) fig. of God as refuge *27*[1] 31[5] 37[89] 52[9] Is. 25[4. 4] Na. 1[7] Jo. 4[16], מ' ישׁוּעֹת Ps. 28[8], צוּר מ' 31[8] Is. 17[10], אלֹהֵי מ' Ps. 43[2]; (3) fig. of human protection מ' רֹאשִׁי 60[9] = 108[9]. *v. 7*[6]. — **2.** [בְּקָרֹב] Qal inf. cstr., בּ temporal, apod. יִשְׁרוּ pf. past experience ‖ יִּפְּלוּ, ו coörd. — [לִי] attached to אֹיְבִי, emphasising the sf., was doubtless original, completing the pentameter. — [הֵמָּה] is a gl. to emphatically resume the subj. (*v. 16*[3]). — **3.** [אִם] protasis of condition, parall. with previous temporal clause, with apodosis בְּזֹאת. — [יִירָא] gl., either emph., to call attention to the object of trust ; or *in spite of this, even then*, as RV., Dr., Kirk., al. — [בֹּטֵחַ] Qal ptc. (*v. 4*[6]) continuous action, with verbal force, and subj. אֲנִי completing the l. — **4.** [אַחַת] emph., *one thing.* — [שָׁאַלְתִּי] Qal pf., emph. present. — [אוֹתָהּ] emph. object, *that thing.* — [שִׁבְתִּי בְּבֵית יהוה] gl. from 23[6b]; שִׁבְתִּי inf. cstr., c. sf. 1 s. from ישׁב without לְ is striking in view of לְ with the subsequent infs. The glossator did not assimilate it to the context. — [כָּל יְמֵי חַיַּי] gl. from 23[6a]. — [לַחֲזוֹת] Qal inf. cstr., obj. of previous vbs.: *behold,* usually c. acc. (*v. 11*[4]), here more intense with בּ, *look intently, gaze on.* — † [נֹעַם] n.m. *delightfulness, loveliness ;* † of יה, in temple here, in His favour 90[17], elsw. Zc. 11[7. 10] Pr. 3[17] 15[26] 16[24]. — [וּלְבַקֵּר] is a second inf. Pi. cstr. of ‡ בקר, Aramaism, rare in Heb., Lv. 13[36] c. לְ *seek, look for ;* Ez. 34[11] c. acc. *seek* flock, to care for it ; Pr. 20[25] is difficult. Toy renders *make inquiry.* The proper mng. of the vb. is improper here. What was he to seek in the temple syn. with *gaze ?* *B*DB. *contemplate* suits context, but Toy says there is no authority for such a rendering. Point it therefore לַבֹּקֶר *in the morning,* the hour of prayer, as 5[4] 59[17] 88[14]. — **5.** [כִּי] is causal and the vbs. are futures. — [סֻכֹּה] Qr. סָכּוֹ [לֹךְ]; *thicket, covert, lair* (*v. 10*[9]) not suited to context ; better Kt. סֻכֹּה *booth,* a refuge in storm, as 18[12]. — [בְּיוֹם רָעָה] *in the day of distress,* as 41[2] (*v. 21*[12]). — [בְּסֵתֶר אָהֳלוֹ] phr. *a.λ.,* but סֵתֶר *hiding-place* (*v. 18*[12]). אֹהֶל *tent,* for the temple. — [בְּצוּר] (*v. 18*[2]) not suited to the situation in the courts of the temple, though 𝕳 is sustained by ancient Vrss. Rd. בַּצַּר *in straits.* An ancient editor interpreted it as צֻר and wrote it fully צוּר. — **6.** [יָרוּם] not temporal, but logical (*v. 2*[10]). — [יָרוּם] Qal impf. 𝕳 ; but 𝕲, 𝕵, PBV., ירים Hiph. more prob. in accord. with previous context, as 3[4] 110[7]. — [סְבִיבוֹתַי] 𝕳 and all Vrss. except 𝕲, 𝖅, as 18[12] 79[8] (*v. 3*[7]). It then has two tones as the complement of the line. 𝕲 rd. vb. סִבֵּב Polel pf. 1 s. *go about in procession,* as 26[6] (*v. 17*[11]), and attached it to next vb., which is then interpreted as ו consec. impf. ; but the obj. of vb. in this sense could hardly be missing, and no adjustment of the measure is practicable. — [וְאֶזְבְּחָה] ו coörd., with Qal cohort. expressing resolution. For זבח vb. and noun, *v. 4*[6]. — ‡ [תְּרוּעָה] n.f. *shout,* in *ψ* (1) *religious shout* in temple, in connection with sacrifices; so here, 33⁸ 47⁶ 89¹⁶; (2) *clashing*, of cymbals 150⁶; cf. vb. רוּעַ, *v. 41¹²*. The l. needs a word to complete its measure. That is probably ליהוה. Then אֲשִׁירָה and וַאֲזַמְּרָה are expansive gls.

XXVII. B.

7. A new measure, trimeter; and doubtless another Ps. begins here, which was pieced on to the previous Ps.; cf. Pss. 19, 24. — שְׁמַע] Qal imv. of petition, sq. acc. קוֹלִי, as 18⁷ 55¹⁸ 64² 119¹⁴⁹; so ⅏, PBV. — קוֹלִי] does not go with אקרא as AV., RV., for this vb. belongs with l. 2. — וְחָנֵּנִי וַעֲנֵנִי] vbs. in emph. coördination preceded by ו of consequence; both Qal imvs. c. sf. 1 s. For חנן *v. 4²*; עֲנֵה *v. 3⁶*. — **8.** לְךָ] emph. — אָמַר לִבִּי] phr. *a.λ.*, elsw. בלב 10⁶. ¹¹. ¹³ 14¹ (= 53²) 35²⁵ 74⁸, בלבב 4⁶; but cf. בטח לב 28⁷. — בַּקְּשׁוּ פָנָי] 2 pl. is striking here in the midst of 2 sgs. referring to God, and 1 sg. referring to the poet. But Vrss. had a different text: ⅏ᴮ ἐξεζήτησα τὸ πρόσωπόν σου, so Roman Psalter *quaesivi faciem tuam*, בְּקַשְׁתִּי פָנֶיךָ; 𝔙 *exquisivit te facies mea*, 𝔍 *quaesivit vultus meus*, so Σ and ⅏ˣ ᶜ. ᵃ. ᵀ. and 98 other codd., HP. Compl., Theodoret, בַּקְּשׁוּ פָנָי. ⅏ has the shorter text בקשו פני פנין and attaches יהוה to the next l. The latter is tempting, but improbable. All but ⅏ agree in this l., which is entirely appropriate to context. All but ⅏ in the oldest codd. agree in בקשו פני which is best explained in 𝕳 and then regarded as a marginal pious gl. — **9.** אַל־תַּט בְּאַף עַבְדֶּךָ] phr. *a.λ.* and difficult. Vb. Hiph. of 𝕳 improb. ⅏, 𝔙, 𝔍, take it as Qal, as if with מֵעַבְדְּךָ, so Horsley. עַבְדְּךָ is prob. a later substitution for בִּי, which is required by rhyme. The vb. is best interpreted as Qal. — עֶזְרָתִי] emph. (*v. 22²⁰*). — הָיִיתָ] aorist of past experience in order to get a basis for plea. It makes the l. too long and is gl. — אַל־תִּטְּשֵׁנִי] juss. with neg., two tones. ‡ נטש, vb. Qal *abandon*, elsw. 78⁶⁰ 94¹⁴. — אֱלֹהֵי יִשְׁעִי] *v. 12⁶*, fuller for original יִשְׁעִי, as v.¹ — **10.** וַיהוה] emph. — יַאַסְפֵנִי] Qal impf. אסף in sense of *take up, care for*, late (*v. 26⁹*). This v. is a general statement, not in accord with the urgent petition of the psalmist in a real situation of difficulty. It has five tones and is not in accord with the rhythm. It disturbs the strophical organisation. It is a generalising gl. to make the Ps. more appropriate for synagogue worship, when such breaking up of families took place as in Maccabean times. — **11.** בְּאֹרַח מִישׁוֹר] phr. *a.λ.*; for ארח *v. 8⁹*, מִישׁוֹר *v. 26¹²*. — לְמַעַן שׁוֹרְרָי] gl. from *5⁹*, which was in the mind of the copyist. The vbs. הוֹרֵנִי, נְחֵנִי, were originally at end of line for rhyme in י, characteristic of the Ps. — **12.** צָרָי] pl. sf. i.p. Rhyme and ‖ יפח require sg. י. — קָמוּ] real pf. 3 pl. c. ב pers., elsw. c. עַל 27⁸ 54⁵ (?) 86¹⁴ 92¹² 124²; evidence of another and later hand. — † עֵדֵי־שֶׁקֶר] as Ex. 20¹⁶ Dt. 19¹⁸. ¹⁸ Pr. 6¹⁹ 14⁵, cf. 12¹⁷ 19⁵. ⁹ (pl.), a legal term of generalisation; there is nothing in the rest of the Ps. similar to it. ‡ עֵד n.m. in ψ elsw. phr. † עֵדֵי חמס 35¹¹, as Ex. 23¹ (E) Dt. 19¹⁶; and of the moon Ps. 89³⁸. This clause disturbs the thought and is a gl. — יָפֵחַ] dub., *B*DB. adj. † יָפֵחַ *a.λ.* √יפה only Je. 4³¹, both dub.; better n. formed by י from פוּחַ, which vb. is used in 𝔅, Pss. 10⁵ 12⁶, in the same sense as here. — **13.** לוּלֵא] marked as doubtful in MT. by extraordinary points (*v.* Intr. § 3). ‡ לוּלֵא *if not, unless;* in ψ elsw. לוּלֵי 94¹⁷ 106²³ 119⁹² 124¹. ². ⅏ has ἑαυτῇ = לִי, and

the measure requires another word with the previous clause. לוּלֵא is probably a conflation of two readings, לוּ לִי and לֵא. But the original was doubtless לִי
in rhyme, as all other lines of this Ps. The Ps. is complete here. The
remaining lines are liturgical additions. — בְּאֶרֶץ חַיִּים] phr. elsw. in 52⁷ 142⁶
Is. 38¹¹ 53⁸ Je. 11¹⁹ Ez. 26²⁰ 32²⁸ (+ 5 t. Ez.) Jb. 28¹⁸. — **14.** חַוֵּה] Pi. imv.
repeated in last clause (*v. 25³*), c. אל here, as in 37⁹⁴ Is. 51⁵; usually c. acc.,
as in 25⁵.

PSALM XXVIII., 3 STR. 4⁵.

**Ps. 28 is a prayer: (1) expostulating with Yahweh for aban-
doning His people in peril of death, and crying aloud for help, with
hands uplifted towards the holy shrine (v.¹⁻²); (2) urging that He
discriminate between them and their enemies, visiting the latter
with retribution for their deeds (v.³⁻⁴); (3) blessing Yahweh, the
strength and shield, and rejoicing in Him as the refuge for king
and people (v.⁶⁻⁸). Glosses give a reason for the imprecation upon
enemies (v.⁵) and a liturgical petition for salvation (v.⁹).**

UNTO Thee I call, my Rock: be not silent (turning) from me;
  Lest, if Thou be still (turning) from me, I be compared to them that go down
    to the Pit.
  Hear the voice of my supplication for grace, while I cry unto Thee for help;
  While I lift up my hands, (my God) unto Thy holy Shrine.
DRAG me not away with the wicked, and with workers of trouble;
  Who are speaking peace with their neighbours, while wrong is in their minds.
  O give them according to their deed, and according to the badness of their doings;
  According to the work of their hands, render them their recompense.
BLESSED be Yahweh, because He hath heard the word of my supplication for
    grace!
  Yahweh, my strength and my shield, in whom my heart doth trust!
  And I am helped, and my heart doth exult, therefore with my song will I praise
    Him,
  Yahweh, the strength (for His people), and the refuge for victorious deeds for
    His anointed.

Ps. 28 was in 𝔇. It received two important glosses: (1) v.⁵, a mosaic
from Is. 5¹² and Je. 24⁶ 42¹⁰ 45⁴; (2) v.⁹, a liturgical addition. The Ps. is a
prayer for help in time of war, closing with a certitude of victory. It resembles
Pss. 20, 21 : משיחו v.⁷ = 20⁷; עֹז v.⁷· ⁸ = 21²· ¹⁴; ישועות v.⁷ = 21²· ⁶; שיר v.⁷ = 21¹⁴.
The lifting up of hands towards the דביר v.², is similar in situation to the
sacrifices offered in 20⁴. The Davidic monarchy was still in existence v.⁸,
and the temple worship was carried on v.². The wicked are foreign enemies
who are treacherous, professing peace, but really bent on mischief v.⁸. The
situation is one of extreme peril. The nation is in danger of perishing.

יורדי בור v.¹ is a phrase, of which no earlier usage can be assigned than Ez. and the exilic apocalypse Is. 14. The Pit is the Pit of Sheol. We are led to think, therefore, of the late Babylonian period shortly before the exile. The king was probably Jehoiakim. The wicked nations were probably the Moabites, Ammonites, and Syrians of 2 K. 24².

Str. I. is composed of two stair-like couplets. — **1.** *Unto Thee*], emph. in position, Thee, and no other, defined by *my Rock*, which in the earlier literature is a divine name ; but which has become in the time of composition of this Ps. a concrete expression for Yahweh as the safe refuge of His people (*v.* 19¹⁵ 73²⁸ 92¹⁶ 144¹), an idea taken up again in syn. phrases in v.⁷⁻⁸. A later editor inserted *Yahweh*, at the expense of the measure. — *I call*], emphatic present, what is now being done, and not as EVʳ. " will call " future action. — *be not silent*], changed in the syn. line into a conditional clause, *if Thou be still;* that is ignoring, neglecting the prayer, and the serious situation of the people. These verbs have a pregnant construction in Hebrew involving the insertion of an appropriate verb *turning from me.* — *I be compared to*], not only become like, resemble, but in the eyes of others, before the enemies, be compared to the other nations they have conquered and destroyed. — *that go down to the Pit*]. The Pit is the deep dark dungeon in Sheol, to which the wicked nations descend, according to Is. 14¹⁵·¹⁹ Ez. 26²⁰ 32²⁵·²⁹·³⁰, cf. Ps. 7¹⁶, and not another name for Sheol itself. So the people of God would lose their national existence, just like the other nations destroyed by the Babylonian empire, unless Yahweh their God saved them. — **2.** *Hear the voice of my supplication for grace*]. The prayer is a supplication for favour and bestowal of gracious deliverance. It is aloud, the voice of the petitioners sounding forth in the court of the temple in plaintive tones ; defined by *while I cry unto Thee for help.* These public prayers, recited aloud by priests and people, doubtless, as always, accompanied the sacrifice of whole burnt-offerings in the courts, and the burning of incense in the temple itself. At the same time, the attitude of supplication is expressed in the gesture, *I lift up my hands*, the ancient and natural attitude of invocation and supplication, stretching forth the hands to call and to receive. So in La. 3⁴¹ " Let us lift up our heart to our hands unto God in the heavens." The heart goes up to the uplifted hands and from them upward to God in heaven. But to the author of La. there was no temple; it had been destroyed. This Ps. was, however, sung in the temple, and the hands were lifted up towards the place where Yahweh was conceived as resident. — *Unto Thy holy Shrine*], the *Debir*, the throne room, otherwise called the Holy of Holies of the temple. The measure requires the insertion of *My God*, which was omitted by copyist's mistake, due to the similarity of the Hebrew word with the preposition that follows.

Str. II. is composed of a synth. couplet and one of introverted parallel. — **3.** *Drag me not away*]. The petition for discrimination between the people of Yahweh and the nations that have perished, or are ready to perish, at the hands of the Babylonian empire, now passes over into a plea for discrimination between them and the minor surrounding nations, who are in similar peril, lest they be involved in the common ruin. Israel would not be dragged along and away as captives with them. — *with the wicked*]. These are, as frequently in the preëxilic Pss., wicked nations ‖ *workers of trouble*, the trouble, mischief, injury that they were doing to the people of God in their extremity. They are also treacherous, *speaking peace with their neighbours*]. They pretended to be friendly and in alliance against a common foe ; but in reality they were hostile, ready to betray Israel on the first opportunity. — *wrong is in their minds*], their real intent was to take advantage of the troubles of Israel, to unite with their enemies and prey upon them. This is exactly what Moab and Ammon, the Syrians and Edomites, did, according to 2 K. 24²; cf. also Ez. 25 for the prophet's denunciation of them. — **4.** *O give them ‖ render them their recompense*], an imprecation, in introverted parallel., not upon individuals, but upon the treacherous, cruel, neighbouring nations, calling upon Yahweh to give them exact retribution. — *according to their deed ‖ the badness of their doings ‖ the work of their hands*], the treachery of which they have been guilty and the trouble which they have wrought upon His people. A later editor feels constrained to add a reason for this imprecation, which was evident enough to the author of the Ps. in the historical situation in which he wrote, but not so evident in later times : — **5.** *Because they regard not the works of Yahweh, nor the operation of His hands,*

He breaketh them down and buildeth them not again]. The first
of these clauses is a free citation from Is. 5¹², contrasting the work
of Yahweh's hands with the work of the hands of the wicked
nations, and His work with their work ; with the implication that,
if they had paid attention to His work they would not have done
their work, and because of this neglect, retribution comes upon
them. The second clause is a free citation of a favourite expression of Je. 24⁶ 42¹⁰ 45⁴. Yahweh will break them down, destroy
their national existence, and not build them up again ; their ruin
will be complete and final.

Str. III. is a tetrastich with introverted parallel. It expresses
certitude that the previous petition has been granted, and that by
using again the exact words of v.²ᵃ. This certitude was probably
due, as in Ps. 20, to some external evidence, given either by a
prophetic utterance, or by some sign of the acceptance of the
sacrifice ; and so the Ps. changes its entire tone to a blessing.—**6-7.** *Blessed be Yahweh*]. Such benedictions subsequently
became the ritual conclusion of every Ps. or liturgical selection
(*v.* Intr., § 40). *Yahweh* is repeated for emphasis in the second
line in order to attach to Him, in apposition, the attributes
already involved in " my Rock " v.¹, namely, *my strength and my
shield*. This phrase, only found here, combines the usual conceptions that Yahweh is the source of strength to His people (*v.* 21¹
46² 84⁶), and that He is the shield, interposing between them and
their enemies (as 3⁴ 7¹¹ 18³). — *in whom my heart doth trust*].
The calm confidence to which the psalmist has now come, is in
striking antithesis to the expostulation for neglect and the cry for
help with which it begins. — *And I am helped*], the help has been
given and is now enjoyed, and as a necessary consequence, *my
heart doth exult*]. The trust of the heart has passed over into
exultation, and the vow, *with my song will I praise Him*], the
song of thanksgiving which is to accompany a thank-offering for
the victory over enemies, now regarded as certain. The whole is
summed up in the common experience of king and people. —
8. *Yahweh*], in apposition with the object of the previous verb,
and not an independent clause ; and therefore having in apposition, as v.⁷, and not as predicates, *the strength*, as v.⁷, explained
more fully as *the refuge. — victorious deeds*], from whom deeds

of victory come as a gift, as in 21². — *for His people*], the nation,
as 𝕲; but 𝕳, by error, has "for them," which must have the
same interpretation, although there is nothing to which the 3d
plural refers. — *for His anointed*], their king, anointed by Yahweh over His people, and so His representative, belonging to
Him as His own.

9. When the Ps. was adapted for public worship, probably in
the final Psalter, a liturgical addition was made in order to gen-
eralise this warlike situation.   This is a tetrameter couplet. —
O save], in the later situation more probable than "give victory,"
which would be necessary in accordance with v.⁸ if original to the
Psalm.   But then we miss the reference to "Thine anointed,"
which would be expected rather than "Thy people," as in v.⁸;
|| *thine inheritance*, which also must refer to the people, conceived
as the special divine possession.   The absence of reference to the
king here can hardly be explained otherwise than that this couplet
was appended when Israel had been so long without a king that
it was not natural to think of him any more. — *And be Thou shepherd*], and as a shepherd lifts up and carries in his bosom the
lambs of the flock, *carry them forever*.   The author probably had
in mind Yahweh the shepherd of Is. 40¹¹.

1. יִהְיֶה] makes l. too long, and is a gl. — צוּרִי] for Yahweh, as *18²;* in early
literature as name, later as archaism, fig. of ⸰ as refuge, *v.* 19¹⁵ 73²⁸ 92¹⁶ 144¹.
𝕲, 𝖸, as usual, ὁ Θεός μου, *Deus meus.* — אַל תֶּחֱרַשׁ] Qal juss. 2 m., with neg.
‡ [חָרַשׁ] vb. † Qal *be silent:* (1) alw. of God keeping silence or neglecting
prayer 35²² 50³ 83² 109¹, c. אֶל 39¹⁸, מִן *28¹;* (2) subj. אזנים Mi. 7¹⁶ (be deaf).
Hiph. *keep silence*, neglecting evil Ps. 50²¹ Hb. 1¹³ Is. 42¹⁴, neglecting repentance Ps. 32³. — מִמֶּנִּי] is pregnant, *turning from me*, cf. 22²² 43¹. — [רֶהֱשֶׁה]
final clause. ‡ [חשׁה] vb. Qal *be silent, inactive, still*, of Yahweh *28¹;* of
waves 107²⁹. Hiph. *exhibit silence, be silent* 39³, כמוב preg. *away from good.* —
וְנִמְשַׁלְתִּי] ו consec., Niph. pf. 1 sg., conj. introducing the apod. of the conditional clause.   † משׁל vb. *represent, be like*, in ψ only Niph. *be like, similar,
be compared;* c. עם *28¹* = 143⁷, c. כְּ 49¹³. ²¹; cf. c. אֶל Is. 14¹⁰; elsw. Hiph.
Is. 46⁵; Hithp. c. כ Jb. 30¹⁹. — **2.** תַּחֲנוּנַי] phr., elsw. ψ v.⁶ 31²⁸ 86⁶ 130²
140⁷, cf. 116¹. ‡ [תַּחֲנוּן] n.[m.] only pl. abstr., *supplication for favour*, alw.
in ψ to God; elsw. 143¹; alw. תַּחֲנוּנֵי, except 86⁶ הַתַּחֲנוּנִים. — [בְּשַׁוְּעִי] Pi. inf.
cstr. sf., c. ב temporal (*v. 5³*). — בְּנָשְׂאִי יָדַי] inf. cstr., ב temporal, cf. for this
gesture 63⁵ La. 2¹⁹; cf. also נשׂא נפשׁ אל Pss. 25¹ 86⁴ 143⁸. — ‡ [דְּבִיר] n.m. the
hindmost room of the temple 1 K. 6⁵⁻³¹; the earlier name for קדשׁ הקדשׁים,
only here in ψ, translated *oracle*, AV., RV., after Σ, Aq., 𝕵, on the incorrect

theory that it was derived from דבר *speak*. "Chancel," Dr., is tempting, but does not really correspond with the mng. of the word. 𝕲 εἰς ναὸν ἅγιόν σου, cf. PBV., is correct, distinguishing the ναός as the inner sanctuary, the shrine, from the ἱερόν, the temple as a whole. — [קָדְשֶׁךְ] might be interpreted of the larger sanctuary, as in 74³; but better, as in 5⁸, as attribute of the דביר. The l. is defective; prob. add אלי omitted because of similarity to אל.— **3.** [אַל־תִּמְשְׁכֵנִי] Qal juss., c. neg. משׁך (*v. 10⁹*) *drag along* and *away*. We must give these two words, though connected by Makkeph, two beats. 𝕲 substitutes for sf. τὴν ψυχήν μου, which is more prob., for then אל־תמשׁך would have but one tone and נפשׁי the other. — [דֹּבְרֵי] Qal. ptc. pl. cstr., verbal force, rel. clause, c. עִם, usage of JED and earlier writers; P and later writers prefer דבר את.— ‡ [שָׁלוֹם] n.m.: (1) *soundness, health* 38⁴; (2) *welfare, prosperity* 73³ 122⁶·⁷·⁸; † רב שׁלום 37¹¹ 72⁷; (3) *quiet, peacefulness, tranquillity, security* 4⁹ 37³⁷; (4) *peace, friendship, alliance*, between men, אִישׁ שׁלומִי *man of my friendship* 41¹⁰, cf. Je. 20¹⁰ 38²² Ob. 7, שׁלֹמָיו (‖ בריח) Ps. 55²¹, cf. 7⁵ 69²³, דבר שׁ׳ עם 28³ 35²⁾ Je. 9⁷, בקשׁ שׁ׳ Ps. 34¹⁵, ‖ צדקה 72⁸; (5) *peace* with God in establishment of covenant relations (common in Je., Ez., Is.², P) 29¹¹ 35²⁷ 85⁹·¹¹, cf. Is. 54¹³ 60¹⁷; invoked upon Jerusalem שׁ׳ על Pss. 125⁵ 128⁶, שׁ׳ רב 119¹⁶⁵; (6) *peace* from war (freq. in hist. and prophet. bks.) 55¹⁹ 147¹⁴, antith. מלחמה 120⁵·⁷.— [בְּרָכָם] long form (*v. 4⁵*), cf. with לבִי v.⁷ short form used twice, is dub.; prob. due to dittog. of ב. — **4.** [הֶן־לְהֶם]. The Makkeph reduces the tones of the l. to four. This is impossible. We would naturally expect here cohort. רָנֶה, as 69²⁸ 86¹⁶. But the txt. must have been changed at an early date, for the same phr. has been inserted by copyist's error in next l. at the expense of the measure. For נהן in the sense of *requite v. 10¹⁴*. — [רֹעַ] a.λ. ψ, but in this phr. found also in Dt. 28²⁰ Is. 1¹⁶ Je. 4⁴ + 6 t. Ho. 9¹⁵, cf. 1 S. 25³, *evil, badness*, for רעה v.³.— [מַעֲלֵליהֶם] pl. cstr. sf. 3 pl. ‡ [מַעֲלָל] n.m. *deed:* (1) of God 77¹² 78⁷; (2) *wanton deeds* of men 28⁴ 106²⁹·³⁹ and passages given above in other Liter. — [מַעֲשׂה ידים] of God, as v.⁵, 92⁵ 111⁷ 143⁵, v. 8⁴; of men, as here, 90¹⁷ 115⁴ 135¹⁵. — ‡ [גְּמוּל] n.m.: (1) *requital, recompense* 28⁴ 94² 137⁸; (2) *benefit* from God 103², v. vb. גמל (7⁵). — **5.** [יְבִינוּ] prob. Hiph., as 33¹⁵, where אֵל is used. Qal in ψ alw. c. acc. or לְ, although Qal form is the same and the mng. essentially the same. — [פְּעֻלֹּת] pl. cstr. of פְּעֻלָּה (*v. 17⁴*) *deeds of Yahweh*, change from פעל of v.⁴. The use of this word together with ידיו מַעֲשֵׂה shows an intentional antith. between human deeds and divine deeds. The sentence resembles Is. 5¹², and is a loose citation from it. — [יֶהֶרְסֵם וְלֹא יִבְנֵם] 𝕲 καθελεῖς, οἰκοδομήσεις, 𝕍, 𝔍 *destrues, aedificabis*. Possibly an older txt. had ptc., as Je. 45⁴. This clause is free citation from Je. 24⁶ 42¹⁰ 45⁴. The v. has most naturally a sentence of 4 + 3 tones from Is. 5¹², and a sentence of 3 tones from Je. The first sentence is too long, the second too short, and they cannot be properly arranged in accordance with the measure of the Ps. They are glosses, so Che. — **7.** [עֻזִּי וּמָגִנִּי] phr. a.λ., but יי as strength of Yahweh bestowed for the defence of His people also 46² 84⁶ (*v. 8³*). — [בּו] defines rel. clause with rel. omitted. — ו [וַיַּעֲלֹז] consec., Qal impf., result of previous pf. † עלז vb. *exult*, only Qal, alw. abs. 28⁷ 60⁸

(= 108⁸) 68⁵ 94⁸ 96¹² 149⁶, elsw. Is. 23¹² Je. 11¹⁵ 15¹⁷ 50¹¹ 51³⁹ 2 S. 1²⁰ Zp. 3¹⁴ Hb. 3¹⁸ Pr. 23¹⁶. Here subj. לב as seat of emotions, cf. 4⁸ 13⁶. — [וּמִשִּׁירִי *with my song*, v. Intr. § 24. — [אֲהוֹרֶנּוּ] strong form of Hiph. impf. 1 sg., c. strong sf. 3 sg. (v. Ges. § 53 R. 7). ירה (v. Intr. § 39) expressing resolution, future purpose of praise. 𝔊 has a variant txt. here: καὶ ἀνέθαλεν ἡ σάρξ μου · καὶ ἐκ θελήματός μου ἐξομολογήσομαι αὐτῷ, so 𝔙. 𝔖 agrees with 𝔊 in the first clause, but with 𝔥 and other Vrss. in the second. 𝔊 had בשרי or שארי for מִשִּׁירי, and prob. לבי was transposed with it, and possibly חלף was read for עָלו. — 8. [יְּךָ־לָמִי] 𝔊, 𝔖, 𝔙 have יָמוֹ, so Horsley, Jebb, Dathe, Köster, Che., Bä., al.; more prob., espec. in view of the use of עם in v.⁹ and its parall. with משיחו, so mentioning both king and people. — [הוּא] emph., at end of l., Str., and Ps., is unnecessary, and as it makes l. too long, it is doubtless a gl.

PSALM XXIX., 5 STR. 4⁴.

Ps. 29 is a hymn, describing the advent of Yahweh in a storm. (1) The angels worship Yahweh in the heavenly temple (v.¹⁻²); (2) the thunder of Yahweh's voice is a great power (*a*) on the waters (v.³⁻⁴); (*b*) upon Lebanon and its cedars (v.⁵⁻⁶); (*c*) upon the wilderness and its forests (v.⁸⁻⁹); (3) Yahweh, enthroned over the Flood, reigns forever and bestows blessings on His people (v.¹⁰⁻¹¹).

ASCRIBE to Yahweh, ye sons of gods,
 Ascribe to Yahweh glory and strength;
 Ascribe to Yahweh the glory of His name;
 Render worship to Yahweh in holy ornaments.
THE voice of Yahweh is upon the waters,
 (The voice of) Yahweh is upon great waters;
 The voice of Yahweh is in power,
 The voice of Yahweh is in majesty.
THE voice of Yahweh breaketh cedars,
 Yahweh breaketh in pieces the cedars of Lebanon,
 And He maketh Lebanon skip like a calf,
 Sirion like a young yore-ox.
THE voice of Yahweh whirleth the wilderness about,
 Yahweh whirleth about the wilderness of Kadesh,
 The voice of Yahweh whirleth about the (terebinths),
 (The voice of Yahweh) strippeth bare the forests.
YAHWEH sat enthroned (over) the Flood,
 Yahweh (will sit) enthroned forever;
 Yahweh giveth strength to His people,
 Yahweh blesseth His people with peace.

Ps. 29 was in 𝕯 and 𝕸 (v. Intr. §§ 27, 31). In 𝕲 a liturgical assignment appears ἐξοδίου σκηνῆς, the עצרת, coming in the Jewish year the
next day after the seventh day of Tabernacles, so Bar Hebraeus. But the
earliest Palestinian tradition knows nothing of this. *Sofrim*, c. 18, § 3, assigns
it to Pentecost. The Ps. for the עצרה is 65 (v. De., *Psalmen*, pp. 266–267).
The advent of Yahweh in a storm may be compared with 18⁸ ˢ𝑞.. The בני אלים
angels, v.¹ = 89⁷, cf. Jb. 38⁷, implies the influence of Persian angelology.
הדרת קדש v.², the holy ornament, or vestment of angelic priests, implies a fully
developed priesthood as expressed in P. The use of מבול v.¹⁰ for the ancient
Flood is also in accordance with P. V.¹⁻² are cited in 96⁷⁻⁹ᵃ except that
מׁשפחות עמים is used for בני אלים, an intentional change. Ps. 29 must be
earlier than this royal Ps., which is used in 1 Ch. 16²³ ˢ𝑞.. The Ps. seems to
belong to the Persian period subsequent to Nehemiah.

Str. I. The parall. of this tetrastich is stairlike; though syn. in
the main, each line gives an additional idea. — **1–2.** *Ascribe to
Yahweh*], thrice repeated; the recognition of Yahweh and the
giving utterance to this recognition in worship. — *Render worship*] expressed usually by bowing down or prostration. — *ye sons
of gods*], a term for angels as belonging to the class of divine
beings; and yet in Hebrew conception the servants and worshippers of Yahweh, cf. Ps. 89⁷ Jb. 38⁷. That which is ascribed
is *glory and strength*, the former intensified in the next line, *the
glory of His name*], manifested in His revelation of Himself in
His name, or that which is made known and is known of Him.
The latter is the theme of praise as 8³, and so in 𝕲 conceived as
the praise itself. — *in holy ornaments*]. The angels are conceived
after the manner of ministering priests in the earthly temple as
clothed in sacred vestments.

Three tetrastichs describe the voice of Yahweh, the thunder-
storm, in its effects upon nature, upon the sea, the mountains, and
the wilderness. **Str. II.** The thunder-storm is first described on
the sea. — **3–4.** *The voice of Yahweh*], eight times repeated in the
original, but omitted by copyists in v.³ᶜ, v.⁹ᵇ, inserted in gloss v.⁷,
leaving seven times, the symbolical holy number. In accordance
with ancient conceptions the thunder is the voice of God. Yahweh
descends in theophany to earth, in a storm, either for vengeance
upon His enemies or for the deliverance of His people, *v.* 18⁸ ˢ𝑞..
— *upon the waters ‖ upon great waters*], in accordance with usage
of the phrase, the waters of the Mediterranean Sea, producing, as

is suggested, by *in power* ‖ *in majesty*, powerful, majestic waves, cf. 93⁴. An ancient scribe inserted an explanatory gloss in different measure : " The God of glory thundered," which destroys the symmetry of the Str. — **Str. III. 5–6.** The thunder-storm is next described in the mountains. — *breaketh*], is intensified into, *breaketh in pieces the cedars*], intensified into *cedars of Lebanon*, the giant trees growing in that region, famed in antiquity. The storm is of such extreme violence that it breaks off the limbs, breaks down the trees themselves and breaks them in pieces. — *He maketh to skip*], implying an earthquake accompanying the storm, as 18⁸ ˢᑫ· 114⁴⁻⁶ as usual in connection with theophanies. It shakes the mountains on which the cedars grew. 𝕳, 𝕲, and all Vrss. make the obj. *them* refer to cedars, which would not be harmonious with breaking them in pieces. The suffix is therefore a copyist's error. Lebanon is the object in this line, as Sirion in the next. — *Lebanon*], the range of mountains along the coast dividing Syria from Phoenicia. — *Sirion*], the Phoenician name for Mt. Hermon, the giant of the parallel range of Anti-Lebanon, as Dt. 3⁹. These great mountain ranges skip and dance about under the power of the earthquake ; *like a calf* ‖ *a young yore-ox*], leaping and dancing about when they are excited.

7. *The voice of Yahweh divideth the flames of fire*], so 𝕲, 𝖁, 𝕵, PBV., AV., referring doubtless to the forked lightning ; but 𝕳, followed by RVᵐ., has " heweth out," which is difficult to understand and is probably erroneous. This line, in any case, interrupts the thought, is isolated, having no place in the strophical organisation of the Ps., and is a gloss.

Str. IV. 8–9*b*. The author now turns to the wilderness to describe the storm there. — *whirleth about*], thrice repeated, an appropriate term for the whirling effect of a severe storm ; so 𝕲. 𝕵 takes the alternate meaning of the vb. " make writhe," in pangs, especially of childbirth, so Dr. for the three. It is improbable that the meaning would change. The difficulty is in the Hebrew word rendered " hinds," which seems to favour the latter rendering, the thought being that the storm so frightens them that it brings a premature delivery. But it is difficult to see why hinds should be mentioned rather than other animals, or why they should be mentioned alone, when this Ps. is so striking in the use of parallelism.

It seems better therefore to read by a different interpretation of the same original form, *terebinths*, and so ‖ with *forests;* the former being the great trees characteristic of this region. This makes the entire Str. simple and harmonious. The power of the storm is emphasised in whirling them about. — *strippeth bare*], the leaves, boughs, and probably also barks of trees. — *the wilderness*], as we would suppose from the antith. to Lebanon would be in the South, the wilderness of the wanderings, when Israel came up out of Egypt; more specifically *Kadesh*, that part of the wilderness which centres in the ancient sacred place, where Israel sojourned a long time prior to their entrance into the Holy Land, elsewhere known as Kadesh Barnea.

9c. A copyist introduced a line, taking up in part the ideas of the first Str.: *and in His temple*, probably referring to the heavenly temple, although this is not certain; especially as *all of them* 𝔥, *all* 𝔊, 𝔍, seems to refer to the angels, and *saith glory* is a repetition of v.$^{1b-2a}$. But the difficulty which then arises is, that this line comes in here without any apparent propriety. It has no manner of connection with the twelve previous lines, making three tetrastichs, and none with the tetrastich that follows. The original author, if he wished to introduce that thought, would have used a tetrastich for that purpose. It is evidently a liturgical gloss, and in that case may refer to the earthly temple. Doubtless the thought is an appropriate one, if it were expressed in the style and method of the author of the Ps. As Umbreit says, "Whilst we still hear the voice of the Lord in the rushing of the storm through the forests stripped of their leaves, the poet snatches us away at once from the tumult of earth, and places us amid the choirs of the heavenly temple, which above, in a holy silence, sing glory and praise to the Eternal." But the difficulty is that this idea is not clearly brought out, and the single line tacked on here is too indefinite to give such a grand conception.

Str. V. **10–11** describes Yahweh on His throne bestowing strength and blessing on His people in a stairlike tetrastich. — *Yahweh*] is repeated four times, once in each line, in accordance with the style of the Ps. — *sat enthroned*], historical aorist. — *over the Flood*], so by an easy emendation of a separable preposition for an inseparable one, regaining thereby the lost tone for the

measure. The inseparable preposition might be rendered, " at
the Flood " RV. ; but 𝔊, 𝕵, give it a local sense which is more
probable. — *will sit enthroned*], future, in accordance with 𝔊, 𝕵,
which is more probable than 𝕳 with ו consec., making the second
use of the vb. of the same tense as the first, which can hardly be
reconciled with *forever*. There is indeed an antith. between His
reigning in the past, at the time of the greatest of all traditional
storms, the Flood, directing and controlling it, as He did the
storm described above, and His perpetual reign in the future.
The reign of Yahweh is here conceived of as on earth, and so we
have an antistrophe to v.¹⁻², the worship in the heavenly temple.
Accordingly as the King of Israel, *He giveth to His people ‖ blesseth
them* with the gifts of *strength* and *peace*. The storm has passed
away and the last word of the Ps. is peace. "The beginning
of the Psalm shows us the heavens open and the throne of God in
the midst of the angelic songs of praise, and the close of the
Psalm shows us on earth, in the midst of the angry voice of Yahweh shaking all things, His people victorious and blessed with
peace. *Gloria in excelsis* is the beginning, and *pace in terris*
the end." De.

1. הָבוּ] Qal. imv. ‡ יהב vb. Qal: (1) *give ;* c. acc. *help*, c. לֹ pers. 60¹³ =
108¹³; (2) *ascribe* glory ; so here and v.², elsw. 96⁷· ⁷· ⁸ = 1 Ch. 16²⁸· ²⁸· ²⁹;
cf. גִּיל Dt. 32⁸. — בני אלים] as 89⁷ (*v.* Intr. § 36) = בני אלהים *angels.* 𝔖, 𝕵,
adferte filios arietum, בני אילים. 𝔊 has conflation of both readings. — עֹז]
𝔊 τιμήν, cf. 8³. — 2. כְּבוֹד שְׁמוֹ] as 66² 79⁹ 96⁸. — הַדְרַת קֹדֶשׁ [הֲדֲרֵת] cstr. of
‡ [הֲדָרָה] n.f. (1) *adornment :* c. קדש always in connection with worship, elsw.
96⁹ = 1 Ch. 16²⁹ 2 Ch. 20²¹; cf. הררי קדש Ps. 110³. Cf. הדר v.⁴, as qualifying
the thunder (*v.* 8⁶). 𝔊 has בחצרות קדש, *in the sacred courts, i.e.* of the temple
(cf. 𝔊 of 96⁹). Ps. 96⁷⁻⁹ᵃ is the same as 29¹⁻², except that משפחות עמים takes
the place of בני אלים, and a line is inserted 96⁸ᵇ. It should be said that חצרות
is more suited to 96⁹, and there is no more impropriety in thinking of the courts
of the heavenly temple, where angels worship, than of the heavenly temple
itself. At the same time there is no usage to justify it. 2 Ch. 20²¹ justifies
𝕳, and as the more difficult reading it is to be preferred. — 3-4. עַל־הַמָּיִם]
‖ עַל מִים רבים; rd. for עַל, אֵלֵי to get the fourth beat, and prefix קוֹל to יהוה in
v.³ᶜ as in 4ᵃ·ᵇ. Then rd. במו כח for בכח, and במו הדר for כהדר, as in v.⁶. אֵל
הכבוד הרעים is a gl. explaining קוֹל יהוה. — 5. שֹׁבֵר] Qal ptc. of continuous action, *breaketh in pieces*, possibly should be impf., repeated in v.⁵ᵇ; but not
ו consec. impf. after ptc. or impf., which would make an emph. change of
tense difficult to explain ; rather simple ו with impf. — ארזי הלבנון] phr.

104¹⁶ +, cf. 92¹³; 80¹¹.   ‡ לְבָנוֹן n. pr., mountain range extending along the coast of Syria; elsw. v.⁶, 72¹⁶. — 6. וירקידם] not ו consec., but ו coörd.; c. Hiph. impf. of רקד with sf. 3 pl. referring to trees; so 現, attaching לבנון to next l., but 𝔊, 𝔙, make לבנון second object of vb. *vitulum Libani*. The sf. was prob. due to disarrangement, and should be regarded as gl.   ‡ רקד Qal *skip*, of mountains 114⁴·⁶. Hiph. only here. — כמו] is a separate word; if it had been meant to be attached, we should have had כעגל. — ‡ שריון] n.pr., name of Hermon among the Sidonians; cf. Dt. 3⁹. — בן ראמים] young of the yore-oxen, ראם (*v. 22²²*). — 7. This v. stands so by itself that it is prob. a gl. of addition. — הצב] after שבר (v.⁵) is become ptc.   ‡ הצב vb. Qal *hew out* stone esp., metaph. *hew in pieces* Ho. 6⁵; here להבות אש dub. because it is difficult to get *divide, cleave* from *hew out*, and there is no justification in usage. Che., Du., think we must emend the text by inserting the word *rocks* and making two lines here, the flames of fire, the lightning, being the instrument of the cleaving of the rocks. But the effect of lightning upon rocks is not that of *hewing out*. 𝔊, 𝔙, 𝕵, 𝔖, prob. rd. הצץ *dividing*, but this is not a good idea. Better originally חצוי להבות אש. This a natural gl. as 18¹⁵ Hb. 3¹¹. — להבות אש] for lightning, also אש להבות 105³²; cf. La. 2³.   ‡ להבה n.f. *flame;* elsw. ψ 83¹⁵ 106¹⁸. — 8. יָחִיל] Hiph. impf.   ‡ חול Qal, (1) *whirl, dance,* 96⁹ 114⁷; (2) *twist, writhe,* as in anguish 55⁵ 77¹⁷ 97⁴. Polel, (1) *dance* 87⁷; (2) *writhe, bring to birth,* 90²; (3) *whirl about* 29⁹. (4) Polal, *be brought forth,* 51⁷. Hiph. *whirl about* 29⁸·⁸. 𝕵 in v.⁸ *parturire faciens,* so Dr., and in v.⁹ *obstetricans;* 𝔊 in v.⁸ συνσείοντος and in v.⁹ καταρτιζομένου, *make to whirl about,* suited to the wilderness. — ‡ קְדֵשׁ] n. pr. only here in ψ, the Kadesh of the wilderness of wandering. — 9. יְחוֹלֵל] is taken by 𝔊 as ptc. καταρτιζόμενου, as if כֵּן; but it is Polel impf. in the mng. *whirl about,* as above. — אַיָּלוֹת] *v. 18³⁴,* so 𝔊 ἐλάφους, 𝕵 *cervas;* but this not suited to the context. Therefore rd. אֵלוֹת *terebinths,* Lowth., Horsley, Secker, Venema, Dy., Che., al. (∥ יְעָרִים *forests*); elsw. alw. single tree. — וַיֶּחֱשֹׂף] the ו cannot be ו consec., but conj. It was, however, a gl., for קול יהוה must be prefixed for measure.   ‡ חשׂף vb. Qal, *strip, make bare,* only here in ψ; cf. Jo. 1⁷ of locusts. — יְעָרוֹת] elsw. pl. = יערים.   ‡ יַעַר n.m. (1) *wood, forest, wooded height;* prob. 72¹⁶; (2) as hiding-place for wild beasts 50¹⁰ 80¹⁴ 104²⁰; (3) as stripped by thunderstorm 29⁹, in metaph. of Yahweh's judgments 83¹⁵; (4) *trees of forest* עצי יער fig. as singing before Yahweh 96¹² = 1 Ch. 16³³ Is. 44²³; שָׂדֵי יער Ps. 132⁶ seems to be n. pr. = קרית יערים. — וּבְהֵיכָלוֹ] used sometimes of heavenly temple, sometimes of temple in Jerusalem; if the former here, a return to v.¹; if the latter, a general statement not congruous to the context, and so a gl. — כֻּלּוֹ] 𝔊 πᾶς τις, rd. prob. כל יאמר for כלו אמר כבוד as in v.². — 10. לַמַּבּוּל יָשָׁב] as לכסא 9⁵, *sit enthroned;* but vb. usually c. acc. or עַל. But another word is needed here. Du. לְ מֵעַל, but עֲלִי is sufficient.   ‡ מַבּוּל elsw. only of the deluge Gn. 6¹⁷ 7⁶ + 9¹¹ + 10¹·³² 11¹⁰ (P); therefore prob. so here. *B*DB regards the etymology as dub. The historic reference to the deluge is suited to a thunderstorm, and is antithet. with לִשְׁאוֹל. — וַיֵּשֶׁב] ו consec., Qal impf. of ישׁב; it is improbable that this refers to past also. Point ו conj. and future as 𝔊, 𝕵, Che., וְיֵשֵׁב. It is prob. that the order was, as in the other lines, יהוה ישׁב.

PSALM XXX., 4 STR. 4⁴.

Ps. 30 is a thanksgiving: (1) **exalting Yahweh for raising
up the nation from death** (v.$^{2.4}$); (2) **contrasting the momen-
tary anger of Yahweh with the lifetime of his favour** (v.$^{6.8}$);
(3) **giving the plea that had been made for deliverance** (v.$^{9-11}$);
in order to the climax; (4) **the contrast of the previous mourning with the present gladness expressed in festal dances and
songs of thanksgiving** (v.$^{12-13}$). **The glosses** (v.$^{3\ 5.\ 7}$) **adapt the
Ps. to more general use.**

I EXALT Thee, Yahweh, for Thou hast drawn *me* up;
    And hast not let mine enemies be glad, even *mine.*
    Yahweh, out of Sheol, Thou hast brought *me* up,
    From among them that go down to the Pit, Thou hast quickened *me.*

A MOMENT (passeth) in anger; a lifetime *in favour;*
    At even weeping cometh in to lodge; but in the morning a shout of joy.
    In favour Thou didst cause (mine honour) to stand firm in strength;
    Didst Thou hide Thy face, I became dismayed.

U NTO Thee I was crying, and unto (my God) I was making supplication for favour:
    " What profit is there in my blood, when I go down to the Pit?
    Will the dust praise Thee, declare Thy faithfulness?
    Hear and be gracious, become helper to me."

T HOU hast turned my mourning into dancing for me,
    Thou didst loose my sackcloth and gird me with gladness;
    That my glory might make melody to Thee and not be still.
    Yahweh, my God, forever will I give thanks to Thee.

Ps. 30 was in 𝔇 and later in 𝔐 (*v.* Intr. §§ 27, 31). A liturgical assignment appears in שיר חנכת הבית. It is evident that this cannot refer to the
house of David, 2 S. 5¹¹, as 𝔊$^{B.}$ τοῦ Δαυείδ (but τῷ Δαυείδ 𝔊$^{N. A. R. U}$);
the texts of 𝔍 also differ); or to the site of the temple, 1 Ch. 21$^{26\ sq.}$ 22¹,
whether the temple of Solomon, or the second temple, Ezr. 6¹⁶, even if the
composition of the Ps. could be put so early; but it is a liturgical assignment
to the Feast of Dedication, instituted by Judas Maccabaeus 165 B.C. to com-
memorate the purification of the temple after its desecration by Antiochus
Epiphanes, 1 Mac. 4$^{52\ sq.}$ 2 Mac. 10$^{1\ sq.}$, mentioned as observed Jn. 10^{22}. This
is indeed the liturgical use of the Ps. according to Sopherim, c. 18, § 2
(*v.* Intr. § 39). 𝔊 has also εἰς τὸ τέλος = למנצח (but not in 𝔊$^{N. A. T}$). Such
an insertion would be more difficult than its omission by scribal error. It is
indeed the kind of Ps. we should expect to be taken up into 𝔇𝔐 (*v.* Intr.
§ 33). The Ps. is exceedingly poetic in conception and also in form, after
the glosses have been removed. It is artistic, arranged on the scheme of

four tones, four lines, and four strophes. The glosses v.[3. 5. 7] make it more appropriate for liturgical use. The Ps. is national and not individual. The use of ירד בור v.[4], and ירד שחת v.[10], is not earlier than Ez., referring to the resurrection of the nation from the death of the Exile. V.[8] resembles 18[34]; v.[10], Is. 38[18], cf. Ps. 6[6]; בכורי, v.[13]=נפשי, characteristic of Pss. 7[3] 16[9] 57[9] 108[2], all 𝔅. V.[8b] = 104[29a]. V.[5b] = 97[12b]; but the latter is probably original, this v. in our Ps. being a gl. It is probable that v.[6a] depends upon Is. 54[7-8]; and v.[12] upon Je. 31[13]; and therefore the Ps. must belong to the Restoration; then not to the earlier days of distress and trial from enemies, but to the more prosperous times subsequent to Nehemiah, when the nation had revived and its perils were past.

Str. I. is a tetrastich, syn. in the first, third, and fourth lines; but the second line is synth. to them all. — **2-4.** *I exalt Thee, Yahweh*], cf. Ex. 15[21] Ps. 34[8], in thanksgiving and praise; resumed in v.[13], the last word of the Ps. "I will give thanks to Thee," thus enclosing the whole Ps. within this resolution, making it a song of thanksgiving. — *for Thou hast drawn me up*], from what, is not mentioned here, so that some think of a cistern, or pit, in accordance with Je. 38[6-13], misled by the gloss v.[3], which separates v.[2] from its syn. v.[4], where this clause is taken up and defined in the clause: *out of Sheol Thou hast brought me up;* the conception being not of peril of death to the individual or nation, from which Yahweh had delivered him; but of real death, the nation having in fact suffered death in its exile and gone down into Sheol, the abode of the nations destroyed by their conquerors, in accordance with the conception of Ez. 37. This is also sustained by the constant usage of the phrase: *them that go down to the Pit*], referring to conquered nations descending to the Pit in Sheol, under the wrath of God against them as His enemies and the enemies of His people. And accordingly we must render the parallel Hebrew word, not "kept me alive " EV[s]., but *quickened*, restored to life, revived; referring to the nation in exile, already dead in Sheol. This Str. has an unusual kind of parall., in that the two lines of v.[4] are syn. with v.[2a] whereas v.[2b] is synth. not only to v.[2a] but also to v.[4] as well. — *And hast not let mine enemies be glad*], because of the final overthrow and death of the Jewish people. — *even mine*], emphasising the enemies as personal enemies to the nation. "Over me," EV[s]., is indeed implied in the sentence, but is not expressed, and certainly is not a proper translation of the original, which I have rendered as above.

3. *Yahweh, my God, I cried unto Thee for help, and Thou didst heal me*]. This is a pentameter line in the midst of tetrameters, and is difficult to adjust to the other lines in any scheme of parall. It mars the beauty of the parall. as stated above. It adds a line to a Str. already complete without it. It interrupts the harmony of the thanksgiving and is doubtless a gloss. It reminds us of 6^3 Is. 38^{9-20}, both of which were probably in the mind of the editor, who conceived that a petition introduced here would be more suited for public prayer.

5. This verse is a trimeter couplet, a call to the pious to make melody in temple worship.

> Make melody to Yahweh, ye pious,
> And give thanks in a sacred commemoration of Him.

It is an anticipation of v.[13], and the second line probably a citation from 97^{12b}. — *in a sacred commemoration*]. This is more in accordance with Hebrew usage than " remembrance of His holiness," PBV., AV., although favoured by 𝕲, 𝔍. This couplet is a liturgical addition, disturbing the order of thought, the measure and the strophical organisation.

Str. II. is composed of two couplets, the first syn., the second antith., but so that the antith. really extends to that which is already given in the antith. halves of the two syn. lines of the previous couplet. — **6.** *A moment*], a single moment of time, the briefest time that is known to usage. — (*passeth*) *in anger*]. So brief is Yahweh's anger against His people ; antith. with a *lifetime*, a long life *in favour*], so long does His favour towards them last. All this is relative and may be compared to Ps. 90^4, where God's measurement of time is so different from that of men. It is a nation's experience the psalmist has in mind, doubtless that given in Is. 54^{7-8}, where the prophet describes Yahweh's dealings with Zion (*v.* Br.[MP 398 sq.])

> For a small moment have I forsaken thee: but with great compassion will I gather thee.
> In a gush of wrath I hid my face from thee for a moment;
> But with everlasting kindness I have compassion on thee, saith Yahweh thy Redeemer.

— *Weeping*], personified as a traveller, a messenger from Yahweh, parallel with anger, *cometh in to lodge* as a guest to pass the
night, when the day is over, *at even;* but another traveller is also
on the way from Yahweh as a messenger of favour. He comes
with the break of day, *in the morning.* He is *a shout of joy*, and
this guest comes to stay. The last antithesis is taken up first in
its application to the salvation of the nation. — **8.** *In favour*],
the favour of Yahweh extended to the nation through its long
history prior to the Exile. — *Thou didst cause to stand firm*]. As
Ps. 18³⁴ king David on the high places of the battle-field, so here
the nation. — *mine honour*], as ⅏, Ʋ, ⅀. The honour of the
nation was in peril through the attacks of the enemy. Yahweh
had restored that honour by bringing them back from exile, and
had made it to stand firm against repeated assaults. — *in strength*],
adverbial accusative intensifying the idea of the vb. ; so as to resist all enemies. AV., RV., attach strength to the " mountain " in
the rendering " made my mountain to stand strong," as essentially
Ʒ, PBV. ; similarly " established strength for my mountain " Dr.
" Perhaps ' Thou didst place a fortress upon my mountain ' " Pe.
" Zion, strong by position and art, may be thought of, partly in
itself, partly as an emblem of the Davidic kingdom " Kirk. The
variant readings of Vrss. and interpreters make the exact meaning
of the passage doubtful. In antith. to " showing favour " is the
alternative, *Didst Thou hide Thy face*], in disfavour, during the
moment of anger. — *I became dismayed*], in the night of weeping, v.⁶ᵇ.

7. An editor inserts here as above v.³·⁵ a pentameter line. —
I, on my part, said in my ease : I shall never be moved]. This
disturbs the strophical organisation, the beautiful parall. of the
Str., as well as the measure. The author thinks of a careless,
sinful ease, because of continued prosperity ; and of the presumptuous assurance that this would continue forever ; and that the
people would never be shaken or disturbed from their strong situation. This doubtless was an experience not uncommon, stated
in order to be rejected in public prayer ; but it is difficult to see
what connection it has with the fine antitheses of this Str.

Str. III. is synth. throughout. — **9.** *Unto Thee*], emphatic, unnecessarily defined by *Yahweh* at the expense of the measure. —

my God], so 𝕲, for which 𝕳 substitutes Adonay, which is not
so probable. — *I was crying ‖ I was making supplication for
favour*], both imperfects referring to the past experience, and
therefore frequentatives implying oft-repeated importunate prayer.
This is referred to in this Str. in order to the strong statements
of its antistr. It was only implied in the first Str. The remaining lines now give the contents of that pleading. — **10.** *What
profit is there*], what advantage or benefit of any kind? implying
a negative answer. — *in my blood*], my death by bloodshed; in
the defeat and slaughter of the battle-field, or of the capture of
the city and extermination of its inhabitants. — *When I go down
to the Pit*], syn. v.⁴ referring to the Pit in Sheol. The profitless-
ness of this is set forth in the expostulation: *Will the dust*],
those whose bodies have returned to dust, *praise Thee*, in the
ritual worship of the temple service as 6⁶ Is. 38¹⁸. This is not an
absolute denial of the possibility of the dead praising God. The
nation is meant here and not the individual. It is the national
ritual worship that would cease if the nation perished. — *declare
Thy faithfulness*], in Pss. of thanksgiving; the faithfulness of Yahweh to His covenant and His people. The prayer now changes
from negative expostulation to positive entreaty. — **11.** *Hear and
be gracious, become helper to me*], by delivering me from the
deadly peril.

Str. IV. is an antistr., composed of two syn. couplets. — **12.** The
first couplet reminds us of that of the second Str., with which
it is parall. The same antith. is drawn. — *my mourning ‖ my
sackcloth*], the garment of sorrow and especially of mourning for
the dead. Mourning is appropriate here, because of the situation
of the nation, mourning over the death of a great portion of the
population. Those remaining in exile, while capable of mourning,
still felt that their nation was dead. Over against this, *dancing ‖
gladness*, imply a festival in celebration of a national deliverance.
This transformation has been accomplished by Yahweh. — *Thou
hast turned for me ‖ Thou didst loose ‖ gird me*]. The psalmist
probably had in mind that great prophecy of the Restoration of
Zion, Je. 30–31, and especially 31¹³: " Then the virgin will rejoice
in the dance, and the young men and old men together: and I
will change their mourning into joy and I will comfort them, and

cause them to rejoice more than their sorrow " (*v.* Br.^[MP 247 sq.]).
This prediction of Jeremiah had been fulfilled in the experience
of the people, and has its recognition in their thanksgiving. —
13. This transformation had a purpose, and indeed the same one
that the people had so much at heart in their expostulation with
Yahweh v.^[10b]: *might make melody to Thee*] with songs in the
temple and synagogue ; || *give thanks to Thee*, in the Hallels of
worship (*v.* Intr. § 35) . — *my glory*], the name for the soul as the
seat in man of honour and glory, peculiar to 𝔅, 7^6 16^9 57^9 108^2.
— *not be still*], or silent ; but keeping these songs of praise ever
resounding, and so, *forever.* — *Yahweh* is here claimed by the
people most appropriately as their own personal God ; *my God.*
The Ps. closes as it began with thanksgiving.

2. [אֲרוֹמִמְךָ] Polel impf. ; present, not future of resolution. — [דִלִּיתָנִי] Pi.
proper perfect † דלה vb. Qal, *draw water* Ex. 2^{16. 19. 19} ; counsel, from mind
Pr. 20^5 ; cf. 26^7. Pi. *draw out* or *up*, prob. from Sheol, so here ; cf. v.^4.
— [אֹיְבַי לִי] strengthens the sf. of אֹיבי and does not go with the vb. —
3. [יהוה אלהי] as v.^{13} ; seldom in ψ, style of D. or late (*v.* 7^2). This l. is a
pentameter and doubtless a gl. — **4.** [הֶעֱלִיתָ] Hipf., proper perfect c. מן, as
40^3 71^{20} 81^{11}. שְׁאוֹל (*v.* 6^6). — [נַפְשִׁי] = *me*, *v.* 3^3. — [חִיִּיתַנִי] Pi. pf. (*v.* 22^{27}),
c. מן pregnant, implying deliverance. — [יׇורְדִי בוֹר] Kt., 𝔊, 𝔙, Θ, 𝔖, Horsley,
Bö., Dr., Kau., as 28^1 143^7 (*v.* 7^{16}) ; better than Qr., Σ, 𝔍, 𝔗, Houb., יׇרְדִי inf.
cstr., sf. I s. for usual יׇרְדִּי v.^{10}, which is improbable. This l. is a trimeter.
A word has fallen out. This is prob. נפשי at close of line for rhyme. —
5. [זֵכֶר קׇדְשׁוֹ] = 97^{12} (*v.* 6^6) *commemoration.* This v. is a trimeter couplet,
a liturgical gl. — **6.** [כִי] causal, prob. not original, but an interpretation. The
new Str. is more independent of the previous Str. — [רֶגַע] *a moment of time*,
v. 6^{11}. — [בְּאַפּוֹ] *during His anger* (*v.* 2^5). Suffix of 3 sg. is strange ; it is an
interpretation due to the gls. v.^{5. 7}, originally without sf. ; so in || ברצונו. —
[וְלִין] should be attached by Makkeph to בֶּכִי. — **7.** [וַאֲנִי] emph. before אמרתי.
— [שַׁלְוִי] sf. I sg. † שֶׁלֶו n.[m.] *ease*, a.λ., cf. שַׁלְוָה 122^7 same ; שַׁלְוֵי pl. cstr.
שַׁלֵו 73^{12}. This v. is a pentameter, if not prose, and is a gl. — **8.** [יהוה] is a
gl., making l. too long. Its insertion was due to previous gl. [ברצונך] emph.
in position, a resumption of v.^6. Prob. the sf. is here also an interpretation.
— [הֶעֱמַדְתָּה] Hiph. pf. 2 m. fully written of עמד. — [לְהַרְרִי עֹז]. 𝔊 makes עז the
object of vb. and renders παράσχου δύναμιν, so 𝔍 *posuisti fortitudinem.* But
they differ as to the indirect object : the former τῷ κάλλει μου = הררי, so 𝔖,
𝔙, *Thou didst prepare strength for my majesty* (either of king or of people) ;
the latter, *monti meo* = לְהַרְרִי as 𝔅, *i.e.* Zion as the firm, sure refuge of the
people of God. Ham., Houb., Lowth, Horsley, al., follow 𝔊 ; Dr., Bä., al., 𝔅.
But 𝔗 has *hast made me stand firm on the strong mountains*, pointing הֲרָרִי ;

so Dy., Hu., Kau. The difficulty with 𝔥 is the failure of an object for the vb. and the use of the prep. ל for על. The prep. may, however, be a scribal interpretation. 𝔊 is less difficult and intrinsically more prob. For הרר *v. 8⁶*; cf. 149⁹ for honour or glory of saints. — סְתָרָךְ חָיֶיךָ] hypothetical clause (*v. 10¹¹*). — 9. אליך] emph. ‖ אל אדני. This divine name improb.; 𝔊 has אלי (*v.* Intr. §§ 32, 36). — יהוה] is a gl. — אֶקְרָא] Qal impf. (*v. 3⁵*), ‖ אֶֽחֱנַן] Hithp. (*v. 4²*), as 142², frequentative of importunate petition. — 10. הי] indirect question expecting a negative answer, as 8⁵ 11³. — ‡ בֶּצַע] n.m. *unjust gain;* elsw. 119³⁶, cf. בֹּצֵעַ 10³. — 11. יהוה] twice in this v.; unnecessary gls., destroying the measure. — עֲזָר לִי] = 54⁶, Qal ptc. — עֹזֵר. — 12. הָֽפְכָה] Qal pf. 2 m. either aorist or proper pf. ‡ הפך vb. Qal: (1) *turn, change, transform,* c. acc. 41⁴ 105²⁵; (2) *turn into,* c. double acc. 114⁸; c. acc. + ל 30¹² 66⁶ 78⁴⁴, cf. 105²⁹; (3) *turn back* 78⁹ Ju. 20³⁹ 2 K. 5²⁶. Niph. *turn aside* Ps. 78⁵⁷; pass. *be turned into* 32⁴. — † מִסְפֵּד] n.m. *wailing:* (1) for the dead Gn. 50¹⁰ (J) Zc. 12¹⁰; (2) for calamity Am. 5¹⁶· ¹⁶· ¹⁷ Mi. 1⁸· ¹¹ Je. 48³⁸ Ez. 27³¹, anticipated Je. 6²⁶ Est. 4³; (3) in contrition Is. 22¹² Jo. 2¹² Zc. 12¹¹· ¹¹; (4) in general; indef. here. — † מָחֹל לִ] n.m. *dancing;* elsw. Je. 31⁴· ¹³ La. 5¹⁵; sacred dance Ps. 149⁸ 150⁴. — ‡ שָׂק] n.m. *sackcloth,* used in mourning and penitence; elsw. 35¹⁸ 69¹². — 13. כָּבוֹד] for כבודי *my glory = soul,* as 16⁹.

PSALM XXXI., 5 STR. 5⁶.

Ps. 31 is a prayer: (1) importunate plea for deliverance of the people from national enemies (v.²⁻⁵); (2) confidence in the deliverance as already accomplished (v.⁶⁻⁹); (3) petition based on complaint of abandonment (v.¹⁰⁻¹³); (4) confidence, with prayer for salvation (v. ¹⁴⁻¹⁷); (5) praise of Yahweh for the salvation (v.²⁰⁻²¹· ²²⁻²⁴ᵃ). There are liturgical glosses (v.²²· ²⁴ᵇ⁻²⁵) and a gloss of imprecation (v.¹⁸⁻¹⁹).

IN Thee, Yahweh, I seek refuge; let me never be shamed, O rescue *me;*
   In Thy righteousness bow down Thine ear unto me, speedily deliver *me;*
   Be Thou to me a rock of *stronghold,* a house of *fortress* to save *me;*
   For Thou art my crag and my *fortress,* therefore lead me and guide *me;*
   Bring me forth out of the net they privily laid for me; for Thou art *my stronghold.*
INTO Thy hand (Yahweh) I commit my spirit ; Thou hast ransomed *me.*
   Yahweh, God of faithfulness, them that regard false idols *I* hate ;
   I will rejoice and will be glad in Thy kindness; and I, on my part, unto Thee do
     I trust;
   Thou who dost see mine affliction, dost know the destitution of *my* soul ;
   And hast not delivered me up into the hand of the enemy, in a broad place hast
     made firm *my* foot.
BE gracious to me, Yahweh, for *I* am in distress; *wastes away* my soul and *my* body,
   For consumed in sorrow is *my* life, my years in (*my*) groaning;

My strength doth fail in *mine* affliction, and my bones *waste away* because of
my distress;
I am become a terror to *mine* acquaintance, in the street they flee from *me ;*
As a dead man out of mind am *I* forgotten, like a lost vessel am *I.*

FOR the defaming of many, terror all around me *I* hear;
While they consult together against me, devise to take *my* life,
I, on my part, upon Thee do trust; Yahweh, Thou art *my* God.
In Thy hand are my times; from the hand of mine enemy and pursuer deliver *me.*
O let Thy face shine upon Thy servant; in Thy kindness give *me* victory.

O HOW great is Thy goodness (Yahweh), which Thou hast *treasured* up for them
that fear *Thee !*
(Which) Thou hast done before the sons of men, for them that seek refuge in
Thee !
Thou *treasurest* them in a shelter from the harshness of men; Thou hidest
them in the covert of *Thy* presence.
I, on my part, said in mine alarm: I am (driven away) from before *Thine* eye.
Nevertheless, Thou didst hear the voice of my supplication, when I cried for
help unto *Thee.*

Ps. 31 was in 𝔇 and 𝔐 and 𝔇𝕽 (*v.* Intr. §§ 27, 31, 33). 𝔊 adds
ἐκστάσεως, doubtless due to ἐν τῇ ἐκστάσει μου, v.²³. The comparison of this
with 1 S. 23²⁰⁾ led to the association of the Ps. with that incident in David's
life. The Ps. has an unusual number of passages showing connection with
other Pss. and prophecies. It has also lost its original metrical and strophical
form. This is due to many glosses, partly explanatory, partly marginal references, partly liturgical. (1) V.²⁻⁴ᵃ are essentially the same as 71¹⁻³, a Ps.
which is a late mosaic without title. Doubtless our Ps. gives the original.
(2) V.⁷ᵃ is essentially the same as Jon. 2⁹ᵃ, and v.²³ᵃ is the same as Jon. 2⁵ᵃ,
where, indeed, the correct text is preserved. Jon. 2 is a mosaic Ps. also, and
doubtless our Ps. gives the original. (3) V.⁴ᵃ may be compared with 18³,
v.⁹ with 18²⁰·³⁴; undoubtedly 18 is original and 31 dependent. (4) V.⁵ is
similar to 9¹⁶, v.⁸ to 9¹⁰·¹⁴ 10¹; probably 31 is dependent on that Ps. also.
(5) V.¹⁶ may be compared with Is. 33⁶ in its use of עתות; v.²¹ with Is. 40⁴ in
its use of the word רכסים; and v.²⁰ with Is. 63⁷ in its use of רב טוב. Is.² is
earlier. (6) V.¹¹ seems to be based on Je. 20¹⁸, and v.¹⁸ in its use of ידמו on
Je. also; cf. Je. 8¹⁴ 48² 49²⁶ 50⁸⁰ 51⁶, and v.¹⁹ in its use of אלם on Ez. 3²⁶ 24²⁷
33²². (7) V.¹⁴ was derived from Je. 20¹⁰. (8) V.²³ᵇ is similar to 28², and
probably derived from it. (9) Moreover, there are a number of uses of other
passages in what seem to be glosses, v.⁴ᵇ from 23³, v.¹⁰ᵇ from 6⁸; v.²², cf. 4⁴ 17⁷
in the phr. הפליא חסד, and 60¹¹ in the phr. בעיר מצור. V.²⁵ is derived from
27¹⁴. (10) V.⁶ in its use of רוח for נפש is not early. (11) The high priest's
blessing, Nu. 6²⁵, underlies v.¹⁷, as Pss. 4⁷ 67² 80⁴·⁸·²⁰ 118²⁷ 119¹³⁵. (12) V.¹¹
כשל כח elsw. Ne. 4⁴ La. 1¹⁴. (13) V.¹² היה חרפה ל, as 79⁴ 89⁴² 109²⁵, is
probably a gloss. The author certainly knew Je., Is., Ez., and many Pss.
of the Persian period. We cannot put the composition earlier than the
troubles of Israel preceding the reforms of Nehemiah. The Ps. is national
and not individual. It is a lamentation reminding us of 22, 69. It is hex-

ameter in three parts, v.[2-9], v.[10-17], v.[20-21. 23-24a]; the first and second of two pentastichs each, the last of a single pentastich. Undoubtedly v.[10-19] seem inconsistent with v.[6-9. 20-24], as Kirk. says, and might be a later insertion. They can only be explained as a resumption of the thought of v.[2-5] on the principle of strophical parallelism. In favour of their originality is the rhyming in *i* which runs through v.[10-19] as well as v.[2-9], changed to a rhyme in *ka* in v.[20-21. 23].

Str. I. is composed of five syn. lines rhyming in *i*. — **2-3.** *In Thee, Yahweh*], emphatic in position. — *I seek refuge*], from enemies, as usual. — *let me never be shamed*], put to shame in defeat by enemies, cf. v.[18]. — *O rescue me*], earnest entreaty, implying real peril from enemies ; ‖ *deliver me* ‖ *save me*. — *In Thy righteousness*], not ethical, but redemptive, vindicatory of the cause of His people, as usual in Pss. and Is.[2]. — *bow down Thine ear unto me*], listening to my plea, in response to my prayer. — *speedily*], there is need of haste ; delay is perilous. — *Be Thou to me a rock of stronghold*], a rock serving as a stronghold, affording strength for defence against the enemy, cf. Is. 17[10], ‖ *house of fortress*], a house fortified so as to serve as a fortress. These terms are repeated singly in the parall. of the subsequent lines, where what is begged, is stated as a fact. — **4-5.** *For Thou art my crag*], syn. term to " rock," ‖ *my fortress* and *my stronghold*. Thus far the Ps. is quoted in essentially the same language in Ps. 71[1-3]. Apparently a new thought begins with v.[4b], *therefore lead me and guide me*]. This is favoured by the insertion of the gloss from 23[3], *for Thy name's sake*, which gives it a more general reference to safe guidance through perilous places. But really the preceding as well as the subsequent context implies the continuation of the plea for deliverance ; and inasmuch as the guidance is connected with Yahweh as the fortress, we must think of a leading and guiding to this fortress, and so we get a suitable transition to the clause : *Bring me forth out of the net*]. The peril is conceived as a net, or a snare which the enemies *privily laid*, as in 9[16], by their intrigues and treachery, out of which Yahweh alone can give an escape by taking them out and conducting them to a sure refuge.

Str. II. is an antistr. to the first Str. It is a pentastich of introverted parall. The first line is a strong statement of confidence in Yahweh, followed by an antith. couplet, emphasising the relation of mutual faithfulness between Yahweh and His people, in order to mediate the advance in confidence, of the final couplet. — **6.** *Into Thy hand*], as a sacred trust. — *Yahweh*] is required by the measure in the first line, and emphasised by *Yahweh, God of faithfulness*, in the second ; because it was just this faithfulness of God to His people, in covenant relation with Him, that was the basis of confidence. — *I commit my spirit*]. The extreme peril of the previous Str. is now summed up in the peril of death. The nation, ready to perish, entrusts to Yahweh its spirit, as that imperishable part which continues to exist in spite of every peril to the body, even if it should be laid in the grave. In the most desperate condition of national depression, even in death and the grave, Yahweh will faithfully keep Israel's trust. Cf. Is. 38[16]. These words, expressing the experience of the nation in extreme peril, were especially appropriate to Jesus when dying on the cross, Lk. 23[46], and have also been found appropriate in all ages to pious individuals, such as Polycarp, Bernard, Luther ; for the generic experiences of Israel were, in the unfolding of the divine purpose of redemption, preparatory to the personal experiences of individuals. This firm and unwavering trust has its immediate reward in the certitude of salvation, which comes at once, enabling the psalmist to say : *Thou hast redeemed me*]. The PBV. " For Thou hast redeemed me," as if it were a reason for the trust, is an interpretation which has no justification in 𝕳 or ancient Vrss. — **7-9.** *them that regard false idols*], cited Jon. 2[9], evidently refers to idolaters, worshipping idols who are not real beings, but unreal and false to their worshippers. This meaning is obscured by the too general and indefinite rendering " lying vanities," AV., RV. PBV., "superstitious vanities," is better. — *I hate*], 𝕳 as the rhyme, and antith. with " do I trust " require ; although 𝕲, 𝕵, 𝕾, followed by many scholars, have " Thou hatest," thinking of God as the subject. — *I will rejoice*, strengthened by *and I will be glad*, as often in the style of the Ps., cf. v.[3. 4. 8b] + ; both, as the antith. implies, to be interpreted of the public worship of Yahweh with songs of praise. — *In Thy kindness*], antith. with the idols, is interpreted by Jon. 2[9] as a name of God ; made possible by a change of the suffix, which prevents that interpretation here.

At the same time the reality and the faithfulness of Yahweh in His kindness is invoked over against the unreality and unreliableness of the idols. — *And I on my part*] emphasises the personal character and the fact. — *unto Thee do I trust*]. The justification for this trust is given in the closing couplet in a progressive relative clause : *Thou who dost see* ‖ *dost know*], the practical, personal, interested, and redemptive seeing and knowing, which advances, therefore, on the negative side into ; *hast not delivered me up into the hand of the enemy*, who had brought the nation into this extreme peril ; explained in the previous line as *mine affliction* ‖ *destitution of my soul;* summing up the more concrete representations of the first Str. — On the positive side, the climax is attained in the statement, *in a broad place*], over against the narrow place, the straits, the net, in which they had been trapped by their enemies. — *hast made firm my foot*], to stand firm, as $18^{20.34}$, so as not to be shaken, or displaced from the position it had taken ; implying, therefore, the defeat of the enemy and the victory of the people.

Str. III. is a syn. pentastich, heaping up terms to describe the miserable condition of the nation. It is certainly out of harmony with the previous Str., which is so firm and assured in its certitude of deliverance. This can only be explained on the principle of the parall. of Hebrew Poetry, which extends to the strophes as well as the lines (*v.* Intr. § 12 *D*). The psalmist goes back to the experiences described in the first Str. in order to strengthen the confidence in God expressed in its antistr. In the first Str. the emphasis was laid upon the place of refuge, with the peril in the background ; here the peril itself is described in detail, the whole introduced by the single word of prayer : **10.** *Be gracious to me, Yahweh*]. All the rest of the Str. is embraced under the clause giving the reason for the plea, *for I am in distress.* This general statement is broken up into a number of specifications. — *wastes away*], a term used elsewhere only v.[11] 6^8, implying the image of the moth eating away garments. The proper subject of the vb. is the comprehensive, *my soul and my body*, comprehending the entire man, his entire nature ; but the influence of 6^8 has brought into the text its own phr., *mine eye in vexation*, which makes the line just these words too long. — **11.** *For consumed is*

my life], in the sense of lifetime, as is shown by the complementary, *my years*. The cause of this consuming away, which
is syn. with the previous "wastes away," is expressed in the
complementary terms, *in sorrow, in my groaning*. It is necessary
to add the second suffix here, because of the rhyme. Ancient
copyists left it off, as unnecessary to the sense. — *in mine affliction*], so 𝔖, 𝔙, 𝚺, in accordance with v.⁸, which is better suited to
the context than "in mine iniquity" of 𝔥, 𝔍, followed by EVˢ.,
which has nothing to suggest it in the context, though doubtless
it made the Ps. more appropriate for public worship. — *my
strength doth fail*], strictly, stumble over an obstacle, implying
such a loss of strength that the man instead of walking steadily
along, stumbles and staggers in his gait. This is intensified by a
reversion to the first line of the tristich, on the principle of inclusion. — *and my bones waste away*], the bones for the framework
of the body. This favours the opinion that we should read here,
because of my distress, the same word as v.¹⁰ᵃ, which in the original
Hebrew so much resembles the word translated "mine adversaries," that this interpretation may be easily explained, especially
in view of the gloss which follows. In any case the "all" is, as
quite frequently in the Pss., an intensifying insertion, making the
measure less easy. — **12**. *I am become a terror to mine acquaintance*], so the original read, in all probability; the acquaintance
being the friendly peoples, a thought which we may compare with
Is. 53¹⁻³. This received an interpretative gloss in terms of later
Pss. 79⁴ 89⁴² 109²⁵, "a reproach and unto my neighbours exceedingly." This can hardly be adapted to the measures or the strophical organisation of the Ps., and indeed, in itself, is difficult
to explain satisfactorily, unless we suppose with many scholars
that "exceedingly," although sustained by 𝔊, 𝔍, is a copyist's
error for some such word as "fear," "wagging of head," or "contention," readings suggested by various scholars. But this difficulty reënforces the other reasons for regarding it as a gloss. —
in the street they flee from me]. These are doubtless the same
persons as those mentioned in the first part of the line ; they flee
from Israel in order not to become involved in the peril, in terror
lest the overpowering enemies may attack them also. The words,
those that see me, are a prosaic gloss, generalising the subject at

the expense of the measure. — **13.** *I am forgotten*], abandonment
leads inevitably to forgetfulness of the person abandoned. — *as a
dead man*], one whose acquaintance was once enjoyed, but whom
one knows no longer, because he is in the realm of forgetfulness.
— *out of mind*], so long dead that the thought of him no longer
comes into the mind. This reaches its climax in, *like a lost vessel*,
which is more suited to the first part of the line, to which it is an
emphatic complement, than the weaker paraphrase " broken vessel " of EVˢ.

Str. IV. is the antistr. to the previous one, and is chiefly petition ; not importunate, but calm and confident, distributing itself
in several phases in the succeeding lines. The psalmist begins
with a synth. couplet, **14**, emphasising the peril. The first line
was taken from Je. 20¹⁰, *for the defaming of many, terror all
around me I hear*]. The enemies were active in slanderous words
and threatening deeds. — *While they consult together against me*],
as in 2² against the king, so here the wicked nations plot against
the people. — *devise to take my life*]. As suggested in the first
Str., the people are in deadly peril, in need of a safe refuge ; here
the purpose of the enemy is nothing less than to utterly destroy
them. But while they are thus plotting, the people are not in
despair ; they have confidence in God, which is affirmed in the
concluding tristich of the Str. — **15.** *I on my part*], emphatic
personal experience. — *upon Thee do I trust*], as v.⁷ᵇ, the object
of trust emphasised, as in v.⁶ᵇ. — *Yahweh, Thou art my God*]. A
later scribe, thinking to make it more emphatic, inserted " I said,"
at the expense of the measure. — **16.** *In Thy hand*], as in v.⁶ᵃ. —
are my times], the " times " for experiences, fortunes, as Is. 33⁶,
doubtless thinking of their issue whether in adversity or prosperity.
The people are in Yahweh's hands here, as their spirit has been
committed to His trust, v.⁶. This resumption of the thought of
Str. II. is in order to the following petition, which in rapid succession adds one thing to another. — *deliver me*], naturally comes
first, resuming the thought of the first Str. — *from the hand of
mine enemy*], with the complementary *pursuer*, in accordance
with the style of the Ps. — **17.** *O let Thy face shine upon*], thinking of the priestly benediction, Nu. 6²⁴ ˢᵠ·, as Ps. 4⁷, the light of
favour and prosperity. — *in Thy kindness*], resuming v.⁸ᵃ. — *give*

me victory], as complementary to the positive favour. The ordinary " save me," EV⁸., is not suited to this line. That victory in war is longed for, is evident from the interpretation of the glossator in v.¹⁸⁻¹⁹. — **18**. *Yahweh, let me not be shamed*], that is, by defeat and disaster ; but, on the other hand, let the wicked nations, the enemy and the pursuer above, be shamed in defeat and slaughter, and so *be made silent, dumb ;* not merely speechless, but helpless, unable to say or do anything, *going down to Sheol* in national death, cf. 6⁶ 9¹⁸. The imprecation is not upon personal enemies, but upon enemies in arms against the people of God. — **19**. *Let lying lips be dumb*]. This suits the citation from Je. 20¹⁰, but not the situation of the Ps. in general. These lying lips are represented as those *that speak arrogantly against the righteous*]. The righteous here do not seem to be righteous Israel, but the righteous as distinguished from the arrogant in Israel. This is still further defined as, *with pride and contempt*, a situation appearing often enough in the Greek period and subsequently. The verse is prosaic, as is the previous one. They can only be made poetic by reductions and other changes.

Str. V. corresponds, in its confidence in God, with the antistrs. of the two previous parts. It rhymes in *ka*, referring to God, the previous Strs. in *î*, referring to the nation. It begins with an exclamation of praise. — **20**. *O how great is Thy goodness*], reminding of Is. 63⁷. This goodness is conceived as a treasure, *which Thou hast treasured up*], reserved in heaven in the divine presence, to be given at the appropriate time ; *for them that fear Thee*], them that have that reverence which constitutes true religion, ‖ *for them that seek refuge in Thee*, resuming v.². That which was treasured up with Yahweh was reserved for a special occasion. — *Thou hast done*], goodness, good, in the bestowal of good things, not in private, but in public ; not before the people of God, but *before the sons of men*, as the context shows, the wicked nations. — **21**. This verse, by glosses and transposition, has lost its measure, rhyme, symmetry, and simplicity, but it is not difficult to restore it to its original form. *The strife of tongues* is suited to v.¹⁹. If that be a gloss, this is a gloss also. This removes the chief difficulty at once. The only other difficulty is removed by transposition of the two clauses. — *Thou treasurest* *them* ‖ *Thou hidest them*]. The thought of the first Str. is resumed ; only what was importunately prayed for there is here taken for granted as a fact. The seeking refuge, of the previous line, passes over into being kept safe in that refuge as a hidden treasure. The place of refuge is *a shelter* ‖ *the covert of Thy presence*. This is probably conceived, as in 27⁵, in the temple courts. The need of this refuge is briefly indicated in the clause, *from the harshness of men*], a term used elsewhere only Is. 40⁴, of rugged places, but sustained by 𝔊, 𝔍. There is no need of any of the changes suggested by modern scholars to avoid this unusual phrase. The previous tristich was supplemented by a later editor in the use of the liturgical phrase : **22**. *Blessed be Yahweh*, the usual form of benediction, with the reason, taken from 4⁴ 17⁷, *For He doth show extraordinary kindness to me*]. The additional phrase, *in a fortified city*, cf. 60¹¹, seems to refer to Jerusalem during a siege, but may be only an explication of the covert of the previous context, extending it to the city of Jerusalem as well as the temple precincts. Such an addition might have been made quite naturally during the Maccabean wars. — **23**. *I on my part*], as v.⁷·¹⁵. — *said in mine alarm*], when so intensely agitated that I hardly knew what I was saying. — *I am driven away from before Thine eye*]. This is quoted in Jon. 2⁵, which undoubtedly gives the true vb. The vb. of 𝔥, mistaking a single letter, gives the weaker meaning, " I am cut off." The people in their extreme peril were at first despairing, feeling that their God had not only forsaken them, but actually expelled them from His presence. The psalmist may be thinking here of the first thoughts of the nation when in exile long before his own time. It is national experience that is here described, and not that of an individual. But this despair as expressed in the alarmed utterance of the people did not stay their prayer nor Yahweh's help. — *Nevertheless*], in spite of all things, strong asseveration of the antith., *Thou didst hear*, in the pregnant sense, implying answer, *the voice of my supplication*, a phrase of 28²·⁶. — *when I cried for help unto Thee*]. With this statement of fact the Ps. comes to its appropriate conclusion.

A later editor, wishing to make a practical exhortation based upon the Ps., for public use, gives a general statement of doctrine and a liturgical conclusion.

> Love Yahweh, all ye His pious ones;
> The faithful Yahweh preserveth,
> But rewardeth the proud doer.
> Be strong and let your mind take courage,
> All ye that wait on Yahweh.

24. *Love Yahweh, all ye His pious ones*]. This is a most appropriate exhortation here, and indeed everywhere. But it has no manner of connection with the context and is really a prose sentence. — *The faithful Yahweh preserveth, But rewardeth the proud doer*]. So probably originally an antith. trimeter couplet, but its measure was destroyed by the insertion of the emphatic "plentifully." — **25.** *Be strong and let your mind take courage, All ye that wait on Yahweh*]. This liturgical addition is essentially the same as 27[14], save that the 2 sg. has been changed into the 2 pl.

2–4 a is cited in the later mosaic Ps. 71 in v.[1-3] with minor variations. V.[2] is identical with 71[1] as far as and including עוֹלב; but 31[2] has two words additional, making the l. overfull; these are in 71[2]. 71[1] is defective by one word and that the one bearing the rhyme. It is easy to find that missing word in פלטני 31[2], which makes that l. overfull and which also appears in 71[2] in juss. [בצרקתך .תצילני || תפלטני. ⅌ of 31[2] also has ῥῦσαί με καὶ ἐξελοῦ με = 71[2]. — **2.** emph. (*v. 5*[9]). This goes into l. 2, as 71[2]. — [הטה אזנך = 71[2b], usually c. ל 17[6] 49[5] 78[1] 88[3] 116[2], only 31[3] (= 71[2b]) 102[3] with אֵל. But one word is needed for measure. 31[3] has מהרה הצילני. 71[2] has יהושיעני, ⅌ καὶ σῶσόν με. ⅌ of 31[3] has τάχυνον τοῦ ἐξελέσθαι με, taking vb. as inf. cstr. without ו and so || with next l. τοῦ σῶσαί με = להושיעני. This fluctuation shows uncertainty of reading. — ‡ [מְהֵרָה] n.f. *haste, speed*, usually adv. *hastily, quickly* before vb., elsw. 37[2] Is. 58[8] Jo. 4[4]; עד מ׳ Ps. 147[15], cf. מהר Ps. 69[18]. — היה לי לצור is the same in both Pss., but it is followed by מעון 31[3], by מעון 71[3]. מעוז *place of refuge*, with צור also Is. 17[10]; apart from צור Pss. 27[1] 28[8] 31[5] 37[89] 43[2] 52[9]. It is better suited to the context here than מעון, which is with צור only 71[3]; but alone 90[1] 91[9] of Yahweh as dwelling place, (⅌ καταφυγή) all dub.: undoubtedly 31[3] is the correct reading. — [לבית מצודות cf. לבית צויה המיר לבוא 71[3], both variations of interpretation of a common original: לבת מצדה; the only difference being the transposition of צ and ד due to txt. err. The pl. is dub. as α.λ., prob. should be מְצוּדָתִי as 18[3] = 2 S. 22[2] = 31[4] = 71[3], cf. 144[2]. לבוא המיר a rel. clause with rel. omitted, referring to מעון. צויה must then be Pi. pf. 2 m. with להושיעני dependent upon it. But ⅌ has here εἰς τόπον ὀχυρὸν τοῦ σῶσαί με, essentially as in 31[3] εἰς οἶκον καταφυγῆς τοῦ σῶσαί με, indicating the same reading as 31[3]. 𝔏 of 71[3] is then txt. err. The form להושיעני in all texts gives the needed rhyme and parallel term, and is undoubtedly original. **4.** [כי. סלעי ומצורתי אתה] is the same in both l'ss., but it closes the v. in 71[3] and begins it in 31⁴. It is derived from *18³* except its framework or construction כי־אתה. The last part of 31⁴ does not appear in 71, for the latter Ps. from this clause on is independent of 31. But this is needed to complete the hexameter l. — ולמען שמך] is derived from *23³* as gl. appended to vb. — ותנו לי] is cognate to הנחני and emphasises it. — 5. ברשת זו טמנו = פרשת זו טמנו] 9¹⁶ᵇ from which it was taken; only put into the frame of רוציאני. — כי אתה מעוזי] cf. v.⁴ 𝔊 ᶜ·ᵉ·ᵃ·ᴬ·ᴿᵃ·λ have κύριος after מעוזי. Prob. יהוה originally preceded בידך of v.⁶. — 6. בידך] emph. — אפקיד רוחי]. For פקד (*v. 8⁵*). רוח *spirit* in sense of ‡ (3) *that which breathes quickly or hard in animation or agitation of any kind = temper, disposition* (this is the distinctive mng. of רוח as cf. with נפש and לבב): courage 76¹³, ההעפף ר׳ 77⁴ 142⁴ 143⁴ (*v.* BD*B*), crushed spirit 143⁷, ‡ *spirit of the living, breathing being, dwelling in the* בשר *of men and animals* ‖ נפש: departing at death *31⁶*. (בשר‖) 78³⁹ ר׳ הולך לא ישוב, cf. 104²⁹⁻³⁰ 146⁴. ‡ (5) *occasionally as seat or organ of mental acts* ‖ or syn. לב, late writers 77⁷ (?). — † (6) *rarely, referring to inclinations, resolutions, determinations of the will =* לב: נכון ר׳ וכון 51¹² (cf. נ׳ לב 57⁸·⁸ (= 108²) 78³⁷ 112⁷); נדיבה ר׳ 51¹⁴ (?) (cf. Ex. 35²¹ and לב 35⁵·²² (P), 2 Ch. 29³¹). ‡ (7) *referring to moral character =* לב: Pss. 32² 78⁸, דכאי ר׳ 34¹⁹ (cf. לב Is. 57¹⁵), ר׳ ושברה Ps. 51¹⁹ (cf. Is. 65¹⁴, לב Pss. 51¹⁹ 34¹⁹ Is. 61¹). For other mngs. of רוח *v. 18¹⁶ 51¹³*. — פדיתה] Qal pf. 2 m. fully written; not aorist, but emph. present (*v. 25²²*). — אותי] emph. acc. sf. in order to measure and rhyme. — אל־יהוה] cf. אלהי אמת 2 Ch. 15¹³, אל אמונה Dt. 32⁴. For אל *v.* Intr. § 32, אשר *15²*. This clause goes with next l. — 7. שנאתי] Qal pf. 1 sg. But 𝔊, 𝔍, 𝔖, 𝔗, 2 pers. שנאת, so Dy., Horsley, Bä., Dr., Kirk., favoured by פדיתה, but opposed by 1 pers. in all lines thus far. 𝔅 is correct, but the vb. should be transposed to end of l. for assonance with other lines. — השמרים הבלי שוא] = Jon. 2⁹ only in latter Pi. משמרים which is a difference of interpretation of original unpointed text. It is doubtful which is original, prob. not Jonah as Du. but our Ps.; although both are mosaics, yet this Str. seems original to the poet in other respects. ‡ הבל n.m. *vapour, breath*, in ψ fig. (1) of man: evanescent, unsubstantial 39⁶·⁷·¹² 62¹⁰·¹⁰ 144⁴, his days 78³³, thoughts 94¹¹; (2) of idols, other gods than Yahweh, הבלי שוא *31⁷* = Jon. 2⁹, cf. הבלים Dt. 32²¹, הבלי זרך Je. 8¹⁹, הבלי הגוים Je. 10⁸ 14²². For שוא *v. 12³*. — ואני] emph. over against השברים. — אל יהוה בטחתי] cf. v.¹⁵ עליך ב׳ יהוה, so here, but without יהוה; בטח of trust in God, c. אל elsw. 4⁶ 56⁴ 86², c. על elsw. 37⁵, for usual ב as 9¹¹ + 21 t. ψ. This clause has been transposed with first clause of v.⁸; making this change of order gives an easier explanation for אשר and also the rhyme characteristic of the lines thus far. — 8. בהס־ך]. The use of this word here in antith. הבלי שוא reminds of Jon. 2⁹. The conception of the Ps. is simpler, for the sf. in Jon. seems to make הסי practically a name of God. — אשר] refers to יהוה and is not causal, although that interpretation is sustained by 𝔊, 𝔍, and followed by most interpreters, owing to the transposition mentioned above. — ראה ‖ ידע] ירעת בצרות נ׳ seems to require that בצרות נ׳ should be ‖ עני, so Σ, 𝔍 take it as obj. *cognovisti tribulationes animae meae*, and the paraphrase of 𝔊 ἔσωσας ἐκ τῶν ἀναγκῶν τὴν ψυχήν μου, favours it. For בצרה *v. 9¹⁰* 10¹

Je. 14¹. The relation of this Ps. to Ps. 9 in other respects also favours it. —
9. רגלי] prob. רגְלִי not רוּגִי as 𝔊; all other lines end in sg. sf. ֶ ָ. This v. is
dependent upon Ps. 18²⁰. ³⁴. — **10.** עשִׁשׁה בכעס עיני=] עשׁשה מכעס·עיני 6⁸, doubtless the original passage from which it is derived here, simply changing the
prep., cf. v.¹¹. This l. has two words too many for measure. The last two
are favoured by v.¹¹, then כעס עיני would be gl. from 6⁸. — **11.** כי כלו חיי is
based on ויכלו בכשת ימי Je. 20¹⁸, which uses in previous context יגון, preferred
by our psalmist to בשת. כלה (*v. 18³⁸*), in sense of exhaustion 71⁹ 73²⁶ 102⁴
143⁷. — באנחה] but rd. for rhyme אנחתי (*v. 6⁷* 38¹⁰). — יְשֵׁל] *totter, fail*, fig. of
כח, also Ne. 4⁴ and Hiph. La. 1¹⁴, but *totter* of knees Ps. 109²⁴ and of persons
105⁸⁷. בַּחֵנִי] has no propriety in this Ps., though supported by Aq., Θ, 𝔗, 𝔍;
𝔊 ἐν πτωχείᾳ, so 𝔙, 𝔖, Du.; Bä., Σ בעוני, as v.⁸. — עשׁשׁו] takes up עשׁשׁה
v.¹⁰. — **12.** מכל צררי] is attached to previous l. by Ew., after 𝔖; if so, rd. צררי,
as 7⁵, for assonance, and not ארי, as 23⁵ 42¹¹ 69²⁰. These words are really
needed to make two hexameters in this v. מן is here παρά in 𝔊, *apud* in 𝔍;
prob. here *at the hands of*, as 74²², not causal, as Dr., *because of* (*v.* BDB מן
2 d). But this is difficult whether we connect with the previous or the subsequent context. It is prob. txt. err. for צר־לי, which suits the rhyme and the
parall. — היִיתי חרפה] as 79⁴ 89⁴² 109²⁵, cf. 69¹¹ (*v. 15³*). — מְאד] is sustained
by 𝔊, 𝔍, but in this case it is better to rd. לשֲׁכֵני at end of l., and sf. 1 sg.
instead of 1 pl., which destroys rhyme. A noun seems necessary. Horsley
suggests מאר *nuisance;* Krochmal מגור; Hi., Ols., Lag. מנור abr. מנור ראש, so
Che.; Gr. מאום. מגור, *terror*, is favoured by v.¹⁴, and רח־, מנוד by usage of
44¹⁵, cf. 22⁸ Je. 18¹⁶. ריב, *object of contention*, is easier, cf. in the same phr.
מדון לשכנינו Ps. 80⁷. But in fact this thought does not suit the context.
היִיתי פחד is prob. a gl. from a later situation, the original being חרפה ולשכני מאר.
— למְידעי] Pu. ptc., sf. 1 pl., so 88⁹. ¹⁹; but rd. מְידע as 55¹⁴. — ראי] a gl., unnecessary and destroying the measure. — **13.** היִיתי should be removed to the
end of the l. for rhyme. — **14.** The l. מסביב . . . כי שמעתי is from Je. 20¹⁰.
The phr. מגור מסביב is peculiar to Je. 6²⁵ 20³. ¹⁰ 46⁵ 49²⁹, cf. La. 2²². שמעי
goes to the end of l. for rhyme. — בהוסדם יהד על] Niph. inf. cstr., *in that;*
cf. 2² נוסרו יחד. — לקחת נפשי] = *take my life*, phr. elsw. 1 K. 19⁴ Jon. 4³
Pr. 1¹⁹. — **15.** אמרתי] is gl., unnecessary and making l. too long. — אֱלֹהַי] for
an original אֵלי required for rhyme and transposed. — **16.** בידֶך] cf. v.⁶. —
עתּתי] *my times, experiences, fortunes*, as Is. 33⁵; 𝔊 οἱ κλῆροί μου is a paraphrase. — הצילני] should go to the end of the l. for rhyme. — אויבי] should
be sg., as v.⁹, and not pl.; so also רדרי, not רדפי. — **17.** האירה פניך] phr.
derived from the high priest's blessing Nu. 6²⁵; so Pss. 67² 80⁴. ⁸. ²⁰ 119¹³⁵,
and in variant form 4⁷ 118²⁷. — הושיעני] should come at the end for rhyme.
— **18.** יהוה אל אבושה] a resumption of v.², to emphasise an imprecation upon
enemies. — ידֻמו] Qal impf. 3 pl. דמם *be still* = *perish*, so Je. 8¹⁴. 48². It is
probable that it should be Niph. ידַלו, as 1 S. 2⁹ *be made silent* Je. 49²⁶ 50⁰
51⁶. 𝔊 has καταχθείησαν, prob. a paraphrase, but Gr. ירדו. — לשאול] is pregnant, cf. 9¹⁸. This l. has eight tones, lacks rhyme, and with following v. shows
a harsher spirit than the Ps. as a whole. — **19.** האלמנה] Niph. impf. ‡ אלם not

[דִּבְרִית] in Qal, Niph. = *be made dumb*, elsw. 39⁹·¹⁰, cf. Ez. 3²⁶ 24²⁷ 33²². — [זֵרֶה] adj. *forward, arrogant;* Qal ptc. f. pl. agreeing with שׁפתי, article for rel. (*v. 5⁷*). — †[בּוּז] n.m. (1) *contempt;* elsw. 119²² 123³·⁴ Gn. 38²⁸ Jb. 12⁵ 31³⁴ Pr. 12⁸ 18³; (2) as poured out by God Ps. 107⁴⁰ Jb. 12²¹. — 20. [רֵה רַב טוּבְךָ] cf. 145⁷ וכר רב טובך ; *goodness* of God, kindness in doing good to one ; cf. Is. 63⁷ רב טוב לבית ישראל. 𝔊 inserts יהוה here, which makes better measure and sense. — אשׁר is needed in l. 2 also to complete the measure. — [חוסים בָּךְ] should be at end of l. for rhyme. — [רִֽכְסִ׃ — 27⁵. ס׳ ס׳ אהלו 32⁷, אתה ס׳ לי 91¹, ס׳ עליון 615, סתר כנפיך cf. [בְּסֵתֶר פָּנֶיךָ. 21. a.λ.; cf. רְכָסִים Is. 40⁴, and vb. יִרְכְּסוּ Ex. 28²⁸ 39²¹ (P), meaning *bind.* But it is difficult to connect either noun with this vb. *B*DB regards both as dubious, and gives no decision as to mngs. 𝔊 renders both the same way, ταραχή, *rough*, so 𝔍 *duritia.* We might then think of *roughness* of places, and *roughness, harshness, hardness, rudeness* of conduct. Ols., Oort, Du., change the text here to רְכִי. This v. is difficult in structure. Its two parts have 5 + 4 tones, and seem to be in syn. parall. It cannot be original in this form. It must either be reduced to 6 tones or enlarged to 12, or else it is a gl. But one l. is needed for measure. פּניך is necessary for rhyme, and must come at close of v. This requires a transposition of clauses. The words מריב לשׁנות are unnecessary, and prob. a gl. — 22. [בָּרוּךְ י׳ ptc. as adj., exclamation (*v. 18⁴⁷*). — 17⁷. 4⁴ [בְּעִיר מצור] *in an entrenched city;* so הפליא הסדו לי 4⁴ הפלה ה׳(ל) so [הפליא הסדו לי] *in an entrenched city;* so 60¹¹ (= עיר מבצר 108¹¹), cf. 2 Ch. 8⁵. If correct, the fortified city is Jerusalem, and the city and its defender have been protected from their enemies by Yahweh. It is possible that they have been besieged by enemies. We would change to עָר, cf. 32⁶ לעת מצא. Du. takes עיר as in 73²⁰ Je. 15⁸ *excitement, terror* (√עור). The v. is, however, a gl. — 23. [ואני] emph. as v.⁷·¹⁵. — [בְחָפְזִי] Qal inf. cstr. sf. 1 s. *in my haste* or *alarm;* so 116¹¹, which has the whole phr. ‡ חפז elsw. in ψ only Niph. *hurry away in alarm* 48⁶ 104⁷. — [נִגְרַזְתִּי] a.λ. Niph. pf. 1 sg. ירז improb.; rd. נגרשׁתי as Jon. 2⁵, which has the same line, omitting the inf. because Jon. 2 is pentameter. ‡ גרשׁ vb. Pi. *drive away* 34¹ 78⁵⁵ 80⁹. — ‡ [אָכֵן] as adv. asseveration, *surely;* in ψ only emphasising a contrast, *but, in fact, nevertheless*, so here, 66¹⁹ 82⁷. — [קול תחנוני] elsw. in ψ 28²·⁶ 86⁶ 116¹ 130² 140⁷; 28² is same as here, save that imv. of שׁמע is used and אכן omitted. The use of אכן is due to the different measure of the Ps. — 24. [אהבו את יהוה כל הסידיו] this is a gl. For v. 5¹², הסיר, 4⁴. — [אֱמוּנִים] is Qal ptc. pl. *faithful*, and not abst., as 𝔊 ἀληθείας, Du.; cf. Is. 26² שׁמר א׳ (*v. 12² 19⁸*). — [עַל־יֶתֶר] *abundantly*, prob. gl. — 25. [חזקו ויאמץ לבבכם] יאמץ Hiph. of אמץ *exhibit strength*, BDB. Hiph. only here and 27¹⁴, where there is a similar l. — [כָּל הַמְיַחֲלִים ליהוה] ה rel. with Pi. ptc. ‡ [יחל] vb. Pi. *wait for, hope for ;* c. ל 31²⁵ 33¹⁸·²² 69⁴ 119⁴³·⁴⁹·⁷⁴·⁸¹·¹¹⁴·¹⁴⁷ 147¹¹; c. אֶל 130⁷ 131³ Is. 51⁵, abs. Ps. 71¹⁴. Hiph. *wait, tarry* (shew a waiting attitude); c. ל 38¹⁶ 42⁶·¹² 43⁵ 130⁵ Mi. 7⁷ La. 3²⁴. This line is dependent on Ps. 27¹⁴, changing 2 sg. into 2 pl., and is a gl.

PSALM XXXII., 2 STR. 5^5.

Ps. 32 was a penitential Ps: (1) proclaiming the blessedness of the one whose sins are forgiven, covered over and not imputed (v.[1-2]), especially in view of the great suffering in body and soul during the long time that Yahweh's punitive hand rested upon him (v.[3-4]). (2) The confession of sin is followed by forgiveness (v.[5]) and the exhortation to the pious to pray to Yahweh in time of distress (v.[6]). Later additions represent Yahweh as the hiding-place (v.[7]); exhort earnestly to walk in the right way and not be stubborn as the mule (v.[8-9]); and contrast the sorrows of the wicked with the joys of the righteous (v.[10-11]).

HAPPY the one whose transgression is forgiven, whose sin is covered!
Happy the one unto whom Yahweh imputeth not iniquity!
When I kept silent, my bones waxed old through my roaring;
For day and night Thy hand was heavy upon me;
I was changed (into misery, as when thorns smite me).

MY sin I make known to Thee, and mine iniquity I do not cover;
I said, "I will confess concerning my transgression to Yahweh";
And Thou forgavest mine iniquity, my sin didst (pardon).
For this let the pious pray unto Thee in time of distress;
At the outburst of many waters, they will not reach unto him.

A משכיל (*v.* Intr. § 26) of 𝔇, not taken up into 𝔇ℜ or 𝔈 (*v.* Intr. §§ 27, 32, 33). It was separated from the Maskelim by the editor of ψ, owing to the fact that the others were used in 𝔈 The Ps. was originally of two pentameter pentastichs v.[1-6]. In this form it belongs to the Persian period. It was enlarged by a series of additions: at first v.[7], then a tetrameter tetrastich of advice v.[8-9], and a liturgical trimeter tetrastich of a general character v.[10-11]. "The influence of the individualising educational movement recorded for us in Proverbs is unmistakable," Che. In v.[8-9] there are Aramaisms: בלם and עצה after 𝔊, required for measure and confused with יעץ. This gloss was of late date, probably in the Maccabean period. The Ps. in its present form is the second penitential Ps. of the church.

Str. I is composed of a syn. couplet, a synth. line, and an emblematic triplet. — **1-2**. *Happy the one*], an exclamation of congratulation, repeated at the beginning of two lines for emphasis. In Ps. 1[1] the righteous man, who was entirely conformed to the Law, was thus congratulated; here, the one who has been a transgressor, but now, after a period of divine chastisement, enjoys forgiveness and reinstatement in the divine favour. The three chief syn. terms for sin are used to comprehend it in all its forms : *transgression*, the violation of divine command whether oral or written in Law ; *sin*, the failure from the normal aim or purpose in life ; *iniquity*, the perverse turning aside from the proper course of life. These forms of sin had incurred the divine displeasure, and had to be removed in order to a restoration to favour. Each term for sin has its appropriate predicate, which is not to be regarded as peculiar to that conception of sin rather than any other, but is in order to balance the threefold sin, with a threefold deliverance from it. — *is forgiven*]. This is, according to the Hebrew conception, the taking up of transgression as a burden, a heavy load, resting upon the sinner and bearing it away from him to a place where it will trouble him no more. The English " forgive," " give away," is syn. to it and sufficiently near to the Hebrew idea of take away, to translate it, agreeing as they do in the essential thing of removal. The same Hebrew term is used v.⁵ᶜ in connection with iniquity ; and probably also in the original, if the proposed change of text is correct, the syn. Hebrew word סלח, having the same essential meaning, which may appropriately be rendered by the syn. English word "pardon." — *is covered*], a syn. term, used also 85³ for the technical Hebrew word כפר, " cover over sin " (*v.* 65⁴ 78³⁸ 79⁹). It is commonly used in connection with sacrifices, where the sin, as staining and defiling the divine altars, was covered over by the application to them of the blood of the victim of the sin-offering. But the word is also frequently used apart from sacrifices, when God is conceived as covering the sin over so as to hide it and obliterate it. This Yahweh does in accordance with His sovereign good pleasure. There can be no doubt that here, as in other Pss., the latter is the true conception ; for there is no hint of any sacrifice in any of these Pss. — *imputeth not*], that is, does not estimate, consider, think of, in connection with the sinner. Far otherwise, Yahweh thinks of him as without iniquity, deals with him as no longer having any connection with it. We should beware of attaching to these terms the technical meanings of modern dogmatic theology. This syn. couplet makes a simple and comprehensive statement. But a later legalist thought that something more was required, and this he supplied by adding :

And in whose spirit there is no deceit. This may be explained
in accord with modern ideas : " Who conceals his sin neither from
God nor from himself," Dr. ; especially if we weaken the term
with EV^s. to " guile " ; but this renunciation of deceit of spirit is
a very high ethical ideal, not appearing elsewhere in the Old Testament. 1 John 1⁸ rises to a higher ethical conception, and may
be cited against self-deception in the matter of neglecting to confess sin, but hardly against one who has so completely confessed
his sin and has been so entirely relieved of it, as stated in the
previous couplet of our Ps. Such an one needs no exhortation
to sincerity of spirit. This clause adds a defective line to a Str.
complete without it ; and also imports a disturbing thought, to
the effect that such a man must not only be accepted by God
as without any more sin attached to him, but must also have the
more positive characteristic of a spirit without deceit. The clause
is a gloss from the school of Hebrew Wisdom. It is probable
that *man* is also a gloss, in order to give the experience, which
was originally national, a more personal and individualistic turn,
in accordance with the glosses, v⁸⁻¹¹. — **3.** *When I kept silent*],
refrained from making the confession, stated in v.⁵, and assumed
as the basis of v.¹⁻². — *my bones waxed old*], as in other Pss. of
penitence and lamentation, aching in sympathy with the distress
of the soul ; cf. 6⁸ 22^{15. 18} 38⁴ 51¹⁰. — *through my roaring*]. The
agony was so great that, although he did not cry to God for help
in penitential prayer, he did cry aloud with so much noise and
so little self-restraint that he lost his manhood and became a mere
animal. This has been intensified by the additional clause, *all day
long*, an insertion probably not designed, but due to dittography
of the following words. — **4.** *For day and night*], continuously,
all day and all night without interruption. — *Thy hand*], God's
hand, put forth in chastisement. — *was heavy upon me*], not
merely by its pressure of weight, but, as the context implies,
heavy because of heavy strokes, smiting him again and again
with His powerful hand, so as to make him roar with the agony
of suffering. Although he did not in fact suffer scourging of his
body, he did in fact suffer from the bruising of his soul by the
experience of the divine anger, so that his bones felt as if they
had been severely scourged. — *I was changed*] ; so 𝔊, 𝔍, trans-

formed from a former condition of comfort *into misery*, by the
severe divine discipline. This is much better suited to the context
than 𝔐, followed by EVˢ., "my moisture is turned into," AV., or
"is like," PBV., or "changed as with," RV., which have no
Hebrew usage to justify them and which are difficult to construct
with the following words. These again are different in 𝕲 from 𝔐.
𝕲 is here also to be preferred in its rendering, *as when thorns
smite me*]. The blows of God's hands are very appropriately compared with the smiting of the body with thorns, especially as in
ancient times thorns were used for the purpose of scourging.
Thus Gideon "took the elders of the city [of Succoth], and
thorns of the wilderness and briers, and with them he threshed
[or taught] the men of Succoth," Ju. 8¹⁶. Jer. and Aug. think
of pricking of the conscience. The reading of 𝔐, "droughts of
summer," is difficult to connect with the previous clause, because
the Hebrew prep. is not appropriate to the verb; and the word
rendered "droughts" is not used elsewhere in 𝔐, though the
meaning is possible, as being in a similar word from the same
stem.

Str. II. is composed of a triplet of two syn. lines, with a third
line synth. thereto, and an emblematic couplet. — **5.** *My sin*],
emph. in position, ‖ *iniquity* ‖ *transgression*, resuming the three
terms of v.¹⁻², in order now to state the confession presupposed in
these verses. The confession is also in three syn. terms, *make
known* ‖ *not cover* ‖ *confess*. The first term is in appropriate
antith. to forgive. The objectifying of the sin, by making it
known, is in order to taking it away. The second term, the
uncovering the iniquity, is that Yahweh might cover it again.
The third, confessing, a term not used elsewhere in ψ, but in
other writings, is properly acknowledging, possibly calling attention to by a gesture, in order that Yahweh on His part might
refuse to look at it, ignore it, not consider it, or think of it. All
this confession is in personal address, *to Thee* ‖ *to Yahweh*, and
meets with the response, *Thou forgavest mine iniquity*, using but
one, and that the oldest, simplest, and most important of the three
terms of v.¹⁻². 𝔐 and the Vrss. all agree in attaching two words
for sin together, "iniquity of my sin." But this is against the
usage of the previous context, and is probably due to the omission

of a verb, which is indeed necessary to complete the measure. This verb is probably the synonym, pardon, which has been omitted by copyist's error, because of its similarity in form to *Selah*, here used at the close of the line. Thus we may perfect the measure, and separate the terms for sin, and render the last clause, *my sin didst pardon.* — **6.** *For this*], namely, forgiveness. — *let the pious*], probably collective in the original text, but made individual by a later editor to correspond with v.[7-11], by prefixing "every." Only the pious, who were in a covenant relation to Yahweh, and so entitled to His kindness, could ask for forgiveness of sin. But all such should be encouraged by past experience to pray for it *in time of distress*, such as that described in v.[3-4]. So the original text should probably read. But it has been changed by copyist's error into "time, when Thou mayest be found." This limits the petition to a particular time, and so is against the context, which exhorts to pray in time of sin and trouble, which would not be usually considered as a time when God would be most favourable. It is probable that the copyist, who made the mistake, was thinking of a fast day, or possibly of the day of atonement, and it suits quite well the Christian use of Ash Wednesday. This mistake of the copyist, seeing two words, where only one was designed, gives the second as an introductory particle to the next clause, sometimes translated "But," PBV., "Surely," AV., RV., for which there is no sufficient reason in the parallelism. — *At the outburst of many waters*]. The distress is compared to a sudden flood, as in Pss. 18[6] 69[16]. — *they will not reach unto him*], because he has been put into a safe refuge by Yahweh, in answer to his prayer. The original Ps. came to an end here, in a most appropriate climax. And this was probably all of the Ps. when it was used in 𝔇.

Later editors made additions to the Ps. for various reasons; and first, **7**, which returns to the first person and is hexameter. — *O Thou, my hiding-place*]. This thought was not suggested by the idea of the Ps. in general, but by the specific thought of the previous line with reference to the flood of waters. The vocative is better suited to the following context than the usual, "Thou art my hiding-place." This phrase has probably come into the Ps. from 31[21]; cf. 27[5] 91[1]. But the reference is here more gen-

eral and later, for we can hardly think of the courts of the temple
in this context. — *From straits mayest Thou preserve me*], not an
expression of confidence in Yahweh, but a jussive of petition. —
O deliverer, mayest Thou encompass me about]. This clause is
thus parallel with and complementary to the previous one. 𝕳, 𝕲,
𝕵, all differ very much. The text has been disturbed by a dittography which caused the insertion of "songs"; 𝕳, EVˢ., more
properly, "jubilation," "shouts of joy"; but 𝕲, 𝕵, have "my jubilation ‖ my hiding-place." The rendering of EVˢ., "Thou wilt
compass me about with songs of deliverance," is to be rejected.
A second gloss was added, v.⁸⁻⁹.

> I will instruct thee and teach thee in the way thou shouldst go;
> I will counsel thee, (I will fix) mine eye upon thee.
> Be not as the horse, the mule, without understanding,
> With bridle and halter, its harness, to be muzzled.

This is a tetrameter tetrastich. It is a warning which most
of the older interpreters and many moderns regard as the words
of God; but most moderns think that they are the words of the
psalmist. In either case they are not suited to the Ps., because
the second person throughout the Ps. has been God, and the
exhortation of the previous context has been addressed to the
pious in the 3d person. It is a supplementary advice of a later
editor to all who listen to the Ps. It is furthermore of different
measure and strophical organisation. — **8.** *I will instruct thee
and teach thee*]. This is in accordance with the legal attitude
of mind subsequent to Nehemiah. — *in the way thou shouldst go*],
the way of the Law, the legal way or course of life and conduct;
more, therefore, in the spirit of Ps. 1 than of Ps. 32. — *I will
counsel thee*], intensifying the previous verbs. — A word is missing
in 𝕳 and also in most Vrss. 𝕾 gives it, instead of the verb preserved in 𝕳, the one using one verb, the other the other verb.
These are, indeed, so much alike that one of them was omitted
in the old codices. This verb is probably original and should be
rendered *I will fix*, which then gives an appropriate construction
to the otherwise difficult phrase, *mine eye upon thee*], the eyes of
the teacher being fixed upon the pupil so as to watch his every
step in the way of life. The positive teaching is followed by an

antith. couplet of warning. — **9.** *Be not as the horse*], intensified
by the more obstinate animal, *the mule.* — *without understanding*],
lacking the capability of receiving instruction and counsel ; therefore they have to be guided by physical means, *with bridle and
halter, its harness, to be muzzled*]. This was the original completion of the tetrastich ; but a brief marginal note, indicating a
reason for the muzzling, has come into the text and given difficulty. 𝔥, followed by most, has "it will not come near unto
thee," but various other renderings are given by ancient and
modern versions, which will not repay consideration.

10–11 are a still later liturgical gloss.

> Many sorrows has the wicked man ;
> But kindness has he that trusteth in Yahweh.
> Be glad and exult, ye righteous,
> And be jubilant, all ye right-minded.

This is a trimeter tetrastich. — *Many sorrows*], as the antith.
of *kindness*, suggests that they were due to divine punishment or
chastisement. The former belong to *the wicked man ;* they are
his by right of earning them ; the latter belongs to the man *that
trusteth in Yahweh.* This was probably the exact antith. of the
original text, but it has been changed by a later editor through
the addition of the verb "compasseth him about," to correspond
with v.[7] ; and so the measure has been destroyed, without any
important addition to the meaning. — **11.** *Be glad and exult* ‖ *be
jubilant*], liturgical terms implying worship in the temple. In
the first line "in Yahweh" is an unnecessary gloss, destroying the
measure. — *ye righteous*], the class of people in Israel living in
conformity to the Law ‖ *ye right-minded.*

1. אַשְׁרֵי] = v.[2] pl. cstr. before rel. clause (*v.* 1[1]); exclamation. — נְשׂוּי]
Qal pass. ptc. נשׂא, for נָשׂוּא, assimilated to כסי as if נשׂה *forgiven*, as v.[5] 25[18]
85[3] 99[8]. ‡ [כסה] vb. † Qal pass. ptc. *covered*, in respect of sin only here.
Pi. (1) *cover, clothe :* earth with great deep 104[6]; heaven with clouds 147[8];
(2) *conceal :* transgressions Jb. 31[33] Pr. 17[9] 28[13]; iniquity Ps. 32[5]; righteousness of God 40[11], cf. 143[9] (?); (3) *overwhelm :* the waters of the sea 78[53]
106[11] Jos. 24[7] (E); waters Ps. 104[9] Jb. 22[11] 38[34]; shame Pss. 44[16] 69[8] Je. 51[51]
Mi. 7[10]; horror Ps. 55[6] Ez. 7[18]; mischief Ps. 140[10], c. על 44[20] 106[17]; (4) *cover
over* sin Ps. 85[3] (by God). Pu. *be covered* Ps. 80[11]. Cf. usage of כפר *cover
over* sin, *v.* 65[4] 78[88] 79[9] BD*B.* — פֶּשַׁע] *transgression,* v.[5] 19[14]. — † חֲטָאָה] n.f.

sin; rare, only in phr. גדולה ה' Gn. 20⁹ (E) Ex. 32²¹·³⁰·³¹ (JE) 2 K. 17²¹ and Pss. *32¹* 40⁷ 109⁷ (*v.* חטאת 25¹⁸, חטא *51⁷*). — **2.** אָדָם] is a gl.; the only other use for individual in ψ, 84⁶·¹³. — יהוה] comes in between vb. and לו in an awkward way and should be transposed. — יַחְשֹׁב] Qal impf. present; חשב (*v. 10²*), here in sense of *impute,* cf. Niph. 106³¹. — עָוֹן (*v. 18²⁴*).—[ואין ברוחו רמיה is a gl.: a denial of sin and the reverse of the confession of sin in its three forms in previous context, and of the forgiveness, the covering over, the non-imputation of it. Besides, the phr. itself is late. רוח (*v. 31⁶*), here in sense of לֵב † for moral character, elsw. ψ 34¹⁹ 51¹⁹ 78⁸. — ‡ רְמִיָה] n.f. *deceit 32² 52⁴* 101⁷, קֶשֶׁת ר' *deceitful, treacherous bow* 78⁵⁷, לשׁון ר' 120²·³, v. מרמה *5⁷*. This can hardly be softened down to internal truthfulness to God. — **3.** כִּי] temporal, but 𝕲, 𝕵, causal.—[הֶחֱרַשְׁתִּי Hiph. perf. 1 sg. aorist; חרשׁ *be dumb, keep silence,* neglecting response (*v. 28¹*). — ‡ [בלה] vb. Qal *wear out:* of garment Dt. 8⁴ 29⁴·⁴; fig. heavens Ps. 102²⁷ Is. 50⁹; bones through suffering here. Pi. causative, *wear out, consume away:* fig. flesh and skin La. 3⁴; form in Sheol Ps. 49¹⁵. — עצמי] for the bones in a similar state of pain *v. 6³* 22¹⁵·¹⁸ 31¹¹ 38⁴ 42¹¹ 51¹⁰ 102⁴·⁶.—[נד־היום] makes the l. too long; dittog. as Du.; cf. כי יומם at beginning of next v. — **4.** † לְשַׁדִּי] ‡ [לְשַׁד n.m. *juice, sap; life blood* a.λ. in this sense; Nu. 11⁸ (J) taste of manna. But 𝕲 has here ἐστράφην εἰς ταλαιπωρίαν; 𝔙 *conversus sum in aerumna mea;* 𝕵 *versatus sum in miseria mea.* These Vrss. rd. שׁד *oppression,* and vb. as 1 sg. which if inf. וַהֲפֹךְ or ptc. וְהֶפֵךְ must have נפשׁי. הפך is followed by לְ in the sense of to *be turned* or *changed* into something (*v. 30¹²*). — † [חֲרבֹנִי n.m. *drought;* only here for usual חֹרֶב. But 𝕲 ἐν τῷ ἐνπαγῆναί ἄκανθαν, 𝔙 *dum configitur spina,* 𝕵 *cum exardesceret messis.* 𝕲 must have read קוץ for קיץ and חרבני, sf. ני and inf. cstr. of חרב *to attack, smite,* as Je. 50²¹·²⁷ (*v. 17¹³*); 𝕵 as inf. cstr. of חרב vb. *be dry.* 𝕾 interprets שַׁד *breast* and חרבני as inf. cstr. sf. 1 sg. חרב *lay waste, destroy.* 𝕲 on the whole seems most probable. חרבני in 𝔋 is late change for חרב, which makes all the readings easy in the different interpretations. — **5.** חטאתי] so עוני, emph. — [אוֹדִיעֲךָ] Hiph. impf. present, ידע. 𝕲 aorist as next vb. improbable. — [נסיתי] emph. present (*v. v.¹*). — [אמרתי is in 𝕲 and 𝕵, and seems to be original, although it would seem more natural at beginning of previous clause. It must therefore be emphatic and express previous resolution. — [עֲלֵי is taken by 𝕲 as κατ᾽ ἐμοῦ, 𝔙 *adversum me,* עֲלָי; but this is certainly incorrect. It is a poetic, archaic prep., lengthened for measure. — אֱלֵי] emph. — [עֲוֹן חטאתי] *guilt of my sin* (*v. v.¹·²*). Du. is prob. correct in reading עוני חטאתי סלחת; the סליה was confused with סלה and so omitted. Then it was necessary to connect the words for sin. This restoration makes the pentameter complete and the construction easy. — **6.** [עַל־זֹאת *for this thing, e.g.* pardon, or *on this account, therefore,* as כן עַל. 𝕲 ὑπὲρ ταύτης, 𝕵 *pro hac.* — לעת מצא cf. Is. 55⁶ בהמצאו; but this is not suited to the context, which emphasises the fact that God is to be found by the penitent, and not any special time of finding. — ‡ [רַק conj. *only,* as 91⁸, or in the sense *assuredly,* does not seem appropriate to the context. Therefore with Du. rd. for מצא רק, מצוק, which has been confused with מָצוֹר and so brought about מברק. לעת מצוק *time*

of distress. † מָצוֹק n.[m.] *straitness, straits:* צר ומ׳ 119¹⁴³ 1 S. 22² Dt. 28⁵³. ⁵⁵. ⁵⁷
Je. 19⁹. This phr. is then further defined by † שֶׁטֶף n.m. *flood, outburst ;* elsw.
Na. 1⁸ Jb. 38²⁵ Dn. 9²⁶ 11²² Pr. 27⁴. — **7.** [רֲנֵי] is a difficult form, pl. cstr. of
† רֹן n.[m.] *a.λ. jubilation =* רִנָּה.— [פַּלֵּט] n.[m.] *deliverance ;* elsw. 56⁸ both
dub. For vb. *v. 17¹³.* But 𝔊 is very different, ἀπὸ θλίψεως τῆς περιεχούσης
με τὸ ἀγαλλίαμά μου λύτρωσαί με ἀπὸ τῶν κυκλωσάντων με. 𝔊 takes הסובבני
and תצרני as alike relative clauses referring to the affliction or distress, צר
being n.f. as if צרה. It points ס׳תר לי ‖ רֹנֵי ; this is most likely, unless with
Houb., Horsley, Hi., Du., רני is dittog. for last letters of תצרני. 𝔍 is somewhat
different, *tu es protectio mea, ab hoste custodies me, laus mea salvans, circum-
dabis me.* צר *= adversary,* פלט is ptc. 𝕳, 𝔍, both take vbs. as expressing
confidence. 𝔊 regards the verse as essentially petition. The vb. תצרני is
‖ ת׳ס כבני, and must be interpreted in the same way. It is improb. that פלט
is a noun. The difficulty with 𝔊 is in taking צר as fem. and in the lack of
prep. מן after פלט. It is better to follow 𝔍 and take פלט as ptc., as 18³ 40¹⁸
70⁶ 144², referring to God, and to regard the impfs. as jussives.—

אתה ס׳תר לי מצר תצרני פלט רס׳כבני

8. [ואורך] ו coörd., emph. addition to previous vb.— [זֽוּ] rel. (*v. 9¹⁶*).— [הֶלֶה]
Qal impf. modal, *should go.—* [אִיעֲצָה] Qal impf. cohort. 1 sg. (*v. 16⁷*). 𝔊 ἐπι-
στηριῶ *=* אֱעֹצָה Qal impf. 1 sg. of עצה, as Pr. 16⁸⁰; so Bä. A word is missing from the measure. עליך implies a vb. which should prob. be that of 𝔊
in addition to that of 𝕳, as Du.— **9.** [אַל־תִּהְיוּ] Qal juss. 2 pl. with neg.—
‡ [מֶרֶג] n.m. *bridle,* as Pr. 26³ Is. 37²⁹. — ‡ [רֶסֶן] n.m. *halter,* as Is. 30²⁸ Jb. 30¹¹.
—‡ [עֶדְיוֹ] n.[m.] *ornament, trapping, harness ;* only here in this sense ; 𝔊 τὰς
σιαγόνας αὐτῶν, 𝔍 *maxillas eorum ;* in ψ elsw. only 103⁵ (dub.). Hu., Pe.,
Moll, take the clause as rel., "*whose harness* consists in bridle and bit to tame
it"; then Moll, "they will not approach thee," Pe. " or else they will not
come nigh unto thee"; Ew., Ri., AV., inf. with ל "must be muzzled, or there
is no drawing near to thee." But vb. כלם is an Aramaic word, not used in
OT., and is late. Du. then takes vb. as Hiph. inf. לחריב. כל בו is dittog., so
we get לחריב.— **10.** [מכאובים] pl. ‡ מכאוב n.m. *pains, sorrows, grief ;* elsw. 38¹⁸
69²⁷ Is. 53³˙⁴ Je. 45² 51⁸ La. 1¹². ¹². ¹⁸. Bi., Du., insert אשר before רשע *wicked
man.* But we might rather omit סובבנו, and so get a trimeter couplet. The
omission of יהוה in v.¹¹ would then give a trimeter tetrastich. — **11.** [הרנינו]
Hiph. imv. 2 pl. requires after it לו as Du. — [כל־ישרי־לב] as 7¹¹ 11² 36¹¹ 64¹¹
94¹⁵ 97¹¹.

PSALM XXXIII., 4 STR. 10³.

Ps. 33 is a song of praise. (1) A call to worship in the temple
with song, music, and shouting (v.¹⁻³), because of the righteousness
and kindness of Yahweh (v.⁴⁻⁵). (2) All mankind are called to
fear Yahweh, the creator of all things, and disposer of all nations

(v.$^{6-10}$). (3) **Yahweh from His heavenly throne inspects all mankind** (v.$^{13-15}$) ; **and victory is not due to armies or warriors** (v.$^{16-17}$). (4) **He delivereth those who fear Him** (v.$^{18-19}$) ; **therefore His people long for Him, are glad in Him, and trust in His name for victory** (v.$^{20-22}$). **A gloss praises the plans of Yahweh as everlastingly secure, and also the happiness of His people** (v.$^{11-12}$).

SHOUT, ye righteous in Yahweh,
    Praise is becoming to the upright;
    Give thanks to Yahweh with the lyre,
    With the ten-stringed harp play to Him;
    Sing to Him a new song,
    Play skilfully with shouting;
    For the word of Yahweh is upright;
    And all His work is with faithfulness;
    He loves righteousness and justice,
    The earth is full of His kindness.
BY His word the heavens were made,
    And by the breath of His mouth all their host;
    He gathereth in a flask the waters of the sea,
    Putteth in treasuries the primeval deep.
    Let all the earth be in fear of Yahweh,
    Let all the inhabitants of the world stand in awe;
    For He spake and it came to pass,
    He commanded and it stood forth.
    He doth bring to naught the counsel of nations,
    He doth make of none effect the plans of the peoples.
FROM heaven Yahweh doth look,
    See all the sons of mankind;
    From the place where He sits enthroned He doth glance,
    At all the inhabitants of the earth;
    He that formed their mind altogether,
    He that discerneth all their works.
    The king doth not gain a victory by his great army,
    The mighty man cannot be delivered by his great strength,
    The horse is a delusion for victory,
    And by his great army he cannot deliver.
BEHOLD, the eye of Yahweh is toward them that fear Him,
    Toward them that hope in His kindness;
    To deliver their life from death,
    And to preserve their lives in famine.
    Our soul doth wait for Yahweh,
    Our help and shield is He;
    For in Him our heart is glad,
    For in His holy name we trust.
    Let Thy kindness, Yahweh, be upon us
    According as we hope in Thee.

Ps. 33 is an orphan Ps. without title, and therefore was not in any of the minor or major Psalters. It was inserted in its present position by the final editor. The τῷ Δαυείδ of 𝔊 is a late conjecture. The Ps. indeed shows the influence of many writings: v.^{3a} of Is. 42^{10}; v.^{3b} of Is. 23^{16}; v.^{7} of Jb. 38^{22}; v.^{9a} of Gn. 1^{3}; v.^{11} of Is. 40^{8} 46^{10} 51$^{6.8}$ 55$^{8\,sq.}$; v.^{13} of Pss. 11^{4} 14^{2}; v.^{15} of Zc. 12^{1}; v.$^{16.\,20b}$ of Dt. 33^{29}; v.^{17} of Pr. 21^{31}; v.^{22} of Ps. 90^{17}. 1 Mac. 3^{19} is probably based on v.^{16}. The use of the participles, v.$^{5.7}$, for the finite verb is in late Aramaic style. The Ps. cannot be earlier than the late Greek period, and probably is Maccabean on account of its reference to divine aid in victories v.$^{16.\,17.\,19.\,20.\,21}$; the joyous temple worship with song, music, and shouting v.$^{1-3}$; and universalism of outlook v.$^{8.\,10.\,13.\,14}$. The Ps. is composed of 22 couplets, corresponding with the number of the letters of the Hebrew alphabet, but without the use of the alphabetic letters at the beginning of the couplets, therein differing from Ps. 34. There is always difficulty in arranging such Pss. in Strs., and scholars differ in this regard. It is probable that the correspondence of the number of couplets with the letters of the alphabet was due to the insertion of two couplets, v.$^{11-12}$, into the original Ps. for that purpose. These couplets may be taken out without being missed — indeed, to the improvement of the course of thought in the Ps., which they interrupt. It is then easy to divide the Ps. into four trimeter decastichs.

Str. I. is composed of five syn. couplets, three of which are a call to worship in the temple, two giving the reason for it. — **1.** *Shout ye*], the sacred shout expressing the enthusiasm of *praise* in the temple worship, which was appropriate to the place and *becoming* to those entitled to worship there. These are the *righteous* ‖ *upright*, in the later sense of those zealous for the Law and institutions of Israel, and living in strict conformity thereto. — **2.** *Give thanks*], implying a song of thanksgiving accompanied with instrumental music of the *lyre* and larger *ten-stringed harp*. The three forms of praise are summed up in **3** : *Sing, play skilfully, with shouting.* That which is to be sung is a *new song*, a fresh outburst of praise ; not in the sense that a new composition was rendered, but that a fresh experience of divine favour had been enjoyed, and was acknowledged in a new festal assembly in the temple for this particular purpose. — **4.** The reason for this summons is *the word of Yahweh* and *His work.* This comprehends all the divine activity, as it has been experienced. The word, in its instruction and promises, *is upright,* as His people who conform to it are upright ; His work in judgment upon enemies and redemption of His people is *with faithfulness* to

His covenant, cf. Dt. 32⁴. But back of all His word and work
is His love in its more ancient form of kindness and its later form
of affection. — **5**. *He loves righteousness*, probably the doing of it
on His part as the context suggests, *and justice*, incorrectly rendered "judgment" in EV⁸. here and elsewhere in this combination.
— *The earth is full of His kindness*] in action, in His work as above,
cf. 119⁶⁴. These divine attributes are conceived as working through
all the earth. That is the background of their particular working
in the experience which calls for the fresh song of praise.

Str. II. is composed of two parts of syn. couplets, giving the
reason for the intervening syn. couplet, summoning the world to
stand in awe of Yahweh. — **6**. The psalmist goes back in thought
to the creation, especially of *the heavens* and *all their host;* that
is, the heavenly luminaries, sun, moon, and stars, in accordance
with the conception of Gn. 2¹ Is. 40²⁶ 45¹², and not the angels as
Pss. 103²¹ 148². These *were made*, the most general term for
creative activity, not implying any particular mode or theory of
creation. — *By His word*], the instrumental means here employed ; that is, by command, as v.⁹ in accordance with Gn. 1.
With this is parallel : *By the breath of His mouth*], the words
breathed forth in speech. Some have thought of the divine Spirit
here in accordance with Gn. 1², the same Hebrew word being
used for "breath" and "spirit" ; but if the reference were to
the divine Spirit it would be Spirit of Yahweh, and not Spirit of
His mouth. — **7**. The creation of *the waters of the sea* is now
described. — *the primeval deep*], probably only the depths of the
sea, in accordance with Jb. 38⁸⁻¹¹· ²², and not the more comprehensive mass of waters, including the subterranean and terranean
waters before their separation, of Gn. 1⁶⁻⁹. — *He gathereth in a
flask*], after 𝔊 and most ancient Vrss., as more suited to the
putteth in treasuries, than 𝔥 followed by EV⁸., "as a heap."
The conceptions of treasuries, where God stores up the snow and
hail, and of a flask, literally water-skin, in which the Orientals
carry their water and wine, where God stores up the waters of
heaven, are in Jb. 38²²· ³⁷. Inasmuch as in Jb. 38⁸⁻¹⁰ the baby sea is
conceived as shut in safely in its place at the creation with bars
and doors, it is most probable that all these terms of Job are at
the basis of this description, rather than the heaping up of the

waters of the Red Sea for the passage through them of Israel, according to Ex. 15[8], which is another and heterogeneous figure of speech to that of treasuries and the permanence of the sea in its place. The verbal forms are participles, but not on that account to be referred to "the continual action of maintenance as well as the original creation," Kirk., because the participles are of the late Aramaic style, used for the finite verb, and refer to the creation itself as in the passage of Job mentioned above. — **8**. The fact of the creation of heavens and sea by Yahweh is a ground on which the psalmist summons mankind to fear such a Creator. — *Let all the earth* ‖ *all the inhabitants of the world*], all mankind wherever they may be. This is an universal summons. — *be in fear of Yahweh* ‖ *stand in awe*]. It is not probable that the psalmist is thinking of fear here in the religious sense appropriate to the people of God, as in v.[18], where the accusative is used; but in the more external sense of awe and submission to the divine sovereignty. — **9**. The reason is reënforced by a return to the conception of the creation, which is stated in terms of the primitive creation of the light, according to Gn. 1[3]. — *For He spake and it came to pass*], the very words of Gn. 1[3], expressing by the Waw consec. the immediateness of the obedience of the creature to the creative word; paraphrased in the syn. clause: *He commanded*, with the same immediateness of result, *and it stood forth*]; that is, it sprang into existence and presented itself, or stood forth as a host, using the imagery of v.[6] and Gn. 2[1], as an army stands forth in array when the sovereign issues the command. — **10**. The creative power has been mentioned as a warning to the nations; it is therefore appropriate in the climax that the providential power should be referred to. This, as we would expect from the purpose of the statement, is on its negative side, with reference to *the nations* ‖ *the peoples*. They may take *counsel* and make *plans* against the people of Yahweh, but in vain; for *He doth bring* them *to naught* ‖ *make of none effect*. He frustrates all their schemes of hostility against His people; and this is the climax which justifies the inclusion of the entire Str. in this Ps. of praise.

A later editor, wishing to emphasise the thought of the last couplet, adds a tetrastich to the Str., and interrupts thereby the progress of thought in the Ps.

The counsel of Yahweh standeth forever,
The plans of His mind to all generations.
Happy the nation whose God is Yahweh,
The people He has chosen for His inheritance!

11–12. *The counsel of Yahweh ‖ the plans of His mind*], the
plans formed in His mind, God being conceived as having a
mind, just as man, His image. These words are in striking antith.
to the counsel and plans of the nations of the previous couplet.
As Yahweh frustrates their counsel and plans, He maintains His
own counsel; it *standeth* firm, not capable of frustration, unchange-
able, permanent, and indeed *forever ‖ to all generations*. This is
a ground for congratulation to the people of Yahweh, for it renders them secure in the hands of their God; therefore they may
sing: *Happy the nation ‖ the people*, antith. to all the other nations
and peoples, because they have the inestimable privilege of one
whose God is Yahweh; and this not simply because they have
chosen Him to be their God, but because *He has chosen* them
for His inheritance, His own special property in accordance with
the original covenant, Ex. 19^5; cf. Dt. 4^{20} $9^{26.29}$ 32^9 Mic. $7^{14.18}$ Is.
19^{25} Je. 10^{16} Pss. 28^9 68^{10} 74^2 $78^{62.71}$ $94^{5.14}$ $106^{5.40}$. A still later editor inserts in the Mss. underlying ⅏ an addition to v.[10], followed
by 𝔙 and PBV., "and casteth out the counsel of princes," which
makes the couplet into a triplet by a third syn. clause. It certainly was not in the original Ps., which was composed entirely
of couplets, although it is an idea entirely appropriate in itself.

Str. III. is composed of three synth. couplets, describing the
divine inspection of mankind, followed by two syn. couplets drawing the consequences, that victory and safety are not due entirely
to human powers. — **13–14.** *From heaven*], emphatic, ‖ *the place
where He sits enthroned*], the divine throne in the heavenly pal-
ace, *v.* 9^8 29^{10} 55^{20} 102^{13} Is. 63^{15} 66^1. — *Yahweh doth look ‖ see
‖ glance*], the divine inspection of mankind, as 11^4 14^2. — *all the
sons of mankind ‖ all the inhabitants of the earth*]. His inspection is universal, a resumption of the thought of the universal
warning of v.[8]. The inspection is a thorough one, nothing escapes
it. — **15.** *He that formed their mind*], created the mind of man,
constructed or formed it as truly as He formed the body; cf.
Gn. $2^{7.8}$ Zc. 12^1 Ps. 94^9. It is possible that the second story of

the creation was in the mind of the psalmist as well as the first, and that he extends the construction of the body of man to that of the mind also. But inasmuch as he thinks of the minds of his contemporaries, the formation of the mind is not that of the primitive man, but that of all men the world over. The psalmist does not, any more than Is.², distinguish the creative activity from the providential. He certainly does not conceive the later distinction between creationism and traducianism. He thought that each and every individual man originates, mind and body, as a result of divine activity; cf. Ps. 139¹³⁻¹⁶. The divine construction of the mind was not partial but total, *altogether*. Therefore Yahweh knows it already in all its powers and activities, its capacities and its limitations. Nothing whatever in the mind of man can escape His inspection. He knows the inner man. He is one *that discerneth all their works*. The result of all this is that the mind and works of men are very much limited; they are under the entire control of Yahweh. — 16-17. *The king*], thinking probably of the king of Syria, the great enemy of the Maccabean times, ‖ *the mighty man*, the trained warrior, ‖ *the horse*, the cavalry of the army. These are conceived as with a *great*, a numerous, *army*, coming up against Israel and relying upon their overwhelming power for *victory*. The renderings of EV⁹., "save," "salvation," or "safety," are too general, and not suited to the context. The beauty of the synonymous thought is spoiled by rendering the same word "host" or "army" in v.¹⁶ and "strength" in v.¹⁷, as if the latter referred to the horse. This would be an exaggeration of the horse, giving it a couplet to itself, and indeed in the climax of the Str., as compared with the king who would have but one line, although he is emphasised by the position of the word in v.¹⁶ᵃ. The king is really the subject of v.¹⁷ᵇ, as well as of v.¹⁶ᵃ. The king thinks he can gain a victory by his great army. His cavalry, in which he chiefly trusted, proves a delusion. Instead of winning victory, he is defeated, and in his defeat the strength of his warriors cannot deliver them, and the king himself cannot find deliverance by his army. The context indicates that all this is due to the divine inspection and interposition so fully stated in the previous couplets. For this situation in history, cf. 1 Mac. 3¹⁹.

Str. IV. is composed of two syn. couplets, setting forth the
experience of deliverance, followed by three synth. couplets of
joyous prayer. — **18.** *Behold*], calling particular attention to what
is to be said. — *the eye of Yahweh*], taking up the inspection of
the previous Str. Yahweh's eye is resting upon His people as
well as upon the nations, only with a different motive. He had
inspected the nations to frustrate their plans and to give them
defeat instead of victory. He inspects His people with favour. —
toward them that fear Him], with the reverential fear of worship,
‖ *toward them that hope in His kindness*], look up to Him for it,
expect it, wait to receive it; recurring to the kindness of v.[5],
praised, as exhibited throughout the earth. That which the people of Yahweh hoped for, looking unto Yahweh in godly fear, they
received. — **19.** His eye had a redemptive purpose when directed
upon them: *To deliver their life from death.* The nation had
been in extreme peril because of the great army of the king of
Syria, threatening to destroy them. Yahweh delivered them by
giving them the victory. — *And to preserve their lives in famine*].
If this is historical, it may refer to the famine of a besieged city
in which the great army of Syria had shut up Israel, and then
probably to a siege of Jerusalem, or else to a peril of famine in
the land, owing to the devastation wrought by the Syrian army.
— **20.** The psalmist now turns to the final prayer. — *Our soul*].
The people are conceived as having but one soul; only they
speak, not as an individual, " my soul," but as an aggregate of
individuals in one nation. — *doth wait for Yahweh*], not here in
the sense of anxiously looking for an exhibition of kindness in
deliverance; but in the temple, in reliance upon His kindness
as already bestowed. — **21-22.** *For in Him our heart is glad* ‖ *we
trust* ‖ *we hope in Thee*, all alike syn. expressions of joyous confidence in their God who had done such great things for them. —
Our help and shield], shield for defence, help to deliver; cf.
Gn. 15[1] Pss. 3[4] 20[3]. — *His holy name*], the majestic name that
secures victory in accordance with 20[6, 8]. The Ps. concludes with
a petition that the *kindness* just experienced in deliverance, v.[18],
and which now fills the earth with its renown, v.[5], may ever abide
upon His people.

1. †[נאוה] adj. (1) *comely :* of woman Ct. 1⁵ 6⁴, so Ps. 68¹³; cf. Je. 6²; face Ct. 2¹⁴; mouth Ct. 4³. (2) *seemly :* of תהלה here as 147¹ (cf. 93⁵); elsw. Pr. 17⁷ 19¹⁰ 26¹. — **2.** [ישור, נבל ,כנור, *v.* Intr. § 34. — **3.** †[שיר חדש] is based on Is. 42¹⁰; elsw. Pss. 40⁴ 96¹ 98¹ 144⁹ 149¹, a fresh outburst of song. — [היטיבו] Hiph. pf. 3 m. pl. ‡ [יטב] vb. Qal, *be pleasing ;* c. ל 69³²; elsw. c. ל· *be well for, go well with,* Gn. 12¹³ (J) 40¹⁴ (E) Dt. 8 t. Je. 4 t. +. Hiph. (1) c. ל *do good to, deal well with,* Pss. 49¹⁹ 125⁴ Ex. 1²⁰ (E) Gn. 12¹⁶ (J) +; c. acc. Ps. 51²⁾ Dt. 8¹⁵ Je. 18¹⁰ +; (2) *do thoroughly,* prob. 36⁴, as Mi. 7³ †(ל)נגן היטיב *play well, skilfully,* here as 1 S. 16¹⁷ Is. 23¹⁶ Ez. 33³²; (3) *do well, right :* ethically Ps. 119⁶⁸. — [וגן] Pi. inf., *v.* Intr. § 34. — [הריעה] *sacred shout, v.* 27⁶. — **4.** [ישר] *right (v.* 7¹¹), as predicate of the דבר only here, but cf. for the commands of the Law in other terms 19⁹ 119¹³⁷. ‡ דבר n.m. (1) *speech, discourse, saying :* ד׳ שפתים 17⁴ 59¹³; ד׳ פה 36⁴; ד׳ שאגה 22²; ד׳ מר *bitter speech* 64⁴; ד׳ טוב *goodly speech* in poem 45²; ענה ד׳ 119⁴² Is. 36²¹ Je. 44²⁰; *spoken command of God* Pss. 33⁴· ⁶ 103²⁰· ²⁰ 105²⁸ 148⁸, prob. 56⁵· ¹¹· ¹¹; ד׳ שלח 107²⁰ 147¹⁸ (cf. v.¹⁵) Is. 9⁷ Je. 42⁵; *promise* Pss. 105¹⁹· ⁴² 106¹²· ²⁴. (2) *Saying, sentence as written, lines of song,* 18¹ 137⁸ Dt. 32⁴⁴; *the Law* as divine sentence Pss. 50¹⁷ 105⁸ 119⁹· ¹⁶· ¹⁷· ²⁵· ²⁸· ⁴²· ⁴³· ⁴⁹· ⁵⁷· ⁶⁵· ⁷⁴· ⁸¹· ⁸⁹· ¹⁰¹· ¹⁰⁵· ¹⁰⁷· ¹¹⁴· ¹³⁰· ¹³⁹· ¹⁴⁷· ¹⁶⁰· ¹⁶¹· ¹⁶⁹ 130⁵ 147¹⁹. (3) *Words, as parts of sentence,* 7¹ 19⁴ 52⁶ 55²² 56⁶ 109³. (4) *Matter, affair,* about which one speaks, pl. 65⁴ 105²⁷ 145⁵ (?); sg. ד׳ רע 64⁶ 141⁴; ד׳ כרמות 35²⁾; ד׳ בליעל 41⁹ 101³; *cause* in judgment 112⁵. (5) Prep. על דבר *because of, for the sake of,* 45⁶ 79⁹ Gn. 20¹¹ (E) Ex. 8² (J). — [כל־מעשׂיהו] should be without Makkeph for measure. — [באמונה] not ב *essentiae,* PBV., Pe., but either *in* as 𝕲, 𝔖, De., Hu., Che., Dr., or *with,* Ew. ‡ אמונה n.f. *firmness, steadfastness, fidelity ;* in ψ only *faithfulness, trust :* (a) of human conduct 37⁸ (?); † (b) as divine attribute 88¹² 89². ³· ⁶· ⁹; shewn in works 33⁴; commands 119⁸⁶; in affliction 119⁷⁵; in oath to David 89⁵⁰; reaching unto skies 36⁶; unto all generations 100⁵ 119⁹⁰; God will not belie it 89³⁴; אמונה מאד 119¹³⁸ (cf. אמן א׳ Is. 25¹); closely associated with חסד 39²⁵ 92³ 98³ (cf. Ho. 2²²), צדקה, צדק 96¹³ 143¹ (cf. Is. 11⁵), salvation Ps. 40¹¹ (elsw. of God only Dt. 32⁴ La. 3²⁸). — **5.** [ארב] Qal ptc. Yahweh subj. — [צדקה] *righteousness (v.* 5⁹). — [משכנ·] *justice (v.* 1⁵). — [חס·] *kindness,* as v.¹⁸· ²² (*v.* 4⁴). — [יהוה] unnecessary gl. — **6.** [דבר ·· is only a variation of ·· אמר of Gn. 1⁶, which the author had in view (v.⁹). This is evident also from the צבא, which in Gn. 2¹ refers to the whole organised creation, but here specifically to the heavenly bodies (*v.* 24¹⁰). — [רוח פיו] (*v.* 18¹⁶ 31⁶) = *breath of his mouth* is syn. with דבר, the uttered word, as most interpreters of modern times. The majority of the older interpreters, however, think of the רוח אלהים of Gn. 1². But this seems excluded by פיו, which is nowhere used in connection with the divine Spirit. Pe. suggests that there is here a usage parallel to Ps. 104²⁹⁻³⁰, where the רוח of God is the source of life as it enters into the animals with quickening power and imparts to them their רוח. So in Jb. 33⁴, the divine רוח and נשמה· are in men the source of life. But this would lead us beyond Pe. to the doctrine of Gn. 2⁷, where the נשמת חיים is breathed into Adam's nostrils by Yahweh, and Gn. 7²² implies that the נשמת רוח חיים of all animals was **also**

imparted by the breath of God. This, however, would lead to the thought that the צבא of heaven are here regarded as living beings, like the morning stars of Job, and the reference here would be to orders of angels. This would widen the doctrine of creation to the extent that all living beings in heaven and on earth owe their life to the breath of the divine mouth. — [כרבר יהוה] is prob. for an original בדברו; otherwise the i. is too long. — **7.** [כֹּנֵס] Qal ptc. † [כנס] vb. Qal, *gather :* people 1 Ch. 22[2] Est. 4[16]; waters here ; stones Ec. 3[5]; wealth Ec. 2[8], cf. v.[26]; portion for priests Ne. 12[44]. Pi. *gather together :* for punishment Ez. 22[21]; for restoration Ps. 147[2] Ez. 39[28]. Hithp. *gather oneself together* Is. 28[2)]. — † [נֵד] *heap ;* as in Ex. 15[8] Ps. 78[13], of Jordan Jos. 3[13. 16] (Is. 17[11] dub.), so 擻, Hu., Pe. ; but Hare, Lowth., Horsley, Houb., Ew., Ols., Che., al., follow the Vrss. (except Quinta) in reading נֹאד = נֹד *bottle* (v. 56[9]). The sea is represented as shut up as water in a bottle or water skin ; cf. Jb. 38[8–11], where the baby sea is shut in with doors and bars. It is tempting to think of the bottles of the clouds ; in this case the upper as well as the lower waters were in the poet's mind. — [מים] (v. *18[12]*) used frequently of waters of the clouds ; but יָם (v. *24[9]*) either of seas on the earth's surface or subterranean. — ‡ [אוֹצָר] n.m., in ψ only pl.f. for the storehouses of God for rain, snow, hail, etc.; elsw. 135[7] Dt. 28[12] Jb. 38[22. 22] Je. 10[13] = 51[16]. — [תְּהוֹמוֹת] pl.f. of ‡ תְּהוֹם n.m. *deep place :* always of waters : (1) of a great sea 36[7] 107[26] 135[6] 148[7]; (2) of the Red Sea at the crossing 77[17] 106[9]; (3) of a river, giving drink 78[15], with waterfalls 42[8. 8]; (4) of subterranean waters 71[20] (?); (5) of the primeval sea here, as 104[6]. — **8.** [ממנו] prosaic gl., makes l. too long. — **9.** [כי הוא] כי here as in v.[4] giving reason of praise. הוא emph. as in parallel line. — [אָמַר וַיֶּהִי] is based on the creation of the light Gn. 1[3], pf. followed by ו consec. impf. immediate result. — **10.** [הֵפִיר] Hiph. pf. 3 m. for usual הֵפֵר, assimilated in form to הֵנִיא ‡ [פרר] vb. Hiph. (1) *break,* the Law 119[126]; (2) *frustrate,* here ; (3) *annul* 85[5] 89[84] both dub. — † [נוא] vb. Qal only Nu. 32[7] Kt. (but Hiph. Qr.). Hiph. (1) *restrain, forbid,* vow Nu. 30[6. 6. 9. 12]; *frustrate,* thoughts here ; *refuse* שבו (but dub.) 141[5]; (2) *restrain from* Nu. 32[7. 9]. — ‡ [מַחֲשָׁבָה] n.f. (1) *thought :* מ' אדם 94[11]; of God, מ' לבו 33[11]; c. אֶל 40[6]; are exceeding deep 92[6]; (2) *device, plan, purpose,* here and 56[6]. — **11–12.** These are tetrameters in their present form. לב of God is as לב of man, the seat of the thoughts and counsels, or plans (v. *19[15]*); cf. Is. 40[8] 46[10] 51[6. 8] 55[8 sq.]. — **13.** [דשמים] emph., cf. 14[2]. — [הִבִּיט] Hiph. pf. emph. present וכט. — **14.** [שִׁבְתּוֹ] Qal inf. cstr. sf. 3 s. ; ישב pregnant sense, *sit enthroned* (v. 2[4]). — [הִשְׁגִּיחַ] Hiph. Pf. † שוה *glance at ;* elsw. Is. 14[16] Ct. 2[9]. — **15.** [יצר לבם] Here God forms the לב, the intellectual and moral nature of man, as in Zc. 12[1] He forms the רוח, the disposition or temper. — [הַיֹּצֵר] Qal ptc.; הַמֵּבִין Hiph. ptc.; both with article and so rel. clauses. — **16.** [אֵין] is constructed with ptc. yb 𝕲, 𝔍, Hu., Dr., Kirk., but with the noun by EV[s].; the former is the better. — [רִכְרֹב] generic article (v. 2[6]). — [וְיִ־־ִי] Niph. ptc. ישׁע (v. 3[8]) has the mng. of *gaining victory,* as Ew., Hi., De., Hu., Pe., Kirk. — **17.** [הַסּוּם] generic article : the horse is שקר (7[15]), *a deception, delusion,* as Pr. 21[31]. — [־־שׁוּעָה] *victory,* for older ישׁוּעָה (v. 3[8]). ‡ תְּשׁוּעָה n.f. (1) *deliverance,* usually by God

through human agency, esp. from oppression and in battle, and so *victory*
here as 144[10]; of deliverance from personal troubles 37[39]; or of national
deliverance under fig. of personal 40[11. 17] 71[15]; ישׁוּעָתִי י׳ 38[23]; of man, תשׁועת
ארם deliverance of or through man 60[13] = 108[13], cf. 146[3]; (2) more exclusively spiritual in sense 51[16] 119[11. 81].—וְיֵמַלֵט] Pi. impf. modal (*v. 22*[6]);
⑮ Niph. pass. These four lines afford a fine example of distributed parallelism. נושׁע of *a* has its parallel in תשׁועה of *c*. ינצל of *b* is balanced with ימלט
of *d*; but רב חיל is in *a* and *d*, although ℨ, EV⁸. regard the second as the
strength of the horse. — **18.** This l. is a pentameter as it stands, but the change
of אל to ל in *b* is improb.; rd. מְיַחֲלִים ואל מיחלים. Pi. ptc. pl., יחל (*v. 31*[25]);
so v.[22]. — **19.** This is also a pentameter line most naturally, but לחיותם is
strange; it is a condensation of להיות חיותם. The trouble of famine is instead
of the battle of v.[16-17]. — [לְהַצִּיל] Hiph. inf. נצל as v.[16], ‖ לְחַיּוֹת Pi. inf. of חיה
(*v. 22*[27]), both expressing purpose. הָיָה in the sense of *life* is only in poetry;
cf. 74[19] 78[50] 143[3]. — **20.** [וַנַּפְשֵׁנוּ] emph. paraphrase of personal pronoun *we*
(*v. 3*[3]). — [חִכְּתָה] Pi. pf. 3 f. ‡ [חכה] vb. Qal, *wait for*, only Is. 30[18] (c. ל).
Pi. *long for* : c. ל here as 106[13], also Is. 8[17] 64[3] Zp. 3[8] +.

PSALM XXXIV., 3 str. 7⁶.

**Ps. 34 is a thanksgiving. (1) A vow of praise in which all
are invited to unite (v.²⁻⁴) ; because Yahweh has answered the
prayer of His afflicted people and delivered them by their guardian angel (v.⁵⁻⁸) ; (2) an exhortation to seek Yahweh, the source
of all good (v.⁹⁻¹¹), with instruction that prosperity depends upon
good conduct (v.¹²⁻¹⁵) ; (3) a contrast of the watchful care of
Yahweh over the righteous (v.¹⁶. ¹⁸⁻²¹) with His destruction of the
wicked (v.¹⁷ ²²). A liturgical gloss was added (v.²³).**

I WILL bless Yahweh at all times, continually shall His praise be in my mouth.
   Of Yahweh will my soul boast; let the afflicted (make it heard) and be glad.
   O magnify Yahweh with me; and let us exalt His name together.
      I sought Yahweh, and He answered me, and from all my terrors He delivered me.
      They looked unto Him and beamed, and their face was not abashed.
      This same afflicted people cried, and Yahweh from all his distresses saved him.
      The angel of Yahweh encamped about them that fear Him, and rescue them.
O TASTE and see that He is good; happy the man that taketh refuge in Him.
   O fear Yahweh, His holy ones; for there is no *lack* to them that fear Him.
   Young lions are in want and they suffer hunger; but they that seek Him *lack*
         not any good.
      O come, sons, hearken to me; the fear of Yahweh I will teach you.
      Who is the man that taketh pleasure in life? loveth days that he may see *good*?
      Keep thy tongue from evil, and thy lips from speaking deceit;
      Depart from evil and do good; seek peace and pursue it.

THE face of Yahweh is against them that do evil, to cut off their memory from the land.

The eyes of Yahweh are unto the righteous, and His ears unto their cry for help;
They cry and Yahweh heareth, and delivereth them out of all their distresses.
Yahweh is nigh unto the broken-hearted, and the crushed in spirit He saveth.
Many are the misfortunes of the righteous: but out of them all Yahweh delivereth him;
He keepeth all his bones, not one of them is broken.
Misfortune shall slay the wicked, and they that hate the righteous shall suffer punishment.

Ps. 34 was in 𝔇, but not in any of the major Psalters. The title has a reference to the life of David, "when he changed" or disguised "his judgment," feigned madness "before Abimelek, and he sent him away and he departed," in accordance with the story 1 S. 21¹¹ᵗ⁹·, except that the Philistine king is there called Achish (v. Intr. § 27). This change might have arisen from defective memory of the editor, or from substituting the common name of the Philistine kings for the specific one. Ps. 56 is also referred in the title to the same period of David's life at Gath. The editor did not mean to imply that David composed these Pss. on that occasion, but that they might be supposed to represent his spiritual emotions at that time. Ps. 34 is an acrostic of 22 hexameters, and like all such poems more or less artificial. There seems to have been a transposition of lines ע and פ. This was due to an editor who changed the earlier order of these letters (v. La. 2, 3, 4, and 𝕲 of Pr. 31) to the later order of his time. The Ps. is original, and shews little dependence on other writings. The conception of the guardian angel, v.⁸, resembles that of 35⁵·⁶ 91¹¹, and is probably an earlier conception of a special angel, having Israel in charge, which subsequently develops into the one named Michael, and implies the Persian period. The term סיר מרש, v.¹⁵, is common to WL., but elsw. only here Ps. 37²⁷ Is. 59¹⁵. The contrition of v.¹⁹ is dependent on Is. 57¹⁶ 61¹ and resembles Ps. 51¹⁹. The Ps. implies the beginning of WL. and the Persian period, but shews no dependence on P. The Ps. omits the line ו, as Ps. 25, in order to get a division into three Strs. of seven lines each. It has also a supplementary liturgical addition which is essentially the same as that in Ps. 25. On account of v.⁹ the Ps. was used in the Holy Communion in the ancient Church; cf. *Apostolic Constitutions*, 8¹³; Cyril, *Cat. myst.* 5¹⁷; Bingham, *Antiq.* V. 460.

Str. I. is a heptastich, composed of a syn. tristich and a syn. tetrastich. — **2-3.** *I will bless Yahweh*], in the benedictions characteristic of Hebrew worship, ‖ *His praise*, the praise of Him, by the use of the hallels, characteristic of festivals (v. Intr. § 35). — *boast*], in these hallels, by describing Yahweh's wondrous deeds of salvation and judgment. This is to be *at all times* ‖ *continually*, perpetual worship in the temple. — *in my mouth*], the sacred

songs, not only written and read, but sung aloud. — *Let the afflicted
make it heard*], namely, the praise of v.[2], taking their share in it ;
so by an easy change of vowel points giving an excellent parall.
instead of the usual " will hear and will be glad " of 𝔥 and Vrss.
— **4**. *O magnify Yahweh*], tell of His greatness and His great
deeds, ‖ *exalt His name*, His supreme majesty as King of Israel
and the nations, cf. 30[2] 99[5. 9] 107[32] 145[1]. — *with me* ‖ *let us together*]. The afflicted are exhorted to unite with the psalmist
in this thanksgiving. It is common praise, worship of the whole
people, and not merely of individuals. — **5-6**. The reason for
the praise is now given as an encouragement to the afflicted. —
I sought Yahweh]. The veteran sage gives his own personal
experience. — *and He answered me*]. His answer was not in
word, but in deed, *He delivered me from all my terrors*], due
probably to the aggression of a powerful enemy. On the basis
of this personal experience, the afflicted taking part in the temple
worship are reminded of their own experience : *They looked unto
Him*], that they might catch the light of His countenance, cf.
27[1. 4], and so *beamed*], their face lighted up by the light from Yahweh's face ; antith. with their condition as the afflicted. — *and
their face was not abashed*], no longer clouded with gloom,
humiliation, and shame. The chief ancient Vrss., 𝔊, 𝔖, 𝔙, 𝔍,
and many moderns, take these verbs as imperatives, in accordance with the jussive at the close of the line. But 𝔥, EV[s]., and
other scholars, rightly regard these verbs as perfects, and the line
as syn. with the previous and following lines. — **7-8**. *This same
afflicted people cried*]. The psalmist points to the nation in its
organic unity, combining himself with all the afflicted. — *Yahweh
from all his distresses saved him*], in response to the nation's
prayer, cf. v.[5]. — The activity of Yahweh now passes over into
that of *the angel of Yahweh*, which might be interpreted as referring to the theophanic angel of the ancient history in accordance
with Is. 63[9], and as implying the conception of the angelic camp
which met Jacob Gn. 32[2]. But it is most probable that the author
here, as in Pss. 35[5. 6] 91[11], is thinking of the guardian angel of
Israel, who in later times received the name of Michael, Dn. 10[13. 21]
12[1]. This angel is represented as chief of an army encamped
about Israel to protect them from enemies, and who, in such

perils as described above, *rescued them;* cf. 2 K. 6¹⁷.— *them that fear Him*], with the reverence of His people for Yahweh.

Str. II. is composed of a tristich of stairlike parall. and a synth. tetrastich. — **9.** *O taste and see*], make a trial, test by experience. — *He is good*], kind, benignant, as bestowing good things upon His people. This is used in 1 Pet. 2³ and applied to Christ as Lord; cf. also Heb. 6⁴⁻⁵, where it is applied to the good things of the Holy Spirit. — *happy the man*], an exclamation of congratulation, as 1¹.— *that taketh refuge in Him*], as 2¹².— **10.** *O fear Yahweh*], taking up v.⁸ and reiterating it in v.¹⁰ᵇ.— *them that fear Him,* ‖ *His holy ones*], His people as consecrated to His service, cf. 16³ Dt. 33³, an idea especially prominent in the Holiness code (*v.* Br.ᴴᵉˣ. ¹⁵²).— *for there is no lack*] of good things, because Yahweh is good to them. This is, then, the basis for the antithesis, **11**, between *young lions* and *they that seek Him;* the former, notwithstanding their strength and greed as active beasts of prey, *are in want,* because they do not always find prey, or cannot, if they find it, take possession of it, and accordingly *they suffer hunger;* but they that seek Yahweh, however feeble and afflicted they may be, and unable to supply their own wants, *lack not any good,* because their wants are supplied by Yahweh, whose characteristic is that He is good. — **12** begins a second exhortation, in the style of a teacher or sage to his disciples; only here in ψ, but characteristic of WL.; cf. Pr. 1⁸ 1 Jn. 2¹.— *O come, sons*], a call to attention, followed by a coördinate imperative, *hearken to me.* He has an important lesson to give: *I will teach you*]. That which is taught is first stated in its summary form, *the fear of Yahweh*]. This is not in the more ancient sense of religion, but in the ethical sense of Pr. 1⁷, characteristic of WL., as the subsequent context indicates. — **13.** The lesson is to be imparted through the answer to a question: *Who is the man?*] as 25¹², *that taketh pleasure in life*], would not only live, but enjoy life; antith. with the afflictions of the afflicted of the previous Str., as suggested by the beaming face of v.⁶. — *loveth days*], days of life, many days, a long life. — *that he may see good*], the vb. "see," based upon the exhortation "taste and see," v.⁹, and the obj. "good" upon v.¹¹, in the sense of good received, prosperity in life. He who would have so good a blessing from Yahweh must have the ethical qualifications, **14–15**. These are both of speech and conduct. — *Keep*], in the sense of " watch," " guard." It concerns both *tongue* and *lips* as the organs of speech, but is only on the negative side of restraint, *from evil ‖ from speaking deceit.* This is not in the older ethical sense, against neighbours to do them injury, but in the later sense of avoiding evil and deceitful speech as such, as in Pr. 4^{24} 13^3 21^{23} BS. 28^{95} Ja. $3^{2 \, sq.}$, based on Persian ethical conceptions. The conduct must be good, both positively and negatively ; negatively, *depart from evil*], a phrase characteristic of WL., Pr. 3^7 13^{19} $16^{6.17}$. The evil is doing evil in an ethical sense, as implied by the antith., *do good*, as in Ps. 37^{27}, where the entire phrase is used. The positive side of doing good is more specifically defined as *seek*, emphasised by *pursue*, — *peace*], with neighbours, probably implying friendship ; cf. Rom. 14^{19} Heb. 12^{14}.

Str. III. encloses five synonymous lines, setting forth Yahweh's salvation of the righteous, between an initial and a concluding line, affirming the destruction of the wicked. The former has been transposed with the following line by a late editor, who wished to follow the alphabetical order of his day, at the expense of the congruity of the lines with their context. The enemies are described, **17, 22**, as *them that do evil*, v.^{17}, in antithesis with the exhortation, " do good," v.^{15}, and also by the ordinary term, *the wicked* and *they that hate the righteous*, v.^{22}, the latter doubtless antith. to v.^{15}. Their punishment is that *the face of Yahweh is against them* in anger, as 80^{17}, with the purpose *to cut off their memory from the land*, v.^{17}, so utterly to destroy them that they will no longer be remembered ; they will pass into oblivion, as 9^7. V.^{22} gives the synonymous *misfortune shall slay*. This is in striking antithesis to v.^{20}, where it is stated that Yahweh will deliver the righteous out of misfortunes, however many they may be. The climax is given in the comprehensive term, *shall suffer punishment*, v.^{22}, which is to be preferred to " shall be desolate," PBV., AV., which is paraphrase and not translation ; or " condemned," RV., which is a possible translation, but is too mild for the climax. — **16, 18–21** set forth the deliverance of *the righteous. The eyes of Yahweh are unto* them, antith. with the face of Yahweh against the wicked, v.^{17}, and so in the syn. clause, *His ears unto* them ;

both eyes and ears are attentive to their necessities, and accordingly He *is nigh unto them*, v.[19]. They are described as in great trouble: *all their distresses*, v.[18], *many are the misfortunes*, v.[20]; they are *broken-hearted* and *crushed in spirit*, v.[19], conceptions based on Is. 57[15] 61[1], cf. also Pss. 51[19] 147[3]; and it is suggested that their *bones* are also in pain, as 22[15. 18] 31[11] 42[11]. All this describes the sufferings of the afflicted of v.[3], whom this psalmist is cheering by his instruction and good counsel. In this situation Yahweh does not disregard *their cry for help*, v.[16]; *they cry and Yahweh heareth*, v.[18]; and this hearing is effective, as in the psalmist's experience, v.[5]. The usual terms describe their salvation: *He delivereth them*, v.[18. 20]; *saveth them*, v.[19]; *keepeth all their bones*, v.[21], and so completely and safely that *not one of them is broken*.

23. The Ps., like 25, has a liturgical addition, which makes it end in salvation instead of punishment. This, in its present form, is composed of two tetrameters, but it may be reduced to a hexameter by omission of unnecessary words inserted in brackets.

> (Yahweh) ransometh the life of His servants,
> And (none) of them that take refuge in Him shall suffer punishment.

This is a general statement, appropriate as a summing up the thought of the entire Ps., and certainly makes a better conclusion for religious use in the synagogue.

2. [בְּכָל־עֵת] *in* or *at all times* (*v. 10⁵*), n. def. by usage. — 3. [תִּתְהַלֵּל] Hithp. impf. 3 f. *make boast* (*v. 5⁶*), as 105³; cf. 63¹². — [נֶפֶשׁ] paraphrase of person, *I* (*v. 3³*). — [יִשְׁמְעוּ] Qal impf. connected by ı coörd. with יִשְׂמָחוּ. But it makes an awkward change in construction and parall. Rd. Hiph. יַשְׁמִיעַ with תְּהִלָּה understood = *make it to be heard*, cf. 66⁸ 106². — [נוּיב] *the afflicted* (*v. 10¹⁷*). — 4. [וְנְרוֹמְמָה] Polel impf. cohort. 1 pl. רוּם, *exalt:* only here *name*, elsw. God Himself 30² 99⁵. ⁹ 107¹² 118²⁸ 145¹. — 5. [דָּרַשְׁתִּי] Qal aorist, past experience. — [וַיְעַנֵנִי] ı coörd. Qal pf. — †[מְגוּרַי] n.f. *terror;* elsw. Is. 66⁴ Pr. 10²⁴; cf. מָגוֹר Ps. 31¹⁴ and vb. גוּר 22²⁴. — 6. [הִבִּיטוּ] Hiph. pf. 3 m. נבט. — [וְנָהָרוּ] ı conj., Qal pf. 3 m. i.p. נהר vb. *beam, be radiant;* elsw. only Is. 60⁵. But 𝕲, 𝔖, 𝔈, 𝔍, imv.; so Che., Bä., Dr., Du., Kirk. This is in accord with אַל יֶחְפְּרוּ, which with this neg. can only be juss. Qal of † חפר, vb. only here with subj. פָּנִים; elsw. with פ 35⁴, בּוּשׁ 35²⁶ 40¹⁵ (= 70⁸) 71²⁴ 83¹⁸. It is then necessary to follow Vrss. and rd. פְּנֵיכֶם for פְּנֵיהֶם 𝕳, unless we suppose that both sfs. are, as often, interpretative of the noun in an original text without them. But a change to imv. is abrupt and impairs the parall. It is more prob. that אל is

an error of transposition for לא, and that the vbs. are aorists as in context. The subj. of vbs. is ענויב, v.[3]. The ו Str. was omitted as in Ps. 25 in order that the alphabetical Ps. might be divided into three heptastichs. — 7. זֶה] emph., pointing to him, this same, referring to the people in whose name the psalmist speaks (v. 24[8]). עָנִי sg. coll. for the people; cf. עָנוים, v.[3] (v. 9[13]). — יהוה] either the divine name or שמע must be a gl. The latter may be explained as adapted to v.[18], and יהוה seems to be needed in the sentence. — צרות] straits, distresses; as v.[18] 25[22] (v. 20[2]). — 8. חֹנֶה] Qal ptc. as finite vb. of late style, encamp (v. 27[3]); but this is not in accord with ו consec. in וַיְחַלְּצֵם Pi. impf. 3 m. sf. 3 pl. חלץ deliver, rescue (v. 6[5]). Either therefore חנה as pf. aorist (as v.[7]), referring to a past deliverance; or else the ו as coörd., referring to a continuous experience. The context and parall. urge the former; so Che. — 9. [מַלְאַךְ‡ n.m. (1) messenger: the winds 104[4], מ׳ רעים 78[49]; (2) angels 103[20] 148[2], having care of the pious 91[11] (all pl.); (3) מלאך יהוה, the angel champion of Israel 35[5, 6]; so here (34[8]) either as the guardian angel of Israel, the Michael of later times, or else as the theophanic angel of J. and Ju. 5[23], constantly called מלאך יהוה. In the latter case it might be a reference to the history of the Exodus, as Is. 63[9], where this angel is called the angel of His presence. But the context favours a more general reference, and then we have to think of the guardian angel of Israel before the time when he received the name Michael, Dn. 10[13. 21] 12[1]. — 9. טַעֲמוּ] Qal imv. 2 pl. ‡טעם vb. Qal taste; in physical sense, 1 S. 14[24], not in ψ, but in psychological sense, perceive by experience, here. ‡טַעַם n.m. not in ψ in physical sense, but only as discernment, discretion תעם טוב‖ דעת 119[66]; שנה טעם change, disguise the discernment, feign madness 34[1] (title) = 1 S. 21[14]. — וראו כי־טוב יהוה] has one too many tones. The divine name is as usual gl. טוב as good in the sense of benignant (v. 25[8]). — 10. יָחְסְרָ‡] [יִרְאֶה־בִּי relative clause Qal impf. frequentative, also v.[23] (v. 2[12]). — קרשׁי] His consecrated ones, of holy men, as 16[3] Dt. 33[3]. — ‡מַחְסוֹר n.[m.] lack, want; α.λ. ψ, but Ju. 18[10] 19[19] +. Vb. הסר v.[11]. — 11. כְּפִירים] emph. (v. 17[12]), young lions, so 𝔍, 𝔗. 𝔊 πλούσιοι, 𝔙 divites, so 𝔖, prob. interpretation as figurative. There is no good reason for emendation here. — רָשׁוּ] Qal pf. ‡רושׁ vb. be in want; elsw. ptc. רשׁ poor man 82[8] 2 S. 12[8] Pr. 13[7] + 15 t. Pr. — וְרֵעֵבוּ] coörd. Qal pf. 3 pl. i.p. ‡רעב be hungry; elsw. in ψ 50[12]: v. רָעֵב n. 33[19]. — דֹּרְשֵׁי יהוה] ptc. cstr. pl. (v. v.[5]); measure requires דֹּרְשׁי as Bä. — טֹּוב] good in the sense of welfare, happiness (v. 4[7]). — 12. לְכוּ בָנִים] Qal imv. 2 pl. of הלך, exhortation to attention, as 46[9] 66[5. 16] 83[5] 95[1]. Sons, not children but young men, addressed by an experienced wise man, as in WL., v. Pr. 8[32]; only here ψ in this sense. — יִרְאַת י׳] the fear of Yahweh, the act of fearing, piety whether religious or ethical, as 5[8] 90[11] 111[10] 119[38] (v. 2[11]). — 15. סור מֵרָע]. This phr. is characteristic of WL. Jb. 28[28] Pr. 3[7] 13[19] 16[6. 17]; in ψ elsw. 37[27]. — עֲשֵׂה טוב] in ethical sense 14[1. 3] (= 53[2. 4]) 37[3. 27] (v. 4[7]). — 16. אֶל] α.λ. ψ. should be אֶל with separate tone and אֶל־שׁוֹעָרם for אֶל־שׁוֹעָה, which makes better measure. Sfs. were often added by scribes. — 17. פְּנֵי י׳] c. בְּ, of hostility, anger, as 80[17] (v. 4[7]). — עֹשֵׂי רָע] antith. with עֲשֵׂה טוב v.[15], עֹשֵׂי variation of writing, not of form. — לְהַכְרִית] Hiph. inf. cstr. with לְ purpose as v.[18], כרת (v.

12⁴), with מארץ also 109¹⁶ Na. 2¹⁴, based on penalty of P., H., מקרב עם Lv. 17¹⁰ 20³·⁵·⁶, זכרם *their remembrance;* cf. Ps. 9⁷ Ex. 17¹⁴ (E) Dt. 25¹⁹ 32²⁶. For word *v. 6⁶.* — **18.** צָעְקוּ] Qal pf. emph., continuation of v.¹⁶. ‡ עֵק vb. *cry out;* as 77² 88² 107⁶·²⁸; v.¹⁷ intervenes and makes the connection difficult. This v. cannot refer to the person of v.¹⁷. In fact, v.¹⁶·¹⁷ have been transposed in order to conform an earlier alphabetical order to a later, at the expense of the thought. For the older order *v.* La. 2, 3, 4 Pr. 31 (𝔊). 𝔊 overcomes the difficulty of change of subj. by inserting οἱ δίκαιοι, but at the expense of the measure.— וייהוח] subj. emph. — **19.** נִשְׂבְּרִי לֵב] phr. elsw. Is. 61¹; cf. לֵב נִשְׁבָּר Ps. 51¹⁹, 147³.— דִּכְּאֵי רוּחַ] cf. לֵב נִדְכָּאִים Is. 57¹⁵, also Ps. 51¹⁹. The dependence upon Is.² can hardly be questioned. As to forms וְשִׁבְּרֵי Niph. ptc. pl. cstr. שׁבר, *v.* also v.²¹: דִּכְּאֵי pl. cstr. of † דַּכָּא adj. elsw. Is. 57¹⁵. — **21.** שֹׁמֵר] Qal. ptc. as v.⁸·²³ of late style. — **22.** וְיֶאְשָׁמוּ] Qal impf. as v.²³, *bear punishment.* Cf. Pr. 30¹⁰ Is. 24⁶ Je. 2³ Ho. 5¹⁵ 10² 14¹ Zc. 11⁵ Ez. 6⁶ (*v. 5¹¹*). — **23** is a supplementary line with פ; cf. 25²².

PSALM XXXV., 3 STR. 10⁵.

The Ps. is a national prayer: (1) petition that Yahweh may interpose as the champion of His people, and especially by His angel, against enemies who without cause have sought to entrap them (v.¹⁻⁶·⁹⁻¹⁰ᵃ); (2) complaint against the neighbours as false friends who reward evil for good, and antipathy for sympathy, with petition for deliverance (v.¹¹⁻¹⁸); (3) petition that these enemies may not be permitted to go on in their treacherous conduct and that Yahweh may interpose in judgment (v.¹⁹·²⁵·²⁷ᵇ⁻²⁸). Each part concludes with a vow of praise. Glosses emphasise the imprecations (v.⁷⁻⁸·²⁶⁻²⁷ᵃ).

O YAHWEH, plead my cause, fight with them that fight *me;*
   Take hold of shield and buckler, and rise up as *my* help;
   Draw out spear (and javelin) to encounter him that pursues *me;*
   Say unto me, (Yahweh): Thy salvation am *I,*
   Let them be ashamed and brought to dishonour together that seek *my* life;
   Let them be turned back and confounded that devise *my* hurt;
   Let them be as chaff before the wind, (thine) angel pursuing *them;*
   Let their way be in darkness and slippery places, (thine) angel thrusting *them* down.
   Then my soul will be joyful in Yahweh, will rejoice in His salvation;
   All my bones will say: "Yahweh, who is like Thee?"
WITNESSES of violence rise up, that of which I am not aware they require of *me;*
   They reward me evil for good, bereavement to *me.*
   But as for me, when they were deadly wounded, I made sackcloth *my* clothing;

I afflicted my soul with fasting, my prayer was upon *my* bosom;

As for a friend, as for mine own brother, I went in procession, in black *I* bowed down.

But when I halted, they rejoiced, and they gathered together (in throngs) against *me*.

Smiters tore me, for that of which I am not aware, without cessation;

In my pollution they mocked, they gnashed upon me with their teeth.

O recover my life from roarers, from lions mine only one;

And I will give thee thanks in the great congregation, among a numerous people I will praise Thee.

LET not them that hate me without cause, rejoice over me, winking with the eye;

For it is not peace that they speak, but against my tranquillity;

Deceitful things they devise, and they open wide their mouths against me;

They said: "Aha, aha! our eye hath seen it."

Thou hast seen, Yahweh; keep not silence, keep not afar off;

Stir up Thyself for my judgment, my God, and awake unto my cause;

Judge me according to my righteousness, my God, and let them not rejoice over me;

Let them not say in their mind: "Aha, our desire! we have swallowed him up."

May Yahweh be magnified, who hath delight in the peace of His servant;

My tongue will murmur Thy righteousness, all day long Thy praise.

Ps. 35 was in 𝕰, but not in any of the other Psalters. They were right. It is not well suited to public worship. It is a pentameter, with many glosses from other Pss. and Prophets. These being removed, it appears to be composed of three symmetrical decastichs, each concluding with a Refrain vowing public praise. V.[26-27] is a gloss from 70[3 sq.]; v.[8] from Is. 47[11]; v.[10b] from Je. 31[11]. In the original Ps., v.[3] is possibly dependent on 3[3]; v.[4] cited from 70[3] = 40[15]; v.[12] reminds of Is. 47[8. 9]; v.[6] of Je. 23[12]; v.[25] of La. 2[16]; v.[18] of Ps. 69[11-12]; v.[18] קהל רב of 22[26] 40[10]. These do not show dependence, but a similarity of situation and language, which suggests nearness of time of composition. V.[10] מי כמוך implies Ex. 15[11], and the singing in the temple some such song of praise. The angel, v.[5], probably the guardian angel of Israel, resembles 34[8], 91[11], and suggests the earlier stages of that idea. The use of חנף, v.[16], for pollution of land is similar to Je. 3[1] Mi. 4[11] Ps. 106[38]. All this favours the situation of the feeble community of the Restoration, owing to the hostility of the neighbouring nations.

Str. I. is composed of a syn. triplet with a line synth. thereto, a syn. tetrastich and a syn. couplet. — **1.** *O Yahweh, plead my cause*], so probably in the original, using the common phrase, which sometimes implies judicial process; at other times, as here, vindication in battle, and so ‖ *fight with them that fight me*. Ancient texts were misled by the last clause to find a parall. with it in the previous clause, and so by a slight change of form made a doubtful word with the meaning "with them that contend," or strive, "with me." The people are in peril from warlike enemies; they are unable to defend themselves, and so appeal to Yahweh to interpose. Yahweh is conceived as a champion, a heroic warrior, as Ex. 15³ Dt. 32⁴¹ Ps. 24⁹. Accordingly, He is implored to arm Himself as a warrior: **2–3**. *Take hold of shield*, as 3⁴; *and buckler*, as 5¹³; || *draw out spear* (*and javelin*)]. The latter word is a conjectural emendation, in accordance with the association of these words in usage, and therefore to be preferred to the emendation of many scholars, "battle axe," which is a foreign word, unknown to Hebrew usage elsewhere, and all the more dubious, that upon it is based an argument for a later date for the Ps. than other evidence will allow. The imperative of 𝕳, "stop," in the pregnant sense, supplying "the way," though sustained by ancient and modern Vrss., is not suited to the subsequent words, which imply, not resistance to attack, but aggression, an advance to meet, *to encounter him that pursues me* || *rise up as my help*. In the climax, the poet turns from the enemies to Yahweh: *Say unto me: Thy salvation am I*]. The personal God and vindicator of Israel is their salvation from the enemies who make the present peril. — **4**. The poet begins his imprecation with a couplet from 70³ = 40¹⁵.

> Let them be ashamed and brought to dishonour together that seek my life;
> Let them be turned back and confounded that devise my hurt.

He imprecates upon the enemies a shameful defeat, involving all the hurt and even death they had planned against Israel. — **5–6**. The psalmist now introduces the angel as in 34⁸. This, in the text, is "angel of Yahweh," but probably in the original was *Thine angel*, because of measure; not the theophanic angel of the ancient tradition, who led up Israel out of Egypt into the Holy Land, overthrowing all their enemies; but the angel of Israel, whom Yahweh had given charge over Israel, cf. 91¹¹, a conception which subsequently developed into the Michael of Daniel. This angel takes up the pursuit of the enemy after Yahweh Himself had defeated them, *pursuing them* || *thrusting them down*. These words have, in all the texts, been transposed, as most modern interpreters think; for pursuit is best suited to the simile *as chaff* *before the wind;* and thrusting down to the *darkness and slippery places* into which in their flight *their way* leads them.

The reason for the petition is now given, in which the groundlessness of their hostility is emphasised, and it is followed by renewed imprecation. This disturbs the course of thought and the structure of the Str., and indeed v.[7] is premature. It is therefore a gloss.

> For without cause they hid for me their net;
> A pit without cause they dug for me.
> Let desolation come upon them unawares,
> And let his net, that he hid, catch him,
> And in the pit let him fall.

7. *For without cause*], with no sufficient reason, gratuitously, implying already, what is more fully brought out in Str. II., that the conduct of the enemies was unreasonable and contrary to what ought to have been anticipated. It was indeed treacherous : *they hid for me their net ‖ a pit they dug for me*], implying the same situation as that in 9[16], the image of hunters seeking to trap animals. — **8.** The imprecation is condensed partly from Is. 47[11] and partly from Ps. 9[16]. The former is, *let desolation come upon them unawares;* the latter probably in the original, *and let his net, that he hid, catch him; and in the pit let him fall,* the last clause of which has been preserved by $, but in , , and other Vrss. has been obscured by a copyist mistaking the word rendered " pit " for that rendered " desolation," and so the texts read either " in the desolation," or " with the desolation let him fall therein."

The Str. concludes with a vow of praise which may be regarded as a couplet of refrain, as it reappears in varied terms at the close of each Str. — **9-10 a.** *Then my soul*]. The conjunction implies temporal consequence with the subject of verb emphatic. The inner nature is syn. with the outer nature, the bodily frame, *all my bones,* which sympathise with the emotions of the soul, and thrill with joy here, as they ache with sorrow elsewhere. — *will be joyful ‖ will rejoice*]. This was doubtless to be expressed in public praise, and is indeed a vow of such praise. The theme is *His salvation,* that is, as wrought by Him, in the defeat of the enemies, and therefore to be celebrated in an ode, as Ex. 15. — *Who is like Thee*], possibly referring to that ode itself, used at the period of the psalmist for this very purpose, in the liturgy of the temple.— **10** *bc*. A later editor, failing to see this reference, and thinking the conclusion of the Str. too abrupt, appends what he thinks an adequate explanation, based on Je. 31[11] :

> Deliverer of the afflicted from him that is too strong for him;
> Yea, the afflicted and needy from him that spoileth him.

Str. II. is composed of a synth. couplet and a syn. triplet enclosing a syn. triplet, concluding with a synth. couplet.—**11.** *Witnesses of violence*], not violent witnesses, but such as testify of violence ; they *rise up* to testify ; *require of me*, demand satisfaction, retribution for violence of which I have no knowledge, *of which I am not aware;* with the implication that it was altogether a false accusation.—**12.** *They reward me evil for good*]. Israel had done his neighbours good, and only good ; and yet they charged him with evil, and, taking for granted that he was guilty, requited him with evil. This evil is emphasised as *bereavement,* not to be generalised into "discomfort" of soul, PBV., or specifically "spoiling of my soul" AV. ; for which there is no authority in Hebrew usage ; but bereavement of children, implying the slaughter of the children of the people by these enemies, as in Is. 47[8.9] ; and this as requited *to me*, as Pss. 41[11] 137[8], the soul here, as elsewhere, being a paraphrase for the person. — **13.** The psalmist now in two triplets brings out the kindness of his people in emphatic contrast with the unkindness of the enemy. — *But as for me*], emphatic assertion of personal conduct.—*when they were deadly wounded*], by their enemies in battle, resulting in the death of the children of their people, antith. with v.[12], and so in mourning and funeral processions. This is weakened into "when they were sick," in MT., which does not suit the context or the thought of the Ps. The context sets forth graphically the ancient method of mourning for the dead. — *I made sackcloth my clothing*], inserting the verb to complete the measure from the cognate Ps. 69[12]. — *I afflicted my soul with fasting*], cf. Is. 58[3.5]. — *my prayer was upon my bosom*], prayer, as the context suggests, of supplication for the bereaved. This was conceived as heartfelt, resting upon the bosom, or upon the heart, while it pulsated with sympathy, as AE., Luther, al. This is certainly an unusual expression ; but it was made more difficult by an ancient editor, who inserted a verb, without regard to the measure, usually rendered " returned," which was probably meant to imply that the prayer, notwithstanding its sincerity, returned to the one who made it without effect, Bar Heb., Ri., al., with the suggestion of a reward from God, instead of a reward from those for whom it was offered. This seems to be the interpretation of 𝕲, 𝕵, Ra., Hu., Ki. The reference to the head bowed down upon the bosom, De., Bä., for which 1 Kings 18⁴² is cited, does not suit the situation or the language. It would be more natural to think of beating the breast, or bosom, as the usual accompaniment of mourning, Na. 2⁷, if the phrase could be so interpreted. — **14**. *I went in procession*], the usual funeral pro- cession, clad *in black*, the colour of mourning. — *I bowed down*], the posture of the mourner, cf. 38⁷, that is, with head bowed and face turned downward. This mourning was as sincere and intense, *as for a friend;* and still more *as for mine own brother*. It has become, however, a little too much by the insertion of " as one that mourneth for his mother," by a later editor, at the expense of the measure, making the line as well as the thought by so much overfull. — **15–16**. In antith. with this sympathetic sorrow of Israel for its neighbours when they were bereaved of their children in war, is the unsympathetic conduct of these neighbours. — *But when I halted*], or limped, as Je. 20¹⁰; as injured in the feet and so in a perilous situation ; intensified by *in my pollution*], pollution of the land with the blood of the slain, cf. Nu. 35³³ Je. 3¹ Mi. 4¹¹. This has been interpreted in MT. as a late adj. with the mean- ing " profane," referring to persons, making the construction and meaning difficult. 𝕲, having either a different text, or else paraphrasing, at all events regarded it rightly as a verb. The conduct of the enemies is graphically described. — *they rejoiced*] antith. the wearing of sackcloth. — *and they gathered together in throngs*]. All were interested in the humiliation of Israel, and none would be absent on this occasion. — *Smiters*], so essentially 𝕵, 𝚺, Pe., Moll., Kirk., better than " smitings," blows, 𝕲, 𝕾. The " abjects " of EVˢ., based on Ki., Calvin, Grot., explained by De. as " dregs of the people," has nothing to justify it in usage. — *They tore me without cessation*]. This v. is antith. with the fasting and prayer of Israel. — *they mocked*], as 𝕲, whether the kindred noun "a mocking" be original or due to dittog. 𝕳, by an early error of text, made a phrase unknown elsewhere, which has ever been regarded as difficult to explain. Ra. first suggested "mockers for a cake," that is, parasites, fawning flatterers, who make jests and witticisms against others, in order to please the rich and powerful, and so secure entertainment from their table. This has been followed by EV*. and most moderns, who have adhered to 𝕳. But it is not suited to the context, and indeed is far-fetched ; so that most recent critics prefer to follow 𝕲 or seek a better text. — *They gnashed upon me with their teeth*], as 37¹²; the mocking passing over into this manifestation of bitterest enmity. This is in fine antith. to the intense grief and mourning expressed by black garments and the funeral procession for a brother of v.¹⁴. — **17 a.** A later editor inserts at this point an appeal to Yahweh, — *Yahweh, how long wilt Thou look on*], that is, with indifference, while such things are happening, such wrong is done. This line not only is apart from the measures of the Ps. and its strophical organisation, but really expresses an impatience which is foreign to its robust confidence. — **17 b.** *O recover my life ‖ mine only one*], as 22²¹ — *from roarers*], an emendation admirably suited to the previous context ‖ *lions*, so We., Du. ; a common figure for powerful and greedy enemies. The "from their desolations" of 𝕳, followed by ancient and modern Vrss., does not suit the context, even if the form of the Hebrew word could be sustained. It requires no greater change in the text to get the appropriate meaning, "roarers," than to get the same word as v.⁸, and the latter is improbable in the original text, if v.⁸ be a gloss. — **18.** The petition for recovery is followed by the refrain, cf. v.⁹⁻¹⁰ : *And I will give Thee thanks in the great congregation, among a numerous people I will praise Thee*], the public thanksgiving in the temple for national deliverance, as in 22²⁶ 40¹⁰.

Str. III. is composed of an introverted tetrastich, a syn. tetrastich in antith. thereto, and a concluding syn. couplet. The common term of both is the prayer : *let not* the enemies *rejoice over me*, v.¹⁹·²⁴, that is, continue to do as they are represented as doing in v.¹⁵ ; and then saying, *Aha*, v.²¹·²⁵. — **19.** *Hate me without cause*], resuming the thought of v.¹¹⁻¹², explained unnecessarily by a late editor through the insertion of the syn. : "mine enemies wrongfully," at the expense of the measure. — *winking with the eye*], a circumstantial clause expressing their malicious insincerity. This is explained as craftiness. — **20.** *For it is not peace that they speak*], as they probably professed, but the reverse of peace; *against my tranquillity*], so probably rather than " the quiet in the land," 𝔥, followed by most interpreters, which is not sustained by 𝔊, and is a phrase unknown elsewhere and improbable in itself, making a distinction between the quiet and others in the land, when the antith. of the Ps. is between the people of the land and their enemies. Omitting " the land," which is not in 𝔊, and maintaining the remaining word of 𝔥 over against that of 𝔊, we get the personal reference to the tranquillity of the people, who speak as usual in the first person, and in fine parallelism to the peace of the previous clause. — *Deceitful things they devise*]; their plans are crafty and deceitful. — **21.** *They open wide their mouths against me*], in much hostile speaking, in accordance with their deceitful plans, in false accusations; resuming the thought of v.[11], and accordingly changing the tense to the perfect, in citing their testimony : *They have said : " Aha, aha ! our eye hath seen it"*], namely, the deeds of violence charged against the people of Yahweh in v.[11]. In striking antith. to this conduct of the enemy Yahweh is exhorted to interpose, resuming the thought of Str. I. — **22.** *Thou hast seen, Yahweh*], an appeal to Him as an eye-witness over against the false eye-witnesses of the enemies. — *keep not silence*], in Thy testimony on my behalf. — *keep not afar off*], in my need, cf. $22^{2. 12. 20}$ 38^{22} 71^{12}. " O Lord " and " from me" are both unnecessary glosses, making the line overfull. On the positive side the plea continues. — **23.** *Stir up Thyself ‖ awake*], strong terms for active, prompt interposition. — *for my judgment ‖ unto my cause*], as v.[1]. A prosaic copyist has, by transposition, attached the verbs together and then the nouns, the latter being separated by the divine name : *My God*, to which " Lord " is added as a gloss. Poetic usage gives each verb its appropriate noun in parall. — **24.** *Judge me*], in the sense of vindication, as above, — *according to my righteousness*], as 𝔍 ; best suited to the context and the course of thought in the Ps., which asserts righteous conduct over against the false charges of the enemy. But 𝔥, 𝔊, and most Vrss. have " Thy righteousness," an appeal to

this divine attribute. Probably here, as often, the original text
had no suffix, so that either interpretation was possible. — **25.** *Let
them not say*], repeated in the next clause for emphasis, but by
editor at the expense of the measure. — *in their mind*], to themselves, in their congratulatory thoughts, antith. with their previous
testimony, which they now suppose has had its effect in the accomplishment of their crafty plans. — *Aha, our desire*]. We have
attained it. — *we have swallowed him up*], implying both the greed
of the enemies and the overwhelming completeness of destruction,
cf. 124[3] La. 2[16].

26-27 *b.* A Maccabean editor inserts an imprecation taken
from 70[3-5] with slight modifications.

Let them be ashamed and confounded together that rejoice in my hurt.
Let them be clothed with shame and dishonour that magnify themselves against me.
Let them shout for joy and be glad (in Thee) that delight in Thy righteousness.
Yea, let them say continually, " May Yahweh be magnified ! "

Besides the desire for an imprecation, the editor was probably
moved to insert this particular one because of the wish — **27** *b.* *May
Yahweh be magnified*, which was probably original to our Ps. and
therefore common to both. This is the beginning of the final
refrain, cf. v.[9-10a. 18]. It is the magnifying Him in the celebration
of His deeds of salvation and judgment in public worship. — *who
hath delight in the peace of His servant*], resuming the thought of
peace of v.[20], and emphasising the fact of the personal relation
of the people to Yahweh, as His servant, in accordance with the
conceptions of Jeremiah and Is.[2]. Yahweh takes pleasure and
delight in His people, as now appears with propriety after the
storm has passed, and the interposition has been triumphantly
accomplished. — **28.** *My tongue will murmur*], give vocal expression in the melody of sacred song. — *all day long*], continuously.
— *Thy righteousness*], the theme as exhibited in the vindication
of the righteousness of His people ‖ *Thy praise*.

1. רִיבָה] Qal imv. cohort. ‡ רִיב vb. Qal (1) *strive :* of battle here ;
(2) *plead a cause :* of God ר׳ רִיב מ׳ 43[1]; without prep. 74[22] 119[154]; abs,
without רִיב 103[9]. — יְרִיבַי] sf. 1 pl. † רִיבַי] n.[m.] *adversary ;* elsw. Is. 49[25]
Je. 18[19] (but dub. in last two ; 𝕲 has רִיב), prob. here also רִיבָה רִיבִי as
1 S. 24[15] Mi. 7[9] Je. 50[34] 51[36] + = *take my part.* — לְחַם] imv. and לֹחֲמַי ptc.

i.p. ‡ לחם *fight, do battle;* in ψ elsw. 56[2.3]. Niph. common in OT., but in ψ elsw. 109[3]. Rd. also יִלָּחֵם (coll.) for 雖 pl. לֹחֲמַי in order to rhyme. — 2. [הַחֲזֵק] Hiph. imv. *take hold of, grasp;* a.λ. ψ, but Na. 3[14] Je. 6[23] Zc. 14[13]. — [מָגֵן] *small shield (v. 3[4]).* — [צִנָּה] *large shield;* elsw. 5[13] 91[4]. — [בִּקְרָאתִי] ב *essentiae,* introducing the predicate (*B*DB.), *as: my help,* as embodied in a person, 27[9] 40[18] 44[27] +. — 3. [הָרֵק] Hiph. imv. ‡ [ריר] vb. Hiph. *empty, draw out,* sword Ex. 15[9] Ez. 5[2.12] 12[14] 28[7] 30[11], possibly in original text of Ps. 18[43], lance, only here. — [הֲנֵית] ו needless gl. — ‡ n.f. *spear, lance;* elsw. ψ, 46[10] and metaph. (lion's teeth) 57[5]. — [סגר] Qal imv. סגר vb. *close up* (the way), *stop;* so 𝔊, 𝔍, Aq., Σ, Θ, Jebb, Ols., De., Bä. Hare, Kenn., Grotius, Street, De W., Ew., Now., Dr., take it as σάγαρις *battle axe.* This is certainly tempting. Du. bases on it argument for late date of Ps. The early date of Ps. is rather an argument against this unknown Heb. word. *B*DB. thinks text corrupt. Schwally חֲגֹר is improbable. Halevy עֻזְרָה (Ps. 59[5]) is too easy. Che. would rd. שְׂכֹר *javelin,* as Ass. *šukûdu.* A change from a common word is improbable. The original was prob. כִּידוֹן *dart, javelin,* Jos. 8[18] 1 S. 17[6.45] Jb. 39[23], usually associated with חנית. In unpointed text כדן might have been mistaken for שבו, if letters were transposed [לְקִרְאַת].—כנר inf. cstr. ‡ קרא *encounter,* enemies here; *meet,* of God 59[5], prob. also 25[18]. — [לִרְדְּתִי] Qal ptc. sf. 1 pl. should be 1 sg. coll., so v.[6].—[לְנַפְשִׁי] *to me (v. 3[3]).* יהוה should be inserted to complete the line. — 4. = 40[15] = 70[3]. Insert in l. 1, after 40[15], יחי to complete pentameter. The second vb. in 40[15] 70[3] is יחפרו, which is transposed here with יכלמו in next l. So also in next l., 40[15] 70[3] have חֶרְפֵּי for הַשָּׁבֵי. This change is probably intentional. The original of 40[15], which is a late addition to that Ps., is in 70[3].—[וְיִכָּלְמוּ] Niph. juss, 3 pl., ו coörd. ‡ [כלם] Niph. (1) *be humiliated, ashamed,* before men 74[21]; (2) *be put to shame, dishonoured,* 69[7]; also here = 40[15] = 70[3]. Hiph. *put to shame = insult, humiliate,* by defeat 44[10]. — [מְבַקְשֵׁי נַפְשִׁי] phr. elsw. 38[13] 40[15] 54[5] 63[10] 70[3] 86[14] Ex. 4[19] (J) Je. 4[30] +. — [יִסֹּגוּ] Niph. juss. 3 pl., *v.* 14[3]. — [חֹשְׁבֵי רָעָתִי] phr. elsw. 41[8] 140[3] Gn. 50[20] (E) Zc. 7[10] 8[17] Je. 36[3] 48[2] Mi. 2[3]. — 5. [וּמַלְאַךְ יהוה] also v.[6b]; so 34[8], cf. 91[11]. יהוה is a later insertion in both verses for מַלְאָכֶךָ *Thy angel.* — [דֹּחֶה] Qal ptc. דחה vb. *push, thrust;* rd. דֹּחֵם as 𝔊, Horsley, Houb., Ols., De., Du., ‖ רדף *(v.* v.[8]). These have probably been transposed, Hu., Bi., Bä. — 6. [יְהִי] prob. a later addition; not necessary, and makes l. too long. — † [חֲלַקְלַקּוֹת] n.f.pl. *slippery places* = Je. 23[12]; elsw. *flattering promises* Dn. 11[21], cf. 11[34]. — 7. [כִּי חִנָּם] so v.[7b]. ‡ חִנָּם adv. (√חנן) *out of favour, gratis, gratuitously;* with vb. שמן 35[7], חפר v.[7], שנא v.[19] 60[5], לחם 109[3], רדף 119[161]. — [חֲמָנוּ־לִי]. The proper obj. is רִשְׁתָּם (9[16]) ‖ חפרו *dig out,* elsw. 7[16]; obj. שחת, which should then be transposed, making two syn. lines; so 𝔖, Hare, Houb., Che., Horsley. This couplet is a tetrameter gl., giving a premature reason. — 8. = Is. 47[11c], which is original: וַתִּבֹא עָלַיִךְ פִּתְאֹם שֹׁאָה שֵׁאָה לֹא־תֵדְעִי, changed here from second to third pers., abbreviated by sf. הו instead of עָלָיו, and omission of פתאם. The change from 3 pl., v. 4-7, to 3 sg., v.[8], is striking. 𝔊 and 𝔖 have pl. correctly; sg. originated from attaching הַ to vb. from noun. — [בְּשׁוֹאָה] rd. בשחת, as v.[7] 𝔊 has

ἐλθέτω αὐτοῖς παγὶς ἣν οὐ γινώσκουσιν,
καὶ ἡ θήρα ἣν ἔκρυψαν συλλαβέτω αὐτούς,
καὶ ἐν τῇ παγίδι πεσοῦνται ἐν αὐτῇ.

παγίς here stands for שואה, which could hardly be mistaken for רשת, possibly for שחת Horsley, or שוחה Gr. θήρα stands for כרף or ציר in 𝕲, but neither suitable here in place of רשת. שואה in v.⁸ᵃ is verified by Is. 47¹¹, but in v.⁸ᵇ one would expect same terms as in v.⁷, רשת and שחת, and the vbs. suggest them. † שׁיאָה n.f. *desolation;* elsw. Ps. 63¹⁰ Is. 10⁸ 47¹¹ Ez. 38⁹ Zp. 1¹⁵ Jb. 30³· ¹⁴ 38²⁷ Pr. 1²⁷ 3²⁵. These are three trimeter lines of gl. — **9.** [נפשי תגיל] = Is. 61¹⁰, cf. כבוד Ps. 16⁹, cf. לב 13⁶. — **10.** [כָּמוֹךָ יִי] cf. Ex. 15¹¹, implying the singing in public praise such a hymn to God (*v.* 4⁷ 29⁶); for this phr. *v.* 71¹⁹ 89⁹. — [חזק ממנו] = Je. 31¹¹, is gl. and עני also, to resume עני with emph. at expense of measure. This v. returns to the sg. for enemy ; not so 𝕲 ; rd. מחזקים מ, מ omitted by slip of eye, and rd. also גוליו. — ‡ [חָזָק] adj. (1) *strong, stout, mighty;* esp. of hand of יי delivering Israel from Egypt ביד חזקה 136¹² Ex. 32¹¹ (JE) Dt. 4³¹ + 4 t. Je. 32²¹; (2) as subst., *a strong one:* c. מן comp. = *one too strong for* Ps. 35¹⁰ Je. 31¹¹; of יי Is. 40¹⁰. Other mngs. not in ψ. — [וגזלו] Qal ptc. verbal force ; ‡ vb. elsw. ψ, 69⁵, noun ‡ גֵּזֶל *robbery* 62¹¹. — **11.** [יקומון] Qal present, archaic form. — [עֵדֵי חָמָס] *witnesses of violence,* who testify to violence that has never been done. — [אשר] rel., unnecessary gl. to make construction more distinct. — [לֹא־יָדַעְתִּי] here in special sense of *not to be conscious of, aware of,* so v.¹⁵; cf. 51⁶. — [יִשְׁאָלוֹנִי] Qal present. שאל in the special sense *demand, require,* cf. 137³. — **12.** [יְשַׁלְּמוּנִי] Pi. present (*v.* 22²⁶), in special sense *require, reward,* cf. 38²¹ with following phr. רעה תחת טובה (*v.* 21¹² 16²); this phr. elsw. 109⁵ Gn. 44⁴ (J) 1 S. 25²¹ Je. 18²⁰ Pr. 17¹³. — † [שכול] *bereavement of children, childlessness,* elsw. Is. 47⁸· ⁹; the more general mng. given here by some, *abandonment,* cannot be shown in language. The vb. is not used in ψ. The proper mng. would not be so bad for a national Ps. ; the slaughter of warriors, the children of the nation, suits the putting on mourning of subsequent context. 𝕲 has כשל *stumbling,* not so good. — [לנפשי] must then be taken as periphrastic personal pronoun (3³). — **13.** [ואני] emph. antith. — [בחלותם] Qal inf. cstr. sf. ‡ חלה vb. *be weak, sick;* only here in ψ, unless we change 77¹¹ חלותי into חליתי, which, though urged by Hu., Pe., Bi., is improb., as 𝕲 sustains pointing of 𝔐, while deriving from other stem חלל in the sense of *begin.* The mng. *sick* is not suited to this context ; point בחליתם, as suggested by 𝕲 παρενοχλεῖν, *when they were mortally wounded.* The vb. ‡ חלל *pierce, wound;* elsw. ψ, 109²². [לְבוּשִׁי שָׂק] cf. for phr. 69¹². A word is needed for measure ; after 69¹² supply יָאֱתוּ. — [עֲנֵיתִי] Pi. pf. 1 s. ‡ ענה vb. III. *be bowed down, afflicted;* in ψ only Qal, † *be afflicted* Ps. 116¹⁰ 119⁶⁷ Zc. 10². Niph. † *be afflicted* Ps. 119¹⁰⁷ Is. 53⁷ 58¹⁰. Pi. (1) *humble, mishandle, afflict:* individual (by imprisonment and bonds) Ps. 105¹⁸; a nation (by war or in bondage) 94⁵; dynasty of David 89²³; † (2) *afflict,* as a discipline (God agent) 88⁸ 90¹⁵ 119⁷⁵ Dt. 8²· ³· ¹⁶ 1 K. 11³⁹ Is. 64¹¹ Na. 1¹²· ¹² La. 3³³; † (3) *humble, weaken:* obj. כֹּחַ Ps. 102²⁴; נפש *oneself* by fasting 35¹³ Lv. 16²⁹ + 4 t. (P)

Is. 58[3.5]; elsw. in this sense Nu. 30[14] (P) Jb. 37[23]. Pu. † *be afflicted*, in discipline by God Pss. 119[71] 132[1] Is. 53[4]. Hithp. † *be afflicted*, in discipline by God Ps. 107[17]. — [בְּצִים נַפְשִׁי] phr. 69[11] with vb. בכה. ‡ צוּב [*fasting*, elsw. מצום 109[24], characteristic of late usage, subsequent to Ne.; cf. Ne. 9[1] Dn. 9[3] Est. 4[3].
— [עַל־חֵיקִי] *resting upon:* not of head bowed on the breast, Bä., Du., the prayer going to the bosom instead of upward or outward; not with Hiph. השיב instead of Qal, and so *requital* as *BDB.* as Ps. 79[12] Is. 65[6.7] Je. 32[18]; but of the prayer resting upon the bosom, as it were pressing upon it while agitated with the pulsation of the heart. The vb. is a gl., which doubtless implied retribution in sense of later editor, but is not suited to context and makes l. too long. Other uses of ‡ חיק n.[m.] in ψ are : c. ב 89[51], with בקרב 74[11]. — 14. [הִתְהַלָּכְתִּי] as in 42[2] for funeral processions. — [רַּאֲבֶל אֵם] ‡ צָבֵל [adj. *mourning*, only here ψ; cf. Gn. 37[35]. ⑤ has אבל, without אם. Phr. is a gl. of explanation, due to adaptation of national Ps. to personal relations. — ‡ [קֹבֵר] as 38[7] 42[10] 43[2], all with הלך in some form, *be in black* as mourner. — 15. [וּבְצַלְעִי] prep. ב temporal; emph. in position, in antith. † צֶלַע n.[m.] *limping, stumbling;* elsw. 38[18] Je. 20[10] Jb. 18[12]. — [וְנֶאֶסְפוּ] Niph. pf. 3 pl. ı coörd., repeated for emph., but improb.; rd. inf. abs. of intensification for second, — [וְנִים. — רֵאָסוּף] pl. of † נֵכֶה adj. *a.λ.; BDB smitten ones* improb.; Ki., EV⁵., Calv., De., al., *abjects* has nothing to justify it ; Ols., Bi., Bä., Kau. נכרים *aliens* seems justified by following vb., but not by antith. triplet; ⑤, 𝔖, μάστιγες *blows, wounds =* נֵכִים for מכים ptc. נכה, so 𝔍 *percutientes,* Σ, 𝔗, Horsley, Hu.³. — [ולא ידעתי] rel. clause, "what I am not aware." — [ולא דָמּוּ] circumstantial clause, *without cessation.* — [קָרְעוּ] Qal pf. ‡ קרע vb. usually *tear* garments, but also various other subordinate mngs.; only here in ψ. Hu., Dr., al., as Ho. 13[8] *tear,* as wild beasts or cruel foes, most probable ; ⑤ διεσχίσθησαν, 𝔍 *scindentes.* Ol., Bä., We., al., *tear with words, rail,* which has no usage to justify it. — 16. [בְּחַנְפֵי] cstr. pl. ‡ חָנֵף adj. *profane, irreligious* persons. This form elsw. Jb. 36[13] חנפי לב; pl. Is. 33[14], sg. Is. 10[6] of nation, 9[16] of a man ; cstr. pl. here before cstr. pl. is strange. Bi., Du., rd. בְּחֹנֶף and attach to previous l. ⑤ ἐπείρασάν με = בחנני, so Gr., tempting, yet not suited to context ; rd. בְּחָנְפִי inf. cstr. ‡ חנף, *in my pollution,* as 106[38]; cf. Je. 3[1.1] Mi. 4[11]. — [לַעֲנֵי מָעוֹג]. The first word pl. cstr. of לַעֵג adj. *a.λ. mockers.* † מָעוֹג *cake,* elsw. only 1 K. 17[1.2] for מְעוֹנ, and so *mockers for a cake;* Greek κνισοκόλακες, ψωμοκόλακες, Mediaeval Latin *buccellarii.* All this is improb. ⑤ ἐξεμυκτήρισάν με μυκτηρισμόν, 𝔙 *subsannaverunt me subsannatione,* לֵיעוּ לִעַג is doubtless correct; so Du.; Bä. לְעֵנִי לָעֵג not so good. It is then prob., as l. is too long, that לעוּ originated in dittog. — [הָרֹק] inf. abs. † הרק vb. *gnash, grind:* c. שׁנִים עַל elsw. 37[12]; also abs. without עַל 112[10] La. 2[16], c. ב Jb. 16[9]. — 17. [אדני] is suspicious. — [כַּמָּה] *how long;* only here in ψ, also Jb. 7[19]. This trimeter l. is a gl. — [מִשֹּׁאֵיהֶם]. ⑤ ἀπὸ τῆς κακουργίας αὐτῶν ; Ols., Dy., Gr., משאגהם *from their roaring;* but neither suited to ‖ מכפירים ; We., Du., משאגים *roarers,* prob. correct ; cf. שׁחל ׃ שׁוֹאה v.⁸, improbable if latter gl. as above. שׁיא *a.λ.* with same mng. is doubtless txt. err.; ס here is possibly dittog. from מכפירים. — 19. ‖ איבי שׁקר שׁנאי חנם. 69[5] has both phrs. (cf. שֹׁנְאַי שֶׁקֶר 38[20]). The one is a gl. to the other.

Probably the latter is original on account of הנב as in v.⁷. — עין [יקרצו]. ⅏ and
𝔍 take it as rel. clause and translate by ptc. קרץ c. עין = *pinch the eye, wink
maliciously*, so Pr. 6¹⁸ 10¹⁰. — 20. כי] causal. ⅏ has לי, doubtless err. for
לא 𝔅, 𝔍, Σ, Aq., ⅏. — [וְעַל רִגְעֵי אֶרֶץ דִּבְרֵי]. ⅏ᴮ has καὶ ἐπ' ὀργῇ δόλους διελογί-
ζοντο (ὀργήν ⅏^{א, c, R}); 𝔙 *et in iracundia terrae loquentes, dolos cogitabant;*
𝔍 *sed in rapina terrae verba fraudulenta concinnant.* These rest on different
texts from 𝔅. רִגְעֵי ארץ *a.λ.* and improb. ⅏ had prob. רגֶז, but not ארץ, which
is explanatory gl., though in ⅏ and other Vrss. Rd. רִגְעִי *my tranquillity.* —
[דברי] not in ⅏, ⅏, and doubtless gl. — [יַחֲשֹׁבוּן] Qal impf. 3 pl. archaic form.
— 21. ו [וַיַּרְחִיבוּ] consec. err. for ו coörd., Hiph. impf. 3 pl. רחב *open wide,*
here of much hostility in speaking, as Is. 57⁴. The last two words of v.²⁰
make with first clause of v.²¹ a complete line. — † [הֶאָח הֶאָח] interject. *aha!*
always introduced by אמר; cf. v.²⁵ 40¹⁶ = 70⁴, also Is. 44¹⁶ Ez. 25³ 26² 36²
Jb. 39²⁵. — 22. [רָאִיתָה] Qal pf. 2 m. fully written, referring to יהוה, antith. to
ראה of adversaries. — [אדני] is gl. — [שמני] is also a gl. — 23. הָקִיצָה] Hiph.
imv. cohort., ‖ הָעִירָה (same form), should go from prosaic order to its noun
לריבי ‖ ולמשפטי‎. — [ואדני] gl. as v.²². — 24. צדקך] so ⅏, 𝔅, but 𝔍 צדקי; prob. sf. not
in original, but must be interpretation. Either יהוה or אלהי gl., prob. the former.
— 25. [האח] is repeated in ⅏, 𝔙, Syr. Hex., but improb. — [נפשנו] = *our desire,*
as 27¹² 41³. — [אל יאמרו] is repeated for emph., but destroying the measure. —
26–28 to be compared with 40¹⁴⁻¹⁸ = 70³⁻⁶. First l. of 70¹ = 40¹⁴ not in 35²⁶,
either prefixed in those passages or omitted here. V.²⁶ᵃ has variation of
מבקשי נפשי, 70³ = 40¹⁵: שמה is in accordance with 35¹⁹. ²⁴ and so better suited
to the Ps.; therefore, if an addition, not a mechanical one without assimilation. V.²⁶ᵇ is not in 70³ᵇ = 40¹⁵ᵇ, but they substitute 35⁴ᵇ, excepting that
חפצי רעתי takes the place of חשבי רעתו. This favours the originality of v.²⁶ᵇ,
which is a good syn. v.²⁶ᵃ. [המגדילים עלי] Hiph. ptc. pl.; of enemies, phr.
of 38¹⁷ 55¹³ Je. 48²⁶. ⁴² Jb. 19⁵, cf. Ez. 35¹³. 70⁴ᵃ is not in 35²⁶⁻²⁷, but אמר
האח האח reminds us of 35²¹. ²⁵. — [וְיִלְבְּשׁוּ] Qal juss. ‡ לבש vb. Qal, *put on* (one's
own) *garment, clothe oneself;* lit. not in ψ, but fig. often: pasture with flocks
65¹⁴; Yahweh puts on majesty 93¹, strength 93¹, honour and majesty 104¹;
priests put on righteousness 132⁹; men put on shame *35²⁶* 109²⁹, cursing 109¹⁸.
Hiph. *clothe, array with;* Yahweh clothes priests with salvation 132¹⁶, enemies with shame 132¹⁸. — ‡ [בֹּשֶׁת] n.f. *shame,* elsw. 40¹⁶ (= 70⁴) 44¹⁶ 69²⁰
132¹⁸ Jb. 8²²; phr. עמה ב' Ps. 109²⁹. — 27. [ירנו] for ישׁישׁו 70⁵; בך 70⁶; has fallen out
of v.²⁷ᵃ by txt. err. חפצי צדקי 70⁵ᵇ here; the change has been
made in 70, for צרק is suited to the context of 35²⁴ and the antith. of v.²⁷ᶜ.
V.²⁷ᵇ = 70⁵ᵇ, except that l. here lacks complement given in 70⁵ᵇ אהבי ישׁועתך,
which takes the place of עברו החפץ שלום‎. — 28. This v. has nothing to correspond with it in 70⁶; but the latter has עני ואביון as 35¹⁰, and concludes with
l. similar to its beginning. — [לשון תהגה] cf. for phr. 71²⁴ Is. 59⁸ Jb. 27⁴.

PSALM XXXVI.

Ps. 36 is composite. (1) A didactic Ps. describing the wicked under the inspiration and flattery of personified transgression, and without terror of God, plotting, speaking, and doing all manner of evil (v.$^{2-5}$). (2) A Ps. of praise: (*a*) comparing the four chief attributes of Yahweh to the four great objects of nature, as a basis for praising Him for saving man and beast (v.$^{6-7}$); (*b*) praising His precious kindness as manifested in the delights of worship in the temple, and in the life and light that issue from Him (v.$^{8-10}$). Glosses (*a*) pray for His kindness, righteousness, and help against the wicked (v.$^{11-12}$), (*b*) and point to the place where the enemies are fallen to rise no more (v.^{13}).

A. V.$^{2-5}$, 6^5.

AN utterance of Transgression (comes) to the wicked man in the midst of his mind:
There is no dread of God before his eyes:
For it doth flatter him as regards the finding out of his (hateful) iniquity.
The words of his mouth are trouble and deceit, he hath ceased to act circumspectly.
To make trouble thoroughly he plans upon his bed;
He takes his stand in a way that is not good, evil he refuseth not.

B. V.$^{6-10}$, 2 STR. 5^3.

YAHWEH, in heaven is Thy kindness,
Thy faithfulness (reacheth) unto the skies,
Thy righteousness is like the mountains of 'El,
Thy justice is a great deep;
Man and beast Thou savest.
YAHWEH, how precious is Thy kindness.
They are refreshed with the rich things of Thy house,
And of the brook of Thy dainties Thou makest them drink;
For with Thee is the fountain of life;
When (Thou shinest, light doth appear).

Ps. 36 was in 𝔇 and 𝔇ℜ (*v*. Intr. §§ 27, 33). The term לעבד יהוה with David corresponds with 18[1]. It seems therefore to suggest some original connection, or association with Ps. 18. This could hardly come from 𝔇ℜ. It must have come from 𝔇, if not already attached to the Ps. when he used it. There is no historical situation suggested in the present title, but it seems probable that the man who proposed these words was thinking of Saul's madness as a suggestion of evil, according to 1 S. 16[14-28] 18[10-11]. But he must have lived at a much later date than the author of these passages, or indeed the author of the similar 1 K. 22[2)-28], where the suggestion of evil is attributed to the divine Spirit; for this editor interprets the story of Saul and David in accordance with v.[1], where Transgression itself as a personified evil makes the suggestion. This conception is certainly earlier than that of Satan, who appears first in Zc. 3[1-2]. The Ps. is therefore probably from the time of Jeremiah, when prophets of falsehood abounded. This does not apply to the whole Ps., but only to the pentameter hexastich, v.[2-5]. The remainder of the Ps. is much later. The original Ps. also is similar in v.[5] to Mi. 2[1]. No other writings have been used, although in some respects the situation and tone of the Ps. resemble 9-10, 14, and on that account it might be referred to the early days of the Restoration. But the wicked here seem not to be enemies of the nation, but wicked men among the people; and the use of mouth and tongue is injurious, and not simply false; and so it implies ethics of speech, earlier than the period of Persian influence. The Ps. in its present form is composite. A Ps. of two trimeter pentastichs has been added, v.[6-10]. This uses the Miktam 57[2] in v.[8] and 57[11] in v.[6]. It also is based on the conception of Eden, Gn. 2[10], in v.[9], especially as applied to the temple in Ez. 47[1 sq.] (upon which also Zc. 14[8] Jo. 4[18] depend). It is also probable that Je. 2[18] 17[13] underlie v.[10]. The humanitarianism of v.[7] is post-Deuteronomic. The author of v.[7] was familiar with Lebanon and Hermon and the Mediterranean Sea, and possibly had his home in northwestern Galilee, where these were ever in view. The similes are so graphic that they could best be explained by an author standing on one of the summits of Lebanon, where all these things would come naturally into his mind. These two Pss. were brought into a sort of unison by a trimeter tetrastich of petition, v.[11-12]. The Ps., as thus constructed, was probably made for 𝕭. A later editor, probably Maccabean, gave the Ps. a reference to national enemies by the addition of v.[13], which was probably based on Ps. 14[5].

PSALM XXXVI. *A.*

The Ps. is composed of two synth. tristichs. — **2.** *An utterance of Transgression*]. Transgression is personified as sin in Gn. 4[7] (cf. Ps. 19[14]). There, like a beast of prey, it tries to get possession of the man and rule him; here it has already taken possession of him, and as the spirit of prophesy, suggests to him as to a prophet. In all other passages this utterance comes from Yahweh to a real prophet; here only, transgression takes the place of Yahweh, and so becomes a god to the wicked man, inspiring him with wickedness, so that he becomes a prophet of transgression. This is all the more impressive to him that it does not come upon him as

an external energy from without, as in the case of Saul, 1 S. 16¹⁴⁻²³
18¹⁰⁻¹¹, but as already within him : *in the midst of his mind,* domi-
nating his mind from its very centre. Thus 𝕲, 𝔖, 𝔙, 𝔍. But 𝔥,
followed by EVˢ., has changed the reading to " *my heart,*" either
by copyist's error, or to avoid the unparalleled conception of an
inspiration of a wicked man in any sense of the term. It is probable that in 𝔥 transgression was originally interpreted as in an objective construct relation, as 𝚺, followed by Ges., De W., al. : "an
utterance concerning the transgression of the wicked is within my
heart," making the psalmist inspired, rather than the wicked man.
But such a construction of the word "utterance " is against all
usage. — *There is no dread of God*], an explanation of the situation by the psalmist, implying that God is not present and will not
call to account, as 10⁴ 14¹ 53². Transgression has taken the place
of God and is become the god of this wicked man. — *before his
eyes*]. He ignores God, can no longer see Him as present ; for
he is so absorbed in the presence of transgression and the experience of its suggestions. — **3.** *For it doth flatter him*]. Transgression does this in its utterance to him ; so most naturally, Ra.,
De., Bä., Kirk. "He flattereth himself," EVˢ., has little to justify
it. — *in his eyes* is a gloss, not in 𝕲. — *as regards the finding out
of his* (*hateful*) *iniquity*], by God, in accordance with the previous
context. He had no dread of God, of His presence, or of His investigation of his conduct ; implying therefore that God would not
find out his iniquity. This iniquity the psalmist emphasises as
something which one is bound to hate, taking it as gerundive,
dependent on iniquity, so essentially, " abominable sin," PBV.
But "to be hateful" AV., "to be hated" RV., emphasise the
discovery of the iniquity by God. It is also difficult to see why
the finding out, which has been pushed into the background of
his mind by the flattering voice of transgression, should now be
emphasised in the climax. The various efforts to improve the
text have all alike proved unsatisfactory. — **4.** *The words of his
mouth*]. The description passes over from the mental state of
the wicked man into his external behaviour : and first his speech,
his words ; these are *trouble and deceit.* His speech, as under the
inspiration of a flatterer, is flattering, and so deceives and makes
trouble to those who depend upon it. The wicked speech is

accompanied by wicked deeds; *he hath ceased to act circum-spectly*]. He has laid aside all prudence in action, because he has no dread of consequences. — **5.** *To make thoroughly*]. The measure requires the attachment of this infinitive to the noun, *trouble;* in accordance with Mi. 7³. This is favoured by the use of Mi. 2¹. The usual rendering, "to do good," as explanation of act circumspectly, Dr., or as dependent upon it, Kirk., not only makes that line too long, but also gives an awkward tautological close to the sentence. — *he plans upon his bed*]. The description goes back to the mental state, the plans suggested by Transgression. These are carefully matured during the quiet of the night, to be thoroughly carried out in the morning. — *He takes his stand*]. The time for action has come, and he is determined to carry out his plans. He takes his position with decision and firmness. — *in a way that is not good*], a way of life, a course of conduct, which is the negative of the good way required by God's Law. This in the climax is: *evil he refuseth not*], which is as much as to say, from no evil does he shrink, he undertakes it all, without reluctance and without remorse.

PSALM XXXVI. *B.*

Str. I. is a syn. trimeter tetrastich, with a synth. monostich. The four chief attributes of Yahweh are compared with the four great objects in nature. Doubtless the psalmist, either in imagination or in reality, stood upon one of the summits of Lebanon, where all these were in full view. — **6.** *Kindness*], the usual meaning of the Hebrew word, especially when in syn. relation with "faithfulness." Yahweh's kindness is *in heaven*, so most naturally, thinking of heaven as at once its source and as illustrating its immeasurable and all-comprehending relations. This is an Old Testament prelude to the knowledge surpassing love of Eph. 3¹⁷⁻¹⁹. The phrase is doubtless based on Ps. 57¹¹ (cf. 103¹¹) "unto the heavens"; but this does not justify us in interpreting the Heb. preposition here in an unusual sense, "to the heavens," as do Bä., Kirk., al., or in paraphrasing, "as the heavens," Pe.; for the author doubtless made the change for the purpose of giving a new turn to the thought. He changes the prepositions for variety of

imagery. — *Thy faithfulness (reacheth) unto the skies*]. Faithfulness is an attribute that may be compared to a long reach, rather
than to comprehensive extent. It is therefore conceived as reaching far up into the expanse of the skies, which extend one above
another in mysterious and sublime heights. There is probably
here an antith. in the poet's mind as in 85¹², kindness coming
down out of heaven, faithfulness ascending the heights of heaven.
— **7.** *Thy righteousness is like*]. This is a real simile — *the
mountains of 'El*], the great, the giant mountains, such as Hermon and Lebanon, whose lofty summits, covered with snow the
greater part of the year, suggest to the pious mind the special
presence and power of God. So the gigantic cedars of Lebanon
are called the cedars of God, 80¹⁰ 104¹⁶. The psalmist is doubtless thinking of the mountains as firm, stable, enduring, everlasting,
majestic, and all-commanding. — *Thy justice*]. As the three other
syn. terms are all singular and all attributes, an attribute in the
singular is required here. But it has been changed by an early
copyist to the plural : " acts of judgment," and so it appears in 𝕳
and 𝕵. — *the great deep*]. A metaphor taking the place of the
similes, so 𝕵. This is more poetical than the sameness of a
particle of comparison here, as urged by We., al., after 𝕲. Although this exact term, *great deep*, is found elsewhere, Gn. 7¹¹
Am. 7⁴ Is. 51¹⁰, in the story of the deluge, yet this does not justify
the rendering " great flood," as Moll., Bä., thinking of that great
historic act of judgment. This might be thought of if the plural
judgments were to be retained, and their irresistible power of
destruction, from which none can escape, might then have been
in the mind of the poet. But that would be inconsistent with the
emphasis upon kindness which characterises this little Ps., and
with the climax of salvation in the last line of the Str. The great
deep is indeed metaphorical of the divine justice, not on its
retributive side, but on its vindicatory side ; because of its un-
fathomable depths, its mysterious movements, and its vastness of
extent. — *Man and beast*], comprehending the animal with man,
in the scope of Yahweh's attributes, cf. 104²⁷⁻²⁸. — *Thou savest*].
The four attributes are all summed up in the work of salvation.

  Str. II. has a syn. tristich and a syn. couplet. — **8.** *Yahweh* is
attached to the previous line in 𝕳, making it too long. It also

appears at the close of this line in 𝔍, where 𝔥, 𝔊 have *Elohim*.
Elohim is improbable in this Ps. The measure allows of but one
divine name, and that in v.^{8a}. — *How precious*], exclamation of
admiration and wonder, explained in subsequent context, — *is Thy
kindness*], resuming the thought of v.^{6a}, kindness at the beginning
of the previous Str. being the most prominent attribute, as shown
also by the climax of salvation. 𝔥 and Vrss. have a tetrameter
line : *And the children of men take refuge in the shadow of Thy
wings.* This is a familiar idea from 57^2, cf. 61^5 91^4 Rev. 2^{12}, with
a subj. which is striking and difficult to explain in this context.
It is doubtless a gloss. — **9.** *They are refreshed*]. The subj. is
general, indefinite, referring to worshippers of Yahweh. It is
unnecessary to supply a subject. — *with the rich things of Thy
house*]. Probably the sacrificial meals of the worship in the
temple at the festivals are in the mind of the psalmist; but these
have certainly been generalised so as to include all spiritual benefits. — *And of the brook of Thy dainties*]. The dainties are regarded as so copious that they are like an overflowing stream.
It may be that the river of Eden underlies the thought, especially
in the form in which it appears in Ez. 47$^{1\,sq.}$, as a river of life
flowing forth from the temple, and similar to the river of the city
of God, Ps. 46^5. — *Thou makest them drink*]. Yahweh Himself
is the host and they are His guests. He gives them their meat
and drink. — **10.** *For with Thee*], that is, in Thy house, Thy
presence, *is the fountain of life*], probably an abbreviation of
fountain of living waters of Je. 2^{13} 17^{13}, a perennial, never-failing
stream flowing forth from Yahweh's presence as a well-spring or
original source. — *When Thou shinest*], lettest the light shine
from Thy face, as Pss. 4^7 44^4 89^{16}, taking the Heb. word as inf.
cstr. in a temporal clause, instead of the usual interpretation as
a noun, " in Thy light," which seems rather tame, and involves the
repetition of the same noun without any new idea. — *light doth
appear*], that is, shine forth upon the worshippers, giving them
light and joy, taking the form as Niphal pf. The usual translation, as Qal, " We see light," introduces for the first time 1st
pers. pl. into the Ps., which everywhere else uses the 3d pers.
This interpretation is doubtless due to the 1st pers. in the gloss
that follows.

O draw out Thy kindness to them that know Thee,
  And Thy righteousness to the right-minded;
  Let not the foot of pride come against me,
  Let not the hand of the wicked make me a fugitive.

11-12. This trimeter tetrastich is a petition which combines the thought of the two Pss. The first couplet is a petition for the *kindness* and *righteousness* of the second part of this Ps., both combined with the same verb, *draw out*, prolong, in the bestowal. — *To them that know Thee*], with the practical, experimental knowledge of worship in the temple and the enjoyment of its good things, cf. v.⁹⁻¹⁰. — *to the right-minded*] as 7¹¹ 11² 32¹¹ +, those whose minds are upright in His worship and in obedience to His commands. The second couplet is a petition for deliverance from the wicked man of the first Ps. — *The foot of pride*], lifted up in haughtiness, strutting along with scornful indifference of others ‖ *hand of the wicked*], the plural taking the place of the singular of v.². — *come against me*]. The petition is that Yahweh will prevent the feet from moving forward to the attack. — *make me a fugitive*], overcome me and put me to flight, so that I will have to wander away in exile from the sacred place.

13. A later editor, probably a Maccabean, wishing to interpret the wicked of the Ps. as national enemies, and justified in some measure by the figurative language of the previous petitions, adds a trimeter couplet setting forth the fulfilment of the expectations of the people in the downfall of the enemy.

There are the workers of trouble fallen;
They are thrust down and cannot rise.

There], pointing to the place, as in Ps. 14⁵, — *are the workers of trouble fallen*], on the battle-field. — *They are thrust down*], by blows from weapons — *and cannot rise*], they have fallen in death to rise no more.

XXXVI. *A.*

2. וְאָם־פֶּשַׁע] phr. α.λ. ‡ וְאָם n.m. *utterance* elsw.: (1) of a prophet Nu. 24³·⁴·⁶·¹⁶ 2 S. 23¹ Pr. 30¹; (2) before divine names (except Je. 23³¹) Ps. 110¹ Is. 56⁸, where alone it begins sentence, elsw. often in middle, but most frequently at the end; found in all the prophets except Hb., Jon., but not in H., D. (except when parall. Kings), Chr., Dn., Job, or Megilloth. פֶּשַׁע is personified, as חטאת Gen. 4⁷, cf. Ps. 19¹⁴. But 𝔊 has ὁ παράνομος, 𝔙 *injustus* = פֶּשַׁע, implying a person, probably an evil spirit, or possibly שטן of the later theology, as Horsley. 𝔥 has the more primitive idea and is more probable in itself. — רָשָׁע] as usual, the person to whom the utterance came, 𝔍 *impii*. 𝔊 has τοῦ ἁμαρτάνειν, 𝔙 *ut delinquat* = לִרְשַׁע, which is against usage and improbable in itself. — בְּקֶרֶב לִבִּי] referring to psalmist, improbable, error of copyist. 𝔊, 𝔙, 𝔖, 𝔍, have לבו, which is favoured by the parall. עיניו and is doubtless correct, as most moderns. רב for the man himself, as 58³. — אלהים] because deity was before the mind, as 14¹. — 3. הֶחֱלִיק אֵלָיו] Hiph. pf. חלק (*5¹⁰*) *flatter;* subj. שׁ׳, explaining the וּאו, c. prep. אל, cf. עַל Pr. 29⁶. 𝔊 has ἐνώπιον αὐτοῦ, which might be a condensation of אליו with בעיניו; but 𝔥 prob. gives us a conflation of two earlier readings, due to the influence of לנגד עיניו above, one of which, prob. the latter, is incorrect. — לִמְצֹא] Qal inf. cstr., may be interpreted either of *finding*, in the sense of *attaining, accomplishing*, or in the sense of *discovery*. Most interpreters take the latter, after 𝔊, 𝔍; cf. Gn. 44¹⁶. — לִשְׂנֹא] Qal inf. cstr., may be taken with 𝔊 as syn. with מצא, and intensifying the discovery of the iniquity by the hating of it, that is, by God, the terror of whom is absent from the wicked man; so RV., and most interpreters; or as gerund *ad odiendum* 𝔍, qualifying the iniquity, *abominable* PBV., *to be hateful* AV., which is preferable if the text be correct. The construction is, however, in either case so awkward that emendation is tempting. Dy., Gr., propose עֲוֹן לשׁנו *iniquity of his tongue;* Du. thinks לשׁנא an Aramaic gl. — 4. אָוֶן וּמִרְמָה] — 138⁴. 78¹ 54⁴ 59¹³, and אמרי פי 19¹⁵ 17⁴ 59¹³ דבר שפתיכ as [דִּבְרֵי פִיו. phr. α.λ. ψ; cf. עמל ואון 10⁷ 90¹⁰, cf. 55¹¹. — ‡ חָדַל] Qal pf. (1) *cease, come to an end, cease to be*, Dt. 15¹¹ Ju. 5⁶·⁷·⁷; (2) *cease, leave off, desist;* here as Ps. 49⁹ Dt. 23²³ Gn. 41⁴⁹ (E) Je. 44¹⁸. — לְהַשְׂכִּיל] Hiph. inf. cstr. objective, *act with circumspection* (*v. 2¹⁰*). Cf. 14² for a similar thought. — לְהֵיטִיב] Hiph. inf. cstr., usually interpreted as syn. with previous vb., so EVˢ., or as a subordinate inf. to it, giving הַשְׂכִּיל the meaning of *consider* or *regard;* so 𝔊, 𝔙, 𝔍, Kirk. But this word makes l. too long and is needed to complete the next l. Give it therefore the sense of *do well, thoroughly* (*v. 33³*), and attach it to אָוֶן, as it is attached to רֵע Mi. 7³. — 5. יַחְשֹׁב] Qal impf. (*v. 10²*), *plan, devise;* cf. Mi. 2¹, where also עַל משׁכב (*4⁵*) is used, making it prob. that the psalmist used the prophet's thought.

XXXVI. B.

The Ps. now changes from pentameter to trimeter, and has an entirely different tone. Another independent Ps. is added. — 6-7. The quartette of attributes הֶסֶד (*4⁴*), אמונה (*33⁴*), צדקה (*5⁹*) favours משׁפט (*1⁵*) also. The pl. משׁפטיך is a later interpretation, not consistent with context. V.⁶ is similar to 57¹¹ (= 108⁶), בהשׁמים for עַד שׁחקים there, is an intentional change, not txt. err. as Du. It is a more difficult reading than שׁ׳, which is in syn. clause and which would have favoured assimilation rather than the reverse. — הַרְרֵי־אֵל] cf. 50¹⁰ *mountains of 'El*, for gigantic mts. which He alone could make and where

He dwelt; cf. ארזו אל 80¹¹. כוכבי אל Is. 14¹³. For אל *v.* Intr. § 32. 𝕲 ὡσεὶ repeats כ before תהום, so We. It is possible that it has fallen off after sf. יְ. — תהום] *v. 33⁷.* — יהוה] makes l. too long, and is needed in next l. — **8.** [יָקָר = *pretiosa* 𝔍, τίμιον Aq., Σ, Quinta, so 𝕿, is a more difficult reading and therefore more probable than יָרֵב, ἐπλήθυνας of 𝕲, *multiplicasti* 𝔈, so essentially 𝕊, which is common with חסד. ‡ יָקָר adj. (1) *precious, highly valued;* usually of stones, in ψ elsw. 45¹⁰ 116¹⁵; (2) *glorious, splendid* (cf. Aram.), in ψ only as subst. 37²⁰, cf. Jb. 31²⁶. — אלהים]. The next clause with ובני אדם (𝕾⁵) is one word too long and is striking in view of אדם above; and אלהים in this Yahwistic Ps. is improbable. 𝔍 had יהוה, showing variant text. Either both glosses or a l. must be found underlying them. Du. rds. אליך יבאו בני-אדם after 65⁸. But we should rather expect something suggested by context, such as אמונתך. Then we might regard אלהים as for an original אל prep. interpreted as אֵל, *God.* But the clause בצל כנפיך יחסיון is similar to 57², cf. 61⁵ 91⁴ Ru. 2¹², and not altogether appropriate to context here; it is probably, with the foregoing, a gl. — **9.** [יִרְוְיֻן] Qal impf. 3 pl. full form, *be refreshed, satisfied.* ‡ רוה vb. Qal only here in ψ, cf. Pr. 7¹⁸. Pi. *saturate, drench,* Ps. 65¹¹, cf. 23⁵. — דֶּשֶׁן בֵּיתֶךָ] *fatness, rich things,* the festival meals in the temple, cf. Is. 43²⁴ Je. 31¹⁴. ‡ דֶּשֶׁן n.m. *fatness, fertility,* 63⁶ 65¹²; spiritual blessings here, as Is. 55², 𝕲 of Ps. 68¹⁶·¹⁶. — נַחַל עֲדָנֶיךָ] phr. α.λ. † [עֵדֶן] n.[m.] *luxury, dainty:* pl. 2 S. 1²⁴ (dub. סרנים Gr., HPS.) Je. 51³⁴ (dub. מַעְרֵי Gie), elsw. only here, 𝕲 τρυφῆς, 𝔍 *deliciarum.* Cf. † [מַעֲדָן] only pl. Gn. 49²⁰ (poem) La. 4⁵ Pr. 29¹⁷. It is possible that there may be a reference to the Eden of Gn. 2¹⁰ and its river of life, if the Ps. is postexilic. For the stream of life from the temple, cf. Ps. 46⁵ Ez. 47¹ ˢᵠ· Jo. 4¹⁸ Zc. 14⁸. — [תַשְׁקֵם] Hiph. impf. 2 m. sf. 3 pl. ‡ [שקה] vb. Qal not used. Niph. Am. 8⁸. Pu. Jb. 21²⁴. Hiph. *give to drink:* abs. Ps. 78¹⁵; c. acc. rei *36⁹,* יין 60⁶, חמץ 69²², ברמות 80⁶; acc. pers. or thing given drink 104¹¹·¹³. — **10.** [מְקוֹר חַיִּים] = Pr. 10¹¹ 13¹⁴ 14²⁷ 16²², *spring* or *fountain of life,* cf. מקור מים חיים Je. 2¹³ 17¹³. ‡ מקור elsw. Ps. 68²⁷ has same mng. חיים (*v. 7⁶*). Yahweh as אור, cf. light of His face 4⁷ 44⁴ 89¹⁶, א:ר החיים 56¹⁴ Jb. 33³⁰. — [נִרְאֶה] Qal impf. 1 pl., 𝕲, 𝔍; introduction of 1 pers. for 3 pers. of remainder of Ps. improbable. Rd. rather Niph. pf. נִרְאֶה. Then it is better to take באורך as Qal inf. cstr. of vb. אור *shine.* — **11.** [לְיֹדְעֶיךָ] *those knowing thee* with the knowledge of righteous adherents. (*v. 1⁶*) ידע || ישרי לב 7¹¹ 11² 32¹¹ 64¹¹ 94¹⁵ 97¹¹, only in ψ, not in prophets. — **12.** [רֶגֶל גַּאֲוָה] *proud foot.* נאוה 10² 31¹⁹· ²⁴ 73⁶ Is. 9⁸ 13¹¹ 25¹¹ Pr. 14³ 29²³. — [אַל-תְּנִדֵנִי] Hiph. juss., נוד *cause to wander aimlessly* as fugitives, as 59¹² (*v. 11⁴*). — **13.** [שם] as *14⁵,* place of defeat. — [דחו] Pu. pf. α.λ. רחה *thrust down.*

PSALM XXXVII., 7 STR. 6⁶.

Ps. 37 is a didactic Ps. — Exhortation (1) not to envy evil-doers, but to trust in Yahweh, who will ultimately make a just discrimination (v.¹⁻⁶); (2) to be resigned and not excited, for in a little while the wicked will be no more and the afflicted will inherit the land (v.$^{7-11}$). (3) Yahweh laugheth at the devices of the wicked. Exact retribution will come upon them; their weapons will be turned against them, but the righteous will be upheld (v.$^{12-17}$). (4) Yahweh knoweth the days of the perfect, but the wicked shall perish, however exalted they may be. They will be cursed and cut off, while the righteous are blessed and enjoy their inheritance (v.$^{18-22}$). (5) A man's steps are established by Yahweh; the righteous are never forsaken, for Yahweh loveth justice (v.$^{23-28a}$). (6) The wicked and their seed are cut off; but the righteous have wisdom and the divine Law, and Yahweh will not let them be condemned (v.$^{28b-33}$). (7) Though the wicked be strong and flourishing, they will be destroyed; while the upright and their posterity will enjoy peace. Yahweh will save all who seek refuge in Him (v.$^{35-40}$). A liturgical gloss was inserted (v.^{34}).

FRET not thyself because of evildoers, and be not envious against them that do wrong;
    As grass they will speedily wither, and like the fresh grass fade.
    Trust in Yahweh and do good, inhabit the land and pasture in confidence;
    And take delight in Yahweh, and He will give thee the requests of thine heart.
    Roll upon Yahweh and trust in Him, and He will do it;
    And He will bring forth as the light thy right, and thy just cause as the noonday.
BE resigned to Yahweh and wait patiently for Him, and fret not thyself (because of evildoers);
    (Be not envious) against him that maketh his way prosperous, against the man that doeth evil devices;
    Desist from anger and forsake heat, fret not thyself at the doing of evil;
    For evildoers will be cut off, but those that wait on Yahweh will inherit the land;
    Yet a little, and the wicked will be no more, and thou wilt attentively consider his place and he will be no more;
    But the afflicted will inherit the land, and take delight in abundance of peace.
THE wicked deviseth against the righteous, and gnasheth his teeth at him.
    The Lord laugheth at him, for He seeth that his day cometh.
    The wicked draw the *sword*, and they tread the *bow* for slaughter;
    Their *sword* shall enter their own heart, and their *bows* shall be broken in their arms.
    Better is a little that the righteous hath than the roar of many wicked men;
    For the arms of the wicked shall be broken, seeing that Yahweh upholdeth the righteous.
YAHWEH knoweth the days of the perfect, and their inheritance shall be forever;
    They will not be ashamed in time of evil, and in days of hunger they will be satisfied.
    Yea, the wicked shall perish, and the enemies of Yahweh (shall be cut off);

Yea, (while in high esteem, while exalted) they do vanish, in smoke they do vanish away.

While the wicked borroweth and restoreth not, the righteous dealeth graciously and giveth;

Yea, those blessed of Him will inherit the land; but those cursed of Him shall be cut off.

OF Yahweh are a man's steps established, and in his way He takes pleasure;

Though he fall, he shall not be cast headlong, for Yahweh upholdeth his hand.

A boy I have been, now I am old, and I have not seen the righteous forsaken;

All the day he dealeth graciously and lendeth, and his seed will become a blessing.

Depart from evil and do good, and abide forever;

For Yahweh loveth justice, and forsaketh not His pious ones.

(THE unjust) are destroyed forever, and the seed of the wicked is cut off;

The righteous will inherit the land, and they will dwell forever upon it.

The mouth of the righteous uttereth wisdom, and his tongue speaketh justice;

The Law of his God is in his mind, and his goings will not totter.

The wicked spieth upon the righteous, and seeketh to put him (to a violent) death;

Yahweh will not forsake him in his hand, and will not condemn him as guilty when he is judged.

I HAVE seen the wicked (terrifying and making himself bare); he was like a luxuriant (cedar);

And then I passed by, and lo, he was no more; and I sought him, but he could not be found.

Watch the perfect man, and see the upright; for (a posterity) hath the man of peace:

But transgressors are destroyed together, the posterity of the wicked is cut off.

The salvation of the righteous is from Yahweh, and their refuge in the time of distress;

And Yahweh will help them, and He will deliver them from the wicked, and He will save them, because they have sought refuge in Him.

Ps. 37 was in 𝔅, but in no other Psalter until the final Psalter. This was because of its didactic character and its length, making it of less value for public worship than many others. It is a series of alphabetical hexameter couplets. As Pss. 25 and 34 omitted the Str. ו in order to get three Strs. of seven letters each, so this Ps. omitted Str. ק in order to get seven Strs. of three letters each. The Ps. is compared by Amyrald to "many precious stones or pearls which are strung on one string in one necklace." Delitzsch says with approval, "Tertullian names this Psalm *providentiae speculum;* Isodorus, *potio contra murmur;* Luther, *vestis piorum, cui adscriptum: Hic sanctorum patientia est.*" The Ps. deals with the same problem as the book of Job; only it takes the earlier position of the friends of Job in their discourses, and does not rise to the higher solution of the discourses of Job himself. The hexameter couplets have for the most part remained unchanged. Strs. ר and כ have been condensed at the expense of the measure, ב and ח have been enlarged. But it is easy to restore them to their correct form. 𝔅 has lost

Str. ׳, but it is given in 𝔊. 𝔥 prefixes ו to Str. ה. There are several passages
similar to those of other writings: אל תתחר v.[1. 7. 8] Pr. 24[19]; v.[2], cf. 90[3] Jb.
14[2]; v.[4], cf. Jb. 27[10]; v.[18], cf. Ps. 1[6]. In all these cases our Ps. was probably
earlier, but in the following cases our Ps. was later: גול על י׳ v.[5] 22[9], cf. Pr.
16[3]; v.[13a], cf. Ps. 2[4]. The language of the Ps. is in some respects peculiar
and original: (1) α.λ. ירק דשא v.[2], רעה אמונה v.[3], ל להתחולל v.[7] in this sense,
הונן ונותן v.[21], חפץ דרך v.[23]; (2) terms elsw. seldom: פה הגה v.[30] Pr. 8[7],
התבונן על v.[10] Jb. 31[1], עשי עולה v.[1] Zc. 3[5. 18], אור = sun v.[6] Hb. 3[4] Jb. 31[26],
חרב פתח v.[14] Ez. 21[33], לטבוח v.[14] La. 2[21] Ez. 21[15], מצערי v.[23] Pr. 20[24] Dn. 11[48],
לא יוטל v.[24] Je. 22[28] Jb. 41[1]. Linguistic evidence favours the same period as
the thought; namely, the situation of the Jerusalem community before Nehemiah, exposed to bitter enemies, who are in prosperity while the people of
Yahweh are in adversity. The people are under the influence of D., and do
not yet know P. They are beginning to be influenced by the principles of
Hebrew Wisdom, but the WL. had not yet been written.

Str. I. is composed of three synth. couplets. — Couplet א.
1-2. *Fret not thyself*], as v.[7. 8] Pr. 24[19], with the heat of passion,
the excitement of anger, indignation, or discontent ‖ *be not
envious*], with the ardour of jealousy, making such comparisons
of one's lot with that of *evildoers* ‖ *them that do wrong*, as to
unduly excite oneself with the sense of injustice and wrong. The
reason why this excitement should be avoided is a practical one :
it is needless ; the situation will be of brief duration. The reason
is stated in the form of a simile. The prosaic insertion of " for "
was unnecessary, especially as it injured the measure. — *As grass ‖
like the fresh grass*], as in 90[6] Jb. 14[2] Is. 40[6-8], a natural image of
frailty and perishableness. — *they will speedily wither ‖ fade*]. —
Couplet ב. **3-4.** The negative warning gives place to the positive
exhortation, turning the attention from the evildoers to Yahweh.
Trust in Yahweh and do good], in antith with " do wrong," v[1].
— *Take delight in Yahweh*], the comfort, satisfaction, and joy
of continued trust. — *inhabit the land*], the land of promise,
the land of inheritance, as v.[9], in possession of the returned
exiles, implying that they would not be driven from it by
their enemies. — *and pasture*], as the flock of Yahweh, partake
of the good things of the land, *in confidence*], in security under
the divine protection. This meaning is given essentially in paraphrase by AV., " so shalt thou dwell in the land and verily thou
shalt be fed." RV. " follow after faithfulness," although sustained

by De., Dr., Kirk., al., gives the Heb. word an unusual meaning, and emphasises the ethical character of the v. at the expense of the parall. with the following context. — Couplet ב. **5-6.** *Roll upon Yahweh*], as 22⁹, cares, anxieties, and troubles. — *Way*, for the whole course of life, is a prosaic addition, at the expense of the measure, and gives the thought too ethical a turn. The climax is reached in: *and trust in Him*], as 31¹⁵, a stronger expression than the idea of personal leaning upon, resting upon Yahweh, without any further care or anxiety. The Str. reaches its climax in v.⁶, which, in a beautiful simile, sets forth the speedy triumph of the righteous. — *And He will bring forth*], from the obscurity in which their *right* ‖ *just cause* had been pushed by the evildoers, the cruel and crafty enemies. — *as the light*], the sunshine ‖ *as the noonday*, the full light of the noontide sun.

Str. II. has a syn. tristich and a tristich in which the second line is syn. with the first half of the first line, and the third line is syn. with its second half. Couplet ד is supplemented by the first line of couplet ה. — **7.** *Be resigned*, quiet, still, calm, and peaceful ‖ *wait patiently for Him*], the steadfast, longing looking unto Yahweh for help, both in antith. with: *fret not thyself*, repeated from v.¹ and given again v.⁸, with its parall.: *be not envious*, also from v.¹; not in 𝕳 or Vrss., but needed for completeness of measure; still further intensified in **8**, *desist from anger and forsake heat*]. The exciting influence here, as in v.¹, was *because of evildoers*, which must be repeated from v.¹ to supply the missing word of the measure, although not in 𝕳 or ancient Vrss. — *him that maketh his way prosperous*, as the context shows, succeeding and prospering in his wickedness ‖ *the man that doeth evil devices*, not only planning them but also accomplishing them ‖ *at the doing of evil*], as the parall. requires. But 𝕳 inserts a particle in order to emphasise its interpretation, "only to do evil," followed by EVˢ.; which thus becomes a warning not to carry their impatient fretting so far as to be evildoers themselves; an idea true and important enough in itself, but an intrusion into this context. — **9-11.** The antith. between the *evildoers* and *those that wait on Yahweh*, in the two parts of v.⁹ appears in the antith. v.¹⁰⁻¹¹, where the former are simply the wicked, the latter the afflicted, as those suffering for righteousness' sake. These antith.

classes have their antith. lots; the former *will be cut off*, by sudden violent death. In a very little while, *and yet a little*, cf. " speedily," v.², they *will be no more*], will pass out of existence, cease to exist; and this so entirely in the emphasis of the complementary part of the line that they cannot be found by the most careful search for them : *thou wilt attentively consider his place*]. In his own place, where he was accustomed to be, and where he could be found if anywhere, he will no more exist. On the other hand, those afflicted for Yahweh's sake *will inherit the land*, will continue to inhabit the land, cf. v.³, as its rightful heirs who cannot be dispossessed; repeated in v.¹¹ in order to the climax, *take delight in abundance of peace*]. The enemies having been destroyed, war has disappeared with them, and there is peace, so full and entire that it is conceived as in abundance, and after the experience of affliction, affording delight, cf. v.³⁻⁴.

Str. III. has two antith. couplets and a synth. one, all describing sure retribution upon the wicked. — Couplet ‫ו‬. **12–13.** *The wicked deviseth against the righteous*], cf. v.⁷ᵇ. His wicked plans are accompanied with such intense hostility that like a beast of prey *he gnasheth his teeth at him*]. This is not an individual enemy, but collective for warlike enemies, nations. — *The Lord laugheth at him*], doubtless a citation from 2⁴, where He laugheth at the nations plotting to overthrow the rule of the Messianic king. The reason for this scorn of the enemy is, *for He seeth*], foreseeth the impending evil. — *that his day cometh*], the day of the judgment upon him, the day of his death. — Couplet ‫ח‬. **14–15.** *The wicked draw the sword* ‖ *they tread the bow*, with the purpose of *slaughter*. This is enlarged, at the expense of the measure, in ancient texts at the basis of ‫ﬠ‬ and the Vrss. to read, " cause to fall," that is, in death, from sword and bow; and the righteous are still further described as " afflicted and needy," ‖ " upright in the way," the latter a phrase only here for the usual " upright of mind," which indeed is given in ⅏. ‫ﬡ‬ has a conflation of both " mind " and " way." All these are glosses, for which there is no place in the measure of the lines or the Str. The retribution is an exact one. Their own *sword* and *bows* will be used against them. — *shall enter their own heart*], pierce them to the heart, and so slay them; *and their bows shall be broken*]. — Couplet ‫ט‬. **16–17.**

The last clause of 16 should be rendered, in accordance with the
previous context, as *the roar of many wicked men*], the noise and
confusion of their multitudes during the attack, rather than with
Vrss. " abundance," or " great riches," wealth, which introduces
a gnome of Wisdom, suitable enough in itself, but intrusive, and
disturbing to the progress of the thought.   Then *the little that the
righteous hath* is not property, but strength and ability to resist
the enemy.   This is *better*, not in itself, but because such men may
rely upon the superabundant strength of Yahweh.   The climax of
the Str. is : *seeing that Yahweh upholdeth the righteous*], a circumstantial clause with ptc., which is more probable in this context
than the usual interpretation, making it an adversative clause.

Str. **IV.** has two synth. couplets, and one introverted couplet.
— Couplet ‛. **18–19.** *Yahweh knoweth*], with a practical interest
and redemptive attention, as 1^6. — *the days*], the duration of life
in 𝕳, but 𝔊, " ways," as 1^6. — *of the perfect*], those who are complete and entire in their conduct ‖ *righteous*, v.^{21}. — *their inheritance*], in the land, repeated v.$^{9. 11. 22. 29}$. — *shall be forever*],
they will never be removed from it by their enemies.   On the
negative side : *they will not be ashamed*], be put to shame by their
enemies, even, — *in time of evil*, when everything is threatening ;
but on the positive side, — *they will be satisfied*], have enough
and to spare even when the times are so evil that they are *days
of hunger*].   When they are besieged, or their enemies have left
them only a devastated land, they will still have plenty. — Couplet ‎ב‎. **20.**   This is in antith. with the previous couplet. — *Yea, the
wicked*, who are at the same time *enemies of Yahweh, shall perish
‖ they shall be cut off*.   The latter is inserted in v.^{20a} for measure,
where it has been omitted by copyist's error ; cf. v.^{22b}, where it is
still preserved. — *while in high esteem ‖ while exalted*], so after
𝔊, which is to be preferred to 𝕳, whether interpreted as the " fat
of lambs," 𝕿, PBV., AV., or " excellence of fields," RV., " splendour of the meadows," Kirk., or " glorying as yore-oxen," 𝕴.   The
reference to animals is not suited to the verb *vanish*, repeated
in the simile, *in smoke vanish away*].   The reference to the
flowers and the glory of the meadows is favoured by v.^{2}, but by
none of the ancient Vrss.— Couplet ‎ל‎. **21–22.**   These verses are in
introverted parall., but at the same time there is antith. between

the halves of both. The reference to the wicked, as one that *borroweth and restoreth not*, in the context, must refer to the humiliation of poverty, which reduces him to the necessity of borrowing and makes it impossible for him ever to repay his debt. This is antith. with the prosperity of the righteous, who are able to give generously to the poor and needy. The righteous are *blessed* of Yahweh, the wicked are *cursed of Him*.

Str. V. has three synth. couplets. — Couplet כ. **23-24**. *Of Yahweh*], emphatic in position. He is the original source from whom *a man's steps* ǁ *his way*, the whole course of his life in which he walks, *are established*, made firm and secure. This is Yahweh's own work, gives Him gratification, and He *takes pleasure* in it. In this walk, though *he fall*, as he may sometimes, owing to stumbling-blocks and impediments of various kinds, yet *he shall not be cast headlong*]. It shall not be a hurtful, dangerous, fatal fall, *for Yahweh upholdeth his hana*]. He has such a hold on his hand that He does not permit him to fall down or suffer injury. — Couplet ל. **25-26**.. The psalmist's experience is now given to fortify his testimony: *A boy I have been*]. He recalls his youth and his long life of varied experiences. — *now I am old*]. In all my life *I have not seen the righteous forsaken*], by Yahweh. Such a thing has never come under his observation, or formed any part of his experience, whether as to himself or others. A later editor, not realising the power of this terse statement, seeks to improve it by the addition, " or his seed seeking bread," which is well suited to the context, it is true, but which is intrusive here, making the line much too long for the measure, and also is premature in its reference to seed, which comes first with propriety in the next line. — *All the day he dealeth graciously and lendeth*]. He is so prosperous, as in v.[21], that he has enough and to spare ; and so can be generous in his dealings with others, and yet leave an abundance to his own children, and so *his seed will become a blessing*. It is probable that the psalmist has in mind the blessings of those who keep the Law of D., and especially Dt. 28[11-12]. — Couplet ם. **27-28** a. On the basis of this testimony and experience an exhortation is appropriate. This is in terms which become characteristic of the piety of Hebrew Wisdom, — *Depart from evil and do good*], both on the negative and positive sides of ethical conduct; with the imperative of apodosis, — *and inhabit forever*, as v.³, *the land*]. The last word was omitted in the text by copyist's mistake, at the expense of the measure. This exhortation is fortified by the reason, which sums up much of the previous context of the Str. and the Ps.: *For Yahweh loveth justice*], that is, the doing of justice, in the vindication of His people, as v.⁶. — *and forsaketh not*], as v.²⁵ — *His pious ones*], another term for the righteous and the afflicted people, as 30⁵ 31²⁴.

Str. VI. has two antith. couplets, with an intervening synth. couplet. — Couplet ע. **28 b–29.** *The unjust are destroyed*], so 𝕲 and many recent scholars, giving the ע of the couplet, missing in 𝕳, and also making a fine antith. The text of 𝕳, "they are preserved forever," though followed by 𝕵 and modern Vrss., is due to the mistake of a copyist, and occasioned many unnecessary difficulties. The retribution of the wicked, as usual in the OT., comes upon their *seed* also; they will *be cut off*, cf. v.⁹. In antith. with the punishment of the wicked is the reward of the righteous in terms of v.³. ⁹. ¹¹. ¹⁸. ²². ²⁷. — Couplet פ. **30–31.** The character of the righteous is more fully described: as to speech; *the mouth* and *tongue*, the organs of speech, on the positive side, — *uttereth wisdom*], the ethical wisdom based on the fear of Yahweh, which is here in its early beginnings, and so associated with *speaketh justice*] as the previous context indicates, that of the Law of D. — *the Law of his God is in his mind*], in accordance with Dt. 30¹⁴ Je. 31³³. Such a man, whose mind and speech are alike ruled by wisdom and the Law of Yahweh, is secure in his course of life; *his goings will not totter*], cf. v.²³. ²⁴. — Couplet צ. **32–33.** The wicked are so treacherous toward the righteous that, like a crafty foe, *they spy upon* him, seeking in every way to entrap him in some kind of violation of Law that will involve a judicial investigation; and so seek *to put him to a violent death*], to involve him in crime and its penalty, capital punishment. The original phrase has been abbreviated by an editor at the expense of the measure, and to the disguising of the technical meaning, which is, however, attested by the following line: *Yahweh will not forsake*] the righteous, as v.²⁵. ²⁸; strengthened here by reference to the specific danger, — *in his hand*], leaving him alone in the hand of his spying enemy, to do what he will with him. On the contrary, Yahweh is with him; He Himself takes control of the proceedings, and *when he is judged*, instead of giving the sentence of death desired by the adversary, — *will not condemn him as guilty*], an emphatic suggestion of the opposite, will declare him righteous.

Str. VII. has a synth., an antith., and a syn. couplet. An early editor, not discerning that the author had intentionally omitted the couplet ק for strophical reasons, and finding the alphabetical structure defective, sought to improve it by inserting **34**, a couplet with ק. But this is prosaic in style and an interruption of the thought, turning it into an exhortation, suitable enough for liturgical purposes, but not suited to the purpose of the original author. — *Wait on Yahweh*, as 25³ 27¹⁴, *and keep His way and He will exalt thee to inherit the land*, as v. ¹¹·²². — *When the wicked are cut off*, as v.³⁸, *thou shalt see it*, as v.²⁵·³⁵. — Couplet ר. **35–36.** *I have seen the wicked*]. This experience is the antith. of that given in v.²⁵. — *terrifying*, so 𝕲, taking it as ptc., cf. 10¹⁸, which is to be preferred to the noun of 𝕳, "as a terrible one," or the paraphrase of EVˢ., "in great power." — *and making himself bare*], throwing away his garments, stripping himself to display his strength and threaten combat, cf. Is. 52¹⁰; or as Dr. paraphrases, "putting forth his strength." "Flourishing," PBV.; "spreading himself," AV., RV., are conjectures without support in the usage of word. 𝕲, "lifting himself" up, had a different reading, which is followed by Du. These and other interpreters are misled by connecting this last ptc. with the simile, when in fact it belongs to the first part of the line; all the terms of which set forth the terrifying strength of the wicked enemy. The simile gives an additional idea, namely, wealth and luxuriance, and in this the enemy is compared to a *luxuriant cedar*, following 𝕲 in the preference for cedar to the "native tree," "tree in its native soil . . . one that has never been transplanted or disturbed, that has therefore struck its roots deep, and shot out with luxuriant strength," Pe. This is certainly a suitable idea of 𝕵, followed by RV., Dr., Kirk., al., although there is no support for this rendering in the usage of the Heb. word. The rendering "green bay tree," PBV., AV., has no authority behind it, but was mere conjecture. — *And then I passed by*, so 𝕲, 𝕾, 𝕵, PBV., which is best suited to the personal experience of the psalmist, and therefore to be preferred to

הֵ, "and he passed away," in death, AV., or as RV., "one passed by," which is an awkward effort to preserve the text of הֵ and at the same time get the meaning demanded by the context. — *and lo, he was no more*], as v.[10]; the experience emphasised by, — *and I sought him*, as in v.[10], but *he could not be found*, so utterly had he perished that no trace of him was left behind. — Couplet ש.

37–38. *Watch ‖ and see*], in order to have the same experience as the psalmist. — *the perfect, the upright*], intensified into *the man of peace*], the man in the possession of peace and in the enjoyment of it, rather than the peacemaker. Such a man *has a posterity* in accordance with v.[26] and the antith. in v.[28]; for the same Hebrew word must have the same meaning in these antithetical lines, v.[37. 38]. But ℐ misled EV[s]. to the rendering, best given in RV., "the latter end of (that) man is peace," introducing an eschatological ideal alien to the thought of the entire Ps., which emphasises, after D., peace and prosperity in this life. It also destroys the fine antith. of the couplet, and cannot easily be reconciled with the syntax of the passage. — But *transgressors*], another term for the wicked of the Ps. — *are destroyed*], as v.[28], — *together*], in one common disaster. And this will extend to their offspring: their *posterity* will be *cut off*, as v.[28]. — Couplet ת.

39–40. *The salvation*], summing up all the benefits of the Ps., and emphasised in the several syn. vbs., *help, deliver, save*. — *is from Yahweh*], as v.[23], the ordering and establishing of their steps. — He is *their refuge*, as 27[1] 31[3. 5]. — *in the time of distress*], as in time of evil, v.[19]. The last word is appropriately : *they have sought refuge in Him*.

---

1. [אַל־תִּתְחַר] so v.[7. 8], Hithp. juss. הרה (*18[8]*). Hithp. *heat oneself in vexation*, elsw. Pr. 24[19], which has same l. except for last two words, for which ברשעים. The Ps. is original. — [אַל־תְּקַנֵּא]. 𝕲 has μηδὲ = ואל required by measure, for אל without conj. would have Makkeph in both cases. ‡ [קנא] vb. denom. Pi. *be envious of;* c. ב pers. here, as 73[3] Gn. 30[1] (E) 37[11] (J); c. ל pers. Ps. 106[16]. † Hiph. *provoke to ardour of jealousy and anger* Ps. 78[58] Dt. 32[16. 21] Ez. 8[3] (?). — [עֹשֵׂי עַוְלָה] *wrongdoers*, phr. elsw. Zp. 3[5. 13]. ‡ עַוְלָה n.f. (1) *deed of violence and injustice;* בן עולה 89[23], cf. Ho. 10[9] 2 S. 3[34] 7[10]; איש מרמה ועולה Ps. 43[1]; עשׂה ע׳ 37[1]; פעל ע׳ 58[3] 119[3] Jb. 36[23]; בעולת ידים Ps. 125[3]; (2) *injustice of speech* 107[42] Mal. 2[6] Is. 59[3] and WL.; (3) *injustice* in general Pss. 64[7] 92[16] Ho. 10[13] 2 Ch. 19[7] and WL. — **2.** [כִּי] causal, dub. dittog. of prep. כ. — [ירק דשא] phr. α.λ. † יֶרֶק n.m. elsw. ירק עשב

Gn. 1³⁰ 9³ (P); ירק השדה Nu. 22⁴ (E); ירק alone Ex. 10¹⁵ (J) Is. 15⁶.—
3. [רעה אמונה] syn. with ירש ארץ v.⁹. Most ancient Vrss. give רעה the usual
mng. of *feed* as a flock; but many moderns think of רעה either as another
stem or as another mng. of same stem, and render as syn. רדף *follow after*,
as 𝔖 (בעה), De., Moll., Hu.³, RV., Dr., Kirk., *cherish* BDB.; but the older
view is preferable (*v.* v.¹¹). אֱמוּנָה adv. acc. *in confidence* (*v. 33⁴*). Secker,
Horsley, Ew., Bä., make אמונה = *security, stability*, as Is. 33⁶ = אמת Is. 39⁸,
and render *feed in security.* 𝔊 has ἐπὶ τῷ πλούτῳ αὐτῆς or חֲמַיְּה v.¹⁶, so
Hare, Houb., Lowth.—**4.** [וְהִתְעַנֵּג] (so v.¹¹) Hithp. † [ענג] vb. Pu. *be daintily
bred* Je. 6². Hithp. (1) *be of dainty habit* Dt. 28⁵⁶; (2) *take exquisite delight
in ;* Ps. 37⁴·¹¹ c. עַל, so Is. 58¹⁴ 66¹¹ Jb. 22²⁶ 27¹⁰; c. ב rei Is. 55²; (3) *make
merry over :* c. על Is. 57⁴.—**5.** [גול דַּרְכֶּךָ] fully written for גל from גלל *roll*,
c. עַל; cf. 22⁹ Pr. 16³, both אֶל for עַל. דרכך is explan. gl., not in other passages;
Ps. 22 certainly oldest of the three. 𝔊 has וְלֹה *uncover*, manifestly wrong.
— [יָּמַח עָלָיו] as 31¹⁵, possibly with meaning אל 4⁶, variation of ב בטח v.³.—
וְהוּא] emph.—**6.** ‡ [צָהֳרַיִם] n.[m.] only pl. *midday, noon :* as time of prayer
55¹⁸; as time of full heat 91⁶; as full sunshine, and so sim. of greatest blessing, here as Is. 58¹⁰.—**7.** [הִתְחוֹלֵל] Hithp. *wait longingly ;* α.λ. in this sense,
cf. Polel Jb. 35¹⁴ (Elihu) (*v. 29⁸*), prob. both a different vb., a variation of
יחל (31²⁵). 𝔊 has ἱκέτευσον, Aq. ἀποπαραδόκει, 𝔍 *expecta.*— [אַל־תִּתְחַר] as v.¹;
we should either prefix ו to get separate accent, or supply בּמֵרעים as v.¹, cf. v.⁸
להרע; in the latter case we should insert, from v.¹, כְּאִישׁ.—אל הקנא is unnecessary, except for measure.—**8.** [אַף] Dr. "only to do evil." 𝔊 has only
ὥστε = ל. אך is gl. of intensification.— [לְהָרֵע] Hiph. inf. cstr. רעע with ל,
either gerundive as interpreted by אף, or better as v.¹·⁸ *at the doing of
evil.* It is not necessary with Gr. to rd. לְמֵרַע.—**9.** [יִכָּרֵתוּן] Niph. impf. full form,
כרת (*v. 12⁴*) *be cut off* by death (from land), so v. ²²·²⁸·³⁴·³⁸ Is. 29²⁰ Ho. 8⁴
Na. 2¹ Pr. 2²². It is the technical phr. of H and P c. מן, but in this Ps. it
is abs. without מן, antith. [הֵמָּה] ירש ארץ.— unnecessary emph., impairs the
measure and is a gl.—**10.** ו [וְהִתְבּוֹנַנְתָּ] consec. Hithp. pf. בין *consider diligently, attentively ;* c. על only here and Jb. 31¹; c. acc. Pss. 107⁴³ 119⁹⁵ Jb.
37¹⁴ +, c. אל Is. 14¹⁶.—**12.** [זֹמֵם] *devise against, plot ;* only here c. ל pers.,
abs. 17³ Pr. 30³², sq. inf. Gn. 11⁶ Dt. 19¹⁹ Pr. 31¹⁴.—**13.** [ארני ישחק לו] cf. 2⁴,
on which it depends.— [יבא יומו] phr. 1 S. 26¹⁰ Ez. 21³⁰·³⁴ Jb. 18²⁰ Je. 50²⁷·³¹,
only here in ψ, day of disaster or death.—**14.** [חרב פתחו] phr. emph. in
position, cf. Ez. 21³³; with other vbs., הֵרִיק Ex. 15⁹ +, שלף Nu. 22²³ +.—
[להפיל עני ואביון]. This clause is a gl.; it makes l. overfull and destroys the
measure.— [לטבוח] ‡ Qal inf. cstr. טבה vb. *slaughter, butcher*, usually of animals, but here poet. of men, La. 2²¹ Ez. 21¹⁵.— [ישרי דרך] phr. α.λ., cf.
יְשַׁר דֹּ Pr. 29²⁷; elsw. יִשְׁרֵי לֵב (7¹¹); so here 𝔊, but it is certainly a gl.—
15. [וקשתותם] has two accents.—**16.** מן [מֵהֲמוֹן] comparative c. ‡ הָמוֹן n.m.
(1) *murmur, roar :* of multitude of people 42⁵ 65⁸; (2) late usage, *abundance, wealth*, Is. 60⁵, cf. Ec. 5⁹; so usually here, cf. 𝔊 of v.³, but the context
favours (1).—**18.** [יָמֵי] so 𝔍, 𝔖; 𝔊 ὁδοὺς = דרכי, so Gr., We., Che., but prob.
assimilated to 1⁶.— [הַתְמִימָם] defective pl. תָּמִים (15²).— [וְנַחֲלָה] unnecessary gl.

— 20. אֹיְבֵי יהוה] phr. α.λ., but idea common (*v. 3⁸*). A vb. is needed for sense as well as for measure, prob. יכרתו, as v.⁹· ²²· ²³· ³⁴· ³⁸, omitted by error, because of similarity to כיקר. — פִּיקָר יְקָר] *BDB.,* Dr., = *like the glory of the pastures,* α.λ. in this sense, dub. 𝔊 ἅμα τῷ δοξασθῆναι αὐτοὺς καὶ ὑψωθῆναι, so 𝔙, taking both as vbs. inf. בִּיקֹר כֹּרִם; Aq., 𝕿, take כָּרִים = *lambs;* Σ, 𝔍, כְּרֵי(אָ)ם. כר in sense of *pasture* is dub. here and Ps. 65¹⁴, elsw. *lamb.* Burgess, We., Bä., rd. בִּיקֹר Is. 10¹⁶, followed by יְקָרִים Burgess, יְקָרִים *ovens* We., Bä. 𝔊 gives the key, ביקר inf. cstr. יקר *while being highly esteemed,* and כֹּרַם also inf. cstr. (*9¹⁴*) *while being exalted* (*v.* v.⁸), prefix כִּי causal as in previous l., omitted by error because of following prep. כ. So essentially Houb., Horsley, " *As soon as they are in honour; as soon as they are exalted.*" — **21.** וְיִשַׁלֵם] Pi. frequentative, *repay,* mng. only here ψ; for other mngs. of vb. *v. 22²⁶.* — חוֹנֵן וְנוֹתֵן] phr. α.λ., cf. v.²⁶ 112⁵. For חנן *v. 4²*. — **22.** כִּי] not causal, 𝔊, 𝔍, and most, for which there is no propriety in context; but asseveration. — **23.** מֵיהוה] emph., כֹּן of source of direction. — כּוֹנָנוּ] † Polal, *be established,* elsw. Ez. 28¹³, both dub. Bi., Du., Polel כּוֹנְנוּ as 7¹⁰, but unnecessary change. — דרכו יחפץ] vb. (*18²⁰*) phr. α.λ.; but vb. c. אֹמֶ 51⁸, כָּל אֹשֶׁר 115³ 135⁶, זְבח(וֹ)ים 40⁷ 51¹⁸· ²¹. — **24.** לֹא יוּמָל] Hoph. ‡ [טוּל] vb. † Hoph. *be hurled, fall;* elsw. Je. 22²⁸ (unto exile), Jb. 41¹ (man, at sight of crocodile), Pr. 16³³ (cast of lot). — יֹרְעוּ מבקּשׁ לחם] expl. gl. making l. overfull. — **26.** לִּבְרכה] *for a blessing* (*v. 3⁹*); that is, source for others, as 21⁷. The l. lacks a word; supply יהיה vb. as usual with ל in the sense of *become.* — **27.** סוּר מרע] phr. of WL. as 34¹⁵ (*v. 6⁹*); also its complement וַעֲשֵׂה־טֹּ֯ב as v.³ (*v. 4⁷*), Makkeph with two accents. — **28.** לְעוֹלָם נִשְׁמָרוּ]. This cannot belong to Str. ס, which is already complete. The ע of the next Str. is missing in 𝕳. 𝔊ᴮ has εἰς τὸν αἰῶνα φυλαχθήσονται ἄμωμοι ἐκδικηθήσονται. This is conflation. 𝔊ˣ· ᶜ· ᵃ· ᴬ· ᴿ· ᵀ· rd. ἄνομοι, so 𝔙. As ἄνομοι = עוֹלִים, this might be a misinterpretation of עוֹלָם, but a word is missing in any case. It is prob. that the original read both words עוֹלִים עוֹלָם, one of which having been omitted by txt. err., 𝔊 and 𝕳 taking different ones; so Lowth., Bä., Dr., Du. The ל of 𝕳 would then be a subsequent addition. † עַוָּל n.m. α.λ. ψ, but Zp. 3⁵ Jb. 18²¹ 27⁷ 29¹⁷ 31³. נִשְׁמָרוּ 𝕳 Niph. pf. 3 pl. pause; but rd. after 𝔊 נשׁמרו as v.³⁸. So most moderns. ‡ [שׁמר] vb. Niph. *be destroyed;* elsw. v.³⁸ 83¹¹ 92⁸. Hiph. *destroy* 106²³· ³⁴ 145²⁰. — **30.** ‡ [חָכְמָה] n.f. *wisdom :* in ψ only (1) *skill,* of sailors 107²⁷; (2) *wisdom, prudence,* in religious affairs, here as 51⁸ 90¹²; (3) *wisdom,* ethical and religious: (*a*) of God, as a divine attribute or energy, 104²⁴, cf. Je. 10¹² = 51¹⁵; (*b*) of man Ps. 111¹⁰, cf. Pr. 15³³ Jb. 28²⁸; ‖ תְּבוּגוֹת Ps. 49⁴. — **31.** לֹא] 𝕳, but 𝔊 ולא required for measure. — **32.** לַהֲמִיתוֹ] Hiph. inf. sf. 3 sg. *put to death, kill,* as 59¹ (*v. 17¹⁴*). A word is missing, probably הָמֵת inf. abs. of the phr. *to put to a violent death,* the penalty as suggested by the judgment of following context. — **34.** קַוֵּה] Pi. imv. (*25³*), c. אל as 27¹⁴. This l. is defective by two words. צדיק is suggested by antith. רשׁע, but prob. the v. is a gl. — **35.** ‡ [עָרִיץ] adj. *awe-inspiring, terror-striking, ruthless;* of formidable adversaries elsw. 54⁵ 86¹⁴; but 𝔊 ὑπερυψούμενον, 𝔙 *superexaltatum,* take it as ptc., which is better suited to the context, *striking with awe,* as 10¹⁸

Is. 47¹². — [מֶתְעָרֶה] Hithp. ptc. ‡ [ערה] vb. Qal *lay bare* foundations Ps. 137⁷·⁷,
life in death 141⁸. † Hithp. elsw. La. 4²¹ *make oneself naked*, of drunken
woman. The word here is dub. 𝔊 ἐπαιρόμενον implies another word; Du.
suggests מִתְעָרֶה *lifting himself up*, form elsw. only Je. 51¹⁸ and dub. there; Gr.
denom. ...; *leaf, foliage*, but not in Bibl. Heb.; 𝔍 *fortissimum* is also dub.,
although possible in implying what Dr. suggests, *putting forth his strength*,
laying it bare ; none of the other suggestions are so good as this. Cf. השׂף זרע
Is. 52¹⁰ as a warrior strips himself for battle. — ‡ [אֶזְרָח] n.m. one rising from
the soil, *native;* common in OT., not in ψ. The word here is usually interpreted of *native tree*, after 𝔍, 𝔗, but this dub.; 𝔊, 𝔙, Houb., Dy., Gr., Bä.,
Du., rd. ארז *cedar*. — ‡ [רַעֲנָן] adj., *luxuriant, fresh:* of trees זית 52¹⁰, ברוש
Ho. 14⁹; of persons Ps. 92¹⁵ (fig. as trees); of oil 92¹¹; here 𝔊 has לבנון, so
Dy., Hi., Gr., Hu.³, Bä., Kau., Du.; but as Dr., We., Kirk., רענן is appropriate to ארז. At the same time these nouns do not suit the ptc. If the image
of the cedar is retained, the two ptcs. go together as making up image of
warrior, and the cedar is a separate image. — **36.** [וַיַּעֲבֹר] Qal impf. ι consec. =
and then, sequence in time ; but 𝔊, 𝔖, 𝔙, 𝔍, Houb., Horsley, Kenn., Bä.,
Du., Dr., Che., ויאעבר, which is certainly correct. — **37.** ‡ [רָם] adj. for noun,
elsw. 64⁵, cf. Jb. 1¹ 8²⁰ 9²⁰·²¹·²² Pr. 29¹⁰. — ‡ [אחרית] as v.³⁸, *posterity*, so 109¹³;
thus Bä., Dr. (‖ זרע), but Du. *future, latter end*, as 73¹⁷ Dt. 32²⁰·²⁹; elsw. ψ
of place 139⁹. — **39.** [ישׁועת] (33¹⁷), ι of 𝔐 error, not in 𝔊, 𝔙, 𝔖, 𝔍, ת Str.
begins here. — **40.** [וַיַּפְלְמֵם] ι consec. Pi. impf.; repeated in 𝔐 without ι, but
not in 𝔍; is gl. or variant. — [וַיּושִׁיעֵם] Hiph. impf. (3⁸), ι coörd. after ι consec. ungrammatical and inconsistent ; 𝔊, 𝔍, all futures and ι coörds., most
probable. — [כי חסו בו] as 2¹².

PSALM XXXVIII., 5 STR. 6³.

**Ps. 38 is a Lamentation : (1) Israel complains of great sufferings
of body** (v.⁷⁻⁹) ; **discouragement and abandonment by friends** (v.¹⁰⁻¹²) ;
**enemies craftily seeking his ruin, while he is compelled to remain
silent** (v.¹³⁻¹⁵). **His only hope is in Yahweh** (v.¹⁶⁻¹⁸), **therefore the
final petition for salvation from his unprincipled enemies, who
repay him evil for good** (v.²⁰⁻²³). **Later additions connect the
suffering with sin, and make it into a Penitential Ps.** (v.¹⁻⁶·¹⁹).

I AM bent, I am bowed down exceedingly;
   I go about in black all the day.
   Yea, my loins are full of that which is contemned;
   And there is no soundness in my flesh.
   I am benumbed and crushed exceedingly;
   I growl with the growling of a lion.
A LL my desire is before Thee,
   And my groaning is not hid from Thee.

My heart in a ferment forsaketh me,
And the light of mine eyes is not with me.
Lovers and friends are at a distance from me,
And my neighbours stand afar off.
THEY also that seek my life lay snares.
Of my distress they speak, of ruin ;
And utter deceits all the day.
But I am like a deaf man that heareth not,
And as a dumb man that openeth not his mouth,
And in whose mouth are no arguments.
FOR in Thee, Yahweh, I hope ;
Thou wilt answer, O my God ;
Lest (mine enemies) rejoice over me,
When my foot is moved, do great things against me :
For I am ready for limping,
And my sorrow is continually before me.
SINCE mine enemies (without cause) are numerous,
And they are many that hate me lyingly,
And are repaying me evil for good ;
Forsake me not, Yahweh ;
O my God, be not far from me ;
O haste to my help, my Salvation.

Ps. 38 was in 𝔻 and then in 𝕸 (v. Intr. §§ 27, 31). It was finally assigned
for the אזכרה of the מנחה (v. Intr. § 39). 𝕲 has εἰς ἀνάμνησιν περὶ σαββάτου,
still more specifically defining the liturgical use as for the sabbath. It is the
third of the seven Penitential Pss. But this is entirely due to glosses : v.²
from Ps. 6² ; v.⁴·⁶ from Is. 1⁶ ; v.³, cf. Jb. 6⁴ ; v.⁵, cf. 40¹³ ; v.¹⁹, cf. 32⁵.
Removing these glosses, the Ps. is a complaint to Yahweh because of perils
from cruel and unscrupulous foes, and is a prayer for salvation. V.⁸ is dependent on Is. 1⁶ ; v.¹² on Ps. 88¹⁹ ; v.¹⁴, cf. Is. 53⁷ ; v.²¹, cf. Ps. 35¹² ; v.²², cf.
35²² ; v.²³, cf. 70⁶. There are an unusual number of α.λ. : נפוגתי v.⁹ ; סחרחר v.¹¹,
but probably error for חמרמר La. 1²⁰ 2¹¹ ; אור עיני v.¹¹, but cf. 4⁷. There
are several unusual words and phrs. : נקשו v.¹³, 109¹¹, but error for יקשו ;
מוט רגל v.¹⁷, Dt. 32³⁵ Ps. 94¹⁸ ; צלע v.¹⁸, 35¹⁵ Je. 20¹⁰ ; מכאב v.¹⁸, as 32¹⁰ 69²⁷.
There is no evidence of late date, apart from glosses. The Ps. is the complaint of the afflicted community of the Restoration, before Nehemiah.

The original Ps. has prefixed to it a gloss of five pentameters,
attributing the sufferings to divine discipline because of sin.

Yahweh, correct me not in Thy wrath, nor in Thy heat chasten me ;
For Thine arrows are gone down into me, and Thy hand resteth upon me ;
There is no soundness in my flesh, because of Thine indignation ;
There is no wholeness in my bones, because of my sin.
My wounds stink, they fester, because of my folly.

2 is a loose citation from 6². — **3.** *For Thine arrows*], Yahweh's visitation, as Jb. 6⁴, — *are gone down into me*], have penetrated my flesh and so gone deep into my body, causing me intense pain and suffering. — *Thy hand resteth upon me*], by elision of the last letter of the Hebrew word, which probably originated from dittography, getting thus a syn. and common conception; whereas the repetition of the same word in the original text is not only tautological, but is inappropriate to the use of the hand of Yahweh, and compels the Vrss. to resort to variations in paraphrase, without any sort of justification in Heb. usage. — **4, 6** are based upon Is. 1⁶ in their description of the wounds resulting from the divine scourging. — *There is no soundness in my flesh*], given again v.⁸ᵇ, where, however, it is without the reason given here, although it probably induced the fuller description here. This, then, has as its syn.: *there is no wholeness in my bones*, which is still further explained by, — *my wounds stink ‖ they fester;* they are become running sores, so foul by mortification that they are offensive to the person himself and to all who come near him. The reason for this state of things is given in three parallel clauses: *because of Thine indignation*], God's hands and arrows, moved by His anger and indignation and wrath, have brought about this serious situation — *because of my sin ‖ of my folly*], the reason on the human side. Their sin and folly have provoked the divine wrath and indignation against His people. — **5.** A later scribe inserts before the last two lines a tetrameter couplet describing the sin from an entirely different point of view. This must have come from a marginal statement, because it is difficult to see how it could have been inserted in this place, except by one who was inattentive to the meaning of what he was copying. This couplet conceives of *iniquities* as a flood of waters which have suddenly overwhelmed the man and *are gone over his head*, so that he is drowning in them, cf. 18⁵⁻⁶ 69³· ¹⁶; and also *as a heavy burden, too heavy for* him, from the point of view that sin rests upon the sinner as an external load which has to be lifted and carried away from him, in order that he may be rid of it; a conception upon which the OT. doctrine of forgiveness rests. This gloss makes the Ps. appropriate for penitence, especially to the nation in its appointed seasons of repentance.

Str. I., in three synth. couplets, describes a terrible condition of suffering, which may have been individual, but more probably was national, as in so many other Pss. of this period. — **7.** *I am bent ‖ bowed down*], by a weight of care, anxiety, and suffering, and this, *exceedingly*, to the utmost degree of intensity. — *I go about in black*], as a mourner, lamenting the loss of dear friends, and especially of children, cf. 35[14]; probably implying just such bereavements at this time of many of the people, because of the enemies described in the third Str. This continues, — *all the day*, because of the prolongation of these bereavements. — **8.** *Yea*], intensive, continuation of the description; and not *for*, as EV[s]., which interpret the description without sufficient reason. — *my loins*], as the seat of strength ‖ *my flesh*, to emphasise the physical side of the suffering, — *are full of that which is contemned*], regarded as ignominious, disgraceful, thinking, probably, of physical weakness in the seat of strength, which is in general accord with the ancient Vrss., and is more suited to the parall. — *there is no soundness*], referring to physical exhaustion and soreness of the flesh from suffering. Many moderns, because of the dependence on Is. 1[6], especially in v.[4-6], think of another and similar verb, and so of the loins as full of "burning," the fever of the festering wounds. But the reference to such wounds is in the gloss, and not in the original Ps.; and there is nothing in the immediate context to suggest divine discipline. Indeed, the description moves in somewhat different lines. — **9.** *I am benumbed and crushed*]. Strength has so departed from him that he has become, as it were, paralysed and incapable of effort; his energy and vital power have been crushed, and this has, as in v.[7], become intense — *exceedingly*. He is altogether helpless, and the only thing he can do is to *growl*, as an animal, in a state of helpless pain, — *with the growling of a lion*], so, by an easy addition of a single letter, which has apparently fallen off the Heb. word, because of assimilation to v.[11a]. The word "heart" is incongruous with "growling," and the various Vrss. based upon it are necessarily paraphrases. "Disquietness of heart," EV[s]., is weak and unjustifiable. This Str. has only to do with the physical frame; the more internal suffering of heart appears as characteristic of the second Str.

Str. II. also has three couplets only describing the sufferings with reference to the soul. — **10.** *All my desire*], for relief, as is evident from the context ‖ *my groaning. — is before Thee*], in Thy sight, altogether seen and known ‖ *is not hid from Thee*. This is a strong appeal to Yahweh's knowledge of the terrible situation of His people, in order to a continuation of the description. There is, indeed, a sort of introverted parall. between the Strs. in that the growling, which closes the previous Str., begins this Str. with its syn., groaning. — **11.** *My heart in a ferment*], so by an easy change of Heb. text, after La. 1^{20} 2^{11}, to avoid an unjustifiable interpretation of the Heb. word used in the text, which is incongruous with its noun in any meaning to be found elsewhere. The various renderings proposed : "panteth," PBV., AV., JPSV., "throbbeth," RV., Kirk., Dr., "palpitates," *B*DB., are purely conjectural. — *forsaketh me*], in extreme discouragement, so that I have no heart any more. — And *the light of mine eyes*], the light that illumines the eyes, enabling them to see what is to be done, giving confidence and courage. — *is not with me*], is no longer in my possession, I am destitute of it. — **12.** *Lovers and friends* ‖ *my neighbours*], those upon whom I could ordinarily rely for sympathy and aid. — *are*, or remain *at a distance from me* ‖ *stand afar off*]. They have, in fact, abandoned him to his lot.

Str. III. now brings the enemies into view, who were in the background of the previous Strs., yet the real cause of the sufferings and terrible situation. They are described, **13**, as *they that seek my life*]. They were mortal enemies. A gloss duplicates it in "they that seek my hurt," which, however, makes the measure overfull. The activity of these enemies is described in a synth. triplet, and the inability of the people to defend themselves in an anti-triplet. The enemies *lay snares*], cf. 9^{17}. — *Of my distress* (*they speak*) *of ruin* ‖ *utter deceits*]. All their activity of speech is treacherous, seeking in every way to destroy the life of the people of God. — **14-15.** The people have become so weak and paralysed, as set forth in the previous Strs., that they are not only incapable of resistance, but they are incapable of speaking in their own defence. — *I am like a deaf man* ‖ *as a dumb man*], not that they are altogether unconscious of the machinations of the enemy, but that their senses are so benumbed and paralysed, with the other parts

of their bodies, that they must behave *as one that heareth not*].
This is repeated in a variant gloss, " I am like a deaf man that
heareth not," making the Str. overfull. — *that openeth not his
mouth*], which is explained in the climax : *in whose mouth are no
arguments*], that is, in reply, in defence against calumnies and
false accusations. The author probably had in mind the suffering
servant of Yahweh of Is. 53[7].

Str. IV., in three synth. couplets, resumes the description of
sufferings, in order to show that the only hope is in God, to whom
the plea is made for salvation. — **16.** *For in Thee*], emphatic,
Thee only, *Yahweh* ‖ *my God*, emphasised by the gloss, " O
Lord." — *I hope*], in a waiting attitude, looking for and expecting
help ; and therefore with its appropriate result : *Thou wilt answer*],
not with words, which were hardly expected, but with deeds of
salvation. — **17.** The motive for this on the negative side was :
lest they rejoice over me. The ancient texts prefix, " For I said,"
at the expense of the measure, in order to put the subsequent
context as a plea in the mouth of the psalmist. 𝕲 retains the
subject *enemies*, omitted by 𝕳, required by context. — *do great
things against me*], as 35[26] 55[13] ; taking advantage of their opportunity, when the people were in grave trouble. — *when my foot is
moved*], as 94[18] Dt. 32[35], and so unstable, insecure. — **18.** *For I
am ready for limping*], about to limp because of injury to the
knee ; and so unable to stand firm in resistance, not to speak of
advance to attack. This is all summed up in the last line of the
Str. : *and my sorrow is continually before me*]. I cannot escape
it, and cannot see or think of anything else. — **19.** A later editor,
probably the same as the one who prefixed v.[2-6], inserted here a
confession of sin, unsuited to the context, which does not suggest
any such thing by any sort of implication. This was in order to
adapt the Ps. to public worship by connecting the sufferings with
sin, and to suggest that their removal could come only through
confession and penitence. — *For mine iniquity I declare*], to Yahweh, cf. 33[5] Is. 3[9]. — *I am anxious*], in a state of anxiety which
involves a dread of the consequences. — *By reason of my sin*].
There is no suggestion of what the sin might be. It is entirely
a general statement. The Ps. is an assertion of the innocence
and guiltlessness of the people over against their enemies. But

this would not be thought of by the glossator, who is moved by general and accepted principles in the worship of his own time.

Str. V. is essentially a petition for salvation, beginning with a reason in a tristich, put in a circumstantial clause. — **20-21.** *Since mine enemies are numerous ‖ are many*]. These are public and not private enemies, cf. 3^{2-3}. They are described in 興, ⅄, and all ancient texts as being "alive" or "lively"; but most recent scholars think this was an error for the Heb. word of similar letters: *without cause*, cf. 35^7 ‖ *hate me lyingly*], that is, in their hatred telling lies, bearing false witness ‖ *repaying me evil for good*, cf. 35^{12}. This latter is emphasised in a gloss, "They are my adversaries because of my pursuing good," so EV⁸., which is explained by ⅄ as "righteousness," all giving the reason of the persecution; which is introducing a later situation into this Ps. — **22-23.** The final petition is now given in a tristich antith. to the previous one. *Forsake me not ‖ be not afar from me ‖ O haste to my help*]. Each one of these vbs. is emphasised by a divine name: *Yahweh ‖ O my God*, and the climax, *my Salvation*. A later glossator, not realising this significant climax, inserts, "O Lord," and thus makes a difficulty in measure and construction.

2. This v. is cited loosely from 6^2. The second אל was either omitted by prosaic scribe as unnecessary, or the measure is pentameter and the l. a gl. The only other change is the use of קצף for the earlier אף. — ‡ [חֵמָה] n.m. *wrath;* elsw. ψ, 102^{11}; only in P of Hex. and Dt. 29^{27}; not in Is.¹, but Je. 10^{10} + 3 t. Je., Is. 34^2 54^8 60^{10} Zc. $1^{2.15}$ 7^{12} +. — **3.** [חִצֶּיךָ] emph. *thine arrows*, for God's visitation of wrath, as Jb. 6^4; similar idea, but so differently expressed that no dependence is evident. — [וַתִּנְחַת] Niph. pf.; cf. Pi. 18^{35} = 2 S. 22^{35} of the bow pressed by the arms (but dub.), Ps. 65^{11} of pressing down furrows of land. Niph. α.λ. *penetrate*, BDB. dub.; Du. rds. Qal וַתִּנְחַת *descend into*, cf. Pr. 17^{10}, which is probable; so v.²ᵇ יְרֻנַח Qal impf. ו consec., subj. hand of Yahweh. But these are differently translated in ⅄, ἐνεπάγησαν for first, but ἐπεστήριξας, 𝖅 *confirmasti*, for second. Du. suggests הכבר as 32^4, but Gr. יְהָנַחַּת; so Che. This Hiph. of נוח with יד, cf. Ec. 7^{18}; but Qal as ותנח Is. 25^{10} is preferable here. The final ה probably originated from assimilation to previous vb. — **4, 6.** V.⁴ has two pentameters and v.⁶ one pentameter. These three lines are based on Is. 1^6 and are glosses. Each end in the same way, מפני (9^4). — ‡ [אֱלֶת] n.f. *folly;* especially guilty, here as 69^6, elsw. Pr. 23 t. — [אֵין מתם בבשרי] same as v.⁸ᵇ; no reason for repetition. † [מְתֹם] n.m. *soundness;* elsw. Is. 1^6. — [אֵין שלום] syn. expression. שׂרוֹב *health;* cf. adj. שָׁלֵם Gn. 33^{18}, vb. Jb. 9^4. — [הִבְאִישׁוּ] Hiph.

pf. ‡ באש vb. Hiph. *emit a stinking odour ;* same idea as Is. 1⁶, but varied expression ; not elsw. ψ, but cf. Ex. 16²⁴ 1 S. 27¹². — [וַיֵּקֻ] Niph. pf. † מקק vb. Niph. *fester ;* a.λ. in this sense ; but *rot* Zc. 14¹². ¹² of plague, and of heavens mouldering away Is. 34⁴, pining away in divine punishment Ez. 4¹⁷ 24²³ 33¹⁰ Lv. 26³⁹. ³⁹. Hiph. Zc. 14¹². — † [הַבּוּרָה] from Is. 1⁶ *stripes, wounds :* elsw. Gn. 4²³ Ex. 21²⁵. ²⁵ Pr. 20³⁰ Is. 53⁵. — **5.** [עֲוֹנִי עָבְרוּ רֹאשִׁי] phr. a.λ., but idea of peril by drowning 69³. ¹⁶⁻¹⁷, so also 18⁵. ⁶. עָוֹן (18²⁴), for great guilt v. 40¹³. — ‡ [יִשָּׂא] n.m. *burden ;* only here of iniquities, but idea familiar in mng. of vb. נשא *remove* sin, conceived as a burden ; noun common elsw. for real burdens as carried by men or animals, but not in ψ. — ‡ [כָּבֵד] adj. *heavy :* a.λ. in ψ, but common elsw. — [כברו] Qal impf. The adj. is only needed for tetrameter. It might have originated from dittog. But this v. looks like two tetrameters, in which case it is a gl. — **7.** [נַעֲוֵיתִי] Niph. pf. ‡ עוה Niph. *be bent, bowed down ;* so Is. 21³ ǁ [יבדר], of לב Pr. 12⁸. — **8.** [יִ] not causal, but intensive, *yea.* — † [כֶסֶל] n.m. (1) *loins* Jb. 15²⁷ Lv. 3⁴. ¹⁰. ¹⁵ 4⁹ 7⁴, so here ǁ בָשָׂר, cf. v.⁴; 𝔊 ἡ ψυχή μου prob. depends upon שׂכל = שֵׂכֶל = *understanding ;* (2) *confidence* Pss. 49¹⁴ 78⁷ Pr. 3²⁶ Jb. 8¹⁴ 31²⁴ Ec. 7²⁵. — [וְקִלָה] Niph. ptc. † קלה vb. *roast,* *B*DB., here *burning,* a.λ., so De., Dr., Du., Kirk., al., the burning of feverish wounds, based on Is. 1⁶. The vb. is used in Qal Je. 29²² Lv. 2¹⁴ Jos. 5¹¹ (P) ; but denom. קלי and improb. here. 𝔊, 𝔘, Aq., Σ, 𝔍, all take it as Is. 3⁵ 16¹⁴, Niph. ‡ קלה *be lightly esteemed.* Cf. ‡ קָלוֹן n.m. Ps. 83¹⁷ Je. 46¹² Ho. 4⁷. ¹⁸ Hb. 2¹⁶, so Bä. This is most probable. — **9.** [וּפוּגֹרִי] a.λ. Niph. pf. † [פוג] vb. Qal, *grow numb :* of hand 77³ (dub.) ; of לב Gn. 45²³, of Thorah Hb. 1⁴ *be ineffective.* Niph. *be benumbed :* of person Ps. 38⁹ (prob. also 88¹⁶ for 𝔐 אָפוּנָה for אָפוּגָה a.λ.). — [ונדכיתי] coörd., Niph. pf. דכה † Niph. *be crushed :* of physical distress here, of contrition 51¹⁹ ; v. 10¹⁰. — † [וַיְזָקֵה] n.f. usually interpreted as *groaning,* but only here in this sense (yet cf. vb. in Pr. 5¹¹ Ez. 24²³) ; elsw. *growling,* Is. 5³⁰ of sea as lion, so rd. here לביא for לבי (א before אדני has fallen off), as Hi., Ols., Gr., Bä., Du., Kau. — **10.** [אדני] not in 𝔊, is a gl. as ל. is sufficiently long without it. — **11.** [סררהר] a.λ. Pilp. סחר *palpitates,* *B*DB., but Qal does not justify this rendering ; improb., rd. after Gr. as in La. 1²⁰ 2¹¹ חמרמר Pe'al'al of חמר, there of bowels, in ferment of distress (ǁ לב). The l. is too long ; either לב is inserted for explanation, or כח is gl., prob. the latter. — [אור עֵינַי] phr. a.λ., but cf. אור פנים *light of face,* of bright, cheerful face Jb. 29²⁴, v. 4⁷. — [וְכ־הֵם] not in 𝔊, is gl. ; makes l. too long. — [אֵין אִתִּי] phr. a.λ. in ψ, but אין with ל and ב frequent. — **12.** [מֶנֶגֶד נִגְעִי יַעֲמֹדוּ] 𝔊 has ἐξ ἐναντίας μου ἤγγισαν καὶ ἔστησαν, so 𝔘, 𝔖 ; this implies a text מנגדי נגשו יעמדו. But only one word of these is needed to complete the l. יעמדו has been inserted as prosaic explanation ǁ עָמְדוּ v.¹²ᵇ ; it is tautological and improbable for a poetic writer. This leaves of 𝔐 מנגד נוֹעי, of 𝔊 מנגדי נגשו ; both נוֹעי of 𝔐 and נגשו of 𝔊 are dittog. The original was prob. מנגדי *at a distance from me,* as 10⁵, ǁ מֵרָחֹק 10¹ 139². — ‡ [וַנֶגַע] n.m. *stroke, plague,* as 39¹¹ 89³³ 91¹⁰ Is. 53⁸. — **13.** [וַיְנַקְשׁוּ] Pi. impf. *B*DB. *strike at,* only here and 109¹¹ (of creditor, c. ל). But obj. is lacking ; cf. Hithp. c. נוקשׁי *strike at my life* 1 S. 28⁹. This is favoured by 𝔊, 𝔍. But most moderns, Bu., Dr., Bä., Du., Pi. of נקשׁ,

lay snares, cf. יקש (*v. 9^{17}*). Bu. thinks the form denominative. This idea is
better suited to the context. There is evidently an ancient corruption of the
text, for 𝔊 supports 𝔐. ו consec. is improb.; rd. ו conjunctive. ודרשי רעתי
is suspicious immediately after בקשי נפשׁ.., the latter a common expression,
the former only Pr. 11^{27} and late. It is a gl., so Bä.] רעתי (*v. 21^{12}*) is in ψ
attached to חובי 35^4 41^8 140^3 or הכן 40^{15} = 70^i, בקש 71^{13.24}. — רברו הֲוַּת] we
should read יְדַבְּרוּ הֲנוּ ‖ (*1^2*). רעתי was put before the vb. for emphasis, as
‖ רְמוֹת. This misled copyist to insert ptc. רשׁ, which made all the mischief.
— הַוָּה] *engulfing ruin, destruction, v. 5^{10}*, so 55^{12}; here as obj. דבר; cf. 52^4
obj. רעה. The subj. cannot be ודרשי רעתי, for that makes the l. too long;
besides, subj. is evident in previous l. Rd. רעתי ידברו הַוּוֹת. — **14.** אני] emph.
— וְלֹא אישׁמע rel. clause. — ‡ חרשׁ] adj. *deaf*, as 58^5, ‖‡ אִלֵּם adj. *dumb;* elsw.
Ex. 4^{11} Is. 35^6 56^{10} Hb. 2^8 Pr. 31^8. — וּכְאִלֵּם יפתח פיו] as in Is. 53^7, which is in
mind of author. — **15.** אהי כאישׁ אשׁר לא שׁמע] is dittog. of v. 14^a, an awkward, prosaic sentence. — תּוֹכָחֹת] pl. ‡ הֵיכָחַ n f. † (1) *argument, impeach-*
ment, here as Jb. 13^6 23^4 Hb. 2^1; (2) *correction, rebuke* Pss. 39^{12} 73^{14} Pr. 29^{15}
Ez. 5^{15} 25^{17}. — **16.** אֲדֹנָי אֱלֹהָי] so 𝔊; one divine name is, however, sufficient.
אדני gl. — **17.** כי אמרתי] this is parenthetical gl. פן ישׂמחו לי] needs subj.
It is given by 𝔊. אֹיבי — **18.** כי אני] emph. — לְצֶלַע] *for limping, stumbling*,
as 35^{15} Je. 20^{10}. — נָכוֹן] Niph. of כון *be prepared, ready;* in this sense only
here ψ. For the phr. cf. איד נכון לצלעו Jb. 18^{12}. — כְּאוֹב] *sorrow*, as 32^{10} 69^{27}.
— **19.** כִּי־עֲוֹנִי אַגִּיד ‖ אֶדְאַג מֵחַטָּאתִי. The l. as it stands is a tetrameter. Du.
supplies יהוה and אלהי to get better measure. For עון *v. 18^{24}*. אגיד Hiph.
impf. נגד *confess*, only Is. 3^9; cf. הודיע Ps. 32^5. We might separate כי and מן
from nouns, and so get trimeters. At the same time, confession of sin interrupts the thought here, is abrupt and isolated. — אֶדְאַג] Qal impf. † דאג Qal
(1) *be anxious for:* c. מן here, as Je. 42^{16}; c. ל I S. 9^5 10^2; abs. Je. 17^8;
(2) *dread:* c. acc. Is. 57^{11} Je. 38^{19}. — **20.** הַיִּים] is not suited to ‖ שֹׂקר (7^{15});
rd. therefore חִיִּם, as 35^7·^{19} 69^5, so Houb., Gr., Bä., Dr., Kirk., al. — יַּעֲצֵמוּ] Qal
pf. i.p. ‡ עצם vb. Qal *be numerous*, here as 40^6·^{18} 69^5 139^7. † Hiph. *be made*
strong 105^{24}. — **21.** וּמְשַׁלְּמֵי] Pi. ptc. pl. cstr. (22^{26}), before רעה not good
usage; rd. רֶע. Cf. 35^{12} for phr. תַּחַת טוֹבָה] should be prob. תַּחַת־שׂוֹב.
יִשְׂטְנוּנִי] Qal impf. 3 m., sf. 1 sg. *be my adversary;* † שׂטן elsw. 71^{13} 109^{4.20.29}
Zc. 3^1. — רָדְפִי] Kt., רָדְפִי Qr. (*v. 7^2*). The latter inf. cstr. *because of my pur-*
suing good, for which 𝔊 δικαιοσύνην, which is probable explanation of שׂוב here
as ethical. The latter is more suited to context, the former a more natural
change in later times. Bä. inserts here l. of 𝔊 in Syr. Hex. 𝔊^{R. ℵ}: καὶ ἀπέρ-
ριψάν με τὸν ἀγαπητὸν ὡσεὶ νεκρὸν ἐβδελυγμένον, which he translates into
Hebrew thus: הַשְׁלִיכוּנִי יְחִיד כְפגר נתעב; so Gr., but Du. objects rightly. It has
a different measure. It is doubtless a l. from some ancient piece, and not a
gl. composed by a scribe. Such a l. is not known elsw. But Is. 14^{19} has
a similar thought with reference to the king of Babylon: וְאַתָּה הָשְׁלַכְתָּ מִקִּבְרְךָ
וְאַתָּה נֶעֱצַבְתָּ לְבֻשׁ הֲרֻגִים מְטֹעֲנֵי חֶרֶב יוֹרְדֵי אֶל־אַבְנֵי־בוֹר כְּפֶגֶר מוּבָס. Doubtless this was
in mind of glossator or author, as we may decide. The former is more prob-
able, because the previous Str. is complete without this l., and the codd. 𝔊

which have it are the old corrupt texts. It is not found in any of the other Vrss. It is too strong for its context, and it is not suited to begin a new Str.— **22.** [אל תעזבני יהוה] closing petition usual in ψ; cf. 27⁹ 71⁹· ¹⁸. — [אל תרחק ממני] = 35²² 71¹². This we may take as two trimeters, especially if we read ואל in l. 2.— **23.** [חושה לעזרתי] cf. 70⁶ חושה לי עזרי, also 71¹² לעזרתי.—[אדני] before העושתי is either *Adonay my salvation* or אלהי תשועתי; 𝔊 κύριε τῆς σωτηρίας μου, 𝔍 *Domine, salutis meae.* Probably אדני is a gl. and the l. the concluding trimeter.

PSALM XXXIX., 2 STR. 7⁵ + RF. 1⁵.

Ps. 39 is an elegy: (1) A resolution to repress complaint for suffering in the presence of the wicked, which can only partly be carried out because of internal excitement, and which therefore takes the form of prayer that Yahweh may make him know the brevity of life (v.²⁻⁶ᵃ). (2) A statement of the unsubstantial character of man in his life and activity, with a petition to Yahweh, the only hope, for deliverance from transgression. He has suffered in silence, recognising that he was afflicted by Yahweh; but now prays for relief lest he melt away under his severe chastisement (v.⁷⁻¹²ᵃ). The refrains assert that man in the presence of God is altogether unsubstantial (v.⁶ᵇ· ¹²ᵇ). Glosses are petitions of a more general character (v.¹³⁻¹⁴).

I SAID, " I will take heed to my ways, that I sin not with my tongue.
   I will take heed to my mouth (that I do no wrong), while the wicked are in
      my presence."
   In stillness I kept silent, apart from comfort, and my sorrow was stirred.
   My heart became hot within me, during my musing the fire kindled.
   I spake with my tongue : " Yahweh, make me know mine end,
   And the measure of my days, what it is, what my duration is."
   Behold, my days are handbreadths, and my duration is as nothing.
        In Thy sight surely altogether vapour every man doth stand.
S URELY as a semblance man walketh about, surely as vapour he bustles about.
   And he heapeth up, and he knoweth not who he shall be that will gather.
   And now what wait I for? My hope is in Thee.
   From my transgression deliver me; make me not a reproach for the impudent.
   I am dumb, I open not my mouth, because Thou hast done it.
   Remove Thy stroke from off me : I come to an end.
   Wouldst Thou chasten a man with rebukes, as a moth Thou dost make him
      melt away.
       (In Thy sight) surely altogether vapour every man doth stand

Ps. 39 was in 𝔇 and 𝔐. It was also taken up into 𝔇ℜ (*v.* Intr. §§ 27, 31, 33), and given the superscription לידותון(ל) (*v.* Intr. § 34). In its original form it was two pentameter octastichs, the last line of each being the same refrain. There are two liturgical additions, — a tetrameter couplet, probably from the editor of 𝔇ℜ, and a trimeter quartette of later date. This last is dependent on Jb. 10^{20-21}. Whether 1 Ch. 29^{15} is earlier or later is not so evident, but probably earlier also. The original Ps. shows no dependence on other literature. (*a*) There are several *α.λ.*: מחסום v.^{2}, נעכר v.^{3}, מדת ימי v.^{5}, הרפת נבל v.^{9}. (*b*) There are also forms not elsw. in *ψ*: החשיתי v.^{3}, but Is. 42^{14} 57^{11}; כאבי v.^{3}, but Is. 17^{11} Je. 15^{18}; טפחות v.^{6}, but 1 K. 7^{26}; יצבר v.^{7}, but Gn. $41^{35.49}$ (E) Ex. 8^{10} (J); תוחלת v.^{8}, but La. 3^{18}, Jb. 41^{1}. (*c*) There are forms rarely used in *ψ*: נאלמתי v.$^{3.10}$ 31^{19} Is. 53^{7}; הגיגי v. ^{4}, elsw. only Ps. 5^{2}; חלדי v.^{6}, 89^{48} Jb. 11^{17}. The vocabulary favours an early date; so does the syntax: (*a*) cohort. v.$^{2.2.5(?)}$; the conditional clause with change of tense, v.^{12}. The sin with the tongue, v.^{2}, is not lying, but, as context indicates, murmuring against God because of afflictions, an early idea of La., Je. The conception of the brevity of life, v.$^{5\,sq.}$, is also characteristic of the age of Je. The idea of v.^{7} implies conscious existence after death, but ignorance of what transpires in the world, such as Jb. 14. The recognition of the divine chastisement, v.$^{10-11}$, is like Jb.; but it is the idea of Is.^{2} also. The Ps. is not earlier than Je., and probably later than La. and Is.^{2} It has the experience of the exile behind it, and is a national Ps., composed just before the reforms of Nehemiah.

Str. I. is composed of a syn. couplet, a synth. couplet, a syn. triplet, and a monostich of refrain. — **2.** *I said*], introducing a resolution, or purpose, the contents of which are given in this couplet. — *I will take heed*], repeated for emphasis, — *to my ways*], moral action and character, as 5^{9} 49^{14} 50^{23}, although, as the context shows, the reference was to watchful restraint of speech, and not to conduct, and so ‖ *to my mouth.* The purpose of this self-control is: *that I sin not with my tongue*], as the context indicates, by murmuring against God on account of sufferings. — *that I do no wrong*]. This, as 𝔖, is required by parallel. But ℌ, by error, has a noun unknown elsewhere, which has occasioned the ungrammatical rendering, "I will keep my mouth with a bridle," EV^{s}. Most moderns who retain the word follow 𝔊 in its use of another verb, and render "put a muzzle to my mouth." — *while the wicked are in my presence*]. This does not imply a contrast of his lot of suffering with the prosperity of the wicked, as many suppose; but that he would not give the wicked any ground for reproaching the God of Israel as unable to save His people. —

3. *In stillness*, intensified by, *I kept silent*, still further intensified in all texts by prefixing, "I was dumb," from v.[10], at the expense of the measure; all this in fulfilment of the resolution of v.[2].
However, he was still *apart from comfort*], so essentially RV.[m],
JPSV., Dr. His self-repression only made him still more uncom-
fortable. But there is room in the ambiguous text for other
explanations: "even from good words," PBV., or "even from
good," AV., RV., after ⅏, explained by Kirk., "speaking neither
good nor bad."—*and my sorrow was stirred*]. He could not
repress his internal excitement.—**4**. *My heart became hot within
me*]. Repression makes the reaction so great that—*during my
musing the fire kindled*]. The effort at self-restraint kept the
attention fixed upon the wrong, and so all the musing tended to
increase the passion. It could no longer be restrained, it must
find vent in the flame of words—*spake with my tongue*]. This
speech is not, however, the murmuring which he had repressed,
but a prayer to God for instruction and guidance, and therefore
not sinful or provocative of the scorn of the wicked, but rather a
mark of righteous resignation.—**5**. *Yahweh, make me know*], cf.
90[12]. This is virtually repeated in the text of ℌ "that I may
know," or "let me know," as the verb may be variously rendered;
but it is an unnecessary addition, making the line overfull.—*mine
end*], that is, the end of my life, how short a time will elapse before
the end ‖ *the measure of my days*, the measure of time comprehended in the days of life.—*what it is*], emphatic reiteration,—
what my duration is], so by a correction of the text to correspond
with the same word of the next clause, cf. ⅏, ℐ, on which is
based, "How long I have to live," PBV. The transposition of a
single letter has given in ℌ a word which is rendered "how frail
I am," AV., RV., for which there is no linguistic authority.—
6. *Behold*], emphatic, calling attention to the fact in the climax:
my days are handbreadths], measured by the shortest measure,
the span of the hand. This is relatively so short that, in the
climax, the psalmist feels justified in saying: *my duration is as
nothing*]. It amounts to nothing at all; it is hardly worth considering. This simple and strong line has been modified at the
cost of the measure by a copyist who inserts the verb, "Thou hast
made," to emphasise divine activity and responsibility as to the

length of human life; and then he softens the assertion that the duration of life was as nothing, by attaching to it, " in Thy sight," making it relative in the point of view of God. But this last word really belongs to the last line of Refrain as necessary to complete its measure. — *Surely*], strong asseveration characteristic of this Ps., v.$^{7, 12}$, also cf. 23^6. — *altogether vapour every man doth stand*]. Man, standing before God, in the divine presence, has no substantial existence. He is, as it were, composed of vapour, which is so slight and unsubstantial that the least wind will drive it away. There is, indeed, a serious irony involved in the very thought of such an unsubstantial vapour standing in the divine presence, and it is just this that makes it so suitable as the Refrain of the elegy, reappearing in v.^{12b}, though a careless scribe has there abbreviated it.

Str. II. has two synth. couplets, a synth. triplet, and a monostich of Refrain. — **7.** *Surely as a semblance*], that is, an image rather than the thing itself, and, as the context shows, a shadowed likeness, — *as vapour*], an unsubstantial, vaporous body. This is so even in his activity, as he *walketh about* ‖ *bustles about.* The change of persons in 𝔊, followed by some Vrss., is exceedingly improbable. It was due to a copyist's mistake in attaching the conjunction ו to the previous verb, so making it 3 pl. — *And he heapeth up*], in his bustling activity. The object is not given ; to supply it makes the line overfull. In the antith., — *he knoweth not who he shall be that will gather*]. The last verb should also be without its object. It has, however, been supplied by a copyist in the suffix " them," which compels its use, in thought, at least, as the object to the previous verb. But the line is more forceful without objects in either case. — **8.** *And now*], the logical consequence of the foregoing, — *What wait I for ?*]. There is no relief through myself or any other to be expected. There is but one thing to be thought of under the circumstances : *My hope is in Thee*]. It is fixed on Yahweh and on Him alone. From Him the relief will come. Accordingly prayer springs forth. — **9.** *From my transgression deliver me*]. The psalmist recognises that the sufferings of the people are due to their transgression against God, so that first of all freedom from transgression must be secured. This is conceived as rescue. This vb. is used ordinarily with reference to enemies and troubles, seldom with reference to sin, elsewhere only 51^{16} 79^{9}, probably also 110^{170}. Doubtless in these cases transgression is conceived in the guilt and the misery that it has involved. — *make me not a reproach*]. If left in his miserable condition of suffering for transgression, he would be exposed to the reproach of the enemies. These enemies are described as *impudent*], cf. 14^{1}. They would also reproach his God. — **10.** *I am dumb* ‖ *I open not my mouth*]. The reason is a different one from that given v.$^{2-3}$, and, indeed, an additional one not inconsistent therewith : *because Thou hast done it*]. The suffering was due to the divine discipline for transgression ; and therefore there was no room for complaint, but only for confession and penitence. — **11.** This is then explained as, — *Remove Thy stroke*], intensified by the gloss, " contention " 𝔥, " strength " 𝔊, " of Thy hand," both at the expense of the measure. — *I come to an end*], I have about reached the limit of endurance ; I am ready to perish. — *Wouldst Thou chasten a man with rebukes*]. The divine discipline, though wholesome in leading to repentance, may yet be carried so far as to be destructive. This is what the psalmist apprehends in the present case. — *as a moth*], who eats away garments and so destroys them. — *Thou dost make him melt away*]. Gradually, but surely, his vital sap is exhausted, and he dies away. The Ps. concludes with the same Refrain as 6^{b}.

13 a. This fine elegy, when taken up into 𝔇𝔎, was probably given a more general application to congregational worship by the petition, *O hear my prayer, and O give ear to my cry for help. At my tears be not silent.* Here three syn. verbs, calling upon *Yahweh* to give help, have three corresponding terms for prayer. It is sufficient to cite Kirk. : " It is a Rabbinic saying that there are three kinds of supplication, each superior to the other, prayer, crying, and tears. Prayer is made in silence, crying with a loud voice, but tears surpass all " ; and De. : " Alongside of the words of prayer appear the tears as a prayer understood by God, for when the doors of prayer appear to be closed, the doors of tears remain open."

A still later editor appended a trimeter tetrastich : **13 b–14.**

> For I am a guest with Thee,
> A sojourner as all my fathers ;
> O look away from me that I may be cheerful,
> Before I depart and be no more.

This addition is elegiac, in the spirit of the original Ps., but from a later point of view. The conception that Israel was Yahweh's *guest* ‖ *sojourner*, and always had been such, the present generation, *as all my fathers*, is emphasised in the prayer of David, 1 Ch. 29[15], which is probably at the basis of this couplet. The last couplet is based on Jb. 10[20-21]. It is a petition for a little respite from suffering before death, which is not altogether in keeping with the original Ps.

---

2. אֶשְׁמְרָה] Qal cohort. 1 sg. repeated in l. 2 in 𝔥. 𝔊 ἔθεμην, so Ols., Dy., Gr., Bä., Du., Che., al., Qal cohort שִׂים which alone is suited to use of לְ, cf. שִׁית לְפִי 141[3]. — מַחְסוֹם] n.m. *muzzle*, *B*DB. α.λ. and dub.; cf., however, † חסם vb. Dt. 25[4] Ez. 39[11]. 𝔊 φυλακήν; 𝔙 *custodiam*, paraphrase; 𝔖 implies inf. cstr. prob. מֵחֲסֹם ‖ מֵחֲטוֹא. This best suits parall. and the vb. of 𝔥. In this case לְ is an interpretative gl., and 𝔥 is to be followed. — **3.** דוּמִיָּה] *silence;* elsw. 62[2] (dub.) 65[2] (dub.) 22[3]; 𝔊 has vb. καὶ ἐταπεινώθην. — הֶחֱשֵׁיתִי] Hiph. pf. חשׁה *be silent;* Hiph. *exhibit* or *keep silence* only here ψ, but Qal Pss. 28[1] 107[29]. — מִטּוֹב] *apart from good*, pleasure, comfort. The l. is overfull; of the three syns. the easiest נֶאֱלַמְתִּי is the most probable gl. — † כְּאֵב] n.m. *pain, sorrow;* only here in ψ, but Jb. 2[18] 16[6] Is. 17[11] 65[14] Je. 15[18]; cf. מַכְאוֹב Pss. 32[10] 38[18] 69[27]. — נֶעְכָּר] Niph. pf. ‡ עכר vb. *stir up, disturb.* Niph. = pass. *be stirred up;* elsw. Pr. 15[6]. but text of latter dub. (Toy, *B*DB., reject it); 𝔊 ἀνεκαινίσθη; 𝔙 *renovatus est*, paraphrase. So Aq., Σ, ἀνεταράχθη, 𝔍 *conturbatus* and 𝔖, 𝔗. — **4.** חַם] Qal pf. ‡ חמם *be* or *grow warm;* here fig., cf. Dt. 19[6] Ho. 7[7] Je. 51[39]. — **5.** הוֹדִיעֵנִי] Hiph. imv. followed by אֵדְעָה Qal cohort. 1 sg. either subjunctive as 𝔊, 𝔍, or apodosis. It is really tautological and impairs the measure. — מִדַּת יָמַי] phr. α.λ., cf. Jb. 11[9] fig. ‡ מִדָּה n.f. *measure;* common Ez., Je. 22[14] 31[39], of garment Ps. 133[2], usually of size, distance. — מֶה־חָדֵל] cf. adj. Is. 53[3] *lacking;* here *si vera, cessation,* but improb.; rd. חֶלֶד (17[14]) as v.[6] *duration* of life, cf. 89[48]. It is possible that we should read חֶלְדִּי as below, v.[6], which takes up both ימי and חלד, 𝔥 using אני because of its mistaken חָדֵל. — **6.** ‡ טְפָחוֹת] *spans, handbreadths;* only here in ψ, but in measures 1 K. 7[9. 26]. — נתתה] is prob. gl., as the l. is overfull and it is unnecessary. — כְּאַיִן] as noun = *as nothing*, rare usage, cf. 73[2] 69[2]; v. 3[3]. — נֶגְדֶּךָ] belongs to next l., where it is needed for measure. It is not needed here. — וְנִצָּב] Niph. pf. (v. 2[2]). נגדך must be attached to this vb., otherwise it is difficult. 𝔊 ζῶν; *B*DB., Dr., "though standing firm." — **7.** ‡ צֶלֶם] n.m. *image;* in ψ only fig. of emptiness, instability, and so prob. semblance of man esteemed by God, here c. ב *essentiae,* and 73[20]. — יֶהֱמָיוּן] Qal impf. 3 pl. full form; pl. in the midst of sg. is strange. ‡ המה] vb. Qal (1) *growl*, like a dog 59[7. 15]; (2) *murmur, moan,* 42[6. 12] 43[5], in prayer 55[18] 77[4]; (3) *roar,* of waves 46[4] (?); *be tumultuous,* of peoples 46[7] 83[3] (also 𝔊 65[9]); (4) *bustle about,* of noise of streets 39[7] Is. 22[2] 1 K. 1[41]. — יִצְבֹּר] Qal impf. † צבר vb. Qal, *heap up;* c. acc. Gn. 41[35. 49] (E) Ex. 8[10] (J),

Hb. 1¹⁰ Zc. 9³ Jb. 27¹⁶; here abs. but wealth implied by subsequent sf. —
8. [וְעַתָּה] *and now*, logical sequence, 2¹⁰ 27⁶. — [אֲדֹנִי] is gl. — † תּוֹחֶלֶת [הוֹחַלְתִּי]
n.f. *hope* (cf. 71⁶); elsw. Jb. 41¹ Pr. 10²⁸ 11⁷ 13¹² La. 3¹⁸. — [הִיא] is emph. for
copula. — **9.** [אֲכָל כַּעֲיֵי] emph.; כָל makes the phr. too long for a single accent,
and is prob. a gl. — [הרפה־נבל] phr. a.λ., but cf. ה׳ אדם 22⁷ (*v. 15³ 14¹*). —
11. [שרגרת ידך] a.λ., as phr.; makes l. overfull and is gl.; and as to form
† הֵרָה n.f. *contention*, as J., but 𝕲 ἰσχύς = גבורה more probable. — **12.** [עַל עָוֹן]
explanatory gl. — [חֲמוּדוֹ] pass. ptc. חמד, elsw. Jb. 20²⁰ Is. 44⁹ *his desired things;*
usually fem. חמודה but later style: 𝕲 נפשׁוּ; prob. both interp. glosses. The
Rf. is abbreviated, but must be restored as in v.⁶. — **13.** [יהוה] not in 𝕲, is gl.
to the v., which is throughout a liturgical gl. Indeed, it shows three stages
of glossification. — [אָזְנִי] fuller form for אני, because needed for euphony. —
‡ [הִישֵׁב] *sojourner* (√ישׁב) only P and late, not elsw. in ψ. — **14.** [הָשֵׁעַ] Hiph.
imv. ‡ שׁעה Qal, 119¹¹⁷, c. ב *look on attentively.* Hiph. a.λ. c. מן *look away from.*
— [אַבְלִיָה] Hiph. cohort. † בלג (1) *look cheerful;* so here and Jb. 9²⁷ 10²⁰;
(2) *cause to flash* Am. 5⁹.

PSALM XL.

Ps. 40 is composite: I. A thanksgiving. (1) After patient
waiting the people have been delivered by Yahweh, and have
praised Him with a fresh outburst of song, to the great encouragement of many (v.²⁻⁴); (2) those happy ones are congratulated
who trust in Yahweh rather than idols; and the impossibility of
adequately setting forth the wondrous deeds and thoughts of Yahweh is asserted (v.⁵⁻⁶); (3) sacrifices of various kinds would have
been offered if acceptable to Yahweh, but the preference has been
given to hearing His Law as prescribed in the book roll, and
preaching it to the great congregation (v.⁷⁻¹⁰ᵃ); (4) the praise
of Yahweh will not be withheld in the congregation, and therefore He will not withhold His compassion and kindness (v.¹⁰ᵇ⁻¹²).
II. A prayer for speedy help against enemies; that they may
be shamed by defeat, while the people rejoice in Yahweh and
magnify His name (v.¹⁴⁻¹⁸). These Pss. are combined by a seam
connecting the great number of evils with the numerous iniquities,
which have brought great discouragement (v.¹³).

A. v.²⁻¹², 4 STR. 5⁵.

I WAITED steadfastly on Yahweh, and He inclined unto me;
 And brought me up from the pit of desolation, from the clay of the mire;
 And set my feet upon a rock; He established my steps;

And gave a new song in my mouth, a song of praise to my God.
Many see and they fear, and they trust in Yahweh.

HAPPY the man who has made Yahweh his trust,
And who hath not turned to (vain idols), or turned aside falsely!
Many things hast Thou done, O Thou, Yahweh, my God.
Thy wonders and Thy thoughts, — there is no setting in order;
Should I tell or should I speak, they are too numerous to be counted.

PEACE offering and grain offering hast Thou no delight in; then had I the covenant;
Whole burnt offering with sin hast Thou not asked; then didst Thou command me.
Lo, I am come, in the book roll it is prescribed to me.
Thy will I delight in, and Thy Law is within me.
I have preached righteousness in the great congregation; behold my lips.

I WILL not withhold, Yahweh, Thou knowest, Thy righteousness;
I have not covered in my mind Thy faithfulness and Thy salvation.
I say, I have not concealed Thy kindness and Thy faithfulness from the great congregation.
Thou, Yahweh, on Thy part, wilt not withhold Thy compassion from me:
Thy kindness and Thy faithfulness (they) will continually preserve me.

B. v.[14-18], 2 STR. 4[5].

YAHWEH, to deliver me, my God, to my help, O haste.
Let them be shamed and confounded together, who seek my life;
Let them be turned back and let them be dishonoured who delight in my distress.
Let them be desolate by reason of their shame, who say "aha, aha!"

LET them exult and let them be glad in Thee, all who seek Thee.
Let them say: "May Yahweh be magnified," those who love Thy salvation.
Since I am afflicted and poor, Yahweh, O haste to me;
O Thou my helper and my deliverer, my God, tarry not.

Ps. 40 is a composite Ps.: v.[2-12], connected by a seam, v.[13], with v.[14-18], which is the same as Ps. 70; so Street, Che., al. Only v.[2-12] belong to the original Ps., with the title stating that it was in 𝔅, and that it was also in 𝔐 and 𝔇ℜ (*v.* Intr. §§ 27, 31, 33). Ps. 70 has its own title, which was original to it before it was attached to Ps. 40 as v.[14-18], stating that it also was in 𝔅 and 𝔇ℜ, but it subsequently received the liturgical assignment להזכיר for the offering of the מנחה (*v.* Intr. § 39). The two Pss. were connected by a seam which explains the evils suffered as due to the great number of iniquities. V.[2-12] show dependence on Je. Is.[2] and Ps. 22: v.[3], cf. Je. 38[6]; v.[7], cf. Je. 7[21 sq.]; v.[9], cf. Je. 31[33]; v.[4], cf. Is. 41[5] 42[10]; v.[6], cf. Is. 55[8-9]; v.[10. 11], cf. Ps. 22[26]. It therefore must be postexilic. V.[14-18] = 70 = 35[4. 26-28] indicates a more troublous time. Both Pss. belong to the community of the Restoration, the latter to the times of trouble due to the persecution of the minor nations before Nehemiah, the former to the more prosperous times, when perils might be looked upon as past, and probably, therefore, subsequent to Nehemiah. The com-

bination of the two Pss. by the seam must have been subsequent to 𝔅, otherwise the two Pss. would not have had separate titles and have existed apart in
that Psalter. Besides, Ps. 70 belongs to 𝔈, which did not use Ps. 40.

PSALM XL. *A.*

Str. I. is a progressive pentastich. — **2.** *I waited steadfastly*],
with intensity of waiting ; not the continuance of it, or the patient
quality of it, but its persistence, the steady adherence to the attitude of waiting until the relief came. — *on Yahweh*], from whom
it would come, — *and He inclined*], usually with ears, which are
doubtless understood here, and implying, therefore, answer. —
unto me]. The answer is a practical one. — **3.** He *brought me
up from the pit*], into which the psalmist conceives the nation as
having fallen, cf. La. 3⁵³·⁵⁵. This is described as *desolation,* a more
probable reading than the similar word of 𝕳, which has usually
the meaning, "roaring," as Ki., Calv., Dr., but is paraphrased in
EVˢ. as "horrible," without any justification in the usage of the
word. — *the clay of the mire*], as 69³ and Je. 38⁶; the pit into
which Jeremiah had been cast, where the foot slips and slides,
and there is no sure footing. — *and set my feet upon a rock*], that
is, a lofty rock, a crag high above danger, in antith. with the pit
into which he had fallen. — *He established my steps*], made them
firm and secure upon the rock. — **4.** The deliverance having been
completed, praise follows : *and gave a new song in my mouth*], a
fresh outburst of song, with a new theme, the deliverance just
experienced, as 33³ 96¹ 98¹ 144⁹ 149¹ Is. 42¹⁰. — *a song of praise
to my God*]. This praise is public praise, in the temple or synagogue, cf. v.¹⁰·¹¹ ; and therefore *many*], not as distinguished from
few, but the many, those constituting the great congregation. —
see and they fear], as the context shows, with reverential fear, *and
they trust in Yahweh*]. The three vbs., joined by ו coördinates,
do not give a sequence of dependence, but a parall. of contemporary
actions.

Str. II. is the anti-str. of the previous one. It begins with an
antith. couplet, congratulating those who have had the experience
described in the previous Str. — **5.** *Happy the man*], cf. 1¹. This
man, collective for the nation. on the positive side, *has made Yah-*

weh his trust], as v.⁴ᵇ, noun for verb; on the negative side, *hath not turned* ‖ *turned aside*], the latter by an easy emendation, to *vain idols*], as 𝔊 ‖ *falsely*. This in 𝕳, by an error, has become a difficult word, only used here, which is variously explained; "unto the proud," EVˢ., referring to wicked men, and the next clause is then interpreted as also referring to these men, in various modes of rendering: "such as go about with lies," PBV.; "such as turn aside to lies," AV., RV.; "fall away treacherously," RVᵐ.; none of which can be regarded as any better than conjectural paraphrases; whereas 𝔊 and the emendation suggested above give us an easy and natural thought appropriate to the context and in accordance with good usage. — **6.** The tristich resumes the new song of v.⁴, and the theme of the song is placed first for emphasis. — *Many things hast Thou done* ‖ *Thy wonders*]. To these deeds are added, *Thy thoughts*, cf. Is. 55⁸⁻⁹. This, in a gloss of 𝕳 (not in 𝔊), is defined as " to usward." That they are Yahweh's and belong to no one else, is emphasised by the use of pronoun *Thou*, the personal name of God, *Yahweh*, and the statement of personal relation to God, *my God*. The "many things," now extended to "wonders" and "thoughts," are *too numerous* for human estimation. — *There is no setting them in order*]. 𝕳, by the insertion of "unto Thee" (not in 𝔊), has given the verb an unnecessary interpretation, followed by EVˢ.; but has also suggested another meaning of the vb. as 89⁷, "there is none to be compared unto Thee," RVᵐ., which, however, does not suit the context. — *should I tell or should I speak*], modal imperfects coördinated, implying that it was venturesome so to do, under the circumstances, demanding a strong determination, which, nevertheless, would fail because they were *too numerous to be counted*.

Str. III. has two synth. couplets and a synth. monostich. **7-8.** *Peace offering*], the sacrifice whose chief characteristic was communion by eating of the flesh of the victim, Yahweh having His part at the altar. This was accompanied by *grain offering*. This offering in some cases consisted of the raw grain, or roasted ears, at others of the meal, but in connection with peace offerings of various forms of cakes or bread, in which also there was communion by eating of the most of it, only a small portion going to the altar for God. — *whole burnt offering*], whose chief char-

acteristic was that the entire victim went up in the flames
to God expressing worship. — *with sin*], associated with sin and
the guilt of sin, as Is. 61[8], where robbery associated with the
whole burnt offering is hated by Yahweh. Sin vitiated all sacrifices ; sacrifices were of value only as expressive of righteousness.
EV[s]. and most scholars, ancient and modern, think of *sin offering*
here rather than sin. This is tempting in order to complete the
enumeration of the great classes of offerings ; but the sin offering
is not known in the Psalter elsewhere ; it is not known to
the literature upon which this Ps. depends, especially in this
verse ; the Hebrew word used here nowhere else has that meaning ; and even with the sin offering the list of offerings would be
incomplete without the *Asham* already used Is. 53[10]. — *Hast Thou
no delight in*]. Protasis of interrogative clause in order to the
apodosis of the last clause of v. This is based on Ho. 6[6]: "For
I delight in kindness and not in peace offering ; and in the
knowledge of God rather than whole burnt offerings ; " cf. Is. 1[11]
Ps. 51[18], and especially 1 S. 15[22]: "Hath Yahweh as great delight
in burnt offerings and peace offerings as in obeying the voice of
Yahweh?" — *Hast Thou not asked*]. This is based on Je. 7[22-23],
"For I spake not unto your fathers nor commanded them in the
day that I brought them out of the land of Egypt, concerning
burnt offerings or peace offerings ; but this thing I command them,
saying : Hearken unto my voice," cf. Ps. 50[8-10] Mi. 6[6-8]. This is
essentially true so far as its antith. is concerned, but it needs
qualification, for not only the code of D, Dt. 12, 16, upon which
this Ps. relies, but also the code of E, Ex. 23[14-19], which antedates
Hosea and Micah, prescribes just these sacrifices as an essential
part of the ritual of worship from the earliest times. At the same
time, all these sacrifices are primitive, and antedate all Hebrew
Law, and are common to the worship of Israel and all his neighbours ; so that they are not as sacrifices in any way distinctive of
the religion of Yahweh, or to be regarded as for the first time
commanded in His Law. They are incorporated in His Law and
given a meaning, and that meaning is His command, rather than
the sacrifices themselves. This is the unanimous consensus of the
prophets from Samuel onwards. These questions as to sacrifices
as such, as external ritual ceremonies, not being required, are in

order to the statement in the apodosis of what Yahweh did require.
— *Then didst Thou command me*]. This, by a slight emendation of form, gives us the appropriate apodosis parall. and in
assonance with, — *then had I the covenant*], which is probably
the original of a difficult passage, in which 𝔊, followed by Heb.
10^5, translates, "a *body* didst Thou prepare for me," which rests
on a text variant from that of H. Θ, Σ have the same verb as
𝔊, which could not have been the same as the verb of 𝔐. 𝔐
and Vrss., however, rd. in the last clause, *Then I said*, which is
tame and unsuited to the context, and the parallel 𝔐, " ears didst
Thou bore me." This strange statement is variously explained.
Some of the older interpreters fancied that there was a reference
to the ancient usage of boring the ear of a slave as the sign of
bondage, Ex. 21^6 Dt. 15^{17}, and therefore with the implication that
Israel was made a slave of Yahweh. But this is improbable. The
reference is rather to the creative power of God, who dug out the
ears and made them organs of hearing, in order that His people
might hear and obey Him, cf. Ex. 4^{11} Mt. 13^9. The emendation
that I have proposed gives fine parall., and is especially appropriate to the book of the covenant in the subsequent context. —
Lo, I am come], calling attention to prompt obedience. — *in the
book roll*], the Deuteronomic Code as written on the roll, cf.
Je. $36^{2.4}$. — *it is prescribed to me*], as RV^m., Bä., Dr., Kirk., al.,
rather than "written of me," concerning me, of 𝔊, 𝔍, EV^s. —
9. *Thy will I delight in*], is in emphatic antith. to the offerings
of v.^{7}. The psalmist delights in what Yahweh delights in, and not
in what He does not delight in. The will of Yahweh is expressed in
the *Law*, which is, as the previous context indicates, recorded in
the book roll. A scribe has made it more emphatic by prefixing,
" To do," which, however, makes the line overfull. It is an unnecessary gloss. The Law of Yahweh was written in the book
roll ; but more than that, the psalmist says, "it is *within me* "],
literally in the midst of my inwards, v. 22^{15} ; the intestines being
the seat of the emotions, affections, and passions, according to the
Heb. conception ; and so, " within my heart," EV^s., in accord
with the teaching of Dt. 30^{11-14}. — **10.** *I have preached*], heralded
as glad tidings, in accordance with the usage of Is.^{2} $40^{9.9}$ 41^{27} $52^{7.7}$,
— *righteousness*], which is interpreted by 𝔐, 𝔍, as Yahweh's, but

by 𝕲 as the psalmist's; the former alone correct as referring to Yahweh's vindicatory righteousness in the salvation of His people, and so repeated in the opening line of the antistr., and ‖ *Thy faithfulness* and *Thy salvation*], which appear again in the concluding tristich in *Thy kindness*, *Thy faithfulness*], repeated, *Thy compassion in the great congregation*, the congregation of Israel assembled in great numbers for worship as in 22²⁶ 35¹⁸. — *behold my lips*], which have moved in preaching, and which give visible evidence of what they have uttered, so that Yahweh is invoked to see the evidence that His people have in fact fulfilled His will.

Str. IV. has a syn. tristich and a syn. couplet antith. thereto. — **10 b**. *I will not withhold*]. The change of tense is in order to a vow as to future action. In antith. with it is: *Thou, Yahweh, on Thy part, wilt not withhold*], the one the exact counterpart of the other. What the people in their worship will not withhold is the praise of Yahweh's vindicatory, saving righteousness. — **11-12**. *I have not covered in my mind*], kept to myself ‖ *I have not concealed*. The psalmist appeals to Yahweh Himself as witness: *Thou knowest*], and parallel therewith makes a solemn asseveration, *I say*. What Yahweh on His part will not withhold, is the use of His attributes in salvation, and that *continually*. They are indeed personified, as often, as guardian angels, and *they will preserve* His people. The Ps. here reaches an appropriate conclusion. But a later editor for liturgical reasons attaches another Ps. to it by a seam.

For evils encompassed me until there was no number.
Mine iniquities overtook me, and I was unable to see.
They were more numerous than the hairs of my head, and my courage forsook me.

13. This v. goes back to the situation described in v.³ and enlarges upon it, in the use, however, of other images. — *Evils*], are here personified, and are represented as innumerable. They *encompassed me*], probably based on 18⁵, and therefore implying the image of a flood. The evils have as their parallel, — *mine iniquities*], because it is in the mind of the psalmist that the evils are due to the iniquities that the people have committed. These are also personified, and represented as *more numerous than the hairs of my head*. They pursued the people, and so *overtook* *them*, and in such a way that they were dazed, paralysed, and *unable to see*, and *courage forsook* them. They had no heart left, as they had no eyes to see.

PSALM XL. *B.*

This was originally a separate Ps., preserved apart in Ps. 70 : an importunate plea for speedy deliverance from mortal enemies, in lines 1, 7, 8, enclosing a tristich of imprecation upon enemies, and an antith. couplet of petition for the righteous. The divine names vary. The original was a Yahwistic Ps., using *Yahweh* for the divine name, with a variation, — *my God.* The uses of "God" in Ps. 70, and *Adonay* 40^{18} are due to editorial changes.

Str. I. is a monostich of petition and a syn. tristich of imprecation. — **14.** *To deliver me*], emphatic in position, because of intense feeling of immediate need ‖ *to my help*, repeated in the climax, v.^{18}, in nominal forms, — *my helper and my deliverer.* This is softened in v.^{14}: "Be pleased," which makes the line overfull, and is improbable in itself, especially as it is not in 70^1. — *O haste*], repeated in v.^{18} with ‖ *tarry not.* — **15-16.** *Let them be shamed*], by defeat. They are public, not private enemies, — *who seek my life*], to destroy it ‖ *who delight in my distress*], disasters of various kinds. — *who say, "aha, aha"*], congratulating themselves, and gloating over the shame of the people of God. Accordingly, the syn. imprecations, — *let them be confounded together, let them be turned back*, forced to retreat, and *let them be dishonoured, let them be desolate by reason of their shame*, defeated, disgraced, made desolate.

Str. II. has two syn. couplets. — **17.** In antith. to the imprecation is the exhortation to the people of Yahweh, described as, — *all who seek Thee*], the worshippers of Yahweh ‖ *those who love Thy salvation*], enjoy it and so love it, and Yahweh, who gives salvation, and is Himself salvation. The exhortation is that these may *exult and be glad in Thee*], in public praise, and so, — *Let them say*], in the songs of praise : *May Yahweh be magnified.* — **18.** The ground of this importunate plea is, — *Since I am afflicted and poor*], the feeble, afflicted community of Yahweh, at the Restoration, encompassed by bitter enemies.

XL. *A*.

2. קַוֹּה] Pi. inf. abs. with קִוִּיתִי Pi. pf. intensifies the idea of waiting, *wait patiently* or *persistently* (*v.* $25^{3.5}$). — וַיֵּט אֵלַי] ו consec. Qal impf. נטה. This is explained by וישמע שועתי, which has crept into text as gl. (*v.* 18^{7}). — **3.** שָׁאוֹן] α.λ. in the sense of *desolation*, improb.; cf. 65^{8} שאון ימים, rd. שואה as Gr. (*v.* 35^{8}). — טִיט] *mud, mire;* cf. 69^{15} Je. 38^{6}. — † יָוֵן] n.[m.] *mire;* elsw. 69^{3}. — כּוֹנֵן] Polel pf. כון instead of ו consec. c. impf. makes an independent parall. clause. — אֲשֻׁרָי] fig. mode of life 4^{5} 17^{5} 37^{31}. The situation is common to Je., La., and the Pss. of lamentation. — **4.** שיר חדש] new, fresh outburst of song Is. 42^{10} Pss. 33^{3} 96^{1} 98^{1} 144^{9} 149^{1}. — אלהינו] for original אלהי, although 𝔊, 𝔍, also have 1 pl.; a liturgical adaptation. — יראו] Qal impf. 3 pl. ראה followed by ו coörd. for emph. coördination. Cf. Is. 41^{5} רָאוּ אִיִּים וְיִירָאוּ; here רבים takes the place of איים. — **5.** אַשְׁרֵי] (*v.* 1^{1}) with גבר 34^{9} 94^{12} 127^{5}. — שָׂם] Qal pf. rel. clause; so 𝔍, but 𝔊, 𝔖, 𝔙, שֵׁם *name.* — מבטח] obj. of confidence, as 22^{10} 65^{6} 71^{5}. — רְהָבִים] α.λ. suspicious; 𝔍 *superbias*, cf. רָהְבָּם α.λ. 90^{10} *pride;* but prob. err. for רחב. רַהַב is a monster of a mythical character 89^{11} Jb. 26^{12} Is. 51^{9}, especially of sea Jb. 9^{13}; and so as name of Egypt Ps. 87^{4} Is. 30^{7}. It is difficult to see any connection with Egypt here. 𝔊 ματαιότητας, 𝔙 *vanitates*, so 𝔖 = הבלים, so Ols., Gr., Che.; cf. Dt. 32^{21} and Ps. 31^{7}, Jon. 2^{9} הבלי שוא. — שָׂטֵי] pointed as Qal ptc. pl. cstr. שׂוט α.λ. similar to שׂטה *turn aside* Pr. 4^{15} Nu. $5^{12.19.20.29}$ (P). The construction is then to be explained as בֹּגְדֵי אָוֶן Ps. 59^{6}, construct of quality, *v.* Ges.$^{128(3)}$. It is then dependent on אֶל, after 𝔊 μανίας, 𝔍 *pompas*, neither of which is easy to understand. It is better to regard the original as ושטה, ו coörd. Qal pf. ‖ פנה, and כזב (*v.* 4^{3}) as acc. of manner. — **6.** רַבּוֹת] emph. position, ‖ נפלאתיך (*v.* 9^{2}). — אתה] emph. — יהוה אלהי] divine name emphasised. — אלינו] is an explan. gl., not in 𝔊. — אליך] is gl. of interpretation, not in 𝔊, but in 𝔍. — עָצְמוּ] Qal pf. 3 pl. (*v.* v.^{13} 38^{20}), c. מן comparative, which should be separated for measure. Is. 55^{8-9} is at the basis of this v. — **7–8.** זבח] *peace offering* (*v.* 4^{6}), ‖ מנחה *grain offering* (*v.* 20^{4}), ‖ עולה *whole burnt offering* (*v.* 20^{4}). It is tempting, therefore, to render חטאה *sin offering*, as most Vrss., Ges., SS., al., but there is no usage to justify it. *Sin offering* is always חטאת, the intensive noun, which, however, is nowhere used in ψ in this mng., not even in the penitential Ps. 51. חטאה is always *sin* (*v.* 32^{1}), so here 𝔖. The ו is the ו of accompaniment, *with*, in both connections. — חפצת] Qal pf., technical term for acceptance of sacrifice, as $51^{18.21}$. — אזנים כרית לי]. 𝔊 and Heb. 10^{6} rd. σῶμα δὲ κατηρτίσω μοι; Aq., Σ, Θ, rd. ὠτία, which has passed over into some Mss. 𝔊. Possibly 𝔊 rd. עצם for אזנים, as Agellus, Che., the latter, however, thinking עצם a corruption of שמנים and so making the same emendation as Gr.; but אזן is more suited to vb. כרה, so 𝔙, 𝔍, 𝔖. Pierce, Lowth, Street, would rd. אז גוה, but this does not explain כרית לי. Gr. would rd. ברותי לי. It is easy to rd. אז ברית לי, "Then had I the covenant." 𝔊 translates as if it rd. כּוֹנַנְתָּ and had supplied the obj. 𝔥 mistook ב for כ, and אז for אזן. This passage is based on Je. $7^{21\,sq.}$

where the prophet tells them that God, when He brought their fathers out of Egypt, gave them no command respecting sacrifices; cf. also 1 S. 15²². הנה שמע מזבח טוב. 頂 of this v., and also Vrss., make this last l. defective; but the next v. is too long just by אז אמרתי. Many changes have been suggested. Rd. אָמַרְתִּי לִי, then we have two lines in assonance, *say to*, in the sense of command, as 106³⁴; cf. 33⁹ 105³¹·³⁴ 106²³ (?) 107²⁵ and 2 Ch. 29²⁴ אמר המלך העולה. וההבאת—. [אז *then*, logical sequence, as 119⁶·⁹². The previous vbs. are then prob. in protasis of interrog. clause.—[הִנֵּה begins the l., calling emph. attention. —[מְגִירַת ספר as Je. 36²·⁴ Ez. 2⁹ *book roll*, ‡ ספר n.m. *book;* elsw. 69²⁹ 139¹⁶. ב not *with*, but as 𝕲, 𝕵, *in*.—[כתוב עלי Qal ptc. not qualifying *book*, but as vb. *it is written, prescribed*, as 𝕲, 𝕵. עלי = περὶ ἐμοῦ, *de me* 𝕵, so 𝕾, 𝖁, 𝕿; better *for me* or *to me*, as Dr., Bä. This is the Deuteronomic roll, setting forth the divine instruction for Israel. ‡ כרב vb. *write;* Qal only ptc. pass. here and 149⁹. Inf. cstr. as *enrolled* 87⁶ (?). Niph. *be written* or *enrolled* עַל in a book, c. עִם with others 69²⁹ 139¹⁶; *recorded* 102¹⁹.— 9. [לעשות emph. in position; Qal inf. cstr. —[כתוב מעי for לב (*v. 22¹⁵*), cf. בתוך לבי v.¹¹. This l. is overfull. אלהי is an unnecessary gl. There is still one word too many. The inf. לעשות is unnecessary, and is therefore prob. the gl. The idea is based on Dt. 6⁶ Je. 31³³.— 10. [בִּשַּׂרְתִּי Pi. pf. ‡ בשר vb. Pi. *herald glad tidings;* so also 68¹² 96², after Is. 40⁸·⁹ 41²⁷ 52⁷·⁷.—[צדק *righteousness*, as vindicated (4²), ‖ צדקה v.¹¹ (which in 頂, 𝕵, has suffix הּ, in 𝕲 יִ־, both probably interpretations), also ‖ אמונתך (33⁴) and תשועתך (33¹⁷). Under these circumstances it is improb. that צדק was original; rd. צדקה.—[קהל רב as v.¹¹, elsw. 22²⁶ 35¹⁸.—[לא אכלא cannot be dependent on previous context, for it makes the l. overfull. The impf. is, however, difficult in the midst of perfects. But it is evidently antith. אכלה, v.¹², and is therefore probably an expression of resolution, at the beginning of a new Str. ‡ [כלא vb. Qal (1) *shut up*, or *in*, antith. with יצא 88⁹; (2) *restrain:* c. מן 119¹⁰¹; (3) *withhold:* c. acc. צדקה here, רחוק 40¹².— 11. [אמרתי is in 頂, 𝕲, 𝕵, attached to תשועתך, but it makes l. too long. Besides there is no usage which justifies such a construction as is given here. It is really an emph. asseveration at the beginning of the next l., where the measure requires it. —[נִחַרְתִּי Pi. pf. ‡ [נחד vb. Niph. *be hidden:* c. מן 69⁶ 139¹⁵. Pi. *hide:* c. מן 78⁴, c. ל pers. 40¹¹. Hiph. *hide, efface, annihilate*, c. מגוי 83⁵.— 12. [אתה יהוה emph. antith. —[וַיְצְרוּנִי Qal frequentative. The l. is defective. Inasmuch as the subjects precede the vb., insert for emphasis הֵמָּה, as 23⁴ 43³. The Ps. ends with this l. — 13. There is a return to the sad condition of v.⁸, which is intensified in description. —[כי causal. —[עַר אין מספר phr. elsw. Jb. 5⁹ 9¹⁰. ‡ מִסְפָּר n.m. *number:* of persons cf. with stars 147⁴ (37 t. P, H); עד אין מ' 147⁵; אין מ' 40¹³ (*v. above*); ואין מ' 104²⁵ 105³⁴ Jo. 1⁶; מתי מ' *few men* Ps. 105¹² Gn. 34³⁰ (J) Dt. 4²⁷ Je. 44²⁸ 1 Ch. 16¹⁹. —[משערות ראשי = 69⁵, not elsw. —[לבי עזבני as 38¹¹, cf. 22¹⁵.

XL. B = Ps. 70.

14. [רְצֵה] Qal imv. is prefixed to the first l., making it a hexameter, which is contrary to the measure of both Pss. ‡ רצה vb. Qal (1) *be pleased with, be favourable to :* (*a*) of God, c. acc. pers., His people 44⁴; those fearing Him 147¹¹; c. acc. rei, land of Israel 85²; † c. ב pers. 149⁴; † c. ב rei 147¹⁰, also Hg. 1⁸; † abs. Ps. 77⁸; (*b*) of men, c. acc. rei 62⁵ 102¹⁵; c. ב rei 49¹⁴, also 1 Ch. 29³; c. עם pers. Ps. 50¹⁸ (?), cf. Jb. 34⁹. (2) *accept :* of God, c. acc. sacrifice Pss. 51¹⁸ 119¹⁰⁸, cf. Mal. 1¹⁰. ¹³ Dt. 33¹¹ (?). † (3) *be pleased, determined :* c. inf. Ps. 40¹⁴, elsw. only c. ב pers. 1 Ch. 28⁴. Other mngs. and parts of vb. not in ψ. — [יהוה] v.¹⁴ᵃ· ¹⁷ for אלהים of 70²ᵃ· ⁵. The יהוה of v.¹⁴ᵇ 70²ᵇ· ⁶ is copyist's substitute for an original אלהי preserved in 40¹⁸. — [להצילני] Hiph. inf. cstr. (*v.* 7²), emph. in position, dependent upon חוּשָׁה Qal imv. cohort. חוּש (22²⁰), which is repeated in 70⁶ with its secondary object עזרתי (22²⁰), changed there into עזרי by txt. err. as it is cited in our Ps. as לְעֶזְרָתִי. — **15 = 70³.** יבשו [ויחפרו] also 35²⁶, where יחדו takes place of יחד, which is lacking in 70³ yet needed for measure, and omitted by txt. err. — [מבקשי נפשי] also 35⁴. — [הָסְפּוּרָֽיְחָ] Qal inf. cstr., not found in 70³, added with same effect as in preceding v. ‡ [ספה] vb. Qal. *sweep* or *snatch away ;* cf. Gn. 18²³· ²⁴ Dt. 29¹⁸ Is. 7²⁰. — [יסגו אחור] also 35⁴, where וילמו is used as well. — [חפצי רעתי] (5⁵) cf. שמחי רעתי 35²⁶. — **16 = 70⁴.** [יָשֹׁבוּ] Qal impf. 3 pl. substituted for ישובו of 70⁴, which is certainly older and original ; the latter is juss., *turn back* in defeat, as 6¹¹ 9⁴ 56¹⁰. ‡ [שָׁמֵם] vb. Qal, *be desolate ;* so here of persons, as La. 1¹³· ¹⁶. Niph. *made desolate* Ps. 69²⁶. Hiph. *devastate :* c. acc. place 79⁷. Hithpolel *be made desolate :* of לב 143⁴. — [האמרים האח האח] also with variations 35²¹· ²⁴. לי is appended to האמריב here. — **17 = 70⁵,** except for use of תשועה for ישועה (3³), due doubtless to the use of the former in v.¹¹ — [יאמרו המיר יגדל] also 35²⁷ ; המיר must be a gl. — **18 = 70⁶.** [יאני] emph. — [אדני] for an original יהוה = אלהים 70⁶, doubtless through substitution of Qr. for Kt. by late copyist. — [יחשב] Qal juss. (10²), for חויבה of 70⁶. — [עזרה] (22²⁰) for עזר (20³) of 70⁶, which latter is probably err. from use of עזרה 70². — [אלהי] for יהוה of 70⁶, the former doubtless original. — [תאחר] Pi. juss. 2 m. ‡ אחר vb. Qal only Gn. 32⁶. Pi. *delay ;* so here Pss. 70⁶ and 127².

PSALM XLI., 4 STR. 5⁴.

Psalm 41 is a prayer : (1) Petition to Yahweh to deliver from enemies and make happy in the land (v.²⁻⁴ᵃ). (2) The enemies look for Israel's utter ruin, and they visit him as false friends to slander him (v.⁶⁻⁷) ; (3) they devise evil, they talk of his speedy death, and violate treaties to do the greatest injury (v.⁸⁻¹⁰). (4) A final petition that Yahweh will raise him up to stand in His presence, and will not permit his enemies to triumph (v.[11-12]). Glosses assert that Yahweh hath restored health (v.[4b]), and attribute sufferings to sin (v.[5]).

HAPPY be he that acteth circumspectly, though weak (and needy)!
    In the day of evil may Yahweh deliver him;
    May Yahweh preserve him, (make him happy) in the land;
    And may He not give him over unto the greed of his enemies;
    May Yahweh support him upon the couch of his illness.
MINE enemies say that it is bad with me:
    " How long ere he die and his name perish."
    Even if one come to see me, falsehood he speaketh;
    His mind gathereth trouble to itself;
    He goeth abroad, he speaketh it altogether.
AGAINST me all that hate me whisper;
    Against me they devise that it is bad with me:
    " A deadly thing is poured out within him;
    He has lain down and he will no more rise."
    Yea, the one in covenant with me (has spoken great things) against me.
BUT, O Thou Yahweh, be gracious to me and raise me up.
    By this I know that Thou delightest in me;
    That mine enemy will not shout over me.
    But as for me, in mine integrity Thou dost hold me fast;
    Thou (on Thy part) wilt station me before Thy face forever.

Ps. 41 was in 𝔇, then in 𝔐𝔯 and 𝔇𝔯 (v. Intr. §§ 27, 31, 33). It shows no dependence upon other Literature, and is therefore doubtless early. It is remarkable for its reference to the treachery of a familiar friend in the expressive איש שלומי v.[10], further explained by glosses as one in whom he trusted, and as eating at his table. This is traditionally referred to Ahithophel, the false counsellor of David, 2 S. 15-17; and is cited by Christ, Jn. 13[18], as applicable to Judas the traitor, cf. Acts 1[16 sq]. Both of these references are quite appropriate. But the Ps. is national, and the false friend is a treacherous neighbour who violated treaties of alliance and friendship, and there is no reference to an individual. The people are dwelling in their land, v.[3], after the Restoration, and lament to God the serious troubles which they suffer from the crafty minor nations of Palestine, in the time of Sanballat and Nehemiah, before the building of the walls of Jerusalem.

Str. I. is a pentastich of petition, as is evident from the negative of the jussive, v.[3b]; and it cannot be regarded as a statement of fact, AV., ignoring this jussive; or as beginning with fact, v.[2], and continuing in petition, v.[3-4], PBV.; or as all fact except the jussive, v.[3b], RV., which is grammatically correct, but disturbs the simplicity and harmony of the Str. — 2-4. *Happy be he*], may he be happy, cf. 1¹ 2¹² 32¹ 40⁵ — *that acteth circumspectly*], as 2¹⁰ 14² 36⁴, taking the preposition as an interpretive gloss. If the preposition be original, it is necessary to interpret as ancient and modern Vrss.: "that considereth the weak," that is, is attentive and considerate in dealing with them; an idea which, however appropriate in itself, is not in accord with anything whatever in the rest of the Ps., and is in a strange sort of isolation, especially as thus introduced. — The *weak*, to which we must add, after 𝔊, the *needy*, are rather in apposition with the previous participle. Notwithstanding they are in this sad condition, they have yet acted circumspectly, and will be happy. — *In the day of evil*, or adversity. This is still further explained as exposure *unto the greed*, the greedy desire of *his enemies*. The nation is so reduced in strength that it is compared to a sick man, *upon the couch of his illness*. The petition continues in the syn. clauses: *May Yahweh deliver him* ‖ *preserve him* ‖ *may Yahweh support him* ‖ *make him happy in the land*]. The land is the holy land of Israel. "Upon the earth," EVˢ., is a misconception. A glossator adds a line stating the fulfilment of the prayer, — *all his bed Thou hast changed in his sickness*]. This is not the tempting thought that Yahweh made his bed over fresh and clean while the man continued to be sick, as would a nurse, which has no usage to justify it; but that He changed the bed of sickness into one of health by giving recovery from sickness. This perf. can be explained as a part of the original Ps. only with great difficulty and arbitrariness. — 5. A glossator adds a distich to make the transition from the third person to the first person easier, and also to explain the affliction as due to sin, in accordance with 38¹⁹. — *I, on my part, said: Yahweh be gracious to me*], taken from v.¹¹ ‖ *O heal me, for I have sinned against Thee*]. Sin is conceived as a disease in its consequences upon the sinner himself, and as guilt to be removed by a healing remedy, cf. 51³⁻⁴.

Str. II. in a synth. pentastich sets forth the peril from the enemy. — 6. *Mine enemies say*]. They talk about him, gloating over his troubles, — *it is bad with me*], I am in a bad way. This condition of the nation is hopeless. — *How long ere he die*]. They hope that he will soon die, and yet long that it may be sooner.

— *and his name perish*]. They wish that Israel may be so entirely destroyed, that no memory of his existence will remain to posterity. — **7**. *Even if one come to see me*], make a visit, ostensibly friendly, but really to spy upon him and report his serious condition. The hostility is chiefly in what they say : *falsehood he speaketh ‖ he speaketh it altogether.* — *His mind gathereth trouble to itself*]. He gathers up every kind of trouble in order to remember it and talk about it ; and accordingly, — *he goeth abroad*, in streets and public places, in order to tell all about it.

Str. III. continues the description of the activity of the enemies in a pentastich of introverted parall. — **8–10**. *Against me all that hate me whisper ‖ has spoken great things against me*]. This latter rendering is better suited to the context than, " hath lifted up his heel against me," AV., RV., which may be explained as endeavouring to kick me or trip me up ; a speculative interpretation without usage to justify it, and which has nothing to suggest it in the context. The word " heel " is a gloss to give the verb an object. The object was omitted in the original on account of measure, as 1 S. 20⁴¹, cf. Ez. 35¹³, and the context suggests words rather than deeds. The other activities were all in order to speech. — *Against me they devise*], meditate, plan, not in order to do anything, but, as the context indicates, in order to say falsely that the people were in a bad condition. — *it is bad with me*]. A repetition of v.⁶ ‖ *A deadly thing*], a ruinous trouble, a mortal injury, — *is poured out within him*], infused in him. — *He has lain down*, on his bed in mortal wounds, and *he will rise no more*, in health and life. — *The one in covenant with me*], not to be interpreted as an individual, Ahithophel or any other, but as nations in covenant, who have treacherously broken covenant and become bitter enemies. This is enlarged upon by glosses, — *in whom I trusted, which did eat of my bread.*

Str. IV. is a synth pentastich, and is essentially petition, in introverted parall. with Str. I. — **11**. *But O Thou Yahweh*], emphatic, — *be gracious to me and raise me up*], in antith. to the hope of the enemies, v.⁹. A marginal gloss of vengeance : " And I will repay them," came into the text at the expense of the measure and the harmony of the thought. — **12–13**. *By this*], defined in the parall. : *that mine enemy will not shout over me*], in

triumph, as they hoped to do in the previous Str. — *I know*],
having such good evidence. — *Thou delightest in me*], dost look
upon me with favour and acceptance. — *in mine integrity*], going
back upon v.². — *Thou dost hold me fast*], keep a firm hold on me
‖ *Thou wilt station me*], place me and make me stand firm, —
before Thy face forever], in Thy presence in the land and in the
temple. The doxology at the close of this Ps., v.¹⁴, does not belong
to the Ps., but indicates the end of the first part of the Psalter. It
was, indeed, the doxology to be used at the close of every Ps. in
the book, and also at the close of any section of the Pss. that might
be selected, at places indicated by *Selah* (v. Intr. § 41).

2. אשרי [pl. cstr. abstr., exclamation of congratulation, *v.* ₁¹ 2¹² 32¹ +.
— [משכיל] Hiph. ptc. verbal force, rel. clause (2¹⁰), c. אל here, for usual acc.,
so Vrss.; but this gives a mng. entirely apart from thought of ψ. אל prob.
gl. for acc., as Ne. 8¹³, due to misinterpretation. — ‡ דל] adj. *weak, lowly ;*
‖ אביון (9¹⁹) in 72³¹ 82⁴ 113⁷ Am. 4¹ 8⁶ +; 𝕲 adds אביון here; and the measure requires it, so Gr., Bi., Ley., Du., Bä. Cf. also Ps. 82³. — ביום רעה] as 27⁵
Je. 17¹⁷·¹⁸ 51². — [ימלטהו] Pi. impf. prob. juss., as all subsequent impfs. in Str.
— **3.** [ויחיהו] ו coörd., Pi. juss. sf. 3 sg. היה (*v.* 22²⁷); not in 𝕲ᴮ, but in
𝕲ˣ·ᴬ·ᴿ·ᵀ from חיה; an evident gl., making l. too long. — [יאשר] Kt. α.λ. Pu.
juss., Qr. יאשׁר, ו consec. pf. ‡ אשר Pu. *be made happy,* as Pr. 3¹⁸, so Σ, 𝕵 ;
but 𝕲 καὶ μακαρίσαι αὐτόν = Pi. ואשׁרהו as 𝕾, 𝔈, 𝕿, changed when חיה inserted
ויחיהו. Cf. 72¹⁷, *pronounce happy,* Gn. 30¹³ (J) Mal. 3¹²·¹⁵ +. — [אל־תהנהו
ו coörd. c. neg. of juss. 2 sg. sf. 3 sg.; but 𝕲, 𝕾, 𝕵, Σ, 3 sg. vb., so Street,
Dathe, Gr., Du., al., which is better suited to the context. The change to
2 pers. might be due to the interpretation of previous impfs. as futures indicative. In favour of the 2 pers. is the difficulty of reconstruction, and so most
adhere to it. — [נפש] in the sense of *desire,* as 27¹² 35²⁵ 78¹⁸ 105²²; 𝕲 εἰς χεῖρας
is prob. a paraphrase. — **4.** [יסעדנו] Qal juss. strong sf. 3 sg. ‡ סעד Qal *sustain,
support ;* elsw. 18³⁶ 20³ 94¹⁸ 119¹¹⁷, with food 104¹⁵. — † דוי] n. *illness,* rd. with
𝕲 דוי ‖ חלי; cf. Jb. 6⁷ (txt. dub.); adj. דוה La. 1¹³ 5¹⁷ Is. 30²² (?) Lv. 15³³
20¹⁸ and דוי Is. 1⁵ Je. 8¹⁸ La. 1²². — [הפכת] *turn* or *change, transform ;* here
bed, not elsw.; *to change* the bed, as maid or nurse, improb.; *to restore to
health* as *B*DB conjectural; change of subj. striking, though sustained by 𝕲
improb.; most likely a txt. err. Previously the whole clause was a gl. —
[בחליו] *in his sickness,* α.λ. ψ, but Dt. 7¹⁵ 28⁶⁹·⁶¹ Is. 38⁹ 53³·⁴, metaphor. of
land Ho. 5¹³ Is. 1⁵ Je. 10¹⁹. — **5.** [אני] emph. with אמרתי of asseveration.
This v. is gl. — **6.** [רע לי] *it is bad with me,* I am in a bad way. Rd. רעה as
v.⁸ for better measure ; so Hare. — [למות] after שחר, final clause. — **7.** [ואם בא
conditional clause, *even if* (pf. in prot., impf. in apod.); indef. subj. — [שוא
emph., *emptiness* of speech, *falsehood* with דבר 12³ 144⁸·¹¹, cf. 24⁴ 26⁴. — [לבו
emph., *his mind* (19¹⁵). — **8.** [יחד] in 𝕲 this goes to previous l., thus making

better measure and leaving the next two lines both to begin with עלי, making assonance; so Hare.— [יחלחשו] Hithp. present † לחש vb. *whisper*. Pi. 58⁶ of serpent charmers. Hithp. *whisper together;* elsw. 2 S. 12¹⁹. — [עלי יחשבו רעה לי]. The vb. is c. על, as Gn. 50²⁰ (E) Je. 48² Na. 1¹¹ ; לי belongs to רעה as v.⁶, and not to vb. as most. — **9.** [דבר בליעל] *ruinous, deadly thing (18⁵)*, so De., Che., Dr., al. — [יצוק בו] Qal ptc. pass. ‡ יצק Qal, usually with על *upon*, here with ב *within*, α.λ. of disease. Hiph. *be poured out:* of anointing Ps. 45³ Lv. 21¹⁰. — [ואשר שכב] J *qui dormivit*, 𝔊 μὴ ὁ κοιμώμενος, Aq. καὶ ὃς ἂν κοιμηθῇ. The rel. is not in 𝔊, and the negative is peculiar to 𝔊. Both are glosses. — [לא] should be ולא for a tone. — **10.** [אשר בטחתי בו אוכל לחמי] is a gl. of exaggeration. — [הגדיל על] elsw. with לעשות 35²⁶ 38¹⁷ 55¹³ Jb. 19⁵ Je. 48²⁶· ⁴², cf. Ez. 35¹³, here inf. omitted because speech is referred to and not doing. — [עקב] is given as obj. in MT. and 𝔊, but this phr. not used elsw., and the noun is not cognate to vb.: *lifted high*, Ges., not elsw.; *gave insidiously a great fall*, De., Now., not justified by usage. עקב is prob. ancient gl. to give vb. an object. — **11.** [ואתה] emph. — [וֹאֲשַׁלְּמָה לָהֶם] is doubtless gl. — **12.** ‡ [רֵעַ] vb. לֹא יִרִיעַ Hiph. *shout:* war cry, signal, not in ψ, but (1) *in triumph*, c. על here, as Je. 50¹⁵; (2) *in public worship*, c. ל, to God Pss. 47² 66¹ 81² 95¹· ² 98⁴ 100¹, לפני 98⁶. Hithp. *shout* (1) *in triumph* 60¹⁰ 108¹⁰; (2) *in joy* 65¹⁴ (meadows). **13.** [ואני] emph. — [וַתַּצִּיבֵנִי] ו consec. Hiph. impf. נצב *station, set*. This l. is too short. The antith. suggests ואתה.

PSALMS XLII.–XLIII., 3 STR. 9⁵, RF. 3⁵.

Pss. 42–43 are the lament of an exile : (1) Intense longing to return to the sacred places of divine presence, saddened by the recollection of pilgrim processions and ritual worship (42²⁻⁵). (2) Description of the condition of the exiles looking back to Jerusalem from the region of the upper Jordan, with the sensation that they were drowning in its depths ; and expostulation with God because of the taunts of the enemy (42⁷⁻¹¹). (3) Petition for vindication, with renewed expostulation, and supplication that Yahweh may restore to the sacred places (43¹⁻⁴). The Refrains are exhortations to confidence in Yahweh (42⁶· ¹² 43⁵).

A S a hind that longeth after channels of water,
  So longeth my soul for Thee (Yahweh).
  My soul doth thirst for Yahweh, for the God of (my) life.
  When may I come to appear in the presence of (Yahweh)?
  My tears are my food day and night,
  While they say unto me all the day : " Where is thy God ? "
  These things I would remember, and I would pour out my soul upon me:

How I used to pass on (to the majestic tabernacle), unto the house of Yahweh,
With the sound of jubilation and thanksgiving, (the roar) of the pilgrim band.

Why art thou cast down, O my soul, and moanest upon me?
Hope thou in (Yahweh), for yet shall I sing His praise;
(I shall sing the praise of) the saving acts of the presence of (Yahweh) my God.

UPON me my soul is cast down; therefore I would remember Thee,
From the land of Jordan and the Hermons and from Mount Mizar.
Deep calleth unto deep at the sound of Thy cataracts:
All Thy breakers and Thy billows are gone over me.
Day by day is with me prayer unto the God of my life.
I would say to the God of my crag: "Why dost Thou forget me?
Why must I go in mourning because of the oppression of the enemy?"
While (the slayer) crushes in my bones, mine adversaries do reproach me,
While they say to me all the day: "Where is thy God?"

Why art thou cast down, O my soul, and moanest upon me?
Hope thou in (Yahweh), for yet shall I sing His praise;
(I shall sing the praise of) the saving acts of the presence of (Yahweh) my God.

O JUDGE me and plead my cause against unkind nations.
From deceitful and unjust ones deliver me (Yahweh).
For, O Thou, the God of my refuge, why dost Thou reject me?
Why must I go in mourning because of the oppression of the enemy?
(While they say to me all the day: "Where is thy God?")
(O) send forth Thy light and Thy faithfulness: let them lead me;
Let them bring me unto Thy holy Mount, unto Thy dwelling places;
I would come unto the altar of Yahweh, to the God of my gladness.
My Rejoicing, I would sing Thy praise with the lyre, (Yahweh) my God.

Why art thou cast down, O my soul, and moanest upon me?
Hope thou in (Yahweh), for yet shall I sing His praise;
(I shall sing the praise of) the saving acts of the presence of (Yahweh) my God.

These Pss. begin Bk. II. They were originally one, as is evident from the dependence of 43 upon 42, the repetition of 42[10] with slight variations in 43[2], and especially from the Rf. 42[6. 12] 43[5], which divides the Pss. into three equal Strs. The separation was made for liturgical purposes. Ps. 43 is accordingly without title, the only orphan in the group of 𝔈: 42–49. This is possibly the reason why 37 Codd. Kenn. and 9 De R. combine them, for the ancient Vrss. give them apart. The title of 42 shows that it was a משכיל, originally in 𝔈, and subsequently in 𝔈 and 𝔇𝔈 (v. Intr. §§ 26, 28, 32, 33). It begins the usage of the group 42–83 of employing אלהים instead of יהוה. This, in the case of the Pss. of 𝔈, was due to 𝔈 and not to the author. The structure of the poem is artistic and elegant. The author uses poetic language, chiefly classic or early. There are an unusual number of cohortatives 42[5. 10] 43[1. 4]. What is peculiar is גוי לא חסיד 43[1], and the stress laid on the combinations of אֶל with nouns: אל חי(ו) 42[3. 9], אל סלעי 42[10], אלוהי מעוזי 43[2], אל שמחת(י) 43[4]. The α.λ. סַךְ and אֶדַּדֵּם 42[5] are txt. errs. for well-known words. There is a close connection with 44: לחץ 42[10] 43[2] 44[25]; תשתוחחי נפש 42[6. 7. 12] 43[7], cf. 44[26] La. 3[20]; זנה Pss. 43[2] 44[10. 24]; but so far as can be traced with no other Literature. ערג 42[2], cf. Jo. 1[20]; אפיקי מים 42[2] 18[16], cf. 126[4]; הָמוֹן, roar of crowd, 42[5] 65[8];

צנוריך 42⁸, as 2 S. 5⁸; משכנות Pss. 43³ 132⁵·⁷; קדר 42¹⁰ 43², as 35¹⁴ 38⁷; שפך נפש 42⁵, cf. La. 2¹²; the taunt Pss. 42⁴·¹¹ 79¹⁰ 115² Mi. 7¹⁰ Jo. 2¹⁷; the conception of tears as food Pss. 42⁴ 80⁶; of divine attributes as messengers 43³ 85¹¹·¹²; and of billows of trouble 42⁸ 18⁵ 69¹⁻²; — all show resemblance with a variety of literature, but without sufficient evidence of dependence. The poet was certainly an independent writer of a high degree of talent. The ancient tradition that David was the author or editor of the entire Psalter, led the older interpreters to think of David as the author of this Ps. in the time of his flight before Absalom. The later theory, that the Pss. of 𝕵 were composed by members of the Davidic choirs, made them contemporaries of David, and thought of the same occasion for our Ps. But Mount Hermon and the sources of the Jordan seem to be the place of sojourn of the poet, v.⁷, and this does not suit the locality of David's flight; and his situation at that time was quite different from that described in this Ps. The internal evidence points to a Levitical singer who had been accustomed to share in the festival processions in the holy places at Jerusalem, 42⁵; who was especially at home in the region of the upper Jordan and Mount Hermon, 42⁷; and whose reminiscences are so fresh and vivid that he could hardly have been long absent from them. The altar and the holy places are still in existence, for the author longs to return to them, 42², and again take part in the ritual of worship, 42⁸·⁶ 43³·⁴. He seems to have been one of the earlier exiles, before the destruction of Jerusalem, one of the companions of Jehoiachin.

Str. I. is composed of an emblematic tetrastich, a synth. distich, and a synth. tristich. — **2–3.** *As a hind*], emphatic. The exiles are compared to the thirsty hind. This is not the subject of verb, as AV., RV., but the verb is in a relative clause : *that longeth after channels of water*], to sate the thirst. AV., RV., "panteth after the water brooks" is sufficiently near, and certainly more poetical, but it is not an exact translation of the original. — *So longeth my soul*], present experience ‖ *doth thirst*], emphatic present. The נפש, in Heb., is the seat of appetites, emotions, and passions, cf. 63² 84³. — *For thee, Yahweh*], so doubtless in 𝕴; but 𝕰 changed *Yahweh* into *Elohim*, here and elsw.; and so it appears in all Vrss. The proper name *Yahweh* is more suited to the context, and so is used here and throughout the Pss. of this group. *Yahweh* is in the same relation to the thirsty soul, as the channels of water to the thirsty hind. — *the God of my life*], as v.⁹; by slip of copyist changed to "God of life," so EVˢ., the latter as the possessor and source of life, the former as the source and sustainer of the life of the people, as the living waters of the rivers sustain the life of the hind. — *When may I come*], longing for the time, in the form of a plea for a speedy return from exile. — *to appear in the presence of Yahweh*], in the courts of the temple, taking part in the ceremonies of public worship, cf. Ex. 34[23] Ps. 84[8]. It is probable that in the original it was, "see the face of Yahweh," in accordance with the conception of His theophanic presence in the temple; but later writers, shrinking from this primitive idea, modified it as above, owing to undue awe of God and the exaggeration of His transcendence. — **4.** *My tears are my food*], taking the place of living water and the living God, who refuses His presence, cf. 80[6] Jb. 3[24] La. 3[15]. — *day and night*], long-continued, uninterrupted weeping. — *While they say unto me*], the enemies, v.[10.11], who have taken the people captive, — *all the day*], constantly taunting with the absence of the God for whom they thirsted. — *Where is thy God?*], as 79[10] 115[2] Mi. 7[10] Jo. 2[17], urging the impotence of the national God of Israel to save His people from their enemies. This taunt is really the occasion of the Ps., repeated in v.[11], and probably also in the original text of 43[2]. — **5.** *These things*], not those which precede, but those which follow. — *I would remember*]. The cohortative form expresses subjective resolution. The only relief is in tearful recollection of the past. — *and I would pour out my soul*], give vent to sorrow of soul, which is here, in connection with tears, conceived as melting in liquid form, cf. 142[3] 1 S. 1[15] La. 2[19] Jb. 30[16], — *upon me*], connected not with verb, and so incorrectly "within me," AV., but with "soul," which in Heb. psychology is conceived as resting upon the conscious self, cf. 142[4] La. 3[20] Jon. 2[8]. — *How I used to pass on*], frequentative, of habitual worship, cf. 55[15]. — *to the majestic tabernacle*], after ⅌, the temple in Jerusalem. MT., "with the throng," the crowd of worshippers; and "go solemnly with them," cf. Is. 38[15]; or, as otherwise pointed, "lead them solemnly," are difficult to justify in etymology, syntax, or usage; and are probably due to errors of early copyists. — *With the sound of jubilation and thanksgiving*], loud festal worship with song and music, cf. 47[2] 118[15]. — *the roar*], as 65[8], of the crowd of people in the procession, — *the pilgrim band*], coming up to the pilgrim feasts and taking part in the processions in the temple which characterised them. — **6.** Rf., as v.[12] 43[5]. *Why art thou* *cast down ?*], under the weight of grief and longing, heavy and grievous though it be. — *O my soul*], vocative; the soul as the seat of sad recollection, present sorrow, and longing for the future. — *and moanest upon me ?*]. The soul is in great pain; cf. v.[11], where the bones of the body ache as if by crushing, and v.[10] 43[2], where one goes about clad in black as in funeral procession; and so the soul moans, groans, and cries out. There is reason enough for all this. And yet there is much greater reason against it, for the expostulation is really based on the antithetical exhortation: *Hope thou in Yahweh*]. Though absent apparently, He will not abandon His people. —*for yet*], the time will surely come again when I will *sing His praise* in the Hallels of temple worship, as above, v.[5]. The verb was probably repeated in the original, as the measure requires it, but was left off by a prosaic copyist. The second object is pl. : *saving acts*, as usual with such plurals, and not abstract, "salvation," Dr., "health," AV., RV. — *of the presence*], the divine interposition for the vindication of His people. The variations in the Rf. of 𝔐 at this point may thus be best explained by taking the form as cstr. rather than as with sf. 3 pers., 42[6], or 1 pers., 42[12] 43[5]. — *of Yahweh my God*]. "Yahweh" is needed for measure, and is more probable in itself, as in accord with usage before "my God." It was left off by 𝔈.

Str. II. is composed of an embl. tetrastich, a synth. tristich, and a synth. distich. It begins with a recognition of the actual state of soul, against which the poet expostulated in v.[6a], and bases on it a resolution.—**7.** *Therefore I would remember*], which reiterates v.[5a], only what would now be remembered is not so much the ritual of worship as Yahweh Himself, who used to accept it and grant favour to His worshippers. In this case also there is a looking back to former experiences in Jerusalem, from the place in which the exiles are now tarrying. —*from the land of Jordan*], the region of the upper Jordan, its sources in *the Hermons*, the several peaks of this giant mountain, more particularly defined as, from *Mount Mizar*, a peak not yet identified, probably a summit in antith. with the giant peaks, known for its littleness, possibly on the West Jordan range (*v.* Guthe, *Palästina*, I. S. 217 seq.). This situation, at the sources of the Jordan, suggests the rapids as a metaphor of the trouble, cf. 18[5] 69[1. 2]. —**8.** *Deep calleth unto deep*]. The deep waters are personified and represented as calling aloud to one another in their noisy descent. — *at the sound of Thy cataracts*], the waterfalls of the upper Jordan. There is no usage to justify " waterspouts," AV., RV., which introduces a novel idea, alien to the context. — *All Thy breakers and Thy billows*]. The waves of the river, in their agitated condition, break over and roll over the man who is struggling against their power. They are all conceived as Yahweh's, because the river of trouble in which the people are struggling is His; and He has agitated it against His people with disciplinary purpose. — *are gone over me*]. The exiles are submerged in their troubles and are drowning. The nation is in deadly peril. — **9.** *Day by day*], day after day, continually, since the trouble came. 𝔥, " By day," followed by EV⁸., was due to the gloss, " by night," to assimilate it to v.⁴. — *is with me prayer unto the God of my life*], as v.³. This is in accord with the painful situation described above. But a scribe probably inserted a marginal petition : " May Yahweh command His kindness," which, when it became a part of the text, had to be regarded as an expression of confidence in God : " will command." A later glossator inserted " His song," a song to Him to correspond with the emphasis on ritual worship, v.⁵. — **10.** *I would say*], in the remembrance of Yahweh, cf. v.⁷. — *to the God of my crag*], the God who is my crag, to whom I resort as a refuge ; doubtless suggested also by the situation in the highlands of the upper Jordan. — *Why dost Thou forget me ?*]. So apparently from the troubles to which He has given them over. — *Why must I go in mourning*], as one bereaved, and clad in dark and dirty garments, 35¹⁴ 38⁷ 43². — *because of the oppression of the enemy ?*] The enemy have defeated the people of Yahweh, have slain them, and carried into captivity a remnant of mourners. — **11.** *While the slayer crushes in my bones*], so, by a conflation of 𝔊 and 𝔍, each of which uses one of two similar forms, both needed for measure, one omitted by mistake by each Vrs. The enemy slays the people of God, crushing their bones by iron maces and other weapons. This is real and not figurative. At the same time *mine adversaries do reproach me*], taking advantage of their victory and of the weakness of their captives in taunting them, as v.⁴ᵇ.

Str. III. is composed of a syn. couplet, a synth. tristich, and a synth. tetrastich. — **43¹**. *O judge me and plead my cause*], both should be cohortatives of urgent petition for vindication. — *deliver me*], jussive, at close of the syn. couplet. The divine name has by a prosaic copyist's mistake been removed from the latter verb, where the measure requires it, and inserted between the two imvs., making the line too long. — *against unkind nations*], in the earlier sense : cruel, vindictive, the enemies of the previous Str. ‖ *deceitful and unjust ones*], not only cruel, but crafty and wicked. AV., RV. give the later sense, "ungodly nation." — **2.** *For O Thou, the God of my refuge*]. Who art my refuge, the same idiom as $42^{3.10}$, suggested by the saving acts of the presence ; cf. Rf. — *Why dost Thou reject me ?*], stronger than *forget*, 42^{10}, the statement of the previous Str., followed by the same line as 42^{10b}, to which should be added 42^{11b} to complete the number of lines of the Str., and also to repeat the significant taunt. — **3.** *O send forth*], probably cohort., as other imvs. of Str. — *Thy light*], shining from the divine presence in the temple, cf. 4^7 27^1 36^{10} 44^4 89^{16}, joined with *Thy faithfulness*, both personified, as angel messengers, cf. $85^{11.12}$. — *Let them lead me* ‖ *bring me*], out of exile, away from the divine presence, back to the divine presence in the temple, — *unto Thy holy Mount*], Zion, the sacred place of Yahweh ‖ *unto Thy dwelling places*], the precincts and various buildings of the temple on the sacred mountain, cf. 84^2 $132^{5.7}$. — **4.** *I would come*], following the lead of Yahweh's messengers, promptly responding to their call, — *unto the altar of Yahweh*], in the temple court, — *to the God of my gladness*], who is my gladness, the source and object of it. This is the same idiom as that in v.². By a copyist's mistake, omitting the suffix, "gladness" has become construct before *my Rejoicing*], making the one line too long, the other too short. The latter is really an epithet of God beginning the last line emphatically. The Str. closes before the Rf. with the same vow as in the Rf. itself, making a proper climax to the Ps., — *I would sing Thy praise*], in the ritual worship of song, — *with the lyre*], to the accompaniment of this musical instrument which is most commonly used in such worship, cf. 33^2.

XLII.

2. [כְּאַיָּל] *a.λ. ψ,* vb. 2 f. requires אַיֶּלֶת 22[1] Je. 14[6] Pr. 5[19], Ols., Bö., Bi., We.,
Oort, Che., Du.; haplog. because of ה of following vb. The l. needs an addi-
tional word; rd. כְּמוֹ for כְּ < עֲרֹג. [תַּעֲרֹג] Qal impf. in rel. clause. †עָרַג elsw.
Jo. 1[20] of שׂדה בהמות. אֲרֵ c. *BDB long for,* ⅏ ἐπιποθεῖ, 𝔙 *desiderat,* 𝔍 *praeparata
ad.* 𝔖, Rabb., Luth., Calv., Ham., al., think of the cry of the animal; cf. געה
of the bull, שאג of the lion; tempting, but dub. — [עַל] ‖ אֶל, error of late style,
which confuses the two preps., *v.* B*D*B. נפש is often elsw. the seat of appetites (*v. 17[9]*), and ‡ of emotions and passions: (*a*) *desire;* with terms expressing desire, הָאֲוַת נ 10[3] Is. 26[8], כלה נ Pss. 84[3] 119[81], cf. v.[20]; used alone
27[12], cf. 35[25] 41[3]; לוֹ *according to one's desire* 78[18] Dt. 21[14] Je. 34[16]; בנ *at
one's desire* Ps. 105[22] Ez. 16[27]; נשׂא נ *lift up the soul, desire,* Pss. 24[4] 25[1] 86[4]
143[8] Dt. 24[15] 2 S. 14[14] Je. 22[27] 44[14] Ho. 4[8] Pr. 19[8]. (*b*) *sorrow and distress*
in various phrs. Pss. 6[4] 57[7] 107[26] 119[28]; עבעה נ 88[4], cf. 123[4]; עֲנָה נ 35[13]
Is. 58[3. 5]; אתככה עלי נ Ps. 42[6], cf. Jb. 30[16] La. 2[12]; תשתוחחי נ Pss. 42[6. 12] 43[5],
(עלי) 42[7], cf. 44[26] La. 3[20]. (*c*) *joy* Pss. 86[4] 94[19] 138[3]; נ הגיל 35[9] Is. 61[10].
(*d*) *love* Ps. 63[9], cf. Gn. 34[3] (J). (*e*) *hatred,* שׂנאה נ Ps. 11[5] Is. 1[14], cf. 2 S. 5[8].
(*f*) *soothing, refreshment,* Ps. 131[2], היטיב נ 19[8] 35[17] (?) Ru. 4[15] Ps. 25[13] La.
1[11. 16. 19], cf. Ps. 23[3]. — **3.** [לְאֵל חָי] *deum fortem viventem* 𝔍, πρὸς τὸν Θεὸν
τὸν ζῶντα ⅏, are condensation; rd. for better measure אֵל חַי as v.[9], cf. 84[3],
so Du., Che. — ו [אֵרָאֶה] subordinate, Niph. impf.; so ⅏, 𝔍, c. acc. פני, cf.
Ex. 23[15] 34[23] Dt. 16[16] 31[11] 1 S. 1[22] Is. 1[12], all regarded by Ges., Bu., SS., Che.,
as for original Qal, *see the face of,* changed for dogmatic reasons to Niph.
appear in the presence of; so Bä., Du., We., al., rd. Qal, *see the face of Yahweh* in the temple. — **4.** [היתה] emph. present. — [דמעתי] sg. coll.; chiefly poetic
in Je. and cotemp. — [בֶּאֱמֹר] Qal. inf. cstr., ב temp., cf. v.[11] באמרם, where sf.
is interpretive and not original. — **5.** [אֶזְכְּרָה] emph. — [אֶזְכְּרָה] Qal cohort. subjective resolution, followed by ו coörd. with cohort. אשפכה, Dr.§ 52. — [עָלַי].. The
נפש in Heb. Psychology is concerned equally with the body as resting upon
the basis of the person, *v.* B*D*B. — [אֶעֱבֹר] frequentative, *v.* Dr.§ 30. — [בַּסָּךְ]
a.λ. in the throng, improb.; ⅏ ἐν τόπῳ σκηνῆς; 𝔙 *in locum tabernaculi* =
סֹךְ *booth,* so Θ, Σ; 𝔍 *ad umbraculum,* so Aq., 𝔗, cf. 76[3] Qr. 27[5]. The complement עד בית favours reference to temple. — [אֶדַּדֵּם] = אֶרְדֵּם Ges.L. 542b √דרה
but sf. unusual and difficult, Ges.L. 121. 4; elsw. Is. 38[15] אֶדַּדֶּה *walk deliberately*
in life, Schnurer; Dy., Bi., Bä., Kau., Dr., would rd. Pi. אֲדַדֵּם *lead slowly,* but
without support in classic Heb. N.H. uses Pi. for *lead slowly.* 𝔍 *tacebo usque*
favours אֶדֹּם. ⅏ θαυμαστῆς as adj. c. σκηνῆς; 𝔙 *tabernaculi admirabilis,* so
Kenn., Street. Du. is followed by Bä. in the conjecture אֹהֶל אַדִּירִים as אַדִּירִים רֹסֹ
16[3]; but more prob. אֲדֶרֶת n.f. *majesty,* Lowth, adj. אַדִּירָה *majestic* tabernacle;
this gives excellent sense and is to be preferred. — [הָמוֹן] (*37[16]*) *crowd, multitude, B*DB; as 𝔍, Aq., 𝔖, Bä., al., not elsw. ψ in this sense; but in Je., Ez.,
Ps. 65[8] + in the primary mng. *murmur, roar,* made by a crowd of people,
so Du. here, as ⅏ ἤχου, 𝔙 *sonus,* Aug. The previous context favours noise.

— חֹגֵג] ptc. ‡ חגג *keep a pilgrim's feast*, celebrated by processions and dances; so prob. 76¹¹ (⑤), also Ex. 5¹ 23¹⁴ (JE) Na. 2¹ +; cf. Ps. 107²⁷ *reel* on sea, as if in festival excesses. — **6.** = v.¹² = 43⁵, Rf. — ־מַה] (3²) = *why* v.¹². ¹² 43⁶. ⁵ 52³, unusual for לכה v.¹⁰ (2¹). — הִשְׁתּוֹחֲחִי] † Hithp. impf. v.⁶. ⁷. ¹² 43⁶; שָׁחָה *be cast down, despairing*, cf. Ps. 35¹⁴ 38⁷. — וַהֱמִי] ı consec. Qal impf. המה after impf. is difficult. It would indicate emph. change of tense, but it is not original. Rf. v.¹² = 43⁵ ומה־תהמי is tempting, as Kö.^{Syntax, § 366 n.}, as ⑤, Ꝑ, Σ, Ƨ, but it would make l. too long; rd. ı coörd. — כִּי עוֹד] two accents required; Makkeph of v.¹² 43⁶ is incorrect. — יְשׁוּעֹת] = יְשׁוּעֹת v.¹² 43⁶, pl. cstr. ישׁועה *saving acts, acts of salvation;* so 116¹³ : 𝕵 pl., but ⑤ יְשׁוּעֹת (*v. 3³*). — פָּנָיו] is due to a mistaken separation of lines, אלהי beginning next Str. V.¹² and 43⁵ have פני ואלהי; but ı was not in text of ⑤ in v.⁶ 43⁵. It is a later insertion. Rd. therefore פני אלהי, then better פְּנֵי than פָּנַי, the latter interpretation of form has forced the insertion of ı. It is difficult to see a good reason for such a short l. We may restore the two missing beats by prefixing אורה, omitted as a repetition, and reading י אלהי י, י having been omitted by Ꝑ. — **7.** הֶרְמוֹנִים] a.λ., pl. הרמון, two or three peaks of Hermon, one of which may be שְׂנִיר (Rob. ^{III. 357}, Bädeker, *Palestine*, 301); יִם־ may have arisen from dittog., as Gr. — מצער] proper name of unknown mountain. ⑤ μικροῦ, 𝕵 *minimo*, as adj. from √צער, *little, insignificant*, Gn. 19²⁰ Jb. 8⁷. It prob. indicates more definitely the locality of the poet, a smaller mt. in the upper Jordan region, of the East Jordan range. Bä. interprets מן as *far from*, and thinks of Zion as the little mountain; but this seems to be far fetched. Bä. also interprets מ of previous clause as *far from*, and thinks of the psalmist as stating his absence from the holy land: Hermon in the north and Zion in the south. But it is most probable that he indicates his temporary sojourn. The following context refers to the rapids of the Jordan. — **8.** † צִנּוֹרֶיךָ] elsw. 2 S. 5⁸ *gutter, water course;* here *waterfall, cataract*, Hu., De., Pe., Du., as ⑤, 𝕵; not *water run* as Gr., Bä., or *water spouts* as Dr. — **9.** יוֹמָם] (1²) *by day*, cf. v.⁴; rd. with Du. יוֹם יום. — יהוה] only here in a Ps. of Ꝑ is a gl. — יְצַוֶּה חַסְדּוֹ] change of subj. from 2 sg. to 3 sg. is suspicious; it is prob. a gl. of confidence of later editor, or possibly of petition, צוה חסד phr. a.λ. This coming into text, it was natural to insert לילה as v.⁴, only in the later style בלילה. This called for another insertion, which acc. to Ꝓ is שִׁירֹה = שׁירו *his song*. The Levitical singer sings the songs of Zion in his banishment. ⑤ δηλώσει = הורה *he instructs, teaches me*, as 25¹⁴ 51⁸ 147¹⁹, is variation of gl. Ols., We., Be., Du., regard the whole as gl. The Str. is just this one l. too long. — **10.** אוֹמְרָה] fully written cohort. Qal אמר *I would say*, as v.⁵ אזכרה. — לְאֵל סַלְעִי] either *God of my crag (18³)* as "God of my life," or as ⑤ paraphrase ἀντιλήπτωρ μου εἶ *thou art my helper*, 𝕵 vocative *petra mea;* or in apposition, as Pe., Dr. — בְּלַחַץ] *amidst* (Dr.) or *because of* (Pe.) *oppression* by an enemy; cf. 43² 44²⁵. ‡ לַחַץ n.m. not elsw. in ψ, but Ex. 3⁹ (E) 2 K. 13⁴. — **11.** † רֶצַח] elsw. Ez. 21³⁷ as noun, both dub. ⑤ ἐν τῷ καταθλᾶσθαι τὰ ὀστᾶ μου, so Ƨ, Θ; 𝕵 *cum me interficerent in ossibus meis.* רצח as vb. always *kill, murder*. ⑤ must have had a different text, prob. ברץ inf. cstr. רצץ *crush*. The reference to bones in agony of suffering is common in ψ (*v. 6³*). רצח is not harmonious with *bones*, and can only be interpreted with suffix as pregnant with another word. The l. lacks a word. It is improb. that this word, so needed for sense and measure, was omitted in original text. If 𝔍 depends on ברצח and 𝔊 upon ברץ, it is easy to find an original ברץ רצח, the רץ being omitted because of its repetition = *while the slayer crushes in my bones*.

XLIII.

1. אלהים] has been transposed from close of v., making l. 1 too long and l. 2 too short. — שגוי] Dr., Bä., pregnant (so as to rescue from); נוי coll. (*v. 2¹*) 105¹⁸ 147²⁾; so איש.— **2.** אלהי מעוזי] dub., cf. אל elsw. 42³· ⁹· ¹⁰ 43⁴. 𝔊 ὁ Θεὸς κραταίωμά μου, 𝔍 *deus fortitudo mea*. אל might be interp. either as constr. or abs., but not so אלהי; therefore rd. אֵל. — זנחתני] Qal pf. emph. present. ‡ זנח Qal, *reject*, in ψ subj. always God; elsw. 44¹⁰ (= 60¹² = 108¹²) 44²⁴ 60³ 74¹ 77⁸ 88¹⁵ 89³⁹.— אתהלך] for אלך; prob. originally the same. This Str. lacks a line. Du. suggests 42⁴ᵇ = ¹¹ᵇ; the same in each Str. — **3.** שְׁלַח] prob. cohort. שלחה, the use of Makkeph without reason crushing out final ה. — הֵבִיאָה] emph. demonstr. summing up. — הר קדשך] 2⁶ 3⁵ 15¹ 48² 99⁹.— **4.** וְאָבִיאָה] cf. אזכרה 42⁵, אומרה 42¹⁰. Is it here the same, or is it apod. of imv., or with ו subordinate? It is dub. whether ו is original, and whether it may not be interpretive.— אֶל שִׂמְחַת] with גילי makes l. too long. גילי is needed in next l. We would expect שמחתי as 42³· ⁹· ¹⁰ 43² *unto God* (of) *my gladness*. But 𝔊 τὸν εὐφραίνοντα τὴν νεότητά μου = שִׂמַּח נעורי; 𝔍 *exsultationis meae*. It is hard to see how 𝔊 and 𝔥 can be traced to same original; prob. 𝔊 paraphrases. The *et* of 𝔍 may be interpretation or be based upon ויגיל, prob. former; but 𝔊 has no conj. before אורך, prob. it was not original any more than *et* of 𝔍 in previous l. Therefore there is no obstacle to reading גילי אורך; then ‡ גיל n. as 45¹⁶ 65¹³ is an ascription to God ‖ שמחתי *e.g. my rejoicing.* — אלהים אלהי] 𝔊 κύριε ὁ Θεὸς μου; 𝔍, 𝔙, *deus, deus meus;* rd. יהוה אלהי as required by measure.

PSALM XLIV., 4 STR. 8³.

Ps. 44 was a national prayer during the Exile: (1) relating the divine favour to the fathers at the conquest of the Holy Land (v.²ᵃ· ³⁻⁴); (2) the present distress from powerful and cruel enemies (v.¹¹· ¹³⁻¹⁵); (3) expostulating with Yahweh for breach of the covenant (v.¹⁸⁻²⁰· ²³); (4) pleading that He will interpose to help (v.²⁴⁻²⁷). To this glosses were added at various times: (a) confidence in God, with the sense of great shame (v.⁵· ⁷ ¹⁶⁻¹⁷); (b) exultation and laudation of God for victory (v.⁶· ⁸⁻⁹); (c) sense of shame from recent defeat (v.¹⁰· ¹²), and plea of innocence of idolatry (v.²¹· ²²).

YAHWEH, with our ears we have heard,
　Our fathers have told it to us;
　Nations Thou didst dispossess, and plant them;
　Peoples Thou didst afflict, and cause them to spread out.
　For not by their own sword did they possess the land,
　Neither did their own arm give them victory;
　But it was Thy right hand and Thine arm:
　And with the light of Thy face Thou didst favour them.
THOU makest us turn back from the adversaries,
　And they that hate us plunder at their will.
　Thou sellest Thy people for no wealth,
　And dost not make great gain by their price.
　We are a reproach to our neighbours,
　A scorn and a derision to them that are round about us.
　Thou makest us a taunt song among the nations,
　A shaking of the head among the peoples.
THIS has come upon us, and we have not forgotten Thee.
　We have not dealt falsely against Thy covenant.
　Our mind is not turned backward,
　And our steps have not declined from Thy path.
　Thou hast crushed us down in the place of jackals,
　And overwhelmed us in dense darkness.
　Yea, for Thy sake we were killed all the day,
　We were counted as sheep for the slaughter.
O arouse Thyself, why sleepest Thou?
　O awake, cast not off forever.
　Why hidest Thou Thy face,
　Forgettest our affliction and our oppression?
　For our soul doth sink down to the dust,
　And our body doth cleave to the earth.
　O arise for help for us,
　And ransom us for Thy kindness' sake.

Ps. 44 was first a משכיל, then in 𝕽, 𝕰, and 𝔇𝕽 (*v.* Intr. §§ 28, 32, 33).
It was regarded as prophetic of Maccabean times by the ancient Antiochean
school, Theodore of Mopsuestia, Theodoret, and Chrysostom; so by an early
Commentary wrongly ascribed to Bede, from which the prefaces of the Paris
Psalter were derived (*v.* Bruce, *Anglo-Saxon Version of the Book of Psalms,
commonly known as the Paris Psalter*, 1894). So also Nicolaus de Lyra, Calv.,
al. Gr., Now., Bä., We., Kau., Venema, Dathe, Ros., Ols., regard the Ps. as
Maccabean. Hi. thinks of the defeat of Joseph and Azarias at Jamnia,
1 Mac. 5⁵⁶⁻⁶², 1 Mac. 5[56-62]; Bu. of the defeat of Judas at Beth Zacharias, 1 Mac. 6[28 sq.].
But neither of these defeats suits the situation implied in this Ps. The
reasons adduced for so late a date are: (1) the reference to the ancient
history of the nation, v.[2-4]. But the reference to the dispossession of the
Canaanites and taking possession of the land was suitable at any date subsequent to it. It is indeed characteristic of D; cf. 2 S. 7[18-24] Is. 63[7 sq.].
(2) The emphasis upon fidelity to God and denial of idolatry. But there is

no evidence of a consciousness of P. The covenant, v.[18], is a term of D. The denial of idolatry, v.[21], is a gloss. (3) Religious persecution, v.[23], which was not before Antiochus, 168 B.C. But the persecution is עליך as in 69[8], and of Israel by the nations, which was true enough in preëxilic as well as in exilic and early postexilic times. It is not a persecution of the righteous by the wicked. There are several phrases which are connected with other literature: (1) פעל פעלת בימיהם v.[26], cf. Hb. 1[5]. This, with its complement בימי קדם, makes a pentameter in the midst of trimeters. Besides, it is too strong a statement at the beginning, making an anticlimax. It is a gloss. (2) V.[10b] ולא רצא בצבאותינו = 60[12] = 108[12]. Doubtless 60[12] is the original, and the couplet is a gloss here; it is not suited to the context. (3) V.[14]

$$\left.\begin{array}{l}\text{תשימנו חרפה לשכנינו}\\\text{לעג וקלם לסביבותינו}\end{array}\right\} = 79^4.$$

The only difference is that תשימנו stands for היינו. But the former has been assimilated by copyist's error to v.[15], and היינו was doubtless original. Ps. 79 is a mosaic of earlier pieces, and it is improbable, therefore, that in this v. it should have the original of 44. The first clause is given in the 3 sg. in 89[42] and in I sg. in 31[12], of which 89 is the earlier. 89[A] and 44 have a similar historical situation, and the phr. is common to them from this common situation. V.[15a] משל, as in 69[12], is based on Je. 24[9]. V.[15b] מנור ראש, cf. 22[8], is based on Je. 18[16]. V.[16] בשת פני phr. of 2 Ch. 32[21] Ezr. 9[7] Dn. 9[7. 8] (but also Je. 7[19]). This is a couplet using I sg. instead of I pl., and is doubtless a gloss. V.[17b] מפני אויב ומתנקם = 8[3]; phr. nowhere else, doubtless derived from Ps. 8 and a gl. V.[19b] ורט אשרנו מני ארחך, cf. Jb. 31[7] אם הטה אשרי מני הדרך. These are similar phrases, but of different construction, and there is no evidence of dependence. V.[20] מעון חנים = מקום חנים Je. 9[10] 10[22] 49[33] 51[37]. V.[22] תעלמות n.f. *hidden things*, elsw. Jb. 11[6] 28[11] (sg.). This v. is a gloss. V.[23] כצאן טבחה = Je. 12[3] כצאן לטבחה. V.[27] למען הסרך = 6[5]; the latter doubtless is earlier. So far as this line of evidence goes, it shows nearness to Je., Ps. 89[A], and favours the early exile. The reference to the ancient history of the nation, v. [2-4], is in the style of 22[5] 80[9-16] 2 S. 7[22-24] Is. 63 and Je.; the reference to the זרוע in style of Is.[2] and Ps. 89[11. 22]; and אור פניך reminds of Is. 63[9]. The selling of Israel, v.[13], as Dt. 32[30] Is. 50[1]. לא שקר ברית v.[18], cf. Is. 63[8]. In Ps. 89[34] it is the covenant with David, here the covenant with Israel at Horeb; but the two are parallel and the situation is similar. The evidence from these references favours a similar situation to Pss. 22, 80, 89, dependence on Je. and connection with Is.[2]. The Ps. is not homogeneous. In its present form it has four parts: (1) v.[2-9], 20 l.; (2) v.[10-17], 16 l.; (3) v.[18-23], 12 l.; (4) v.[25-27], 8 l. There are many glosses. We have already seen that v.[16] is a gloss; it changes the I pl. of Ps. to I sg. Two other couplets having I sg. are likewise glosses, v.[5. 7], the latter a tame repetition of v.[4]. These three glosses doubtless came from the same hand. But these glosses carry with them several others: v.[16] has v.[17] dependent upon it, which for another reason may be regarded as a gloss. These two couplets, v.[5. 7] and v.[16-17], with 1 pers. express deep shame for the situation in which the people is placed and a confidence in the divine King. These may have come from 𝔈. V.[5. 7] as gl. carry with them the intervening v.[6], which must have been inserted between the two halves of this tetrastich. Indeed, this v. is of a different tone from that of the Str., introducing the triumphant and defiant strain which appears in v.[8-9] also. These three verses doubtless were inserted by the same hand. We have seen that the pentameter v.[2b] is also a gloss of intensification which may have come from the same hand. Thus Part I. is reduced to a simple, homogeneous octastich, just the same as Part IV. It is altogether probable, therefore, that the intervening parts have been enlarged from this normal length to their present form. A critical examination makes this evident. As we have seen already, v.[10. 16. 17] are glosses. V.[12] is a pentameter; either it is a gloss or a word is missing, probably the former. Thus Part II. is reduced to an octastich. V.[10. 12] have a different tone from the glosses just considered, and imply a recent defeat, possibly the defeat of Judas the Maccabee. In Part III. v.[21. 22] are complementary and interrupt the simple order of thought by a conditional clause, which reminds us of the protestations of innocence characteristic of the book of Job and without analogy in early Literature. It is probably Maccabean. Thus the Ps. has four equal parts: (1) Historical retrospect of divine favour to Israel. (2) Experience of present disaster. (3) Protest and appeal based on the covenant. (4) Petition for speedy help. The original Ps. is best explained from the troublous times of the late Persian period, as Ew., RS.

Str. I. has four syn. couplets. — **2.** *Yahweh*], for which 𝔈 substituted *Elohim*, — *with our ears we have heard*], oral instruction over against written; not, however, depreciating the latter, or implying ignorance of such narratives. — *Our fathers have told it to us*], the story of the conquest of the Holy Land, v.[3-4]; cf. Ex. 10[2] 12[26 sq.] Dt. 6[20 sq.] Pss. 22[31] 78[3]. This was emphasised by the insertion by an editor of the clause: "The work Thou didst work in their day," after Hb. 1[5], victories, as Ps. 74[12], wrought by divine power in the lifetime of the fathers of the nation, the story having been transmitted orally through their posterity. This editor also added, — *in days of old*], as Mi. 7[20] Is. 37[26] Je. 46[26], the forefront of the history of Israel. The same editor prefixed, — *Thou, with Thy hand*, to v.[3a] to emphasise that it was God's hand that did it. But this is premature. A term of J and Is. is used instead of those of v.[4] and the measure is destroyed. — **3.** *Nations* ‖ *Peoples*], the inhabitants of Canaan at the Conquest. — *Thou didst dispossess* ‖ *afflict*], by defeat and slaughter, as the context suggests. — *and plant them*], the fathers of the nation, as a vine, 80⁹·¹⁶, or as a tree in the ground, cf. Am. 9¹⁵. — *cause them to spread out*], continuing the figure as 80¹². It is possible, however, to regard the nations as the obj. of the verb with 𝕲, 𝕵, and translate, " send forth," " cast them out," as PBV., AV. — **4.** *For not by their own sword ‖ their own arm*], the strength, number, and discipline of their armies, cf. 20⁸ 33¹⁶⁻¹⁷, strongly stated. — *Thy right hand*], phr. of Ex. 15⁶·¹² Is.² ‖ *Thine arm*], phr. of D, Je., Is.². — *did they possess the land*], win the victory, by which the land became theirs. — *And with the light of Thy face*], 2 subj. of following verb, as 3⁵; wrongly attached to the previous line by Vrss., destroying the measures. — *Thou didst favour them*], the divine face shining with the light of favour upon His people, cf. 4⁷ 43³ 80⁴ 85².

5-9 are insertions between v.¹⁻⁴, telling of the conquest of Canaan, and v.¹⁰⁻¹⁷, telling of present distress. Their strain is victory in the present and future, and not in the past; and so is inconsistent with the following context. The one using 1 sg. belongs to a period of renewed confidence, possibly 𝔈, the other, using 1 pl., to times of victory, probably Maccabean.

> Thou art my King, O God,
> Commander of victories for Jacob.
> For not in mine own bow do I trust,
> And mine own sword cannot give victory.

5. *Thou art my King, O God*]. Elohim here is probably original. God is King of Israel, frequently in ψ; cf. 10¹⁶ 29¹⁰, and especially the royal Pss., 96–100; ‖ *Commander*], as 𝕲, more probable than the imv. " command " of 𝕳 and other Vrss. — *of victories*], as the context implies, of God in the long history of Israel until the Exile, cf. 18⁵¹ 28⁸ 74¹². — *Jacob*], poetic name for Israel frequent in 𝕰 and 𝔄. **7** is a needless repetition of v.⁴, without its fine antith.

> In Thee will we butt our adversaries;
> In Thy name will we tread under foot those who rise up against us.
> For Thou hast saved us from our adversaries,
> And them that hate us Thou hast put to shame.
> Yahweh we praise all the day,
> And Thy name we laud forever.

6. *In Thee ‖ in Thy name*], instrumental, for presence, as 20[6. 8] 33[21] 89[13 17. 25], — *will we butt*], as a bull or ram, cf. Dt. 33[17] Ez. 34[21]; ‖ *tread under foot*], trample; probably continuing the figure, as in the rush of a herd of cattle, cf. Ps. 60[14] Is. 14[25] 63[6]. This boastful confidence in victory seems to imply the Maccabean successes.— **8**. *Thou hast saved*], implying victory; *put to shame*, by defeat, cf. 14[6]. The enemies are national and not personal. — **9** uses liturgical phrases of national thanksgiving for victories, implying continuous musical service of God in the temple.

Str. II. 10-17 shows evidence of three hands. The original was four syn. couplets, v.[11. 13-15]. — **11**. *Thou makest us turn back from the adversaries*]; the armies of Israel have been defeated disastrously. — *And they that hate us plunder at their will*], none can resist them. — **13**. *Thou sellest Thy people*], a phr. of Ju. 2[14] 3[8] Dt. 32[30] Is. 50[1], giving them into the hands of their enemies as captives, who, in accordance with ancient usage, sell them for slaves. — *their price*], paid for them in the sale. — *for no wealth*], for a price which was not wealth, so poor was it. — *And dost not make great gain*], so trifling that it amounted to nothing. This implies the captivity of the people, after they had been thoroughly defeated and plundered, which suits their situation in the great Exile. — **14**. *We are a reproach*], for so we must correct the text after 31[12] 79[4] 89[42]; ‖ *a scorn and derision*], original here, cited by 79[4], cf. Je. 20[8]. — **15**. *Taunt song*], as 69[12], sung by their adversaries to torment them for their weakness and dishonour. — *A shaking of the head*], as 22[8] Je. 18[16], a gesture of contempt and mocking. Those who indulge in these manifestations of bitter hostility are the *neighbours*, the lesser nations of Palestine, who rejoiced in the misfortunes of Israel; such as Moab, Ammon, the Philistines. — *The nations ‖ peoples*], probably refer to the greater nations, such as Babylon and Egypt.

An early Maccabean editor, in times of defeat and disaster, inserted the following three lines at what he supposed to be appropriate places in this Str.

> But now Thou dost cast us off and put us to shame,
> And Thou goest not forth with our armies,
> Thou makest us meat like sheep, and among the nations dost scatter us.

10. *But now*], an additional statement of a new and antithetical situation. — *Thou dost cast us off*], reject, as 43² 60³. — *and put us to shame*], the shame of defeat; some Maccabean disaster, which was the occasion of this gloss. — *Thou goest not forth with our armies*], citation from 60¹². The armies of Israel, going forth without their God as the supreme commander, went to certain defeat and dishonour. — **12.** *Thou makest us meat*]. War devours the people, as 14⁴ 27² 79⁷. — *like sheep*], weak, helpless, and incapable of defence, cf. Is. 53⁷. — *and among the nations dost scatter us*], captured and sold as slaves wherever their purchasers would take them.

The earlier editor, possibly 𝔈, who inserted v.⁵·⁷, also inserted v.¹⁶⁻¹⁷.

> All day long mine ignominy is before me,
> And the shame of my face doth cover me;
> Because of the voice of him that reproacheth and revileth,
> Because of the enemy and the avenger.

16. *All day long*], continually, — *mine ignominy*], or sense of insult, as 69⁸ Je. 51⁵¹ ‖ *shame of my face*], late phr. implying probably Greek period. — **17** gives the reason of v.¹⁶. The enemy is one that *reproacheth and revileth*, or blasphemeth, suggesting to many Antiochus, the great oppressor of Israel, who provoked the Maccabean revolt; but more probably collective of the enemies of Israel ‖ *the enemy and the avenger*, cited from 8³.

Str. III. has two syn. tetrastichs, v.¹⁸⁻²⁰· ²³, with gloss inserted v.²¹· ²². — **18.** *This*], referring to the distress of previous Str., intensified by a later copyist by the prefixing of "all," which injures the rhythm; defined more fully again, v.²⁰· ²³. — *has come upon us*], from without, coming up against, attacking as a calamity that could not be resisted. — *and we have not forgotten Thee*], fidelity, not previous to the affliction, but subsequent to it, in spite of it, and therefore one which continues in the present ‖ *have not dealt falsely against Thy covenant*], the covenant with the nation at Horeb, Ex. 24 Dt. 4¹³, renewed Dt. 28⁶⁹ 29 30, cf. Pss. 25¹⁰ 50⁵· ¹⁶ 78¹⁰· ³⁷. The people in captivity and affliction have not forsaken Yahweh their God; but have remained faithful notwithstanding all their disadvantages. — **19.** *Our mind*], the internal thought and purpose ‖ *our steps*], the external walk and

conduct. — *is not turned backward*], away from Yahweh and His
covenant ∥ *have not declined*], bent aside from the *path* of the Law
of D, cf. Is. 2³ Ps. 119¹⁵ Jb. 31⁷. — **20.** *Thou hast crushed us
down*], the nation, by the heavy weight of disasters which, though
coming from their national enemies, have yet been inflicted by
their God; ∥ *and overwhelmed us*], as a drowning man with a
flood, or one going down to death, covered over by the earth, cf.
106¹⁷. All this is not of a disaster long ago experienced, but of
one which has come upon them and still abides with them. The
introductory "though" is due to dittog. — *in the place of jackals*],
a variation of a phr. of Je., implying a desert place, the resort of
these wild animals. — *in dense darkness*], a place where dense
darkness dwells. The people are in a desolate wilderness and in
a dark, gloomy waddy, cf. Pss. 23⁴ 107¹⁰·¹⁴ Is. 42⁷·²² 49⁹. — **23.** *Yea,
for Thy sake*], because of fidelity to Yahweh and His covenant, as
69⁸, emphatic to indicate that this was the chief, if not the only
reason, they were killed. — *We were counted as sheep for the slaughter*], a phr. of Je. 12³; defenceless as sheep, whose only use is to
be slaughtered for meat, cf. Is. 53⁷. — *all the day*], continuously,
and not merely on some historic battle-field.

21-22. A late Maccabean editor emphasises the fidelity in
accordance with the conception of his own times, by putting it
in the protasis of a conditional clause, and appealing to the divine
vindication in the apodosis after the manner of Jb. 31.

> Have we forgotten the name of our God,
> Or spread forth our palms to a foreign god?
> Will not Yahweh search this out?
> For He knoweth secrets.

21. *Have we forgotten the name of our God*], that is, to honour
His name in worship, and so somewhat different from the forgetting of v.¹⁸. — *spread forth our palms*], the gesture of invocatory
prayer, cf. Jb. 11¹³ Ezr. 9⁵, — *to a foreign god*], as 81¹⁰, implying
idolatry. The question is asked only to be answered in the negative by an appeal to the knowledge of God Himself. — **22.** *Will
not Yahweh search this out?*], implying a positive answer, cf.
Jb. 5²⁷, 28²⁷ Ps. 139¹; — *For He knoweth*], that is, practically, by
such searching of men. — *secrets*], hidden from men, but which
cannot be hidden from God.

Str. IV. is a final appeal to Yahweh Himself to interpose, in four syn. couplets. — **24.** *O arouse Thyself*], from silence, inattention, and apparent slumber ; || *Why sleepest Thou* || *O awake*]. It is quite true that Yahweh does not, and cannot sleep, 121⁴ ; yet He seems to sleep, when inattentive to His people's necessities ; and awakes as one out of sleep, 78⁶⁵, when He interposes as a warrior in their behalf. — *cast not off forever*]. Thou hast cast us off, now a long time ; let it not continue, lest it be forever. — **25.** *Why*], continuation of the plea, with variant verbs, — *hidest Thou Thy face*], awake, indeed, but not seeing and not being seen, cf. 10¹¹ 22²⁵. — *forgettest*], having seen, but so long ago that Thou hast forgotten, — *our affliction*], as 9¹⁴, *and our oppression*], as 42¹⁰ 43² ; that described in the previous Str. and now emphasised. — **26.** *For our soul*], the seat of internal distress || *our body*, the seat of external suffering, — *doth sink down to the dust*], in prostration ; || *doth cleave to the earth*], unable to rise up again, cf. 119²⁵ — **27.** The final plea, — *O arise*], stand up from sitting, an inactive posture, to interpose, — *for help for us*], specific application of the help ; || *And ransom us*], that is, from enemies and distresses, v.¹³. — *For Thy kindness' sake*], as 6⁵.

3. אַתָּה יָדְךָ] emph. gl. of intensification. 𝔊, 𝔙, 𝔖, omit אתה. Prob. there is here a conflation of two readings, as Street. — תָּרֵע] Hiph. impf. רעע used of God Ex. 5²² Je. 25⁶ Zc. 8¹⁴; between pf. and dependent ו consec. impf. improb.; ו consec. omitted by copyist's error. There is no justification in txt. of Vrss. for תגרף Lag., or תָּרַע We., Du., or תָּרִיץ Che. — **4.** לָמוֹ] archaic sf. for rhythm. — כִּי רְצִיתָם] dittog., הָ making an awkward clause, forcing the attachment of פניך אור to previous l. at the cost of the measures of both lines, when it really is second subj. of רציתם as 3⁶, Ges.§144. 4. — **5.** הוא] dem. for copula. — צַוֵּה] Pi. imv. 𝔅, 𝔍, Σ, 𝔗; but 𝔊, 𝔖, מצוה ptc. is to be preferred with Kenn., Horsley, Bi., We., Che. — **9.** הִלַּלְנוּ] Pi. usually *praise*, as 𝔊, 𝔍, but with acc. pers.; here only with בְ as Hithp. and Qal *boast;* cf. 10³ c. עַל. Prob. בַ is interp. of late copyist. The parall. הודה favours *praise*. — **10.** אַף] usually addition, *also, even, yea;* 𝔊 ννὶ, 𝔍 *verum;* rarely antith. *nay, but*, as 58³. — **11.** מְנִי] archaic form of מִן for euphony. — לָמוֹ] archaic sf. for euphony: *at their will*, BDB, cf. 64⁶ 83¹⁸. — **13.** מְחִירֵיהֶם] obj. sf. *the prices paid for them*, cf. Je. 15¹³. — **14.** תְּשִׂימֵנוּ] tautological of v.¹⁵; probably assimilated by ocular error ; 31¹² 79⁴ 89⁴² all favour הֱיִינוּ, so Du., Che. — **19.** מִנִּי] makes one beat too many for measure ; error of assimilation to Jb. 31⁷, for מארחך. — **20.** כִּי] prob. gl., dittog. after הָ, difficult in context. — תַּנִּים] *jackals*, as Je. 9¹⁰ 10²² 49³³ Is. 34¹³; but 𝔍 *draconum* תנינים, referring to monster nations, tempting, but improb.; **ⓖ** κακώσεως, doubtless interp. — צַלְמֶוֶת] here as elsw. error for צַלְמוּת, place of *dense darkness 23⁴*. — **22.** † הַעַלְמוֹת] n.f. pl.; elsw. Jb. 11⁶, sg. 28¹¹. — לֵב] gl. of definition, making l. too long. — **25.** אֲדֹנָי] is gl. making l. too long. — **27.** עֶזְרָתָה] old acc. ending for euphony, in order to retract accent before לָּנוּ, as 63⁸ 94¹⁷, cf. 2¹².

PSALM XLV., 3 str. 2⁴ 6³ 18⁴· ᵒʳ ³, RF. 1⁴.

Ps. 45 is a song celebrating the marriage of Jehu. (1) **The king is the fairest of men** (v.³ᵃ· ᵇ). (2) **He is a warrior who rides forth in his chariot and pierces the heart of his enemies with his arrows** (v.⁴⁻⁶). (3) **He embodies all precious ointments in himself.** He and his queen at his right hand are royally arrayed (v.⁸ᶜ⁻¹⁰). She is urged to forget her people, and in her beauty be satisfied with her godlike lord and the homage of the people (v.¹¹⁻¹³). Her virgin companions, arrayed in all their glory, are conducted to her in the king's palace (v.¹⁴⁻¹⁶). Rfs. congratulate the king on the divine blessing (v.³ᶜ) and his anointing (v.⁸ᵇ), and everlasting praise (v.¹⁸ᵇ). Glosses set forth the perpetuity of the throne of God and His sceptre of righteousness (v.⁷⁻⁸ᵃ), and wish the king a goodly posterity of kings (v.¹⁷⁻¹⁸ᵃ). An Introduction states the emotions stirred by such a theme (v.².)

THOU art very fair, above the children of men;
 Grace has been poured on thy lips;
  Therefore Yahweh hath blessed thee forever.
GIRD thy sword on thy thigh,
 O hero, thy splendour and thy majesty;
 Tread the bow, have success, ride on;
 And thy right hand will shew thee terrible deeds.
 O hero, thine arrows are sharp,
 In the heart of the king's enemies.
  Therefore Yahweh thy God hath anointed thee.
O OIL of joy above thy fellows,
 Myrrh and aloes, cassia (thou).
 All thy garments are from ivory palaces,
 Whence kings' daughters gladden thee.
 In thy costly things the queen doth stand at thy right hand,
 In golden attire, her clothing of embroidery.
 Hear, see, and incline *thine* ear,
 And forget thy people and *thy* father's house:
 For the king desires *thy* beauty.
 Worship him for he is *thy* sovereign lord.

The daughter of Tyre will do homage with a gift for *thee;*
The richest peoples will court *thy* face.
In all glorious things the king's daughter is within;
Inwrought with gold is *her* clothing.
In embroidery are conducted to the king *her* attendants;
Virgins, her companions, (are brought to *her*);
With gladness and exulting they are conducted (to *her*);
Into the king's palace they are brought (to *her*).
Therefore the peoples will praise thee forever.

Ps. 45 was originally in 𝔼, and was then subsequently taken up into 𝔻𝔼 (*v.* Intr. §§ 28, 33). It belonged to the class משכיל (*v.* Intr. § 26). But prior to this was an older title שיר ידידת, a song of marriage love, an *epithalamium* (*v.* Intr. § 24), which is an exact designation of its contents. It was adapted for public use when it was included in 𝔼. It may have received then the liturgical addition, v.¹⁸ᵃ, and the gloss referring to the reign of Yahweh, v.⁷⁻⁸ᵃ. When it was used in 𝔻𝔼 it was assigned for rendering after the melody *Lilies* (*v.* Intr. § 34). Messianic significance was given to the Ps. because of v.⁷⁻⁸ᵃ, which, when applied to the king, ascribes to him godlike qualities, such as the Messiah alone was supposed to possess. But this gloss was later than the Ps., and its Messianic interpretation later still. There are two Aramaisms in the Ps.: (1) one of etymology, v.², רחש only here as verb in OT.; (2) one of syntax, v.², אמר אני, also late Heb. However, both of these might be explained from the dialect of North Israel, which was tending to the Aramaic earlier than the dialect of Judah, owing to proximity to Syria and constant association with Syrians in war and commerce. There are several words which are urged as late: מעשי, v.², *my work*, of lines of poem, a.λ. in this mng. It is not certain whether this is a usage late or early, or peculiar to North Israel. סופר מהיר, v.², elsw. only Ezr. 7⁶. These evidences of late date heaped up in v.² suggest that the Introduction may be a later prefix to the Ps. ענוה, v.⁵; this is dubious, and is probably interpretive by error of late scribe. שגל, v.¹⁰, in late Heb. and Aram.; but probably Ju. 5³⁰ by emendation. It belongs to the dialect of the North. כתם אופיר, v.¹⁰, elsw. Is. 13¹² Jb. 28¹⁶, but misinterpretation of late scribe. 𝔊 preserves the earlier text. Thus the language does not favour a late date, but the dialect of North Israel. The Ps. shows no dependence on other Scriptures. This favours an early date, and also North Israel as a place of composition. The Ps. is referred by Ols. to the Syrian king Alexander and his marriage with Cleopatra, 1 Mac. 10⁵⁷⁻⁵⁸, by Du. to Aristobulus I., by Ros. to a Persian monarch; but of none of these could the poet say, *Yahweh, thy God, hath anointed thee*, v.⁸. The older view, still maintained by Kirk., held it to represent the marriage of Solomon with Pharaoh's daughter, 1 K. 3¹; but there is no support in the Ps. for this opinion. De. thought of the marriage of Joram and Athalia; Hi., of Ahab and Jezebel; Ew., of Jeroboam II. V.⁴⁻⁶ favour a reference to Jehu, 2 K. 9–10. He was a well-known hero, v.¹ᵇ·⁶ᵃ, anointed by a prophet of Yahweh, v.⁸ᵇ, to overthrow the house of Ahab and the worship of Baal,

and right the wrongs of the people ; cf. v.⁵ᵇ. He was at once proclaimed by
the army, showing his popularity and probable grace of form and speech, v.³.
He rode forth in his chariot to meet the king and overthrow him, v.⁵. He
was a famous charioteer, and killed the king by piercing his heart with an
arrow, v.⁵ᵃ ⁶ᵃ. He wrought fearful deeds upon Jezebel, the royal household,
and the worshippers of Baal, v.⁵ᶜ. No more graphic presentation of the victorious ride of Jehu could be composed than v.⁴⁻⁶. We know nothing of the
wife or marriage of Jehu, but the marriage of such a hero might well be the
theme of a poet of the time of Elisha. There is, moreover, in the descriptions of the marriage, reference to ivory palaces, which were first erected by
Ahab, 1 K. 22³⁹, and mentioned elsewhere only in Am. 3¹⁵ in reign of Jeroboam II., both in North Israel. A poet of Jehu's court would be most likely
to mention them, v.⁹ᵇ. Am. 6⁴⁻⁶, speaking of the luxury of the nobles of the
North in the reign of Jeroboam II., alludes to ivory beds, to their anointing
themselves "with the chief ointments," cf. v.⁸⁻⁹, and to their singing songs to
the accompaniment of musical instruments, evidently as court poets and musicians. There is nothing in the Ps., apart from the two glosses, that is opposed
to this time of composition, and there are many striking coincidences with
Jehu's career. In the Roman, Sarum, and Anglican uses, the Ps. is assigned
to Christmas ; in the Gregorian, to the Annunciation.

A late editor, who regarded the Ps. as Messianic, and probably
the final editor of the Psalter, gave this ancient Ps. an introduction in a syn. tristich, expressing the emotions of the poet in composing such a poem.

> My mind moves with a goodly word;
> I am saying my poem of a King;
> My tongue is the pen of a ready writer.

2. *My mind moves*], "is astir," Dr., so after Aram. usage, of
movement of lips, to be preferred to "overfloweth with," RV.,
a speculative interpretation after cognate Heb. stems. — *With a
goodly word*], a choice, excellent, beautiful song, and not "matter,"
AV., RV., as if it were the theme or subject matter of the poem.
— *My poem*], literally, "my work," RV.ᵐ. — *of a king*], without
article in Heb., and so emphatically indefinite. — *My tongue is the
pen*], metaphor for rapid movement, as we say the "tongue runs."
— *ready writer*], elsw. only of Ezra the scribe Ezr. 7⁶.

Str. I. is a synth. couplet, with the Rf. — **3.** *Thou art very
fair*], in form and stature. — *above the children of men*], surpassing
all men, all kings, superhuman, cf. v.⁷. — *Grace has been poured on
thy lips*], grace of speech as a gift of Yahweh, added to beauty of

face and form. — *Therefore Yahweh hath blessed thee forever*]. 𝔈 has changed an original *Yahweh* into *Elohim*, which change has been perpetuated by the texts and Vrss. Grace of speech and beauty of person are evidences of a perpetual blessing of Yahweh.

Str. II. has three synth. couplets and a line of Rf. Glosses make two of the couplets triplets. — **4.** *Gird thy sword on thy thigh*], arm for battle. — *O hero*], attached to second line on account of assonance, which extends to the three words of the couplet. The king is a renowned warrior. — *thy splendour and thy majesty*], the royal state; usually of God, 96^6 104^1 111^3; but of the king 21^6. — **5.** *Tread the bow*], so 𝔊, which suits the context v.^{6a}; the MT., "in thy majesty," followed by EV^s., is dittog. of previous word. — *have success*], prosper. — *ride on*], in the chariot. The three imvs. without conj. are an emphatic expression of rapidity of action, as also the trimeter measure of the Str., which here, as elsw. in Ps., takes the place of the usual tetrameter for that purpose. We are reminded of the chariot ride of Jehu after he had been anointed king by a prophet and acclaimed by the officers of the army, 2 K. 9^{20-24}. — *Because of faithfulness and the afflicting of righteousness*]. So, by an easy change of a letter of text, cf. Ps. 18^{36}. 𝔥 gives an interpretation of a late scribe, thinking of the ענוים of his own time; but the absence of a conjunction after "humility" in 𝔥 (supplied in 𝔊) and the unexampled form render it suspicious. — *And thy right hand will shew thee terrible deeds*]. This probably refers to the terrible deeds described in the killing of Jezebel, all the royal seed of Ahab, and the priests of Baal, 2 K. 9^{30} 10^{30}. — **6.** *O hero*], so 𝔊, as required by measure, omitted by copyist of 𝔥; a term aptly fitting Jehu. — *thine arrows are sharp*]. Jehu was a famous charioteer and bowman. — *in the heart of the king's enemies*]. So Jehu's arrows pierced the heart of Joram, 2 K. 9^{24}. — *peoples fall under thee*]. This implies victory over various nations. It does not suit the history of Jehu, and it is probably a gloss of a later writer who desired to give the Ps. a universal reference. — **8 b.** *Therefore Yahweh thy God hath anointed thee*]. This is the second Rf. The blessing of Yahweh passes over into his anointing by Yahweh. The anointing is not thought of as subsequent to the victorious ride; but, as in v.^{3c}, as the ground or reason for the whole Str.

Yahweh was especially the God of Jehu over against Baal; and Jehu was anointed by the prophet of Yahweh, and commissioned by Yahweh to do the work he did.

The description of the victorious chariot ride of the king is followed by a syn. tristich before the Rf., **7–8 a**. There is nothing in the context that has any relation whatever to the thought of these lines. When they are removed they are not missed. The reference of this throne to the king of the Ps. has given endless difficulties of interpretation.

> Thy throne, Yahweh, is forever and ever;
> A sceptre of equity is the sceptre of Thy royalty;
> Thou dost love righteousness and hate wickedness.

7. *Thy throne, Yahweh, is forever and ever*]. The divine name *Elohim* stands for Yahweh, as throughout the Ps. All the Vrss. regard *Elohim, God*, as vocative; all refer it to the king except $\mathbb{C}$, which thinks of God. The reference to God has against it the 2 pers. v.$^{5-6}$, and again v.^{8}, "Yahweh thy God." None of the many explanations of scholars satisfy, and so new opinions are constantly emerging, equally unsatisfactory. Yahweh's throne is a common theme in Pss. $9^{5.8}$ 11^{4} 47^{9} 89^{15} ($= 97^{2}$) 93^{2} 103^{19}; that of the king of Israel, $89^{5.30.37.45}$ 122^{5} 132^{11}. — *a sceptre of equity*] phr. a.λ.; but uprightness of divine reign, 67^{5} is similar, cf. 75^{3} 96^{10} 98^{9} 99^{4}. — *is the sceptre of Thy royalty*], cf. 103^{19} $145^{11.12.13.13}$ for royalty of Yahweh. — **8 a.** *Thou dost love righteousness*], always of God, 11^{7} 33^{5} 37^{28} 99^{4}, — *and hate wickedness*] ; for hatred of evil by God cf. 5^{6} 11^{5}; by men, cf. 26^{5} 31^{7} 36^{3} (?) 97^{10} 101^{3} $119^{104.113.128.163}$ $139^{21.22}$.

Str. III. is composed of three times the number of lines of the previous Str., and may be subdivided into three parts, v.$^{8c-10}$ v.$^{11-13}$ v.$^{14-16}$, each of six lines. Part I. has two syn. couplets enclosing a synth. couplet. — **8 c.** *O oil of joy*], vocative, cf. Ct. 1^{3} 4^{10}; the king addressed by metaphor as "oil of joy"; and not obj. of verb in previous clause of Rf., "with the oil of joy," and so attached to the previous Str., which referred to the anointing of a king to reign, and not to the anointing of him for feast or festival. — *above thy fellows*], fellow kings, cf. v.^{3a}, "above the sons of men."—**9.** *Myrrh and aloes, cassia*], the three chief spices, mixed with the oil and making it more precious. The king is addressed as himself the embodiment of such precious oil, because he had been anointed with it for the bridal feast. For a similar profusion in the anointing of Aaron, cf. 133². Amos reproves the nobles of Samaria for their luxury, and mentions their anointing themselves with the chief ointments, Am. 6⁶. — *Thou*]. This pronoun has been condensed with the previous noun into a fem. pl. of that noun by error of copyist. This occcasioned the usual interpretation, "myrrh and aloes, cassia are all thy garments," or "all thy garments smell of myrrh," making it the beginning of a new Str. But this makes the line too long, and is an awkward way in which to begin a Str. — *All thy garments are from ivory palaces*]. Ivory palaces are mentioned in OT. only 1 K. 22³⁹, as built by Ahab; and Am. 3¹⁵, as in Northern Israel in the time of Jeroboam II., suiting, therefore the intermediate time of Jehu. The king's garments have been brought to him from these ivory palaces. — **10**. *Whence kings' daughters gladden thee*]. These were the princesses, the secondary wives and concubines, who dwelt there, and they gladden their lord and king. "Whence" is the interpretation of a difficult form as given by 𝕲 and 𝕵. But most moderns think of a defective form of a word used elsewhere only in Ps. 150⁴, meaning "stringed instruments," and they attach "kings' daughters" to the next line. Such a term for stringed instruments is, however, doubtful. Am. 6⁵ speaks of the nobles of Israel singing songs to the accompaniment of the harp. We would expect the same word here, if music of stringed instruments was referred to. Such a word is all the more excluded if the Ps. be an early one. — *In thy costly things*], a term referring usually to precious stones and jewels, but which may be referred to persons, and attached to kings' daughters. "Kings' daughters are among thy honourable women," RV., "thy precious ones, dear ones," *B*DB. 𝕲 and 𝕵 understand it of the reverence given their husbands by women. But such an arrangement spoils the measure of lines and Strs., and introduces the kings' daughters prematurely before the queen in a principal clause; whereas in the interpretation given above they are mentioned with the ivory palaces and the king's garments, and so make up the closing line of a tetrastich referring to the king. — *the queen doth stand at thy right hand*], adorned with the precious stones and jewels the king has given her. — *in golden attire*], so 𝔊, 𝔖 (golden crown, 𝔍), adding, to complete the line, *her clothing of embroidery*, as v.¹⁴ᵇ⋅¹⁵ᵃ. The last clause is omitted by ℌ, and the word rendered attire is read "Ophir," and so "gold of Ophir," followed by AV., RV.; elsewhere Is. 13¹² Jb. 28¹⁶ only. These two words attached to previous line make it too long. The arrangement and interpretation adopted above give four lines of the Str. to the king and two to the queen, all describing their adornment for the marriage.

In Part II. three syn. couplets are addressed to the queen. — **11.** *Hear, see, and incline thine ear*]. The assonance of the three imperatives is destroyed by the insertion of "daughter," after "hear," to make the reference to the queen more evident. It gives ground for the opinion that the poet was a venerable court official. Such alone would address the young queen in this way. But it is error of a copyist who was not capable of such nice distinctions. — *And forget thy people and thy father's house*]. She was a foreign princess who had left her people and her father to become queen of Israel. It was doubtless jealousy of foreign religious influence which was the basis of this exhortation. — **12.** *For the king desires thy beauty*]. Her beauty had won the love and desire of the king, and as his queen she has in him a great admirer and proud possessor. — *For he is thy sovereign lord*]. As in the previous line the beauty of the queen is praised, so here the majesty of the king. — **13.** *The daughter of Tyre will do homage*]. So 𝔊, but ℌ, 𝔍 attach the verb to previous line referring to the queen, *and worship thou him;* but that leaves the next line without verb. The verb really belongs to both lines, only in the second it has no direct object. — *With a gift for thee*], supplying the suffix, because assonance in 2 fem. sg. is characteristic of the closing words of this Str. in every other line. It is improbable that this would be the only exception in six lines. This gives the queen an interest in the gift; it is for her, and as the bride, and so a special act of homage to the king also. 𝔊 has "daughters of Tyre," suggesting that the queen is a Tyrian princess. 𝔍 also takes it as pl., "daughters of the mighty" ‖ "richest peoples," but ℌ makes it sg., referring therefore to the city or nation. — *The richest peoples will court thy face*]. Some who interpret the sg. as "people," think of the rich merchants of Tyre ; but 𝕲 adds "of the land," referring to the land of Israel. The parall. with "the daughter of Tyre," of 𝕳, favours a reference of the phr. to neighbouring commercial nations, the richest peoples, taking the sg. as collective.

Part III. has two syn. and a synth. couplet. — **14.** *In all glorious things*], by an easy emendation of the text to bring the form into assonance with the other lines : not "in all her glory," 𝕲; "in his glory," 𝕵, or "all glorious," EVª., none of which can be well sustained by usage of Heb. words. — *The king's daughter*], the queen as the daughter of a foreign king, cf. v.^{11b}. — *within*], within the palace, where she stands at the right hand of the king. — *in-wrought with gold*], cf. Ex. $28^{11 \text{ sq.}}$ $39^{6 \text{ sq.}}$, for the setting of stones on the shoulder piece of the high-priest. — *is her clothing*], cf. v.^{10c}. — **15.** *In embroidery*], cf. v.^{10c}. — *are conducted to the king*], pl., so 𝕲; MT., "is conducted," referring to the queen, is against the context, which represents her as already within, and v.^{10}, where she stands at the right hand of the king, and therefore could not be conducted to him now. The subj. is therefore *her attendants*, those following after her, which also on the ground of the assonance in *-ah*, $14^{a. b}$, belongs to this line and closes it. 𝕳 has transposed this word with "virgins," which begins the next line, thus continuing assonance in *-oth*. — *Virgins, her companions, are brought (to her)*], so assonance requires, and parall. *to the king*, and *into the king's palace :* "to thee," of 𝕳, 𝕲; EVª., involving a change of person without reason, is copyist's error. — **16.** *With gladness and exulting they are conducted (to her)*], continuing the double assonance. — *Into the king's palace are they brought to her*]. — **18 b.** The Rf. represents that the people of coming generations will praise the king forever.

An editor, probably the one who arranged 𝕯𝕽, thinking that the Ps. should conclude with a reference to the perpetuity of the dynasty, inserts **17**, a wish that the king may have a numerous posterity, and that he may be a universal king, with his sons reigning as princes in all the earth.

> Instead of thy fathers may thy sons appear,
> Whom thou wilt set princes in all the earth.

A still later liturgical addition was made, **18 a**, probably by the final editor of the Psalter, to make the Ps. suitable for the congregation, which continues to exist in all generations. — *I will celebrate Thy name in all generations*]. This was not suited to a poet speaking for himself or addressing the king at the time of his marriage.

2. רָחַשׁ] a.λ. N.H. *be moved*, Aram., Syr., of movement of lips. רְחִישׁ, cf. רחשׁוּה, *thoughts* that move within ; מַרְחֶשֶׁת n.f. Lv. 2⁷ 7⁹, *boiling-vessel, stewpan.* The reference seems to be to the movement of the לב in sympathy with the lips. — אֹמֵר אָנִי] ptc. with pron. for tense, Aramaism. — מַעֲשַׂי] a.λ. in mng. *lines* of a poem. — לְמֶלֶךְ] ל *with reference to*, and not *to, unto.* — † עֵט] n.m. *stylus*, the reed pen of the Orient ; elsw. Je. 8⁸, iron pen for use on stone or metal Je. 17¹ Jb. 19²⁴. — **3.** יָפְיָפִיתָ] a.λ. ⅏, Ƀ, Aq., Σ, Ƨ, Ɉ, Quinta, had two words יפי יפית. Rd. יָפָה יָפִיתָ inf. abs. with Qal pf. יפה, which indeed is required by the measure. — כִּשְׂפָתוֹתֶיךָ] has two poetic accents, cf. 59⁸. — עַל־כֵּן] as v.⁸ᵇ· ¹⁸ᵇ Rf. — **4.** זַל־יְרֵכֶךָ] rd. יְרֵכֶךָ for assonance with הֲדָרֶךָ, as גִּבּוֹר at beginning of second l. in assonance with חָמוּר, and indeed הַרְנֵן with חֶרֶבְּךָ. — **5.** וְהֲדָרְךָ] הוֹדְךָ assimilated in 𝔐 to previous word. ⅏ ἔντεινον, Ƀ *intende* = וְהִדְרְךָ Hiph. imv. דרך, *span the bow*, is better suited to the context, so Horsley. Ɉ, Ƨ, omit it, and it is regarded as dittog. by Street, Ols., Gr., Now., al. But it is needed for measure and these Vrss. are rather guilty of haplog. — עַל דְּבַר] either *because of* Gn. 20¹¹· ¹⁸ (E) 12¹⁷ 43¹⁸ (J) Nu. 17¹⁴ (P) Ps. 79⁹, or less frequently *on behalf of* Ex. 8⁸ (J). — וְעַנְוָה־צֶדֶק] dub., usually explained as shortened because of Makkeph for עֲנָוָה, but improb. עֲנָוָה, *humility*, is a rare and late word, Pr. 15³³ 18¹² 22⁴ Zp. 2³ Ps. 18³⁶ (txt. err. for עֹנְתְךָ 2 S. 22³⁶), so prob. here err. for צֶדֶק. — וְתוֹרְךָ] ו subordinate, *that*, or ו with apodosis of imv. — נוֹרָאוֹת]. ⅏ θαυμαστῶς, Ɉ *terribiliter ;* elsw. of God 65⁶ 106²² 139¹⁴ 145⁶. — **6.** חִצֶּיךָ שְׁנוּנִים] dimeter improb., ⅏ δυνατέ = גִּבּוֹר is demanded for measure. — **7.** כִּסְאֲךָ אֱלֹהִים] Vrss. take אלהים as vocative referring to the king, except Ƭ, which rightly refers it to God. If v.⁷ is original to Ps. the 2 pers. v.⁵· ⁶· ⁸ urge the former; the latter can be sustained only by regarding it as a gl. Hu., Moll., regard כִּסְאֲךָ as cstr., *thy divine throne*, notwithstanding sf., cf. 1 Ch. 29²³; but such usage improb.; there is no sufficient evidence for it, *v.* Ges.ᴸ· ¹²⁸· ᴬⁿᵐ· ᵇ. AE., Ew., Hi., Bä., make אלהים predicate, *thy throne is divine* || עוֹלָם וָעֶד, "a throne of God," JPSV. Bruston, Giesebrecht, We., Du., think that אלהים represents an original יהוה which should be interpreted, not as the divine name, but as Qal impf. *will be* יִהְיֶה. This is rather tame, and we would expect יכון in that case. The usage of the terms of this v. favour a reference to God. — מִישׁר] for the usual מֵישָׁר (9⁹). — **8.** שֶׁמֶן שָׂשׂוֹן] elsw. Is. 61⁸, referring to marriage ; usually taken as second obj. of משׁח, making a long prose sentence and prolonging the Rf. against other examples in Ps. It is really vocative, cf. Ct. 1⁸ 4¹⁰. — ‡ חָבֵר] adj. *associate, fellow*, cf. 119⁶³. — **9.** † מֹר] *myrrh*, as perfume elsw. Ct. 1¹³ 4⁶· ¹⁴ 5¹· ⁵· ⁵ Pr. 7¹⁷, incense Ct. 3⁶, ointment Est. 2¹², ingredient

of sacred oil Ex. 30²³ (P). — † [אֲהָלוֹת] pl. *aloes*, elsw. Ct. 4¹⁴ of bride as odo-
riferous tree, pl. יט Nu. 24⁶ of trees, Pr. 7¹⁷ of perfume of bed. — [קְצִיעוֹת] a.λ.
cassia; pl. form may have arisen from assimilation, but prob. represents a
missing אֶקָּה, needed for measure and distinctness of reference of these lines
to the king. Its compression into the previous word caused the misinterpretation of v.⁸ᵇ. — [כָּל־בִּגְדֹתֶיךָ] is suspicious ; pl. f. *a.λ.,* pl. m. 155 t. OT.
Talm. *Pea* 1¹⁶ᵇ interprets it by בְּגִידָה √בגר of *treacherous* actions, cf. Zp. 3⁴.
But this does not suit context. 𝔊 ἀπὸ τῶν ἱματίων σου, 𝔍 *in cunctis vesti-
mentis tuis*. Pl. f. prob. originated from assimilation to previous words. —
[מִנִּי] archaic form of מֵן, as 44¹¹. ¹⁹ 68³² 74²² 78². ⁴² 88¹⁰ ; before rel. clause
whence, 𝔊 ἐξ ὧν, 𝔙 *ex quibus,* 𝔍 *quibus*. According to Ew., Hu., De., Rä.,
Pe., Du., Bä., Kirk., *B*DB., it is defective pl. † מִנִּים *stringed instruments;*
Aramaism elsw. 150⁴. 𝔗 n.pr. *Armenia*. 𝔖 rd. prob. רִישׁוֹן *principal,* for שֶׁן
and regarded מני as prep. with sf. 1 sg. Ainsw., Bö., regard מן as comparative, *more than,* but it is improb. 𝔊 is simpler and to be preferred, as Ra.,
Calv., Ham., Genebr., al., after all ancient interpreters. — 10. † [כֶּתֶם אוֹפִיר]
phr. elsw. Is. 13¹² Jb. 28¹⁶. 𝔊 ἐν ἱματισμῷ διαχρύσῳ περιβεβλημένη πεποικιλ-
μένη, 𝔍 *diademate aureo,* shew that אפר was in the original text and that
𝕳 has serious omissions. 𝔍 rd. פאר; 𝔊, 𝔖, אֵיּר, *covering, attire,* as in 1 K.
20³⁸. ⁴¹, cf. Ass. *êpartu, garment, B*DB. The original was doubtless as in 𝔊
בכתם אֲפֵר לבושה לרקמות. — 12–13. [וְיִתְאָו] ו of apod. of imv., shortened juss.
Hithp. אוה. 𝔊 ὅτι ἐπεθύμησεν implies כִּי which is needed for measure; rightly
followed by Gr., Du. — [כִּי הוּא אֲרֹנַיִךְ] goes to the end of the l. for assonance
in ־ךְ. — [הִשְׁתַּחֲוִי־לוֹ] belongs to the next l. וּבַת־צֹר according to 𝔊. It prob.
belongs to both, and has been once omitted by haplog. ו with בת is therefore
dittog. 𝔊 rd. pl. vb. and בנת for בַת; cf. בת בבל 137⁸, בת ציון 9¹⁶ referring to
the nation. Aq., 𝔍, take בת as vocative, 𝔍 *filia fortissimi,* Σ θυγάτηρ ἡ κρα-
ταιά. — [וְשִׁירֵי] pl. cstr. superlative. 𝔊 interprets οἱ πλούσιοι τοῦ λαοῦ τῆς γῆς,
𝔍 *divites populi*. — [כְּמִנְחָה]. 𝔊, 𝔍, have pl. Homage to the king is improb.
here, where all else refers to the bride. Rd. מִנְחָךְ *with a gift for thee,* which
then gives all the lines the same ending in ־ךְ : מִנְחָךְ, אֲרֹנַיִךְ, יְחֵר, אָבִיךְ, אֶזְנֵךְ,
and then by change of order פָּנַיִךְ. — 14. [כָּל־כְּבוּדָּה] is dub. 𝔊 πᾶσα ἡ δόξα
αὐτῆς θυγατρὸς = בְּבְדָה, so 𝔙 *omnis gloria eius filiae,* but sf. with cstr. is dub.
𝔊ᴺ. ᶜ. ᵉ. ᵃ. ᴬ. ᵀ. λ, 𝔍, have it not. † [כְּבוּדָּה] adj. f. elsw. only Ez. 23⁴¹ of a bed. As
we shall see, every other line of Pt. 3 of Str. begins with a form in יְ, so prob.
here. Rd. כבדות, *glorious things,* referring to her ornaments ; cf. נכבדות Ps.
87³. — ‡ [פְּנִימָה] *within,* after vbs. of motion Lv. 10¹⁸ 2 Ch. 29¹⁸, and so of
being within 1 K. 6¹⁸ 2 K. 7¹¹. 𝔊ᴮ· ᴺ Ἐσεβών, *v.* Jer. Ep. LXV., err. for
ἔσωθεν 𝔊ᴬ· ᴿ· ᵀ· ᴮ· ᵃ· ᵇ· ᴺ· ᶜ· ᵃ· There is no sufficient reason to rd. פנינה, *her
corals or pearls,* as Krochmal, Gr., Bu., Du. — [מִמִּשְׁבְּצוֹת] two accents. †The
word elsw. *setting* of the onyx stones on the high priest's shoulders Ex.
28¹¹. ¹³. ¹⁴. ²⁵ 39⁶. ¹³. ¹⁶. ¹⁸ (P). — 15. [הוּבָל]. 𝔊 ἀπενεχθήσονται, as v.¹⁶ᵃ, תּוּבַלְנָה,
is doubtless correct ; and the subj. is אַחֲרֶיהָ, which has been transposed with
בְּתוּלוֹת, which should begin the next l. — [לָךְ] is altogether improb.; rd. לָה, as
Street, in assonance. — 16. [בְּשִׂמְחָה] should begin l. for assonance. — [תְּבֹאֶינָה]

rd. as above מוּבָאוֹת for assonance, followed by לה, which is needed at the end
for the same reason. Pt. 3 of this Str. as restored is as follows:

כל כבדות בת־מלך פנימה
ממשבצות זהב לבושה
לרקמות תובלנה למלך אחריה
בתולות רעותיה מובאות לה
בשמחות וגיל תובלנה לה
מובאות בהיכל מלך לה

—**18.** הִשִּׁיחֲמוּ] archaic sf., but without sufficient reason, and improb.

PSALM XLVI., 3 STR. 6⁴, RF. 2⁴.

Ps. 46 is a national song in the early days of Josiah : (1) expressing confidence in Yahweh, the sure refuge, in troubles that can
only be compared to the effects of an earthquake (v.²⁻⁴) ; (2) asserting the sure refuge in the city of Yahweh, gladdened by His
gracious presence, and unshaken by the tumultuous nations (v.⁵⁻⁷) ;
(3) a call to behold the wonders of Yahweh, especially in causing
wars to cease (v.⁹⁻¹¹). The Rfs. assert that Yahweh is with His
people as their high tower (v.⁸·¹²).

(YAHWEH) is ours, a refuge and strength,
 A help in troubles to be found abundantly;
 Therefore we will not fear though the earth (roar),
 And though mountains totter into the heart of the sea:
 The (seas) roar, their waters foam,
 Mountains shake with the swelling (of its stream).
   Yahweh (God of) Hosts, is with us,
    The God of Jacob is our high tower.
HIS brooks make glad the city of (Yahweh),
 The holy place of the tabernacle of (Yahweh) 'Elyon.
 (Yahweh) is in her midst; she cannot be made to totter;
 (Yahweh) will help her, at the turn of the morn.
 Nations roared; kingdoms tottered;
 Has He uttered His voice, the earth melteth.
   Yahweh (God of) Hosts, is with us,
    The God of Jacob is our high tower.
COME, behold the works of Yahweh,
 What desolations He hath set in the earth;
 He is causing wars to cease unto the ends of the earth,
 The bow He breaketh, and cutteth the spear in sunder.
 Desist and know that it is I, (Yahweh) ;
 I shall be exalted among the nations, I shall be exalted in the earth.
   Yahweh (God of) Hosts, is with us,
    The God of Jacob is our high tower.

Ps. 46 was composed as a שיר, exceedingly artistic in structure. It was then taken up into 𝕰, and subsequently into both 𝔇𝕽 and 𝕰 (*v*. Intr. §§ 28, 32, 33). In the former it received the assignment על עלמות (*v*. Intr. § 34). In the latter יהוה was changed to אלהים or omitted, except in refrains (ʾ v⁹. txt. err.). V.⁹ is cited 66⁵. The language is early. אנכי v.¹¹, ו consec. pf. v.¹⁰ צבאות (א׳) יʾ v.⁸·¹², מפעלות, v.⁹, txt. err. for earlier פעלות. The author was familiar with the effects of an earthquake on mountains and sea, probably at the base of Mt. Carmel, v.³⁻⁴. The city of God was still the secure refuge against the nations, v.⁵⁻⁷, cf. Zp. 3¹⁵⁻¹⁷. The song may well express the confidence with which the young Josiah began his reign amidst the commotions among the nations due to the Scythian invasions of Western Asia as described in Zp. The destruction of the instruments of war is in the style of Ho. 2²⁰ Is. 9⁴ Mi. 4¹⁻⁴ = Is. 2²⁻⁴, and עמנו, v.⁸·¹², reminds of Is. 7¹⁴. The poet has been influenced by the early prophets. The נהר v.⁵ᵃ, according to 𝕳 and Vrss., is the river of Zion, with its canals, פלגים, and reminds of Is. 8⁵ˢᵍ· and 33²¹; but it was prob., as attached to v.⁴, the stream of the sea, and the פלגים were used figuratively, as Ps. 1³, although the watercourses of Hezekiah, 2 K. 20²⁰ were prob. in the poet's mind. This Ps. is used in the Latin Church in the ritual of the consecration of a church or altar. Luther's choral, *Ein feste Burg ist unser Gott*, is based on it.

Str. I. has three couplets; the second line of each, starting from the syn. idea, amplifies and intensifies it in stairlike advance. — **2.** *Yahweh*], original divine name of Ps., for which *God* was substituted in 𝕰, also v.⁵·⁶ᵃ·ᵇ·¹¹. — *is ours*], belonging to us, our own; weakened in EVˢ. into " our," which, moreover, obscures the force of the cæsura in the middle of the line. — *a refuge*], to whom His people may resort, ‖ *strength*], the place of it, the source of it, ‖ *help*]. Yahweh Himself is all this, in *troubles*, as subsequently explained, first as caused by a severe earthquake, and then by warlike commotions of the nations. — *to be found abundantly*], that is, not to be anxiously sought and difficult to reach, but accessible, to the full extent of the need. — **3.** *Therefore we will not fear*], because there is a sure resort from all danger. — *though the earth roar*], with the loud rumbling sound of earthquake. By an early coypist's mistake, the verb was mistaken for another, meaning " change," 𝕳, EVˢ., moved from one place to another ‖ *mountains totter*], so severely shaken that they totter and fall *into the heart of the sea*. The poet had probably witnessed such an earthquake, and seen portions of Mt. Carmel falling into the Mediterranean Sea. — **4.** *The seas roar, their waters foam*], by the effect of the earthquake itself, and the masses of rock and soil falling into them. By an ancient copyist's mistake the measure has been destroyed by the omission of "seas," because of its closing the previous line ; and the remaining noun has thus become the subject of both verbs, as in EV⁸. — *Mountains shake*], those portions that have not tumbled into the sea. — *with the swelling of its stream*]. Great waves come in from the sea, produced frequently by such an earthquake, and, swelling up against the mountains, dash against them with so much power as to shake them to their foundations. An ancient copyist has made an error in dividing the verses, attaching "stream" to the following verse, destroying the measure of both verses and changing their thought.

The Rf. has been omitted after v.⁴, because unimportant in liturgical use ; but it was originally at the close of this Str. as well as of the others, v⁸·¹². — *Yahweh*] has been preserved in the refrains by 𝔈, though changed for God in the Strs. ; but *God of Hosts*, the older form, is also needed for the measure. *God* was probably omitted by the editor of 𝔎, otherwise 𝔈 would have preserved it. — *God of Jacob*], the ancient poetic title of God, characteristic of 𝔎, 𝔄. — *is with us*], companionship, especially for help. Indeed, that was the original meaning of the divine name, " Yahweh," acc. to Ex. 3¹²⁻¹⁵ (E), BD*B*., cf. Is. 8¹⁰, and " Immanuel," Is. 7¹⁴. — *our high tower*], as Pss. 9¹⁰ 18³, RV.ᵐ. The "refuge" of EV⁸. weakens the metaphor.

Str. II. has also three couplets which are stairlike in character. —**5.** *His brooks*], not those of the stream, which latter really belong to the previous Str., as the stream of the sea ; but those of Yahweh Himself ; and thus figurative of the rich blessings of His favour to His city. The poet had in mind the watercourses built by Hezekiah, bringing water from the Wady Urtas to Jerusalem, and distributing it into several brooks and ponds, cf. Is. 8⁵ ˢᵉ𝓺· 2 K. 20²⁰, also Ps. 1³. — *make glad the city of Yahweh*], Jerusalem, the capital of the Davidic dynasty and of Yahweh Himself, whose temple, or palace, made it sacred. — *The holy place of the tabernacle*], combining the two ideas of the dwelling-place and the consecrated place. — '*Elyon*], most High, the poetic divine name, as 47³, cf. 57³ 78⁵⁶. — **6.** *Yahweh is in her midst*], dwelling in her in His palace and capital. The poet has the same thought here as

Zp. 3[15], and the historical situation is probably the same. — *she cannot be made to totter*], resuming the thought of the earthquake of v.[36], preparatory to that of the commotion of the nations. — *at the turn of the morn*], as the morning turns in to take the place of the night. The night is the time of gloom, the morn of redemption, as 30[6] 90[14]. — **7.** *Nations roared*]. The Scythian hosts, by their rapid invasion of Western Asia, were like the waves of an earthquake in the effect upon the nations, Zp. 1–2. — *kingdoms tottered*], falling into ruins. It was all the work of Yahweh Himself, as Zp. declares. — *Has He uttered His voice*], in this the great day of His historic judgment upon the nations, cf. 68[34]. — *the earth melteth*], in terror, as Am. 9[5], cf. Ez. 21[20], Pss. 75[4] 107[26].

Str. III. has three couplets of the same stairlike parall. — **9.** *Come, behold*], emphatic summons. — *the works of Yahweh*], the works He has wrought, the deeds He has done. These are defined as *desolations* in the earth, the destruction of kingdoms and nations by the invading hordes. All this is preparatory to a better future, in which universal peace will prevail. — **10.** *He is causing wars to cease*], by destroying the warlike nations and the kingdoms which have waged war against the city of God in the past. — *unto the ends of the earth*], to remote regions this destruction has extended. The instruments of war are destroyed, as in earlier prophets, Ho. 2[20] Is. 9[4] Mi. 4[1-4], cf. Ez. 39[9-10], which refers to an eschatological invasion of a similar kind. An additional line has been added by a later editor to emphasise this destruction, but at the expense of the measure and symmetry of Str., *Wagons He burneth in the fire*. — **11.** *Desist*], that is, from war. These are the words of Yahweh addressed to the nations, — *and know*], the fact *that it is I, Yahweh*, who am doing all this, and it is vain to resist me. This is not a recognition of God as God, which in Vrss. is due to the substitution of "Elohim" for Yahweh by 𝕰. — *I shall be exalted*], repeated for emphasis; that is, in majesty, and the exhibition of it in the deeds above described, — *among the nations* ‖ *in the earth*], among all nations and throughout the entire world.

2. וְמָצָא] Niph. ptc., Ew., De., Moll., Bä.; but Hu., Pe., Du., pf. 𝕲 ταῖς εὑρούσαις ἡμᾶς is paraphrase. — **3.** בְּהָמִיר] inf. cstr. מור not used in Qal; Hiph. *change, alter,* BDB. Bä. supplies in thought *ihre Stätte;* Du. גֵּוָיָה. Aq., Σ,

ἀλλάσσεσθαι, 𝔍 *cum fuerit translata terra.* But 𝕲 ἐν τῷ ταράσσεσθαι τὴν
γῆν favours בְּהֵמֹת here as יהמו v.⁴, המו v.⁷. This gives a better mng., the *roar*
of the earthquake. — בְּלֵב] *into the midst,* as Ex. 15⁸ Ez. 27²⁷, cf. Jon. 2⁴. —
4. יֶהֱמוּ] Qal impf. concessive, carrying on inf. with בְּ. For המה *v.* 39⁷. —
יֶחְמְרוּ] in emph. coördination. † חמר vb. Qal, *ferment, boil, foam,* elsw. of
wine 75² (?). Pe'al'al of *bowels* La. 1²⁰ 2¹¹. The l. is defective in measure.
Both vbs. need subjs. in tetrameter. ימים has been omitted by haplog. because of its occurrence at close of previous l. — בְּגַאֲוָתוֹ] for בגאות נהר, necessary for measure. נהר has been attached by error to next l., making it too long.
נהר is the stream of the sea, as 93³ 98⁸. — **5.** קֹדֶשׁ] *holy place,* for קְרֶשׁ, as Σ, 𝔍;
𝔖 קְרֹשׁ as adj. ; 𝕲 ἡγίασεν = חֵרֵשׁ, *consecrate,* with עֶליון subj., so Bä., Du., is
opposed by usage of Pss. — מִשְׁכָּנָי] *a.λ.* for מִשְׁכְּנֹת improb. 𝕲, 𝖁, Houb.,
Horsley, Bä., Du., משכנו still leaves l. defective; rd. משכן יהוה; יהוה omitted
by 𝕰. — **6.** לִפְנֵיה] inf. cstr. לְ temporal. — **7.** נָתַן בְּקוֹלִי] as 68³⁴ for usual
נתן קול 18¹⁴. — **8.** יהוה צבאות] so v.¹², shortened by 𝕰 from older י׳ אלהי צבאות,
which the measure requires. — **9.** לְכוּ חֲזוּ כְּפְעֻלֹּת יהוה] cited by 66⁵ לכו וראו
מִפְעֲלוֹת אלהים. Imv. without copula more emphatic. חזו more graphic than
ראו. † מִפְעֲלִית not used elsw. אלהים was probably in text of 46⁹ 𝕰 when cited
by 66⁵; but in 𝕴 it was יהוה, and singularly enough a later copyist restored it,
doubtless because of its use in Rfs. — שַׁמּוֹת] ‡ שָׁמָה n.f. (1) obj. of astonish-
ment and horror, Dt. 28³⁷, 𝕲 τέρατα, 𝖘, Hu., Ew., Pe., Bä. ; (2) better, *desolations* Ps. 73¹⁹ Is. 5⁹ Ho. 5⁹ Je. 2¹⁵, 𝔍, Calv., Dr. — **10.** עֲגָלוֹת] *carts,* always
for transportation, *B*DB., dub. 𝕲 θυρεούς, 𝖁 *scuta,* 𝕮 עֲגָלין, cf. Aram. עֲגִיל,
round shield. This l. is trimeter and excessive to the Str. and is doubtless a
gl. of intensification.

PSALM XLVII., 5 STR. 4³.

Ps. 47 is a temple hymn for the Feast of Trumpets : (1) **a call
to the festival in praise of Yahweh, the great King (v.²⁻³),** who has
subdued the nations and chosen Jerusalem as His inheritance v.⁴⁻⁵).
In triumphal procession He enters the temple, with singers and
musicians (v.⁶⁻⁷). The call is renewed to make melody to the
enthroned King of nations (v.⁸⁻⁹). The nobles of the nations unite
with the people of Yahweh in exalting Him (v.¹⁰).

> A LL ye peoples, clap the hand,
>   Shout to (Yahweh) with the sound of jubilation ;
>   For 'Elyon is awe-inspiring,
>   A great King over all the earth.
> H E subdued peoples under (Him),
>   And nations under (His) feet.
>   He chose (His) inheritance,
>   The excellency of Jacob which He loves.

(YAHWEH) came up with a shout,
    Yahweh with the sound of the horn :
    Make melody to (Yahweh), make melody;
    Make melody to our King, make melody.
MAKE melody to Yahweh with a Maskil;
    For He is King of all the earth.
    (Yahweh) reigns over the nations.
    He is enthroned on His holy throne.
THE nobles of the people assemble,
    (With) the people of the God of Abraham;
    For to (Yahweh) belong the shields of the earth,
    Greatly exalted is ('Elyon).

Ps. 47 was in 𝕽, 𝕸, 𝕰, and 𝕯𝕽 (*v.* Intr. §§ 28, 31, 32, 33). It was prob. composed for the procession in the temple at the Feast of Trumpets. V.⁴ depends on 18⁴⁸ = 144²; the Aramaism ירבר, prob. a substitution for an earlier יורד, as in 18⁴⁸, cf. 2 S. 22⁴⁸. גאון יעקב. V.⁵ depends on Am. 6⁸ 8⁷ Na. 2⁸. בחר, אהב, v.⁵, are terms of D. שופר, תרועה, v.⁶, the new moon of seventh month, cf. Lv. 25⁹. זמר משכיל, v.⁸, implies a kind of Ps. known only to the earlier Minor Psalters, before 𝕰, 𝕯𝕽. כסא קרשו, v.⁹, cf. Pss. 89¹⁵ (= 97²) 93² 103¹⁹. אלהי אברהם, v.¹⁰, phr. of 𝕵 elsw. 1 K. 18³⁶ 1 Ch. 29¹⁸ 2 Ch. 30⁶. מגני, v.¹⁰, for nobles cf. 89¹⁹. The עמים take part in temple processions, as Ps. 87. The conception of Yahweh as king of nations is as Pss. 96–100. The hymns of Is.² are at the basis of all these. The Ps. implies peaceful times of friendliness with the nations, subsequent to Nehemiah, but in the Persian period. It is the New Year's Ps. of the Synagogue, the proper Ps. for Ascension day of the Church.

Str. I. has two syn. couplets. — **2.** *All ye peoples*], vocative, Israel calling upon the foreign peoples, cf. v.⁴ᵃ˙¹⁰ᵃ ; ‖ *nations*, v.⁴ᵇ˙⁹ᵃ, to unite with him in celebrating the triumph of *Yahweh*, for which 𝕰 substituted the divine name *Elohim*. The celebration is to be in the temple, with rhythmic accompaniment, expressed by, — *clap the hand* ‖ *shout with the sound of jubilation*], 42⁵ 66¹ 81² 95¹˙² 98⁴ 100¹ 118¹⁵. — **3.** The reason for this festival is that *'Elyon*, the poetic name of Yahweh, as Most High, is exalted in majesty, and indeed *over all the earth*. He is *awe-inspiring*], to be revered and regarded as majestic. — *A great King*], not only of Israel, but of all nations, universally, cf. 95³ 97⁹ 98⁶ 99⁴.

Str. II. also has two syn. couplets. — **4.** The nations are to celebrate a recent victory of Yahweh, which He has won, doubtless, in overcoming some great oppressor of His people, and of other nations also, who are now rejoicing over their deliverance from the yoke. — *He subdued peoples under Him ‖ under His feet*], so probably in 𝔎, as more suited to the context than "under us," "under our feet," 𝔥, making the triumph that of the people of Israel, which certainly would have been no ground for the rejoicing of foreign nations, and which in fact had no historic realisation until the Maccabean times. Then the victories were so exclusively national and hostile to other nations, that no one would have thought of asking them to share in Israel's triumph. — **5**. *He chose ‖ He loves*], terms of D, Is.[2], to indicate Yahweh's free, sovereign choice of Israel and Zion, out of love. — *His inheritance*], which He would occupy as His residence, changed by the editor to "our inheritance," "for us." — *excellency of Jacob*], as in Am. 6[8] 8[7]; the Holy Land as a land of which Jacob, the poetic name of Israel, might be proud, because of its association with the majestic exaltation of Yahweh Himself.

Str. III. has two syn. couplets. — **6**. *Yahweh came up*], the ascent of the hill of Zion into the temple in triumphal procession, cf. 24[7-10] 68[25-28]. — *with the sound of the horn*], blowing the summons to take part in the triumph. — **7**. *Make melody*], five times repeated to emphasise the instrumental accompaniment.

Str. IV. has a tetrastich of three syn. lines, synth. to the first. — **8-9**. *With a Maskil*], a contemplative song (*v.* Intr. § 26); describing graphically and contemplatively, with practical reverence and praise, the triumph above referred to. The lines in v.[8] have been transposed by copyist's error. The first line resumes the thought of v.[7], the last introduces that of v.[9]. — *King of all the earth*], as v.[3b], ‖ *reigns over the nations ‖ enthroned on His holy throne*]. It is not clear whether the poet is thinking of the heavenly throne, or the throne room of the temple; probably the latter, because of the procession up into the temple of v.[6], and the assemblage in the temple of v.[10].

Str. V. has two synth. couplets. — **10**. *The nobles*], foreign nobles, ‖ *shields*], for shield bearers, the princely warriors, cf. 89[19]. — *with*], together with, omitted by early copyist because of identity of letters with following word, and so the connection became difficult, and is variously, but unsatisfactorily, explained. — *the people of the God of Abraham*], the people of Israel, who by inheritance serve the God of their first father, Abraham. — *'Elyon*], in the last line has been omitted by prosaic copyist at the expense of the measure. — *He is greatly exalted*], as the great King, v.³, victorious, v.⁴, and making His triumphant entrance into His sanctuary, v⁶, and to His throne, v.⁹.

3. יהוה עליון] יהוה in 𝔈 is always suspicious. It is not needed for measure, and is doubtless a later insertion. So also in v.⁶ᵇ it was substituted for אלהים of 𝔈 by the same hand. The יהוה of the original Ps. of 𝕽 elsw. v.²ᵇ·⁶ᵃ·⁷ᵃ·⁸ᵇ·⁹ᵃ·¹⁰ᶜ was changed to אלהים. — **4.** יַדְבֵּר] Hiph. juss. Aram. רבר, *lead*, elsw. 18¹⁸, txt. err. for Hiph. ירד as 2 S. 22¹⁸ Ps. 144², so here יירד. — וַחְתִּינוּ] later Maccabean change for the original הֹהַיר which the context demands; so רַגְלֵינוּ for רגליו. — **5.** נַחֲלָתֵנוּ] 𝔅, 𝔍; 𝕲, 𝔙, have preserved נחלתו the original form. — **7.** אלהים] 𝕲 אלהינו, was assimilated to מלכנו. The original of 𝕽 was יהוה. — **9.** אלהיב]. The first is for an original יהוה as usual, but the second is gl., making l. too long. — יְחֵא קָרְשׁוֹ] phr. a.λ. — **10.** נְם אֱלֵהֵי אַבְרָהָם] 𝔅, 𝔍, but 𝕲 μετὰ = עָם; both needed for sense and prob. original, the texts, because of identity of letters, retaining variously one of them. — קָוְגֵי־אָרֶץ]. 𝕲 οἱ κραταιοί, 𝔙 *fortes*, the warrior shield-bearers, for the shields themselves, doubtless correct. — מְאֹד נַעֲלָה]. The measure requires another word, prob. a divine name, which must have fallen out very early, for 𝕲, Aq., 𝔍, translate vb. as pl. agreeing with מגני ארץ. Gr., Bi., Bä., Du., add from 97⁹ עַל כל אלהים; but this could have been omitted with difficulty, and would make the l. too long.

PSALM XLVIII., 4 STR. 4⁵.

Ps. 48 is a temple song of the late Persian period : Praise of Yahweh, the high tower, in His royal city (v.²⁻⁴) ; who in olden times had put to flight hostile kings, giving assurance that He establisheth it forever (v.⁵⁻⁹) ; praise, extending throughout the earth, of His kindness and righteousness, giving joy to the city and its daughters (v.¹⁰⁻¹²) ; admiration of its fortifications, telling to posterity that such is Yahweh forever (v.¹³⁻¹⁵).

GREAT and highly to be praised in the city is our God.
　His holy Mount is beautiful in elevation, the joy of the whole earth ;
　Mount Zion on the northern ridge is a royal city ;
　Yahweh doth strive in her citadels, is known for a high tower.
FOR lo, the kings assembled ; they passed on together ;
　They saw, so they were amazed ; they were dismayed, they fled in alarm.
　Trembling seized them there, writhing as a woman in travail.
　We heard, so we saw ; Yahweh establisheth it forever.
WE ponder Thy kindness, Yahweh, in the midst of Thy palace.
　As is Thy name, so is Thy praise unto the ends of the earth.

Thy right hand is full of righteousness; Mount Zion rejoices,
The daughters of Judah exult because of Thine acts of judgment.
Go about Zion and encircle her, count her towers,
Set your mind upon her ramparts, distinguish her citadels;
That ye may tell (this) to the generation following,
That such is Yahweh our God forever and ever.

Ps. 48 was originally a שׁיר, then used by 𝕱, 𝕽, and subsequently by 𝕰 *v*
Intr. §§ 24, 28, 31, 32. In 𝕲 it is assigned to the second day of the week for
the Jewish Egyptian rite. V.² is cited in 96⁴ 145³, v.¹² in 97⁸. V.³ is dependent
on La. 2¹⁵, v.⁷ on Ex. 15¹⁵ Je. 13²¹, but Is. 33¹⁴ is probably later. V.⁹ יכוננה =
Ps. 87⁵, of similar date if not same author. V.¹⁴ = 78⁴, both dependent on Dt.
29²¹. It is therefore subsequent to D and Je. It is a royal Ps., as 46–47 and
96–100, but earlier than the latter group. The terms v.²⁻³· ¹⁰· ¹²· ¹³· ¹⁴ indicate that
the temple was standing and the city well fortified and strong. The phrases v.³
imply an author accustomed to admire the temple mount from the south. The
city had been in peril from kings who had been thrown into a panic and disastrous flight, v.⁵⁻⁷. This is an historical reference to the army of Sennacherib,
2 K. 19. There is no ground for descending later than the late Persian times.
The Ps. is a proper Ps. for Whitsunday.

Str. I. has a syn. and a synth. couplet. — **2-3.** *Great*], in the
magnitude of His power and authority, and, as v.³ implies, in His
royalty, cf. 47³ 95³. — *and highly to be praised*], as 96⁴ 145³,
for reasons to be assigned. — *in the city* ‖ *Mount Zion* ‖ *royal
city*], v.³, cf. v.⁹· ¹²· ¹³; Jerusalem, the capital and residence of
Yahweh. By misinterpretation, at an early date, *our God*, the
proper subject of the clause, was connected with the city in 𝕳
and all Vrss., probably owing to the influence of the gloss, v.⁹;
and so it became necessary to insert a new subject, " Yahweh,"
which in 𝕰 is always dubious. The capital city suggests the royal
residence in the palace or temple, cf. v.¹⁰, and so *His holy Mount*,
the sacred mountain on which the temple was situated, — *Mount
Zion on the northern ridge*], the temple being on the northeastern
corner or back of Mount Zion, — *is beautiful in elevation*], looked
at from the south. The temple rises up in lofty majesty and
lordly beauty, the royal city by eminence, because it was the exact
place in the city where Yahweh Himself resided in the throne-room
of the temple. There are no good reasons for thinking of spiritual
elevation, as Is. 2² = Mi. 4¹, or of a comparison with the Oriental
Olympus, Is. 14¹³, as Hi., Ew., Kirk. — *the joy of the whole earth*],
cf. La. 2¹⁵ Is. 60¹⁵, giving joy to all nations, and invoking praise unto

the ends of the earth, v.[11]; not to be confined to the land of Palestine. — 4. 𝔥 and Vrss. all have "great king," but such a phr. is unknown elsewhere with רב, and there was no sufficient reason to abandon the usual phr. with גדול. The word is indeed needed for the measure of the next line, and so it is best explained as Qal pf. of verb. — *doth strive*], of the warlike king striving with the hostile kings, and so introductory to Str. II. — *is known*], not by reputation, but practically by valiant deeds in defeat of the enemy and in defending His people, — *for a high tower*], in which they have obtained sure refuge and defence, cf. 46[8. 12], where the same metaphor is used in the same circumstances. — *in her citadels*], where the real defence is made by warlike bravery and skill, cf. v.[14].

Str. II. has a synth. tetrastich. — **5.** *For lo*], introducing graphic description of the campaign of hostile kings against Jerusalem, doubtless referring to the siege by the army of Sennacherib, 2 K. 19. The several stages of the campaign are represented by the several verbs, which follow one another in rapid succession. — *assembled*], by appointment, gathering from different parts at a designated place to undertake the campaign. — *passed on*], of the onward march, — *together*], as a united, organised host, moving under one direction and with one purpose. — **6.** *They*], the very ones, emphatic, demonstrative, — *saw*] the city, its defences, its defenders, and something more which is not indicated, that made them pause. — *so they were amazed*], the amazement is balanced with the seeing, corresponding with it, implying that they saw with amazement something that seriously alarmed them, some manifestation of Yahweh. The author is thinking of a theophany that frightened them and threw them into a panic. — *they fled in alarm*], cf. Cæsar's *veni, vidi, vici*, Calv., of which this is the very reverse. The poet has in mind panics caused by theophanies, cf. Ex. 15 Ju. 5, as is evident also from his dwelling on their terror. — **7.** *Trembling seized them*], as it did the nations of Canaan, Ex. 15[14-16]. — *writhing as a woman in travail*], as it did Damascus, Je. 49[24], and Judah before the conquering armies of Babylon, Je. 13[21]. The description is complete and perfect ; but a glossator thought to enrich it by another exhibition of the power of Yahweh, not connected with the previous history. — **8.** *With the east wind Thou breakest the ships of Tarshish*], which, how-

ever, is the use of God's power on the sea, rather than in warlike
deeds. — **9**. *We heard*], that is, by tradition from our fathers;
strengthened by prosaic copyist by prefixing " as," or " according
as," to emphasise more strongly the resemblance in present experience as described in v.²⁻⁴. — *so we saw*]. The past and the
present entirely correspond. — *Yahweh establisheth it forever*], as
in the past and in the present, so in the future, the city of Yahweh
will stand firm and be a sure stronghold against its enemies. A
late editor, at the expense of the measures, inserts, *in the city of
Yahweh Sabaoth ‖ in the city of our God.*

Str. III. has a synth. and a syn. couplet. — **10–12**. *We ponder*], literally, compare things that are like, and so consider them.
— *Thy kindness*], as exhibited to the people, for it is *in the midst
of Thy palace*, the temple ; and yet the renown of it extends *unto
the ends of the earth*], throughout all the earth, cf. v.³. — *As is
Thy name*] ; the divine honour and glory as celebrated, balanced
as coequal and coextensive with *Thy praise.* — *Thy right hand*],
as stretched forth to bestow, its palms filled, *full of righteousness*,
probably vindicatory and redemptive of His city, antith. *acts of
judgment* against the enemies, so comprehending as the grounds
of praise both Strs. I. and II., and thus the reason why *Mount
Zion ‖ the daughters of Judah*, the dependent cities, *rejoice ‖
exult.*

Str. IV. has a syn. and a synth. couplet. — **13–14**. *Go about*]
round about ‖ *encircle*, make a complete round of the city. The
reason for this circuit is the inspection, the thorough examination
of the defences, *her towers ‖ her ramparts*, or bulwarks ‖ *her citadels*, as v.⁴. The inspection is graphically described as, — *count*],
their number, — *set your mind upon*], give close attention to, —
distinguish], give separate consideration to each one, noting its
special characteristics, so probably the original, as 𝕲 or 𝕵. But
owing to textual error a form appears in 𝔥 which is variously
explained as " traverse," RV.ᵐ ; " pass between," *B*DB. ; " go to
and fro between," Dr. But some such word as *consider*, of AV.,
RV., Kirk., is required by context. — *that ye may tell*], relate, as
22³¹. This is required for measure and sense, referring to previous
contents of Ps. — *to the generation following*], as Dt. 29²¹ Ps. 78⁴·⁶
102¹⁹ ; transmit it from one generation to another. As the poet's

generation has heard it from the fathers, cf. 44², so they are to
tell it to their children. — **15.** *That such is Yahweh our God*],
such as has been described above, — *forever and ever*], a sort of
Rf., as v.⁹. The closing words of 𝔥, " He will be our guide unto
death," are not in 𝔊, and are a gloss.

2. [יהוה] in 𝔈 as usual, late insertion. — [בְּעִיר] should not be cstr. before
אֱלֹהֵינוּ, but abs. and pointed בָּעִיר. אלהינו was the original subj., displaced by
יהוה. And so the pentameter is restored. — [הַר קָדְשׁוֹ] begins second l. —
3. [יְפֵה נוֹף] phr. a.λ. 𝔊 εὐριζῶν, Aq. καλῷ βλαστήματι, 𝔍 *specioso germini* as
Aram. נוֹף, *branch of tree, bough*. It might be rendered *beautiful plant*, cf. צמח
for the fertile land Is. 4², and for the king Je. 23⁵ 33¹⁵ cf. Zc. 6⁹⁻¹⁵; but more
prob. in accord. with context נוֹף is *elevation*, *B*DB. after Arab. analogies ;
cf. כלילת יפי La. 2¹⁵. — [יַרְכְּתֵי צָפוֹן] cf. Is. 14¹³, where הַר מוֹעֵד is the Oriental
Olympus ; here most prob. *northern back* of Mt. Zion, the seat of the temple,
contemplated from the south. — [רָב] 𝔥, Vrss., adj. with מֶלֶךְ, but without support in usage and against the measure. It is needed as Qal pf. vb. רִיב, *strive*,
in the next l. — **4.** ‡ [אַרְמְנוֹתֶיהָ] *her citadels*, rather than palaces, as v.¹⁴, cf.
122⁷ Am. 6⁸ La. 2⁵·⁷ Ho. 8¹⁴ Mi. 5⁴. — **5.** [הַפְּלָכִים] 𝔈 *reges terrae* is interpretation. — **8.** [אֳנִיּוֹת תַּרְשִׁישׁ] as Is. 2¹⁶ 23¹ +, destroyed by divine judgment ;
not ships belonging to or bound for Tarshish, but great ships such as made
this distant voyage. This v. is a gl. — **9.** [כַּאֲשֶׁר] prosaic addition, injuring
the measure ; no more needed here than in v.⁶. — [בְּעִיר יהוה צְבָאוֹת] is a gl.
enlarging the l. without reason and introducing the divine name יהוה against
the usage of 𝔈. — [בְּעִיר אלהינו] also a gl. — **10.** [דִּמִּינוּ] Pi. pf. דמה, *compare*,
liken, ponder, 50²¹ (prob. *17⁴*) Is. 10⁷. — [בְּקֶרֶב הֵיכָלֶךָ] 𝔥, 𝔍 ; but 𝔊 ἐν μέσῳ
τοῦ λαοῦ σου improb. ; λαοῦ early error in 𝔊 for ναοῦ. — **11.** † [קַצְוֵי אֶרֶץ]
n.[m.] only this phr., elsw. 65⁶ Is. 26¹⁵, both with כל. — **12.** [יִשְׂמַח הַר־צִיּוֹן] belongs to previous clause ‖ תגלנה בנות יהודה, phr. elsw. 97⁸ which has cited this
l., adding יהוה, given here also by 𝔊, but not by 𝔥, 𝔍. — **13.** [סֹבּוּ] Qal imv.
סבב in sense of *go about*, only here and *17¹¹* in ψ ; elsw. *turn about* 114⁸·⁵,
surround 18⁶ 22¹⁸·¹⁷ 49⁶ + ; in Po. however, *march, go about*, 55¹¹ 59⁷·¹⁵, in
processions 26⁶. — **14.** [חֵילָה] a.λ. err. for חֵילָהּ ; 𝔊 εἰς τὴν δύναμιν αὐτῆς. —
[פַּסְּגוּ] a.λ. *traverse, pass between*, *B*DB., cf. Aram. פסע, *tread ;* but 𝔊 κατα-
διέλεσθε, 𝔍 *separate* = הפלו, Hiph. פלה, *distinguish ;* Gr., Che., פקרו improb.
— **15.** [הוּא יְנַהֲגֵנוּ עַל מוּת] 𝔥, 𝔍, but not 𝔊 ; is a gl. עַל מוּת might be for
עַל עֲלָמוֹת as 46¹, a musical direction, appended as Hb. 3 ; but this Ps. was not
in 𝔻𝔎, which alone makes these additions. It might belong to Ps. 49 𝔻𝔎,
as Horsley, Bä., Che., al., if it could be thought suitable. The other words
would then be expl. addition.

PSALM XLIX., 2 STR. 14³, RFS. 2³.

**Ps. 49 was a lament of the pious over the riddle of death.
(1) Complaint to God of experience of the iniquity of the rich
(v.⁶⁻⁷), who yet cannot ransom themselves from death (v.⁸·¹⁰); the
wise and the foolish alike die and their graves become their everlasting home (v.¹¹⁻¹²). (2) Those who are self-satisfied are assigned
to the dominion of death in Sheol, and continually waste away
(v.¹⁴⁻¹⁵); therefore the rich should not be feared, for they must
abandon their wealth in death, however much they may have congratulated themselves on their possessions; and never more shall
they see the sunlight (v.¹⁷⁻²⁰). The Rf. states the enigma: man
like the beasts abideth not (v.¹³·²¹). An introductory gloss calls
all the world to meditation upon the enigma (v.²⁻⁵). Intermediate
glosses represent that the ransom from death is too costly for man
to pay (v.⁹), but that Yahweh will ransom the righteous (v.¹⁶).**

WHY should I fear in evil days,
 When my deceitful (foes) encompass me with iniquity;
 They that trust in their wealth,
 And boast of the abundance of their riches.
 Man cannot at all give ransom,
 Cannot give to Yahweh His price,
 That he should live forever,
 (And) not see the Pit.
 The wise die together,
 The stupid and brutish perish,
 And abandon to successors their wealth;
 Their graves are their homes forever,
 Their dwelling places to all generations,
 Theirs whose names are upon lands.
  Man in worth abideth not,
  He is to be compared to beasts that are no more.
THIS is the way of them that have self-confidence,
 And the latter end of them that are pleased with their portion.
 They are as a flock that are put in Sheol,
 Death is their shepherd and their ruler;
 Every morning their form wasteth away,
 In Sheol, far from the lofty dwelling.
 Fear not, when one groweth rich,
 When the glory of the house is increased;
 For he cannot take it all in his death,
 His glory cannot descend after him.
 Though in his life-time he congratulated his soul,

> And lauded it because it was doing well to itself;
> It will go to the generation of his fathers,
> Who forever see not daylight.
>> *Man in worth abideth not,*
>> *He is to be compared to beast. hat are no more.*

Ps. 49 was taken up into 𝔐, then into 𝔈 and 𝔇𝔎 from 𝔎 (*v.* Intr. §§ 28, 31, 32, 33). It resembles 73: (*a*) שׁחת √ שׁתת v.[15], elsw. only 73[9]; (*b*) (ים)רָבְקָר v.[15], prob. same use as 73[14]; (*c*) אֲחֲרִיהֶם v.[14], p.ob. error for אַחֲרֵיהֶם = 73[17]; (*d*) use of בַּעַר v.[11] = 73[22]; (*e*) בְּחֵמוֹת v.[13, 21], cf. 73[22]; (*f*) use of לָקַח v.[16], for taking of righteous by God, prob. a gl.; cf. 73[24]; (*g*) besides, there is the same essential tone and situation throughout the Ps. V.[1-5] also resemble 78[1-3] in the general appeal, and especially in the use of מָשָׁל and חִידָה, although in the former the appeal is to the world, in the latter to the people of God. This introductory Str. has also terms of WL. הַכְמוֹת, תְבוּנוֹת, v.[4]; but חֲכָמִים, כְּסִיל, כֶּסֶל, v.[11, 14] do not imply WL. V.[2] חֶלֶד as in 17[14], the antith. of בְּנֵי אָדָם and בְּנֵי אִישׁ as 62[10]. But these are in introductory Str., which shows most of the evidence of dependence on other Literature. The only other case of dependence is v.[7], which implies 52[9] 𝔇. Ps. 49 is so different from all others of 𝔎 and so much more like Pss. of 𝔄, that it would be classed with the latter rather than the former, were it not for לִבְנֵי קֹרַח in title. But it is quite possible that an early copyist unconsciously made this mistake, because this Ps. followed 42–48, all 𝔎, notwithstanding that it was followed by 50 of 𝔄. The antith. between the wicked rich and th⸱ pious poor implies a commercial situation, either the Greek period, if the writer lived in Palestine, or possibly a late Persian period, if he lived in the Diaspora. The latter is more probable, if it be a Ps. of 𝔄. The former is difficult to reconcile with the date of 𝔎 as determined from a study of all the other Pss. of 𝔎. 𝔍 inserts in title appropriately *vox ecclesiae super lazaro et divite purpurato.* The use of שׁחת v.[10] for the Pit of Sheol with ראה as 16[10] is not earlier than Ez.; but זְבֻל v.[15] is an early word, I K. 8[18] Hb. 3[11] Is. 63[15]. On the whole the Ps. is best explained as originally of 𝔄.

The Ps. has an introductory Str. of a later date. It is composed of two syn. tetrastichs.

> Hear this, all ye peoples!
> Give ear, all ye inhabitants of the age!
> Both sons of mankind and sons of men,
> Rich and poor together!
> My mouth will speak holy wisdom,
> And the meditation of my mind will be sound understanding;
> I shall incline mine ear to a parable,
> I shall open upon the lyre mine enigma.

— **2–5.** *Hear this, all ye peoples,* ‖ *all ye inhabitants of the age*], of the duration of the world, 17[14]; analysed in antith. classes; *both sons* *of mankind*, the common people, ‖ *poor; and sons of men*, those of position and station, ‖ *rich*, cf. 62[10]; and all these *together*, in a like situation, needing common instruction. They are summoned to *hear this*], that which is to follow, ‖ *give ear to* — the *holy wisdom*], wisdom in its abstract, intensive sense, as summed up in sacred things and relations, ‖ *sound understanding*], complete, entire, and perfect, to be set forth in a *parable*], which, in the OT. sense, is a comparative, emblematic, shrewd saying, ‖ *mine enigma*], one that involves a difficult, puzzling question, such as the Rfs., v.[13. 21]. The poet is about to give utterance to such a poem. — *My mouth*, emphatic, *will speak*, ‖ *the meditation*], not internal of the mind, but the murmur of the voice in giving expression to the reflection of the mind. On the one side, the poet himself says : *I shall incline mine ear*], to catch the inspiration from the parable, and on the other side, — *I shall open*], explain it, render it as a song to the accompaniment of *the lyre*, with instrumental as well as vocal music.

Str. I. is divided, as usual in fourteen-lined Strs. (cf. Ps. 18), into two parts, of eight and six lines, the former having two tetrastichs, the latter two tristichs. — **6.** *Why should I fear*], remonstrance with oneself. While fear has apparent justification, it has no real basis, as is now to be explained, cf. v.[17]. — *in evil days*]. It is quite true that the times are bad ; *when my deceitful foes encompass me with iniquity*], so essentially 𝔖, Origen, Hi., De., Bä. ; "iniquity of them that would supplant me," RV.[m], JPSV., Dr., Kirk., in accordance with context ; but 𝔊, 𝔍, 𝔖, PBV., AV., refer the iniquity to the singer as a confession of sin, "iniquity of my heels." It is possible that this may have been the interpretation in later Heb. liturgical use ; for such confessions of sin are not uncommon as glosses to Pss. ; but certainly this idea is altogether foreign to the context and thought here. An intermediate position is taken by RV., Pe., "iniquity at my heels," which is a possible translation of MT., but not probable in itself. — **7.** *They that trust in their wealth*]. They had become wealthy by craft and deception, as well as by their iniquity, and having been successful, as such men always are, they had an unlimited confidence in their ability to purchase any and every thing. Accordingly they *boast of the abundance of their riches*], cf. 52[9]. If the rich were correct in their self-

confident boasting (*v.* v.[19]), the poor would have sufficient ground
for fear ; but they are not correct, for wealth cannot purchase the
most essential thing, the life of its possessor, or the ability to enjoy
wealth, or to direct who else shall enjoy it, cf. Ec. 5[13-17]. — **8.** *Man
cannot at all give ransom*], emphatic denial by adding inf. abs. to
the impf. tense of verb. This has been generalized by an early
copyist through the interpretation of "man" as the object of the
verb ; which then seemed to require the insertion of the subj.
"brother" ; but this is awkward, and most moderns give various
unsatisfactory explanations. Man might pay ransom according to
the Law for his life, Ex. 21[30], when his carelessness had been the
occasion of the death of his neighbour. And it was not uncommon
for the rich to purchase exemption from the crime of murder,
though it is prohibited in the Law, Num. 35[31] ; but when Yahweh
demands his life from a man, no ransom is possible : *He cannot
give to Yahweh His price*]. Yahweh cannot be purchased by any
price whatever to relinquish His purpose. — **10.** *That he should
live forever*], continue to live and enjoy his riches in this life,
— *and not see the Pit*], the Pit in Sheol, 16[10] 30[10] 55[24] 103[4], the
dark, gloomy abode of the wicked dead, who suffered punishment
there. EV[s]. perpetuate ancient mistakes in regarding the term
as abstract, "corruption," AV., RV., or "grave," PBV. — **9.** A
later gl., wishing to emphasise this still more, inserted : "Indeed,
the ransom of life is too costly," even for the rich man to pay ; and
therefore he warns him : "desist forever" from such a vain effort
and from confidence in its success. If this v. came from the author it must be parenthetical, but no good explanation of it has
been given. It is of a different measure from the previous and
subsequent lines, and makes the Str. too long. — **11.** *The wise
die*] = not the wise rich men, but the pious wise. This is as much
as to say, that even those possessed of holy wisdom die, and that
— *together*], all together, all alike in a death common to all. A
prosaic copyist, wishing to bring this statement of fact in closer
connection with the rich men of the previous context, prefixed :
"for He seeth that," namely, the wise die ; but this spoils the
measure of both lines, forcing MT. and Vrss. to attach "together"
to the next line, thus making it a tetrameter. — *Stupid and brutish*], in antith. to the wise, those who are stupid and dull, and

so, gross and dumb like the brute, they *perish*], probably in the sense of descending to Abaddon, a syn. of the Pit in Sheol ; and they *abandon their wealth*], cf. v.[18]. They cannot take it with them, can no longer use it ; it has become of no value to them. — *to successors*], any one that may succeed to their property ; not even defined by a suffix, as it might have been, to indicate their own successors, their descendants. — **12**. *Their graves*], so after ᵹ, 𝔙, 𝔖, 𝔗, and most moderns ; "their inward thought," of 𝔥, 𝔍, followed by EV⁸., is due to a copyist's transposition of letters of Heb. word. The former is so suited to the context, and the latter is so unsuitable, that there should be no doubt as to the original. — *are their homes forever*], taking the place of their temporary earthly homes, cf. Ec. 12[5] Tobit 3[6]. — *Their dwelling places to all generations*] ; and this not merely for the poor and pious wise men, and the dull, dumb, brutish men, who have no ability to acquire wealth ; but also for those who have been so exceedingly rich, that they have become great landed proprietors ; *whose names are upon lands*], having their names attached by public recognition to their lands. This has been strengthened, at the expense of the measure, by prefixing the verb "call." — **13**. The Rfs. here and v.[21] sum up the real enigma of the situation : *Man*], the general term for mankind, comprehending all of the race ; and no longer men, as v.[8], referring to men of position and wealth. — *in worth*], preciousness ; carrying on the idea of price of v.[8], and not honour, EV⁸., which is less exact and from a different point of view. — *abideth not*], does not continue to lodge or abide in his lodging place in the world, so 𝔥, Σ, 𝔍, 𝔗 ; but ᵹ, 𝔖, "understandeth not," as v.[21], 𝔥, and all Vrss. It is improbable that the Rf. would differ in this verb. The difference in Heb. is of a single letter, which is an easy copyist's mistake. Though the weight of external testimony is strongly for the latter rendering, the former is supported by still stronger evidence ; for it is much better suited to the context and thought of the entire Ps., and it gives the less frequent Heb. word, and on that account the most difficult reading. — *He is to be compared*], or likened in a simile, — *to beasts*]. In the matter of death the difference between them is slight, if at all. — *that are no more*], both man and beast alike are cut off from life in the world, and have no further existence apart from the abode of the dead.

Str. II. has the same structure as Str. I., save that, on the principle of inclusion, the first six lines are in general correspondence with the last six lines of Str. I. — **14.** *This is the way of them*], the course of life which they pursue, leading on to its goal, — *And the latter end of them*], as 73[17], best suited to the context. But a copyist's error of a single letter, ה for ל, made a difficult text, which is explained in various ways by Vrss., all unsatisfactory ; EV[s]., "their posterity," after Σ, least of all. — *that have self-confidence*], as RV.[m], JPSV., Dr., Kirk., the earlier and usual meaning of Heb. word, more suited to the context than the later meaning, "folly," of EV[s]. — *that are pleased with their portion*], literally their mouthful, the portion for their mouth to enjoy as a delicious morsel ; a conception more frequent in the phrase, "double portion," assigned usually to the first-born son, Dt. 21[17]. The Vrss. and interpreters generally, overlooking this meaning of the Heb. word, and thinking of the more usual meaning, "mouth," paraphrased, as 𝔊, or thought of speech of the mouth, as EV[s]. after Σ ; or interpreted the Heb. verb as another form, with the meaning "run," as Aq. ; all thinking of others than the wicked rich men of the previous line, and so impairing the strength of the syn. couplet. — **15.** *They are as a flock*], simile, as 42[1], followed by relative clause. — *that are put in Sheol*], the abode of the dead being conceived as their fold, in which they are shut up for the night. — *Death*], personified, — *is their shepherd*], as 𝔊, RV., JPSV. ; possibly antith. to Yahweh Himself, as the shepherd of His people, 23[1] 80[2] 95[7]. AV., "feed on them," is a slight improvement on PBV., "gnaweth," which, though possible, as justified by a rare usage of the verb, 80[14], with the conception that death is a wild beast, is not suited to the context, and is improbable in itself. — *and their ruler*], having dominion over them. A later glossator, misled by a copyist's mistake in writing sg. "morning," for pl. "mornings," and thinking of the morning of the Messianic day of the redemption of Israel, and then interpreting the verb as referring to the dominion of the righteous over the wicked, inserted his explanation in the text, at the expense of the measure and the syntax, making the passage a crux to all subsequent interpreters. The original was really, *every morning*, continually, as 73[14], belonging to the next line to complete its measure. — *their form*], figure, the shape and appear-

ance of their disembodied being; not to be paraphrased into
"beauty," EV⁸., or to be regarded as a poetic reference to their
bodies, mouldering in the grave, Kirk. — *wasteth away*], becoming old and worn out by age and decay, cf. Jb. 14¹⁰⁻²². — *Sheol*]
belongs to the following line, 𝕲, 𝕵, PBV., AV., as the measure
requires; and is not the subject of verb, as RV., Pe., Dr., Kirk.
— *far from its lofty dwelling*], that of the form; paraphrased
by 𝕲, 𝖁, and referred to the glory of the rich men themselves.
The dwelling in Sheol, where they are doomed to waste away, is
contrasted with the lordly dwelling of the rich in this life, as in
v.¹², with which v.¹⁵ is parallel. RV., "that there be no habitation
for it," is not justified by the usage of the Heb. word or the context. — **16**. A later editor, possibly 𝕰, wishing to make the Ps.
more useful for public worship, inserted this gloss, asserting the
antithetic beatitude of the righteous, in what is really a prose sentence : "But God will ransom my life from the hand of Sheol, for
He will take me." The interpretation of this passage depends in
great measure upon the view taken of its relation to the context.
The first clause may be interpreted either of ransom from death,
or of ransom from Sheol after death ; but the last clause defines it
as a taking by God, which is suited not to the former, but only to
the latter. The verse probably is based on 73²⁴, and both Pss. on the
story of Enoch, Gen. 5²⁴ (P), which preceded both Pss. in its date
of composition ; cf. also 2 K. 2⁹·¹⁰ Is. 53⁸. It implies the assumption of the righteous dead by God to Himself, to the paradise of
the departed, which developed in later Judaism in antith. to Abaddon or the Pit. Du. and Charles agree with De., among recent
commentators, in this opinion. Most moderns, even A. B. Davidson and Salmond, minimise the Eschatology of the ancient Hebrews, so as to reduce it much below the level of that of the
ancient neighbouring nations. — **17**. Resuming v.⁶ with a selfexhortation, — *Fear not, when one groweth rich ‖ when the glory
of the house is increased*], as the context indicates, and as good
usage occasionally allows, referring to wealth, which indeed is substituted in RV.ᵐ, but without sufficient reason. — **18**. *For he cannot take it all*], with him in his death, when he dies and descends
to Sheol. — *His glory cannot descend after him*], in his train, as
baggage, as it would in his travels in this world. The text resumes

the word "glory" in this clause, and this favours the opinion that
all, the whole, of the previous clause, refers to all his riches ; not
with the implication that he might take some of it with him, but
that he must leave it all behind as no longer of any real worth to
him, as v.⁷⁻⁸,¹¹. — **19.** *Though in his life-time*], in antith. to his death-
time, v.¹⁸ ; resuming the thought of v.⁷. — *he congratulated his soul*],
cf. 62⁵ ; blessing himself for what he had acquired in the wealth in
which he trusted, v.⁷ᵃ ; ‖ *lauded it*], the soul, the self, as such men
usually do, taking all the praise to themselves for their success in
life. — *because it*], the soul, the self, — *was doing well to itself*].
This had been and continued to be its habit during its life-time,
boasting of the abundance of riches, v.⁷ᵇ.   All this really amounts
to nothing, so far as prevention or consolation is concerned ; it
only makes the antith. all the more striking and distressing. —
20. *It*], this very soul, or self, — *will go to the generation of his
fathers*], not simply to the ancestral tomb, for this was not always
the case ; but to the gathering of the fathers in the realm of the
dead, who were regarded as living as nations, tribes, and families,
a shadowy existence, reflecting the associations of this world, cf.
Gn. 15¹⁵. — *Who forever*], these fathers, all departed souls. — *see
not the daylight*], which shines in this world, but does not shine
in the dark and gloomy cavern of Sheol, or its Pit, whither the
wicked rich must go.

2. כָּל־יֹשְׁבֵי־חָלֶד] combined for two tones. חלד, *v. 17*¹⁴. — **3.** בני־איש . . .
בני אדם] men of low degree, common men, antith. men of high degree, of position and influence, as 62¹⁰, *v. 4*³. — **4.** הגות] *a.λ. meditation, musing*, as הגיון 19¹⁵;
why not הגיה Qal inf. cstr. vb.? *v. 1*². — הבונית, חכמות] abstr. intensive pls., terms
of WL., *v.* ‡ תְּבוּנָה n.f. in ψ only (1) *act of understanding* 78⁷² 136⁶; (2) *object
of knowledge*, here and 147⁵.   For חכמה *v. 37*³⁰. — **5.** מָשָׁל] may refer to Ps.
as a whole, the original conception of its author, cf. 78² Nu. 21²⁷⁻³⁰ 1 K. 5¹²,
or to the proverbial saying in Rf. v.¹³,²¹, *v. 44*¹⁵. — ‡ חִידָה] n.f. *riddle, obscure
saying, enigma*, such as the Rf.; elsw. 78² Nu. 12⁸ (JE) Ez. 17² Pr. 1⁶. —
6. וְיֵי רָע] as 94¹³; but 𝔊, Du., יוֹם as Am. 6⁸, prob. only inexactness of translation. — עֲוֹן וְרֵבִי יְסִנֵּי .]. 𝔊, 𝔍, Σ, PBV., AV, יְרֵבִי, *my heels*, with עוֹן cstr.
of subj., *iniquity of*, or *attached to my heels*, implying confession of iniquity ;
an unexampled phr., difficult to understand, modified by RV., Pe., as cstr. of
obj. *at my heels*, in vindictive pursuit, no less unexampled.   *B*DB interprets
עָקֵב adj. vb. *overreacher*, but while possible as a form, it is not used elsw.
Origen, followed by Bä., Ecker, ακουββαει = עֲקֻבַי, *my insidious, deceitful*
(foes), as Je. 17⁹, paraphrased by 𝔖, *mine enemies*, is most probable.   Origen

gives also ιεσουββουνει יִסְבְּנִי 3 pl. for 3 sg. עֵין is therefore, as the context suggests, the iniquity of these enemies. — **7.** עֲלֵי־חֵילָם] is needed for measure. חֵילָם, *their wealth*, as v.¹¹ 62¹¹ 73¹². — **8.** אָח] is suspicious. Usage requires אח . . . אח or אִישׁ . . . אִישׁ. Houb., Ew., Du., Bä., Che., rd. אַך as v.¹⁶, but it is probably a gl. due to the interp. of אִישׁ as obj. of vb. Moreover it makes l. too long. — יִדֶּה] inf. abs. to intensify vb. לא is uncommon before the combination, but cf. Gn. 3⁴ Am. 9⁸. 𝕲 has two clauses, ἀδελφὸς οὐ λυτροῦται, λυτρώσεται ἄνθρωπος, taking אח ‖ אִישׁ. — **9.** וַיֵּחְר] intensive, asseverative with Qal impf. [יֵקַר] *be precious*, of life 72¹⁴ I S. 26²¹ 2 K. I¹³·¹⁴; here its *redemption*. 𝕲 τὴν τιμήν, 𝔍 *pretium* = יְקָר n., so 𝔖. — [וְחָדַל] so 𝔍, but 𝕲 וְנַפְשׁוֹ; both sfs. interpretations. — וְחָדַל] 1 consec. pf. after יֵקָר, but improb. It should be pointed as imv. of exhortation, as 𝔖. The whole l. is a prose gl. or pentameter, which Du. makes into two trimeters by adding from v.¹⁰ ויחי עוד at the cost of syn. parall. of next couplet. — [וִיחִי] 1 subord. with juss. of purpose, dependent on v.⁸. — **11.** [כִּי יִרְאֶה] introductory gl. to connect the two ll. more closely, makes this l. too long. — [וְיֵזְבוּ] 1 consec. pf. — **12.** [קִרְבָּם] 𝕲, 𝔍, 𝔖, ℭ, קברם, so Houb., Kenn., Lowth, Street, Bä., Du., Dr., Kirk., Charles, alone suited to context. — [בָּתֵּימוֹ] archaic sf. for euphony. — [קָרְאוּ] interpretive and expansive gl. inconsistent with לֵמוֹ, archaic and euphonic for לָם, which therefore is original. — **13.** [וְאָדָם] 1, not in v.²¹ and not suited to Rf., is a gl. — † יְקָר] n.m. *preciousness*, as Pr. 20¹⁵ Jb. 28¹⁰ Je. 20⁵ (om. 𝕲) Ez. 22²⁵, of *price* Zc. 11¹³, not *honour* as Est. 1⁴ + 9 t. Est. — [יָלִין] so Σ, 𝔍, ℭ ; but 𝕲, 𝔖, Cap., Houb., Kenn., Lowth, Horsley, Dathe, Ew., יָבִין, as v.²¹. Rfs. must have been alike. External evidence favours the latter, internal the former. — [וְנִדְמוּ] Niph. pf. rel. clause. ‡ דמה, *cut off*, early word Ho. 4⁶ Zp. 1¹¹ Ob.⁵ of people, Ho. 10⁷ of king, Is. 15¹·¹ Je. 47⁵ of city. — **14.** [זֶה] emph. subj. — [לָמוֹ] archaic sf. euphonic. — ‡ [כֵּסֶל] 𝔍 *insipientiae, folly*, as Ec. 7²⁵; cf. v.¹¹; not so prob. as *self-confidence* Ps. 78⁷ Pr. 3²⁶ Jb. 8¹⁴ 31²⁴. 𝕲 σκάνδαλον, 𝔍 *scandalum* = כשׁל improb. — [אַחֲרֵיהֶם]. 𝕲 μετὰ ταῦτα, 𝔍 *postea*, 𝔍 *post eos*, Σ οἱ δὲ μετʼ αὐτοὺς, all improb. Rd. with We., Du., אחריהם ‖ דרכם, as 73¹⁷ Dt. 32²⁰·²⁹ Je. 12⁴ 31¹⁷. — [בְּפִיהֶם] 𝕲 ἐν τῷ στόματι αὐτῶν, 𝔍 *juxta os*, Aq. כפיהם פה is usually interp. as referring to speech, after λόγον of Σ. It is rather *portion*, as mouthful. שְׁנַיִם פּי Dt. 21¹⁷ 2 K. 2⁹ Zc. 13⁸. — [יִרְצוּ]. 𝕲 εὐλογήσουσιν, interp. of רצה as 119¹⁰⁸, but 𝕲^{A.R.T}, Σ, εὐδοκήσουσιν ; Aq., 𝔍, *current*, יָרֻצוּ √רוץ. — **15.** [כַּצֹּאן] simile, followed by rel. clause, as 42². — [שַׁתּוּ] Qal pf. † שׁתת, elsw. 73⁹, = שׁית. 𝕲 ἔθεντο, 𝔍 *positi sunt*, so Aq., Ki., al. — [וַיִּרְדּוּ בָם יְשָׁרִים לַבֹּקֶר] 𝕲 καὶ κατακυριεύσουσιν αὐτῶν οἱ εὐθεῖς τὸ πρωί, so 𝔍. This sentence is tetrameter and leaves the previous and subsequent lines defective, therefore improb. Rd. יִרְדֵּם, and attach it to previous l. to complete it. ‡ רדה, *have dominion*, c. ב Gn. 1²⁶ (P) Ez. 29¹⁵, c. בקרב Ps. 110², acc. pers. Ez. 34⁴, רָדָם Ps. 68²⁸, abs. 72⁸. The change was due to the insertion of the interpretative יְשָׁרִים as gl., and the interp. of לבקר as the morn of the Messianic day when the righteous would rule, an idea much later than our Ps. לבקר, then, belongs to the next l. to complete it, and we should rd. pl. לבקרים, as 73¹⁴ 101⁸. — [צִירָם] Kt. † [צִיר] n.m. *image, idol*, Is. 45¹⁶. Qr. צוּרָם = צוּרָתָם,

their form, ‡ n.f. as Ez. 43¹¹, so 𝔖, 𝔍, *figura*. 𝔊 ἡ βοήθεια αὐτῶν, Σ τὸ κρατερὸν = צור, *rock*, is improb. — לְכַלּוֹת] Pi. inf. cstr. *purpose*. 𝔊 παλαιωθήσεται, 𝔙 *veterascet*, 𝔍 *conteretur*. Rd. prob. Qal, for שׁאול is not connected with this vb. and is needed for next l., as 𝔊, 𝔍, *in Sheol.* — מִזְּבֻל לוֹ]. 𝔍 *post habitaculum suum*. † זְבֻל n.m. is *elevation, lofty abode*, of sun and moon 1 K. 8¹³ = 2 Ch. 6² Hb. 3¹¹, of God in heaven Is. 63¹⁵. It is improbable that it could refer to the abode in Sheol. It probably refers by antith. to the glorious abode of the rich in this world ; so that 𝔊 ἐκ τῆς δόξης αὐτῶν, 𝔙 *a gloria eorum*, in their paraphrase are essentially correct. מן in the sense of *far away from*, v. B*D*B. — לוֹ] 3 sg. refers to צורם. 𝔊, 𝔙, pl. interpret as referring to the rich למו, so Street, Horsley, Ew., Hi., al. — **19.** וַיִּרְדְּ]. The 3 pl. between 3 sg. m. and f. is awkward and improb. דְ is dittog. of כי. Rd. יִּרְדָּה; so לָהּ for לָךְ, which has been assimilated.

PSALM L., 3 STR. 6⁶, RF. 2⁶.

Ps. 50 is a didactic poem. (1) God shines forth from Zion in theophany, summoning earth, and heaven, and His godly ones to be present at the judgment of His people for infidelity to the covenant at Horeb (v.¹⁻⁷). (2) He declines to accept their ritual sacrifices, which they had offered in sufficient numbers, for He has no need of them ; the animals belong to Him already. He will accept, however, thank-offering and votive-offering, and will rescue His people in their trouble (v.⁸⁻¹⁵). (3) He convicts them of professing fidelity to the covenant, while at the same time they were violating the seventh, eighth, and ninth Words. He warns them not to forget Him ; but rather to glorify Him by thank-offerings ; and then He will let them see His salvation (v.¹⁶⁻²³).

YAHWEH doth speak, and call the earth from the rising of the sun unto the
    going down thereof.
  Out of Zion, the perfection of beauty, Yahweh cometh shining forth ;
  Fire devoureth before Him, and round about Him it storms exceedingly.
  He calleth to the heavens above, that He may judge His people :
  " Gather my godly ones to Me, they that made a covenant by peace-offering ;
  And let the heavens proclaim righteousness, that (Yahweh) Himself is about
    to judge."
      " *Hear, My people, and I will speak ; Israel, and I will protest to thee ;
      I, (Yahweh) thy God, (who brought thee up from the land of Egypt)*."
" NOT for thy peace-offerings will I reprove thee, nor for thy whole burnt-offerings
    which are before Me continually ;
  I will take no bullock out of thine house, nor he-goats out of thy flocks ;
  For Mine are all the beasts of the forest, the cattle upon mountains where
    thousands are ;

I know all the birds of (the heavens), and that which moveth in the field is in
My possession.
If I were hungry, I would not tell thee; for the world is Mine and the fulness
thereof.
Shall I eat the flesh of the mighty bulls, or drink the blood of he-goats? "
" *Sacrifice to (Yahweh) thank-offering, and pay thy vows unto 'Elyon;*
And call upon Me in the day of trouble; I will rescue thee and thou shalt
glorify Me."

" WHAT hast thou to do with telling My statutes, and taking My covenant by
thy mouth?
Seeing thou hatest discipline, and hast cast My words behind thee.
When thou sawest a thief, thou wast pleased, and with adulterers was thy
portion;
Thy mouth thou hast put forth for evil, and thy tongue frameth deceit;
Thou sittest down to speak against thy brother, against thy mother's son thou
allegest fault.
These things thou hast done, and I have kept silence; thou didst deem that
I was like thee."
" *I will convict thee, and set it forth before thine eyes ; consider this, ye*
forgetters of Me.
Whoso offereth a thank-offering glorifieth Me. I will let him see the
salvation of (Yahweh)."

Ps. 50 was in 𝕬 and 𝕳𝕳 before it was taken up into 𝕰 (*v.* Intr. §§ 29, 31, 32).
The author uses in v.[1], Dt. 32[1 sq.] Is. 1[2]; in v.[2-3], Dt. 33[2], cf. Ps. 80[2-3] (𝕬);
the Ten Words (7, 8, 9) in v.[18-20]; the preface of the Ten Words in v.[7];
דברים for the Ten Words in v.[17]; the חקים of E, D, in v.[16]; כרת ברית in v.[5], phr.
of J, E, D, not used in P; על זבח of Ex. 24 in v.[5]. The limitation of sacrifices
to זבח, עולה, תודה, נדר, v.[5, 8, 14], is Deuteronomic. All this favours dependence
on D and priority to P. V.[1] מזרח שמש עד כבאו = 113[3] Mal. 1[11], but earlier,
because it refers to the earth in antith. to the heavens, and not to its own
inhabitants in a universalistic sense. V.[2] מכרר יפי is related to La. 2[15], and is
probably a proverbial expression used of Zion in preëxilic times, and so
attached to it that it persisted in postexilic usage, even though the later temple could not compare in beauty or grandeur with the former, cf. Ps. 48[8].
V.[7] is related to 81[9] in its citation of the preface to the Ten Words, and v.[2-3]
to 80[2-3], v.[11] to 80[14] (both 𝕬) and v.[9] מכלאה to 78[70], cf. Hb. 3[17]. עליון in v.[14] is
characteristic of 𝕬. The Ps. is thus similar to others of 𝕬. The heaping up
of divine names v.[1] as Jos. 22[22] is redactional; אנכי v.[7] is in citation; אליה v.[22]
is a late gl.; פן אטרף v.[22] is a gl. citing from 7[3]. These give no evidence of
date. מוסר v.[17] is used in the earlier sense of Je., and not in the later sense
of WL. The syntax is early: ו consec. impf. v.[1, 17, 18], cohort. v.[7, 8]. The other
examples, v.[3, 6, 7], are glosses or misinterpretations of MT. The judgment is
of the people of Yahweh as Dt. 32, and not of the nations. The people are
apparently dispersed in the earth, though the temple is standing and Yahweh
is present there. The Ps. was prob. composed in the Eastern Diaspora in the
late Persian period subsequent to Nehemiah.

Str. I. has a tetrastich with introverted parallelism, and a synth.
couplet. — **1.** *Yahweh*], doubtless original to the Ps. throughout,
for which 𝔈 substituted *Elohim*, which by dittog. became *El
Elohim;* finally a later editor restored *Yahweh*, thus heaping up
divine names, as elsewhere only Jos. 22²². This destroyed the
measure and induced various explanations. — *doth speak and call*],
in the sense of summon to attend at the seat of judgment. — *the
earth*], personified, and repeated in gloss after *the heavens above*],
v.⁴; based on Dt. 32¹⁻² Is. 1². They are summoned as witnesses
or assessors at the judgment, they taking their part in commotions
such as usually accompany theophanies. — *from the rising of the
sun unto the going down thereof*], from the extreme East to the
extreme West, for the entire earth between these two extremities ;
and not as 113³ Mal. 1¹¹, for the nations inhabiting the entire earth ;
for they have no place whatever in this judgment of Israel. —
2–3. The theophany for judgment is now described : *Out of Zion*],
the royal residence of Yahweh, implying that the temple was standing and the ceremonies of worship were carried on there. — *the
perfection of beauty*], the proverbial description of Zion as it appears in La. 2¹⁵, not, however, implying a preëxilic situation. That
the second temple was not equal in beauty to the first might well
have been the feeling of the old men who had seen the ancient
temple and could compare them ; but not of their posterity, still
less of the Diaspora to whom Zion was a glorious ideal, cf. 48³ (𝔈)
1 Mac. 2¹². — *Yahweh cometh shining forth*]. The measure requires
this combination. The coming is the theophanic coming forth
from the throne-room of the temple ; it is a shining forth of the
light of the Glory, cf. 80² (𝔄) Dt. 33². A copyist inserted in the
margin, " let Him not keep silence," in a time when the advent
of Yahweh was longed for by His people. This eventually became
a part of the text, and occasioned the separation of " come " from
the previous line and the insertion of its subject, " our God," giving
four tones of an incomplete line additional to the Str., and making
the negative jussive in its context a crux of Heb. syntax. — *Fire
devoureth before Him*], as frequently in theophanies ; the light of
the glory accompanied by devouring fire, cf. 97³. — *and round
about Him it storms exceedingly*], cf. the advent in a storm, 18⁹⁻¹⁶
Jb. 38¹. — **4.** *that He may judge His people*]. The theophanic

advent, the summoning of the witnesses, is, as the subsequent context shows, for testing them by the covenant to which they had pledged allegiance. The nations are not to be judged at this advent, as in the royal Pss. 96–100, cf. 9–10; but the people of Israel alone, as Dt. 32[36]. — 5. *Gather to Me*], assemble from various places. Yahweh Himself speaks, addressing the heavens, Hu., Bä.; not the angels understood, Moll., Kirk., which do not appear in this Ps. — *My godly ones*], usually referred to pious Israelites, scattered about over the earth, which is apparently favoured by the addition of the gloss, " earth," to " the heavens above," in the previous clause. If, however, the heavens are the agents, it is more probable that others than pious Israelites are in view, especially as it is the people as a whole that are to be judged, and not merely wicked Israelites. It is probable that the ancient worthies, Moses and the elders, are summoned from the gathering place of the departed to witness this judgment of Israel. This best suits the context, for they were the ones *that made a covenant by peace-offering*], at the institution of the covenant at Horeb, Ex. 24[5]. The later generations inherited the covenant with its obligations, but did not share in the peace-offerings in connection with which it was made. — 6. *Let the heavens proclaim righteousness*], make the solemn, public proclamation that righteousness is about to be administered, ‖ *that Yahweh Himself is about to judge*], decide the case of His people as regards their fidelity to covenant obligations. Even 𐤉 attaches the suffix " his " to righteousness, although it is not suited to the words of Yahweh, which continue here and throughout the Ps. The suffix is an interpretation, as probably also in the previous verse, in both 𐤉 and 𐤂, the one using the 1st pers., the other the 3d pers. — 7. *Hear, My people*]. Now for the first time, in presence of the witnesses and assessors, Yahweh addresses His people. This is a couplet of Refrain, as v.[14-15] v.[21c-23]. — *And I will speak*]: what I have to say as judge of the case in hand ‖ *and I will protest to thee*], solemnly bear witness. — *I, Yahweh, thy God*], asserting His right as the God who had taken them into covenant at Horeb, *who brought thee up from the land of Egypt*, reaffirming, therefore, the introductory sanction of the Ten Words. The measure requires this clause, which is indeed cited in 81[11], and which was probably omitted here by an

early copyist as an abbreviation, the introductory words sufficiently
suggesting it to the pious Jew.

Str. II. has three syn. couplets. — **8.** *Not for thy peace-offerings*]
emphatic in position, the festal offerings with their communion
meals, ‖ *whole burnt-offerings*], those entirely consumed on the
altar, expressive of worship. — *which are before Me continually*],
because offered daily in the Levitical ritual, morning and evening,
so that in later times these offerings gained the name *Tamidh;* cf.
Nu. 28³, which Kirk. thinks is alluded to here ; but this is improbable, because the Ps. depends on J, E, D, and shows no knowledge of
the institutions of P. — *will I reprove thee*], that is, because these
were insufficient or not in proper form, in accordance with the
ritual Law. The reproof has, as the subsequent context shows, not
ritual, but ethical reasons. — **9.** *I will take*], in the sense of accept as satisfactory. — *no bullock*], the most valuable of the offerings of the herd. — *nor he-goats*], the most valuable of the offerings
of the flock. — *out of thine house*], in the larger sense, including
the out-houses where the cattle were stalled. These, the most
valuable of all offerings, were not acceptable because they were
not offered by a people in right relations with their God. —
10. *For*], giving as a reason of the previous couplet, that God has
no need of such offerings, preparatory to the chief reason, which is
reserved for Str. III. — *Mine*], emphatic in position and statement,
— *are all the beasts of the forest*], the wild animals roaming there
in free and vigorous life. — *the cattle*], grazing *upon mountains
where thousands are*], so Aq., 𝕵, RV.ᵐ, and most moderns ; in
vast numbers, and not " thousand hills," as PBV., AV., or, " and
oxen," 𝕲, 𝖀. — **11.** *I know*], as a shepherd knows his herd and
flock ‖ *in My possession.* — *all the birds of the heavens*], as 𝕲, 𝕾,
𝕿, more probable than "of the mountains," 𝕳, 𝕵, EVˢ. ‖ *and that
which moveth in the field*], as 80¹⁴ ; possibly reptiles, but uncertain
in reference. All kinds of animals belong to God, and He can
use them at His pleasure without receiving them from men. —
12. *If I were hungry*], a conditional clause implying a negative
answer. — *I would not tell thee*], as if I had need of anything the
people could give me ; *for the world is Mine*], all belonging to
me, as its proprietor. — *and the fulness thereof*], all its inhabitants,
all living things and all vegetation, everything in it that could be

eaten. — **13.** *Shall I eat* ‖ *drink*], implying an indignant negative, — *the flesh of the mighty bulls*], those of Bashan, the strongest and most valuable, — *the blood of he-goats*], as offered in sacrifice and given to God as His share, in the flame of the altar. If God accepted His share of the sacrifices in this way, it did not imply the gross idea that He, like men, ate and drank these things. — **14.** The Rf. is a couplet of exhortation, after the previous remonstrance. — *Sacrifice to Yahweh thank-offering*], usually interpreted of thanksgiving expressed in prayers and songs, in antith. to a sacrifice of animals ; but this is improbable, as the ‖ *pay thy vows unto 'Elyon*], can only be understood of votive offerings ; both characteristic of 𝔻, and regarded as voluntary offerings, expressive of a real, pious disposition of the offerer ; as distinguished from prescribed ritual offerings, which too often become perfunctory, and merely empty ceremonial forms. This is as much as to say : make real, sincere, and voluntary offerings, and pay the votive offerings you have vowed ; get into right relations with your God ; and then, — **15.** *Call upon Me*, in petition or intercession, — *in the day of trouble*, when divine help is especially needed ; *I will rescue thee*, from the trouble, and then *thou*, on thy part, *shalt glorify me*, in public thanksgiving and praise.

Str. III. has all its lines in synth. relations with their predecessors, in pressing home one serious charge after another, until the climax is reached. — **16.** A glossator, wishing to separate this Str. more distinctly from the previous one, prefixes the clause : " and to the wicked God said," which gives but half a hexameter, and one line too many for the Str., or else, if attached to the first line, make that much too long. The context makes the address sufficiently obvious without this prosaic addition. — *What hast thou to do*], an idiomatic phrase : is it thine affair, or business ? — *with telling My statutes*], the brief, terse sentences of Law, usually with the penalty attached (*v.* Br.[Hex. 239]) ; proclaiming them and teaching them, when they do not obey them themselves, addressing the people in their solidarity, as in the Ten Words, and not as individuals. — *taking My covenant by thy mouth*], taking up the ancestral covenant, renewing it by oral assumption of its obligations, as was done by the nation in the times of Hezekiah and Josiah. — **17.** *Seeing thou hatest discipline*], instead of loving it as a true child of God, in the earlier sense of prophetic instruction, as in Je. 17[23] 32[33] 35[13] Zeph. 3[2. 7]. — *My words*], as v.[18-20], the sentences of the Ten Words, Ex. 20 Dt. 5 (*v.* Br.[Hex. 181]). — *hast cast behind thee*], of positive, scornful, and determined rejection. The specifications of the charge follow rapidly : — **18**. (*a*) *When thou sawest a thief*], instead of visiting him with punishment according to the Eighth Word, *thou wast pleased*], accepted him with gratification. — (*b*) *and with adulterers*], the violators of the Seventh Word, *was thy portion*, sympathising with them in their unlawful acts, instead of putting them to death as the Law required. — **19**. (*c*) *Thy mouth thou hast put forth*], in utterance ; let it loose in speech, — *and thy tongue frameth*], deliberate construction ; — *evil ‖ deceit*], to the injury of neighbours, by false witness in violation of the Ninth Word ; and this even against near kindred. — **20**. *Thou sittest down*], of deliberate action, — *to speak against ‖ allegest fault*], of complaint before the ministers of justice, in false witness, — *against thy brother*], the son of the same father, and, still worse in a polygamous society, — *against thy mother's son*]. These three Words were doubtless taken as specimens of violation of the primitive tables of the Covenant, just as in the discourse of Jesus, Mt. 5[21-37]. They are sufficient to lead to the summary statement, — **21**. *These things thou hast done, and I have kept silence*], not visiting them with punishment, apparently not noticing them or caring for them ; and so, from this seeming neglect ; *thou didst deem that I was like thee*], in caring for none of these things, or in being pleased with them. A kind but firm rebuke is now given in the climax. — *I will convict thee*], make the matter so plain and distinct that it cannot be evaded, — *and set it forth before thine eyes*], so clearly that it must be seen. — **22-23**. The Rf. summons to serious reflection : *Consider this, ye forgetters of Me*]. Only forgetfulness of Yahweh could let them think that He would act so contrary to His covenant as to overlook the persistent violation of its fundamental Words. A later editor, dissatisfied with the mildness of the rebuke, inserted at the expense of the measure, from 7[3] : "lest I tear you in pieces and there be none to deliver " ; and at the same time makes the previous word more objective by substituting " God " for the suffix " Me." — The Ps. concludes with essentially the same thought as v.[14]; only the exhortation is changed into a statement of fact: *whoso offereth a thank-offering glorifieth Me*]. The last clause is made more difficult by the insertion of a sentence evidently designed to make it more definite : "There is the way wherein " ; as 𝔊, 𝔖; otherwise explained by other Vrss., ancient and modern, but without agreement or satisfactory results. The clause is indeed essentially the same as v.[15]. If Israel, on his part, offers the acceptable thank-offering, Yahweh, on His part, *will let him see*], look upon with gratification, *the salvation of Yahweh*.

1. אֵל אֱלֹהִים יהוה] three distinct divine names, cf. Aq., Σ, Θ, 𝔍 ; but 𝔊, 𝔙, 𝔖, אֵל cstr. θεὸς θεῶν κύριος. יהוה in 𝔈 improb. אלהים is a simple variant of the poetic אֵל. — [עֵד־] 𝔊 יָעֵד, makes a separate tone. — 2. מִכְלַל יפי] a.λ. כְּלִילַת יפי La. 2[15] of Zion, Ez. 27[3] of Tyre ; final ת has been elided by txt. err. ם is prosaic repetition of מן. — [הוֹפִיעַ] rightly attached by 𝔊 as adv. ἐμφανῶς to יבא, as the measure requires. — 3. [וְאַל־יֶחֱרַשׁ] no good explanation of neg. juss. here, except as gl. of petition. It is rendered by Vrss. ancient and modern as indicative with לא. — [נִשְׂעֲרָה] Niph. pf. 3 m. impersonal, *it storms*. † שֵׂעַר for סֵעַר, elsw. Qal 58[10], Pi. Jb. 27[21], Hithp. Dn. 11[40]. — 4. [יָעֵל] for מֵמַעַל, as Gn. 27[39] 49[25] (JE) ; so Houb., Lag., We., Che., here. — [ואל הארץ] is a gl. — 5. [אִסְפוּ־לִי] elsw. c. אֶל. 𝔊 לו or אליו, so 𝔖. The difference of sfs. extends to הסידי or הסידיו, בריתי or בריתו. צדקו v.[6] 𝔐, 𝔊, favours 3 sg. ; but all these sfs. are prob. gls. of interpretation, the originals being without any of them. The interp. of 𝔐 is, however, correct in all save צדק; for God is speaker. — 6. [וַיַּגִּידוּ] ו consec. impf. must go back to pfs. of v.[1], as the response of heaven to the divine call. But 𝔊 rd. simple ו, as apodosis of imv. It is best to take it as ו coörd. and the vb. as juss. — [הוא] is a copula in 𝔊, 𝔍. Ew., Pe., take it as emph. demonst., *self*. — [שֹׁפֵט] Qal ptc. may have nominal force, as 𝔊, 𝔍, Bä., Du., or verbal as Dr. — 7. [וַאֲדַבְּרָה] ו apod. of imv., cohort. impf. 𝔊 has σοι = לְךָ, against the measure. — [אָנֹכִי] older form in citation from Ex. 20[2]. — 9. [מִמִּכְלְאֹתֶיךָ] has two accents. † [מִכְלָאָה] *enclosure, fold*, √כלא, 78[70] Hb. 3[17]. — 10. [לִּי] ל of possession, emph. — [חַיְתוֹ־יָעַר] as 104[20] Is. 56[9], cf. Gn. 1[24] (P) Pss. 79[2] 104[11], v. Ges.§ 90m; archaic case ending, merely euphonic. — [הַרְרֵי־אָלֶף] fuller form cstr. for הֲרֵי, poetic and euphonic. Cstr. before number is unexampled ; so Du. הרים אלח. But Aq., 𝔍, *in montibus milium ;* so De., Bä., RV.m, al. 𝔊 καὶ βόες, 𝔙 *et boves*, so 𝔖, = וָאֶלֶף, elsw. always pl. Ps. 8[8], cf. 144[14]. Ols., Oort, Bi., We., Ecker, rd. הַרְרֵי אֵל. — 11. [עוֹף הָרִים] 𝔐, 𝔍, improb. phr. due to error of eye of copyist taking הרים from previous l.; given correctly הַשָּׂדֶה 𝔊, 𝔖, 𝔗, Street, Du., Che. — [וְזִיו שָׂדַי] † = 80[14], cf. As. *zizânu*, coll. *reptiles*, BDB. *moving things*. — 15. [וּתְכַבְּדֵנִי] as v.[23]; the l. is defective, prefix ואתה. — 16. [וְלָרָשָׁע אָמַר אלהים] is expl. gl. — [וַיִּקָּח] ו consec. impf. after inf. makes both aorist. — 18. [וַתִּרֶץ] ו consec. impf. Qal. רצה Dr., Du.; but 𝔊, 𝔖, 𝔗, Luther, Gr., Oort, Bä., וְהָרֵץ, רוץ *run*. — [עִמּוֹ] is prob. dittog. of the

וַעַם that follows; it makes l. too long. — **19.** הַצְמִיר] Hiph. impf. † צשׁר vb.
Niph. c. לְ, *attach oneself to*, 106²⁸ Nu. 25³·⁵ (JE). Pu. *be bound*, of sword on
loins 2 S. 20⁸. Hiph. *bind together, frame*, here. Gerber thinks it is denom.
of צֶמֶר. — **20.** חֵשֵׁב] impf. frequentative; variation from previous aorists. —
† דֳּפִי] i.p. elsw. BS. 44¹⁹, cf. N.H. יֹובִי, *blemish, fault :* 𝕲 σκάνδαλον, Aq., Σ,
𝕵, *opprobrium*. — **21.** וְהֶחֱרַשְׁתִּי] coörd. emph. antith. of man's actions and
God's. — הֱיֹות] Qal inf. cstr. with vb. unexampled and improb. There is
conflation of two variants, as l. is one word too long. Inf. cstr. as more difficult is prob. original. One only is known to 𝕵. 𝕲, Θ, 𝕾, ἀνομίαν ὅτι ἔσομαι
= הֱיֹות = ἀνομία 57². — וְאֶעֶרְכָה] txt. err. for אֶעֶרְכָה, 𝕾. — **22.** שֹׁכְחֵי
אֱלֹיהַּ] makes the l. too long. אֱלֹיהַּ is a late insertion ; rd. שֹׁכְחֵי. — **23.** זֹבֵחַ]
ptc. MT., 𝕾, Σ, 𝕵; but 𝕲 יֶרַח n. subj. vb. — יַּכַּבְּדָנְנִי] cf. v.¹⁵ יּרִכַּבְּרָנִי. The
second נ is dittog. The נ of the energetic form is improb. — וְשָׂם דֶּרֶךְ] 𝕲, 𝕾,
Luther, Lowth, *there is the way*. De., Dr., expl. וֹ consec. pf. שִׂים, *and prepare
a way*. Hare, Street, Gr., Oort, Kau., יַּרְאֵּם. It makes l. long, and is doubtless
an expl. gl.